I

THE MANUSCRIPTS[1]

The first version of *Piers Plowman* is known to have survived in seventeen manuscripts and one fragment:

A *MS Ashmole 1468*[2] *Bodleian Library (S.C.7004)*

Paper, a composite volume assembled in the seventeenth century, comprising three distinct manuscripts. The third of these, consisting of 36 leaves numbered 307–78, contains *Piers Plowman* **A** I 142–XI 313. Size of page 11½ to 11¾ × 8 inches, with 22–30 lines per page.

COLLATION

a imperfect; it lacks i–iv, vi and its conjugate, and the conjugates of i and ii. It survives as pp. 307–8 (v) and pp. 309–14 (conjugates of iii–v).

b a six: pp. 315–38; signatures *b*j–*b*iiiij.

c imperfect and incorrectly rebound; it lacks i and the conjugate of vi; v, which apparently broke away at the fold, is pasted in as first leaf of the quire; the conjugate of i is pasted in; the stub of v is visible; signatures run *c*v (p. 339), *c*ij (p. 341), *c*iij (p. 343), *c*iiij (p. 345). The present p. 339 should follow p. 346.

d a five: pp. 359–78.

CONDITION

From the colour of the paper, this manuscript lay unbound for a long time. The ruling of frames has scored the pages, some of which have broken along the lines. Probably very few folds are intact. The text lacks the following: Prologue—I 141 (*a*i–iv); II 18–145 (*a*vi and its conjugate); III 114–229 (conjugates of *a*i and *a*ii); VII 33–85 (*c*i); and VIII 32–80 (conjugate of *c*vi). In addition *c*v has been bound in the place of lost *c*i, so that VII 237–86 follows VII 32 and is followed by VII 86.

DIVISIONS OF TEXT

II Passus secundus de visione
III Tercius passus de vissone
IV Passus quartus de visione *and so forth to*
IX Hic incipit vita de dowel dobet & dobest
X Primus passus de dowel

[1] From considerations of expense the publication of full descriptions of these manuscripts must await some other occasion. The present section restricts itself to information about them with a possible bearing on the textual problem. Nor is their language examined here; a linguistic analysis of all manuscripts of the three versions will form part of the fourth volume of this edition.

[2] See *A Descriptive, Analytical and Critical Catalogue of the Manuscripts Bequeathed unto the University of Oxford by Elias Ashmole Esq.*, W. H. Black, Oxford, 1845, cols. 1275–7; also *The Vision of William concerning Piers Plowman, . . . the 'Vernon' Text; or Text A*, ed. W. W. Skeat, EETS 28 (London, 1867, and reprints), p. xxi. Henceforth referred to as 'Skeat, *A-Text*'.

XI Passus secundus de dowel

at end Amen Amen

HANDWRITING

A skilful but ugly bastard hand.[1] The scribe inconsistently distinguishes *þ* and *y* by dotting.

DATE

From the hand, and general character of the manuscript, third quarter of the fifteenth century.[2]

HISTORY

There is no evidence for determining the origin and early movements of the manuscript.

Ch *Chaderton MS*[3] *Liverpool University Library F.4.8*

Vellum, 103 leaves, average size 10½ × 8 inches, with 30–36 lines per side. Pages numbered 1–202 (fols. 102 and 103 are unnumbered). Contains *Piers Plowman* **A** Prologue—XI 313 plus a **C** conclusion, on pp. 1–202. The manuscript is intact except at the end.

DIVISIONS OF TEXT

Four parts of *Piers Plowman* are distinguished by roman numerals at the tops of pages: *i* **A** Prologue–VIII; *ij* **A** IX–**C** XVIII; *iij* **C** XIX–XXI; *iiij* **C** XXII and XXIII. In addition there are divisions as follows:

A *I* Primus passus de visione

II Passus secundus de visione *and so forth to*

VII Passus septimus de visione vt prius

VIII Passus octauus de visione vt prius

IX Explicit visio willelmi de petro le plouȝman Eciam incipit vita de dowel dobet et dobest secundum witte and Resoun

X Passus primus de Dowelle

XI Passus secundus de Dowelle

after **A** *XI 313 the tag* Breuis oracio penitrat celum *from* **C**, *followed by* Passus tercius de Dowel *and then* **C** *XII 297 ff.*[4]

C *XIII no division*

XIV no division

XV Passus quartus de Dowel

XVI Passus quintus de Dowel vt supra

XVII Passus sextus de Dowelle

XVIII Passus septimus de Dowel et explicit Incipit Dobet

XIX Passus primus de Dobet *and so forth to*

[1] In the sense defined by N. Denholm Young, *Handwriting in England and Wales*, Cardiff, 1954, pp. 37–8.

[2] This is not, however, the indication of the watermarks. There are several, of which I have identified two: hillock like Briquet 11689 or Zonghi 1276 and 1277; and horn somewhat like Briquet 7666. The hillock of this type was in use from the last quarter of the fourteenth century to 1500; the horn is commonest in late fourteenth-century paper.

[3] See J. H. G. Grattan and R. W. Hunt, 'The Text of "Piers Plowman": A Newly Discovered Manuscript and its Affinities', *MLR*, xlii (1947), pp. 1–8.

[4] References to the other versions of *Piers Plowman* in this volume employ the line numbering of Skeat's editions. Subsequent volumes will contain the information needed to convert Skeat's numbering to that of the present edition.

XXII Explicit dobet Et incipit de Dobest
XXIII Passus secundus de Dobest
at end Explicit liber Willelmi de petro le plowȝman

HANDWRITING

An expert English vernacular hand, written with attention to speed and legibility rather than beauty. The letters *þ* and *y* are carefully distinguished, *u* and *n* are not.

DATE

From handwriting, about 1425.

HISTORY

The origin and the movements of the manuscript before the sixteenth century, when it appears to be connected with Oxfordshire, are not known.

D *MS Douce 323*[1] *Bodleian Library (S.C.21897)*

Paper, a book of 167 leaves numbered in pencil, average size 11 to $11\frac{1}{8} \times 8\frac{1}{4}$ inches. On fols. 102*a*–140*a* are copied *Piers Plowman* **A** Prologue–XI.[2] There are 28–34 lines per page of its text.

CONDITION

Except for loss of the last three leaves the manuscript is intact. Dislocations of *Piers Plowman* content on fol. 111 (where III 137–61 are copied after line 77) and on fols. 137*b* and 138*a* (where XI 128–66 are misplaced after line 206) occurred in an antecedent copy.

DIVISIONS OF TEXT

I Primus passus de visione
II Passus secundus de visione *and so forth* (*IV, VI, VII, VIII omitting* de visione) *to*
IX Vita de dowel dobet and dobest secundum wyt and resoun
X Primus passus in secundo libro
XI marked by a capital letter
at end Explicit liber petri plouman

HANDWRITING

One semi-cursive hand throughout the manuscript. The letters *þ* and *y* are distinguished; *u* and *n* are not.

DATE

From handwriting, late fifteenth century.[3]

HISTORY

Although the origin and early history of this manuscript are not confidently determinable, a fifteenth-century association with the eastern counties is not unlikely.

[1] See Skeat, *A-Text*, p. xxi.

[2] The other contents are: *The Brut of England*, prose, fols. 1–101*b* (see J. E. Wells, *A Manual of the Writings in Middle English*, New Haven, 1926, pp. 206–7); *The Charter of the Abbey of the Holy Ghost*, fols. 140*b*–159*b* (see Wells, *Manual*, p. 369 and H. E. Allen, *Writings Ascribed to Richard Rolle*, London, 1927, pp. 336 ff.); *Ipotis*, imperfect at end, fols. 160*a*–167*b* (see C. Brown and R. H. Robbins, *The Index of Middle English Verse*, New York, 1943, no. 220).

[3] Watermarks are a unicorn's head, like Briquet 15841–43 and Zonghi 783–91, found on paper used after 1410.

E *Trinity College, Dublin, MS D. 4. 12*[1]

Paper, 72 leaves so numbered, with subsidiary numberings beginning on fols. 1 and 27. Size 8½ to 8¾ × 5¾ inches. 27–34 lines per page. On fols. 1–26*b* are copied *Piers Plowman* **A** Prologue–VII 44 and VII 70–213a.[2]

COLLATION

a a thirteen: fols. 1–26. Sewing visible.

b lost.

c a six: fols. 27–38. On fol. 27*a* the signature *c*; on fol. 38*b* the 'catchword' 3, which also appears on fol. 39*a* top margin.

d indeterminate:[3] fols. 39–53. Sewing visible between fols. 46 and 47; fols. 39–46 bear the signatures *d*j–*d*viij.

e indeterminate and imperfect: fols. 54–66; lacking a leaf between present fols. 65 and 66. Sewing visible between fols. 59 and 60; signatures *e*j–*e*vij on fols. 54–60.

f six leaves of fifteenth-century paper; originally more. At least three stubs are visible.

CONDITION

i. *Piers Plowman* VII 70–213a are misplaced, beginning on fol. 6*a* after I 182, that is, one line before the end of the passus, and occupying fols. 6*b*, 7, 8*a* and part of 8*b*. At the end of the misplaced passage I 180–2 are recopied.[4] *ii*. *Piers Plowman* is defective at the end.[5] *iii*. *Alexander* is defective at the beginning, lacking, by comparison with MS Ashmole 44, its first 677 lines. *iv*. *Alexander* is defective in *e*, lacking a leaf after fol. 65. *v*. *Alexander* is defective at the end.

DIVISIONS OF TEXT

I Primus Passus de Visione

II Passus Secundus de Visione

III Passus tercius de Visione &c

IV Quartus Passus De Visione Petri &c

V Passus quintus de Visione

[1] See W. W. Skeat, *The Wars of Alexander*, EETS ES 47 (London, 1886), pp. xv–xix; also T. K. Abbott, *Catalogue of the Manuscripts in the Library of Trinity College, Dublin*, London, 1900, no. 213; E. St John Brooks, 'The *Piers Plowman* Manuscripts in Trinity College, Dublin', *The Library*, fifth series, vol. vi, December 1951, pp. 141–4.

[2] The other contents are: a page of monastic accounts on a leaf between the front flyleaves and fol. 1; *The Wars of Alexander*, fols. 27*a*–66*b* (Brown and Robbins, *Index*, no. *74, ed. Skeat, EETS ES 47); another page of accounts, fol. 67; a Latin tale or exemplum, imperfect, fol. 68*b*; a short prose life of Alexander, imperfect, fols. 70*b*–72*a*.

[3] Sewing and signatures point to an original quire of eight, but the second half has only seven leaves. Agreement of the text in this second half with that of MS Ashmole 44 (See Skeat, *Wars of Alexander*, pp. 115–45) forbids assumption of a lost leaf. The indication of watermarks is that fol. 39 is a single leaf.

[4] A similar dislocation is found in R and U, and possibly also in the Pembroke fragment (see below, pp. 14, 16, 13).

[5] The conclusion of *Piers Plowman* and the beginning of *Alexander* apparently occupied an original second quire. The size of this is not palæographically determinable. From the point, however, where *Piers Plowman* breaks off in E to the end of XI is about 1100 lines of which some 140 are already copied (see *i* above); in E, as in R and U, these were probably not copied again. The 960 remaining lines of *Piers Plowman* VII–XI, with the 677 presumably missing from the beginning of *Alexander*, at an average of 32 lines per side, would occupy 51 sides, very nearly a quire of 13 like the first in the manuscript. For genetic reasons (see p. 85 below) it is probable that the text of E continued originally to the end of XI, and that loss of such a quire should be inferred.

VI Sextus Passus de Visione

VII Septimus Passus de Visione

HANDWRITING

A common scrivener's hand of the fifteenth century throughout the manuscript. The letters *þ* and *y*, and *u* and *n* are not distinguished.

DATE

From the watermarks[1] and its general character, 1475–1500.

HISTORY

Identification of various names in the manuscript indicates that it was in Durham Priory round about 1500.

H *MS Harley 875*[2] *British Museum*

Vellum, 22 leaves so numbered, size 10¼ × 6½ inches; 36–41 lines per page; containing *Piers Plowman* **A** Prologue–VIII 142.

COLLATION

a and *b* fours: fols. 1–16.

c originally a four, now lacking the outer fold: fols. 17–22.

CONDITION

The manuscript lacks a leaf from the beginning of *c* (VI 48–VII 2), and its conclusion. In addition its text is defective where patches applied to original perforations before copying have broken away. See Apparatus at IV 76 ff., 118 ff., V 2 ff., 42 ff., 82 ff., 122 ff., 160 ff., 197 ff., corresponding to fols. 12, 13, 14 and 15. The skin is elsewhere perforated, without loss of text, as e.g. at fols. 2, 4, 7, 9, 10, etc.

If *c* were intact it would presumably contain the remainder of VIII. There is no indication in the manuscript whether *c* was its last quire. For genetic evidence that it was not, see below, pp. 39, 85.

DIVISIONS OF TEXT

Prologue a rubricated capital

I a crude rubric

II Tercius passus de visione *and in the margin* passus 3us

III Passus tercius de visione *with marginal guide*; *and so forth* (*except for defects*) *to*

VIII Passus Octauus de visione *with marginal guide*

HANDWRITING

Two main hands, one in *a*, and the other in *b* and *c*. Hand *a* is a coarse English vernacular hand, ugly and angular. The form of its *þ* is true, but *y* is variable, often resembling *þ*. Hand *bc* is a rounder type of vernacular hand, influenced by bastard; here *þ* is clearly distinguished from *y*. Neither hand distinguishes *u* and *n*.

DATE

Skeat (*A-Text*, p. xvii) thought this manuscript 'of early date, about 1400'. But the handwriting, especially in *a*, is distinctly later. It is to be dated 1450–1475.

[1] In *a*, flower, nearest Briquet 6452; in *c*, tower, nearest Briquet 2328–9; in *d*, dog, resembling Briquet 3625, 3626; in *e*, chalice, nearest Briquet 4589; in *f*, chalice, and also ox-head, resembling Briquet 15042, 15054, 15092.

[2] See *A Catalogue of the Harleian Manuscripts in the British Museum*, London, 1808, i, p. 466; also Skeat, *A-Text*, pp. xvii–xviii.

HISTORY

There are no indications of the origin and early movements of this manuscript.

H² *MS Harley 6041*[1] *British Museum*

Paper, 102 whole leaves and fragments of distinct leaves, size 8¾ to 9 × 5½ to 5⅞ inches, numbered 1–102,[2] containing 31 lines per page. On fols. 1–96*a*, *Piers Plowman* **A** Prologue–XI plus **C** XII 297–XXIII.[3]

COLLATION

This is not determinable by the usual means, since the manuscript has been restored from loose leaves by trimming their inner edges and pasting these to modern paper. From catchwords on the *verso* of fols. 12, 35, 39, 47, 59, 71, 83 and 95, and from signatures, the following reconstruction is conjectured:

a a six: fols. 1–12.

b a six: fols. 13–24. The lower part of 24, with any catchword that it may have contained, is lost.

c a six, imperfect: fols. 25 (numbered 26)–35. A leaf after fol. 33 was lost before the folios were numbered.

d a two: fols. 36–9. (This departure is indicated by a catchword. On fol. 36 the faint note *iiij quaternio*. The **A** version ends two lines short of the bottom of fol. 39*b*.)

e a four: fols. 40–7.

f probably a six: fols. 48–59.[4] At bottom right of fol. 48*a*, *v qtn.*

g–j sixes: fols. 60–95, marked as *vi*, *vij* and *viij qatn* or *qtn.*

k seven leaves: fols. 96–102.

This reconstruction, based on surviving catchwords, will be seen to conflict with an ancient numbering of some quires. The probable explanation of this circumstance is that the numbering of quires took place before copying, and that during copying the gathering of six which was the projected fourth quire was divided into present *d* and *e* in order that *d* should be no larger than was needed to accommodate the **A** version.

CONDITION

The manuscript is broken at the folds throughout, and has been repaired by pasting to modern paper. Five leaves survive as fragments only: fols. 23 and 24 as triangles from the upper inside corners; fols. 25 and 26 as the lower inside corners; fol. 35 has lost its lower outside corner. A whole leaf is missing after fol. 33. These deficiencies have occasioned

[1] See *A Catalogue of the Harleian Manuscripts in the British Museum*, iii, p. 313; also Skeat, *A-Text*, pp. xx–xxi.

[2] After fol. 24 several fragments of lower portions of leaves were at first missed, but the omission is corrected after fol. 27 (numbered 25).

[3] In addition, on fols. 97*a*–102*b*, a manual of confession, beginning *Herst or thow go to schrifte be in a priuey stede* and ending *that I trespasid haue in my lyf tyme Amen*; cp. Wells, *Manual*, p. 360

[4] Within *f*, after the last line of fol. 51*b*, some 370 lines (**C** XV 202–XVII 23) are wanting, an amount to cover six leaves. At the foot of fol. 51*b* in a very early ink and hand, probably the same which has noted the absence of a rubric at the beginning of **C** XIII (below, p. 7), and not unlike that of the main scribe, there is the note *deficit*. In view of the general collation by sixes this loss seems to me more likely to have occurred in an exemplar which also had about 30 lines a side than in the present manuscript. But this cannot be conclusively shown, for although the signature *v* occurs on fol. 52*a* as if the quire were intact, signatures were added in this manuscript after copying, and the loss may have intervened between the two processes. The trimming of inner edges deprives us of the evidence of the watermarks on this point.

NOTE

The present edition of *Piers Plowman* owes its conception to the late Professors R. W. Chambers and J. H. G. Grattan who, in 1909, embarked upon an edition of the A version, and later encouraged others to examine the textual problems of the B and C versions. Work on the project, by themselves and under their direction, continued until prolonged ill-health and the outbreak of the second world war caused their plans for publication to be suspended and eventually abandoned. Professor Chambers died in 1942, and Professor Grattan in 1951. But two younger scholars, A. G. Mitchell and George Kane, who had been introduced to the *Piers Plowman* project as postgraduate students of Professor Chambers in 1937 and 1938 respectively, continued to assemble materials. By 1950 sufficient progress had been made for the Board of Management of the Athlone Press to consider and accept proposals for the eventual publication of a full edition.

The edition is planned in four volumes as follows: I, the A version, edited by Professor George Kane; II, the B version, edited by Professor Kane and Professor E. Talbot Donaldson; III, the C version, edited by Professor A. G. Mitchell and Dr G. H. Russell; IV, Glossary and linguistic apparatus. Professor Kane has undertaken at the invitation of the Board of Management of the Press to act as co-ordinating general editor of the work as a whole.

The relation between the edition of the A version as it now appears and that projected by Professors Chambers and Grattan is defined in the editor's preface to this volume.

PIERS PLOWMAN: THE THREE VERSIONS

General Editor

GEORGE KANE

D1278821

PIERS PLOWMAN: THE A VERSION

WILL'S VISIONS OF PIERS PLOWMAN AND DO-WELL

AN EDITION IN THE FORM OF TRINITY COLLEGE CAMBRIDGE MS R.3.14 CORRECTED FROM OTHER MANUSCRIPTS, WITH VARIANT READINGS

BY

GEORGE KANE

UNIVERSITY OF LONDON
THE ATHLONE PRESS
1960

Published by
THE ATHLONE PRESS
UNIVERSITY OF LONDON
at 2 Gower Street, London WC1
Distributed by Constable & Co. Ltd
12 *Orange Street, London* WC2

Canada
University of Toronto Press

U.S.A.
Oxford University Press Inc
New York

Printed in Great Britain by
WESTERN PRINTING SERVICES LTD
BRISTOL

PREFACE

ALTHOUGH I am in some degree the successor of the great initiators of this edition, and although I have enjoyed unrestricted access to their materials, I cannot claim the honour of collaboration with them. I was privileged, at various times, to learn from both Professor Chambers and Professor Grattan, and it is hardly possible for me today to distinguish my own findings from what they taught me, by writing and by word of mouth. But because opinions about textual criticism are much changed since their time, with an inevitable effect upon me, I cannot claim that they would have approved of the direction which my conclusions have taken.

Independence has, indeed, been forced upon me. When I undertook to edit this version of *Piers Plowman*, Professor Grattan was still alive; the plan then was that my uninformed energy would be guided by his great experience. But with his death all responsibilities fell upon me; at the same time I was deprived of any source of interpretation of the materials collected by my predecessors. If I was to continue with the work, no course seemed possible except to treat it as my own. For, in a situation of this kind, although credit can be shared, responsibility is indivisible. Therefore I recollated in full that part of the poem already examined by them, instead of simply completing their collations as was originally planned; I reviewed all editorial decisions taken by Chambers and Grattan or by Grattan and myself; and I replanned this volume as the present state of the subject seemed to require. I did not let considerations of piety affect my decisions; that is, I know, the last thing they would have wished. True piety seemed to me to lie rather in following to the utmost of my ability the high tradition of scholarship which they represented. They would at all costs have wished me to obey the direction of the evidence. Still, it remains a fact that their interpretation of this evidence might not have been the same as mine. Therefore, while my relation to them is one of obligation in almost every respect, and they must share in any credit attached to my performance, the responsibility for this volume is mine alone.

I am also under many other obligations, for help and support. The Leverhulme Research Fellowships Advisory Committee in 1948 awarded me a grant towards the expenses of preparing the edition; a substantial grant from the Central Research Fund of the University of London in 1950 enabled me to visit Ann Arbor and consult the files of the Middle English Dictionary; a further grant from this source paid for visits to libraries in Great Britain and Ireland to examine manuscripts. I have especially to thank the Provost and Professorial Board of University College, London, for permission of access to the Chambers and Grattan papers in the library of that college; Professor Hans Kurath of the Middle English Dictionary for most handsomely putting the unpublished materials of that project at my disposal; the Librarian of the National Library of Wales for depositing a *Piers Plowman* manuscript in the British Museum for my use; and the Librarian of Pembroke College, Cambridge, for lending me the *Piers Plowman* fragment discovered in the library of that college. The Librarians of University College and Royal Holloway College have given me unfailingly cheerful help; the Librarian of Liverpool University has most generously lent me *Piers Plowman* photostats in his charge. I have enjoyed, on a number of occasions, the hospitality of the libraries of Trinity College, Cambridge, Lincoln's Inn, and the Society of Antiquaries of London. Dr R. W. Hunt of the Bodleian Library patiently answered many questions. Mr David Masson, then of Liverpool University Library, Mr William O'Sullivan of Trinity College, Dublin, and Dr John Plummer of the Pierpont Morgan Library most kindly checked and supplemented information gathered during all too hasty visits to their libraries. Dr C. E. Wright of the British Museum Manuscript Room gave me information about Harleian manuscripts. For their patience and co-operation I am greatly obliged to the officers of the Athlone Press.

For permission to publish from *Piers Plowman* manuscripts in this edition I am happy to thank the Trustees of the British Museum, the Curators of the Bodleian Library, the Master and Fellows of Trinity College, Cambridge, the Board of Trinity College, Dublin, the Treasurer and Masters of the Bench of the Honourable Society of Lincoln's Inn, the University of Liverpool,[1] the Keeper of Manuscripts

[1] Professor Grattan would have wished to name as a friend and benefactor of this edition the late Mrs Clara Hornby, who presented the Chaderton manuscript to the University of Liverpool.

and Records in the National Library of Wales, the Pierpont Morgan Library, the Society of Antiquaries of London, and the executors of the late Duke of Westminster.

Several scholars upon whom I had no claim have been most generous of their time and interest. I am especially obliged to the late Sir Walter Greg and to Dr Kenneth Sisam, who read my introduction; their expert comments and criticisms invariably resulted in improvement. Professor Francis Wormald undertook to examine and date the hands of the manuscripts of the A version. It has been immensely reassuring to have the benefit of his professional opinion, and the dates in my description are his, or confirmed by him. My friends, Talbot Donaldson, Morton Bloomfield, Alex Mitchell, Randolph Quirk, and Stanley Hussey have helped me in various ways, with checking, with stimulating discussion, and with constructive criticism. To Professor Hugh Smith I am particularly indebted. But for him this undertaking would never have been realized. He supported it when to do so was an act of faith; his patient confidence and sustained encouragement have heartened a much protracted and often lonely task. I cannot exaggerate the value of his experience and advice, from which I have benefited at every turn.

For defects and errors, which I cannot hope to have avoided, I alone am to blame. I must confess to a lively consciousness of fallibility. The responsibility for accuracy in a work of this size has weighed heavily upon me, and my best hope must be for friendly correction.

Royal Holloway College
Englefield Green

G.K.

CONTENTS

ABBREVIATIONS

DNB *Dictionary of National Biography*, ed. Leslie Stephen and Sidney Lee, London, 1885–1901.

EETS Early English Text Society, 1864–.

MED *Middle English Dictionary*, ed. H. Kurath and S. M. Kuhn, Ann Arbor and London, 1952–.

MLR *Modern Language Review*, 1906–.

MP *Modern Philology*, 1903–.

NED *New English Dictionary on Historical Principles*, ed. J. A. H. Murray *et al.* Oxford, 1888–1933.

PMLA *Publications of the Modern Language Society of America*, 1884–.

SP *Studies in Philology*, 1906–.

TLS *Times Literary Supplement*, 1902–.

losses in the following passages: **A** VII 53–293; X 107–68; XI 34–71. About 370 lines are wanting after fol. 51 (see above).

DIVISIONS OF TEXT

A *I* Passus primus

II Passus secundus de visione *and so forth to*

VI Passus sextus de uisione ut prius *and so forth to*

IX Explicit hic visio willelmi de petro the plouȝman Eciam incipit uita de dowel. dobet and dobest secundum wit & reson

X Passus primus de dowel &c

XI Passus secundus de do wel et c

at the end of **A** *XI, as one line,* Passus tercius de dowel Breuis oracio penetrat celum *followed by* **C** *XII 297*

C *XIII in margin, an early hand and ink,* primus passus deficit hic

XIV Passus quartus *in margin*

XV Passus quintus de dowel

XVIII Passus octauus hic finitur de do wel Incipit primus passus de dobetere

XIX Passus primus de do bet *and so forth to*

XXII Explicit de dobet Incipit primus passus de do best do best

XXIII Secundus passus de do best

HANDWRITING

An English vernacular hand of good character. The letters *þ* and *y* are distinguished, but not *u* and *n*. There are many corrections in a mid-sixteenth-century hand.

HISTORY

From shields of arms,[1] the original owner of the manuscript was a member of the Bedfordshire family of Hoo. At an early date it seems to have passed into the possession of a monk of St Augustine's without Canterbury, and eventually to the William Holyngborne whose name appears on fol. 96*b*.

DATE

From the above, from handwriting, and from watermarks,[2] not long after 1425.

H³ *MS Harley 3954*[3] *British Museum*

Vellum, 126 leaves, average size 11½ × 5¾ inches,[4] containing on fols. 92*a*–123*b* *Piers*

[1] These are found on fols. 1*a*, 1*b*, 2*b*, 3*b*, 4*b*, 5*b* and 96*b*. All but the last and possibly the first seem to have been drawn by the original scribe. That on fol. 1*b*, *quarterly sable and argent*, was borne by Sir William Hoo, an officer of Richard II, before 1399 captain of the castle of Oye near St Omer, from which district his wife came. He died between 1412 and 1415. A connexion of the Hoo family with the vicinity of Canterbury was established in 1385 when Sir William and members of his family were, by royal licence, granted tenure of the manors of Threvely, Chilham and La Molesshe, property of the abbey of St Bertin near St Omer in royal custody during hostilities. William Holyngborne was a senior member of the community of Black Monks of St Augustine's during the period 1510–39, appearing in documents as a petitioner to the king, as the abbot's chaplain, and as a signatory of the instrument of surrender.

[2] They are incomplete, but it is possible to see part of a hillock like Briquet 11851–3, 11861–3, 11889–90, 11894, and a unicorn very like Briquet 9956. These occur on paper in use from 1376–1430, and in the first years of the fifteenth century respectively.

[3] See *A Catalogue of the Harleian Manuscripts in the British Museum*, iii, p. 98; and Skeat, *A-Text*, pp. xxiii–xxiv.

[4] On other manuscripts of this shape, see below, p. 11, fn. 2.

Plowman **B** Prologue–V 105 (approximately) plus **A** V 106–XI.[1] The number of lines per page varies from 39–42 but is most often 40. Folios are numbered 1–88, then two are missed, thereafter 89–124.

CONDITION

The conjugates, fols. 109 and 114, and 111 and 112, have been torn at the folds but are correctly repaired. Loss of *Piers Plowman* **A** VIII 116–IX 96 did not occur in the present copy; the point of loss is between the fourth and fifth lines of fol. 116*b*.

DIVISIONS OF TEXT

Title Perys Plowman

B *I* Thys is þe fryst part of þis book perys plowman

II þis is þe secunde part of þis book. Perys plowman

III Thys is þe thryede part of þis book ho þe kyng concelyt mede to be maryid

at end of IV Here endyt þe ferd part of þis book plowman

A *at end of V* Here endyth þe v part of þis book pers plowman

at end of VII Here endyth þe sexte part of þis book pers plowman

at end of X Here endyth þe seueth part off þis book

finally Explicit tractus de perys plowman quaþ herun
Qui cum patre et spiritu sancto viuit & regnat
per omnia secula seculorum Amen.

HANDWRITING

The main script is a distinctive vernacular hand, heavily sloped and angular; *þ* and *y* are not distinguished; *u* and *n* sometimes are. *Filius Regis* (fols. 90*a*–91*b*) is in an unremarkable fifteenth-century English vernacular script.

DATE

From the handwriting and the shape of the manuscript, third quarter of the fifteenth century.[2]

HISTORY

There are no indications of the origin and early movements of the manuscript.

J *Ingilby MS*[3] *Pierpont Morgan Library of New York M 818*

Paper, 54 leaves so numbered (a subsidiary numbering begins on fol. 16*a*), size 8½ to 8¾ × 5 to 5¾ inches, containing 29–38 lines per page. On fols. 16*a*–54*b* are copied *Piers Plowman* **A** Prologue–XII 88.[4]

[1] The manuscript also contains: *The Travels of Sir John Mandeville*, fols. 1–69*b* (see J. W. Bennett, *The Rediscovery of Sir John Mandeville*, New York, 1954, p. 291); *The Childhood of the Saviour*, fols. 70*a*–74*a* (Brown and Robbins, *Index*, no. 250); *The Merit of Hearing Mass*, fols. 74*a*–76*a* (op. cit., no. 1986); *The Virtue of the Mass*, fols. 76*a*–78*a* (op. cit., no. 1988); *The Seven Virtues and the Seven Deadly Sins*, fols. 78*b*–81*a* (op. cit., no. 2059); *The Seven Works of Mercy*, fols. 81*a*–82*b* (op. cit., no. 2062); *The Seven Sacraments*, fols. 82*b*–85*b* (op. cit., no. 1901); *The Seven Principal Virtues*, fols. 85*b*–86*b* (op. cit., no. 2045); *An A B C Poem on the Passion*, fols. 87*a*–88*a* (op. cit., no. 1523); and *Filius Regis Mortuus Est*, fols. 90*a*–91*b* (op. cit., no. 404).

[2] The main hand is not unlike one in B.M. MS Arundel 327, Osbern Bokenham's *Legends of Holy Women*, dated 1447. See fols. 75*b* and ff.

[3] See W. W. Skeat, *The Vision of William concerning Piers Plowman*, part iv, section ii, EETS 81 (London, 1885), pp. 856–9.

[4] Other contents are *The Pistill of Susan*, fols. 1–5*a* (Brown and Robbins, *Index*, no. 3553); *The Form of Perfect Living*, fols. 5*b*–15*b* (see H. E. Allen, *Writings Ascribed to Richard Rolle*, p. 262).

CONDITION

The *Piers Plowman* copy is intact: Passus XII breaks off with a single line copied at the head of fol. 54*b*.

DIVISIONS OF TEXT

I Primus passus
II Passus secundus de visione
III Passus quartus de visione
IV Passus quartus de visione
VIII Passus octauuus de visione
IX Explicit visio willelmi de Petro Plowhman Hic incipit vita de dowele dobet & dobest secundum wit & resoun
X Primus passus de dowele
XII Passus tercius de dowele

The headings for I, II, III and VIII are in the margin.

HANDWRITING

A nondescript fifteenth-century informal hand which varies enough to suggest the possibility of several writers.

DATE

From handwriting and general appearance, mid-fifteenth century. One watermark (type of Briquet 11664–728) has been identified, but not precisely enough to help with the dating.

HISTORY

The origin and movements of this manuscript are obscure.[1]

K *MS Digby 145*[2] *Bodleian Library (S.C.1746)*

Paper, a book of 180 leaves, size 11½ to 11¾ × 7¾ inches; folios are numbered *i–iii*, then 1–159, thereafter 9 leaves unnumbered, then 160–70; there are also various subsidiary numberings. Fols. *i* and 170 are flyleaves. The number of lines per page varies from 24–28. On fols. 2–130*a* are copied *Piers Plowman* **A** Prologue–XI plus **C** XII 297–XXIII.[3] The manuscript is intact.

DIVISIONS OF TEXT

A *Prologue* Primus passus de Visione Petri plowghman *at end* finis
I Passus secundus de visione *at end* finis *and so forth to*
VIII Passus nonus de Visione *at end* Explicit visio
IX Hic Incipit Vita de dowell dobett & dobest secundum Witte & Reson *at end* finis

[1] Names in sixteenth-century marginal entries appearing to connect the manuscript with Leicestershire (the fullest is on fol. 34*b*) have resisted identification. The reliability of Skeat's information that the manuscript once belonged to Fountains Abbey (op. cit., p. 856) is now not determinable. Dialect and orthography, however, suggest a northern scribe.

[2] See G. D. Macray, *Catalogi Codicum Manuscriptorum Bibliothecae Bodleianae Pars Nona: Codices a Viro Clarissimo Kenelm Digby . . . Donatos Complectens*, Oxford, 1883, col. 143; also Skeat, *A-Text*, p. xxiv.

[3] Other contents are: Sir John Fortescue's *The dyfference betweene Dominium Regale et Dominium Politicum & Regale*, fols. 133*a*–159*a* (printed in *The Works of Sir John Fortescue, Knight*, ed. Thomas, Lord Clermont, London, 1869, pp. 449 ff.); a collection of proverbs, fols. 160*b*–161*b* (printed in *A History of the Family of Fortescue* by Thomas, Lord Clermont, London, 1869, pp. 177–8).

X Secundus Passus de dowell *at end* finis
XI Passus tercius de dowell
on fol. 56b, at end of **A** *XI 313, in the main hand and ink, and cancelled in the same ink,* amen; *thereafter, partly erased and obscured by show-through, but legible under ultra-violet light* Finis de dowell
C *after XII 313* finis
XIII Passus quartus de dowell *at end* finis
XIV Passus quintus de dowell *at end* finis
XV Passus sextus de dowell
XVI Passus septimus de dowell *at end* finis *and so forth to*
XIX Passus primus de dobett *at end* finis *and so forth to*
XXII Primus passus de dobest *at end* finis
XXIII Passus secundus de dobest *at end* finis totaliter

In addition running titles: *de Visione* fols. 3–43*b*; then *dowell* to fol. 91*b*; then *dobett* to fol. 113*a*; thereafter *dobest*. All by the main scribe, in a larger form of his usual hand.

HANDWRITING

A practised, cursive sixteenth-century free hand. The text was copied from an exemplar or exemplars in which *þ* and *ȝ* were used. Substitution for these letters is general but not invariable; when *þ* is kept it is sometimes written like *y* and sometimes preserves its true shape.

DATE

1531–2[1]

HISTORY

The manuscript was copied by Sir Adrian Fortescue.[2]

L *Library of the Honourable Society of Lincoln's Inn no. 150*[3]

Vellum, 125 leaves so numbered, with various subsidiary numberings, size 12 × 5¼ inches, containing 50–55 lines per page. On fols. 109*a*–125*b* are copied *Piers Plowman* **A** Prologue–VIII 155.[4]

COLLATION

a and *b* imperfect:[5] fols. 1–13.

[1] On fol. 1*b* appears the note: *Iste Liber Pertinet Adriano Fortescu Militi Sua manu propria Scriptus Anno Domini 1532 & Anno Regjs h. viij^ui xxiiij^to*. The *2* in *1532* is altered from *1* by over-writing, and *xxiiij* altered from *xxiij* by erasure and addition. The date 1532 appears again on fol. 159*a*, at the end of *Dominium Regale*.

[2] See *DNB*., vii, pp. 476–7.

[3] See J. Hunter, *A Catalogue of the Manuscripts in the Library of the Honourable Society of Lincoln's Inn*, London, 1838, pp. 143–6; Skeat, *A-Text*, pp. xxii–xxiii; E. Kölbing, 'Vier romanzen-handschriften', *Englische Studien*, vii (1883), pp. 194–5; E. Kölbing ed., *Arthour and Merlin*, Leipzig, 1890, p. xvii; M. Kaluza ed., *Libeaus Desconus*, Leipzig, 1890, p. ix; M. E. Barnicle ed., *The Seege or Batayle of Troye*, EETS 172 (London, 1927), pp. x–xiv; G. V. Smithers ed., *Kyng Alisaunder*, ii, EETS 237 (London, 1957), pp. 3–4.

[4] The manuscript also contains: *Libeaus Desconus*, imperfect, fols. 1, 4–12*b* (Brown and Robbins, *Index*, no. 1690); *Arthour and Merlin*, imperfect, fols. 2, 3, 13, 14*a*–27*b* (op. cit., no. 1162); *Kyng Alisaunder*, fols. 28*a*–90*a* (op. cit., no. 683, and ed. G. V. Smithers, EETS 227 (London, 1952); *The Seege or Batayle of Troye*, fols. 90*b*–108*b* (Brown and Robbins, *Index*, no. 3139).

[5] These quires were originally sixes; their surviving leaves are now incorrectly assembled.

c–l sixes: fols. 14–121.
at end four leaves: fols. 122–5.

There are no formal divisions of *Piers Plowman.* At the head, in a much later hand and another ink, is the title *Plowman Piers.* Passus I is set off only by one of the frequent paragraph marks; II–VII by single or double oblique strokes in the left margin, in the main ink or one very like it.

CONDITION

On fol. 125*b* *Piers Plowman* ends at VIII 155. The four leaves at the end of the manuscript, fols. 122–5, contain about 400 lines; if they belonged to an original quire of six, like those in the rest of the manuscript, the leaves lost from that quire could easily have accommodated the remainder of the **A** version, even including Passus XII. In view of the condition of the manuscript at the beginning[1] it is not hard to assume that there were substantial losses at its end.

HANDWRITING

A nondescript hand of the sort found in late fourteenth- and fifteenth-century provincial guild or corporation documents and private correspondence, expert but unpretentious.

DATE

From handwriting, first quarter of the fifteenth century. The shape of the manuscript, also, is more characteristic of the fifteenth and sixteenth centuries than of the earlier period.[2]

HISTORY

There is no clear evidence for the early history of this manuscript.[3]

M *Library of the Society of Antiquaries of London no. 687*

Paper, a book of 279 leaves, size $8\frac{3}{8}$ to $8\frac{1}{2} \times 5\frac{1}{2}$ to $5\frac{3}{4}$ inches, containing in the *Piers Plowman* portion 28–35 lines per page. The fourth flyleaf is numbered 1; an odd leaf

[1] There the following losses are to be inferred: *Libeaus* 1–215 (original *a*i and *a*ii); 430–555 (original *a*v); 793–906 (original conjugate of *a*v); 1126–461 (original conjugates of *a*ii, *a*i and original *b*i); 1579–695 (original *b*iii); 1936–2166 (*b*vi and its conjugate); *Arthour and Merlin* 339–436 (conjugate of *b*i). Leaves at the beginning and end are much discoloured; the *verso* of the last leaf is largely illegible.

[2] It is a 'holster book'. Others like it are Harley 3954 (above, p. 7); Bodley Eng. poet. b 5 ($15\frac{1}{4} \times 6\frac{1}{4}$ inches), collections of recusant poetry; Ashmole 61 ($16 \times 5\frac{1}{2}$ inches), a late fifteenth-century minstrel's book; Harley 1239 ($15\frac{1}{2} \times 5\frac{3}{8}$ inches), poetry of Chaucer; Sloane 4 (12×5 inches), fifteenth-century medical recipes; Additional 37658 ($15\frac{7}{8} \times 6\frac{7}{8}$ inches), Royal Year Book of Edward II; Yates Thompson *Talbot Hours* ($10\frac{3}{4} \times 4\frac{1}{2}$ inches); Yates Thompson *Hours of Margaret Beauchamp* ($8\frac{3}{4} \times 4\frac{1}{2}$ inches); Additional 27879 (as now bound $15\frac{1}{4} \times 5\frac{1}{4}$ inches), the Percy folio manuscript; and Balliol College Oxford 354 ($11\frac{1}{2} \times 4$ inches), Richard Hill's commonplace book. See *Bodleian Library Record*, iii, p. 50; also J. M. Manly and E. Rickert, *The Text of the Canterbury Tales*, i, Chicago, 1940, p. 191; and on the date of Ashmole 61, A. J. Bliss, *Sir Orfeo*, Oxford, 1954, p. xii. Dr R. W. Hunt and Dr G. S. Ivy were kind enough to discuss 'holster books' with me. I have not examined the Yates Thompson manuscripts.

[3] Previous suggestions must be discounted. Hunter inferred from a mention of Beverley on a vellum fragment bound as a flyleaf, and from 'the fact that at Beverley there was in the times when this manuscript was written a noted fraternity of minstrels' (pp. 145–6), that 'the contents of this book were originally transcribed for their use'. But this is made to seem unlikely by the dialect of the manuscript in the first instance; ignores the presence of names on the flyleaf from another part of England; and assumes what cannot be shown, that the manuscript and this flyleaf have the same origin. Miss Barnicle's theory that the manuscript belonged to Wenlock Priory and passed in the reign of Henry VIII to an Anthony Foster of Trofford or Trafford (*Seege or Batayle*, pp. xii–xiv) is based on a questionable transcription: the placename may well be not Trofford but Trotton, as Kölbing read it ('Vier romanzen-handschriften', p. 194).

serving as title page is 2; thereafter pages are numbered *recto* 3–67, one unnumbered, 69–557. At the end is a paper supply numbered 559, 561. On pp. 470–549 is copied *Piers Plowman* **A** Prologue–XI.[1] The manuscript is intact except for early loss of three leaves after p. 358.

DIVISIONS OF TEXT

I and II paragraph marks in the main ink
III Passus tercius de visione
IV Passus quartus de vsione
V Quintus passus
VI Passus vj^us^
VIII a double oblique stroke in the margin, main ink
IX Explicit visio de petro plouthman hic incipit prologus de dowel dobet ⁊ dobest
X, XI a double oblique stroke
at end Explicit prologus de dowel dobet ⁊ dobest

HANDWRITING

A hasty, practised free hand tending to cursive writing. The distinction between *þ* and *y* is generally maintained; *u* and *n* are not distinguished.

DATE

From combined indications of watermarks[2] and handwriting, about 1425.

HISTORY

There is no evidence for the manuscript's movements before the seventeenth century, when it appears connected with Lincolnshire.[3]

N *National Library of Wales no. 733B*

Vellum, 88 leaves, size 7¼ × 5¼ inches, with 29–35 lines per page; the pages numbered 1–176. Contains *Piers Plowman* **A** I 76–VIII 184 plus **C** IX–XXII.

COLLATION

Fours throughout. No signatures.

CONDITION

The manuscript is defective at beginning and end. Assuming an original **A** prologue like that of its genetic fellow, W (see below, p. 31–3), it lacks at the beginning about 180 lines which, at 30 lines per side, would cover three leaves. Taking into account the uniform composition of the surviving portion of the manuscript it thus appears that *Piers Plowman* was not originally the first item. At the end, as far as the faded last leaf

[1] Other contents are: English Paternoster and Creed, p. 3; *The Prick of Conscience*, an augmented version, pp. 5–358 (cp. R. Morris ed., *The Pricke of Conscience*, in *The Philological Society's Early English Volume*, London, 1865); a manual of confession in English prose, pp. 359–81 (cp. Wells, *Manual*, p. 360); a treatise on the deadly sins in English prose, pp. 383–411 (cp. Wells, *Manual*, pp. 350 ff.); a treatise on the ten commandments in English prose, pp. 412–30 (cp. Wells, *Manual*, pp. 354, 456, 471); *The Vision of Edward the Confessor*, in Latin prose, pp. 431–68 (cp. Wells, *Manual*, p. 220); instructions to the clergy about ecclesiastical censure, in English prose, pp. 552–8, a new hand; definitions of common law terms in legal Latin and French, followed by notes on medieval English historical events, in a third, seventeenth-century hand, headed *Ex libro vetusto legum et consuet: Angl: in archivis Dmi de Heling*, pp. 559 ff.

[2] These are: hillock, resembling Briquet 11678, 11685, 11696; hillock in circle resembling Briquet 11851–4, 11856, 11862, 11872, 11886.

[3] The entries in the third hand (pp. 559 ff.) are possibly by the Lincolnshire antiquary Gervase Holles (1607–75) or one of his amanuenses.

allows one to estimate, about 400 lines, from **C** XXII 457 to the conclusion, are wanting. The first surviving leaf is also very badly faded.

DIVISIONS OF TEXT

A *II* Passus secundus de visione. vt supra
III Passus tertius de visione. vt prius *and so forth to*
VIII Passus octauus de visione. vt prius
at the end of **A** *VIII, before*
C *XI* Passus nonus de visione & vltimus et hic desinit Et de cetero tangit auctor de inquisicionibus de Dowel Dobettre & Dobest sicut patebit speculantibus. Inquisicio prima.
XII Primus passus de Dowel
XIII Passus secundus de dowel *and so forth to*
XVIII Passus septimus de Dowel & hic desinit. Et hic incipit Inquisicio prima de Dobet
XIX Passus primus de Dobet
XX Secundus Passus. De Dowel
XXI Tercius Passus De Dobet
XXII Quartus passus de dobet et hic desinit & incipit dobest

HANDWRITING

A somewhat unusual English vernacular hand. The letters *þ* and *y* are carefully distinguished; *u* and *n* are not.

DATE

From handwriting and general appearance, early fifteenth century.

HISTORY

I have no information about the early history of the manuscript.

Pembroke College, Cambridge

A fragment, vellum, discovered in a binding in Pembroke College Library by Messrs M. J. C. Hodgart and N. R. Ker, brought to my attention by Dr G. S. Ivy. It is a single fold, measuring when open 8 × 11¼ to 11½ inches, originally the outside member of a quire of four. The contents are: IV 106–45 (omitting 112–14, 139–40, 146–7) on the first page; IV 148–V 29 (omitting V 10, 21) on the second; VII 84–93 followed directly by VII 212α–41 (omitting 225–6, 233) on the third; and VII 242–82 (omitting 251, 260, 269, 270, 272, 278, and transposing 267–8) on the fourth. Although the text in this fragment is so corrupt that I have not thought its variants worth recording in the apparatus, it is interesting in one respect. On the third page, after the tenth line (VII 93), with no physical interruption, comes VII 212α. This omission of VII 94–212 is very similar, although it does not correspond exactly, to the omission of VII 70–213a in RUE after the appearance of these lines in Passus I of those manuscripts (see pp. 14, 16 and 4). The absence of VII 94–212 from P, like that of VII 70–213a from their right place in RUE, is probably to be explained as caused by loss of an inner fold of an unbound quire in an antecedent.

R *MS Rawlinson Poetry 137*[1] *Bodleian Library (S.C.14631)*

Vellum, 41 leaves so numbered, size 9½ × 5¾ to 6 inches, with 30–34 lines per page, containing *Piers Plowman* **A** Prologue–XII.

CONDITION

Apart from cropping, which has caused no loss of text, this copy is physically intact. Like E and U (cp. also the Pembroke fragment) it misplaces a passage of 145 lines (VII 70–213a), which are copied in Passus I after line 179, on fols. *5b–7b*, and do not appear on fols. *24b* ff., where they belong in the sequence of the poem. The dislocation did not take place in R, but in an unsewn ancestor, where the misplaced lines were copied on an inner fold of a quire containing 36 lines to the side, which fell out of place *as lance leueȝ of þe boke þat lepes in twynne*, and was later stuffed carelessly into the middle of the first quire. In R the last line of the dislocated passage, VII 213a, is followed immediately by I 180. In E and U there are signs of tinkering. In E, after the misplaced passage, three lines of the text which preceded it (I 180–2) are recopied. In U, where the misplaced passage follows II 23, the text returns to I 180 after VII 213a. Evidently a scribe in the tradition of E, having copied mechanically to the end of VII 213a, now perceived that something was amiss, and from his own manuscript or from comparison with another copy, gave Passus I at least a few lines of its own conclusion. The situation in U is harder to account for, but the return of U's text to I 180 rather than II 24 at the end of the misplaced passage shows that, whatever the attempts at adjustment, the point of dislocation in a near antecedent, as in the case of E, was after I 179.

DIVISIONS OF TEXT

Prologue Hic incipit liber qui uocatur pers plowman. prologus
I Passus primus de visione *and so forth to*
IX Explicit hic visio willelmi de petro &c Et hic incipit vita de dowel. dobet. & dobest secundum wit & resoun
X Passus primus de dowel *and so forth to*
XII Passus tercius de dowel
at end Explicit dowel

HANDWRITING

An English bastard hand, distinguishing *þ* and *y* but not generally *u* and *n*.

DATE

From handwriting and general appearance only, mid-fifteenth century.

HISTORY

The evidence for the early history of this manuscript resists interpretation.[2]

[1] See Skeat, *A-Text*, pp. 142*–4*.

[2] The scribe signs himself *Tilot plenus amoris* after the *explicit*. I have found no Fullaloves in the published national records of the fifteenth and sixteenth centuries, and *plenus amoris* may be no more than a jingle (cp. W. D. Macray, *Annals of the Bodleian Library*, 2nd edn., Oxford, 1890, pp. 21–2 fn.). The name does, however, occur in Norfolk (see *An Essay towards a Topographical History of the County of Norfolk*, ii, by F. Blomefield, London, 1805, p. 356; op. cit., viii, by C. Parkin, London, 1808, p. 536; *Index of Wills Proved in the Consistory Court of Norwich 1370–1550*, i, Norfolk Record Soc., 1943, p. 160) and Suffolk (Macray, op. et loc. cit.).

T *Trinity College, Cambridge, MS R.3.14*[1]

Vellum, 74 leaves, size 11¼ to 11½ × 6½ to 6¾ inches, containing 41–46 lines per page. Folios are correctly numbered in arabic; in addition an early, roman numbering, top left *verso*, beginning on fol. 1*b* as *xxiij*, continues correctly to fol. 67 and thereafter is out because of a mistaken alteration. The manuscript contains *Piers Plowman* **A** Prologue–XI plus **C** XII 297–XXIII on fols. 2–74.

CONDITION

From the roman numbering of folios it appears that the manuscript is defective at the beginning. There have been no losses within the surviving portion.

DIVISIONS OF TEXT

A *I* Primus passus de visione

II Passus secundus de visione *and so forth to*

VI Passus sextus de visione vt prius *and so forth to*

IX Explicit hic visio willelmi de Petro de Plouȝman. Eciam Incipit Vita de do wel do bet & do best secundum wyt & resoun

X Passus primus de dowel &c

XI Passus secundus de dowel &c

at end of **A** *XI* Passus tercius de dowel. Breuis oracio penetrat celum *followed by* **C** *XII 297 ff.*

C *XIII* Passus secundus de dobet

XIV a capital letter only

XV Passus quartus de dowel

XVI Passus quintus de visione vt supra

XVII Passus sextus de dowel

XVIII Passus septimus de dowel & explicit

XIX Passus primus de dobet *and so forth to*

XXII Explicit de dobet Et incipit de dobest

XXIII Secundus passus de dobest

at end Explicit

HANDWRITING

One good English vernacular hand throughout. The letters *þ* and *y* are carefully distinguished; *u* and *n* are generally not.

DATE

From handwriting and the appearance of the manuscript, about 1400.

HISTORY

The manuscript was one of over a hundred given to Trinity College by Thomas Nevile, Master from 1593–1615. I can find no indications that it came from the conventual library of Christ Church, Canterbury.[2]

[1] See Skeat, *A-Text*, pp. xviii–xix; M. R. James, *The Western Manuscripts in the Library of Trinity College, Cambridge*, ii, Cambridge, 1901, pp. 64–5; G. S. Ivy, *The Make-Up of Middle English Verse Manuscripts*, University of London doctoral dissertation (1953), pp. 154–62.

[2] For the suggestion that this was one source of Nevile's gifts see James, op. cit., i, p. viii; also C. E. Woodruff and W. Danks, *Memorials of the Cathedral and Priory of Christ in Canterbury*, London, 1912, pp. 386–7.

U *University College, Oxford, MS 45*[1]

Vellum and paper, an early miscellany of five distinct items, of which the first, consisting of 36 leaves, contains *Piers Plowman* **A** Prologue–XII 19α. Folios are numbered 1, 2, 4–32, 32, 33–6. Size of page 8¼ × 5½ to 5¾ inches; number of lines on the vellum pages 30–8, on the paper generally 28.

COLLATION

a–d fours: 1–32 (1); *a* is defective, lacking iii.	Vellum. Catchwords on *a* and *d*; sewing visible in each quire.
e originally a four, now defective: fols. 32 (2)–36. Lacks i, the conjugate of i, and the conjugate of ii.	The paper portion. The original composition is deduced from the contents.

CONDITION

The manuscript lacks I 33–99 (*a*iii); X 211–XI 47 (*e*i); and XII 20 onwards (conjugates of *e*ii and *e*i). Like E and R (above, pp. 4, 14) this manuscript misplaces VII 70–213a. As in E and R, the dislocation did not occur in the present copy, where the misplaced portion begins within a page (fol. 5*b*). In U, VII 70–213a follow after II 23, occupying most of fols. 5*b*, 6, 7*a* and part of 7*b*. At line 13 of fol. 7*b* the text returns to Passus I, recopying I 180–3 and thereafter continuing normally with II. The original point of dislocation in the U tradition was thus after I 179 as in E and R, and the present character of the text of U here is the result of cobbling.

DIVISIONS OF TEXT

I Passus primis de visione

II Passus secundus de visione *and so forth to*

IX Explicit hic visio willelmi de petro plowman Et hic incipit dowel dobet & dobest secundum wit & resoun

X Primus passus de dowel

XII Passus tercius de dowel &c

HANDWRITING

On the vellum portion an English vernacular hand which distinguishes *þ* and *y* invariably, but does not consistently distinguish *u* and *n*. On the paper quire an excellent example of bastard hand. Here *þ* and *y*, and *u* and *n* are sometimes distinguished, and sometimes not.

DATE

Hand I belongs to the first quarter of the fifteenth century; Hand II to the second.

HISTORY

The early history of the manuscript is not known.[2]

[1] See H. O. Coxe, *Catalogus Codicum MSS. Qui in Collegiis Aulisque Oxoniensibus Hodie Adservantur*, Oxford, 1852, i, pp. 13–14; also Skeat, *A-Text*, pp. xix–xx.

[2] It is believed to be the gift of Obadiah Walker, Master from 1676–89. See R. W. Hunt, 'The Manuscript Collection of University College, Oxford: Origins and Growth', *Bodleian Library Record*, iii, pp. 13 ff., esp. pp. 26–7.

V *MS English Poetry a. 1 Bodleian Library (S.C.3938–42)* *The 'Vernon Manuscript'*[1]

Vellum, 341 leaves,[2] size $21\frac{1}{2}$ to 22×15 to $15\frac{1}{2}$ inches; folios numbered in roman, top left *verso*, with various errors; a subsidiary arabic numbering, top right *recto*, begins after *cccx*. Contains *Piers Plowman* **A** Prologue–XI 183 on fols. *cccxciiij–cccxcxj*, with 160 lines per page in two columns.[3]

CONDITION

What survives of this manuscript is well preserved, but it appears to lack 73 leaves, lost either as whole quires when unbound, or subsequently when illuminated pages were cut out.[4] *Piers Plowman* is physically intact except for loss of its last leaf (fol. 402). This could have held 320 lines, that is the 135–40 lines needed to finish Passus XI and at least 180 more. It could thus have accommodated the 117 lines of Passus XII as well as a beginning for the next item, *Joseph of Arimathea.* But since the Vernon text of the alliterative life of Joseph appears to be unique there is no way of determining how much of fol. 402 was originally occupied by *Piers Plowman.*

DIVISIONS OF TEXT

A space of one line is left at the beginning of each section of the poem, presumably for the later insertion of a rubric, except at the beginning of Passus IX where, in the hand and ink of the text, is the legend *Incipit hic. Dowel. Dobet. and Dobest.*

HANDWRITING

An expert English vernacular hand. The letters *þ* and *y*, and *u* and *n* are carefully distinguished.

DATE

The manuscript is dated 'about 1370–80' by Skeat (*A-Text*, p. xv), and 1380–1400 by others (Serjeantson, p. 222). But the scope of the collection, the character of its *Piers Plowman* text, presupposing a considerable number of stages of transmission, and the lateness of Harley 875, the genetic twin of the Vernon *Piers Plowman* text, argue that the Vernon manuscript was copied nearer 1400 than 1380.

HISTORY

Dialect study of the index to the manuscript associates this with Staffordshire.[5] Recent investigations connect Colonel Edward Vernon, who presented the manuscript to the Bodleian Library in 1677, with Houndhill, Staffs.[6]

[1] This manuscript is often noticed, but the only authoritative account of it is by Mary Serjeantson, 'The Index of the Vernon Manuscript', *MLR*, xxxii (1937), pp. 222–61; even this is concerned mainly with its content.

[2] According to my count, including the surviving half of fol. 406 but not the index of 8 leaves.

[3] For a list of the contents of the manuscript see Serjeantson, op. cit., pp. 228–61.

[4] See Serjeantson, op. cit., and add loss of original fols. 88 (lxxxviij), 248 (ccxlviij), and probably also two leaves from the end of the final quire.

[5] Serjeantson, op. cit., pp. 222–7.

[6] Rev. J. Quinn, S.J., 'Earlier Owners of the Vernon Manuscript', *Bodleian Library Record*, iv, pp. 133 ff.

W *The Duke of Westminster's Manuscript, Eaton Hall*[1]

Vellum, 78 leaves, numbered in roman i–lxxvj, and in arabic 1–78; size 11 × 7½ inches; with 40–42 lines per page. Contains *Piers Plowman* **A** Prologue–XI plus **C** XIII 1–XXIII on fols. 1–76*a*. The manuscript is intact.

DIVISIONS OF TEXT

A *Prologue* Capitulo primo, *upper right-hand margin in the ink of the roman folio numbering*
I Passus primus de visione *and in left margin* Cap[i] ij
II Secundus passus de visione *also* Cap[i] iij
III Passus tercius de visione *also* Cap[i] iiij
IV Quartus passus de visione *also* Cap[i] v
V Passus quintus de visione *also* Cap[i] vj
VI Sextus passus de visione *also* Cap[i] vj *altered from* vij
VII Septimus passus de visione *also* Capi vij (*? altered from* viij)
VIII Passus octauus de visione *also* Capi viij
IX Sequitur prologus de dowel dobett & dobest *also* Capi ix
X Primus passus de dowel *also* Capi x
XI Passus secundus de dowel *also* Capi xj *altered from* xij
after XI 166 Tercius passus de dowel *also* Capi xij
after **A** *XI 313, in another hand the rubricator's guide* passus iiij de dowel *and a line left blank (the last of fol. 31a)*
C *opposite* **C** *XIII 1 (at the head of fol. 31b)* Cap xiiij
XIV a blank line, the guide passus v[us] de dowel *in another hand, and in the margin* Capi xv
XV similarly a blank line, the guide Passus vj de dowel *and* Capi xvj
XVI a blank line, the guide vij passus de dowel *and* Capi xvij
XVII a blank line, the guide viij[us] & vltimus passus de dowel *and* Capi xviij
XVIII a blank line, the guide Explicit vltimus passus de dowel & incipit primus passus de dobet *and* Capi xix
XIX a blank line, the guide ij passus de dobet *and* Capi xx *then so forth to*
XXII a blank line, the guide Explicit vltimus passus de dobet & incipit primus de dobest *and* Capi xxiij
XXIII a blank line, the guide ij passus de dobest *and* Capi xxiiij & vltimo
at end Explicit tractatus[2] piers plowman nominatus

HANDWRITING

A script closely resembling official court hand of the fifteenth century. The letters *þ* and *y* are always, *u* and *n* generally distinguished.

DATE

From the general appearance of the manuscript, 1450–75 or even later.

HISTORY

There is no indication of the movement of this manuscript before 1600, when it appears connected with Chester.

[1] See W. W. Skeat, *The Vision of William concerning Piers Plowman*, part iv, section ii, EETS 81 (London, 1885), pp. 853–6.

[2] After *tractatus* three minims with *i* above the second and third. Skeat (*Piers Plowman*, part iv, p. 853 and fn.) reads this as *uiri*. It is perhaps a false start for *nominatus*.

II

MANUSCRIPTS AND VERSIONS

The manuscripts discussed in the preceding section differ markedly in length and content. Nevertheless they agree in reading a considerable number of lines and passages, not found in other copies of *Piers Plowman*, which give an altogether distinctive character to the first twelve sections of the poem. The uniformity with which this distinguishing material is attested in these manuscripts, notwithstanding their diversities of shape, is remarkable. Its absences are haphazard, occurring without significant relation to the varieties of shape. On grounds of this common possession of characteristic material a substantive version of *Piers Plowman*, consisting of twelve sections, that is Prologue and Passus I–XI, is to be identified in these manuscripts.[1]

Some of the seventeen manuscripts are variously differentiated in shape from the rest by possession of material characteristic of other versions of *Piers Plowman*.[2] In a sufficient number of instances this additional material is found in circumstances that require us to ascribe its presence to some other agency than an author.

General agreement in possessing distinctive material thus positively indicates the presence of an independent version of *Piers Plowman* in these manuscripts; omissions of this material fail to disturb that identification. Differentiations of shape by possession of material characteristic of other versions prove on examination to be the work of compilers. In addition, the genetic groups into which these manuscripts fall do not correspond (with one exception which does not affect the argument) to the arrangements of the manuscripts by shape, but cut across them; the descent of the hypothetical genetic groups from their

[1] As has been known for nearly a century: see Skeat, *A-Text*, pp. xii–xxvii, especially pp. xviii–xix. Contrary opinions (an anonymous reviewer in *TLS*, 10 February 1950, p. 87, and Gertrud Görnemann, *Zur Verfasserschaft und Entstehungsgeschichte von 'Piers the Plowman'*, Heidelberg, 1915, pp. 119–20) will be found not to survive examination of full evidence.

[2] Two other versions are clearly identifiable by distinctive content, and established by substantial attestation: one (called **B** by Skeat) represented with striking uniformity in eight manuscripts and a black letter edition, and with less uniformity but still marked agreement in seven more; another (called **C** by Skeat) in nineteen copies.

respective exclusive common ancestors thus bears no relation to the various shapes of the manuscripts. Finally, some manuscripts of differentiated shape show physical signs of cobbling which establish them as compilations.

Despite diversities of shape and content these manuscripts, then, preserve in varying degrees of purity and completeness a version of *Piers Plowman* consisting of a prologue and eleven passus, distinguished from the corresponding parts of the **B** and **C** versions by a substantial number of lines and passages. Some manuscripts with a text consisting of a prologue and seven or eight passus only, are shown to belong to this version by their agreement with the longer manuscripts in possession of the characteristic lines and passages as far as they go. These shorter manuscripts are all imperfect at the end, and show no sign that they did not originally contain a prologue and eleven passus. The shapes of the six manuscripts containing long conclusions generally similar in form and content to the latter part of the **C** version are the products of scribal compilation.

This is a firm conclusion, and has indeed been generally accepted by informed opinion. Nevertheless full evidence in support of it has not hitherto been presented. Therefore it seems advisable here to define the version of the poem represented in our seventeen manuscripts.

In the following discussion it will be useful to have in mind the shapes of these manuscripts in which the material distinct from the **B** and **C** versions occurs:

1. Prologue and I to VII[1]: E (imperfect at end)
2. Prologue to VIII: LH (imperfect at end)
3. I to VIII augmented from **C** or **B** and **C**, with a **C** conclusion: N (imperfect at beginning and end)
4. Prologue to XI: DVAM (V imperfect at end)
5. V 105 to XI after a **B** beginning: H³
6. Prologue to XI, with a twelfth passus: RUJ (UJ imperfect at end)
7. Prologue to XI with a **C** conclusion: TChH²
8. Prologue to XI augmented from **C** or **B** and **C**, with a **C** conclusion: KW.

The variety of shapes among these manuscripts is great enough. Nevertheless, of the seventeen manuscripts twelve agree, apart from

[1] For the sake of brevity the reference 'Prologue and I to—' is henceforth given as 'Prologue to—'.

physical imperfections and two major contaminations (Prologue and Passus VI in K), in the general content of Prologue to XI, four more agree with these for Prologue to VII or VIII, and one for V 106 to XI. Within this considerable area of concurrence all manuscripts contain a substantial amount of material absent from **B** and **C** or markedly distinguished from the corresponding passages in **B** and **C**. For convenience of classification this material may be divided into three kinds:

i. Lines or passages not found in the **B** and **C** versions;

ii. A few lines or passages which may be echoed in the **B** and **C** versions, but differ in sense from the lines or passages which echo them;

iii. Lines or passages which have recognizable equivalents in the **B** and **C** versions, revised by expansion, compression, rearrangement of content, or appreciable modifications of sense, with substantial changes in the form of expression.

The following tables will serve to indicate the principal lines or passages of these types, as well as any failures among the seventeen manuscripts to read them. Each reference is accompanied by information about manuscripts which omit the material in question; manuscripts there defective; and substitutions of **B** or **C** material at or near the point of occurrence.

i. Lines or passages not found in the **B** *and* **C** *versions*

PASSUS I 110[1] [omitted L; here A is defective]

PASSUS II 20 [omitted E and once U (the passage occurs twice); followed by two **C** lines WN; defective A] 30–1 [separated by a spurious line H (see below, p. 45); defective A] 36–42 [36 sophisticated and followed by a spurious line L (see below, p. 47); defective A] 45–8 [after 45 a spurious line H; after 45 five **B**/**C** lines W; after 45 seven **B**/**C** lines N (see below, p. 30); defective A] 50–3 [53 sophisticated EM; defective A] 87 [defective A] 165–6[2]

PASSUS III 222–4 [defective A] 243 [omitted TUDChH²] 274

PASSUS IV 67 108 [followed by three **B** lines W (see below, p. 30)] 141–3 [142 omitted U; after 143 five **B** lines W (see below, p. 30)]

PASSUS V 12 69–72 [71 omitted, 70 and 72 combined A; 69 sophisticated L] 74–5 [omitted AM] 154 176[3] [omitted LK; wrongly divided from following TChH², RU, D] 186[4] [omitted A] 239–40 252 [omitted A]

PASSUS VI (K substitutes a **C** passage for VI 18–94) 32 [omitted N] 35 79–81 [after 81 EAMH³ insert three **B**/**C** lines (see below, p. 31); defective H] 94 [omitted A; defective H]

[1] Possibly an accidental omission from **B**. Compare **C** II 107.

[2] Line 166 resembles **C** III 248.

[3] Not in **B**, but compare **C** VII 385.

[4] This line appears as **C** VII 395.

Passus VII (E breaks off at VII 213) 12–13 127–8 [misplaced (see description of manuscripts, above, p. 14) RUE; defective H^2] 165–9 [misplaced RUE; defective H^2] 180–3 [misplaced RUE; defective H^2] 210–12 [211 omitted TRUDChE; 212 and 212α transposed H; defective H^2]
Passus VIII (L mostly illegible after 130, breaks off at 155; H breaks off at 142) 40–1 [defective A] 48 [defective A] 62 [defective A] 116 [absent H^3] 150–1 [149 and 150 transposed U; absent H^3]
Passus IX (N assumes a **C** character) 45 [absent H^3] 71 [absent H^3] 93 [omitted VA; absent H^3] 95
Passus X 14–15 [15 occurs twice in A] 23 25 34 46–7 [47 run together with 49, omitting 48 M] 50–79 [therein omissions: 64 W; 67 RW; 74 D; 77 U; wrong divisions: 52–7 W; 66–7 J] 83–130 [omissions: 94 TD; 94α VJ; 99 A; 100 A; 107 Ch; 111 U; 112 V; 118 R; 120 UCh; 120α U; 121 W; 123–5 A; wrong divisions: 86–7 W; 89–90 VW; 94–94α W; 108–8α V; 109–110 W; 114–15 A; 119–120α V; 120–1 W; 123–5 TRUDChKWMH^3; transpositions: 90, 91 M; 108, 108α W; 108α, 109 M; 113–15, 112 H^3; a spurious line after 85 J; 104 expanded ChM; 107–30 defective H^2] 141–8 [142 omitted U; 145 omitted V; defective H^2] 152–6 [156 omitted R; 155–6 as one line U; defective H^2] 163 [defective H^2] 177 206–8 [wrongly divided VAKMH^3]
Passus XI (V breaks off at line 183) 22 [defective U] 28 [defective U] 32 [defective U] 60–3 154–154α [a different Latin line substituted U; misplaced D] 161 [misplaced D] 165 [omitted A; misplaced D] 168 177–8 [omitted RDW] 182–203 [omissions: 196 and 196α U; 203 W; wrong divisions: 183–7 W; 185–6 A; 191–192α A, W; 191–2 M, H^3; 194–6 TRDChH^2, J; 197–9 W; transpositions: 192α, 193α U; 193, 193α M; 196α, 197 A] 214–18 221–4 [223 omitted U] 241–9 [245 mostly omitted TRUDChH^2JK; wrong quotation at 242 U; wrong divisions: 243–245α TRUDChH^2; 244–245α J, K] 269 272–5 293 [omitted U] 297

ii. Lines or passages echoed in the **B** *and* **C** *versions, but with major changes in the sense*

Passus I 178 [omitted V]
Passus II 19 [defective A] 138 [defective A]
Passus III 89 [W has a **B** reading]
Passus IV 29–30 [preceded by three **B** lines W] 105 [followed by three **B** lines W] 116 [W reads the **B**/**C** equivalent] 133 [followed by a **B** line W]
Passus V 102
Passus VIII 107 [omitted AW]

iii. Lines or passages substantially altered in the **B** *and* **C** *versions but still recognizable as equivalent*

Prologue 90–5 [92–3 wrongly divided W; defective A, N; K reads the **C** equivalent for 84–102]
Passus I 112–13 [four **B** lines in place of 112 W; defective A] 136–8 [defective A]
Passus II 11–14 [11 omitted RU (in U the passage occurs twice); 12–13 sophisticated

H] 17 22–4 [24 omitted RU; defective A] 26 [defective A] 29 [omitted VH; defective A] 32 [omitted N; followed by a spurious line H; defective A] 35 [omitted U; defective A] 43–4 [followed by a spurious line H^2, W; defective A] 49 [defective A] 58–66 [63–4 omitted J; 63–4, 65 transposed E; twelve **C** lines inserted after 65 WN; defective A]

Passus III 50–1 [as three lines E; 50 as two lines L; omitted and twelve **B**/**C** lines in their place N] 54–64α [64α omitted R; 57–9 sophisticated A] 246–53 [248–50 omitted U] 272–3

Passus IV 60–1 [wrongly divided J, L, N] 96 [sophisticated L; W reads the **B** version] 134–6 [a **B** reading for one word of 136 AM; two spurious lines after 134 E] 144

Passus V 11 23 [omitted WN] 104 109[1] [wrongly divided TChH^2, U, RDM; EAMH^3 resemble the **B** equivalent] 206 213 254[1] [W echoes the reading of **B**]

Passus VI 50 [defective H] 71 [omitted N; EMH^3 have a **B**/**C** reading; defective H] 103[1] [defective H]

Passus VII 10–11 [11 omitted V] 60 [? an echo of **B**/**C** MH^3; defective H^2, A] 115 [defective H^2; misplaced RUE] 125 [defective H^2; misplaced RUE] 130–8 [132 omitted UVHN; 137, 138 transposed A; defective H^2; misplaced RUE] 170 [defective H^2; misplaced RUE] 178–9 [178 omitted TDCh; 178 expanded VHJN; defective H^2; misplaced RUE] 184 [defective H^2; misplaced RUE] 192 [defective H^2; misplaced RUE] 209 [defective H^2; misplaced RUE] 227 [defective H^2] 232 [omitted U; defective H^2] 235–6 [236 misplaced after 232, and a sophisticated line in its place N; defective H^2] 281 [omitted W; defective H^2]

Passus VIII 13–18 [15 omitted A; 15 as two lines Ch] 32–3 [wrongly divided J; defective A] 37–9 [38 omitted MH^3; defective A] 43–4 [defective A] 45–7 [after 45 a spurious line H; 46 sophisticated N; defective A] 55–8 [defective A] 61 [omitted H^3; defective A] 123 [as two lines H; absent H^3] 134 [absent H^3] 152 [absent H^3]

Passus IX 47 [absent H^3] 53–4 [54 omitted A; absent H^3] 78 [absent H^3] 102–3 [103 omitted A]

Passus X 28 35–6 80–2 [81–2 omitted W; 81 omitted V; 81 and 81α as one line H^3] 131–7 [defective H^2] 149 [as one line with following VW; defective H^2] 151 [defective H^2] 158–60 [159–60 wrongly divided W; defective H^2] 175 179–81 [180 omitted M; wrongly divided W] 201 [omitted A] 204 [omitted A; as one line with following W]

Passus XI 30 [defective U] 37 [defective U, H^2] 40 [sophisticated H^3; a **B** reading K; defective U, H^2] 72–3 [73 omitted Ch] 87 180–1 209 213 [J echoes the **B** reading] 219–20 [220 omitted A] 230–1 252–4 [254 omitted M; 252, 253 as one line A; 253–4 wrongly divided W] 258–61 267 295 [omitted UA; as one line with 296 W] 298–301 310 313

In the above tables some 240 lines have been listed which occur in the manuscripts under discussion but not in the **B** or **C** versions, as well as about 190 lines markedly distinguished in form or sense or both from their recognizable equivalents in the **B** and **C** versions.

[1] These lines occur in **C**.

The seventeen manuscripts distinguished by possession of these lines vary in length; while the majority break off with an eleventh or twelfth passus or even earlier, six have a conclusion of more than 3000 lines, longer by nearly a half than the Prologue–XI which precede it. Nevertheless, these six exhibit in this lengthy conclusion no comparably distinctive characteristics.[1] The individual character of the text exhibited by these manuscripts is in fact confined to the prologue and first eleven passus of the poem.

Within this limitation (which affects only TChH²KWN) that individual character is fully established by the material noticed above. In quantity this amounts to a generous sixth of the 2400 lines of Prologue–XI. That proportion by no means includes all differences between these manuscripts and the **B** and **C** versions of the poem and could easily be increased; the amount of material in *iii* above (pp. 22–3) could be doubled if examples of less striking but still substantial differences between these manuscripts and the **B** and **C** versions were included. The examples listed are, however, enough to demonstrate the individual character of the form of Prologue–XI of *Piers Plowman* represented in these seventeen manuscripts.

The distinctive material, or material in distinctive form, noticed above is found in these manuscripts without relation to their shapes. This is immediately clear from consideration of the omissions of the lines and passages listed above. Such omissions fail to correspond in any way to the length of the manuscripts, to their being augmented or not augmented, or to their having or lacking a **C** conclusion. They have therefore no bearing on the question of versions.

The largest combination of manuscripts agreeing in omission of *i*, that is non-**B**/**C** lines, namely TRUDChH²JK omitting XI 245, includes representatives of four shapes: D (Prologue to XI); RUJ (Prologue to XII); TChH² (Prologue to XI *plus* **C**); and K (augmented Prologue to XI *plus* **C**). The line meanwhile occurs in AM (Prologue to XI); W (augmented Prologue to XI *plus* **C**); and H³ (Passus V to XI after a **B** beginning). Neither the presence nor the absence of the line can be related to any classification of the manuscripts by shapes. The next largest combination, TRUDChE

[1] When allowance has been made for scribal variation. I am given to understand by the editor of the **C** version that there is no evidence for regarding TChH²'s later portions as an early draft or version of **C**, and that the later portions of TChH², K, W and N belong to the **C** form of the poem and descend from its archetype.

(omitting VII 211), contains one Prologue to VII manuscript, E; one Prologue to XI manuscript, D; two Prologue to XII manuscripts, RU; and two Prologue to XI *plus* C manuscripts, TCh. The group TUDChH[2] (omitting III 243) consists of a Prologue to XI, a Prologue to XII and three Prologue to XI *plus* C manuscripts; the group RDW (omitting XI 177–8) consists of a Prologue to XI, a Prologue to XII and an augmented Prologue to XI *plus* C manuscript; the group RW (omitting X 67) of a Prologue to XII and an augmented Prologue to XI *plus* C manuscript; the group TD (omitting X 94) of a Prologue to XI *plus* C manuscript and a Prologue to XI manuscript; the group UE (omitting II 20) of a Prologue to XII and a Prologue to VII manuscript; the group UCh (omitting X 120) of a Prologue to XII and a Prologue to XI *plus* C manuscript; the group LK (omitting V 176) of a Prologue to VIII and an augmented Prologue to XI *plus* C manuscript; the group VJ (omitting X 94α) of a Prologue to XI and a Prologue to XII manuscript. Two instances occur of manuscripts with the same shape agreeing in omissions: VA (IX 93); and AM (V 74–5). The remaining omissions occur in single manuscripts.

In the same way omissions of lines or groups of lines listed in *ii* and *iii* are not material to the question of shape. Among the omissions from *iii* eight combinations of manuscripts occur, of which only one corresponds to agreement in shape. They are UVHN (omitting VII 132), composed of a Prologue to XII manuscript, a Prologue to XI manuscript, a Prologue to VIII manuscript, and an augmented Prologue to VIII *plus* C manuscript; TDCh (omitting VII 178), composed of a Prologue to XI and two Prologue to XI *plus* C manuscripts; VH (omitting II 29), composed of a Prologue to XI and a Prologue to VIII manuscript; WN (omitting V 23), composed of an augmented Prologue to XI *plus* C, and an augmented Prologue to VIII *plus* C manuscript; MH[3] (omitting VIII 38), composed of a Prologue to XI and a Passus V to XI manuscript; VW (omitting X 81), composed of a Prologue to XI and an augmented Prologue to XI *plus* C manuscript; UA (omitting XI 295), composed of a Prologue to XII and a Prologue to XI manuscript; and RU (omitting II 11 and 24) composed of two Prologue to XII manuscripts. Thus, on the infrequent occasions when several manuscripts agree in omitting any of the material which distinguishes the seventeen as a whole, the variant groups so formed fail to correspond in any significant way to classification of the manuscripts by shape.

At the same time the amount of omission of these characteristic lines is inconsiderable; they are in fact handsomely attested.[1] There is no indication that their omissions are anything but scribal. Indeed, if the omissions of characteristic lines have any significance it is in relation to the quality of the manuscripts where they occur. Thus, for instance, the manuscripts A and U, which most frequently omit the lines listed in *i* and *iii*, also omit the largest numbers of lines generally in Prologue to XI. There are various other indications of the scribal character of many of these omissions. The classic *homœoteleuton* was apparently the cause of a number;[2] others were occasioned by the occurrence of the same or similar beginnings in adjacent or nearby lines;[3] others by the presence of the same or similar words within adjacent or nearby lines.[4] Some may have been occasioned by the grammatical structure of the passage.[5] Omissions in the immediate vicinity of rubrics are probably scribal.[6] The number of omissions for which no explanation suggests itself is not large.[7] Taking into account the relatively small total number of omissions, and that a considerable number of omissions are evidently, or at least very probably palæographic errors, it can be maintained that the attestation of the characteristic passages in these manuscripts is practically complete.

The agreement extends to the order of content of the manuscripts. The instances where characteristic lines are disordered (II 63–5 E; VII 137, 138 A; 212, 212α H; 236 N; VIII 149, 150 U; X 90, 91 M; 108, 108α W; 108α, 109 M; 112–15 H[3]; XI 192α, 193α U; 193, 193α M; 196α, 197 A) probably have a scribal origin. The agreement among these seventeen manuscripts in the arrangement of

[1] In both *i* and *iii* the number of omitted lines is about two per cent of the number of times of writing necessary to produce these lines in the surviving copies only.

[2] For a discussion of such omissions see p. 123 below.

[3] See p. 123 below.

[4] See p. 123 below.

[5] See p. 125 below.

[6] See p. 125 below.

[7] Of those not palæographically accounted for, several can be explained by reference to scribal sophistication of copy (below, pp. 129 ff.). An instance of a crude form of this is A's omission of V 251–2 so that a passus may finish at the end of a leaf. I 110 is omitted from L because its sense has been incorporated in a rewritten 109. The manuscript V omits I 178, which has occurred before, perhaps on stylistic grounds. U omits IV 142 so that the text should run on easily from a corrupt 141. WN omit V 21–3 perhaps because the poet's *occupatio* is taken at its word (perhaps simply because 23 practically repeats 11 above). At X 123–5 A appears to have suppressed one of several illustrations. W's omission of XI 203 is a bowdlerization. The force of such explanations of omissions is, however, not pressed at this point. It will become more apparent in the discussion of scribal treatment of copy below, pp. 115 ff.

all their content is marked. Apart from transpositions occurring through scribal error,[1] the only serious discrepancies are RUE's dislocation of VII 70–213 and D's dislocation of III 137–61 and XI 128–66, which patently have no bearing on the question of versions of the poem.

A form of Prologue and I to XI of *Piers Plowman* distinct from that exhibited in the corresponding parts of the **B** and **C** versions is accordingly established by possession of this substantial number of characteristic lines and passages, attested with remarkable uniformity in the seventeen manuscripts. This may now without begging the question be called the **A** version. It is exhibited without qualification in the manuscripts DVAM and without serious qualification in RUJ, which contain a whole or part of a Passus XII. The shape of the remaining manuscripts will now be considered in terms of the **A** version.

The manuscripts E and HL are copies of part of this version which break off in VII and VIII respectively. Except in length, these copies do not differ materially from the representatives of the **A** version already named, DVAM and RUJ, which contain IX to XI. E, H and L lack VIII to XI, or IX to XI, but within Prologue to VII or VIII they are, allowing for scribal error and sophistication, as unmistakably representatives of the **A** version as are DVAM or RUJ. Whether their shorter form is a palæographical accident or a literary event is not surely determinable, but the former seems more likely. All are defective at the end, so that one is denied possible guidance from explicits. A circumstance affecting conclusions about their original character is that the poem reaches an organic point of division at the end of VIII, a fact which was evident to scribes.[2] The essential evidence, however, is the general conformity of the text of these manuscripts as far as they go to the **A** version represented in DVAM and RUJ. It is close enough in the case of H and E to permit hypotheses about their genetic relation.[3] There are, then, indications that H, L and E are copies of the **A** version lacking IX to XI, and there is no evidence that they preserve a separate version of the poem.

Thus a form of *Piers Plowman* exists, characterized by content not

[1] See below, p. 126 and fn.

[2] See above, pp. 1, 2, 3, 7, 9, etc. It has been common knowledge in our time since Skeat (*A-Text*, pp. xxiv–xxvi), and became sensational only during the 'authorship controversy'.

[3] See below, p. 85.

found in the **B** or **C** versions, which is represented in the manuscripts DVAM, RUJ and HLE. As has been shown above this characteristic material occurs also in seven other manuscripts. But these differ from the ten just named in containing additional matter which corresponds to that found at approximately equivalent points in the **B** and **C** versions. It will now be shown that these seven manuscripts received this **B** or **C** material, and their present shapes, through scribal compilation, and that they are actually contaminated and augmented copies of the **A** version.

TChH² are the simplest of the mixed manuscripts in form. They present the **A** version to the end of XI with great fidelity, omitting very little characteristic material; thereafter they follow the **C** version. They have almost no characteristically **B** or **C** material before the end of XI; thereafter they present a **C** text in unmixed descent from the archetype of the **C** manuscripts.[1] The change of character in these manuscripts at the end of XI is sharp and clear. There are then two alternatives: that the portion of TChH² after XI is an author's continuation, following on from the **A** version represented in Prologue to XI of these manuscripts, made without touching this earlier part of the poem; and that the second portion of TChH² is from the **C** version and was combined with an **A** beginning by someone else than the author. That TChH² are compilations appears from two considerations. The first is literary: in these manuscripts the poem after **A** XI proceeds as from a different preparation than that found in **A** IX–XI, and the juncture at the end of **A** XI is mechanical, not organic.[2] The second is genetic: there is, as will be shown (below, pp. 85 ff.), evidence for treating TChH² as a close genetic group which, for **A** Prologue to XI, is in further genetic relation with RUD, manuscripts having the form Prologue–XII or Prologue–XI. It is thus probable that Prologue–XI of TChH² descend from the same exclusive common ancestor as three unmixed **A** manuscripts, and that a single act of compilation created their shapes.

H³ poses a curious rather than important problem. This manuscript begins as a copy of the **B** version. At some indeterminate point

[1] See above, p. 24, fn.

[2] So Skeat observed (*A-Text*, p. xix): 'Though the junction of the texts has been effected as well perhaps as it could have been effected, there are certain differences of arrangement of the subject-matter in texts A and C, which interfere with the continuousness of the story, so that patching becomes at once obvious upon comparison.'

between V 100 and 150 it becomes an **A** text, containing thenceforward almost all the distinctive **A** lines and very little material from **B** or **C**, until it ends with XI. It is not possible to do more than speculate about the reasons for the change of character in this manuscript.[1] For present purposes the important point is that the second part of H³ is a normal **A** text, showing no signs of authorial revision, and falling into a genetic group which includes manuscripts of other shapes.[2]

The manuscripts so far discussed are relatively simple cases because their **A** portions are largely free from material characteristic of the other versions. This is not true of W, N and K. The shapes of these three manuscripts have several broad common features. While in Prologue–XI (Prologue–VIII in the case of N) they read a very high proportion of the characteristic **A** lines and passages, all have long conclusions from the **C** version, that of N beginning after **A** VIII, those of W and K after **A** XI. Before the change of character all contain passages of various lengths resembling **B** or **C**. Nevertheless in Prologue–XI (W and K) and Prologue–VIII (N) these manuscripts belong to the **A** version; their shapes are the results of conflation and compilation.

In general the motives of conflation are a hard subject, and attempts to recover them may well appear too complex to be convincing, even though in actual fact, if knowledge of the circumstances of a case were available, the shape of a conflated manuscript might be very simply accounted for. But the fact of conflation is another matter, which can be established, since the officious copyist tended to leave signs of his activity in the character of the text produced by his conflation. Such signs are to be found in W and N and K, and they are happily unambiguous.

Before discussing them it must be stated that the conflation which produced Prologue–XI or Prologue–VIII in these manuscripts was clearly from the other versions into copies of the **A** version. This statement is based on the amount of material in a manuscript recognizably from one or another version. The attestation of distinctive **A** material in all the seventeen manuscripts has already been shown (above, pp. 21 ff.). The following list of the occurrences of distinctive

[1] The relation of H³'s earlier passus to **B** will be examined in the appropriate volume of this edition.

[2] See below, pp. 70, 75, etc.

B and **C** lines and passages will indicate, by the way, how infrequently such material actually occurs in Prologue–XI of W and K, and Prologue–VIII of N.

Prologue after 4 K adds **C** I 5
after 12 K adds **C** I 10–13
after 14 K adds **C** I 16
after 83 E adds a version of **B** Prol. 112 or **C** I 139
for 84–102 K reads **C** I 85–223
for 96–7 E reads **B** Prol. 92, 94, 98–99 or **C** I 90, 92–3, 126–7
I after 31 K adds **B** I 32 or **C** II 31; W adds **B** I 31α–33
after 111 N adds **C** II 112–22 and adjacent Latin lines
for 112 W reads **B** I 113–16
after 129 WN add **B** I 139 or **C** II 140 and Latin
after 132 WN add the Latin as after **C** II 144
after 139 N adds **C** II 147–8 and 150–61
after 150 H adds the Latin from **B** I 176 or **C** II 175
after 152 WN add the Latin from **B** I 176 or **C** II 175
after 161 WN add the Latin from **B** I 185 or **C** II 184
II after 20 WN add **C** III 28–9 and Latin
after 21 N adds **C** III 31–40 and Latin
after 45 W adds **B** II 59–63 or **C** III 60–4; N adds **B** II 59–65 or **C** III 60–6
after 56 WN add the Latin from **B** II 73 or **C** III 78
after 65 WN add **C** III 84–7, 89, 92, 98–100, 102–4
after 83 N adds **C** III 121–5, 127–36
for 131 WN read **C** III 185–8
after 194 WN add **C** III 243–8
III after 33 WN add **C** IV 32–3
after 45 K adds **B** III 52–4, 56–8 or **C** IV 56–8, 60–2
for 50–1 N reads **B** III 51–62 or **C** IV 55–66
after 75 N adds **C** IV 86–114
after 98 N adds **C** IV 134–6, 138, 140, 141–2, 143–5
after 141 WN add the Latin from **C** IV 189
IV after 17 EAWM add **B** IV 17–18 or **C** V 18–19
after 23 W adds **B** IV 25
after 28 W adds **B** IV 31–3
after 48 W adds **B** IV 62
after 105 W adds **B** IV 119–21
after 108 W adds **B** IV 123–5
after 133 W adds **B** IV 151
after 143 W adds **B** IV 152–6
after 145 W adds **B** IV 165–70
V after 31 JEAM add **B** V 32–3 or **C** VI 135–6
after 33 W adds **B** V 36–41
after 39 K adds **B** V 51–2 and 49–50; W adds **B** V 49–56

after 42 EKWM add **B** V 60 or **C** VI 201
after 68 W adds **B** V 87–93
after 99 W adds **B** V 120–1 or **C** VII 86–7
after 110 MH³ add **B** V 194–5 or **C** VII 201–2; E adds **B** V 194 or **C** VII 201
after 162 VHEANMH³ add **B** V 321 or **C** VII 367
for 164–5 A reads **B** V 324 or **C** VII 373
for 165 E reads **B** V 324 or **C** VII 373
after 165 VHNMH³ add **B** V 324 or **C** VII 373
after 188 EAMH³ add **B** V 347 or **C** VII 398
after 198 UEMH³ add **B** V 358–63 or **C** VII 409–14; A adds **B** V 358, 360–3 or **C** VII 409, 411–14
after 219 K adds **C** VII 423–VIII 62 (omitting some lines)
after 250 K adds **C** VIII 70–154 (omitting some lines)
VI for 18–94 K reads **C** VIII 175–260
after 81 EAMH³ add **B** V 601–2 or **C** VIII 240–1
after 109 K adds **C** VIII 276–7
after 123 K adds **C** VIII 292–306 (with additions)
(It might be possible to treat the whole of K's Passus VI as **C** text with conflation from **A**; here I have noted only the identifiable **C** portions.)
VII after 74 H³ adds the Latin from **B** XI 88 or **C** XIII 31, or **B** XII 91, or **B** XIV 290
VIII after 54 MH³ add the Latin from **B** VII 51
IX Henceforward N has a **C** character
X after 200 J adds **B** IX 175
XI after 152 H³ adds the Latin from **C** VI 58
after 229 H³ adds the Latin from **B** XIV 211 or **C** XII 203
after 313 TChH², K and W attach conclusions from the **C** version

This list of **B** and **C** material in the seventeen manuscripts will have shown that the amount is at all considerable only in W, N and K. K has the most, over 400 lines at thirteen points before the end of XI; N has about 150 lines at twenty-one points before the end of VIII; W has 95 lines at twenty-eight points before the end of XI.

WN

At twelve points in I–III W and N contain the same material distinctive of another version than **A**. A hypothesis of exclusive common ancestry for the earlier portions of these manuscripts is suggested by this circumstance. But W and N differ strikingly in shape. The following considerations apply: both manuscripts contain a majority of the characteristic **A** lines and passages; for part of their length they appear to be of exclusive common ancestry (see also below, pp. 77–8); each has **B**/**C** readings not present in the other; in Passus IX–XI they differ markedly in character. The simplest explanation of this situation is the likeliest: that these two manuscripts descend from an exclusive common ancestor which was a manuscript of the **A** version augmented from another version; and that intervening ancestors of W and N were subjected to further augmentation and compilation.

This explanation receives support from scrutiny of the additional **B** or **C** matter in the manuscripts, both that common to W and N, and that which is independently read. At a number of points the character of the text created by the presence of this additional matter shows clearly the effects of manipulation of an **A** copy by a scribe imperfectly familiar with the poem and ignorant of the purposes behind the revisions which he was conflating with their unrevised originals. The effects of his activities show themselves in the presence of both primitive and revised forms of the same passage; in inappropriate or misplaced augmentation; in broken syntax; and in broken or inferior sense.

For instance, after II 20 WN read lines like **C** III 28–9 and their Latin.[1] In WN these **C** lines follow a verse (**A** II 20) no longer present in **B** or **C**; in the revision it has been replaced by the point which **C** III 28–9 are intended to drive home. Without this purpose, in WN, these lines are in the air. They can have been inserted only in ignorance of the local differences of meaning between the versions.

After II 45 WN read lines like **C** III 60–4 or **B** II 59–63. These occur in the middle of a distinctive **A** passage, which at once suggests augmentation rather than revision. At the same time the additional passage reflects lines also present in the unrevised form: the *brocours of chaffare*, *Forgoers* and *vittlers* of the **B**/**C** passage are the *selleris* and *beggeris* of **A** II 44. Finally the additional passage interrupts the syntactical relation between **A** II 45 and 46. This is unskilful augmentation.

After II 65 WN read **C** III 84–7, 89, 92, 98–100, 102–4. The disjointed and inconsequential effect of this passage is striking, and shows a failure to grasp the content which must not be imputed to the author of the poem. It appears that when **C** III 84–104 were chosen for insertion certain lines in that passage were rejected because it was seen that lines corresponding to them occurred in the **A** copy

[1] Any points of textual interest in this and the other interpolated passages will be treated in the edition of the version from which they come.

before the point of insertion: **C** III 88, equivalent to **A** II 60; **C** III 91, to **A** II 63; and **C** III 93–7 because lechery and gluttony had been named in **A** II 61 and 64. The compiler failed to notice that **C** III 84 corresponded to **A** II 59 which he had already copied. The effect of the additional matter is to make the passage incoherent. **C** III 85–7, which in **C** have for climax the assignment of the earldom of Envy, fall flat in WN because that assignment has already been made at **A** II 60. **C** III 98–100 and 102–4 which are the **C** expansion of the idea contained in **A** II 66 grievously weaken **A** II 66 by preceding it, when as particularizations of its general statement they ought to follow.

For II 131 WN read **C** III 185–8. In **C** this passage follows from a protestation by Simony and Civil Law corresponding to that in **A** II 133 (**C** III 181). Since WN retain **A** II 133 unaltered, the substance of the protestation comes before the protestation. The augmenter, probably guided by 'notary' in **A** II 131 and **C** III 185, chose the wrong point for the insertion. Scribes in the W and N traditions tried to smooth the awkward break in the flow of sense, but in both manuscripts the noun clause of **A** II 132, originally governed by the ousted line 131, was troublesome.

After III 33 WN read **C** IV 32–3. In **C** these two lines follow the **C** equivalent of **A** III 29. As they stand in WN they are syntactically unrelated to the text before and after. This is misplaced augmentation.

The texts created in WN by the presence of **B**/**C** lines at the above points owe their character to ignorance of differences of meaning between the versions and imperfect acquaintance with their content, qualities not to be imputed to the author of the poem. The outward signs of these qualities are inappropriate or misplaced augmentation, inconsequence, and the presence of unrevised and revised forms of the same line(s) within a passage. These establish that the exclusive common ancestor of WN was subjected to clumsy scribal interpolation. That an author would use a manuscript so interpolated as a basis for revision is unlikely. But we need not rely on this unlikelihood to define the character of W and N. Both manuscripts contain further passages resembling the other versions, which bear similar traces of scribal activity. These will now be considered and it will appear that, being descended from a manuscript of the **A** version which contained a small number of **C** passages in I–III, more immediate ancestors of W and N independently received further augmentation.

W

In the case of W this shows itself in resemblances to **B** or **B**/**C** at sixteen points. Their extent is not great and they occur spasmodically, twice in I, nine times in IV and five times in V. Sufficient traces of scribal activity are to be discerned in a number.

After IV 28 W reads **B** IV 31–3. These lines come from a longer passage which is the revision of **A** IV 29–30; W nevertheless reads **A** IV 29–30.

After IV 133 W reads **B** IV 151, recognizable as a scribal insertion because it does not follow on from the unrevised **A** line before it. After IV 143 W reads **B** IV 152–6. Three of these lines contradict the statement of **A** IV 141–2, no longer present in **B** or **C** but retained by W. After IV 145 W reads **B** IV 165–70. But the additional matter should properly follow **A** IV 140. In W it interrupts the king's speech, of which the third line (**A** IV 146) is now meaningless, the reference of *herto to bringe it* (*herto it bringe* W) being lost. These three insertions clearly reveal failure to understand the purpose of the revision from **A** to **B** and the consequent difference between the two versions. At the end of IV **A** depicts an unqualified triumph over Wrong. Reason is supreme; Meed held to scorn for a light woman; Warren Wisdom and Witty are stunned and speechless. In the corresponding part of **B** there are shadows: Reason doubts the integrity of clerks, and rightly, since they serve the king's material advantage, and not his soul's welfare, while Meed still has charms for the lawyers. W has introduced some elements of the **B** situation, but ineptly, so that the passage as he reads it achieves neither effect clearly.

After V 99 W adds **B** V 120–1. This is the revised form of a longer **A** passage (V 69–72), not found in **B** and **C**, which W has, however, faithfully preserved.

These passages make it sufficiently clear that W's agreements with **B** are of scribal origin. This manuscript, it now appears, owes its character to a number of relatively slight augmentations made on at least two separate occasions in the course of its transmission, before it underwent the major one of receiving a **C** conclusion. Matter from **C** was first inserted into an **A** manuscript which was the exclusive common ancestor of WN. Matter from **B** was inserted into a copy intervening between this ancestor and the immediate original of W

Prologue–XI. The twice augmented **A** copy was finally given a **C** conclusion[1] by someone unacquainted with the difference between **A** XI and **C** XII. Except for the last process, however, none of the operations of conflation was extensive, and the prologue and first eleven passus of W remain substantially an **A** text, exhibiting nearly all the distinctive **A** lines, and genetically related to **A** manuscripts of other shapes.[2]

N

The independent resemblances of N to the **C** version likewise bear the marks of the conflating scribe.

After I 111 N adds **C** II 112–22. This additional material occurs in the midst of distinctive **A** lines. Its intrusive character is apparent on examination of the form of the passage in the two revisions. On such comparison **A** I 112–16 proves to be the original of **B** I 113–25, from which, in turn, **C** II 120–9 was developed. In N, although part of this product of revising **A** I 112–16 is present, the original, unrevised passage (**A** I 112 ff.) follows directly upon **C** II 122.

After I 139 N reads **C** II 147–8 and 150–61. This is an unskilful insertion. First the two groups of **C** lines are brought together by omission of **C** II 149 which, the compiler saw, corresponded to **A** I 137–8, already copied in N. But bringing the two passages together produced an incongruous mixture of images. Properly **C** II 147–8, as the equivalent of **A** I 135–6, should have followed **A** I 134, and **C** II 150 ff. come after **A** I 137a. The compiler's difficulty was in managing equivalent material or the same material in two forms; his mistake was retaining **A** I 136–7, which had been developed in **B** and **C** into a different figure. The result in N is confused and weak in meaning, with a distressing interruption of the definition begun in **A** I 139, and resumed at the end of N's interpolation.

After II 45, in addition to the **B**/**C** lines shared with W, N reads two more, **C** III 65–6 or **B** II 64–5, independently. Of these the first is the revised equivalent of **A** II 49 which N nevertheless copies in its correct place three lines after the insertion.

After II 83 N reads **C** III 121–5, 127–36. The augmenter omitted **C** III 126 because he saw its resemblance to **A** II 85, but he missed

[1] Genetically related to one of the families of surviving **C** manuscripts, the 'p' group.
[2] See below, pp. 85, 90, 95, etc.

other correspondences, with the result that material in both primitive and revised form occurs in N's text of this passage. The whole of **C** III 125b–136a is an expansion of **A** II 84 by insertion of matter between its half-lines. Nevertheless N retains **A** II 84. In the revised form the argument of **C** III 130–6 has replaced that of **A** II 87; N has both. **C** III 127 echoes **A** II 90; **C** III 129, **A** II 86. Both forms of these lines are present in N.

After III 98 N reads **C** IV 134–6, 138, 140–5. Presumably **C** IV 137 was omitted because of its resemblance to **A** III 96; in any event the inserted passage is treated as a unit. It is not a unit and resists treatment as one. **C** IV 134–6 ought to follow **A** III 95 and come before **A** III 96; **C** IV 138–45 ought to have replaced **A** III 97–8. As N's text stands, the retention of **A** III 97, equivalent to **C** IV 134, makes the passage contain three statements of forgiveness, one unnecessary to the king's relations with Meed in N's text; while **C** IV 138b–144, which in the revision replace the simple injunction of **A** III 98 by a threat, now follow soon after **A** III 98, with consequent weakening of effect. The source of the muddle is failure to understand the pattern of Meed's conduct as described by the king in terms of the whole passage.

The character of the text of N at these points, recording imperfect understanding of the material handled, together with the similar indications of the common WN insertions, and N's very faithful attestation of distinctive **A** lines and passages to the end of **A** VIII, direct us to regard Prologue–VIII of N as a copy of the **A** version with identifiable augmentations from **C** and **B**/**C**.

K

Of the three manuscripts under discussion K contains the largest number of lines resembling other versions, apart from its **C** conclusion which is genetically related to the 'i' group of **C** manuscripts. The shape of K is then markedly distinguished from that of the remaining manuscripts which contain the distinctive **A** lines. There is, however, in the character of the text formed by the presence of this additional material in K, striking and conclusive evidence that the shape of Prologue–XI of this manuscript is not authorial but scribal.

After I 31 K adds a line like **C** II 31 or **B** I 32. This has been crowded into the text between **A** I 31 and 32, which are normally spaced, in the hand of the main scribe. It is conceivable that he was simply making good an omission of his own from his main copy, but at least as possible that he was augmenting his text from another source.

After V 219 K reads a long passage which, except for a number of condensations, expansions, omissions and additions, resembles **C** VII 423–VIII 62. The form of this additional matter conclusively establishes the shape of K in Prologue–XI as scribal, confirming the suggestion of the physical evidence of augmentation after I 31.

This additional matter in K after **A** V 219 falls into four parts: Glutton's oral confession (**C** VII 423–37); Glutton's resolution of amendment (**C** VII 438–41); Sloth's appearance and confession (**C** VIII 1–55); Sloth's swoon and the admonition to repent (**C** VIII 56–62). Two of these parts correspond to passages in the **A** version: **C** VII 438–41 to **A** V 209–12; and **C** VIII 56–62 to **A** V 213–19. K's form of the passage records two mistakes by the augmenter: treatment of the additional matter (**C** VII 423–VIII 62) as a unit, and the choice of the wrong point of insertion for it. In consequence Glutton's resolution of amendment appears twice in K, both at **A** V 208–12 and as the **C** lines VII 437–41; and Sloth's swoon is present in two forms, first adapted to fit Glutton at **A** V 213–19 (*And than this gloton for sorowe fell down in a swowne*); and then describing Sloth at **C** VIII 56–62. *Vigilate* thus awakens two despairing sinners by the identical means and gives them the same counsel; Glutton, having confessed once, and made resolution of amendment, is never-theless overcome by Wanhope and must confess again, as well as make a second resolve to change his ways.

A passage where such lack of insight into the form and meaning of the poem is exhibited cannot be ascribed to the author. K's shape is then scribal, and the positive determinant of its character in Pro-logue–XI is its possession of the distinctive **A** lines; in this part it descends from an **A** manuscript. K Prologue–XI is an **A** text, conflated with **C** in Prologue and VI,[1] very slightly augmented from **C** in I and III, and more considerably so in Passus V.

[1] In Prologue the main copy was an **A** manuscript. In this section of the poem, when **A** and **C** have distinctive forms of lines, K with few exceptions follows the **A** version. Its agreements with **C** in the Prologue appear principally as augmentations. The opening of K's equivalent of **A** VI appears to be from the **A** copy; the first line may have a **C** reading, *wight none*, but at 6, 16 and 17 K follows the **A** version. Thereafter, however, it follows a **C** copy until some point between 95 and 100 when its readings again appear as predominantly **A** with augmentation from **C**. K's beginning and end of this passus are made like those of **A**, which differ from **C**.

The **B** or **C** lines in E, M, A, H^3, U, H, V and J (see above, pp. 30–1) need receive only brief notice since they do not seriously affect the shapes of the manuscripts. The often inferior quality of the text of these lines suggests that they were supplied from memory; their infrequency argues that they do not owe their presence in these manuscripts to systematic conflation. Occasional agreements, as of VH, or $EAMH^3$ in reading them, are poor indications of possible authenticity because they may well reflect genetic relations. The manuscripts where these lines occur are clearly copies of the **A** version, and their interpolations are unlikely to be the consequence of comparison of versions.

Such comparison, which must be assumed to account for the shapes of W, N and K in particular, was, nevertheless, a primary likelihood in the circumstances of composition of *Piers Plowman*. The poem was current in several forms, one markedly shorter than the others. Its content held the liveliest interest for readers, who would thus be jealous for the completeness of their copies. There is then a probability of comparison which implies another, that, after comparison, the shortest version would be augmented. The **A** version was multiplied both before the general currency of **B** and **C**, and, subsequently, by men unaware of the existence of these fuller versions or lacking access to them. The effects of comparison would be determined first by what was accessible to copyists, and second by the extent of their acquaintance with the content of the several versions, and their energy and leisure. There would, presumably, be a difference of attitude between professional copyists and amateurs of the poem who were making, or directing the making of copies for themselves. A mechanical combination like that of $TChH^2$ might well be a professional product; more minute or complicated additions or substitutions seem rather ascribable to enthusiasts. Comparisons involving the **A** manuscripts were evidently never systematic or complete.[1] Augmentation of these manuscripts is occasional in the early part of the poem, more general and frequent in Passus V which appears to have been a favourite, and practically ceases after Passus VI, when the poem becomes obscurer and the longer versions begin to differ markedly from **A** not

[1] A marginal entry in T illustrates their character. On folio 20*b*, in the right-hand margin at the end of Passus VII a sixteenth-century hand writes *here is lefte ovte v versis which is in the olde coppi ꝥ ar set be nethe*; at the foot of the page the same hand has copied **B** VI 328–32. The difference was noticed because of its prominent position.

merely in the quantity of statement on any topic but also in the tendency of meaning. After Passus VI the problem of harmonizing was evidently found too difficult.

Further confirmation that the shapes of certain **A** manuscripts are scribal modifications of a single version is to be found in the genetic relation of these manuscripts, discussed in the following section. I have not advanced this as a primary argument because of the qualified nature of my findings about **A** manuscript genealogy. Nevertheless it deserves some attention, since the available genetic information, however limited, has a bearing on the question of shapes.

Among the variational groups formed by the **A** manuscripts the following seem to be genetic:

(VH): well established
(WN): well established in the earlier part of the poem
(EAWMH^3): containing E up to VII, H^3 from Passus V onwards, and W after the end of its relation to N, that is, after a change of exemplars; this group is not susceptible of further definition because of conflation and coincident variation
{⟨[(TH^2)Ch]D⟩RU}: well established.

These genetic classifications do not conform to the arrangement of manuscripts by their shapes. Each of the two genetic pairs consists of manuscripts of different shapes; the large group {⟨[(TH^2)Ch]D⟩RU} contains manuscripts of three shapes; and the indeterminate but well-attested group (EAWMH^3) contains manuscripts of four shapes. More precisely, the likelihood of H representing an authorial shape is minimized by its genetic relation with V; the earlier evidence for the scribal origin of the shapes of both W and N is confirmed; the composite character of TChH^2 is affirmed by the genetic relation of their earlier portions with manuscripts of other shapes; the necessity of positing only one operation to produce the shapes of TChH^2 is shown; and E and H^3 are made to appear not as distinct, authorial versions of the poem, but as variously imperfect descendants of the manuscript that also produced M, which is of the standard **A** shape.

This evidence has little or much force depending on acceptance of the above groups as genetic. As the following section will show, my conclusions about the family history of the **A** manuscripts have had mainly negative force. Therefore it seems to me wrong to treat as primary evidence the bearing of the few positive results on the question of the shapes of the **A** manuscripts and their authenticity. In my view the **A** version is satisfactorily defined without recourse to evidence from genetic relation. Nevertheless the confirmation afforded by this evidence is obviously not unwelcome.

There are, finally, physical features in several manuscripts, which have a bearing on the question of versions.

The three shortest manuscripts, E ending in VII, and H and L ending in VIII, are imperfect at the end. There is no indication in any of these that its form before loss or mutilation was necessarily short. No perfect specimen of a form of the poem ending with VIII has survived; the suggestion that there was such a form arises only out of the circumstance that there is an organic division of the poem after VIII. If this were not so, E, H and L would simply be accounted imperfect manuscripts of **A**. And so they should be considered: the existence of the structural division at the end of VIII is, after all, known only because it can be observed in manuscripts of the longer form, which continue with IX–XI. Its significance with respect to the forms of E, H and L must primarily be that it would encourage separation of an unbound copy after VIII for purposes of reading or lending, or even cessation of copying from a longer exemplar at the end of VIII.

The present form of H allows the possibility that H originally contained IX–XI. A reconstruction of the collation of E, whereby it would contain VIII–XI and the missing portion of its next item, seems encouraged by the evidence. That the reconstructed collation of L reveals an original uniform composition of quires of six encourages the inference that four leaves at its end are survivors of a last quire also of six, which could have accommodated IX–XI. The heavily damaged beginning of L further suggests that any loss at its end was serious. In the case of E and H genealogical considerations should probably be decisive: both manuscripts seem to belong in genetic groups descended from ancestors in the **A** version containing IX–XI.

T, Ch and H² show their composite nature by disturbance of the divisions of the poem at and after the point of juncture with the **C** version, a sign, I think, of preoccupation or uncertainty in their compilers. All make the normal divisions of the **A** version up to XI, their last **A** passus. Then confusion sets in because the numbering of divisions in the earlier part of **C** has not corresponded (equivalent matter for matter) to that of **A**, and because the endings of **A** XI and its equivalent **C** XII are dissimilar. (After **C** XII 296, corresponding to the last line of **A** XI, **C** continues this passus for nearly 20 lines.) The simple effect of this condition is seen in T, which heads these last few lines of **C** XII *Passus tercius de dowel*, and makes a fresh division, *Passus secundus de dobet*, after the end of **C** XII. The *dobet*, which is wrong, is a further sign of the compiler's anxiety, as is also probably the absence of an incipit at the beginning of **C** XIV. Ch likewise dignifies the last few lines of **C** XII by an incipit, *Passus tercius de Dowel*. In this manuscript the absurdity of starting a new division less than 20 lines later is avoided by denying **C** XIII an incipit. But thereafter confusion follows: the compiler also omits to give an incipit to **C** XIV; then he calls **C** XV *Passus quartus de dowel*, so that his subsequent titles are out. The juncture in H² has apparently a relation to the collation of this manuscript. The quires in this copy are generally sixes, but that on which **A** XI ends two lines short of the end of a leaf is a two (as if the amount of paper needed to accommodate **A** has been estimated) and the next quire is a four (as if it were the rest of a quire originally made up of six folds). Here too the divisions are confused. Before **C** XII 297, which follows the end of **A**, is the incipit *Passus tercius de dowel*, and there is no incipit at the beginning of **C** XIII. A very early marginal note drawing attention to this deficiency very significantly reads *primus passus deficit hic*, where *primus* means the first of the recognized additional matter.

The case of W is plain: in this manuscript **A** XI is followed directly by **C** XIII, with a space for the incipit, and a rubricator's guide, *passus iiij de dowel*. The **C** lines following *breuis oracio penetrat celum*, which complete **C** XII, are not copied. No studied combination of W's earlier and later portions would have omitted this matter essential to the narrative. It is wanting in W because the juncture between the two parts of W or an ancestor was mechanically made by someone aware that **C** XII corresponded to **A** XI but unaware that **C** XII had developed the account considerably beyond the point where it broke off in **A**. The attempt to adjust the numbering of divisions is also crude: a preposterous incipit, *Tercius passus de dowel*, is inserted before **A** XI 167.

Finally there is K. A suggestion of its composite character appears early in this manuscript: in Passus I a verse from **B** or **C**, in the main hand, is squeezed between two **A** lines which are normally spaced (above, pp. 36–7). But the clearest physical evidence that K's shape is composite, and its combination of **A** and **C** material artificial, is afforded by the condition of the text at XI 313 (fol. 56*b*), to which notice was drawn long ago by Skeat.[1] Here Fortescue originally wrote *without penaunce at her partyng into hye blisse amen / Finis de dowell.* Subsequently he cancelled *amen* by drawing several heavy lines through it, and partly rubbed out *Finis de dowell.* Despite show-through, increased by the thinning of the paper where the erasure was made, *Finis* can still be read by ultraviolet light, and *de dowell* by natural light. *amen* alone would have had the value of an explicit here, since nothing in **A** XI 313 itself calls for the pious response. The additional *Finis de dowell* (compare *finis* at the ends of other divisions of K and *finis totaliter* at the end of the poem) puts it beyond doubt that in K a division of the poem once ended with **A** XI 313. That is a characteristic of the **A** version but not of **C**. When, sooner or later, Fortescue decided to continue with copying the **C** supplement, he had to remove the indications of this division before writing **C** XII 297, which follows as the next line.

The definition of the **A** version is now complete and may be summed up. Among the more than fifty manuscripts preserving the work called *Piers Plowman* two distinct versions are handsomely attested by substantial numbers of copies of uniform shape. The remaining manuscripts have various shapes, but seventeen of them are distinguished by the common possession of some 400 lines not found in the other two versions. These distinctive lines are confined to the first twelve sections of the poem, that is **A** Prologue to XI. Those twelve sections are represented in four manuscripts, DVAM; they are represented in three more which contain as well the whole or part of a thirteenth section (**A** XII), namely RUJ. They are represented partially in three manuscripts, E, H and L, which break off in the eighth or ninth section shortly before a natural point of division in the poem, but otherwise conform to this third version, which is then established on the attestation of ten manuscripts, DVAM, RUJ, and HLE. The question is next whether the seven other manuscripts possessing the distinctive lines and passages belong to this

[1] *A-Text*, p. xxiv.

version. These seven manuscripts exhibit four shapes. Of these shapes one (TChH²) conforms without qualification to the **A** version up to the end of its twelfth division; and thereafter conforms, again without qualification, to the **C** version. From the point of view of content and meaning this combination is forced and inorganic. Therefore it is concluded that the shape of TChH² is not authorial, and represents a scribal combination of two versions. A similar argument applies in the case of H³. The remaining manuscripts, W, N and K, while conforming handsomely to the **A** version by possession of its distinctive lines, differ from it in containing additional matter characteristic of **B** or **C**. Nevertheless the presence of this matter in them often creates a text of a kind not to be ascribed to the author, but likely to be produced by a compiler. These positive and negative arguments together require the conclusion that the first nine sections of N and the first twelve sections of W[1] and K belong to the **A** version, having suffered augmentation by scribal editors. As to the **C** conclusions, in the case of W and K again these create a text for the whole manuscript with a violent breach of meaning and content. As with TChH² their latter portions follow on, not from **A** XI which precedes them, but from a highly revised form of this part of the poem. For these various reasons the portions of W, N and K which contain the distinctive **A** lines and passages are to be identified as copies of the **A** version augmented from **B** or **C**, to which the latter part of the **C** version has been added. Genetic groupings identifiable among the **A** manuscripts support the conclusion that the authorial **A** version consisted of a prologue and eleven passus containing the distinctive lines identified above, from which all of the seventeen manuscripts are descended whatever their shape. Certain manuscripts, finally, exhibit physical signs that they owe their present shape to an artificial juncture of texts.

This definition may at first sight seem to require explanations of an unduly complicated and speculative character. That is not a valid consideration for several reasons. To reject an explanation because it is complicated would suggest the improbability of complicated situations in the history of texts, which is manifestly false. But the complexity of such explanations may well be merely apparent. The major conflation in these manuscripts is, I believe, mainly a record of the availability of copies at various times and places. It seems to me very

[1] Ignoring W's misdivision noticed on p. 41 above.

probable that if we could recover the circumstances in which the compilations occurred the explanations would appear essentially simple. But, whether complicated or not, to account for the shapes of some **A** manuscripts by conflation and compilation is in fact the simplest explanation of their origin. Readers to whom its relative simplicity is not apparent are recommended to consider the assumptions which would be required by any hypothesis that the shape of W, or N, or K, for instance, is other than of scribal origin.

In connexion with the problem of manuscript shapes one consideration remains: that of the manuscripts which differ from other **A** copies by including individual material not directly or closely resembling the corresponding parts of the **B** or **C** version. Passus XII, as represented in R, J and U, will be the best known of such material; the additional lines in H, many of which Skeat printed, will also be familiar. All such lines and passages except Passus XII are now here printed, after a list of their occurrences. Passus XII, as of a somewhat different character, appears elsewhere (below, pp. 427 ff.).

Prologue after 54 R adds 2 lines; E adds 4 lines (2 agreeing with R); H² adds 2 lines
I after 28 H one line
after 49 H one Latin line
after 58 L one line
after 82 L one line
after 161 H one line
after 175 H 2 lines
II for 12–13 (moved to another point) H 2 lines
after 30 H one line
after 32 H one line
after 36 L one line
after 44 H² one line; W one line
after 45 H one line (cp. H² II 44)
after 75 H² one line; H one line
after 76 E 4 lines
between 91 and 92 (transposed) H one line
after 112 H one line
after 129 H 4 lines
after 130 H 3 lines
after 168 H one line; H² 2 lines (one agreeing with H)
after 172 A one line
after 190 H² one line; L one line
after 192 L one line
after 194 H 3 lines (one a form of 187); L 3 lines
III after 18 H 2 lines
after 29 A one line (cp. III 192)
after 32 L one line
after 49 M one line
after 64α H one line
after 89 H 4 lines
after 92 H² one line; H one line
after 228 H one line
IV after 134 E 2 lines
V after 28 A 2 lines
after 31 L 2 lines
after 41 H one line
after 55 H² 4 lines
after 92 RU one line
after 105 A one line
after 156 A one line; L 2 lines
after 179 H one line

after 196 N one line
after 204 L one line
after 205 L 2 lines
VI before 1 H 2 lines
after 2 H one line
VII after 25 L one line
after 77 H^3 one line
after 148 A one line
after 150 M one line
after 224 H one Latin line
after 227 H a Latin tag
after 230 H^3 one Latin line
after 282 V one line
VIII after 45 H one line (cp. VIII 60)
after 54 HW one Latin line
after 125 H 2 lines
IX after 47 M one line
X after 13 J 2 lines
after 22 J one line
after 85 J one line
XI after 101 J one line
after 192α H^3 2 lines
after 257 H^3 a Latin tag
after 311 H^3 4 lines
after 313 M 6 lines; R a twelfth passus; J a fragment of a twelfth passus; U a fragment of a twelfth passus.

H

after I 28
For luste of lykerousnes his lycam to plese

after I 49
Reddite ergo que sunt cesaris cesari et que sunt dei deo

after I 161
þat is to sokoure þe sorowful ⁊ haue charite to alle

after I 175
ȝoure grace ⁊ ȝoure good happe ȝoure welþe for to wynne
⁊ þerwiþ knoweþ me kyndely of þat I ȝou sende

for II 12–13
of reed gold so ryche redilyche Idyȝte
wiþ precyouse stoones so stoute stondynge þer ynne

after II 30
lerne his lawe þat is so lele ⁊ siþþe teche it furþer

after II 32
When heo was me fro I loked ⁊ byhelde

after II 45
⁊ for þe flaterynge freeris alle þe foure orders
(*compare* H^2 *after* II 44)

after II 75
taberes ⁊ tomblers ⁊ tapesters fele
(*compare* H^2)

between transposed II 91 *and* 92
at oo ȝeris ende whan ȝe reken schul

after II 112
For where falsenes is oft fownden þere feiþ fayleþ

after II 129
for falsenes aȝeyn þe feiþ sisoures he defouleþ
þoruȝ comburance of coueytyse clymben aȝeyn truþe

þat þe feiþ is defouled & falsly defamed
& falsnes is a lord Iwoxe & lyueþ as hym lykeþ

after II 130
for feire speche þat is feiþles is falsnes broþ*er*
& þus sysoures ben sompned þe false to serue
& feir*e* speche fauel þat moche folke desceyueth

after II 168
I bydde þee awayte hem wele let non of hem ascape
(*compare* H²)

after II 194
Spicers aspieden hi*m* & speken wiþ hi*m* feyre
& pr*e*yeden him p*ri*uely to putte forþ her ware
& he asured hem forsoþe to serue hem for euer

after III 18
þat þou schalt haue boþe myȝt & maystrye & make what þe likeþ
wiþ þe kynge & þe comyns & þe courte boþe

after III 64α
Here forsoþe þei fongon her mede forþwiþ

after III 89
Now beoþ ȝe war if ȝe wole ȝe mayst*ur*s of þe lawe
for þe soþe schale be souȝte of ȝoure soules so me god helpe
þe suffraunce þat ȝe suffre suche wrong*us* to be wrouȝt
while þe chaunce is in ȝour*e* choyse cheose ȝe þe best

after III 92
wiþ myrþe & wiþ mynstrasye þei pleseden hir ychoone

after III 228
þat here riȝthond is hepid ful of ȝeftis

after V 41
& bringe ȝow to þat ilke blisse þat e:::::::stende

after V 179
for he shulde p*re*ise þe penyworþes as hym good þouȝt

before VI 1
Now riden þis folk & walken on fote
to seche þat seint in selcouþe londis

after VI 2
for while þei wente her*e* owe*n* wille þei wente alle amys

after VII 224
Auferte ab illo mnam & date illi

after VII 227
Omni habenti dabitur

after VIII 45
To mote for mene me*n* but ȝif þei hadde money

after VIII 54
Qui facit hec non mouebitur in eternum
(*compare* W)

after VIII 125
slynge awey þese scorners he seiþ wiþ her*e* shrewid fliting
for wiþ hem redely y kepe not to rest

L

after I 58
Heo saide segge sikerly þeo soþe for to say
after I 82
þan þat louely lady wiþ laghynge chere
after II 36
To ȝeue al his lordschipes with londes & leodes
after II 190
And when he had dwelled wiþ heom on half ȝere
after II 192
Maden on heore maner him in abyt as afrere
after II 194
For as longe as he lyues he is w*ith* heom bylefte
with fees of flatery þ*at* faile wol heom neuer
For kyng no for knyght corouned vndur heouen
after III 32
Of chirches of chapels chese of þe beste
after V 31
For hit passed apound þe pletes weore so monye
And his hood hyghely yholde hit worth a grote
after V 156
& þou kepest bote þe coos of aknyues haft tofore þe:::::
For I wot in my wit what þy wombe wilneth
after V 204
þan his wif at his word wratthede sore
after V 205
And for to leden suche lif þat leosed wel monye
And made heom haue heore home in helle for euer
after VII 25
how y schal my lif lede & libbe þer after

H[2]

after Prologue 54
who so ȝeueth for godes loue wyl nat ȝeue his þankis
But þ*ere* his mede may be most and most m*er*ytorye (*compare* **C** X 66–8)
after II 44
And for flat*er*yng freres alle four*e* orderys
(*compare* H *after* II 45)
after II 75
Taylo*ur*s tapsters and tau*er*ners many
(*compare* H)

after II 168
Sette him on þe pelorye for any preioure I bidde
wayte hym wel late hym not ascape
(*compare* H)
after II 190
To ben of here consel whan þei cayren aboute
after III 92
In to þe priuyest place þe prince hadde euere
after V 55
And chastite to seke as a chyld clene
The lust of his likam to leten for euere
And fle fro felyschipe there foly may a rise
For that makith many man mysdo ful ofte

A

after II 172
And crep in a cope & held hym þer Inne
after III 29
The lest brolle of here blod a baronys pere
(*compare* **A** III 192)
after V 28
And bynde hem to gedur schrewys to techyn
willyam he wysid wollis to wynde
after V 105
Also wilsum in hert & pensyue in hert & thouth
after V 156
Ha ha quot gloton gowe in and drynk
after VII 148
And bid hem go werchyn what he best likith

H³

after VII 77
And In þe name of our lord myn testament make
after VII 230
Quod videtur habere auferetur ab eo et dabitur ei qui decem &c
after XI 192α
And ȝyff þin frend be sory be þou þe same
And wyt hem þat be mery loke þou mery make
after XI 257
Reddam unicuique iuxta opera sua (unicuique *one extra minim*)
after XI 311
For þei leuyn as þei be leryd & oþer wyse nouth
Musyn in no materes but holdyn þe ryth beleue
He þat redyth þis book & ryth haue it in mende
Preyit for pers þe plowmans soule

M

after III 49

woldyst þou helpyn þ*er*to a pound or tweyne

after VII 150

To werchen & to wynnen his his lyfelode with swynke

after IX 47

To wisse & to wise þe þe þy v wittis had he g*ra*untid

after XI 313

For þey I rede alle men þat on crist be leuyn
Asken m*er*cy of god for her*e* misdedes
And coueiten no*n* clergie ne catel on þis erþe
But alwey to s*er*uen god & hendy*n* in hise werkys
And þat he g*ra*unte vs þe Ioie þ*at* euer*e* schal lastyn
wit*h* pers þe plowma*n* to wonyn in his blysse Amen Amen

J

after X 13

Dobest is in hir*e* bowre & boldyth þat leuedy
and berith a batte on his honde lyche a byschoppys mace

after X 22

as dobest & dobet & dowele acordyn

after X 85

and also ȝerde to take ȝeme is ȝouy*n* to done bet

after XI 101

As long as I lyffe bothin late & rathe

after XI 313

(see below, pp. 427 ff.)

E

after Prologue 54

P*er*sons with þair p*ro*curases p*er*mutyn þair chirches
With al þe besynes of þair body þe bett*er* to haue
Vicars on fele halue fandyn þaim to Done
Leders þai ben of lovedays & with þe lawe mellyth
(*compare* R)

after II 76

Sym þe semer out of sumud (? *for* sumu*ur*) sete
And haukyn þe hunter of hold*er*nes
And hudde þe hulour of holand aswa
Milners & michers for þai er all fals

after IV 134

Þ*er* is no euyll vnpunyshyd of owr lord
Ne na ded þ*at* is wele done bott dowele shal it qwyte

R

after Prologue 54

on fele halue fonden hem to done

lederes þei be of louedays and *with* þe lawe medle

(*compare* E)

after V 92

and al þe wele þat he haþ greueþ me wel sore

(*compare* U)

after XI 313

(see below, pp. 427 ff.)

W

after II 44

For beggers for borwers & for many oþer

after VIII 54

Qui facit hec non mouebitur in eternum

(*compare* H)

U

after V 92

and al þe wele þat he haþ greueth me wol sore

(*compare* R)

after XI 313

(see below, pp. 427 ff.)

V

after VII 282

From þat tyme þat þulke weore eten take he schulde his leue

N

after V 196

& made endentures of þe brode worlde

The absence of manuscript support for all these lines is in itself sufficient ground for denying them admission to the text. It will have been seen how seldom any is attested by more than one copy. Only the following agreements occur: RE after Prologue 54; H²H after II 44 and 45; II 75; and II 168; RU after V 92; HW after VIII 54. The RE agreement is partial only and explicable in terms of genetic relation between these manuscripts or ancestors; in any case it could scarcely argue authenticity. The three H²H concords are curious rather than weighty. That of RU is to be referred to the common origin of these manuscripts; that of HW probably reflects no more than independent insertions of an appropriate quotation.

A second important consideration against the authenticity of such lines generally, and a demonstration of scribal meddling, is afforded by the manuscripts H and L. There the intrusive lines are most numerous, and there also scribal alteration of an unmistakable character in authentic lines is very often apparent. The two phenomena are clearly related, and the possibility of scribal 'improvement' of copy strongly established. There is thus a strong presumption of the spurious character of such poorly attested lines generally. In addition their literary quality is of a kind to make their authenticity improbable: they are often unmetrical, sometimes ungrammatical, often clumsy. To argue the genuineness of any of them would require several difficult demonstrations: the undisputed excellence and purity of transmission of the manuscript concerned; the reasons for the omission in all the remaining copies; and the evident necessity and appropriateness of the line in question.

Indeed the only important material of this kind, and the only difficult case, is 'Passus XII', attested in R and imperfectly in U and J. Some of this 'Passus', written as by another person (106–17) is evidently spurious; more (99–105), describing the death of the Dreamer-Narrator in the third person, should probably also be rejected out of hand. What remains after those subtractions (1–98) does follow on after a fashion from **A** XI and, although its general character makes this seem unlikely, may be wholly or partly authentic, representing wholly or partly an imperfect or abortive continuation of the poem by the author.

The most serious doubts about its authenticity are raised by its poor manuscript support. Knott and Fowler argue,[1] rightly in my opinion, that it was probably not in the archetype of the extant manuscripts. They add the caution, however, that the imperfect ending of the manuscript V and the concealment of the original form of the ending of TChH²KWN by the various **C** additions obscure the evidence and stand in the way of a firm conclusion. Another interpretation of the state of TChH²KWN would be that the possession of a **C** conclusion is evidence for the original absence of a Passus XII from these manuscripts because, with a Passus XII, they would have been less likely to attract augmentation at the end. It seems as if textual evidence

[1] Thomas A. Knott and David C. Fowler, *Piers the Plowman: A Critical Edition of the A-Version*, Baltimore, 1952, pp. 148–9.

by itself is insufficient to close this question, or to exclude, for the present, the possibility that some at least of Passus XII is authentic.

The literary examination of this Passus must be reserved for another occasion. 'Passus XII' must in any case make an appearance somewhere in an edition of the **A** version of *Piers Plowman*, if only as a manuscript variant. Because the possibility of its authenticity has not yet been confirmed or dismissed it is printed in this edition, as by Knott-Fowler, after the end of XI, its dubious character being indicated by describing it as an appendix. Since, for some of its length it exists in several manuscripts containing enough variants to suggest how the text of R should be corrected, it has been edited as far as the limited evidence permits.

III

CLASSIFICATION OF THE MANUSCRIPTS

If, as has been argued, the seventeen manuscripts under discussion represent one version of this poem they are ultimately descended from a single archetypal ancestor. It has generally been assumed[1] that editing the **A** version would take the form of recovering this archetypal ancestor's readings by recension, that is, the systematic application of knowledge about the genetic history of the manuscripts to the rejection of unoriginal readings.[2] Recension is, however, no longer an unquestioned method. Concern has rightly fixed on its practicability, in view of the frequent difficulty or impossibility of recovering with any precision the genetic history of manuscripts. The literature of textual criticism in the last generation records the attempts to control the subjective factor in this process.[3] A French school of editors appears

[1] Thomas A. Knott, 'An Essay toward the Critical Text of the A-Version of "Piers the Plowman"', *MP*, xii (1915), pp. 389–421; R. W. Chambers and J. H. G. Grattan, 'The Text of "Piers Plowman"', *MLR*, iv (1909), pp. 357–89; 'The Text of "Piers Plowman": Critical Methods', *MLR*, xi (1916), pp. 257–75; 'The Text of "Piers Plowman"', *MLR*, xxvi (1931), pp. 1–51; R. W. Chambers, 'The Original Form of the A-Text of "Piers Plowman"', *MLR*, vi (1911), pp. 302–23; 'The Three Texts of "Piers Plowman", and their Grammatical Forms', *MLR*, xiv (1919), pp. 129–51; J. H. G. Grattan, 'The Text of "Piers Plowman": A Newly Discovered Manuscript and its Affinities', *MLR*, xlii (1947), pp. 1–8; David C. Fowler, *A Critical Text of Piers Plowman A-2*, unpublished University of Chicago dissertation (1949); 'Contamination in Manuscripts of the A-Text of "Piers the Plowman"', *PMLA*, lxvi (1951), pp. 495–504; Thomas A. Knott and David C. Fowler, *Piers the Plowman: A Critical Edition of the A-Version*, Baltimore, 1952, pp. 20–8.

[2] There is a concise account of the process by Paul Maas, 'Text-kritik', in *Einleitung in die Altertumswissenschaft*, ed. A. Gercke and E. Norden, 3rd edn., Berlin, 1927, i §2, pp. 1–18. The outstanding recent illustration is found in Sir Walter Greg's edition, *Jonson's Masque of Gipsies in the Burley, Belvoir, and Windsor Versions: An Attempt at Reconstruction*, London, 1952, p. 69.

[3] I do not know of a satisfactory bibliography of textual criticism. For my own part I have found the following works profitable reading (and would take this opportunity of stating my obligation to them all):

Bédier, J., *La Tradition Manuscrite du Lai de L'Ombre. Réflexions sur L'Art d'Éditer les Anciens Textes*, Paris, 1929.
Chaytor, H. J., *From Script to Print*, Cambridge, 1950.
Collomp, P., *La Critique des Textes*, Paris, 1931.
Fourquet, J., 'Fautes Communes ou Innovations Communes?', *Romania*, lxx (1948–9), pp. 85–95.
— *Le Paradoxe de Bédier*, (Publications de la Faculté des Lettres de l'Université de Strasbourg fasc. 105), Paris, 1946.
Grattan, J. H. G., 'The Text of *Piers Plowman:* Critical Lucubrations with Special Reference to the Independent Substitution of Similars', *SP*, xliv (1947), pp. 593–604.
Greg, Sir W. W., *Jonson's Masque of Gipsies in the Burley, Belvoir, and Windsor Versions: An Attempt at Reconstruction*, London, 1952.

to have made a sweeping rejection of recension;[1] even Sir Walter Greg, whose *Calculus of Variants* will not be lightly set aside, observes in the Preface to that book how he has been 'unable to avoid the question altogether' whether the 'central problem of textual criticism', the construction of a genealogy, is 'completely soluble'.[2] It is, then, impossible to accept earlier conclusions about the genealogy of the manuscripts of the **A** version without further scrutiny.

There is in print a genealogy of these manuscripts which has never been substantially questioned, and was recently used, as it appears, to construct a 'critical' text of the **A** version.[3] This is not to be rejected on theoretical grounds, or grounds of present fashions in textual criticism; it must be tested by fresh examination of the evidence. But as one faces this examination the problem ceases to be simple: the test of the published genealogy must be an attempt to make a genealogy without reference to the one already in existence. That raises the vexed question what kind of evidence is to be employed in the process. Nor can simple conclusions be necessarily expected. Knott's genealogy

Greg, Sir W. W., Review of E. Vinaver, 'Principles of Textual Emendation' (q.v.) in *The Library*, fourth series, xx (1939–40), pp. 426–9.
— *The Calculus of Variants: An Essay on Textual Criticism*, Oxford, 1927.
— 'The Rationale of Copy-Text', *Studies in Bibliography*, iii (1950–1), pp. 19–36.
Griesbach, J. J., *Novvm Testamentvm Graece*, i, 2nd edn., London, 1796.
Housman, A. E., *D. Ivnii Ivvenalis Satvrae*, London, 1905.
Kantorowicz, H., *Einführung in die Textkritik*, Leipzig, 1921.
Maas, P., 'Textkritik', in *Einleitung in die Altertumswissenschaft*, ed. A. Gercke and E. Norden, 3rd edn., Berlin, 1927, i, §2, pp. 1–18. (English trans. by B. Flower, *Textual Criticism*, Oxford, 1958.)
Manly, J. M. and E. Rickert, *The Text of the Canterbury Tales*, ii, *Classification of the Manuscripts*, Chicago, 1940.
McKerrow, R. B., *Prolegomena for the Oxford Shakespeare: A Study in Editorial Method*, Oxford, 1939.
Moore, E., *Contributions to the Textual Criticism of the Divina Commedia*, Cambridge, 1889.
Pasquali, G., Review of P. Collomp, *La Critique des Textes* in *Gnomon*, viii (1932), pp. 127–34.
— *Storia della Tradizione e Critica del Testo*, Florence, 1934 and 1952.
Quentin, Dom H., *Essais de Critique Textuelle*, Paris, 1926.
Sisam, K., *Studies in the History of Old English Literature*, Oxford, 1953.
Vinaver, E., 'Principles of Textual Emendation', in *Studies in French Language and Mediæval Literature Presented to Professor Mildred K. Pope*, Manchester, 1939.
Westcott, B. F. and F. J. A. Hort, *The New Testament in the Original Greek*, Cambridge and London, 1881.

[1] Vinaver, in 'Principles of Textual Emendation' (p. 351) observes: 'Recent studies in textual criticism mark the end of an age-long tradition. The ingenious technique of editing evolved by the great masters of the nineteenth century has become as obsolete as Newton's physics, and the work of generations of critics has lost a good deal of its value. It is no longer possible to classify manuscripts on the basis of "common errors"; genealogical "stemmata" have fallen into discredit, and with them has vanished our faith in composite critical texts. . . . Nothing has done more to raise textual criticism to the position of a science than the realisation of the inadequacy of the old methods of editing.'

[2] p. v.

[3] Thomas A. Knott, *MP*, xii, pp. 389–421. The edition is Knott and Fowler's *Piers the Plowman*. See its introduction, pp. 26–8.

might be sustained; or it might be shown to be partly right; or it might be supplanted; or the evidence might resist interpretation, and the genetic history of these manuscripts be denied to us.

The present section is the result of attempts to discover whether a genealogy of these manuscripts useful for recension could be recovered, and to test the authority of the one hitherto proclaimed. The conclusions are firm, and seem to me beyond doubt: first, that convergent variation (whether correction or coincident error) has so obscured the evidence by which common descent might be ascertained that no clear or unquestioned genealogical picture takes shape; second, that any 'family tree' of these manuscripts, or any description of their agreements in variation less detailed than a line-by-line account is grossly oversimplified and useless for purposes of recension; and last that while some genetic groups, in the main those of Knott, can be detected, there is no clear evidence to indicate their ultimate relationship and thus to form a stemma, previous 'demonstrations' of such relationship having been achieved entirely by *petitio principii.*

These conclusions are hard-won. It was quickly apparent to me that, in terms of Knott's genealogy, much convergent variation had taken place in the tradition of the **A** manuscripts, and that random groupings were extremely numerous. The experience of other editors made it seem likely that in these circumstances it would be very difficult, if not impossible, to determine, to any useful degree of accuracy, the genetic history of the **A** manuscripts.[1] Moreover, there was no longer any question of simply using the older, traditional method of classification. Yet an attempt had to be made, since there was no way of

[1] Housman, *Juvenal*, p. xxiv: 'Authors like Juvenal, read and copied and quoted both in antiquity and in the middle ages, have no strictly separated families of MSS. Lections are bandied to and fro from one copy to another, and all the streams of tradition are united by canals'; Moore, *Contributions*, p. xliii, expresses a similar view. Kantorowicz, *Einführung*, pp. 45–6: 'Überall wo wir . . . Übereinstimmung zwischen Hss. verschiedener Gruppen feststellen und hieraus auf die Lesart der gemeinsamen Stammschrift, namentlich der Urschrift selber, und die Unechtheit abweichender Lesarten schliessen, kann die Verschiedenheit der Gruppen blosser Schein gewesen sein und die Übereinstimmung der Lesarten einfach auf der gemeinsamen Abhängigkeit von irgend einem Stammvater einer der Hss. beruhen. . . . Auch kann man in diesen Fällen nicht mehr von einem bestimmten Verwandtschaftsgrade und von einander unabhängig gegenüberstehenden Abschriften sprechen.' Pasquali, *Storia*, p. 133, seems to echo Housman. Fourquet, 'Fautes Communes ou Innovations Communes?', pp. 86–7, suggests that genealogy is determinable only if 'Une leçon nouvelle, une fois apparue dans la tradition (1) se transmet désormais sans changement, n'est plus récouverte; (2) n'apparaît pas une seconde fois, indépendamment, dans un autre mss.' Greg, *Calculus*, pp. 11–12: 'Should it be found that all possible arrangements occur with much the same frequency the grouping in general may be described as *random*, and, of course, no inference as to the relation of the manuscripts is possible.' Compare also op. cit., pp. 43–4.

determining the amount of convergent variation other than to study the groupings of the manuscripts.

But to study these groupings presented difficulties of method at the outset. Classification of manuscripts has been attempted in various ways, but always upon one of two broad principles: either analysis of all agreements in substantive readings; or the scrutiny of agreements in selected 'common errors, deviations, and omissions'. An extreme example of the first method is that of Quentin,[1] which fails to recommend itself for a variety of reasons, principally because it is so complicated that it can be applied only to a selection of variants.[2] The second, once traditional method, is that employed by Knott in his classification of the **A** manuscripts. It has been frequently described,[3] but since this introduction is concerned with Knott's conclusions, it seems fittingly illustrated by his own exposition:

> Two or more MSS, or two or more groups of MSS, are assigned to an identical, hypothetically reconstructed ancestor, or archetype, if they possess in common a number of clear errors, omissions, and additions. Common errors, deviations, and omissions in two or more MSS must be due to coincidence, or to contamination, or to their existence in the MS from which copies were made. If there are more than a very few significant errors, the laws of probability forbid attributing them to coincidence. If two MSS, copied from two entirely different archetypes, were afterward compared, and a number of erroneous readings were transferred from one to the other by the collator, the position of descendants of the contaminated MS in the family tree would be very difficult to determine. For these descendants would contain the erroneous readings and deviations which were their legitimate inheritance, and also those which resulted from the contamination, and the text critic would find it difficult, if not impossible, to determine the real position of the MSS. But one characteristic will enable him to locate such MSS with some degree of certainty, and thus to determine which are contaminations, and which are legitimately descended errors. *Omissions* are not the result of contamination. We have a number of A-text MSS . . . which contain readings inserted or substituted in different or later hands or inks than the original hand and ink. In several of these MSS lines or words are inserted which were omitted by the original scribe, or lines are inserted from the B-text. *But in no case is any line or word or passage expunged.* Possessors of MSS who compared them with other MSS seem to have thought that their own MSS were defective or wrong whenever they

[1] See p. 54, fn., above.

[2] Quentin, *Essais*, pp. 61–2.

[3] E.g. by Pasquali, whose *Storia della Tradizione e Critica del Testo* recounts the experiences of various editors who have attempted to use it. See also H. J. Chaytor's sketch of the history of textual criticism, *From Script to Print*, pp. 148 ff.

differed or omitted anything, but not when they contained lines, words, or passages which the other MSS omitted. The possession of any considerable number of common omissions, therefore, unless they can be accounted for on some other definite grounds, makes a very strong case for common descent.

Common ancestry is of course rendered more certain if all the MSS of a group possess also a considerable number of other variants (not necessarily errors) different from the readings common among the MSS of other groups.[1]

In this method the editor's judgement operates at all stages, first to identify erroneous readings, then to determine what are 'significant errors', and then to distinguish between 'legitimately descended errors' and 'contaminations'. The editor will not be human who can avoid the early formation of preconceptions about relationships, and subsequently the dismissal of apparently conflicting groups by reference to convergent variation, before their character has actually been established.

Between the two extremes lie various attempts to control the subjective element. The most notable, in *The Calculus of Variants*, postpones and limits the exercise of the editor's judgement. Nevertheless, in the application of the calculus 'judgements concerning the originality of readings, which are incapable of logical proof', are an indispensable function.[2] Manly and Rickert, in the earlier stages of classification, relied on numerical persistence of agreements to make decisions for them. Arguing that the amount of evidence in the manuscripts of *The Canterbury Tales* justified 'a trust in the regular operation of the laws of probability' they based their classification upon the 'whole body of variants',[3] these being, presumably, departures from Skeat's 'Student's Edition', their 'basis for collation'.[4] The groups formed by these departures (apparently including agreements in right readings on the occasions when the basis for collation had a wrong reading) they recognized as '*prima facie*, merely variational groups'.[5] The genetic groups would be determined by the relative persistent and consistent appearance of the same sigils together:

That is, that no sigil usually present should be often absent without an assignable reason and no extra sigil should often appear without assignable reason. The most frequent causes of the absence of a MS from the group to which it belongs genetically are: (1) individual variation on the group-variant, which is common enough

[1] *MP*, xii, pp. 393–4.
[2] pp. 47–8.
[3] *The Text of the Canterbury Tales*, ii, p. 23.
[4] op. cit., p. 5.
[5] op. cit., p. 20. The terms 'variational' and 'genetic' are Greg's. See *Calculus*, p. 13.

in perhaps all members of all groups; (2) correction, real or supposed, to conform to the reading of some MS of another group.[1]

The establishment of genetic groups would be achieved in the first instance without the exercise of personal judgement, by arithmetic according to the relative frequency of agreement in variation from the 'basis of collation'. Lateral transmission and coincident error would presumably occur so seldom that the groups produced by them would never rival the genetic groups in persistence. The inclusion of agreements on original readings necessarily produced by collation with an arbitrarily chosen text of unestablished originality would presumably not often introduce misleading groups of sigils formed because the manuscripts which they represented happened to have been uncorrupted at the points in question:[2]

The law of probability is so steady in its working that only groupings of classificatory value have the requisite persistence and consistency to be taken as genetic groups.[3]

If, however, contamination was to be reckoned with, or in the case of manuscripts which 'have few variants and do not group themselves readily', judgement must be employed, in the one case to determine which variants should be attributed to vertical, and which to lateral transmission, in the other to estimate the value of the infrequent variants 'for classificatory purposes'.[4]

It seems that, so far at least, no purely mechanical process for classifying manuscripts genetically has been devised. Judgement, however strenuously excluded at the outset, is sooner or later admitted. In the case of the calculus its rôle is so crucial that, by its justice, albeit 'incapable of logical proof', the editor's whole interpretation of the evidence stands or falls.[5] In Manly and Rickert's method judgement decides a matter of vital importance if the genealogy is to be used for recension: whether readings are the product of vertical or lateral transmission.[6]

Nevertheless an attempt to discover the genetic relation of the manuscripts of the **A** version of *Piers Plowman* remains necessary as a test of

[1] *Canterbury Tales*, ii, pp. 20–1.

[2] By the principle that agreement in right readings does not establish genetic relation. I hope I am not unjust to the editors of *The Canterbury Tales* about this matter. They evidently accept the principle, and once (p. 24) refer to 'the nonclassificatory fact' that two manuscripts are 'nearly always in agreement in having the right readings', but I cannot find any place where they allow for the effect of this element in their method.

[3] op. cit., ii, p. 22.

[4] op. cit., pp. 23–7.

[5] Greg, *Calculus*, p. 47.

[6] *Canterbury Tales*, ii, pp. 24–7.

the genealogical hypothesis about these manuscripts published by Knott. The question is, then, at what stage in the process of classification the exercise of judgement should be admitted. The length of the poem, the number of manuscripts, the evident frequency of both lateral transmission and 'the chance coincidence of error', and the number of complex variants, make the application of the calculus to these manuscripts seem impracticable.[1] As for Manly and Rickert's method, the question would arise whether seventeen was a sufficient number of copies to ensure 'the regular operation of the laws of probability'. Must judgement, then, operate in the selection of 'significant errors' as Knott[2] employed it?

Nothing in the experience of subsequent editors or the circumstances of this particular text seems to recommend the adoption of Knott's method. The reliability of 'striking' variants as evidence of genetic relation is very doubtful. Greg writes:

> What usually happens is that collation and 'correction' are confined to some of the more striking variants. . . . Where conflation is suspected, the value of variants as an indication of ancestry is in inverse proportion to their intrinsic importance. To the herd of dull commonplace readings we must look for the genetic source of the text, to the more interesting and striking for the source of the contamination. Nothing can be more misleading than to seek to 'place' a manuscript on the evidence of a few 'test' readings.[3]

Equally, however, the 'herd of dull commonplace readings' is an unreliable source of evidence for genetic relation. Certainly conflation is unlikely to extend to such variants. But another factor in the transmission of manuscripts, especially those in Middle English, is likely to produce agreement in readings of the more trifling kind, namely coincident variation. The frequency of substitution of one 'dull commonplace' reading for another can be seen in the apparatus; the number of random agreements in such readings suggests that convergence of variation by coincident substitution of one 'dull commonplace' reading for another was also frequent.[4]

[1] Greg, *Calculus*, pp. 43–4, 56–8.

[2] See p. 56 above.

[3] *Calculus*, p. 57. Manly and Rickert follow Greg: 'Striking variants and variants that are *prima facie* preferable are especially subject to borrowing. The original text-tradition of a contaminated MS is generally indicated by the presence of many individually trifling variants.' (*Canterbury Tales*, ii, p. 26.)

[4] It will be shown in Section IV below that many readings are the products of well-defined scribal tendencies of variation, and that these tendencies produce insignificant as well as striking variants. There is, then, an inherent probability of coincident variation. This is implied in Pasquali's axiom (*Storia*, p. xvi): 'Coincidenza in errori ovvi e in "trivializzazioni" non prova parentela.'

No rule about the reliability of one or another kind of variant as evidence of genetic relation survives application to the manuscripts of the **A** version of *Piers Plowman*. The danger of generalizing about the selection of variants for classification becomes clear once the whole body of variants is accessible. Thus Knott laid it down that '*Omissions* are not the result of contamination. . . . The possession of any considerable number of common omissions, . . . unless they can be accounted for on some other definite grounds, makes a very strong case for common descent.'[1] Of omissions resulting from physical imperfections in manuscripts this statement is probably true. It may also be true as a principle that a 'correcting' scribe would not expunge matter from his own copy because it was wanting in the copy that he was consulting. But many, if not most omissions of lines and passages in these manuscripts can be accounted for on palæographic grounds, by reference to circumstances as likely to operate with one scribe as with another. Omissions are thus likely to occur coincidentally, and are therefore not necessarily evidence of genetic relation.[2] While, then, it may be correct to say that agreements in omissions do not indicate contamination, it by no means follows that such agreements make any necessary case for genetic relation.[3]

The inadvisability of choosing any particular type of variant as the evidence for classifying these manuscripts will have appeared. There is, moreover, a great practical difficulty in the way of accepting the results of any classification attained by a selective treatment of evidence. Whatever type of variant is treated as reliable, the subsequent classification will force the editor to ignore or to explain away a large amount of evidence which, by his own choice and definition, is significant.

The full force of this difficulty was quickly brought home to me when, after finishing the collation of the manuscripts, I made my first attempt to classify them. This attempt was made independently, as a test of Knott's conclusions, but employed the traditional system. *A priori* judgements were made about originality wherever the character

[1] *MP*, xii, pp. 393, 394. Compare Manly and Rickert, *Canterbury Tales*, ii, p. 26.

[2] Compare Greg, *Calculus*, p. 20, n. 1: 'The easier it is to explain how an error arose, the less valid the assumption that it only arose once.'

[3] The agreements of **A** version manuscripts in omissions are given below (pp. 111–12). It will be seen that by Knott's genealogy some of them are necessarily random and coincident. Pasquali (*Storia*, pp. 33–4 and 182) makes important qualifications of the value of omissions for classification.

of the variant readings made this seem possible, and the groups were determined in relation to these *a priori* judgements. Many of the results seemed to confirm those of Knott. But information came to light which had not been revealed in Knott's article: *first*, the evidence for classifying these manuscripts was grievously obscured by the existence of many random groups which must signify conflation or coincidence of error; *second*, the agreements which would have to be dismissed as insignificant in order to establish a genealogy differed little if at all in character or weight, and only in relative persistence from those on which the classification would be founded; *third*, some well-attested groups must be viewed with suspicion because they were products of traditions in which corruption, and therefore presumably also correction, were especially frequent; and *fourth*, as my classification was tending, if, like Knott, I were to treat the more persistent groups as genetic, to use such groups in recension would not infrequently require the preference of an easier reading, a reading repugnant to the context, or a reading from which the variants rejected by recension could not conceivably have originated.

It was thus immediately evident that Knott's genealogy was a most dangerous instrument to employ for recension since, even if it did sketch the genetic history of these manuscripts, they contained so many variants necessarily not produced by vertical transmission that the applicability of the genealogy to any given reading could not safely be assumed. Tested by the method employed to form it, Knott's genealogy was found inadequate.

The limitations of the method of classifying by selected variants made it, however, impossible to rest on this negative conclusion. The question was now whether an analysis attempted from all variants (except of course those of spelling, dialect and grammar merely) would produce more satisfactory results: either another genealogy, or a clear demonstration of the impossibility of recovering one.

The tendency of the first attempt to classify these manuscripts had been to suggest with some emphasis that no method of analysis would produce usable results. It therefore seemed advisable, before making another attempt at classification, to scrutinize the variants themselves. It appeared to be a necessary inference that not all the variational groups of the first analysis were produced by vertical or lateral transmission, but that some of them were produced by coincident variation.

There was the possibility that in some cases, where originality was not seriously in doubt, the reasons for the variation might be ascertained.

As it turned out the scrutiny of variant readings had far-reaching results that determined my subsequent approach to the editing of the **A** manuscripts. Comparison and analysis of the variant readings brought to light a number of well-defined tendencies of variation which acted to produce coincident variants. The discovery of such tendencies seriously diminished confidence in the possibility of distinguishing between genetic groups, groups produced by conflation, and those produced by coincident variation. It was, meanwhile, clear that if coincident variation was an appreciable source of variational groups among these manuscripts,[1] there was little likelihood that Knott's genealogy or any other would prove trustworthy when employed for recension.

While removing the last grounds for belief that a genealogy of these manuscripts serviceable for recension could be recovered, study of the variant readings as types of substitution had useful positive results. Clearly, if tendencies of variation could be established, the knowledge of those tendencies would afford means of distinguishing original from unoriginal variants where originality might not otherwise be immediately apparent. The text could now be fixed by a direct method, in effect by applying widely and with some confidence the second of the principles described by Greg for determining originality without recourse to recension: 'To show that a reading is original two main lines of argument are available: that the reading is itself satisfactory, and that it explains the origin of the erroneous alternative.'[2]

I am bound to admit to a sense of relief on reaching the conclusion that knowledge of the scribal tendencies of substitution[3] was a better instrument for determining originality with these manuscripts than recension based upon a dubious genealogical hypothesis. For, had one

[1] The attitude of textual critics to this phenomenon seems to depend more on their experience than on theoretical considerations. Thus Fourquet ('Fautes Communes ou Innovations Communes?', pp. 89–90) regards the chances of coincident variation as small. Manly and Rickert (*Canterbury Tales*, ii, p. 21) suggest that coincidence of error in any but the most trivial variants will 'not often produce groupings which by their persistence and consistency impose themselves as genetic'. Chambers and Grattan ('The Text of "Piers Plowman" ', pp. 14, 15) discuss the possibility of coincident variation. Grattan ('The Text of *Piers Plowman*: Critical Lucubrations', pp. 593–604) proposes instances from the **A** manuscripts. Greg, as usual, goes to the heart of the matter: 'As a rule, the easier it is to explain how an error arose, the less valid the assumption that it only arose once.' (*Calculus*, p. 20, n. 1.)

[2] *Calculus*, p. 20, n. 1.

[3] They are set forth at length below, pp. 127 ff.

been obliged to rely on recension, there would have been the greatest difficulty at the very beginning of an attempt to determine a genealogy by modern methods. I could not accept that collation upon an arbitrarily chosen standard of indeterminate originality like Dom Quentin's *Clementine Bible*[1] or Manly and Rickert's Skeat's 'Student's Edition' would produce a genuine result, since the variant groups formed by such collation would of necessity include many agreements in right readings, which are not evidence of descent from an exclusive common ancestor and would grievously mislead. In fact it was not clear to me how the classification of these manuscripts could be successfully attempted in ignorance of the original readings, and in any case, from observation of the variants I was convinced that whatever method were employed, the resulting genealogy would be an arbitrary structure, producing in recension a text which was original or otherwise only as, indeterminately, the genealogy chanced to correspond to the history of the manuscripts at that point.

Therefore I welcomed the direction of my interest to the variant readings, and the results obtained by studying them. Since these made it possible to determine originality at a large number of points the need for a genealogy (evidently difficult or impossible to recover) ceased to be pressing, even if I had not reached the position described by Greg where 'the relation of the manuscripts ceases to be of any interest whatever'.[2] I would fix my text without using recension, and would treat genetic evidence as only one of a number of available indications of originality.

I was, at the same time, finally equipped to demonstrate what was becoming increasingly clear to me, that the character of the groupings of these manuscripts made the recovery of their genetic history to any extent useful for recension impossible. My text, determined with the aid of information about scribal tendencies of substitution, contained, as I believe, the original readings in something more than 'a few cases, sporadically'. I now made a second analysis of the variant groups of the **A** manuscripts, in relation to this text. The results were as follows:

i. certain very persistent groups took shape;

ii. a large number of relatively less persistent groups, frequently in conflict among themselves or with the groups in *i*, could not be ignored;

[1] *Essais de Critique Textuelle*, p. 25.

[2] *Calculus*, p. 54. For the use to which I put the available genetic information about the **A** manuscripts, see p. 151 below.

iii. more than a thousand random groups testified to the existence of either abundant conflation, or extensive coincidence of variation, or both;

iv. no stemma of these manuscripts could be reconstructed.

It was thus evident, even omitting from consideration all the cases where my determination of originality might be disputed, and my grouping therefore described as unreal, that both kinds of convergent variation had played a major part in forming the character of the surviving copies of the **A** version of *Piers Plowman*. The results of this second classification fully authorized the rejection of recension as a means of establishing the text of this version.

Unhappily, in the circumstances of the subject, it is not possible merely to state this conclusion and leave my apparatus to support it. Since it amounts to plain contradiction of the published findings of other editors I am obliged to devote the rest of this section to presenting, in full, the main variational groups assumed by the **A** manuscripts, together with the hypotheses of Knott and Fowler which I reject as untenable, and my reasons for rejecting them.

Certain differences of presentation are now indicated for greater ease of reference:

Difference of sigils

for *E* (Erin) Knott-Fowler use T^2

for *K* (Kenelm) Knott-Fowler use *Di*

for *J* (adopted by Chambers and Grattan to avoid confusion with the personal pronoun in the critical apparatus) Knott-Fowler use *I*

Difference in the order of citing the sigils

Unless for a stated reason, I invariably cite sigils in the order TRUD ChH^{2}VHJLEAKWNMH^3. This order, adopted by Chambers and Grattan as they became acquainted with manuscripts, is arbitrary and reflects no genetic relation. I fell in with it in the early stages of my work with the **A** manuscripts and used it in the layout of my collations. Had the manuscripts been amenable to classification, and had I employed recension, it would have been necessary to replace it with a series reflecting the classification. As things are the only alternative is the equally arbitrary order of the alphabet. The main requirement is that sigils should be consistently cited in one order; this I have tried to fulfil. The only exceptions are given below at p. 171. Knott-Fowler, in accordance with their genealogical findings, cite sigils in the order TH^{2}ChDUREAMH^{3}JLWNKVH, or, using their sigils, TH^{2}Ch DURT^{2}AMH^{3}ILWNDiVH.

In the following discussion, to enable quick reference to the critical apparatus, I use my sigils when citing Knott-Fowler.

Knott knew of fourteen manuscripts when he made his classification; he did not know of Ch, M and N. He found[1] that these manuscripts were to be classified in the following relation:

i. The manuscripts fell into two main groups
 group *x* containing V and H
 group *y* containing TRUDH^{2}JLEAKWH^3
ii. Group *y* comprised four subgroups
 L
 J
 KW
 TRUDH^{2}EAH^3
iii. The subgroup TRUDH^{2}EAH^3 fell into two further subgroups
 one containing TDH^2 throughout
 one containing EAH^3 nearly throughout
 from Prologue I to about I 183 (Knott's reference) and VII 69a (Knott's reference) to VII 209 (Knott's reference) E went with RU, while AH^3 formed a sub-subgroup of equal genealogical weight with TRUDH^{2}E
 within the subgroup TDH^2 there was a further subgroup TH^2
 RU formed a separate subgroup throughout, both when they went with TDH^2 and when they belonged with EAH^3

This classification professed to describe the relations of these fourteen manuscripts to VIII 130, where Knott's interest ended because, in his words, 'it is at this point that Mr Manly (and I) believe the work of A 1 ceases'. Throughout his presentation he gives an impression of setting forth firm conclusions clearly directed by the evidence. Contrary indications are made to seem not material. They can be dismissed by describing them as the 'result of contamination or of emendation by a scribe' (p. 401); another useful explanation is 'that different parts of the same MS were sometimes copied from different ancestors' (p. 403). Such reference to these possibilities suggests that the occasions when they might arise with the **A** manuscripts are never troublesome. So

[1] His results appear in *MP*, xii (1915), pp. 389–421.

does the observation, made while discussing conflation, that 'the modern text editor would perhaps encounter considerable difficulty in placing such a contaminated MS in his tree' (p. 416). The 'Essay' nowhere indicates that Knott in fact encountered such difficulty.

Knott's work was supplemented by Fowler, who examined the relations of the manuscripts Ch, M and N in Prologue–VIII, and the relations of all known manuscripts for Passus IX–XI, the Manlian **A** 2. Fowler's conclusions,[1] presumably formed by the method which Knott described (above, pp. 56–7), presented in two stages, are very briefly as follows:

i. In Prologue–VIII (where he undertakes to place Ch, M and N in Knott's genealogy for **A** 1)

Ch is grouped with TH^2 as [(TH^2)Ch]

M is grouped with A, E and H^3, depending on the presence of these three manuscripts, thus (the references are Fowler's):

EM	Prologue–I 142	(A defective, H^3 **B** text)
	II 18–145	
	III 112–226	
EAM	II 146–III 111	(H^3 **B** text to V 105)
	III 227–V 106	
$EAMH^3$	V 106–VII 69	(all represented)
AMH^3	VII 69–VII 209	(E otherwise grouped)
AMH^3	VII 210 to 'the end of A–1'	(E defective)

within a genetic group $EAMH^3$ deduced from this classification he further identifies as genetic

EA	to VII 69	(A defective at beginning)
MH^3	V 106–VIII 111	

N gives trouble, since its most persistent grouping is with W, which Knott had classed with K as a subgroup of *y*. (In *Piers the Plowman: A Critical Edition* (p. 26), however, Fowler's stemma contains the group [(WN)K], which presumably represents his final opinion. In that stemma, therefore, N is part of *y*.)

Fowler amplifies Knott's classification by drawing attention to a variational group RUD (see also *PMLA*, lxvi, pp. 495–504). This group, he concludes, is the result of contamination, and D is genetically related to $TChH^2$.

ii. In IX–XI

'For the most part the *y* MSS in A-2 maintain the same relationships which they had in the middle portion of A-1. . . . An exception to this rule is W, which joins the minor group AMH^3, while retaining a superinduced relationship with Di [K], its former

[1] David C. Fowler, *A Critical Text of Piers Plowman A-2*, unpublished University of Chicago dissertation (1949), pp. 10–40. The library of University College, London was permitted to buy a microfilm of this dissertation through the courtesy of the University of Chicago Library.

associate' (Thesis, p. 28). The two main groups persist, *x* being represented by V, *y* comprising all the remaining manuscripts.

y now consists of J, K and TRUDChH^{2}AWMH^3, including Ch and M unknown to Knott, and having received W by change of exemplar.

Ch continues in [(TH^2)Ch], the relation (TH^2), [(TH^2)Ch], ⟨[(TH^2)ChD]⟩, and {⟨[(TH^2)Ch]D⟩RU} persisting throughout IX–XI.

In the new family AWMH^3, the groups AW and MH^3 are genetic.

In this part of the poem there is evidence of contamination between D and RU, W and K, U and J.

It will be seen that Fowler's conclusions are somewhat more qualified than those of Knott. Fowler not only allows the possibility of contamination, but actually identifies examples of its occurrence, and refers to the importance of detecting it (Thesis, pp. 39, 40). He is also aware of the possibility of coincident variation. Nevertheless his conclusions are presented as firm ones, and it must be presumed that he considers his propositions to be fully demonstrated, and a genetic classification of the **A** manuscripts to have been accomplished. That is certainly the impression conveyed in the two pages, with stemmata, devoted to the genetic relations of the **A** manuscripts in Knott and Fowler's recent edition.[1]

The following presentation of the main variational groups assumed by the **A** manuscripts will show:

i. That certain of the smaller groups described by Knott and Fowler may well be genetic.

ii. That there are, meanwhile, many more well attested variational groups than Knott and Fowler lead one to believe, and that these very often conflict with the presumably genetic groups.

iii. That the explanations of anomalous groups invoked by Knott and Fowler sometimes beg the question of relationship.

iv. That some of the smaller, but well attested groups are not stable enough to allow more than a general admission of their genetic character.

v. That the larger groups, TRUDH^{2}EAH^3 (Knott), equivalent to TRUDChH^{2}EAMH^3 (Fowler supplementing Knott), TRUDCh H^{2}AWMH^3 (Fowler), and *y* (Knott and Fowler) cannot be established from the evidence available, and that, therefore, no stemma can be formed.

vi. That for this reason in particular, as well as generally because an

[1] *Piers the Plowman*, pp. 26–7,

enormous amount of convergent variation qualifies all conclusions about genetic relations, the use of recension for determining this text is unauthorized.

From the groups which follow I have excluded all variants involving no addition or substitution of words, or change of meaning, or metrical change, or error of copying, in fact all certainly orthographical and dialectal variants, even though they need not necessarily record the education or origin of the most recent scribe, and may be traditional.[1] Variants arising from substitution of *and* or *but* for *ac* have been excluded; so also substitutions of *carien* for *cairen*, and *lere* for *lerne* or the reverse. Variants of wholly Latin lines have been excluded as especially liable to correction. I have, further, made the following exclusions, because independent substitution seems particularly likely there:

I 48
II 13
II 116
IV 120 be] for
IV 127
V 59 comsiþ he]
V 87 *omissions*
V 126 pleit]
V 134 pilewhey]
V 198 þrumblide]
VI 6 weþewindes]
VII 178 blereyed]
VII 223 nam]
VII 282 peysen]
VIII 6 *insertion of* him
VIII 112 þat . . . not]
XI 64 vs . . . made]
XI 186 toille]

But for these exceptions, and for any unintentional omissions, all material variants have been included. Since a full critical apparatus accompanies the analysis it is within the power of anyone who would add or exclude further instances to do so. He may then study how far my conclusions have been affected.

There is one more, important consideration. It has not seemed wise, in the case of these manuscripts, to limit the analysis to what Greg calls 'simple' variants.[2] It is doubtful whether in their case the 'natural variants of type 2' would 'prove sufficient to establish the manuscript relation'.[3] The contingency to which Greg referred, where 'variation

[1] Greg, *Calculus*, p. 44: 'The minuter the collation the greater will be the number of abnormal variants, not only absolutely but relatively.' Compare *The Play of Antichrist from the Chester Cycle*, Oxford, 1935, p. xxvi, where Greg describes as 'of little evidential value', 'small scribal errors in single manuscripts, slight differences of grammatical form, and certain common alternatives, such as *you* and *ye*, or *thy* and *thine*.'

[2] *Calculus*, pp. 18–20.

[3] op. cit., p. 42.

has advanced to such a point, that practically all variants are of complex type'[1] has not actually arisen; simple variants do occur, but complex variants are extremely numerous. Every effort was, however, made to give value to the groupings at discernible stages of successive variation.[2] Where successive variation has obscured earlier agreement this was not always possible.

Since the agreements between pairs of manuscripts are of striking persistence, and since any larger groups would presumably be built up of smaller subgroups, the demonstration begins by presenting the evidence for the main variational groups of two manuscripts. Membership of larger groups is left until the occurrences of a manuscript in smaller groups have been examined. The presentation which follows is alphabetical.

Variational Groups of Two Manuscripts

1*a*. *The manuscript* A *in some* 50 *agreements with* M

I 143 pyne] tene.[3] 147 miȝtful] mygthi. II 6 feris] f. vnfeythful to knowyn. 193 likiþ] wolde. III 6 þat] *om.* 50 þere . . . auter] I schulde it so makyn M; I wold it grauyn A. 56 or deliþ] *om.* 61 in] i. ȝoure. 235 maner] more. 244 þe] to þ. 260 knowe] schal k. 264 be dyademid] bigge dyademys. IV 82 pees . . . purid] pens in presens ⁊ pecis of. 129 þou] *om.* 136 resoun] mekenes. 157 he faille] elles. V 24 go] to. 30 He] And. 49 affaiten] afeyntyn. 74–5 *ll. om.* 95 *expanded.* 101 dryue] drawe. 201 he] hym. VI 33 ⁊(1)] *om.* VII 95 pote] staf. 213 not] *om.* VIII 3 ⁊ *a*] *om.* 127 And . . . I] *tp.* 136 a] þe. 174 What] And how. IX 3 And] I. 7 þis] þat. 20 alwey . . . hom] *tp.* 28 stif] fast. 36 watris] wawis. 47 wile suffre] sufferith. 50 ȝow] þe to. 60 doute] drouth. 64 wiȝt] man. 82 haþ] *om.* 85 for] *om.* X 35 ymage] like. 52 ⁊ . . . gode] to goode and heryng also A; to goode þy*n* eryng to þe same M. 58 In] w*ith*. 73 cheuisshen] clense. 91 accordyng] acordith w*ith*. XI 4 sterneliche . . . studie] schornely dam stodie sternely A; scornynge dam stodie st*er*neliche M. 12 wexiþ] growith. 14 erþe] erde. 18 it] ȝif it. 53 þe] here. 247 heiȝly] holy. 257 but] but ȝif. 280 wiþ] in.

1*b*. *The manuscript* A *in some* 40 *agreements with W*

II 168 Er . . . put] Put hym. III 271 robe] robis. IV 2 sauȝte] acorde. 111 robberis] robbyng. V 88 crist] god. 95 hy] þat þai A; þat he W. VI 66 heiȝ] holly. 75 kirnelis] corneris. 91 For] *om.* 100 þe] ȝou. VII 91 to . . . ȝede] *tp.* 131 me god] *tp.* 133 hem] *om.* 181 to kepe] and cepte. 183 Al] *om.* 235 hondis] hand. 254 ek] *om.* 298 curse] Thay c. VIII 23 for] *om.* 107 *line om.* 143 how] of. 176 founde] *om.* IX 33 here on] of þis. 105 þre] *om.* 117 in] i. þis. X 20 a] *om.* 30 of(2)] *om.* 88 clene] *om.* 89 Wilne . . .

[1] op. cit., p. 43.
[2] op. cit., pp. 24–5.
[3] The following lists are intended only to show points of common variation. The apparatus should be consulted for information about details of form and spelling.

neuere] Whil . . . wonyst A; Whil . . . art W. 94 so] *om.* 97 counseilliþ] techith. 117 porcioun] possessioun. 218 þat is] his. XI 6 wittis] witte. 21 conne] do can. 38 lewid] l. men. 48 hunsen] hold. 85 þou] he. 111 gold haþ] *tp.* 158 þat] þis. 181 siþen] *om.* 191 & . . . oþere] *om.* 200 &] in. 264 And] *om.* 270 wrouȝte] wrote W; wretyn A. 272 werkis] clerkis. 275 And] *om.*

1*c*. *The manuscript* A *in some* 30 *agreements with* E

I 165 ben auauncid] *tp.* 179 graiþ] grettest. II 9 Ipurfilid] Ipurid A; Puryd E. 15 þus] þat is þus. III 51 writen] þerin w. 91 as swiþe] *om.* 230 it] i. full. 262 happe . . . somme] hap for hisse grett synne E; rygth so schal synne A. IV 21 ȝet] *om.* 23 swyþe] in hast. 24 on waryn] an warnyd E; warnyd A. 38 gadelynges] goslynges. 39 fer] ferd. 75 maynprise hym] *tp.* 98 boþe] als. 148 on] vppon. V 17 segges] I say. 48 þere] þerin. 69 Venym] Wyrmys (? Wyriuys) A; Wormes (? Wermes ? Weriues) E. 77 tunge] talys. 94 wepe] wepyd E; wepte A. 95 þere] in my hert. 102 shope a] stoppe it wer. 126 pakke nedle] bat nedil A; bat nedyls E. 163 dykere] Drinker. 165 *line om.* 188 ygulpid] gobbyd E; gabbid A. VI 2 baches] bankes. 66 And] *om.* 68 freþid] fetterd E; federid A. 91 þe] þat. VII 15 wile] biddes. 31 to(*both*)] at. 99 Dikeris] Diggers. 103 to plese] pleasyd.

1*d*. *The manuscript* A *in some* 30 *agreements with* H^{3}

V 106 ne . . . me] may not. 109 bleride] blereyd A; blere eyid H^{3}. 137 bummide] bybbyd H^{3}; bubbith A. 153 he] herry. 198 He] And. VI 11 for] þat. 21 wy] wyte A; wyth H^{3}. 77–8 *wrong division.* 89 weue] weyn. 110 is] be. VII 11 it] *om.* 112 And] *om.* 121 sone] *om.* 161 þe(1)] so þe. 178 brokelegged] bedrede A; bedderede H^{3}. 187 erde] lond. him] *om.* 243 wilnest] woldis hauyn. 300 þere] *om.* VIII 20 hadde] han. 92 al] *om.* 97 no . . . fynde] non oþer pardoun. 109 manye oþere] *tp.* X 74 for] and. 149 it] *om.* XI 15 rentis] rent. 89 to] *om.* 91 wile] schal. 93 þat] *om.* 153 hotiþ] biddyth. 157 wel] ful. 159 many] *om.* 183 it is] *tp.* 190 hem(2)] *om.* 207 þe(1)] *om.* 304 for] in.

1*e*. *The manuscript* A *in some* 20 *agreements with* J

III 19 merciede] myrthed. 20 &] *om.* V 143 chaffare] crafte. 195 asid . . . arere] *tp.* VI 92 And] *om.* VIII 2 his] him. 101 And] *om.* 174 dedist] dost. IX 86 &] *om.* X 56 For] *om.* 68 And] *om.* 94 And] *om.* 101 For] *om.* 164 it] *om.* XI 55 And] *om.* 56 kete] cowrte J; courte A. 72 prechide] precheris. 116 And] *om.* 206 þat] *om.* 264 &] *om.* 269 in(2)] *om.* 272 And] *om.* 276 And] *om.*

1*f*. *The manuscript* A *in a few agreements with* U

V 136 lay] lith. VI 76 oþer] or elles. VII 273–275 *ll. om.* 291 haue] hadde. VIII 30 *line om.* IX 74 *line om.* 76–77 *ll. om.* X 26 And] *om.* 37 al] *om.* 132 it] þat. 156 hatide] h. hem. 175 eiȝte] seuene A; souen U. XI 66 a] *om.* 172 þe] *om.* 219 wiþ] and. 224 þat] *om.* 246 to] *om.* 295 *line om.*

1*g*. *The manuscript* A *in a few agreements with* V

II 149 gyede] gilede V; begylith A. V 34 prelatis . . . prestis] *tp.* 49 fers] Frele. 82 hail-side] heilede. 219 þat] *om.* VI 95 þat wykkide] for he is a. 117 Wyte god] Iwis. VII 180 And] *om.* VIII 87 loue of] *om.* 108 prophet] prophetes. 114 vs] *om.* 128 euene . . .

sitte] s. euyn south A; s. souþ euene V. IX 10 hailside] heilede. 80 or] o. eny of. 93 *line om.* X 154 hem] *om.* 179 And] *om.* XI 6 flatereris] Fayturs. 132 garte] gon.

1*b*. *The manuscript* A *in a few agreements with* H

IV 31 þanne] *om.* 90 *line om.* 126 þe man] *om.* V 42 mote] *om.* VII 6 were] come. 119 *line om.* 134 al þe] *om.* 175 An] & an. 187 Hom] *om.* 297 ywrouȝt] bycome. 304 wat*er*] watr*is*. VIII 142 men] lordis.

[Knott found that A formed a group with E from I 143 to VII 69; so Fowler. After VII 69 Knott grouped A with H[3]. Fowler groups A with W in IX–XI.]

2. *The manuscript* Ch *in some* 20 *agreements with* T

Prologue 22 Wonne] Whom. 69 hym] it. 71 bleride] bleriþ. 86 poundide] poynteþ. I 4 clyf] kiþ. 18 wollene . . . lynene] *tp.* 30 him] hem. II 96 a maiden] of maides. III 193 *line om.* 257 him] þat king. IV 72 *line om.* VI 42 riȝt] þe r. way. VII 67 shulde] ne s. 139 wasto*ur*] þe w. 158 wastours] wasto*ur*. shendiþ] apeiriþ. 195 nediþ] of nedide. 210 fare . . . betere] at ese. 212 Make] And m. 236 hem] *om.* 279 þis] a. VIII 48 penyworþ] peny. X 115 ȝe begg*ere*] þe bigg*ere*. 118 and] *om.* 130 þat] as. 131 Formest] And f.

[Other, less persistent groups of two manuscripts including Ch are noted on p. 93 below.]

3*a*. *The manuscript* D *in some* 20 *agreements with* M

Prologue 77 þe boy] þey boþe. III 34 þ*ere*] *om.* V 107 hym nouȝt] not hym. 194 gan he] *tp.* 200 his] *om.* VI 24 in] here i. 103 þoruȝ(2)] *with.* VII 116 wiþ] *om.* VIII 106 pen*au*nce] pena*un*ces. 165 ȝow] ȝe. 177 haue] *om.* IX 65 art þou] *tp.* 75 drunkelewe] dronken. 77 as(1)] *om.* 88 pungen] put. X 69 hem] hym. 194 hem] *om.* XI 25 þe] *om.* 52 Mendynauntȝ] Many pore men. 87 &] *om.* 184 &] or.

3*b*. *The manuscript* D *in some* 10 *agreements with* T

Prologue 100 tolleris] tokkeris. I 138 mery] m*er*cy. II 19 heo] it. 66 sese] set. 172 falsnesse] falnesse. 185 hy] be T; ben D. III 93 Curteisly] Certis. 188 marchal] march*a*unt. VI 76 best] worst. VII 205 to] *om.* 277 bake] blake. X 94 *line om.* 107 it telliþ] techiþ eu*ere*. 123 þat . . . and] *om.* XI 53 gorge] þrote. 151 biddiþ] *om.*

4*a*. *The manuscript* E *in some* 80 *agreements with* M

Prologue 81 parissh] kirkes. 95 cuntre] peple. 96, 97 *misplaced.* I 35 þat . . . is] no blysse E; lesse M. 37 wolde] þat w. 39 set . . . herte] be war *with* þair wyles E; be war of her*e* wyles M. 41 wel] *om.* 44 seide] made. 46 Ȝif] Wheder. 57 þat dredful is] swa d. 69 wyt] hert. 86 telliþ] trow þou. 94 taken] t. al. 95 t*er*mined] det*er*minyd. 98 ap*er*tly] *om.* 99 fyue score] fyftene. 102 his] *om.* 112 felawis] felaship. 117 wenden . . . shuln] w. s. aft*er* M; s. aftir hym w. E. 118 Aftir . . . day] To þat Pyne endles. dwelle] won. 119 word] werke. 123 siȝte of] *om.* 127 haue I] *tp.* kenne . . . bet] lerne bet*ere* M; bett*er* to lere E. 133 I . . . treuþe] is t. for sothe. 138 ȝedde] syng. 141 wiþ loue] kyndely. 164 is] *om.* 180 tixtes] text. 183 þe] you. II 16 haþ . . . me] at me hase g. 23 forgid] fanged E; fongid M. 24 begon . . . so] ben forthganger E; ben forgor*e* M. 29 þ*ere*] *om.* 32 coueitise] þing. 36 any] on. 37 mede] m. þat maydyn E; þat maydyn M. 38 hous] boure. 46 þe . . . wolde] þai write wald. 47 feffid] sesyd. 51 fulfille] do. 52 buxum . . . hende] qwilse þair lyue last. 53 *another line substituted.* 65 delites] likyng. 81 weddyng] werk*es*. 101 And] *om.* 103 his] *om.* 117 þi . . . wyf] weddytt E; wendyd M. 121 for euere] toged*er*. 122 fals] falshed. 131 hadde] h. þe. III 22 *line om.* 30 callen] to c. 35 mekeliche] myldely. 74 on] *om.* 99 beȝonde] b. see. 105 consience . . . kyng] befor þe k. c. M; before k. c. E. 129 Heo] And. 143 ofte] *om.* 144 Barouns . . . bringeþ] Offt sho bringgeȝ barons & burgeȝ. 146 leiþ] allegg*es*. þe treuþe] hym þe gate. 147 floreynes] gold. 150 Lawe] Hir l. 154 þat . . . hire] maynteners of hir E; hire meyntenours M. 158 *line om.* 159 þe king] And he M; And E. 174 kilde] begylyd E; gylede M. 178 caban] cabons. 185 merþe] mery men. 192 þe] Ya þe. 201 ȝeftis] gyfteȝ enow. 206 bidding] mede. 209 of hem] þair. 211 alse] at þe male tyme. 212 Alle kyn] *om.* 214 *the line rearranged.* 216 worþi] best w. IV 46 *the line similarly corrupted.* 50 manye] *om.* 124 me god] *tp.* 146 be . . . it] to me to bryng þaim toged*er*. 155 redy] al r. M; als r. E. V 39 ȝe . . . betere] þai be storyd wele E; ȝoure stor bettere M. 64 leyn] ben. 132 dede] *om.* 148 And] Bot. 177 acorden] a. welle E; wele a. M. VI 47 ȝe] if ȝ. 83 for] *om.* 103 aȝen] *om.* VII 101 þere were] *tp.* M; was þ. E. 195 hem(2)] þai.

4*b*. *The manuscript* E *in some* 30 *agreements with* A (*see* 1*c above*)

4*c*. *The manuscript* E *in some* 20 *agreements with* R

Prologue 11 þanne] þer. 14 toft] coste (E*'s reading doubtful*). 22 Wonne] *om.* wastours] w. now. 28 holden hem] lyuen. 48 Wenten] and w. 54 *hereafter additional lines.* 62 Manye] Fele. 66 a bulle] bullys. 78 parissh . . . pardoner] *tp.* 79 haue] departyn. 98 bocheris . . . breusteris] *tp.* I 17 hiȝte] lyȝthe into. 39 þi] þ. sely R; þ. sory E. 40 *line om.* 52 riȝtfulliche] ryȝthful. II 6 many] alle. III 64 it] *om.* V 139 cuppemel] coppe ale R; copnale E. 220 seynide] shryued R; schraffe E. 229 leten] l. ȝut R; ȝet l. E. VI 85 me] *om.* VII 160 wombe] mawe. his] her.

4*d*. *The manuscript* E *in a few agreements with* H

Prologue 24 comen] þei conen hem. 97 here] seen. II 193 likiþ] luste H; list E. III 89 or ȝerisȝiuys] amysse H; wrangwysly E. 130 harmide] harme dide. 165 And] *om.* IV 3 hote] bid. 131 lef] self. V 16 Piries] Peretrees. 39 ȝoure] here. 60 pale] *om.* 83 He] but he. 104 wel] ful. 111 age] old. 116 *line om.* 201 And] *om.* VII 38 &] *om.* 75 & hor] *om.*

4*e*. *The manuscript* E *in a few agreements with* L

I 25 driȝeþ] thyrstes. 49 se] s. hit. 87 ille] eouel. II 11 frettid] fetred. 31 lord] bote lord. 107 signes] s. of notories L; notary s. E. 118 wiþ] þorgh. 127 þanne] And. 174 wiþ hym] *tp.* 175 in] *om.* 192 copide] þey c. IV 50 pes] *om.* 71 woo] muche w. V 132 aunsel] *om.* 223 dere] *om.* VI 8 ampollis] saumples L; ensaumples E. 99 out] *om.*

4*f*. *The manuscript* E *in a few agreements with* U

Prologue 1 whanne] as. 3 of] *om.* 9 lenide] l. me. 49 lif] lyues. I 25 þe] ȝow. 102 þat] þis. 182 is] *om* (U(2) *only*). II 20 *line om* (U(1) *only*). 145 fariþ] goþ. V 25 maner] kynne. VII 112 þeiȝ] ȝif. 131 as(1) . . . I] as I seie U; as I sayd as E. 163 He] And. 190 þou] ȝe.

[Knott grouped E with A from I 143–VII 69. Fowler groups E with M to I 142, from II 18–II 145, from III 112–III 226; he calls EA a subgroup in Prologue–VII whenever A is present. He finds signs that E is 'not completely stable' in its relations to AMH[3] 'through the middle of A–1'.]

5a. The manuscript H *in some* 230 *agreements with* V

Prologue 10 swiȝede] sownede. 14 triȝely] wonderliche. 21 settyng] Eringe. 32 þriuen] scholden. 41 bely . . . bagge] *tp.* bratful] faste. 50–1 *ll. om.* 53 from oþere] for breþeren. 58 as . . . wolde] ille V; ful yuel H. 62 fallen] bifalle. 63 ⁊ hy] biginne. 76 His . . . sent] Heo scholde not beo so hardi. disseyue] d. so V; bigyle so H. 82 licence . . . leue] *tp.* 99–100 *ll. om.* 107 osay . . . gascoyne] *tp.* 109 *line om.* I 4 clyf] loft. 9 holde] ȝeueþ. 21 Arn . . . þo] Heore nomes beþ neodful. 22 And . . . hem] Bi Rule and. 23 is vesture] Cloþing is. 34 gut] bodi. 36 a] *om.* 39 set] seo V; I see H. 46 þe] heore. 54 tut*our*] tour. 66 Eldir] Ellerne treo. 68 on his] in heor. betraid . . . sonnest] þer no truþe is Inne. 70 writ] w. me. 72 wisside] techeþ V; tawght H. 78 my] vr. 80 I . . . wil] *tp.* 87 wilneþ] doþ. 88 a . . . be] acounted to. 90 kenne] techen. 93 riden . . . doun] Rihtfuliche Ray- men V; ryȝtfullyche rule H. 98 p*ro*fessioun ap*er*tly] perte p. V; p*ar*fyt p. H. 101 neue*re*] *om.* 102 whoso] he þat. 105 miȝt] maystrie ⁊ m. V; honour*e* ⁊ m. H. 121 wende] *om.* 134 lere] teche. aftir] forþ*ur*e. 135 wytnessiþ] techeþ us. 139 miȝt] Fitte. 155 lelly] trewely. 156 Of] And. goodlyche] Treweliche. 162 worþ . . . helle] wite þou forsoþe. 163 It] *om.* 168 cheynid] claymed. 169 ȝe] *om.* 170 coueitise] care. 171 haþ] heo beoþ *with.* II 4 Kenne] Teche. sum] kuynde. 6 feris manye] hole Meyne. 8 And was] þ*en*ne w. I. 9 pureste] ricchest. 23 forgid] brouȝt. 28–9 *ll. om.* 30 ȝif] Bote ȝ. 48 is] was. 50 falshed] Falsnesse. 51 boun] Boxum and B. 55 fals] Falsnes. 57 Wyten] HIt w. 58 falsnesse] Fals. mede] þat Mayde*n* m. V; þis mayden m. H. 63 al] *om.* 64 togid*ere*] Ifeere. 66 *signiure*] seruyse. 70 synken] senden. 80 bokes] lokkes. 81 wraþþe] teone. 83 of . . . engendrit] a Mayden of goode. 84 g*ra*untide] graunte vs. mede . . . treuþe] hire þer t. wol asigne V; hir þere t. wol assente H. 89 *similar lines have been substituted.* 97 wolde] schulde. 104 ȝow in] such. ⁊] þat ȝe. 127 Þanne] Bote. 128 shirreue] schirreues Bak. 131 hadde . . . none] Notaries none Hors hedde*n* V; notaries had noo*n* horses H. 132 on . . . gange] go on foote. 143 of] *om.* 144 As] *om.* here] *om.* 145 Fals] Now F. 161 I hote] *om.* 168 I hote] *om.* 171 alle] eke. 172 falsnesse] Fals. 182 wypide] wrongen. 190 dayes] wykes. III 10 mede] þe Mayden. 14 dwelliþ] was Inne. 15 be . . . leue] and made hire good chere V; ⁊ made hir at eese H. 19 mede þanne] *tp.* 24 lordis] lordynges. 26 And] we. hire] þe. 30 callen] to tellen. 31 lede] lewedeste. 32 ferst] *om.* 33 clokke] Couche. 39 sem] su*m*me. 60 lordis] lordynges. 62 men] folk. 70 biggen] abuggen. 71 wel] and. 79 or] *with.* richesse] Rubyes. meynteyne] fauere. 82 Salamon] Bote S. 86 lettride] lewede. 109 Quaþ] Nay q. 132 hise] þe. 145 Bi Ie*su*] Heo Buggeþ. 146 þe treuþe] so faste V; it so fast H. 164 þat] *om.* 168 half] Nekke. 177 ofte] þere. 185 leue] lete. 186 boldite] to bolden. 193 Cowardly] Soþliche V; but soþely H. 194 his] þat. 197 hise . . . mede] m. to men. 208 haþ . . . of] Meedeþ. 211 alse] eke. 214 No] þer may no. miȝte] *om.* 216 þe] Muche. 220 werchen wel] *tp.* 221 p*re*chiþ it] hit p*re*chede. 235 a] *om.* 236 is] nis. 245 fulfille] worche. 254 seide] sende. 260, 261 *misplaced.* 268 who so] heo þat. IV 1 leng*ere*] more. 7 Rape] þat þou R. 12 þe(1)] my. 17 calde] clepte. 19 let] loke þou. wytful] swiþe feole. 24 on waryn] on a wayn. 34 into] to. 35 How] H.

þat. 50 manye] forþ Moneye. 53 wan] wente. also] *om.* 58 it make] *tp.* 61 For . . . hise] Him for his. to paye] Rediliche he payede. 66 wel] *om.* 69 catel] Meede. 77 þat] his. 78 seide] s. him. 89 sey no more] *tp.* 97 Summe] þenne s. 106 oþer . . . it] and vsun hit no more V; & no more it vsen H. 112 signe . . . shewiþ] bereþ s. of þe kyng. 114 forfaiture] Forfet. 116 þe pope] Popes. 118 þe] eny. 119 *line om.* 128 confessour] Clerk V; clerkis H. 140 nose] Eres. 144 sawis] Connynge. 153 shalt . . . raike] Rydest not. V 3 &] *om.* 6 I . . . fote]Forþer mihti not a fote V; ferþer ne mi3te y one fote H. 8 babelide] blaberde. 20 shal] schulde. 22 shal] *om.* 33 no . . . hem] hem wonte non ei3e. 43 his] þis. 44 wil] william. 50 hei3] liht. 57 dyne] eten. 66 þat] *om.* 67 And] *om.* to . . . þou3te] he þou3te him awreke. 70 Walewiþ] walleþ. 73 nei3 me] me neih V; many H. 76 don] make. 96 wi3t] w. in þis world. 99 bolniþ] Bolleþ. 100b, 101b *transposed.* 117 lef] lessun. 118 Wykkidly] & w. 121 Ne hadde] Bote nedde. 123 drapers] þis d. 129 My] And m. was a wynstere] at westmunstre. &] þat. 130 And] *om.* 136 my] þe. 137 And] *om.* 139 þat] such. 146 glotoun] þe G. 156 for] f. þis. 159 waffrer] warinar. 163 dykere] disschere. 167 glotoun] þe g. 168 Clement] ÞEnne C. 169 nempnide] he leyde. 174 in rape] Raply. 180 Hikke . . . þanne] *tp.* 208 liþer] wikkede. 219 more] wel m. 232 wile] schal. 242 wiþ] for. VI 6 ywounden] Iwriþen. 24 er] bote. 30 al] *om.* fourty] fiftene. 35 beter] more. 48 men . . . wyues] Mon . . . wyf. VII 3 poule] peter. 6 til] And wissen ou þe rihte weye t. V; & teche 3ow þe ri3te weye t. H. 19 it] *om.* 24 tau3t] þus t. V; so t. H. 26 poule] peter. 47 wiþ none] not wiþ H; not þou with V. 62 crafty] Craftus. 67 I . . . hem] *om.* 68 For] *om.* 77 bequest] Testament. 95 putte] posschen V; posse H. 114 Some] And s. 116 lord] vr. l. ygracid . . . 3e] we hit þonken. 121 I . . . sone] sone I schal. 128 cowes] Crowen. 131 ete] haue. 136 flessh . . . fend] Fend and heore flesch. 161 þe(2)] boþe his. 166 hise] boþe h. 183 cacche] caste. 199 beggeris . . . bigge] Bidders . . . Beggers. 203 swettere] þe s. 247 sit] Faste. 251 maner] *om.* 256 hym] *om.* 282 Grene] *om.* 285 hy] and. 300 here maister] *tp.* 304 shal] wole. VIII 10 in . . . rewliþ] Rulen þe Reame. 32 wiln] wolde. 34 skynes] oþer. 44 mede] þonk. 53 a] worþ a. 61 3if] wher. 62 it] þat hit. þus] so. sewiþ] serueþ. 72 ne] þat. 74 vp] *om.* 78 mysshapen] mis happes V; myshappis H. 81 he . . . man] þei weore Men. he] þei. shal] schul. 90 þe] *om.*

5b. The manuscript H *in some* 20 *agreements with* W

Prologue 57 good] silf. I 13 And] he. III 83 meires] þise m. 231 Prestis & personis] *tp.* 244 & hotiþ] to say. 263 shal(2)] *om.* IV 15 sente] bade. 121 wiþ croune] crowned. V 73 hym] hem. 74 hym(2)] hem. fame] defaut. 127 pressour] presse. 133 hire] h. also. 182 þe hostiller] *om.* VII 106 Shulde] þei s. 188 3et] *om.* 193 my . . . breþeren] b. of one blood H; b. of blood W. 209 nedy ben] *tp.* 227 his] hym to þat h. H; hym also þat h. W. 237 quaþ . . . *charite*] *tp.* 238 my] *om.* 260 it] *om.* 297 he . . . werkman] þei were werkmen. VIII 18 passe] wende. 54 *hereafter the same Latin line.* 130 metelis] meting.

5c. The manuscript H *in a few agreements with* L

I 1 merke] deope. 180 seide er] *tp.* III 30 constory . . . court] *tp.* H; þe courte of constory L. 164 gret] most. 246 kille] quelle. IV 95 reste] *om.* 157 graunte] g. wel. V 77 don] mad L; I made H. 78–80 *ll. om.* 92 I wysshe] *tp.* 139 vside] vsiþ. VI 1 þider] *om.* 42 ri3t] r. home. VII 193 bou3te] made. 294 fissh] fresch f. VIII 32 Pore] & pore.

5d. *The manuscript* H *in a few agreements with* A (*see* 1*b above*)

5e. *The manuscript* H *in a few agreements with* E (*see* 4*d above*)

[Knott-Fowler find that H forms a genetic pair with V.]

6. *The manuscript* H^2 *in some* 40 *agreements with* T

I 122 hem] hym. 126 on] her*e* o. T; her*e* in H^2. II 7 my] þ*at*. 110 non] non ne. 192 For] Fro. III 36 And] A. he. 91 fette] fecche. 92 boure] borugh. 212 Alle] Of a. 227 seiþ] seide. 258 cas] clause. IV 24 on waryn] vnwary. 53 wan] w. to. 141 witty] no wyt. V 7 adoun] in my bedis T; on my bedis H^2. 29 hom] *om.* felis] f. his wyf. 69 or(1)] ⁊. 174 rowneden] rombeden T; romeden H^2. 181 shulde] þe coup*er*e s. 214 þe veil] þ*er* while. VI 6 ywounden] he bond hym. 120 hem] *om.* VII 84 he] I. 306 and] oþ*er* þoruȝ. VIII 21 hem] hym. 28 myseise] myseises. 44 copiede] coupide. IX 7 ne] n. þe. 33 it] *om.* 39 siþes] tymes. 70 fer] for. 79 bigerdlis] breigerdlis. X 4 wittiliche] wiȝtliche. 7 heo hatte] he haþ. haþ] *om.* 39 as] þ*at*. 191 pliȝt] piȝt. 215 hem] hym. XI 54 mene] *om.* 97 grayn] gayn. 102 while] þ*er* whiles. 121 Fro] For. 126 I] þou. 136 hem] hym. 149 whoso] who. 164 to] for to. 192 beþ] bed þe T; bad the H^2. 201 þo] þe. 266 him] hem. 293 haue] any. ferþer] for.

[Knott-Fowler find that H^2 forms a genetic pair with T.]

7a. *The manuscript* H^3 *in some* 60 *agreements with* M

V 108 ⁊ . . . lokide] he loketh s*er* heruy ⁊ holowe. 117 Ferst] For. 127 hem(2)] hym. 147 cairiþ] koueryth H^3; kouerereth M. 151 wile] shal. 177 þei] Tweyne H^3; ⁊ tweyn M. 227 And . . . I] Qwat eu*er* I namm H^3; And eu*er*che man M. 233 þe] *om.* VI 2 baches] dales. 3 long] till longe. 20 callen] clepeth. 28 siþþe] sothe M; sothenesse H^3. 47 wilneþ] þenkyn M; thenke H^3. 117 Wyte] I vowe to. VII 15 wile] comandeth. 19 it . . . is] wha it is tyme. 26 for] ⁊ f. 35 conseyuede] rehersede. 59 any . . . swynke] hewe *with* þe hatchet H^3; he with his hachete M. 60 haue . . . þe more] haue leue . . . to leuyn. 61 wiþ . . . corn] þer mydde mauggre. it] *om.* 89 my] her*e*. 99 balkis] Rotes. 142 pilide] pyned. 171 Faitours . . . fer] For ferede this faitours. 223 vsen] wise M; wysse H^3. 233 crist] cryst hy*m* selue H^3; as crist hi*m* self M. 235 of . . . hondis] *om.* 237 *pur* . . . kenne] þat þou me techi*n* woldist. 275 þe] me. 285 gart] getyn M; gat H^3. VIII 23 god . . . hem] mote he*m* god H^3; he*m* god M. 32 wiln . . . wyues] wyues willen none be*n* M; wyuys wyl be H^3. 38 *line om.* 41 graiþ] heye. 57 þise . . . ben] For þe tresouris be*n* oure aldiris M; For þe tresour be*n* thrall*es* þ*at* is H^3. 73 þei] For þ. 80 lyuen] ledyn. 84 here] in h. 110 þat] He þ. H^3; For he þ. M. lelly] treuly. IX 111 ne] *om.* 118 Here . . . wolde] To hery*n* hys wytt wold I H^3; To heryn fawen woldy M. X 13 lelly] treuly. 17 wit*h*alle] *om.* 25 calle] clepe. 32 shap] schaft. 68 ⁊ cateles] of catel. 89 neu*er*e] al woi*e* M; al wey H^3. 93 comist] gynnyst H^3; gynnyt M. 104 þat] And. 122 fruyt] frend. 139 þeuis] schrewys H^3; schewis M. 146 constellac*ioun*] tyme. 175 Outtake] but take. 205 derne] *om.* do . . . shulde] xuld no ma*n* do H^3; schuld not be don M. 212 ȝif] þat. XI 21 conne] kan do. 32 More] ⁊ m. 47 ne] ⁊. 48 hunsen] comau*n*di*n*. 56 kete] grete. 57 mene] fewe. 77 lelly] treuliche. 100 whanne] w. þat. 111 þe] a. 115 Boþe] b. in. ⁊] ⁊ i*n*. 130 boke] scole. 151 And] He. 173 gome] man. 182 lele] trewe. 213 Poperiþ] Ridit. 238 lele] trewe. 252 To] Neiþ*er* t. 268 techiþ] tellit.

7b. The manuscript H³ *in some* 30 *agreements with* A (*see* 1*d above*)

[Knott found that H³ formed a genetic pair with A after VII 69. Fowler groups H³ with M from V 106 to the end.]

8a. The manuscript J *in some* 40 *agreements with* U

Prologue 69 wel] *om.* his] wel h. I 13 And] þat. 104 such . . . anoþer] & seuen moo oþere J; and siche mo oþere U. 122 troniþ hem] tryeste of. 123 Forþi] þerfore. 139 in herte] *om.* 180 Forþi] þerfore (U(1) *only*). II 154 mi3te] mowe. III 187 Dede] & dide U; And didyn J. 213 go] mete. IV 90 mede] he. V 75 be] with. VII 60 here] mede. 225 his] þat. 243 wilnest] desirest. 245 hote] bidde. 264 to] with t. VIII 4 aftir] þeraftir. 24 catel] ware. 74 wiþ] þat w. 79 of] *om.* 80 loþe] curse. 100 shalt þou] *tp.* 112 besy] b. ben. 130 metelis] matere U; mater meteles J. 132 loue þe] lyf. wel pensif] pitously. 135–6 *similar wrong division.* 136 Daniel] d. þe prophete. 149 on] mochil o. 160 leue] byleue it. 161 do] togidres mown. 165 renkes] lordes. 170 To] For to. IX 96 But] & but 3if. X 52 eggiþ] eggide U; eggyd J. 194 3if] *om.* 210 &(2)] *om.* XI 100 gan I knele] i knelyd. 166 mekly] meche U; mychel J. 229 in] to comen i. U; to com to J. 284 wi*th*] be.

8b. The manuscript J *in some* 20 *agreements with* M

I 74 þi . . . þe] þe þi faythe. III 141 barnes] childeryn. 164 Þere] For þ. IV 13 þe frek] co*n*sciens. 124 my] no. V 96 wi3t] man. VII 9 shedyng] spyllyng. 25 conne] gynne to J; gy*n*ne M. 245 ete] 3it. VIII 160 forbede] forbode. IX 6 wi3t] man. 85 And] *om.* 95 pite or] ony. 100 nou3t] *om.* 115 To] and. X 131 Formest . . . ferst] *tp.* to folk] t. men J; þise men M. XI 6 to(2)] *om.* 43 þe] *om.* 107 þat] &. 139 And] *om.* 165 q*u*aþ she] *om.* 170 þe gode wyf] stody. 189 ben] *om.* 241 cristene] þei. 278 þe wyt] *om.* 282 hadde . . . saluac*io*u*n*] was he sauid M; was sauyd J.

8c. The manuscript J *in some* 20 *agreements with* A (*see* 1*e above*)

[Fowler finds contamination between U and J in **A** 2.]

9. The manuscript K *in some* 40 *agreements with* W

Prologue 10 slepyng] sclepe. 34 giltles] gylefully K; gylously W. 36 hem(1)] hem in. 44 knaues] hewyn K; hyne W. 63 hy] charite. 64 vp faste] on hye. 74 leniþ] levyth K; leuen W. I 21 nedful] so n. 163 lewid] l. a thyng. þat . . . inne] wi*th*out light. II 34 two] *om.* 80 bokes] chek*es*. IV 45 but] *om.* V 67 hym] hem. 126 Brochide] Prycked. 129 made] worched K; wroght W. 146 shrift] chirche. 244 so] *om.* VI 101 Happily] And h. 118 a]no. VII 77 Forþi] And yet. 79 þat . . . haþ] he haþ best W; he hath it best K. 114 cunne] done. 168 defendite] fett. 170 be(2)] er W; or K. al warm] in erthe K; ful depe W. 196 3if . . . wistest] of the. 224 *line om.* VIII 16 here] to her. 55 bigge] sell. 63 here] yo*ur*. 149 Al] and a. 154 le*tt*res] seles W; *after cancelled* seales K. IX 26 watir] wawes. 27 stande] stomble. X 1 dwelliþ . . . wyt] *tp.* 96 þe] the thou. 159 sed] seth. XI 42 forþ] a. 49 leniþ] levith K; leueþ W. 53 of] among*es*. 81 his] her. 184 sout*er*is] towkkars. 220 &(1)] *om.* 261 markid] maked K; mad W. 269 in(3)] i. the. 290 to] t. the.

[Knott found that K and W formed a subgroup of *y*. Fowler (Thesis, p. 40) treats KW agreements in **A** 2 as the product of contamination; in *Piers the Plowman*, p. 26, a family tree apparently for **A** 1 indicates the relation [(WN)K].]

10*a*. *The manuscript* L *in a few agreements with* E (*see* 4*e above*)

10*b*. *The manuscript* L *in a few agreements with* H (*see* 5*c above*)

11*a*. *The manuscript* M *in some* 80 *agreements with* E (*see* 4*a above*)

11*b*. *The manuscript* M *in some* 60 *agreements with* H³ (*see* 7*a above*)

11*c*. *The manuscript* M *in some* 50 *agreements with* A (*see* 1*a above*)

11*d*. *The manuscript* M *in some* 30 *agreements with* W

Prologue 78 parissh] *om.* 80 ⁊ . . . prestis] and vicaries. 86 Pleten] To p. I 25 And] The þredde. 43 me] me lady W; me madame M. 171 ȝow] hem. II 56 heiȝe] loude. 196 þe] þat. III 224 his] *om.* 232 ⁊] or. IV 21 many] *om.* V 33 forwanye] wanye W; wanyn M. 73 neiȝ] by. 232 seke] s. þerwiþ. VI 105 þe(2)] þat. 109 Largenesse] And largesse. VII 43 wel] *om.* 62 crafty] Cristen. 120 mowe noþer] ne mow W; ne may M. 133 sellis] selle. 295 ⁊] or WM. VIII 58 ⁊] and to. 61 ⁊] of. 67 bulle] bill. 74 wiþ] *om.* 108 *line om.* 184 day of] dredful d. at M; dredful W. IX 15 here] *om.* 36 ⁊] and þe. 100 oþere] non o. 112 of a softe] s. of his. X 135 here] *om.* XI 2 of louȝ] *tp.* 33 seint] *om.* 36 Leccherie . . . losengerie] *tp.* 43 at here] a. þe. 195 is he] *tp.* 218 al] *om.* 252 hem(1)] hym.

11*e*. *The manuscript* M *in some* 20 *agreements with* D (*see* 3*a above*)

11*f*. *The manuscript* M *in some* 20 *agreements with* J (*see* 8*b above*)

11*g*. *The manuscript* M *in some* 20 *agreements with* V

I 168 chastite . . . charite] *tp.* III 131 heo] *om.* IV 30 wiþ] bi. 35 hadde . . . wyf] *tp.* V 84 wolde m*u*rdre] Morþerde V; mordred M. 205 ⁊] ⁊ of. VI 99 as dew] *om.* 114 any] þat. VII 106 Shulde] He s. 234 The . . . seiþ] For so s. þe Sauter V; And so s. þe sautir M. VIII 51 þat] his. 109 Be þat] As. 182 whiles] while þat. IX 24 fore-bisene] ensau*m*ple. 43 doþ] *om.* 44 Ay] Euer. 80 Erl] *om.* 95 hem] him. X 67 whiles] whil þat. 134 of] in. XI 85 yworsshipid] Iheried. 117 wit*h*] to. 123 wiȝt] mon. 125 signe] tokene.

[M was unknown to Knott. Fowler groups it with E from Prologue 1 to I 142, II 18 to II 145, and III 112 to 226. He groups M with H³ from V 106 to the end.]

12*a*. *The manuscript* N *in some* 130 *agreements with* W

I 107 Tauȝte] he t. 123 Forþi] F. ȝit. er] *om.* 129 *hereafter additional matter.* 131 loue] l. lelly. 132 *hereafter additional matter.* 141 on] vpon. 152 *additional matter.* 153 ȝe . . . ȝo*ure*] þow . . . þi. 161 *additional matter.* 165 none] no man. 171 haþ] now h. 179 graiþ] gracieuse. 180 Forþi] f. ȝit. II 20 *additional matter.* 22 Tomorewe] Now. þe] a. 31 lord] now l. N; now oure l. W. 45 *additional matter.* 53 as sire] right a. 56 *additional matter.* 65 *additional matter.* 66 In al] Wiþ. 86 þe] Thi. 87 to] wel t. 91 ȝe ⁊] And also

W; Also N. 103 For] *om.* 120 wolde] will. 123 And] Thei. 124 And alle] To her bodes to W; Til here bodis N. 131 *a substitution from the* C *version.* 132 þat] *om.* 134 þat] *om.* 135 And] Thei. 137 denis] Erchedeknes. 143 And . . . lyere] Of l. make N; Of liars make W. 151 But] He. 152 And] He. 160 comaundite] called. 164 And]*om.* 194 *additional matter.* III 2 to] afore. 4 To] *om.* 11 þere was] *tp.* 25 to . . . same] wiþ confort and game. 27 For to] To. þi(1)] alway þ. 29 lordis] gret l. hem(2)] *om.* 33 *additional matter.* 40 ek] also. 47 wyndowe . . . werching] w. ywroght. wile stonde] stont W; stant N. 61 To writen] *om.* of] in waunting of N; in wastyng of W. 75 certayn] seure. 79 or] of. 104 Before] Aforn. 105 Knelynge] K. þan. 127 And] She. 132 For] *om.* 139 prestis] styfly. she] hem. 140 holde] h. here. & lotebies] *om.* 141 *additional matter.* 142 þere] Whan. 143 is . . . to] fauoreþ (þe). 146 þe treuþe] him eure N; hem euere W. 150 Lawe] The l. 155 For] The. 160 more] bettre. 162 Nay] ȝe. 173 before] afore. 180 And] þou. 185 merþe] wiþ m. W; with my m. N. 196 kepiþ] kepe shal. 198 with] for. 199 Mede] For m. 202 wiþ] of. 203 here] þe. 207 here] *om.* asken] taken. 208 *line om.* 214 wiþoute . . . libbe] may leue w. mede W; lyue w. mede N. 216 worþi] wel w. 217 Nay] *om.* 220 werchen] ay w. 223 Loue] But l. 253 wiþ] forþ. 257 *line om.* IV 7 Raþe] Now r. 20 Hange] And h. 22 þanne] *om.* 30 to] aforn. 42 murþre . . . hynen] robbe and to slee. 47 for . . . vnneþe] for hym ones forth W; for hem onis for N. 51 And seide] For. 81 gan mede] *tp.* 90 For] *om.* 99 þat . . . be] To make mede. 128 Let] Do. þe] *om.* 134 among . . . renkis] in a rude wraþ N; and angre W. 143 stoden] s. stille. 144 be . . . to] anon t. 145 reherside] sayd. 147 ledis] lordes. 156 So] ȝif. V 6 I . . . fote] A f. ne myght I ferþer. 21–23 *ll. om.* 33 Let] That. 35 þat] Al þ. þe peple] *om.* 37 And siþþe] *om.* to] wel t. 40 And ȝe] Tho. 43 and reherside] to reherce. 46 And . . . &] She sighed soryfu & saide W; And syked ful sorowfully & seide N. criede] *om.* 55 make] gete. 66 His . . . bolnid] Al forbolne. wraþþe] angre. 79 meyne] wyf. I haue] *tp.* 84 maistrie] þe m. 97 And] *om.* 100 May . . . swage] Ther is . . . may s. 106 ne . . . me] may me not. 108 heruy] henri. 109 He] *om.* 135 hym] it. 151 I wile] *tp.* VI 1 þere were] *tp.* 20 þou] *om.* 54 Forto] Til. 68 fees] foos W; foes N. 105 And] *om.* VII 49 For] *om.* 52 perkyn] Piers. 106 ben hirid] haue hyre. 143 Wilt] For w. 154 countide] sette. 178 leyȝe] hadde l. 187 erde] hous. 192 werchiþ] now w. N; w. nowe W. 216 Go to] In. 233 oþer] &. 262 nile] wil. 266 an hauer] an hote W; an hot N. 276 peple] p. þan. VIII 6 to (2)] *om.* 118 to perkyn] þo.

12*b. The manuscript* N *in a few agreements with* V

II 47 feffid] *om.* III 94 melis þise] Melodyes V; melioudiouse N. 98 þou] *om.* 186 bateride] Battede. V 35 proue] to p. 203 wakide he] *tp.* wynkyng] wynk. 219 is] nis. VI 65 loke] l. hem. þere] *om.* 76 oþer þou] wher þorw. 95 be] b. wel. 109 let] ledeþ. 116 be] for. VII 41 þou] ȝe. VIII 155 þe . . . dome] Domesday. vndirfongen] Ipreiset V; praised N.

[Fowler (Thesis, pp. 11 ff.) does not seem to reach a conclusion about N. In the printed edition (p. 26) he groups it with W.]

13*a. The manuscript* R *in some* 210 *agreements with* U

Prologue 10 swiȝede] sweuenede. 36 Fonden] gon fyndyn. 38 þat] þ. þ. 70 vp knelynge] *tp.* 72 rauȝte] r. hym U; r. hem R. 85 þat] *om.* seruide] pletede. 86 Pleten] þei pleted.

92 Archideknes] I saw þ*er* a. 94 Ben] þey b. be] þorw. 102 dede] werk. 106 to hem] tolled he*m* and. I 1 bemeniþ] may mene. 3 yclo þid] was y. 21 ⁊] to. 26 Þat] so þ. þou . . . shuldist] ȝe swynke schulde. 152 wende] goþ R; gon U. 168 cheynid] schryned. II 11 *line om.* 24–25 *ll. om.* 42 teldit] tyȝth. 45 þropis] þrepis. 53 segge] *om.* wille] heste. 54 forþ] vp. 58 feffe] haue. 62 hem] ȝou. 63 vsurie] vsur*es*. 70 to(2)] and. 101 ȝif] *om.* 121 ioye] lawe. 160 þat] he. 164 to me] forþ. 168 p*re*your] treso*ur*. 172 Þanne] þo. III 1 ⁊ . . . mo] name. 2 Wiþ] And w. 13 somme] to sompne R; to sowpen U. 29 hem(1)] ȝou. 30 here] ȝour*e*. 53–4 *wrong division.* 63 here] ȝour*e* gode. 75 burgages] bargayns. 91–2 *wrong division.* 122 myselis] many tyme. 126 prisone*rs*] þe p. 142 wel] *om.* 166 dep*ra*ue] dispyce. 171 menske] mylde. 176 my sake] me. 177 soþly] sykerly. 185 mo*ur*nyng . . . leue] fro morwe*n* til eue. 187 me at] at his. 195 reaume] of rewmys. 230 it] ful. 234 louȝ] lond. 251 sente] bad. 262 happe . . . so*m*me] hap me*n* schuld se su*m* tyme. 268 his wille] ryȝth. 270 houue] gowne. IV 20 to] and. 24 on waryn] on were U; ton wer*e* R. 30 rombide] rowned. 47 for . . . vnneþe] onys for hy*m* R; ones on hym U. 60 hym . . . helpe] to h. h. at nede. 106 it] hit he*m* selue. 120 so were] *tp.* 130 afeld] to f. 131 lef] best. 143 stoden] s. forþ. V 21 I miȝte] *tp.* 36 we] for w. 60 in . . . palesie] and paltyk. 73 ofte] wel o. 86 techiþ] me t. 88 þat] *om.* crist] our*e* lady. 92 *additional matter.* 93 lauȝe] smyle. it liȝtiþ] þ*er*of lauȝeth. 102 shope] were. 113 wandre] slyde R; slideren U. 114 *expanded.* 115 I s*er*uide] *tp.* 118 weiȝe] wynne. 124 semide] semeþ. 128 *line om.* 132 aunsel dede] almesdede. 135 ⁊] for. 143 ne] n. no. 166 an heþ] *om.* 176–7 *wrong division.* 177 not] n. ȝut Iuge ne. 178 to] vp t. 183 aftir] afore. 214 þe veil] wile R; wol U. fet] fecche. 219 *line om.* 221 tofore] to veri. 223 dere] parysch. 229 lakke] fayle. 237 þe] hi*m*. 251 men] m. and mo. VI 29 sowe . . . sette] now and siþe. 35 he] hi*m*. louiþ] lykeþ. 62 þin] ȝo*ur*. 67 berwe] bak. 89 wif] wyȝt. 97 pokiþ] lokith U; loke R. 98 þi] þat. 104 sistris] douȝtr*es*. 108 *line om.* 120 is] had. VII 5 þat] my*n*. 10 faste] ȝe shole. 28 ek] *om.* 29–30 *wrong division.* 30 wasto*urs*] water*es* R; watris U. 39 assent] acorde. 50 seide] seyþ. 52 me] *om.* 56 a] his. 77 bequest] bequest*es*. 120 seknesse] febelnysse. 144 and] *om.* vs] so v. 237 *pur*] for. 242 hem] *om.* 283 chepyng] towne. 287 in come] *tp.* VIII 21 hem] *om.* 84 bed-rede] blereyde. 121 betere] moche more. 169 Þat] þei. IX 3 And] a. I. ful] wel. 5 askide] frayned. 14 among] at hom *with*. 18 I] he. 22 sone] sawe. 23 þe . . . day] *tp.* 34 liknid] lyk. 36 Þat] and. 41–2 *wrong division.* 41 aȝens] of alle a. 42 For . . . þe] *om.* 57 lerne] lyþen. 60 dremide . . . doute] *tp.* 78 helpiþ] delyþ. nede] most n. 80 or] and. 89 waiten] haunteþ. 94 shulde . . . kyng] *tp.* 105 q*ua*þ] *om.* 109 wiþ] *om.* 112 softe] sad. 117 beþ] were. X 21 And] *om.* 23 þise] *om.* 26 what] of w. is kynde] *om.* 29 þat] þ. he. 40 *line om.* 44 in] *om.* 53 good] *om.* 55 ȝif] hot. 56 Inwit] þe wit. 58 ȝonge] *om.* wiþ] in. 61 braynwod] brayned. 63 miȝt] myȝtis. 68 to] and. 80 It] and. 86 þ*er*of] þ*er*. 91 Be] *with*. 94 writ boþe] cherche after. 97 his teching] þis þing. 104 marbil] m. mosy R; m. mose U. 114 seluen] soule. 119 þoruȝ] þus þ. U; þ*us* in R. 121 his] our*e*. 124 a] as a. 125 Sp*ri*ngeþ] þat s. 135 kynde] kyn. 157 to] he*m* t. 172 on] to. 174 oþ*ere*] þe. 179 eiþ*er*] her*e* e. 185 þe] þis. 194 don] hiden. 199 macche . . . ysamme] ȝow to same takyn. 201 And] *om.* 206 As] Ac. 207 iche] eu*er*y. XI 77 lore] lord. 85 be þou] *tp.* 87 a] *om.* 90 degre] day. 92 oþ*er*] day. 131 to arguen] furst to a. 134–5 *wrong division.* 134 contreuide] construed. tolis] her*e* to lerne Tolus. 135 keru*er*is] kerue. 136 lyuel ⁊ lyne] *tp.* loke] lokede. 139 derkere] depper*e*. 156 gynful] greful R; gryfful

U. 168 foretolde] fayre tolde. 179 seide] s. hi*m* R; s. hem U. 185 foode] craft. 197 Forþi] For þis. 206 it] hi*m*. þei] me*n*. 209 roileþ] roxleþ U; roxlet R. 219 þat] *om.* kinghed . . . kniȝthed] king*es* . . . kniȝt*es*. 220 of] ou*er*. 221 it(2)] *om.* 229 riche] þe r. 230 penaunce] pacience U; pacient R. 231 Hauen] h. her*e*. 236 so(2)] þat. 237 þat] *om.* 241 þe] our*e*. 257 Eche] eu*ery*. 262 were] ded were. 263 wykkid] wiled. 278 vnwisly] vnwittily. 281 kneuȝ on] kneled to. 288 who] *om.* 291 souereynes] so fer. 302 or] *om.*

13*b*. *The manuscript* R *in some* 20 *agreements with* E (*see* 4*c above*)

[Knott-Fowler find that RU form a genetic pair.]

14*a*. *The manuscript* T *in some* 40 *agreements with* H² (*see* 6 *above*)

14*b*. *The manuscript* T *in some* 20 *agreements with* Ch (*see* 2 *above*)

14*c*. *The manuscript* T *in some* 10 *agreements with* D (*see* 3*b above*)

[Knott-Fowler find that T forms a genetic pair with H².]

15*a*. *The manuscript* U *in some* 210 *agreements with* R (*see* 13*a above*)

15*b*. *The manuscript* U *in some* 40 *agreements with* J (*see* 8*a above*)

15*c*. *The manuscript* U *in a few agreements with A* (*see* 1*f above*)

15*d*. *The manuscript* U *in a few agreements with* E (*see* 4*f above*)

15*e*. *The manuscript* U *in a few agreements with* W

I 183 lenge] duelle. IV 77 þe] do þ. VI 31 sewide] kepid U; siþ kept W. 36 pay] plese. VII 27 swynken ⁊ sweten] *tp.* 163 hem] hym. VIII 31 nonnes] wyues. IX 5 he] it. 20 at hom] *om.* 29 ⁊ sound] *om.* 108 on] of. X 58 ⁊] and in. XI 154 it] *om.* 170 I] and. 277 ⁊ . . . wyt] *om.* 294 *line om.*

[Knott-Fowler find that U forms a genetic pair with R, and that there is contamination between U and J.]

16*a*. *The manuscript* V *in some* 230 *agreements with* H (*see* 5*a above*)

16*b*. *The manuscript* V *in* 30 *agreements with* W

IV 85 to] *om.* V 100 ne . . . þing] so swete. VI 96 in . . . sitteþ] *tp.* VII 3 seint] *om.* 21 þe] *om.* 31 go] g. þou. 53 fynde treuþe] *tp.* 153 liȝt] luytel V; litil W. 162 þat] *om.* VIII 72 nouȝt in] in no. 79 mane*r*] *om.* 127 waitide] lokede V; loked me W. 132 And] *om.* 143 þe . . . sonne] *tp.* 156 pardou*n*] pardou*n*s. 172 to] *om.* IX 24 a] *om.* X 2 þat] of. 27 bestis] best. 46 a] and a. 81 *line om.* 89–90 *as one line.* 126 out of (2)] on W; vppon V. 127 gynneþ] doþ. 194 but . . . helpe] *om.* XI 24 ay] euer. 60 þat] þei. 71 musen] leeuen. 97 hise] hire. 180 þere] *om.*

16*c*. *The manuscript* V *in some* 20 *agreements with* M (*see* 11*g above*)

16*d*. *The manuscript* V *in a few agreements with* A (*see* 1*g above*)

16*e*. *The manuscript* V *in a few agreements with* N (*see* 12*b above*)

[Knott-Fowler find that V forms a genetic pair with H.]

17*a*. *The manuscript* W *in some* 130 *agreements with* N (*see* 12*a above*)

17*b*. *The manuscript* W *in some* 40 *agreements with* K (*see* 9 *above*)

17*c*. *The manuscript* W *in some* 40 *agreements with* A (*see* 1*b above*)

17*d*. *The manuscript* W *in some* 30 *agreements with* M (*see* 11*d above*)

17*e*. *The manuscript* W *in* 30 *agreements with* V (*see* 16*b above*)

17*f*. *The manuscript* W *in some* 20 *agreements with* H (*see* 5*b above*)

17*g*. *The manuscript* W *in a few agreements with* U (*see* 15*e above*)

[Knott found that W formed a genetic pair with K. Fowler (*Piers the Plowman*, pp. 26–7) pairs W with N in **A** 1 and with A in **A** 2.]

In these demonstrations of agreement no selection other than that specified above (pp. 68–9) has been practised. The variants in every group are of widely differing kinds: synonyms more or less obvious; roughly equivalent words not synonyms; additional words or phrases; omitted words or phrases; changes in word order; wrong divisions of lines; omissions of one or more lines; and additions of lines. All substantive variants, both striking, and dull and common-place were included in the hope that thus the misinterpretation that might result from selection would be avoided.

The groups may then be reviewed:

A

AM : 50
AW: 40
EA: 30
AH^3: 30
JA: 20
UA: 10
AH: 10
VA: 10

Ch

TCh: 20

D

DM: 20
TD: 10

E

EM: 80
EA: 30
RE: 20
HE: 10
LE: 10
UE: 10

H

VH: 230
HW: 20
HA: 10
HE: 10
HL: 10

H^2

TH^2: 40

H^3

MH^3: 60
AH^3: 30

J

UJ: 40
JA: 20
JM: 20

K

KW: 40

L	N	U	W
LE: 10	WN: 130	RU: 210	WN: 130
HL: 10	VN: 10	UJ: 40	KW: 40
		UA: 10	AW: 40
M	R	UE: 10	WM: 30
EM: 80	RU: 210	UW: 10	VW: 30
MH^3: 60	RE: 20		HW: 20
AM: 50		V	UW: 10
WM: 30	T	VH: 230	
DM: 20	TH^2: 40	VW: 30	
JM: 20	TCh: 20	VM: 20	
VM: 20	TD: 10	VA: 10	
		VN: 10	

In the above analysis three variational groups of exceptional persistence came to light: VH; WN; and RU. Other variational groups of relative persistence emerged: EM; MH^3; UJ; KW; and TH^2. In addition the number of variational groups persistent enough to require inclusion was substantial.

Even the manuscripts composing the most persistent groups very often appeared in conflicting groups. Thus, against the variational group VH must be set four groups in which H appears with another manuscript than V, and four groups in which V appears with another manuscript than H, comprising together more than 120 agreements which, if VH is genetic, must be random. Similarly the very persistent group WN, resting on 130 agreements, is qualified by more than 170 agreements of W with another manuscript; and the very persistent group RU, resting on 210 agreements, is qualified by more than 70 agreements of U with another manuscript, and more than 20 of R with another manuscript.

The majority of manuscripts do not form strikingly persistent variational groups of two manuscripts, but do occur in conflicting groups with striking frequency. On the whole the amount of convergent variation, whether conflation or coincident error, necessarily assumed to account for this situation, is very large.

In these circumstances the difficulty of forming even preliminary opinions about the genetic character of any of the groups of two manuscripts is evident. Inferentially the manuscripts must be in some genetic relation, but actually its character altogether fails to emerge at this stage. The majority of the variational groups of two set out above must be random. In addition to these groups there are about 1500 further agreements of two manuscripts, which, although they fail to form variational groups of serious persistence, must nevertheless be taken into account in assessing the amount of convergent variation that occurred in the transmission of this poem.

The substantial number of variational groups shown above does not begin to indicate the extent of random agreement among these manuscripts, since it fails to show the further agreements of pairs of manuscripts which have attracted notice as variational groups, within larger groups. Such agreements in company have not been treated as evidence in the analysis above. They are not in fact primary evidence, and to admit them as such at the stage of distinguishing genetic groups from variational groups would beg the question. Of course, once a group is treated as genetic, its sigils, appearing within a larger group, must reflect that genetic relation. But the converse applies equally, and in the present instance. For example, in distinguishing a genetic group RU, or a genetic relation between A and M, or W, or E, or H^3, relatively infrequent groups like RA[1] are dismissed as random. To appreciate the amount of divergence from RU, and from AM, or AW or AE or AH^3 (whichever of the latter is regarded as genetic), the occurrence of RA in larger groups must be observed.[2] The same applies to other, presumptive genetic groups.

[1] IV 89 *line om.* V 53 had] h. of. 59 cope] counte A; compte R. VII 185 And] *om.* 238 lere] ken. VIII 90 kenne] telle. 120 abbesse] aunte. IX 4 wiȝt] *om.* 30 þe] *om.* X 38 þat(2)] of. 111 chirches] cherche. 141 þat] *om.* XI 21 craftis] *om.*

[2] *The sigils* RA *occur in about 50 groups where* U *is missing:* III 47 wel] *om* (*with* J). 84 hym] hem (*with* ChVJLEKWNM). IV 107 it] *om* (*with* DJEWNM). 134 whanne] *om* ($TDChH^2$). V 13 þise] þe (HLEKW). 56 þeraftir] after (DVEM). 88 hym] hem (VHLEWN). 91 beholde] byhelde (EM). 198 þrew] fel ($TDChH^2HMH^3$). VI 28 to] forto (D). for] *om* (DMH^3). 47 to] *om* (E). 71 þat] *om* (W). VII 86 holden] byholde (H^3). 95 putte] pyke (EH^3). 226 before] þer b. (TH^2K). 227 his] þat h. ($DLKMH^3$). 238 lef] lyf ($TChVMH^3$). 245 ete nouȝt] *tp* (H^3). 283 þat] and (WNM). 286 And] *om* ($WNMH^3$). 298 þanne] *om* (VHH^3). VIII 6 or] and (HLN). 11 wel] ful ($VHNH^3$). 25 hem] him ($TChH^2J$). 26 hem(1)] him ($TChH^2M$). hem(2)] him ($TChH^2M$). 120 þe] myn (L). 121 kennide] tauȝthe (VH). 123 þat] *om* (VJWN). 125 seldom] litel ($TChH^2VHJ$). 141 deuinide] demed ($TDChH^2M$). 147 his] þe (VM). 178 patent] p. of þi pardoun (DK). 181 er] her e. (DJKN). IX 8 befel] fel (VJ). 16 comside] gan (M). 29 is he] *tp* (DH^2VJK). 30 stere] sterne (VKWM). 34 þe] þis (K). 67 þo] *om* (ChW). 84 ȝe] þe ($TDChH^2W$). X 11 þise] þe (WMH^3). 53 þe] *om* (DW). 54 is he] *tp* (H^2VKW). 140 on] of (JWM). 175 þe] *om* (V). XI 3 so] þus me (W). 4 And] a. al (VJWM). 5 wisdomis] wisdam (VKWM). 113 to] of (H^2). 195 so] And s. (KWM). he] *om* (JK). 230 in] and (WM). 264 on(2)] *om* (JKW). 298 or of] and (KWH^3).

The sigils RA *occur in more than 30 groups where* E, W, M *and* H^3 *are missing:* III 47 wel] *om* (J). IV 11 crist] god (UDVH). 23 rit] ryȝth (UH^2). 55 þo] *om* (U). IV 134 whanne] *om* ($TDChH^2$). V 15 poynt] þing (U). 36 leue] loue (UDVHJLK). 85 to(2)] byfore (UV). 230 iche] euery (UH). VI 6 *line om* (U). 28 to] forto (D). 54 Forto] Forþ til (U). 67 at] *om* (U). VII 226 before] þer b. (TH^2K). 257 lord] god (UCh). VIII 6 or] and (HLN). 90 For] *om* (N). 120 þe] myn (L). 121 kennide] tauȝthe (VH). 125 seldom] litel ($TChH^2VHJ$). 178 patent] p. of þi pardoun

The difficulty of attempting to distinguish variational from genetic groups of two manuscripts should now be apparent. Any genetic hypothesis simple enough to be used for recension leaves a residue of groups not accounted for. To conceal or dismiss this as immaterial is misleading. To explain some of it by conflation only increases the complexity of the hypothesis, diminishing its usefulness for the simple and uncompromising logic of recension. Ascribing the unstable relations of some manuscripts to their descent from different exemplars in different parts of the poem has the same effect.

The character of the problem is shown by the manuscripts E, A, W, M and H^3. Among these Fowler distinguishes EA as one of 'three branches of the minor group' EAMH^3 (Thesis, p. 20; see also the stemma on p. 26 of *Piers the Plowman*). For this decision 14 variants are his authority (see p. 70 above for the agreements of EA). It is not impossible that EA is a genetic group. But any hypothesis that makes it such is severely tested by 26 agreements of AM, 15 agreements of AW, and 15 agreements of AH^3, to the point where E breaks off, as well as by 25 agreements of EM where A is available. Moreover, the usefulness of such a hypothesis is very doubtful in these circumstances. Similarly the proposed genetic group MH^3 is tested by 30 AH^3 agreements, as well as by 8 EM agreements between V 105 and the point in VII where E breaks off. E, meanwhile, for Prologue–I 142 where A begins, is found in some 20 agreements with M, as, from the hypothesis of a genetic group EAMH^3 (below, p. 92), might be expected in the absence of A and H^3. But at the same time, for this part of the poem E occurs 15 times in agreement with R, 6 times in agreement with U, and (below, pp. 86–7) some 20 times in agreement with RU in a variational group of three manuscripts. The agreement RUE is explained by assuming a change of exemplar, so that for Prologue–I 183 the genetic relation is {[(EA)M]RU} (Fowler, Thesis, p. 15). Again, change of exemplar is an undeniable possibility, but the genetic hypothesis which requires its inclusion is so much the less useful for recension.

The conclusions permitted by the evidence of variational groups of

(DK). 181 er] her e. (DJKN). IX 8 befel] fel (VJ). 16 comside] gan (M). 29 is he] *tp* (DH^{2}VJK). 34 þe] þis (K). waniþ ⁊ waxiþ] *tp* (U). 35 grete] *om* (UDJ). 78 ouȝt] *om* (U). X 53 ⁊] a. of (UV). 64 ne in] and (UK). 151 hatid] h. he*m* (UVK). 166 ⁊] a. of (UK). 175 þe] *om* (V). 176 shynglid] sengle (UD). XI 154 for] of (UJK). 195 he] *om* (JK). 198 chaste] teche (U). 224 wyes] weyes (UDH^{2}JK). 268 writ] cherche (TUDH^2).

two manuscripts are typical of those at all stages in this demonstration: that there is some ground for distinguishing genetic groups, but so much contradictory evidence that the distinction cannot extend to all the manuscripts; and that such genetic information as can be recovered is not clear, simple and unqualified enough to use for recension.

We can allow that the persistence of the groups RU, VH and WN probably establishes their genetic character. In addition there are strong indications of a genetic relation between E, A, M and H³, but there is little likelihood that the exact nature of this relation is recoverable: no clear arrangement of these four manuscripts in groups of two or otherwise emerges. Several of the remaining groups of two manuscripts attract notice: TCh as the only persistent group of two in which Ch appears; DM as the only persistent group of two in which D appears; TH² as the only persistent group of two in which H² appears; UJ as the most persistent group of two containing J; KW as the only persistent group of two containing K. About these it is necessary to defer judgement. On the negative side there are the qualifications already noted regarding EAMH³; the conflicts RU : UJ; KW : WN in particular; and generally the abundance of conflicting agreements, most of which, by exclusion, must be random. At this stage, then, where conclusions ought to be easiest, it begins to seem as if a useful genetic hypothesis will not be attainable. The remainder of the examination will put this beyond doubt.

VARIATIONAL GROUPS OF THREE MANUSCRIPTS

Persistent variational groups of three manuscripts are, as might be expected, less numerous than those of two. A number, however, attract notice. They are now given in order of persistence.

1. *The manuscripts* TChH² *in some* 90 *agreements*

I 59 þat] þ*ere*. 78 to] *om.* 101 hem] hym. 103 kingene king] king of kinges. 110 of siȝt] to loke on. 135 wytnessiþ] askiþ wytnesse. II 59 or for] oþ*er*. 131 þo] þ*ere*. 142 of] fro. III 72 richen] risen vp. 79 þise] þat. 95 wy] ywys. 109 me] *om.* 139 persones . . . prestis] *tp.* 251 him] *om.* 259 noiȝide me] *tp.* 268 aȝeyn . . . wille] to þe wrong. IV 23 swyþe] ȝerne. 24 on waryn] on wary Ch; vnwary TH². 53 wan] w. to TH²; went to Ch. 73 shal] shulde. 106 it] i. w*ith* tungis. 112 shewiþ] shewide. 119 oþer] forsoþe. 129 it in] þis. V 17 segges] sent god. 25 craft] of c. 57 Drinke] Shulde d. 60 in] ⁊ on. 81 market] a m. 93 Of] And o. 98 lyk] as. 109 babirlippid] b. boþe TCh; bit*ur*browed bothe H². 119 wente] was sent. 132 whanne] ⁊. 176–7 *wrong division.*

177 þei] þanne þ. TH^2; bot þen þ. Ch. couþe not] ne c. 196 foules] larkes. 214 þe] þ*er*. 232 se] seke. 250 aunte] hyne. VI 22 me god] g. mote m. 29 and sette] his seed. 37 I] And. 53 brok] bank. 67 berwe] bo*ur*ne T; burne H^2; borne Ch. 104 seruen treuþe] t. louf T; t. loueþ ChH^2. VII 5 akir] a. so me god helpe. 25 conne] lerne to. 30 and . . . men] *om.* 32 to(1)] þe. 48 suche] for s. 52 pilgrymys] pilgrym. 196 Now . . . I] I wolde. VIII 7 man*er*] m. of. 8 þat] þe. 32 Pore] *om.* aftir] helpe hem þ*ere* a. 45 lettrid] lewid. 61 ȝe(2)] *om.* 73 Þei] Þ. ne. 100 shalt] ne s. TH^2; Sne s. Ch. 122 likide] likiþ. 129 Meteles . . . moneyles] M. on m*er*ueilles TH^2; Mynnyng on þe mervailes Ch. 134 nay] *om.* 139 vncouþe] an vnkynde. 158 to . . . Ioye] *a pena ⁊ a culpa.* 159 a lef] þe lif. techiþ] shewiþ. 169 welþe . . . world] world at wille. 179 to] *om.* IX 7 lesse] þe l. 85 hiȝte] bit hym. 113 I] I ne. X 12 douȝter] sistir. 17 inwit] þouȝt. 47 allie] halle. 78 roten] roren. 176 Þat] Put þ. TH^2; Putte Ch. shynglid] same. shal] þat s. TH^2; þat I s. Ch. 178 Þus þoruȝ] *tp.* 180 leiȝen] ley hem. 193 betwene] togid*ere*. 207 mariage] man*er*. 208 werche] do þat werk. 210 leiȝeris] folis. 212 as wolues] *om.* ȝif] what þat. XI 2 louȝ] loþly. 7 and . . . hym] bitt*er*ly. 19 deseites] þe d. 55 seke] se. 56 kete] kid. 77 on þe] of. 80 whyes] werkes. 82 þat(2)] *om.* 97 grayn] graunte Ch; gayn TH^2. 110 as(1)] *om.* 129 to knowe] k. alse. 183 husbondis] lewide men. 211 be stretis] aboute. 246 ben lyche] beleuiþ. 260 wrong] *om.* 301 alle] at wille.

[Fowler identifies TChH^2 as a genetic subgroup.]

2. *The manuscripts* EAM *in some* 50 *agreements*

I 145 pite] *om* AM; *deferred* E. 151 mete . . . ellis] to oþer men m. AM; tyll other m. E. 152 Ȝe] *om.* weiȝe] mett E; metyn AM. þ*er*wiþ] vnto you E; to ȝou AM. 157 masse . . . houres] heuenriche blys. 160 fait] fewte. 161 dede] ded*es*. 180 siȝte of] *om* (E(1) *only*). II 5 Loke . . . ⁊] *om.* 16 haþ . . . me] at me hase grevyd EM; þat greuyth me A. 146 mene] men. 154 I . . . cacche] I hym c. myght E; I kacche mythe M; I hem caut may A. 161 To] For to. 193 hi*m*] he. 197 fere] ferde. III 5 wile] sal. 11 m*er*þe] moche. 21 pecis . . . siluer] other gyfteȝ mony. 33 *line om.* 65 mene] þe menes EM; þece menis A. 78 Or] As. 89 ȝouþe . . . elde] thoght . . . dede EA; word . . . dede M. 112 She] And. 273 leute] loue. IV 21 And] For. 31 in to] agayns. 33 a . . . wisly] *tp.* wel] ful. 50–1 *wrong division.* 58 mede] I. 65 wot] it w. 67 euere] *om.* 75 mowe] may. 82 pees . . . purid] pe*n*nys for p. ⁊ pecys of E; pens in presens ⁊ pecis of AM. 84 wile] *om.* 85 Pes . . . pitousliche] *tp.* 92 I] we. 96 more] bett*er*. 100 not] *om.* 129 wedde] gyff þe. 130 Þat] Bot. shal] *om.* 146 be . . . it] to me to bryng þaim toged*er* EM; to brynge togederis A. 147 ledis] londis AEM. V 23 How] When. 46 lord] *om.* 48 Heo] þat sche. 70 Walewiþ] Walk*es* E; walkyt M; Walkyn A. 77 And] To EM; Tho A. 78 gode happis] godnes. 79 hym] men. his] þair. 90 Awey] Also AM; And also E. turne] t*ur*ned. 95 *expanded.* 103 to] *om.*

[Fowler finds EAM a genetic group to V 106.]

3. *The manuscripts* RUE *in some* 40 *agreements*

Prologue 1 softe . . . sonne] I south wente. 7 ⁊] I. 13 an heiȝ] vp. 14 Imakid] ontyrid R; atired U; entyred E. 16 ⁊(2)] *om.* 17 þere] *om.* 21 settyng] seedtyme. 29 Coueite] And c. in] i. þe. 30 likam] lykamys. 32 semiþ to] ys sene in. 37 ȝif] what. 42 Flite þanne] þei flyteþ. 47 at] in. 52 þat . . . were] loth for. 67 þat] *om.* 71 bunchide] blessed. 72 And] *om.* 77 It is] I trowe hit be R; y trowe i. i. U; I trow . . . it be E. 87 nouȝt] non. ones] *om.* 107 Whit] wiþ white. 109 Al] *om.* I 23 vesture] v. verylyche. 24 at] a. ȝo*ur*. 101 ne] n. for. ȝeftis] syluer. 126 triȝest] þe t. 132 diȝe . . . þou] þeȝ þ. d. RU; yf þ. d. E. 175 dele] may d. 180–3 *similar dislocation of* VII 70–213a *here.* II 120 þat] þ. þe. 141 cartesadil] sadle. 171 hym] hem. III 30 at] a. þe. 260 kynde] resou*n*. 270 a] no. V 37 holde] kepe. VI 117 forsoþe] þe sothe. VII 70–213a *similarly misplaced.* 93 in] by. 95 pote] *om.* 102 Eche] euerey. 103 vp] out. 108 hey . . . lolly] dusada*m*-meme. 151 ordre] lord. 163 he(2)] and. 173 on] onys o. RU; onys of E. 177 bedrede] blereyed RU; blered E. 195 aftir] what. 201 bollnyng] swellyng. 210 or] ne. 213 I] *om.*

[Knott found that RUE were a subgroup in Prologue 1–I 183 and VII 69a–VII 209. Fowler (*Piers The Plowman*, p. 26) observes that 'the UR manuscripts reveal that in different portions of the text they (or rather an ancestor) were copied from different exemplars, or "parent" MSS'. In the stemma on that page they appear as {[(EA)(MH^3)]RU}.]

4. *The manuscripts* AMH^3 *in some* 20 *agreements*

V 116 loke] wayten. 153 he] herry AH^3; heruy M. 159 waffrer] bereward. VI 3 longe] to l. A; till l. MH^3. 37 oþerwhile] sumtyme. 100 þeroute] wi*th*oute. VII 86 mynde] messe. 122 ⁊] *om.* 139 arise] *om.* 142 pilide] pyned MH^3; foule pyne A. 168 þe . . . ferst] *tp.* 171 Faito*urs* . . . fer] *tp.* 187 erde] lond AH^3; lord M. 190 I . . . wel] *tp.* 193 blody] *om.* 233 Actif . . . contemplatif] *tp.* 235 wiþ] Thorow. 237 *transposition.* 270 cole plantis] *tp.* VIII 18 passe] partyn. 20 hadde] han AH^3; þey han M. 100 to . . . wende] þe deuyl schal haue þi soule. IX 102 sauo*ur*iþ] sauerid. X 18 haþ] had. 19 hende] thride. 101 comsist] begynne A; gynnyst MH^3. 168 hem] h. brymme AH^3; h. breme M. XI 18–19 *as one line.* 19 Þat . . . deseites] *om.* 94 mele] speke. 170 þe] þat. 184 sout*er*is] toucheris.

[Fowler finds AMH^3 a genetic group from VII 69a to VII 209.]

5. *The manuscripts* RUD *in some* 20 *agreements*

Prologue 11 mete] to m. 41 bratful] bred ful. II 53 as . . . wile] at . . . wille. 61 lord-sshipe] worschep. III 29 hem(2)] ȝou. 179 han] *om.* 262 happe] hap me*n* RU; happed ende D. 270 þat] h*is*. IV 51–2 *wrong division.* 72–3 *as one line.* 72 ⁊ . . . cunstable] *om.* 119–21 *as two lines.* 124 þoruȝ] wi*th*. 146 it(2)] *om.* V 17 segges] seyþ god RU; sayd god D. 135 louȝ] loþ. 176 an] on an. 196 wiþ] wilde. VI 34 waytide] to wayte RU; wayten D. VII 212 Make] lat make. 247 to] *om.* IX 11 *pur*] for. 42 þi] þe. 56 a(1)] *om.* X 29 þe] *om.* 64 miȝt] wit. XI 56 kete] ked D; kedde RU. 82–3 *wrong division.*

[Fowler, Thesis, pp. 21–6, 39–40, as well as 'Contamination in Manuscripts of the A-Text of *Piers the Plowman*', *PMLA*, lxvi, pp. 495–504, finds contamination between RU and D.]

6. *The manuscripts* VHW *in more than* 10 *agreements*

Prologue 7 forwandrit] of wandringe. 95 And] To. 102 As] *om.* I 17 helpe] seruen. 94 teiȝen] bynden. 130 in] þe i. II 60 for euere] *tp.* III 11 to] wi*th* t. 239 þe] þat.

252 kilde] slouh. IV 20 holde] bere. 142 nouȝt] *om.* 146 to(2) . . . it] hit bringe. V 25 he] þei. 77 And] *om.* 174 in] *om.* VII 60 Shal] He s. 128 Cacche] Gaste. 152 now] ȝit VH; And ȝit W. VIII 79 þis] *om.*

7. *The manuscripts* TDCh *in more than* 10 *agreements*

Prologue 71 bunchide] bunchiþ. III 195 ouerhouiþ] ouer on. IV 118 mote] mo T; moo D; many Ch. V 174 risen] r. þei. VI 33 doluen] deluen. 89 vp] out. VII 75 now] *om.* 101 þat] &. 120 noþer] not. 164 wiþ] but. preyede] þei p. 175 An hep] In helpe. 178 *line om.* 195 aftir] *om.* 222 mouþiþ] nempniþ T; nempned Ch; nemened D. 266 an hauer] non oþer. 282 *line om.* VIII 156 of] at. IX 54 And] *om.* X 26 *line om.*

8. *The manuscripts* AWM *in more than* 10 *agreements*

II 161 tresour] þing. 168 preyour] thyng. V 40 at] of. 45 hire] *om.* VI 63 but] *om.* 114 ingang] in. VII 294 yfried] fryed or rostid. VIII 151 a] *om.* 176 þe(2)] *om.* XI 33 neuere] neþer. 36 Leccherie] Losengerie. 47 Is] I. þer. 61 &] ȝif þat. 167 And] I. 257 make] lette. 264 on(1)] it wel be. 277 wende to] wynne me.

9. *The manuscripts* WMH³ *in more than* 10 *agreements*

V 243 for] of. VII 29 þat] *om.* 149 þe . . . þanne] *tp.* 285 to] on. IX 110 lyk] and l. X 202 vntyme] no tyme WH³; non t. M. 204 also] leuyng W; lyuende M; leuedyn H³. XI 21 yclepid] called. 22 serue] sewit M; sweyn of H³; folweþ W. 87 And] But. 119 half] hande. 126 bible] bille. 132 garte] made. 149 techiþ] telleþ. 175 heo] þai. 193 singe] and s. 217 þis(2)] þe.

10. *The manuscripts* TDH² *in more than* 10 *agreements*

I 112 his] *om.* II 95 And] *om.* III 208 mede] nede. IV 60 wepid] wepiþ. 95 in] hym i. 153 raike] wende. V 251 þo] þe. VI 120 is] haþ. VII 35 þe] þise. VIII 171 dede] þe d. X 191 pliȝt] piȝt TH²; put D. 201 þanne] *om.* XI 60 feiþ] false T; face D; fase H². 263 vnwriten] vndirwriten. 277 here(2)] for h.

11. *The manuscripts* VHJ *in more than* 10 *agreements*

Prologue 22 Wonne þat] þ. monie of. wiþ] In. I 59 care] c. quod heo. 77 I knelide] *tp.* 105 þe . . . þouȝte] *om.* II 26 as I] soþ as I VH; soth I J. 159 on] of. III 75 wel] *om.* 225 Þere] Bote þ. 268 takiþ] doþ. IV 100 no] *om.* V 104 for] f. heore VH; of her J. VII 5–6 *wrong division.* 6 I . . . ȝow] *tp.* VIII 46 For] *om.*

12. *The manuscripts* VHM *in about* 10 *agreements*

Prologue 59 Manye] For m. I 62 falshed] Falsnes. 170 Ȝe] þei VH; þe M. II 16 maide] m. quod heo VH; med quod sche M. 87 mede] hure. III 116 false] Feire. IV 39 fer] dreede. V 17 segges] to Men. 70 &] or. 196 leide] leiþ. VI 46 long] gret. VII 41 Nyme] Takeþ. 71 shal] wol. 257 lord] vr l. VIII 122 piers] *om.*

13. *The manuscripts* VHN *in about* 10 *agreements*

III 6 of] in. 97 þe(2)] þis. 238 þou(2)] þat. V 18 grounde] eorþe. 153 Hast þou] Hastou ouȝt I þi pors. 200 hym] h. hom. 204 bolle] Cuppe. 219 goodnesse] Merci.

VII 69 auntir] þrift. 189 begg*er*is & bidderis] *tp* VN; bedrede*n* & beggeris H. 278 &] *om.* VIII 58 &] or to. 67 Begg*er*is & bidd*er*is] *tp.*

14. *The manuscripts* RUJ *in about* 10 *agreements*

Prologue 96 bondage] bondeagys. III 146 treuþe] t. ofte U; hem ofte RJ. 259 it] ʒif hit. IV 133 þis] þe. V 204 was] what. VII 283 Be þat] by þa*n*. VIII 117 Haue þei] *tp.* IX 64 þou wost] *tp.* X 106 ben þei] *tp.* XI 233 pistil] postel RU; apostel J. *After* XI 313 *additional matter.*

15. *The manuscripts* RUM *in about* 10 *agreements*

Prologue 24 comen] þey c. II 42 beside] þ*er* b. 135 þise] þe. 161 atache] take. V 57 doke] goos. 136 wouʒ] wowes UM; walles R. VI 55 þ*ere*] þ*er*inne. 103 gift] thing. VIII 50 is Innocent] *tp.* X 76 þ*at*] and. 161 suche] þese. XI 216 found*ours*] fou*n*d*our*.

16. *The manuscripts* VHE *in about* 10 *agreements*

I 117 werchen . . . wrong] wrong worchen. 155 loue] liuen VH; leve E. II 88 fastnid] feffet. 131 Þo] þe*n*ne. 158 þis] *om.* 161 tirauntis] Traytours. IV 156 So] S. þat. V 96 I] For I. 123 drouʒ I] *tp.* 253 Criede] Criʒinge. VII 9 þe(1)] *om.*

17. *The manuscripts* RUV *in a few agreements*

I 2 I . . . faire] *tp.* V 89 broken] brode. VII 56 hals] bak. IX 42 &] he. 47 þi-self] þou. 87 men] hem U; hi*m* RV. 111 *line om.* XI 69 here(2)] þat. 135 kende] tauʒþe.

18. *The manuscripts* AWH^{3} *in a few agreements*

VI 3 þ*at*] *om.* 74 þeroute] oute. VII 229 And] *om.* VIII 21 non] *om.* X 119 sou*er*aynes] souereynte. XI 82 to] *om.* 86 so] s. euere W; sum eu*er* A; eu*er* H^{3}. 120 Til] Whan AW; And qwa*n* H^{3}. 136 And . . . lyne] Leuel & lyne I hem lernyd. 291 none] þer non.

With this information it would be possible to extend the genetic hypothesis beyond the point allowed by the evidence of the variational groups of two manuscripts. Thus the very persistent group of three manuscripts, TChH^{2}, would confirm the suggestion of the group TH^{2} (p. 75 above), and might be used to explain the group TCh (p. 71 above), if the genealogist took into account occasional defections, or assumed correction in the absent member of the trio, whether H^{2} or Ch. He would then posit a genetic group [(TH^{2})Ch]. There would also be confirmation of a genetic relation EAMH^{3} in the groups EAM, AMH^{3}, WMH^{3} and AWH^{3}, although, as with the pairings of these manuscripts, clear and uncontradicted evidence of the exact nature of their relation would be lacking. Meanwhile a genetic group EAMH^{3} would be questioned by the relatively persistent group RUE.

This would, however, seem to be the limit of permissible inference, and the hypothesis could not be carried even so far without recourse to the type of explanation which would make it less useful for recension, such as reference to copying from different exemplars in different parts,[1] or to conflation.[2] While such expedients might seem to account for some of the disagreements implied in the various groups set out above, they would not remove these, any more than they would account for them all; and still there would remain some 300 variational groups of three manuscripts not set out above, representing agreements necessarily discrepant from any hypothesis rather more often than once in four lines, having regard to groups of three manuscripts alone. The descriptive accuracy, and therefore the usefulness of any genetic conclusions authorized by the evidence so far, are thus very seriously qualified.

One group of three manuscripts proposed as genetic by Fowler,[3] namely KWN (his WNDi), has not appeared in the above demonstration. KWN is evidenced by the following agreements:

I 170 out crepe] *tp* KN; crepe ought W. III 102 ellys] in haste. IV 150 it] *om.* V 39 steward] stiwardes WN; stiwarden K. 54 Lecch*our*] Lechery. VII 214 seide . . . þanne] *om.*[4]

It will be seen that this group is less persistent than all those cited above, many of which are excluded from his genetic structure. It should also be noted that it is no more persistent than the following groups of three containing K or W or N:

JWN: II 137 & southdenis] *om.* III 52 iche] eu*ery*. 261 regne] r. ȝit. V 17 segges] *om.* 53 enuye] p*ri*de. 84 & miȝt] *om.* VII 16 For] And. 284 was] w. þe.
ChKW: III 255 shendfully] schamfully. VII 7 scleire] chayere K; chare Ch; share W. 296 But] And b. IX 19 mowe] may. 30 arise] ros ChW; rose K. X 209 gatis] wise. XI 248 good] godes.

As long as the evidence of manuscript agreements is observed without preconceptions there is no more authorization for treating KWN as genetic than there is for the other groups just now noticed. Study of these groups of three manuscripts, therefore, has not removed the discrepancy between the groups KW and WN (above, pp. 76 and 77–8).

[1] Fowler (Thesis, pp. 15–16) proposes this explanation for RUE.
[2] Fowler (Thesis, pp. 21–6) proposes this explanation for RUD.
[3] See the stemma, *Piers the Plowman*, p. 26.
[4] To these Fowler (Thesis, p. 11) adds I 163, where, however, KW differ markedly from N, and VI 27 where KN appear to be following the **C** version.

Variational Groups of Four Manuscripts

Among the more than 350 variational groups of four manuscripts persistent groups are few. They are the following.

1. *The manuscripts* TDChH^2 *in about* 60 *agreements*

I 171 harde] faste. II 51 boun] bounde. 82 And] *om.* 86 texte] textis. 94 and] *om.* 123 in . . . abouten] *tp.* 165 sende] sente. III 83 meiris and] *om.* 102 *line om.* 118 Is] I. 165 to] for to. 171 menske] au*aun*ce. 241 al] *om.* 257 for euere] *om.* IV 24 on waryn] on wary Ch; on warry D; vnwary TH^2. 47 for . . . vnneþe] v. on hym f. 58 þi] *om.* 106 to] *om.* 114 at douere] do eu*er*e. 126 þe man] he may. 145 hadde] *om.* 148 rauȝte] deiȝede. V 16 plumtres] plantes. 41 seint] at hom s. 56 shulde] *om.* 93 it liȝtiþ] þerof. 113 walsshe] w. scarlet. 114–15 *wrong division.* 119 wente] was sent TChH^2; sende D. 157 glotou*n* in] *tp.* 181 shulde . . . fille] þe coup*er*e shulde felle þe cuppe TH^2; þe cobeler*e* schuld *etc.* DCh. 191 Þat] And. 236 cros] rode. 251 þrongen] wrong. VI 29 and sette] his seed TChH^2; ⁊ seden D. 68 fees] flouris. 69 Loke] And l. 82 gateward] porter. 106 humylite] meknesse. 122 two] *om.* VII 29–30 *wrong division.* 116 lymes] hondis. 144 þi(1)] þis. 196 Now] *om.* 304 þoruȝ] þis. 306 and] oþ*er* T; or DChH^2. VIII 26 hem best] þ*a*t h. D; þ*a*t hym TChH^2. 36 And] *om.* 70 defraudiþ] gyleþ DChH^2; kiliþ T. 117 to go to] þerto. 140 lowere] lewide. 152 be pure] before. 153 demide] he leuide. 170 *line om.* IX 15 as] *om.* 30 rauȝte . . . stere] ariȝt sterede. 75 is] *om.* X 64 fend] deuil. 181 were] *om.* 202 man . . . wo*m*man] men . . . wo*m*men. XI 44 gorge] þrote TDH^2; þrotes Ch. 129 knowe] k. alse TChH^2; k. aft*er* D. 134–5 *wrong division.* 145 scole] skile TChH^2; skele D. 192 beþ] bad Ch; byt D; bad the H^2; bed þe T. 227 heueneward] heuene. 232 wiþsigge] wisse. 280 þefte] þeftis. 298 Whanne] Wheþ*er* TChH^2; whar D.

[Fowler finds that TDChH^2 is a genetic group, but that D is contaminated from RU.]

2. *The manuscripts* AWMH^3 *in about* 30 *agreements*

VII 157 þat] he. 176 ditte] holdyn. 213 wolde] ne wold A; nold WMH^3. 294 yfried] fryed or rostid. VIII 101 asondir] on tweyne AH^3; atwynen M; a two W. X 53 going] good dede. 69 helpe] kepe. 70 folies] falsed ⁊ f. A; falsnesse ⁊ f. M; falsnesse ⁊ fro f. W; falsnesse from f. H^3. 88 self] soule. 94 goddis . . . writ] *tp.* 160 godis hest] þe h. of g. 168 hem] h. breme M; h. brymme AH^3. boot] bote brime W. 186 vncomely] vnkendely AWH^3; vnkende M. 215 *line om.* XI 4 staringe] scornyng WM; skorn-fullych H^3; schornely A. 13 werkis] wordis. 18 as . . . wolle] *om.* 21 conne] kan do MH^3; do can AW. 22 deuil] deuels lore WH^3; deuelis loris A; lore M. 29 lessou*n* techiþ] sermoun schew*ith.* 61 ⁊] ȝyf H^3; ȝif þat AWM. 100 *expanded.* 144 Leue] L. nowe WMH^3; Now l. þu A. 145 scole] lore. 146 I . . . catou*n*] in c. þu may rede. 151 enemys] fomen. 153 god] so g. WM; ⁊ so g. AH^3. 154 seide] schewid AM; sheweþ W; swew*ith* H^3. 164 Foundit . . . formest] *tp.* Foundit] f. in feth. 171 his] þe. 213 a] his. 226 for] be. 228 lordis] londis. 239 an heiȝ] a man þat is AWH^3; he þat is M. 245 suche] *om.* sewiþ] sone s. 284 *line om.* 311 Souteris] Saweris.

[Fowler finds AWMH^3 to be a genetic group from IX 20 to the end.]

3. *The manuscripts* EAMH^3 *in about* 20 *agreements*

V 108 ⁊ . . . lokide] he l. *ser* heruy ⁊ holowe MH^3; he l. so heri ⁊ so ille A; he l. as an hotte of hell E. 109 eiȝen] eyn as a blynd hagge AM; eyne blynd as an hagge H^3; ene like a blynd asse E. 110 lollide] lokyd AMH^3; likerd wer E. *Thereafter* **B/C** *additions.* 115 symme . . . nok] synne it þouth me mery A; synne it semed me merthe M; synne me thoght it semyd wele E; symony it semyd to me myrthe H^3. 130 softe] out AM; þ*er* owt EH^3. 146 for] *om.* shrift] his wey AEH^3; his wyse M. 147 kirkeward] þe kirke E; chirche AMH^3. 159 waffrer] bereward AMH^3; bewer E. 176 who . . . herde] ouere þe hode ⁊ þe cloke MH^3; for þe h. ⁊ þe c. A; ouer þe hude swornne E. 188 *hereafter a* **B/C** *line.* 215 flattide] platt. VI 1 fewe men] nane. 3 longe] to l. A; till l. MH^3; so l. E. 28 sure] swere. 42 his] his awne. 44 swere] s. fast. 48 þoruȝ] be. 68 He] Þ*at.* 81 *hereafter* **B/C** *lines.* VII 5 akir] a. ⁊ sawyn it after. 12 be] b. on E; b. an A; be ony MH^3. 15 wile] bidd*es* EA; comandeth MH^3.

[Fowler finds EAMH^3 to be a genetic group where all are present.]

4. *The manuscripts* VHWN *in a few agreements*

II 78 signes . . . notories] Notaries signes. 196 no mo] no mon. III 217 erþe] grou*n*de. IV 92 er] til. V 16 erþe] grou*n*de. 198 erþe] grou*n*de VWN; g:::::: H. VII 109 Be] Now be. 244 dyne] haue dynet. VIII 58 where] wheþer.

5. *The manuscripts* VHJN *in a few agreements*

V 91 cote] C. and his wyf anoþer. 142 shal] wol. VII 6 til] And wissen ou þe rihte weye t. V; And wysse ȝow riȝt wel t. N; ⁊ teche ȝow þe riȝte wey t. H; And techyn ȝow riht forth t. J. 108 to] him t. þe . . . akir] *om.* 178 *expanded.* 261 be þou] þe b.

6. *The manuscripts* EAWM *in a few agreements*

I 157 in(1)] of. II 177 þennes] þen E; þanne AWM. IV 17 *hereafter* **B/C** *lines.* 91 haþ] hed E; had AW; þat hadde M.

The difference in persistence between groups 1 to 3 and the other groups of four manuscripts here cited is substantial. Therefore it might appear that the results of this stage of the investigation were unusually satisfactory. The group [(TH^2)Ch] might now be extended to include D thus: {[(TH^2)Ch]D}; and confirmation of W's change of exemplar at VIII might be claimed, so that a group (EAMH^3) could be hypothesized for Prologue–VII, and a group (AWMH^3) for the remainder of the poem. But the impression of firmness created by the marked persistence of these groups of four fails to survive a recurrence to the grouping of the component manuscripts.

Thus, while {[(TH^2)Ch]D} may possibly, as a formula, describe a broad genetic relation of these manuscripts, as a description of their relation in particular lines it is less useful because of the omissions and simplifications necessary for its determination. Its inadequacy in this respect is of utmost importance in connexion with the use of recension, where every delinquency of a manuscript from its hypothetical family ought to test the propriety of employing the method. To illustrate in the present case, acceptance of {[(TH²)Ch]D} as a genetic group involves disregarding, or explaining by processes hostile to recension, the groups TD (p. 71); TCh (p. 71); DM (p. 71); RUD (p. 87); TDCh (p. 88); RUDE,[1] as well as any larger groups[2] in which, while TDChH² seem to be represented as a family, one or several of the members fail to agree, to say nothing of the following, where members of this proposedly genetic group appear in discrepant groups of two manuscripts:

ChA: V 4 sadd*ere*] hardere A; hard Ch. 135 lay] liþe. VII 32 bukkes] bolis A; bole Ch. 252 þe] *om.* VIII 105 be] me. IX 78 he(2)] *om.* X 19 ⁊(1)] and sir. XI 87 cacche] wete. 89 which] what. 134 contreuide] contrewed Ch; contrued A. 275 here(2)] *om.*
ChE: II 156 ille] euel. III 73 þat] *twice.* V 142 lete] neuer. VI 57 se] *om.* VII 73 it] *om.* 109 þo] al.
ChH²: I 176 lok] boke. II 150 hem] hit. V 132 myn owne] þe. VI 78 as . . . wombe] of herte. VII 2 we] *om.* VIII 15 as] And. 36 sende] s. hem. 106 shal] mot. X 106 þei] *om.* XI 123 þe to] for to. 149 techiþ] t. it. 207 or] of.
ChH³: VII 16 ȝif] *om.* 109 q*ua*þ] þo q. 228 to] and. 306 fruytes] froite Ch; fruth H³. X 184 weddyng] mariage Ch; maryages H³. XI 160 of] and. 199 he is] is. 251 hem] hym.
ChJ: I 99 nouȝt] *om.* IV 16 araye] rape. V 49 affaiten] endaunten Ch; dawntyn J. 119 to(2)] *om.* XI 121 speche] speches. 127 ⁊] *om.* 135 Of] *om.* 172 hire] hem. 276 shal] schuld. 277 wende] þei went.
ChL: Prologue 27 haue] h. after. III 111 fikel] and f. 209 of hem] after. V 95 I do] *tp.* 201 þis] his. VI 118 ferþ*ere* a foote] *tp.* VII 252 armes] hede.
ChM: II 188 go*m*mes] gynnes. V 117 lef] lesing. 142 þat] *om.* VII 170 þei] he. VIII 42 þanne] And þ. IX 35 þe(2)] to. X 104 *expanded.* 123 swet] *om.* XI 59 proude] poure.
ChV: II 181 pulden] putte. IV 38 hise] þe. V 17 ȝe] we. IX 38 þe(2)] his. 44 þou] ȝef. X 188 Or] Or to. XI 122 simplite] sympel.
ChW: VII 229 he] *om.* 262 I(2)] I nauȝt. 270 cole] colde. IX 36 watris] water. X 75 he] *om.* XI 22 ben] *om.* 126 þat] *om.* 205 morals] morale.
DA: V 175 þe peneworthis] a penyworth. VII 213 greue god] *tp.* 260 forȝelde] ȝelde. VIII 161 ⁊(2)] *om.* XI 7 hym(1)] hem. 87 And] *om.*
DCh: III 97 þe(2)] þy. IV 5 But] B. yf. 73 feet] fote. 157 he] I. VII 85 I] And I.

[1] Prologue 41 bratful] bred ful RUD; *with* bred full E. III 75 ȝe] þou. VII 208–212 *redivision, with omission of* 210b *and* 211.

[2] See below, p. 96, for some examples of such groups.

306 and] or. VIII 42 many] & m. 139 kniȝtis] kyng. 160 leue] loue. IX 43 Þat] For.
DH^3: VI 119 hym] he*m*. VII 243 þin] *om.* VIII 81 shal] *om.* X 193 & choppis] *om.* XI 42 forþ] *om.* 141 þe] *om.* 204 þe] a. 209 steruiþ] stereþ.
DJ: I 139 þ*er* comsiþ] þou co*n*seyuys J; conseyue þou D. V 78–80 *dislocated.* 88 Þanne] *om.* VI 93 wel] wil. VII 292 a day] *om.* XI 106 þise] *om.* 113 And] *om.* 135 ferst] &.
RD: III 247 choppe] schep R; schap D. V 228 wan] bywan. VII 85 hym] hem. 245–8 *wrong division.* 245 I . . . þe] *om.* VIII 45 lettrid] lered. X 82 dred] for d. XI 67 wy] wey. 196 & techiþ] *om.*
UD: VII 25 conne] lere to. 205 suche] s. men. 245 ete] *om.* IX 47 so] *om.* X 15 þis(2)] þe. 140 on] and. 153 &] & of. 169 dayes] *om.* XI 121 speche] *om.* 158 þat] þe. 282 he] *om.*
DV: IV 75 mowe] *om.* V 110 as] lik. VI 64 be] b. hem. VIII 5 hym(1)] *om.* 123 þi] my. IX 7 lede] ladde. XI 46 for(*both*)] of.
DW: II 100 Leaute] liau*n*ce. III 79 þese] *om.* 267 leaute] lyaunce. IV 122 wyte miȝte] *tp.* VI 68 Floreynes] floures. 81 not] *om.* VII 5 *line om.* VIII 23 muste] *om.* X 148 hym] hem.
H^2H: I 41 madame m*er*cy] *tp.* II 44 (H^2), 45 (H) *additional matter.* 56 heiȝe] an h. 75 *additional matter.* 83 molere] medlere. 168 *additional matter.* 185 Þanne louride] Therof herden. IV 34 bille] bulle.
H^2W: Prologue 22 wastou*rs*] w. in þe worlde. 93 pore] the p. IV 18 suffre] suffraunce. V 10 I sauȝ] *om.* 187 so] *om.* VIII 93 lynes] leues. IX 94 hem] hi*m*. X 103 how] ȝou. 189 neu*er*e shal] *tp.* XI 69 þe] that.

To assess the force of these agreements it must be borne in mind that TDChH^2 is a relatively stable group, whose members appear less often in disagreements than do those of, for example, the group EAMH^3. Therefore the sum of these discrepant groups is impressive as indicating how imperfectly, even under the most favourable circumstances, a genealogy of these manuscripts would describe their relations.

The group AWMH^3, next in persistence of these groups of four manuscripts, appears only in VII–XI. The evidence of the groups of two manuscripts, where W agreed some 40 times with A, and some 30 times with M[1] might seem to support the genetic character of this group. W's persistent agreement with N to the end of VII might be explained by a hypothesis of change of exemplar on the part of W at the end of this passus. But evidently the matter is not so simple. About half W's agreements with M occur before the end of VII, and its agreements with A were not confined to VIII–XI. It is also

[1] Above, pp. 69–70, 77. Compare also W's agreements with H^3: V 137 bouȝte] paied. VI 17 my] þe. VII 119 of] *om.* 296 ellis] ȝit. X 146 knewe] k. hem. XI 15 or(2)] and. 19 &] To. wrongis] wrong. 78 in] here i. 83 sathan] S. vnsaght W; s. þe vnsaut H^3. 202 riȝtful] right.

occasionally found in agreement with E.[1] Thus it might appear that W, as well as being in a common vertical relationship with AMH^3 in VII–XI, is in some indeterminate relation to a manuscript of their kinship for the earlier part of the poem, while it persistently agrees with N. Attempts to determine W's relation to AMH^3 in the earlier part of the poem would serve only to demonstrate further the unstable relations of these three manuscripts. Meanwhile, throughout the poem W maintains agreement with K (above, pp. 76–7). Evidently, then, calling AWMH^3 a genetic group for VIII–XI can be only the most general of descriptions.

So also, explaining away the small number of agreements by reference to the defective character of E and to H^3's absence to the middle of Passus V, one might call the group EAMH^3 genetic. But again such a description would establish no point of great use for recension, in view of the number of conflicting groups in which these manuscripts appear. Whatever ingenious explanation were put forward (the possibilities are by no means exhausted) it would remain glaringly evident that convergent variation had affected the character of all these manuscripts.

Thus, at the stage of groups of four manuscripts, any genetic hypothesis which relative persistence of agreement might seem to authorize would be subject to severe qualifications. The genetic character of the most persistent groups is questioned by substantial contradictory evidence. Therefore, even if a genetic hypothesis hits upon the ultimate relationship of the manuscripts, it does not describe their present relation with any accuracy. Nor, if the actual amount of contradictory evidence is taken into account, can such a hypothesis be trusted to apply to any given line.

VARIATIONAL GROUPS OF FIVE MANUSCRIPTS

Some 250 variational groups of five manuscripts occur, of which none is persistent, and none likely to be genetic. Only the three following attract attention:

[1] Prologue 90 bolde] *om.* II 33 regniþ] wonnys. III 6 of] on. 229 And] *om.* IV 61 For . . . hise] And pr*a*ed hym for of hys. 106 to . . . harlot*rie*] all h. to here. 117 I shal] *tp.* 143 for] forth. V 31 Þat] *om.* 106 so] *om.* 124 along] of lenth E; on lengh W. 131 by] for. 247 to] fast to E; ⁊ fast on W. VI 50 hertis] hert. 51 next] *om.* 77 hallis] bath h. E; boþe alle W. VII 19 it . . . is] it in tyme. 82 reles ⁊ remissiou*n*] *tp.* 152 not(1)] neu*er*.

1. *The manuscripts* TRDChH² *in a few agreements*

I 153 For þeiȝ ȝe] For þi. III 253 telliþ] tolde. IV 111 alle] a. þe. 126 þe man] þ. may R; he may TDChH². VII 227 herde] hadde. VIII 2 tilien . . . erþe] *tp.* 101 pure] *om.* 119 lettrid] lernid. X 185 þat] as. XI 47 noye] anguyssh.

2. *The manuscripts* TRUChH² *in a few agreements*

II 88 lawe] lawes. 163 gerdiþ] gederiþ. III 122 monkis] mynstrelis. IV 19 wytful] riȝtful. V 175 aparte] apertly TRUH²; pertely Ch. X 89 wy] why. 202 vntyme] my tyme.

3. *The manuscripts* TRUDCh *in a few agreements*

III 97 my] *om.* 121 alle] monk TRUCh; monkes D. IV 71 *line om.* VI 39 wiþhalt] ne halt. VII 165 heȝede hem] he hadde TRU; he had DCh. 183 cacche] chase. 217–18 *wrong division.*

These three apparently conflicting groups may presently seem explicable as agreements of a larger group when one or another of its members is absent (below, p. 97 and fn.). Meanwhile they have no positive value in any attempt to reconstruct a genealogy. The great majority of groups of five manuscripts do, however, have negative force in the present examination by their suggestion of the occurrence of convergent variation among these manuscripts.

More than 400 variational groups composed of more than five manuscripts occur. Of these only one is at all persistent:

The manuscripts TRUDChH² *in more than* 30 *agreements*

I 127 kenne . . . bet] me b. k. TUDChH²; me b. teche R. II 83 mendis] frendis TRDChH²; frendis of frendis U. III 89 or ȝerisȝiuys] for here seruice. 139–40 *wrong division.* 257 him] þe king RUDH²; þat k. TCh. 260 wit] it. 269 Leaute] his wykkide l. TRUChH²; His wikyd liaunce D. IV 4 Crist] god. 48 Þe . . . kneuȝ] Þo kneuȝ þe king TRUChH²; That knewe þe k. D. 84 wile] shal. 114 at douere] do euere TDChH²; dygnere R; diuerse U. 154 lete . . . nile] loue . . . wile. V 16 puffid] put. 17 segges] sent god TChH²; seyþ god RU; sayd god D. 34 preyide] prechede RUChH²; prechet D; prechiþ T. 43 ran] *om.* 66 lippes] lippe. 91–2 *as one line.* 92 and . . . aftir] *om.* 110 And] *om.* 114 ben] ylouid. þat caitif] he al my lyue D; he al my lif tyme TRCh; al my lif tyme UH². 176 who . . . herde] *om.* VI 33 Dyked] Dyken. VII 18 longe] louely. 25 conne] lere to UD; lerne to TChH²; leye þer to R. 31 to(1)] þe. 84 tiþe] tiþes. 144 fecche] f. awey. IX 6 wente] wene. 17 synneþ] falliþ. 36 walwen] wawen TDChH²; wawes RU. 57 foulis] briddis. X 48 þe(2) . . . Inwyt] *tp.* 186 me þinkeþ] I wene. XI 56 kete] kedde RU; ked D; kydde Ch; kid TH². 78 in] be. 108 as] *om.* 134–5 *wrong division.* 134 Of] And. 243–5 *wrong division.* 244 pore] p. men. 250 creature] man. 251 heþen] hem TRUDH²; hym Ch.

[Fowler finds that TRUDChH² form a genetic group in **A** 2.]

The persistence of this group, and its concordance with the previously suggested groups (TH^2), [(TH^2)Ch] and {[(TH^2)Ch]D} argue its genetic character and suggest the further hypothesis of a family ⟨{[(TH^2)Ch]D}RU⟩. That tidy organization of evidence is the most convincing piece of genealogical reconstruction authorized by the groupings of the **A** manuscripts. But a review of the groups presented earlier in the discussion will show that its neat and plausible representation is at best an imperfect description of the relationship of these manuscripts.

The hypothesis is progressively constructed upon about 470 agreements, among which those of RU amount to nearly half. This is impressive evidence, and the explanations of the two major discrepant groups, RUE and RUD, by change of exemplar and conflation respectively, are altogether possible. But the body of contrary evidence is also very substantial. Apart from their presence in the hypothetical group, these six manuscripts appear in more than 20 discrepant groups of two manuscripts persistent enough to attract notice,[1] and in four relatively persistent discrepant groups of three manuscripts;[2] they also form, with other manuscripts of their hypothetical family, six groups of two[3] and three groups of three[4] which conflict with the hypothesis. The agreements in support of these discrepant groups are together as numerous as those supporting the hypothesis, occurring on an average of once in five lines. Explanations have been offered for RUE and RUD; a number of the discrepant groups among the six manuscripts are accounted for by the defections of other manuscripts.[5] But when these are subtracted there is still a very substantial disagreement. In any case, when it becomes necessary to make assumptions of change of exemplar or conflation, the simplicity of recension is lost; the admission of personal judgement, moreover, defeats its purpose. The bulk of the discrepancies cannot be so explained. These must diminish confidence in the descriptive accuracy of the genetic hypothesis, since evidently this can show only some of the sources of readings in the surviving manuscripts, and therefore lacks authority as a test of originality.

[1] ChA; ChE; ChH^3; ChJ; ChL; ChM; ChV; ChW; DA; DH^3; DJ; DM; DV; DW; H^{2}H; H^{2}W; RA; RE; UA; UE; UJ; and UW. See pp. 70, 71, 72, 76, 80, 83, 93, 94 above.

[2] RUE; RUJ; RUM; RUV. See pp. 86–7, 89 above.

[3] ChH^2; DCh; RD; TCh; TD; UD. See pp. 71, 93–4 above.

[4] RUD; TDCh; TDH^2. See pp. 87, 88 above.

[5] Thus, for instance, some TCh agreements which occur where H^2 is wanting would include H^2 if H^2 were undamaged.

It may nevertheless appear that, despite these qualifications, a stemma has begun to take shape. The next step in the analysis is therefore of prime importance: are there persistent agreements of larger groups, comprising those which have already attracted notice, and conceivably indicating the more remote relations of descent? Of the more than 400 larger variational groups remaining none is persistent. Larger genetic groups have, however, been proposed, and the evidence for them must now be considered. In 'An Essay toward the Critical Text of the A-Version of "Piers the Plowman"' Knott instanced nine passages between Prologue I and VIII 130 as evidence for a group TRUDH^{2}EAH^{3}, which he calls TH^{2}DURT^{2}AH^{3}.[1] He did not then know of Ch, N or M. If he had he might have argued for a group TRUDChH^{2}EAMH^{3}; this may be inferred from the fact that his continuator, with access to Knott's papers,[2] undertook to 'place' Ch, N and M in Knott's 'trees'.[3] The passages adduced by Knott may then without injustice to him be scrutinized as evidence for TRUDChH^{2}EAMH^{3} in Prologue–VIII 130. For the rest of the poem Fowler proposes a corresponding group TRUDChH^{2}A WMH^{3}, E having broken off in VII and W transferred to an exemplar in the AMH^{3} tradition.[4]

These proposals are without foundation. One is prepared for the agreements supporting larger groups to be fewer than those supporting, say, genetic pairs. The remoteness of the act of copying their exclusive common ancestor establishes a probability that further variation will have obscured many of its errors, or correction have removed them. But an indispensable requirement of evidence for grouping manuscripts is actual agreement, and particularly, agreement in the same unoriginal variant or in unoriginal variants demonstrably stemming from a common variation. Where no agreements are found, the process of classification cannot begin.

Such agreement is not forthcoming in the nine instances proposed by Knott in support of a group TRUD(Ch)H^{2}EA(M)H^{3}, except in two cases where he seems to me to have preferred an unoriginal reading. It is not forthcoming in any of the instances proposed by Fowler to support the corresponding group in IX–XI. The groups TRUD(Ch)H^{2}EA(M)H^{3} and TRUDChH^{2}AWMH^{3} are therefore

[1] *MP*, xii, pp. 400–2.
[2] *Piers the Plowman*, pp. vii–ix.
[3] Fowler, Thesis, pp. 10 ff.
[4] Fowler, Thesis, pp. 31–2, and *Piers the Plowman*, pp. 26–7.

not proven. They are, in my opinion, not provable; and, even if they were presumptive, this would not be authorization for applying them to recension. The nature of the evidence for them must now be examined; the means by which Knott and Fowler came to their conclusions will then appear.

1. *Knott's evidence for a group* TRUDH^{2}EAH^3 (TRUDChH^{2}EAMH^3)

a. I 153

For [þeiȝ ȝe] be trewe of ȝo*ur*e tunge ⁊ treweliche wynne

þeiȝ] H; þeighe U; þei JN; though K; þouth M; Thow AW; þof (*corrected same hand from* þi) E; þauȝ V; þagh L; þi TRDChH^2. ȝe] UVHJLEAKM (*altered to* þou H; *above line same hand* E); þow WN; *om* TRDChH^2.

There is no agreement here, since UAM and probably E fail to support the proposed group. The locus is therefore not evidence. The explanations that E's correction is 'a contamination or conjectural emendation'; that A's *Thow* originated in 'the same sort of reason'; and that U's reading 'must be a result of contamination or of emendation by a scribe' beg the question. In any case the corruption is easy and might have occurred independently. E's reading might very well be the scribe's correction of his own error, made from his exemplar.

b. II 83

For mede is molere of [m]endis engendrit

mendis] mendes JLK; me*n*nis N; ma*n*nys M; frendis TRDChH^2; frendis of frendis U; fendes E. *Missing* AH^3; *line om* W.

There is no agreement here. M's error is from an original *mendis*; E's *fendes* is by no means 'obviously' an attempt at 'an emendation on the basis of' *frendis*. More likely, E's scribe set out independently to put the worst character upon Meed, having, in the way of scribes, failed to look beyond the line. In the absence of AH^3, and with M erring independently, no relation is established here between TRUDChH^2 and EAMH^3.

c. III 260

[I] consience knowe þis for kynde [w]it me tauȝte

kynde] resou*n* RUE. wit] VHJLAWNM; it TRUDChH^2; hase it E; *om* K. me] *om* E. H^3 *absent*.

There is no agreement here. The teacher is *kynde wit* in AM; *kynde* in TDChH²K and *resoun* in RUE. Two manuscripts of the group proposed have the original reading, and that of RUE is not demonstrably related to the reading of TDChH².

d. IV 84

For I wile wage for wrong he [wile] do so no more

wile] wil JEAWN; wol VHLK; wolde M; shal TRUDChH². H³ *absent.*

Knott did not know of M, and omitted to mention that E clearly reads *will.* It is therefore not true that 'lack of alliteration characterizes the subgroup'. There is no agreement here.

e. V 161

hogge þe [nede]lere

nedelere] nedeler*e* JAKWMH³; neldere VH; meller*e* D; melner*e* R; myllere TChH²; mylner UE; *om* N. L *sophisticated.*

There is no agreement here, since AMH³ have the original reading. Knott argued that 'AH³ must show contamination' because of their close connexion with E. He would now have to extend this argument to include M. This is a striking illustration of *petitio principii.*

f. V 239

Þi wil w[orþ]e vpon me as I haue wel des*er*uid

worþe] worthe JM; worþ VHLKWH³; worch Ch; wurche U; werche TH²A; wirche RD; wirke E. (worþ *Knott.*)

There is no agreement here, and the support of M for H³ has split the EAMH³ group. As the reading of this group is not determinable without appeal to the proposition under proof, it cannot be maintained that H³ 'is undoubtedly restoring conjecturally, or perhaps has a contaminated reading'. In any case independent *th*><*ch* corruption is easy and probable (see below, p. 120).

g. VI 94

And lere þe for to loue & hise lawes holden

loue] TRUDChH²EH³; louyn him JLWN; loue hi*m* wel V; leuen M. *Line om* A; *contaminated* K; *defective* H. (loue hym *Knott.*)

By my text this is agreement in an original reading, which does not prove relationship. See below, p. 160.

h. VII 116

We haue none [lymes] to laboure wiþ lord ygracid be ȝe

ygracid . . . ȝe] gyff vs grace E; Ithanked be ȝe L; we hit þonken VH. ygracid] T; ygraced RUChKN; gr*a*cyd H[3]; graced D; gr*a*cied M; grace A; þankyd J; þonked W. *Defective* H[2]. (þankid *Knott, but Fowler reads* ygracid.)

Knott's choice of reading is here determined by recension, employing the genetic hypothesis for which the present case is supposed to be proof: 'The genealogical positions of the MSS attesting "þonked, þonken", in A render the C[ritical] T[ext] of that version certain.'[1] Thus Knott argues that K's reading 'must be a result of contamination'. He would, presumably, have explained N's reading in the same way. This is agreement in an original reading, which is not proof of genetic relation.

i. VII 212α–213

Facite vobis amicos

I wolde not greue god quaþ peris for al þe gold on ground

TRUDChEA *divide after* god; JLM *copy* 212α *in the margin*; VHJKWH[3] *augment the Latin*; N *divides as above.*

There is no agreement here: the various arrangements of M, H[3] and TRUDChEA are not demonstrably related corruptions, but if anything the contrary.

2. *Fowler's evidence for a group* TRUDChH[2]AWMH[3]

a. VIII 140

Among l[ower]e lordis þi londis shuln be dep*ar*tid

lowere] RUVHJLWN; lowar K; hyere A; lewide T; lewid H[2]; lewed D; lewde Ch; lether M. H[3] *absent.*

There is no agreement here: RUW have the original reading; the reading of A is derived from *lowere*; and it would be hard to show that M's *lether* was more likely derived from *lewide* than from *lowere*.

b. VIII 141

As daniel deui[n]ide in dede it fel aftir

deuinide] deuyned WN; dyuynyd J; diuinede V; dyuyned UK; deuysed H; demide T; demyd A; demed RDChH[2]; dymde M.

[1] *MP*, xii, p. 401, n.

There is no agreement here, since U and W have the original reading. Fowler (Thesis, p. 31) explains their defection by reference to conflation of U with J, and W with K. More likely the readings *demide* etc. are independent palæographical errors. See p. 121 below.

c. IX 56

And vndir a lynde vpon a launde lenide I me a stounde.

me] TRUChH²M; *om* DVAKW. H³ *absent.* (*Fowler excludes* me.)

This is a typical minor crux; see pp. 151–2 below. But whichever reading is adopted there is no agreement of the proposed group.

d. X 104

Þat selde m[os]seþ þe marbil þ*a*t men ofte [t]reden

mosseþ] mosseth K; Moseþ VW; mosyth JAH³; men seþ TH²; men sen D; me*n* se . . . mosy RU; men se . . . Be ouermolded with mosse Ch; men seyn . . . Is wol seldyn Isein wit mos begrowyn M.

There is no agreement here, since AWH³ preserve the original reading. It is better to explain their disagreement with M by reference to the ease of an *o*><*e* corruption (see p. 119 below) than to assume that AWH³ must have been corrected, as the hypothesis of the proposed group would require.

e. X 156

And alle þ*a*t couplide hem w*ith* þ*a*t kyn crist hatide [dedliche]

dedliche] VJKWH³; eu*ere* TUD; after ChAM. *Line om* R; *defective* H².

There is no agreement here, WH³ having the original reading. It cannot even be maintained that *after* and *euer* are related variants.

f. X 176

Þat in þe [shynglid] ship shal ben ysauid

shynglid] schynglid KM; shyngled W; schynglede V; schyngelyd J; sengle RUDA; sollyd H³; same TChH².

There is no agreement here, WM having the original reading. The variants do not demonstrably go back to the same substitution. Fowler's explanation of WM's reading by conflation 'since they are elsewhere closely related to A and H³, which agree with TH²ChDUR in deviating from the correct reading' (Thesis, p. 31) both begs the question of relationship and suggests, incorrectly, that mere 'agreement in deviating from the correct reading' is evidence of genetic relation.

g. X 202

For in [vn]tyme treweliche betwyn m[a]n & wo*m*m[a]n

vntyme] VJK; no tyme WH³; no*n* tyme M; my tyme TRUChH²; tyme D. *Line om* A.

Here the proposed family agrees only in unoriginality, not in the readings. The scribal efforts to make *vntyme* into something easier are sharply distinguished. That of TRUChH² originated in reading the four minims of *un* as *mi* (cp. p. 121 below). That of WMH³ may be aural, as M's *non* suggests, or merely an effort to make sense of a difficult expression. No necessary connexion between these errors exists, and therefore they are not evidence of genetic relation. At best they show that *vntyme* was difficult.

h. XI 4

And sterneliche staringe dame studie seide

So TRDChH². staring d. s. ste*r*nelyche JVK; scornynge d. s. ste*r*neliche MA; skornfullych d. s. to vs bothe H³; scornyng sternly she W. U *absent*.

There is no agreement among these arrangements to support the pro-posed group. If the text adopted has the original word order, which is not determinable, then AM agree outside the proposed group with VJK by removing *sternelyche* to the end of the expression. But which-ever arrangement is preferred TRUDChH²AWMH³ fail to behave as a genetic group agreeing in an unoriginal reading.

i. XI 52

[Mendynaunt3] meteles mi3te go to bedde

M. meteles] Wiþ Mony defauti Meeles V. Mendynaunt3] Mendicans J; Manye me*n*-dynau*ns* RUKW; Many pore men DM; Manye men TChH²H³. *Line om* A. (Manye m. *Fowler*.)

Here there is no agreement of the proposed group except in unorigin-ality. RUW (and, incidentally, K) have increased the emphasis of the statement while retaining the apparently difficult *Mendynaunt3*. DM have glossed this, at the same time making a very natural addition to preserve alliteration. Conceivably the still weaker reading of TCh H²H³ is related to that of DM, but this does not amount to agreement of the proposed group. More likely TChH^{2}H^{3} have made a substitution of a kind typical when the original is difficult. See p. 133 below.

This inspection of the evidence for TRUDChH^{2}EAMH^{3} and TRUDChH^{2}AWMH^{3} has shown how there is not a single instance of these manuscripts agreeing in the same, clearly unoriginal variant, or in unoriginal variants demonstrably related. There were some agreements in readings which, for reasons other than genetic, seem to me to be original: 1 *g* and *h*; and others where the manuscripts agreed in failure to preserve the original reading but not in their variants: 1 *b* and *i*, and 2 *g* and *i*. In the remaining instances the manuscripts of the proposed group simply do not agree. Of eighteen passages adduced to prove a genetic relation twelve actually argue against that relation. Their failure to support it by agreement is explained away as the result of convergent variation. If there were otherwise a substantial number of agreements in support of the proposition this explanation might do, but as things are it merely begs the question, since the identification of the convergence is carried out by means of the hypothesis which is in the course of being proved. Convergent variation may account for the divergence of manuscripts from a genetic relation, but recourse to it as an explanation does not convert the passages where divergence occurs into proof of such a relation.

This process of reasoning is most frequently applied to manuscripts from the unstable group EAMH^{3}. In five cases where one of these fails to support the hypothetical larger group its disagreement is accounted for by conflation or correction: in 1 *a* of A; in 1 *c* of A; in 1 *e* of AH^{3}; in 1 *f* of H^{3}; and in 1 *i* of H^{3} (Knott, pp. 400–2). The assumption is made that the reading of the group EAH^{3} (EAMH^{3}) is determinable, and that therefore a failure to fall in with the hypothesis argues a reading not the product of vertical transmission. But the group reading of EAH^{3} is being determined by the preconception that readings of EAH^{3} should agree in unoriginality with those of TRUDChH^{2}. A simple instance is 1 *e* where AH^{3} depart from the proposed group reading 'miller' to read 'needler'. Knott maintained that AH^{3} 'must show contamination, for they are here, as elsewhere . . . closely connected with T^{2}' [E]. E, like TRUDChH^{2}, reads 'miller'. He evidently began by assuming that there is a genetic group TRUDH^{2}EAH^{3}; went on to reason that since 'miller' is the majority reading of these manuscripts it must be the reading of the exclusive common ancestor of the assumed group; and finally viewed the failure of AH^{3} to conform, not as a test of his first assumption, but as evidence of contamination in AH^{3}. He was undoubtedly handicapped by ignorance of M, which here (as often elsewhere) sides with the delinquent manuscript(s). But it seems very much as if his argument for this group was determined by preconceptions rather than evidence.

It cannot, meanwhile, be denied that the descent of TRUDChH^{2}EA(W)MH^{3} from an exclusive common ancestor is possible, or, for that matter, that the absence of certain selected variants in JLKN and in W for Prologue–VIII may suggest this. The possibility is not, however, demonstrable from the available evidence, for the variants in question are neither at all uniformly present in TRUDChH^{2}EA(W)MH^{3} nor uniformly absent from JLK(W)N (see 1 *c*, *h*, and 2 *i*). And, as the critical apparatus abundantly shows, there are many groups formed on variants both striking and trivial, which conflict with the hypothetical genetic group proposed by combining various of its elements with one or more of VHJLN. The conclusion is plain that if TRUDChH^{2}EA(W)MH^{3} are descended from an exclusive common ancestor, their descent is now so grievously obscured that to employ its possibility for recension is without justification.

Finally Knott[1] and Fowler[2] propose a group *y*, comprising all the known manuscripts of the **A** version except VH, which, by possessing many common errors, are distinguished as a second 'main' group *x*. That VH are probably cognate is well attested (see pp. 73–4 above). In addition to their many individual variants these two manuscripts have a large number of variants in common. But the absence of these variants shared by VH from the remaining manuscripts means in the first instance no more than that an exclusive common ancestor of VH was at some stage subjected to intensive corruption. It proves nothing about the rest of the manuscripts. To establish exclusive common ancestry for TRUDChH^{2}JLEAKWNMH^{3} it would be necessary to show that these manuscripts agree in unoriginal variants, absent from VH, which are identical or demonstrably the product of the

[1] *MP*, xii, pp. 397–9. [2] Thesis, pp. 28–30.

same act of variation. How far such agreement actually exists will now be shown:

3. *Knott's evidence for* y

a. I 148

To hem þ*a*t hongide hi*m* [heiȝe] & his herte þirlide

hongide . . . heiȝe] hym hangyd E. hi*m* heiȝe] V; hym hyȝe H; hym eye M; him on cros L; him by TRUDChH²JKWN; on hym A.

There is no agreement here in the same error or in error that can be related to one variation. M's variant is probably a personal spelling of the original reading. That of L is more likely to derive from *heiȝe* than from *by*, as is E's *hym hangyd*. A's *on hym* cannot be shown to relate to either *heiȝe* or *by*. Moreover the reading *by* is not, as Knott maintained, 'unintelligible' and therefore difficult, but easy and natural in the particular context as well as because of the likelihood of *h*><*b* corruption (see p. 120 below). This line is not evidence for *y*.

b. II 87

Worþi is þe werkman his mede to haue

mede] hir*e* M; hure V; huyre H. (hure *Knott*.)

M, of which Knott did not know, breaks away from *y*, so that there is no agreement whichever reading is preferred.

c. V 100

May no sugre ne swet þing swage it an vnche

swage . . . vnche] dryue hit from myn herte VH, *but they read* aswagen hit vnneþe *as the second half of* 101. (an vnche] vnneþe *Knott*.)

The manuscripts of Knott's *y* here agree in an original reading. His emendation is unauthorized: see p. 442 below.

d. V 153

Hast þou quaþ he any hote spices

Hast þou] TRDChH²EKMH³; Ye but hastow W; hastow ought UJLA; hast þou ouȝt in þy pors H; Hastou ouȝt I þi pors V; ȝe hastow ought in þi p*ur*se N. (Hastou ouȝt I þi pors quod he *Knott*.)

Even if Knott's insertion, apparently made because of the agreement between VH and the **B** version, were authorized, there would not be agreement of *y* here, since N sides with VH. Moreover the four other variants of *y* are not demonstrably cognate. This line is not evidence for *y*.

e. V 162

Hereafter VHEANMH³ *add*
Sire Pers of pridye and pernel of Flaundres.

Treating this line as genuine, Knott regarded its absence from the remaining manuscripts as evidence for *y*; it was present in EAH³, he argued, by restoration from the **B** version. He would now have to extend this explanation to M and N, which also read it. My reasons for rejecting the line are given on p. 443 below. In any case there is no agreement here.

f. VI 88–9

Biddiþ amende ȝow meke hym to his maist*er* ones
To weue [vp] þe wyket þat [þe wif] shette

Line 88 *om* A; *correctly divided* VEMH³; *divided after* maist*er* TRUDChH²JLN. ones] *om* W. *Defective* H; **C**-*text here* K.

There is no agreement of *y* here, since EMH³ divide correctly and W goes its own way. Knott argued that 'The presence of the correct reading in the minor subgroup T²H³ [EH³] means nothing but contamination from B, or perhaps conjectural restoration in their ancestor'. The logic of applying this explanation has already been indicated.

g. VIII 62

Siþen ȝe sen it is þus sewiþ to þe beste

þus] this K; so VH; soþ W. (so *Knott.*)

This is agreement (except for W) in an original reading. Knott emended, apparently, because *so* 'is the reading of *x* and *z*' (the **B** version), and because he regarded the text given above as unmetrical. His reason for emending depends on the genealogical proposition for which this instance is supposed to be evidence. The line is metrical without *so*, which is the more likely intrusive variant. See p. 142 below.

4. *Fowler's evidence for* y

a. IX 52

And [g]iue þe g*ra*ce on þis erþe in good lif to ende

giue] gif RW; geve K; ȝiue TUV; ȝif DH²JA; ȝeue M; ȝef Ch. erþe] erde A; grou*n*de VK. H³ *absent.* (erþe] grounde *Fowler.*)

There is no agreement here. Fowler explains K's delinquency as 'the result of contamination or scribal emendation'. Reasons for preferring *erþe* are given below, p. 452.

b. X 123–5

Riȝt as a rose [þ*a*t red is and] swet
Out of a raggit rote and a rouȝ brere
Sp*ri*ngeþ & sprediþ þ*a*t spice*r*is desiriþ

Correctly divided as here VJ; *as two lines divided after* rote TRUDChKWMH³; *lines omitted* A; *defective* H². 123 þ*a*t . . . and] riseth Ch; *om* TD. swet] *om* ChM. 124 and . . . brere] *om* M.

There is no agreement of *y* in error here, since J divides the line correctly. Fowler offers the usual explanation of contamination or conjectural emendation for J's correct division.

c. X 159

And siþen se[þ] & his suster [sed] wern spousid to kaymes

suster sed] V; suste*r*ys seede JH³; sustre seth KW; suster TRDChM; sister UA.

The manuscripts of the proposed *y* disagree, since JH³ side with V, and KW's variant is independently derived from *suster sed.*

d. XI 163–4

Alle þise sciences sikir I myself
Foundit hem formest folk to desceyue

Correctly divided as here VJK; *divided after* foundit TRUDChH²; *after* formed W; *after* formest AH³; *after* forme*r*st M. 163 myself] m. made K.

Again the manuscripts of *y* fail to agree. JK do not support the proposed group; moreover the misdivisions of TRUDChH² and AMH³ are by no means necessarily related to a single act of variation. This passage is not evidence for *y*.

Among these eleven passages there is only one where the manu- scripts of the proposed genetic group *y* agree, namely 3 *c*. Agreement there is in an original reading, and without significance of genetic relation. In five instances, 3 *a*, *f*, 4 *b*, *c* and *d*, the manuscripts of the proposed group simply do not agree. In the remaining instances, where I have preferred another reading than Knott-Fowler, there is in either case no agreement of *y*: 3 *b*, *d*, *e*, *g* and 4 *a*. Thus the necessary agreement in unoriginal variation is absent.

Since the passages adduced are not instances of agreement in error they are not evidence for *y*. If *y* were otherwise demonstrably a genetic group it might be permissible to interpret disagreements like those of 3 *a*, *f*, 4 *b*, *c* and *d* as caused by conflation or correction. To apply this interpretation when these passages are actually being put forward as evidence for the genetic character of *y* is to beg the question. Above all, to determine the text by the genetic hypothesis which is being proved, and then to adduce variants from the text so determined as evidence of the genetic relation, as Knott apparently does in 3 *d* and *e*, is illogical. Nor does it serve to prove the genetic character of *y*, since the manuscripts of *y* in any case disagree at these points. The pre- sumption of a genetic group *y*, suggested by the many agreements of VH in variations not found in TRUDChH²JLEAKWNMH³, therefore remains unproven.

There is, in fact, a substantial amount of evidence against it, and it would not be hard to make a better case for other genetic hypotheses relating to VH. Groups of three manuscripts containing VH were noticed above: VHE (p. 89); VHJ (p. 88); VHM (p. 88); VHN (pp. 88–9); and VHW (pp. 87–8); also groups of four: VHJN (p. 92); and VHWN (p. 92). Among these VHJ is interesting because its third member, J, does not appear in any group of sufficient relative persistence to encourage a genetic hypothesis. Why not enter- tain the possibility of a genetic relation between VH and J? The postulate of universal variation (particularly applicable to VH, V and H), and a hypothetical correction of J might be invoked to account for the relatively small number of agreements. The main evidence would be the group VHJ (above, p. 88). There is a variational group VJ, not poorly attested:

III 257 for] *om.* IV 87 wel] w. amendis J; amendes V. VI 111 He] *om.* VIII 107 me] *om.* IX 65 he] I. 87 on] *om.* X 15 þis(2)] þat. 85 þe] *om.* 94α *line om.* 122

þe(*both*)] *om.* 185 þe] þat. 203 were boþe] *tp.* XI 19 can construe] counterfetyn J; Conterfeteþ V. 32 almiȝt] *om.* 69 alle] *om.* 134 contreuide] counterfetyd J; con Coun- terfeten V.

This group would be explained by defection of H or by independent variation in H. Similar explanations would account for a variational group HJ:

III 51 make . . . mende] *tp.* 253 telliþ] techiþ. IV 31 com in to] welcomed. 59 his] here. VII 5 half akir] *om.*

If from these agreements a hypothesis of a genetic group VHJ were set up, then the presence of VHJ in larger variational groups would assume genetic significance. The number of such groups where VHJ occur is considerable. In addition to VHJN (p. 92 above) there are the following:

Prologue 26 Al] *om* (*with* RUE). 60 here(1)] *om* (M). 70 Comen] and c. (U). 94 bisshop] Bysschopes (H²LE). 102 dede] dedes (H²EM). I 14 ꝧ] þat (UWM). 22 in] by (UH²LWM). 25 þe] þou (RDKWM). 61 wy] wiht (RChEKWM). 120 perfite] profitable (UW). 129 dotide] dotest (L). II 5 half] hond (D). *add* quod heo (UH²W). lo] seo (UDKN). 21 for] *om* (LK). 128 Sette] And s. (K). 141 þe] vr (U). 144 iotten] rennen (RUDLKWNM). 151 forþ] *om* (WNM). 182 cloþis] cloutes (EWNM). 198 wrang] w. hire hondes (LA). III 27 þi(2)] vr (RULKWNM). 53 alle] to a. (LEAKWNM). 58 þi] *om* (RUDChEWNM). 79 oþer] *om* (UH²E WNM). 87 forbrenne] brenne (LEAWM). 101 lord] God VH; goddes J (ChLE AKW). 111 feiþ] Flesch (RE). 114 techiþ] heo t. (ENM). 119 ꝧ(2)] In (DN). 155 men] *om* (ChWN). 169 my] of m. (WN). it] *om* (ULEWNM). 187 hym] hem (LENM). 206 of] *om* (RLEKM). 242 here] his (RUDLEKWNM). 258 cas] *om* (RULKW). IV 10 mo oþere] *tp* (DEM). 12 þe(2 *and* 3)] *om* (RUM). 14 renneþ] Rod VJ (K); rideþ H (H²LEAWN). 21 And] *om* (WN). 33 wel] *om* (W). 42 hynen] hewyn J; owen H; owne V (LEAKM). 57 my] þi (LEWM). 61 penys . . . proffride] *om* (RUDLEAKWNM). 76 for] of (A). 77 Amende] And a. (EW). 83 man] *om* (EM). 91 king] k. þo (ChEANM). 113 coyn] Coroune (EAKWNM). 136 he] *om* (ChLWM). 150 be(1)] b. so (RU). V 36 leue] loue (RUDLAK). 59 cope] gylt J; gultus VH (L). 93 liȝtiþ] likeþ (K). 94 of] for (EW). 95 þere] *om* (LKWN). 130 spynstere] spinsters (EAWNMH³). 135 hym] hem (TRUDH²LEH³). 156 And] *om* (EKWNM). 164 ꝧ] *om* (RUEKWNH³). 173 of . . . cloke] *om* (WN). 194 And] *om* (DEA). 207 make] to make (LWN). 210 wombe] mawe (RUWH³). 215 it] *om* (UChAM). 217 synne] sunnes (LEAKNMH³). 241 *reddere*] no Red (DW). 242 I owe] I knowe (EAKWMH³). VI 2 baches] valeyes (TRUDChH² KN). 21 wy] he (RUDW). 27 kende] tauȝte (MH³). 46 For] *om* (LEANMH³). VII 10 wyues] ȝe w. (LEKNH³). 12 oþer] or elles (ULN). 56 at] on (RUMH³). 66 forþ] forþer (RULM). 68 tiþes] tiþe (UH³). 76 with] w. þis (LKNMH³). 114 leg] legges (LAKNMH³). 128 cowes] Crowen VH; crowys J (LKNM). 136 flessh . . .

fend] *tp* (UW). 144 and] And of (LAKNMH³). 178 brokelegged] for b. (LN). by] Vppon softe sonenday b. VH (N); On softe segys on sonndayes b. J. 190 For] *om* (WN). 199 breed] mete (UWH³). 222 wiþ] *om* (UN). 229 shal nouȝt] *tp* (H²L KWH³). 230 þat he] *tp* (DNH³). 258 it] *om* (RMH³). 262 god] þe (UChLNH³). 266 A] And a (UChA). 288 or(1)] and (RWNM). VIII 23 ⁊] *om* (U). 31 also] *om* (UANH³). 36 sende] s. ow (KWMH³). 38 soule] soules (UChN). 54 sauf sykirly] *tp* J (ULH³); siker saaf VH (N). 112 aboute . . . ioye] while we woneþ in þis world to make vs wombe Ioye V (*cp.* U); In no maner wise aboute oure wombe ioiȝe H; aboute Ne trauellyn to myche to makyn þe wombe Ioye J. 125 seldom] luitel (TRChH²A).

It does not seem necessary to labour this demonstration further by adding more than 100 agreements of VJ in larger variational groups, to say nothing of about 40 such agreements of HJ. There would clearly be more evidence for a genetic connexion between VH and the unattached manuscript J, than for a genetic group *y*, since there is none for *y*. The agreements of VH and J, which incidentally illustrated the unrealistic character of the *y* hypothesis, have been noticed by Fowler, who seems to account for them by assuming conflation between J and *x* (VH).[1] Scrutiny of the evidence for *y* might suggest that it would be more correct, if the VHJ agreements had any weight, to entertain the possibility that they reflect a genetic relation obscured by universal variation, and perhaps by correction as well. But this could only remain a possibility, in view of the amount of conflicting evidence, and would be useless for recension.

In the last analysis the conflict of evidence, not only here but in every other instance where a variational group begins to look persistent, is the most important circumstance revealed by examining the variational groups among the manuscripts of the **A** version. No attempt to determine their genetic relation made without preconceptions of the result can fail to take the abundance of conflicting agreements into account. The impression given by Knott and Fowler that their genetic hypotheses are undisturbed by the contradictory evidence does not survive scrutiny of the full body of variants, but is shown to be altogether misleading.

Knott's exposition of his principles suggests no doubt or qualification of his results.[2] Indeed, his reference to the availability of common omissions as a sure test of genetic relation implies the

[1] Thesis, p. 30. The question arises through the defection of J from *y* in 4 *b* (p. 108 above). Fowler cites Chambers and Grattan 'The Text of "Piers Plowman": Critical Methods', p. 262 and footnote. They merely noted, however, that VH and J have common errors.
[2] See pp. 56–7 above.

contrary, that the agreements in omission confirm his findings. This is not, however, the case, as the following list of such agreements shows:

Prologue 50–1 VH; 99–100 VH; 109 VH. I 29 TChE; 40 RE; 103 VE; 106 VHL; 168 AWN; 177 UV. II 11 RU; 20 U(1)E; 24–5 RU; 28–9 VH. III 22 EM; 23 VEM; 33 EAM; 102 TDChH^2; 158 EM; 193 TCh; 206 UWN; 208 WN; 233α HN; 243 TUDChH^2; 257 WN. IV 71 TRUDCh; 72 TCh; 89 RA; 90 HA; 106 AN; 119 VH. V 10 TChHN; 21–3 WN; 38–9 LA; 74–5 AM; 78–9 HL; 80 HJL; 96 DWN; 116 HE; 128 RU; 165 EA; 175 HLK; 176 LK; 177 LAK; 219 RU. VI 6 RUA; 70 AN; 108 RU. VII 5 DW; 74 VE; 119 HA; 132 UVHN; 178 TDCh; 211 TRUDChE; 224 KW; 255 UNH^3; 273–5 UA; 282 TDCh. VIII 30 UA; 38 MH^3; 103 HH^3; 107 AW; 108 WM; 170 TDChH^2. IX 74 UA; 76–7 UA; 83α UJ; 93 VA; 111 RUV. X 26 TDCh; 40 RU; 67 RW; 81 VW; 94 TD; 94α VJ; 120 UCh; 215 AWMH^3. XI 148 TUChH^{2}VAH^3; 177–8 RDW; 284 AWMH^3; 294 UW; 295 UA.

Of these 80 agreements in omission nearly half conflict with Knott's 'family tree', and at least one of the conflicting groups, UA, begins to seem persistent. The picture of simply determinable genetic relationships is, in this respect, as in others, false. The same misleading impression of editorial capacity to deal with all the evidential complexities of this problem is given in the two pages allotted to 'Classification of the MSS' in Knott and Fowler's published edition (pp. 26–7). 'No single diagram', we read, 'can account for all of the complexities that we inevitably find in a study of this kind.' This ought to read '*No* diagram'; as it stands it suggests to the reader who lacks access to the facts that, indeed, not one, but a number of neat diagrams, excluded from the book on considerations of space, do in fact account for these complexities.

The suggestion arises from the absence of full evidence, and it would be wrong to see a disingenuous connexion between it and that circumstance. More likely the assurance was genuine and originated in confusion of principle and of practice. Two unjustified assumptions seem to underlie this attempt at classification: that because of the existence of certain strongly attested variational groups of **A** manuscripts, the remaining copies must also fall into discernible groups; and that the genetic history of these manuscripts is necessarily recoverable. With a full apparatus of variant readings available, these assumptions can now be tested.

My conclusions reject them. They are: that the genetic history of the

A manuscripts is not recoverable in any form useful for the editorial process of recension; that the combination of the two types of convergent variation, correction or conflation on the one side, and coincident variation on the other, so obscures the relation of these manuscripts as to make general, clear and unqualified deductions about their genetic relation impossible; and that the genetic hypothesis put forward by Knott and Fowler has not only not been proven, but is challenged at every stage by a great deal of contradictory evidence.

Thus, although the relative persistence of certain variational groups suggests a genetic relation {⟨[(TH^{2})Ch]D⟩RU}, it is clear that a great many variants in these manuscripts are not the product of that relation. Similarly, while it seems likely that EAMH^{3} in Prologue–VII and AWMH^{3} in IX–XI are somehow genetically related, the evidence fails to authorize a more precise description than this, and often points to a many ⟩ one relation.[1] And while the many unoriginal variants common to V and H make it appear altogether likely that VH are a genetic pair, the evidence necessary to determine the relation of VH to the remaining manuscripts is wanting. WN may, from its persistence, seem a genetic group in Prologue–VIII, but if its genetic character is accepted, a variational group KW is unaccounted for, to say nothing of many random agreements of W in Prologue–VIII. Certainly there is no evidence for a group [(WN)K].

If these possibilities are formed into a genetic hypothesis further assumptions become necessary: of conflation to account for the variational groups RUD, UJ and KW; of change of exemplar to account for the variational group RUE and the appearance of W with AMH^{3} in VIII–XI; and of correction to account for many defections of members of the group {⟨[(TH^{2})Ch]D⟩RU}.

Nor is the hypothesis tenable without recognition of the extreme frequency of convergent variation. Meanwhile the distinction between genetic groups and groups arising through convergent variation will have been made solely on grounds of persistence,[2] since the variants establishing the groups acceptable to the genetic hypothesis do not differ in character from those establishing groups that require additional assumptions.

[1] Cf. Greg, *Calculus*, p. 44.

[2] This distinction requires an assumption of the necessarily limited character of convergent variation, which is difficult. It is not true, for instance, of the manuscripts of the *Iliad*, or of Juvenal or of *The Divine Comedy*.

Finally, if the formation of a genetic hypothesis on these possi bilities, and accounting for discrepancies from it by the numerou assumptions required, continues to retain its attraction, there is n evidence on which to proceed with the further relation of the group {⟨[(TH^2)Ch]D⟩RU}, (E)A(W)MH^3, VH, WN, and the manu scripts J, L and K, to enable the exercise of recension. Even if ther were, the propriety of recension would be doubtful because of th evident frequency of convergent variation in the tradition of thes manuscripts.[1]

Thus the comfort and the appearance of authority afforded b recension are denied to the editor of the manuscripts of the **A** versio of *Piers Plowman*. He can neither evade the responsibility for decision about originality by referring them to a genealogy, nor put his tex beyond criticism by calling it 'critical'. Recension might be a per missible method if the whole history of these manuscripts could b recovered. But the accuracy of its results must depend primarily on th accuracy of the genetic information available. Here we have at bes some uncoordinated possibilities of genetic relation. Evidently then i is necessary to seek some other means of determining originality o readings. The history of transmission of the poem was not one o mechanical copying; it was, indeed, very much the contrary. Thu the method of editing cannot be mechanical.

[1] There is fairly general agreement on this point. Compare Maas, 'Textkritik', p. 4: 'Wen . . . einzelne Schreiber mehrere Vorlagen kontaminiert haben, so ist in dem Bereich diese Kontaminationen die eliminatio stark behindert, wenn nicht unmöglich'; Pasquali, *Gnomor* p. 131: 'Wo die Überlieferung nicht rein mechanisch ist, wo die Kontamination viele ode auch alle Zweige der Überlieferung ergriffen hat, muss man, wenn man überhaupt ein Resulta erreichen will, diese Methode stark verfeinern. Die Verfeinerung, Vervollkommnung besteh aber nicht etwa in einer grösseren Mechanisierung des Verfahrens, sondern umgekehrt in eine intensiveren Benutzung der sachlichen und sprachlichen Kriterien, darunter des usus scribenc und der lectio difficilior'; the same author in *Storia*, p. xvii: 'Quanto alla *recensio*, solo nei cas relativamente rari, di tradizione meccanica è possibile . . . applicare i criteri, essi stessi meccanic della recensione chiusa, formulati dal Lachmann; dove la recensione è aperta, valgono sol criteri interni'; Manly and Rickert, *Canterbury Tales*, ii, p. 25: 'The value of mixed texts fc genealogical purposes is comparatively slight. Some scholars regard them as unusable'; Fourque 'Fautes Communes ou Innovations Communes?', p. 94: 'Il ne faut pas que la contaminatio vienne tout brouiller'.

IV

EDITORIAL RESOURCES AND METHODS

Recension is not a practicable method for the editor of the **A** manu- scripts. Nor is the creation of a hierarchy, with some one copy elevated to a rôle of authority: while some of these manuscripts are certainly more corrupt than others, all are corrupt to an indeterminate but evidently considerable extent. The sole source of authority is the variants themselves, and among them, authority, that is originality, will probably be determined most often by identification of the variant likeliest to have given rise to the others.

Piers Plowman was especially subject to variation as a living text with a content of direct concern to its scribes.[1] Its relevance to contem- porary circumstances would not merely distract them from the passive state of mind ideal for exact copying, but actually induce them, whether consciously or subconsciously, to make substitutions. Pro- fessional copyists 'just able to take an unintelligent interest in what they were doing' as well as educated amateurs taking copies for their own use might be so affected. In this *Piers Plowman* resembles the *Divine Comedy*.[2] In one respect the Middle English poem was even more susceptible to corruption than the Italian. Because it was written in non-stanzaic, unrhymed lines with an indeterminate number of syl- lables, little skill or ingenuity would seem to be required of those who set out to alter their copy. Indeed, scribes ignorant of the practice of alliterative poetry, or with an imperfect grasp of it, might receive an altogether false notion of freedom from formal control. The copyist's sense of obligation to follow his exemplar might be further relaxed by awareness that the poem was current in several shapes, or from knowledge of discrepancies between copies, whether of the same or different forms of the poem. If the exemplar before a scribe was evi- dently corrupt in parts he might cease to respect it as a whole. These conditions: the liveliest personal interest in the theme and content, the

[1] Compare Kantorowicz, *Einführung*, pp. 30, 40 ff.
[2] Moore, *Contributions*, pp. vii–viii; compare Quentin, *Essais*, pp. 43–4.

apparent absence of technical discipline, and the suggestion that form and expression were to some extent fluid, combined to make the scribes of *Piers Plowman*, in many cases if not all, 'amateur, uncritical and anonymous editors, unchecked by the editor's sense of responsibility'.[1]

In these circumstances it might seem that substitution would be not merely frequent but also wild and wayward.[2] In fact this is not generally the case. A study of the effects of substitution on the text at points where originality can be determined with reasonable certainty argues strongly that scribes[3] treated their copy in a number of characteristic ways, and in so doing expressed several clear tendencies of substitution, distinct from mechanical errors of transmission. Such treatment of the text, implying a process of comparison, preference and rejection absent from mechanical error, whether it was deliberate and careful, or casual and habitual, or even subconscious, generated the type of variant which poses the editor's most serious problems.

By contrast with the variants produced by scribal editing of this kind, those originating in mechanical error hardly seem problematic. Mechanical errors can often be identified without difficulty. For this reason, although they are numerous enough, it will be sufficient to

[1] Moore, *Contributions*, p. viii.

[2] Supposing that Chaytor's 'considerable and almost systematic individualism' were applicable (*From Script to Print*, p. 129).

[3] In this discussion I write, of necessity, as if 'scribes' were a body of persons of uniform and consistent habits, which is clearly not so. Since all the surviving **A** manuscripts plainly represent the accumulated errors and substitutions of at least several processes of copying there is little means of distinguishing clearly the traits of individual scribes. For one thing there were almost certainly two kinds of scribes, professional scriveners, and amateurs taking copies for themselves or others (for the latter see W. Wattenbach, *Das Schriftwesen im Mittelalter*, Leipzig, 1896, pp. 487–8). But there is little to show even that any manuscript is the product of a succession of copyists entirely from one or the other class. If anything the evidence is to the contrary. Some manuscripts in formal hands, for instance, show signs of confusions of letters unlikely to have occurred in such hands, but probable in cursive or intermediate hands. Broadly speaking it may be true that professional scribes were less ready editors, and that errors related to the physical aspect of a page, such as lines truncated or otherwise shortened for the sake of symmetry are to be attributed to them, whereas amateurs would care more about the substance of what they wrote than the layout of the page. But this is only a generalization, and as unsafe to maintain as that amateurs would not be able to write a formal hand. (On this point compare S. H. Steinberg, 'Medieval Writing Masters', *The Library*, fourth series, xxii, pp. 1–2; also H. C. Schultz, 'Thomas Hoccleve, Scribe', *Speculum*, xii, pp. 71–81.) Nevertheless, while the qualities of individual copyists are generally obscured by the process of incremental error and substitution, certain broad tendencies of substitution are suggested by the recurrence of variants for distinct reasons probably unoriginal, which have similar effects on the poem and, therefore, presumably originated in similar intentions. To identify them is, admittedly, the most general kind of observation, true of the individual copyist only in so far as he was typical. But the evidence for these tendencies is markedly persistent, and it seems tenable that they were present, more or less strongly, in many of the copyists of this poem at least. They are fully illustrated below, pp. 128 ff.

illustrate[1] here some forms which they take in the **A** manuscripts, before passing to the more serious problem of the variants originating in substitution.

Mechanical errors, where the scribe, at the moment of writing, was unaware of his departure from copy and would presumably have admitted the mistake if shown it, seem to arise mainly from inattention through fatigue, momentary external distractions, or internal distractions of memory or verbal association. Such inattention can give rise to simple aberrations, of which the following (allowing for the possibility of some bad spellings) are probably examples.

Prologue 11 m*er*ueillous] nerwelous R. 13 Est] west Ch. 20 putte] butty*n* M. 90 bacheleris] bacheris J. 96 burgeis] bugeys M. I 12 treuþe] trew M. 33 ȝerne] ȝeore V. 48 standis] stodid J. 97 Dide] De M. 115 lucifer] lucificer N. II 43 kniȝtes] kyȝthy*s* R. 142 fetten] fethem W. 157 mayntenip] meynt L. III 3 king] kyn L. 19 hem] vs E. 112 manye] my E. 131 countiþ] count*er*yth J. 171 miȝte] mgthe M. 180 cloud] knowde R. 242 eldren] eldes Ch. 269 shal] sha M. IV 48 tolde] tolle H². 76 biggen] beingen H². 87 wagid] waieg N. V 31 worþ(1)] wor A. 47 behiȝte] bieght N. 57 doke] doge L. 86 p*re*ye] p*ri*ye H². 223 chirche] chrche A. 238 sake] salke M. VI 11 v*er*nicle] vernache A. 40 louȝ] lown H³. 76 beleue] eliues A. 106 anoþ*er*] the tohere M; þe oþr H³. 122 þoruȝ] þorou*r* A. VII 25 kniȝt] kyng D. 77 bequest] lyqueste N. 110 ȝe] ȝ A. 193 my] may E. 254 calabre] alabre R. VIII 163 þinkeþ] þinkeþs W. IX 16 clerk] clek W. 105 dwellen] dulli*n* M. X 32 mark] mar D; martl J. 51 reccheles] recches A. 139 feiþles] feithes U. 156 couplide] cowled D. 196 forsworn] forswon R. XI 89 Siþen] Sþe A. 251 amende] amen W.

Occasionally the aberration takes the form of repeating the copy, as in the following examples:

Prologue 9 ⁊] *twice* M. 35 ⁊ iangleris] *twice* D. I 21 none] *twice* E. 88 a god be] accounted accounted to H. 175 *Date . . . vobis*] *twice* J. II 3 bar þe] *twice* E. 83 of mendis] of frendis *twice* U. III 91 as swiþe] *twice* H². seriauntis] a sergaunt þe sergaunt M. IV 145 þ*at* resoun] *twice* A. V 28 to take] *twice* R. 57 doke] goos *twice* U. VI 116 þ*at*] *twice* M. VII 26 seint] *twice* E. 146 to þe] *twice* E. VIII 131 mad] *twice* T. 142 king] *twice* D. IX 58 me a] me on me D. 106 lyue] lyfe lyue J. X 59 þ*at*] *twice* H². sitten] *twice* U. XI 58 questiouns] questiou*n*ou*n*s M. 157 werche] *twice* T. 211 rid*er*e] ridedere A.

Such errors probably occurred when a scribe mistook, after being distracted, the point where he had left off. Repetition of whole lines, or of

[1] None of the lists of examples in the present section is exhaustive. Considerations of space have made it necessary to limit severely the evidence adduced in support of any observation. Nor are differentiations of spelling and grammatical or dialectal form as full as in the critical apparatus, to which reference may be made for further details.

several lines, in some cases probably because the point of resumption was mistaken, is relatively infrequent but does occur.[1]

Whatever confusion such errors may have created in lost, intermediate copies, they are generally detectable in the surviving manuscripts. This is not always true of a special form of aberration which, not infrequently, results in the copying of a plausible reading, namely the transposition of letters in a word. This phenomenon, with which anyone who uses a pen or typewriter is familiar, seems to result from a combination of fatigue and unconscious suggestion. The following are examples from the **A** manuscripts (the starred forms suggest hypothetical intermediate variants):

Prologue 10 so] os E. 17 folk] flokke E. 29 cuntre] court L. 107 osay] asoye J. I 20 þre] þer J. 21 nempne] *nemyn] meny*n* *or* meuy*n* R. II 29 Knowe] Kawne E. 71 while] wlysse E. 163 gerdiþ] ged*er*iþ TRUChH^{2}. III 40 arnede] erdene J. 103 callid] glad M. 111 freel] frely Ch. 159 g*ra*ce] garce E. 180 cloud] colde J. IV 132 couplide] clepedy*n* M. V 49 fers] fresch RUHL. 194 glemans] gelmannys A. 201 surfet] suffird E. 204 spak] sapke E. VII 136 foulide] folowed UHE. VIII 35 Releue] Reule WUVM. 70 fals] flas H^{3}. 163 triste] *trost] storn A. IX 39 Synnes] *Synneþ] syþ*en* R. 113 durste] drost H^{3}. X 33 warp] wrap KH^{3}. 47 desiriþ] sedireth H^{2}. 75 wrong] worng A. 111 witnessid] wyttens A. XI 47 nymen] meuen D. 86 worþ] wrouth A. 87 my] *þyn] þuy H^{3}. 209 steruiþ] streueþ Ch. 294 was hit] what is TRH^{2}.

A certain number of mechanical errors doubtless resulted from scribes reading their copy aloud to themselves and writing from auditory memory of it, or, possibly, of writing from dictation.[2] I do not profess to identify many with assurance; possibly variants like III 130 *harmide*] *harme dide* HE; V 27 *at*] *hadde* M; VII 82 *rental*] *trentale* ChL; VIII 85 *takiþ þis*] *takiþ his* TDH^{2}; XI 241 *degre*] *decre* KH^{3} have such an origin.

Likewise, scribes must have made numerous mistakes in reading their copy simply by forming a wrong visual impression of it. How little the recognition of words depends on spelling is well known. A scribe looking carelessly at a word, so that his memory retained a picture of only part of it, or a scribe taking in too much copy at a glance, could receive a false impression, especially if guided by unconscious preconception or memorial suggestion. Sometimes it is difficult to see how he was not pulled up by the inappropriateness of the

[1] As, for instance, at I 173 (T); II 23 (E); II 67 (L); III 192 (A); IV 1 (W); VII 221 (L); VII 282 (A); X 15 (A); X 129–31 (Ch); XI 108–9 (J).

[2] See Chaytor, *From Script to Print*, chapter ii, esp. pp. 14, 19 ff.

mistaken form; at others it fits without jarring into an evident train of meaning or a preconceived syntactical pattern. In the latter case we may ask how far such suggestion emerged to consciousness and amounted to deliberate substitution of a seemingly apt word of similar shape. Some variants, with the appearance of visual errors merely, may well have been consciously substituted. In estimating this possibility it is necessary to study how far the suggestion of improvement in an intrusive variant might have been strong enough to outweigh such sense of fidelity to copy as the scribe possessed. If, however, the ousted readings are not difficult, and do not seem to encourage substitution, or the intrusive readings are not necessarily easier, and have an appearance of waywardness, there seems a strong likelihood that the variants came into being through visual errors, and record unconscious substitutions. The following are examples:

Prologue 20 ful selde] for þe sede E. 91 acountis] a courte E. I 5 sone] soon M. 21 nedful] medful E. 60 he] here M. 67 lett*ere*] leder D. 119 word] world D. 176 lok] boke ChH^2. 182 what] *qwat] q*ua*þ U. II 46 þe writ wolde] þai write wald EM. 146 mene] men EAM. 173 agast] ꝥ gessid A. III 24 mede] nede D. 36 softely] sothly H^2. 92 boure] borugh TH^2. 118 Is not] I not TDChH^2. 185 mo*ur*nyng] morwen RU. 194 lordsshipe] worschep R. 206 mede] mete VEM. 253 bible] bylle R. IV 10 wedde] weld E. 30 riȝt] rauȝt H. 83 skaþe] state J. V 11 com] *con] bygan H. 50 hente] haunte D. 98 loueles] lawles E. 127 p*re*ssour] pryson M. 164 ribibo*ur*] bribo*ur* LJ; ribaud R. 223 dere] derne H^3. 249 lepe] kepe D. VI 28 sure] swere EAMH^3. 71 manis] man*ere* W. 103 gift] gilt E. VII 8 wo*m*men] wy*n*ne R. 74 his woord] þys world M. 85 hym p*re*stly] þe p*ri*st E. 179 helide] halsyd E. 245 ete] ȝet AH^3; ȝit JM. 270 cole] colde ChW. VIII 40 oþes] oþere H^3. 85 myselis] me selfe A. 152 be pure] before TDChH^2. 173 leddist] haddest D. IX 1 yrobid] Roberd M. 25 brood] brok A. 109 ywar were] war werey D. X 21 gowel] dowel R. 89 Wilne] whil AW. XI 31 haue god my] to haue good In W. 57 mene] many R. 77 lore] lord RU. 166 mekly] meche U; mychel J. 215 fet] feyth A. 252 god hiȝte vs] good hit is Ch. 291 none] now TChH^{2}K.

That scribes did not always look closely at their copy, and that they could register it incorrectly is made quite clear by a large number of variants originating from a more confidently determinable cause, the similarity of various letters in the handwritings, whether formal or intermediate, of the fifteenth century. The following are examples:

Confusion of e *and* o

Prologue 11 sweuene] swouene R. 69 leuide] loued L. I 54 tresour] troso*ur* R. II 192 copide] kepten V. III 12 woniþ] went N. 157 menide] mowed N. IV 158 libbe]

*leue] loue H. V 223 dere] dore V. 254 moten] meten H². VI 68 fees] foos WN. 101 eft] ofte M. 113 hed] hod R. VII 34 croppiþ] crepen H. 169 benis] bones L. VIII 60 mene] mone U. IX 7 lengide] longeþ R. X 104 mosseþ] men seþ *etc.* 193 cheste] chost R. XI 145 scole] skele D. 182 lewide] lowed W. 210 cloistre] cleyster A. 281 shrof] shref TDH².

Confusion of þ *and* y

Prologue 77 boy] boþe DM. I 36 liȝ*er*] liþ*er* TRDCh. II 85 gyuen] þif W. 178 manye] mouthe L. III 89 ȝouþe] þouth A; thoght E. 94 melis þise] *melid þes] Melodyes V; melioudiouse N. 185 m*er*þe] merie HChEM. VI 68 freþid] frayd W. VII 4 eren] *erye] erþe Ch. 163 boþe] þe Boyes V. 220 tilie] tylthe K. VIII 55 þridde] y rede U. IX 66 raþ*ere*] raye A. 67 þouȝt] youth M. X 115 ȝe] þe TCh. 157 seþ] sey(e)(n) TRUCh. XI 121 liþer] liȝeris TRUDChH²V. 243 ȝiue] þeue U.

Confusion of t *and* c

Prologue 14 toft] coste R. I 12 toft] cost R. 172 treccherie] tretherye D. II 79 tale] call J. 142 vitailes] vicail*es* H². III 91 fette] fecche TH². IV 38 Boþe] Boche D. V 79 wraþþe] wreche A. 239 worþe] worch *etc.* VI 15 At] ac R. VIII 163 to triste] be crist D. X 63 suche] swethe H³. XI 2 lich] lithe K. 87 cacche] kaithe K.

Confusions involving w

Prologue 2 shroud] schrubb*es* K: w] bb. 3 abite] whit M: *tall* a + b] w. 44 robertis] rowt*es* E: b*er*] w. I 72 wisside] hailised Ch: w] ha. V 70 Walewiþ] Walk*es* EAM: lw] lk. 148 breust*ere*] bribester L: w] b. VII 177 botind] *ibotned] wotned N: ib] w. IX 36 walwen] walkyn A: lw] lk. XI 44 gnawen] gabby*n* H³: w] bb.

Confusion of f *and* s

Prologue 14 toft] coste R; twist M. I 12 toft] cost R; testre J. 35 lef] lesse M. II 47 feffid] sesyd EM. III 168 half] halse EKN; Nekke VH. VII 305 fyue] syn L. VIII 142 les] *lost] lafte V. XI 142 lat] *laft] last UH³.

Confusion of b *and* h

II 185 hy] be TD. IV 80 bote] hote A. VI 95 be] he M. X 52 heryng] beryng W. XI 72 olde] *hold] bold W.

Confusion of long r *and* y

Prologue 75 eris] eyen K. II 149 gyede] gredde R. VIII 7 man*er*] many U. 60 resceyueþ] res*er*uit M.

Other confusions of a similar nature:

round s *and* c

Prologue 102 As] ac R. VII 103 su*m*me] come Ch. X 206 As] ac RU.

l *and* s

IX 10 ylernid] serued D. XI 128 lerid] servyd K. 142 lat] set V.

long r *and* þ

VIII 165 renkes] þenke DRWM. XI 89 Siþe] Sire V.

h *and* l

I 17 hiȝte] lyȝthe RE. XI 247 heiȝly] leely Ch.

b *and* v

III 274 banisshit] vanshed N. VI 53 bowiþ] vowe H².

Confusion over minims

Prologue 3 vnholy] my holy E. I 36 Leue] *Lene] Gyff E. II 83, 96 molere] mulere] Iuweler V. III 145 Iuelx] wylys M. 152 coupliþ] compliþ H²; compellit M. 264 daunten] damnen D. 274 Vnkyndenesse] wykkednysse RUHEM. IV 104 holynesse] *(h)alinesse] almesse R. V 69 *verious*] vernisch VKWN. 115 symme] synne EAM. 211 aunte] amyte J. VI 62 bowis] bonys W. VIII 130 *mamelyng] Mony elynge V. 136 deuinide] demide (*after loss of* m *suspension*) TRH²M. IX 113 meue] mene W. X 66 fauntis] fautys *various*. 202 vntyme] my tyme TRUChH². XI 2 lene] leef M. 145 louis] lowest A. 212 lond] lowde Ch.

Confusion over contractions or suspensions

Prologue 23 ap*ar*ailide] ⁊ playde J. 42 here] he M. I 68 *bet*ray*id] tyid J. 95 *ter*mined] *tur*nyd J. II 28 longiþ] logyn M. 162 Fet*er*iþ] Fetteþ D. 176 p*re*ntice] Prynce E. III 83 amende] mede A. 93 Curteisly] Certis TD. IV 115 *let*tres] hors K. V 16 plumtres] plantes TDChH². VI 8 ampollis] apples H². VII 93 þerewiþ] þe *with* D. VIII 176 frat*er*nite] fruyte D. IX 102 sauo*ur*iþ] saide D. X 15 man*er*] mare R. XI 31 harlotrie] harlot D. 63 fantasies] fawtys J. 90 degre] day RU. 141 þerein] þrynne D. 274 in] ⁊ RH³.

Confusion over division of words

Prologue 14 a tour] autour E. III 185 to leue] *til leue] til eue RU. V 251 þrongen] þe wrong TDH². VI 95 wraþþe] *wraþ þe] wrathe þe N. 116 apeward] a peward E. VII 267 A lof] al of H. VIII 152 inpugnid it] enpugnedid M. X 180 leiȝen] ley hem TChH². XI 188 bakken hem] bachem U.

Mechanical errors of copying also occurred through 'attraction' to the whole or part of an adjacent or nearby word in the line being copied or in a nearby line. Presumably the scribe's attention either returned inadvertently to matter already copied, or was distracted by copy to come, his pen being misdirected accordingly. The following examples illustrate this familiar error in the **A** manuscripts. Scrutiny of the critical apparatus will indicate how often it occurred.

Attraction to a word or letter previously copied

Prologue 44 robertis] Rybald*es* K. 52 lobies] globis M. 69 likide] lykyk J. I 53 welþe] witte Ch. 62 falshed] falfhede R. 78 pitously] precyusly M. II 20 to] out M. 86 texte] tyxtest Ch. 165 warne] warde R. III 7 wil] witte W. 43 shrewidnesse] mysdedes H². 234 þat] Thaþ R. IV 35 wyf] wille A. 65 skaþe] gate skate H². 71 woo] wrong A. V 76 belowen] Bylowlen N. 95 ȝet] ȝiȝt N. 171 bette] bede K. VI 81 Deþ] daye M. 90 bane] hane E. VII 18 longe] louely TRUDChH². 199 Bolde] Hold E. VIII 1 peris] trewthe H³. 33 loue] loues H². 61 lawieris] lawisteris TD. IX 32 were] with H². 65 Wot] wost A. 112 softe] sad RU. X 55 his bour] brayn Ch. 95 werchist] werchif H². 195 fecche] flicche M. XI 65 crabbide] crappede M. 137 tymes] tynne A. 144 lelly] leuely J. 261 mercy] merke A.

Anticipation of copy

Prologue 9 lokide] kokyd J. 24 cloþing] glothyng H². 73 þus] ȝus M. I 3 lynene] lynned H. 110 was] wat R. 128 compsiþ] domseth K. II 75 rutelondis] Rokelandes URJ. 82 weddyng] wreddynd M. 163 giles] giled N. III 14 burde] berthe R. 111 freel] frethil R. 186 bak] bak bod U. IV 26 dischargid] disgargid H². 80 bet] bute E. V 64 lek] led N. 104 synne] synneþ H. 183 repentiþ] repentist U. 246 his] hie A. VI 31 sewide] kepid UW. 62 breke] plokke A. 90 eten] heten AM. VII 28 And] Ac T. 130 beddrede] Bredred M. 278 ripe] riche T. VIII 15 bere] bernyn J. 137 nempne] memned R. 142 king] lord U. IX 80 þat] The D. 109 wyt] wtite A. 110 long] lond A. X 7 hatte] haþ TH². 56 bounde] wanton W. 169 flood] folood H². XI 89 wilneþ] wiþneth W. 213 fro] to T. 258 haue walkid] hawed W.

Variants which, according to the text adopted, appear as omissions, bring us to the border between mechanical error and deliberate alteration of copy. The most numerous and difficult of such variants are the small ones, such as the presence or absence of: the conjunction *þat* before an object clause; *and*, within a line or at its head; an article; a possessive adjective or demonstrative adjective where the reference is not in doubt; the resumptive object pronoun; a conjunctive or prepositional element in a second or third parallel construction. Many such variants doubtless occurred through inadvertent omission, but many others, also, probably occurred through scribes substituting their personal habits of speech for the wording of their copy, or through indolent (perhaps even habitual) pruning of unessential words. As a class this type of variant resists analysis.

The omission of some whole lines or groups of lines is identifiable as mechanical, the features of the text which occasioned the omission being preserved in surviving copies. Other omissions of lines or groups of lines have a convincing look of being the work of scribal editors. But between the two clear types are doubtful cases, omissions of lines or larger units for which explanations can be conjectured but not demonstrated, and omissions for which no cause is apparent.

One frequent occasion of mechanical omission of a line or several lines is *homoteleuton* or *homœoteleuton*. A few examples are given.

Prologue 50–1 VH (*aftir*, 49, 51). I 24 Ch (*saue* 23, *selue* 24). 40 RE (*herte* 39, *beste* 40). 135 N (*aftir* 134, 135). II 24–5 RU (*togidere* 23, 25). 28–9 VH (*alle* 27, 29). 63–4 J (*togidere* 62, 64). III 248–50 U (*hem to depe* 247, 250). IV 78–80 N (*þe betere* 77, 80). V 74–5 AM (*ofte* 73, 75). 175–7 LK (*togideris* 174, 177). VI 83–4 A (*forsoþe* 82, *þe soþe* 84). VII 279–81 W (*manye* 278, 281). IX 111 RUV (*oþer* 110, *noþer* 111). X 107 Ch (*euere* 106, *euere* as TD 107). 180 M (*togedere* 179, *togideris* 180). XI 177–8 RDW (*stodie* 176, 178).

Omissions were also occasioned by the proximity of lines with the same or similar beginnings (*homœoarchy*). Such a feature of the copy seems to have had two distinctive effects. It might make a scribe mis‑take his point of resumption when his eyes returned to the exemplar to pick up more material. This appears to have happened in the fol‑lowing cases where the earlier of two or several lines with similar beginnings is omitted.

Prologue 82 D (*To* 82, 83). I 101 M (*And* 101, 102). III 165–6 M (*þou . . . consience* 165, 167). IV 32 H (*And* 32, 33). V 32–3 A (*He* 32, 34). VI 70–1 N (*And þanne* 70, *þanne* 72). VII 202–3 A (*ȝif* 202, 204). 255 UNH[3] (*And be* 255, *And le‑* 256). X 67 RW (*þei* 67, 68). 118 R (*þus* 118, 119). 145 V (*In* 145, 146). XI 102 A (*For to* 102, *To* 103). 165–6 A (I 165, 167).

Or, in other instances where lines with the same or similar beginnings occur in proximity, this feature of the copy appears to have made the scribe omit the second or third of these lines because he was conscious of having already copied a line with such a beginning. This seems to have happened in the following cases.

I 103 VE (*And* 101, 102, 103). II 92 V (*ȝe* 91, 92). V 40 E (*And be* 39, *And ȝe* 40). VII 124 W (*wastours* 122, 124). 178 TDCh (*Blynde* 177, *þat leyȝe blynde* 178). 211 TRUDChE (*Wiþ* 210, *Or with* 211). 289–90 H (*Ne* 287 *But* 288, *Ne* 289 *But* 290). VIII 38 MH[3] (*þat* 37, 38). IX 42–3 A (*þat* 41, 43). X 156 R (*For alle þat* 155, *And alle þat* 156).

When the same or similar words occurred in the body of adjacent or nearby lines similar processes of mistaking the point of resumption or thinking of the line as already copied were apparently possible. The following omissions are found in such circumstances.

Prologue 79 M (*parissh* 79, 80). II 20 U(1)E (*wrong* 19, 20). 84 E (*gyue* 84, 85). III 71–2 M (*peple* 70, 73). 206 UWN (*for here* 206, 207). IV 93 E (*awey* 92, 93). V 71–72a A (*waxiþ* 70b, *wexiþ* 72b). 185–6 A (*rise* 183, 186). VII 132 UVHN (*good, god* 131, *god* 132). IX 4–5 V (*Men* 3, *man* 5). 108 Ch (*dayes* 107, *day* 108). X 47b–49a M (*helpe* 47, 49). 81–2 W (*drede* 80, 82). 142 U (*best* 142, *haste* 143). 155b–156a U, 156 R (*alle . . . caym* 155, *alle . . . kyn* 156). XI 141 U (*loue* 141, 142). 171 R (*wyf* 170, 171).

The arrangement of these illustrations according to the location of the words presumed to have caused omission will be recognized as a convenience of classification only; clearly scribes could be distracted by the recurrence of a word at any point in a line. Thus the presence of *peple* at the end of I 5 and again at the end of 7a was probably responsible for the loss of 6 and 7a from W. The scribe of A, a frequent offender, probably omitted V 117, which begins with *Ferst*, because his eye was caught by *ferste* within 118. X 26 was omitted from TDCh because of the presence of *What . . . kynde* in X 25 and *And what . . . kynde* in 26, although the two lines are not otherwise similar in shape. W probably omitted X 64, ending with *mi3t*, because he had just written this word in copying line 63, where it appears in the middle. Even the occurrence of a whole line like one in the text preceding could apparently occasion omission. Thus the loss of V 21–3 by WN probably resulted from the similarity of 23 to line 11 above. Apparently when the scribe's eye was caught by 23 he concluded from its familiar appearance that he must have copied both it and what went before it, and so passed on to something which he knew he had not yet written. By another process the omission of VIII 51–2 by R may also result from the similarity of 53 to 37 above, but here it appears that the familiar words attracted the scribe's eye and pen, making him overlook 51 and 52.

Thus a variety of physical features of the copy could occasion omission of lines. When such features are preserved or can be reconstructed it is within the power of the editor to make a good guess at the cause of omission. But where the omission occurred in a lost, intermediate copy, detection of its cause may well be made impossible by further variation. Thus physical features of the text, obscured by subsequent copying, may have caused omission in a number of cases where (to me at least) no satisfactory explanation now suggests itself.[1] For it seems a primary likelihood that the omission of lines essential to the sense, and not evidently difficult, occurred mechanically, for physical reasons, despite my inability to recover these.

[1] Such as V 90 (L); 119–20 (A); 171 (H³); 175 (H); 177 (A); 194 (W); 244–5 (H); VI 28 (W); VII 177 (K); 273–5 (UA); VIII 122 (K); XI 220 (A).

There are a number of omissions apparently caused not by physical features of the text, but by a combination of grammatical structure and sense. The common elements in such omissions, apart from the absence of evident physical reasons in the surviving copies, are that each amounts to a jump over a syntactical unit which appears to delay or interrupt the flow of sense, and that the text, after the omission, still reads plausibly.[1] Such omissions were certainly made easier by the frequent paratactic structure and the absence of control in the form of a rhyme or stanza scheme. Many are probably mechanical, and occurred because the scribe took in too much copy at a time and forgot some of it as he wrote, or because his interest in the substance of his copy made him write hastily and without attention to detail. But some may be the work of lazy scribes deliberately pruning their copy to save themselves work. A sure means of determining whether these omissions were generally mechanical or deliberate does not, however, suggest itself. Thus the editor is brought to the difficult borderline between mechanical and conscious variation.[2]

The distinction between mechanical and conscious variation depends on the possibility of discovering motives for any variation. Errors of copying, on the one hand, are clearly unconscious. Instances where comparison of alternative readings shows difference in the meaning, force or metrical form of the expression are possibly conscious. Where neither an occasion of mechanical inaccuracy nor a possible motive for substitution can be recovered the editor is powerless (see below, pp. 151–2). One such type of variant, the small omission, has been noticed (above, p. 122). Others are variants of dialect, construction, tense, mood or number, word order and vocabulary equivalents, which do not materially alter the substance of the communication in any way now determinable. Many such substitutions may well have been deliberate, as of moment to the scribe. Others were almost certainly instinctive substitutions of a more familiar or habitual locution. Some probably originated in careless reading of the exemplar, with the result that an equivalent expression, supplying the defect of visual

[1] As, for instance, at Prologue 37 (J); 54 (U); I 156 (M); II 6 (K); 11 (RU); 149 (J); 157 (H); 182 (K); III 6 (J); 15 (Ch); 23 (V); 27 (A); 80 (U); 110 (E); 115 (K); 158 (EM); 176 (E); 243 (TUDChH[2]); 245 (N); 257 (WN); IV 43 (A); 71–2 (TCh); 89–90 (A); V 97 (V); 164–5 (A); 165 (E); 185–6 (A); 207 (M); 217 (U); VI 94 (A); VII 11 (V); IX 93 (VA); X 74 (D); XI 236 (A). A number occur in connexion with a Latin line or quotation, as, for instance, at VIII 97 (M); 110 (N); X 81 (VW); 94 (TD); 111 (U); 120 (UCh); XI 23 (R); 73 (Ch); 295 (UA).

[2] Omissions probably deliberate are discussed in the treatment of scribal editing which follows below (p. 129, fn.).

impression, took the place of the one in the original. Such substitutions, of which the deliberate character cannot be shown, are very numerous.

Nevertheless there remain many variants which, in all likelihood, were deliberately substituted. There is a *prima facie* improbability that all variants, whether substitutions, additions or omissions, were merely careless or erratic. The majority of scribes did, after all, copy a very large number of words in a great many lines faithfully, often to the extent of keeping spelling and dialect forms of the exemplar. When they caught themselves writing the wrong word, or copying a word wrong, they often left a trace of their state of mind by writing the correct word immediately after the mistake.[1] When they omitted words, or substituted others for them, they not infrequently contrived to work in the omitted or supplanted words more or less smoothly at some point soon after.[2] When they were quite defeated by a word, they often substituted another of similar shape (see p. 133 below). When they caught themselves jumping a line they sometimes copied the omitted line after the one which should properly have followed it, or as soon as the omission was remarked.[3] That scribes thus recognized and tried to fulfil an obligation to follow the exemplar is an argument that much substitution affecting the meaning, force or metric form of

[1] As in the following instances: Prologue 23 pride] þe play & p. J. 65 a p*ar*don*er*] of p*ar*don a p. E. III 1 no mo] Inome*n* & n. m. V. 72 regratrie] regatris regratrie A. 250 Barnes] burwes & bernes H. IV 21 wehe] wey & whehe A. 109 assigne] asyng asyne Ch. 129 eris] heres er*es* U. V 29 wyuene] heuene wyuene U. 238 on . . . man] o. hym þ*at* m. D. VI 67 blenche] see b. U. VIII 9 chirche] chirke c. A. 12 p*ar*adis] purgatori in paradidice A. 78 hede] ende h. U. 120 myn] þe a. b. myn U. 130 metelis] mat*er* meteles J. X 32 mark] martl m. J. 111 chirches] clergyes c. J. The first writing is sometimes cancelled.

[2] As in the following instances: Prologue 69 wel UJ (*previously omitted*). 100 tokkeris TD (*after previous substitution*). I 61 þerin E (*after previous substitution*). 70 so wysely E (wise *previously omitted*). II 48 feffyd E; fessyd M (*after substitution in* 47). 180 huntyd E (*after previous substitution*). III 111 feiþ H (*after previous substitution*). 239 vpon his children of þe man saul A (*after omission of* saul & on). 245 And hoteþ þe W (*after substitution in* 244). 254 Samuel V (*after previous substitution*). 273 waxen E (*after previous omission*). IV 120 for J (*after previous omission*). V 75 hem W (*pronoun object previously omitted*). 101 aswagen hit vnneþe VH (*after substitution in* 100). 147 shriftwarde W (*after substitution in* 146). 248 efte sonys A (*after substitution in* 247). VII 270 pores W (*after previous substitution*). VIII 146 defaute M (*after substitution in* 145). IX 42 aȝen synne D (*after omission from* 41). 109 wenty*n* & M (*after omission of* ȝeden *from* 107). X 57 bounden W (*after substitution in* 56). XI 139 Mistiloker V (*after substitution in* 138).

[3] As in the following instances: Prologue 59 after 60 E; 71 after 72 L; 96 after 97 W. I 100 after 101 L; 166 after 167 H. II 10–11 after 12 H; 63–4 after 65 E; 65–6 after 67 which is then recopied L; 91 after 92 with a spurious line between to smooth the broken sense H. III 198 after 199 R; 234 after 235 W; 260–1 after 265 VH. IV 55 after 56 A. V 74–5 after 76 H; 78–9 after 82 with omission of 80 to smooth J; 78–80 after 84 D. VI 46 after 47 U; 62 after 63 A. VII 137 after 138 A; 212 after 212α H; 233–5 after 236, rounded off with a spurious line N; 266 after 267 W; 276 after 277 A; 278 after 281 H; 279–81 after 282 A. VIII 59 after 60 W; 83 after 84 Ch; 95–6 after 99 H; 108 after 109, but 107, also omitted, is not there copied A; 109 after 110, but 108 lost M; 149 after 150 U. X 90 after 91 M; 108 after 109 W; 112 after 115 H^3. XI 81 after 83 J; 115 after 116 R; 193 after 193α M. The correct order of lines is sometimes indicated.

the text was deliberate. The explanation of this seeming paradox lies in the existence of several, identifiable motives for deliberate substitution. These motives, revealed by comparison of variants where originality seems determinable with some assurance, appear to have overriden the sense of obligation to copy *verbatim*. Thus, in addition to mechanical error, and careless or unconscious substitution, deliberate alteration is a source of textual corruption.

Motives of substitution were inferred from comparison of the variant readings where the distribution of support gave a *prima facie* suggestion of the direction of variation. For instance, it was observed that of two available readings one was sometimes more and one less explicit. Until direction of variation was fixed the situation was ambiguous, and the motive of substitution might have been either to increase or diminish the explicitness of statement. Acceptance of the majority variant as probably original pointed, in many instances, to a wish for more explicit statement as the motive of substitution.

Such identification was strengthened by logical considerations as instances were multiplied. For, when a variant was supported by one manuscript only, there was a probability that it was unoriginal because it was easier to assume one substitution than to assume several independent, coincident substitutions, as would be necessary if the variant supported by one manuscript were treated as original and the alternative majority variant as unoriginal. But such probability would approach certainty only if the number of substitutions required to account for the alternative were very large. As soon, however, as further occurrences of minority variants with a similar effect on the text were noted the situation changed. For, while a single improbability could not be ruled out with any confidence, the likelihood that such a less probable operation, in similar circumstances and with similar consequences, should recur a number of times, diminished with each new instance.

Thus the minority variant which made the text more explicit was at first presumed to be unoriginal because supported by one or only a few manuscripts. Meanwhile it remained possible, if less likely, that the more explicit variant was the original, and that the less explicit variant had been several times independently substituted. But as further cases of more explicit readings attested in a minority of manuscripts were noted, support for presuming originality to lie with the less explicit majority reading increased. Now it was no longer a question whether to accept a somewhat less probable occurrence in a single instance, but whether to accept the great improbability involved in assuming numerous substitutions by a majority of manuscripts, all resulting in a less explicit statement, in other words, the frequent recurrence of the unlikelier possibility with similar effects. Thus, the choice was between deducing a scribal tendency to make the text more explicit, instanced often enough, usually but not always in a minority of manuscripts, and an overwhelming tendency to make the text less explicit (or more difficult, or less emphatic) instanced usually in a majority of manuscripts.

Therefore, although the recognition of a tendency of variation depended in the first place on the possibility of identifying the direction of variation solely from the relative support for variants, as soon as sufficient instances were to hand, presumption of originality began to be strengthened. Thereafter, the identification of patterns of scribal behaviour could be made with increasing confidence, to rest, finally, on the sufficiently numerous cases where indications of originality by the manuscript representation and the character of the variation agreed.

In general scribes set out to produce what seemed to them a more correct, or a more easily intelligible, or a more emphatic, or a more elegant text. Their substitutions seem designed to make the meaning clearer, or to express it more forcibly, or to embellish the form of its expression. While they evidently understood that they should copy word for word, and evidently tried to do so as a rule, they were jealous for the best presentation of the matter, in which, as will be apparent, they took a lively interest. They seem to have been determined that what they wrote should make good sense, if possible that of their original as they understood this, in the best form that they could supply; but if they found the original unintelligible, or considered that it made inferior sense, they were prepared to alter the substance of their copy.[1]

A governing impulse of substitution was apparently desire to make intelligible copy as the scribe understood this. One application of this general principle of textual criticism to the **A** manuscripts can be observed in the frequent attempts of their scribes to make the copy read smoothly when either it was corrupt in their exemplar or they

[1] It will be seen that these observations correspond to the experience of editors of classical texts, as described, for instance, by F. Madan, *Books in Manuscript*, London, 1920, ch. vi, or by Griesbach in his Introduction.

themselves had made a mistake which they noticed before passing on out of the context. The two situations are, strictly speaking, distinct. A scribe who perceived that his original was corrupt might not have access to a second copy; he would have no recourse but smoothing (in effect, conjectural emendation) to make what he wrote intelligible. But a scribe who caught himself out in a mistake might more properly have corrected that mistake by cancellation or erasure than covered it by smoothing. Thus substitution in the latter case is in fact stronger evidence of readiness to take liberties with the text. However, in frequent default of the genealogical information necessary to reconstruct a scribe's more immediate original, the two cases cannot often be confidently distinguished. Therefore they are here illustrated together, by the following representative examples:

Prologue 22 that many H²; þat monie of VHJ; þan þer y sygh L: *padding after loss of* Wonne; *cp.* RE *variant.* 93 W *pads after wrong division.* 98 *and* 99 *run together after an omission from* 98 M. I 17 þe] into *after* hiȝte] lyȝthe *confusion* RE. 93 biddyn ⁊ techyn *making the sense follow on after loss of* 92 M. 176 loue] lif *after* lok] boke *substitution* Ch. II 126 for] forþ *after* caride] cariede *error* T. 162 faste] forth *after* Feteriþ] Fetteþ *error* D. 180 trusse] þorow þe lande *after* yhote] huntyd *substitution* E. III 74 *insertion of* not *after* on trewely] vntrewly *confusion* K. 89 elde] dede *after* ȝouþe] thoght *confusion* E; *so probably* AM. 143 fouliþ treuþe] t. pursueþ *after* fouliþ] foloweþ *corruption in original* W. IV 24 on waryn] on asent weore *smoothing corrupt original* L. 115 þat wiþ hym beriþ *covering his first substitution* H. 154 þe I nile] we sall togeder *after* lete] *leve *substitution* E. V 29 pyne] pyment *after* wyuene] wyne *confusion* J. 69 *insertion of* than *after* Venym or] Venymour *confusion* K. 115 it þouth me mery *etc. after* symme] synne *corruption in their original* AEM. VI 32 kepide] layd on and lad *after* sewide] kept *substitution in* 31 W. 76 not] *om after* oþer þou] wher þorw *confusion* VN. 113 be myn] to ben *to smoothe* hed] had *confusion in his original* D. VII 126 dryue] dyne *after* tem] tyme *confusion* H³. 266 ⁊] I can *smoothing* an hauer] non oþer *confusion in original* Ch. VIII 35 renten] rede *after* Releue] Reule *confusion* U. 55 *addition of* ydel *smoothing* þridde] y rede *confusion* U. 93 lettre] litel *after omission of* nouȝt L. IX 89 wikkidnesse] wikkedly *after* any] ay *confusion* Ch. X 85 ben ywar] drede *after* dobet] dowel *substitution* U. 104 *additions and redivision after* mosseþ] men se(y)(n) *confusion* ChM. 123 riseth *supplying omission in original* Ch. XI 128 Logik] Long *probably smoothing* lerid] servyd *confusion* K. 243 *omission of corrupt reading of original* R; *cp.* U'*s variant* þeue ⁊. 263 writen *smoothing* vnwriten] vndirwriten *corruption in original* Ch.

Scribes wanted the text to run smoothly and were prepared to substitute, add and omit[1] for this purpose, whether they themselves had

[1] As far as reliance can be placed on genetic evidence, they seem to have gone so far as to omit whole lines which were corrupt in their original. The following may possibly be examples of such omission: I 128 E (*cp.* M *variants*). II 188 E (*cp.* E'*s corruption of* 187 *and* M'*s* gommes] gynnys *in* 188). III 259 H (*cp.* H'*s corruption of* 258 *and* V'*s* noiȝide] munged *in* 259). IV 46 A

been at fault and were covering up their mistake, or whether there were errors in the exemplar. In addition they very often found mistakes in their exemplar where, so far as can now be discerned, none actually existed. Through carelessness, ignorance or lack of intelligence, they evidently often mistook the author's meaning. Then, in their understanding of what they had read while they copied, the wording of the exemplar seemed less good than they themselves could make it. On such occasions they sometimes substituted expressions which, according to their misinterpretation, were required by the context.[1]

Readiness to make changes in the copy for the sake of greater intelligibility was not confined to occasions when scribes were recovering from their own mistakes or trying to improve an exemplar which, with or without good reason, seemed unsatisfactory to them. It extended to many cases where, as can still be deduced, the exemplar was good, and where the scribe evidently understood or nearly understood it. Throughout the poem and in most copies variants are found which must be interpreted as recording the writers' desire for greater intelligibility, a wish to make the text easier.[2]

Many variants of the **A** manuscripts suggest that the scribes of this poem tended to remove even slight obscurities by addition or

(*cp.* EM *variants*). 142 U (*cp.* U'*s corruption of* 141). VI 11–13a E (*cp.* A's vernicle] vernache *in* 11). VII 69 M (*cp.* M'*s corruption of* 68 *and additions to* 68α). 74 E (*cp.* E'*s corruption of* 73 *and* M *variant for* 74). VIII 30 UA (*cp.* R *and* MH^{3} *variants for* bynde). 107 AW (*cp.* beloure] beloue M). 165 A (*cp.* renkes] þinkyn M). IX 79 A (*cp.* M *variant*). X 121 W (*cp.* AM *variants*). XI 43 A (*cp.* H^{3} *variants*). 251 A (*cp.* MH^{3} *variants*).

They also, evidently, omitted lines in the course of extensive smoothing. Examples of such omission are: I 109–10 L (a spurious line in their place); III 30–3 A (he has inserted after 29 a form of III 192, and 30–3 no longer follow on); 59 A (its loss part of the sophistication of 57–8); 93 L (two spurious lines in its place); 124 U (to smoothe after his *sompnours*] *schereues* substitution in 123); V 68 A (inconsequent after the rewriting of 67); IX 56, 57 J (58 remodelled from recollection of the **B** version).

[1] The following variants, originating in detectable misunderstandings of the line or passage, illustrate the many substitutions of this kind: Prologue 34 giltles] gylefully K; gylously W; synfullyche H^{2}. 48 wise] vayn H. I 104 such . . . anoþer] and such seuene oþere REM; ⁊ seuen moo oþere J; and siche mo oþere U; ⁊ alle þe foure ordres HVK. 116 þat he] he was HJ. 169 body] soules H. II 20 Out of] Into V; And wyt M. 149 gyede] gilede V; begylith A. III 5 soþly] softly E; slyhly M. 78 wiþoute] oþer UM. 151 Wiþoute . . . fewe] w*ith* . . . manye M. IV 56 be] not by N. 80 bet] Ilete K. 99 meynp*er*no*ur*] maynprysyd ⁊ E. V 63 fore] two H. 118 my ferste lessou*n*] þe þridde H. 185 louryng] lurkynge U; loteri*n*g V; lenyng E; Inowe M; *om* H. VI 35 he] hi*m* RU. 74 wil] foule W. 111 welcome . . . faire] vnwolcome . . . vnfair U. VII 39 but treuþe] þ*at* trewly E. 168 defendite] fett KW. 247 sit] Faste VH. VIII 20 in . . . margyn] ⁊ her meyne H^{3}. 45 lettrid] lewid TChH^{2}. 120 abbesse] au*n*te RA. IX 108 on] w*ith* H^{3}. 114 I bad þouȝt] þouȝt bad V. X 22 sixe] fyue ChMH^{3}. 49 in þe heuid is] is þe heuyd J. 89 neu*er*e] allwey H^{3}. XI 78 in] be TRUDChH^{2}. 227 ȝeris] heres KWMH^{3}. 246 ben lyche] beleuiþ TChH^{2}.

[2] This bears out the experience of earlier editors. Compare Griesbach's rule for the treatment of variants in New Testament manuscripts: *Difficilior et obscurior lectio anteponenda est ei, in qua omnia tam plana sunt et extricata, ut librarius quisque facile intelligere ea potuerit*, and *Durior lectio praeferatur ei, qua posita, oratio suaviter leniterque fluit.* (*Novvm Testamentvm Graece*, p. lxi.)

substitution. The reasons for their evident close interest in the intelligibility of what they wrote were probably mixed (see pp. 136–7 below) and admit of speculation only, but the interest itself is abundantly shown. Although the intrinsic difficulty of some of the readings which they replaced or altered can be inferred, many do not seem hard. The majority of substitutions tend not so much from a hard to an easy reading as, broadly and in various ways, to an easier one.

The tendency of scribes to make their text easier expressed itself in two main ways: addition or substitution designed to produce a more explicit statement, and substitution of equivalent or nearly equivalent expressions for those which, in the original, were themselves difficult, or were put to a difficult use. Evidence of both is common.

Variants designed to express the sense of the text more fully are an important indication of the copyist's state of mind. They may show his concern for the convenience of readers, but may also record an active interest in the subject matter (see p. 136 below), or, by contrast, record a probably unconscious protest against the necessity for unremitting, intelligent attention to meaning. They tend to more complete grammatical representation of meaning, more explicit reference, and more precise designation. The following examples will show the character and frequency of such substitution:

III 2 ⁊] ⁊ wiþ H. 5 self] s. seyd þe kyng H. apose] hir a. HAM. 7 be] b. my UVHLNM. 12 Þat] Þo þ. M; þei þ. H; Heo þ. V; and þo þ. R; And þai þ. W. worsshipeþ] thay w. K. 16 mo*ur*ne] m. þow ChVEAW; m. ȝe L; ne m. þou H. 24 hy] þei her ChHE. 30 callen] don c. JKWN. 32 beknowe] þer Iknowe W. 44 Tolde] Heo t. VHEWN. a(2)] in hond a L. 46 he] to her*e* UVH. 48 þe] owr E. 61 in] i. ȝoure AM. of] in waunting o. N. 63 ȝe] þ*at* ȝ. E; lest ȝ. H; ȝif ȝ. J. 65 mene] þe menes EM; þece menis A; mad m. L; ordeyned meenes H; menene dwelly*n* H^{2}. 73 þat] þ. þ. ChE. 75 bouȝte] shulde bye H. 82 Salamon] Bote S. VH; Forþi S. W. 83 amende] a. wiþ HN; amendyng of E. 90 fro] f. þe HAW; f. his K. 97 Ac] But ȝit N. þe(2)] þ*at* RJLEKM; þis VHN; þy DCh; in þi A. 99 consience] hatte c. TRChH^{2}VHEKW. beȝonde] b. see EM. 100 wilneþ] w. wedd E. 101 þat lady] Mede þo M. forbede] it f. U; f. it DV. 102 honge] lat hangyn JLAWNM. 104 clerkis] of c. JK; bothe c. L. 106 What] to wyte w. HLW; To heryn w. M; ⁊ askyd qwat J. 109 Quaþ] Nay q. VH. 111 She] For s. UH^{2}HM. fikel] and f. ChL. 114 techiþ] heo t. VHJENM *and the late corrector of* H^{2}. 116 fadir] F. Adam V. 121 to alle] a. other E. 125 land] l. be her*e* M. 127 þe] to þ. L. 131 To be] þeiȝ heo b. HJ. 133 hire] she h. *corrector of* H^{2}. 137 þe] her*e* RDJLEKN; hem here W; alle þ. M. 146 And] Sche UVWN. 147 forþ] forth for LK. 148 makiþ] m. agayn right W. 150 Lawe] Hir l. EM; The l. WN. so] now s. W. lordlich] l. proud *corrector of* H.

This selection will have illustrated the type of variation designed to make the meaning more explicit, and its frequency. Substitution to make the meaning easier in other ways usually takes more substantial forms, and occurs somewhat less often; nevertheless it is also very frequent.

The confident identification of expressions found difficult by scribes is made possible by a substantial body of variants of a particular type. These are readings which preserve something of the shape of the supplanted, original words or phrases, but little or nothing of their meaning or relation to the context. The majority (a few may be visual errors) probably result from complete inability of scribes to interpret, in the given context, the original expressions for which they are substitutions. It appears from these variants that scribes, confronted with a word of which they could make nothing, tended to do one of several things with similar effects. They might consciously write in its place a word of similar shape; they might mistakenly identify it with a word of similar shape but distinct, sometimes quite inappropriate meaning with which they were acquainted, and write that; they might set down in distraction a meaningless group of letters of shape similar to the supplanted word. It is not always possible to say which of the first two processes generated a particular variant, or the exact nature of the third process. But it seems as if scribes were, on occasion, reluctant to copy faithfully, letter by letter, something that they could not understand. The sources of difficulty could be words in themselves hard, like those belonging to the alliterative vocabulary, regionally restricted words, obsolescent words, or new words, but they could also be expressions not intrinsically difficult, used with a difficult meaning in the context, or key words in a passage difficult and liable to misunderstanding as a whole.

Such variants are found in all the manuscripts. Their frequency suggests how quickly scribes could find the text difficult, and the strength of the impulse to correct, which persisted even when the resources for correction were lacking. These variants are of importance in another connexion (pp. 162 ff. below). In the present exposition, by indicating typical sources of difficulty, they form the basis for the proposition that scribes tended to make their text easier by substantive alterations. I assume that this type of variation is not confined to *Piers Plowman* manuscripts, but I know of no technical term for it. For convenience I venture to call such substitutions homœographs. The following are examples:

Prologue 10 swiȝede] sweiued E; sweuedy*n* J; sweuenede RU; semede M; schewed D. 14 triȝely] trewlich DChJLM. 29 cairen] caryen RUDChVHKW; carry E; scayr*e* J. 41 bratful] bredful RUD; *with* bred full E. 86 poundide] pond*er*ys E; poynteþ T; pointen Ch. I 122 troniþ] trowen RH²; turnyt M. 128 compsiþ] comeþ R; coueitid M. 160 fait] fewte EAM; Fey V; faitour Ch. 171 haspide] happyd JLEA. 179 graiþ] gret K; grettest EA. II 11 frettid] freten K; fetred L; fetterd E; federid A. 63 Ile] ilde M; ill K. 66 *signiur*e] segoury E; synge J; synnes M; seruyse VH. 83 molere] medler*e* H²H. 147 tom] tunge UChEAM. III 13 somme] sone TChH²EW; soone VH; to sompne R; to sowpen U. 19 m*er*ciede] myrthed JA. 39 sem] su*m*me VH. 94 melis] mengyd J; myd M; mekely D. 95 wy] ywys TChH². IV 13 frek] feytȝ R. 19 wytful] riȝtful TRUChH²; full wyght E; swiþe feole VH. 24 on waryn] on a wayn VH. 134 renkis] reules D. 147 ledis] landes E; londis AM. V 17 segges] sent god TChH²; seyþ god RU; sayd god D; I say EA. 39 stewid] storyd E; stylet H²; stor M. 49 affaiten] afeyntyn AM; afaute*n* R; frete E. 59 cope] counte A; compte R. 214 þe veil] þ*er* while TH²; þ*a*t wille E; þer wol Ch; wile R; wol U. VI 2 baches] bankes EA. 8 ampollis] saumples L; ensaumples E. 67 berwe] bo*ur*ne T; borne Ch; burne H²; brok VMH³; bak RU; brige E. 98 bienfait] buffet R; lyffe fett E. 114 ingang] in ȝong L. VII 7 scleire] clere E; chare Ch; chayere K; share W. 128 cowes] Crowen VH; crowys JLKNM. 177 botind] aboute RUEH³. 201 abaue] bayte R; batten Ch; Ba*m*me V. 223 nam] name R; man AH³; ilman W. VIII 41 graiþ] grete RUH; grace of V. 57 þrowe] sowe*n* H³; þriuen V; p*ro*ued R. 108 payn eet] peyne haþ R; peyned TVK; peyne H; peynes H²; pyned A; fayn D. 147 faraos] fargos H². 159 lef] lif TChH². IX 30 rauȝte] ariȝt TDH²; riȝt Ch. 60 driȝt] wyth A; I ȝit J. 79 þe bagges & þe bigerdlis] To bidderis & beggeris M. bigerdlis] begg*er* doles D. 81 mammones] mani mannis M. X 47 allie] halle TChH². 56 brem*er*e] brent U. 60 helde] holden DH²JAH³. 89 wy] why TRUChH²K; weye J. 212 wolues] walwes D. XI 18 cardit] carket V; caried W; carpyd H³. 56 kete] kedde RUD; kid TChH²; cowrte JA. 70 motifs] motyngys J; motetys H³; motes U; notes R; maisties A. 156 gynful] gynn*er* J; gryfful U; greful R; synful ChAW. 177 collide] callide TUAKMH³.

Such expressions, difficult in themselves or in their use, were the occasion of persistent substitution throughout the poem in all the manuscripts. Not all substitutions for difficult readings, however, resulted in homœographs. There are many cases where scribes were evidently not altogether perplexed by their original, but nevertheless made substitutions; comparison of the original and substituted readings suggests that even relative difficulty was enough to cause variation. The effect on the text is, in general, to remove from it: terms of the esoteric vocabulary of alliterative poetry; words of regionally restricted use which may not necessarily belong to this vocabulary; words falling into disuse; new words, presumably not yet in general currency; punning words; words used allegorically or otherwise figuratively; ambiguous expressions; or expressions otherwise difficult in the context. The change is in the direction of flat statement, simplifying not only language but also connotation, and sometimes losing or altering denotation. It favours the obvious and the colourless, and rejects language pregnant, or mannered, or fanciful.[1] The results of this tendency are a prosy utterance and loss of force in the communication of meaning, weakening of poetic tension, dilution of the archaic flavour of the style, and general loss of efficiency. It should be remarked that many of the variants are adequate readings in the sense that they would pass muster if not exposed to comparison. Some are near or exact glosses of the supplanted readings. The following are examples of such substitutions, made when the scribes had a more or less exact notion of the meaning of the original:

Prologue 10 swiȝede] sownede VH. 26 streite] harde VE. 32 þriuen] chewen L. 41 ycrammid] filled Ch. 60 meten] macchyn M. I 33 ȝerne] desyre RM. 71 halside] assched R; askyd M; axed J. 138 ȝedde] syng EM. 148 þirlide] þerssed W. 176 lok] lesson L. II 42 teldit] tyȝth RU. 56 gomes] gromes DH^{2}JWN. 63 þe faste] þe false DVH. 83 molere] maydyn M. 147 tom] tyme RLN *and corrector of* H. III 31 lede] ladde D. 91 ofsente] sent for EK; sent aftur HJWM. 95 wy] wo*m*man LN. 132 cotiþ] cloþiþ TRUChH^{2}M. 191 kiþ] cu*n*trey H. IV 102 hucche] chiste M. 128 confessour] Clerk V; clerkis H. 147 ledis] lordes WN. 148 rauȝte] reste LEW; rest hym H. V 5 hente] hadde TRDH^2. 8 babelide] badde M. 39 stewid] stayed K. 48 serke] shert HLM; smok VK. 167 hansele] drynke RUH. VI 3 lede] ladde D. 21 wy] wyte AH^3. 49 wyte] knowe V. 99 as dew] at dore K. 119 pukide] pullid H^2; plocked LA. VII 112 doel] defaute VHL. 116 ygracid] þankyd JVHLW. 128 Cacche] kepyn J. 132 gare] graunte JL. 176 ditte] dryue RUChE. VIII 30 bynde] Beete VKNH^3. 88 pur] pley*n* R. 90 kenne] knowen V. 115 fynt] feedeþ V. 155 digneliche] derly A. IX 88 pungen] pycche R; put DM. X 37 lynage] kynne J. 114 stable] strong J. 168 Busken] Bringen VW. 191 pliȝt] put D. 193 cheste] chiding TChH^{2}H^3. XI 94 mele] speke AMH^3. 177 collide] Clupte V. 213 Pop*er*iþ] Prykyth J. 311 iottis] peple J. 312 P*er*cen] Pasen U.

The process of debasing the expression and meaning illustrated in these substitutions might, perhaps, be explained as no more than an easy, natural, and thoughtless preference for the obvious sense or the more familiar or habitual mode of expression. Examination of the variants for stave words which destroy alliteration, however, argues

[1] The effect of some substitutions to increase emphasis of statement is a separate matter. See pp. 138–9 below.

that substitutions of easier for more difficult expressions were predominantly deliberate. Such substitutions in a metrical position are very numerous. The disturbance of the metre indicates their importance to the scribe, who would presumably have substituted an expression that preserved the metre, had he had one at his disposal or given thought to the prosody in that instant. This follows from the general tendency of scribes to increase the alliteration of the line (pp. 141 ff. below). Thus the variants which destroy alliteration should demonstrate the strength of the tendency of scribes to make their text easier and reduce its language to an average mode of communication even where they had some idea of its meaning. The following are examples:

Prologue 14 triȝely] wonderliche VH. 28 holden hem] lyuen RE; dwelle W. 30 likam] body M. 41 bratful] full JW; fully K; faste VH. 45 sewiþ] folwyth M. 87 vnlose] open HE; opnyd RU. 89 mom] word M. 102 dede] werk RU. I 20 comaundite] hete W. 34 gut] bodi VH. 42 molde] werld JEM. 72 wisside] tawght H; techeþ V. 128 cors] body HM. 135 wytnessiþ] techeþ us VH. 160 fait] werk UH. 179 graiþ] redyeste RH. 183 lenge] duelle UW. II 3 barn] chyld M. 16 noiȝede] grevyd EAM. 31 lette] dwelle D. 56 gredde] criddyn J; crye EM. 70 synken] dwelle W. 123 segges] men V; pepul *corrector of* H. 147 tom] while V. 153 carpide] told A. 159 lokis] wele DA; bit M. III 24 lauȝte] toke ChVA. 29 lelly] truly HM. 47 in werching] at hom M. 62 grede] crien JEM. 79 regrat*ou*ris] sellerys M. 142 is wel] dwellys E. 157 menide] pleyned RUHEWM. 171 menske] au*au*nce TDChH². 214 wiȝt] man N. 247 choppe] dryue H. 258 *culorum*] ende D. IV 2 sauȝte] acorde AW. 13 þe frek] co*n*sciens JM. 23 rapiþ] hastid H. 33 wordiden] speken HAW. 64 panne] hode H. 108 drawe] bring Ch. 133 declynede] distinkte V. 135 mothalle] court H. 142 warpen] seie H. wiþsigge] aȝenseie H. 145 reherside] sayd WN. 148 rauȝte] henge M; deiȝede TDChH². V 3 wynkyng] slep E. 4 sadd*ere*] hardere A; hard Ch. 13 pur synne] S. alonly E. 15 poynt] þing RUA. 39 stede] lond M. stewid bet*ere*] amendid H. 49 affaiten] endaunten Ch; dawntyn J. 59 cope] gylt JL; gultus VH; synnes Ch; wilis M. 82 hailside] Grette M. 88 criȝe] p*ray* U; bidde H. 110 lollide] honged W. 123 Þanne drouȝ I me] I was M. 125 rendrit] lerned ChVHH³. 126 Brochide] Prycked KW. 128 tollide] drow A. 170 hitte] caste ChHAMH³; threwe J. 184 grete] presente M. 206 shrapide] robbed H. 208 liþ*er*] wikkede VH. 210 defie] rist E. 223 dere] parysch RU. 249 lepe] go H. VI 38 presteste] rediest H. 39 hyne] man WHA. 45 fonge] take HMH³. 53 bowiþ] wende A. 82 gateward] porter TDChH². 89 weue] put E. 100 ycliket] Ihoked M. 114 ingang] in AWM. VII 35 conseyuede] answeryd J; rehersede MH³. 37 foreward] counand E. 41 Nyme] Takeþ VHM. 83 caroyn] body E. 111 glade] helpe A. 132 gare] make KMH³. 138 bu*mm*iþ] etyth H³. 157 houpide] clepid M; wyschid A; wepyd H³. 165 heȝede] busked L; wente A. 183 cacche] chase TRUDCh. 187 erde] lond AH³. 201 bollnyng] swellyng RUE. 275 dere] wel W. 297 ywrouȝt] bycome HA. VIII 30 bynde] amendyn M. 44 couden] ȝeue TDChH²W. 47 penc*iou*n] mede W. 57 þrowe] yȝeu*en* H. 68 suggestiou*n*] cause M; destenye U. shapiþ hem to] þei fore TChH²HW. 80 loþe] curse UJ. 110 lelly] treuly MH³; wel U. 117 garn*er*] berne U; fode J. 127 waitide] lokede VW. IX 24 forebisene] ensau*m*ple VM. 28 stif] fast AM. 32 lacchesse] sleuþe V. X 17 inwit] þouȝt TChH². 52 eggiþ] tisit M. 67 witen] kepyn JMH³. 73 cheuisshen] kepyn J; clense AM. 146 constella-c*iou*n] tyme MH³. 171 banne] curse V. 186 copil] weddyng A. 209 gatis] wise Ch KW. XI 6 frentyk] wilde M. 30 dauncelid] honourid A. 44 gorge] þrote TDChH². 47 noye] disease M; anguyssh TRDChH². 56 kete] grete MH³. 71 musen] leeuen VW. 80 whyes] p*ri*uytes M. 87 cacche] wete ChA. 138 muse] studie V. 188 bakken] coue*r*yn J; happi*n* M. 239 an heiȝ] a man þat is AWH³; he þat is M.

To sum up: while scribes evidently had a sense of obligation to reproduce their exemplar *verbatim*, they departed from this as readily when there was need to cover up their own mistakes as when their original was corrupt. If they mistook the meaning of this exemplar they did not refrain from substitution to bring what they wrote into line with their misconception. In general they were anxious to make the text more easily intelligible. To this end they very often made its utterance more explicit, changing its wording so that relationships of meaning were more fully expressed. They were quick to find the poem difficult; sometimes they were unable to do more than make an approximate visual substitution for the expression which baffled them. They made many other substitutions which glossed difficult expressions more or less precisely. The deliberate character of such substitutions is shown by their readiness to sacrifice the metre of a line in the course of making its meaning easier.

It does not seem probable that these substitutions originated simply or wholly in concern on behalf of possible readers. Another factor to account for them was almost certainly a lively, but not necessarily intelligent participation by many scribes in the poem that they were copying. *Piers Plowman* was a living text; its content was a matter of immediacy to a man reading, or reading and copying it during the fourteenth or fifteenth century. He would be likely to associate himself with its sentiments and to identify himself to some extent with its author. Thus the text of a contemporary document, transmitted by copyists to whom it was of direct, personal moment, could not fail to be variously affected by the reactions of that medium. Related in the first instance to the undisputed difficulty of the poem, this consideration suggests that the many substitutions designed to produce an easier text record not anxiety that others should find it easy, but a primarily selfish interest, resulting in an actual working out of the meaning in the mind of the scribe. In these substitutions his interest in what he was copying took the form of a desire to define and express, as clearly as his resources allowed, the sense of his text.

Certain other variations bear this interpretation out. Two types of these are especially interesting evidence of the participation of scribes in the meaning of the poem. Neither is very frequent or systematic, but both are found often enough to establish them as characteristic. One occurs where the text reads a proper name, or an expression instancing a type, whether of a person or an abuse under criticism;[1] then another name or type or instance is sometimes substituted or added. The scribe thus seems to be relating the matter under discussion to his own immediate experience, once even to the point of replacing the name of Margaret with Maud. Such substitution is not made out of concern for a reader, but occurs because the scribe, whether knowingly or not, is re-enacting the composition of the poem in his own person. It is, as will be seen, more frequent where the content of the poem refers clearly to contemporary life. The following examples illustrate it:

Prologue 54 E'*s additional lines*; *see above*, p. 49. 98 manye] & kokys R. 100 tokk*eris*] tau*er*nere*s* RCh; tann*er*is T; tynkelers E; tornors L; thackers J; Souters D. tolleris] ty*n*kere*s* R; Tapsters Ch. II 74 Bette] Bernard E. 75 H^2 *and* H'*s additional lines*; *see above*, p. 45. 76 & . . . o*þere*] of malwiche strete U. *Also* E'*s additional lines*; *see above*, p. 49. 137 denis] officyales H. southdenis] officyall*es* K. III 41 clerkis . . . kniȝtes] courteors & þe comyns H. 122 monkis] Preostes V. IV 37 marg*er*ete] molde H. V 91 heyne] herry Ch; hoge J; hyk K. 119 wynchestre] wynchelsey Ch; ware E; sleytforth H^3. wy] wellis H; woborne L. 148 Betou*n*] bele H. 153 he] herry AH^3; heruy M. 158 Cisse] Sy*m*me H; kytte L. 159 Watte] bratram E. 160 tynkere] Trumpour M. 162 clerk . . . chirche] c. . . . werkis H. 164 ribibo*ur*] redylle maker E. 165 rose] kitte W; rafe K. disshere] kempstere W. VI 9 synay] asyce AM; sissel E. 16 armonye] Ynde V. alisaundre] Assye V. 117 waffrer] brewst*er* J. VII 108 hey . . . lolly] dusada*m*meme RUE. VIII 61 legistris] Registres M. XI 184 sout*er*is] towkkars KW; toucheris AMH^3. 298 p*r*inces] kynge*s* K. 311 Sout*er*is] Saweris $AWMH^3$.

The second type indicates another kind of association with the substance of what is copied. Scribes, it suggests, regarded themselves as responsible in various senses for what they wrote, and accordingly departed from their copy to censor or to bowdlerize it.[2] They appear

[1] Kantorowicz (*Einführung*, p. 30) remarks on a similar type of variation in late medieval legal manuscripts; Pasquali (*Storia*, pp. 18–19) observes that proper names are certain to be corrupted. But their cases are not fully analogous to the present one.

[2] Compare Pasquali, *Storia*, p. 119.

to have been exercising political caution by removing or rendering innocuous references to the king, or removing expressions with a flavour of treason; or religious discretion by suppressing criticism of the pope, or a suggestion that the monastic orders might be expropriated; or they modified expressions of violence; or they omitted or toned down oaths, such as the unlucky one 'By the peril of my soul'; they omitted gross expressions, or the mention of a sacred thing in a ribald context. Again such treatment of the text is not systematic, and lets plenty of inflammatory matter, as well as many oaths and gross expressions stand, but it seems clearly to originate in the scribe's consideration of himself as well as his reader. The following examples illustrate substitution of this kind:

I 92 *line om* M. II 25 liȝen] leuen VHL; ledeþ hem W. III 86 lordis] me*n* RUVH WM. 122 monkis . . . mynstrelis] mynstrelis . . . messang*er*is TUChH²; menstralis . . . meselys R. 145 Be I*esu*] Heo Buggeþ VH; *om* W. 174 kilde . . . king] gylede . . . k. M; Miskaried . . . k. Ch; begylyd . . . man E; agult hym H. 184 lif] worschepe M. 202 pope] peple M. 246 wo*m*men to kille] þe cu*n*tre to quelle H. 256 þe kyng] þ*at* man E. IV 51 *line om* H. 70 swor] seith M. crist] hymselfe A. 74 God wot] Nay sire W. 117 be . . . rode] *om* L. 144 be crist to] anon t. WN; wel t. M; ꝧ kneow soth L. 148 to . . . king] þan W. 149 rend . . . ribbes] þou sall noght wele like E. V 38–9 *ll. om* LA (*another substituted* L). 189 paternost*er*] litel M; *om* W. 250 *line om* M. leiȝe] lyve E. VI 44 Nay be þe p*er*il of my soule quaþ piers] Piers sone seyde nay M. 58 god] *om* H³. 87 *line om* A. 110 so me god helpe] sothely to telle K. 117 Wyte god] Iwis VA. VII 50 be seint Iame] þe same N. 72 suffre . . . wille] Sufferance to suffurre in tyme E. 142 pisse] *om* J. 156 þe peril of my soule] goddis pyte N. 269 be crist] *om* A. VIII 157 pope] peple M. IX 74 *line om* U. X 180 leiȝen] spowsyd J. XI 40 how two slowe þe þridde] a tale or twoo K. 58 Freris . . . faitours] *erased* H³. 81 ars] taile K. 203 *line om* W. shryue] serue A. 204 pope] clerk M; busshop *corrector of* H³. *To these examples should perhaps be added omissions of lines where the term 'simony' occurs, at* II 35 (U); 78 (K); 136 (V).

But the most striking of the variations originating from the scribe's association of himself with what he copied are those designed to increase the emphasis of statements. These are not confined to passages where zeal for religious reform might have given rise to them. Nor are they likely to have resulted simply from a naïve preference for vehement statement.[1] Such variation took place because scribes were enthusiastic for the poem, and consciously or unconsciously, if sometimes without intelligence or taste, strained to participate in the experience that it

[1] As Griesbach seems to imply: *Erudituli enim librarii, ut commentatores, emphases amabant ac captabant* (*Novvm Testamentum Graece*, p. lxii).

recorded, as well as to contribute to its purpose. This variation is persistent throughout the poem, but most frequent where the content is easy, and the copyist was able to enter into it most fully. Where the text is difficult, or the matter less lively, variation increasing emphasis is not so marked, but continues to occur. The following selection of examples will illustrate it:

I 1 mounteyne] fayre m. R. 4 me] m. ful W. 12 tour] ryche t. M. 57 dale] deope d. V. 63 ille] helle R. 70 writ] w. so wysely E. 90 knowe] k. wel W. 94 faste] ful f. E. 96 kniȝtes] mony k. L. 98 ap*er*tly] prop*ur*lich L. 105 miȝt] maystrie & m. V; honour*e* & m. H. 106 his] al h. UJEW. 110 lord] l. der*e* J. 121 heuene] h. blysse E. 131 loue] l. lelly WN. 133 bet*er*e] best E. 136 oure] euer o. Ch. 138 bidde þe] þ. faste b. D. 163 lewid as] lewedore þen L. 166 Vnkynde] Vnkyndar nane E. 167 here] al þair E. 169 kepe ȝow] arn contynent & L. III 13 ioye] gret i. W. 27 þi(1)] alway þ. WN. 28 hem] þaim all E. 29 lordis] gret l. WN. 38 fiftene] fo*ur* score U. 95 ofte] wel o. RUDA; full o. E; right o. K; many tyme and o. W. 102 ellys] sone VEAM; in haste KWN; hye L. 133 self] dere M. 145 Iuelx] riche I. W. 146 treuþe] t. ofte U; hem ofte RJ; hem euere WN. 148 as] rith a. W. 164 gret] most HL. may] m. ofte L. 168 enleuene] mony feole L. 177 ofte] ofter E; ful o. W. 185 m*er*þe] mychel m. JL; m. ful muche V. 192 Þe] Ya þ. EM. 203 men] gretly m. H. 213 nede] alweys n. L. 220 wer-chen] ay w. WN. 230 it] i. full EA; hit wel LKN; ful RU; wel JM. 246 wo*m*men] alle w. L. 252 here] feir V. 258 not] neu*er* A. 267 loue] lele l. W. V 4 more] muche m. E. 14 southwestryne] grete s. M. on . . . eue] þat so loude blewe W. 20 dedly synne] deth U. 30 to] mychel t. J. 44 wiþ] riht at bothe J. 47 made] m. with his myght L. 55 hym] his pore soule V. 64 þe] the hote L. 72 er I dyne] alway W. 75 wel ofte] feole sithes L. 80 tunge] wikkyd t. A. 89 bolle] bolles LN. 94 weile] werys E. 97 angriþ] gretly a. E. 103 goode] þe best HEAM. 104 Sorewe] Oft s. W. 108 & . . . lokide] he l. as a hotte of hell E. 111 twelue] twenty L. 114 here] h. befor*e* crist and his swete moder R; h. byfore crist & his clene modir U. 121 gon] g. aye E. 128 þrittene] xv M. 138 A] Ay a W. 141 elleuene] wel e. L; long e. A; þis xv M; al þis xxx[ti] H. wynt*er*] w. lang E. 151 synne no] neu*er* s. E. 154 Ȝa] ȝhe god wot H. 172 Þ*er*e] Thus sone W. 180 cloke] c. in rape A. 182 ys*er*uid] ful serued W; wel Iseruet V; wel apaied H. 184 grete] sone g. A. 185 lauȝing] myche l. H. 187 euesong] mydnyȝt H. 188 a galoun] to galons L. 200 brouȝte] þrow W. 202 he . . . sonneday] al a somer he slepe N. 211 aunte] adu*er*sarij E. 225 non ale] no riot H. 247 to] fast t. E; fast on N. eftsones] ofte sythis A. 248 he shulde] apertly s. h. J. newe] al n. H; efte sonys A. 251 men] m. and mo RU. XI 12 p*re*cious] p*re*ciousest J. 52 Mendynaunȝ] Manye m. RUKW. 68 whiche] wykkyd J. 86 so] s. euere W; sum eu*er* A. 111 Gladd*er*e] ȝa g. M. 137 ten] ofter*e* þan x M. 141 þat] þe more þ. W. 186 any] alle H^3. 191 oþ*er*e] alle o. H^2. 215 fet] blode his f. W. 290 Cristene] Mychel c. J. 291 sou*er*eynes] more sou*er*eyn D.

The general and persistent interest of scribes of the **A** version in what they were copying apparently extended beyond the content of this poem to its form. Precisely how much substitution was prompted by unmixed desire to embellish the form cannot be determined. A number of variants have such a look; especially, some of the many changes in word order or phrasing which do not alter the sense may originate in this desire. But simply the absence of another motive for substitution is not enough to put a variant into this class. A case like V 10 where the reason for substitution, scribal objection to two lines ending with the same word, can be identified as stylistic, is the exception.[1] Substitution from a stylistic motive may have played a larger part in forming the character of H, W and L than of the other manuscripts. It may account for a number of cases in all manuscripts when lines have been reshaped for no evident reason; if so, the variant forms of the lines in question record scribal confidence that the gist of the copy could be expressed in more satisfying form.[2] The possibility of a general impulse to make substitutions on stylistic grounds must be noted because there is substantial evidence of a more particular kind that scribes were concerned to improve the expression of the poem. This relates to their treatment of its metre.

As might be expected scribes attempted to smoothe or restore the metre of lines received in corrupt form, or lines which they had themselves, by substitution, rendered unmetrical.[3] Their attentions of this kind included lines which now seem to have been left unmetrical by the poet, or else were unmetrical in the archetypal ancestor of the **A** manuscripts, as well as lines where the metre might be called difficult, which they probably took to be unmetrical.[4] These processes are

[1] Other possible examples are: V 9 tolde] shewid H. 26 pernel] dame p. N. 114 I . . . caitif] I am caytif coueitous W. VII 93 treuþe] sent t. A. 172 flappide] flyp flapt W. 174 peris] piers wif W. hadde] h. gert E; let H. 215 ȝe . . . hungir] Therof be þou wel bold W. 238 my dere] anone L. 283 neiȝide ner heruest] to h. hiȝede V. VIII 126 perkyn] sire p. W. IX 53 dowel] sere d. M. 112 of a softe] s. of his WM. softe] sad RU. X 8 *Princeps*] sire *p*. H². XI 94 becom so confus] lost so his cowntenaunce J. 98 studie] dame s. K. 211 religioun] sire R. M. 213 toune(1)] parkes Ch.

[2] Possible instances are: Prologue 32 (J); I 103 (L); 172 (H, W); II 36 (L); 56 (M); 115 (L); III 64 (H); V 167 (W); VII 107 (W); 120 (A).

[3] As for example, in the following: Prologue 22 wastours] w. in þe worlde H². II 96 of gode] ful gent V. V 205 þanne . . . ⁊] blyue for his wykked W; þat he wolde ay beon so bold to L. VII 116 laboure] harowȝe Ch. XI 173 ground] moolde M.

[4] For example: Prologue 106 to hem] tolled h. and RU; titly Ch (*substituting a stronger stave for one consisting of a preposition*). I 8 kepe] willyn KW (*see p. 154 below, for a possible scansion*). 23 Þat on] þe furste L. vesture] v. verylyche RUE; v. of cloþe W; cloþing DL. chele] cold DLW (*see critical note, p. 434 below*). II 16 noiȝede] marred V (*substituting a stronger stave for* me). 65 lust] deedly synne H ('*improving' a two-stave line*). II 87 mede] hure VHM (*the line unmetrical in the archetype*). III 6 world] molde RUHEKW (*see critical note p. 437 below*). 21 pecis . . . siluer] wel clanliche ywroghte L (*an unmetrical line: discussed on p. 158 below*). 62 giue] *ȝiue] dele *etc*. (*the metre lost through dialect variation*). 75 be . . . certayn] so richeliche arayed M (*objection to* be *as a stave*). 216 worþi] wel w. WN. þe] Muche VH. haue] welde L (*a two-stave line in the archetype*). IV 91 god] crist U (*the archetype either unmetrical or* aa bb

extensions of the desire to produce smooth copy already illustrated (above, p. 136). The copyist's impulse to correct his own mistakes or those he found in his exemplar extended beyond its sense to its form.

Scribal interest in the form of expression did not stop with correction. A substantial number of additions and substitutions affecting the metrical character of the lines suggest that scribes took an active interest in the versification of the poem.

Most often these variants increase the number of staves in the line. Sometimes, however, they introduce secondary alliteration, or replace the classical form of two staves in the first and one in the second half-line with an *aa bb* alliteration; or with cross-alliteration, which was perhaps regarded as especially elegant. A few actually make the alliteration more exact, in lines where the poet was, seemingly, content to make a simple consonant sound alliterate with the first element in a consonant group. A substantial number of such variants seem to have been introduced solely for adornment; but others also make the meaning clearer or more emphatic, especially the latter. The motives are often hard to disentangle, but one of them was clearly to embellish the metrical form of the text by increasing alliteration.

This is most strikingly illustrated in the variants of L, as the following examples will indicate:

Prologue 3 vnholy] vnworthy. 4 here] wayte. 8 side] brymme. 14 Imakid] ytymbred. 18 of(2) . . . riche] mest*er* men makid vppon molde. 19 askiþ] wilnyth. 21 harde] sore. 27 heueneriche blisse] heouene to huyre. 28 cellis] houses. 30 plese] like. 33 conne] meleden. 34 I trowe] god graunte. 36 ⁊ . . . make] for . . . feynen. 37 list] wolde. 45 Slep] Sory s. 47 seintes] rerykes. 50 staues] s. hyeden. 56 wombe] paunche. 57 good] leof. 58 as . . . wolde] aȝeyn kynde. 59 cloþe . . . lyking] wiþ couetise heom cloþen. 69 speche] leodene. 73 helpe] gladen. 106 tolde] t. treoweliche. I 53 kepe] wayte. 54 nede] tyme. 56 made] formed. 66 siþen] hasted him. 80 wrouȝte] made.

type). 151 quaþ] seiþ N (*a two-stave line*). V 55 mysdede . . . hym] sowle . . . m. A. betwyn . . . hym] in mendyng of his soule N (*the line has an advanced cæsura*). 107 com] c. sone A; c. sire W (*interposing an unstressed syllable between staves*). 221 tofore] to veri RU (*substituting a stronger stave*). 232 treuþe] sir t. K; seynt t. VHLE *and correctors of* H^2 *and* N (*a two-stave line*). 254 seke] gon . . . to s. L; gon to AEKMH^3 (*a two-stave line*). VI 22 me god helpe] G. glade me V (*a two-stave line*). 23 pik] sclaveyn W (*a two-stave line*). 45 for . . . shryne] not for fyften shillyng W (*substituting a stronger stave*). 71 loke . . . nouȝt] in na maner ellys EMH^3 (*see critical note p. 445 below*). 78 as . . . wombe] of hert ChH^2; also E; echon oþer W (*shortening an unusually long line*). VII 6 til] And wissen ou þe rihte weye til V; And wysse ȝow riȝt wel til N; ⁊ teche ȝow þe riȝte wey til H (*substituting a stronger stave*). 15 wile] comandeth MH^3 (*the line has an advanced cæsura*). 59 any . . . swynke] he(we) with his hachete MH^3 (*substituting a stronger stave*). 61 wiþ . . . corn] þer mydde mauggre M; þ*erwith* mawgry H^3 (*the line unmetrical in the archetype*). 139 gan] wald E (*a two-stave line*). X 130 wiþ] wel M (*substituting a stronger stave*). 187 ȝiuen] weddyn M (*unmetrical in archetype?*). XI 34 value] ȝift J (*the scansion difficult*). 61 ⁊ . . . riche] Brothel an oþer V (*substituting a stronger stave*). 252 harme . . . slen] hirtyn . . . h. J (*a two-stave line*).

133 can . . . betere] treuly hit techeth. 154 chirche wepiþ] cradel crieth. 160 nouȝt] a fache. 164 aweye] a. charred. 165 hardere] h. holders. II 17 lakkide] l. lodlich. 35 assent] sone sent. 55 ymakid] yformed. 70 pyne] sorwe. 98 be(2) . . . aftir] wayfe away wronge. 100 Ȝif] Lokith ȝ. 108 ynowe] ful feole. 111 ynowe] feole. 113 gret . . . þonking] graunt mercy þey gradden. 116 *certis*] c. in same. 124 alle] vche beorne. 126 caride] karkeden. 127 fette] f. forth. 145 togidere] on foles yfere. 155 oþer(2)] þat flaterer or. 168 I hote] or for poundes. 170 wente] w. on his way. 177 Liȝtliche liȝere] L. launced lightly. 190 wiþheld] wolde haue withholden. half . . . dayes] to þe worldis eynde.

This tendency to embellish the form by increasing alliteration, exhibited so strikingly by L, appears, to a lesser extent but markedly, in the other manuscripts. There seems no doubt that such substitutions, unmistakably directed to altering the form of presentation, seemed improvements to those who made them. But as presumed improvements of form rather than content (especially when they merely increased alliteration) they cannot have been made for the benefit of readers, and seem primarily to have been for the satisfaction of those who introduced them. They are then important as further evidence of the active interest taken by scribes in their copy, and the liveliness of their participation in it. The following examples illustrate such substitutions:

Prologue 14 Imakid] atired U; entyred E; ontyrid R. 21 harde] sore H²HKW. 37 list] wolde H. 55 Freris] f. forsothe J. 62 Manye] Fele RE. 70 knelynge] k. vppon kneys E. I 4 callide] clepte VHK. 31 wyn] drynke M. 36 techiþ] ledith HJ. 39 soule] sely s. R; sory s. E. 45 peny . . . temple] prece of a p. M. 47 lettre] scriptur E. 110 of siȝt] to loke on TChH². II 8 war] worthily w. A. 26 telle] treuly t. W. 58 mede] þat Mayden m. VH. 97 kysse] komlyche . . . k. J. 116 seide *certis*] sikerly . . . s. Certes W. 124 beggeris] bath b. E. 127 fette] f. fourty H². 152 tolde] callyd E. 161 I hote] tried E. 165 warne] seye H. III 6 man] wiȝt N. 15 Counfortide] Curteisly c. U. clergies leue] clergey clene E. 60 wrytyng] lernyngus H. 69 harm] wrong E; wo M. 71 peple] pore p. H. 77 selleris] s. of sythes E. 108 make] fere W. 111 feiþ . . . speche] fleische . . . feiþ H. 131 risshe] crosse H. 135 sel] s. sire M. IV 27 rede] reule hem & r. H. 55 tale] wordes E. 143 stoden] s. stille WN. 144 sawis] Connynge VH. 152 Erlis] kniȝtis H. 153 redily] Ryht r. J. V 26 pernel] p. þe prowde JW. 56 þeraftir] sykerly þ. J. 71 auȝte] miȝte TRUDChH²J. 79 hym] man J; men EAM. 86 techiþ] prechiþ H. 89 bolle] blake b. H². 94 tyme] while A. 105 enuye] þat sherew NM. 129 made] worched K; wroght W. 154 gossib] good g. W. 177 consience] clene c. U. 184 grete] gaynly g. W. ale] good a. A. 187 seten so] sa still sammen þai s. E. 216 war] wel w. N. 218 beet] b. bittyrly W. 220 faste] sore V. 233 lokide] reufulli . . . l. AMH³. 250 aunte] lemman J. VI 2 bestis] blynde b. H. 21 dwelliþ] walkeþ H. 30 ben . . . folewere] folwed forth W. 48 go þoruȝ] mete wiþ W. VII 28 ek] lelly W. 62 conne lyue] trauail W. 68 asken] taken RVW. 118 grace] grete g. JL. 159 mawe] wombe A.

168 ferst] f. fast K. watir] fresh w. W. 170 al warm] ful depe W. 201 wombe] belyes N. 205 men] folk V. 213 on ground] þ*at* groweþ on g. RDCh. VIII 6 sowen] s. or sette W. 37 shal] xal don H^3. 62 þus] so VH; soþ W. 63 hondis] landys M. 64 wynnen] tiþen V. 104 harde] sore KM. 116 fresiþ] f. fast W. 142 men] lordis HA. 143 m*er*ueillously] Metels ful Meruilous V. IX 3 ofte] faste K. X 17 wys] wondir w. M. 23 kepe] k. wele J. 70 folies] falsed & f. $AWMH^3$. 81 tale] sawe K. 128 kynde] milde M. 135 nempnid] callyd J. 207 of wedlak] and Matrimoyne IMedlet togedere V. 210 leiȝeris] folis $TChH^2$. XI 10 wille] heore w. V. 23 seide] s. . . . for a sawe K. 29 techiþ] lerith J. 48 þenne] hennys K. 83 sathan] sory s. J; þat schrewe s. M; S. vnsaght WH^3. 90 lyue] l. lely U. 92 oþ*er*] day RU. 134 contreuide] con Cou*n*ter-feten V. 146 in catou*n*] my self K. 155 hard] h. heuy A. 164 Foundit] f. in feth AW MH^3. 240 god] c*r*ist J. 245 sewiþ] sone s. $AWMH^3$.

The many variants in the **A** manuscripts thus originated in two main ways, sharply distinct in principle even if the results are not always clearly distinguishable. First, the scribes of these manuscripts were evidently subject to many of the typical unconscious errors of copying. Variants created by such errors can often be identified, because the conditions that caused them have been preserved. The occurrence of others no longer identifiable is probable, although further variation will have removed or concealed their causes. The number of detectable mechanical errors in these manuscripts is large, but by no means accounts for all or most of the variants.

Second, many variants originated not in mistakes by scribes, but in the exercise of scribal preference. In some instances this process may have been unconscious. That is probably true of many purely linguistic variants, but not necessarily of all such. It is probably also true of some substitutions other than linguistic, which produced variants of more or less equivalent value. It is probably not true of most readings where the sense or force of the communication is affected by the variation.

The frequent recurrence of presumably unoriginal variants with similar effects on the substance of the poem, and therefore presumably made from similar motives, allows the editor to deduce the existence of several general tendencies of scribal substitution. An interest in the subject matter of the poem moved scribes to present this more clearly, as it seemed to them. Enthusiasm for this subject matter, and association of themselves with it caused them to increase the emphasis of its presentation. Beyond that, they satisfied a desire to participate in the poem by adding to its expression formal metrical adornment. Such circumstances both account for the large number of material variants and afford a means of interpreting these in crucial passages.

They affect the character of the editorial problem by representing that, although the number of variant readings in the manuscripts of the **A** version is very great, these were in the main introduced by copyists writing from an exemplar. It has been proposed that a more likely source of variants was oral transmission in the tradition of manuscripts.[1] But a distinction should be made of this term. Certainly *Piers Plowman* will have been recited, and learned by heart for that purpose. But the extreme possibility, that even the worst of the surviving **A** manuscripts was set down from memory, or is descended from a manuscript so set down, seems altogether remote. None of these manuscripts has the characteristics which, from knowledge of Middle English texts preserved in several versions, one connects with true oral transmission. By such I mean compression at one point and expansion at another, dislocation of matter other than palæographic, large omissions evidently made for abridgement or from defect of memory, and marked unevenness in the accuracy of reproduction.[2] On the other hand, that some, perhaps many readings of the **A** manuscripts are the products of unconscious substitution prompted by memory, or are unconscious substitutions of equivalent expressions supplying defects in the scribe's visual or aural recollection of his copy, is probable. Such processes are, however, not related to oral transmission, but are normal features of manuscript copying. Moreover their operation can be theoretically defined. The first will account for variants referable to other parts of the **A** version, or to **B** or **C**; the second for the generally slovenly character of the copy in a manuscript like A. Neither process satisfactorily explains the recurrent substitutions with a similar effect on the text, which are more likely to be the products of scribal editing. To insist that variation is frequent in the **A** manuscripts because of oral transmission would not only ignore the character of the variants, but also require the difficult assumption that men copying from an exemplar did not usually or often make substitutions. Strictly speaking, then, oral transmission in any accurate sense of the term is an unlikely source of corruption in these manuscripts. Departure from copy through the various operations of the memory of

[1] *TLS*, 10 February 1950, p. 87. The idea seems to be H. J. Chaytor's (*From Script to Print*, p. 129).

[2] Compare Chaytor, *From Script to Print*, pp. 127–8.

copyists, a very different matter, most probably is a source of much variation. Its effects can often, but not always be identified.

The establishment of characteristic scribal reactions to the substance of the poem also bears on the question of 'author's variants'. In the case of *Piers Plowman* the two fuller versions may be treated as author's variants. Within the **A** version the manuscripts KWN and to a lesser extent others might seem at first sight to have acquired their present form by authorial revision. I have shown above how unlikely this is. As for individual, smaller variants, it is certainly possible that some may have resulted from the author correcting or making revisions in copies of the **A** version, or in his own copy, or that copies of this version were made before he finished with and 'published' it, if he ever did so.[1] Where two variants leave nothing to choose between them the possibility of both being authorial may be allowed, however little it helps the editor.[2] But the number of such instances is diminished by knowledge of the several typical scribal responses to copy. The frequency of variation in the **A** manuscripts is, as a principle, to be explained without reference to the undemonstrable hypotheses of oral transmission or of extensive revisions by the author, in terms of the attitude of its scribes to the poem.

Substitution in these manuscripts appears to have been anything but 'wild and wayward'. Indeed it tends to take several clearly defined forms determined by the relationship set up between the scribe and the matter that he was copying. This is not to suggest that it was systematic. The evidence is to the contrary. Scribes did not see their alterations in any large relation to one another. Their view of the copy seems generally to have been limited to the single line, and seldom extended to any appreciably larger unit. They were likely to understand what they read in an obvious and *prima facie* sense, without the exercise of reflection.[3] Thus their activity as editors would take now one form, now another. The tendencies of substitution that can be observed in their variants represent broadly typical impulses aroused by the matter being copied. The regularity with which these tendencies were expressed

[1] The difficult question of publication is discussed by H. S. Bennett, 'The Production and Dissemination of Vernacular Manuscripts in the Fifteenth Century', *The Library*, fifth series, i (1946–7), pp. 167 ff., esp. pp. 172, 177. See also Chaytor, *From Script to Print*, ch. vi.

[2] Compare Pasquali, *Storia*, pp. 419–20: 'Le "varianti d'autore" sono l'ultima *ratio* della critica testuale, e non è lecito ricorrere a esse, finchè le divergenze si possano spiegare in qualsiasi altro modo.'

[3] Moore, *Contributions*, pp. xvi, xvii.

was determined by the momentary liveliness of the scribal sense c
obligation to the exemplar, the degree of understanding of it, and th
extent of response (or, for that matter, attention) to the poem as a docu
ment of personal moment.

Despite these qualifications the identification of typical scrib
substitutions is, in default of recension, the main resource of the edito
of these manuscripts. To the cruces of his text he must apply the know
ledge of characteristic scribal behaviour gained from passages whe
the direction of variation is scarcely in doubt, hoping by this means t
establish presumption of originality among available readings, or, les
often, to reconstruct the original reading from the variants.

In carrying out these operations as editor, I act on the postulate tha
presumption of originality can be established often enough to justif
a process of editing. This postulate is by no means generally accepte
at present; indeed opinions on editing are sharply divided. It is some
times maintained that 'The surest and most realistic method of editin
a text would seem to be to choose very carefully a "base" MS. an
reproduce it in its entirety, excepting when it gives a reading that i
obviously nonsense and when it is reasonably certain what the *scrib*
intended to write.'[1] That undoubtedly easiest course might be author
ized with the **A** version if there were a 'best' manuscript which coul
never be corrected with assurance from the variants of other copies
This is, however, not so: there are only less corrupt manuscripts. T
print one of these without editing it would invest it with quite un
merited authority.[2] Moreover to refrain from correction to somethin
more than 'what the *scribe* intended to write', when this was evidentl
possible, would be to shirk a serious obligation.[3] If the obligation t
correct occasionally is accepted, the scope of textual criticism canno
thereafter logically be restricted, but will have to extend to all variants
since to set a limit to it at any point requires an exercise of judgemen

[1] The author of the sentence quoted is Chaytor (*From Script to Print*, p. 129), but this opinio
is widely held.

[2] Compare K. Sisam, *Studies in the History of Old English Literature*, p. 39: 'To support a ba
manuscript reading is in no way more meritorious than to support a bad conjecture, and so fa
from being safer, it is more insidious as a source of error. For, in good practice, a conjecture i
printed with some distinguishing mark which attracts doubt; but a bad manuscript reading, i
it is defended, looks like solid ground for the defence of other readings.'

[3] Again compare Sisam, op. et loc. cit.: 'The difference between a better reading and a wors
is, after all, a matter of judgement; and however fallible that faculty may be, the judge mus
not surrender it to the witness.'

at least as arbitrary as any undertaken during comparison of variants. The circumstances in the present case do not seem to warrant mere publication of a manuscript. At any point in the text of the **A** version two major possibilities exist: that among the available **A** variants[1] one is the original of the rest; and that all the variants are unoriginal.[2] I do not see how the editor can avoid the responsibility of examining these possibilities as far as lies in his power.[3]

The results of the present examination are published in the form of a corrected basic manuscript. A manuscript is chosen as the base because it appears the most suitable when the number of its obvious errors and deficiencies is weighed against the character of its spellings, dialect forms and grammar. This manuscript is allowed to determine the linguistic form of the edited text, with the important qualification that such linguistic form is not at all necessarily that of the original.

In the comparison of variants which may lead to correction of the basic manuscript, the readings of this manuscript are not treated as more authoritative than those of any other. Every variant in any manuscript tests the originality of corresponding variants in other manuscripts. Thus the reading of the text adopted is ideally not affected by the choice of the base (although in practice when originality is not determinable the reading of the base may be allowed to stand). Since the basic manuscript does not have superior authority the adoption of a reading from another manuscript as more probably original is not a violent course. The basic manuscript contains some evident errors;

[1] The limitation to **A** variants is unavoidable, since this is an edition of the **A** version. In theory all variations of corresponding lines in the three versions might afford indications of a common, presumably unrevised original form of such lines. In practice the intrinsic likelihood that the authorial revision responsible for the major differences between versions will also have introduced smaller differences, makes it impossible to say of many lines whether their various forms in the three versions originated with scribe or author. The editor of any version is thus restricted to the evidence of the variants in manuscripts inferentially descended from the archetypal copy of that version. He will employ the evidence of variants from other versions only in certain special circumstances (for one type of these see below, p. 157). This restriction is to be regretted, since it cannot fail to have some effect on the quality of the text of each version. But it is inherent in the nature of this textual problem.

[2] There is, of course, the third and last possibility, that because of authorial revision several variants are original (see above, p. 145). But I do not know of an instance where this can be shown conclusively of **A** variants.

[3] Compare Greg, 'The Rationale of Copy-Text', p. 26: 'It is impossible to exclude individual judgement from editorial procedure: it operates of necessity in the all-important matter of the choice of copy-text and in the minor one of deciding what readings are possible and what not; why, therefore, should the choice between possible readings be withdrawn from its competence? . . it may not be too optimistic a belief that the judgement of an editor, fallible as it must necessarily be, is likely to bring us closer to what the author wrote than the enforcement of an arbitrary rule.'

all manuscripts as instruments of multiplication were prepared by individuals prone to error. Therefore the suggestion of the variants about originality must be followed, whether this involves correction of the basic manuscript or not. Editing, that is correction of a selected basic manuscript, is finally justified by presentation of all the variants, by indication of the points where correction has taken place, and by discussion of the evidence.

It must be emphasized that presumption of originality is never strictly equivalent to proof, and varies greatly in strength. Even when all manuscripts agree no proof of originality exists, since the unanimity may relate to an unoriginal reading in an archetypal manuscript. In practice unanimity of support must be accepted as establishing the strongest presumption of originality, unless the reading attested by all the manuscripts is patently unsatisfactory. In that case the editor has commonly no recourse and must content himself with pointing out the character of the text forced on him by the evidence.

The agreement of a considerable majority of manuscripts must, *in the absence of all other considerations*, be taken to indicate presumption of originality. This is because the assumption of the smaller number of substitutions necessary to account for the existence of the minority reading is the easier. Identification of originality in such cases rests on relative probability only. For practical purposes it must obviously be accepted, but it cannot be regarded as sure, since the degree of difference of probability is not very great, and the operation of probability may have been disturbed by circumstances unknown to the editor. Where, then, the choice is between perfectly equivalent, or equally good readings, the limited character of the authority conferred by majority support is to be appreciated.

The strength of presumption of originality when a reading is supported by a majority of manuscripts is affected by genetic considerations. The results of the genealogical analysis, limited as they are, may help to estimate the strength of the majority support. The support of a genetic group is equivalent to the support of the single manuscript which is their hypothetical exclusive common ancestor. Therefore, even having regard to the qualified value of genetic evidence in the case of the **A** manuscripts, the term majority is not to be simply understood.

But, since allowing majority support to indicate presumption of originality assumes the undisturbed operation of simple probability, any external circumstance which might disturb this operation is important. Such a circumstance is one which might suggest, or encourage, or direct substitution. When there is such a potential inducement to coincident variation, support of a majority of manuscripts is a poor indication of originality. Thus, as an aid to identifying original readings, knowledge of typical scribal substitutions becomes more reliable than considerations of manuscript representation, for, although a variant may be well attested, if it appears to originate in a scribal tendency of substitution this may explain the frequency of its occurrence.

Broadly speaking, identification of the scribal tendencies of substitution equips the editor with his final means of determining originality. The knowledge of repeated, similar reactions of scribes to copy, deduced from variants poorly attested and, therefore, on a first argument probably unoriginal, is applied to interpreting the evidence at points of difficulty. This is not to say that a set of rules is drawn up; it means that when the editor is obliged to identify originality among several variants in a crucial passage he is conscious that elsewhere, when direction of variation was suggested by the manuscript representation, the unoriginal variants often stood in certain typical relations to the presumptive original readings. He then interprets the readings of his crucial passage in terms of those typical relations, and not infrequently discovers by this means some indication of originality.

The authority of the text reconstructed by these means must vary with the character of the evidence available; it cannot be uniform any more than it can be exactly determinable. In the last analysis all decisions about originality are provisional only, subject to modification or rejection if further manuscript evidence should come to light. For these reasons some illustration of the variety of problems and the varying degrees of confidence with which these can be attempted seems necessary.

At the outset a number of T's readings could be rejected as evident errors immediately on comparison with those of other manuscripts. The following are examples:

Prologue 39 his. 88 Tho. I 31 þe. 46 wile. 49 þanne. 170 mowe. II 34 bedale. 126 cariede forþ. III 47 of. 72 regratie. V 1 *omission of* his. 27 kepte. 38 apeiriþ. 146 *omission of* go to. 155 peynye. 156 felkene. VI 58 A. VII 77 wyte. 129 brod.

164 Nhadde. 168 þi. 191 hym. VIII 70 kiliþ. 174 *omission of* by day. X 67 ȝouþ. 157 sende. XI 65 carpide. 94 becomiþ. 179 seiȝe. 213 to toune &.

In the same way variants in the other manuscripts could be confidentl dismissed, as, for example:

Prologue 3 vnworthy; 4 wayte; 14 ontyrid *etc*; 21 sore: *examples of scribes increasing allitera tion.* 29 caryen: *perhaps a bad spelling for* cairen, *but more likely a homœograph.* 107 with wiþ white; wiþ good: *mistakes of reading and attempts to improve them.* II 127 Fauu fette forþ: *increasing alliteration.* 147 tong: *a homœograph.* III 6 molde: *improvement alliteration.* IV 24 vnwary *etc.*: *attempts to improve a misunderstood line.* 76 bringen *mistake of reading.* 114 do euere *etc.*: *misreading and attempts to improve.* V 30 wite: *increasin alliteration.* 60 polet; piller; pelled: *homœographs.* VIII 62 so; soþ: *improvements alliteration.* X 104 men seþ *etc.*: *attempts to improve a misunderstood text.*

Many variant readings in all manuscripts could be rejected a evident palæographic errors; these have been sufficiently illustrate above (pp. 117 ff.). A very large number of readings in various manu scripts were excluded because they were in the first instance minorit readings; many such were not intrinsically inferior to those adopted but were simply less well attested. The employment of this standar was inevitable when rival readings were of equal intrinsic value, an neither contained an argument for originality over the other. Th frequency of such situations can be illustrated by the following ex amples from the first hundred lines of Passus V:

1 his] the H². 3 wiþalle] þerfore H. 7 sat] sett me E. 8 þei] it AN; that H²VH. 9 tolde] shewid H. 10 before] furst H². 12 on] of DVAN. 18 blowen] bowed Ch 19 in] for J. 20 er] on EK; at A; aforn W. hem alle] þe world H. 21 Of] On A vpon H; In M. 24 go] to AM. 25 wiþ] be EK. maner] kynne UE. 26 preyede] prechid U. 31 Þat] for K. 33 Let] That WN. wynnyng] welthe U. 34 He] and A. 36 wile] schul DA; shal W. ȝow] hem HEAM. 37 religioun] religyus RU. holde] kepe RUE. 38 ȝour] her ChHE. 39 ȝoure] here HE. til] or D; so þat U. 40 at] in U; of AWM. 41 ȝou] vs R. 43 and reherside] to reherce WN. his] þis VH. 44 made] gart A wiþ] of E; riht at J. 45 erþe] grounde VHAN. 46 lord mercy] to vr ladi V. 49 fers] Frele VA. 50 hente] hold A. me] it A. 52 But] And VJ. 54 Lecchour] Lechery KWN. to . . . lady] lord mercy H. criede] gradde L; bad H. 55 for] of LW. 60 in þe palesie] paltyk RU. 61 descryue] deuise W. 66 for] *with* AK. 74 to bringe] & brouht J. fame] defaut HW. 75 be] with UJ; in E. 76 And] I haue A. 77 don] made HL; gar E. þoruȝ] *with* DVHA. tunge] wordes L; talys EA. 78 sore] ofte A. 79 hym . . . his] men . . . þair EAM. wraþþe] striffe E. 80 þoruȝ] be M. 81 most] so muche L. 84 murdre hym] him mayme L. 85 to] byfore RVA; afore U. 89 broken] brode RUV. 91 heyne] herry Ch; hoge J; hyk K; he H. cote] cloke A. 92 and] *with* E. 94 of] for VHJEW. 95 ille] euele DHLEN. 96 iche] euery J; euerilke E. 99 bittir] bitternes E.

Although it had proved impossible to recover the genealogy of the A manuscripts, and there was no question of using recension as a nethod of editing, such information about genetic groupings as merged from the study of manuscript relations was a useful aid in letermining originality because it enabled more exact assessment of he strength of manuscript support (compare p. 148 above). In this ssessment the limiting factor was the amount of information available; t is possible to imagine circumstances where a fuller knowledge of nanuscript descent would permit more extensive interpretation of nanuscript support, still short of recension, which, as a method, is listinct. With the **A** manuscripts the most elaborate hypothesis of enetic relation is the group {⟨[(TH^{2})Ch]D⟩RU}; this will therefore erve well as illustration. The following cases, which affect the correc- ion of the basic manuscript, show how, although a variant appears in everal copies, it is treated as having the support of only one because he manuscripts where it occurs are in hypothetical descent from an xclusive common ancestor. A glance at the apparatus will show that he illustration could easily be extended to other groups.

59 þat] þere TChH^{2}. 78 to] *om* TChH^{2}. 101 hem] hym TChH^{2}. 110 of siȝt] to oke on TChH^{2}. 126 on] here on T; here in H^{2}. 153 þeiȝ ȝe] þi TRDChH^{2}. 171 arde] faste TDChH^{2}. II 59 or for] oþer TChH^{2}. 82 And] *om* TDChH^{2}. 86 texte] extis TDChH^{2}. 123 in shires abouten] abouten in shires TDChH^{2}. 165 sende] sente TDChH^{2}. 192 For] Fro TH^{2}. III 72 richen] risen vp TChH^{2}. 118 Is] I TDChH^{2}. 39 persones . . . prestis] prestis . . . persones TChH^{2}. 257 him] þat king TCh; þe ing RUDH^{2}. IV 4 Crist] god TRUDChH^{2}. 48 king kneuȝ] kneuȝ þe king TRUDChH^{2}. 58 þi] *om* TDChH^{2}. 148 rauȝte] deiȝede TDChH^{2}. 154 lete . . . ile] loue . . . wile TRUDChH^{2}. V 16 plumtres] plantes TDChH^{2}. puffid] put TRUDChH^{2}. 25 maner] m. of TChH^{2}. 56 shulde] *om* TDChH^{2}. 66 lippes] lippe TRUDChH^{2}. 69 or] & TH^{2}. 98 lyk] as TChH^{2}. 110 And] *om* TRUDChH^{2}. 57 glotoun in] in g. TDChH^{2}. 196 foules] larkes TChH^{2}. VI 22 me god] g. mote n. TChH^{2}. 120 hem] *om* TH^{2}. VII 18 longe] louely TRUDChH^{2}. 144 þi] þis TDChH^{2}. VIII 7 maner] m. of TChH^{2}. 21 hem] hym TH^{2}. 26 hem best] þat em D; þat hym TChH^{2}. 158 to passe to Ioye] *a pena & a culpa* TChH^{2}. IX 6 wente] vene TRUDChH^{2}. 15 as] *om* TDChH^{2}. 33 it] *om* TH^{2}. 57 foulis] briddis TRUD ChH^{2}. 75 is] *om* TDChH^{2}. 85 hiȝte] bit hym TChH^{2}. X 4 wittiliche] wiȝtliche TH^{2}. 78 roten] roren TChH^{2}. 181 were] *om* TDChH^{2}. 186 me þinkeþ] I wene TRUDChH^{2}. 207 mariage] maner TChH^{2}. 215 hem] hym TH^{2}. XI 78 in] be TRUDChH^{2}. 211 be stretis] aboute TChH^{2}. 227 heueneward] heuene TDChH^{2}. 250 creature] man TRUDChH^{2}. 280 þefte] þeftis TDChH^{2}. 301 alle] at wille TChH^{2}.

Where, however, readings seemed of equal value, and none received the support of a clear majority of manuscripts, even after the application of genetic information, there was no choice but to let the text of the basic manuscript stand.[1] This situation is not infrequent, but the instances vary markedly in importance. There are, for one thing, many where the choice of reading has no effect on the meaning and little or no effect on the style of the passage. The following examples will suffice to illustrate them.

Prologue 10 into] in; on. 12 wiste I] I wyste. 88 myst] þe m. I 22 in] by. II 3 blisside] blisful. 15 þus] so. 84 g*ra*untide] g*ra*untith. 138 at] to. III 3 callip] callyd. 96 þo] whan. IV 28 harm] harmes. V 54 to] on. 130 spynst*ere*] spinsteres. 206 þat . . . asshamide] he a. þat schrewe. VI 49 into] to. 112 ȝe] he. VII 114 leg] legges. lorell*is*] loselys. 160 watride . . . eiȝen] hys eyne watteryd. VIII 54 sauf sykirly] sikerly sauf. X 73 for] fro. 158 couplide] couple. XI 4 sterneliche . . . studie] staring dame stodye st*er*nelyche. 69 suffride] suffryn. 122 simplite] symplenesse. 162 þerewi*th*] wi*th* hem.

Here determination of originality is impossible because of the balance of representation and the equivalence of the readings. A similar situation exists when various arguments for and against originality come to mind, and none of them clearly outweighs the rest. This again is not always serious, but cases do occur where it is impossible to determine originality as between two variants with fairly distinct meanings, and the reading of T must be allowed to stand. Important cruces of this kind are discussed in the critical notes; since, however, such balance of evidence is probably the editor's worst problem, I give a few examples here.

II 182 Wysshen hym & wypide him & wounde hym in cloþis

cloþis] cloutes VHJWNM; clott*es* E

At first sight it might seem that *cloutes* in the sense 'clothes' (*NED Clout* sb.[1] 4b) was the original, and that *cloþis* was substituted as an easier synonym. But scribes might have taken an original *cloutes* in the more general sense of 'rags, shreds', and preferring to interpret the allegory as signifying that pardoners dressed Liar up in fine style, altered their copy to *cloþis*. Or, on the other hand, precisely this may have been the sense of an original reading *cloþis*, and scribes may have thoughtlessly expressed their antipathy to pardoners and to Liar by

[1] Compare Greg, 'The Rationale of Copy-Text', p. 31: 'Suppose that the claims of two readings, one in the copy-text and one in some other authority, appear to be exactly balanced: what then should an editor do? In such a case, while there can be no logical reason for giving preference to the copy-text, in practice, if there is no reason for altering its reading, the obvious thing seems to be to let it stand.'

dressing him in rags like a beggar. This would be in accordance with the scribal tendency to increase emphasis, a consideration that weighs against the slight preponderance of manuscript evidence in favour of *cloutes*.

IV 34 Þanne com pes into þe p*ar*lement & putte vp a bille

þe] *om* RDChVJLEKM

Here considerations of sense fail to disturb the balance of manuscript evidence. Without the article *parlement* should mean the Great Council of England. While this is conceivably what the poet intended, it seems equally possible that as he proceeded with his allegory he had no particular assembly in mind. I can see no way of determining whether he wrote or did not write the article before the word.

VII 20 Chesiblis for chapell*is* chirches to honoure

chapell*is*] chapleynes ChVJLEKNMH[3]

The readings are of equivalent value and the support of the manuscripts is fairly divided. Arguments from the sense are not decisive. Scribes might have substituted *chapellis* because of the suggestion in *chirches to honoure*; or *chapleynes*, denoting the actual wearers of the chasubles, might have seemed preferable to them because it was more explicit.

X 86 And þ*er*of seiþ þe saut*er* þe salme þou miȝt rede

þe salme] þi selue JVAKWMH[3]

The two variants are similar in shape and either could have been substituted carelessly for the other. Neither is difficult; in other passages *salme* is generally correctly copied. Two considerations apply without producing a decision: *þe salme* is attested only in the probably genetic group TRUDChH[2]; against that, *þi selue* is the more emphatic expression, and therefore somewhat likelier to be of scribal origin.

X 93 For ȝif þou comist aȝen consience þou combrist þiseluen

comist] co*m*sest RDKW; gynnyst H[3]; gynnyt M; do JA

It is hard to determine how difficult fifteenth-century scribes would have found an original *comist aȝen* here (for the sense of this expression see *NED* s.v. *Again* B prep. 5, 6, 8). The manuscripts which here read *comist* have previously kept an original *comsen* uncorrupted, e.g. at I 128, V 23 (except U), and IX 16, and do so again at X 101. This makes it unlikely that in them *comist* is a homœograph for *comsist.* But the words are very similar in shape, and careless reading of an original *comsist* may have resulted in substitution of *comist.* No decision about originality seems possible, and the reading of T there-fore stands.

There are, further, cases where it might seem that the editor has sufficient means of determining originality, but where he may well be uneasy about the authority of the text adopted. The first line of the poem affords an example in the variant *as I south wente.* This reading, attested in only three manuscripts of indifferent quality, which un-doubtedly stand in some genetic relation, vertical or lateral, is hard to account for. If it is a scribal insertion, how did it seem superior to the copyist who substituted it? If it is original, why was it generally lost? These unanswered questions cast doubt on the originality of both variants. In addition the reading adopted, with two staves in the second half-line, has a look of scribal versification by comparison with the classical pattern of *as I south wente.* While no one would be likely to complain if an editor silently passed over this poorly attested variant, it seems right to point out that its existence is very hard to account for.

In Prologue 79 the form of text adopted is that authorized by manu-script evidence. But the metre, with three staves coming before the cæsural pause, is unusual. The line would be improved by the omission of *peple* as in RH, and the substitution of *departyn* for *haue* as in RE. Indeed, one could argue that *departyn* had been removed from it by scribes who objected to the occurrence of this word in two successive verses. These considerations must be allowed even while the line stands as adopted on strong manuscript authority.

In I 8 the text, following manuscript direction, reads *þei kepe no betere*; for *kepe* two manuscripts read forms of 'will', which seems the obvious reading and makes the line conform to the expected metrical scheme. But because I cannot explain how 'will' would have been lost; or how, supposing it to have been the original reading, sub-stitution would be so uniform, *kepe* must stand, and the line (unless scanned *þéi þís þéi*) remain unmetrical.

In I 105 it is said that Christ in His majesty conferred power on the angelic orders, *þe meryere hem pouȝte.* There is a variant *hym* which could easily pass unremarked as a careless minority substitution of no importance. In fact it challenges *hem*, and if admitted to the text would give the difficult meaning that this conferment of power, presumably as a fulfilment of the act of creation, was a source of joy to the Creator. Thus the apparently secure text is actually seriously questioned.

In I 137 the expression *plante of pes* occurs as the centre of an image both striking and difficult. In the **A** manuscripts this has the substantive variants *plente* and *playnt*, neither demonstrably original from **A** evidence. But my confidence in the originality of *plante* is seriously disturbed by the possibility that it might stand for an original *planete.* Indeed a case could be made out for the 'planet of Peace', since this was Mercury, and Mercury symbolizing Christ was the psychopomp,[1] an idea perhaps reflected in **B** I 157, *leder of the lordes folke of heuene.* No **A** manuscript has a trace of an original *planete* here, but the **B** manuscript Y (Newnham College, Cambridge) reads *planetes* as a variant at **B** I 150. Far from the text of **A** here being secure, as a glance at the critical apparatus might suggest, it is actually seriously in doubt.

The crux *doom dyne* at II 169 is another case in point. But for its rôle in the authorship controversy *doom* might have stood as the unquestioned original. The manuscripts support it well enough, since VJL which read various forms of *dyne* have no great authority alone or in combination. But the arguments from sense adduced by Chambers and Grattan to show that *dyne* was the harder reading[2] must lessen confidence in the originality of *doom.* I retain *doom* because the overriding consideration seems to me the ease with which *dyne* might gain admittance to **A** manuscripts as a memorial contamination from **C.** But it seems necessary to call attention to the other arguments.

In III 223 the text adopted is *Loue hem & le[n]e hem*, less an emendation than a different interpretation of the ambiguous *lene-leue* from that of the scribe of T, who clearly writes *leue* (in most manuscripts *n* and *u* are not here distinguished). *Loue & lene* is indicated by the context in VII 207, and very possibly the poet meant it here as well. But not necessarily or certainly; I have in mind his statements at **B** III 313–15 and **C** IV 471–3, which suggest also for the present

[1] I owe this information to Morton Bloomfield, who produced it in support of my suggestion that the original reading here might have been *planete.*

[2] The discussion appears in *MLR*, xxiii, p. 4, and xxvi, pp. 31–4 and 336–7. See also Critical Notes below, p. 437.

A passage the transcription *leue*, 'leave in peace, do not tax or threaten with the processes of law'.

In VIII 110 Piers says, *þat louiþ god lelly his liflode is þe more.* Of the **A** variants for this line *þe more* is the best supported; as more pregnant than *wel muche* it is also the harder reading. On the face of it the line is then straightforward; *wel meth* (L) and *ful mete* (A) might, without more ado, be rejected on the ground of the poor authority of these manuscripts. But **B**'s reading *ful esy* suggests a possible original *ethe* for **A**. It would take a bold editor to adopt this reading, but the possibility that all the **A** variants are here unoriginal must be noticed.

In IX 107 for *þre dayes we ȝeden* V reads *þroly w. ȝ.* The overwhelming manuscript support for *þre dayes*, the greater emphasis in *þroly*, and the sophisticated character of V fully authorize the editor to reject *þroly* as unoriginal. But it is not manifestly an inferior or easier reading; thus it is impossible to be altogether confident of the originality of *þre dayes.*

In XI 67, *Þat he gilide þe womman & þe wy aftir*, manuscript support for a reading *(be)gilide* leaves no doubt that this was in the archetype of the surviving manuscripts. In a sense the editor's obligation ends there. But it is hard to avoid thinking that the poet wrote *wilide* (*NED Wile* v. 1), a form sufficiently difficult to invite substitution. This is scarcely a crux, since the sense of the line is not affected. But the existence of the possibility is an indication of the limits of textual criticism.

The lines discussed stand in the text as the evidence of the manuscripts seems to require. But the text there cannot be regarded as fixed. How is it to be determined whether at some points the author has shown lack of skill or resource, whether some alternative readings are author's variants, or whether it is a case of errors in the archetype of the **A** manuscripts? There are, thus, occasions when the editor, following the direction of the evidence, has little choice but to read what seems to him a text of doubtful originality.

Between the extremes illustrated, where the editor is confident, and where he cannot decide originality or the evidence fails him, there is a wide range of instances where he can determine originality as surely as is ever possible with Middle English texts preserved in several manuscripts. The means at his disposal will now be illustrated.

The original form of a small number of lines or expressions can be recovered by reference to **B** or **C** at corresponding points. This is not to treat **B** as another branch of the **A** genealogy.[1] Such a course might be authorized if it could be determined with any certainty when a difference of reading between **A** manuscripts and those of the **B** version arose through corruption of **A** or **B** manuscripts, and when through authorial revision. But since this is evidently often impossible the readings of the **B** version, and *a fortiori* those of **C**, can never be treated as primary authorities in determining originality for **A**. There is, however, a situation in which they serve as guides to conjecture: when most or all of the **A** variants for a passage are unsatisfactory in ways which cast doubt on their originality, and when, at the same time, the reading of another version could easily and naturally have given rise to the **A** variants if it had been the original of **A** as well. This applies at II 144 (*fobbis*); V 90 (*Awey*); V 198 (*þrumblide*); XI 268 (*Demde*), where I have adopted a form or reading from **B** or **C**.

In a number of cases metrical considerations supported one variant against another. The simplest examples were merely choices between different forms of the same word, usually on the assumption that the metrical variant was the more probably original. Applied to such cases this assumption does not seem difficult; it is a fairly safe inference that the author, whatever his native and literary dialects, would write *þe king & his kniȝtes to þe kirke wente* rather than *þe king & his kniȝtes to þe chirche wente.* Thus, where manuscript evidence permitted and no other consideration forbade it, the metrical variant was adopted. For example, in Prologue 63 *hy* was adopted, both for metrical reasons and because it was the likeliest common original of *he* and *þei*; in II 37 *þermyd* was adopted both as the metrical and as the older form of the adverb; in III 20 *gaf*, and III 62 *giue* were adopted in preference to *ȝaf* and *ȝiue*; so in V 1 and 85 *kirke*; in V 95 *hy*; in VII 29 *kirke*; in XI 153 *agens*. The possibility that these forms were inserted by scribes making good the deficiencies of a major alliterative poet might, of course, be maintained, but I think it slight. The adoption of *raþer* against *erst* (IV 5), or *peple* against *folk* (VI 108), or the restoration of *fro* (VI 13), are in a different category. Metrical considerations also play a part in the restoration of V 132.

[1] As do Knott (*MP*, xii, pp. 396, 409–10) and Fowler (*Piers the Plowman*, pp. 26, 27).

I refrain, however, from emendation on metrical grounds where all support is lacking. For example in II 87, *Worþi is þe werkman his mede to haue*, there is no manuscript authority for the obvious *wage* (the variant *hire* being probably a scribal attempt to make a metrical line of another type); in III 21 *pecis of siluer* should perhaps read *coppes of siluer*, 'copes of silver thread', but authority other than W's variant is lacking; in III 49 it is hard to see why the poet did not write *saluacioun* for *heuene*, but there is no indication that it was ever present in the **A** tradition; in IV 63 a change of *wiþ* to *myd* would make the line metrical but lacks authority; in IV 91 adoption of U's variant *crist* for *god* of the other manuscripts would provide a stave in the second half line, but since no reason for the loss of original *crist* appears, *god* must stand; in XI 159 reading *fele* for *many* would complete the metre but lacks support from any manuscript.

The most generally useful means of determining originality is the application of knowledge about scribal tendencies of substitution to the variant readings. How these tendencies were deduced has already been described;[1] now their use will be illustrated. For instance, because a great many variants, supported by one or only a few manuscripts, and therefore probably unoriginal, have the effect of making the text more emphatic, it is inferred that preference for a more emphatic statement was a broad characteristic of scribal substitution. Many examples were given above[2] of more emphatic minority readings treated as unoriginal. Where manuscript balance is less decisive, knowledge of this characteristic enables the editor to treat the more emphatic variant as probably unoriginal; this has been done, for instance, at II 26 *as I*] *soþ as I*; III 113 *wel*] *ful*; IV 71 *woo*] *muche wo*; V 65 *foule*] *full f.*; VI 109 *wel*] *ful*; VII 29 *kepe*] *k. wel*; 100 *payed*] *wel p.*

Similarly, because study of variants with minority support has indicated that scribes tended to make the expression of their copy more explicit,[3] the less explicit reading is treated as more probably original in cases of balance or near-balance of manuscript support, and in the absence of conditions that might lead to omission. Thus, for example, in Prologue 75 *Were*] *But w.*; 83 *synge*] *s. there*; 101 *mynours*] *& m.*; I 47 *he*] *god*; 63 *eggide*] *e. hem*; II 138 *reste*] *here r.*; III 99 *consience*] *hatte c.*; IV 149 *But*] *B. ȝif*; VII 10 *wyues*] *ȝe w.*; IX 41 *þat*] *And þ.*; XI 3 *so*] *þus me*; *me þus*.

[1] pp. 127 ff. above. [2] pp. 138–9. [3] p. 131 above.

Substitutions and insertions which make the text more explicit are part of a general tendency to make it easier that takes a variety of forms. One frequent example is the replacement of original *ac* by *but* or *and*, or its omission. This conjunction appears to have been losing currency fairly early in the fifteenth century; there are indications that some scribes of the **A** manuscripts did not know its values. Except in a few cases I have treated *ac* as the probable original. Examples of the type of exception are VII 28 where T's reading *Ac* is evidently a palæographic error induced by the following word; XI 24 and 35 where the variants are not those characteristically produced by original *ac*; and XI 155 where I think that *ac* was scribally introduced on the model of the constructions in 137 and 149.

The term 'harder reading' has various senses in determining originality.[1] If it is true that a scribe would not knowingly or wilfully introduce a more difficult or less straightforward reading, the problem is to identify the harder reading with confidence, dismissing variants that make nonsense or present 'some perverse and distorted grammatical complication'. The editor of a Middle English text is particularly bedevilled by the lexicographical question, and by the lack of comprehensive studies of Middle English syntax. When he attempts to compare usage or currency in the mid-fourteenth century and, say, a hundred years on, he is bound to make judgements on insufficient evidence. Some examples will illustrate my attempts to determine originality by identifying the harder reading.

In Prologue 31 originality must be determined between *chosen hem to chaffare*, *chosen to chaffare*, and *chosen chaffare*. Here it seemed to me that the first variant was the more difficult because of its less obvious meaning 'betook, devoted themselves to'; cp. *NED* s.v. *Choose* v. 10 and add to the parallel example there c. 1394, *Wars of Alexander*, ed. W. W. Skeat, EETS ES 47 (London, 1886), (Dublin) 1773, *Ay a childe most hym chose vnto childer gammez*, and *Parlement of the Three Ages*, ed. I. Gollancz, London, 1915, 255, *And chese me to the chesse that chefe es of gamnes*. Compared with the meanings 'took their way, proceeded to go', (*NED*) s.v. *Choose* v. 8b), or 'selected, made a

[1] Compare Moore, *Contributions*, p. xxxvi: 'If a *word* or *expression* be strange or unfamiliar, either in itself or in the sense implied in the passage—if the *form* of a word be unusual or archaic —if the *order* of the words be apparently unnatural or uneuphonious—if the *construction of the sentence* be long, complicated, or grammatically anomalous—in all these and other similar cases that might be added, there is a natural tendency to substitute simpler, more obvious, more familiar words, inflexions and constructions.'

choice of', the variant adopted seems distinctly the harder and less likely to have been inserted by scribes.

In Prologue 42 where the choice is between *Flite* and *Fayted*, *Flite* seems to have the more difficult meaning in the context, whereas it is hard to see why an original *Fayted* should have been corrupted. Original *Flite*, however, a regionally restricted word, with the sense that beggars and such were obsequious until they had full bellies and wallets, but then made insolent demands and brawled over their drink (cp. VII 115 ff. and 139 ff.) might well have been missed. Accordingly I adopt *Flite*, and explain *Fayted* as substitution on the suggestion of 40–1 above, or perhaps as a homœograph.

In I 104 the reading adopted, *such seuene & anoþer*, is harder than the alternative *and such seuene oþere* because it presupposes a knowledge of the reason for *tene* in 103, as well as the ability to count to ten (see W. W. Skeat, *The Vision of William concerning Piers the Plowman*, part iv, section i, EETS 67 (London, 1877), pp. 33–4). The reading *and such seuene oþere*, introduced by scribes who knew only nine orders of angels, is in fact ruled out by the undoubtedly original *tene* of the preceding line. The scribes of REM failed to relate this to their total of nine in 104; J altered *tene* to *þat tyme*.

In V 35, *Þat þei preche þe peple proue it hemselue*, a number of manuscripts read *& proue*. This is probably the easier reading: consisting of two paratactic clauses, it is grammatically inferior to the single, taut construction of the adopted text, with its closer logical relation of ideas. It seems more probable that an original as adopted would be relaxed by addition of the conjunction than that the force and meaning would be improved by a copyist.

In VI 94 the choice between *loue* and *loue hym* is determined by the greater difficulty of *loue* in the context. If the pronoun is admitted to the text the sense is that the pilgrim will be taught to love God; without the pronoun it is, less obviously, that he will be taught Charity, perfect love, after he has achieved moral perfection (cp. I 155 ff.). A scribe, failing to grasp the full meaning of an original *loue*, would very naturally insert *hym*. In the absence of occasion for omission of *hym* this consideration is decisive.

In VIII 30, *And bynde brugges aboute þat tobroke were*, the decision about originality between *bynde*, *bete* and *bigge* is made on lexicographical grounds. *bynde*, which might at first sight seem a nonsense variant, proves to have the difficult, technical sense 'reenforce by attaching lateral beams' (see *Cursor Mundi*, part ii, ed. R. Morris, EETS 57 (London, 1875) and ff., (Cotton) 8783 *þe balk þat mast þe werk suld bind*; and op. cit., (T) 18087 *ȝoure brasen ȝatis spere ȝe wele And byndeþ hem wiþ barres of stele*; also *NED* s.v. *Bindbalk*). Assuming such a difficult original, *bigge*, *bete*, *boten*, *amendyn* are substitutions guided by the context, and *þinke on* probably a gloss of a homœograph or misreading *mynde*.

In X 91 the choice is between *accordyng holy chirche* and *accordyng with h. c.*; the nominative absolute construction, adequately attested but not very frequent (e.g. *Cloud of Unknowing*, ed. P. Hodgson, EETS 218 (London, 1944), p. 49, line 4; *Sir Gawain and the Green Knight*, ed. J. R. R. Tolkien and E. V. Gordon, Oxford, 1936, line 450; and further E. Einenkel, *Geschichte der Englischen Sprache*, ii, *Historische Syntax*, Strassburg, 1916, pp. 59–60), is treated as the harder, and therefore probably original reading.

Four readings adopted as the harder and therefore more probably original may be discussed together. The first, in III 201, is *ȝerne* against *renne*. The form adopted is metrically satisfactory, that rejected unmetrical, but this alone would not be enough. *ȝerne*, as an obsolescent form of restricted currency is the harder reading, and the more likely to have been supplanted (see *NED* s.v. *Yern* v. where the latest example is 1425). The original presence of *ȝerne* in the **A** tradition is attested by the variant *þey desiryt* of M, a mistaken scribal attempt to gloss. A harder reading, which was successfully levelled to a more usual form by most scribes, but confused at least one scribal modernizer, is thus restored to the text.

The others are *heþyng* against *hyne* (IV 104); *raike* against *ryde* (IV 153), and *mynchons* against *martires* (X 136). These stand or fall as a group. All are directly attested in one authority only, Ch. They must be considered first with this in mind. They may be original readings uniquely preserved, the variants of the other manuscripts being groups of coincident substitutions that give a false appearance of unanimity against Ch; or original readings restored by correction in Ch (for possible evidence of correction in this manuscript see the variational group TDH² above, p. 88); or author's variants; or brilliant scribal emendations. Each of these readings is harder than its alternative, and therefore can be rejected outright only if the fourth possibility is accepted. To do this seems to make nonsense of the basi of textual criticism by assuming a scribe capable of improving on th poet's work, who nevertheless confined his archaizing to three point in the **A** version. Therefore the editor must at the outset allow th possibility of originality to these readings.

As it turns out two of the three have in fact further manuscript sup port. At IV 153, TDH²'s unmetrical variant *wende*, an obviou scribal guess from the context, is quite unlikely to be a substitutio for an easy, metrical, original *ryde*. Thus the attestation of *raike*, more difficult reading, in a single manuscript, is supported by th character of the substitution in this manuscript's genetic fellows, whicl suggests a more difficult original than *ryde* in their exclusive commo ancestor. At X 136 the unmetrical *nonnes* of TRUD (H² is defectiv here) most probably goes back to original *mynchons*; and betwee *mynchons* and *martires* the latter is the likelier substitution because of th suggestion of the common phrase of liturgy and ecclesiastical calendar The harder reading here proves to have support outside the singl manuscript which preserves it intact, and there is a source of suggestio for the easier variant. Finally the authority of Ch in respect of *raik* and *mynchons* extends to *heþyng*. I adopt all three readings because the are the harder; because two have more substantial manuscript suppor than the sigils in the apparatus indicate; and because there is no sug gestion outside these readings that a scribe in the tradition of C might have been an archaizer.

Perhaps the most useful means of determining originality is, finally afforded by the variant readings which I have called *homœographs*. Where these occur they often suggest which of the available variant most probably gave rise to the others, and where originality probabl lies. A good example is found in I 179, where there are available th variants *graiþ* (*greytheste*, *grethed*); *gret* (*grettest*); *geynyist*; *graciouse redyeste*. On the necessary assumption that, to generate this corruption the original was difficult, *graiþ* etc. and *geynyist* are singled out. Th easy *gret* etc. is an unlikely original because its corruption to *redyest* or *graciouse* is almost inconceivable; *graciouse* is unlikely because excep in *geynyist* (*NED* s.v. *Gain* a.2), no trace of its meaning is found in th other variants. Thus *graiþ* and *geynyist* only are difficult enough to hav presumptive originality. Neither, indeed, is manifestly more difficul

[1] pp. 132–3 above.

than the other. But since *graiþ* stands in a central position to both a homœograph *gret*(*test*) and a gloss *redyeste*, whereas *geynyist* is supported only by glosses (*graciouse* and *redyeste*) originality is presumed to lie with *graiþ*.

This line of reasoning, where identification of the variant likeliest to have given rise to the remainder is made easier by homœographs, is employed at a large number of points. The variants with the appearance of homœographs suggest a hypothesis of originality; those which seem to be glosses (often they are unmetrical) help to support it. If on such a hypothesis all the variants at a crux can be explained, originality is regarded as determined to the limit of certainty possible in textual criticism. Some further illustrations may be of interest.

In Prologue 14 the variants are *triȝely*, *trewlich*, *wonderliche*, the last unmetrical. The similarity of shape and lack of sense-correspondence between *triȝely* and *trewlich* point to one being a homœograph for the other. Judging by the relative currency of the words *trewlich* is the likelier substitution. A hypothesis that *triȝely* is original allows the other variants to be explained: *trewlich* as a resourceless substitution for a difficult original, keeping some of its shape and saving the alliteration but losing most of the sense; *wonderliche* as a gloss that comes somewhere near the sense of the supplanted original, but at the expense of the metre.

At XI 80 the difficult original *whyes* is confirmed by the occurrence of the homœograph *weyes* and the near-gloss *priuytes* among the variants. To begin with, the variants *werkes*, *wordes* and *weyes* are to be rejected as unoriginal, since none seems hard enough to have set extensive corruption afoot, and certainly none is likely to have given rise to the unmetrical *priuytes*. Hypothesis of an original *whyes*, suggested by K's *whyys*, the least obvious of the metrical variants, explains the other readings satisfactorily. Its difficulty accounts for the existence of three variants, *werkes*, *wordes* and *weyes*, all resembling it in shape, and none comparably hard, as homœographs; and *priuytes* appears as a tolerably successful attempt to gloss, at the expense of the metre. Indeed, the hypothesis is even satisfactory in terms of the genetic information which we possess: for the exclusive common ancestor of TChH² (*werkes*), D (*wordes*) and RU (*weyes*), certainly read something harder than any of these three variants; likewise the original reading in a common ancestor of AWMH[3] is likely to have been harder than *weys* to generate *priuytes* in M.

On several occasions a variant identifiable as a homœograph allows recovery of an original reading not actually preserved in any **A** manuscript. In III 95 the homœograph *ywys* of TChH[2] points to an original reading *wy*. *ywys* itself is probably unoriginal because it is unlikely to have generated the variants *mayde*, *mede*, *womman*. Of these, in turn, *mayde* and *mede* are both unmetrical and too easy to be widely corrupted; *womman*, as both easy and altogether apt, would hardly be generally lost. Hypothesis of an original *wy*, as a mid-point between *ywys* and *womman*, and a possible source of both, accounts for all the variants. Such an original, doubly hard in a feminine reference (*NED* s.v. *Wye*[1]3) would produce the homœograph *ywys* (in its turn glossed *Certis*) or be replaced, according to the direction of the context, by *mede*, *mayde*, *womman*. No other original would, it seems to me, have given rise to this pattern of variation.

At V 142 the variants are *so mote I the*, *so þike*, *so I think*, *to þe*, and *soþely*. No special penetration is needed to see that the original of these variants must have been *so þe y*, or, as T would spell it, *so þe I*. This form in the original could have produced the paraphrase *so mote I the*, the homœographs *soþely* and *to þe*, and by way of a dialect variant like *so þike*, the misguided correction *so I think*. The longer expression *so mote I the* is a less likely original because it would less easily have given rise to *soþely*; *soþely* itself is least likely, for it is so apt that as an original it would hardly have been seriously corrupted. As a probable homœograph, however, it suggests the exact form of the original asseveration.

At X 47 the variants are *help* and *halle*. Despite the impressive weight of support for *help*, this is unacceptable as the original unless *halle* can be fairly accounted for. But *halle* cannot have originated from *help* by any conceivable process of error, and so the likelihood of an original *help* is minimized. In its turn *halle* seems to be rejected by the sense of the passage and the allegory. Original *hale*, 'remedy, specific' (*NED* s.v. sb.[1]), or even *hale*, 'secret place, refuge' (ibid., sb.[2]) are only remotely possible; *hale(þ)*, which would do very well for sense, seems historically too difficult. Neither available reading is thus a likely original. The crux, however, admits of solution on the hypothesis that one of these variants is a homœograph and the other an attempt to gloss a difficult original not preserved. As the less acceptable to the sense of the passage *halle* is the probable homœograph; the original may then have been a word resembling *halle* in shape, with something of the sense of *help*. Such a word is *allie* (*MED* s.v., n. 1 (b)). If this was the original reading both the unsatisfactory variants are accounted for, the one as a homœograph, the other as a guess-gloss, very probably directed by line 49 below.

The examples set out above will have shown my use of the various resources for determining originality. I have tried to prevent any of them from becoming rules, or arranging themselves in a hierarchy. Each crux is unique, and often several considerations must be weighed in its solution. It will then be evident that the authority of a text of this kind must vary from line to line; the assurance with which originality is determinable, and, indeed, has been determined by its editor, must depend on the arguments available in any given case and his ability to perceive them. It has seemed to me right in honesty to make this clear. If a 'critical' text is one in which the editor has compared the variant readings, then mine is critical, but it is not critical in any Lachmannian sense of being invested with a mysterious authority that sets it beyond question by its users. Therefore I have laid my decisions open to examination by full presentation of the evidence and an exposition of my grounds for determining originality.

An account is now required of the presentation of text and critical apparatus.

The basic manuscript or copy-text is T, MS Trinity College, Cambridge R. 3. 14. This was chosen for several reasons. First, it is one of the few **A** manuscripts without large omissions or physical imperfections. Of the seventeen copies four, H, L, E and N are short forms; H^3's **A** portion begins only in Passus V; R, U, D and A have serious dislocations and large omissions; H^2 is physically imperfect; V is imperfect at the end and manifestly corrupt throughout; K and W both interpolate and substitute from other versions. Four complete copies remain: J, M, Ch and T. Of these, J and M are corrupt and badly spelled; J is relatively late. The choice is thus between T and Ch, which are both complete and not demonstrably inferior copies.

Comparison of T and Ch sustains the independent decisions of Knott, and Chambers and Grattan, before Ch was known, that T was the best basis for an edition. Neither manuscript omits many lines, but Ch omits more than T; both spell fairly well, but Ch not quite so consistently as T. Finally, T needs to be corrected somewhat less often than Ch. For these reasons the choice of the earlier editors can stand.

In the transcription of T the following practices have been adopted. Initial letters of the line are treated as capitals. The scribe of T was not entirely consistent, but wrote capital forms of letters at the beginnings of lines often enough to show his intention. This I fulfil. His capital letters within the line are preserved except where a capital would result from correction of a wrong line-division in T. To remove T's occasional capitals within the line would logically necessitate capitalizing throughout according to modern usage, which does not seem authorized in an edition like the present one.

Suspensions and contractions are expanded, the letters so produced being printed in italic type. Expansions are carried out as far as possible according to T's spelling of similar unabbreviated forms elsewhere; when such are not available they are given the common value of the suspension or contraction.[1] The contraction *Ihu* is expanded to *Iesu* (e.g. III 145 and XI 27); *qp* is expanded to *quap* on the model of II 154, III 109, IV 3 etc. The scribe of T does not always place his *er*/*re* suspensions carefully, and sometimes in words like *here*, *pere*, etc. there is doubt whether to print -e*re* or -*ere*; I adopt the former transcription because a substantial number of instances where -e*re* can be determined exists.

Superior letters of simple value, for example the ^{e} in *p*^{e} or *treup*^{e}, are not distinguished in transcription. Where T's uncontracted spellings suggest that a superior letter indicates contraction, as in *p*^{u}, uncontracted *pou*, I have shown the expansion in the usual way. A curled flourish after final *m* or *n* has not been treated as a suspension, since there is no indication from uncontracted forms that the scribe spelled with a double final nasal. A convex line over final *p* is not expanded (Prologue 45 *slep* etc.); nor are suspension marks something like the *es*/*is* suspension after final *f* (Prologue 61 *chief* etc.); after final *g* (Prologue 19 *Worching* etc.); after final *k* (Prologue 84 *silk* etc.); nor is an angular suspension resembling Tironian 7, attached to final *t*

[1] Contractions and suspensions are sources of corruption in transmission and sources of error in editorial transcription. To expand them silently is to withhold information about both possibilities.

(Prologue 71 *breuet* etc.); nor is a horizontal stroke through final *h* (Prologue 78 *parissh* etc.).[1]

Latin lines and tags are printed in italic letters. Expansion of the manuscript abbreviations in these is silently made. When Latin lines contain English words or are evidently part of the syntactical structure they are numbered like the English lines; when they are detachable (and might have made their way into the text by way of the margin) they are referred to by the number of the preceding English line followed by a Greek letter. Unmistakably French words are printed in italic type.

The transcription does not preserve the word-divisions of T, which are markedly inconsistent. The scribe of T makes false joins, e.g. Prologue 16 *Wiþdepe*; 53 *beknowen*; 87 *forloue*; I 3 *oflire*; 73 *toknowe*; III 98 *nomore*; IV 109 *besouȝt*; XI 7 *bestille*; 247 *beholde*. He makes false divisions, e.g. II 35 *a sele*; 112 *a maistrien*; 178 *to luggid*; III 91 *of sente*; IV 49 *a ferd*; 142 *wiþ sigge*; V 33 *for wanye*; 251 *þou sand*; VII 124 *werk men*; IX 8 *be fel*. Since no purpose would be served by keeping such arrangements I have treated word-division arbitrarily. I have joined, where they are not joined in T, all *-self* compounds; the indefinite pronouns *whatso* and *whoso*; the adverbs *forthy*; *hereafter*; *hereto*; *thereafter*; *therefore*; *therein(ne)*; *thereof*; *thereon*; *thereout*; *thereto*; *therewith*; *wherewith*; *withal* etc.; as well as expressions which do not seem to be free forms, but have limited contexts, such as *bondemen*; *ȝerisȝiue*; *heueneriche*; *madame*; *redyngking*; *riggebones* etc. I have separated *forto* when used purposively or as the infinitive particle (see *MED* s.v. 1, 3). I have joined or separated *into* according to modern usage. I have joined *dowel*, *dobet* and *dobest* when these expressions denote the allegorical characters (rather than hyphenate them) since the scribe frequently joins them in such cases, but I have separated, or left them separate when they have literal value.

I have shown every substitution or addition to which the text of T is subjected. But in this connexion I must insist that my use of the square bracket is not intended to display the whole editorial process. To observe this in detail it is necessary to consult the apparatus. The following general procedure is employed. Substitution of another

[1] See C. Johnson and H. Jenkinson, *English Court Hand*, Oxford, 1915, i, p. xxiii: 'In late hands, where English is the language used, suspension marks over a final consonant (such as *d*, *g* or *n*) are very common; and frequently mean little more than that the ending, had the language been Latin, could only have been that of a suspended, or incomplete, word; i.e. that the scribe is acting from force of habit, and that the abbreviation is little more than formal.' See also op. cit., p. 70.

reading for that of T, or addition to the text of T, or rearrangements of T's matter in the line, or omissions of one or several letters from a word of T, are indicated by the presence of square brackets. These brackets are, however, primarily intended to be the 'distinguishing mark which attracts doubt'. When the nature of the emendation could be indicated by the manner of placing the brackets I have done this, but the types of correction are very numerous, and the precise character of some cannot easily be shown in this way. I therefore reserve discretion in the manner of using the brackets, but guarantee their presence in every case specified above.

Omissions of whole words, word-equivalents (e.g. *N* in *Narn*, I 21) and phrases, although invariably shown in the apparatus, are not indicated in the text. Typographical experiments failed to produce any satisfactory means of showing them. The square bracket is itself unsightly enough, but at least it is now so familiar that the reader unconcerned with editorial problems has become expert in ignoring it. No second sign could be devised to show omissions, which did not seem offensively obtrusive. Some effort is therefore required of the reader interested in my omissions from the text of T. I give here a list of the lines where these occur, and where attention has not been directed to the apparatus by square brackets in the immediate vicinity. The reader may mark this information in his own copy as he pleases.

Prologue 5; 75; 77; I 21; 22; 37; 63; 97; 126; 172; 173; II 104; 110; 138; 186; 189; III 36; 99; 117; 165; 212; 255; 260; 269; IV 45; 47; 53; 77; 89; 94; 95; 97; 106; 111; 135; 147; 149; V 25; 29; 35; 41; 46; 57; 81; 93; 102; 109; 113; 120; 148; 174; 177; 209; 230; 238; VI 28; 41; 42; 64; 66; 69; 115; VII 5; 48; 67; 79; 110; 137; 139; 144; 150; 163; 164; 195; 212; 213; 217; 224; 226; 236; 251; 262; 274; 275; 280; 296; VIII 4; 7; 19; 29; 32; 44; 73; 90; 100; 113; 126; 171; IX 7; 41; 65; 94; 113; X 67; 81α; 131; 139; 150; 157; 176; 178; XI 19; 39; 60; 75; 99; 129; 134; 149; 157; 164; 213; 244; 277; 289.

Additions and substitutions were made to conform as far as possible to the spelling and grammar of T. To save space in the apparatus, however, the form of variant of another manuscript was adopted if this did not differ markedly from the practice of T's scribe. When whole lines or large parts of lines had to be restored they were taken from the manuscript nearest in form to the usual orthography of T at that point.

The grammatical and orthographical forms of T have generally been preserved. No attempt has been made to restore the morphology of the author's copy from manuscript evidence. To follow the direction of the manuscripts in this respect on the infrequent occasions when this might be possible would be to depart from the principle of copy text: that in ignorance of the author's linguistic habits the best course is to publish his poem in an authentic Middle English form. Even though such a form, as afforded by T, is relatively late, and probably consists of layers of dialect accretions and spelling conventions, that is no justification for adding further to the mixture.

Thus I have, for instance, retained the following forms peculiar to T or to T and a minority of manuscripts.

Prologue 59 may; 61 Siþen; 68 auowes; 94 ylope; I 3 lire; 51 *oþer*; 66 Eldir; 68 tresten; 85 derworþi; 107 trouþe; 129 þine; 173 lering; II 35 assent; 44 beggeris; 83 molere; 95 kynde; 116 cesse; 137 southdenis; 146 mene; 182 Wysshen; III 22 ricchesse; 31 louye; 62 *Oþer*; 69 þise(2); 113 trist; 148 let; IV 30 rombide; 41 plete; 66 kneuȝ; V 65 lourande; 105 selde; 141 Sheo; 171 bed; 181 felle; 213 fil; VI 58 almiȝt; VII 60 here; 177 botind; 190 ywent; VIII 65 louȝ; 125 beholdis; X 2 skenis; 23 þise(1); XI 48 hunsen; 68 wille; 180 lere.

On the other hand, for various reasons I have altered such forms of T as the following:

Prologue 63 *þei* to *hy* as required by the metre; compare II 25; 126; III 24; 65 etc. where T preserves *hy*. Prologue 73 *ȝouen* to *gyuen* as required by the metre; compare II 84 *gyue*; 85 *gyuen*; III 169 *gyue*; 219 *gyueþ*; IV 88 *forgyue* etc., where T preserves the alliterating form. I 62 *foundit* to *foundide* as an anticipation of the following word. I 72 *he* to *heo* as a thoughtless substitution; compare I 73; II 20; 24; 198 etc. where T preserves *heo*. II 51 *bounde* to *boun* as probably not a true form, since *bode* later in the line may have induced the -*de*; also cp. II 124 where T reads *boun*. III 63 *hire* adv. to *here* as probably not a true form, but induced by *hire* n. earlier in the line. III 67 *pynnyng* to *pynyng* as probably not a true form in T, but induced by the double consonant in *pillories*. V 1 *chirche* to *kirke* as required by the metre; the preservation of the Northern form in various manuscripts here, and e.g. at V 147; VII 29 and 83 argues its original presence in such metrical positions. V 109 *bittirbrowid* to *betilbrowid* because the form *bittir*- does not appear to be attested outside *Piers Plowman* manuscripts; because in its context there it might have been induced by *babir*- later in the line; and because among the **A** manuscripts it occurs only in TRUDH[2], members of a probable genetic group. V 110 *liþerene* to *leþerene* as probably not a true form, but influenced by the suggestion of *liþer* in a context of unfavourable description. VII 212 *permiþ* to *permid* as probably not a true form but an unconscious mixture of *mid* and *wiþ*.

The effect of this treatment is, as I hope, to restore the form of T, respecting accidentals, to what it would have been if the scribe or his immediate predecessors had made no spelling mistakes for palæographic reasons, and if he had consistently instead of occasionally preserved forms like *giue*, *hy*, *heo*, *agens* etc. where they seem metrically necessary, and where, whether as part of his native dialect or as items of his literary equipment, the poet seems to have used them.

Finally I have supplied modern punctuation. I regret the necessity for this, as our customs of punctuation are ill suited to the form of Middle English sentences and paragraphs generally, and to the grammatical structure of this poem in particular. Since, however, I have reached many decisions about originality on grounds of meaning, I am obliged to indicate my interpretation of the poem in the conventional manner by punctuation.

The text is supported by a critical apparatus. This records all substantive variants from the text, all morphological variants which may possibly be substantive, the majority of grammatical variants, the majority of dialect variants, and a great many orthographical variants.

The apparatus is thus unusually full, and sets out a more minute collation than is at present in favour.[1] Several circumstances have combined to require this. First, as this introduction will have shown, the nature of the textual problem calls for the full presentation of substantive variants. A 'judicious selection', on whatever principle, is not good enough. In addition, because in the course of *Piers Plowman* studies various theories have been supported by argument from linguistic forms, it seems advisable to record not merely substantive variants, but also linguistic variants to indicate the character of this evidence. The critical apparatus thus serves a second purpose over and above its relation to the textual problem, by exhibiting the variety of linguistic and orthographical forms to be found not merely in different manuscripts, but within individual manuscripts. Finally the nature of the problem of determining the original language of this poem must be shown; this seems best done by a certain increase in the size of an apparatus already made bulky by its other functions.

The apparatus is, on the whole, set out after the conventional practice. The lemma, closed by a square bracket, is followed by its variant readings. The authority for these is shown by the sigils after them, distinct variants being set off by semicolons, and the variants for any lemma by a full stop. This use of punctuation in the apparatus, making it easier to read quickly, seems permissible because no variants of punctuation are recorded.

[1] Compare Greg, 'The Rationale of Copy-Text', pp. 30 ff.

When the text in the lemma follows the reading of T, no sigils are shown in support of it. This means that the reading of the lemma is found in T and in any manuscript whose sigil does not appear among the variants, *except* (*a*) manuscripts there defective; (*b*) manuscripts that omit the line in question; (*c*) manuscripts that omit or vary from a larger phrase of which the lemma forms a part. For instance, at I 24 *þi*] *ȝour* RE; *ȝow* U, positive variation is limited to RE and U, but since (*a*) the manuscripts A, N and H³ are not available here; (*b*) the line is omitted from Ch; and (*c*) the manuscript W varies from the larger lemma *of . . . selue*], support for *þi* is confined to TDH²VHJLKM.

When the text providing the lemma does not follow the reading of T, the lemma is supported by the sigils of all the manuscripts where its reading occurs, the variant of T then appearing as a variant. Thus in Prologue 57 the text reads *hem*; support for this reading against T's *him* is shown by the sigils following the lemma (as, of course, by the variants *heom*, *þaim* and *them*); the sigil of T takes its place after the variant *him*. The same principle applies at Prologue 7 *forwandrit* where T is corrected. Although no sigil follows this lemma because no manuscript reads the adopted variant in this spelling, which has been made to conform to the usage of T, the authority for its adoption is shown by the variants of UJM and RH²L.

Sigils of manuscripts supporting a variant are cited in or from the order TRUDChH²VHJLEAKWNMH³, unless the spelling of the first manuscript in this order where the variant is found is untypical; in such a case the variant is given from a manuscript with a more representative spelling, the sigil of this manuscript is promoted for the occasion, and the customary order thereafter resumed to cite the rest of the manuscripts which have the variant in question. For instance, in Prologue 81 *paryschenes* URHK, the normal order RUHK has been altered to avoid suggesting that a spelling anything like R's *parryssenys* was found in U, H and K. Here, then, only the substantive variation is being recorded.

The support of a variant by several sigils does not guarantee its spelling form in the manuscripts denoted by any other than the first of these sigils. It guarantees, in the first instance, substantive agreement only. This is a natural consequence of the impossibility of citing all variants of all kinds.

It is important to note that the order of sigils in the apparatus signifies no differences of authority. The position of a sigil at the beginning of a series means only that the variant is given in the spelling of the manuscript denoted by that sigil. The arrangement of the variants after a lemma is determined not by the order of citing sigils but by the relation of the variants to the reading adopted in the text and shown in that lemma. This practice serves the main purpose of the apparatus, namely to give the evidence for determining originality with the greatest clarity possible. At the same time it makes easier a more rapid use of the large apparatus; the reader will, I think, easily distinguish substantive variants from accidentals, and recognize the points where only the former are recorded.

Transcription of variants follows, in general, the practice governing transcription of T. Any expansions of contractions or suspensions are printed in italic letters. Where *þ* and *y* are identical I distinguish them if the intention of the scribe is clear. Where the unabbreviated forms of any manuscript are consistent its abbreviations are expanded accordingly. If a manuscript is inconsistent, like, for instance, E and K, which have unsuspended verbal and noun plural endings in *-es*, *-is* and *-ys*, I expand the terminal flourish sometimes used for these endings arbitrarily. I regularly expand the contraction *wᵗ* to w*ith*. As with the text of T, I treat the joins and separations of words in the apparatus arbitrarily, from the point of view of economy of space, but after consideration of the editorial problem. I generally but not invariably reproduce capitals in manuscripts other than T, the main exceptions being certain forms of *M*[1] and *R*[2]. The second of these at least was patently often intended as an undistinguished letter, particularly in the manuscripts Ch and K.

The critical apparatus, then, shows all the evidence available for determining originality; abundant evidence for tests of earlier theories based on inference about the poet's original language; a generous display of the linguistic and orthographical forms in which the poem appears; and sufficient indication of possible sources of linguistic and palæographic information, not directly relevant to the textual problem, to be found in these manuscripts.

[1] Compare Johnson and Jenkinson, *English Court Hand*, i, p. 32 no. 8.
[2] Compare op. cit., p. 43 no. 13.

WILL'S VISIONS OF PIERS PLOWMAN AND DO-WELL

PROLOGUE

IN a som*er* sesoun whanne softe was the sonne *fol.* xxiiij *a*
I shop me into a shroud as I a shep were;
In abite as an Ermyte, vnholy of werkis,
Wente wyde in þis world wondris to here.
But on a may morwenyng on malu*er*ne hilles 5
Me befel a ferly, of fairie me þouȝte:
I was wery [for]wandrit ⁊ wente me to reste
Vndir a brood bank be a bo*ur*n[e] side,
And as I lay ⁊ lenide ⁊ lokide on þe watris
I slom*er*ide into a slepyng, it swiȝede so m*er*ye. 10

1 sesoun] sesyn J; season K. whanne] whenne R; when ChHL; whon V; as UE. softe . . . sonne] I south wente RUE.
2 shop] schaped L. into] in UEM; to D; vndur H; *om* R. a shroud] schroudes DH^{2}L; a shrowedes W; schrubb*es* K; þe schropbys J; schregges Ch. as . . . shep] a schep as y M; a schepe as I J; A scheep as I V. shep] schepe ChHEK; scheep UH^2.
3 abite] an abyte DH; whit M. as] of ChVHJK. Ermyte] *after a* k H^2; herment E. vnholy] von holy R; my holy E; vnworthy L. of] *om* UE. werkis] workes DCh; warkus H.
4 Wente] Y wente RUHJEKW; wente I M; wende I V. wyde] wydene V. in] into L. þis] þe ChWM. world] wordle R; werlde JE. wondris] wond*er*ys EM; wondres ChUH^{2}VLW; wonderes D; wonders JK. here] heare K; hure R; wayte L. *Here* K *adds a line like* **C** I 5.
5 on(1)] vpon R; apon E; in DChV. a] *om* L. may] Mayes VHJ. morwenyng] Morwnynge V; mornynge UDChHJ KWM; morwe RH^2; morn LE. on(2)] RUVHJLEKWM; vpon TDChH^2. mal*ue*rne] maluarne ChL; malu*e*ron J. hilles] hulles DVL; hullis H; hellys M.
6 befel] byfeol L. ferly] farly H; farley case K. of . . . þouȝte] ⁊ fayr*e* me it thowte J. of] A V. fairie] fayre D; feirey Ch; ferrom E.
7 *line om; supplied marginally in another hand* W. wery] weori V. forwandrit] forwandryd UJM; forwandred RH^{2}L; for wandryng D; for wand*er*yng E; of wandringe VHW; of wandrit T; of wandred ChK. ⁊] I RUE; *om* H^2. reste] rist E.
8 Vndir] Vnderneth J; Opon W. bo*ur*ne] burne RDChVHLKWM; bo*ur*nis TU H^{2}E (*a caret below* ur T); broke J. side] brymme L.
9 And] But RE; *om* ChW. as] als J. lenide] lenyd K; lenede RH^{2}W; lenedde D; lened ChLM; leonede V; leoned H; laynyd J; lened me UE. ⁊] *twice* M; I J. lokide] lokyd EK; lokede UH^{2}VM; loked DChHLW; luked R; kokyd J. on] in H. watris] water ChJLW.
10 slom*er*ide] slomeryd DE; slomered LW; slomerde M; slomerd Ch; slombride U; slombryd R; slomberyd J; slombred H^{2}H; slumberde V; sclombrid K. into a] into J; in a RVH; on a UH^{2}LEM; a KW. slepyng] slepe W; sclepe K. it] I RUE; and J. swiȝede] swyed H^{2}LW; swyyd K; swede Ch; sweiued E; sweuedy*n* J; sweuenede R; sweuenyd U; semede M; sownede VH; schewed D. so] ful J; os E; me M. m*er*ye] myrie UH; murie VL.

Þanne gan I mete a m*er*ueillous sweuene,
Þat I was in a wild*er*nesse, wiste I neu*er*e where;
Ac as I beheld into þe Est an heiȝ to þe sonne
I saiȝ a tour on a toft triȝely Imakid;
A dep dale beneþe, a dungeoun þ*er*einne 15
Wiþ depe dikes & derke & dredful of siȝt.
A fair feld ful of folk fand I þ*er*e betwene
Of alle maner of men, þe mene & þe riche,
Worching & wandringe as þe world askiþ.
Su*m*me putte hem to plouȝ, pleiȝede ful selde, 20
In settyng & sowyng swonke ful harde;

11 Þanne] þenne V; þen H; And þan (And *cancelled*) W; And þenne Ch; Than forthw*ith* K; Þer RE. gan] gon VE; gun J; can H. mete] meten H²; metyn M; Meeten V; to mete RUD. a] *om* L. m*er*ueillous] nerwelous R. sweuene] sweue M; swouene R; sweuenes L.
12 a] *om* UChJ. wiste I] wuste I V; I wyste RUHEKW. where] were ChM; ware J; qwer E. *Here* K *adds lines like* **C** I 10–13: *see above*, p. 30.
13 Ac] But RUChJEK; And H²V; *om* HWM. as] *om* H²LM. beheld] beo heold V; by heold L. into] in U; to JKW; vnto E. þe] þo J. Est] eest UH²E; hest M; west Ch. an heiȝ] an hey W; on hey DM; an hiȝe H; on hygh L; an hie Ch; on hye H²K; on heght J; vp RUE. þe(2)] þo J.
14 saiȝ] say H²J; sauh V; sagh L; saw RUDChEW; sawe HK; seyth M. a tour] a t*ur*ret J; autour E. on] in RUH²JEM. toft] twist M; coste R; cost (? coft *or even* toft) E. triȝely] triely UE; tryelyche H²W; tryly R; trylich K; trewlich DCh; treweliche M; trulyche J; treoweliche L; wonderliche V; wondurly H. Imakid] Imaked DChH²; Imakett V; makyd J; maked HW; ontyrid R; atired U; entyred E; ytymbred L. *Here* K *adds a line like* **C** I 16: *see above*, p. 30.
15 A] And sawe a K; *om* J. dep] Deop VHL. dale] dalys J. beneþe] bineoþe VL; beneþyn M; beneght E; þ*er*e benethe H²; al benethe W; bynethen & H; *om* K.
16 depe] deop VHL. dikes] dykys RK; diches UH²L; dychis JM; dyke E; diche H; dich V. derke] darke HL; dyrke E. & dredful] þat dredeful was H. &(2)] *om* RUE. of] to L. siȝt] siht VH²; syȝth R; syth JM.
17 folk] Folkes D; flokke E. fand I] I fonde H. fand] fonde RUDH²VJLEW; found K; fon M. þere] *om* RUE.
18 of(2) . . . riche] mest*er* men makid vppon molde L. of(2)] *om* D. mene] meane K; pore J.
19 *line om* H. Worching] werchyng M; wirching Ch; wyrkyng JE. wandringe] wondringe V. as] als J; so D. þe] þis RJ. world] werlde J; wordle R. askiþ] askys RE; wilnyth L.
20 Summe] But so*m*me H. putte] putten UVH; butty*n* M. hem] þem J; þaim E; hemself M. to] to þe UChH²VHJLEKM. plouȝ] plouth M; ploght E. pleiȝede] pleyed DCh; pleiden U; plaied L; and pleyde RH²E; & pleyden H; & playȝid J; & playeden W; & playyd K; & plydy*n* M; & pleiden he*m* V. ful] but H; for þe E. selde] seelde UH; seilde L; seldene V; seldy*n* M; seldome J; sede E.
21 settyng] seedtyme RUE; sowing J; Eringe VH. &] an H²; And in VW; of R. sowyng] sawyng E; harowing J. swonke] swonken VL; swonkyn RK; þei swonken UW; þei swanke E; & swonken H; and swynkyd J; swynkyn M. ful] wel DLK; wol M; for E. harde] sore H²HLKW.

[Wonne] þ*at* þise wastou*rs* wiþ glotonye destroiȝeþ.
And su*m*me putte hem to pride, ap*ar*ailide hem þ*er*eaftir,
In cunten*au*nce of cloþing comen disgisid.
In p*re*you*rs* & pen*au*nce putten hem manye, 25
Al for loue of oure lord lyuede wel streite
In hope [for] to haue heueneriche blisse,
As ancris & Ermytes þ*at* holden hem in [here] cellis,
Coueite not in cuntre to cairen aboute
For no likerous liflode here likam to plese. 30
And so*m*me chosen [hem] to chaffare, þei cheuide þe bet*ere*

22 Wonne þ*at*] wo*n*nyn þat M; Wan that K; and wonnen þat UW (*over erasure* W); whanne þat D; Whom þ*at* TCh; Þat RE; that many H^2; þ*at* many of J; þat monie of VH; þan þ*er* y sygh L. þise] þies J; þis E; þese UDH; þes RChK; þeos V; *om* H^2LW. wastou*rs*] wastorys now RE; wastours in þe worlde H^2W (in þe worlde *cancelled* W). wiþ] In VHJ. destroiȝeþ] destroyen RU; destroye J; distroyen HKW; distroie Ch; distroy E; dystroeth H^2; dystroith M; distruen V; destruyed L.
23 And] *om* RUEW. su*m*me] *om* M. putte] putten UVH; puttyn M; putt E; put ChH^2JKW. hem(1)] heom L; þem J; þaim E; *om* M. pride] pruide VL; þe play & p*r*ide J. ap*ar*ailide] aparayldyn M; apparaylde*n* VL; parayled E; & apparelid K; & aparayleden H; and p*er*alyde R; aparayleth H^2; & playde J. hem(2)] þem J; þaim E; *cancelled* W; *om* D. þere] *om but added in margin* D.
24 cunten*au*nce] quoyntyse H. of] and K. cloþing] glothyng H^2. comen] comyn J; þei comen U; þey comyn R; þey kemy*n* M; comen in W; came in al K; þei conen hem H; þai can þaim E; queinteliche V; crafteliche L. disgisid] degysed L; de-Gyset V; disgyse H; degyse E.
25 In] To RUH^2VEW. p*re*you*rs*] prayere RVJE. &] and to RUV. putten] puttyn K; putte W; putt E; put ChH^2J; þ*er*e puttyn M. hem] heom VL; þem J; þaim E. manye] monye VL; ful many J; to manyse E.
26 Al] and H^2W; *om* RUVHJE. for] *in margin, another hand* H^2. loue] þe loue RUH^2HJEW. lyuede] lyueden UVH LW; lyvyden K; lyfuyd J; leued Ch; leueden D; leuedy*n* M; lyvelode E; leuen-den H^2. wel] ful RUChH^2VHJE; *om* M. streite] strayte RDHJ; strayght K; harde VE.
27 In] Al in H^2. for] RUDH^2VHJEW; *om* TChLKM. haue] haue after ChL; haue þ*er* for W; haue for her mede M. heueneriche blisse] heouene to huyre L.
28, 29 *touched up, another hand* H.
28 As] Als J. holden hem] lyuen R; leven E; dwelle W. holden] holdyn K; holde H^2; holdeþ V; hold*ith* H; hody*n* M; helde J. hem] heom L; þem J. here] her*e* RUDH^2W; her ChHJK; heore VL; þair E; *erasure* T; *om* M. cellis] houses L.
29 Coueite] Couet J; Coueyten DH^2; Coueytyn M; Couetyn K; and coueyte U; And coueyty*n* R; And couette*s* E; Comen Ch. not] nouȝt DRChJM; noght ULE; nauȝt H^2. in] in þe RUE; to H^2. cuntre] court L. to] forto J. cairen] karyn M; caryen RUDChVHKW; carry E; scayre J. aboute] abowtyn M.
30 no] none RVM; *om* W. likerous] lycoras K. here] her ChHK; heore VL; þer J; þair E. likam] lykham H^2; lykames U; lykamys RE; lyh*a*m J; lyke hem D; body M. plese] plesen DM; please EK; like L.
31 And] *om* RH^2JEW. chosen . . . to] RUD; chosyn þaim to E; chese hem to J; chosen to TCh; chosen H^2VHWM; chosyn K; chesen L. þei cheuide] þey cheuyd RE; þei cheueden Ch; þey cheuen DH^2LM (s *added to* þei *above line, same hand* L); þei cheue J; to cheuen W; to chevyn K; to cheeuen V; to preue H. þe] wele þe J.

As it semiþ to oure si3t þ*at* suche men þriuen.
And so*m*me mer*þ*is to make as mynstral*is* conne,
And gete gold wiþ here gle giltles, I trowe.
Ac Iap*er*is & iangleris, Iudas children, 35
Fonden hem fantasies & foolis hem make,
And haue wyt at wille to wirche 3if hem list.
Þat poule p*re*chiþ of hem I dar not p*ro*ue it here:
Qui loquitur turpiloquium [is] luciferis hyne.
Bidd*er*is & begg*er*is faste aboute 3ede 40
Til here bely & here bagge were bratful ycrammid;

32 J *corrupts to*: Os semyth be þe marchaundys þat mychil welth haue. semiþ to] ys sene in RUE. to] in H. þat] *cancelled* W; *om* M. suche men] þei so H. suche] siche UE; swyche W. þriuen] thryvyn K; thrive W; þryueth D; chewen L; scholden VH.

33 *divided from following after* Menstrals M. so*m*me] su*m*me men R. mer*þ*is] myrthis J; myrthes RUDH²HEK; murthes L; Murþhes V. make] maken VM. as] als J. mynstral*is*] Minstralles ChE; mynstrals HJL; mynstrell*es* K; menstralys R; menstrales D; menestralles W; Munstrals V; thys Menstrals M; munstralle *changed to* mynstralle H². conne] connyn K; kone J; kanne E; meleden L.

34 *line om* V. And] þat HK; *om* RUEM. gete] geten H²HLW. gold . . . gle] wiþ heore gleo gold L. gold] þem gode J. wiþ] whyth M. here] her RHK; þair E; þ*er* J. gle] glee EKWM; gleo H. giltles] gylelas L; gylefully K; gylously W; synneles RUDHJE; senles M; synfullyche H². I trowe] god graunte L. I] þai E.

35 *line om* K. Ac] Bot ChH²VHJL; And E; For W. & iangleris] & Ianglers & Langlo*urs* D. Iudas] iudacys R; Iudases U; ben Iudas (ben *cancelled*) H; & iudas E. children] chyldryn RDCh; childer J.

36 Fonden] Fondyn K; Founden VLWM; Foundes J; Fynden H²; Fyndon E; gon fyndyn RU; þa feynen H. hem(1)] heom L; þaim E; hem in KW; hem to D; hem on M; meny R. fantasies] fantesy J. &] for L. hem(2)] þem J; þaim E; heo heom L. make] maken UChH²HEWM; makyn RK; makes J; maaden V; feynen L.

37 *line om* J. haue] hauen M; han RUH² HLW; hase E; habbeþ V. wyt] her*e* whyttes M. at] atte M; at her RUH; at heor V; at þair E. wirche] worche RChHLW; worchen H²V; wurche UD; werche M; wirke E; work K. 3if] 3ef ChL; what RUE. hem] þaim E; hy*m* DCh; þei HL. list] liste ChK; lust H²; luste V; lykys RE; liketh U; like M; wolde HL.

38 Þat] What H; þ*at* þat RU. poule] paul DE. p*re*chiþ] prechyt M; prechet H; p*re*chys E; p*re*ches J; p*re*chid K. of hem] hem of H². hem] heom L; þaim E; þam J. dar] may W; wol U. not] nou3t ChM; noght UE; nau3t H²; *om* KW; p*ro*ue] p*ro*uen U; p*ro*uyn R; preue ChH²; preouen V; tell E; sey H. it] *om* RUV HEM. here] heere V.

39 *as two lines divided after turpiloquium* V. *Qui*] Bote *Qui* L. *loquitur turpiloquium*] *turpe loquitur* DM. *turpiloquium*] *turpeloquium* W. is] ys RUDChH²HJLEKWM; his T; Hee is V.

40 Bidd*er*is & begg*er*is] beggere*s* and byddere*s* RUEK. Bidd*er*is] Than bidders W. aboute] abouten M. 3ede] 3eden HW; 3edyn UK; 3eode L; eoden V; ryden E; Rennen M.

41 Til] To E; And L. here(1)] her RHK; heor VL; þ*er* J; þair E; þe W. bely] belyes RUJ; belyys K; balies L; byllys E; Bagges VH. here(2)] her ChRHK; heore VL; þ*er* J; þair E; þe W. bagge] bagg*es* RUJLEK; Balies VH. were] were*n* VH; ware RM; weore L; was DH²; *om* E. bratful] bretful H²LM; bretfulle Ch; bred ful RUD; wi*th* bred full E; full JW; fully K; faste VH. ycrammid] Icrammed H²; ycro*m*med LW; Icro*m*met V; crammyd U; crammed RD; cramed JM; cro*m*med H; be cromed E; filled Ch.

Flite þanne for here foode, fouȝten at þe ale.
In glotonye, god wot, go þei to bedde, |
And risen vp wiþ ribaudrie as robertis knaues; *fol.* xxiiij *b*
Slep ⁊ sleuþe sewiþ hem eu*er*e. 45
Pilgrimes ⁊ palm*er*is pliȝten hem togid*er*e
For to seke seint Iame ⁊ seintes at rome;
Wenten forþ in here wey wiþ many wise talis,
And hadde leue to leiȝe al here lif aftir.
Ermytes on an hep, wiþ hokide staues, 50
Wenten to walsyngham, ⁊ here wenchis aftir;
Grete lobies ⁊ longe þat loþ were to swynke
Cloþide hem in copis to be knowen from oþ*er*e;

42 Flite þanne] Fliten þan Ch; þei flyteþ R; þei fliten U; Þai Flyte E; Flytteden ⁊ D; And flytyd fast K; Fayted J; Fayteden HM; They faited W; Fayto*urs* H^{2}L; Feyneden hem V. here] her RChHK; heore VL; þ*er* J; þair E; he M. fouȝten . . . ale] at þe nale foghten L. fouȝten] fouten D; and foughten UHWM; ⁊ fowghtyn K; and fiȝten Ch; and fyȝthen R; ⁊ fyght E. at . . . ale] atte alle V; atte hale M; at þe nale UChHEW (the *cancelled* W); at nale H^{2}K.
43 wot] whote M. go] gon ChH^{2}VHLM; goon K. þei] þai JE; thay K; heo V. bedde] bedd*es* E.
44 And] an H. risen] rysyn EK; riseth DV; risyth L; rys J. vp] *om* DKM. ribaudrie] rybaldre E; rybaldy L; rybaudye RDH^{2}VHW; rebaudy Ch; rebaude M. as] tho H^{2}LM; þis V; þese H; *om* J. robertis] Robertes ChRM; Roberdes UD H^{2}VHJLW; Rybald*es* K; rowt*es* of E. knaues] knafvys E; hewyn K; hyne W.
45 Slep] Sleep UVH; Sclep R; Also sclepe K; Sory slep L; Slogardie W; Slouth J. sleuþe] sleuȝþe V; slouthe URDL; sclowth K; mochull slouthe M; sorye *inserted before* sleuthe *by late corrector* H^2; slep J. sewiþ . . . eu*er*e] euer heom sywith L. sewiþ] seweþ DH^{2}HW; suweþ V; sueth U; sewen Ch; sewyn K; sewys E; sewes J; folwyth M. hem] þaim E; þame J. eu*er*e] hewere M. *Here* J *leaves space for about* 5 *lines.*
46 Pilgrimes] Now pylgrymes K; Pylgrymers H. pliȝten . . . togid*er*e] togedres heom plyghten L. pliȝten] plihten V; plight E; plyten M; plytyth R; pyghten H; pight W; pyke J. hem] þaim E.
47 For] *om* RH^{2}EKWM. seke] sekyn K; seche VHLM. Iame] Iames M; Iamys EK; Ieme V; ȝame Ch. seintes] rerykes L. at] in RUE; of WM.
48 Wenten] wente H^2; went DChJL; They went W; and wente RE; Wentyn hem K; wendyt M. in] on JLK. here] her RChHJK; heore VL; þair E. many] mony VLE. wise talis] tales wyse L. wise] vayn H.
49 And] At E; þan J. hadde] hadden UHM; haden L; hedden V; hedde E; had þei J. to] for to HJEM. leiȝe] lyȝe H^{2}Ch; lyȝen V; lye RUHJW; lyen DLKM; lee E. here] her ChHK; heore VL; þ*er* J; þair E. lif] lyues UE. aftir] tyme VL.
50 *line om* VH. Ermytes] hernyt*es* R. on an] on a D; a grete H^2. an hep] hepys J. hokide] hokyd JKM; hokede RW; hoked DChLE; hogete H^2. staues] staues hyeden L.
51 *line om* VH. Wenten] Wentyn KM; wente RDH^{2}JE; To wende L. to] unto J. here] heore L; þ*er* J; þair E.
52 Grete] w*ith* grete J. lobies] lobres V; lob*urs* H; losels E; globis M; polys J. þat . . . were] loth for RUE. were] weren HM; weryn K; weore VL. swynke] worche K; werche M.
53 Cloþide] Clothid JK; Cloþed RDChW; Cloþeden VH; Clothen L; Clothys E; Claddyn M; Gloseth H^2. hem] heom L; þem J; *om* E. be] ben UJM; beo VL. knowen] knowyn JEKM; knowe RUH^2 LW. from oþ*er*e] for breþeren VH.

Shopen hem Ermytes here ese to haue.
I fond þ*er*e Freris, alle þe foure ordris, 55
Prechinge þe peple for p*ro*fit of þe wombe;
Gloside þe gospel as h[e]m good likide;
For coueitise of copis construide it as þei wolde.
Manye of þise maistris may cloþe hem at lyking
For here mony & here marchaundise meten togid*er*e. 60
Siþen charite haþ ben chapman & chief to shryue lordis
Manye ferlis han fallen in a fewe ȝeris.
But holy chirche & [hy] holden bet togid*er*e

54 *line om* U. Shopen] schopyn REK; Schope Ch; Schapen L; And schopen H; And schapyn M; And su*m*me schopen V; They shopen W; And madyn J. hem] heom L; þaim E; hem to DH; to V. Ermytes] such clothis K. here] her ChHK; heore VL; þeir J; þair E. ese] eese H; ease EK; ayse L. to] for to HJE. haue] hauen L. *Here* RH^{2}E *read additional lines; see above*, pp. 47, 49, 50.
55 I] But I D; *om* M. fond] fand E; Font V; foundyn K; Fondy*n* M. Freris] þe frere*s* RDHL; of freris M; freris forsothe J. alle] of alle H^{2}K. þe] *om* H^{2}M.
56 Prechinge] P*re*chand J. þe(1)] to þe W; to H^2. peple] pepyl J; pepule H; people LK. p*ro*fit] profyght W. þe(2)] her*e* RUD; her HJK; heore V; þair E; hem M. wombe] wombes UV; wombys RHJE; paunche L; selue*n* M.
57 Gloside] Glosid UJK; glosede R; Glosed Ch; Gloseden L; Glosedyn M; And glosed H^{2}W; Gloseth D; Glosys E; Glosynge VH. þe] þeo L. hem] RUChH^2 VHJKM; heom L; them W; þaim E; him TD. good] leof L; self W; silf H. likide] lykyd JK; lykede RM; liked H^{2}W; likyth L; lyketh DVH; lik*es* E; þouȝt Ch.
58 *line om* E. coueitise of] q*ua*yntnes of her J. construide] construyd K; construed UH^{2}W; construd R; constrewed Ch; co*n*strudyn M; construeth DV; construen H; þey co*n*struen L; constru J. it] *om* H^{2}JWM. as . . . wolde] at wille D; ille V; ful yuel H; aȝeyn kynde L. wolde] woldyn M.
59, 60 *transposed* E.
59 Manye] Mony L; For many M; For monye VH. þise] þis VW; þese UDH^{2}H; thes ChK; þo R; þ*er* J; þir E; heore L; *om* M. maistris] masters K. may] mown R; mow U; mowe H^2; mowe*n* VH; ben M; *om* L. cloþe . . . lyking] be clothed the better H; wiþ couetise heom cloþen L. cloþe] cloþen RUVKW; close H^2; cloþid M. hem] þem J; þaim E; hym D; *om* M. at] at her K.
60 For] *om* W. here(1)] her RChK; heore L; þair E; *om* VHJM. here(2)] her ChR HK; heore V; þair E; *om* DH^{2}JLM. marchaundise] marchandises D; Marchau*n*die V. meten] mety*n* RUEK; mete D; meete*n* ofte V; metten H; mettyn J; macchyn M.
61 Siþen] sythe R; Syth H^{2}HW; Sethen D; Sethyn J; Sethe M; Seþþe V; Seþ Ch; Sen L; Sir E. charite] Freeris HM. haþ] hase E; han H; *om* M. ben] be RDH^{2}VW; byn K; beo L; aryn M. chapman] chapmon VL; chapmen H. &] *om* V. chief] chosyn M. shryue] schryff K; schriue*n* V; schryuy*n* M; scriuen J.
62 Manye] Mony VL; Fele RE. ferlis] farlyes H; farleys K. han] haue JK; hath DE. fallen] fallyn JEM; falle RDH^{2}W; bifallen H; bifalle V; Ifall K. in] ryȝt in H^2. ȝeris] ȝerus R.
63 But] An but H. chirche] cherche R; churche DH. & hy] biginne VH. hy] he UDH^{2}JM; þei TRChL; þai E; charite KW. holden bet] þe better to holde H. holden] holdyn RJKM; holde UDV. bet] bett*er* K; *om* RUJLE.

Þe moste meschief on molde is mountyng vp faste.
Þ*ere* p*re*chide a p*ar*done*r* as he a prest were; 65
Brouȝte forþ a bulle wiþ bisshopis selis
And seide þ*at* hymself miȝte assoile hem alle
Of falsnesse of fastyng & of auowes broken.
Lewide men leuide [hym] wel & likide his speche;
Comen vp knelynge to kissen his bulle. 70
He bunchi[de] hem wiþ his breuet & bleri[de] here eiȝe[n]
And rauȝte wiþ his rageman ryngis & brochis.
Þus [ȝe gyuen ȝoure] gold glotonis to helpe

64 on] vpo*n* H; on þis U; of W; of þis R; of þe E. is mountyng] mou*n*teþ RV; mountith U; mount*es* E; is toward M. vp faste] vp wel faste DH^2H (wel *over erasure* H); wol faste M; on hye K; an hie W.
65 p*r*echide] p*r*echeth D; p*r*echys E; priked ford J. a p*ar*don*er*] of p*ar*don a p*ar*don*er* E. as . . . prest] a p*r*est as he UJ; prist as he E; a p*r*est as it H; a prest as þouȝ he R. prest were] preost weore L.
66 Brouȝte] brouȝthe R; Brouthe M; And broughte UVHJKW. forþ] vp V. a bulle] bullys RE. bisshopis] bisscoppes J; bischopp EW; mony bysschopes L. selis] seaulles E.
67 þat] *om* RUE. hymself] he H^2. hym] hem W. self] seolue L; silf H; selfe he E. assoile] asoylen VH; asoylyn JKM; soile L. hem] heom L; þaim E. alle] vchon L.
68 falsnesse] falshode W. of(2)] and VW. fastyng] fastynges L; fastyng*us* H. &] of lesynges H^2; *om* RUDJLM. auowes] wowes H^2E; vouwes VHJLWM; a wow D. broken] brokyn RE; Ibroken VJL; Ibrokyn M; ybroke H^2KW; breking Ch.
69 Lewide] Lewyd H^2; Lewed DJL; lewde ChKM; þe lewid UE; þe lewede V; The lewed W; þe lewde R; These lewyd H. men] folk W. leuide hym] hit loued L; it lyked W. leuide] levyd EK; leued RDChH; leueden J; lyueden U; likede V; likedyn M; lyked H^2. hym] RUVHJEM; it TCh; *om* DH^2K. wel] *om* UJ. likide] lykyd RE; liked DChL; lykeden H; leued H^2W; leuedy*n* M; leeueþ V; allowyd K; lykyk J. his] hyse M; wel his UJ; *over original* him, *another ink* H. speche] leodene L; wordys M; *over original* wel, *another ink* H.
70 Comen] Co*m*myn KM; come RD; Com E; Thei comen W; and comen UVH; & kemyn J. vp knelynge] vp kneolynge HL; knelyng vp RU; knelyng vppon kneys E. to] and VHEM. kissen] kyssyn RJE; kussen U; kusse L; kessen D; kyssede*n* H; cusseden V; kestyn M. his] þe J. bulle] bulles HK; bullys RM.
71, 72 *transposed* L.
71 He] And he Ch. bunchide] bunchyd K; bunchede M; bunched H^2; bonchede V; bonched LW; bunchiþ T; buncheth Ch; bonches D; blessid U; blessed R; blyssyd E; blessud (*over erasure*) H; blenchet J. hem] heom L; þaim E; *om* J. breuet] breued L; brevett*es* K. &] *om* DL. bleride] blerid UH^2HJKM; blered RDVLW; blerett E; bleriþ TCh. here] her ChHJK; heore VL; þair E. eiȝen] V; eyeȝen Ch; eyen UDH^2KW; eyȝnen L; eyes RE; yȝen H; yen J; eiȝe T; eye M.
72 And] And he L; he M; *om* RUE. rauȝte] rauhte V; rauthe M; raut J; rauȝthe he*m* R; Raughte hym U. rageman] ragman DChHJEKW; raggeman U; Ragemon VL. ryngis & brochis] broches and rynges RUDEM.
73 Þus] ȝus M. ȝe] RUH^2VHJLWM; þei TDCh; þai E; thay K. gyuen] geven E; ȝyuen H; ȝiueþ V; ȝeuen RUDChH^2 LM; ȝeuyn JK; ȝeve W; ȝouen T. ȝoure] HRUH^2JWM; oure VL; here TD; her ChK; þair E. gold] goulde J; gode Ch; good*us* H. glotonis] Glotonye V. helpe] helpen V; helpyn RM; gladen L; please K.

And leniþ it loselis þat leccherie haunten.
Were þe bisshop yblissid ⁊ worþ boþe hise eris 75
His sel shulde not be sent to disseyue þe peple.
It is not be þe bisshop þat þe boy prechiþ,
Ac þe parissh prest ⁊ þe pardoner parte þe siluer
Þat þe pore peple of þe parissh shulde haue ȝif þei ne were.
Personis ⁊ parissh prestis pleynide hem to here bisshop 80
Þat here parissh w[ere] pore siþþe þe pestilence tyme,
To haue a licence ⁊ leue at lundoun to dwelle,

74 leniþ] leneth H[2]VL; lenyn RUJ; lenen ChHM; levyth K; leuen W; lattes E. it] hit to RUDVE; hyth to (yth *over erasure another ink*) H; at W; þese M. loselis] lorelles K. leccherie] lecchorie Ch; lychery J; lichory E; lechories H. haunten] hauntyn JK; haunteth DH[2]; hauntyt M; hauntes E.
75 Were] DH[2]JKM; weore VL; where W; But were TRUChHE. þe] þeo L. yblissid] yblessid UH[2]K; yblessed RChL; Iblesset V; blissyd JEW; blessyd DH. ⁊] *added above line* W; or D; *om* M. boþe] boþen M. hise] hese W. eris] eares H; heres W; eryn M; eyen K.
76 His . . . sent] Heo scholde not beo so hardi V; þei schulden not be so hardy H. sel] seel DH[2]J; seal ULKM; selys R; seaules E. shulde] suld E; sold J; schul H[2]. not] nat ChH[2]; noght UE; nouth M. be] ben M; beon L; be so Ch. sent] send E. to . . . peple] þeo people to deseyue L. disseyue] disseyuyn M; disave E; seyuyn J; deceyue so V; bigyle so H; sustein Ch. peple] people K; *after* l Ch.
77 It . . . not] I trow noght it be E. It is] y trowe it is U; I trowe hit be R; Saue hit nis V; He is D. not] RVJLW; nouȝt H[2]; noght U; nouth M; not al THK; nat al Ch; nouȝt al D. be] for RUE; born M. bisshop] bishop will (will *above line, similar hand*) W. þe boy] þey boþe D; þey boþin M. prechiþ] precheþ RUDChVHLW; prechyt JM; prechys E; preched H[2].
78 Ac] But UDChH[2]VHLKW (*over original* Ac, *another ink* H); but for RE. parissh . . . pardoner] pardoner and þe parichsprest RE. parissh] *om* WM. prest] preost L. þe pardoner] he VL. parte] parten UChHL; partyn JKM; parteth D; partiþ W; departe V; departen E; departyn R; departid H[2]. þe] þair E. siluer] syluur J; seluer VM; seoluer L; monoye W.
79 *line om* M. þe(1) . . . haue] haue schulde þe pore parisschens V. þe(1)] *om* H[2]. pore] *om* W. peple] people LK; men E; *om* RH. of . . . parissh] *om* RUJEW. shulde] suld J. haue] hauen J; depart E; departyn R. ȝif] ȝef L; ȝif þat RUV; nyf W. þei] þay LE; thay K; heo V. ne were] ne weore V; nere K; hem pilden W.
80 Personis] Than persons W. ⁊ . . . prestis] ⁊ prouenders H; and vicaries WM; prestly J. parissh] parsch Ch. prestis] preostes L. pleynide] pleynyd J; pleyned DChW; pleynyden K; pleynen U; pleyne E; pleynyt M; plenyth H[2]; playneþ V; playnen RL; han playned H. hem] þaim E; *om* RH[2]VHLKW. here] her HRJ; heore V; þe DChLKWM; *om* E. bisshop] Bisschops V; Bischoppis E; bisschoppus H.
81 Þat] At E. here . . . tyme] sen þe furste pestilence heore parysch weore pore L. here] her RChHJ; heore V; þair E; their K. parissh] parsch Ch; parisches H[2]; paryschenes URHK; cherchys M; kirkes E. were] DH[2]EK; weryn M; was TChW; ben RUJ; haþ ben V; han ben H. pore] pure E. siþþe] sithe H[2]; sith HW; syþen RU; syþyn M; seþþe V; seþe D; seþ ChE; syns K; seyn J. þe] *om* HJ. tyme] *om* V.
82 *line om* D. To haue] And han H; And askeþ V; Thay asked W; To E. a] *om* ChVHJLEKM. licence] licance E; leue VH. ⁊] and a RU; *om* W. leue] lyve E: lycence VH; *om* W

To synge for symonye for siluer is swete.
Þere houide an hundrit in houuis of silk,
Seriauntis it semide þat seruide at þe barre; 85
Pleten for penis & [poundide] þe lawe, |
A[c] nouȝt for loue of oure lord vnlose here lippes ones. *fol.* xxv *a*
Tho[u] miȝtest betere mete myst on maluerne hilles
Þanne gete a mom of here mouþ til mony be shewid.
I sauȝ bisshopis bolde & bacheleris of deuyn 90
Become clerkis of acountis þe king for to serue;
Archideknes & denis þat dignites hauen

83 synge] syngen U; syngyn M; synggyn J; synge there H²VHLKW. symonye] Sir symonye E. siluer] seluer VM; seoluer L. *Here* E *adds two lines derived from* **B** Prol 112 *or* **C** I 139: *see above*, p. 30.
84–102 no collation from K: *see above*, p. 37.
84 Þere] Than W. houide] houyd RUE; houed DChH²HL; houedyn JM; houeþ V; hoved þer W. an] a HEM. hundrit] hundrid UM; hundret V; hundreth E; hundred ChRH²JL; hondred DHW. in . . . silk] in sylkyn houuys M; of silkyn howfys E; alle with selk howes L. houuis] howys R; howes Ch. silk] selk UH²V.
85 Seriauntis] Seriaundes J; Seriauns V; Sergans M; Sariawntis H. it] þo R; þei U; thay K; þaim E. semide] semyd JE; semede R; semed ChH²HLW; semeden U; semedyn DM; semeþ V. þat] at E; to DVH; *om* RU. seruide] seruyd E; serued ChLW; seruyn DJM; seruen H²V; serue H; pletede R; pletiden U. at þe] atte V; at ChH².
86 Pleten . . . poundide] For penyes & for powndis pladden H. Pleten] Pleden V; þat pledeyn J; To pleden W; to pletyn M; Pletand E; þei pleted R; þei pletide U; Pleded en DL. for . . . lawe] þe lawe for penyis & powndes J. penis] panyes L; pons V. poundide] U; poundyt R; poundys M; poundes DH²VLW; ponderys E; poynteþ T; pointen Ch.
87 Ac] RU; But HW; And TDChH²JLM; Wald E; *om* V. nouȝt] nouth M; nauȝt H²; Not VL; non RUE; *om* HW. loue] lof J; þe loue RUHW. vnlose] vnlouse L; vnlese M; vnlesyn J; vnloseþ V; not vnlese W; vnclose Ch; opyn E; not open H; opnyd RU. here] her HJ; heore VL; his UE. lippes] lyppus H; leppys M; lippe J. ones] onus H²; oonus H; *om* RUE.
88 Thou] þou RUDChH²VJLEWM; For þou H; Tho T. miȝtest] might EW. betere] bettur HJ; bet M. mete] meten V; metyn JM; meouen L. myst] þe myst RH²VHEM; a myst W; *om* L. on] of E; *om* L. maluerne] maluarne L. hilles] hellis M; hulles DVL; hullus H.
89 gete] geten VL; getyn RJM. a . . . mouþ] of hys mouth a mum E. mom] mombe W; word M. here] her RChHJ; heore VL. mouþ] mougth W; mowȝt R. til] or ChJEM; but H². be] beo L; were H; wer E; weore V. *Here* EM *copy ll.* 96–7.
90 I] *om* W. sauȝ] saw ChE; say DH²JL; seyth M; sauh þer V; saw þer RUH; *om* W. bisshopis] erchebisschopes U. bolde] bysy L; *om* EW. &] *om* J. bacheleris] bacheris J. deuyn] þe deuyne J; dyuine boþe W.
91 Become] Bekomyn JM. clerkis] *twice, second cancelled* T. acountis] acounptys M; acomtes H²; countes Ch; acount RUVH; a courte E. þe] þeo L. for] *om* W. serue] seruen V; seruyn RM.
92 *divided from following after* preche W. Archideknes] Erchedenes M; I saw þer archedeknys RU. denis] dekenes H²V. þat] & E; the M. dignites] dignyte RUVJE; dignyty H; diuine W. hauen] hauyn R; haue DJ; han H; haueth L; havys E; haddyn M; *om* W.

To preche þe peple ⁊ pore men to fede
Ben ylope to lundoun be leue of hire bisshop,
And ben clerkis of þe kinges bench þe cuntre to shende. 95
Barouns [and] burgeis ⁊ bondage also
I sauȝ in þat sem[b]le as ȝe shuln here aftir,
Baxteris ⁊ bocheris ⁊ breusteris manye,
Wollene websteris and weueris of lynen,
Taillours, t[okk]eris ⁊ to[ll]eris boþe, 100
Masonis, mynours, ⁊ manye oþere craftis,
As dikeris ⁊ delueris þat doþ here dede ille
And driueþ forþ þe longe day wiþ *dieu saue dame emme*;

93 To] For to EM; shold W. preche] prechen U; prechyn JM. peple] people L. pore] pure E; the pore H^{2}W. to] eueremore to W. fede] feede V.
94 Ben] Beon VL; Beth DW; þei ben U; þey beþ R; Or E. ylope] Ilopyn M; lope L; lopen UH^{2}VHW; lopyn R; loppyn E; lepyn J. be] þorw RU; to E; for J. leue . . . bisshop] byshopes leue W. leue] lofe J. of] on E. hire] here RUD H^{2}M; her ChHJ; heore VL; þair E. bisshop] Beschop M; byschopes H^{2}VJL; Bischoppis E; bisschopus H.
95 And ben] ȝe M. And] To VHW. ben] be DW; beon L; beþ R; er E; become H. clerkis] clerke H^2. þe] *om* M. kinges bench] chauncellery L. bench] benke E; huntch (?) M. cuntre] contreys L; comune W; peple E; people M. shende] schenden M; schynde R.
96, 97 *transposed* W; *misplaced after line* 89 EM; *in their place here* E *reads a passage containing lines like* **B** Prologue 92, 94, 98–9 *or* **C** I 90, 92–3, 126–7: *see above*, p. 30.
96 and(1)] ⁊ RDChH^{2}VHLEWM; *om* TUJ. burgeis] burgeysys R; burgeises H; burches E; bugeys M. bondage] bondeagys RUJ; Bonde men VHLEM. also] alse RL; als JEW.
97 I sauȝ] Than sawe I W. sauȝ] saw RUE; sawe ChH; say DH^{2}JL; seyth M. in þat] þat in Ch. in] on L; *om* W. þat] a J; *om* E. semble] UDChH^{2}VHJ LEWM; semele T; symple R. as] als JE. shuln] schul RUDChH^{2}VH; scholyn J; shal EWM. here] heren UV; herin JM; see E; seen H. aftir] herafter R; heraftur V.
98 *run together with following* M. Baxteris] Bakeris UChH^{2}VHW; Bachers E; I saw þer bakesteres R. ⁊(1)] *om* VJM. bocheris] bouchiers L; brewesteres R; brewers EW; *om* M. ⁊(2)] *om* R. breusteris] brewstars H; browsteres D; bocheres RE. manye] monye VLE; boþe U; ⁊ kokys R; *om* M.
99 *line om* VH. Wollene] wollen DJW; Wolne E; Wullen UCh; And eken wollen L; *om* M. websteris] webbes W; *om* M. and] aswa ⁊ E; *om* U. weueris] weouers L. of] *om* E. lynen] lynene RM; lynnen L; lynnene U; lynyn Ch; lennyn E; lyne J.
100 *line om* VH. tokkeris] Tokers W; and towkers H^2; toucheris U; ⁊ toucherys M; and Taucheris (*cancelled for* and thackers, *similar hand*) J; tauerneres RCh; tanneris (? tauneris) T; ⁊ tynkelers E; ⁊ tornors L; ⁊ Souters D. tolleris] UH^{2}JLEWM; tokkeris TD; tynkeres R; Tapsters Ch. boþe] *cancelled for* of merkettes *by late corrector* H^2.
101 mynours] ⁊ mynours DH^{2}HJLEM. manye] mony VLE.
102 As] Als E; and UH^{2}J; ac R; *om* VHW. dikeris] Dichers HL. doþ . . . dede] heore dedes don L. doþ] don RUChH^{2}VW; done JM; doon H; doys E. here] her HJ; er Ch; heore V; þair E. dede] werk RU; dedes H^{2}VEM; dedys J; dedus H. ille] hille M; euel Ch; euyl E; yuol H.
103 Here collation from K **resumes.** And] And heuere M; þat ULK; To R. driueþ] dryuen UChH^{2}HL; dryvyn K; dryue RDJEWM. longe] *om* M. wiþ] *om* D. *dieu*] dieuȝ H; deu vus V; douce M; duke (uke *altered to* iu *and* vous *added above line by late corrector*)H^2. *saue*] salve K; sa RU; saynt E; gard D; *om* M.

Cookis & here knaues crieþ 'hote pyes, hote!
Goode gees & gris; go we dyne, go we!' 105
Tauerners to hem tolde þe same:
'W[hit] wyn of osay, & wyn of gascoyne,
Of þe ryn & of þe rochel, þe rost to defie!'
Al þis I sauȝ slepyng & seue siþes more.

104 *divided from following after* pyes J. here] her RChHJK; heore VL; *om* E. knaues] knaffys E; knawys R. crieþ] crien ChH²VHJLM; cried E; criede W; cryden RU; cryyd K.
105 gees . . . gris] grys & gees L. gees] geys W. &] & eke M.
106 Tauerners] And tauerners H²J; Than tauerners W. to . . . same] þe same to þe folk told W; hem tolde þilke same tale H. to hem] to heom L; til hem D; vnto þaim E; on tyll hym M; tolden to hem (tolden *cancelled*) J; tolled hem and R; tollid hem and U; titly Ch. tolde] toldyn J; tellyd E; tolde hem RUChH² (*late corrector cancels* hem *and adds* n *to* tolde H²); tolde treoweliche L. same] same tale VK.
107 Whit] L; White KW; wiþ white UR; Whit qwyte E; with DH²JM; Wiþ TCh; wiþ good V; Good H. osay] asay DL; asoye J; Gaskoyne V; gaskyne H. &] & þe H; *late corrector* adds whyte H². wyn(2)] *om* RUEM. of(2)] *om* U. gascoyne] gasconne E; Oseye VH.
108 Of þe(1)] Of VW; þe HM; And þe J; And L. ryn] Ruyn V; rene E; ryuer W. &] ad V; *om* DChM. of þe(2)] þe RH²HJ; of DVEW; *om* L. to] to do M. defie] defyȝe H.
109 *line om* VH. Al] *om* RUE. I sauȝ] saw I RUW. sauȝ] sawe ChE; say DJL; seigh K; sey M. slepyng] sclepyng K; my selue slepynge U; my self R. seue] seuen RUChJ; seuene DH²W; sevyn K; sewyn M; seoue L; vij E. siþes] siþe DW.

I

What þe mounteyne [be]meniþ, ⁊ ek þe [m]erke dale,
And ek þe feld ful of folk I shal ȝow faire shewe.
A louely lady of lire in lynene ycloþid
Com doun fro þ*at* [clyf] ⁊ callide me faire,
And seide 'sone, slepist þ*ou*? sest þ*ou* þis peple, 5
How besy þei ben aboute þe mase?
Þe moste p*ar*tie of þis peple þ*at* passiþ on þis erþe,
Haue þei worsshipe in þis world þei kepe no bet*ere*:
Of oþ*er* heuene þanne here holde þei no tale.'

1 What] wat M; Qwat J; Now what RE W. þe(1)] þ*is* RUVHEK. mounteyne] montane E; mounte J; fayre mou*n*teyn R. bemeniþ] bemenyth JK; bemeneth H^{2}V HLW; meniþ T; meneþ DChM; menys E; may mene RU. ek] *om* RUVHKW. þe(2)] þ*is* RVH. merke] M; merk W; myrk JE; derke TRUChH^{2}VK; dyrke D; deope HL. dale] dalys R.
2 ek] all W; *om* RVE. þe] þ*is* RH; that K; þis feire V. feld] feild L. folk] folkes D. I . . . faire] fai*re* y schal ȝow U; feire I schal ow V; fayre wil I R. shal] sal JM.
3 lady] leuedy J. of] on VJ. lire] lyre E; lere RUDJWM; leer LK; leor VH; lo*re* H^2. lynene] lynen DH^{2}W; lynnene UV; lynnen ChJL; lynnyn K; ly*n*nyng E; lynned H. ycloþid] Icloþed ChH^{2}VH JLWM; cloþed D; clethyd E; was ycloþed R; was clothid U.
4 Com] cam RK; Kem J. doun] adoun VHWM. fro] *om* W. þ*at*] þe RUDH^2 VHEM; *om* W. clyf] UDH^{2}LEKM; cleffe J; chyf R; kiþ TCh; loft VH; *om* W. callide] callyd E; called RDChH^2 JLW; calde M; clepid HK; clepte V. me] me ful W.
5 *run together with* 7 W. sone] soon M. slepist] sclepyst RK; slepis JE; slepes Ch. sest] seest UDHK; seyst R; seys E; sixt V; seo L. þou(2)] þou nout M. peple] peeple M; people LK.
6 *line om* W. How] Al hou V. besy] bysy RUH^{2}VHL. þei] þai E; thay K; þat þei RDH^{2}HJM. ben] be R; ben al H; beon alle L; ben ⁊ al D; ben now JE. aboute] abowten J.
7 Þe . . . peple] *om* W. Þe] þeo L. p*ar*tie] p*ar*te H^{2}HK; p*ar*t EM. þis(1)] þe RUVH. peple] people LK. passiþ] passys E. on þis] on þe ChE; on RW; vppon UH; in M; here on D; here in L; nou on V. erþe] eorþe VL; lyue R; hye J.
8 Haue] Hauen V; han L. þei] þai E; thay K; heo V. worsshipe] worschepe U; worchep JM; worschupe V; worchope W; worsciped L; worschipes H^2; worschepys R; welþe Ch. in] of RUDH JEWM. þis] þe UEW. world] wordle R; werld J. þei kepe] kepe þei UDChV; kepyn þei J; ne kepe þei HW; þey woll M; ne willyn thay K. no] non L. bet*ere*] bettur HJ; more K.
9 Of oþ*er*] Of M; for ofþer H. oþ*er* heuene] heuen oþer Ch. heuene] heuy*n* JK; hewen M; heouene L. þanne] þen VHLE. here] her L; heer VJ; here is H. holde þei] holdyn hey J; hald þai E; not holdyn thay K; ȝeueþ þei V; ȝyue þei H.

I was aferd of hire face þeiȝ heo fair were, 10
And seide 'm*er*cy madame, what is þis to mene?'
'Þe tour [on] þe toft,' q*ua*þ heo, 'treuþe is þ*er*einne,
And wolde þ*at* ȝe wrouȝten as his word techiþ.
For he is fadir of feiþ & fou*r*mide ȝow alle
Boþe wiþ fel & wiþ face, & ȝaf ȝow fyue wyttes 15
For to worsshipe hym þ*er*ewiþ whiles ȝe ben here.
And þ*er*fore he hiȝte þe erþe to helpe ȝow ichone
Of [woll]ene, of [lyn]ene, of liflode at nede |
In mesurable man*er* to make ȝow at ese; *fol.* xxv *b*
And comaundite of his curteisie in comou*n* þre þinges; 20

10 I] Ich V. aferd] aferid U; ferid J. hire] hir HE; here UDH²LWM; her ChJK. þeiȝ . . . were] so faire was here lyre W. þeiȝ] þouȝ DChH²K; þoghe U; þof J; þow R; þou M; þauh V; þagh L; al if E. heo] sche RUDChH²KM; che J; sho E. were] weore VL.
11 And] I W. seide] *om* E. madame] my dame E. what] wat M; qwat JE. is . . . mene] may þis bymene RUHE. þis] *om* J.
12 Þe(1)] þis V. tour] ryche tour M. on . . . heo] q*uo*d she on þe toft W. on] DH²HLK; in RU; of TChJEM; & V. þe(2)] þis V; *om* R. toft] testre J; cost (?) R. heo] sche RUDChH²KM; che J; scho E. treuþe] trouþe RChLE; truthe HK; trew M. þ*ere*] here H².
13 And] þat UJ; he HW; *om* RD. wolde] wald E; woldyn M. þ*at*] at E. ȝe] þou R; you (? þou) E; me*n* M. wrouȝten] wroughtyn K; wrouȝt ChE; wroghte LW; wrouth H²; wrouten DM; wrouȝtest R. his] þys M. word] wode M. techiþ] techit JM; teechithe H; techys E; teches D; schewys R.
14 feiþ] Fei V; fath E. &] þat UVHJWM. fou*r*mide ȝow] ȝow formed W. fou*r*mide] formyd EK; fourmed H; formed RD ChH²VJLM. ȝow] ow V; vs REM.
15 Boþe] Bothyn J; *om* REM. wiþ] wyt M; in W. fel] flesse & felle M. wiþ face] whyt face R; with fleche E; in flesh W. &(2) . . . ȝow] & a R; w*ith* owr E; & ȝour*e* M. ȝaf] ȝaue H; gave K. ȝow] ow VL. fyue wyttes] fyn wyt R. wyttes] wyttys J; witt*us* H.
16 For to] Forte V; To W. worsshipe] wurschipen U; worschepe RChH²; worchepe M; worcheppyn J; worschupe*n* V. þ*er*ewiþ] w*ith* DE; *om* VK. whiles] wiles Ch; qwylis J; qwylse E; while VKW; wyll M; whyl þat R; þe whyle þat H. ȝe] we EW; he M. ben] beon L; beoþ VH; dwelle E. here] heere V; on erthe M.
17 And] *om* RDE. þ*er*fore] for V. he] *om* H. hiȝte] heet M; hooteth H; byhyghte L; heten W; hyed J; hiȝte ȝou DH²; hetyth yow K; bad ȝow U; lyȝthe R; light E. þe] into þe E; into R; *om* UH². erþe] eorþe VL; *om* U. to . . . ichone] eche on helpen oþer (on *above line same ink*) U. helpe] helpyn JM; serue HW; seruen V. ȝow] ow V; vs REW; *om* K. ichone] icheon J; echone RDChH²W; vchone VHL; ilkon E; *om* K.
18 *line om* J. Of(1)] And D. wollene] RUV; wollen DH²HLW; wollyn EKM; lynene T; linen Ch. of(2)] and UDK; and of H²W. lynene] R; lynen H²W; lynnene UV; ly*n*nen DHL; lynnyn EK; lynenyn M; wollene T; wollen Ch. of(3)] to UDH²VLEKW; & HM (*over erased* to H; *after cancelled* to M). liflode] help yow E. nede] neode VH.
19 In] In a H. mesurable] neesurale (?) M. make] maken RVJ; makyn M. ȝow] ow V; vs REW. ese] ease EK.
20 And] He W. comaundite] comandide U; co*m*maunded RDChH²JLM; co*m*maundyd K; Comau*n*det V; co*m*maundeth H; co*m*mande*s* E; hete W. of] in E. his] *om* M. in] of E. þre] þreo VL; þer J. þinges] þingeȝ E; þing*us* H; thynkes H²; ȝinges J; yinȝis M.

Arn none nedful but þo & nempne hem I þenke,
And rekne hem in resoun; reherse þou hem aftir.
Þat on is vesture fro chele þe to saue;
Þ*at* oþ*er* is mete at meel for myseise of þiselue;
And drink whanne þe driȝeþ, ac do it nouȝt out of resoun 25
Þat þou worþe þe wers whanne þ*o*u werche shuldist.
For loth, in his lyf dayes, for lykyng of drink
Dede be his douȝt*er*[n] þ*at* þe deuil lykide,
[Delyted hy*m* in drynke as the deuyl wolde],

21 Arn . . . þo] Heore nomes beþ neodful V; her naames beoþ neodeful H. Arn] ULM; Aru*n* J; Are RH²; Eron W; Er E; Ther ar K; Narn T; Ne arn D; Beþ Ch. none] *twice* E. nedful] so nedefull KW; medful E. but] as W; *om* K. þo] þei U; þai E; *om* K. &] to RU; *om* Ch. nempne] nempnen VL; nemen D; nemyn JM; nembe W; neuen E; name K; meny*n* R. hem] heom L; hym D; þaim E; them K. þenke] thynke DChKM; thyng J; woll E.
22 And . . . hem] Bi Rule and VH. rekne] rekene H²; rekkene R; rekenen D; reken ChEW; rekken J; rekon K; rykene L. hem] þa*m* E; hem ȝow U; *om* L. in] by UH²VHJLWM. reherse] Rehersen V; & rehersen J. þou] þe L; þe (? ye) EK; ȝe RUWM; ȝow H²; *om* VHJ. hem] heom L; them K; þaim E; hym D. aftir] URDChJLEWM; hereafter H²K; heraftur VH; þeraftir T.
23 Þat on] þe ton U; þe furste L; That on of þis W. is vesture] Cloþing is VH (*marked for transposition* H). is] *above line, same hand* W. vesture] vesture verylyche RUE; vesture of cloþe W; cloþing DChL. fro] þat from L; for DJ. chele] cheele H; cheld J; cold UDLWM; cald E. þe] þe nou J; þat it may þe D; ȝou RUHLE; ow V. to saue] kepeth L. to] *om* D. saue] sauen M; hele W.
24 *line om* Ch. Þat oþer] þe toþ*er* U; And þat oþur V; And E. is] *om* RDVEM. at] at ȝo*ur* RUE. meel] meyle E; male J. for] fro W; from E. myseise] mysease K; myshese W; myschef RUHE. of . . . selue] þe to helpe W. þi] ȝo*ur* RE; ȝow U. selue] seluen VE; seoluen L; silue H²; syluen H.
25 And] *om* RUH; The þredde WM. drink] dryngke H²; dryng J. whanne] qwan J; quan M; whon V; when RL; qwen E. þe] ȝow UE; þ*o*u RDVHJKWM. driȝeþ] drieth UChH²; dryest RDHJM; dryyst K; druiȝest V; drye art W; thriste*s* E; thyrstes L. ac] but UChH²VHJKWM; & LE. do] *om* W. it] *om* H²JLEWM. nouȝt] nouth J; not RDVHLEKWM; nat Ch. out] outȝ H². resoun] reason (*same hand after cancelled* mesure) K.
26 Þat] At E; so þ*at* RU. þou(1)] the H²; ȝe RULE. worþe . . . wers] þe worse worthen (? worchen) L. worþe] weore V; worche Ch; wurche U; wyrche RJ; wirke E; werke M; do W. þe] noght þe E; *om* J. wers] wors DRChH²VHKW. whanne] qwan JM; whon V; when RChHL; qwen E. þ*o*u(2)] ȝe RULE. werche] worche DChVHLKW; wyrchyn J; wyrk E; werke H²M; swynke RU. shuldist] schuldest DChH²HK; scholdist J; scholdest VW; schulde R; scholde UL; suld E.
27 loth] lot V; lott K; lote Ch; loot RH. his] *om* U. lyf dayes] lifday J. for] þorouȝ H. drink] dring J.
28 Dede] Dide UH; Did JEK; Deode L; Dude V; Dide ly (ly *added above line*) W. douȝt*ern*] douȝtern Ch; douhtren V; douȝtryn R; dowtryn M; douȝteres H²HLEKW; douterys D; doughter*e* U; douȝt*er* TJ. þ*at*] as REK. þe] þeo L. deuil] dyuel M; deouel L. lykide] lykyd REK (*after cancelled* would K); likidde Ch; lykede M; liked DH²HJLW; louede V. *Here* H *adds a line: see above*, p. 45.
29 RUDH²VHJLKWM; *line om* TChE. Delyted] he delyted HW. hy*m*] hem D; *om* J. drynke] dring J; drynken L. deuyl] deuol H; deouel L.

And leccherie h[i]m lauȝte ⁊ lay be hem boþe; 30
And al he wytide it wyn þ[at] wykkide dede.
Dred delitable drynk ⁊ þou shalt do þe bet*ere*;
Mesure is medicine þeiȝ þou muche ȝerne.
Al is not good to þe gost þ*at* þe gut [ask]iþ,
Ne liflode to þe lykam þ*at* lef is to þe soule. 35
Leue not þi lycam for a li[ȝ]*er* hym techiþ,
Þ*at* is þe wrecchide world [wolde] þe betraye.
For þe fend ⁊ þi flessh folewiþ togid*ere*,
[And þat] shend[iþ] þi soule; set it in þin herte;
And for þou shuldist be war I wisse þe þe beste.' 40

30 leccherie . . . lauȝte] laght hym wiþ lecherie W. leccherie] lechorye UH; lichery J; lichory E; with lecherie Ch. him] hym RUDH²VHJLEKM; hem TCh. lay] he lay HE. hem] heom L; them K; þaim E. boþe] boþyn M; bathe E.
31 wytide] wytyd K; witede UV; wyted RDHJL; wittyd E; witted ChH²; witte WM. it] it þe W; þe RH²EM (*above line, late corrector* H²); *om* UChJK. wyn] drynke M. þat] þ*at* RUDChH²VHJK WM; of þ*at* E; þe T; þeo L. wykkide] wykyd EK; wikkede VW; wyckede R; wykked DChJ; wyked M; wyckud H²H; worchyng of þe L. *Here* K *adds a line like* **B** I 32 *or* **C** II 31; W *adds lines like* **B** I 32–3 *and the preceding Latin: see above*, p. 30.
32 Dred] Dreed UV; But drede D. delitable] delicable J; delectable EK. drynk] drynkes D. ⁊] *om* HJ. shalt] schal JE. do] don J. 33–99 *om* (**a leaf missing**) U.
33 Mesure] For mesure DWM. þeiȝ] þey RH²M; þouȝ DChK; þauh V; þagh L; þof J; if W; al yf E. muche] myche H; meche DH²; muchel L; mochel K; mochyl M; mykel J; mekyl E. ȝerne] ȝeore V; desyre RM; crave E.
34 is] nis V. not] nouȝt ChH²; noght E; nouth M. good] gude E; worth, *above it* good *in contemporary script* H². to] for J. þe(1 *and* 2)] thy D. gost] gast E; gotte L. þat] at E. gut] gutt*es* K; gost L; bodi VH. askiþ] askyt R; askeþ DH²HWM; askys E; axyt J; axeth L; likiþ T; likeþ ChV.
35 Ne] No Ch; Neo L. liflode] lif fode L; lyfful R. þe(1)] þy D; *om* R. lykam] body M. þat] *om* EM. lef is] is lef W; no blysse E; lesse M. lef] leof VHL; lyf R. þe(2)] þy D; þo J. soule] saule E.
36 Leue] lef RH²; Leef DVM; Gyff E. not] nouȝt ChH²; noght E. þi] þis E. ȝut R. lycam] body M; *glossed* flesch K; for] *om* W. a] *joined to following* RH²; *om* VH. liȝer] lyȝere V; lyere H²; liere LW; lyer JM; lyar HK; lear E; lþer R; liþ*er* T; leþer Ch; led*er* D. hym] hem RM. techiþ] techit K; techeþ ChH²VL WM; techetȝ (*cancelled for* ledis *similar hand*) J; techys RE; teches D; ledith H.
37 is] *om* R. þe(1)] þis RDEM. wrecchide] wrechid H²; wretchid K; wrechede L; wreched RDJWM; wrychyd E; wikked ChVH. world] word V; wordle R; werlde JE. wolde þe] þat wold þe M; þat wald þe E; þe to TRDChH²VHJLKW.
38 For] *om* H. þe fend] *defective* L. þi] þe EW. folewiþ] folowyn K; folwyn RJ; folewen VH²; folowe D; folow Ch; flowen W; foloweþ þee H; folows þe E; fowtyn þe M.
39 And þat] And þ*at* DH²HJKW; And VL; For to TChM; to RE. shendiþ] schendith K; schendeþ VHJW; shent DH²; shende TRChEM; ::::::::t L. þi] þi sely R; þi sory E; þe W. soule] saule E. set . . . herte] be war of here wyles M; be war *with* þair wyles E. set] ⁊ set D; and seith H²K; ⁊ sent L; seo V; I see H; take W. herte] harte HK; heorte L.
40 *line om* RE. And] *om* W. for þou] *defective* L. shuldist] schuld*es* K. be] ben HJ; beo VL. war] ywar H. I wisse] I wesse M; *corrected from* wysseth, *late hand* H². þe(2)] *om* L. beste] bettre V.

'A madame *mercy*,' q*ua*þ I, 'me likiþ wel ȝoure wordis.
Ac þe mone on þis molde þ*at* men so faste holdiþ,
Tel me to whom þ*at* treso*ur* apendiþ.'
'Go to þe gospel,' q*ua*þ heo, 'þ*at* god seide himseluen,
Þo þe peple hym aposide w*ith* a peny in þe temple 45
Ȝif þei [shulde] worsshipe þ*er*wiþ cesar þe king.
And he askide of hem of whom spak þe l*ett*re,
And þe [Image ilike], þ*at* þ*er*einne standis.
"Cesar," þ[ei] seide, "we se wel ichone."
"*Reddite cesari*," q*ua*þ god, "þat *cesari* befall[iþ], 50

41 A] A a Ch; *om* EKWM. madame m*er*cy] m*er*cy madame H²H. m*er*cy . . . I] q*uo*d I m*er*cy Ch. likiþ] lyk*es* RE. wel] *om* EM. ȝoure] oure L; þi VHKW.
42 Ac] But H²ChVHLKW (*late corrector alters to* as H²); Of E. mone] mony E; monye KW; money RDChH²VHL; monoye W. on] in H; of RH²JLEKWM. þis] the Ch. molde] world M; werld JE. so] swa E. holdiþ] holdeth LK; holdes D; holdys R; hald*es* E; holdyn M; holden ChH²VH; holde W; helden J.
43 Tel] telleþ RDH²J. me] me lady W; me madame M. whom] hom J; wham DH; qwame E. þ*at*] þe E. apendiþ] appendit Ch; apendys R; apendes D; apent*es* E.
44 Go] Ga E. heo] sche RDChH²JKWM; sho E. þ*at*] þer H. seide . . . seluen] him seolf saide L. seide] seith H²V; made EM. seluen] selue RDH²JM; self ChEKW.
45 Þo] whan KW; whon V; when H; *om* JE. þe(1)] þeo L. peple] peepele M; people LK. a . . . temple] þe prece of a peny M. a peny] þe peny W; penys J.
46 Ȝif] ȝef LK; Ȝhif W; Wheder E; wether*e* M. þei] þai E; thay K; hy J; heo V. shulde] schulde RDChH²; scholde L; shold W; suld E; schulden VHK; scholden JM; wile T. worsshipe . . . king] therw*ith* Cesar the kyng worshipe K. worsshipe þ*er*wiþ] ther*e*w*ith* worschipe H². worsshipe] worschepe DChM; worschep R; worschupe V; wrchepyn J. cesar] kayser *cancelled for* cesar *same hand* L. þe] her H; heore V.
47 he] god RH²JLEKW. askide] askyd H²K; asked RDChVLWM; axed HJ; sayd E. of] to E. hem] heom L; them K; hym H²E (*altered same hand to* hem, *and by late corrector to* them H²). of(2)] *om* J. whom] qwome E; wham DL; as (*cancelled, and* of qwo*m* *added above line by corrector*) J. spak] spekyth J. l*ett*re] letture H; lecture J; letter*er*is M; scriptu*r* E.
48 And] And whom VH; And qwom to E; And vnto whom L; And to hem (to hem *cancelled for* wat *same hand*) J; It M. þe Image] JW; þe ymagis T; þe Image is ChL; is þe ymage E; þe ymage was VH; an Image KM; ymage RDH². ilike] y lyke W; lyke RChH²HLEK; lik TDVM; k lykyth (*cancelled for* was *by corrector*) J. þ*at*] at E. þ*er*e] other H²; þroude (?) M. inne] *om* M. standis] standes DE; stondes Ch; standith K; standeth H²; stondyt M; stondeth HLW; stod V; stodid (*cancelled for* standis *by corrector*) J.
49 Cesar] Sesaris M; To cesar E. þei] þey RDChH²VHJLWM; þai E; thay K; þanne T. seide] seiden H²VH; seydyn M; sayde REW; saiden LK. se] sen RM; seen JK; seoþ VH; ssee it E; seon hit L. ichone] echone RDChH²K; vchone VHL; ilkon E. *Here* H *adds a Latin quotation: see above*, p. 45.
50 *Reddite*] Redde H²; þenne *Reddite* V; Ȝeldeþ H. *cesari*(1)] cesaris TRM (*final* s *erased* T); to cesar H; *om* V. *cesari*(2)] cesar DRJEW; to Cesar VHL; to sesari M. befalliþ] byfallyþ RH²E; byfalleth K; befalleþ W; befallet Ch; befalle T; falleþ VL; fallit M; he longeþ D; apendiþ H.

Et que sunt dei deo oþ*er* ellis ȝe don ille."
For riȝtfulliche resoun shulde rewele ȝow alle,
And kynde wyt be wardeyn ȝoure welþe to kepe,
And tuto*ur* of ȝo*ur* tresour, ⁊ take it ȝow at nede;
For husbondrie ⁊ he holden togid*er*is.' 55
Þanne I fraynide hire faire for hi*m* þ*at* hire made,
'Þe dungeon in þe dale þ*at* dredful is of siȝt:
What may it [be]mene, madame I þe biseche?'
'Þ[at] is þe castel of care; who[so] comiþ þ*er*einne
May banne þat he born was to body or to soule. 60
Þ*er*einne woniþ a wy þat wrong is yhoten;
Fadir of falshed, he foundi[de] it hymselue. |
Adam ⁊ Eue he eggide to ille, *fol.* xxvj *a*

51 *line marked with cross in margin* D. *Et . . . deo*] ⁊ to god his deel H. *deo*] *digno* D. oþ*er*] or RDChH^2VHJLEKWM. ellis] *om* DJ. ȝe don] don ȝe L; do ȝe V; you (? þou) do E; þe don M. don] do RE. ille] eole L; euel Ch; euyll E.
52 riȝtfulliche] rytfulleche M; rightful E; ryȝthful R. shulde rewele] schal reule R; rewlys E. rewele] rewlyn J; rule HK; rulen V. ȝow] ou V.
53 kynde] kende RD; kuynde V. wyt] wit*h* (*late corrector alters to* wyt) H^2; *om* M. be] ben JM; beo L; schulde be H; ȝoure H^2K. ȝoure] oure VL. welþe] weolþe VL; weale for E; witte Ch. kepe] kepy*n* M; wayte L.
54 tuto*ur*] þe tutour Ch; tour V; toure H; *om* E. ȝo*ur*] vr V. tresour] troso*ur* R. ⁊] to RVHLE; ac H^2. take] taken M; takyn J. it ȝow] you it E. it] *om* JM. ȝow] *om* V. at] in L; *om* E. nede] neode H; tyme L.
55 he] ȝe E; witte H. holden] holdy*n* M; shold hold W; holdeth boþe L; hald*es* wele E.
56 Þanne] ÞEnne VCh. I fraynide] frayned I HJW; freynnyd I M. hire(1)] hir H; here DH^2WM; her ChJK; hur*e* R. faire] ferrer E. þ*at*] at E. hire(2)] hir HEM; here DH^2 W; her ChJK; hur*e* R. made] formed L.
57 Þe(1)] þeo L; þat VJK. dungeon . . . dale] dale ⁊ þe dongown H; doun in þ*at* deope dale V. þe(2)] þat J. þ*at*] so M; swa E. is] *om* EM. of siȝt] to se H^2.
58 What] wat M; Qwat JE. may it] may þat H; it may DE; hit myghte L. bemene] JRHK; bemenyn M; mene TDChH^2VLEW. madame . . . biseche] þat ȝe me wolde telle L. madame] dame E. I] Ich V; I wold W. þe] ȝou DJE; it þe M. biseche] beseke H^2J. *Here* L *inserts a line: see above*, p. 47.
59 Þat] RDVHJLEKWM; Þ*ere* TChH^2. þe] a Ch. care] care q*uo*d heo VH; car*e* q*uo*d che J; *late corrector adds* qod she H^2. whoso] RWM; ho so DCh; hose V; qwo so J; wha so E; for whoso L; ⁊ who so K; who þat TH^2H. comiþ] co*m*mys E. þereinne] þarin E; þerto R.
60 May] he may H. banne] bannyn JM. he] her*e* M. born was] bore was RD ChH^2JLWM; was borne H. or] oure Ch. soule] saule DE.
61 inne] *om* E. woniþ] wonyt M; wonnys E; dwelleþ W. wy] wyȝe L; wey D; wiȝt Ch; wyght KW; wighte H; wyȝth R; wiht VJ; wyth M; wight þ*er*in E. wrong is] is wrong W. wrong] wrang E; *om* R. is] was R. yhoten] yhote RDCh VHW; Ihotyn J; hotyn M; callyd E.
62 falshed] falfhede R; Falsnes VHM. foundide] foundyd H^2; foundede VM; foundit T; found K; fondid Ch; fonded H; fonde RDJW; fond L; fand E. it] *om* H^2VHM. hym] his L. selue] seluen V; seluy*n* M; syluen H; seoluen L.
63 Adam] Boþe Adam W. eggide] Eggyd H^2EK; eggede VM; egged DCh HLW; heggede R; heggyd J. to] H^2H JEWM; to don V; hem to TRDCh; heom to L; them to K. ille] euyll EK; helle R.

Counseilid kaym to kiln his broþer,
Iudas he iapide wiþ Iewene siluer, 65
And siþen on an Eldir hongide him aftir.
He is lettere of loue, leiȝeþ hem alle;
Þat tresten on his tresour betraid arn sonnest.'
Þanne hadde I wondir in my wyt what womman it were
Þat suche wise wordis of holy writ shewide, 70
And h[a]lside hire on þe heiȝe name, er heo þennis ȝede,
What he[o] were witterly þat wisside me so faire.
'Holy chirche I am,' quaþ heo, 'þou auȝtest me to knowe;

64 Counseilid kaym] Caym he cownseyled H. Counseilid] and conseyled RJLWM; He Counseld E. to] fo to M. kiln] kyllen DChH²EK; kyllyn J; kylle RH; kyll W; cullen VL; slen M. his] his owne L. broþer] brodere J.
65 iapide] beiapede M. wiþ] þorogh H. Iewene] þe Iewes VHEKW. siluer] seluer VM; seoluer L.
66 siþen] siþyn M; sethen DCh; syyn J; siþ W; hasted him L; *om* VH. an] a RJ. Eldir] eldere R; Eldre Ch; eldren H²; elderine J; elrne L; yllern D; eller E; aldre W; hellarn (*same hand after cancelled* eller) K; Ellerne treo V; ellarne tree H. hongide] hongyd K; hongede V; honged H; hangyd E; hanged D; heng R; hing Ch; he hong W; heng vp M; hangyn J; to hongen L. him] hymself RK; him selue Ch; hym seluen E; hym selfyn M; hem self W. aftir] *om* ChEWM.
67 *line om* Ch. lettere] a lettere V; a lettar H; swyche a letter J; leder D. loue] loue and RVHEKWM; lof he J. leiȝeþ] lyeth DV; liys E; lyygh on K; bylyȝeth H; seyueth R; gillith J; gylyd M; lithers W; laccheth L. hem] heom L; þaim E; hym D.
68 tresten] treston J; trusten ChW; trustyn R; truston H²; trusteþ VHL; trustyth K; thrustnyn M; trastes E. on his] in his E; to his J; in her H; in heor V. tresour] trosour R; tresoun M. betraid . . . sonnest] þat no trewth is ynne H; þer no truþe is Inne V. betraid] betrayed DChH²LK; betrays W; tyid J. arn] ar RCh; is E; buþ D; he W. sonnest] sunnest M; sannest L; so fast J; sonered (? *touched up*) R.
69 Þanne hadde] þenne hedde V. wyt] hert EM. what] wat J; qwat E. womman] wommon VHL. it] þis H; sho E; þat sche M. were] war K; weore VL; was HE.
70 suche] syche E; swych JWM. wise] *om* E. writ] wryth M; writ me VH; writte so wysely E; chirch K. shewide] schewyd H²JEK; schewede VM; schewed DLW; schewde R; schewd Ch.
71 And] I HJKW. halside] halsyde E; halsede H²V; halsed DHW; hailside T; hailsyd K; hailised Ch; *con*iured L; askyd M; axed J; assched R. hire] hir HEK; here DChH²; her R. on] in VH. þe heiȝe] cristes L. heiȝe] hey D; hye RCh H²JEKWM; hiȝe H. name] nome V. er . . . ȝede] to telle me hire name L; *om* M. er] ar K; or DChH²JE; or þen R. heo] he (*late corrector prefixes* s) H²; sche RDChJEKW. þennis ȝede] ȝede þenne J. þennis] þenne R; þeonne V. ȝede] ȝeode V; yode E.
72 What] wat M; Qwat JE; And what L. heo] VHL; he TH² (*late corrector prefixes* s H²); sche RDChJEKWM. were witterly] witerly was L. were] where W; weore V; ware H²; war K; was JEM. witterly] wyturly H²H. wisside] wysed DL; wisse W; tawght H; techeþ V; hailised Ch. so faire] she wolde W.
73 *as two lines in* L: Owgh segg heo saide þou aghtest me to knowe For ycham holychirche & cheosed þe ones. chirche] churche RDVH; cherche W; scherche M. I am] Icham V; *om* M. heo] sche RDChJKWM; sho E. þou] þat E. auȝtest] auȝtes H²; auȝtys R; augtest (h *added before* t(1) *another ink*) W; ouȝtest DChHK; ouhtest V; outyst M; aught E; axist J. me] ye E. knowe] knowyn M; knaw E.

I vndirfang þe ferst and þi feiþ [þe] tauȝte.
Þou brouȝtest me borewis my biddyng to werche, 75
To loue me lelly whiles þi lif duriþ.'
Þanne I knelide on my knes & criȝide hire of *gra*ce;
Preiȝede hire pitously [to] preiȝe for my sennes,
And ek kenne me kyndely on crist to beleue,
Þat I miȝte werchen his wil þ*at* wrouȝte me to man: 80
'Teche me to no treso*ur* but tel me þis ilke,
How I may sauen my soule, þ*at* seint art yho[ld]en.'
'Whanne alle treso*ur*s arn triȝed treuþe is þe beste;
I do it on *Deus caritas* to deme þe soþe.

74 I] Ich V; And L. vndirfang . . . ferst] þee furst undurfonge H; þe vndurfong furst V. vndirfang] vndurfong L; vnd*er*fong RDChW; vnderfangyd E; vnderfonged J. ferst] furst RL; first DChH² JEKW. þi . . . þe] VHW; the faith the K; þe þi faythe J; þe þyn feyth M; ȝut feyþ þe R; þi feiþ TDH²L; þi fath E; the feith Ch.
75 brouȝtest] browghtist K; brouthyst M; broutest D; brouȝt*es* RJ; broght E. borewis] borwys RH²M; Borwes VW; borowys K; borowes DChH; borowhes J; borows E. werche] wyrche RJ; worche ChVHLKW; wirke E.
76 To] And to VHL; And M. loue] louen JM. me] *in margin, same hand, to go after* lelly L. lelly] leely VJ; lefly H²; trewely M; truly (*over erased* lelly) H. whiles] wilse E; qwylys J; while VHL WM; þe whylys R. lif] lyue JE. duriþ] durede VM; induryt E; lasted H.
77 Þanne] þe*n*ne V; þen H. I knelide] I knellyd E; y kneoled L; knelede I VHJ; I courbed W. knes] knees ChH²HW; kneys RE; kneos V; kneoes L; knee K. criȝide] *cri*ȝed V; Cryyd K; cryede M; cryed RDChH²JLE; p*ra*yed H; asked W. hire of] on here M. hire] hir HE; here DChH²J; her K; hur*e* R.
78 Preiȝede . . . pitously] to haue pytee on þe pepul & H. Preiȝede] Preyde M; Prayede RH²; Prayed DL; I praied W; And preied ChVE; & p*ra*yed J; And p*ra*yyd K. hire] here DChH²M; her JK; hur*e* R; hir ful E. pitously] petously DCh H²J; p*re*cyusly M. to] RDVHJLEKWM; *om* TChH². preiȝe] preye V; p*re*yen M; praye RH; pray DChH²LEKW; prayen J. my] vr VH. sennes] se*n*niys M; synnes DRChH²HJLEKW; su*n*nes V.
79 ek] als it J; sho E; *om* ChHWM. kenne] ken Ch; kenyn J; kend E; teche RD; techyn M; to teche VH. kyndely] kuyndely V; kendely DChWM; knowlech L. crist to] cristes W.
80 I . . . wil] I his wylle myȝt wurche H; Ich his wille mihte worche V. miȝte] may M. werchen] werchyn J; werche M; worchen H²L; worchyn K; worche W; worch Ch; wirche D; wyrke RE. wrouȝte . . . man] to mon me made L. wrouȝte] made M; broght E. me] *om* M. man] Mon V.
81 Teche] Techit J. to] *om* HJLE. treso*ur*] troso*ur* R; tresoure quoþ I H. tel] tellit J; teche H; kenne W. þis] þat LEM.
82 How] whou (? whon) M. may] myghte L; shuld E. sauen . . . soule] my soule saue HL. sauen] saue RDChH²VE KW; sauyn JM. soule] saule D; synfull saule E; self M. þat . . . yholden] fro synnes in þis eorþe L. þat seint] þat senne D; for þerto E. art] arn R; am E; had D. yholden] D; Iholdyn K; yholde RVHWM; I haldyn E; yhoten T; Ihotyn J; Ihote ChH². *Here* L *inserts a line: see above*, p. 47.
83 Whanne] whe*n*ne RH; whon V; Qwan JE; Saide when L. treso*ur*s] tresoure DV. arn] aru*n* J; er E; beþ W; is DV. triȝed] tryed DChH²JLEK; Itriȝed V; tryȝed quod heo H; tryed q*uo*d sche RW; tr*i*id q*uo*d sche M; *late corrector adds* quod she H². treuþe] than truth K.
84 to] for to E. deme] demen W; demyn J; deeme V; tryen M.

It is as derworþi a dreury as dere god hymseluen. 85
For whoso is trewe of his tunge, telliþ non oþer,
Doþ þe werkis þerwiþ & wilneþ no man ille,
He is a god be þe gospel on ground & on lofte,
And ek lyk to oure lord be seint lukis wordis.
Þe clerkis þat knowe it shulde kenne it aboute, 90
For cristene & vncristene cleymeþ it ichone.
Kinges & kniȝtes shulde kepe it be resoun,
And riden & rappe doun in reaumes aboute,
And taken trespassours & teiȝen hem faste
Til treuþe hadde termined here trespas to þe ende. 95

85 *line om* M. as] als E; a H²J (*added by late corrector* H²); *om* D. derworþi] derworþe RDH²VH; derworth ChJLKW. a] & D; *om* H²HJ. dreury] drywery L; drurie VEK. dere] deore VL; dere as Ch. seluen] selue RDChJ; selfe E; self W; seoluen L.
86 For] *om* JM. whoso] ho so ChJ; hose V; whos L; he E; Qwere he M. trewe] treowe L; trowe J. telliþ] tel hit RW; & tellith H²H (& *erased or rubbed* H; *inserted by late corrector* H²); & teleth L; tell he euel of J; trow þou EM. non oþer] not elles V.
87 Doþ] & doþ H; And doys E; Þat dot M; Bot dothe ChK; And do J; Do W. þe] his VH (*over erasure, another ink* H); gode J; *om* M. werkis] workes ChK; warkes H. þerwiþ] þor wit M; of god E. &] *om* RDLKWM; at E. wilneþ] willeþ DCh; wyllyþ RH²; willit M; wil JEW; doþ VH. man] mon VHL. ille] non ill W; euell E; eouel L.
88 a . . . be] acounted to VH (acounted *twice, but second cancelled* H). a] in J; on Ch; *om* H². god] good H²M (*late corrector alters to* godd H²). be] *om* M. þe] *om* H²M. gospel] gospelles K. on(1) . . . lofte] in heuen & in erþe H. on(2)] a R. lofte] lofthe R.
89 ek] also W; alsa E. lyk] Iliknet V. lukis] lucas H²; Lucus V; Iamys R.
90 Þe] *om* RChVH; *cancelled* J. knowe it] knowyn it (*after cancelled* kennyn a *same hand*) J; hit knoweþ R; it knowe wel W. knowe] knowen DVHL; knowyn K; knoweth Ch; knowyt M; knawys E. it] *om* K. shulde] schulden H; schud J. kenne] kennyn JM; techen V; teche H. aboute] abowten J.
91 cristene] cristenemen H². vncristene] vncrystned H; heþen W. cleymeþ] cleymyt M; cleymen D; cleymyn J; cleyme W; claymeþ Ch; claymen HK; him cleymeþ V; shuld clame E. it] *om* RV. ichone] echone RDChK; vchone VL; uchoone H.
92 *line om* M. kinges] kyngus H; kynkges W. kniȝtes] knyȝtus H; knihtes V; knygtes W; knyȝthes R; knytes H². shulde] schulden H. kepe] kepen V; kepyn JK. it] hem V; *om* J.
93 riden . . . doun] Rihtfuliche Raymen V; ryȝtfullyche rule H; biddyn & techyn M. riden] rydyn JK; ryde RChE. & . . . doun] at randoun D; rapely to rensake E. rappe] rappen H²W; rape ChK; rapen L; rapyn J. doun] adoun RChK. in] the ChVE; her H. reaumes] reames DW; rewmes H; rewmys J; remes Ch; remys R; Realmes VLEM; realmys K. aboute] abouten V; abowtyn M.
94 And taken] Alle toillors and L. And] For to J; To E. taken] takyn JK; take RDH²VH; takyn alle M; take al E. trespassours] hem þat trespassen H. teiȝen] teyen DChJ; teyn M; tyȝe R; tyen H²K; tye E; eke tye L; bynden VW; bynde H. hem] heom L; them K; þaim ful E.
95 treuþe] truþe RH; trouþe M. hadde] hedde V; haue REW. termined] Itermyned H; Itermynyd K; Itermynet V; determinyd EM; turnyd J. here] her HK; heore L; þair E; þe V. trespas] trispas E; truþe R. þe] an R; *om* H²K. ende] hende M; eynde L.

For dauid, in hise dayes, dubbide kniȝtes,
[Di]de hem swere on h[ere] swerd to *ser*ue treuþe eu*er*e.
Þat is þe p*ro*fessioun ap*er*tly þat apendiþ to kniȝtes,
And nouȝt to fasten a friday in fyue score wynter,
But holde wiþ hym & wiþ hire þ*at* aske þe treuþe, 100
And neu*er*e leue h[e]m for loue ne lacching of ȝeftis;
And whoso passiþ þ*at* poynt is apostata in his ordre.
And crist, king[ene] kin[g], kniȝtide tene, |
Cherubyn & seraphyn, such seuene & anoþ*er*; *fol.* xxvj *b*

96 dayes] lyfdayes D. dubbide] dubbyd H²JK; dubbit E; dubbede RDM; dubbed L; dobbed W; he Dubbede V; he dubbed ChH. kniȝtes] mony knyghtis L.
97 Dide] Dude V; Deode L; He dide W; & did J; and dude R; And dyddyn K; Made TDChH²; & made H; And E; De M. hem] heom L; þaim E. swere] swer*e* RChVJLEKWM; to swere TDH²H. here] WJM; h*er* RH; heore L; heor V; he K; a D; his TChH²E. swerd] sweord L; swerdys R; swerd*us* H; sword*es* K. to . . . euere] trouþe euer to *ser*ue L. *ser*ue] seruen JM. treuþe] trupe RJ; trouþe ChE.
98 Þat . . . þe] For þat M. Þat(1)] This RJE. p*ro*fessioun ap*er*tly] perte p*ro*fession V; p*ar*fyt professyou*n* H. p*ro*fessioun] prophecye RE; p*ro*feace M. apertly] aperlich K; aperty H²; apert W; propurlich L; *om* EM. þat(2)] at E; *om* M. apendiþ . . . kniȝtes] to a knyȝt apenteth L. apendiþ] apendit ChM; appent*es* E; dependit H²; pendeþ W; longith J.
99 nouȝt] nout M; not VHLKW; *om* ChJ. to] *om* J. fasten] faste RDVHLKM; fast ChEW; Fastyn J. a] oon H; one K; on L; *om* H². fyue score] foure skore L; fyftene E; xv M. wynter] wynt*ur* H; wynt*er*ys E; ȝeres V.
100, 101 *transposed* L.
100 Here U resumes. holde] holden ChVJ; holdyn K; haldyn M; to holde HE. hym] hem VH; hire L. & wiþ] & M; or w*ith* E; and hym H². hire] hir E; here DJW; her ChK; heore V; hur*e* R; hers H; hi*m* L. þat] at E. aske] asken UVHWM; askyn K; askeþ RChH²L; askys E; axedyn J. þe] *om* H²HJ.
101 *line om* M. And] No ChL. neu*er*e] neither U; nowder E; *om* VH. leue] leuen VJ; leef U; lett E; let W; lach Ch. hem] RUDJK; heom L; hym TChH²; *om* VHEW. for] for no VH. loue] luffe J. ne] ne for RUE; ne no H; no L. lacching] lakkynge UEK; lachesse D. ȝeftis] yeftes K; ȝiftys J; ȝiftes ChH²LW; ȝiftus VH; gyftes D; sylu*er* RUE.
102 And] for HW. whoso] ho so DJ; qwo so E; whos L; he so þ*at* R; who þat WM; he þat VH. passiþ] passeþ DChH²VLW; passet J; passys E; pasid M; pursewyt R. þ*at*] þis UE; *om* R. poynt] *om* R. is apostata] apostota he is E. is] he is R. in . . . ordre] for euere W. his] þe V; that K; h*er* R; *om* EM.
103 *line om* VE. L *substitutes* For crist creato*ur* cried and kraftely made. And] For H. crist] kyng U. kingene king] kyngene kyng RU; king of kinges TChH²; kyndede kyng M; knyttene kyng *cancelled for* kyng of knyhtys *same hand* J; kyng of knyȝtes DK; kynge of knyȝt*us* H; knyght & kyng W. kniȝtide] knyhtide U; knyȝted D; knighted KW; knyȝthede R; knythtede M; knytide Ch; knitede H²; knyttid J; knytted H. tene] *cancelled for* þat tyme? *same hand* J; somtyme H; in tyme K.
104 Here N becomes legible. L *substitutes* Of Aungles and archangles ordres nyne. such . . . anoþ*er*] and such seuene oþere RE; & sweche vij other*e* M; & seuen moo oþere J; and siche mo oþere U; & alle þe foure ordres HK; an al þe foure ordres V. such] shuche W. anoþ*er*] on oþer Ch; oþ*er* D.

ȝaf hem miȝt in his mageste, þe meryere hem þouȝte, 105
And ouer his meyne made hem archaungelis;
Tauȝte hem þoruȝ þe trinite þe trouþe to knowe:
To be buxum at his bidding; he bad hem nouȝt ellis.
Lucifer wiþ legionis leride it in heuene,
And was þe louelokest [of siȝt] aftir oure lord 110
Til he brak buxumnesse þoruȝ bost of hymseluen.
Þanne fil he wiþ [his] felawis ⁊ fendis bicome;
Out of heuene into helle hobelide þei faste,
Summe in eir, summe in erþe, summe in helle depe.
A[c] lucifer lowest liþ of hem alle; 115
For pride þat he put out his peyne haþ non ende.

105 ȝaf] and ȝaf RUVHJ; And ȝef L; And gaf E; He ȝaf W. hem] heom L; þaim E. miȝt] myȝth R; myth H^{2}M; maystrie ⁊ miht V; honoure ⁊ myȝte H. his] *om* W. þe . . . þouȝte] *om* VHJ. meryere] myriere U; murier L. hem] hym DEM.
106 *line om* VHL. And] *om* E. his] al his UJEW. meyne] meynye K; mayne R; mene E; mene meyne M. hem] þaim E.
107 Tauȝte] he tauȝt NW; And tauȝte UVH. hem] heom L; *om* VE. þe(2)] *om* VJW. trouþe] truþe H; trwþe N; treuþe RUDChH^{2}VJKWM. to] for to VHE. knowe] knowen V; knowyn M; knaw E.
108 To] And UVE. be] ben JM; beo VL. at . . . ellis] ⁊ boun his biddyng to werche M. at] to L. bidding] heste U; bone W. hem] heom L; þaim E; *om* Ch. nouȝt] not VHLW; o nouȝt (*late corrector changes* o *to* owe) H^2.
109–110 L *substitutes* And þe lyght lucifer illumyned ouer heom alle.
109 leride] lerid H^{2}HE; lerede V; lered RChWN; lernyd UJKM; lerned D. it] *om* DCh.
110 And] He VHWN; þat UM. was . . . louelokest] louelyerst was M. was] wat R. þe] *om* H^{2}VHJ. louelokest] louelekyst R; luflikest J; loveliest EK; lofliest W; louelyst UN. of siȝt] DRUVHJEKWNM; to loken on Ch; to loke on TH^2. aftir] eftir N; next vnto E. lord] lord seluyn M; lorde dere J.
111 Til] To E. brak] brek D. hymseluen] hys pride M. seluen] selue RUDChJ; selfe EKWN; seoluen L; sillue H^2. *Here* N *inserts a passage like* **C** II 112–22 *with the preceding and following Latin: see above*, p. 30.
112 *for this line* W *substitutes a form of* **B** I 113–16: *see above*, p. 30. Þanne] þen HLK; þenne V. fil] fel RUChVHJEKNM; feol L. wiþ] ⁊ E. his] RUChVHJLEKN M; *om* TDH^2. felawis] felaus DL; felowys K; felaship E; felaschepe M. fendis] feondus H; feondes L. bicome] bicomen VHL; becomyn M.
113 Out] Ouȝt H^2; And oute W. heuene] heouen L. hobelide] hobeled WN; hobeleden J; hoblide U; hobblid K; hoblede R; hobled DChE; hobleden VHL; hobledyn M. þei] þai EW; hy (*after cancelled* many *same hand*) J; wol M; wel (*over erasure another hand and ink*) H; *om* V.
114 eir] eyer D; ayre JN; þe Eir V; erþe REM. summe(2)] and some RVKW. erþe] eorþe L; þe Eorþe V; eyre RE; þe eyr M. summe in(3)] doun in to R. summe(3)] ⁊ summe VKWN. depe] deope VHL.
115 Ac] UJN; But ChVHLEKW; And TRDH^{2}M. lucifer] lucificer N. lowest] lawest E. liþ] lithe Ch; lyyth K; liȝþ V; lyȝthe R; light UE; liþ hit H^2. hem] heom L; þaim E.
116 pride . . . out] his pompe ⁊ his pruyde L. pride] pruide V; þe pride U; his pryde (his *cancelled*) H. þat] at E; *om* UHJ. he] him W; he was H; he was *þus* J. out] out was D; out of H^{2}W. peyne] payne RHJE; pyne L. haþ] hat M. non] no E. ende] eynde L.

And alle þ*at* werchen w*ith* wrong wenden þei shuln
Aftir here deþ day & dwelle wiþ þ*at* shrewe.
Ac þo þ*at* werchen þe word þ*at* holy writ techiþ,
And enden as I er seide, in p*er*fite werkis, 120
Mowe be sikur þ*at* here soule shal wende into heuene,
Þ*ere* treuþe is in trinite & tron[iþ] h[e]m alle.
Forþi I seye as I seide er, be siȝte of þise textis:
Whanne alle treso*urs* arn triȝed treuþe is þe beste.
Leriþ it þus lewide men, for lettrid it knowiþ, 125

117 And] So W. alle] *om* J. þ*at*] at E. werchen . . . wrong] wrong worchen VH; wrong werk*es* E. werchen] werchyt M; worchen ChL; worche H²WN; worchet K; worken U; wrchyn J; wurche D; worschepe R. wrong] wronges D. wenden . . . shuln] shal aftir hym wend E. wenden] wendyn M; wende RUChH²VH WN; þedyr *added later hand* H. þei] thay K; hy J; hij N; *om* M. shuln] schulen VL; schule H; schullen ChH²; schulle UD; schull KW; schulde R; sholde N; schall J; scholy aft*er* M.
118 Aftir . . . day] To þ*at* Pyne endles E; To þ*at* peyde endeles M. here] her ChHJK; heore VL; þe W. dwelle] dwellen DV; dwellyn JK; won E; wonyn M. þ*at*] þe W.
119 *line marked with cross* D. Ac] But ChHKWN; And LE. þo] þei ChL; þay H; heo V; ho D. þ*at*(1)] at E. werchen] werchyn M; worchen ChH² VHLKN; worche RW; wurchen U; wrchyn J; wyrkis E. þe . . . þ*at*] *in* þis world as (*another ink over erasure*) H. þe] þat RChVKM. word] werke EM; world D. writ] chirche L; cherche RM; kirke E. techiþ] techit KM; techys RE; teches D.
120 enden] endyn DJ; endeþ RVH; end*es* E; end K; hendyt M; eynden L. I] Ich V. er] are ChE; ore K; her D; here N. p*er*fite] p*ro*fitable UVHJW; p*ro*pletys (? *for* p*ro*phetys) M. werkis] workys RH² K; workes Ch; warkis H.
121 Mowe] Mown L; Mouwen V; Mou*n* J; May EM; þey may (þey *cancelled*) H. be] ben UJM; beo L. sikur] syker RUVHLK; sikre W; sykyr J; seker DChH²N; sekyr EM. þ*at*] at E; *om* U. here] her RHJKW; heore VL; þair E. soule] soules UChVHJLWM; saules E. shal] sal JE; schul UChW; schule L; schulen H; schull*en* V; scholy*n* M. wende] wenden JW; wendyn KM; *om* VH (wende in *supplied in margin another hand* H). into] to UDH²VHJLEM. heuene] heouen L; heuen blysse E.
122 Þ*ere*] Thar W. &] to L; *om* UJM. troniþ] troneþ N; tronen T; treonen L; turnyt M; trowe H²; trowen R; crowneþ HKW; Corouneþ V; crownen DCh; techys E; tryeste UJ. hem] RDChVHK WNM; heom L; þaim E; hym TH²; of UJ.
123 Forþi] þ*er*fore UJ; For VHLE; For ȝit WN. seye . . . er] sigge sikerli V. seye] sey ChH²J; saye H; say DLEKW. I(2)] *om but inserted by late corrector* H². seide er] er sayde HJL; are sayd E. seide] sayde RDW; said K. er] are Ch; arst K; her D; *om* WN. be] right be E. siȝte of] *om* EM. siȝte] sent (? seut) R. þise] þis N; þese RUH²; thes ChJ; þeose L; þe DVHEK WM. textis] tyxt*es* RH²JL; text EK; tyxt M; d tixstes Ch.
124 Whanne] wanne M; Qwan J; Whon V; when HL; Qwen E. treso*urs*] trosur*es* R; tresoure DVWN. arn] aru*n* J; ar E; ben H; be R; is DVWN. triȝed] tryed RUD ChH²HJLEKWN; tryd M; Itriȝet V. treuþe] truþe RH; trwþe N; trouth E; trowþ Ch.
125 Leriþ] Lerneth K; lernyt M; lere HE; To leryd J. it] *om* RDJM. þus] þis DVM; these K; þe W; þe (? ye) E; to HJ; *om* UN. lettrid] lettride U; lettred DChKWN; let- trede V; letteryd RJ; lettered men H; *late corrector inserts* men H²; leryd E; lered L. knowiþ] knowyt M; knowyn RJ; knowen UWN; knawys E.

Þat treuþe is þe tresour triȝest on erþe.'
'Ȝet haue I no kynde knowyng,' quaþ I, '[ȝe mote kenne me bet]
Be what craft in my cors it compsiþ, & where.'
'Þou dotide daffe,' quaþ heo, 'dulle arn þine wittes.
It is a kynde knowyng þat kenneþ in þin herte 130
For to loue þi lord leuere þanne þiselue;
No dedly synne to do, diȝe þeiȝ þou shuldist.
Þis I trowe be treuþe; who can teche þe betere,
Loke þou suffre hym to seyn & siþþe lere it aftir.

126 Þat] At E. treuþe] trouth E; truþe RHW; trwþe N. þe] a HW; *om* RUCh H²VEM. triȝest] tryest DChH²JKWN; þe tryeste RU; triedest VHL; þe tridest E; trustirst M. on] RUDChVJLK; vpon HEW; on on N; in M; here on T; here in H². erþe] eorþe VL; *same hand after cancelled* ered J.
127 Ȝet] ȝit UDChVHJEWN; ȝut R; *om* M. haue . . . knowyng] ne know I W. haue I] I haue EM. kynde] kuynde V; kende ChM; *om* R. knowyng] knawyng E. quaþ I] *om* UDJE. ȝe mote] ȝe mot RUChH²; ȝe motyn J; ȝet mote ȝe TK; þou most VH; þe most W; ȝit mot N; ȝit must I M; but ȝe D; bote L; me byhofis E. kenne . . . bet] kenne me better KWN; kennyn me bettur J; kenne me bet : : : L; teche me betere V; me bet kenne TDH²; me betere kenne UCh; me betere teche R; me teche better H; lerne betere M; better to lere E.
128 *line om* E. what] wat NM; qwat J. craft] kynne craft U. in my] þat myn M; or W. cors] corps DH²VKN (p *inserted by late corrector* H²); cours W; body HM (*over erasure another hand* H). it . . . where] I may hit ay knowe (knowe *after cancelled* fynde *same hand*) L. compsiþ] comseth UH²WN; cumseþ V; comsit DCh; bicomseþ H; comsin J; comeþ R; domseth K; coueitid M. &] or W. where] were ChM; whare UDHN; ware J.
129 Þou] A W. dotide] dotyd UChH²; dotede RM; doted DKWN; dotyst J; dotest VL; dootest H; dol E. heo] he RH² (*altered to* she *late corrector* H²); sche UDChJEKWNM. arn] arne K; arun J; are RVN; ar W; er E; ben UH; be D. þine] þy RUDChH²VHJLEKWN. *Here* WN *insert a line like* **B** I 139 *or* **C** II 140, *and the Latin: see above*, p. 30.
130 kynde] kuynde V; kende DChM. knowyng] knawying E. þat] þe L. kenneþ] kennyth JK; kennet D; kennes L; comseth U; cometh Ch; komyt M; comes R; kyndellys E. in] þe in VHW; *om* J. þin] *om* V. herte] heorte L; harte K.
131 For] *om* WN. loue] louen J; louyn M; loue lelly WN. lord] louerd V. leuere] leouer L; betere U. þanne] þen VE. selue] self H²KWM; seluen VHEN; seluyn R; seolue L.
132 H² *substitutes* Ne no wrong to worche to no man in erthe. No] Non JM; Na E. synne] senne M; sunne V. to] for to ChE; þat þou H. do] don DJ. diȝe . . . þou] þeȝ þou deye R; þoghe þou deye U; yf þou dye E. diȝe] die ChLKW; deie N; dey D; deyen J; to deth M. þeiȝ] þouȝ DChKW; þouth M; þauȝ V; ȝof J; raþer L. shuldist] sulde E. *Here* WN *insert a Latin line as after* **C** II 144: *see above*, p. 30.
133 I . . . treuþe] is trouth for sothe EM. I] as I W. trowe] trowhe J. be] beo VL. treuþe] trouth K; truþe RH; trwþe N; trewe W. who] ho DCh; who so HL; ho so J; qwa sa E; hose V. can . . . betere] treuly hit techeth L. can] con V. teche] techyn JM; ken W. þe] *om* H²E (*supplied by late corrector* H²). betere] best E.
134 *line om* M. seyn] seyne J; seye UVH; sey Ch; sayn L; say RDEKW. siþþe] syþe RU; siþ H²W; seþþe V; seþ Ch; sithen HKN; sethen L; seþin J; syne E; seche D. lere] leret D; lerne UJK; teche VH. it] *om* RDE. aftir] further H; forþure V.

For þus [wytnessiþ] his woord, werche þou þeraftir, 135
Þat loue is þe leuest þing þat oure lord askiþ,
And ek þe plante of pes; preche it in þin harpe
[Þer] þou art m[er]y at mete, ȝif men bidde þe ȝedde.
For in kynde knowyng in herte þer comsiþ a miȝt,
And þat falliþ to þe fadir þat fourmide vs alle, 140
Lokide on vs wiþ loue, & let his sone deiȝe
Mekliche for oure misdedis to amende vs alle.
And ȝet wolde he hem no woo þat wrouȝte him þat pyne,
But mekly wiþ mouþe mercy he besouȝte

135 *line om* N. For] *om* D. þus] *om* W. wytnessiþ] witnessith UDJK; witnessit M; witnesseþ RL; wittnes E; askiþ wytnesse TChH²; I wole wettenesse W; techeþ us VH. his] þis JW. werche . . . aftir] wryten in þe bible L. werche] wercheþ D; werck M; worche RChHW; worch VK; wurche U; wyrche J; wroche E. þou] *om* D.
136 Þat] At E; For N. loue] loffe J. þe] *om* M. leuest] leouest HL; leuerest M. þat(2)] at E. oure] euer oure Ch. askiþ] asket D; askys E; axith J; axeþ HN.
137 ek þe] also þe W; also U; ȝe R; in E; I M; is L. plante] plaunte H²H (u *over erased* y H); plonte D; plente REKM; playnt V. pes] peace K. preche it] priche it J; prechet V; prechyd RM; preche þou it E; put it U; precke it (*from* preche it *another ink*) H; proche hit L. in] þe V; *om* E. þin harpe] ofte E. þin] myn M. harpe] p *erased and* t *inserted another ink* H; arpe (h *another script*) W; herte UDJ.
138 Þer] Ther RUDVHJLEKWN; ȝif TH²M; when Ch. art] is E; sittest W. mery] ChH²EKNM; merye R; myri J; myrye UH; mury L; Murie V; mercy TD; *om* W. at] at þe U; at þi V; at þin JM; a W. ȝif . . . ȝedde] in þi most myrthe (*over erasure another hand*) H. ȝif] ȝef L; whan RU; whon V; & JM (& men *above line replacing cancelled* yif J). men] me ChV; heny R. bidde þe] þe bydde M; þe faste bydde D. bidde] biddeþ V; byddyt R. ȝedde] ȝedden U; ȝeddyn J; ȝede K; syng EM; *om* D.
139 in(1)] by UV; *om* HLM. kynde] kuynde V; kende DChM; *om* W. knowyng] knawyng E; kennyng W. in(2)] of R; *om* UJ. herte] heorte L; hart K; *om* UJ. þer . . . miȝt] kenneth þe þeo sothe L; þou conseyuys a myrth (*after cancelled* þer comsyt aryht *same hand*) J. þer comsiþ] Cumse þer V; conseyue þou D. þer] *om* HENM. comsiþ] comsit Ch; comseth UKWN; begynnys E; bygynne H; comeþ RH²; coueitid M. a miȝt] myȝte D; it right U; a merthe R; alle merthe M; al myrth E; a Fitte V; suche a fytt H. *Here* N *inserts lines like* C II 147–8 *and* 150–61: *see above*, p. 30.
140 And] *om* VHKM. þat] *om* L. falliþ] fallit M; falleþ RDChVHWN; fallys E; fallid J; ful L. to] *om* H². þat] at E. fourmide] formyth J; comsed W. vs] ȝow M.
141 Lokide] lokede R; Loked DChL; he lokyd K; He lokede V; he loked HWN; þat lokide U; He logh E; And leykyd J; he dede M. on] vpon WN; for M. wiþ loue] kyndely E; kendly M. &] he HM. let] dede M. deiȝe] deye RUDH²M; diȝe H; die ChVJLEKWN.
142 **Here** (*page* 307) A **begins** He ::::: for vs:::::::ly he deyd for vs alle. Mekliche] Meokelich L. misdedis] misdede VM; dedis J. to] forte V. amende] amenden DJLW; amendyn M.
143 ȝet . . . woo] *illegible* A. ȝet] ȝit UDChH²VE; ȝut R; *om* HJLWM. wolde he] he wolde H; he wald E; ne wolde N. he] *om* RDChJKW. hem] heom L; þaim E; hym RUD. no] non M. woo] wae E; *om* U. wrouȝte] wroughten K; wrouthe M; wrout A; wrouuhtyn J; wolde V. þat(2)] *om* A. pyne] peyne DChN; tene AM; ill W.
144 mekly] meokelich L. wiþ] by R; be UEW. he] *om* RUChHJAM. besouȝte] bysouȝthe R; besouth H²M; besoutht W; gan seche A.

To haue pite on þat peple þat pynede hym to deþe. 145
Here miȝt þou sen ensaumplis in hymself one |
Þat he was miȝtful & mek & mercy gan graunte *fol.* xxvij *a*
To hem þat hongide him [heiȝe] & his herte þirlide.
Forþi I rede þe riche haue reuþe on þe pore;
Þeiȝ ȝe ben miȝty to mote beþ mek of ȝour werkis; 150
For þe same mesour ȝe mete, amys oþer ellis,
Ȝe shuln be weiȝe þerwiþ whanne ȝe wende hennes.

145 line *om* H. haue] hauyn A. pite . . . peple] of þat peple pite (pite *above line similar hand*) E. pite] pete J; pety K; *om* AM. on] of LN. þat] þe UDJKWN. peple] people LK; puple A. pynede] pyned RUDChLA; pynyd JEK; pyne H²; peyned W; peynid NM. deþe] deye R; dede EA.
146 *line om* H. miȝt þou] þou miht V; men might K. miȝt] mygth A; myth M; may JE. þou] we Ch; *om* U. sen] se RUChH²; seen N; see EK; seon V; seo L. ensaumplis] exaumples RJ; ensaumple ChVEKWNM; example A. in] of LM; on A; by K. hymself] himselfen N; hymseluyn M; þiself V; þe selfe A. one] on DCh; ane E; al one LK; onys A.
147 *line om* H. Þat] Hou V. he] he þat L; *om* W. was] is E. miȝtful] mercyful R; mygthi A; mythy M. &(2)] þat V; *om* LE. gan] gon V; for to E. graunte] grauntyn U; craue M.
148 To] For H. hem] heom L; þaim E; hym WNM. hongide . . . heiȝe] hym hangyd E. hongide] hongyd K; hongede H²; honged HLW; hangid N; hengyn RJA; hengen D; heng M; heengen V; hyngen U; hyng Ch. him heiȝe] V; hym hyȝe H; hym eye M; him on cros L; him by TRUDChH²JKWN; on hym A. &] whan þey M. herte] harte K; heorte L. þirlide] thirlede E; þirled HKN; þerled RDCh; þurleden V; þurled L; thrillyd JA; þrillede H²; þrellydyn M; þerssed W.
149 *run together with following* V. Forþi] For why K; þerfore UHJEWN. þe] þee H; ȝe H²J; ȝow ANM; þe þou R. riche] ryȝte H; Mihtful of Mayn V. haue . . . pore] *om* V. haue] hat M; to haue U. reuþe] ruth K; mercy W. on] of HJN.
150 Þeiȝ . . . mote] *om* V. Þeiȝ] They H²; þouȝ DK; þoghe U; þouth M; þof J; Thou A; Thow RChW; þagh L; Yf E. ȝe] þou HEW; he A. ben] be RDChH² HEAWNM; beon L. miȝty] mygthi A; myhty J; mythy M; myȝte D; myȝtful H. to] of H. mote] mute E; mete J; mayn H. beþ] be DVHEAWM; ben K. of] in AN. ȝour] oure L; þi VHEW. werkis] workys RChK; warkys H; wordes V; hertes D. *Here* H *inserts the Latin after* **B** I 176 *or* **C** II 175: *see above*, p. 30.
151 þe same] what W. mesour] mesuris A. ȝe] þat ȝe VHJLEANM (þou *another ink over* ȝe H); þe W. mete . . . ellis] to oþer men metyn AM; tyll other metes E. mete] meten DVHL (*altered to* metest H); metyn J; metyn here U. amys] ariȝt (*over erased* amysse) H. oþer] or W.
152 Ȝe] þou (*over erased* ȝe) H; *om* EAM. shuln] schule L; schul RChV; schullen U; schollyn J; schal DAKWNM; Sal E; schalt *over erasure* H. be] ben JAKM; beo L. weiȝe] weyȝen U; weye RD; weyen VW; wey Ch; weyn JN; weyed HL; weyyd K; mett E; metyn AM. þerwiþ] vnto you E; to ȝou AM. whanne] whon V; whenne RDChHLW; qwan J; qwen E; whan þat U. ȝe wende] þou wendest *over erasure* H. wende hennes] henys wende A. wende] wenden VLK; wendyn JM; goþ R; gon U. hennes] hyne E. *Here* N *inserts the Latin from* **B** I 176 *or* **C** II 175, W *the same in margin: see above*, p. 30.

For þ[eiȝ ȝe] be trewe of ȝoure tunge & treweliche wynne,
And ek as chast as a child þat in chirche wepiþ,
But ȝif ȝe loue lelly & lene þe pore, 155
Of such good as god sent goodlyche parteþ,
ȝe ne haue no more meryt in [masse] ne in [houres]
Þanne malkyn of hire maidenhed þat no man desiriþ.
For Iames þe ientil ioynide in his bokis
Þat feiþ wiþoute fait is feblere þan nouȝt, 160
And as ded as a dorenail but ȝif þe dede folewe.

153 For] *om* AWNM. þeiȝ] H; þeighe U; þei JN; though K; þouth M; Thow AW; þof (*corrected same hand from* þi) E; þauȝ V; þagh L; þi TRDChH² (*late corrector alters to* though H²). ȝe] UVHJLEAKM (*above line in same hand* E; *erased and* þou *written over* H); þow WN; *om* TRDChH² (*late corrector adds* ye H²). be] ben VHJAKM (n *erased* H); beon L; beþ RCh. trewe] treowe L; trowe J; trwe HN (*touched up* H). ȝoure] oure L; þi WN; thy *on erased* ȝoure H; *om* VAM. tunge] tong*es* RDK; tong*us* (*same hand after cancelled* wordus) L. wynne] wynnen L; wynnyn M; wynnes D; wynnest (st *over erasure*) H.
154 ek] *om* AWN. as] als E; be R; *om* U. chast] *om* U. a] *om* J; *above line same hand* U. chirche] cherche UWM; churche DH; þe chirche H²N; þe cherche R; þe kirke E; cradel L. wepiþ] wepit AM; wepys RE; wepes D; crieth L.
155 ȝif] ȝef ChL; *om* RUVEAM. ȝe] ȝow (*altered to* þow *another ink*) W; þou HAN (*over erased* ȝe H). loue] louen JLM; lyue H; liuen V; leve E. lelly] leally K; trewely VH; wel god M. &] and eke V; *om* R. lene] lenen J; lend K; ȝeue to lone H²; loue (? lone) DV; loue (? lone) wel HA (*altered from* louen ek H); releue þe meseise & L; succurre E; ek M; *om* R.
156 *line om* M. Of] And VH; wiþ L. such] swiche UJ; sweche A; syke E. good] god A; gude E; goodes HK. sent] sente H²; sendeþ H; sendith K; haþ sent UJ; ȝou sent L; þe send*es* E; hath þe sent A. goodlyche] Treweliche VH; loueliche A; frely E. parteþ] partith H²; parten V; partene J; parte DLKWN; departyn R; departe HEA.
157 ȝe] þei R; Tho A; þou (*in corrector's ink*) H. ne haue] naue V; haue RDJEKM; haueþ L; han A; hast (*over erased* nabb:::) H. no] na U. more] *om* N. meryt] merites K. in(1)] of EAWM; *om* Ch. masse . . . houres] heuenriche blys EAM. masse] RDVHKN; messe W; messes L; matynes TUChH²J. ne in] ne W; no Ch; no in JL. houres] hour*es* RUDVHL KWN; masse TChH²; oures (*cancelled for* messe *same or similar hand*) J.
158 Þanne] þen ChV; *om* E. malkyn] makyn J. hire] hir HN; here UDAWM; her ChH²JK. maidenhed] maidenhode Ch H²VHLEWNM. man] Mon VL. desiriþ] desirit M; desyr*es* R; deser*is* E; desired U.
159 ioynide] ioyned Ch; bond hit V; Iugyd R; Iuggid UJ; iuged N; iugged W; Iuggit M; Ivgyth K; Iuggeth L; he iuggith A; demys E; hath wryten D; Seyth it (Seyth *over erasure in corrector's hand*) H. bokis] bukeȝ E; book UVHK WN; pistle L.
160 feiþ] fay D; Treuþe V. wiþoute] wiþouten UVJW; withowtyn EM. fait] fet R; fete N; feet DL; feate (*altered from* fette) K; þe feete J; þe fect W; fewte EM; feute A; werk U; warkis (kis *touched up*) H; Fey V; faitour Ch. is] *om* E. feblere] febelore V; febelare E; werse M. þan] þen VLE; þat J. nouȝt] nouȝth R; nouth JM; nout A; nougȝ (*late corrector adds* te) H²; a fache L.
161 And] *om* DAM. as(1)] als ChE; *om* RUVHJW. ded] deffe J. as(2)] os J. a] *om* M. nail] nale E. ȝif] ȝef ChL; þe ȝif U; *om* VEAM. þe] þine A; gode M. dede] deede V; ded*es* E; dedis AM. folewe] folwen M; folwyn A. *Here a spurious line* H; *the Latin after* **B** I 185 *or* **C** II 184 WN: *see above*, pp. 45, 30.

Chastite wiþoute charite worþ cheynide in helle;
It is as lewid as a laumpe þ*at* no li3t is inne.
Manye chapelleins arn chast ac charite is aweye;
Arn none hard*ere* þan [hy] whanne [hy] ben au*au*ncid, 165
Vnkynde to here kyn & ek to alle cristene,
Chewen here charite & chiden aftir more.
Such chastite wiþoute charite worþ cheynid in helle.
3e curato*urs* þ*at* kepe 3ow clene of 3o*ur* body,
3e ben acumbrid wiþ coueitise, 3e [conne] not out crepe; 170

162 *line marked with cross* T. Chastite] Castite A; for chastitee H. wiþoute] wiþoute*n* UVJN; w*ith*owtyn E; s*a*unce K; san3 WM. worþ . . . helle] wite þou forsoþe VH. worþ] wors H². be E; schal L. cheynide] cheynid H²K; cheyned ChW; chenyd ENM; chaynyd J; schryned RU; schryned beon L; shewed D; tenyd A. in helle] RUDChH²JLEAKWNM; *another script and ink* T.
163 It] For hit L; þ*at* U; *om* VH. as(1)] als E; *om* H²L. lewid . . . laumpe] a lamp lewde N. lewid] lewyd a thyng KW; lewedore L. as] þen L. þ*at* . . . inne] w*ith*out light KW. no li3t] no*n* lyth M. inne] w*ith*Inne J.
164 Manye] Mony ChVL; Now many U. chapelleins] chapelynes N; chapelanys H²E. arn] aru*n* J; ar H²N; ar*e* R; er E; ben ChVH; beon L; beþ D. chast] chrafti & chast A. ac] but UVHJLKW; & EANM. is] *om* EM. aweye] awey charred L.
165 Arn] Aru*n* J; Ar N; are R; Er E; Beþ DCh; þer beoþ H; Beo V; Is W. none] noon H; nane E; no men RDVJK; no man WN. hard*ere*] hardore V; hardo*ur* K; hardar EN; hardyere D; hardede A; hardur holders L. þan . . . hy] þat þey þat M. þan] þen ChVLE. hy] hij N; hey (e *cancelled*) J; þei TUDH² VHW; þey RChL; þai EA; thay K. whanne] whon V; when ChHLE; qwa*n* J. hy] J; heo V; þei TUH²WN; þey RDChL; þai EA; thay K; þe H. ben au*au*ncid] beoþ avaunset V; avaunsid ben A; au*a*unced be E.
166, 167 *transposed* H.
166 Vnkynde] Vnkende DA; Vnkuynde V; Wonkynde R; vnkynde men N; Vnkende men J; Vnkyndar nane E. here] her RChHJN; heore VL; þair E; their K. kyn] kun V; ken M; kynrede A; kynge H². &] *om* W. ek] also W; als E; *om* VHAN. cristene] oþir L.
167 Chewen] Chewyn DJK; Chiwen U; þei chewen HW; Thei chewyn N; he chouhen A; schewen R; þei schewyn M; Thai shew al E. here] her ChHKN; heore VL; þair E. chiden] chidyn AKM; chide WN; chyd*es* E. more] mare E.
168 *line om* AWN. Such] Swich UJM; Swa E. chastite] Charite VM. wiþoute] wiþoute*n* UVJ; w*ith*owtyn E; saun3 M. charite] Chastite VM. worþ . . . helle] cheue schal ille L. worþ] wrth J; be E. cheynid] chenyde J; cheyned Ch; cheneyd M; chynyd E; schryned RU; shewed D; claymed VH.
169 3e] For þi 3e A; The W; For EM; *om* VH. curato*urs*] creatours L; createrus M; creat*ur*es J; creaturis A. þ*at*] at E; *om* D. kepe 3ow] schulde 3ou kepe H; arn contynent & L. kepe] kepen UCh; kepyn JAKM; kepys E; schulde*n* kepe V. 3ow] 3e J; hem V; hemself M. of] i*n* H. 3o*ur*] oure L; heore V; her*e* M. body] bodies ChVLAWN; bodyis M; bodis JK; bod*es* E; soules H.
170 3e] þei VH; þe M. ben] bene Ch; beon L; be A; beþ RW; beoþ V; er E. acumbrid] encombrid U; cu*m*bred VLW; comberyd JAK; combyrd E. wiþ] in VKW. coueitise] care VH; synne R. 3e . . . crepe] creopen out 3e ne konne L. 3e] þei HM; & V. conne] ChH²W; konny*n* M; con HKN; konyne J; cu*n*ne U; cunnen V; cou*n*ne R; can DEA; mowe T. not] nou3t RUChWN; nouth J. out crepe] crepe out KN; crepe ought W. out] ou3t H². crepe] crepyn UD; Icrepe (*altered to* Icrepyn *same hand*) J.

So [harde] haþ auarice haspide ȝow togid*er*is.
Þ[at] is no treuþe of trinite but treccherie of helle,
And a lering to lewide men þe latt*er*e to dele.
For þise arn þe wordis writen in þe Eu*aun*gelie:
Date & dabitur vobis for I dele ȝow alle. 175
Þ*at* is þe lok of loue þ*at* letiþ out my grace
To counforte þe carful acumbrid wiþ synne.
Loue is þe leueste þing þ*at* oure lord askiþ,
And ek þe graiþ gate þ*at* goþ into heuene.

171 So] Swa E. harde] URVHJLEAK WNM; faste TDChH^{2}. haþ] hase E; now haþ WN; þei ben wiþ H; heo beoþ *with* V. haspide] haspid UH; hasped RDWN; Ihaspet V; hapsed K; hesped Ch; happyd JEA; happed L; Iclept M. ȝow] hem WM; *om* VH.
172 W *corrupts to* Al trouþ ȝe haue tinte & treches ȝe hante; H *to* þat þe trewe tresoure of trouþe is almost forȝete. Þat . . . treuþe] Ye trow noght E. Þat] þ*at* RUDVLAKNM; Þ*ere* TChH^{2}J. is] nis V. no] no*n* M. of(1)] of þe UDLAKN; in þe E. trinite] trenite A. but] RDCh VJANM; but a TUH^{2}LK; bott of E. treccherie] trechory ChEK; tricherie VL; tretherye D.
173 *copied twice but the second cancelled* T. And] *om* LW. a . . . to(1)] ȝe lere E. a] *om* A. lering] lernynge UChHAKW NM; leornyng VL; begy*n*nynge R. to(1)] RUH^{2}HLANM; to þe TDChJW; for VK. þe latt*er*e] the lighter K; þe wors W; þer A. to(2)] for to DA; forte V; do (*late corrector adds* to) H^{2}. dele] delyn M; lere E; worche W; dwelle A.
174 þise] þis RJW; þese UDH^{2}A; þes ChK; þees E; þeose L; þeos V; þo M. arn . . . wordis] wordes arn W. arn] arne K; aru*n* J; aryn M; ar N; ar*e* R; er E; beþ DVH; ben Ch. þe(1)] *om* RUVJLK. writen] writyn JKN; writtyn E; wreten DW; wretyn AM; ywryten RUV. in] on H^{2}. þe(2)] *om* JN. Euaungelie] ewa*n*gelye RV; wangelie W; vangelie A; *euangelio* N; eu*aun*geliste K; gospel L.
175 *divided from following after* loue J. *Date . . . vobis*] *twice, same hand, in margin opposite* 174 J. &] *om* A. *vobis* for] *vobis* &c for NA; *uobis* ȝyueþ to myne of ȝo*ure* good*us* for H. dele] deale K; may dele RUE; shal dele W; *cancelled for* gyff *similar hand* J. ȝow] ow V. alle] also K; alle q*uod* he (q*uod* he *cancelled*) J. *Here* H *adds two lines: see above*, p. 45.
176 *line om* V. þ*at* . . . grace] *with line* 177 J. þe lok] lok AM; þe boke ChH^{2} (*late corrector alters to* loke H^{2}); þe lesson L; a leche J. loue] lif Ch. þ*at*(2)] & EW. letiþ] lettith K; letteþ N; lete E; lette A; lateþ RW; latet D; lat M; I lete J; lyth H. out] ought W; ouȝt N; oute of J; in HM. my] ȝoure H.
177 *line om* UV. counforte] counfortyn M; comforte RDChH^{2}HLK; comforthe J; comforth EA. þe] of W. acumbrid] acomerid A; combryd E; & cu*m*berid J; þat arn combred L. wiþ] in HJLW.
178 *line om* V. Loue] Luffe J; for loue H. þe] *om* M. leueste] leuyste RUChA; lefest D; leouest HL; leu*er*ist M; *same hand after cancelled* leef J. þ*at*] at E. askiþ] askyt M; asket D; askys E; axith J; axeþ N.
179 *line om* V. ek] also E. graiþ gate] gate grethed J. graiþ] greithe L; greytheste U; geynyist M; redyeste RH; gret K; grettest EA; gr*a*ciouse N; gracieuse W. gate] waye H. goþ . . . heuene] into heuene ledeþ W. goþ] got M; goyth K; goys E. into] vp into L; vnto E. heuene] heouen L.

Forþi I seiȝe as I seide er be siȝte of þise tixtes: 180
Whan alle tresouris arn triȝede treuþe is þe beste.
Now haue I told þe what treuþe is, þ*at* no treso*ur* is bet*ere*,
I may no leng*ere* lenge; now loke þe oure lord.'

180–3 *After* I 179 R *copies* VII 70–213a *and then carries on with* I 180. *After* I 182 E *copies* VII 70–213a, *but recopies* I 180–2 *before going on with* 183. U *inserts the misplaced passage after* II 23, *but returns thereafter to* I 180, *recopying* I 180–3 *and* II 1–23. *See above*, pp. 14, 4, 16.
180 *line om* V. Forþi] For þey M; þ*er*fore U(1)J; For ChA; for ȝit WN. seiȝe] seye RU(*both*)H²HNM; sey ChJA; say DL E(*both*)KW. I(2)] *om* H². seide er] er seyde H; er saide L. er] ar E(*both*)K; here D; *om* U(2)WN. be] ben H². siȝte of] *om* E(1)AM. siȝte] sith H²W; sent (*or* seut) R. þise] þis JE(2); þese RU(*both*)H²; þes ChK; þe DHLE(1)AWNM. tixtes] tyxtis A; textes U(1)DKWN; textis U(2); tyxt M; text E(*both*).
181 *line om* V. Whan] when ChHLE(*both*); Qwan J. alle] alle þ*er* (þ*er cancelled*) J. tresouris] tresoure DAN. arn] are RH²; er E(*both*); ben ChHJ; be W; is DAN. triȝede] triede U(1); tried U(2)DChH²HJLE (*both*)AKWNM; tryde R. treuþe] trouth E(*both*); truþe RH; trwþe N; þane truthe M.
182 *line om* V. haue] *om* H². I] *om* U(2). told þe] þee tolde H. told] teld M; telde E(2); tald E(1). þe] yow E(2); *om* DJE(1)AM. what] qwat JE(*both*); q*ua*þ U(2). treuþe] trouth E(*both*); truþe RH; trwþe N. þat . . . is] is non tresor A; ne is no*n* tresur*e* M. þat] and Ch; *om* U(2) HE(*both*). no] non JA. is(2)] *om* U(2)E (*both*).
183 *line om* V. leng*ere*] leng*ur* HA; lengor L; lengyr J; longer R; lang*er* E. lenge] lengen D; lende HEA; lendyn J; lette RN; lettyn M; duelle U(2)W; duellen U(1). now] but H; *om* DA. loke . . . lord] oure lord þe mote loke L; lord loue ȝou alle A. loke] luke E. þe] you EM; þou loue H; by D.

II

ȝet knelide I on my knes ⁊ criȝede hire of grace,
And seide, 'mercy madame, for marie loue of heuene
Þat bar þe blisside barn þat bouȝte vs on þe rode,
Kenne me be sum craft to k[now]e þe false'. | *fol.* xxvij *b*
'Loke on þi left half, ⁊ lo where he standis, 5
Boþe fals ⁊ fauel ⁊ hise feris manye.'
I lokide on [my] left half as þat lady me tauȝte,
And was war of a womman wondirliche cloþide,

1 ȝet] ȝit U(*both*)ChVHJWM; ȝut R; it E; And ȝet A. knelide I] y knelid U(*both*)JAM; I kneled N; I knellyd E. knelide] knelyd DChK; kneled RH²VH W; kneoled L. my] *om* W. knes] knees U(*both*)ChH²HN; kneys R; kneos V; kneoes L; knene K; kney E. criȝede] criede H²W; cryed DChVJLEKN; cride U(1); praide U(2)H; preyd AM; souȝþe R. hire] hir HEN; here DH²AW; her ChJK; hure R.
2 mercy madame] Madame Merci V. marie] Maries VHWM. loue] sone W. heuene] heuyne JAK; heouen L.
3 bar þe] bare þe *twice but second* bare *cancelled* E; þe(1)] þat RHLA. blisside] blissyd JEKWM; blessyd D; blessede R; blisful U(1)ChVHLAN; blesful H². barn] barun J; baron A; chyld M. vs] *om* U(1). on . . . rode] wiþ his blood H. þe(2)] *om* JLEM.
4 Kenne] Teche VH. be sum] sum JA; kyndly be sum E; by kynde H; þe kuynde V. to] for to HEA; forte V. knowe] RU(*both*)DChVHAKWN; knowyn M; knowene J; knaw E; kenne TH²L. þe] þeo L; by þe M; *om* E. false] falsyde E.
5 *as one line with following* E; *divided from following after* fauel A; *after* faylande M. Loke . . . ⁊] *om* EAM. þi] þe U(1)V. left] lifte HL; lyfþe R; laft J; luft V. half] half quaþ he H²; half quod she W; hand D; hond quod heo VH; hande quod sche J; quod sche U(1). ⁊] *om* LW. lo] loke R; see U(*both*)DHJKN; seo V. where] were N; qwere JEM; whare U(1)H. he] heo V; ho L; hy J; þei U(1)HAM; *om* E. standis] standes U(2)D; stondes W; standith H²; standeþ ChN; stondith K; stondeþ VL; standyn A; stonden H; stondyn JM; stonde U(1).
6 *line om* K. Boþe] boþyn M; *om* E. fals] þe false M. ⁊(1)] *om* E. fauel] fikill W; þe faylande M. hise . . . manye] many of here ferys vnfeythful to knowyn M. hise] al his V; here A; alle her H. feris manye] hole Meyne VH. manye] alle RE; many vnfeythfully to knowe A.
7 lokide] lokid U(1)EAKM; lokede DV; loked RChH²HJLWN. my] RU(1)DH JLEAKWNM; þe U(2)ChV; þat TH². left] lyft HLA; lyfþe R; luft V. half] alf N; hond H. as] als JLE; and Ch. þat] þe RU(*both*)DVHEA. me] *om* WM. tauȝte] badde W.
8 And was] And I was U(1); I was M; þenne was I VH. war] worthily war A. womman] wommon VL. wondirliche] was wondurly H; fayre A; worthliche M. cloþide] clothid U(2)H²EA (*after cancelled* Icho A); cloþed DChVHLW; Iclothid KNM; ycloþed R; atired U(1). *Here* H *adds a form of line* 13

Ipurfilid wiþ pelure, þe pureste [o]n erþe,
Icorounid in a coroune, þe king haþ non bet*ere*; 10
Alle here fyue fyngris were frettid wiþ rynges
Of þe pureste p*er*reiȝe þ*at* p*ri*nce werde eu*ere*;
In red scarlet robid & ribande wiþ gold.
Þ*ere* nis no quen queynt*ere* þ*at* quyk is o lyue.
'What is þis wo*m*man,' q*ua*þ I, 'þus worþily atirid?' 15
'Þat is mede þe maide, haþ noiȝede me ful ofte,
And lakkide my lore to lordis aboute.

9 Ipurfilid] Ipurfuled Ch; P*ur*filed U(1)H; Purfylet V; Ifurryd M; Ipelurid J; Ipurid A; Puryd E. pelure] Piloure E; peolour L; pelury K. þe] *om* ChE. pureste] puyrest L; finest J; ricchest VH; worthiest E. on] RU(*both*)DChEKWNM; vppon VH; apon L; in TH^2; of J; *lost in repairing* A. erþe] eorþe VL; erde A. *Here* H *adds a form of line* 12.
10 Icorounid] ycorouned RU(2)VW; Icrownyd K; Icrowned ChN; Corounyd JEM; Corowned U(1); Crouned DHL; Croundid A. in] *altered to* with *by late corrector* H^2; wiþ U(*both*)DChVHLEAK NM. coroune] crown ChHKN; trone W. þe] þat D; at þe E. haþ] hat M; hase E. non] no RU(*both*)DChH^{2}VHE AK.
11 *line om* RU(*both*). here] her ChHK; hire JLM; hir VE. were] weren H^{2}K; weryn JM; weore V; *om* W. frettid] frettyt J; fretted HN; frettet DV; frette Ch; fryttid H^2; yfretted W; freten K; fetred L; fetterd E; federid A.
12 *Copied after line* 9; *in its place here a spurious line* H. *See above*, p. 45. L *substitutes:* Of riche rubies wel rede and oþir feole stones. Of] pyȝte ful of H. þe] þe þe M; *om* H. pureste] preciousest V; *om* H. perreiȝe] perreye RU(2)ChW; perrye HK; perry DH^{2}J; perre U(1)VEANM. þat . . . euere] & of preciouse stoones H. þat] þe DH^2 AM. p*ri*nce] princes Ch. werde] weride U(1); weryd H^{2}JEAKM; wered RU(2) DChVWN.
13 *Copied after line* 8; *in its place a spurious line* H. *See above*, p. 45. In] In a H^{2}JEKM. red] reed U(2)H^{2}HM; roed U(1); *om* E. scarlet] scarlate H^2; scharled A. robid] robed DChL; yrobed WN; robe H^{2}EK; roobe M; round robe A; cote J; heo rode H; heo Rod V. &] *om* RU(1)ChVHE WM. ribande . . . gold] wiþ gold rebended L. ribande] rybanyd U(*both*); Rebaned Ch; rebaund A; IRybaunt V; rybaynyd aboute R.
14 nis] is RU(*both*)ChHJLEAK. quen queyntere] quoyntre qwene L. queynt*ere*] queyntur H^2; qweyntore V; qwaynt*our* K; koynter H; so queenlike E. o lyue] on lyue RU(*both*)DChH^{2}HJLWM; alyue VKN; on lyfe A; on erthe E.
15 What . . . wo*m*man] wat woman is þat M. What] Qwat J. þis] þat RA. wo*m*man] wommon VHL. þus] so RU(*both*)DJLKWNM; þat is þus EA. worþily] worthly Ch; wortly (*late corrector supplies* h) H^2; wonderly RU(*both*)VN; wondurly H; gentely M. atirid] atyryde JE; atired U(*both*)DChH^{2}HLAKWN; atyret V; ateryd M.
16 Þat] Þis E. mede þe maide] a maydyn hyth med q*uo*d sche M. maide] made W; maiden U(1)JLE; mayde q*uo*þ heo H; Mayde*n* q*uo*d heo V; mayde qod she (qod she *added by late corrector*) H^2. haþ . . . me] þat me hat greuyd M; at me hase grevyd E; þat greuyth me A. haþ] þat haþ RVHW. noiȝede me] me marred V. noiȝede] noyede H^{2}J; noyed RU(*both*) DChLW (*in margin, same hand, for cancelled* Inored L); noyyd K; niyed N; anoyȝed H. me] *om* L. ful] fol L; wel U(2)DChK; *om* VHEANM.
17 And] Ad V; And eke A; And also M. lakkide] Ilakked VH; hase laykd E; lakked lodlich L; lackith A. lore] lare E. aboute] aboutyn M.

In þe popis paleis heo is *pre*uy as myselue;
And so shulde [heo] not be for wrong was hire sire;
Out of wrong heo wex to wroþ*er*hele manye. 20
I au3te ben hi3ere þanne heo for I com of a bet*ere*.
Tomorewe worþ þe mariage mad of mede & of fals;
Fauel wiþ fair speche haþ forgid hem togid*ere*;
Gile haþ begon hire so heo g*ra*untiþ alle his wille;
And al is li3eris ledyng þ*at* hy li3en togid*er*is. 25
Tomorewe worþ þe mariage ymad as I þe telle;

18–145 missing A; *see above*, p. 1.
18 In . . . as] heo is more pryue wiþ þe pope þan y am L. In . . . is] She is in þe popes paleys (in *added above line*) W. popis] poopis H; papes (*touched up*) K; papis E; pope V. heo] he (*late corrector prefixes* s) H²; sche RU(*both*)DChKN; *om* JEM. is] *om* JEM. preuy] priue U(*both*); pryuei N; as preuy M; als preve E; as priue VHW. as] als E. selue] seluen VE; seluyn M; seolue L; sylue H.
19 so] swa E. shulde] suld E. heo] VHL; he (*late corrector prefixes* s) H²; sche RU(*both*)ChJKWNM; sho E; it TD. not] nou3t DChH²VHN; noght U(*both*) EW; nouth J. be] be*n* J; beon L; *om* U(1)VHW. was] is K. hire] hir VHEN; here U(*both*)DH²JW; her ChK; hur*e* R. sire] fadir L; si3te Ch.
20 *line om* U(1)E; *marked with a cross* N. Out of] Ou3t of H²; Into V; And wyt M. heo . . . to] wente sche U(2). heo] he DH² (*late corrector prefixes* s H²); sche RChJKWNM. wex] wax DH²HL; wox VK. to] out M. wroþerhele] wrotherhele *same hand after cancelled* wrotherel U(2). manye] monye V. *Here* WN *add lines like* **C** III 28–9 *and the adjacent Latin: see above*, p. 30.
21 I] Ich V; Bot I E. au3te] au3the R; awte J; haute M; ou3te DN; owght K; ouhte V; oght L; oute W. ben] be RU(2)Ch; to ben U(1)DJM; to be HEK; to beo L. hi3ere] hyere RJEW; hey3er HK; heyere U(*both*)D; herre VLN; bet M. þanne] þen V; þe E. heo] he (*late corrector prefixes* s) H²; sche RU(*both*)D ChJKWNM; sho E. for] *om* VHJLK. com] cam U(1)ChJM. a] an H; þe M; *om* RU(*both*)ChE. betere] *over erased* herre H. *Here* N *adds lines like* **C** III 31–40 *and their Latin*; *see above*, p. 30.
22 Tomorewe] To morn ChH; To þe more E; Now WN. worþ þe] worþ a WN; worthy E; woth L; shal þe (shal *another hand over erased* worþe) H. mad] ymad U(2)V; be made H. mede] Meede V; hyre M. fals] falshed E.
23 *Copied here and after line* 26 E. fair] feir VCh; þe fayre DE(2); his feyre HM. haþ] hat M; hase E(1); haue E(2). forgid] forgit (*late corrector alters to* forgid) H²; forged RU(1)DJLWN; forget E(2); forgett K; fanged E(1); fongid M; brou3t VH; ioyned Ch. hem] heom L; þaim E(*both*).
24 *line om* RU. Gile] And Gile VHWN. haþ] hase E. begon . . . so] so begon her*e* J; ben forgor*e* M; ben forthganger E. hire] hir HN; here DH²L; her ChKW. heo] he H²; sche DChJKWN; & EM. grauntiþ] grauntes E; graunted J; grantyd M. alle] *om* JEN. his] her*e* M. wille] welle M.
25 *line om* RU. al is] al his DH²W; is M; al is it Ch; herewi*th* hys E. li3eris] lie3ers Ch; ly3ars H; lyeris J; lyeres DH²; liers LWM; liars KN; *om* E. ledyng] lore W. þat] *om* E. hy] heo V; þey DChHNM; þay LE; thay K; *om* H²W (*late corrector supplies* they H²). li3en] lie3en Ch; lyen DJK; lye E; shal lye N; schal lygge M; leuen V; lyuen L; lyue so (*small* o *above* yu) H; ledeþ hem W.
26 Tomorewe] To morowene J; Tomorne UChHN; Now W. worþ þe] worht þere a W; be þis E; schal þei make þe H. mariage] marage (*corrected from* made) D. ymad] mad L; maad U; made ChH²JEK WNM; *om* DH. as I] soþ as I VH; soth I J. þe] þe treuly W; er of L; *om* RM. telle] tolde LK.

Þ*ere* miȝte þ*ou* wyte ȝif þ*ou* wilt whiche þei ben alle
Þ*at* longiþ to þ[at] lordsshipe, þe lasse ⁊ þe more.
Knowe hem þ*ere* ȝif þ*ou* canst and kep þe from hem alle
ȝif þou wilnest to wone wiþ treuþe in his blisse. 30
I may no leng*ere* lette, lord I þe bekenne,
And become a good man for any coueitise, I rede.'
Alle þe riche reten*aun*ce þ*at* regniþ wiþ false
Were beden to þe b[ri]dale on boþe two sides.
Sire symonye is assent to asele þe ch*art*res 35
Þ*at* fals ⁊ fauel be any fyn halden,

27 Þ*ere*] þ*at* V. miȝte þ*ou*] þ*ou* miht V; may þ*ou* LE; thow mayht J; mightestow W; mayst þ*ou* H. wyte] witen JLN; wete DE; wetyn M; seo V. ȝif] *twice, second cancelled* T; ȝef L. wilt] wolt RVHLK; will EW. whiche] wiche ChJLNM; whuche VH; what E. þei] þai EW; thay K. ben] beon L; beþ H; se E.
28 *line om* VH. Þ*at*] And D. longiþ] longyn J; longen Ch; longon L; langeþ D; lang*es* E; longe (th *added above line similar ink*) W; logyn M. þat] þ*at* RUChJEK WNM; þe TDH^{2}L (*late corrector alters to* þat H^2). lasse] lesse RChJEWM; fals K. ⁊] an R. þe] *om* E.
29 *line om* VH. Knowe] Knowen K; Kawne E. hem(1)] heom L; þaim E; hym M. þere] *om* EM. ȝif] ȝef ChL. canst] can E. hem(2)] heom L; them K; þaim E. alle] euere L.
30 ȝif] ȝef L; Yf þ*at* E; Bote ȝif VH. wilnest] wilne V; willest DChH^2; will E; wilt M; wolt K; couet J; þenkest R. to] *om* DEKM. wone] wonyn M; wonye K. treuþe] trouth E; truþe RH; trwþe N; crist Ch. in] ⁊ in K; *corrected from* and W. *Here* H *adds a line: see above*, p. 45.
31 lengere] lengore VL; leng*ur* H^{2}H; langer E. lette] lettyn M; lete E; letyn J; lende H; dwelle D. lord] our lorde ChV HM (our *over first stroke of an* l Ch); now oure lord W; now lorde N; bote lord LE; *late corrector adds* god the H^2. I] Ich V. bekenne] byteche R; bytake H; bekepe E.
32 *line om* N. And] *late corrector adds* to H^2; Loke þou H; *om* W. become . . . coueitise] for any couetise bycom a goode mon L. good] goud R; gude E. man] mon V. for . . . rede] I rede þe for any coueitise W. any] eny RV; ony UDEM. coueitise] þing EM. I rede] Ich rede V; *om* H. *Here* H *adds a line; see above*, p. 45.
33 Alle] For al E; Now al WN; ⁊ sawe al H. þe] þis V; þat H. retenaunce] Retenaunces N; Retenau*n*tes V; retenu J; retenew E. regniþ . . . false] with false reigneth U. regniþ] regnyt M; reignyn J; Regneden V; regned H; ryneþ R; woneþ W; wonnys E. false] þe fals WNM; falsehed E.
34 Were] weren ChH^{2}JM; Weryn K; weore L; weoren V. beden] bedyn D; bede V; ybede R; boden HLN; bodyn JKM; bode H^2; yboden U; bidde Ch; byddyng E. þe] þis LK; þ*at* J. bridale] UDChH^{2}HJ LKN; brydhale M; brydell E; bredale RW; Bruytale V; bedale T. on] opon W. boþe] boþin JM; Bo VL. two] þe two ChE; two þe VL; *om* KW.
35 *line om* U. is] was HJM; was sone L; *om* E. assent] *late corrector adds* for H^2; sent L; of asseent M; of sent RVN; after sent J; aftur sent H; sent for K; Isent W. to] te H. asele] ensele H^2; enseale K; sele RDLW; selen M; selyn J; seele HN; seyll E. þe] þo J; þeo L; þees E. chartres] chatures (*late corrector supplies* r *after* a) H^2; charter JW.
36 L *corrupts to* How false wold a fyn rere ⁊ not wold he faile; *then adds a line: see above*, p. 47. Þat] Of all þat W. fals] fayvell E; *om* N. ⁊] oþ*er* RUHWN; oþur V. fauel] faufelle H; falshed E. any] eny VN; ony RUDHJ; on EM. fyn] peyne V. halden] holden UDHEN; holdyn JKM; heolden V; holdeþ RW.

And feffe mede þer[myd] in mariage for euere.
þer nas halle ne hous to herberwe þe peple,
þat iche feld nas ful of folk al aboute.
In myddis a mounteyne at mydmorewe tide 40
Was pi3t vp a pauyloun proud for þe nones,
And ten þousand of tentis teldit beside
Of kni3tes of cuntr[e], of comeres aboute,
For sisours, for somenours, for selleris, for beggeris,
For lerid, for lewid, for laboureris of þropis, 45
Alle to wytnesse wel what þe writ wolde,
In what maner þat mede in mariage was feffid; |
To be fastnid wiþ fals þe fyn is arerid. *fol.* xxviij *a*

37 And] to HM. feffe] feoffe L; enfeffyn M; feffyd E; feffeþ W. mede] Meede V; *om* M. þermyd] þermyd LUKN; þer wiþ T RDChH²VHJW; þer wyt M; þat maydyn E. mariage] maryage þat maydyn M.
38 þer] Bote þer V. nas] ne was JM; is nowder E. hous] boure EM. to] þat miht V. herberwe] herberwyn J; herborwe V; herborw3 H²; herbarowe Ch; herbery E; harborowe HK; *in margin, same hand, the original word erased* L; resseyue M. þe] þeo L; þat E; alle þe J; in þe D. peple] pepule H; people LK.
39 iche feld] ichon M. iche] ech RUD H²KW; vche V; euery Ch. feld] feild L. nas] ne was UWN; no was L; was DJEM. ful of] filled wiþ H. of folk] of folkes D; *om* E. al] alle 3erde (*late corrector alters to* alle the yerde) H²; *om* R. aboute] abowtyn M.
40 In] In þe W; I D. a] an H²; on a V; of a DHKW. mounteyne] montane E. mydmorewe] mydmorne E. tide] tyme RL.
41 pi3t] py3þ R; pyt J. vp] upon H²; vpp *corrected from* vpon W. proud] a proud H²VHKW; was proud D; prow U. nones] nonys RJKNM; nons E; noonus H.
42 And] *om* W. ten] ton U. þousand] 3owsyng J. of] *om* R. tentis] teltys M. teldit] telded WN; teilded L; Itelded Ch; Iteldyde (*altered another ink to* Ibeldyde) H; telt M; Itald E; telden K; telid J; teled D; tight U; ty3th R; Itilled V. beside] besydes VKWN; bysedes D; þer byside UM; þer by sydes R; forþ bisydes H; by þer sides L.
43 Of] For H²VHLM. kni3tes] kni3tghes N; ky3thys R; *om* L. cuntre] UH²VM; þe Contre DHLE; cuntres TChJKWN; cortyeres R. of] and VHLEM. comeres] comuners LKWN; commons al E.
44 somenours] Somondours E; sompnours H²HL. selleris] sellars KN; seollers L; sullers V; sillers (*late corrector changes* i *to* e) H². for(4)] ⁊ JL. beggeris] beggers Ch H²E (*late corrector changes to* byggers H²); biggeris J; biggers H; biggars N; byggeres RUW; Buggers V; byars K; buyers L. *Here* H²W *add a line: see above*, pp. 47, 50.
45 lerid] lernyd M; lewed L; lewede V. for(2 *and* 3)] fo M. lewid] lawed D; lerid L; lerede V. laboureris] laborars K; labores DHJ; laboreys M. of þropis] many E. of] for R. þropis] þropes ChH²VHKN; thorppys JM; þorpes D; þrepis RU; werkes W; kraftes L. *Here* H *inserts a line;* W *adds a passage like* **B** II 59–63 *or* **C** III 60–4; N *one like* **B** II 59–65 *or* **C** III 60–6. *See above*, pp. 45, 30.
46 Alle] And al N. to] *om* J. wytnesse] wytnesseyn M. wel] *om* W. what] qwat J. þe . . . wolde] þey wrytyn woldyn M; þai write wald E. writ] write K.
47 what] wat M; qwat JE. þat] ⁊ howe þat H; *om* E. in . . . feffid] was feoffed in mariage K. in mariage] *om* H. in] in stout N; wiþ W. was] *om* N. feffid] feoffed L; Ifeffed H; sesyd EM; *om* VN.
48 To be] was N. be] ben M; beo VL. fastnid] fastned LWN; fastnet V; fastenyd K; fastened DH; festened Ch; feffyd E; feffed U; fessyd (*for* feffyd) M. fals] þe fals D; falshede E. is] was VH.

Þanne fauel fettiþ hire forþ & to fals takiþ
In foreward þat falshed shal fynde hire for euere, 50
And he[o] be bou[n] at his bode his bidding to fulfille,
At bedde & at boord buxum and hende,
And as sire symonye wile segge to sewen his wille.
Symonye & cyuyle stondiþ forþ boþe
And vnfolde þe feffement þat fals haþ ymakid; 55
Þus begynne þe gomes & gredde wel heiȝe:
'Wyten & wytnessen þat wonen vpon erþe,
Þat I, fauel, feffe falsnesse to mede,

49 Þanne] þenne V; þen ChH; Now N. fettiþ] fetteþ Ch; fette ULM; fet VHJ; feccheþ N; feheþ W; fecchet D; fechyd E. hire] hir HE; here DJM; her ChKWN; *om* L. &] & hir N. takiþ] takeþ RChH² VLWN; taket D; hir toke H; hir knytt E; tauthe M.

50 In] I M. þat] at E. falshed] falsed M; falsede LW; false U; Falsnesse VH . shal] schuld H; suld E. fynde] fynden V; fyndyn J. hire] hir HEN; here DH²JW; her ChK.

51 And] *om* V. heo] H; he TH²; sche RDKWNM; che J; scho E; *om* UChVL. be] beo L; ben J; To be VEK; to ben M; *om* N. boun] LKW; bowen N; bounde TDChH²; Boxum and Boun VH; buxoum RUJEM. at . . . bode] *om* VHEM. bode] bede D. bidding] hest N; dyddyng M. fulfille] fulfulle L; folfulle V; do E; done M.

52 At(1)] In V; Boþyn at M. &] *om* ChH² (*late corrector inserts* H²). buxum . . . hende] whil here lyf lasten M; qwilse þair lyue last E. buxum] be buxum K. hende] heende H.

53 E *substitutes* In wittnes of Simony & siuile his brother; M *substitutes* In wytnesse of syre syuyle & symonye is broþyr. And] *om* KN. as . . . wile] at sire symonyes wille RUD. as sire] right as WN. wile] wole H; wol VLK. segge] sigge V; seye H; sey Ch; seyn DJN; say K; sayn W; *om* RU. to . . . wille] his bidding to fulfille W. to] *om* V. sewen] sewyn K; suwen H; suen N; suyen U; schewen VL; schewyn RJ. wille] heste RU.

54 Symonye] Now Simonye VWN; þo symonye H. cyuyle] gyle H². stondiþ] stondeþ VLK; standith U; standeþ D; standes RE; stonden ChW; stonde N; stondeth ȝe H²; stodyn JM; stoden H. forþ] vp RU. boþe] bothin JM; togedir E; in fere H.

55 And] *om* V. vnfolde] vnfolden DCh JLKN; vnfoldyn M; vnfoldeþ R; vnfoldith U; vnfalden E; vndoþe W; VnFoldyng V; vnfoldeden H. feffement] Feoffement L; vestyment R. fals] Falsnes VH. haþ] had H; hade E; hadde M; *om* V. ymakid] Imaked ChH²N; makyd R; maked D; made VHEW; Imakyn M; yformed L.

56 *line om* V. Þus . . . gomes] þe cryurs begunne M. Þus] & þus HLW. begynne] bygynnen L; begynnyn J; begynneþ RUDChW; begynnys E; begonne K; bygonnen H. þe] þise N; þis REW; thes K; þeose L. gomes] gome R; goom U; gromes DH²JWN (r *added above line* W). &] for to E; to N; *om* M. gredde] grede N; greden ChLKW; gredeþ D; gredith U; gradden H; gretyþ R; criddyn J; crye E; crye þe chartre M. wel] wol U; wil D; ful J; *om* E. heiȝe] hyȝe L; hiegh N; hye UDChJK; an hyȝe (an *cancelled*) H; an hye H²; he E; loude WM; eche R. *Here* WN *add the Latin line after* **B** II 73 *or* **C** III 78*: see above*, p. 30.

57 Wyten] Wityn K; Weten D; wete E; Witeþ W; wytyth J; Wytyt M; weteþ Ch; Now witen N; HIt witen VH. wytnessen] witnesse UE; witnesseþ ChW; wytnessyth J; wytnessit M. wonen] woneþ RDVN; wonyth J; wonyt M; wonnes E; wonyen K. vpon] apon L; on K. erþe] eorþe VL.

58 Þat] At E. feffe] feff H; haue feffyd E; fastne M; haue RU. falsnesse] Fals VH; falshede EW; falsed N. to] with J; to þat Mayden V; to þis mayden H. mede] me M.

To be p*re*sent in pride for pou*er*e [or for] riche,
Wiþ þe Erldom of enuye for eu*er*e to laste, 60
Wiþ alle þe lordsshipe of leccherie in lengþe & in brede;
Wiþ þe kingdom of coueitise I croune hem togid*er*e;
And al þe Ile of vsurie, & auarice þe faste,
Glotonye & grete oþes I gyue hem togid*er*e;
Wiþ alle þe delites of lust þe deuil for to s*er*ue, 65
In al þe s*igniur*e of slouþe I se[se] hem togid*er*e;
Þei to haue & to holde & here eires aftir
Wiþ alle þe p*ur*tena*un*ce of p*ur*catorie into þe pyne of helle;
ȝeldinge for þis þing at o ȝeris ende
Here soulis to sathanas to synken in pyne, 70

59 To] For to E. be] ben J; beo L; *om* WM. pride] pruyde V; p*r*ide to ben M; pres W. or for] RUDVHJLEKWNM; oþ*er* TChH^2.

60 of] on N. for eu*er*e] euer for VHW; for eu*er*e more M; eu*er*e RUN; euer more ChLE.

61 *line om but supplied in margin by corrector before rubrication* H. Wiþ] *om* M. alle] *om* H^2HJEWNM. þe] *om* J. lordsshipe] lordechip N; lordechepp JM; lordschupe V; worschipe UD; worschep R. of] *om* V. leccherie] lecchory Ch; lichery J; lichory E; *om* V. in(1)] of V; on EM. lengþe] lenth EW; leynthe L; lenght H^2K; lengh N. in(2)] of VE; on M; *om* Ch.

62 kingdom] kyngdam DHJM; kyndome H^2; kyndam L. I] & E; *om* M. croune] coroune ULEK; corouny*n* M. hem] heo*m* L; þaim E; ȝou RU. *Here* E *copies line* 65.

63 *line om* J; *marked with a cross* N. And] wiþ UVHEN. al] *om* VH. Ile] isle H^2N; ilde M; ill K; euell E; vycys RU. vsurie] vsure VENM; vsur*es* RU. þe faste] þe laste Ch; þe false DVH; þe þ*er* wyth H^2; alse LWM; al hale E.

64 *line om* J. oþes] oþus V; ooþ*us* H; athes E. I gyue] ȝeue I M. I] Ich V. gyue] gyf REN; geue DCh; ȝiue VH; yeve K; graunte L. hem] heom L; þaim E; ȝow U. togid*er*e] Ifeere V; i*n* fere H. *Here* L *copies line* 67.

65 *copied before line* 63 E. alle] *om* H^2E. þe] *om* DVLW. delites] delices UK; delicis J; lyt*es* R; likyng EM. of] and V. lust] lustes VL; deedly synne H. deuil] deuol H; deouel L. for] fo M. s*er*ue] seruen DK; s*er*uyn M. *Here* WN *insert lines like* **C** III 84–7, 89, 92, 98–100, 102–4: *see above*, p. 30.

66 In al] Wiþ WN. þe] þeo L. s*igniur*e] siegnyo*ur*ie K; seignourie URDChH^2LWN; segoury E; synge J; synnes M; seruyse VH. slouþe] slewþe H^2ChEWNM; scleuþe R; sclouth K. sese] RUH^2VJLW; seyse ChEN; ceese H; sesen K; lese M; set TD. hem] heom L; þaim E. togid*er*e] yfere L; for eu*er*e M.

67 *appears both here and before line* 65 L. Þei] Þai E; thay K; þat H; here D; *om* VJWN. haue] haue*n* M; hauyn J; habben V. to(2)] *om* RHL(*both*). holde] holden V; holdy*n* M; hould K; hald E. &(2)] to Ch. here] her ChK; heore L(2); þ*er* J; all heore V; all here WN; alle her H; all þair E; to heore L(1). eires] arys E. aftir] for euere L.

68 alle] *om* VEWNM. p*ur*tena*un*ce] ap*ur*tinaunce LM; portunanc*es* R. p*ur*catorie] purgatorye RUChH^2VHJEKWNM; pugatorye D; penaunce L. into] & H; & wiþ W. pyne] peyne DNM; payn K.

69 ȝeldinge] ȝeildyng L; Yeldand E. þis þing] þeose thyngis L; þis D. at] atte J. o] on RChLNM; oon H; one UH^2K; þe DVE; *om* J. ende] eynde L.

70 Here] her ChHJ; Heore VL; Þ*er* E. soulis] saules DE; soule K. to(1)] vnto E. to(2)] and RU. synken] synkyn DJKNM; synke RUH^2E; senden V; sende H; sogerne L; dwelle W. in] into RUVHEM. pyne] *after cancelled* hell K; peyne DWN; sorwe L.

þere to wone wiþ wrong while god is in heuene.'
In witnesse of whiche þing wrong was þe furste,
And piers þe pardoner, poulynes doctor,
Bette þe bedel of bukyngham shire,
Randolf þe reue of rutelondis sokne, 75
Munde þe myllere, & manye mo oþere.
In þe date of þe deuil þe dede is asselid
Be siȝte of sire symonye & signes of notories.
þanne tenide hym theologie whan he þis tale herde,
And seide to cyuyle, 'now sorewe on þi bokes, 80
Such weddyng to werche to wraþþe wiþ treuþe;

71 *line om* U. þere] And þer E. wone] wonen V; wonyn J; wonne E; wony DK. wiþ] *om but added above line another script* W. wrong] þat wyght L. while] wil NM; whiles K; whilys RJ; wlysse E. heuene] heuyne J; heouen L.
72 witnesse] witnessyng Ch. of] of þe H. whiche] wich ChLN; qwych J; whilke E; whuche VH; weche M. þing] þynges D; *om* J. wrong] wrang E; þis wrong W. furste] fyrste RUDChH²JEKWN.
73 *run together with following* J. And] *om* RUVJ; A E. þe] a L. poulynes] paulynes URDVLKWNM; & paulyns HE; *om* J. doctor] douȝter RVHN; *om* J.
74 Bette] and bette RUN; And bedde W; Bernard E. bedel] bedyl UK; bedul H²; bydel M; bydul R; beodil L; Budul VH. bukyngham] Bokynghames V.
75 Randolf] Randof J; Randalf D; Rondulf V; Rondol (f *added another ink*) H; Randor (r *over erasure*) Ch; Reynald M; And ranald E. of] oute of H. rutelondis] Rotelondes V; Rokelandes U; Rutelonde K; Rotelonde H; Rotlond M; Roteland L; Rutlond Ch; rutland EW; Rutteland D; rotolonde N; rokelond RJ. sokne] *om* H. *Here* H²H *add a line: see above*, pp. 47, 45.
76 Munde] Mounde H; Monde VM; Mundy R; and munde U; Maclum L. myllere] myllar K; Mellere D; mylnere RUHJEW; Mulnere V; melleward M; meoleward L. & . . . oþere] of malwiche strete U. manye] mony DVHL; ony E. mo] moo H; an M; *om* E. *Here* E *inserts four lines: see above*, p. 49.
77 þe(1)] *om* D. deuil] deouel L. þe(3)] þis RUDEKWNM. is] was ChH²VHL; I RUNM; here þai E. asselid] aselyde J; asseled Ch; aseled H²; aselet V; aseelid L; seled D; yseled W; Insealid K; asele RUNM; seyll E.
78 *line om* K. Be] In Ch. siȝte] seyt R. & signes] in seals D. &] vndur L; wiþ W. signes . . . notories] Notaries signes VW; notarie sygnes HN.
79 þanne] þEn VHL; þo M. tenide] tenyd UE; tenede M; tened DChJWN; teonede V; teoned HL. hym] *om* DE. theologie] tealogy þat J. whan] whon V; when RHL; qwan J; qwen E. he] þe (*altered to* she *by late corrector*) H². þis] ys M. tale] call J. herde] hurde R.
80 to] vnto W. cyuyle] sir ciuile E. now] *om* RUChVEWM. sorewe] sorwe RUH²WM; sorowe HK; sorow DChEN; sorw L; serwe V; sorowyn J. bokes] bukes E; lokkes VH; chekes KW (*same hand after cancelled* bokes K).
81 Such] Siche a U; Swyche JM. weddyng] weddyngis N; werkes EM. werche] worche RH²VLKN; wurche UDH; wirche ChJ; wirke E; make W. to . . . wiþ] þerwith to wreth E. wraþþe] wrathyn JM; wreþen Ch; wreþthe W; werre R; teone VH. wiþ] herewith J; *om* Ch. treuþe] trouth E; truþe RHK; trwþe N; syre treuþe H².

[And] er þis weddyng be wrouȝt wo þe betide!
For mede is molere of [m]endis engendrit
God *gra*untide to gyue mede to treuþe,
And þou hast gyuen hire to a gil*our*, now god ȝiue þe sorewe! 85
Þe text[e] tell[iþ] not so, treuþe wot þe soþe:
Dignus est operarius mercede [*sua*].
Worþi is þe werkman his mede to haue,
And þou hast fastnid hire wiþ fals, fy on þi law[e]!
For al be lesinges þou lyuest, & leccherous werkis;

82 And] RUVHJLEKWNM; *om* TDCh H[2]. er] or RDChE; ar VKN; her M. þis] þat H; þyn (*same hand above cancelled* þu) M. weddyng] wreddynd M; *om* L. be] beo VL. wrouȝt] wroth (*altered to* wrowght *by late corrector*) H[2]; ywrouȝþ R. wo] woo DHK; wa E; sorwe M. þe] þe now J. betide] beotyde V.
83 *line om* W; *marked with a cross* N. molere] muliere RUCh; mulyer D; moillere N; moill*our* L; a mulier E; a moyler*e* J; a mewliere K; medler*e* H[2]; a medeler H; a maydyn M; a Iuweler V. of . . . engendrit] a Mayden of goode VH. of] for M. mendis] mendes JLK; me*n*nis N; mannys M; frendis TRDChH[2]; frendis of frendis U; fendes E. engendrit] engendritȝ H[2]; engendrid UDN; engendred ChLK; ingendred E; gendered J; engendryng M. *Here* N *inserts lines like* C III 121–5, 127–36: *see above*, p. 30.
84 *line om* E. God] And god M. *gra*untide] *gra*untyd K; grauntede M; graunted W; *gra*untith J; grauntеþ RUDLN; graunt ChH[2] (*late corrector suffixes* it H[2]); graunte vs VH. to(1)] for to J. gyue] geue DChKW; ȝiue VH; ȝiuen M; ȝeue L; ȝeuyn J. mede . . . treuþe] hire þer treuþe wol asigne V; hir þere truþe wole assente H. to(2)] menskelich to L; for JN. treuþe] truþe RK; trwþe N; þe trewe W.
85 And] for H; Now K; *om* D. þou] *om* E. hast] has J; hase E. gyuen] geue*n* DE; gevyn K; ȝiuen VHJM; ȝeuen L; ȝeue Ch; ȝif R; þif W. hire] hir HEN; here UDChW; her K; hur*e* R; mede her*e* (mede *cancelled*) H[2]. to] *om* VJ. a gil*our*] gile W. now . . . sorewe] *om* R. now] *om* DVHJEKWM. god . . . þe] ȝiue þe god H[2]. god] oure lord H. ȝiue] ȝeue DChM; ȝef L; gyve K; gife W; gyf JN; gyff E. sorewe] sorowe DHJK; sorow ChEN; sorwe UH[2]LW; serwe V; sorweyn M.
86 Þe] Thi WN. texte] UHEKWN; tyxte RVJLM; textis TH[2]; textes D; tyxtest Ch. telliþ] tellith UHJLK; tellit M; telleþ RChVWN; tellys E; telle TDH[2]. not so] now J. not] nouȝt DChN; noght U; the not H[2]W (the *by late corrector* H[2]); þee not H; þe noȝt E; þe nout M. so] swa E; *om* D. treuþe] truþe RHKM; trwþe N; god E. wot] wate E; wotith K.
86α *in margin* R; *run together with line* 87 M; *om* W. *operarius*] *mercenarius* K. *mercede*] *om* M. *sua*] UDChH[2]VHJK; *sua &c* LEN; *om* TRM.
87 Worþi . . . werkman] *om* M. Worþi] worth (*late corrector adds* i) H[2]. is] es J. þe] a K. werkman] workman ChK; werkmon V; warkmon H; warkeman N. his] *om* R. mede] hir*e* M; hure V; huyre H. to] for to HLE; wel to WN. haue] hauyne J.
88 fastnid] fastned RDJW; fastynyd K; fastened ChLN; fastinde H[2]; festnyd U; fasted M; feffyd E; feffed H; feffet V. hire] hir HEN; her*e* UDW; her ChK; hur*e* R. wiþ] to KWM. fals] falshed E. fy] now fye HEW. lawe] DVHJLEKW NM; lawes TRUChH[2].
89 V *substitutes* For lechours & lyȝers lihtliche þou leeuest; H *substitutes* for lesyngis & lecheryes suche warkes þou louest. be] ben H[2]. lesinges] lesyng DE. lyuest] lyvyst KM; leuest DChH[2]J; leuys E. leccherous] licherous E; lechores L; lecherours D; liccherours J. werkis] workes ChH[2]K.

Symonye & þiself shenden holy chirche; | 90
3e & þe notories noye þe peple; *fol.* xxviij *b*
3e shuln abigge boþe, be god þat me made.
Wel 3e wyte, wernardis, but 3if 3oure wyt faile,
Þat fals is a faitour [and] feyntles of werkis,
[And] as a bastard yborn of belsab[ubb]is kynde; 95
And mede is a mulere, [a maiden of gode];
She mi3te kisse þe king for cosyn 3if he[o] wolde.
Werchiþ be wysdom & be wyt aftir;
Ledíþ hire to lundoun þere lawe is yhandlit

90 Symonye] Synonye Ch. self] selue UJ; seolf L; silf H. shenden] schendeþ R; schendyt M; schend H2; shendes E. chirche] cherche RJWM; Churche DHE. **91, 92** *transposed with a spurious line between them* H: *see above*, p. 45.
91 3e &] And also W; Also N. 3e] for 3e H; hit is noted 3e L; He V. þe] þese H; þees E; þise NM; þis W; þeose V; 3e U; *om* Ch. notories] Nataries V. noye] noien UDJKWN; noy3en RChH2; noys E; anoyen HM; anuy3en V; ney3en L. þe] ofte þe J. peple] pepul HJ; people LK.
92 *line om* V. 3e] Bot 3e E. shuln] schul RUDW; schulen L; schule H; schullyn M; schulle Ch; scholyn J; shal EKN. abigge] abyggen JK; abyggyn M; abugge L; aby3e R; abye EWN. boþe] boþyn M; it boþe HK; it bath E; *late corrector inserts* it H2; *om* J. god] criste JM. þat] at E.
93 Wel] For wel VL; wyl N. wyte] witen VL; wyton H; wytyn J; witte W; wyttyn K; wete Ch; weten D; wetyn M; wate E. wernardis] weornardes L; wyrnardes H; warnardes N; warnerdys R; warnerdes K; werlardys M; I warand E; warnarde *cancelled for* & wytterly *same or similar hand* J. 3if] 3ef ChL; *om* UJM. 3oure] or V; ow L. wyt] wittes E; wittis N; wittus H. faile] wante L.
94 fals] falshed E; falsnesse Ch. a] *om* R. faitour] fautor E. and] RUHJLEKWNM; a V; *om* TDChH2. feyntles . . . werkis] Falsly wirkes E; defowlys many werkys J. feyntles] feytles M; feythles UHN; faithles KW; faylere V; fals R. of] of his RD. werkis] workes ChK; warkes H.
95 And] RUChVHJLEKWNM; *om* TD H2. as] als E; *om* ChVHL. a] *om* R. yborn] Iborun J; Iboryn M; ybore RHW; born DCh; is borne E. belsabubbis] belsabubbes UDVJEKWN; belsabubus H; bealsabubbes L; belsaboukis T; belsa-buckes RCh; bessabukes M; belsabouris H2. kynde] kende M; kynne RUHJN; kyn DW; kunne V.
96 a(1)] *om* RUDKWN. mulere] muliere RCh; mulyer DE; moliere U; mewlyar K; moillere WN; meylere J; maiden LM; mened H2; medelar H; Iuweler V. a maiden] URDH2VJEKN; a mayde W; of maidens Ch; of maides T; a moiller L; amonge men H; engendryd M. of gode] RUDH2HJLEKNM; of gode mynd W; ful gent V; engendered Ch; engendrit T.
97 J *corrupts to* komlyche for cosyn þe kyng myht sche kysse. She] Sho E; Heo VHL. kisse] kyssyn M; Cusse VHL. cosyn] *om* R. 3if . . . wolde] y trowe L. 3if] 3ef Ch; & KNM. heo] VH; he TDH2K (*late corrector prefixes* s H2); sche RUChEWNM. wolde] wald E; schulde VH.
98 Werchiþ] Worchith K; Worcheþ RUDVN; wurche M; wirche Ch; worche 3e L; Wirke 3e E; þerfore worcheþ H; And þerfore do (fore *above line similar hand*) W; wolde sche wyrche J. wysdom] wisdam ChDVL; wytte H. be(2) . . . aftir] by wysedam boþe H; wayfe away wronge L. aftir] eftir E.
99 Ledíþ] ledyt M; lede DE; And lede W. hire] hir HEN; here UDH2W; her ChK; hure R. lawe] þe lawe L; wit M. yhandlit] yhandlyd U; Ihandelyd K; Ihandeled ChWM; Ihondlet V; yhondeled H; handlyd RD; handled L; yhanled N; Ihauntith *altered by late corrector to* Ihaunditd H2; Ihaunted *cancelled for* Ihandelyd *same hand* J; haldyng E.

3if any Leaute wile loke þei ligge togid*ere*. 100
And 3if þe iustice iugge hire to be ioyned *with* fals,
3et be war of þe weddyng for witty is treuþe.
For consience is of his counseil ⁊ knowiþ 3ow ichone,
And 3if he fynde 3ow in defaute, ⁊ wiþ fals holden,
It shal besette 3oure soulis wel sore at þe laste.' 105
Hereto assentiþ Cyuyle, ac symonye ne wolde
Til he hadde silu*er* for his selis ⁊ signes.
Þanne fette fauel forþ floreynes ynowe,
And bad gile go gyue gold al aboute,
'And nameliche to þe notories, þat hem non fail[e]; 110

100 3if] 3ef ChK; Giff E; Lokith 3ef L. any] ony UDHEM; eny RVN; *om* L. Leaute] lealte LM; laute (*late corrector alters to* lawe) H^2; liaunce DW. wile] wole H; wol ChVLKM. loke] loken V; lokyn M; like L. þei] þat þei VH (þat *above* if (?) *another ink* H); at þai E; hem D; to W. ligge] liggen ChVK; liggyn JM; legge DH^2; lybbe H; lengen L; lye hym W.
101 And] *om* EM. 3if] 3ef Ch; Giff E; þei JNM; þagh L; though KW; *om* RU. þe] the *after cancelled* ye K; ony E; *om* RULWM. iustice] Iustises LWN. iugge] iuggen UJL; Iuge W; iugyn RK; wol Iugge VH; will iuge E; wolde Iugge M. hire] hir HN; here UDH^{2}J; her ChK; hur*e* R; *om* EM. to . . . fals] to þat fals ioyne L; to Ioyniy*n* hyr*e* to false M; at he be to hir in ionyd E. to] *om* W. be] bien J. ioyned] Ioynet V; Ioynyd RK; ioynide H^2; Iuned J. *with* fals] to false JW; for euere U.
102 3et] 3it UChVJN; 3ut R; ⁊ 3itte H; Swa þat fals E; *om* WM. be] beo L; beþ HWN. þe] þat RUL; þis H; youre D; *om* ChJKN. witty] wytet M.
103 For] And M; *om* WN. is] *om* M. of] on of V; *om* H. his] *om* EM. counseil] counseloure H; *om* V. ⁊ knowiþ] ⁊ knowit H^{2}M; ⁊ knowth K; ⁊ knawys E; þat kenne3 W. 3ow] ou VL. ichone] echone RUDChH^{2}K; vchone VLN.
104 And] *om* W. 3if] 3ef ChL; *om* E. 3ow in] 3ow with Ch; such VH. defaute] þe faute RM. ⁊] þat 3e VH; *om* W. wiþ] with ChVHJLEW; wyt M; wiþ þe TRUDH^{2}KN. holden] holdyn RM; holde DJLKN; holdeþ U; haldyng E; þat 3e holde W.
105 *line om* H^2. besette] beset RD; be set on U; besytt K; bisitten V; sitte LWN; sittyn M; sitt H; be sene of E; *om* J. 3oure] oure V. soulis] sawles DE. wel] wol UM; ful HLEW; *om* VN. sore] sare E; soure LWNM; sower K; sour*e* abyggyn J. at þe] atte VJWNM; at Ch. laste] *corrector adds* ende H.
106–21 *om* V.
106 to] *om* H^2. assentiþ] assentit M; assent E; assencit H^2; assentid DHJ; assented N. ac] but ChHLKW; ⁊ N; *om* DEM. ne wolde] ne wald E; nolde RUDW; it nold K. ne] no L.
107 silu*er*] seoluer L. his] *om* RUJWN. selis] sealle3 E; seale K; sawes H. signes] syngnes togeder*e* M; signes of notories L; notary signes E; his seeles *altered to* his selynge *another ink and hand* H.
108 Þanne] and þanne U. fette . . . forþ] fet forth fauel JL; fauuel fochyd furth E. fette] fett HN; fet KW; fecchide U. forþ] *om* WNM. floreynes] florenys E; florens JLK; florynes U; floryns DM; floreyne H^2; floure*s* R. ynowe] ful feole L.
109 go] to N; for to J; go to ⁊ H; *om* K. gyue] gif N; gyfe LW; geve K; geuy*n* M; 3yue UH; 3eue Ch; 3euyn J; belyue ⁊ gyff E. gold] *rubbed* H; *om* M. al] anon al R; to vche gome L; *om* ChH^{2}HE.
110 þe] þis H; þees E; *om* ChJLWM. þat] latt E. hem] þaim E; þei J; thay K; he Ch; þer L. non] RUDChHJLKWN; non ne TH^2; not E; no gold M. faile] fayle DH^{2}EWM; failiþ T; failed ChJLKN; faylede RU; lacked H.

And feffe false wytnesse wiþ floreynes ynowe,
For he may mede amaistrien and maken at my wille'.
Þo þis gold was gyue gret was þe þonking
To false & to fauel for here faire ȝeftis,
And comen to counforte fro care þe false, 115
And seide, '*certis* cesse shuln we neu*ere*
Til mede be þi weddit wyf þoruȝ wyt of vs alle,
For we haue mede amaistried wiþ oure m*er*y speche
Þat he[o] g*ra*untiþ to gon wiþ a good wille
To lundou*n* to loke ȝif þ*at* lawe wolde 120
Iuggen ȝow ioyntly in ioye for eu*ere*'.

111 And] Bott E. feffe] feoffe L; festene M. false wytnesse] falsnesse ChKM. floreynes] florens HK; floryns UD; floure*s* R. ynowe] feole y praye L; mony E.
112 he] she W. mede] medyn (yn *over original* e) J. amaistrien] amaysteren H; amaistre N; amastrye RU; amastren K; maystryen DH²; maystrie W; maistryn M; maist*er* E; and maistren Ch; & mays-t*er*yn J. maken] makyn J; make RUHE WN. at] hir at HE; her*e* at U; h*er*in at J. my] our U; his DHL; hire W; *om* J. *Here* H *adds a line: see above*, p. 45.
113 Þo] Þoo H; Bote þo L; To (*late corrector alters to* when) H²; Whan KWN; When E. þis] þe HJKWN. gyue] gefe W; geuen D; gevyn EK; ygyue RUL; ygyuen N; ȝeuen ChM; ȝouen H; Iȝouyn J. gret . . . þonking] graunt mercy þey gradden L. gret] miche M. was] were H. þonking] þankyng RUDChJE; thonkes HW; thanke*s* K; þanke M.
114 here] her ChHJM; heore L; their K; þair E. faire] grete R. ȝeftis] ȝiftes UDJ NM; ȝifthes R; ȝyftus H; giftes W; gifteȝ E.
115–17 *as two lines divided after* saiden W.
115 L *corrupts to* And þenne fals from kare konne þey faste comforte. And] many H; Thay K. comen] come REW; comyn NM; kemyn J. to . . . false] from care to cou*n*forte þe false (*over erasure another hand and ink*) H. to] for to JE; forth to M. counforte] cou*n*fortyn JM; comforte RCh K; Comforten DH²; comforth E. fro . . . þe] *om* W.
116 And] And þei J. seide *cer*tis] certe*s* sayde R; saide *cer*tes in same L; certys seydyn to hym M; cert*es* sothly E; sikerly þay saiden Certes W; sworen on þe hoolydom þat H. seide] seiden ChJN; sayden K. cesse] cese URDChLW; secyn JK; ceese H; slepe M. shuln] schul UChH² HM; schull K; schulle R; sulden J; schal DLEWN. we] I E. neu*ere*] newr*e* N.
117 Til] Till at E; or H. mede . . . wyf] ȝe haue mede wedded W. be] beo L. þi . . . wyf] weddytt E; wendyd M. weddit] weddid UH²JKN; wedded RD ChL; weddud H. þoruȝ . . . alle] *om* W.
118 haue] han UH²HLM. amaistried] amaistred LN; amaysterd H; amayst*er*yd J; amastred K; maystryed D; maistred Ch; maistrede W; maystryd M; maistird E. wiþ] þorgh L; þorow E. m*er*y] meory L; myri H; faire UEM. speche] wordis H.
119 *line marked with cross* Ch. Þat] Þan Ch. heo] L; hee H; he TChH²; sche UDJK WNM; sho E; *om* R. grauntiþ] g*ra*untes E; g*ra*untyd J; graunted Ch. to] w*ith* vs to H²L. gon] go RUChH²M; goo H; gay E; come W.
120 *line om* M; *divided from following after* þere J. lundou*n*] londo E. to(2)] and R. loke] loken DLN; lokyn JK; luke E. ȝif] ȝef ChL; for J. þ*at*] þ*at* þe RU; at þe E; þe ChHJLKN. lawe] lawe þere J. wolde] wold Ch; woulde K; wald E; wole H; will WN.
121 Iuggen] Iugge DHLEWN; Iugen R; Iuge K; Ioyne UCh; Ioynyn J; To Ionye M. ȝow] hem Ch. ioyntly] Ioynly M; gentely JN. in ioye] w*ith* Ioye M; to be Ioyned H; in lawe RU. for eu*ere*] toged*er* EM.

Þanne was fals fayn, & fauel als bliþe,
And let somoune alle þe segges [in shires abouten],
And alle be boun, beggeris & oþere,
To wende wiþ hem to westmynstre to wytnesse þ[is] dede. 125
Þanne car[i]de hy fo[r] capelis to carien hem þider;
Þanne fette fauel folis of þe beste,
Sette mede on a shirreue shod al newe,
And fals sat on a sisour þat softeliche trottide,
And fauel vpon fair speche, fe[int]liche atirid. 130

122 Here V **resumes**. Þanne] þenne V; þen H. was fals] fals was H²; was falshed EM. als] alse (e *altered to* o *another ink*) H; also VWN; as RUDChJM; wel L. bliþe] bylythe E; bliue Ch.
123 And] Thei WN. let] leet U; bad H. somoune . . . segges] Symonye seche D. somoune] somne H²; somnen Ch; somen J; sompne VHLM; Somond E. alle] *om* UChEM; *cancelled* H. þe] *om* VLM. segges] men V; pepul *another hand over erasure* H; schyreues M. in . . . abouten] in schires aboute URHJLEKWN; of schyris aboute M; abouten in shires T; about In scheres ChH²; al aboute in Shires D; in Cuntre aboute V. shires] scheres R.
124 V *substitutes* To Arayen hem redi Boþe Burgeys and schirreues. *Divided from following after* wende J. And alle] To her bodes to W; Til here bodis N. And] *om* UHL. alle] alle to ChH²; þaim al E; bad hem alle M; þat alle U; þat alle þei myȝten H; þat vche beorne L. be] beo L; ben K; beþ R; þe J. boun] bon R; bounde D; bolde J. beggeris] beggars KN; buggers M; bath beggerys E; begger L.
125 wende] wenden W; wendyn M; weende V. wiþ hem] al E; *om* WNM. hem] heom L; them K. westmynstre] westmunster VL; westmenstre M; westmester ChN; london E. wytnesse] wytnessyn JM. þis] þis RUJLEKWNM; *after cancelled* þe H; þe TDChH²V.
126 Þanne] þenne V; þen H. caride] karidyn JM; carede H²W; careden V; caryd RE; cared UDChKN; caareden H; cariede T; karkeden L. hy] he H²; heo VL; þey RUDChHJWNM; þai E; thay K. for] RUDChH²VHJLEKWNM; forþ T. capelis] capelus H²; capyllys E; capuls Ch; caples UVHJLKWN; cables D. carien] caryyn R; carry E; karyn M; kairen N. hem] heom L; þaim E; them K. þider] þidyre JM; þidur H; þeder RChEW; thether K.
127 Þanne] And þan JKNM; And LE; Bote VH. fette fauel] fauel fette M; Fauuel fette forþ VHL; fauuell fochis forth E. fauel] fauel forþ U; fauel fourty (*late corrector alters* fourty *to* fourthe) H². folis] florens M. of] þer of R.
128 Sette] And sette VJK; & setten H; *om* W. shirreue] schirref LW; shiryue N; shereue UDH²M; sheroff E; schreue Ch; schriff K; schirreues Bak VH. shod] schoȝed L; yschod RKM; Ischood V; rode shodde W. newe] neowe L.
129 *line om* V. And] *om* W. fals sat] sett fals K. sat] set D; *om* RUHLE. sisour] sesoure Ch; seyssour E; sysoures backe H. þat] ful W. softeliche] sotely Ch; fetiliche H²; stoutliche M. trottide] trottyd K; trottede M; trotted RChHLN; trotdyd J; troddide *altered same ink to* trotdide H²; gan trotte W; trotteþ D; wald trott E. *Here* H *adds four lines: see above*, pp. 45–6.
130 And] *om* HEW. vpon] apon L; on W; vppon a UH²; vp a R; on a DVH. feintliche] Feyntliche VM; fayntely E; ful feyntly H; quentyliche H²; sotely Ch; fetelych J; fastlyche D; fetisliche TUK; fetysly RN; fetosly L; ful fetisly W. atirid] atired UDChH²HLW; atyret V; tyryd K. *Here* H *adds three lines: see above*, p. 46.

Þ[o] hadde notories none; anoyed þei were
Þat symonye & cyuyle shulde on *here* fet gange.
Þanne swor cyuyle & seide be þe rode |
Þat somen*ours* shulde be sadelit & *ser*ue hem ichone, *fol.* xxix *a*
'And let app*ar*aille þise p*ro*uisou*rs* in palfreis wise; 135
Sire symonye hymself shal sitte on here bakkis;
And alle þe denis & southdenis, as destreris hem diȝte,
For þei shuln bere þise bisshopis & b*ri*nge hem at reste.
Paulynes peple, for pleyntes in constorie,

131 *line om and a passage like* **C** III 185–8 *substituted* WN. Þo] RUDJLKM; þe*n*ne VH; Than E; Þ*ere* TChH². hadde . . . none] Notaries none Hors hedde*n* V; notaries had noo*n* horses H. hadde] hadde þe M; hed þe E. notories] notarye M. none] nane E; non hors H². anoyed] anoyd E; anoyȝed R; anuyed V; annuyed L; anewed Ch; anieuyd (? amenyd) D. þei were] þei weore V; thay weren K; wer þai E; sore þey weoren L.
132 Þat] And eke þat L; and RK; *om* WN. symonye & cyuyle] syuyle & symonye H. shulde] schulden VH; schuldyn JM; suld E; schulen L; shal N; dide W. on . . . gange] go on foote VH. h*ere*] her ChKW; heore L; *om* H²JE. fet] fote H²JEN. gange] gangyn D; go E; gon ChW; gone K.
133 Þanne] þe*n*ne V; þen HL. swor] sware EK; seyde RUVHN; said W. seide] syde M; swor*e* RUVHN.
134 Þat] *om* WN. somen*ours*] somnars K; Somondo*urs* E. shulde] schulden H; schuldy*n* M; suld E; schule L; shal WN. be sadelit] sadyld be E. be] beo L; ben VJK. sadelit] sadelet V; sadelyd J; sadeled DChH²HLK; sadlyd RM; sadled UWN. *ser*ue] seruen VK; *ser*uyn RDJM; beren U. hem] heo*m* L; him W; vs E; ȝow N; *om* DJK. ichone] echone RUDCh H²JK; vchone VLN; yhone H; ilkane E.
135 And] Thei WN. let] lete ChWN; leet U; lat H²J; gart E. app*ar*aille] apparaylen DL; app*ar*aylyn M; ap*ar*elyn J; hem p*ar*ayle R. þise] þis JL; þese DH²; þes ChK; þe RUM; *om* VEWN. proui-sours] p*ro*visoners EK; professours Ch. in] on UV. palfreis] palfreyen L; palfreyne U; palfrey D; palfray RK.
136 *line om* V. Sire] and seyde M. self] seolf L; silf H. shal] sall E. sitte] sitten UDH; syttyn RJM; sette H². here bakkis] hym oone H; þe best J. here] heore L; þair E; their K. bakkis] bakys E; backe M.
137 alle] *om* M. þe] þise HWN; þes JK; þees E; *om* VLM. denis] Erchedeknes W; archedekenes N; officyales H. &] *om* DJWN. southdenis] soutȝdenys H²; suddenes Ch; sudenes UL; sodenys D; Sodenes V; subdenys RE; deenys H; officyall*es* K; *om* JWN. as] to D; on W. destreris] destroiers Ch; distrers E; dextrers WN; destrys M; palfreyes (*over erasure*) H. hem diȝte] he*m* diȝt *over erasure another hand* H. hem] heom L; be E; I M; *om* V. diȝte] dyȝthe R; diȝth N; dighten K; dihten V.
138 For . . . shuln] to H. þei] he J. shuln] schul UDChH²; schule L; schullen V; schullyn J; schulle R; scholyn M; shall EKWN. bere] beren VK; beryn J; bern M. þise] þis M; þese RUH²H; þes ChK; þees E; þe DLW; *om* VJ. b*ri*nge] bringen V; bryngyn M. hem] heom L; þaim E. at] to UVHLEKWM. reste] UDVHLKWNM; rist E; h*ere* reste TRChH²J.
139 Paulynes] pauly*us* R; Paulun (*followed by space for* 3 *or* 4 *letters*) J. peple] people LK. pleyntes] pleynt J; pleytes H²; pletyng E. in] In þe ChH²HL; of M. constorie] constarye JW; consistory EK; constrye H; constories M.

Shuln *ser*ue myself þ*at* cyuyle hatte; 140
And let cartesadil þe Comissar*e*, oure carte shal he d*ra*we,
And fetten oure vitailes [of] fornicat*our*is;
And makiþ of lyere a lang carte to leden al þis oþ*ere*,
As fo[bb]is & faitou*rs* þ*at* on here feet iotten.'
Fals & fauel fariþ forþ togid*ere*, 145
And mede in þe myddis, & al þis mene aftir.
I haue no tom to telle þe tail þ*at* hem folewiþ
Of many man*er* of m[e]n þ*at* on þis molde libbeþ.
Ac gile was forgoere and gyede hem alle.

140 Shuln] Shul DCh; Schule L; Schullen U; Schullyn M; schulle R; Schollen J; Schulden K; Schal VWN; þei schul H; Þai sall E. *serue*] serue*n* V; seruyn M; ber E. self] selue UH²; silf H; seolf L. cyuyle] seuyle R; symple M. hatte] hette V; hote K; hihte J; am Ihoten M; is haldyn E; am cleped L.
141 N *corrupts to* þe carter shal þe comissarie in þe carte put. And] *om* VHWM. let . . . Comissare] Oure comessar*e* wiþ Cart sadle W. let] lat RJM; late D; he gart E. cartesadil] cartsadely*n* J; cartsadlen L; sadyll E; sadle RU. þe] the *same hand for cancelled* our K; þe þe M; our UVHJ; *om* E. Comissar*e*] comysaries HEK. oure carte] for vs M. carte] cart*es* K; long carte H. shal he] he schal V; schal they K; sall þai E; þei schul H; schal be D; sal ben J. d*ra*we] drawyn M.
142 fetten] fettyn M; fet JL; fecchen UN; fecche HK; fette in R; fethem W; shall fett E; setten D. oure] al oure L; our all K. vitailes] vicail*es* (*altered by late corrector to* vitail*es*) H². of] RUDJLEKWNM; of þe V; fro TChH²; at H. fornicat*our*is] fornycacio*u*n*s* D.
143 And . . . lyere] Of liar make N; Of liars make W. And] Bott E. makiþ] makyt M; makyn RJ; make DChVHE. of] *om* VH. lyere] lier ChH; liȝere H²V; lyars K; leyers E; her*e* R; hem J. lang] long RUVHJLKWNM; large Ch. leden] ledy*n* M; lede RChH²HEKN. þis] þise N; þes JK; þese UH; þees E; *om L*.
144 As] Als J; *om* VH. fobbis] fobbars K; Fabulers V; folis TRUDChH²JM; fals E; flat*er*ers H; Freres LWN. faito*ur*s] fauto*ur*s E; flatoure*rs* W. here] her ChK; heore L; þair E; *om* VH. feet] Fote VHE; fot M. iotten] Iotton H²; trotten Ch; rennen VHWN; rennyn J; renneth DL; rennes UM; rennys R; rynnen K; gang*es* E.
145 *line om* R. Fals] Now Fals VH; Than falsed W. fauel] fauyel L. fariþ] fareþ H²VN; faret M; faryn J; faren ChHLK; fare DW; goþ U; goys E. togid*ere*] on foles yfere L.
146 **Here** A **resumes**. in] *om* R. myddis] meddes W; myddyl M; Middel V; middeward E; maydyn R. al] *om* A. þis] þise N; þese AM; þe RUChVHJEW. mene] meyne UChH²VHLWN; meyney K; meyny J; mayne RD; men EAM.
147 I] I ne H. tom] tome *altered to* tonge D; tome *altered another ink to* tyme H; toom H²W; tyme RLN; tong ChE; tunge UAM; while V. to] for to H. telle] tellyn JM. þe] þat Ch; of þe L. þ*at*] at E. hem] heom L; þem AK; *om* E. folewiþ] folowith K; foloweth DH; folwyt M; folewede J; folowed ChN; folwyd RUA; folwed W; come aftir E.
148 many] mony L; meny R; so many H; so mony V; alle UWN. of(2)] *om* RDVK. men] RUChVHJLEAWNM; man TDH²K (*late corrector alters to* men H²). þis] *om* VHEAM. molde] erthe EM; erde A. libbeþ] libbith JA; lybbet D; libbes U; lybbys R; lyvyth K; levys E; liuen VHWNM.
149 *line om* J. Ac] And H²M; But DCh VHLEKWN; *om* A. forgoere] forgoar K; forngoer*e* M; foregange*r* E; forgere D. gyede] gyed DChLWN; gydyd EK; gydys M; bygyed (by *partially erased*) H; gilede V; begylith A; gredde R. hem] heom L; them K; þaim E.

Soþnesse sei3 hem wel & seide but litel, 150
But prikede forþ on his palfray & passide hem alle,
And come to þe kinges court & consience tolde,
And consience to þe king carpide it aftir.
'Be crist,' quaþ þe king, '& I mi3te cacche
Fals oþ*er* fauel oþ*er* any of his feris, 155
I wolde be wroken of þise wrecchis þ*at* werchen so ille,
And do hem hange be þe hals & alle þ*at* hem mayntenip.
Shal neu*ere* man of þis molde meynprise þe [l]este,
But ri3t as þe lawe lokis let falle on hem alle.'
And comaundite a cunstable þ*at* com at þe ferste 160

150 *line om* E. Soþnesse] Sotnesse M; And sothenesse Ch. sei3] sey3e Ch; sëye U; see K; say DJLAN; saw3 H; sauh V; seiþ WM; seþ R. hem] hym UHN; hit ChH²; *om* L. wel] *om* D. seide] seyþ R; *om* L. litel] luyte V; a litil UChH.
151 *line om* E. But] He WN. prikede] pryked HJ; p*r*ikyde H²; prykkyd K; p*r*eked DCh; prikeþ WN; prikith L; prekith A. forþ] *om* VHJWNM. passide] passid H²K; passede VM; passed DChHJ; pasid A; pasede R; passeth LN; paseþ W. hem] heom L.
152 And] He WN; To he E. come] cam RJAKNM. court] hous A. &] þ*er* E. tolde] tolle *altered to* tollde H²; it tolde M; he callyd E.
153 to] til Ch. þe] *om* J. carpide it] it carpyd E; & told it A. carpide] carpyd H²HJK; carpede RV; carped DChLWN; karpit M. it] *om* RJ.
154 *divided from following after* false L. Be] Now by UVHN. crist] god M. king] kyng þo JW; kyng þanne A. &] 3if UV WN. I . . . cacche] I kacche mythe M; I hym cache myght E; kacche mowe I L; I hem caut may A. mi3te] mowe UJ. cacche] chacche RV; cacchyn here J.
155 Fals] Falshed E. oþ*er*(1)] or UDHJLE AM. oþ*er*(2)] or UDChVHJEAWM; þat flaterer or L. any] eny RVN; ony UDHEAM. his] her*e* JAW; her ChHKM; þair E.
156 wolde] shuld EAM; wile J. be . . . wrecchis] of hem ben awreke W. be wroken] bewreke me R. be] beo L; ben UJ. wroken] wrokin ChEK; wreken UVH; wrekyn DAM; wreykyn J. of] on UDVHAM. þise] *altered to* þo H²; þis V; þes Ch; þoys E; þo RUDHLAN; þe JKM. wrecchis] *om* U. werchen] werchyn D; werkyn EAM; worchen ChH²VHLK; worche WN; wyrkyn J; wroughten U; wrou3thy*n* R. ille] euel ChE.
157 *line om* H. do] don RUDVJAM; done KN; gerr E; I shal W; *om* H². hem] heom L; þaim E; hym D; *om* W. hange] hangyn J; honge LK; hong Ch; hongen VW. þe] *om* E. &] *om* W. alle] þey D. þat hem] hem that K. hem] heo*m* L; þem A; þaim E. mayntenip] meyn*t*en*t* M; mayntene JWN; Meyntenen V; meynt L; helpis E.
158 Shal] Sall E. neu*ere*] no HEAM. man] mon L; non V; *om* U. of . . . meynprise] meynp*r*ise on moolde M. of] on RUDChHAKWN; vppon VE. þis] *om* VHE. molde] mound Ch. meynprise] manprise WH²; mayprisyn J; neynpryse R; Meyntene VL. leste] ChH²VHLEAKN; beste TRUDJWM.
159 ri3t] *om* W. þe] *om* A. lokis] lokith UH²JLK; lokeþ RChVN; luk*es* E; loke W; wole loke H; wele D; wole A; bit (*twice, but second cancelled*) M. let . . . alle] on hem shal it falle W. let] lat RUEA; schal M. falle] fallen V; fallin JAM. on] of VHJ. hem] heom L; þaim E.
160 And] He EWN. comaundite] comandide U; Co*m*mandyd EM; comaunded DHK; comaunde ChVJA; comandyþ RL; called WN. a] þe V. þat] he RU; to Ch. com] cam JAKM. at þe] atte DH²JLM. ferste] firste URChH²JEWNM; furste VHL; fryst A; laste K.

To atache þis tiraunt[is] ‘for any treso*ur*, I hote;
Fet*eri*þ falsnesse faste for any skynes ȝeftis,
And ge[rd]iþ of giles hed; let hym go no ferþ*ere*;
And bringeþ mede to me maugre hem alle.
Symonye & cyuyle, I sen[d]e hem to warne 165
Þat holy chirche for hem worþ harmid for eu*ere*;
And ȝif ȝe lacche leiȝere let him not askape
Er he be put on þe pillorie, for any p*re*your, I hote.’
Dreed at þe dore stood & þat doom herde,
And wiȝtliche wente to warne þe false, 170
And bad hym fle for fer & hise feris alle.

161 To] For to EAM. atache] atachyn J; attachen K; atayche H; take RU; takyn M; cache EA; cachen W. þis] þes Ch; þese UD; þo JEAK; þe RVHLN; *om* M. tirauntis] tirauntys J; tyrau*ntes* RUChKW M; tirraundes L; terauntes A; Tyrans D; tiraunt TH^{2}N; Traytours VH; tratours E. for . . . hote] as tid as he myghte L. any] eny RDVN; ony UHEAM; non J. treso*ur*] þing AWM. I hote] tried E; *om* VH.
162 Fet*eri*þ] Feterit M; Fetter*e* H; Fett*er* E; Fettre Ch; Fetre W; Ich hote ȝe Fet*ere* V; Federith A; Fetteþ D. falsnesse] falsnysse R; falnese J; falnes E; fals ChVH; falshed M. faste] faste he saith L; forth D; *om* A. any] eny RDVKN; ony UHEAM. skynes] skynnes H^2; skynny*s* RM; kyns LN; kynnes DChHEK; kynnys A; kyn W; kynne U; kenys J; kunnes V. ȝeftis] yeftes K; ȝyftys RAN; ȝiftes UDChH^{2}J; ȝiftus VH; giftes W; gyfteȝ E; þynges M.
163 *line marked with cross* N. gerdiþ] gerdit M; gyrdith AKN; gyrde JW; gyrd E; gurdeþ VL; gurde DH; ged*eri*þ TH^2; gedereþ Ch; gaderyþ R; gadereth U. giles] giled N. hed] heued UChH^{2}JM (*altered to* hedde *by late corrector* H^2). let] lat RUD; & let JN; & lat EA. go] *om* L. no] no*n* M. ferþere] forþer VENM; forthir L; further H; farther K; firþer Ch.
164 And] Bot E; *om* WN. bringeþ] bring ChHEWNM. to me] forþ RU. maugre] maugry ChJE; magrey A; Maugret M. hem] heom L; þaim E; to hem J.
165 Symonye] symoy L; Sey symonye N. cyuyle] seuyle R. I] *om* A. sende] RUHJLEAKWNM; seende V; sente TDChH^2. hem] heom L; þaim E. warne] warde R; seye H.
166 chirche] churche DH; cherche W; kirke E. hem] heom L; þaim E. worþ] is E; wroch (? wroth) M. harmid] harmed RUDHJLWN; harmet V; armed Ch.
167 And] *om* W. ȝif] ȝef ChL. ȝe] þou HLM; þou maight W. lacche] lacchyn J; take HK; chacche V; chache E. leiȝere] leyer Ch; liȝere H^{2}V; lyere RUDJLAW; lyer HE; lyar KN; her*e* M. let] lat RJEA; letyth K. not] nouȝt DChH^{2}EN; nouth J; nauȝth R. askape] scape Ch; aschape RJA; chape E.
168 Er . . . put] Put hym AW; Sette h*im* H; Set hem M; Bott sett E; To ben set V. Er] Or DChH^{2}K; Til UJN. be] beo L; *om* R. put] set U. on] to Ch. pillorie] pylary JL; pelorye H^{2}AKW. for . . . hote] yf he be wode wrath E. any] eny RDVN; ony UHAM; *om* L. p*re*your] treso*ur* RU; thyng AWM. I hote] i hete J; or for pou*n*des L; *om* VH. I] ich K. *Here* H *adds a line,* H^2 *two lines: see above*, pp. 46, 48.
169 at þe] atte JM. stood] stant RU. þat . . . herde] hard þe dom A. þat] al that K; þis HW; þe UVEM; grete J. doom] dom DM; dome RUChHEKWN; deone L; dune V; dyne J. herde] harde K.
170 And] *om* HA. wiȝtliche] wytthly M; wytely A; whytelych J. wente] wentyn J; he wente awey A; went on his way L; went he þo H; he he wente M; he went for E. warne] warne*n* M; warnyn J. þe false] felshed E.
171 And . . . hym] *om* W. hym] hem RU; þaim E. fle . . . fer] fast fle A; faste to fle V. fle] flee EKN; fleo HL; flen M; flene J; To fle W. for fer] forferd E; forþ swyftly W; fast H; *after erasure same hand* N. hise] here U. alle] eke VH.

Þanne fal[s]nesse for feer flei3 to þe Freris;
And gile doþ him to go agast for to dei3e.
Ac marchauntis mette wiþ hym ⁊ made hi*m* abide;
Besshette hym in here shoppis to shewen here ware; 175
Ap*ar*ailide hym as a p*ren*tice þe peple to se*r*ue. |
Li3tliche li3ere lep awey þennes, *fol.* xxix *b*
Lurkyng þoru3 lanes, toluggid of manye.
He was nowhere welcome for his many talis,
Oue*r*al yhuntid ⁊ yhote trusse, 180

172 Þanne] þe*n*ne VH; And þanne MK; þo RU. falsnesse] RUChH^2JLEAWNM; falnesse TD; Fals VH; falshode K. for feer] for ferd M; for ferde A; for feryd H^2; forth ferd E. flei3 . . . Freris] to þeo freres fledde L. flei3] fleih V; fley RUDJ; flew3 Ch; flewe KM; fledde W; fled A; ⁊ fled E. to] tille Ch. þe] *om* (*late corrector inserts*) H^2. *Here A adds a line: see above*, p. 48.
173 gile] gyll E. doþ . . . to] to hym ga*n* (*erasure after* to) W. doþ] dede M; dide HE. to go] awey U. to] for to M. go] goo K; ga E. agast . . . dei3e] for to dye agast E. agast] he was agast M; ⁊ gast D; ⁊ gessid A. for to] to DM; lest he L. dei3e] deye RUM; dey JA; dy3e ChVH; dye DLKWN.
174 Ac] Bot ChVHLKW; And AM; Vnto E; A N. marchauntis] marchaundis ChHJEAWM; m*er*chaunte*s* K; marchande N. mette . . . hym] hem mette W. mette] mette*n* VHL; mettyn JM; mett E. wiþ hym] hi*m* wit*h* LE. made] maden HL; maaden V; bad A. hi*m*] hem W. abide] onbyde J; to abide UH^2HLEM; to abyden V; to bide W.
175 *run together with following* R. Besshette] Beschetty*n* J; Byschetten L; Byschitten U; Byschuttyn K; he schetty*n* M; ⁊ busscheden H; And shette W; And sett E; And syttyn A; Bisou3ten V. hym] hem W; *om* A. in] *om* LE. here(1)] her HJKN; heore VL; þair E. shoppis] schoppus H^2H; Shoppe D. to . . . ware] *om* R. to] ⁊ J. shewen] schewyn JAM; shewe W; shew men E; sewen (*late corrector alters to* sellen) H^2; sellen UK; sullen V; syllen H. here(2)] her ChHAKN; hir*e* J; heore VL; þair E.
176 Ap*ar*ailide . . . p*ren*tice] *om* R. Ap*ar*ailide] Apparailed WUN; Apparalyd E; Apparaylede*n* V; App*ar*ailden L; Apareyldyn J; Peraylid A; And apparailyd K; ⁊ aparelde*n* H; And app*ar*aildy*n* M. hym] hem DW; *om* AK. as] has A. a p*ren*tice] apprentyse UDM; a Prynce E. peple] people LK; puple JA. to] for to VEA. se*r*ue] seruen UM; deseyue L.
177 Li3tliche li3ere] Lyer launced lightly ⁊ L. Li3tliche] ly3þlyche R; Lytely A. li3ere] ly3er Ch; lyere RUDAWM; lyer HJE; liar KN. lep] lepe DChKWN; leep U; leop VHL; lepyd E; lepte R; went A. þennes] þen E; þanne AWM.
178 Lurkyng] Lourkyng K; Lorkyng LDW; lurkande R; Lurkyd A; Lurked N; Lurkede V; And lurked J; He lurkyd E; And lokyd M; *om* H. þoru3] in M. lanes] hyrnes ⁊ lan*us* H; lones V. toluggid . . . manye] wer*e* he mythe duellyn M. toluggid] tolugged DChH^2HKN; toluggide U; tologged V; lodly tologged L; luggyd J; logged W; to be logged R; to be luged E; to lyen A. of] on A. manye] Monye VChE; monoie W; mouthe L.
179 He . . . nowhere] Nowre qware was he E. He] And AM. was] ne was J; nas VH. nowhere] nou3wher V; neqwer*e* J; neue*r* D. welcome] wolcome UA; wilcom E. many] mony VLE; meri W.
180 Oue*r*al] Bot oueral ChVWN; Bote ouer al foule L; but H. yhuntid ⁊ yhote] abowtyn þey comaundy*n* hym M. yhuntid] yhunted UChVL; yhonted RD; huntid A; hunted WN; was he hatyd E; honsched as an hounde H. yhote] hote DVL; hooten H; hoted W; Ibodyn J; bad hym A; huntyd E. trusse] to trusse DVHK; for to trusse W; go trusse U; trusse ferþere A; to tresse (? *touched up*) L; þorow þe lande E.

Til p*ar*done*r*s hadde pite & pulden him to house,
Wysshen hym & wypide him & wounde hym in cloþis,
And senten hym on sundais wiþ selis to chirche,
And ȝaf p*ar*doun for panis poundmel aboute.
Þanne louride lechis & lettris [hy] sente 185
For to wone wiþ hem, watris to loke.
Spiceris speke wiþ h[i]m to aspie here ware,
For he coude on here craft & kneuȝ manye go*m*mes.
Mynstral*is* & messang*er*is mette wiþ him ones,

181 Til] To E; *om* VH. hadde] hadden H²H; haddyn JKM; had EA; haden L; hedden V. pite] pete DEA; pety K; pite on him Ch; pytee of hi*m* H. pulden] puldyn M; pulleden L; pulled RHW; pullid UEKN; putten V; putte Ch; pylledyn J; tollid A. him] hem D. to] i*n*to M.
182 *line om* K. Wysshen] wisshe N; wyschyn (*cancelled for* weschen) J; weschen Ch; whuschen H²; wosschen VHL; washe W; Weschid A; Waschede R; Waschid U; wyssin M; Þai weshyd E. hym] *om* E. &(1)] *om* H. wypide] wipyd EA; wyped RUDN; wyptyn J; wipten ChM; wypt W; wypen L; wrongen VH. wounde] wounden ChVNM; woundyn J; wonde H²; wonden D; wand UE; wryen L; leyden H; put A. hym in] hem in D; wiþ L. cloþis] cloutes VHJ WNM; clott*es* E.
183 And] Thai E; *om* W. senten] sentyn JM; sente RH²A; sent UChEWN; senden DVHL; sendyn K. hym] hem D; *om* A. sundais] sonendayes VHJ; a sonday L. chirche] cherche R; churche D; þe churche H; chirches ChJKN; cherches W; churches V; kirkes E.
184 And] To EW. ȝaf p*ar*doun] pardou*n* ȝaf D. ȝaf] gaf UL; gaue N; gyff EW. p*ar*doun] p*ar*dones Ch. panis] *late corrector alters to* penis H²; pans H; pens RUDA WN; penys JE; penyes ChLKM; pons V. poundmel] poundme U; poundelmele J; poundel M; penymel L; & pound*es* all E. aboute] abouten J; aboutyn AM.
185 Þanne louride] þis leornden þis V; Therof herden H²H. Þanne] þen LN; Tho A. louride] louryd U; lourede R; loured DChW; louredyn AM; lowryd E; lowred KN; lowreden L; lowredyn J. hy] he U; þey LWNM; þai E; þo R; him H²VHK; to him Ch; for him J; be T; ben D; *om* A. sente] sentyn A; sende H; send E; senden VL; sendyn M.
186 For to] þat he schuld H; þat he wolde L; For lyer shuld E; To come and W. wone] wonyn JM; wonne EN; wonye K; wony DCh; dwelle W; ben V. hem] heom L; þaim E; hym U; him (i *over erasure*) V. watris] water*es* RUChVHJ LEAKWNM; & watris TDH². to] for to D. loke] loken M; lokyn J; see E.
187 *line om but a corrupt version with two spurious lines inserted after line* 194 H: *see above*, p. 46. speke] speken UL; spekyn K; speeken V; spoke Ch; spoken N; spokyn JAM; spak REW. wiþ him] wiþ hym UDChH²VLKWN; wiþ hem TR; to hym AM; to þaim fast E; hi*m* w*ith* for J. aspie] aspien UDVJLAM; aspiȝe Ch. here ware] þ*er* he was E. here] her RJAKN; heore VL; þ*ere* W.
188 *line om* E. he] þei Ch. coude on] couthe on UChJLN; cowld of K; knewe H; ke*n*nede him in V; kenneþ W. here] her RChHJN; heore VL; their K; þe H²A. kneuȝ] knewȝ H²; knew ChAM; knewe UKN; kneow L; know J; knoweþ RW; knowith D; couþe H. manye] mony VL. go*m*mes] gomes W; gynnes Ch; gy*n*nys M; Iapes H.
189 Mynstral*is*] Mynstralis U; Mynstralles ChN; Minstrals W; Mynstrelis A; Menstralys R; Mu*n*strals V; And mynstral*is* T; And mynstrales DH²J; Bote mynstrals LE; But mynstrell*es* K; But Menstrales M; Messangers H. messang*er*is] messager*es* RUDH²VWM; massengeris A; mynstrels H. mette] metten VHL; mettyn JM. him] he*m* J. ones] oones H; onus H²; anes E.

And wiþheld him half [a] ȝer & elleuene dayes. 190
Freris wiþ fair speche fetten hym þennes;
F[or] knowing of com*er*is copide hym as a Frere.
Ac he haþ leue to lepen out as ofte as hi*m* likiþ,
And is welcome whanne he wile & woniþ wiþ he*m* ofte.
Alle fledden for fer & flowen into hernis; 195
Saue mede þe maiden no mo durste abide.
Ac trewely to telle heo tremblide for fere,
And ek wep & wrang whan heo was atachid.

190 *line marked with a cross* N. wiþheld] wiþhelden H; wythheldyn JAM; witheld H²; held E; helden DN; ofheeld U; fast heldyn K; wit*h*heode*n* V; wolde haue withholden L. him] *om* N. half . . . dayes] to þe worldis eynde L; wit hem terme of her*e* lyues H². half a] DVJEA KW; half TRUNM; an half ChH. elleuene] alleuen Ch; enleue R; a ellevyne E; xv M. dayes] wykes VH. *Here* H²L *add lines: see above*, pp. 48, 47.
191 Freris . . . speche] wiþ faire speche freres U. Freris] Fryers K; But freris M. fair] her*e* fayr M; heore fair L. speche] speches V. fetten] fettyn KM; fette W; fecchin J; fechyd EA. hym] hem W. þennes] þine E.
192 For] RUDChVHJLEAKWNM; Fro TH². knowing] knawyng E; knoweris A; *om* R. com*er*is] co*m*mars K; inco*m*mers J; corners L. copide] copyd RDAK; copeden H; kopedyn JM; coped Ch WN; þey coped L; þai capyd E; kepten V. Frere] brother L. *Here* L *adds a line: see above*, p. 47.
193 Ac] Bot ChVHLKM; And EAWN. he haþ] gaf hym W. haþ] has L; hed E; had AM. lepen] lepyn UDH²JAK; lepe RChHEWNM. out] outȝ H²; in and out R. as(1)] als ChE. ofte as] ofty*n* as JK; *om* M. him] he EAM. likiþ] lykys J; lyked W; list E; luste H; wolde AM.
194 is] ȝit is M; *om* E. welcome] wolcome DAWM; wolcum E. whanne] whe*n* RHL; whon V; qwan J; qwen E. wile] wele M; wole V; wol RChK; cometh UHL; comyth A; cu*m*mys E. woniþ] woneþ RUChVHKWN; wonetȝ H²; wonet D; wonnys E; duellit M; is L. wiþ he*m*] þer A. he*m*] heo*m* L; þaim E; hym D. ofte] ofthe R; efte E. *Here* H *reads a form of line* 187 *with two additional lines;* L *reads three spurious lines;* WN *insert lines like* **C** III 243–8. *See above*, p. 30.
195 *marked with cross* N. Alle] And alle V; Alle oþur H; This oþer W; Alle þei N. fledden] fleddyn RDJAK; fledde HWN; fled H²E; flowyn M. for fer] for ferd HEA. flowen] flowyn RD; flowe WN; flow E; floyn A; flewen Ch; heddy*n* M. into] he*m* in M. hernis] hyrnis A; hyrnes UHJW; hirnnes K; huirnes VL; henes N.
196 Saue] But A. þe] þei U; þat WM. maiden] maydy*n* M; madyn E; maide UDChH²HJAKWN. no . . . durste] durst no mo D. no mo] na mo U; na ma E; no mon VH (*altered to* none H); no man WN; none K. durste] dursten J. abide] abyden L; abydyn M; onbyde J.
197 Ac] But VChHLEKW; And AM. trewely] treowely L. to telle] I tell you E. to] for to R. telle] tellyn JM. heo] he H²E (*late corrector prefixes* s H²); sche RUDChJKWNM; ȝhe A. tremblide] tremblyd EM; tremblede V; trembled HLWN; tremlyd J; tremled DCh; tremelyd RH²A; trymbeled K. fere] feare K; ferde EAM; drede RUHN.
198 *line om* E. And ek] Boþe W; *om* JA. wep] wepe DChH²HW (*second* e *altered to* t H²); weep U; wepyd A; wept JLN; wepte VKM. wrang] wrong RDChK WNM; wrong hire hondes VHL; wrong her*e* handdes JA. whan] when RChHL; who*n* V; qwan J. heo] he (*late corrector prefixes* s) H²; ho H; sche RUDChJK WNM; ȝhe A. atachid] atached RDCh LKN; atachet V; atayched H; atired W.

III

Now is mede þe maide, & no mo of hem alle,
Wiþ bedelis & baillifs ybrouȝt to þe king.
Þe king calliþ a clerk—I can not his name—
To take mede þe maide & make hire at ese.
'I wile assaie hire myself, and soþly apose 5
What man of þis world þ*at* hire were leuist;
And ȝif heo werche be wyt & my wil folewe
I wile forgyue hire þe gilt, so me god helpe.'

1 maide] maiden ChH²VHL; maydyn M; madyn E. & . . . mo] & na ma E; no mo JWN; nomme (*late corrector alters to* nomor) H²; name RU; Inomen H; Inome*n* & no mo V. of] on H². hem] heom L; þaim E; *om* M.
2 Wiþ] And w*ith* RU. bedelis] bideles H; Beodeles VL. &] & wiþ H. baillifs] baylifys R; bailyfuus H²; bailȝeffes E; baillys UChJ; balies A; bayles H. ybrouȝt . . . king] to þe kyng ybroghte L. ybrouȝt] ybrougȝ H²; brouȝt DUEKWNM; brouȝth R; brout A; brohut J; & brouȝt H. to] befor A; afore WN. þe] *om* (*late corrector supplies*) H².
3 king] kyn L. calliþ] Calleþ DWN; callitȝ H²; callyd JEK; callide U; called RChH; cald M; callid in A; clepet V. clerk] Cler V. can] con H; conne K; knowe ChV; knaw E. not] no (t *supplied another ink*) H²; nouȝt ChN; noght UE. name] nome V.
4 To] & bade him H; *om* WN. take] taken M; takyn J; Take hym W. mede] vpp E. þe] that K. maide] maiden ChH²VHLK; maydyn M; madyn JE. &] to W. make] maken UV; makyn M. hire] hir HEN; here UDH²JAW; her ChK; hur*e* R. ese] easse E; hese M; eyse K.
5 I wile] Ichulle V. wile] wole HLK; wolde RU; schal AM; sal E. assaie] assayen VM; asayn A; asayne J; say LN. hire] hir HJEN; here DAW; her ChK; hur*e* R; *om* M. my] me A. self] seolf L; self seyd þe kyng H. and] *om* A. soþly] softly E; slyhly M; *om* (softly *supplied in margin contemporary hand*) H. apose] aposen V; opose W; here apose A; hyr*e* appose M; hir appose H; appoyse E; avise R.
6 *line om* J. What] Qwat E. man] Mon V; wyhe L; wiȝt N. of] on EW; in VHN. world] *late corrector cancels for* molde H²; werld A; molde RUHEKW. þat] *om* AM. hire were] were here A; sche is M. hire] hir HEN; her*e* UDH²W; her ChK; hur*e* R. were leuist] leuest were D. were] war ChK; weore VL. leuist] leouest VL; loouest *altered to* leouest *same ink* H; most leve K; most leefe E; leuer*e*st M.
7 And] *om* AW. ȝif] ȝef ChL; *om* H. heo] he (*late corrector prefixes* s) H²; sche RUDChJKWNM; sho E; ȝhe A. werche] worche ChH²VHLKWN; wurche U; wirche DJ; wyrke RE. be] be my UVH LNM. wil] witte W. folewe] fulfille H².
8 wile] wol UChHL; wele M; schal V. forgyue] forgyf RLE; forgeue DK; forgefe AW; forȝiue V; forȝyuen (*after cancelled* forȝif) J; forȝeue ChM. hire] hir HE; her*e* UDH²JA; her ChKN; hur*e* R. þe] þis DHLKWN; her*e* M; my JEA. gilt] gult VHL; mysgilt D. so] sa E. me god] god me A.

Curteisliche þe clerk þanne, as þe king hiȝte,
Tok mede be þe myddel & brouȝte hire to chaumbre. 10
Ac þ*ere* was m*er*þe & mynstralcie mede to plese;
Þat woniþ at westmenstre worsshipeþ hire alle;
Ientily wiþ ioye þe Iustices so[mm]e
Buski[de] hem to þe bour þ*ere* þe burde dwelliþ,
Counforti[de] hire kyndely be clergie[s] leue, 15
And seide, 'mo*ur*ne nouȝt, mede, ne make þou no sorewe,
For we wile wisse þe king & þi wey [shape]

9 Curteisliche] Curtesye D. þe . . . þanne] þan þe clerk WNM (þe *above line another hand and ink* W). clerk] Clerkes D. þanne] þen H; þo VJ; come E. þe king] his kynde H. hiȝte] hihte V; hyȝþe R; hygth AM; hete W; hett K; hote Ch; hoted L; hutte J; wolde H.
10 Tok] And toke E. mede] þe Mayden VH. myddel] myddyl DAK; myddile U; mydil N; myddul H²; mydle W; meddel Ch; medyll E; mudel J. brouȝte] brouȝthe R; brougthe M; brout A; brougȝ H²; led E. hire] hir HEN; here DH²JW; her ChAK; hur*e* R.
11 Ac] Bot ChLEK; and RAM; þan WN; *om* VH. þ*ere* was] was þere WN. m*er*þe] mirthe UH²HJKN; murþe DVL; moche E; meche A; myche M; good W. &] *om* EAWM. mynstralcie] mynstrasie RU; mistralsy E; menstralcy M; Munstralsye V; mynstrales D. to] for to EAK; w*i*th to VHW. plese] please EK; ple U.
12 Þat] Þo þat M; þei þat H; Heo þat V; and þo þ*a*t R; And þai þat W. woniþ] woneþ DV; wonyn AM; wonen ChH; wone R; wonneth K; wonne W; wonyen U; woned J; woneden L; wonnyd E; went N. at] to N. westmenstre] westmester Ch; westmu*n*stre V; westmyster N. worsshipeþ] worschipet H²; worschipen UD; worschip W; worschepen Ch; worschepyn RM; worscypen H; worschipeden L; worchipedyn J; worshippyd E; worchepid AN; thay wurschippyn K. hire] hir HEN; here DH²JW; her ChAK; hur*e* R. alle] ychoone H.
13 Ientily] Ientile H²; Corteysly M. ioye] Ioyȝe H²; gret ioye W. þe] of þe L; of M. Iustices] Iustice is Ch; Iustyse RUVHJEK (s *added* H). somme] LN; some D; summe AM; su*m*me *cancelled for* icchone *same hand* J; to sompne R; to sowpen U; sone TChH²W; soone V; sonne K; sone come E; wel soone H.
14 Buskide] U; busked RDChVHAWN; Buskedyn JM; Boskeden L; And Buskyd E; Buskiþ TK; Busketh H². hem] heom L; hym RUH²VHEK (*altered to* hem *another ink* H). to] in to V. þe bour] þe chaumb*ur* H; be bowne E. burde] Buyrde V; byrde UKW; bierde N; birde E; berde DChJAM; beorde L; berthe R. dwelliþ] dwelleþ D; duellet M; dwellyd JEA; duelled ChLWN; was Inne VH.
15 *line om* Ch. Counfortide] Conforted WN; Counfortedyn M; cowmfortyd H; Comfortid A; Cumfortede V; Comforteden L; Counfortiþ TRH²; Comfortyth K; Comforteþ D; Curteisly confortide U; And co*m*forthdyn J; He comforth E. hire] hir HE; here DH² AWM; her KN; hur*e* R; mede U; *om* J. kyndely] kuyndely V; kendely D; *om* U. be . . . leue] and made hire good chere V; & made hir at eese H. clergies] clergyes RUDJLAKWNM; clergie TH²E. leue] tene (? cene) J; clene E.
16 And seide] *om* W. mourne] morne þow ChVEAW; ne mowurne þou H; morne ȝe L. nouȝt] not RVHLAK; nat Ch. mede] *om* E. ne] no Ch; neo L. þou] ȝe L; *om* Ch. no] no*n* M. sorewe] serwe V.
17 For] *om* A. we] *twice* M; *om* L. wile] *in margin, same hand* J; wilen M; wol ChLW; woll K; wolen VH; shall E; *om* N. wisse] wissyn (*an* h *above the* i, *same hand*) J; wyse M; wysen V; spek to A. þi] þei U. shape] schape HJWN; schapen VL; schapyn M; make TRUDChH²E; maken K; makyn A.

For al consiences cast a[nd] craft as I trowe'. |
Mildeliche mede þanne m*er*ciede hem alle *fol.* xxx *a*
Of here grete goodnesse, & [g]af hem ichone 20
Coupis of clene gold [and] pecis of siluer,
Rynges wiþ rubies & ricchesse manye;
Þe leste man of here mayne a mutou*n* of gold.
Þanne lauȝte hy leue, þise lordis at mede.
Wiþ þ*at* come clerkis to conforten hire þe same, 25
And bidden hire be blyþe, 'for we ben þin owene
For to werche þi wil while þi lif lastiþ.'

18 For] And L. consiences] concience DChVHJLEAKWN. cast] caste H; Craft VJL. and] RVKWNM; or UE; o Ch; a TDH²HA (or *above line, late corrector* H²); is J; *om* L. craft] cast J; Casten V; forcasten L. as . . . trowe] as we trowen L; can we schewe H. *Here* H *adds* 2 *lines: see above*, p. 46.
19 Mildeliche] Mekely H. mede þanne] þenne Meede VH; þe mayde þan W. þanne] *om* U. merciede] þankede M; myrthed JA. hem] heom L; them K; vs E.
20 Of] And of J; For A. here] her ChH; hire J; heore VL; þair E; their K. grete] *om* U. goodnesse] gudeȝ E. &] *om* JA. gaf] DAWNM; gaue EK; ȝaf TUChH² VJ; ȝaue H; giftes gaf L; *om* R. hem] heom L; þaim E; them K. ichone] echone RUDChH²AK; vchone VHLN (*altered to* echone *another ink* H); ilkane E.
21 Coupis] Coupes UChVHW; Cowpys E; Cowpes J; Cuppes K; Coppis AN; Coppes D; Couered coupes L. of] and R. clene] *om* L. and] RUDVHEAKWNM; *om* TChH²JL. pecis . . . siluer] oþer ȝiftis many AM; other gyfteȝ mony E; wel clanliche ywroghte L. pecis] coppes W. siluer] syluure J; seluer V.
22 *line om* EM. Rynges] Riches A. wiþ] and UChA. rubies] rubeys R; rybyes HW; ryngys A. ricchesse] riches L; rychesses RUDH²VHJN; rybies A. manye] Inouwe V.
23 *line om* VEM. leste] menest L. man] mon L; *om* W. here] her ChHK; hire W; heore L. mayne] meyne UChL; meynee H; meynye K; meny A; menye N; men W; moynie J.
24 Þanne . . . hy] And þey laugthen her*e* M. Þanne] þenne V; þen H. lauȝte] lauȝthe R; lauȝten DHK; laghten L; lahutten (h *above line after* a) J; toke ChVA. hy] hij (*late corrector alters to* they) H²; þei RUDVLWN; þai A; thay K; þei her ChH; þai þair E. þise] þis DVW; þese UH; þes RChJK; þeose L; þeis N; þir E; þe A. lordis] lordis aboute A; lordynges V; lordyng*us* H; wordes (*late corrector alters to* lordis) H². mede] nede D.
25 Wiþ þ*at*] wiþ þat þer V; Than A. come] comen UD; comyn AM; kemyn J. clerkis] clerc (*late corrector adds es*) H². to . . . same] wiþ confort and game W; wiþ conforme & game N. conforten] co*n*forte RUH²; cou*n*fortyn JM; comforten DK; comforte L; comfort ChA; comforth E; Cu*m*forte V. hire] hir E; here DJA; her ChK; hure R; *om* VH. þe same] eken L; þanne R. þe] in the K.
26 And] we VH; *om* A. bidden] biddyn M; beden LN; bedyn D; bodyn J; bode R; bad UEAW; biddeþ VH. hire] hir EWN; her*e* UDH²A; her ChK; hur*e* R; þe VH. be blyþe] blithe be J. be] boen L. ben] beon L; be DH²JAN; beþ RCh; beoþ VH; er E; arn W; bynnen K. þin] all yo*ur* E. owene] awne JE.
27 *line om* A. For to] Forte V; To WN. werche] worche H²VHWN; worchen LK; wurche U; wyrche RCh; wirchin J; wirke E. þi(1)] alway þi WN; oure L. while] wil N; qwylys J; þe while H; qwylse þat E. þi lif] we E. þi(2)] oure RUVHJLKWNM. lastiþ] lastet M; lastes L; last H²; may last E; durith J; dureþ UV.

Hendely þanne heo behi3te hem þe same,
To loue hem lelly & lordis hem make,
And in constory at court callen here names. 30
'Shal no lewidnesse hym lette, þe lede þat I louye,
Þat he ne worþ ferst auauncid for I am beknowe
Þere cunnyng clerkis shuln clokke behynde.'
Þanne com þere a confessour ycopid as a frere;
To mede þe maiden mekeliche he loutide, 35
And seide [wel] softely, in shrifte as it were,
'Þei3 lerid & lewide hadde lei3e be þe ichone,

28 Hendely] kendelich Ch; Myldeliche A. þanne . . . hem] sho hight þanne þaim all E. þanne heo] sche þanne RChKN; sche þen (þen *cancelled*) J; Mede M. þanne] þenne VH. heo] *late corrector prefixes* s H[2]; *after cancelled* he *same hand* L; 3he A; sche UDW. behi3te] behy3þ R; behygth A; behyte J; behete K; byhatte L; highte UWM; hieght (*or* bieght) *altered to* biheght N. hem] heom L; þem AK; me W; *om* N. same] sane A. **29** loue] louen VHLKM; louyn JA; lenen (? leuen) N. hem(1)] heom L; þaim E; 3ou RU. lelly] lelle *altered to* lelly R; leyly E; leally K; truly HM. lordis hem] þaim lordes E. lordis] gret lordes WN. hem(2)] 3ou RUD; to VJL; *om* WN. make] maken VHK; makyn M. *Here* A *inserts a version of* III 192. **30** *line om* A. And] *om* HWNM. in] in þe J; *om* L. constory . . . court] courte & in constrye H; þe courte of constory L. constory] consistory E. at] at þe RUE; in H[2]; & in M. callen] calle RUCh (*followed by one minim* Ch) to callyn M; to call E; do callen N; don callen J; do call K; to don calle W; þat calles L; to tellen VH; telleþ D. here] her HJKN; heore V; har Ch; þair E; 3oure RU; my L. names] name L. **31** *line om* A. Shal . . . lewidnesse] lewidnesse schal not M. Shal] Scal J; þer schal RUHE. no] non J. hym lette] letten him Ch. hym] hem RUVHK; you E; *om* DJNM. lette] lettyn JM. þe] þeo L; þat W. lede] leod LN; ladde D; lewedeste VH; leste K; clerk M. þat] at E. louye] loue DChH[2]VHLEKWNM; luffe J. **32** *line om* A. Þat] For D. he] þei H. ne] no L. worþ . . . beknowe] wer auaunced first qwar I be knawyn E; worth thorgh myn help hyghly auaunced L. ferst] first UDChH[2]JKWN; furste R; *om* VH. auauncid] avaunset V. I am] Icham V. beknowe] beknowen N; knowe H[2]; Iknowe VH; þer Iknowe W. *Here* L *adds a line: see above*, p. 47. **33** *line om* EAM. Þere] þere as H; wher LW. clerkis] clerkis of clergy L. shuln] schul RUDChVHJN; schal LKW. clokke] clokken Ch; klockyn JK; go clokkyng W; Couche VH. *Here* WN *add lines like* **C** IV 32–3: *see above*, p. 30. **34** Þanne] ÞEnne VH. com] cam RJA; comeþ ChH[2]; comyt M. þere] *om* DM. ycopid] Icoped DL; Icopet V; copyd UH[2]JAK; coped ChHWN; capyd E. **35** To] And to EK. þe] þat M. maiden] maydyn M; maydeyn J; madyn E; mayde RUDChH[2]AKWN. mekeliche] meokelich L; mykeliche U; ful Mekeliche V; & mekely N; loweliche A; myldely EM. loutide] louteþ W. **36** And] RUDChVHJLEAKWNM; And he TH[2]. wel] RJLK; wol UAM; wil D; ful TChH[2]VHEW; *om* N. softely] soflych J; Myldely M; sothly H[2]; faithly E. in] a R. shrifte] scryfte M. were] weore V. **37** Þei3] þeyhe U; They RDH[2]JM; þow3 ChK; Thow A; þauh V; þagh L; 3if W; Gyff þe E. lerid] lerned M. lewide] þe lewyd E; lawed R. hadde] haddyn M; hedden V; haue EKW; han L. lei3e] ley3en Ch; leyen VL; leyn HWM; leyne N; ley UDH[2]J; ly E; lyen K; loy A; loyn (n *over erasure*) R. ichone] echone DChH[2]AK; ilkane E; alle UVJL; walle (*the* w *cancelled*) R; boþe HNM.

And þeiȝ falshed hadde folewid þe þis fiftene wynter,
I shal assoile þe myself for a sem of whete,
And ek be þi baudekyn, & bere wel þin arnede 40
Among clerkis & kniȝtes consience to felle'.
Þanne mede for hire mysdedis to þat man knelide,
And shrof hire of hire shrewidnesse shameles I trowe;
Tolde hym a tale, & tok hym a noble
For to be hire bedeman & hire baude aftir. 45
Þanne he assoilide hire sone, & siþen he seide,
'We haue a wyndowe [in] werching wile stonde vs wel heiȝe;

38 And] *om* W. þeiȝ] þei RDH²J; þowȝ ChK; þow A; þou E; þauȝ V; þagh L; ȝif W; *om* NM. falshed] Fals V; falsnesse RUH; falnesse J. hadde] hedde V; haue EKW; *om* M. folewid] yfolwed R; Ifolwyd M; yfolowed N; felewyd H². þe] *om* E. þis] *om* D. fiftene] *altered to* fiftye *by late corrector* H²; fyueten J; xj R; four score U.
39 shal] sall E. assoile] asoylyn JM; soile H². myself] my seolf L; my silf H; *om* M. sem] somme H; summe V. of] *om* RUJN. whete] qwete E.
40 ek] als J; also WN; *om* E. be] ben JA; beon L. baudekyn] baude DChV; bawdstrot H; bedman alswa E. &] to W. bere] berin JM; beore L. wel] *om* A. arnede] arnde R; arende U; arunde H²; erande DHAWN; erand EK; herand Ch; ernde VL; hernde M; erdene J.
41 Among] Emang E; amonges KN; Amongis A; To M. clerkis . . . kniȝtes] þese courteors & þe comyns (or clerkes and knyȝtes *in lower margin, another hand*) H. felle] falle V; fele K.
42 Þanne] ÞEnne V; þen H; Tham A. for] of J. hire] hir N; here UDH²AWM; her ChHJK; hure R; hys E. mysdedis] mysdede UVEAM. þat] þe RA. man] Mon V; frere A. knelide] knelyd RH²A; knelede VM; kneled DChHJKN; kneoled L; knellyd E; kneles W; lowtide U.
43 shrof] schroue ChK; scrof M; shraue E. hire(1)] hir HJEN; here UDH²LA; her ChK; *om* R. hire(2)] hir VHJEN; here UDA; her RChK; *om* W. shrewidnesse] sherewdnesse N; shrowdnes E; synne U; sunnes V; mysdedes (*late corrector alters to* synnys) H². shameles] schemelas L; schomeliche V.
44 Tolde] And told Ch; She told WN; Heo tolde VH; Sho tald E. tale] tale þer W; tokne RU. tok] took UDH²; tuke E. a(2)] in hond a L.
45 be] ben VANM; bene J; beon L. hire(1)] hir HJEN; here UDH²AW; her ChK; hure R. bedeman . . . aftir] bawde & bere wel hir erand H. bedeman] beodemon VL. hire(2)] hir EN; hyere M; here UDH²A; her ChK; hure R. *Here* K *inserts a passage like* **B** III 52–4, 56–8 *or* **C** IV 56–8, 60–2: *see above*, p. 30.
46 *line om* A; *marked with cross* N. Þanne] þene V; þen H; And þan W; And M. he assoilide] assoilled he W. assoilide] assoile U. hire] hir HJEN; here UDH²W; her ChK; hure R. siþen] sythn E; syþyn M; siþe W; siþ H; sethen DChL; seþin J; swyþe R; *om* V. he] to hire V; to hir H; to here U; *om* D.
47 haue] han UVHLAWM. a] *om* E. wyndowe . . . werching] werchyng a wyndowe D; wyndowe ywroght WN. wyndowe] wyndowne A. in] *in* UVHJLEAK; of T; at RM; on H²; a Ch. werching] worching ChH²VLK; wurchynge H; wyrchyng RUJ; wirkyng E; hom M. wile] wele M; wol UChVHLK; & wil A; *om* WN. stonde] stonden UVL; stondyn JM; stont W; stand EA; stant N. vs] *om* E. wel] wol U; ful DVHEWM; *om* RJA. heiȝe] heye DM; hyȝe RChHL; hie UH²JEAKW; hiegh N.

Woldist þou glase þe gable, & *gra*ue þ*er*e þin name,
Sikir shulde þi soule be heuene to haue'.
'Wiste I þat,' q*ua*þ þe wom*m*an, 'þ*er*e nis wyndowe ne auter 50
Þ*at* I ne shulde make or mende, & myn name writen
Þ*at* iche segge shal se I am sistir of ȝo*ur* hous.'
Ac god alle good folk such g*ra*uyng defendiþ
And seiþ *Nesciat sinist*[*ra*] *quid faciat dexter*[*a*].
Let not þi left hond, late ne raþe, 55

48 *line om* M. Woldist þou] woldestow LN; woldustow V; Woldis þu A; wildys tow J; Wald þou E; Wilt þou W. glase] glace DA; glasen J; glasse E. þe] owr E. gable] gabul H²; gauyll E. *gra*ue] grauyn J; wrygth A; sette L. þ*er*e] þ*er*In ChH²VHLEK; *om* J. name] nome VL.
49 Sikir] Siker UVH²HNM; Sikere K; Sekir EA; Seker DCh; And syker W; wel siker L. shulde] suld E; shal W. soule] saule DE. be] ben VAM; beo HL. heuene... haue] for to dwellen in heuene V. heuene] hefne R; heuyn J; heuyn blis A; heouen blisse L. to] for to HE. haue] hauen M. *Here* M *adds a line: see above*, p. 49.
50–1 *as three lines divided after* sayde: amende E. N *omits, substituting a passage like* **B** III 51–62 *or* **C** IV 55–66: *see above*, p. 30.
50 *as two lines divided after* þanne L. Wiste] wust V; Wost A; ȝe wiste L. þat] *om* R. þe womman] Mede M; ȝhe A. þe] þat J. womman] wommon V; wenche W; womman wel weore me þanne L; woman at þou south sayde E. þ*ere* . . . auter] I schulde it so makyn M; I wold it grauyn A. þ*ere*] For þer L. nis] ne is J; nes no Ch; is no REK; nis nouþ*ur* V. ne] no ChL. auter] weoued wroght in ȝour wones L.
51 Þat . . . mende] bot I þaim suld amende E; And ame*n*dy*n* auters M; *om* A. ne] *om* DH. make] maken V; mende H; mendyn J; g*ra*ue U. or] oþ*ur* V; & RUH². mende] ame*n*de RChW; make HJ. &] And wysely gar wirke it & þ*er*in E. name] nome V. writen] wryte RChH²VHW; wryty*n* J; writte E; þer inne wrytyn A; on write L.
52 Þat] þerto L. iche segge] I say E. iche] eche UDK; ech R; vche V; ech a Ch; euery JWN; alle HA (*cancelled* H); *om* LM. segge] segg L; ma*n* DW; mon V; men HM; folke A. shal se] y schewe me now L. shal] sal J; sall E; schuld A; schulde UVK; schulden HM; myght W. se] sen A; see JK; seen N; sey H; seye V; seyn M; sayn W; wite U; be done E. I] Ich V; þat I DHKN; *om* L. am] ame K; were UVHAWM; *om* L. sistir] suster RH² VLAKW; sustur H; soster U; a suster ChM. ȝo*ur*] oure L; þe H; *om* V.
53 *divided from following after* seyþ RU. Ac] Bot ChVHJLEAKWN; And R; As M. alle] to alle VHJLEAKWNM; *late corrector supplies* to H²; & alle (*after cancelled* & god) U; & D. good] gude E; *om* H²AM (*late corrector supplies* H²). folk] men EAKM. such] syche E; swich UDJWM; sweche A; schucȝ H². grauyng] wrytyng JAM; writtyng E. defendiþ] defendit H²; defe*n*det V; defende*s* E.
54 And seiþ] *om* N. seiþ] says E; seyde M. *Nesciat*] *Nescit* D. *sinistra*] RUChVHLA KM; *sinistra tua* W; *sinister* TDH²JN; *senister* E. *faciat*] *facit* DJLW. *dextera*] RUChVH; *dextra* LM; *dextera tua* K; *dextra &c* AW; *dexter* TDH²JEN.
55 *divided from following after* wete E. Let] Lete VN; Lett K; Lat UJLEA; late DH²HW. not] nouȝt DChNM; noght UE. left] lyfte HLAK; lyȝft R; luft V. hond] hand DChH²EWM; half RUJAN. late . . . raþe] lete ny*m* (? ny*n* *or* uy*n*) raye M; in ony wyse E. ne] no ChJL.

Be war what þi ri3t hond werchiþ or deliþ,
A[c] so p*re*uyliche parte it þ*at* pride be not sei3e,
Neiþ*er* in si3t ne in þi soule, for god hymself knowiþ
Who is curteis or kynde or coueitous, or ellis.
Forþi I lere 3ow lordis, leuiþ such wrytyng, 60
To writen in wyndowis of 3oure wel dedis, |
Oþ*er* to grede aftir godis men whan 3e [g]iue dolis, *fol.* xxx *b*
An aunter 3e haue 3oure hire þ*er*of h[e]re;
For oure sauio*ur* it seide & hymself p*re*chid:

56 Be war] Beo war VL; Ben wel I war M; wite RU; wytyn J; wete E. what] qwat JE. ri3t] rith JM; ryt R. hond] hand DH[2]EAKWM; half RUJ. werchiþ] werchit KM; wercheþ D; werchis A; worchit3 H[2]; worchyt R; worcheþ Ch VHN; worches L; woorche W; wurchith U; doys E; thinkyth J. or deliþ] in stede or in strete E; *om* AM. or] ne U. deliþ] dealith K; deles L.
57–9 A *corrupts to* For it is pride for soþe as I sey For þi merite is lost in syth & in sowele I sey þe verili so god hym selfe knowith.
57 Ac] DJM; Bote VLEK; And TRUCh H[2]N; *om* HW. so . . . it] parte hit so priueli V. so] *om* H[2]EM. parte it] dep*art* þ*er*witt E; be it parted H. pride] pruide V. be] beo VL. not] nat H[2]; nou3t DChN; noght UE; nougtht M; nouth J. sei3e] se3en V; seye RDHM; seyn U; seyne JN; sene EWM; Isee K; schewed L.
58 Neiþ*er*] Neþer ChH[2]; Nouþer VHL; Nowd*er* E. in] in thy K. si3t] syth RH[2]. ne] no ChL; nor W; ner E; neiþ*er* N. þi] *om* RUDChVHJEWNM. soule] saule DE. god] c*r*ist E; *om* M. self] silf H; seolf L. knowiþ] knowyt M; wate E.
59 Who] Ho V; Qwo J; ho so D. curteis] curteys *same hand above cancelled* covetise K; cu*r*tasse E; coueytous M. or(1)] & JLN; of Ch. kynde] kuynde V; kende DW. or(2)] *om* UDVHLWN. coueitous] co coueytes R; couett*es* E; couetise K; curteys M. or(3)] other K; oght E.
60 Forþi] For þey D; For whi A; þ*er*for JWN; Tharfor E. lere] lerne J; rede RUHWM. 3ow] þese A. lordis] lordynges V; lordyng*us* H; wordis A. leuiþ . . . wrytyng] such wrytynges leuyþ R; such writynge 3e leue V; swych wrytyng to leuen M; swyche writyng to lete W; suche lernyng*us* to leue H. leuiþ] leueth DLK; leue ChE; to leue UN. such] swiche UJ; sweche A; swilke E. wrytyng] writynges LK; writingis N.
61 To writen] Writte noght E; *om* WN. writen] wryte RChH; wrytyn AKM. in] in 3oure AM. of] in waunting of N; in wastyng of W; *om* A. wel dedis] wylddedes D; wel worchyng L; gode ded*es* EK; gode dedyes J.
62 *as two lines divided after* 3erne A. Oþ*er*] Oþyr M; or RUDVHJLEAKWN. to] for to H[2]; *om* ChJWNM. grede] greden UDVL; gredyn RA; crien JM; cry E. godis] Godus V; goodes W; gudes E. men] folk VH; *om* E. whan] whon V; when RHLW; qwan J; qwen E; 3erne of 3oure wele dedis whan A. giue dolis] dole deles L; shall o3t dele E; 3ou*re* good deles W. giue] gyue N; geuen ChK; 3iue T; 3yuen UH; 3eue DH[2]; 3eyue R; 3iuen or V; dele JA; delyn M.
63 An] On DL; In HJEAWN; And M; Par V. aunter] auenture VJNM. 3e] þat 3e E; lest 3e H; 3if 3e J; 3he & he A. haue] hauen DM; han VH; haue þore J; haue here U; hauen her L. 3oure] oure V; þe W. hire] huyre L; hure VH; here A; mede UM. þerof] þ*er*fore VHEA; for U; *om* JLM. here] DChH[2]VHEKW NM; hire T; rith here J; 3ou*re* gode RU; resceyued L; *om* A.
64 H *corrupts to* for of suche men oure sauyoure seiþ in þe gospel. it] *om* RE. seide] seiþ V; seth A; says E. &] as W; *om* E. hym] hem D; hys awne E. self] selue UJ; seluen V; seolf L; selfe & E. p*re*chid] p*re*cheþ V; p*re*chys E; prchid A.

Amen Amen [*dico vobis receperunt mercedem suam*].
Meiris ⁊ ma[ce]ris, hij þat ben mene 65
Betwyn þe king ⁊ þe comunes, to kepe þe lawis,
As to punisshen on pillories ⁊ on py[n]yng stolis
Breweris ⁊ bakeris, bocheris ⁊ cokes,
For þise arn men of þise molde þat most harm werchiþ
To þe pore peple þat parcelmel biggen, 70
For þei poisone þe peple preuyly wel ofte,
And ri[chen] þoruȝ regrat[r]ie ⁊ rentis hem biggen

64α *line om* R. *Amen . . . vobis*] UJE; *Amen dico vobis* VHKM; *Amen dico vobis vobis* L; *Amen Amen* TDChH^2AN; *om* W. *receperunt*] UVHLEKWNM; *reciperunt* Ch; *recipiebant* TDH^2JA. *mercedem suam*] VHJKWM; *mercedem suam ⁊c* UE; *mercedem et cetera* ChL; *mercedem* N; *⁊c* TDH^2A. *Here* H *adds a line: see above*, p. 46.
65 Meiris] ȝe meyres HW. maceris] macerys UA; macers JL; masers N; mercers E; maistris TM; Maystres DCh H^2VW; maysteres R; maysters H; masters K. hij] þei UD; ⁊ thay K; ȝe RJLN; and ȝe V; hem Ch; *om* HEAWM. ben] bene JK; be N; beon L; beþ RW; beoþ VH; er E. mene] meane K; menes W; þe menes E; þe menys M; þece menis A; mad mene L; ordeyned meenes H; menene dwellyn H^2.
66 Betwyn] Betwyxen J; Bitwix E; by twythe R. þe(1)] þeo L. þe(2)] his U; *om* A. comunes] comune N; common R; commen K; comen J; comouneris A. to . . . lawis] þe lawe forto kepe H. kepe] kepyn JM. þe] þese A. lawis] lawe N.
67 As to] as R; to HAM; For E. punisshen] punysche UN; puneschun J; punesch Ch; punschin RM; ponyschin A; ponysche HKW; ponschen (y *added after* n *by late corrector*) H^2; punyshyng E. pillories] pileries H^2; pylorie UHK; pelory AW. ⁊ on] and UNM; or on ChV; or EW. pynyng] pynynge UDHJLEAKN; pynnyng TRChV; pynnyg H^2W; kuckyng M. stolis] stole W.
68 Breweris] Breworis U; Brewars K; Brewstres ChVHA; Breowesters L; Bakers WN; Baksters EM. ⁊(1)] *om* RV. bakeris] bakars K; baxsters LA; bowchers E; brewers WN; breusters M. bocheris] bochars K; ⁊ bocherys M; brewsters E. cokes] Cookes V; kukeȝ E.
69 For] *om* AW. þise(1)] þis JW; þese UDH^2HM; Thece A; þes RCh; þees E; þeose VL; thay K. arn] arun J; aryn M; ar N; are R; er E; ben DHW; be V. men] þe men DA. of] on RDHLAKW; in U; vppon V. þise(2)] þis UDChH^2JLE AKWNM; *om* RVH. molde] mounde Ch; world UM. þat] *om* A. harm] wrong E; wo M. werchiþ] wircheþ Ch; worchiþ H^2; werchis A; wirkes E; werchen D; wyrchyn J; worchen VHLKW; worchyn M; worche N; wurchen U; werkyn R.
70 To] Tharfore E. þe] þeo L; þis R; *om* E. pore] pure E. peple] people VLKM; puple RA. þat] þair E. parcelmel] parcemel N; partymel L; part E; al schal V; al most H. biggen] biggyn NM; bigge A; buggen L; beggen RCh; Beggyn DK; biggeth H^2; abyggen H; abuggen V; sare abysse E.
71 *line om* M. For] *om* V. poisone] poysene ULN; poson E; poysyn J; appose *altered, similar ink, to* appresse W; punisschen V; pylen H; prechyn A. peple] people LK; puple RA; pore pepul H. preuyly wel] ful priuily W. preuyly] preualy ChE; pryuyly RH^2J; priueliche VLN; priueyly U. wel] wol U; full EN; fol A; and VH.
72 *line om* M. richen] UDLKN; richyn J; riche E; rechyn RA; recheþ V; beþ riche W; waxen ryche H; risen vp TChH^2. þoruȝ] by W; *with* A; þer J; *om* H. regratrie] UDH^2JLEKWN; regratie T; Regatorie V; regratyng R; regatris regratrie A; regratoures H; Regalrye Ch. ⁊] *om* E. hem] þaim E; þey L. biggen] byggyn A; bygge J; buggen RL; beggyn D; byen K; buggeþ V; byes E.

Of þat þe pore peple shulde putte in here wombe.
For tok h[y] on trewely h[y] tymbride not so heiȝe,
Ne bouȝte none burgages, be ȝe wel c*er*tayn. 75
Ac mede þe maide þe mair heo besouȝte
Of alle suche selleris silu*er* to take,
Or p*re*sauntis wiþoute panis as pecis of silu*er*,
Ryng[es] or oþ*er* richesse, þ[ise] regrato*ur*[is] to meynteyne.
'For my loue,' q*ua*þ þat lady, 'loue hem ichone, 80
And suffre hem to selle sumdel aȝens resoun.'

73 Of] with ChVHE. þat] þat þat Ch; þat at E. þe] *om* D. pore] *om* E. peple] people LK; puple RA. shulde] suld E. putte] putt HK; putten U; putty*n* JAM; put ChEN; puten V; pote R. here] her RChJKN; heore VL; hor H; þair E. wombe] wambe E; wo*m*bes RUH.
74–5 *over erasures in another hand* H.
74 For] for ne RUW; For no (no *cancelled*) E; *om* A. tok hy] if þei toke*n* H. tok] tokyn JM. hy(1)] he TRChH^{2}JM; þei UDVLWN; þai EA; thay K. on trewely] vntrewlych D; not vntrewly K; w*ith* trouthe H; so wrongwisly U. on] *late corrector changes to* but H^2; *om* EM. trewely] trwly N; treowely L. hy tymbride] tymbred þey D. hy(2)] he TR ChH^{2}J; þei UVHLWNM; þai EA; thay K. tymbride] tymbrydyn M; temberd E. not] nat H^2; nouȝt DChN; noght E; nouth J; nout M. heiȝe] heye D; hiegh N; hyȝhe L; hye RUChH^{2}VHJEAKW; eye M.
75 Ne] No L. bouȝte] bouȝþe R; boute A; bougthyn M; bowhtyn J; boghten L; shulde bye H. none] no ChHLAKW; hem no J; þai no E. burgages] Borgages VN; bargages H^2; Burgage EW; burgace A; burges J; borgates L; bargayns RU. be . . . c*er*tayn] so richeliche arayed M. be . . . wel] be wel ȝe H^2; þis is A. be] beo VL. ȝe] þou RUDE. wel] wol U; full E; *om* VHJ. c*er*tayn] certan E; seure W; sure N. *Here* N *inserts lines like* C IV 86–114: *see above*, p. 30.
76 Ac] BOte VHLEKWN; and RA. þe(1)] þat M. maide] mayde*n* RVHJ; maydyn M; madyn E. heo] *late corrector prefixes* s H^2; sche RUDChJKWN; heo haþ (haþ *cancelled*) H; ȝhe hath A; hat M; hase E. besouȝte] besowȝthe R; besougte H^2; besouth A.
77 alle] *om* E. suche] swyche JM; sweche A; swilke E; *om* U. selleris] sellars KN; sullers VL; sellers of sythes E. silu*er* . . . take] for to take syluer H; mede to make (m *in* make *partly erased*) H^2. silu*er*] seluer DV; seoluer L; sumwhat M. to] *twice* N; for to LEA. take] taken VM; takyn K. *After this line* D *copies lines* 137–61: *see above*, p. 3.
78 Or] Oþ*er* U; As AM; Als E; of RCh. p*re*sauntis] p*re*sandes E; p*re*sens N; p*re*sent UA. wiþoute] wiþouten WV; w*ith*owtyn E; oþ*er* U; or M. panis] pans DChHL; penys JEK; pens RUAWNM; pons V. as] os H; or UM; and Ch. pecis] bedys M. silu*er*] seluer V; seluyr M; seoluer L.
79 Rynges] UDVLEWNM; Rynggys JA; Or rynges H; Ryng TRChH^{2}K (*late corrector suffixes es* H^2). or] & A; of WN; w*ith* VH; *om* ChK. oþ*er*] *om* UH^{2}VHJE WNM. richesse] riches LA; richeȝ E; rychesses RUDM; Rubyes VH. þise] þese UH; þes R; þe VJEKN; þeo L; euyr þe A; þat TChH^2; swych M; *om* DW. regratouris] regr*a*tours URDChH JLEAKWN; regrato*ur* TH^{2}V; sellerys M. meynteyne] mayntyne A; fauoure H; fauere V.
80 *line om* U. loue(1)] lofe E. þat] the ChVHLEW; *om* M. lady] mayden J; mede M. loue(2)] leve K; soffre W. hem] heom L; þaim E; hem wel V. ichone] echone DChAK; vchone VLN; ilkane E.
81 And . . . hem] To byggen and W. And] *om* A. hem] heom L; þaim E. selle] sellen W; sellyn JM; sulle V; sylle H. sumdel] sumwhat A; soundely E. aȝens] aȝen DN; aȝeyn VHL; ageyn RAK; agayne JEW.

Salamon þe sage a sarmon he made
For to amende [meiris and] men þat kepiþ þe lawis,
And tok hym þis teeme þat I telle þenke:
Ignis deuorabit tabernacula eorum qui libenter accipiunt munera. 85
Among þise lettride lordis þis latyn amountiþ
Þat fuyr shal falle ⁊ forbrenne at þe laste
Þe hous and þe hom[e] of hem þat desiren
To haue ȝeftis [or ȝerisȝiuys] in ȝouþe or in elde.
Þe king fro counseil com ⁊ callide aftir mede 90
And ofsente hire as swiþe; *ser*iauntis hire fe[tt]e

82 Salamon] Bote Salamon VH; Forþi Salemon W. a] in a A. sarmon] *ser*mou*n* RDChHLEAKWN.
83 For to] For E; to RUVHJWNM. amende] amenden U; amendyn JM; amende wiþ H; mende wiþ N; amendyng of E; mede A. meiris . . . men] meyr*es* and men RUVJLEKNM; men ⁊ meyris A; þise meyres ⁊ men HW; men TDCh H^2. kepiþ] kepeþ V; kepit H^2; kepys E; kepe RDAWM; kepen ChHK; kepyn UJ; kepte L; kept N. þe] *om* JLEKWN. lawis] lawe V.
84 And . . . þis] Lo þis was his H. tok] tolde VLAWM; tould K; telde N; telyd J; he tald E. hym] hem RChVJAKW NM; heom L; þaim E. teeme] theme E; teone L. I telle] tellyn ȝow I M. I] I þe W; I wol V. þenke] thinke RDChH^2 JLEAKWNM; nouþe V.
85 *deuorabit*] *deuorabitur* (*ur* erased) H. *libenter*] *libenter sic* (?) J. *munera*] *munera* ⁊*c* LE.
86 Among] Emong E. þise] þis DVJL WM; þese RUH^2; þece A; þes ChK; *om* E. lettride] lettrid WM; lettred DL KN; letterid H^{2}JA; lettered RCh; leryd E; lewede VH. lordis] lordyes J; me*n* RUVHWM. amountiþ] amou*n*thyþ R; amount*es* E; amountyd M.
87 Þat] The DA. fuyr] fure L; fyer DH K; fyre RH^{2}JEN; fere A; fer UChWM (*altered to* fyr W). shal] sall E. falle] fallen H^2; fallyn JAM; felle L; afall W. forbrenne] brenne VHLEAW; brenny*n* JM. at þe] atte VJNM; at Ch. at] al at H^2; right at U.
88 hous] houses VHJLEAKNM. home] W; hame E; homes TRUDChH^{2}VJLA KNM; hoomes H. of . . . þat] þat suche ȝeftes L. hem] þem AK; þaim E; hym M; men R. þat] at E. desiren] desyryne J; dyshyryn A; desyreþ VLN; desirit M; deser*es* E.
89 To] For to V; *om* M. haue] take HA; ȝerne L; *om* M. ȝeftis] yeftes K; ȝift*es* RDChH^{2}VHJAWNM; gyft*es* E; mede U. or ȝerisȝiuys] or ȝerisȝeuys JN; or ȝeresȝeftes L; or ȝeriuys A; ⁊ ȝerius M; or presentes K; or mede W; amysse H; wrangwysly E; of her*e* *ser*uises R; for here seruyses D; for here *ser*uice TUChH^2; *om* V. in . . . elde] because of here office W. ȝouþe] ȝougþe DCh; ȝyngthe J; þouth (? youth) A; thoght E; word M. elde] olde D; dede EAM. *Here* H *adds four lines: see above*, p. 46.
90 Þe] þeo L; þan þe D; Then ca*m* þe HW N. fro . . . com] com from Counseyl V. fro] þo fro J; fro þe W; from þe HA; fro his K; for his R; ⁊ his U. com] cam JAM; *om* RHWN. ⁊] *om* R. callide] callid H^{2}JEKM; called DChHLWN; calde R; cleped V; cryed A.
91 *divided from following after* hire (2) RU. And . . . hire(1)] For to haue A. And] He E. ofsente] assent Ch; sent aft*er* JWM; sent aftur H; sent for EKN (for *in margin, another hand* N). hire(1)] hir HEN; here UDJ; her ChK. as swiþe] *twice, but the second is cancelled another ink* H^2; aswiþe V; also swithe ChJN; swythe LKW; swyþe w*ith* RU; w*ith* a *ser*gaunt M; *om* EA. *ser*iauntis] Seriauns V; sergauns L; seriau*n*te H^2; a *ser*iaunt EAW; þe sergaunt M; *ser*uau*n*tes DK. hire(2)] hir HJEN; here UDAWM; her ChK. fette] RUDChHLKWNM; fetten J; fecche TH^2; to fette V; for to fette A; for to feche E.

And brouȝte hire to bo[ure] wiþ blisse & wiþ ioye.
[Curteisly] þe king compsiþ to telle;
To mede þe maide melis þise wordis:
'Vnwittily, [wy], wrouȝt hast þou ofte; 95
Ac wers wrouȝtest þou neu*er*e þan þo þou fals toke.
Ac I forgyue þe þe gilt & g*ra*unte þe [my] g*ra*ce;
Henis to þi deþ day do þou so no more.
I haue a kniȝt, consience, com late fro beȝonde;

92 brouȝte] brouȝþe R; brouthe M; browte D; brout A; broght EW; brouȝten H; browhty*n* J. hire] hir HEN; here UAM; her ChK; *om* D. to] to þe HM; into J; out of N. boure] RUDChVHJ LEAKWN; borugh T; borugȝ H[2]; bourth M. wiþ . . . ioye] *with* ioy & *with* blysse E; þere þe king was ynne H. blisse] merþe W. *Here* H[2]H *insert lines: see above*, pp. 48, 46.
93 L *substitutes two lines* And on hire kneoes heo kneoled when heo þe kyng sygh Bote he hire tok vp by þe hond & hailsed wel faire. *Run together with following* HK. Curteisly] URH[2]VHJ EAKWNM; Certis T; Certes D; Connyngly Ch. þe] þan þe DW; þen þe E. king] kyng þan JAK; kyng þoo HM. compsiþ . . . telle] *om* HK. compsiþ] comsiþ H[2]; comsit Ch; comseþ RUD WN; Cumseþ V; comensit M; began for JEA.
94 To . . . wordis] seyde to mede H. To . . . maide] *om* K. To] And to LW. þe] þat M. maide] mayden RH[2]VJL; maydyn M; madyn E. melis] melus R; melleth K; he mellyt E; meled LW; Melodyes V; melioudiouse N; he mengyd J; moueþ U; & mevede A; myd M; mekely D. þise] þis JW; þese RUDA; þes ChK; þees E; þeose L; *om* VN.
95 Vnwittily wy] Vnwittily ywys T; On witly I wis Ch; Ful wyckedely Iwis (*late corrector adds* woman) H[2]; Vnwittily mayde J; Vnwyttily þu mede M; vnwitly wo*m*man N; wo*m*man vnwittely L; vnwittily UDKW; Won wyttyly R; Vnwisly EA; Certis unwysely H; Qweynteliche quaþ þe kyng V. wrouȝt . . . þou] hastow wroght W. wrouȝt] wrouȝþ R; wrouȝg H[2]; wrouht VJ; wrouth A; Iwroughte K; wroug M. hast] þan hase E. ofte] oftyn JM; wel ofte RD; wol ofte UA; full ofte E; right ofte K; many tyme and oft W.
96 Ac] Bot ChVLEKWM; and RAN; *om* H. wers] worse RDChVHLEKW. wrouȝtest þ*o*u] destow W. wrouȝtest] wrouȝþest R; wrougtyst M; wroutest D; wroutist A; wrouht J; wroght E; wraghtest L. þan] þen ChVH; but A. þo] whan ULAWM; whon V; qwen E; *om* (whane *in margin, another hand*) H. toke] tuke E.
97 *run together with following* H. Ac] But RChHLEKW; But ȝit N; And A; *om* M. I forgyue] forgif I N. forgyue] forgiff EW; forgeve D; forȝiue VH; forȝif A; forȝeue ChJKM. þe(1)] *om* U. þe(2)] þat RJLEKM; þis VHN; þy DCh; in þi A. gilt] gult VL. & . . . grace] *om* H. g*ra*unte] graunte*s* E. my] H[2]VJLEAK WNM; *om* TRUDCh.
98 Henis . . . day] *om* H. Henis] Heyne E; Hene A; hen M; So þat hennes L. deþ day] deday E. deþ] det M; ded H[2]AW. do . . . so] þou do so L; so þu do so A; so do þou M; so þou do so (*second* so *erased*) H. do] doþ U. þou] *om* VN. so] swa E. no more] namore UH[2]; no mare E. *Here* N *adds a passage like* **C** IV 134–45; *see above*, p. 30.
99 I haue] Ichaue V. a] *om* M. kniȝt] lyȝt D; *om* M. consience] conscience UDJLANM; hatte consience TChH[2]; hate consciens E; hette Concience VH; hyght consience KW (hiȝt *above line same hand* W); hyȝþ conciens R. com] cam JAN; come RDHEKW; I come M. beȝonde] be ȝou*n*den J; beȝondyn A; beȝende Ch; beyonde see E; beȝondyn see M.

ȝif he wilneþ þe to wyue wilt þ*o*u hym haue?' 100
'ȝa lord,' q*ua*þ þat lady, 'lord forbede ellis;
[But I be holly at ȝo*ur* heste honge me ellys].'
Þanne was consience callid to comen & aperen
Before þe kyng & his counseil, clerkis & oþ*er*e.
Knelynge, consience to þe kyng loutide, 105
What þ*a*t his wille were & what he do shulde. |
'Wilt þou wedde þis womman ȝif I wile assente? *fol.* xxxj *a*
For heo is fayn of þi Felasshipe, for to be þi make.'
Quaþ consience to þe kyng, 'crist it [me] forbede!
Er I wedde such a wif wo me betide! 110

100 ȝif] ȝef L. wilneþ] wilne VL; wylleþ D; willyth H[2]; wil RA; will W; wele M; wol ChHK; will wedd E; ȝerne J. to] *om* A. wyue] wyfe AEKWN. wilt þ*o*u] wiltow H[2]JN; wolt þ*o*u UVHK; woltow L; þou shal E. hym haue] assente H.
101 ȝa] ȝea H; ȝe RDVJLWN; Yee K. þat] þe HW; *om* M. lady] leuedy J; lady þo Ch; Mede þo M. lord] god ChVHLEAKW; goddes J. forbede] forbeode L; forbyd E; it forbede U; forbede it D; forbeode hit V; forbode J.
102 RUVHJLEAKWNM; *line om* TD ChH[2]; *preceded by a corrupt version of itself* (*shown thus: A*) A. But] Bot ȝef L. I] Ich V. be holly] hoolly be H; holde me V. be] beo L; ben J; *om A*. holly] holy ULA*A*K; haly E; holely N; *om* WM. at ȝo*ur*] to oure V. honge me] lat me hange A; gurd off my nek H; god forbede *A*. honge] hange UE; lete honge W; let hange LNM; lat hangyn J. ellys] sone VEAM; in haste KWN; hye L; *om* H.
103 Þanne] þ*e*nne V; Then HL. consience] *om* D. callid] Called DChHL; cald RA; ycallid U; ycalled W; ycalde N; Iclepet V; glad M. to . . . &] and cam to R. comen] comyn UDJ; come ChH[2]H LEKW; com A; knowyn M. aperen] Apere DHJLAKWN; apeeren V; apeyren R; appeire E; apsperyn (?) M.
104 Before] Beforyn J; afore N; Aforn W; Tofore V. kyng . . . his] kynges W. clerkis] of clerkys JK; bothe clerkus L; knygthis M. &] & of J.
105 Knelynge . . . kyng] Kneland before kyng consciens E; & knelyng befor þe kyng concience M. Knelynge] kneolynge VL; Knelyng þan WN; knelyd þo J. to] & to (& *above line*) J; þen to H; befor A. loutide] loutid A; loutede VM; louted R; lowtyd JE; lowted DChHN; saide (*another hand*) W; he carped L.
106 *line om* V. What þat] What at E; what RUN; to wyte what HLW; To heryn what M; & askyd qwat J. wille] *in margin another hand* N. were] weore L. what(2)] qwat J. he] þat he L; sche M. do] don RUDJM; doy E; *om* L. shulde] suld E.
107 Wilt þou] Wiltow WN; wittow J; Woltou V. Wilt] wil RA; Will E; wolt UHLK. wedde] weddyn M. womman] wommon V. ȝif] ȝef L; q*uod* þe kyng ȝif VJM. I] he D; *om* E. wile] wele M; wole DH; wol UVL; will E. assente] assentyn AM.
108 For] *om* VAN. heo] he (*late corrector prefixes* s) H[2]; sche RUDChEKWNM; che J; ȝhe A. is . . . for] wol fayn vnderfonge þe W. is fayn] fayneþ N. of . . . þi(2)] & gladly desyrit þe to M. þi] þis D. Felasshipe] felaschep RDChH[2]JA; felawschupe V. for to] & wolde N. be] beo VL; ben J. make] fere LW.
109 Quaþ] Nay quaþ VH. to] vnto E. þe] *om but supplied by late corrector* H[2]. kyng] kyng tho (tho *by late corrector*) H[2]. crist] god E. it me] URDVHJLA; me it EK; me WNM; it TChH[2]. forbede] forbeode VL; forbydde E.
110 *line om* E. Er] ar KN; Or DChA. I] Ich VL. wedde] weddyd J; wolde D. such] siche U; swyche JM; sweche A. wo . . . betide] crist it me forbede A.

She is freel of hire feiþ, fikel of hire speche;
She makiþ men mysdo manye score tymes;
In trist of hire treso*ur* she teniþ [wel] manye;
Wyues & wydewis wantonnesse techiþ,
Leri[þ] hem leccherie þ*at* loui[þ] hire ȝeftis. 115
Ȝoure fadir he[o] fellide þoruȝ false behest,
Apoisonide popis, apeiride holy chirche;
I[s] not a bet*er*e baude, be hym þ*at* me made,

111 She] Sho E; Heo VL; ȝhe A; For sche UH^{2}M; For heo H. freel] frel H^2; frele DVJLWN; freil E; freyle H; frayle K; frely Ch; frethil R; fals M. hire(1)] hir HJEN; here UDAW; her ChK; hur*e* R. feiþ] feth A; fait M; Flesch VE; fleische H; fleys R; flexe J. fikel] fykil UJM; fykul H; fekyl DH^{2}EA; and fikel ChL. hire(2)] hir HEN; here UDH^{2}AWM; her ChK; hur*e* R. speche] tonge V; feiþ H.
112 She] Heo VHL; And EAM. makiþ] makit A; makeþ RDChH^{2}VHWN; maket M; mak*es* E. mysdo] mysdon D; mysdone Ch; mysse do H; to misdoy E; to done amysse J. manye] moni VHLN; my E. score] schor A; scoris M. tymes] tyme DJE; siþys M.
113 In] Be A; For W. trist] trust RUDH^2 VHEKWNM; trost A; tr*o*yste J; treost L. hire] hir HEN; here DJAW; her UCh JK; hur*e* R. she] sho E; ȝhe A; heo HL; *om* V. teniþ] tenyt M; teoneþ VHL; tenys E; tenes D; troyteth U. wel] RDH^2 JLKWN; wol UA; ful TChVHEM. manye] monye VLE.
114–229 *om* A (**two leaves wanting**).
114 Wyues] wif Ch. wydewis] wydowys H; wydowes UDJLKN; wedewes H^2; wedowes W; wedows E; wedues R; wedow Ch. techiþ] techeþ RDChLW; teches U; sche techyth JN; she techitȝ (she *by late corrector*) H^2; she techet M; she techys E; heo techeþ VH.
115 *line om* K. Leriþ] H; Lereþ V; And lereþ W; Al lerith L; Sho lerys E; lerneþ ChN; lernyt M; Sche lernyth J; Leride T; lerid UH^2; lered RD. hem] heom L; þaim E; hem to H; *om* W. leccherie] lechorye Ch; liccherye J; lichory E. þ*at* . . . hire] & lecching of H. louiþ] loueþ VL; louet M; louen ChJW; loue N; lufys E; louiden T; louedy*n* RU; loueden H^2; loued D. hire] hir Ch; here UDH^{2}JW; her N; heore L; hur*e* R; wele E. ȝeftis] ȝiftes RUDChH^{2}VJNM; gyfteȝ E.
116 Ȝoure fadir] Our Father K; Vr Fader Adam V; fele men H. heo] VHL; he TH^2 (*late corrector prefixes* s H^2); sche RUDChJEKWN; sir*e* sche M. fellide] fellid H^{2}E; felled WN; felde RDJL; filled Ch; fylyd K; falde V; falliþ H; begylede M. þoruȝ] þorow EN; þorowhe J; þorgh L; þurw U; þorþ R; þrogh W; through K; w*ith* DVHM. false] Feire VHM behest] behest*es* RUDChH^{2}HL EKM.
117 Apoisonide popis] & popis heo poiseneþ H. Apoisonide] Apoysoned D; Apoysende V; Apoisou*n*de H^2; Apo-sowned U; Appoysonyth K; Apoyseneþ N; Poysonede R; Sho poysond E; Sche hath poysynhyd J; Sche poysenet M; She poysou*ns* W; Enpoiseneth L. popis] papes E. apeiride] apeyrid H^2; apeyred RUD; appaired Ch; apeyryt M; appaireth W; enpeyreth K; enpaires L; peireþ N; & peyrid J; and peyreþ VH; & parys E. holy] RDChVHJLEWNM; al holy TU H^{2}K. chirche] cherche UWM; Churche DH; kirke E.
118 Is . . . a] Ys not a KW; Is nouȝt a RUEN; Is no M; þer is not a L; þ*er* ne his a J; þer nis no VH; I not a TDChH^2. bet*er*e] bitterer J. baude] boude (? bonde) J. hym þ*at*] cr*is*t at E.

Betwyn heuene ⁊ helle, ⁊ erþe þeiȝ men souȝte.
She is tykil of hire tail, talewys of hire tunge, 120
As comoun as þe cartewey to knaue ⁊ to [alle],
To [monkis], to [mynstrelis], to myselis in heggis.
Sisours ⁊ sompn*ours*, suche men hire p*re*isiþ;
Shirreues of shires were shent ȝif heo ne were.
She doþ men lese here land ⁊ here lif boþe; 125
And letiþ passe prison*ers* ⁊ paieþ for hem ofte,
And [g]iueþ þe gaileris gold ⁊ grotis togid*ere*

119 *marked with cross* N. Betwyn] bytwen RUDChH^{2}K; Bytweone L; Betwix EW; Betwyxn J; At twix N. heuene] helle RUDL; halle (e *above* a *in original ink*) H^2. ⁊(1)] or E; *om* M. helle] heuene RUDL. ⁊ erþe] y holde L. ⁊(2)] in DVHJN; or E. erþe] eorþe V. þeiȝ] þey DH^{2}HJNM; þowȝ ChK; þoghe U; þauȝ V; ȝif W; yf E; ȝef L. souȝte] souȝþe R; sougthe M; souhte V; soghte UE; soght W; soghten L.
120 She] Sho E; Heo VHL. tykil] tykel RUVHLW; tekyll E; tekel Ch; tekul H^2. of] on Ch. hire(1)] hir EN; here UHW; her ChJK; hure R; he D. tail] taille *above line similar hand* W. talewys] talle wys R; talows J. hire(2)] here UDHM; her K; hure R; *om* ChJLEWN. tunge] wordes L.
121 As] Als ChLE; Also N. comoun] comen ChJM; comyn H^{2}HL; Comuyn V. [þe a U; *om* DJ. knaue] knaues DVHJLE KWNM. to alle] H^{2}VHJKWNM; othir L; al other E; to monk TRUCh; to monkes D.
122–61 D *omits lines* 122–36, *and misplaces lines* 137–61 *after line* 77 *above.*
122 *marked with cross* N. monkis] HJLK WNM; monke E; Preostes V; mynstrelis TRUChH^2. to(2)] ⁊ to EKWN; and RUChM. mynstrelis] mynstrell*es* K; minstrall*is* J; mynstrales LN; mynstr*alus* H; mynstrals WV; menstrall*es* M; mynstral E; messangeris TUChH^2; meselys R. to] ⁊ to E; and ChM; *om* RU. myselis] myssales N; meseles LW; mesels HV; messeles Ch; meseyls J; mesalles E; many tyme RU. heggis] hedgys K; heges W.
123 Sisours ⁊] To sysou*rs* to J. sompn*ours*] somnours ChJLKW; sou*m*ner*es* R; somonou*rs* N; Somonders E; schereues U. suche] siche U; swych JM. hire] hir EN; here U; her ChK; che J. p*re*isiþ] preiseþ ChL; preysit M; preysen UVH; preyse R; praysen WN; praysyne K; p*ri*yseth H^2; prasys E; p*ro*resid (?) J.
124 *line om* U. Shirreues] Shiryues N; Schreues Ch; Schryffes K; Sherofes E; Schrewes H^2; Schererys M. of] and R. shires] schyryn J. were(1)] were*n* H; weryn KM; weore V; weoren L. ȝif] ȝef ChL. heo] he H^{2}M; sche RChJKWN; sho E. ne were] no weore L; nere VHW.
125 She] Sho E; Heo VHL; *om* M. doþ] gers E; And M. lese] lesyn RJM; leosen VH; lose E; to lese H^2; to leose L; sell K. here(1)] her ChHJKN; heore VL; þair E. land] lond RChH^{2}VLKWN; londes J; londed (? londes) H; lond be her*e* M; lyf U. here(2)] her ChJK; hir*e* H^{2}HW; heore VL; þair E. lif] liue E; lyfes H; lyues V; lond U. boþe] boþyn M; bathe E; aftir UChVLN; eke H.
126 And] Ant L; She WNM. letiþ] letyyȝ R; lettyt M; let U; lateþ W; lat (*originally* lath; h *erased*) J; latt*es* E. passe prison*ers*] p*ri*sou*n*s passe H. passe] passyn J. prison*ers*] p*ri*sons VJWM; þe prysoner*es* RU. paieþ] payet M; payȝeth J; pays E; preyeþ R. hem] heom L; þaim E. ofte] often M; oftyn J; ofthe R.
127 And] Heo V; She WN. giueþ] gyueþ UN; gyffeȝ E; gyf R; geueþ Ch; ȝiueþ T; ȝyuet H^2; ȝifeth J; ȝeueþ VHL; yevyth K; ȝefeth W; ȝeuyt M. þe] to þeo L; *om* M. gaileris] gaylours KR; gailer ChV HW; iauelers E. gold] golt M. ⁊ . . . togid*ere*] oþir seoluer L. togid*ere*] among H.

To vnfet*ere* þe fals, fle where hym lykiþ.
He[o] takiþ þe trewe be þe top, tei3eþ hym faste,
And hangiþ hym for hattrede þ*at* harmide neu*ere*. 130
To be cursid in constorie heo countiþ not a risshe;
For heo copiþ þe Comissarie and c[ot]iþ hise clerkis
Heo is assoilid [as] sone as hireself likiþ.
She may nei3 as muche do in a moneþ ones
As 3oure secre sel in seue score dayes. 135
She is p*re*uy wiþ þe pope, p*ro*uisou*rs* it knowiþ;
Sire symonye & hireself seliþ þe bullis;

128 To] For to L; And R; She N. vnfet*ere*] vnfeteryn M; vnfettren J; vnfetereþ R; vnfeteriþ N. þe] *om* KW. fle] flee KN; to fle RE; to fleo L; to flene J; and fle ChHW; and fleo V; *om* (*late corrector supplies* goe) H[2]. where] wer*e* JN; qwar E. hym] hem ChVJ; þaim E. lykiþ] lykyt M; lik*es* E; luste R.
129 Heo] VHL; He TRH[2]; Sche UChJK WN; And EM. takiþ] takyt M; takys E. þe(1)] *om* RUHJEM. trewe] treowe L; true K; treuthe UHJEM; truþe R; trwþe N. tei3eþ] tey3et3 H[2]; and tey3eþ R; and teieþ U; and ti3eth ChV; & tieþ HLWN; & fettreth JK; & feteryt M; and fetter*es* E. hym] heom L; hym vp U.
130 And] *om* M. hangiþ] hangyt M; hang*es* E; hongiþ H; hongeth ChVW. hym] *om* EW. hattrede] hateredyn J; haterydyn E; hatrahede M; hate V. þ*at*] hym that W. harmide] harmyd JK; harmede H[2]V; harmed RChLWN; harmyd hir*e* M; harme dide HE.
131 To be] To ben M; To beo L; þei3 heo be H; þow sche be J; Heo þ*at* ben V. cursid] Curset V. in] in þe E. heo] he RH[2] (*late corrector prefixes* s H[2]); sche UChJKWN; sho E; *om* VM. countiþ] countyht M; count*es* E; count*er*yth J; 3yueþ U. not] nou3t ChH[2]N; nou3th R; noght UE; nouth J; nout M; noþ W; hit not at V. risshe] Russche VJM; resche E; crosse (*rubbed*; ? cresse) H.
132 For] *om* WN. heo] he RH[2] (*late corrector prefixes* s H[2]); sche UChJKWNM; sho E. copiþ] capyd E. þe] þeo L. cotiþ] HJ; Coteþ VLKWN; cotid E; cloþiþ TU; cloþeþ RH[2]; cloþes Ch; cloyth M. hise] þe VH.
133 Heo] he (*late corrector prefixes* s) H[2]; Sho E; Sche RUChJKWNM. as . . . self] agayn as sho E. as(1)] RUH[2]VHLWM; als ChE; also K; so T; þ*us* JN. as(2)] als L. hire] hir WN; here UH; her ChK; hur*e* R; she hir*e* (she *by late corrector*) H[2]. self] selue UJ; seol L; der*e* M. likip] liket M; lik*es* E.
134 *marked with cross* N. She] Sho E; Heo VHL. may] *cancelled for* myth *same hand* M. nei3] ney3e H[2]; negh L; ney R; nigh KW; ni3e Ch; ny UJ; nere E; *om* VHM. as . . . moneþ] don in a monyth as myche M. as . . . do] do as myche H; doy als much E. as] als ChL. muche] myche H[2]N; mychel JK. do] don RL; done ChJKN; doon W. moneþ] monyth J; Mooneþ V; mowth N. ones] onys RHJ; onus H[2]; anys E; one N.
135 3oure] vre V; þe U. secre] secret RUChH[2]JLEKN. sel] seal sir*e* M. seue] seuene RChH[2]VE; vij U; viij[xx] M; four*e* H; syxe JLK; sex WN. dayes] 3erys M; 3eres *cancelled for* dayes *same hand* H[2]; wintr*is* H.
136 She] Sho E; Heo VHL. p*re*uy] p*re*vay E; p*ri*uey RN; p*ri*ue UVHLW; pryuy MK. pope] pape EK. knowiþ] knowit3 H[2]; knowyt M; knowyn K; knowen UVWN; knawys E.
137 **Here** D **resumes**, *lines* 137–61, *however, appearing after line* 77 *above.* Sire] *om* EWN. hire] hir EKN; here UDHJW; her Ch; hur*e* R. self] seolf L. seliþ] seleþ RCh; sealeþ D; seallys E; selyn JK (*same hand after cancelled* sellyn K); selen UHWN; seollen L; aselyn M; asselen V. þe] her*e* RDJKN; heore L; þair E; hem her*e* W; alle þe M.

She blissiþ þise bisshopis ȝif þei be lewid;
P*ro*uendrou*rs*, [persones], & [prestis] she mayntenip
To holde le*m*manis & lotebies alle here lif dayes, 140
And bringen forþ barnes aȝens forboden lawis.
Þ*ere* she is wel wiþ þe king wo is þe reaume,
For she is fauou*r*able to fals & fouliþ treuþe ofte;
Barouns & burgeis she bringeþ in sorewe;
Be I*esu*, wiþ hire Iuelx ȝou*re* Iustice she shendiþ, 145
And leiþ aȝen þe lawe & lettiþ þe treuþe

138 She] Sho E; Heo VHL. blissiþ] blissit M; blisseth Ch; blessith UN; blesseþ RD; blessitȝ H²; blesses L; blyssid W; Blessede V; examyneþ H; gyff*es* E. þise] þies J; þese UD; þes Ch; þees E; þeo L; þe VHKWM; þus R. bisshopis] bischoppes b*e*nefyces E. ȝif] yef (? þef) J; þif W; þeigh N; þagh L; though K; þeigh þat U; þey þat R; þouȝ þat V; þo þat D; þere þat M; of all E. þei] þai EW; thay K; þi H²; *om* RD (he *above line similar hand* R). be] ben UDVJKM; bien J; beon L; beþ H.
139–40 *divided after* mayntenip VHJLE KWNM; *after* holde TRUDChH².
139 P*ro*uendrou*rs*] Prouendrers L; Prouendreres V; Prouandrise & E; P*ro*uendris H²; prouendr*es* RH; P*ro*uendours DCh; Prouend*er*ys J; P*ro*vendreth KW; Prouendriþ N; Prouendrit M. persones] p*er*sones RUDVHJLEKWNM; prestes Ch; p*re*stis T; p*re*stus H². &] *om* UDVJ. prestis] p*re*stis H; prest*es* RUJK; prist*es* EM; preostes V; p*er*sones TChH²; prouest L; styfly WN; *om* D. she] sho E; heo VHL; hem WN. mayntenip] mayntenes E.
140 holde] holden K; holdy*n* M; howldyn J; hald E; holden here WN. &] *om* WN. lotebies] loteboyes K; lotobies H²; lutebyes U; lutbyse E; luttebys J; lubytens D; *om* WN. here] her ChN; hir*e* H; heore L; heor V; their K; þair E. dayes] dawes R; dawys M.
141 And] To EKWN. bringen] brynge RW; bryng H²EN; bringgyn JM; bringeþ VH. barnes] barons U; childeryn JM; fruit (*above line same hand*) E. aȝens] aȝen RDH; aȝeyn VJLN; ayanys E; ageynst K; aȝen þe M; al agayn þe W. forboden] forbodene V; forbodyn JM; forbodon E; forbodone K; forbode RUChHN; *om* W. lawis] lawe W; hestes L. *Here* WN *copy the Latin of* **C** IV 189: *see above*, p. 30.
142 Þ*ere*] Whar E; Whan WN. she] sho E; heo VHL. is wel] is RU; dwellys E.
143 she] sho E; heo VHL. is fauou*r*able] fauoreþ WN. to] and R; þe W; *om* N. fals] falshed E. fouliþ treuþe] truþ pursueþ W. fouliþ] fouleþ RUV; defoulyt M; fileþ Ch; falliþ H; destruys E; foloweþ DN. treuþe] trouthe L; truþe R; trwþe N; þe trewthe M. ofte] oftyn J; *om* EM.
144 Barouns . . . bringeþ] Ofty*n* sche bryngyt barou*ns* & burgeys M; Offt sho bringgeȝ barons & burgeȝ E. burgeis] burgeyses R; bachelers H. she] heo VHL. in] to RUH²VHW. sorewe] serwe V; sorwy*n* M; slouthe L.
145 Be I*esu*] heo biggiþ H; Heo Buggeþ V; *om* W. hire] hir EN; here UDHW; her ChK; heore V. Iuelx] riche Iowelles W; wylys M. ȝou*re*] vr V; owr E; þe M. Iustice] Iustyces RVHLM. she] sho E; heo VL; & hem H. shendiþ] schendyt M; chendiþ N; shend*es* E.
146 *divided from following after* is D; *after* forthe K. L *substitutes* And combreth heom with hire kraft þat crist ȝef heo*m* kare. And] Sche UWN; Heo V; *om* H. leiþ] leyyth K; lyth W; lihþ V; lyȝt H²; lieȝth Ch; lieþ N; allegget M; allegg*es* E; doth lityn J; makiþ hem liȝe H. þe] ȝoure M. & . . . treuþe] *om* DK. lettiþ] lettyt M; lett*es* E; lefteþ R. þe treuþe] treuthe ofte U; hem ofte R; hem oftyn J; hem euere W; hi*m* eure N; hym þe gate EM; so faste V; it so fast H.

Þat feiþ may not haue his forþ, hire floreynes go so þikke.
She let lawe as hire list & louedaies makiþ;
Þe mase for a mene man þeiȝ he mote euere. | *fol.* xxxj *b*
Lawe is so lordlich & loþ to make ende, 150
Wiþoute presentis or panis he plesiþ [wel] fewe.
Clergie and coueitise he[o] coupliþ togidere.
Þis is þe lif of þat lady, now lord ȝif hire sorewe!
And alle þat meynteniþ hire men meschaunce hem betide!
For pouere men mowe haue no power to pleyne [þeiȝ] hem smerte, 155

147 Þat] So þat L; Þer E. feiþ] *om* E. may . . . forþ] no forth hat M; may no man it haue E. not . . . his] haue no H. not] nat H²; nouȝt ChN; nouth J. haue] han V. his] is D. forþ] forth for LK; For D. hire] hir V; here UDJ; her KN; his RCh; þe E; *om* L. floreynes] florens N; florence K; floryns UVHL; florans Ch; false floryns D; gold EM. go] gon VL; goþ RH; goot M; goys E; gone K; walke D. so] so faste & therwith so K. þikke] þinke M.
148 *as two lines divided after* list W. She] Sho E; Heo VHL. let] ledeþ RDVN; ledyt M; ledith UChHJLKW; hase (*same hand after cancelled* as) E. lawe] þe lawe VEKWN; þe lawis H. as] rith as W. hire] hir EN; here UJM; her ChK; hure R; here self W; sche D; heo H. list] lust RH²LN; luste V; lest M; wol H. louedaies] ladiys loue M. makiþ] makyt M; maket D; makes E; makeþ agayn right W.
149 *line om* W. Þe mase] A mayse E. Þe] þeo L. mene] meyn E; pore U. man] mon V. þeiȝ] þey M; þouȝ DK; þowȝ Ch; þoghe U; þow R; ȝof J; þauȝ V; þagh L; if E. mote] mute E; plede H.
150 Lawe] Hir law EM; The lawe WN. so] now so W; now D. lordlich] lordliche proud (proud *above line another ink*) H; lordschipe D. loþ] lath E. make] maken RUVW; makyn JM. ende] eende V; an ende KN; an eynde L.
151 Wiþoute] wiþouten UVJWN; with M. presentis] presens EWN; present UL. or] oþer H; & M; of LEW. panis] pans ChL; penys E; pens RUDWNM :penyes HJK; pons V. he] heo VHL; sche UChJWNM; sho E. plesiþ] pleciþ N; plesit M; pleasys E. wel] RHJLKWN; wol M; ful TUDChH²VE. fewe] manye M.
152 Clergie] Clergies JM. and] an V. heo] VHL; he TH² (*late corrector prefixes* s H²); sche UDChJKWNM; þai E; *om* R. coupliþ] coupleth UChVLW; couplet D; cowpellith JK; copleþ N; coupyll E; coupleþ hem R; compliþ H²; compellit M.
153 Þis] þeys M. þe] þeo L. lif] liȝf N. þat] þis LE; þe V; þy H. lady] leuedy J. now] oure RUChVHM; now our K; *om* L. lord] louerd J; god LE. ȝif] ȝyue UH²M; ȝeue H; ȝef ChW; gif N; gyff E; gyfe L; geve K. hire] hir EN; here UDJWM; her ChK; hure R. sorewe] serwe V.
154 alle] *om* D. þat . . . hire] þat here meynteneþ H; þat here mayntene WN; maynteners of hir E; hire meyntenours M. meynteniþ] meintene UK; maynten ChJ; manteyne R. hire] here UD; her ChK; hure R. men] meny (y *added another script*) Ch; now DW; *om* VHENM. meschaunce . . . betide] vr lord ȝiue hem care V. meschaunce] sorwe W. hem] heom L; þaim E.
155 For] for þe H; The WN. men] *om* ChVHJWN. mowe] mown L; may VHEK; now H²; *om* RUJWNM. haue] han UM; haþ WN. power] pith E. pleyne] pleynyn JM; playne VW. þeiȝ] þey RHM; þouȝ DKN; þof J; þauȝ V; þagh L; hem þeiȝe U; ȝif TH²EW; ȝef Ch. hem smerte] hem smert ChH; hem smarte K; þei smerte U; þai smert E; him smert W; hem nede R; þey sterue L; him scholde N.

Such a maister is mede among men of goode.'
Þanne mournide mede & menide hire to þe king
To haue space to speke, spede ȝif she miȝte.
Þe king grauntide hire grace wiþ a good wille:
'Excuse þe ȝif þou canst; I can no more seiȝe, 160
For consience acusiþ þe to cunge [þe] for euere.'
'Nay lord,' quod þat lady, 'leu[iþ] him þe wers
Whanne ȝe wyte wytterly where þe wrong liggeþ;
Þere þat meschief is gret mede may helpe.
And þou knowist, consience, I ca[m] nouȝt to chide, 165
Ne to depraue þi persone wiþ a proud herte.
Wel þou wost, consience, but ȝif þou wilt leiȝe,

156 *run together with following* W. Such] schuche R; Siche H; Swiche UJM; Swilke E; Shche W. maister] master K; maistres E. among . . . goode] *om* W. among] emong E. goode] gude E.
157 *marked with cross* N. Þanne . . . mede] Than mede mornyde H²; *om* W. Þanne] ÞEnne V; þen H. menide] menyd J; Menede V; mened DChL; mevyd K; mowed N; pleynyd M; pleynede U; pleyned RHW; plenyd E. hire] hir N; here UD; her ChK; hure R; *om* H²EWM.
158 *line om* EM. space] leue W. to] forto H; and R. speke] speken V; speykyn J; speche R; *om but late corrector supplies* H². ȝif] ȝef ChL. she] heo VHL; he H².
159 Þe king] þenne þe kyng V; And he M; And E. grauntide] grauntid HJM; graunted RDChVKN; graunt E; grauntith L; graunteþ W. hire] hir EN; here UDW; her ChK; hure R. grace] garce E. good] gude E.
160 Excuse] Escuse L; Ascuse Ch. þe] *om* E. ȝif] ȝef ChL. canst] const V; can E. can] con V; will E. no . . . seiȝe] sey no more H. no] na U. more] bettre WN. seiȝe] seye V; sey Ch; say EW; seyn N; sayne K; segge RJL; sigge UD; siggyn M.
161 acusiþ . . . cunge] konygliche acusith J. acusiþ þe] þe acuseth L. acusiþ] acusit M; acuset H²; accuseþ RDChKWN; accusis E; haþ accused H; haþ acuiset V. cunge] congeie NV; conieye H; congyn M; hange K. þe] RUDChHJLEKWNM; *om* TH²V.
162 Nay] Ȝe WN. þat lady] Mede þo M; sche þoo J. þat] þe DChHW; *om* E. leuiþ] leuyth JK; leueþ W; leues L; levys E; leue TRDChH²HN; leef UV; ac leue M. wers] worse DChVHLK.
163 Whanne] when ChHLE; whon V; Qwan J. wyte] witen VHL; wytyn J; witte W; wyttyn K; wete Ch; wetyn M; weteþ D; wot N; wate E. where] wer M; qwere J; qwar E. þe] þeo L; *twice* M. wrong] wrang E. liggeþ] liggyþ H²J; liþ HWM; lihþ V; liȝthe N; lyes E; duelliþ U.
164 Þere] For þer JM; Whare E. þat] as M; a E; *om* VH. is] it W. gret] gret lord V; most HL. mede] *twice* H²; mede mayde D; ȝett mede E. may] it may H; may ofte L. helpe] helpyn JM; amende H.
165 *line om* M. And] *om* HE. knowist] knowist wel H; knowes wele J; knawys wel E. I] at I E. cam] ChH²J; com UDVL; com *altered to* cam R; come HKWN; can TE. nouȝt] not DVHLKW. to] RUVHJLKN; for to TDChH²; heder to W; *om* E.
166 *line om* M. Ne] No L; *om* R. to] for to R; *om* JE. depraue] deprauyn J; dampne H²L; disprayse E; dispyce RU. a] no E; *om* K. proud] prout H. herte] heorte L; harte K.
167 Wel] And wel M. þou] þowȝ Ch. wost] wate E; wotest K. consience] þi seluen E. ȝif] ȝef ChL; *om* RW. wilt] wolt UVHL; will E; woldest R. leiȝe] lyȝe H²VH (*cancelled for* gabbe *by late corrector* H²); ly RUDChLEKWNM; lyen J.

Þou hast hongid on myn half enleuene tymes,
And ek grepe my gold & gyue it where þe likiþ.
Why þou wraþþest þe now wondir me þinkiþ. 170
ȝet I may, as I miȝte, [menske] þe wiþ ȝeftis,
And maynteyne þi manhod more þan þou knowist;
And þou hast famid me foule before þe king here.
For kilde I neu*ere* no king ne counseilide þ*er*aftir,
Ne dide as þou demist; I do it on þe king. 175
In normandie was he nouȝt anoyed for my sake,
Ac þou þiself, soþly, asshamidest hym ofte;
Crope into a caban for cold of þi nailes;

168 Þou] þat þou J. hast] hase E. hongid] honged DChH²VL; hangyd EM; hanged N; hongen W; hangyn J; hange*n* RU. half] halse EKN; Nekke VH. enleuene] Enleue V; endleue M; elleuene RDChHJ EKWN; mony feole L. tymes] tyme RJ.
169 ek] eken L; also HWN; als E; *om* RH²JM. grepe] grepyn R; gripen UCh H²HN; Igripen V; griped W; grypyd E; groped K; haste grope L; hast gropyn J. my] of my VHJWN. gold] gold wyt þyn hand M. &] to JEM; *om* LN. gyue] gyfe L; gif N; gyff E; gyue*n* RH²; geue D; gef W; geuen Ch; ȝyuen UV; ȝifen J; ȝeue HM; yevyn K. it] *om* UVHJLEW NM. where] were JN; qwar E; þer ChV. þe] þou EW. likiþ] liketh DChL; lik*es* E; likid U; lyked JKWNM; lykede V; list H.
170 Why] Qwy J; And why L. þou wraþþest] wrethys þou E. þou] *om* HN. wraþþest] wrathys J; wrothist H². þe] me ChEM; *om* DK. þinkiþ] þynkyt M; thynkys J; thingeȝ E; þenketh W.
171 ȝet] ȝit RUDChH²HJM; For ȝit VWN; Yf E. I may] may y L. miȝte] myȝthe R; myyth N; mgthe M. menske] VHLEKWNM; manschippyn J; mylde RU; au*au*nce TDChH². ȝeftis] yeftes K; ȝyftys JM; ȝiftes RUDH²VLN; gyft*es* E.
172 manhod] monhode L; Monhede V. more] mare E. þan] þen VHE. knowist] knowest RDChVHLKWN; knowes U; knawys E.
173 And] but HEWNM; ac J. hast] hase E; hat M. famid] famed RUDChH² VHLEKNM; defamed W. foule] falsly Ch; *om* W. before] afore WN. þe king] þy kyn L. here] heere V; nowþe H; *om* W.
174 *marked with cross* N. H *corrupts to* & I agult hym neu*er* ne his counsel neþ*er*. For] Ne W; *om* Ch. kilde I] I begylyd E. kilde] kylled RKWN; kyllid J; Culde V; kulled L; kelled D; kyde (*late corrector alters to* kylde) H²; gylede M; Miskaried Ch. I] *om* H²N (*late corrector supplies* H²). no] þe N; *om* DEW. king] man E. ne] no LM. counseilide] Counsald E; counseile Ch; conseylyd hy*m* M.
175 Ne dide] for I dede neu*er* H. Ne] No L. dide] did JEKN; dede RD; dude L; dede nouth M; ded I Ch; dude i neu*ere* V. demist] demys E; dost R; dust V; didest H. it] *om* D. on] o J. þe king] oure kyngis mouthe L; þy silue H.
176 *line om* E. was] nas VHWN. nouȝt] not UVJK. anoyed] anoȝede (a *above line same ink*) H²; anuyȝed V; noied UChW; noyede J; noyȝed RH; nuyed L; agreuyd M. my sake] me RU. my] *altered to* þy L.
177 Ac] Bot ChHLEKWNM; And R. þou] *om* ChH. þi] *om* U. self] seluen J; seolf L. soþly] suthly E; sykerly RU. asshamidest] ashamyd H; aschamed Ch; schamedyst J; shamedest N; schamyd K; schamed RDLEW; aschamyst H²; þou schamedyst M; schomedest V; conseiledest U. hym] hem W. ofte] often M; ofter E; ful oft W; þennes U; þere VH.
178 *marked with cross* N. Crope] crepe RH²K; Creep U; Creptest V; þou crope LW; þow crepe JN; Þou crepyd E; þou creptest H. to] *om* DCh. a] *om* LEM. caban] cabans M; cabons E. nailes] nales E.

Wendist þat wynter wolde han last euere;
And dreddist to be ded for a dym cloud, 180
And hastide[st] þe homward for hunger of þi wombe.
Wiþoute pite, pilour, pore men þou robb[ed]est,
And bar here bras on þi bak to caleis to selle,
Þere I lefte wiþ my lord his lif for to saue,
And made hym merþe mournyng to leue, 185
And bateride hym on þe bak, boldite his herte,
Dede hym hoppe for hope to haue me at wille.
Hadde I be march[al] of his men, be marie of heuene,
I durste han leid my lif & no lesse wed

179 Wendist] þou wendest HJWN; And wendest L; For þou wend E; wenest þou R. þat] whar L; *om* E. wolde] wald E. han . . . euere] euere haue Ilastid M. han] haue ChVHJLEKWN; *om* RUD. last] laste UJLN; lasted ChW; lasten R; ylast H. euere] for euer L.
180 And] And þou L; þou WN. dreddist] dreddest RChVKWN; dredest D; draddest UL; dred E. to] for to D; þe to UHEKM. be] beo L; haue be HW; haue ben VJE; ha ben M; haue bi N. a] on Ch. dym] lityl J; don Ch. cloud] knowde R; colde J.
181 And] þou H. hastidest] U; hastedest ChVHLW; hastedyst JM; hastide TH²; hasted DKN; hastest R; hast E. þe] *om* VL. homward] hamward VHLEW. wombe] wambe E.
182 Wiþoute] *with*oute*n* VJ; Withowtyn EM. pite] pyte þou RULNM; pete þou EK; pete þan J; ri3t þou H. pilour] pelour RDE; *after cancelled* robbe L. pore] of pore D; þore J. robbedest] RChVHLN; robbedist UJ; robedest W; robidyst H²; robbed EK; robbest TD; Robbist M.
183 And] Thou W. bar] bore R; bere L; beere V. here] her UChM; heor VL; their K; þair E; out R. on] at LK. caleis] Cales K; calys E. selle] sellen M; seolle L; sille H; sulle V.
184 Þere] Þair E; and R. lefte] lafte RDVHJLN; lefete M. wiþ] at home *with* R. lif for] worschepe M.
185 And] And I E; *om* V. made] Maade V. hym] his E; alle hise M. merþe] myrthe H²K; merþes R; mirthes U; mychel myrthe J; muche murthe L; murþe ful muche V; wiþ myrþe W; *with* my myrthe N; mery Ch; merie H; mery men EM. mournyng] his mornyng J; þair murnyng E; fro morwen R; fro morwe U. to] til RU; till Ch. leue] leeue H²; leyuyn (*touched up* ?) M; lete VH; eue RU.
186 And] I RUDKWN; *om* V. bateride] baterid H²; batered Ch; batride U; batrid H; batrede LM; batred RDJKW; Battyrd E; Battede V; batted N. hym] hem VJWNM; þaim E; men H. þe] *above cancelled* my D; here H. bak] Bakkes VHE; bak bod (bod *cancelled*) U. boldite] boldide U; boldede R; bolded DL; and bolded ChJKWNM; & baldyd E; to bolden VH. his] here HWM; her N; heore VL; þer J; þair E. herte] harte K; hertes VEW; hertis HJNM; heortes L.
187 Dede] Dyde H²; dyd K; Dude V; Deode L; I dede WM; I did E; & dide U; And didyn J; I made H; I bad N. hym] hem VHJNM; heom L; þaim E; *om* W. hoppe] hoppyn JM; *om* DE. for] for to E. hope] ioi3e H. haue] han U. me] *om* RU. at] at here H; at his RU.
188 Hadde] Hade LE; Hedde V. be] ben DJENM; beon L; byn K; *om* U. marchal] RUChH²VHJLEWNM; merschall K; marchaunt TD. of] ouere UChH². men] oost H. marie] marie loue RU; maries loue H. heuene] heouene L.
189 han] haue RUDChVHJLEKWN. leid] leide ChRH²LN; leyyd K; layd EW; Ileid V. my] al my W. lif] heed U. lesse] lasse RVHJLM; wors D.

He shulde haue be lord of þ*at* lond in lengþe & in brede, 190
And ek king of þ*at* kiþ his kyn for to helpe,
Þe leste brol of his blood a barouns pere. |
[Cowardly þou consience conceiledest him þennes]
To leuen his lordsshipe for a litel siluer, *fol.* xxxij *a*
Þat is þe riccheste reaume þ*at* re[yn] ou*er*[houiþ]. 195
It becom[iþ] a king þat kepiþ a reaume
To ȝiuen hise men mede þ*at* mekly hym s*er*uen,
To alienes, to alle men, to hono*ure* hem w*ith* ȝeftis.
Mede makiþ hym be louid & for a man holde.

190 shulde haue] suld haue E; had WN; hadde M; hedde V. be] beo V; ben UDNM; byn K; beon L; *om* E. lord] a lord R. of] of al W; in R. lond] land E. in (*both*)] on M; of E. lengþe] lenkþe V; lenght K; lenketh J; lenthe W; lenth E; leynthe L.
191 ek] als E; *om* H²W. of] of al W. þat] *om* M. kiþ] cuþþe V; ketthe M; cuntrey H; lytȝ R. kyn] cun V; ken M. for] þer wiþ W; *om* E. helpe] helpyn M; haue holpyn E.
192 Þe] þeo L; Ya þe EM. leste] leeste V. brol] brothel J; barn RVH; Baron W; braunche M. his] here A(1; *see above, line* 29).
193 LRUDH²VHJEKWNM; *line om* TCh. Cowardly] Þere cowardly M; Soþliche V; but soþely H; Þan Come E. þou] *om* U. conceiledest] counceiled D; counceilid K; consailled W; þou counseyledest RUVH; þou counseld E. him] hem W. þennes] þannes H; þine E.
194 To] For to E. leuen] leuyn RJKM; leue VH; lefe E. his] þer his L; þat VH. lordsshipe] lordschep Ch; lordchepe M; lordschupe V; worschep R. litel] litil UE KWM; litul H²; luitel V. siluer] seluer V; seluyr M; seoluer L; disese H.
195 þe] *om* D. riccheste] ricchesd J; Richerste M. reaume] reame V; realme EK; rewme HJLNM; Reme DChH²; of rewmys RU. reyn] UVHL; rayn JK; regniþ T; regneþ DWN; reigneth Ch; regnet (*late corrector alters to* reyne) H²; regnes R; rengnit M; is E. ouerhouiþ] ou*er*houyth J; ouerhoueþ VH; ouerhoues RU; ou*er* oveþ (oveþ *cancelled for* erthe) K; ouer hongeth L; ou*er* one D; ou*er* on TCh; vnd*er* heuene H²WNM (*late corrector alters to* overhangyth H²); ouer qware E.
196 It] For it J; Bot it E; Þat M. becomiþ] becomyth JK; bycometh UDChVHLWN; becommys E; bycome R; becom TH²; besemet M. a] For a V; to a ChHLEK WNM. kepiþ] kepeþ RDChVLK; kepit M; kepys E; kepe shal W; kepe sal N.
197 ȝiuen] ȝiue V; gyue N; gyff E; ȝeuen LM; yevyn K; ȝeue RDChH; gefe W. hise . . . mede] meede to men VH. hise] hese W. þat] at E. mekly] meokely L; manlyche R; menskly H. hym] *om* D. seruen] seruyn J; s*er*ue H²KWN; serueþ DChL; s*er*uis E.
198–9 *transposed, but the error noted in margin* R.
198 To] and UCh; *om* JM. to(2)] & UChJEM. alle] alle othir L; oþ*er* M. men] *om* L. to(3)] & L; *om* DJM. honoure] honouren L; honowry*n* J; haue honour W. hem] heom L; him H²NM (*late corrector alters to* hem H²); hure R; *om* UEW. with] for WN. ȝeftis] ȝiftys JM (*after cancelled* wyttys *same hand* J); ȝift*es* RUDH²VLN; gyft*es* E.
199 Mede] For mede WN. makiþ hym] hym maketh K. makiþ] makeþ RDCh VHWN; makyt M; makys E. hym] hem DChJW; *om* U. be] beo VL; to be UEK; *om* RHWN. louid] loued DCh LEK; yloued R; biloued HN; bilouet V; *om* W. man] Mon VL. holde] holden RUChEN; holdyn K; yholde HL; Iholden V; Iholdy*n* M; be holde (be *cancelled*) H²; ben holdyn J.

Emp*erours* ⁊ Erlis ⁊ alle man*er* lordis 200
Þoruȝ ȝeftis han ȝonge men to [ȝerne] ⁊ to ride.
Þe pope wiþ his p*re*latis p*re*sentis vndirfongiþ,
And mediþ men hymself to mayntene h*ere* lawis;
Seruauntis for here s*er*uyse, we se wel þe soþe,
Takiþ mede of here maistris as þei mowe accorde; 205
Begg*er*is for here bidding biddiþ of men mede;
Mynstral*is* for here m*er*þis mede þei asken;
Þe king haþ [m]ede of his men to make pes in londis;
Men þ*at* [kenne] clerkis crauen of h[e]m mede;

200 Emp*erours*] dukis H. ⁊(1)] *om* RUDJKWN. Erlis] Eorles VL; elrs E. man*er*] man*er* of RL; other E.

201 Þoruȝ] ȝorow N; For W. ȝeftis] ȝeftes ChLKW; ȝeft*us* H; ȝiftis UJ; ȝift*es* RDH^2VN; ȝyftis Inowe M; gyfteȝ enow E. han . . . ⁊] þey desiryt M. han] haue RDChJEN; haven K. to(1) . . . ⁊] *om* E. ȝerne] renne TRChH^2VHKN; rennen UDLW; rennyn J. ⁊ . . . ride] abowte L. ride] riden JK; rede *altered to* ryde *another ink* W.

202 Þe] þeo L; þe*n* M. pope] pape EK (*touched up* K); peple M. wiþ] and VHLM; of WN. his] þys M. p*re*sentis] p*re*sand*es* E; ȝifthis R. vndirfongiþ] vnderfongen RVH; vndirfonges D; vnd*er*faungeȝ E.

203 mediþ] medeþ DChW; medyn JM; mede*n* HLN; Meedeþ V; mede is E. men] mene E; gretly me*n* H; hem U. hym] hem VJNM; heom L; here D; hir E; *om* H. self] selue U; seluen VK; seluyn J; seoluen L; *om* H. mayntene] maynteygne W; meyten J. h*ere*] her ChJ; heore VL; hur*e* R; þair E; his U; þe WN.

204 Seruauntis] Seruauns VL; And s*er*uandes J; Seriauntes H^2EN (*line marked with a cross* N). here] her ChJKN; heore VL; þair E; to W. s*er*uyse] seruyces D; s*er*ue W. we . . . soþe] wite ȝe forsoþe H; wete wel þe soþe M. we] ȝe V. se] sen RUDWN; seen JK; seon VL.

205 Takiþ] Takeþ V; Takyn JKM; Taken UChHLWN; Take RD; Takes E. here] her ChKN; hire H^2; heore VL; þair E. mowe] mowen UVJM; mowyn K; mown RW; may DL; can E. accorde] acordy*n* M.

206 *line om* UWN. here] her ChK; heore V; *om* EM. bidding] beggyng Ch; bedis H; mede EM. biddiþ] byddeþ RDV; bidden H; bidde Ch; askyn M; þai beg E; bedith K; bedyn J. of] *om* RVHJLEKM. men] mennes E; hem H^2; me R. mede] me*n*de H; mete VEM.

207 Mynstral*is*] Mynstralles ChH^2LEN; Mynstrals W; Munstrals V; mynstrels HK; Mynst*er*elis J; Menstrales DRM. here] her ChK; heore L; heor V; þ*er* E; *om* WN. m*er*þis] merþes W; myrthis J; mirthes ChH^2KN; murþes DL; m*er*þe RM; myrthe UE; Murþe VH. þei] þai EW; thay K. asken] aske E; askyn M; axen U; axin RJ; sechen L; taken WN.

208 *line om* WN. L *corrupts to* And for to reule þe rewme þe kyng mede ȝefes. haþ . . . of] Meedeþ VH. haþ] hat M; hase E. mede] RUChJEKM; nede TDH^2 (*late corrector supplies missing minim* H^2). his] *om* Ch. make] maken V; makyn JM. londis] londe UVHJM; land E; his londe K.

209 Men þat] ⁊ þese H. kenne clerkis] clergye konnen L. kenne] kennyn J; ken WN; techyn M; ku*n*nynge H; knoweþ V; ben TRUDChH^2E; byn K. clerkis] childryn M. crauen . . . mede] mede of hy*m* crauytȝ R; Meede hem craueþ V. crauen] crauyn JK; craue H^2N; craues E. of hem] KWN (*but cancelled* K); of hym TUDH^2; hem of J; þair E; her*e* M; after ChL; vpo*n* H.

Prestis þ*at* preche þe peple to goode 210
Asken mede ⁊ messe penis ⁊ h*ere* mete alse;
Alle kyn crafty men craue mede for h*ere* p*re*ntis;
Mede ⁊ marchaundise mote nede go togid*ere*;
No wiȝt as I wene wiþoute mede miȝte libbe.'
Quaþ þe king to consience, 'be crist, as me þinkiþ, 215
Mede is worþi þe maistrie to haue'.
'Nay,' q*ua*þ consience to þe king ⁊ knelide to þe erþe,
'Þ*ere* arn to man*er* of medis, my lord, be ȝ*our* leue.
Þ*at* on god of his g*ra*ce gyueþ in his blisse

210 *divided from following after* mede DEM. Prestis] Preostes L. preche] p*re*chen UDChHLW; prechin RJKN; p*re*cheþ V; prechys E; techyn *after cancelled* the M. þe . . . goode] *om* E. þe] þeo L. peple] people LK; puple H. to goode] of god M; crist for to pleese L.
211 Asken] Askeþ V; axen DN; axin RJ; askyn here M; cravys also E. ⁊(1)] And eke D; of R; *om* EM. messe] masse RVL KM; mas HJ. penis] penyes ChHJ; pens RUDKWM; pans LN; pons V. h*ere*] her ChJK; heore VL; þ*er* E. alse] als J; also UDChHH^{2}KWN; eke VH; atte mel tyme M; at þe male tyme E.
212 L *substitutes* Alle maner mester men moten medlen with mede. Alle kyn] alkyn K; Alle kynne U; Alle ku*n*ne V; alle kinde R; Alle kende D; Alle kinnes ChN; Alkens W; ⁊ alle kyn J; Of alle kyn TH^2; ⁊ alle maner*e* H; *om* EM. crafty] craftis H; craftes VEK; craft W. craue . . . p*re*ntis] for craft taken mede W. craue] crauen UDHKM; craueþ V; craves E; haue J. for] to H; of E. h*ere*] her ChKN; heore V; þair E. p*re*ntis] prentyȝs M; prentasse E; p*re*ntices K.
213 *line om* E. Mede ⁊ marchaundise] Marchaundise and mede J. Mede] for mede HW. marchaundise] m*er*chaundise HK; Marchau*n*die V; marchaundises L. mote] moten LK; mot RUVM; most HW; *om* J. nede] nedes ChK; not V; alweys nede L; *om* J. go] gon DM; goon K; com R; mete U; metyn J; holde H; *om* Ch.
214 E *substitutes* Now þus *with*owtyn mede may no man be blyth; M *substitutes* As I wene witowty*n* Mede now may no man libbe. No] þer may no VH; Ther is no W; Miȝte no N. wiȝt] wiȝth D; wyt R; whyte J; man N. I] ich K. wiþoute . . . libbe] may leue wiþoute mede W; lyue *with*oute mede N. wiþoute] *with*outen VJL. mede] mete D. miȝte] may J; *om* VH. libbe] lyue H.
215 Quaþ] þo *quo*þ H; NOw *quod* V; Quod consience (consience *cancelled*) H^2. as . . . þinkiþ] as I wene M; þat me made H. þinkiþ] þinke E; þenkeþ W.
216 Mede is] Now is mede L. worþi] wel worþi WN; best worthy EM. þe] þo J; Muche V; myche H. haue] welde L.
217 Nay] Na E; Than W; *om* N. q*ua*þ] saide W. to . . . king] *om* W. knelide] knelyd RDH^{2}HJEK; knelede V; kneled ChNM; kneoled L; knelyþ W. þe] *om* V. erþe] ereth J; eorthe L; grou*n*de VHWN.
218 arn] aru*n* J; ar K; er E; beth DChHW; beoþ V; be N. to] too DW; two RUHL EN; twey V. man*er*] man*er*s D. of] *om* W. medis] mede DE. my] *om* UJW. lord] sire J. be] *with* DLN. ȝ*our*] þi VL. leue] *same hand after cancelled* wille J; liue E.
219 Þ*at*] Thet H^2; Þe UE; þo J. on] one K; ton UJ; tone E. god] good God V; is god Ch; is good D. his(1)] *om* D. gyueþ] giffyth J; gyff*es* E; geuyþ RK; geue vs D; ȝiueþ V; ȝeueþ Ch; grantyt M; haþ g*ra*untid H. in] of D. his blisse] heuen E.

To hem þat werchen wel whiles þei ben here. 220
Þe prophet prechiþ it & put it in þe sauter:
Qui pecuniam suam [non] dedit ad vsuram.
Tak no mede, my lord, of [men] þat ben trewe;
Loue hem & le[n]e hem for oure lordis loue of heuene;
Godis mede & his mercy þerwiþ miȝte þou wynne.
Þere is a mede mesurles þat maistris desiriþ; 225
To mayntene mysdoeris mede þei taken,
And þerof sei[þ] þe sauter in a salmis ende
In quorum manibus iniquitates sunt; dextera eorum repleta est muneribus.
And he þat gripiþ here giftes, so me god helpe,
Shal abiȝe it bitterly or þe bok liȝeþ. 230

220 hem] heom L; them K; al E. werchen wel] wel werchen H; wel worchen V. werchen] werchyn M; worchen RChH[2] LK; wurchen UD; wyrchin J; wirkes E; ay worche W; ay wyrche N. wel] well K; wele ChJE; his welle M. whiles] qwylys J; qwilse E; while ChHW; wil N; whil þat V; þe wyle þat M. þei] þai EW; thay K. ben] bene J; beon L; beþ H; er E; lyue W.
221 prechiþ it] it prechid H; hit prechede V. prechiþ] prechitȝ H[2]; precheþ R; prechys E; prechyd JKM; prechide U; preched DCh WN; prechede L. it(1)] so W. put] putte LW; puttes E; preued H. it(2)] *om* E.
221α *non . . . vsuram*] *&c* W. *non*] RUChV JLEKNM; *om* TDH[2]H. *dedit ad*] *dat in* H. *vsuram*] *vsuram &c* UHLE; *vsuram & munera super innocentem* N; *vsuriam* (i *cancelled*) Ch.
222 Tak] Tac þu M. my . . . men] of hem my lord H[2]. men] RUDVHLK WN; hem TChJM; þaim E. þat . . . trewe] at trew ben E. ben] beon L; beþ RW; beoþ V. trewe] treowe L; trwe N.
223 Loue] Lof J; Luffe E; But loue WN. hem(1)] þaim E; hym R; *om* L. &] ad Ch. lene] W; lenne E; lene *or* leue RUDChH[2] HJLKNM; leue T; leeue V. hem(2)] heom L; þaim E. oure] þe ULEKN; *om* JWM. heuene] heouene L.
224 mede . . . mercy] mercy & his mede J. his] *om* WM. wiþ] *om* L. miȝte þou] mahytow J; þou maiht V. miȝte] myȝth RH[2]; mytht L; myth M; mightyst K; may E.
225 Þere] Bote þer VHJ. maistris] masters K; Maystrie VH; maistries Ch. desiriþ] desireth DH[2]HLN; desiryt M; desyret V; desyren RUChKW; deserris E.
226 mede] þat mede M; mony E. þei] þai EW; thay K; ofte þey L. taken] takyn RJ; take DLEN.
227 H *corrupts to* & þat witnessiþ wel þe sauter of wicked men. And] *om* JM. þerof] Of hem M. seiþ] seyþ RUDChV LKWN; seys J; Says E; seide TH[2]; spekyt M. a] þe VE; *om* M. salmis] psalme E; spalmus N. ende] eende V; eynde L.
228 *In quorum*] *Inimicorum* H. *sunt*] *&c* W. *dextera . . . muneribus*] *om* WM. *dextera*] *dextra* RK. *muneribus*] *muneribus &c* L. *Here H adds a line: see above*, p. 46.
229 And] But H; *om* EW. he] heo V; þai E; thay K; ho D; ȝe M. þat] so D. gripiþ] grypytȝ R; grypit M; gripeth UDChVHLWN; grypis E; grypes H[2]; grepyn K. here giftes] mede so J. here] her K; heore VL; oure R; þe N; siche H; suche E; *om* Ch. giftes] gift N; ȝiftis M; ȝiftus V; ȝeftes LW; ȝeftis H; gold U. so] sa E. me] *followed by first strokes of a* g Ch.
230 **Here A resumes.** Shal] Sall E; he schal H; Schul A; Schallen K; Schulun J; Scholyn M; þei schullen V. abiȝe] abye RUDChH[2]EWN; abyen J; aby A; abigge HK; abiggyn M; aBugge VL. it] it full EA; hit wel LKN; ful RU; wel J; wol M; *om* ChV. bitterly] biturly H[2]; bytter LEM; bitere U. or] or ellis HLA; ar N; as E. bok] buke E. liȝeþ] lyeth DH[2]HJLAKWN; lieȝth Ch; liet M; lyes RU; tellis E.

Prestis & personis þat plesing desiriþ,
Þat take mede & money for massis þat þei synge,
Shal haue mede on þis molde þat mattheu haþ grauntid:
Amen Amen rec[eperu]nt mercedem suam.
Þat laboureris & louȝ folk taken of here maistris | *fol.* xxxij *b*
Is no maner of mede but a mesurable hire; 235
In marchaundie is no mede, I may it wel auowe;
It is a permutacioun apertly, a peny[worþ] for anoþer.
Ac reddist þou neuere *Regum*, þou recreiȝede mede,
Why þe vengeaunce fel on saul & on his children?
God sente hym to segge be samuels mouþ 240

231 *line om* N. Prestis & personis] Persouns & prestis HW. Prestis] Preostes VL. þat] at E. plesing] pleasyng E; plesynges RULM; presentȝ W; penyes H; prechit and A. desiriþ] dishirith A; desyren RUHLKW; deserys E.
232 *line om* N. Þat] And VEK; To RHM; Or W; Schal U; *om* A. take] taken LK; takyn JAM; takeþ V; takys E. mede] medis A. & money] or mony MW; for her money Ch; *om* D. massis] Massen V; messes RUChEA; masse DH²; messe W. þat] at E; or J. þei] þai EA; he J; the K. synge] syngen UDVHL; syngyn JAKM (*same hand after cancelled* sygnyn J).
233 *line om* N. Shal] Sall E; Schul UA; Schulyn J; Schullen V; Scholyn M; Schallen K; þei H. haue] hauen HM; han RV. mede] þe mede RUWM; here mede H; that mede (that *by late corrector*) H². on] in VE; of RUJLM. þis] his DH² (*late corrector prefixes* t H²); þe R. molde] mounde Ch. þat . . . grauntid] wiþouten eny more H. haþ] has E; *om* DM. grauntid] grantide H²; graunted RChL EW; ygrantid UK; Igrauntet V; hem graunttid M; graunteþ D.
233α *line om* HN. *Amen*(2)] *amen dico vobis* EAK; *dico vobis* UVLWM. *receperunt*] VLEAKWM; *reciperunt* R; *recipierunt* Ch; *recipiebant* TUDH²J. *suam*] *suam &c* E.
234 *transposed with following* W. Þat] Thaþ R. laboureris] labores EM. louȝ] louh V; low DJLKN; lewed W; lewid HEAM; lewd Ch; lond RU. folk] folkes DK; men HM. taken] takyn JAM; take DW; takeþ R; takys E; lacchen N. here] her ChKN; hire H²; heore VL; þair E.
235 Is . . . a] An oþer mede þer is W. Is] Nis V; hit is RUDJAKNM; hit nys H. no] non M. maner] more AM. of] *om* UDVH. a] *om* VH. mesurable] musarable (?) Ch. hire] huyre VHL; hure N; heyre D; here ChW.
236 marchaundie] marchandise UDChV HJLEAKWN; mariaundise H². is] nis VH. may] maw E. it] *om* A. wel] *om* L. auowe] awowe N; awoye E.
237 It is] but H. a . . . apertly] apertly a permutacioun U; apert permytacioun as H. apertly] pertly DCh; aperly A; *om* VJE WM. penyworþ] penyworth URDJLE AKNM; peny TChH²VHW.
238 Ac] Bot ChVLEAKM; Ne WN; *om* H. reddist] Raddest VK; redde WN; redd E; redest Ch. þou(2)] þat VHN. recreiȝede] recreyede RU; recreyed HJ LN; recreyde DW; recreyd A; recrayeȝed Ch; Recrayed K; recrayd E; recride H²M.
239 Why] Qwy JE; how RHW. þe] þeo L; þat VHW; *om* J. fel] fyl DH²; worched L. on(1) . . . children] vpon his children of þe man saul A. on(1)] vpon M. saul] *corrected from* soule Ch. on(2)] eke on DJM; on al R; *om* VHEWN. children] chyldryn RM; childrine J; childern K; childre WN; chylder E; chidren V.
240 God] How god W. sente] sent DChJEAWN; sende VHL. hym] hem W; *om* V. to] *om* E. segge] seye RUVJ; seyn NM; seyne A; say HKW; sayn L; sayne D; saw E. samuels] samuel (*late corrector adds es*) H².

Þat agag of amaleg & [al] his peple aftir
Shulde diȝe for a dede þat don hadde h*er*e eldren
[Aȝens isra[e]l and aaron and moyses his broþer].
Samuel seide to saul, "god sendiþ þe & hotiþ
To be buxum & boun his bidding to fulfille. 245
Wende þidir *with* þin ost wom*m*en to kille;
Children & cherl*is*, choppe hem to deþe.
Loke þ*o*u kille þe king; coueite nouȝt hise godis;
For any mylionis of mone murdre hem ichone;
Barnes and bestis brenne hem to deþe." 250
And for he kilde not þe king as crist [him] bode sente,

241 agag] agas RChE; agagye K; agax J; achaz U. of] and RUChVJE; for D. amaleg] amalech UH^2KWM; Amalec DVHJLEAN; amelek R; amules Ch. al] RUVHJLEAKWNM; *om* TDChH^2. his] her Ch. peple] people LK; puple RHA. aftir] eft*er* E.
242 Shulde] Schulden V; Schuldyn M; Scholdyn J; Sall E. diȝe] dye DChVL EKWN; deyȝe H^2; deye RUH; dey A; deyen M; deyn J. þ*a*t] & E. hadde] haddyn M; haden L; hedde V; hed E. h*er*e] her Ch; his RUDVHJLEKWNM. eldren] elder*e* J; eldres UD; eldris H^2M; elders EW; eldars K; elderis A; heldres N; aldres L; eldes Ch.
243 RVHJLEAKWNM; *line om* TUDCh H^2. israel] VHJEAKWNM; isral R; yraels L. and(1)] *om* W. his] *om* W; here A. broþer] broder*e* J; brether E.
244 sendiþ] sendyt M; sendeþ RDCh; sendes L; sende H; send K; sent EAW; seendeþ V. þe] to þe AM. &] to HW. hotiþ] hotit (*final* t *corrected from* d) M; hoteþ RDChVLKN; highte E; say HW.
245 *line om* N. To] And hoteþ þe W; Bot þou E. be] beo VL; ben JAM. &] *om* W. boun] bone Ch; bownde K; bold RU; boner E; *om* W. bidding] biddyngis A. fulfille] fulfillyn D; fulfellyn M; fulfulle L; werche H; worche V.
246 Wende] weend V; Wendyt M; wyndith A. þidir] þider UVLNM; thidur H^2; þedir E; þeder RDChW; þedur A; thither K; þou to amalek H. wom*m*en] wymme*n* DChVJKWM; wy*m*man R; alle wymmen L; þe cu*n*tre H. to] for to A; þou L. kille] killen Ch; Culle V; quelle HL.
247 Children] Childe E. cherl*is*] cherles UDH^2WN; Cheorles VL; churles E; chorles R; clerkys J; clerkes Ch; clark*es* K. choppe] Chop VJM; chope E; chopen (*corrector prefixes* s) H^2; schap D; schep R; dryue H. hem . . . deþe] of here hedis A; of heore hedes L. hem] þaim E; them K. deþe] dede EM; deye R; þe deþ N.
248 *line om* U. Loke] Luke E. kille] kile M; culle VL. þe] *om* E. coueite] & coueyte L; bot couett E; take W. nouȝt] not RDV HJLAKW. godis] gudeȝ E; gode ChN.
249 *line om* U. any] ony EAWM; eny RDHN; *om* V. mylionis] meliounis AK; multitude L. mone] Monye Ch; money DH^2HLEKN; Moneye V; monoye W; gold A. murdre] murþer ChJE; morder H^2; morþ*er*e RV; loke þou morþre W; muldre D; moldre N; molde H; dismembre A. hem] heom L; þaim E. ichone] echone DChH^2HAK; vchone VLN; all E.
250 *line om* U. Barnes] Bernes VEW; Bernys JA; Beornes L; Biernes N; Barnet D; burwes & bernes H; Gerdis M. brenne . . . deþe] þou brenne H. brenne] bren DJ; brene R; bryng E; brutne L. hem] heom L; þaim E. to] to þe N; al to V. deþe] *after cancelled* dede *same hand* J; dede EAM; gader*e* H^2; askes V.
251 And] *om* HJA. kilde] kylled DChHN; kyllyd JEAK; culde V; kulled L; quelled W. not] nouȝt RChN; noght UE; nouth J; nout M. as . . . sente] bot covett hys goodeȝ E. him] hy*m* RUDVHJLA KWNM; *om* TChH^2. bode] boþe D; self VH; selue U; *om* R. sente] sende HL; bad RU; hihte V.

Coueitide here catel, kilde nouȝt hire bestis,
But brouȝte wiþ hym þe bestis as þe bible [telliþ],
God seide to samuel þat saul shulde deiȝe,
And al his sed for þat synne [shend]fully ende. 255
Such a meschef mede made þe kyng [to] haue
þat god hati[de him for euere] & alle hise heires aftir.
þe *culorum* of þis [cas] kepe I not to shewe;
An aunter it [noiȝide me non] ende wile I make.
[I] consience knowe þis, for kynde [w]it me tauȝte, 260
þat resoun shal regne & reumes gouerne,

252 Coueitide] Coueitid M; Coueytede H²V; coueyted RDChLKN; Coueyte A; And Couett E; but coueyted UHJ; For coueitise of W. here] her ChKN; heore L; *þer* E; his D; þe H; feir V; *om* W. catel] good A. kilde] kylled DChN; killid AK; kulled L; and kylde U; & kyllyd JE; slow W; & slow H; and slouh V. nouȝt] not DVHLAKW. hire] here RUH²HJAWNM; her ChK; heore L; *þer* E; his DV.
253 But] & HE. brouȝte] brouhte V; brouȝthe R; brouth A; broghte L; browte D; drof W. wiþ] forþ WN. hym] hem RUHA; *om* WN. þe] here H. bestis] bestaile L; goodis H. as] als E. bible] bibille ChE; bylle R. telliþ] tellith UN; tellit AM; telleþ VLKW; tellys E; techiþ HJ; tolde RDChH²; hym tolde T.
254 seide] sende VH. samuel] say H; seye V. saul] sowle J; Samuel (m *rubbed or erased*) V. shulde] suld E. deiȝe] deyȝ H; deye RUDJM; dey A; die ChVLE KWN.
255 his] he A; *om* U. sed] seyde A. þat] hys E. synne] sunne V; senne M. shendfully] schendfulliche UDVH; schenfullyche RLNM; schamfully ChKW; senfully T; synfully H²EA; schent ben J. ende] RUVHKWN; endy*n* M; eynde L; endid A; shulde ende TDChH²E; for euere J.
256 Such] suych R; siche H; Swich UJM; Sweche A; Swilke E. a] an W. meschef] mysdede U; mysse A. mede made] made mede M. þe kyng] þat man E. to] RUDChVHKW; for to H²JLEAM; *om* TN (*supplied in margin* N).
257 *line om* WN. hatide] U; hatid HJA; hatede VM; hated RH²LK; hatiþ T; hateth DCh; hat*es* E. him] VHJLEAKM; þe king RUDH²; þat king TCh. for euere] RUHLEAKM; eu*er*e VJ; *om* TD ChH². alle] *om* VJA. heires] eiȝers Ch; ayres L; sede E.
258 þe] Thou R. *culorum*] colour*e* HJE AK; ende D. cas] NChEAM; clause TH²; terme D; *om* RUVHJLKW. kepe] ne kepe W; no kepe L; *om* D. not] nouȝt ChH²KN; noght UE; nouth JM; oute D; neu*er* A. shewe] schewen M.
259 *line om* H. An] On DL; O N; en R; In VJEA; And an W; And Ch. aunt*er*] auenture VJNM. it] þat it E; ȝif hit RUJ; if I W. noiȝide me] noiede me UJ; noyed me RDAKW; noyd me E; nuyed me L; annuyed me N; me noiȝide T; me noyȝede H²; me noiȝed Ch; greuede M; munged (? *for* nuuiged) me V. non] LANM; nane E; now J; now an D; nygh an K; an TUChV; and H²; *om* RW. ende] eynde L; hende M; amende W. wile] wol ChVLK. make] makyn M.
260, 261 *misplaced after* **265** VH.
260 I] HJLAWNM; In TRUChH²EK; yf D; *om* V. knowe] knaw E; knew H; knoweþ V; schal knowe A; schal knowyn M. þis] DVHJWNM (*preceded by erasure* N); þat A; hit L; I þis TRUChH²K (I *above line another ink* K); *om* E. kynde] kuynde V; kende Ch; resou*n* RUE. wit me] VHJLAWNM; it me TRUD ChH²; me K; hase it E. tauȝte] tauȝthe R; tauth A; thaught E; tould K.
261 þat] And E. resoun shal] resonis schul A. regne] regny*n* M; reynge K; reine ChH²A; rene E; reygne ȝit JWN. reumes] Reames DV; remes ChH²; realmis A; realmeȝ EK; regnes N; regnys M. gouerne] gouernyn M; defende E.

And riȝt as agag hadde happe shal somme:
Samuel shal slen hym, & saul shal be blamid,
And dauid shal be dyademid & daunten hem alle,
And o cristene king kepe vs ichone. 265
Shal no more mede be maister on erþe,
But loue & louȝnesse & leaute togideris;
And whoso trespassiþ [to treuþe, or] takiþ [aȝeyn his wille],
Leaute shal do hym lawe [and no] lif ellis.
Shal no seriaunt for þat seruyse were a silk houue, 270
Ne no ray robe [wiþ] riche pelure.

262 *line om* H. as] so as W. agag hadde] fel of agag M. agag] agas RUChE; agagx J. hadde] hedde V; hauyd A; happed L; *om* W. happe . . . somme] happe sum schulden haue K; hap men schul se som tyme U; hap men schuld se sum tyme R; hap for hisse grett synne E; rygth so schal synne A. happe] happen L; happyn J; hapne V; happed W; happed ende D. shal] schul D; schule L; schulyn J; schulle V. somme] of summe M; newly somme H[2]
263 Samuel . . . hym] þen samuel slowe agag H. slen] sle A; sleen Ch; scle R; scleen K; slae E. shal(2)] sall E; *om* HW. be] beo L; ben JM; was H. blamid] blamyde J; blamed RDChLKWN; blamet V; yblamyd H.
264 And] *om* VE. shal be] was H. be] beo L; ben V; bene J; bigge A; biggyn M. dyademid] dyadem Ch; dyademys AM. daunten] dauntyn JAM; daunte E; daunted HW; damnen D. hem] heom L; þaim E; of W.
265 o] on DChVHLANM; one UJK; vn E. king] kyngeȝ E; kyngis A. kepe] kepen V; kepyn KM; schal kepe A; schal kepyn J; to kepen U; clepe E; kept H. vs] ȝou A; hem HM; þaim E. ichone] echone UDChHAK; vchone VLN; ilkane E; alle R.
266 Shal . . . mede] And mede shal nomore (de *above line another script*) W. Shal] Sall E; Now shal N. no] na UE. more] mare E. be] beo L; ben UJ. maister] master K. on] in J; vppon VHEAM; apon L; of N. erþe] eorþe VL; erde A.
267 loue] luff E; lele loue W. louȝnesse] louhnesse V; lownesse RUDH[2]HJLAK NM; lufsumnes E; leute W. leaute] lewȝte Ch; laute H[2]J; lovte M; lyaunce DW.
268 whoso] ho so DJA; qwa so E; who U; heo þat V; he þat H. trespassiþ] trespace M; trespas A; trispas E; trespaced D. to treuþe] HAM; to trouþe VLE; treuþe DKN; aȝeyne trewthe JW; trewely TRUChH[2]. or] VJLEKWNM; & TRU DChH[2]HA. takiþ . . . wille] aȝeyn him takith L. takiþ] takyt M; takes E; doþ VHJ. aȝeyn . . . wille] VHJEAKWNM; agaynes ryȝth RU; ony þyng D; to þe wrong TChH[2].
269 Leaute] Leute VHJLEAKN; lealte M; Leelte W; His wykkide leaute TU ChH[2]; his wikke lewte R; His wikyd liaunce D. shal] sha M. do . . . lawe] leggen him lowe L. do] don RUDVJA WM; done KN. and] RUDEAKWM; or TChH[2]VHJLN. no lif] no lyfe AWM; no lyve E; lese his lif TRUDChH[2]HKN; lesyn his lif J; leose his lif L; leosen his lyf V.
270 *marked with cross* N. Shal] Sall E; *om* W. seriaunt] seriaunȝ N; seruaunt RUH[2]K (*late corrector alters to* seryeaunt H[2]). þat] his RUD; here A. were] weryn J; wern M; weare K; weore L; shal were W. a] þe A; no RUE; *om* Ch. silk] selk UH[2]V; seolk L; silken ChAK; sylkyn WM; selken H. houue] houfe E; howe ChWN; owue JM; houys A; gowne RU.
271 Ne] No L; Na ȝit E. no] non A; noon K. robe] robis AW. wiþ . . . pelure] rechely yforred L. wiþ] with RUVEAKWM; with no DN; with so J; of TChH[2]H.

Mede of mysdoeris makiþ hem so riche
Þat lawe is lord waxen & leute is pore,
Vnkyndenesse is comaundo*ur*, & kyndenesse is banisshit.
Ac kynde wyt shal come ȝet, & consience togid*ere*, 275
And make of lawe a labourer, such loue shal arise.'

272 of mysdoeris] wiþ her*e* mysdedis H. makiþ] makyt M; mak*es* E. hem] heom L; men VE; many W. so riche] lordes W. so] to ChLAM.
273 Þat] þe H^2. lord] a lord UH^2LEM (a *by late corrector* H^2). waxen] waxin M; Iwaxen V; woxin R; *om* E. &] *om* H^2. leute] lelte W; lyaunce D; loue AM; luve E. is] is ful A; is to M; is waxen E. pore] pure E.
274 *marked with cross* N. Vnkyndenesse] Vnkuyndesse V; vnkendenesse ChAW; wykkednysse RUHEM. is(1)] is a L. kyndenesse] kyndenysse R; kuyndenesse V; kendenesse ChAM. is(2)] *om* E. banisshit] banyschid U; banysshed K; banyschede E; banschid DM; bansched RChHW; Banescht V; banychisted J; vanshed N; blamichid A; banned L.
275 Ac] Bot ChHLEKWNM; and RVA. kynde . . . ȝet] ȝet schal kynde wit come L. kynde] kuynde V; kende Ch. come] comy*n* JM. ȝet] ȝit $RUDChH^2VHJENM$; aȝen W.
276 make] makyn JM. lawe] wo lawe A. labourer] loburer R; labore H^2; labrerer (? *a patch in the vellum*) H. such] siche H; swich UJM; sweche A; swylke E; schuche R; schuhc H^2. loue] luve E; lawe R. shal] sal E. arise] arisyn M; areyse R; rice A.

IV

'Sessiþ,' seide þe king, 'I suffre ȝow no lengere.
Ȝe shuln sauȝte, forsoþe, & serue me boþe. |
Kisse hire,' quaþ þe king, 'consience, I hote!' *fol.* xxxiij *a*
'Nay be [Crist],' quaþ consience, 'cunge me raþere!
But resoun rede me þerto [raþer] wole I deiȝe.' 5
'And I comaunde þe,' quaþ þe king to consience þanne,
'Rape þe to riden, & resoun þat þou fecche.
Comaunde hym þat he come my counseil to here,
For he shal rewele my reaume & rede me þe beste
Of mede & of mo oþere, what man shal hire wedde, 10

1 *also copied at the head of* VII W. Sessiþ] Sesith H^2H; Seseth UDChV; Sessyþ now RJW; Es ȝe (*capital wanting*) E; Sekyr A; Kysset M. seide] seiþ N; quod W. king] kyng þo M. I . . . ȝow] ne mote ȝe H. lengere] lengur H^2; leyngre L; langer E; more VH.
2 shuln] schul RUDChH^2HJN; schulle V; scholyn M; schal AW; sal E; schulden K; *om* L. sauȝte] sauȝten K; saghten D; sawtyn J; sauȝtene V; saȝtene HL (*glossed* acoorde *similar hand and ink* H); saughtle N; saghtlyn U; sawtlyn R; saghtyll E; sautalyn M; acorde AW. forsoþe . . . me] & serue me forsoþe A. &] her & E. serue] seruen J; seruyn M. boþe] boþin M.
3 Kisse] kys DEA; kusse UVL; cus R; kesse M. hire] hyr HE; here DA; her ChK; hirre (*for* hure) R; me here W; *om* N. quaþ] coth E. I] Ich V; I the KW. hote] bydde E; bid þee H; rede J.
4 Crist] VHJLEAKWNM; god TRUD ChH^2. quaþ] I quoþ H. cunge . . . raþere] confoundyd wrthe I rathere J; coueytid no more A. cunge] Congeye VLN; counge (*a fifth minim added above line original ink*) H; hang E. me] *om* R.
5 But] But yf D; Bot ȝef Ch. rede me] me rede W. rede] red A; radde H; rewle D. me] mede (de *cancelled*) E. þerto] þertille RDLAK. raþer] rather EAWNM; leuere H; erst TH^2JK; arst RDChVL; first U. wole] wil RDH^2JE AKWNM; hadde H. deiȝe] deye RUM; dey JEA; dye DChVLKWN.
6 And] *om* H^2HEW. þe(1)] *om* RDJLKM. to] *om* E. þanne] þenne UV; þen E; as swiþe H.
7 Rape] rap R; Now rape WN; þat þou Rape VH. þe] *om* M. to] *om* DK. riden] ride UChH^2VHEKWNM; ridyn A. &] *om* HEW. þat] to HEW; *om* RUCh VANM. þou] þou me U; þe D; *om* HEAW. fecche] facche L; fette V; fecche to councell A.
8 Comaunde] & comaunde H. þat he] to LE; for to A; *om* W. here] hure H.
9 shal] sall E. rewele] rewlyn J; rydyn A. my] me J. reaume] Reme ChH^2A; realme EK; *om* J. rede] redyn J; red EA. me] e *rubbed* W. þe] for þe HM.
10 & . . . oþere] þe maiden L. of(2)] *om* ChN. mo oþere] oþer mo DVHJM; other ma E. mo] many Ch. what] qwat JEM; and what VHLKN. man] mon VL. hire] hir VE; here UDAW; her ChKN; hure R. wedde] weddyn M; weld E; haue H.

And counte wiþ [þe] consience, so me crist helpe,
How þou lerist þe peple, þe lerid ⁊ þe lewid.'
'I am fayn of þat foreward,' seiþ þe frek þanne,
And riȝt renneþ to resoun ⁊ rouniþ in his ere;
Seide hym as þe king sente ⁊ siþþe tok his leue. 15
'I shal araye me to ride,' quaþ resoun, 'reste þe a while,'
And calde catoun his knaue, curteis of speche:
'Sette my sadil vpon suffre til I se my tyme,
And let warroke hym wel wiþ [wy]tful gerþis.
Hange on hym þe heuy bridel to holde his hed lowe, 20
And ȝet wile [h]e make many wehe er we come þere.'

11 counte] counpte L; aCounte VHE; acountyn JM. þe] ChHJLKWNM; *om* TRUDH²VEA. so . . . crist] as crist me E. crist] god RUDVHA.
12 *line om* A. L *corrupts to* How bothe lered ⁊ lewed þou lerest þe people. þou] he E. lerist] lerest DH²N; lernyst J; lernest ChHK; ledest V; Reulist M; reulest W; rewliste U; loses E. þe(1)] my VH. peple] people K; puple H. þe(2 *and* 3)] *om* RUVHJM. lerid] lettred K.
13 *line om* A. of . . . foreward] now þer of W. þat] þis E. seiþ] seytȝ R; saith LKW; says D; seide ChVM; sayd E; quoþ H; quod J. þe frek] consciens JM. þe] *om but late corrector supplies* the H². frek] freek U; Freike V; frayk D; feytȝ R. þanne] þenne RV; þen HE.
14 And] He AWN. riȝt renneþ] rideþ riȝt HWN; rydeȝ right E; rytte rygth A; ryd right L; Rod riht VJ; rode K; wendith M. renneþ] rennes RU; rydyth H². to] vnto W; after M. resoun] Concience V. rouniþ] rownes RUDE; Rouned V; rownyd JK. ere] here LM; eare K.
15 Seide] ⁊ seide HWN. hym] *om* UVH. as] that K. sente] sende V; him sente U; seide ChH²J; bade HW. siþþe] siþe H²W; sythen KN; sythyn EM; seþþe V; seþ Ch; sethen D; sethyn J; seothe L; swyþe R; aftir A. tok] took U; tuke E.
16 shal] sal E. araye] arayn A; rape Ch; rapyn J; *om* E. me . . . ride] ryde þider E. ride] rydyn A. reste] reest W; ⁊ rist E; now rest N. þe a] þe the W; þe M; þe þer A; þare a E.
17 And] he HWN. calde] called DChL WN; callyd H²JEK; callith A; clepte V; cliped H. catoun] on caton E; conscience U. knaue] knawe AW; kanue R. curteis . . . speche] þat com at þe furste L. curteis] curtaysie A. *Here* EAWM *add lines like* **B** IV 17–18 *or* **C** V 18–19: *see above*, p. 30.
18 *marked with cross* N. Sette . . . vpon] Late sadle me W. Sette] Sat L. sadil] sadel RDChVHLN; sadul H²; sadeyl M. vpon] apon LE. suffre] suffre quoþ he H; suffraunce H²W. se] see JEKN; seo VL. tyme] teme N.
19 And] *om* A. let] lete N; lat JL; late W; Bad E; loke þou VH; *om* K. warroke] warrokyn JAM. hym wel] wele hym A; him H². wiþ] wit M. wytful] DJLK WN; wittful A; full wyght E; riȝtful TRUChH²; swiþe fele H; swiþe feole V; to goode M. gerþis] gyrthis A; girthes UH²EKM; gurþis H; gurthes L; gurþhes V; garthes WN; gartys D.
20 Hange] hang UDJLE; honge HK; hong RChV; And hange N; And hong W. hym] hys heued M; hem W. þe] an RUVWM; a E. bridel] bridyl JEANM; bridul H². to] and RU. holde] holdyn JAM; hald E; bere VHW. his . . . lowe] doun his hed M. hed] heued UE. lowe] law E; *same hand above cancelled* down K.
21 And] For EAM; *om* VHJWN. ȝet] ȝit UChH²VHJWNM; ȝut R; *om* EA. wile he] MH²JW; wol he ChVHLK; schal he U; he will EAN; wile we T; we wil RD. make . . . wehe] weheen ⁊ wynch L. make] makyn JM. many] mony E; many a RH; moni a V; *om* WM. wehe] wey D; whi V; wey ⁊ whehe A; wiche *altered another ink to* viche E. er] or DChHJLEAK; ar N. we] he ChH² VHAKW. come] comyn [M; be N. þere] þare D; þeder Ch.

Þanne consience on his capil cairiþ forþ faste,
And resoun wiþ hym rit & rapiþ hym [swyþe].
Ac [o]n wary[n] wisdom, and witty his fere
Folewide hem faste for hy hadden to done 25
In cheker & in chauncerie, to be dischargid of þinges,
And riden faste for resoun shulde rede hem þe beste
For to saue hemself from shame & from harm.
Ac consience com arst to court be a myle wey
And rombide forþ wiþ resoun riȝt to þe king. 30
Curteisliche þe king þanne com in to resoun,

22 Þanne] ÞEnne V; þen H; *om* WN. capil] capul ChH²V; caple þo W. cairiþ] cayreth H²L; careþ N; caryd EA; caryeth RUChVJ; caried DHKWM. forþ] forþ*er* N.
23 *line om* D. rit] rideþ ChVHWN; ryd L; ryte K; to ryde E; ryȝt H²; ryȝth R; right U; rygth A. & . . . swyþe] redeliche nyghe L. &] *om* VE. rapiþ] rapeþ Ch; rapit M; rapyd EAK; raped J; rapide U; Rappynge V; hastid H; rouneth W. hym] hem H; *om* VWN. swyþe] RVH JM; faste UK; in hast EA; ȝerne TChH²; in his ere W; aftre N. *Here* W *adds a line like* **B** IV 25.
24 Ac] Bot ChVKWNM; Bod E; & HJA; at U; a R. on waryn] N; one waryn KW; on warry D; on wary Ch; vnwary TH²; þo waryn J; on warynd M; an warnyd E; warnyd A; on were U; ton wer*e* R; on asent weore L; on a wayn V; in a wayn H. wisdom] wyd V. witty] witthy M; wyt D; wisdame V. his] is H²; his ovne D; *om* V. fere] felawe A; Ifeere V.
25 Folewide] folewede*n* HL; Folewedyn M; Folowed DChN; Folowyd K; Folowd E; Folwide U; Folwede R; Folwed W; Folwedy*n* J; Felewyd H²; Folwe A. hem] heom L; þaim E; hy*m* RDM; ȝe A; *om* U. faste] full fast E; faste forþ U. for] or (*late corrector prefixes* f) H². hy] hij H²; he R; þei UDChVHJ LNM; þai EW; thay K; we A. hadden] haddyn J; hadde RUH²H; haden L; had DChWN; hedden V; hed E; han A; done] do E.
26 In] In þe RULK. cheker] chekyr*e* RU; chekerie M; Esscheker V; chauncellery L; court H. & in] in A; and VK; and þe RL; and in þe U. chaunc*er*ie] Chauncelrie VH; chekere L. to] *om* W. be] ben UVJK; beo L; *om* HWM. dischargid] discharged RDChEKN; deschargid U; descharged L; descharget V; disgargid H²; dischargyn he*m* M; dischargen hem H; discharge hem W; charchid J. of þinges] of iugis A; þai þink W.
27 And] þei N. riden] ryde RH²; rydes E; redyn JAM (*altered to* rydyn J); *om* H. faste] *om* HWM. for] forth for H²; to J; after W. shulde] suld E; to W; shulde reule he*m* & H. rede] Rede*n* VLK; redyn JM. hem] heom L; þaim E; hem for HM; hem to K.
28 For to] To W; how to N; & H. saue] sauen VJLKNM. hem] heom L; þaim E; hym W. self] seolf L; selfue*n* M; for silu*er* W; *om* H. from(1)] fram H. shame] schome V; schamys JA; harme H. from(2)] fram H; *om* JA. harm] harmes RUDLKW; harmys JANM; shame also H. *Here* W *adds lines like* **B** IV 31–3.
29 Ac] Bote VJLKWNM; And ChE; An A; *om* H. com] cam RH²AKM; comeþ W. arst] erst DHK; first UJEN; ferst WM; frist A. to co*ur*t] to þe court RUA; *om* K. a . . . wey] a Myle VHLA WNM; lang mile E; halue a myle J.
30 rombide] romyd AK; Romede VM; Romed DChH²HJLEW; rowmed N; rowned RU. forþ] riht J; tho W. wiþ] bi VM; *om* D. riȝt] forth J; & rauȝt H. to] afore N; aforn W.
31 þe . . . þanne] þan þe kyng D. þanne] þenne V; þoo JM; *om* HA. com . . . resoun] to reson he romeþ W. com] cam A; welcomed H; welcomyd J. in to] to V; vnto LK; on to Ch; toward N; agayns E; aȝenys A; aȝen M; *om* HJ.

And betwyn hymself & his sone sette hym a benche,
And wordiden a gret while wel wisly togid*ere*.
Þanne com pes into þe p*ar*lement & putte vp a bille
How wrong aȝen his wil hadde his wyf take, 35
And how he rauisshide rose, reynaldis loue,
And marg*er*ete of hire maydenhed maugre hire chekis.
'Boþe my gees & my gris hise gadelynges fecchen;
I dar not for fer of hym fiȝte ne chide.
He borewide of me bayard & brouȝte hi*m* neu*ere* aȝen, 40
Ne no ferþing þ*er*fore for nouȝt I couþe plete.

32 *line om* H. And] *om* UVJEA. betwyn] Betwix EW; Be twyxin J; atwix N. self] seolf L; *om* RUJAWN. sette] hett set E. hym] hem W. a] on RUDH²VJL KWNM; on þe ChEA. benche] benke E.
33 And] Than W. wordiden] wordyd E; wordeden DChVLK; wordedy*n* RJ; wordyn N; spokyn A; speken H; spak þai W; taledyn M. a . . . togid*ere*] togidere wysely a whyle D. a . . . wisly] ful wysly a gret while M; ful wyssely a gret qwyle E; fol wittely a gret while A. a] *om* Ch. wel] wol U; *om* VHJW.
34 Þanne] þe*n*ne V; þen RH; þo M. com pes] pees com UV. com] cam JAK; *om* WNM. into] vnto W; to VH; in JENM. þe] *om* RDChVJLEKM. &] *om* WNM. vp] hup J; forþ U; for A. bille] bulle H²H (*late corrector alters to* bylle H²).
35 How] whou M; Hou þat VH. wrong] wrang E; he (*late corrector alters to* wronge) H². aȝen . . . take] hed hys wif takyn al ayayn his wille E. aȝen] aȝeyn VJLN; aȝens RUChH²HW (against *late corrector* H²); aȝenys A; ageyn K. hadde . . . wyf] his wif hadde M; his wyf hedde V. hadde] *om* D. wyf] wille A. take] taken UHLW; takyn JAKNM; Itake V.
36 And] *om* N. how] *om* VL. he] he had J. rauisshide] rauyschid JK; Rauischede VM; rauysshed DLEN; raueschid A; rauaschid H; rauesched RChW. reynaldis] reignaldis HL; reyngnaldes H²; reynoldes UChKW; Ranaldeȝ E; Regynoldis N; regnoldys D; raynald J. loue] lufe E; lemmon V; lemman L; douȝt*er* H.
37 *marked with cross* N. margerete] mergarete ChH²; Mergrete VJ; molde H. hire(1)] hir JEN; here UDHA; her ChK; hur*e* R. maugre] mawgreyth J. hire(2)] hir E; here DHAW; her ChKN; hur*e* R.
38 Boþe] Boþin M; Bath E; Boche D. gees . . . hise] gris & my gees & here A. gees] geys R. gris] grises JK. hise] þe ChV; wi*th* E. gadelynges] gadeling*us* H; gadlyng D; goslynge*s* E; goselyngis A. fecchen] fecchyn A; fecheyn J; fetten ChV; feccheth L; fecches RD; he fechys E; fecchedy*n* M.
39 I dar] Ȝit dar I W. dar] ne dar J; durst H; þer D. not] nouȝt ChNM; noght U; noughȝ H²; nowther E; neyþ*er* W; *om* J. fer of] feer of DH²; ferd of A; ferde wi*th* E; dreede of VHM; *om* UW. hym] hem H²VHNM; her*e* W. fiȝte] fyghten K; fyhtyn J; fytht N; fytthen R; fygthy*n* M; feght EW; ne fyte A. ne] no ChL. chide] chiden AKM; chidyn J.
40 borewide] borewed L; borowid A; borowed DChJKN; borowd E; borwide UH²; borwid HM; borwede V; borwed RW. of me] ones W. &] he UEM. hi*m*] hem A. neu*ere* aȝen] me neu*er* JAM (*same hand after cancelled* neuer aȝeyne J). aȝen] aȝeyn VHL; ageyn UK; agayn REWN.
41 Ne] No Ch; Ny L. no] na E. ferþing] ferthyngworth U. þ*er*fore] him fore VL; for hym HK. nouȝt] nouth JM; nowgh W; not A; ought UH. I] þat I ChVHL; at E. couþe] coude RUChH²HAM; could K; con V. plete] pletyn M; plede DVLKWN; pleden H; pledyn J; mote plete U.

He mayntenịþ his men to *mur*þre myne hynen,
Forstallịþ my feiris, fiȝteþ in my chepyng,
Brekịþ vp my berne doris, berịþ awey my whete,
And takịþ me but a taile for ten quart*er*is otis, | 45
And ȝet he betịþ me þ*er*to & lịþ be my maiden. *fol.* xxxiij *b*
I am not hardy [for hym vnneþe] to loke.'
[Þe king kneuȝ] he seide soþ for consience hym tolde.
Wrong was aferd þo & wisdom he souȝte
To make his pes *with* his panis & p*ro*fride hym manye, 50

42 mayntenịþ] may*n*teynes R; meynteth J; moynteit A; mey*n*tene M; mayntened E; mayntide H². his] al his W. to] forto H. m*ur*þre . . . hynen] robbe and to slee WN. m*ur*þre] murþur Ch; Morþere V; morthore E; mortheryn JA; murdre UK; mordre L; mordren D; m*ur*dy*n* M; sle H. hynen] hyne U; hynes R; hinden Ch; hewen K; hewyn J; hewys M; yowes E; owen H; owis A; owne VL.
43 *line om* A. Forstallịþ] Forstalleþ DChV LWN; Forstallys M; forstall*es* RU; he forstallịþ H; And forstallyd E. feiris] fayres DChE; feire UV; faier K; chepyng W. fiȝteþ] fightith KN; fygthit M; fytith H²; fightes U; fyttes R; & fiȝteþ HL; & fytyth J; and fighteȝ E; & flyteþ W. my(2)] *om* Ch. chepyng] chepinges ChVL; fair W.
44 Brekịþ] brekeþ RDChH²V; he brekịþ H; He brekeþ WN; He brek*es* E; & breykyth J; Breke M. vp] *om* W. berne] barne KN. doris] durres Ch; dore VNM. berịþ] bereþ DCh; berth M; beres K; and beryþ RHJA; and bereth UVW; & berys E; & beoreth L. whete] qwete E; qwhete J.
45 And] Ant M; He EWN. takịþ] takyt M; tak*es* E; maketh L. but] þen H; *om* KW. taile] tayle of nowght K; tale E. for] of VHA. ten] xv M. quart*er*is] quart*er* DChVHJWN. otis] H²DJNM; otes UChK; hotis A; ootis H; oten V; of otis TR; of otes LW; of qwete E.
46 *line om* A. M *corrupts to* And whan he hadde my*n* wif bad me go*n* to my*n* maidy*n*; E *to* And also treth me to lye by my maden And bad me thare to lye by my maden. ȝet] ȝit UVHJWN; ȝut R. betịþ] bat V. lịþ] liþe Ch; lyȝþ H²V; liggith JK. maiden] Mayde DChH²HW N.
47 I] ChVHJLEAKNM; And I TRUDH² W. am] ame K; nam VH. not] nouȝt DChN; nougth M; noght H²E; not so RVH; noght so U. for . . . vnneþe] for him vneth JLK; for hym vneþis H; for hym ones forth W; for hem onis for N; for hym to wynkyn ne AM; for hym to wynke ne E; for him vp for V; vnneþe on hym for TChH²; onneþe on hym D; onys for hy*m* R; ones on hym U. loke] lokyn JM; luke E.
48 Þe . . . kneuȝ] þe kyng kneuh V; þe kyng knewe JEAKWNM; þe kyng kneow L; þe king seide H; Þo kneuȝ þe king T; þo knew þe king RUChH²; That knewe þe kyng D. he . . . soþ] soth he said K; & sayde forsoþe D; þis is soþ H. for] *om* D. consience] cocience M. hym] hit me H. tolde] toulde K; tald E; tolle H². *Here* W *adds a line like* **B** IV 62: *see above*, p. 30.
49 Wrong] Wrang E; And wrong D. was] *om* A. aferd þo] þan aferd W. aferd] aferid UH²A; afard L; affert V. þo] þan E. wisdom] wisdam RVLM. he] *om* UVW. souȝte] souȝthe R; sougthe M; south A; bysoughte UK; besoght W.
50 *divided from following after* sayd EAM. make] makyn AM. his(1)] *om* UJLEA WN. pes] *om* LE. his(2)] *om* VHLK. panis] pans RDChLN; penys H²; penyis M; penyes HJ; pens UAKW; pons V; pins E. &] he E; *om* A. profride] p*ro*frid H²HM; p*ro*frede R; profred W; proferid AK; p*ro*fered DL; p*ro*fird E; p*ro*ferde V; proferd ChJN. hym] *om* RUVHEA. manye] monye LA; mony Ch; forþ Moneye VH; *om* EM.

And seide, 'hadde I loue of my lord þe king, litel wolde I recche
þeiȝ pees & his power pleynide hem eu*ere*'.
Wysdom wan þo & so dede wyt also
For þ*at* wrong hadde wrouȝt so wykkide a dede,
And warnide wrong þo wiþ suche a wys tale: 55
'Whoso werchiþ be wil wraþþe makiþ ofte.
I sey it be myself, þou shalt it sone fynde,
But ȝif mede it make [þi] meschief is vppe,
For boþe þi lyf & þi lond liþ in his g*race*.'
Wrong þanne on wysdom wepi[de] hym to helpe, 60

51 *line om* H; *divided from following after* king RUD. And seide] For WN. I . . . king] he þe kynges loue W. hadde] Hedde V. I] I þe R; I I J. loue] luve E. my lord] *om* VJM. litel . . . I] I wold litil A. litel] litil UEKM; litul H²; lyte D; luite V. wolde I recche] wald I rake E; me roghte L. I] he W.
52 þeiȝ] Thei H²J; þowȝ ChK; þow DW; Tho A; þauh V; þagh L; if U; Gyf E; but HM; þat R. pees] *om* L. & . . . power] *om* D. &] wiþ H. his] hese W. pleynide] pleynyd JENM; pleynede H²; pleyned RUDChHLAW; playnyd K; playneden V. hem] heom L; hy*m* UD ChH²N; on hym H; on me V; for E.
53 wan] RUKWM; wan to TH²; wan out (out *above line with caret same hand*) L; qwan he heryd J; ran D; wente VH; went to Ch; wrethed E; wept N; *om* A. þo] þan E; þan *with* a wyse tale A. &] *om* JN. so] swa E. dede] ded A; dide UH²HW; dyd JEKN; dude RVL. wyt] hym witt H; wytty K. also] alse RJLN; als EW; bothe Ch; *om* VH.
54 For] And for V. þat] þat þat D; *om* VAM. wrong] wrongh L; wrang E. hadde] hedde V. wrouȝt] ywrouȝt RHL KN; don U; Ido VM. so] swa E.
55 *transposed with following* A. warnide] warnyd UH²JM; warnede RV; warned DChHEKWN; warneden L; warnyth A. wrong] wrang E. þo] þer E; *om* RUA. wiþ] wit M; & *with* E; wyt*es* R. suche] swych RUJM; siche H; swilk E; *om* A. a] *om* DEK. tale] tal*es* (*after cancelled* wordes) K; talys D; wordes E.
56 *marked with cross* N. Whoso] Ho so J; Wha sa E; whose V; Qwo A; and who R. werchiþ] werchit AM; wercheþ R; werkyth H²; wurchith U; wurchyt D; worcheþ ChVKWN; worches L; wyrchith J; wirkes E. be] w*ith* EK; not by N. wil] wel N. wraþþe . . . ofte] makiþ wraþþe oft HK; makes wrethe ofte E; sone wraþthe makyth H²; woo wakeneth ofte L. wraþþe] wreþþe ChAW. makiþ] makeþ RDVJN; he makit A; he makeþ ChW. ofte] oftyn M; *om* Ch.
57 I] we H. sey] seye UM; say DHLE KW; sigge V. it] *om* AN. my] þi VHJL EW; þi*n* M. self] selue UH²A; seluen VE; seolf L; silue*n* H. þou . . . sone] þe sothe þou schalt J. þou] wrong þou M. shalt] schal D; sall E. it sone] þe soþe A. sone fynde] fynd sone E. fynde] yfynde L.
58 But] For bott E. ȝif] ȝef ChL; *om* RUEK. mede] I EAM. it make] make hit VH; hit made Ch. it] þi pees U; thy mend*es* K. þi] UVHJEAKWNM; þis L; þ*er* R; *om* TDChH². meschief] myschep AN. vppe] huppe A.
59 For] *om* A. boþe] boþin M; bath E. þi(1)] þey D. lyf] lyue DE; self R. &] in D. lond] lande ChH²LEN; lyme H. liþ] lithe J; liȝt D; liȝþ V; lyis E; lyen AK; ben U. his] her*e* H; hir*e* J; þe kynges VW; kyng*es* N.
60 *divided from following after* sore L; after praied N; *after* his J. Wrong] Wrange E; Wrog V. þanne] þe*n*ne V; þen H; *om* EAWNM. on] vppon VHEAWNM. wysdom] wisdom & A; wisdom þo W. wepide] wepyd EAK; wepede J; weped Ch W; wepit M; wepte UVH; wept N; wep R; wepiþ TH²; wepeþ D; weoped wel sore L. hym . . . helpe] To helpe him LK; to helpy*n* hi*m* J; to helpe hym at nede RU; & praied to helpe hi*m* N; fast W. hym to] to hym D. hym] *om* VHAM. to] for A.

For of hise penys he *pro*ffride handy dandy to paye.
Þanne wisdom ⁊ wyt wente togid*ere*
And tok mede wiþ hem m*er*cy to wynne.
Pees putte forþ his heued ⁊ his panne blody:
'Wiþoute gilt, god wot, gat I þis skaþe.' 65
Consience ⁊ þe king kneuȝ wel þe soþe,
And wisten wel þ*at* wrong was a shrewe eu*ere*.
Ac wisdom ⁊ wyt were aboute faste
To ou*er*come þe king wiþ catel ȝif þei miȝte.
Þe king swor be crist ⁊ be his croune boþe 70
[Þat wrong for his werkis shulde woo þole,
⁊ comau*n*did a cu*n*stable to caste hy*m* in yrens]:

61 *line marked with cross in margin* U. For . . . hise] And of his Ch; For ryȝt þ*er* of is RU; Him for his VH; For his K; Sum what for of his M; And pr*a*ed hym for of hys E; And prayed hym for his W; And wisdom in A. penys . . . *pro*ffride] *om* RUDVHJLEAKWNM. handy dandy] *om* E. to paye] payed RUDLNM; rediliche to be paid K; Rediliche he payede VH; hastely he payed A; ⁊ sone had he payd E; I wisse he payed him þanne J; help hym at his nede W.
62 Þanne] þe*n*ne V; þen H; Tho A; *om* J. wisdom] wysdam RVM. wyt] witte þo J. wente] wente*n* RUChHK; wentyn JM; went forth E; wenten hom L.
63 tok] toke DChH²HJW; token U; tuke E; nome LA; nomen VKNM. mede . . . hem] with hem repentaunce K. hem] heom L; þaim E; hym H. wynne] wynde ⁊ wynne A; axe N.
64 *divided from following after* panne D. putte] VL; put UChH²HEAKWNM; putte hym (hym *cancelled*) T; put hym RD; þo put J. heued] hede RJKW; hed DVLAM; heed HN; had H². panne blody] blody panne U. panne] ponne V; hode H. blody] all blodi (all *by late corrector*) H²; *om* R.
65 Wiþoute] wi*th*outen VJ; Wi*th*owtyn E; witoutyn M; Redly wi*th*oute*n* R. gilt] gult VHL; gilt q*uo*d he J. wot] it wot M; it woot A; it wate E. gat I þis] þ*at* is R. gat] gatte M; hent H. I] he A. skaþe] schaþe DA; gate skate (*late corrector cancels* gate *and alters* skate *to* skathe) H².
66 *line om* U. Consience . . . king] þe king ⁊ conscience H. ⁊] þo ⁊ J. kneuȝ] knew ChH²EAWNM; knewe RDK; knewen VH; knewy*n* J; kneow L. wel] *om* VH. soþe] suthe E.
67 *marked with cross* N. And] *om* V. wisten wel] full wel vnd*er*stude E. wisten] wisty*n* J; wiste R; wist WN; wusten V; wisdom wist A. wel] ful wil M. þ*at*] at E; *om* K. wrong] wrang E. was . . . eu*ere*] euer was a schrewe L. shrewe] cherewe N. eu*ere*] *om* EAM.
68 Ac] Bot ChVHLKWNM; and RU; Bot þan E; *om* A. wisdom] wisda*m* RVLM. wyt] wi*th* þo J. were] weren HM; weryn JA; weore*n* VL; waren K; was E. aboute] abowty*n* J; abouȝte D; ȝeorne aboute V.
69 ouercome] ouyr A. catel] Meede VH. ȝif] ȝef ChL; ⁊ K. þei] þay LE; thay K; heo V; he J. miȝte] mihten V; mythyn M; mowht J.
70 Þe . . . crist] Be crist seith þe kyng þo M. Þe . . . swor] Than swore þe kyng E. swor . . . crist] be crist swore W. be] þo bi V. crist] *crist* þo J; hymselfe A. his] *om* R. croune] coroune UVLE. boþe] bath E.
71 HH²VJLEAKWNM; *line om* TRUD Ch. wrong] wrang E. werkis] work*es* K; werke A; werk E; wyckidnesse H². shulde] suld E. woo] wo H²VWNM; qwoo J; muche wo L; mekyl wa E; wrong A. þole] tholyn JAM; soffre L.
72 HH²VJLEAKWNM; *line om* TCh; *run together with following* RUD. ⁊ . . . cu*n*stable] *om* RUD. ⁊] he N. comau*n*did] comaunded LKWN; Comau*n*dede V; co*m*mand E; comande A. caste] caste*n* UVL; castyn JM. hy*m*] hem RVW. yrens] Ironnes K; ernys D; p*re*son H².

'He sh[al] not þis seue ȝer se hise feet ones!'
'God wot,' quaþ wysdom, 'þat were not þe beste.
And he amendis mowe make let maynprise hym haue, 75
And be borugh for his bale & b[ig]gen hym bote;
Amende þat mysdede, & eueremore þe betere.'
Wyt accordiþ þerewiþ & seide þe same:
'Betere is þat boote bale adoun bringe,
Þanne bale be bet & bote neuere þe betere.' 80
Þanne gan mede to meke hire, & mercy besouȝte,
And profride pees a presaunt al of purid gold;

73 He] And A. shal] HRUDJLEAKW NM; ne schal V; shulde TChH². not] nouȝt ChE; nouth M; *om* UV. þis] þese Ch. seue] seuen ChVHE; seuene H²A WN; seuyn JK; seouen L; vij RUD; viij M. ȝer] ȝeir L; yeres K. se] see EK; sen UDAWM; sene JN; seon VL. hise] hese W. feet] fote D; foot Ch. ones] anys E.
74 God wot] Nay sire W. wot] wate E; it wote K. were] weore VL; wer þe E; nere W. not] nat H²; nouȝt ChN; noght UE; nouth J; nout M.
75 *marked with cross* N. And] ȝif N; ȝef H; But M. amendis . . . make] mow amendes make Ch; may make amendes N. amendis] amendese K; mendes L. mowe] may EAM; wol H; *om* DV. make] makyn M. let] lat REA; late WN. maynprise hym] menprisyn hym M; hym maynprise him N; hym meinpris A; hym maynpres E. haue] raþer W; þanne M.
76 *here* (*fol* 12) *a hole in* H. And] to H. be] ben J; beo VL; brynge W; *om* A. borugh] borow DChN; borowe JK; borw UV; borwe R; borwes W; borewid M; brouȝth H²; brouȝt H; brout out A; boght E. for] of VHJA; from E. his bale] *defective* H. biggen] UK; biggyn N; bigge HAW; buggen VLM; beggyn DJ; als bye E; bringen TR; bring Ch; beingen (?) H². hym] hem W. bote] to bote Ch.
77 Amende] Amendyn M; & amende HEW; And aMenden V; & amendyn J; To amend K. þat] RUDJEKNM; þis W; þe A; þat he TChH²L; his VH (*then defective to* euer) H. mysdede] mysdide H²; mysdude L. þe] be E; do þe UW.
78 *line om* N. Wyt] we D. accordiþ . . . seide] *defective* H. accordiþ] acordeþ RL M; acordyd JK; acorded ChW; aCordede V; acorde D; acord E. þerewiþ] þer to U; herwith V. seide] seide him VH.
79 *line om* N. Betere is] Hit is betere V; Bettere M; Bottre is L. þat . . . bringe] *defective* H. þat] thet H²; *om* U. boote] bute E. bale] þat bale A. adoun] doun DEK. bringe] bryngyth A.
80 *line om* N. Þanne] þen VH; Than maken W; And E. be . . . neuere] *defective* H. be] beo L; be full E; *om* D. bet] beten VL; Ibete D; Ibetyn J; Ibette Ch; bote RUAW; bute E; Ilete K. bote] boote V; bute E; hote A.
81 *marked with cross* N. Þanne] ÞEnne V; þen H; *om* N. gan mede] mede gan WN. gan] began Ch; come H; *om* V. mede . . . hire] mekyn here mede A; *defective* H. to] *om* VJLEM. meke] mekyn JKM; meoken L; Meokede V; megen N. hire] hir EN; here UDW; her ChK; hure R. besouȝte] besowhte J; besougthe M; bysoughte U; bisouhte V; bysoghte L; bysouȝthe R; besouȝt ChK; besoght EW; besougȝt H²; besouth A; bysouȝt H.
82 profride] profrid HM; profrede H²V; profred UW; proferyd JAK; profered RDL; proferd ChEN. pees . . . purid] pennys for pes & pecys of E; pens in presens & pecis of A; penies to present & peces of M. presaunt] *defective* H. of] *om* W. purid gold] gold purid H. purid] pured D; puyred L; pure Red V; pure RUChKWN; pewre J.

'Haue þis of me, man,' q*ua*þ heo, 'to amende þi skaþe,
For I wile wage for wrong, he [wile] do so no more.'
Pees þanne pitousliche p*re*yede to þe king 85
To haue m*er*cy on þ*at* man þ*at* mysdede hym ofte:
'For he haþ wagid me wel as wysdom hym tauȝte
I forgyue hym þ[at] gilt wiþ a good wille;
So [þat] ȝe assente I can sey no more,
For mede haþ mad my mendis; I may no more axen.' | 90
'Nay,' quaþ þe king, 'so god ȝiue me blisse, *fol.* xxxiiij *a*
Wrong wendiþ not so awey er I wyte more.
Le[þe] he so liȝtly awey, lauȝen he wolde,

83 of . . . man] man of me AWN. man] mon L; *om* VHJEM. quaþ heo] *om* LEWN. heo] *late corrector prefixes* s H[2]; he R; sche UDChJKM; ȝhe A. amende] amendyn J; mende DL; Amende w*ith* VH; amendy*n* wit M; mende wiþ WN. skaþe] skate (*late corrector alters* te *to* the) H[2]; schathe A; scaþis H; state J.
84 I wile] I wol UChHLK; Ichul V; I EAM. wage] wagyn J; plegh E. wrong] wrang E. he] þat he L. wile] wil JEAWN; wol VHLK; wolde M; shal TRUDChH[2]. do so] so do Ch. do] don M; *om* L. no more] namor*e* UCh; no mare E.
85 *line om* R. Pees . . . pitousliche] Pytously þan pes EM; Petousely þan pes A. þanne] þenne V; þe*n* H; *om* W. pitousliche] petusly ChJW; pytuously K. to] *om* VW. king] kyng þanne W.
86 *line om* R. haue] haue*n* M. on] of ChJLEN. man] Mon VL. mysdede] mysded J; mysdide UH[2]; mysdyd EKN; mysdeode L; misdude V; mysse dede A. hym] *om* L. ofte] oftyn J.
87 *line om* R. haþ] hat M; has E; hadde H. wagid] wagyde J; waged DH[2]LW; wagytt E; waget V; wached Ch; waieg N. me] hym H. wel] wele amendis J; amendes V. as] *in margin, another hand* N. tauȝte] tauth A.
88 *line om* R. I] And I W. forgyue] forgyff E; forgeue DCh; forgefe A; Forȝiue V; forȝif J; forȝeue HKWM. hym] þee H. þat] UDVJLEAKN; þis H; þe TChH[2]W; his M. gilt] gult VL; gult q*uo*þ pees H. good] gude E.
89 *line om* RA. So] Swa E. þat] VHJLEKWNM; *om* TUDChH[2]. ȝe] he E. assente] DK; assent EWN; assenten L; assentyn JM; assente þ*er*to TUH[2]; assent þerto Ch; assent my lord H; assented beo V. can] con V. sey no more] no more say H; no more sigge V. sey] seyȝe ChH[2]; say LEKW. no more] namore UCh; no mare E.
90 *line om* HA. For] *om* WN. mede] he UJ. haþ] hase E. mad] maad V. my] myn KM; me my Ch; me UVJEWN. mendis] amendys JM; amendes UVEKN; amende W. may] can K. no more] namore U; nomare E. axen] axe DM; axyn RJ; asken ChK; aske VEW; *illegible* L.
91 king] king þo ChVHJANM; kyng þan E. so] sa E. god] crist U. ȝiue] ȝif JA; ȝeue DChHLWM; gyve K; gif N; gyff E.
92 Wrong] Wrang E. wendiþ] wendeþ RChL; wendit M; went V; wendes DEWN. not] nat H[2]; nouȝt ChN; noght E; nouth M. so] swa E. awey] *om* WNM. er] or DChH[2]JEAK; til VHWN. I] ich V; we EAM. wyte] wit N; wete DChE; wytyn M; wetyn A; wot W.
93 *line om* E. Lepe] DJLKWN; lep RH[2]; Leep TCh; lope UVAM; for yf he lept H. he] *om* H. liȝtly] *om* M. awey] wey M; þe losel L; *om* UHWN. lauȝen . . . wolde] he wolde vs alle scorn H. lauȝen] laughen M; lawȝen Ch; lawghen K; lawhen DAN; laghen UL; laugȝen H[2]; lauȝwhen V; laqwyn J; laghyng W. he wolde] wolde he loude L.

And ofte þe bold*ere* be to bete myn hynen.
But resou*n* haue reuþe on hym he shal reste in þe stokkis 95
As longe as I lyue but more loue it make.'
Su*m*me redde resoun to haue reuþe on þ*at* shrewe,
And to counseile þe king & consience boþe;
Þ*at* mede muste be meynp*er*nou*r* resoun þei besouȝte.
'Rede me not,' quaþ resoun, 'no reuþe to haue 100
Til lordis & ladies louen alle treuþe,
And p*er*nelis purfile be put in hire hucche;
Til childris cherisshing be chastisid w*ith* ȝerdis;

94 *marked with cross* N. And] *om* W. ofte] oftyn M; oftere U; eft VJL; after R; eftirward E; eke AN; Alwey W. þe . . . be] be þe bolder*e* HN; be þe baldore V; ben þe baldir M; beo þe balder L. þe] *om* E. bold*ere*] balder RUEA. be] RUD ChEW; ben H²JK; to be TA. to] forte V; and R. bete] beten H²VL; bety*n* RJ AM; mysdo H. hynen] hyne DW; hynes E; hynys M; hynden Ch; hyen J; hewyn K; hewys A; heuene N; puple H; buxume L; *om* V.
95 But] For bott E. haue] haþ W; *om* J. reuþe] reouthe L; reugthe M; ruþe R; rewe J. on] of VEN. hym] hem W. shal] *om* VJEAWM. reste] resten U; resteþ VW; restith J; restit AM; rest*es* E; *om* HL. in] RUChVJLEAKWNM; into H; hym in TDH². þe] my JANM; *om* RUH²W.
96 As] Als LE; Also VN; lie as H. longe] lang E. I] he W. lyue] lyfe J; leue DCh LEANM; lyueþ W. but . . . make] but lownesse hym borwe W; with leautees leue L. more] þe more Ch; bett*er* EAM; ȝif JN. make] makis A; may make (may *cancelled*) J.
97 Summe redde] þanne was resou*n* redde N. Su*m*me] Somme JLAKWM; þe*n*ne su*m*me VH; Su*m*me men TRDChH²E; þanne U. redde] reddin JA; rede D; red E; reden K; Radde VLW; radden H; raddyn M. to . . . shrewe] rewth for to haue E. to] þo to W. reuþe] ruþe R. on] of VJLN. þat] þe D.
98 to . . . king] þe kyng conseilled N. to counseile] to counseylyn J; þo co*n*seilede U; conseilled W; consailde M; concelid A; counseld E; concelyng L. boþe] als E; alce A.
99 Þ*at* . . . be] To make mede WN. muste] mostyn J; might EK. be] beo L; ben a JM. meynp*er*nou*r*] maynprysyd & E. þei] þai EW; thay K; heo V; þe A. besouȝte] besowthi*n* M; soght E; p*re*ied H.
100 Rede] Red DLAN; Rediþ H. me] I W; *om* L. not] nouȝt DChN; nout R; *om* EAM. no] þan na E; *om* VHJ. reuþe] reouthe L; ruþe RK. to] for to HEA.
101 Til] til þat HE. ladies] ladis M; ladeȝ E; leuedys J. louen] love EW; louyn JA. treuþe] trowthe LW; truþe R; trwþe N. *Here* W *copies line* 106: *see apparatus, line* 105 *below.*
102 And] til R. p*er*nelis] peornels L; Parnell*es* K; pirnelis U; p*er*onelys R; alle here p*er*leys J; pelurs E. purfile] purfle K; & purfels E. be] beo L. hire] here UD H²HAW; her ChKN; heore V; þair E; he R; p*er*kyns L. hucche] whucche V; whicche H; chiste M; pouche L.
103 childris cherisshing] chefysyng of chyld*er* E. childris] childres RW; childerys JA; childrens H; childrenes U; Children DChVLN; childern K. cherisshing] Chereschinge V; cherissyng JN; chersyng RWM; chiresschenge D; chersynges Ch; chere cheryschest L; chiding H; chastisyng A. be] beon L. chastisid] chastised ChHLKW; chastesyd J; chastid U; chasted RDN; chastet V; castyd E. ȝerdis] yardes K; ȝerde W.

And harlotis holynesse be holde for an [heþyng];
Til clerkis & kniȝtes be curteis of here mouþes, 105
And haten [to] h*ere* harlot*rie* oþ*er* mouþe it;
Til p*re*stis here p*re*chyng p*re*ue it hemselue,
And do it in dede to drawe vs to goode;
Til seint Iame be souȝt þ*ere* I shal assigne,
Þat no man go to galis but ȝif he go for eu*ere*; 110
And alle rome renn*er*is, for robberis of beȝonde,
Bere no silu*er* ou*er* se þ*at* signe of king shewi[þ],
Neiþ*er* grotis ne gold ygr*au*e wiþ kynges coyn,

104 *line om* N. And] Til V. harlotis] harlatys J; harlot D. holynesse] holinis A; halynes E; almesse R; harlotrie U. be] beo L; ben A. holde] holde*n* RUChVLK; holdyn AM; howldyn J; halden DE; preised H. for . . . heþyng] ful hiȝe H. for] *om* J. an] a E; any D. heþyng] Ch; heuene M; hyne TRUDH²VJLEAKW.
105 Til] To N; And L. clerkis] kniȝtes H. kniȝtes] knytes DA; knythis M; kyȝtthes R; kynges W; clerkis H. be] ben DChVJ AKM; beon L; beþ W. curteis] curtaise Ch; c*ur*tase E; co*ur*tys D. here] her RCh JN; hire H²W; heore VL; þair E; their K. mouþes] mouþe RUDLEWM. *Here* W *adds lines like* **B** IV 119–21: *see above*, p. 30.
106 *line om* AN; *copied after line* 101 W. haten . . . harlot*rie*] haten al harlotrie to heren W; hate all harlottre to here E; alle harlotrie haten to heryn M. haten] hate RU; hatyn JK. to] RUVHJLK; *om* TDChH². h*ere*] her Ch; heren L; heryn J; don heor V; do H. harlot*rie*] herlatry J; harlet*ries* H; of any harlotries ȝelpyng L. oþ*er* . . . it] oþ*er* hit mouþen D; and vsun hit no more V; & no more it vsen H; *om* L. oþ*er*] or RUH²JK; or to EWM; to Ch. mouþe] mowþen ChK; mowthin JM. it] K; it for eu*ere* J; hit he*m* selue RU; it w*ith* tungis TH²; hit with tong Ch; *om* EWM.
107 *line om* U. prestis] preostes L. here] her ChKN; heore VL; þair E. p*re*chyng] p*re*chenge D. p*re*ue] p*re*uen VN; preuyth A; preoue L; p*ro*ven KWM; p*ro*ueþ R; p*re*ued D; it p*re*uyth J; p*ro*fers E. it] hit in VH² (in *supplied by late corrector* H²); *om* RDJEAWNM. hem] heom L; þaim E. selue] seluen VHEM; selfen K; seoluen L; silue H².
108 do] don UChVJAWM; done HKN. it . . . dede] hem self as þei say W. it] *om* N. to] & E. drawe] drawen UV; drawyn JAM; bring Ch. vs] me*n* H. goode] god E. *Here* W *adds lines like* **B** IV 123–5: *see above*, p. 30.
109 *line om* H. Til] To E. Iame] Iames EK; iamis A; Iemys J. be] beo VL. souȝt] sougth M; south A; Isouȝt ChUL; Isouht V; ysouȝth R. þ*ere*] as M. shal] sall E. assigne] assynge E; assyne DRK; syngne J; asyng asyne Ch.
110 *line om* H; *marked with cross* N. Þat] And V. no] na E. man] mon VL. go] goo K; ga E. to] *om* N. galis] gales DH²W. ȝif] *om* UChVLAWM. he . . . for] hit be to Ch.
111 And] til H; Ne E. alle] UVHLAK WNM; alle þe TRDChH²; no E; *om* J. renn*er*is] rynners E; ronnars K. robberis] Robbeours V; robbyng AW. of] *om* ChEW. beȝonde] beȝendyn J.
112 *same hand after cancelled* Beore no signe of seoluer þat of kyng L. Bere] Beryn M; Beore L. silu*er*] seluer ChV; seoluer L. ou*er*] ouer þe JAWM. signe . . . shewiþ] bereþ signe of þe kyng VH. signe . . . king] kyngis signe M. signe] syng J; coyn U. of] of þe ChA. king] coyn W. shewiþ] schewith UDJK; schewit M; scheweþ RL; schewys E; shewide T; schewyd H²; schewed Ch; schewt A; beris N; haþ W.
113 *line om* L. Neiþ*er*] Neþer DChW; Nother H²HK; Nouþer VE. ne] neþ*er* D; y ne E. ygr*au*e] Igrauen Ch; graue DAW; graven E; g*ra*uyn J; grauyd M. wiþ] wit M; w*ith* þe VHAKW; *om* J. coyn] Coroune VEWM; crou*n* HJAKN.

Vpe forfaiture of þat fe, who fynt hym [at douere],
But it be marchaunt, oþer his man, oþer messang[er] with lettres,
Oþer prouisour, or prest þat þe pope auauunciþ.
And ȝet,' quaþ resoun, 'be þe rode, I shal no reuþe haue
Whil mede haþ þe maistrie to mo[te] in þis halle.
Ac I may shewe ensaumplis as I se [oþer],
For I seiȝe it be myself, & it so were 120
Þat I were king wiþ croune to kepe a reaume,
Shulde neuere wrong in þis world þat I wyte miȝte

114 *line om* L; *marked with cross* N. Vpe] Vppe M; vp RUChH²JN; Vppon VHEAK; I W; *om* D. forfaiture] þat forfeture M; Forfet VH; For faytour DN. þat] þe HJW. who] who so HKNM; ho so JA; wha sa E; hose V. fynt hym] hit fynde V. fynt] fynte ChH²A; fynd E; fynde JKN. hym] *late corrector alters to* hem H²; hem JAWNM; hit HEK. at douere] VHJKM; at douyr A; at douorre WN; do euere TDChH² (*corrected, late hand, to* at doverr H²); dygnere R; diuerse U; may E.
115 But] But if H²AM; Bote ȝef L. it] he W. be marchaunt] be marchaunȝt N; merchaunte be K; be be messingere H. be] beo V; beo a L. oþer . . . man] *om* W. oþer] oþur V; or RUDChH²JLEANM. man] men V. oþer(2) . . . with] þat wiþ hym beriþ H. oþer(2)] or RUDChH²VJLEAKWNM. messanger] ChJLKN; messenger EA; messager UDH²VWM; myssager R; messangeris T. with] of W. lettres] letter J; hors K.
116 Oþer] Or RDVLAKWNM; Or ellis JE. prouisour] Prouisours V; prestis H. or] oþer UH; or ony A. prest] preest D; preost L; Preestes V; prouisours H. þat . . . auauunciþ] or penant for his synnes W. þat] at E. þe] *om* VH. pope] pape E; Popes VH. auauunciþ] avaunseþ RUDChLNM; avaunset V; auaunceȝ E; avauncydh J; doþ auaunce H.
117 ȝet] ȝit UChH²VHJWM; ȝut R; *om* DEAN. quaþ . . . rode] by þe Rode quod resoun N. quaþ resoun] *om* W. be . . . rode] *om* L. þe] *om* E. rode] rude E. I shal] shal I W; sall I E. shal] scal J; wol UL; nel R. no] na E. reuþe] reowthe L; rouþ W; ruþe RK.
118 Whil] wil N; Whyls E; Whiles K; qwil J. haþ] hat M; hase E. þe] eny VH. maistrie] maistre E; ? maistris A. mote . . . halle] *defective* H. mote] RKWN; moten UL; motyn JAM; mot H²; Mooten V; moute E; mo T; moo D; many Ch. þis] þe RL.
119–21 *as two lines divided after* selue RUD.
119 *line om* VH. Ac] Bot ChLEKWNM; and R; *om* A. may] *om* E. shewe] schewyn JM; schewe ȝou RUE; schewyn ȝou A; seyn in N. ensaumplis] ensaumple RChEK; an ensample W; þe ensaunple M; examplis J; example AN. as . . . oþer] *om* U. as] als E. I] ȝe A. se] see K; sen A; seo L. oþer] oþer RJLEAKWNM; forsoþe TChH²; *om* D.
120 For] For ȝef Ch; *om* RUDJLEAKWNM. seiȝe] seie U; sey RChJLANM; say DHEKW; sigge V. it(1)] *om* UWN. be] for RDVJLEAWNM; *om* ChH. self] selue RUDJAK; seolf L; soule V. &] yf E; ȝif WN; for and J. it(2)] *om* E. so were] were so RU. were] weore VL; war K.
121 Þat] And JA; ȝif W; *om* U. I] Ich V; *om* E. were] weore VL; war K. king . . . croune] corounyd a kyng M. king] a kyng UHAW. wiþ] wiþ a L; *om* HW. croune] coroune ULEA; crowned HW. kepe a reaume] goue : : : : : : : H. kepe] kepen UH²VLN; kepyn JAM. a] þe E. reaume] realme EKM; reame DV; rewme RUJLN; Reme ChH²; rem A.
122 *marked with cross* N. Shulde] Suld E; Schul H²; ne shulde H; Ne shol W; Schuld þer A. neuere wrong] wrong neuer H². neuere] no DM. wrong] wrang E; *om* U. in . . . world] in þe word R; more W; *om* H. world] werlde JEA. I] Ich V. wyte miȝte] myght wytte W; myȝte wete D; *defective* H. wyte] wit N; Iwite V; wete ChEA.

Be vnpunisshit at my power for peril of my soule,
Ne gete my grace þoruȝ giftes, so me god helpe!
Ne for no mede haue mercy but meknesse it made, 125
For *nullum malum* [þ]e ma[n] met[t]e *with Inpunitum*
And bad *Nullum* [*bonum* be] *irremuneratum.*
Let þi confessour, sire king, construe it þe on englissh,
And ȝif þou werche [it in] werk I wedde myne eris
Þat lawe shal ben a labourer & lede afeld donge, 130
And loue shal lede þi land as þe lef likeþ.'

123 Be] Ben VJAM; Beon L. vnpunisshit] vnpunyshyd E; vnponyschid A; onpunschid H[2]; vnpunschid HJM; vnponysht W; vnpunysched UVLN; vnponyssched DK; onponesched Ch; vnpunsched R. at] by RDL; be U; beo V; in JEAKNM; for W. my(1)] *om* L. of . . . soule] *defective* H. soule] saulle E; seluen M.
124 Ne . . . grace] Neo my grace geten L. gete] getyn JM; gett EK. my] no JM; *om* VEWN. þoruȝ] þorow ChJEAKN; þorw V; þourth M; þrow W; *with* RUD; by H. giftes] geftes Ch; gifte LEANM; ȝiftes RUH[2]; ȝeftes WK; ȝeftis H; ȝifte J; ȝift V. so] sa E. me god] god me E; gad me M; me gold V.
125 H *substitutes* for loke what þese wordis seyn þat writen beþ in latyn. Ne] Neo L; But A. for . . . mercy] haue mercy for mede W. no] *om* VJKM. meknesse] meknysse R; meokenes L. made] make H[2]VEKW.
126, 127 *divided after* wyþ R; *as one line* H.
126 For] *Quia* H. *nullum malum*] *multum bonum* L. þe . . . *Inpunitum*] *inpunitum* þe may mete with U; *erit* to man *inpunitum* E. þe man] JKWN; þe Mon VL; þat man M; þe may R; he may TDChH[2]; *om* HA. mette] VLWN; mett K; met A; mete TRDChH[2]J; made M; *om* H. with] withouten V; *om* H. *Inpunitum*] *Impunitum* DChKW; *irremuneratum* L; *infinitum* A.
127 L *corrupts to Nec multum malum* lawe wolde þat schulde beo *Inpunitum.* And] *nec* H. bad] bad þat W; bad *quod* D; also E; *om* H. *Nullum*] *vllum* H. *bonum*] RUDChH[2]VHJEKWNM; *malum* TA. be] VAKN; ben M; bene J; shold be W; *om* TRUDChH[2]HE (*late corrector supplies* H[2]). *irremuneratum*] *inremuneratum* JA.
128 Let] Lete H[2]H; lat ChJLE; Late A; Do WN. confessour] Clerk V; clerkis H. sire] sere A; *ser* KM. construe] constru D; constrew Ch; constreu E; *construyn* J. it þe] þe hit ChLK; it WN; þe þis J; þis VHEAM. on] in RUVHLEKM. englissh] englys RH[2]; engelis A; englesch Ch; ynglysh W; ynglyss E.
129 ȝif] ȝef ChL; *om* A. þou] *om* AM. werche] werch A; werchest H; werke H[2]; wirche ChJN; wirke R; wyrk E; worche ULKW; worchest V; wurche D. it in] DRUVLAKWNM (it *cancelled for* as I said *same hand* K); it in þi J; þis in E; þis TH[2] (? *altered from* in T); þes Ch; þerafter H. werk] worke K; workes Ch; wit V; *om* H. I] Ich V. wedde] lay H; gyff þe E; gefe þe A; ȝeue þe M. myne] boþe myn UVHLWN; þerto myn J; boþe his R. eris] heres eres (heres *cancelled*) U.
130 Þat] Bot EAM. shal] *om* EAM. ben] bien J; be RUChH[2]HEAKWNM; beo L. lede] leden V; ledyn J. afeld donge] dong on felde W. afeld] afelde ChH[2]KN; on feld A; on felde DJ; on feild L; ofilde M; to feld U; to felde R.
131 And . . . shal] þanne schal loue M. loue] luffe J. shal] sal E. lede] leden VM; ledyn JA. þi] al þi N. land] lond RUChVHJLAKWNM. as . . . likeþ] in leynthe & in brede L. as] als E; *om* M. þe] hym E. lef] leue ChJAWN; leof V; best RU; self HE. likeþ] likyt M; lykes RDE.

Clerkis þat wern confess*our*s couplide hem togid*er*is, 132
For to construe þis clause declynede faste,
Ac [whanne] resoun among þise renkis reherside þise wordis, |
Þ*er*e nas man in þe mothalle, more ne lesse, *fol.* xxxiiij *b*
Þat he ne held resoun a maist*er* & mede a muche wrecche.
Loue let of hire liȝt & louȝ hire to scorne,
And seide it so loude þat soþnesse it herde:
'Whoso wilneþ hire to wyue for welþe of hire godis,

132 Clerkis . . . confessou*rs*] þo alle þe grete clerkis H. wern] weren K; werin JM; were RDChH²VWN; wer E; weore L; ben U; arn A. couplide] couplid H; coupled RDVLW; cowplide H²; cowplid A; cowplede J; cowpled ChN; coplyd E; copled K; couple U; clepedy*n* M. hem] þaim E; *om* L.
133 For to] Forte V. construe] construe*n* M; *construyn* J. þis] þe RUJ. clause] cause W. declynede] declyned DKN; declyneden H²; þai declyned EA; þey declinid M; he declinedy*n* J; þai clined W; and declyned RL; & declyne U; declynand Ch; & distinkte V; & wite H. faste] it faste D; it aftir UV; what it mened H. *Here* W *adds a line like* **B** IV 151: *see above*, p. 30.
134 Ac . . . renkis] amonge hem þo þei J. Ac] Bot ChHLK; And AM; *om* VEWN. whanne] whan UKWN; whe*n* HE; whon V; whan þat M; þo L; *om* TRD ChH²A. among . . . renkis] i*n* a rude wraþ N; and angre W. among] emong E; to V. þise renkis] hem HM. þise(1)] þis V; these H²; þes Ch; þeose L; þo A; þe RUDK; *om* E. renkis] Reynkes V; renges U; reules D. reherside] hadde rehersid AE; hadde rehersed RUDK; haddy*n* rehersyd J; rehersen had W. þise(2)] þis JWM; these H²H; þees E; þeose VL; þes Ch; þo RAK; alle þise N; þe UD. *Here* E *adds two lines: see above*, p. 49.
135 *marked with cross* N. Þere nas] Þan was þ*er* no E. Þere] And þ*er* L; *om* V. nas] ne was J; was RLA. man] RUHA WNM; mon L; non V; no man TDChH²; *om* JEK. in] *om* E. þe] þat RV; this H²; *om* E. mothalle] mote alle (*error noted and corrected, another hand*) N; mote W; court H. more] mare E; neyþ*er* more W. ne] no Ch; ny L; ne no E; noþ*er* H. lesse] lasse RVHJLKM.
136 Þat . . . held] Þen held þai E. he] *om* ChVHJLWM. ne] no L. held] heeld U; huld L; hulde H. resoun] mekenes AM. a(1)] *om* Ch. maist*er*] master K; Mayster þo V. a(2)] *om* L. muche] myche H²HJM; mochel K; mychel N; meochel L; mekyll E; *om* A. wrecche] wryche E; shrewe H.
137 Loue . . . &] *Simul invnum diues & pauper* A. Loue] Luffe J; And loue M. let] lete HJEWN; lette V; leet U; lat L. hire(1)] hir EN; here RDW; her ChK; Meede V. liȝt] ligth M; lyȝth D; liȝtly H; luite V. louȝ] louh V; louȝh H²H; lowgh KN; lowh DJ; lowȝe Ch; lowhe U; loghe E; low R; lawid A; lauwidh M; laght W. hire(2)] hir EN; here DH² AW; her ChK; hur*e* R. scorne] schorne A.
138 seide] gredde U. it] þis W. so] swa E; with so L; *corrected from* to D. loude] loude steuene L. þat] at E. soþnesse] sotnes A; sothfastnes L. it] *om* L. herde] harde AK.
139 Whoso] Ho so JA; Hose V; Wha E; þat who R; For who so U. wilneþ] willet M; wyllith H²K; wyll E; wold A; ȝernyth J; wynne R. hire(1)] hir EN; her*e* UDAW; her ChK; hur*e* R. wyue] wynne (*late corrector alters to* wyve) H²; welþe] weolþe V; weole L. of . . . godis] or for worschipe L. hire(2)] hir EN; her*e* UDJAW; her ChK; hur*e* R. godis] gudes E.

But he be cokewald ycald, kitte of my nose.' 140
War[yn] wisdom þo, ne [witty] his fere,
Couþe nouȝt warpen a word to wiþsigge resoun,
But stari[den for] stodyenge [and] stoden as bestis.
Þe king acordite, be crist, to resonis sawis
And reherside þat resoun [hadde] riȝtfulliche shewide; 145
'Ac it is wel hard, be myn hed, herto to b*ri*nge it.
And alle my lige ledis to lede þus euene.'

140 But] But ȝif A; Bote ȝef L. be] beo L; be a W; beo a V; *om* R. cokewald ycald] cald cokewald M; mad cokewald A. cokewald] cokewold UVHJLKN; cokwolde W; cokold ChH²; Cukkold D. ycald] ycalde RN; Icalled Ch; Icallid H²J; called D; callyd E; Iclepid K; ykyd H; Ikore V; of kynde L; *om* W. kitte] kyt HM; kutte LEAW; Cutt K; cut RUD VJN. my nose] my*n* nase M; myne eeris H; boþe myn Eres V.
141 Waryn] LWN; waren JK; Warne TDH²; War ne E; wary Ch; On warned R; Vnwar was U; I warne þat H; Than boþe A; was nouþer V; Reyth her M. wisdom] wisdam ChVM; witte A. þo] wer þ*er* E; *om* UHAN. ne] ny L; ꝧ UD ChEAK; *om* R. witty] witti VHJLK WN; wyt DM; witte ChE; ynwit U; on witt*es* R; no wyt TH²; wysdom A. his] his owne D; in A; *om* R.
142 *line om* U. Couþe] kouthen L; coude RDChH²AKM; Þai couth E; þat couþe V; ne couþe H. nouȝt] nout M; not RDH²JLAK; *om* VHW. warpen] werpyn KN; werchin J; carpen ChLM; carpyn A; carpe E; seie H. a] o Ch; þo a W. wiþsigge] wi*th*siggen VM; wi*th*segge RChH² LAN; wi*th*seggen D; withsay KW; withseyn J; aȝenseie H; witte sayd E.
143 But] And E. stariden] starede*n* RVHLN; staredyn JM; staryd EA; stared KW; staring TDChH²; starende U. for] VJLAKNM; forth EW; ꝧ TRUD ChH²H. stodyenge] studyeng LK; studiing VW; studeing N; stodiynge M; stodynge DCh; studiande U; stodiede R; studede*n* H; stondyng H²J; stridyng E. and] RVHJLEAKWNM; *om* TUDChH². stoden] stodyn DJAM; stode E; stooden V; stode forþ RU; stode stille WN; stonden Ch. as bestis] al stonyed L. as] like E. *Here* W *adds lines like* **B** IV 152–6.
144 acordite] acordytt E; acordide U; acordyd DH²JAKNM; acordede V; acorded RChLW; acord H. be . . . to] anon to WN; wel to M; ꝧ kneow soth L. resonis] resou*n* JEW. sawis] sawas L; Connynge VH.
145 reherside] rehersid H²HJEA; rehersede VM; rehersed RDChLK; seid N; sayd W. þat resoun] *twice* A; he (*added another hand*) W. hadde] HJLM; had RUKWN; hed E; hedde V; hath A; *om* TDChH². riȝtfulliche] rightwysly E. shewide] schewid UH²HJEAKN; schewed RDCh LWM; Ischewet V. *Here* W *adds lines like* **B** IV 165–70.
146 Ac] Bot ChVHLEKNM; *om* AW. wel] wol U; ful RDA; *om* VHEWNM. hard] herd EN. be . . . it] to me to bryng þaim togede*r* E; to me to bryngge hem to togeders (to *over cancelled* þo, *same hand*) M; to brynge togederis A. hed] heued U; hed q*uo*d þe kyng W. her . . . it] to bryng þis abowte L. herto] here Ch; it þerto U. to(2) . . . it] hit bringe VHW. b*ri*nge] bringyn J. it(2)] *om* RUD.
147 And . . . to] þat eny lyuy*n*g men shulde H. And] *om* UVA. alle] *om* M. lige] ligge A; leige E; lege DChH²LW NM; lyche RK; riche J. ledis] leodes VL; lordes WN; londis AM; landes E. to] for to A; *om* K. lede] leden UK; ledyn RJ. þus] VJLEKWNM; hem þus TRUD ChH²H; *om* A.

'Be hym þat [rauȝte] on þe rode,' *qua*þ resoun to þe king,
'But I reule þus þi reaum rend out my ribbes,
Ȝif it be þ*a*t buxumnesse be at myn assent.' 150
'And I assente,' quaþ þe king, 'be seinte marie my lady,
Be my counseil ycome of clerkes and Erlis.
Ac redily, resoun, þou shalt not [raike] henne,
For as longe as I lyue l[et]e þe I [n]ile.'
'I am redy,' *qua*þ resoun, 'to reste wiþ ȝow eu*er*e; 155
So consience be of ȝo*ur* counseil, kepe I no bet*er*e.'
'I g*r*aunte,' *qua*þ þe king, 'godis forbode he faille!
As longe as I lyue libbe we togid*er*is.'

148 rauȝte] raughte U; rauhte V; rauȝt N; rawght K; rauȝþe R; rawt J; reste L; ryst EW; was rauth A; rest hym H; henge M; deiȝede T; deyde DH²; died Ch. on] vppo*n* EA. þe] *om* ChA. rode] rude E. *qua*þ] seyde A. to þe king] þan W. to] te R.
149 But] UVHLEAWNM; But ȝif TRDChH²JK. I] þou E; ȝe AK. reule] reoule L; Rule VKN. þus . . . reaum] þi realme þus E. þi] my R; ȝoure DJAKN; oure L. reaum] realme KM; Reame DV; rewme RUHJLWN; rem A; Reme ChH². rend . . . ribbes] þou sall noght wele like E. rend] rendith J; rent RDChLK. out] outȝ H²; of RUWM. ribbes] ribbe W.
150 Ȝif] ȝef LKM; But H²; Swa E. it . . . þ*a*t] at þou lat E. it] þat hit L; *om* KWN. be(1)] beo L; be so RUHJ; beo so V; so be KWNM. buxumnesse] buxumesse D. be(2)] beo VL; ben J. at] of RUDHLKWNM. myn] þi E; ȝoure A.
151 L *corrupts to* By goode god *quod* þe kyng y graunte wel þanne. And] *om* VHAM. I] Ich V. quaþ . . . king] *om* H. quaþ] seiþ N.
152 Be] Beo VL. ycome] ycomen UW NM; Icomyn J; come LA; comon E. and] and of RUDVHEAWM. Erlis] eorles L; kniȝtis H.
153 Ac] And H²; Bot ChVHLEKWNM; Bit (*cancelled*) J; *om* A. redily resoun] reson redyly (*marked for transposition same ink*) H². redily] redly RD; Ryht redyly J; I say þe W. shalt . . . raike] Rydest not VH. shalt] sall E. not] nat H²; nouȝt ChN; noght E; *om* D. raike] Ch; ryde REAKWNM; riden UL; rydyn J; wende TDH². henne] hennes ChLNM; hennys RHJ; henys A; hens KW; heonnes V; hyne E.
154 H *corrupts to* for into my deþday we nele not dep*a*rt. For] *om* A. as] als E. I lyue] me is lant the lyf L. lyue] lyffe J; leue DChH²EAWNM. lete . . . nile] thy lyfelode I þe thonke M. lete] JW; leten N; leete VL; letten K; leuyn A; loue TRU DChH²E. þe I nile] we sall toged*er* E. nile] nylle JAKW; nulle VL; nelle N; wille RUDH²; wile T; wol Ch.
155 *line om* A. I] Ich V. am] ame K. redy] al redy M; als redy E. reste] restyn J; rist E. ȝow] þe VHM.
156 So] So þat VH; Swa þ*a*t E; Ȝif WN. be] beo VL. of] *om* V. ȝo*ur*] our UVHM; *om* EWN. counseil] counseiler V.
157 I g*r*aunte] Yit g*r*auntt I E. I] And I N. g*r*aunte] g*r*aunte wel HL; graunte gladly V; graunte þat W. godis . . . faille] so me god helpe L. godis forbode] god forbede DHEAKWN; God forbeode V. he faille] he feile H; he failed U; I fayle DCh; elles AM.
158 As] Als L; Also N; for as H; And also V; Bott als E. I] we HKM. lyue] lyuen M; lyffe J; leue DChEW; libbe schal L; leue may A. libbe] lyue L; leue VJA; abyde E; dwelle M; be W; loue H. we] we sall E. togid*er*is] the gederys M.

V

þe king & [his] kniȝtes to þe [k]ir[k]e wente
To here matynes & masse, and to þe mete aftir.
þanne wakide I of my wynkyng, & wo was wiþalle
þat I ne hadde yslepe sadd*ere* & yseyn more.
Er I hadde faren a furlong feyntise me h[ent]e 5
þat I ne miȝte ferþ*ere* a fote for defaute of slepyng.
I sat softely [adoun] & seide my beleue,
And so I babelide on my bedis þei brouȝte me aslepe.

1 þe] he E. king . . . kniȝtes] *defective* H. his] RUDChVJLEAKWNM; the H^2; *om* T. kniȝtes] knyȝt*us* H^2; kniȝtghtes N; knytis A. þe] *om* H. kirke] LEN; kyrk J; chirche TChH^2AK; cherche RUW; Churche DVHM. wente] wenten UVLM; wentyn J; *þer* þei wenten H.
2 To] For to A. here matynes] *defective* H. here] hear K; heere V; he D. masse] messe UChH^2EAWN. to] sithe to U; gon to Ch. þe] *om* UChH^2LAKN. aftir] eft*er* E. *After this line:* Quintus passus M.
3 þanne] þe*n*ne VL; þen H; Tho AW. wakide . . . my] *defective* H. wakide] wakid UJAK; wakede V; waked RDL WN; wakenyd E; wakened Ch; wakende M. my] *om* H^2WM. wynkyng] wink V; slep E. &] *om* VH. wo was] me was wo V. wo] wa E. was] was me HLE. wiþalle] þerfore H.
4 ne hadde] nadde M; nedde V. ne] no L; *om* A. hadde . . . sadd*ere*] *defective* H. hadde] hed E. yslepe sadd*ere*] sadder yslept N; saddere slept W; sadloker Islept V; saddar sclept K; rather I slepte M. yslepe] slepe UDH^2; slepyn JA; sleped ChL; slepyd E; sclepte R. sadd*ere*] hardere A; hard Ch; : : : enger H. yseyn] Isey DChAW; yseyen L; yseye RUH^2 NM; Isee K; Iseȝe V; sene E. more] nomore (no *cancelled*) D; muche mare E.
5 Er] Or DChH^2EAK; Ar LN; But or J. hadde . . . furlong] a Furlong hedde Ifare V. hadde] hed E; hadde*n* R. faren] fare RDH^2H; faryn JA; farn N; fared W; faryd E. feyntise] fayntis J; Fantyse N; A Feyntise VA; a fayntnes E; fantasye RDKW (a(2) *altered from original* e R); swiche fantesie U. hente] UVHJLAKW NM; hynt E; kauȝt Ch; hadde TRDH^2.
6 *line om* L. þat] *om* WN. I . . . fote] A fote ne myght I ferþer WN; Forþer mihti not a fote V; ferþ*er* ne miȝte y one fote H. ne miȝte] mygth no A. ferþ*ere* a fote] a fote forthere D; a fote ferther M; o fote ferþer Ch. ferþ*ere*] forthere J; ferrer E; forth K. a fote] a fute E; *om* A. defaute] defauȝte Ch. slepyng] sclepyng K; slepe DHEW; sleep V.
7 *line om* D. sat] sate HM; sett me E. softely] sotely H^2. adoun] adou*n* RUCh VHJAKWNM; doun LE; in my bedis T; on my bedis H^2. & . . . beleue] *om and* 7a *copied with* 8b, *then* 7b *supplied above line and* 8a *marginally in original or similar hand and ink* H^2. seide] sayde RLEKW. beleue] beoleeue V.
8 *line om* D. so] swa E; also W; *om* A. I] *om* A. babelide] babelyd H^2; babeled Ch; bablide U; bablede J; bablyd EK; babled RLWN; babbid A; blaberid H; blaberde V; badde M. bedis] Beodes VL. þei . . . me] I was broght E; til I was W. þei] thay K; it AN; that H^2VH. brouȝte] brouȝþe R; brouth H^2; brout A; broughten U; browty*n* J. aslepe] on slepe RChH^2 JLEKM.

þanne sauȝ I meke[l] more þan I before tolde,
[For I [sauȝ] þe feld ful of folk þat I before tolde], 10
And consience wiþ a cros com for to p*re*che,
And p*re*yede þe peple haue pite on hemselue,
And p*ro*uide þat þise pestilences wern for pur synne,
And þe southwestryne wynd on satirday at eue
Was ap*er*tly for pride & for no poynt ellis. 15
Piries & pl[umtr]es wern pu[ffid] to þe erþe
In ensaumple, se[gges], þ*at* ȝe shulde do þe bet*ere*;

9 þanne] þen VH; & þan M. sauȝ I] y sawe H; I say DM. sauȝ] sauh V; saw RUChLEWN; sey JA; see K. mekel] mekyll E; meche A; mochel K; moche UCh; muche DH^{2}V; mychel JLNM; myche H; meke T; a mekel (a *cancelled*) R; a muche W. þan] þen ChVHE. before tolde] fortelle DL; can of telle K; may ȝow telle W. before] beofore V; aforn A. tolde] tald E; shewid H.
10 DRUH^{2}VJLEAKWM; *line om* TCh HN. For] *om* RUH^{2}JEW. I] *om* H^{2}W. sauȝ] sauh V; saw RULE; say DM; segh K; sey JA; *om* H^{2}W. þe] Al þe H^{2}W; a A. þat] as A. I] ich V. before] of bifore V; aforn A; furst H^2; *om* W. tolde] toulde K; telde A; I tolde (I *cancelled*) H^2; of tolde LW; of tald E; sayde R; nempnyd U; nemede M; nemyde J; schewede V.
11 And] & how H; & I sey J; how N. cros] croyse J; Crois V. com] cam JAKM; bygan H. for to] for the L; forþ to R. preche] p*re*chen K; p*re*chyne J; p*re*chynge L.
12 And] he RUVEWN. p*re*yede] preied ChHL; preide VM; preyȝede H^2; preyȝed J; praiede W; prayed DKN (*same hand after cancelled* proved K); prechede R; prechide U; p*re*chid EA. þe] þeo L. peple] peeple M; people LK; puple HA. haue] to haue RUEN; to hauyn A; ha M. pite] pete A; petie KM. on] of DVAN. hem] heom L; þaim E. selue] seluen EKN; seoluen L; silue*n* H; seuyn M.
13 And] Bote he L. p*ro*uide] p*ro*uyd JA; prouede R; p*ro*ued UDChLKW; preuede V; p*re*ued HNM; *om* E. þat] at E; *om* R. þise] þis UVJ; þese DH^2; þes Ch; þe RHLEAKW; *om* NM. pestilences] pestelence RUHJLEAWNM. wern] wer ChK; weren H^2; were D; wery*n* J; weore V; was RUHLAWNM; fell E. pur synne] Synne alonly E. pur] puire V; pore W; heore L; *om* D.
14 þe] þis V; an K; for a E; *om* R. southwestryne] sowþwestren Ch; southwest*erne* H^{2}VHLE; souþwest RUDJKWN; grete southeweste M; southerne A. wynd] wynt V. on . . . eue] þat so loude blewe W. on] on þe A; on a VHJM; at L. satirday] sat*er*day UJ; sat*ur*day H^{2}AK; seterday ChVE; saterysday RL; sat*ur*days M. at] *om* M. eue] euen RUDChH^{2}VHE; euene JLN; euyn AK; eueyn M.
15 ap*er*tly] ap*er*tily N; apartely K; ap*er*ty JA; inp*er*ty E. pride] pruide VL; synne U. for(2)] *om* W. poynt] þing RUA.
16 Piries] Peryes DJW; Peretrees HE; Perys K. plumtres] UJEAWM; Plomtres VN; plomtrees HL; plomtreys RK; plantes TDChH^2. wern] wer ChK; were RUDH^{2}HJLAWN; weryn M; weore V; war E. puffid] puffyd JAK; puffed WN; poffet L; possid HE; possed M; passchet V; put TRDChH^2; putte U. erþe] eorthe L; erde A; grou*n*de VHWN; grounde erthe (grounde *cancelled*) H^2.
17 In] I H^2. ensaumple] example JAM; exsaumple RE. segges . . . ȝe] that ye segges K. segges] L; to Men VHM; sent god TChH^2; seyþ god RU; sayd god D; I say for E; I sey A; *om* JWN. þat] *om* RUEANM. ȝe] ȝe alle J; we ChV; þei HM; *om* (*late corrector supplies* we) H^2. shulde] schulden K; schuldyn J; sholden M; suld E; schul R. do] don A; done JK. þe] *om* D.

Bechis & broode okis wern blowen to [þe] grounde,
And turnide vpward here tail in toknyng of drede
Þat dedly synne er domisday shal fordon hem alle. | 20
Of þis mater I miȝte mamele wel longe, *fol.* xxxv *a*
Ac I shal seiȝe as I saiȝ, so me god helpe,
How consience wiþ a cros cumside to p*re*che.
He bad wast*our* go werche what he best couþe
And wynne þ*at* he wastide wiþ sum man*er* craft, 25
And p*re*yede p*er*nel hire purfil to leue
And kep[e] it in hire coffre for catel at nede.

18 broode] brade E. okis] hokis A; hookys J; akes E. wern] weren UChH^{2}M; weryn JK; wer*e* RDHWN; weore VL; where A; was E. blowen] blowe RDH^{2}HLW; blowyn AK; blawyn E; bowed Ch; possed M. þe] RUDChH^{2}VHJLEAKWNM; *om* T. grounde] erþe HN; eorþe V.
19 And] þai W. turnide] t*ur*nyd UJEA; t*ur*ned RDChVHKWM; torned LN. vpward] vp RUDAKWM. here] her ChN; þe RUVLEWM. tail] tailes HN; talys E. in] for J. toknyng] takenyng E; tokyn A; tokne W.
20 dedly synne] synne W; deth U. er] or DChH^{2}VHJM; ar LN; on EK; at A; aforn W. shal] sal JE; schulde VH. fordon] fordo RHE. hem alle] þe world H. hem] heom L; þaim E.
21 *line om* WN. Of] On A; vpo*n* H; In M. þis] þis ilke H. mater] *touched up* T. I miȝte] myght y U; myȝthe I R; I mought M; y H. mamele] mamel Ch; mamelyn JA; mamle U; mamble K; Momele V; muche mamele & L; momelid H; manle (*for* mamle) D; m*er*vell E. wel] wol U; ful VHEAM; *om* ChL.
22 *line om* WN. Ac] Bot ChVHLEAKM. shal] sall E; *om* VH. seiȝe] seygh M; seie U; seyn DJ; sey A; say RChHEK; sayn L; sigge V. saiȝ] sayhe J; say H^2; saye M; sauȝ H; sauh V; saw D; sawe ChE; seegh K; sygh L; seyde RUA. so] sa E; as so A.
23 *line om* WN. How] When E; Whan AM. a] his K. cumside] comsyd D; co*m*sede RV; comsed ChK; com for U; comyd A; began M; bygan for HJE; kraftyliche kan L. to] *om* L. p*re*che] prechen DLK.
24 He] and RHA. wast*our*] wastors VHEW. go] to AM; *om* E. werche] worche RVLKWN; wurche DM; wirche UChJ; wirke E. what] wat N; qwat JE. he] þei VH; þai EW. best] be E. couþe] coude RUA; coulde K.
25 *line om* A. wynne] wynnen W; wy*nn*yn J; whynne M. þ*at*] what KM. he] þei VHW. wastide] wastyd DJEK; wastede M; wasted ChHLWN; had wasted R; ne wasteden V. wiþ] be E; by K. man*er*] kynne U; kyn E. craft] RUDVH JEKWNM; of craft TChH^2; werke L.
26 And] And he E; he RUVN. p*re*yede] preied ChHN; preyde M; p*re*yȝede H^{2}V; p*ra*yed DLW; p*ra*yyde K; p*ra*yde R; praed E; p*ra*yȝed J; p*re*chid U; bad A. p*er*nel] peornel L; pyrnel U; peronell E; pyronell K; to p*er*onel R; dame p*er*nel N; p*er*nel þe prowde JW. hire] hir E; here UDHAWM; her ChJKN; hure R. purfil] purfele K; purfelle ChE; ppurfuyll M; proude porfile L. leue] leuyn J.
27–34 *rearranged and augmented thus in* A: 27–30–31—*two extra lines*—28—*two extra lines*—29—(*om* 32, 33)—34.
27 kepe] RUDChH^{2}HLEAKWN; kepen VM; kepyn J; kepte T. hire] hir EN; here UDH^{2}HJWM; her ChK; hur*e* R; *om* A. coffre] cophre W; cofyr*e* JA; cofore H^2; whicche H. for . . . nede] lest rattis hit eten H. at] hadde M. nede] neode V.

Thomas he tauȝte to take two staues
And fecche [hom] felis fro wyuene pyne.
He warnide watte his wyf was to blame 30
Þat hire hed was worþ a mark & his hod not worþ a grote.
He chargide chapmen to chastice here children:
'Let no wynnyng forwanye hem whiles þei ben ȝonge'.
He pre[yide] prelatis & prestis togidere,
Þat þei preche þe peple proue it hemselue, 35

28 M *corrupts to* And Thomas þe tannere a whippe to take. Thomas] Tomme of stowe J. tauȝte] tauȝþe R; tawte J; taut A. to . . . staues] twa staffes to take E. to take] *twice* R. to] *om* H^2. take] takyn JA. two] too D; to JAW; twey V; toughe L. staues] stauenes V. *Here* A *adds two lines: see above*, p. 48.
29 And] To R. fecche] fecchen DWM; fecchyn JA; fette V; facchen L. hom felis] felys hom RL. hom] UDChVHJEAK WNM; *om* TH^2. felis] felice UDChVJ EAKWNM; felis his wyf TH^2; his wyf H. fro . . . pyne] wyfes to spynne A. fro] fram H; fro þe ChJN. wyuene] wyuen DChHKW; heuene wyuene (heuene *cancelled*) U; wyueyn M; wifes E; wymmen L; wyne J. pyne] peyne M; pyment J.
30 *marked with cross* N. He] And als he E; And AM; *om* N. warnide] warnyd UH^2 JE; warnede RV; warned DChLKW; warned also H; warne N; was to warne A; waryede M. watte] wattes W. his wyf] wyf þat she W; *cancelled for* that he *by late corrector* H^2. his] þat his JN; þat is A; witerly his L. to] for to N; mychel to J. blame] wite L.
31 *as three lines divided after* state: monye L. Þat . . . hed] *late corrector alters to* his wifes hoode H^2. Þat] for K; *om* EW. hire] Hir EN; here UDHAWM; her ChK; hure R. hed] heued UE; hode M; hoode K. worþ(1) . . . not] of hygher pris þan feol for hire state For hit passed a pound þe pletes weore so monye And his hood hyghely yholde hit L. worþ(1)] wrth J; wor A. a] half N. mark] merke K. &] *om* W. his] *twice* A. hod] hed H^2; *om* E. not] nat H^2; nouȝt N; nauȝt Ch; noght E; *om* VWM. worþ(2)] *om* RUCh JEK. *Here* JEAM *add lines like* **B** V 32–3 *or* **C** VI 135–6: *see above*, p. 30.
32 *line om* A. He] Als he E. chargide] chargyd H^2HM; chargede V; charged DChJLKW; charched N; chargytt E; chargeþ R. chapmen] chepmen E. chastice] chastisen L; chastysyn JM; Chasten VK; chaste RH; chasty E. here] her ChJKN; hire H^2; heore VL; þair E. children] childeryn J; childern K; childre W; childer E; childris M.
33 *line om* A. Let] lat ChJE; & lete H; That WN. no . . . hem] no wynnyng for wanyyn hem *cancelled for* hem want no wande *similar hand* J; hem wante none eyȝe H; hem wonte non eiȝe V. wynnyng] wonnyng L; welthe U. forwanye hem] hem weny N. forwanye] forwany UCh; forwanyen L; forwane K; forweny R; forweyne E; wanye W; wanyn M. hem] heom L; þaim E. whiles] qwylis J; whils W; qwilse E; while DVLNM. þei] þai E; thay K; þat þei UV. ben] be DCh H^2JN; beon L; beþ RW; er E. *Here* W *adds lines like* **B** V 36–41: *see above*, p. 30.
34 He] And A; *om* M. preyide] preyede V; preied HA; Preyde M; praied LKWN; prayȝed J; praed als E; prechede R; prechide UH^2 (*late corrector alters* to prayde H^2); preched Ch; prechet D; prechiþ T. prelatis] Preestes VA. prestis] pristes ChE; prestes eke W; preostes putten heom L; Prelates VA.
35 Þat] At E; Al þat WN; And L. þei] þai E; thay K; he JA; *om* L. preche] prechen DChVK; prechyn JAM; shulde preche H; preched W. þe] to þe M; to *inserted by late corrector* H^2; *om* WN. peple] people LKM; puple HA; *om* WN. proue] W; proven K; prouyn M; preue A; to preue N; to preuen V; & proue TRU E; & prouen D; & prouyn J; and preue ChH^2H; & preoue L. it] hit in V; *om* D. hem] heom L; them K; þair E; hym H; *late corrector puts* on *before* H^2. selue] seluen VEM; seoluen L; siluen H.

'And libbe as ȝe lere vs, we wile leue ȝow þe betere'.
And siþþe he redde religioun here rewel[e] to holde
'Lest þe king & his counseil ȝour comunes apeir[e]
And be steward of ȝoure stede til ȝe be stewid betere.
And ȝe þat seke seint Iame & seintes at rome, 40
Sekiþ seint treuþe for he may saue ȝou alle
Qui cum patre & filio; Faire mote ȝow befalle.'
Þanne [ran] repentaunce [and] reherside his teme
And made wil to wepe watir wiþ his eiȝen.

36 *marked with cross* N. libbe] lyue RHW (*altered from* leue W); leve E; libbeth LN; libben UV; libbyn D; lyven K; lyuyn J; leuyn A; *om* M. as ȝe] ȝhe as (*late corrector cancels* ȝhe *for* you) H². as] als E. ȝe] yow K; þei HWM; þai EA. lere] leren DL; leryn JM; lerne UChAKWN; lereþ V; tauȝte H. vs] hem H. we] for we RU; þei H. wile] wol UCh; wolle K; woln L; wolen V; wolde H; schul DA; shal W; *om* JEM. leue ȝow] it leue W. leue] leuyn M; trast E; lowe N; loue RUVH LAK; louen D; louyn J. ȝow] ow V; hem HAM; þaim E.
37 And] *om* WN. siþþe] sithe H²L; sithen UK; siþin M; sytthen A; seþþe ChV; sethe D; sethin J; syne E; swyþe R; *om* WN. redde] red JEA; radde RUVH LWNM; rad K. religioun] religyus RU. here] her ChJKN; heore L; þer E; þe V. rewele] rewle UJ; reule RAWM; Rule VHKN; reoule L; reweles TDChH²E. to] for to VA; wel to WN. holde] holden D; holdyn M; helde A; kepe RUE.
38 *line om* A; L *substitutes* And lyue with a lowe heorte oure lord for to serue. Lest] last RU; Latt noght E; þat J. king & his] kingis HWN. ȝour] here H; her Ch; þair E. comunes] comen J; countenaunse Ch. apeire] apeyre RUDH²V KM; appeiren Ch; apaire WN; apare E; apeired H; apeiriþ T; not apayre J.
39 *line om* LA. be(1)] ben JK; beo V; were H; *om* R. steward] stewerd E; stiward RUH²VHM; stiwardes W; stwardes N; stiwarden K. of] in RUVH KWN. ȝoure] oure VM; here H; þair E. stede] stide H²; stude VH; stedes EKN; stedis J; lond M. til] for R; or D; so þat U; & tillyn M. ȝe . . . betere] þai be storyd wele E; ȝoure stor bettere M; þei were amendid H; ȝe cheue þe betere U be] ben JK. stewid] stiwed Ch; stywed R; stowed D; stouwet V; stow it N; stayed K; stylet H²; cattelld W. *Here* K *adds lines like* **B** V 51–2 *and* 49–50; W *adds a passage like* **B** V 49–56: *see above*, p. 30.
40 *line om* E. And] *om* WN. ȝe] Tho WN; nout M; *om* R. þat] *om* M. seke] seken UDChWN; sekyn JAM; sechen LK; secheþ V; sechiþ H; *om* R. Iame] Iames KM; Iamys J. &] ne M. at] in U; of AWM.
41 Sekiþ] Sekit M; Seket D; Seke E; sechiþ HL; Secheþ VK. seint] seynt RU VHJLEAKWNM; at hom seint TD ChH². treuþe] treouthe L; truþe RK; trwþe N; troth E. saue ȝou] ȝou sauen L. saue] sauen VM; sauyn J. ȝou] ow V; vs R. *Here* H *adds a line:* *see above*, p. 46.
42 *patre*] *om* L. *filio*] *filio &c* A. Faire] þat fayre RUHWN. mote ȝow] ȝou mote RU; mote ȝe LM; ȝe mot J; ȝou AH; might hym E. befalle] falle VLK; hendyn M; *defective* H. *Here* EKWM *add a line like* **B** V 60 *or* **C** VI 201: *see above*, p. 31.
43 Þanne] ÞEnne V; þen H; And þan W. ran] HJLEAKWNM; Ron V; *om* TRU DChH². and] VHJLAKM; to WN; *om* TRUDChH²E. reherside] rehersid H²H JEK; rehercede U; rehersed RDChVLM; rehersis A; reherce WN. his] þis VH. teme] theme E; *defective* H.
44 made] gart to A; *om* D. wil] will EK; wille RUChAN; william VH; wylkoc H². to] for to D; *om* N. wepe] wepen DH²W; wepyn JM; weope V; weopen L. watir] watur VAK. wiþ] with boþe VA; of E; riht at bothe J. his eiȝen] *defective* H. eiȝen] eien UDKWN; eyghnen L; eyne M; eȝen V; ene E; Ien J; yne A; eye R.

Pernel proud herte plat hire to þe erþe 45
And lay longe er heo lokide, & 'lord mercy' criede,
And behi3te to hym þat vs alle made
Heo shulde vnsewe hire serke & sette þere an heire
For to affaiten hire flessh þat fers was to synne:
'Shal neuere hei3 herte me hente, but holde me lowe 50
And suffre to be misseid, & so dide I neuere.
But now wile I meke me & mercy beseke
Of alle þat I haue had enuye in myn herte.'
Lecchour seide 'allas!' & to oure lady criede

45 Pernel] Peronel REK; Peornel L; pirnel U; Pernelys M. proud] prout H; þe proud A. herte] harte K; *om* A. plat] platte DVKM; fel plat W. hire] hir EN; here U; her DChJK; hure R; *om* AWM. to] doun to A. þe] *om* ChVA. erþe] eorthe L; grounde VHAN.

46 And . . . &] She sighed soryfu & saide W; And syked ful sorowfully & seide N. longe] lange UE. er] her M; or DH²HJLEAK; ar ChV. heo] *late corrector prefixes* s H²; 3he A; sche RUDChJEKM. lokide] U; lokyd JA; lokede VM; loked RDHLK; lokide vp T; lokyd vp H²E; loked vp Ch. lord mercy] to vr ladi V. lord] oure lord L; *om* EAM. criede] cryed RDChJLK; cride UH; heo cryed (*late corrector prefixes* s) H²; sho cryed E; gan crie AM; *om* WN.

47 *line om* J; *marked with cross* N. And] And sho E. behi3te] behythe M; behyth A; beohi3te V; hight EW; bieght N. made] maade V; maked DK; makyd A; maked with his myght L.

48 *as two lines divided after* scherte M. Heo] s *prefixed by late corrector* H²; he L; sche RUDChJKWN; That 3he A; Þat Sho E; þat sche M. shulde] suld E; wolde VHLA. vnsewe] vnsewen D; vnsewyn J; vnsowe UW; vnsow E; vnsowen HLN; vnsouwen V; on sewe Ch; onsowe K; vnschewyn M. hire] hir E; here UDHAW; her ChJKN; heore L. serke] syrke A; shert HM; schorte L; smok VK. sette] setten V; settyn M. þere] þerin EA; þer on NM; *late corrector adds* on H². an] a EN; *om* M. heire] hayre ChJA; heare K; here VHL; hare E.

49 For to] Forte V; Fort N; To RUW; Tho A. affaiten] affaite W; fayten V; affeyten L; afeyntyn AM; afauten R; frete E; endaunten Ch; dawntyn J. hire] hir E; here UDHAW; her ChKN; heore L. flessh] fleche J; fleys R. fers] Fyrse K; fiers N; fresch RUHL; Frele VA. synne] senne M. *A cross in margin opposite this and following line* N.

50 Shal] Sall E. neuere] neuere me (me *cancelled*) H²; nere R. hei3 . . . hente] my hert be so heyh W. hei3] hey RA; heith M; hiegh N; hyghe L; hye UDChJEK; li3t H; liht V. herte] heorte L; harte K. hente] hentyn JM; hynt E; hende U; hente quoþ heo H; haunte D; hold A. holde] holdyn JM; hald E; euer holdyn A. me] it A. lowe] law E.

51 suffre] suffryn M. be] ben M; bien J; beo VL. misseid] myssayd DJEWN; myssayde H²JLK; missede A; nysseyd R. dide] did JEN; dude RVL; dede DCh A.

52 But] And VJ; *om* H. wile I] I wil RJ; I con wel V. wile] wele M; wol ChHLK; *om* A. meke] mekyn JM; meoke L. me] myself H. beseke] byseke RN; besekyn J; beseche VA; byseche UHL; besechyn M; bysechen K.

53 alle] alle þing J; *om* L. I haue] Ichaue V; I D. had] hed E; Ihad V; had of RA. enuye] pride JWN. herte] heorte L; harte K.

54 *divided from following after* bad H. Lecchour] Lichour E; Lycchere þo J; Þe lechour ChL; þe lechours H; þe leccherouse M; Lechery KWN. seide] sede A. to . . . lady] lord mercy H. to] on RUDJLEKWN. lady] lorde Ch; *late corrector alters to* lorde H². criede] cried JEAN; cryde RUM; cri3ed Ch; gradde L; bad H.

To make m*er*cy for his mysdede betwyn god & hym 55
Wiþ þ*at* he [shulde] þe satirday, seue ȝer þ*er*aftir,
Drinke but wiþ þe doke & dyne but ones.
Enuye wiþ heuy herte askide aftir shrift,
And carfulliche his cope [comsiþ] he to shewe.
He was as pale as a p[e]let, [in] þe palesie he semide; 60
He was cloþid in a caurymaury, I [couþe] it nouȝt descryue;
A kertil & a courtepy, a knyf be his side,
Of a Freris frokke were þe foresleuys. |

55 *as two lines divided after* misdede V. To . . . m*er*cy] *om* H. To] Tho A. make] makyn JA; gete WN; maken him han V. m*er*cy] amendes UM; m*er*cy mene (mene *above line another hand*) J. for] of LW. his . . . hym] god in helpe of his soule W. his] hi*m* M. mysdede] mysdedis HJN; sowle A; *om* M. betwyn . . . hym] in mendyng of his soule N; *om* J. betwyn] bytweone L; bitwix E; bytweþe R. god] god almihti V. hym] hym silue*n* H; his soule LKM; hys seaulle E; his pore soule V; hym of mysdede A. *Here* H[2] *adds 4 lines: see above*, p. 48.
56 Wiþ] And A. þ*at*] thi J. shulde] schulde RUVHJLAKWNM; suld E; *om* TDChH[2]. þe] on Ch; *om* RUJWN. satirday] saterday ChH[2]WNM; saturday DAK; seterday VE; setteresday L; sat*er*dayes U; sato*ur*dayes R; *om* J. seue] seuen ChVHJLE; sevyn K; seuene DH[2] AWN; vij RUM. ȝer] ȝeer D; ȝeir L; yer*es* K. þ*er*aftir] after RDVEAM; sykerly þ*er*after J.
57 Drinke] Drynke RUDHLEAKWN; Drinken V; Drinkyn J; Drynky M; Shulde drinke TChH[2]. but] *twice* M; *om* ChH[2]EAKW. wiþ] wit M; mid N. doke] duke EW; doge L; goos RUM (*twice* U). dyne] dynyn J; ete H; eten V. ones] anys E.
58 heuy] hiȝe H. herte] heorte L; hart K. askide] askid UEAK; askede M; asked RDChHLW; asket V; axed JN. aftir] aftur V. shrift] schreft Ch; schrfte A.
59 And] *om* W. carfulliche] caryfully E; gretliche V. cope] coupe UDEN; coulpe W; Culpe K; counte A; compte R; gylt J; gult L; gultis H; gultus V; synnes Ch; wilis M. comsiþ he] com for A; he couett*es* E; begynnyth he K; begynneþ he TH[2]LWN; begynnyth JM; begynneþ DChVH; he gynnyþ RU. to] for to ChJ.
60 He was] þe pelou*r*r was H; *om* VWNM. as(1)] Also N; *om* RHEK. pale] *om* HE. as(2)] als E; *om* H. a] *om* HJ. pelet] RVAKW; pelat UM; pelot N; palet TH[2] (*late corrector alters to* pellet H[2]); palette Ch; polet DL; piller E; erthe J; pelled H. in] VHJLAWNM; & in EK; on D; & on TChH[2]; and RU. þe] a VKWN; *om* RUDJM. palesie] palasie W; p*ar*lesy E; paltyk R; palatik U. he] *om* RUChE. semide] semyd HAKN; semede RM; semed DChH[2]EW; seemede V; semyth (th *cancelled for* d) J; semeth L.
61 He was] He E; And L; *om* VHNM. cloþid] cloþed RDChL; Icloþed VK; clad AW; Cladde N; cled E; Iclad M. a] *om* ChHM. caurymaury] cawremawre Ch; toury mowry E. I couþe] coude y L. couþe] couthe UVHJEWN; coude RAK; can TDChH[2]M. it nouȝt] nout it D. it] hym UVH; *om* ChEA. nouȝt] not RUH[2]VHJLAKWM. descryue] descreue N; discreue V; discrie RUChLA; discry E; discr*i*en J; discryn M; dese*r*ne K; deuise W.
62 *line om* V. kertil] kertel H; kirtil UJE AWN; kirtel LR; kirtelle Ch; kyrtul H[2]; curtil kurtell K. &] *om* M. courtepy] courteby ChJAKW; courtby E. a(3)] & M. knyf] kneuet A.
63 *line om* V. Of] And of E; As **A.** a] *om* E. Freris] frere DJLEN. frokke] frogge U; frog RA; freyke J. were] wern M; weryn A; weoren L. þe] his HLEAKW. fore] forne JKM; forme UA; two H. sleuys] scleves K.

As a lek þat hadde leyn longe in þe sonne, *fol.* xxxv *b*
So lokide he wiþ lene chekis, lourande foule. 65
His body was bolnid for wr[aþþe] þat he bot his lippe[s],
And wroþliche he wroþ his fest, to wreke hym he þou3te,
Wiþ werkis [or wiþ] wordis whanne he sai3 his tyme.
'Venym, [or] verious, or vynegre I trowe,
Walewiþ in my wombe & waxiþ as I wene. 70
I mi3te not many day do as a man [au]3te,
Such wynd in my wombe wexiþ er I dyne.

64 As] Als E; Os N; like as H. a] *om* HN. lek] leek UH²VJL; leyke A; lyk R; led N; he H. þat] *om* HLWM. hadde] had ChJAN; hedde V; hed E; *om* L. leyn longe] longe leyen L. leyn] leie H; layn A; layne Ch; lay H²; lyen J; yleye RU; yley W; Ileizen V; Ilay K; ben E; Iben M. longe] lang E. þe] the hote L.
65 So] Swa E. lokide] lokyd JAKM; loked RDChVHLWN; lukyd E; lekyde H². he] *om* E. wiþ] wiþ his H. lourande] lowrynge RUDHJLAKWNM; lourede he V. foule] full fowll EKN; ful lowe H.
66 His . . . was] Al WN. bolnid] bolned RDChK; bollid H; Bolled V; bolne A; ybolned L; forbolned N; forbolne W. for] *with* AK. wraþþe] VHJLKM; wreþþe ChEA; wroþ TRUDH²; angre WN. þat . . . bot] bote he on A. þat] and Ch; *om* VH. bot] boot U; bate E. his] boþe his H. lippes] VHJLEAKWNM; lippe TRUDChH².
67 A *substitutes* He lokyd vndur his browis as a bond dogge. And] *om* VH. wroþliche] wrathly E. he(1)] *om* E. wroþ] *altered another ink to* wrong W; wrong RVHLKNM; wrang E. his] hisse Ch. fest] fyste RUDChH²JKWN; fust VHL; handes E. to . . . þou3te] he þou3te hym to wreke H; he þou3te him awreke V. wreke] wreken ULN; wrekyn M; wreykyn J; wroken K. hym] hem KW. he] *om* D. þou3te] þou3þe R; thowth J; þouþt W; þoug M.
68 *line om* A. werkis] workes K; werk UEW. or wiþ] UVHEKWM; or DLN; and with R; & TChH²J. wordis] word UE; woord W. whanne] when RChHL; whon V; qwan J; qwen E. sai3] say H²; sei3 VN; see3 K; sey RUDJ; se W; seith M; saw3e Ch; sawe HLE. *Here* W *adds a passage like* **B** V 87–93: *see above*, p. 31.
69 L *substitutes* Of leosardes or of lobbes venym hath me laghte. Venym] Venymour K; Wyrmys (? Wyriuys) A; Wormes (? Wermes ? Weriues) E; Vermyn Ch; And seyde weriuis M. or(1)] RUDChVHEAWM; & TH²; than K; *om* JN. verious] wynagre E; vernisch VK WN; verdegrese H; veniym M; vermyn A; vernycchith J. vynegre] venegre M; venagre Ch; vinegre or wyriuis (? wyrmis) A; wenom E.
70, 72 *as one line* A.
70 Walewiþ] walowyth K; waloweþ N; Walwyþ RJ; walweþ UCh; walwet D; walliþ H; walleþ V; And walweth L; waldeþ W; walkyt M; Walkyn A; Walkes E. &] or VM; quoþ he or H; *om* A. waxiþ] waxeþ RUChVHWN; waxit H²M; waxet D; waxis E; worcheth L; werkyn A. as I wene] me wrathe L; *om* A. as] *om* RDVHM. I] Ich VK. wene] trowe W.
71 *line om* A. I mi3te] Myght I W. I] I ne V; þat I L. not] nou3t ChEN; nouth J; noth M; *om* V. many . . . do] leve mony 3eres E. many] mony VL. day] a day RHK. do] don DChVL; done KN; doon J; *om* M. a man] I *corrected same hand* H². man] mon V. au3te] aughte L; ou3te HKN; ouhte V; sholde WM; suld E; mi3te TRUDChH²J.
72 Such . . . wexiþ] *om* A. Such] Swche N; swych RJM; siche UH; Swylke E; Suche a W. wynd] wynt V. wexiþ] wexit H²; wexeth Ch; waxyþ RJK; waxit M; waxeþ VHLWN; waxes E; waxed D. er I dyne] alway W. er] or ChH²HJEAK; ar LN. dyne] dye V.

I haue a neiȝebo*ur* neiȝ me, I haue noiȝed hym ofte,
And blamide hym behynde his bak to bringe hym in fame;
To apeire hym be my power I p*ur*suide wel ofte, 75
And belowen hym to lordis to don hym lese silu*er*,
And don hise frendis ben hise fon þoruȝ my false tunge.
His g*ra*ce & hise gode happis greuide me wel sore.
Betwyn hym & his meyne I haue mad wraþþe;
Boþe his lyme & his lif was lost þoruȝ my tunge. 80
Whanne I mette hym in market þ*at* I most hatide

73 *marked with cross* N. I haue] Ichaue V. a] *om* H. neiȝebo*ur*] neihȝebor V; nehebo*ur* R; neyȝbo*ur* UKW; neyȝborow Ch; neyebore J; neythebor AM; nextbur E; neȝeboris H. neiȝ me] me neih V; many H. neiȝ] neyȝe H[2]; nyegh N; nygh L; ney UD; ny RJA; nye Ch; nere EK; by W; be M. I] þ*at* I JN; *om* A. haue] hath A; *om* REN. noiȝed] noyed RUD KW; noyd A; noyde E; nuyed L; anoied H; anoyd M; anyed N; anuyȝed V; neiȝede H[2]. hym] hem HW; me A; *om* JN. ofte] wel ofte R; wol ofte U; full ofte E. *Here* H *copies line* 76.

74 *line om* AM. And] *om* VE. blamide] blamyd UH[2]JK; blamed RDChHLWN; Iblamed E; Ablamed V. hym(1)] hem H. his bak] *om* W. his] her*e* H. to] & J. bringe] bry*n*gen U; brouht J; putte W. hym(2)] hem HW. in] into L. fame] defame L; disclau*n*dre V; defaut HW.

75 *line om* AM. To] And V. apeire] apeiren UH; peire N; appaire ChK; apayryn J; payren W; pare E; peired V. hym] hem H; *om* W. be] with UJ; in E. p*ur*suide] p*ur*sued RDH[2]JWN; pursewed ChK; p*ur*suyed U; p*er*sewed E; haue p*ur*sued L; punissched V; p*re*ued H. wel ofte] feole sithes L. wel] ful DChH; hym E; hem W; hi*m* ful V; *om* UJN.

76 *copied after line* 73 H; *marked with cross* N. And] & eke HLKM; And als E; I haue A; *om* VWN. belowen] belowyn AM; bylowe R; belowȝ D; belowed K; Bylowlen N; yley on U; mislou*e*d E; apayryd (a(1) *above line same script*) J; ybulled H. hym(1)] hem H; *om* A. lordis] þe lord H. to(2)] do N. don] done JKN; do RDH[2]; make VH; gar E. hym(2)] hem H; *om* E. lese] lesyn J; leose VL; lose K; losse E; lost M. silu*er*] seluer VM; seoluer L; hys sylu*er* E.

77 And] To EM; Tho A; *om* VHW. don] done KN; Idon V; mad L; I made H; gar E. hise(1 *and* 2)] here H. frendis] freondes L. ben] be ChH[2]HE; byn K; beon L; to be*n* R. fon] foes E. þoruȝ] wi*th* DVHA. my] his U. tunge] wordes L; talys EA.

78–80 J *misplaces lines* 81–2 *after* 77 *thus:* 77–81–82–78–79—(*om* 80)—83; D *misplaces* 81–4 *after* 77 *thus:* 77–81–82–83–84–78–79–80–85.

78 *line om* HL. gode happis] godnes EAM. happis] happe ChVKW. greuide] greuyd UEK; greued RDChH[2]; greuyth AM; greueþ V; greuyn J; greuen W; greue N. wel] wol M; ful DVEW; *om* UJA. sore] sare E; ofte A.

79 *line om* HL. Betwyn] Betwix EW; Betwyxin J; Atwix N. hym] man J; men EAM. his] here A; ȝere M; þair E. meyne] meynye K; meigne M; mayne R; wyf WN; wyffes E. I . . . wraþþe] wratthe made ofte R. I haue] Ichaue V; haue I WN. mad] maked DK; makid A; Imad V; Imakede M. wraþþe] ofte wratthe U; striffe ofte E; wreche A.

80 *line om* HJL. Boþe] Bath E. his(1 *and* 2)] *om* EAKWNM. lyme] leme D; lyf VA. lif] leme A; leome V; lith E. was] *om* W. þoruȝ] be M. tunge] wikkyd tonge A.

81 Whanne] whon V; when ChLE; Qwan J; wahan M; And whan W; but whe*n* H; *om* N. mette] mete H[2]JWN. hym] *om* DWM. market] RUDJLKW NM; þe Market VHEA; a market TChH[2]. þ*at*] him þat M. most] so muche L. hatide] hatid HEA; hatede DM; hated RChLK; hate VJWN.

I hailside hym as hendely as I his frend were:
He is dou3tiere þanne I—I dar non harm don hym,
Ac hadde I maistrie & mi3t I wolde m*ur*dre hym for eu*ere*.
Whanne I come to þe [k]ir[k]e & knel[e] to þe rode, 85
To p*re*ye for þe peple as þe prest techiþ,
[For pilgrymes, for palmers, for all þe peple] aftir,
Þanne I cri3e on my knes þ*at* crist gyue hym sorewe
Þ*at* bar awey my bolle & my broken shete.
[Awey] fro þe auter myn ei3e I turne 90

82 I] Ich V. hailside] hailsed UHJ; halside H²; halsyd E; halsede D; halsed RChLK; hailse N; hals W; heylid A; heilede V; Grette M. hym] *om* W. as hendely] *defective* H. as(1)] als ChE; so L; *om* J. hendely] frendly DEAW. as(2) . . . frend] his frend as I V. as(2)] so L. frend] freonde L. were] weore VL; ware R; war K.
83 He] but he HE; 3yf he M. is] þ*at* is E; was HA; were M. dou3tiere] dou3thier R; dou3tiore V; dowhtyar J; strengere M; *defective* H. þanne] þen V; *defective* H; *om* E. I(1)] *om* E. I(2)] *om* R. dar] durste RHM. non . . . hym] bede hym none harm H. non] no ChEK; do W. don hym] hym done L. don] done JKN; do ChEW.
84 Ac] Bot ChVLKWNM; And E; 3if H; *om* A. hadde I] I hed E; y had had H. hadde] hedde V; haddy*n* R. I(1)] I þe WN. maistrie &] *defective* H. maistrie] mastrie K; maistre E. & mi3t] *om* JWN. &] or REK; oþer U. I(2) . . . eu*ere*] morthere hi*m* I wolde N. wolde] wald E; hadde H; *om* VM. m*ur*dre . . . eu*ere*] hym al at fort morthere W. m*ur*dre hym] him mayme L. m*ur*dre] murthre U; mourþre R; murþer ChE; mordre H²; mortheryn J; Morþerde V; mordred M; maymed H; a dystroyed A.
85 Whanne] when ChHLE; whon V; Qwan J. come] came KM; cam A. to . . . kirke] :::::::::::::che H. to(1)] tho H². þe] *om* M. kirke] ChLEAN; chirche TUH²JKW; cherche RM; Churche DV. &] to HW; & suld E; I M. knele] RUChH²VHJEWN; kneole L; knelide T; knelid A; kneled DKM. to(2)] byfore RV; beforn A; afore U. rode] rude E.
86 To] I JLA; And scholde V. p*re*ye] preyn M; prei3e V; praye RW; pray DHJLEKN; p*ri*ye H²; preyd A. peple] pepele M; people LK; puple A. prest] preost L. techiþ] techeþ ChLWNM; techys E; teches D; vs techeþ V; me techith U; me techys R; p*re*chiþ H.
87 For . . . peple] EAWM; *om* TRUDCh H²VHJLKN. pilgrymes] pilgrames E. for all] & for A; & alle M. þe] *om* M. peple] puple A. aftir] *with line* 88 TRU DH²K; eft*er* E; & aft*er* (*with line* 88) J; *om* ChVHLN.
88 Þanne . . . knes] On my knes þan I cryed A. Þanne] þan LEKM; þenne ChV; þ*en* H; Aftre þat W; þat U; *om* DJ. I cri3e] crie I L; kryed I M; bidde I H; knelyd I E. cri3e] crye RDChH²VJKW; cried N; p*ra*y U. on . . . knes] on mekely K; wiþ my mouþ H; as cof W. on] vppon VE. knes] knees UDChH²JNM; kneys RE; kneoes L. þ*at*] & praed E; *om* RU. crist] god AW; oure lady RU. gyue] gyf REWN (*altered from* 3yf R); 3yue UV; 3if JAM; geue DCh; 3eue HK; 3ef L. hym] he*m* RVHAWN; hom L; þaim E. sorewe] serwe V.
89 bar awey] brokyn A. bar] baar D; bere K; beryn M; haþ Ibore V. bolle] blake bolle H²; bolles LN. my broken] borne awey my A. broken] broke DJKN; brode RUV. shete] schetes L.
90 *line om* L; *divided from following after* turne K; *after* t*ur*ned EAM; *after* cast W; *after* beholde TRUDChH²VJN; *after* heyne H. Awey] Also AM; And also E; þan W; & N; *om* TRUDChH²VHJK. fro] to forne A. myn . . . turne] y turne myn ei3e UV; y t*ur*ne me H; I myn eien cast W. myn] 3it myne A. ei3e] eye RD; nye J; eyen K; eyne AM; ene E; hiegh N. I] down than I K. turne] t*ur*ned EM; turnyd A.

⁊ beholde how heyne haþ a newe cote;
[Þanne] I wysshe it were myn [and al þe webbe aftir].
Of his lesing I lauȝe; [it liȝtiþ] myn herte,
Ac of his wynnyng I wepe and weile þe tyme.
I deme men *þere* [hy] don ille, ⁊ ȝet I do wers; 95
I wolde þ*at* iche wiȝt were my knaue;
And whoso haþ more þanne I, þ*at* angriþ myn herte.
Þus I lyue loueles, [lyk] a lyþ*er* dogge,

91 *as one line with following* TRUDChH². ⁊] y L. beholde] byholde byholde L; byhelde REAM; byholde heyne H; beholdith K. how . . . cote] byhynde me on a neowe kote haue L. how] *om* M. heyne] hayne RUN; hane W; hyne A; herry Ch; hoge J; hyk K; he H; an hyne M; mony E. haþ] had AW; hed E; þat hadde M. a] *om* E. cote] coteȝ E; cloke A; Cote and his wyf anoþer VHJN.
92 Þanne] LN; þan JEAKM; þe*n*ne V; þen H; Anon W; *om* TRUDChH². I wysshe] wische y HL. I] Ich V. wysshe] wussche V; wyschid A; wischede M; wissyd E; wissed Ch. it] þat þai E. were] weore VL; war K. myn] DVHJLEAKWNM; myn owne Ch; my*n* owen U; my owne H²; my*n* owe R; myn howne (howne *in another hand*) T. and . . . aftir] AVHJLEKWNM; *om* TRUDChH². and] w*ith* E. þe] his H. webbe] *same hand after cancelled* wed K; webbeȝ E; wele H. *Here* RU *add a line: see above,* p. 50.
93 Of] RUVHJLAKWNM; At E; And of TChH²; And alwey aft*er* D. his] þair E; þat M; *om* H². lesing] losyng D; leosinge VL; loysyng E. lauȝe] lawhe JA; lawgh N; lagh W; lauȝhe H; lauhwe V; laghwe L; lugh E; laught M; smyle RU. it liȝtiþ] it liȝteþ NW; hit lightenes L; ⁊ light was E; hit likeþ VHK; it likith J; ay lykeng*e* M; a lytil A; and þerof lauȝeth RU; þerof TDChH². myn] my*n* RUHJLKWN; in myn TDChH²AM; me in myn V; *om* E. herte] heorte L; harte K.
94 Ac] But ChLKWM; And RHN; *om* EA. of] for VHJEW. his] þair E; *om* M. wynnyng] willyng*e* M. wepe] weope L; wepyd E; wepte A. weile] waile UHK; weylid A; weyld D; wailed Ch; werys E. tyme] while LA.
95 *as two lines divided after* ille A; *after* euyll E. I . . . ille] *om* M. I] And I E. men] *om* EWN. þ*ere*] in my hert EA; *om* VHJLKWN. hy] þei TRDChH²HL; þat VJK; þat he W; þat þai A; þ*at* men N; at mony E; y U. don] do RUChN; doþ W; doys E. ille] euele D; euyll E; eouel L; yuel HN. ⁊] But A. ȝet] ȝit ChVHJEAWM; ȝut R; ȝiȝt N. I do] I done K; do I ChL. wers] worse DHLKWN; wel wors ChV; werse be dom of my selfe AM; me wel wers I do me on my seluen (me(1) *cancelled*) E.
96 *line om* DWN. I] For I VHE. wolde] wald E; couet J. þat] *om* L. iche] eche H²KM; ech RU; vche L; eche a A; ech a Ch; vch a V; alle H; eu*er*y J; eu*er*ilke E. wiȝt] wyȝth R; wythe A; wyȝe L; man JM; wiht i*n* þis world V; wiȝtes in world H. were] weore L; wer*e* becomy*n* J; wer becomon E. knaue] knawe AW; knaffe E; knaues H; knaue in þis world wonyng L.
97 *line om* V. And] *om* WN. whoso] hoso A; qwasa E; Who þat W; qwo þat J; whad þat L. haþ] hase E; haue A. more] mare E. þanne] þe*n* HE. þat] it HAWM; he L; þan Ch; *om* E. angriþ] angreþ RChKWN; angret D; angereth L; hangerth M; gretly angers E; greuyth A. herte] heorte L; harte K. *Here* U *repeats line* 96.
98 Þus] Bot þus E; And þus AWN. lyue] lif J; leue DChH²EAW. loueles] lofles J; lawles E. lyk] RUDVHLEKWNM; liche JA; as TChH². lyþ*er*] leþer DChH; lethir E; luþer V; leother L; lyder M; ledur A.

[Þat] al my brest bolniþ for bittir of my galle.
May no sugre ne swet þing swage it an vnche, 100
Ne no dyapendyon dryue it fro myn herte.
ȝif shrift shulde, it shop[e] a gret wondir.'
'ȝis, redily,' quaþ repentaunce & redde hym to goode:
'Sorewe for synne sauiþ wel manye.'
'I am sory,' q*ua*þ enuye, 'I am but selde oþ*ere*, 105
And þat makiþ me so ma[t] for I ne may me venge.'
Þanne com coueitise; I can hym nouȝt descryue,

99 Þat] þ*at* RUVHJLEKNM; And TD ChH²A; Than W. al] *om* J. my . . . bolniþ] bolnyth my breste U. bolniþ] bolneþ RChLKWNM; bolnet D; bolnes E; bolliþ H; Bolleþ V. bittir] bitt*er* DCh VHJAWNM; bittre LK; byter RU; bit*ur* H²; bitt*er*nes E. my(2)] *om* E. *Here* W *adds lines like* **B** V 120–1 *or* **C** VII 86–7: *see above*, p. 31.
100 *marked with cross* N. May] þ*er* may J; þ*ere* nys N; Ther is W. sugre] sugor H²; sucre U; sewkyr J. ne] ne no DAM; nor K; no ChL; so VW. þing] *om* VW. swage it] swagit A. swage] swagen U; asswage K; aswagy*n* J; may swage WN; swete R; dryue VH. it] me E. an vnche] an Inche DChJLKWM; on ynche E; an vche N; from myn herte VH.
101 Ne] Ny L; Nor K. no] no*n* RH²JA. dyapendyon] Diopendion V; diapondiou*n* J; diapenydion UDH²WN; dyapendron A; dyapodyou*n* M. dryue] driuyn J; drawe A; draugh M; aswagen VH. fro . . . herte] vnneþe V; vneþ H. herte] heorte L; hart K.
102 ȝif] RDVHJN; And ȝif AE; And þanne ȝef L; ȝif þ*at* TUH²M; And ȝif þat WChK. shrift] scryfte H²J; schrit V; any schryft L; ony schiryfte M. shulde] suld E. it shope] aswage it H; *om* W. it] me þinke it N; hit þe*n*ne V; me J. shope] schope ChKNM; schepe D; shop T; wer*e* RU; stoppe H²EA; saue JL; swopen out V. a] semed hit a L; nowe a W; it were A; it wer E; *om* RHJ. gret] *om* HJW. wondir] wonder hit were VW; wonder me þinkeþ H; me thingith it wer*e* wonder*e* J.
103 ȝis] ȝus VL; Yes K; A ȝis A; Þus E. redily] redly R; rede I E. redde] rede H²; red DEA; radde UVHLKNM; rad J. hym] hem W. to] *om* EAM. goode] þe best HEAM.
104 Sorewe] Sorowe DChK; Sorow JEN; sorwe RUA; Sorwȝ H²; Serw V; Oft sorwe W; And saide sorwe L. for] for his D; for her*e* H; for heore V; of her J. synne] synnes EKNM; synnys JA; su*n*nes V; synneþ H. sauiþ] saueþ RUCh H²VHLWNM; saves E; saue D. wel] wol UM; ofte wel L; ful HE; men ful V; *om* A. manye] Monye V; many on A.
105 Here collation of H³ **begins.** I] Ich V; And I K. am(1)] ame K; *om* M. enuye] þat sherew N; þat scharewe M. am(2)] ame K; ham M; nam HW; ne am V. but] *om* KH³. selde] selden KN; seldyn J; seldene V; seilden L; sylden M; seldom UEAWH³. oþere] þ*er* E. *Here* A *adds a line: see above*, p. 48.
106 And] *om* U. þat] it H³; *om* L. makiþ] makyt H³; makeþ RDChVLKWNM; mak*es* E. so] ful H³; *om* EW. mat] NH³; mate JK; mad TRUDH²VHLAW; madde ChEM. for] þat JLA; *om* W. ne . . . me] may me not W; may me nouȝt N; may not AH³. ne] no L; *om* Ch. venge] venge*n* H; wenge R; avengyn J; awe*n*ge N; be vengyd H³.
107 Þanne] þenne V; þen H. com] cam UK; cometh M; cam sone A; come sire W. coueitise] Couetous M; co*n*cyens H³. can] couþe V. hym nouȝt] not hym DM. hym] *om* U. nouȝt] not RVHA KW. descryue] discryue DChH²HLKW; descreue N; discreue V; descrye U; discrye RAM; discry E; discr*i*yn J; dyscryȝe H³.

So hungirly ⁊ holewe sire heruy hym lokide. 108
He was [betil]browid ⁊ babirlippid | wiþ two bleride eiȝen,
[And] as a l[e]þerene purs lollide his chekis. *fol.* xxxvj *a*
In a torn tabbard of twelue wynter age,
But ȝif a lous couþe lepe, I may it nouȝt leue
He shulde wandre on þat walsshe, so was it þredbare.

108 *marked with cross* **N**. So] Bote L. hungirly] hongurliche L; hungryly N; hungrely E; hongrely DW; hungry UV HJAKMH³; angrey R. ⁊ . . . lokide] he lokede syre heruy ⁊ holwe H³; he loketh ser heruy ⁊ holowe M; he lokid so heri ⁊ so ille A; he lukyd as a hotte of hell E. ⁊] and so RUVWN; so K. holewe] holowe DChKN; holwe RUHJ; holgh W; lowe L. heruy] henri WN; heuy (? heny) Ch. hym] he ChLW; þanne N. lokide] lokyd J; loked RDCh VHKN; loketh LW.

109–10 *divided after* eiȝen VHJLKWN; *after* baberlypped RDM; *after* boþe TCh H²; *after* biterbrowed U. EAMH³ *copy expanded* 109b *as a separate line.*

109 He] *om* WN. was] *om* EWN. betilbrowid] betyllbrowyd E; betilbrowed ChKM; bedilbrowyd J; bittilbrowid AH³; Bitilbrowed WN; bitelbrowid H; bitelbrowed L; bitelbrouwed V; bittirbrowid T; byterbrowed R; betterbrowed D; babirlippid U; baburlippud H². ⁊] and eke RUDAMH³; ⁊ alswa E; *om* V. babirlippid] HJAH³; baberlypped RDL WM; baberlippid N; babirlippid boþe TCh; blaberlipped K; blaburlepyd E; biterbrowed U; biturbrowed bothe H²; *om* V. two] to AM; too D; twei VL; twa E. bleride] blerid UH²JEK; blered RDChV LWNM; blereyd A; blere eyid H³; brode H. eiȝen] eyen RDKW; eyn N; iȝen H; Ien J; yghnen L; eyn as a blynd hagge AM; ene like a blynd asse E; eyne blynd as an hagge H³.

110 *divided from following after* purs RU. And] VHJLEAKWNMH³; *om* TRUD ChH². as] also E; eken as L; lik DV; *om* A. a] *om* M. leþerene] letherene H³; leþeren DChW; letheryn J; letherne H²VHN; lethern U; lethren L; leþer RK; letheron E; ledren M; lederend A; liþerene T. lollide . . . chekis] *om* U. lollide] lollid H²HK; lolled RDChN; lolleden L; lolledyn J; lullede V; lokede H³; lokened M; honged W; so lokyd A; likerd wer E. his] bothe his L. chekis] chekyn J. *Here* MH³ *add lines like* **B** V 194–5 *or* **C** VII 201–2; E *adds one line like* **B** V 194 *or* **C** VII 201: *see above*, p. 31.

111 A *substitutes* Had an hatte on his heed ⁊ is hood also (*cf.* **B** V 195). a] *om* K. torn] toren V; torun M; tore RUH³; to torne K; nold turned E; broun H. twelue] twefue W; twenty L. age] old H; alde E.

112 L *substitutes two lines* A lous myghte not launce þer on for failyng of fote Bote he hadde beo schod with forstnaile schrap al abowte. ȝif] ȝef Ch; *om* U. couþe] coude RUDChH²JAMH³; could K. lepe] renne J. I . . . leue] I leue nouth I trowe H³; leue þou for soþe W; or flee as I trow E; ⁊ schippe as I trowe A. may] con V. it] *om* H²N. nouȝt] not RUDH²VHK; wele J. leue] leuen M; lleue VHN; trowe RUDJK.

113 He] Heo V; Sho E; She WM; he ne Ch; þat he ne RU; how heo H. shulde] suld JE; xuld H³; myght M. wandre] not wandre AW; not wanderyn H³; nat wandre H²; noght wandir E; not haue wandred L; walke H; renne J; slyde R; slideren U. on . . . walsshe] þeron RU; þer vpon M; þeron ȝerne J; or walke ther K. walsshe] welche N; walsshe scarlet TDChH²; wede HLEH³; walk V; wolde A; lugh W. so . . . bare] for wantyng of wolle L. so . . . it] hit was so VHMH³. it] *om* U. þredbare] bare R.

'I haue [ben] coueit[ous],' quaþ [þat caitif], 'I [bi]knowe [hit] h[e]re,
For sum tyme I *seruide* symme at þe nok 115
And was his *prentis* ypliȝt his *profit* to loke.
Ferst I lernide to leiȝe a lef o*þer* tweiȝe;
Wykkidly to weiȝe was my ferste lessou*n*.
To wynchestre & to wy I [wente] to þe feire
Wiþ many man*er* marchaundise as my maist*er* me hiȝte. 120

114 *marked with cross* N; *divided from following after* tyme TChH[2]; *after* lyue D; *as two lines divided after* tyme RU. I haue] Ichaue V; I W. ben . . . caitif] q*uod* þat kaityf couetouse beo L; am caytif coueitous q*uod* he W. ben] VJEAMH[3]; be HN; byn K; yloued R; ylouid T; loued DChH[2]; louyd U. coueitous] Couetous VHJA NH[3]; coutous M; coueitise TRUDH[2]K; couatyse E; conscience Ch. quaþ] *om* UH[2]. þat caitif] HH[3]; þat caytefe A; þ*at* katyf EN; þis Caityf VK; þe caytefe JM; he al my lyue D; he al my lif tyme TRCh; al my lif tyme UH[2]. I(2)] well I E; and R. biknowe . . . hire] am it wel aknowe W. biknowe] byknowe H; beknowe VJAKMH[3]; byknewe N; knowe TRUDChH[2]L; knaw E. hit] h*it* RUVH JLEKNMH[3]; *om* TDChH[2]A. here] DHJE AKNMH[3]; her Ch; heere V; hire TH[2]; now here L; her*e* befor*e* crist and his swete moder R; here byfore crist & his clene modir U.

115 E *corrupts to* And qwen I *ser*uyd synne me thoght it semyd wele. I *ser*uide] serued I U; serwed I R. I] whan I W. *ser*uide] seruid H[2]JAKMH[3]; seruede V; serued DChHLWN. symme . . . nok] synne it þouth me mery A; synne it semed me merthe M; symony it semyd to me myrthe H[3]. symme] Syme K; symou*n* H; to symond L. at þe] atte DH[2]VJLW; at ChN.

116 *line om* HE. And] I AWNMH[3]. prentis ypliȝt] pliht prentys V. ypliȝt] Iplygte M; Iplyth H[3]; yplyȝþ R; plight LKN; aplight UW; aplite JA. his] it **þout me** mery is A. loke] wayte M; wayten A; waytene H[3].

117 *line om* A. Ferst] First UChJEKWN; Furst RH[2]VH; And furste L; For MH[3]. I lernide] lernyde y U. lernide] lernyd H[2]JKH[3]; lerned RDChHWN; lerened M; leornede V; leorned L; leryd E. to] of E. leiȝe] liȝe ChH[2]VHH[3]; lye RUD KWNM; lyen JL; leyng E. lef] leef UH[2]JN; lessun VH; lesing ChM. oþer] oyþ*er* J; or ChVLM; or elles E. tweiȝe] tweye UH[2]JL; twey ChW; tweyne RD VM; twayne K; two HN; twa E.

118 Wykkidly] wyckudly H[2]; & wickedly HV. to weiȝe] towrie Ch. to] for to VHKN. weiȝe] weygh N; weie VHW; weyen DLM; weyn A; wey E; way K; wynne RU; wirke þo J. was . . . lessou*n*] formest I lerned W; c*er*tis was þe þridde H. ferste] firste UChEK; furste RH[2]L; fryst AH[3]; oþer V; nexst JN.

119 *line om* A. To] Fro H[3]. wynchestre] wenchestr*e* H; wynchelsey Ch; ware E; wy M; sleytforth H[3]. &] *om* H[3]. to(2)] *om* ChJ. wy] wey K; wych V; wynchester ChEMH[3]; wellis H; woborne L; wyrcetr*e* J. I wente] went I E. I] Ich V. wente] RUVHJLWNMH[3]; wente me K; was sent TChH[2]; sende D. þe] *om* K. feire] faire ChJLKW; fare E; feires H.

120 *line om* A. Wiþ] to R. many] mony V. maner] RUVHJLKWNMH[3]; man*er* of TChH[2]E; *om* D. marchaundise] m*er*chau*n*dise HEK; marchau*n*die RM; marchaundeys J; marchandises D. as] þat L. maister] Master K. me] myd L; *om* VJEKWNMH[3]. hiȝte] hyth H[3]; hytt J; hieght N; heghte M; het R; hote K; bad H; tauȝte UChH[2] (*altered from* touȝt Ch); aght E; medled L.

Ne hadde [þe] gr*a*ce of gile gon among my ware
It hadde be vnsold þis seue ȝer, so me god helpe.
Þanne drouȝ I me among drap*er*s my donet to lere,
To drawe þe list along, þe leng*er*e it semide;
Among þe riche rayes I rendrit a lessoun; 125
Brochide hem wiþ a pakke nedle, & pleit hem togid*er*e;
Putte hem in a p*re*ss*our*, & pynnede hem þ*er*einne
Til ten ȝardis oþ*er* twelue tollide out þrittene.
My wyf was a wynst*er*e & wollene cloþ made,

121 Ne hadde] hadde not M. Ne] No L; Bote VH. hadde] had JLAKWNH^3; hed E; nadde H; nedde V. þe] RUVHJLEKW NH^3; *om* TDChH^2AM. gile] god *corrected same hand to* gile U; gyle good A. gon] gone JKM; go RH^3; goon W; gane E; Igon VN; ygo H; ben A. among] aye emang E. **122** hadde] hedde V; hed E; nad W. be vnsold] vnsold beon L. be] ben UDV JEANMH^3; byn K; ofte be H. vnsold] onsolde ChH^2; onsould K; vnsald E; vnseld H^3; onselde M; sold W. þis . . . ȝer] *om* HM. þis] thes K. seue] seuen VJE; seuene ChH^2AWN; sevyn K; seouen L; vij RU DH^3. ȝer] ȝeer D; ȝeir L; yer*es* K. so . . . helpe] Iwys E. helpe] saue L; *defective* H. **123** Þanne . . . me] I was M. Þanne] þenne V; *om* HE. drouȝ I] I drouȝ V; I drowe HE. drouȝ] drow RUDChJANH^3; drewe K. me] *om* E. among] emang E; to UWN. drap*er*s] þis drap*er*s V; þese drap*er*es H. donet . . . lere] *defective* H. to] for to JA. lere] lerne WMH^3; leorne V. **124** To] & M. drawe] drawyn J; drowe RM. list] listes L; lyser J; lysour U; leser RN; lesour WH^3. along] o long J; on longe AH^3; a lang D; on lengh W; wel along V; of lenth E. þe(2) . . . semide] on teyntre we hit tileden L. leng*er*e] leng*ur* H^2A; lengore V; langer E. it semide] *defective* H. semide] semyd JEAKNH^3; semede V; semed DChH^2W M; semyth U; semeþ R. **125** Among] Emong E; And among A. þe] þis V. rayes] rayȝes J; raynes L. I rendrit] rendred I M; lernde I V; lerned I H; þ*er* lernyd I H^3. rendrit] rendrid U; renderid JAK; rendred RDLWN; rendrede H^2; renderd E; lerned Ch. a] þe same L; my fyrst A. **126** Brochide] Brochid H^2HEAH^3; Brochede V; broched RDChJN; And broched L; I broched M; prochid U; Prycked KW. hem] þaim E; him M; he*m* on H^3; *om* L. a] *om* E. pakke nedle] pak neelde V; pacneld HL; bat nedil A; bat nedyls E; bety*n*g nedyl H^3; prikede nedele M; nedel D. &] *om* U. pleit] pleited HN; playted RK; playtyd JE; pletede V; plite Ch; plited WM; plytyd H^3; platte A; platted L; ypleyted U; pleyȝt H^2; plyȝte D. hem] heo*m* L; þaim E; hym M. **127** Putte] & putte HJEMH^3; And puppe A. hem(1)] heom L; þaim E; him M. p*re*ss*our*] p*re*sse HW; pryson M. pynnede] pyn*n*ed RUDChW; pyn*n*yd KH^3; pinde *inked by late corrector* H^2; pyned AM; pynyd J; peyned HLN; pilyd E. hem(2)] heom L; þaim E; hym MH^3; hem to A. þ*er*einne] þere W. **128** *line om* RU. Til] to E. ȝardis] ȝardes LK; ȝerdis HJAH^3; ȝerdes ChH^2VENM; ȝerde DW. oþ*er*] or DChJLEAKW NMH^3. twelue] twelf E; twelw W; thwelfe A; twolue L. tollide] tollid H^2; tolled ChKWN; tylyd E; telled D; tolde H; tolden VLM; toldyn JH^3; drow A. out] *om* DH. þrittene] þrettene DCh VLK; thretene JA; þreten W; tretene E; thertene H^3; xiij HN; xv M. **129** *marked with cross* N; *run together with following* L. My] And my VH. wyf] self Ch. was a wynst*er*e] at westmynst*r*e H; at westmu*n*stre V. wynst*er*e] wy*n*nestre RDL; vy*n*nestre N; wyndster E; weuester (? wenester) Ch; wevest*er* K; webbester*e* M; webstere AWH^3; webst*er* J; webber*e* H^2; breust*er*e U. & . . . made] *om* L. &] þat VH. wollene] wollen RUDH^2H JEKWN; wullen Ch; wolnon M. cloþ] clath E; clothys H^3. made] maked D; wroght W; worched K.

And spak to þe spynst*ere* to spynnen it softe. 130
Þe pound þ*at* heo [payede] by peisid a quart*er* more
Þanne [myn owne] aunsel dede, [whanne] I weiȝede treweþe.
I bouȝte hire barly; heo breuȝ it to selle.
Penyale & pilewhey heo pouride togid*ere*.
For labo*ur*eris & louȝ folk þ*at* lay be h[y]mselue; 135
Þe beste in my bedchaumbre lay be þe wouȝ.
And whoso bu*m*mide þ*er*of, bouȝte it þ*er*eaftir,

130 And . . . spynst*ere*] *om* L. And] And sho E; Ȝhe A; She N; I H^{3}; *om* VH. þe] here H; *om* DENM. spynst*ere*] spinster ChH^{2}; spynnestre R; spynstre K; spinsteres W; spinsters VHE; spynestres N; spynst*er*ys JMH^{3}; spynneris A. to] for to VLA. spynnen] spynny*n* J; spynne RDChVLEAKNH^{3}; spyne M. it] *om* A. softe] so softe R; out AM; þ*er* owt EH^{3}.

131 *divided from following after* qwarter LEAMH^{3}. Þe] two H. þ*at*] at E. heo] *late corrector prefixes* s H^{2}; he R; ȝhe A; sho E; sche UDJKWNMH^{3}; I Ch. payede] paied LWN; payid H^{3}; payd E; payde A; payȝed J; paysed K; peysed H; peysede V; weid T; weyed UH^{2}; weyȝed Ch; way DM; weyes R. by] hem by KH^{3}; heom by L; hi*m* by M; to hym D; hem A; for EW; *om* VH. peisid] peysed DCh; peisede (*added by original scribe at end of line*) V; paysed KN; pysed M; it peysid A; passyd EH^{3}; passed L; weied HW; weyeþ R; was U. quart*er*] quatar E; quartrun V. more] Mare E.

132 Þanne] þen VHE. myn . . . dede] it is dede by myn ansere W; it augthe H^{3}. myn owne] L; my*n* awn J; my awne E; myn VHNM; my A; ony RUD; any T; þe ChH^{2}; *om* K. aunsel dede] almesdede RU. aunsel] Aunser DKN; hauncer M; poundur A; selfe J; *om* LE. dede] ded K; dide H^{2}H; did JN; deode L; dude V; *om* EM. whanne . . . weiȝede] þat was lytil A. whanne] whan UDKWNM; whon V; when HL; whem R; qwan JH^{3}; qwen E; & TChH^{2}. I] sche U. weiȝede] weyede UV; weyed RHKW; weye L; waye M; wey ChJE; way D; weygh N; waugh H^{3}. treweþe] trewþe DLAM; treuthe UH^{2}VHJWH^{3}; trowþe ChN; trothe E; truþe RK.

133 I] My wyf M. bouȝte] brouȝt N; broght W; browt A. hire] hir JENH^{3}; her*e* UDA; her ChK; hure R; hir*e* also H; here also W; *om* M. barly] barlich LW; barly malt JN. heo] ȝhe A; sho E; sche RUDChJKWNH^{3}; and heo (*late corrector prefixes* s) H^{2}; & M. breuȝ] breuh V; brew RUDChH^{2}HJANMH^{3}; brewed LK W; browyd E. selle] sulle V; seolle L; sale RJ; seluen M.

134 Penyale] Pany hale M; Boþe penyale W. pilewhey] pilwhay H^{2}; peleway*e* ChE; pelawey A; pigwhey R; pilwyle J; pylewile LN; pylqwyt H^{3}; piriwhit V; periwhit H; pilewhew U; pele was D; pewe W; spilawaye M. heo pouride] put sche H^{3}. heo] *late corrector prefixes* s H^{2}; ȝhe A; sho E; sche RUDChJKWNM; ofte heo L. pouride] pourid N; pourede V; poured L; powrid HJA; powred ChE; pored DM; pured RK; poured it W.

135 labo*ur*eris] labouros U; laborelis A. &] for RU. louȝ] litel L; lewid HEA; pouere M; lond W; lowd H^{3}; loþ RUD. folk] folkes D. þ*at*] it ANM; she W. lay] layne J; liþe Ch; lyth A; layd it W; lyued L; lyueþ R; lyuen UVH; hym] ChKM; it WN; þe A; hem TRUDH^{2} VHJH^{3}; heom L; þaim E. selue] seluen VEM; seluy*n* H^{3}; seoluen L; silue*n* H.

136 my] þe VH. bed] *om* H. lay] þat laye Ch; lith U; it lyth A. wouȝ] wowe DChVHJAWNH^{3}; walle EK; wowes UM; walles R; benche L.

137 And] *om* VH. whoso] ho so JAH^{3}; Hose V; qwa sa E. bu*m*mide] bu*m*myd DJ; Bu*m*mede V; bu*m*med UChH^{2}KWN; bybbyd H^{3}; bubbith A; boused R; dronke H; drong L; drange M; boght E. þ*er*of] hereof E. bouȝte] bout A; he bouȝt U; shulde bye H; paied W; payid H^{3}. it þ*er*eaftir] for a grote E. it] *om* WH^{3}.

A galoun for a grote, god wot no lasse,
Whanne it com in cuppemel; þ*at* craft my wyf vside.
Rose þe reg*ratour* was hire riȝte name; 140
Sheo haþ yholde huxt*er*ie elleuene wynt*er*.
Ac I swere now, so þ[e I], þat synne shal I lete,
Ne neu*er*e wykkidly weiȝe ne wykkide chaffare make,
But wende to walsyngh*am*, ⁊ my wyf alse,
And bidde þe rode of bromholm bringe me out of dette.' 145
Now begynneþ glotoun for to [go to] shrift,
And ca[iriþ] hym to [k]ir[k]eward hise [coupe] to shewe.

138 A] Ay a W. no] ⁊ no A. lasse] lesse RUDChEKWNMH^3.
139 Whanne] whon V; When RLE; qwa*n* H^3; And so W. com] cam AKNM; cometh UH. in] to E; *om* W. cuppemel] coppe ale R; copnale E; coppis medelid A. þ*at* . . . wyf] it ȝhe ⁊ þat craft A. þ*at*] þis J; þe N; such V; siche H. craft] craftes V. my wyf] heo H; me V. vside] vsyd EAH^3; vsede V; vsed RUDChH^2 KWN; vsiþ H; vseth L.
140 þe] *om* N. was] is UV; wyttyly I wote was J; whos rykeneth right was L. hire] hir JEKNH^3; here UDAWM; her Ch; hur*e* R. riȝte] *om* JL.
141 Sheo] Heo VHL; Ȝhe A; Sho E; sche RUDChH^2JKWNMH^3. haþ] hat H^2; had JKN; hade E; hadde A; *om* R. yholde] holde DChHH^3; holden UVJL KWN; holdyn AM; haldyn E; haldeþ R. huxt*er*ie] hockestrye K; hukstrerye D; osterye U; hostrye M; ostrye RA; ostryȝe H^3; ostre E. elleuene] wel elleoue L; long eleue A; þis elleuen ChV; þis xj RU; þis xv M; al þis xxx^{ti} H. wynt*er*] wynt*er*es lang E.
142 Ac] Bote VJLEKM; but now H; And RNH^3; Now wil W; *om* ChA. swere] assure E. now] you E; *om* HAW MH^3. so þe I] so þike N; so mote I the AMH^3; als mot I the E; so I think J; to þe L; soþely ChHK; soþly TRUH^2W; soþliche D; *om* V. þat] þis A; *om* ChM. synne] sunne V; sum tyme M. shal I] schal be A; dyd she E; to W. shal] xal H^3; wil JN; wol VH. lete] lette K; leue HLW; leuen M; lafte A; neuer ChE.
143 Ne] And VHJLEKWN; I schal A; *om* MH^3. neu*er*e] Neyþ*er* H^3. wykkidly weiȝe] weye wyckedely RW; weyȝyn wikkedly J; wynne wykkidly U. weiȝe] weygh N; weye DVLK; wey Ch; to wey E; forto weye H; werke A; to wynne M. ne] no ChL; ne no RU. wykkide] wiked ChL; wikke NM; wik (? k *imperfect*) J; fals VHA; c*ur*syd E; *om* RUW. chaffare] chaffer ChE; cheffar*e* H; chaffre KN; c*ra*fte JA. make] makyn J; vse H; vsen V; vsyn A; myschaunge W.
144 wende] wenden LK; wendyn JM; weende V; wyndyn A; I wil wend E; wend I wil W. alse] als WH^3; also DCh HK; alswa E; after RJN; boþe A.
145 bidde] bidden M; byddyn J; byd DLAN; pray E. þe] to þe W. rode] good rode A. bringe] bringgy*n* J; to brynge U. me] vs UAWH^3; *om* E. out] outȝ H^2. dette] that dette K; deth A; synne L.
146 Now] But now D; Than W. begynneþ] begynnys E; ginneþ V; by gille L. glotoun] þe Gloton VH; glotony E. for] *om* EAMH^3. go to] RUDChH^2VH JLKWN; gon on MH^3; gang on E; gon A; *om* T. shrift] schreft Ch; chirche K; cherche W; his wey A; hys weyȝe H^3; hy way E; his wyse M.
147 cairiþ] kaireth LN; carith A; karyd E; caryyth J; carieþ RChVK; caried UD; cariede TH^2; koueryth H^3; kouerereth M; wendiþ H; shope W. hym] *om* EAKMH^3. kirkeward] ChN; þe kirke E; chircheward TUDH^2VHJLK; churcheward R; chirche AH^3; Cherche M; shriftwarde W. coupe] N; culpe KH^3; cowlpe E; countis A; gilt J; synne RU; synnes TDChH^2WM; schrift VHL. to] for to UHJLEAW; forte V. shewe] telle V; lete W.

And Betou*n* þe breust*er*e bad h[ym] good morewe,
And heo askide of hym whidirward he wolde.
'To holy chirche,' quaþ he, 'for to here masse, 150
And siþen I wile be shriuen & synne no more.'
'I haue good ale, gossib,' q*ua*þ heo; 'glotou*n*, wilt þou assaie?'
'Hast þou,' quaþ he, 'any hote spices?'
'ʒa, glotoun gossib,' quaþ heo, 'god wot, wel hote: | *fol.* xxxvj *b*
I haue pepir, & p[ye]nye, & a pound of garlek, 155

148 And] þe*n*ne V; Bot EM; Sone W; *om* HN. Betou*n*] bele H. breust*er*e] brewer*e* M; bribester L. bad] ChH²VLE AKWN; badde M; sche bad H³; þ*er*e bad TRUDJ; þen bade H. hym] hy*m* RUChVHLEWNMH³; he TDH²JK; here A. good] goud R; gude E. morewe] morowe DChJKN; morwe RUH²VHA WMH³; morwen L; morne E.
149 And] And seþþen V; And eke L; Fast W. heo] *late corrector prefixes* s H²; she RUDChJEKWNMH³; *om* LA. askide] askid UHEAH³; asked DVLK; axid M; axede R; axed ChH²J; axed þanne N; frayned W. of] *om* ChJAW. hym] him þoo J. whidirward] whiderward UH²; whiderworde N; whedirward D; wheder-ward RChW; whetherward K; whideward L; wyderword J; qwedyrward H³; woderward M; wheþ*er* H; whedur A; qwede*r* E; whoder V. he] þat he VHEA. wolde] walde AE; fared W.
150 To] Tho A. chirche] cherche WNM; churche H; kirke E. for] þ*er*e N. here] heryn M; heare K. masse] messe UEAW NH³; a masse L.
151 And] *om* W. siþen] Siþ W; sytthy*n* H³; sytthe R; siþþe H; sethen D; sethin J; seþþen ChV; seothen L. I . . . shriuen] beo schryuen wol y L. I wile] Ichule V; wil I WN; sall I E; *om* A. wile] wol UHK; shal M; xal H³. be shriuen] shreuen be E; shrive me W; chryue me N. be] ben V. shriuen] schreuen Ch; schreuy*n* H³; shreue R; Ischriuen V; be scheeuyn (?) A. synne no] neue*r* synne E. synne] synnen LM; sy*n*ny*n* JH³; sunge V. no] na U. more] mare E.
152 I . . . heo] A gossib q*uo*d she I haue good ale W. I haue] Ichaue V. good] goud R; gude E. gossib] gosseb Ch; goseppe A; gosop EK; Cossip N; glotyn J; *om* UDLM. q*ua*þ . . . glotou*n*] gloton q*uo*d sche K. q*ua*þ heo] *om* EANH³. heo] *late corrector prefixes* s H²; she RU DCh; che J; syb M. glotou*n*] to glotoun L; gossyb D; gossyp J; *om* HWMH³. wilt þ*o*u] wylt tow H²; wyttow J; wolt þou HK; woltou V; with good heorte L; com ner & M.
153 Hast þou] hauest þou D; Hafeʒ þou E; Ye but hastow W; hastow ought U; hastow oght L; Hastow oute JA; hast þou ouʒt in þy pors H; Hastou ouʒt I þi pors V; ʒe hastow ought in þi p*ur*se N. quaþ he] *om* N. he] he þan W; herry AH³; heruy M. any] eny VHN; ony RUDH²EAM; of any L. hote] hate E. spices] spyce E.
154 *divided from following after* haue H. ʒa] ʒe RDVJKN; ʒhe god wot H; A W. glotoun gossib] gossyp glotoun A. glotoun] *om* HWNM. gossib] gossip VJN; Gossop K; good gossib W; *om* DHE. quaþ heo] ʒhe quath A; ʒa U; *om* R. heo] *late corrector prefixes* s H²; sho E; sche DChJKWNMH³. god . . . hote] wel hote god wote K; ful hote H; I am not al boute L. god] ʒe god D. wel] wol AH³; ful VJEM. hote] goode V.
155–6 L *corrupts to* I haue garlek & greyn de Parys & fenelsed for me::::::.
155 I haue] Boþe W. pepir] pip*er* HE. &(1)] *om* E. pyenye] pienye R; pyeny D; piany UChHKNH³; pionye W; piane V; pyan J; pyonis H²; pyanes A; pyou*n*s M; peynye T; *om* E. a] *om* M. pound of garlek] pomgarnade H; poudr*e* of the beste M. garlek] garlyk RUH²JEAKN; leke H³.

And a [ferþingworþ] of [fenelsed] for fastyng dayes.'
Þanne goþ [glotoun in], and grete oþis aftir.
Cisse þe so[wes]tere sat on þe bench,
Watte þe waffrer & his wyf boþe,
[T]ymme þe tynkere & tweyne of his knaues, 160
Hikke þe hakeneyman & hogge þe [nede]lere,
Claris of cokkislane & þe clerk of þe chirche,
Dawe þe dykere & a dusȝeyn oþere,
A ribibour, a ratoner, & a rakiere of chepe,
A ropere, a redyngking, & rose þe disshere; 165

156 And] *om* VHJEKWNM. ferþingworþ] RUDChH²VHJEAKWNMH³; pound T. fenel] DChH²VHJKWNM; fenill E; fenkel AH³; fenkil U; fynkele R; felkene T. sed] RUDVHJAKWNMH³; sedis TChH²E. for] for þis V; for þese H. *Here* A *adds one line;* L *adds two: see above,* pp. 48, 47.
157 Þanne] þene V; þen H. goþ] geþ V; goyth K; goþ þe HM; commys E. glotoun in] RUVHJLEAKWNMH³; in glotoun TDChH². oþis] oþus V; athes E.
158 Cisse] Cesse UDVN; Sissot E; Sybbe A; Symme H; And sisse M; And kytte L; And fond sisse W. sowestere] sowester L; soustere U; sowestre R; sewster H²; sewistere A; Sewstere DCh JE; soweresse K; semstere W; soutere THNM; sewtere H³; souters wyf V. sat] sate HM; sittyng W; þat sat softe L. þe] hire L. bench] benke E.
159 *marked with cross* N. Watte] what N; And bratram E. waffrer] warynere H; warinar V; weuer JL; webster N; wollen webbe W; bereward AMH³; bewer E. boþe] bath E; after H.
160 Tymme] Tymkyn Ch; Tynne J; Thomme UAKWM; Tomme LN; Tom E; Tomlyn H; Tomkyn V; Symme TR DH²H³. tynkere] tyn:::::: H; tyngkere H³; tynkeler E; Trumpour M. tweyne] twey W; two RUChHN; twoo K; twa E; tewyn M. knaues] knawes L; knaffes E.
161 *marked with cross* N. þe(1)] & þe H³; *om* H². hakeneyman] hakeneymon V; hoper his hors N; *defective* H. & . . . nedelere] þat coude wel heue þe coppe L. &] *om* M. hogge] hobbe RUH; hough M; hugh E; hewe KWH³; hwe J; hyne N; lawe A. þe(2)] *om* N. nedelere] nedelere JAKWMH³; neldere VH; mellere D; melnere R; myllere TChH²; mylner UE; *om* N.
162 Claris] Clares Ch; Claresse D; Clerys H³. cokkislane] ? korkes lane R; Cokkes lone V; *defective* H. & . . . chirche] þat klatre can faste L. &] *om* JN. clerk . . . chirche] pariche clerke E. chirche] cherche RUM; churche V; kyrke N; werkis H. *Here* VHEANMH³ *add a line like* **B** V 321 *or* **C** VII 367: *see above,* p.31.
163 Dawe] Dave K. þe dykere] þer was & dolfyn L. dykere] dychere W; disschere VH; Drinker EA. dusȝeyn] dusseyn H²; doseyn RUDChVHLKWNH³; dosen AM; dosenne E; dosyn J.
164 *line om* A. A ribibour] Robyn H; Alban M. A] Þe E; And V; Harry L. ribibour] bribour L; bribure J; rebauderere H³; ribaud R; redylle maker E. a(2)] þe VHM (*twice but second* þe *cancelled* M); of E. ratoner] retoner M; rotynor K; ratonraw E. &] *om* RUVHJEKWNH³. a(3)] þe N. rakiere] rakere RUH²VK WM; raker LN; rakar JE; baker Ch; ȝekere H³. of] of þe WN (þe *cancelled* N). chepe] schepe K; shyp H³; ryse E.
165 *line om* EA. a(2)] & a HL; of M. redyngking] redekyng KW; Redan king Ch. rose] kitte W; rafe K. disshere] dyȝsshere H²; dissheres N; dystere M; dychere JH³; dysare K; kempstere W; ribbere H. *Here* VHEANMH³ *add a line like* **B** V 324 *or* **C** VII 373 (*that of* N *is marked with a cross*)*: see above,* p. 31.

Of vphold*er*is an hep, erliche be þe morewe,
Ȝeue glotoun wiþ glad chiere good ale to hansele.
Clement þe cobeler cast of his cloke
And at þe newe feire nempnide it to selle.
Hikke þe hostiler hitte his hood aftir 170
And bed bette þe bocher be on his side.
Þ*er*e were chapmen chosen þ*a*t chaffare to p*re*ise;
Whoso hadde þe hood shulde haue amendis of þe cloke.
Þo risen vp in rape & ro[wn]eden togid*er*is,
And p*re*isiden þe peneworthis [aparte] be hemseluen. 175

166 Of] And of VH^3; And RUHJA. vphold*er*is] ephalders E; vpholsters Ch. an hep] *om* RU. erliche . . . morewe] arele amorne E. erliche] þat erly N. be] on W. morewe] morowe DChKN; morwe RUH^{2}VHJWMH^3; morwen L; morne A. **167** W *corrupts to* Eche man for hansel to gloton drank a galon ale. Ȝeue] ȝeuen DChLKM; Ȝefe A; ȝeuyn R; Ȝiue V; Geuen N; Gaf U; Gaff E; Þei geuy*n* H^3; þei ȝauy*n* (ȝauy*n* *after cancelled* ȝaff, *same hand*) J. glotoun] þe gloton VH. glad] gode ChVHA; gude E. chiere] wille ChVH. good . . . hansele] to hansel a galon of good ale L. good] a galon of E. to] *om* D. hansele] hansale H^3; honsel V; drynke RUH. **168** Clement] ÞEnne Cleme*n*t VH. cast] kest EA. of] doun D. **169** And] *om* A. at þe] atte V; atte þe WM; att K; þ*er* at þe E. newe] neowe L. nempnide] nempned ChLK; nemyd JMH^3; namyd E; ne*m*pneþ R; ment D; he nemyd N; he nemeþ W; he leyde VH; he must A. it] hire V; *om* H^2. to] *om* A. selle] seolle L; sulle V; sille H. **170** Hikke] And Hikke V. hostiler] hoper N. hitte] hutte V; caste ChHMH^3; kest A; threwe J; hynt E. aftir] sone after L. **171** *line om* H^3. bed] bad ChH^{2}VLEAW; bade H; badd K; badde M; *om* RUDJN. bette] bede K. bocher] bochiere D; brocher J. be] ben VAWM; beon L; to be RU; to ben D; to bene J; shulde ben N. side] bi syde V; by halue L. **172** Þ*er*e] Thus sone W. were] wern M; weore VL. chapmen] chepmen E. chosen] chosyn EA; ychosen NM; Ichosyn JK; ychose RUVH^3. þ*a*t] þe RUChVHEAWNH^3. chaffare] cheffar*e* HE; chaffre N. p*re*ise] preysen LKM; prayse WN; p*ra*ysyn J; prase E; p*ri*se H^3; prysyn A; p*ri*ise H^2. **173** *as two lines divided after* haue L. Whoso] ho so DJAH^3; Wha sa E; Hose V; An who so W; and ho so R; For who so LN; þ*a*t who so U. hadde . . . hood] þe hod hadde L. hadde] hedde V; hed E; haue H^3; hath M. þe] þo J. hood] hude E. shulde] suld E; xuld H^3. haue amendis] amendes haue L. haue] make N. amendis] mendis AH^3; mendes ChK; þe mendes W. of . . . cloke] Of him þat þe cloke had & þat heom thoghte skille L; *om* VHJWN. of] to E. **174** *marked with cross* N. Þo] Thei RUVHMH^3; Thay A; To N; Two J; Twoo K; Twa E. risen] UH^{2}VHLKWNM; rysyn JA; resyn RH^3; rase E; risen þei TDCh. in] *om* VHW. rape] RUChJLANMH^3; a rape TDH^{2}K; Raply VH; a rowte E; þo radde W. rowneden] DVL; rownede RU; rownedyn J; rounden M; roundyn A; rouned ChHW; rovnned K; rounyd H^3; rownen N; rownys E; rombeden T; romeden H^2. *In margin, original hand* & could not accorde K; *see line* 177 *below*. **175** *line om* HLK. preisiden] preysydyn J; preyseden DH^{2}V; preysede RU; preised Ch; preysden AM; praysed W; prasyd E; p*ri*syd H^3; praisen N. þe] þo J; a DA. peneworthis] peniworþ*us* V; penworþes Ch; penyworth DA. aparte] M; ap*a*rte (? aperte) ANH^3; aparty J; ap*a*rty (? aperty) D; inparty (? inperty) E; apert W; ap*er*tly TRUH^2; pertely Ch; & parted*e*n V. be] betwen Ch. hem] þaim E; hym A. seluen] selue RUDChJA; self W; seluy*n* H^3.

Þ*ere* were oþes an hep, [whoso it herde];
Þei couþe [not] be here consience acorden togid*ere*
Til robyn þe rop*ere* was red to arisen,
And nempnide hym for a noump*ere* þ*at* no debate nere.
Hikke þe hostiller þanne hadde þe cloke 180
In couen*aunt* þ*at* clement [shulde þe cuppe felle],
And haue hikkes hood þe hostiller, & holde hym ys*er*uid,
And whoso repentiþ raþest shulde rise aftir

176 *line om* LK; *divided from following after* couþe TChH[2]; Iuge RU; nouȝt D. were] weren H[2]; weryn JAH[3]; weore*n* V; was E. oþes] athes E. an hep] *late corrector inserts* grete *after* an H[2]; mony E; for to heryn A. an] a M; on an RUD. who . . . herde] hoso it herde J; whoso it harde N; hose þat hit herde V; ou*er* þe war*e* H; ou*ere* þe hode & þe cloke MH[3]; for þe hood & þe cloke A; ouer þe hude swornne E; on aftre oþer W; *om* TRUDChH[2].
177 *line om* LAK. Þei couþe] þen cowde þey D; ȝit cowthen he J. Þei] RUVHN; Þai EW; þanne þei TH[2]; bot þen þei Ch; Tweyne H[3]; & tweyn M. couþe not] VHEW; couthe nouȝt N; coude nought MH[3]; ne couþe TChH[2]; couthe not ȝit iugge Ne U; cu*n*ne not ȝut Iuge ne R. not] nouȝt DJ. be . . . consience] *om* M. here] her ChJ; heore V; here clene U; *om* HEW. acorden] acordy*n* JH[3]; acorde DVHWN; acord welle E; wele acorden M. togid*ere*] to kyderes H[2].
178 Til] To Ch. robyn] Roberd H; robard J. þe] þo J. rop*ere*] ropar J; rap*er* E; Ropier*e* H. was] were J; weore V. red] redde Ch; rad RUVN; radde HWM; Irad JL; preyede K; redy E; *om* H[2]. to] for to AWMH[3]; forte V; vp to RU. arisen] arise ChVH; rysen KM; rysyn J; ryse RULEAWNH[3].
179 And] þei H; Thai E. nempnide] nempnyd RU; nempned ChVLK; nemyd JN; ne*m*myd H[3]; namyd A; named HE; niempned (? mempned) W; nemend D; becomen M. hym] hem W; *om* RUDVJ ANM. for] to H[2]; *om* DHEM. a] an ChK; *om* L. noump*ere*] nounper*e* DJM; nounpiere L; vmper ChK; omper*e* H[3]. þ*at* . . . nere] non baddere was neuyr A. debate] lite E. nere] neore V; were UDH[2] HJEKH[3]; ware RM; aros L. *Here* H *adds a line: see above*, p. 46.
180 Hikke . . . þanne] þe*n*ne Hikke þe Ostiler VH. Hikke] hichkok N. hostiller] hoper N. þanne hadde] had than K. þanne] þen E; *om* H[2]JAN; *added in margin same hand* U. hadde] had JAWN; hedde V; hed E. cloke] cloke in rape A.
181 In] I H[2]. couen*aunt*] counand E; conant W; þ*at*] at E. shulde . . . felle] shulde þe coppe fille HN; schulde þe Cuppe fulle V; þe cuppe schulde fille RUJAKW; þe cuppe suld fille E; þe coppe xuld fylle H[3]; þe cuppe shuld fellyn M; scholde fulle þe coppe L; þe coup*ere* shulde felle þe cuppe T; the coup*ere* schulde fille the cuppe (the(2) *added by late corrector*) H[2]; þe cobelere schuld fille þe cuppe DCh.
182 haue] han UA; habbe V; he shold haue W; klement hadde H; *om* D. hikkes . . . hostiller] þe hostilers hode M; þe hop*er*is hode N. hikkes] hicke LE. hood] hude E. þe] *om* HLAWH[3]. hostiller] *om* HW. holde] holdyn JA; hald E; held H. ys*er*uid] yserued RUChLN; seruyd JAH[3]; serued D; seruiyd M; swa s*er*uyd E; ful serued W; wel Iseruet V; wel apaied H.
183 And] *om* H. whoso] ho so RDJAH[3]; wo so M; qwa sa E; who that H[2]N; he þat V; *om* L. repentiþ] repenteþ ChH[2]V; repente DAM; repent W; repentist U; repentid L; repented RN; repente hy*m* H[3]; repent hym E; repentid hym HJ. raþest] raþes R; ratherest M; raþ*ere* U; sonnest J. shulde] suld E; xald H[3]. rise] arise ChHLKWNMH[3]; arysen V; arysyn J; rysyn rathest A. aftir] afore RU; *om* E.

And grete sire glotoun wiþ a galoun ale.
Þere was lauȝing & louryng & 'lete go þe cuppe!' 185
Bargoynes & beuerechis begonne for to arise,
And seten so til euesong & songe [vmbe]while
Til glotoun hadde ygulpid a galoun & a gille.
He pisside a potel in a *paternoster* while,
And bleuȝ þe rounde ryuet at þe riggebones ende 190
[Þat] alle þat herden þat horn held here nose aftir
And wisshide it hadde be wexid wiþ a wysp of firsen.

184 grete] greten V; gretyn J; greete K; grett E; sone gretyn A; gaynly grete W; presente M. sire] *om* A. ale] of ale RU VEMH³; of good alle A.
185 *line om* A. lauȝing] lawȝing Ch; lawghynge DKH³; lawhynge U; laghyng L; lauȝwhing V; laqwyng J; lawegyng M; boþe laghyng W; myche lauȝhing H. & louryng] Inowe M; *om* H. louryng] lurkynge U; lotering V; lenyng E. lete] let RUChVL; lette M; lett K; late W; lat DH³; lattyng E. go . . . cuppe] of þe cupp ga E.
186 *line om* A. Bargoynes] Bargaynes UD ChHJLWNMH³; Bargeynes RVK; Bargans E; Barkeynes H². beuerechis] beueraches D; beueragys K; Beuerages VChH LWN; berage E. begonne] bygonnen L; begunnyn J; began DEK; gan W. for] þo H; *om* RUChH²VJLKM. arise] ryse RUDHJEWNH³.
187 And] He A. seten so] sa still sammen þai satt E. seten] setyn R; seeten V; setten Ch; sytyn J; sytten N; syttyn KH³; sotyn A. so] þus A; *om* H²W. euesong] euensong UH²VEWN; evynsonge K; euynsong tyme A; mydnyȝt H. &] *om* E. songe] songen ChVHW; songyn MH³; songon LK; sunge H²; sungen U; sungyn JA; was songen E. vmbewhile] vmbeqwyle J; vmwhile N; sumwhile TRUD ChH²VHAWM; somqwyle H³; sumtyme K; wel murie L; *om* E.
188 Til] til þe H; Til sire W. hadde ygulpid] þorgh þe golet let glide L. ygulpid] Igulped Ch; ygolped RU; gulpyd JK; golped W; ygloppid H; Igloupet V; gluppid H²; glupped D; glowpyd N; Iclobbyd H³; gobbyd E; gabbid A; Ibibbed M. a] to L. galoun] galons L. & a gille] of gyle A; of ale RN. a(2)] *om* (*late corrector supplies*) H². *Here* EAMH³ *add a line like* **B** V 347 *or* **C** VII 398: *see above*, p. 31.
189 L *corrupts to* Vche tyme þat he pissed more þen a potel þer passed. He pisside] Than pised he sone W. He] And H³. pisside] pyssyd þoo J. *paternoster*] litel M; *om* W. while] qwyle JEH³.
190 And] He JAMH³; And with þat he L. bleuȝ] Bleuh V; blewe UChHJKNM; blew RDH²LEAWH³. þe(1)] a E. ryuet] reuet DChAKH³; rewet HJL; Ruwet V; ruet H²WNM; rowet RE. at þe] atte H²V (*late corrector adds* his H²); at his LN; atte his M; wel atte W. riggebones] rigges W; bakkes M. rigge] rydge K; ryge E; rig JH³; Rugge V; rugg L; ryng A. bones] bone E. ende] hende JM; eynde L.
191 *as two lines divided after* horn M. Þat] þat RUVHJLEKWNMH³; And TDChH²; Til A. herden] herdyn JMH³; herde RDChVLN; herd E; hardyn A; hard K. þat(2)] þe VAW. horn] noise W. held] heldyn JMH³; heeld U; heold L; heolden V. here] her ChJKN; heore VL; þair E. nose] neose V; noses M.
192 wisshide] wisschid KH³; wyschedyn J; wischeden Ch; wisshed RDLN; wyisschedyn M; wyȝschid H; wysht W; wissyd E; wyssedyn A; weschte V. it] þat hit VLEH³; *om* A. hadde be] were JN; weore V. hadde] *om* E. be . . . firsen] wit a wisp ben on feere M. be] ben DEA; byn K; beon L; *om* U. wexid] waxid UH³; waxed RDChHLW; wyxid K; wipyd E; Iwipet V; waschid A. wysp] wesp V; wips ChH. firsen] firsyn N; firses L; firsys K; fersen RCh; ferse H; fursyn D; þornys J; brerys E; fyre UWH³: fere A.

He hadde no strengþe to stonde er he his staf hadde,
And þanne gan he to go [lik a glemans bicche],
Sum tyme asid, & sum tyme arere, 195
As whoso leide lynes to lacche wiþ [foules].
Whanne he drouȝ to þe dore þanne dymmede hise eiȝen;
He [þr]umblide on þe þresshewold & [þrew] to þe erþe |
Þat wiþ al þe wo of þe world his wyf & his wenche *fol.* xxxvij *a*
Bere hym to his bed & brouȝte hym þ*er*inne. 200

193 *as two lines divided after* stondyn M. He] he ne U. hadde(1)] had K; hedde V. no strengþe] streyngh non W. no] no*n* M. strengþe] strenth E; strenght K; streynthe L. to] for to E. stonde] stondyn JM; stondon L; stande UDChE. er] or DChJEK; ar L; til UVHANM. his . . . hadde] had is stafte A. his] a E. staf] staaf M. hadde] hedde V; hent J.
194 *line om* W; *as one line with following* TRDChH^{2}JK. And] *om* DVHJEA. þanne] þe*n*ne V; þen H; *om* D. gan he] He gan DM. gan] gon V; can L; bygan HE; goþ N. he] *twice* A. to go] forþ N. to] for to V; *om* RUChH^{2}JLAMH^3. go] gon DLAMH^3; ga E. lik . . . bicche] lik a glewma*n*nys bicche UVHEANMH^3; god wot þe sothe L; *om* TRDChH^{2}JK. lik] as HA. glemans] H; glewmans EM; glewma*n*nys H^3; glewma*n*nes N; gleo monnes V; gelmannys A. bicche] bytche H^3; beche E.
195 L *corrupts to* hiderward & þedirward auaunt & arere. Sum tyme] But sone he sayllеþ W; *om* K. asid] o syde R; on side DH^3; of syde E; auau*n*t H; arere JA. &] *om* D. sum tyme(2)] *om* K. arere] o rere R; on rere H^3; of arere E; asyde JA.
196 As] And as H^3. whoso] ho so RDA H^3; qwa sa E; hose V; whos L; who UKM; ho J; he Ch. leide] layde RLEKW; leiþ VHM; schuld ley J; leynd H^3. lynes] a lyne H. to . . . foules] foules to cache W. lacche] lacchen J; lache *altered to* kache Ch; take EMH^3; cacche VHA. wiþ] wilde RUD; alle L. foules] RUDVJLEA KNMH^3; briddis H; larkes TChH^2. *Here* N *adds a line: see above*, p. 50.
197 Whanne] whon V; whe*n* RChHL; Qwan JH^3; Qwen E; And whan KWM; But wha*n*ne N. drouȝ] drouh V; drogh LW; drow RUDChHJEANH^3; drewe K. to] toward H^3. þanne] þenne Ch; þen VHL. dymmede] dy*m*med RDChH^{2}H LNM; dy*m*myd JEKH^3; dummyd A; dymmes W. hise eiȝen] *defective* H. eiȝen] eyen RUDKWN; eyghnen L; eyne H^3; ene E; een M; Ien JA.
198 He] And AH^3. þrumblide] þrompelde V; stumblide TU; stu*m*blid H; stu*m*bled R; stombled DJKWN; stombelid H^2; stombeld E; stumbuled M; stomblod L; stomelid AH^3; stumles Ch. on þe] atte V. on] at H^{2}EKN; atte WM; to H. þresshewold] threswold J; þrexwolde V; þreschfold ChH; þresfold RN H^3; thresschold K; throschfold U; throsfold H^2; þresshald D; threswald A; freswald E; þrosschald L; therschold M. þrew] threw LEKN; þreuh V; þrogh W; threw hi*m* J; stey U; fel TRDChH^{2}H AMH^3. to] on A. erþe] eorthe L; erde H^3; grou*n*de VWN; g:::::: H. *Here* UEMH^3 *insert versions of* **B** V 358–63 *or* **C** VII 409–14; A *of* **B** V 358 *and* 360–3 *or* **C** VII 409 *and* 411–14: *see above*, p. 31.
199 Þat] and Ch; *om* UHJEAWMH^3. wo] waye (? waþe) E. þe(2)] þis UChV JLEANH^3. world] word RM; werlde JEAH^3. his wenche] *defective* H. his] her K; þe Ch. wenche] douȝ*ter* R.
200 Bere] Beren UL; bery*n* RHK; Beeren V; Bare ChE; Bare*n* J; Baryn M; Boryn H^3; Born A. hym] hi*m* hom VHN. his] *om* DM. &] *om* W. brouȝte] brouȝþe R; brouth A; brouhten V; browhtyn J; broghten UL; browty*n* H^3; broweten M; þrow W. hym þerinne] *defective* H. hym] *om* (*late corrector supplies*) H^2.

And aftir al þis surfet an axesse he hadde
Þat he slepte satirday & sonneday til sonne ȝede to reste.
Þanne wakide he of his wynkyng & wypide his eiȝen;
Þe ferste woord þ*at* he spak was 'where is þe bolle?'
His wyf [wit]ide hym þanne of wykkidnesse & synne. 205
Þanne was þ*at* shrewe asshamide & shrapide hise eris,
And gan grete grymly & gret doel ma[k]e
For his liþ*er* lif þ*at* he lyued hadde,
And auowide to faste, for hungir or þrist:

201 And] *om* HE. aftir] Eftir E. al] *om* ChEAMH^3. þis] þ*at* RM; his ChL. surfet] he suffird E. an] ane E. axesse] accidie UH^3. he] hym AM. hadde] hedde V; hede E; toke M.
202 *marked with cross* N. Þat] *om* M. he . . . sonneday] al a somer he slepe N. slepte] sleped Ch; slepyd E; slep RDJM; sleep U. satirday] saterday ChJ; sat*ur*day RH^{2}AKMH^3; sett*er*day E; set*ur*day V; settresday L; til satirday D; *om* W. &] þe W. sonneday] sone*n*day V. til] til þe AKH^3; to þe E; þe D. ȝede] yode E; wente VHA; was M. to] at M. reste] rist E; softe L.
203 Þanne] þe*n*ne V; þen H; whan N. wakide he] he wakede V; he waked N. wakide] wakid UJAKH^3; wakede H^2; waked RDChHLWM; wakynnyd E. his] *om* ChKM. wynkyng] wynk VN. &] he N. wypide] wypid H^{2}JEAKH^3; wypidde Ch; wypede V; wyped RDHL WNM. eiȝen] eye*n* RDKWM; eyn N; eygnen L; eyne H^3; ene E; yȝe*n* H; Iȝene J; yen A.
204 *marked with cross* N. ferste] first UCh JEKWN; furste RH^{2}VHL; fryst AH^3. þat] was þat H; *om* E. spak] sapke (?) E; warpe W. was] what RU; qwat J; *om* DVHEAMH^3. where] were NM; whare U; qwere JH^3; qwar E. bolle] Cuppe VHN. *Here* L *adds a line: see above*, p. 47.
205 His wyf] And L. witide] wytyd EA; wyssyd H^3; warnede V; blamide TU; blamyd JK; blamed RDChH^{2}LWNM; blamy H. þanne . . . &] blyue for his wykked W; þat he wolde ay beon so bold to L. þanne] þo VMH^3; *om* A. of] of hys H^3; his A. &] & of VM; & eke is A; of RH. synne] synnen L. *Here* L *adds* 2 *lines: see above*, p. 47.
206 Þanne] þe*n*ne V; þen H. was] wax W; *om* E. þat . . . asshamide] ashamed þ*at* sherewe N; Shamed þat schrew E; he aschamyd þat schrewe AK; he aschamed þat schrewe L; he aschomed þ*at* schrewe V; he asschamed þe schrewe DM; he shamed þe shrewe W. þat] þe RUChH^2 HJ. asshamide] aschamyd H^{2}JH^3; ashamed RUChH. & . . . eris] & gan for to smert W. shrapide] schrapid UH^{2}AK; schraped RDVM; gan schrapen L; gan sharape N; robbed H; scharped Ch; gan sharpe E; ga*n* xarpe H^3; gan to scharpyn J. eris] earys K; eren VH; heren M; eyne L.
207 *line om* M. gan] gon V; bygan HL; *om* E. grete] greton K; to grete U; to grety*n* RJ; to grede DVL; wepe H^3; to be sory H. grymly] ful gremly E; greuously A; *om* H. doel] deol VHL; dele ChH^2; dol RAH^3; dole DKN; dool UJ; dule E. make] ChEA; maken KH^3; to make VHJLWN; made TRUDH^2.
208 For] And forswor W. his] þe UHW. liþer] lythir J; lyth*ur* H^2; lyder M; leþer Ch; lethyr REH^3; ledur A; luther L; wikkede VH. lif] lyve E. lyued] lyuyd JK; lyud H; Iliued V; leued Ch; levyd EAH^3; so longe lyued L. hadde] hedde V.
209 *marked with cross* N; V *corrupts to* FOr hung*ur* oþer for Furst I make myn Avou. And . . . faste] þo to fast he made a uow H. And] an R. auowide] avowyd H^{2}JEKH^3; avowed UDChLWM; awowed N; vowed R; voued A. to] wel L; *om* W. faste] fasten M; fastyn J. for] RUH JLEAWMH^3; for any TChH^{2}KN; for ony D. hungir . . . þrist] thrist or for hungere J; first or hu*n*ger N. or] & A. þrist] þrest Ch; thruste K; þurste D; for þriste UEAH^3; for thirste L; for þurst HM; for þherste R; elles W.

'Shal neuere fissh on þe Friday defie in my wombe 210
Er abstinence myn aunte haue ygyue me leue,
And ȝet haue I hatid hire al my lif tyme.'
Sleuþe for sorewe fil doun a swowe
Til *Vigilate* [þe veil] fet watir [at] his eiȝen,
And flattide it on his face & faste on him criede 215
And seide, 'war þe for wanhope wile þe betraye;
"I am sory for my synne," sey to þiseluen,

210–212 *occur twice in* K (*see line* 219 *below*).
210 Shal] Sall E; Xal H³; Shold W. fissh] fyche JE; *om* V. þe] *om* RVHLE K(2)WNM. defie] defien UVK(*both*)N MH³; defyȝin J; fyen W; quoþ he defien H; rist E. my] his W. wombe] mawe RUVHJWH³ (*cancelled same hand for* wombe H³).
211 Er] Or DChEA; Ar L; Til JK(*both*)N; Er þat W; er into tyme þat H. myn aunte] *om* H. myn] his W. aunte] haunte NM; amyte J; aduersarij E. haue] hath A; hat H³; had W. ygyue] ygif R; gyf W; gyfyn E; Iȝiue V; ȝyuen U; ȝyuyn J; geue DCh; yȝeue H; ȝeue ANM; ȝeuen LK(2); yevyn K(1); ȝouyn H³. me] hym W.
212 ȝet] ȝit UDChVHJAWN; ȝut R; it E. haue . . . tyme] I here al my lyfe tyme haue I here hatid A. haue I] y haue HLK(1); Ichaue V; hadde he W. hatid hire] hire hatid H. hatid] hatide U; hated RDChLWNM; Ihated V. hire] hir NH³; here UDH²WM; her ChK (*both*); hure R; him J; *om* E. my] his W. lif] lyue J.
213 Sleuþe] Sloupe RUDJL; Slawth AH³; þo sleuþe HM; Than sleuþ W; And than this gloton K. sorewe] sorowe DChK; sorow JEAN; sorwe RUH²HLWH³; serwe V; sorewen M. fil] fel RUDChH² VHJEAKWNH³; feol L. doun] adoun ChW. a swowe] aswoune UH²WM; on swounne H³; on sowen R; in swowe N; yswowe L; in swoune E; Iswowene V; in a swowe J; In a swouȝe Ch; in a swowne K; in sweye A; to grounde a swoun D.
214–19 *occur twice in* K (*see line* 219 *below*).
214 *marked with cross* N; *expanded to two lines divided after* iȝen H. Til . . . fet] til he woke & wept H. Til] To E; Tyl þat M. þe veil] VJLAK(*both*)NH³; þer while TH²; þat wille E; þer wol Ch; wile R; wol U; *om* DWM. fet] fett EK(*both*); fette DChH²VM; had fet W; fecche RU. at] VJLAK(*both*)WNH³; atte M; to TRUDE; of Ch; for (*late corrector alters to* from) H²; wiþ H. his] here M. eiȝen] eien UDK(*both*)WM; eyn N; eyghnen L; eyne REH³; Iȝine J; yen A; iȝen & vigilate þe wakere warned hym þo (wakere *twice but second cancelled*) H.
215 And] heo H. flattide] flattid J; flattede H²; flatted DCh; flatte VK(1); flat UHLK(2); flapte R; flapt N; flascht W; plattyd M; platte H³; platt E; plat A. it] hym W; *om* UChVHJAM. on] in NM; ful al W. his] here U; þe W. faste] flast H. criede] cried RDChLEAN; cryyde K(1); cryyd K(2)H³; criȝede V; cride UHM.
216 *line om* Ch. And seide] and syde M; *om* N. war . . . for] þat H. war] warre M; be ware J; Be wel war N. þe] *om* RJWN. for] fro UDAH³; from EK (*both*)M; of JN. wanhope] wonhope V. wile] he wil UK(1); he wol L; þat wol V; wolde H; he wolde JN; þat wolde MH³; þat would K(2); þat wald E. þe] hym H. betraye] betraysse E.
217 *line om* U. I am] I ame K(*both*); Icham V; I ham M; If þou be W. for] of JLWN. my] þi W. synne] synnes HLEANM; synnys JK(*both*)H³; sunnes V. sey] say HLEK(*both*)W. to] þou M; so EAH³. seluen] selue DAK(2)H³; selfe JK(1); self ChWN; seoluen L; syluen H²H; self þanne R.

And beet þiself on þe brest & bidde hym of *gra*ce,
For is no gilt here so gret þ*at* his goodnesse nis more'.
Þanne sat sleuþe vp & seynide hym faste, 220
And made auowe tofore god for his foule slouþe:
'Shal no sonneday be þis seue ȝer, but seknesse it make,
Þat I ne shal do me er day to þe dere chirche
And here masse & matynes as I a monk were;
Shal non ale aftir mete holde me þennis 225
Til I haue euesong herd, I behote [to] þe rode.

218 And] *om* N. beet] bet RDVWN; bett E; bete ChH²HJAK(*both*)MH³; *om* L. þi . . . on] bittyrly W. self] seluen MH³; seolf L. on] vppon EK(2). þe] þi RHLW. brest] best (*late corrector supplies* r) H². bidde] abyde E; p*r*ay H³. hym] god VHK(1)WNH³.
219 *line om* RU. For] *om* HA. is] nis VN; þ*er* is DJE; is þ*er* L; þ*er* nys HM. no] *om* M. gilt] gult VL; gelte M. here . . . gret] so grett here E. here] her V; hir*e* H²; *om* HJK(2)M. þ*at*] bott EK(1) W; but þ*at* K(2); þan Ch; *om* VA. his] *om* ChHW. goodnesse] grace E; Merci VHN. nis] is DChJLEAK(*both*)WMH³. more] mare E; wel more VH. *Here* K *inserts a passage like* **C** VII 423–VIII 62, *containing lines corresponding to* **A** V 210–12 *and* 214–19: *see above*, p. 31.
220 Þanne] þ*e*nne V; þen ChHK. sat] sate HM; satte AK. sleuþe] sleweth M; sclewth K; slouþe RUDJLN; slawth AH³; sire slouþ W. seynide] seynyd K; seynede H²; seined D; saynede U; sayned ChW; signed L; shryued R; schraffe E; sikede V; siked N; syhede H³; syhed AM; seide H; crowchid J. hym] himself Ch; hem W; to hym siluen H; *om* VANMH³. faste] full fast EA; ofte K; sore V; *om* H.
221 *marked with cross* N. made auowe] awowed N. auowe] awoye E. tofore] before H²VM; afor N; to HAW; vnto E; to veri RU. foule] faule U; vile W; wicked H; saule D. slouþe] slewþe DCh VHEW; sleweth M; sclewth K; slawth AH³.
222 *marked with cross* N; *as two lines divided after* ȝere J. Shal no] Eche W. Shal] Sall EN; Xal H³; Schuld A; þ*at* þ*er* schal J. no] na E. sonneday] sonenday V. be] beo L; ben J; be in K; *om* ChVHEA WMH³. seue] seuen VHJEW; seuene ChH²N; seuyn A; seouen L; vij RUDK MH³. ȝer] ȝeer D; ȝeir L; yer*es* K; *om* U. but] For sorwyn of my sy*n*nys but J. seknesse] syknesse RH²HKM. it make] make it E. it] *om* H³. make] made A.
223 Þat] But A; *om* W. ne] no L; *om* DJAWM. shal] sal JE; xal H³. do . . . dere] vppe eueryday & dygte me to M; eu*er*y day rise erly to H. do] dighte LW. er day] *om* Ch. er] or DJEKW; ar VLN. to] & do me to L. dere] derne H³; dore V; parysch RU; *om* LE. chirche] cherche RJWNM; churche DVH; kirke E; chrche A.
224 *marked with cross* N. And] To N. here] heren M; heare K. masse] messe AWH³; matyns UH²VEKM; maytynes N. matynes] matyn*n* H³; Masse VKM; messe UH²EN. as . . . monk] a monk as I H. as] als L.
225 *marked with cross* N. Shal] Sal JEN; Xal H³. non ale] no ale M; no riot H. aftir mete] *om* Ch. mete] none W. holde] holde*n* RL; holdyn JA; hald E. me] me fro Ch. þennis] þannes H; þine E.
226 Til] To E. I haue] ichaue V. euesong] euensong UH²VLKWN; euynsong A; eunensang E; euesond H³. herd] hard K; yherd UNH³. behote] byhote N; beohote V; hote ChJLAWM; hett E; swer*e* H; sey H³. to] DChH²VJLWN; be MH³; by H; þe be EA; *om* TRUK. rode] rude E.

And ȝet wile I ȝelde aȝen, ȝif I so muchel haue,
Al þat I wykkidly wan siþen I wyt hadde,
[And] þeiȝ my liflode lakke leten I nille
Þ*at* iche man shal haue his er I hennis wende, 230
And wiþ þe residue & þe remen*aun*t, be þe roode of chestre,
I wile seke treuþe er I [se] rome.'
Robert þe robbo*ur* on *reddite* lokide,
Ac for þ*er*e was nouȝt wherew*ith* he wepte swiþe sore.
And ȝet þe synful shrewe seide to hymselue: 235

227 *line om* A. And . . . ȝelde] Qwat eu*er* I na*m*m ȝelde it H³. And] Als E; *om* JW. ȝet . . . I] euerche man M. ȝet] ȝit DUChVHJN; ȝut R; *om* E. wile I] I wol UE; Ichulle V; I wold H. wile] wol RChL; shal N. ȝelde] ȝelden VJLM. aȝen] aȝeyn VJLN; ageyn KMH³; agayn E. ȝif] ȝef L. muchel] much ChVLWM; mochil U; moche RN; mychel J; mychil K; myche H; mechel D; mekell E; mekyl H³.
228 Al] *om* UM. wykkidly wan] wan wikkydly A. wykkidly] wikked D; wokedly W. wan] won V; bywan R; bewan D. siþen] siþ W; siþþe H; syn RAH³; sethen DE; seþin J; seþþe V; seth M; sen Ch; seothe L. I] þat I D. wyt hadde] lyf hadde or wytt H³. wyt] whit M. hadde] hade VE; had K.
229 And] RUVHJLEKWNMH³; *om* TDChH²A. þeiȝ] þei RDH²JM; þowȝ ChHK; þogh W; þof E; þow H³; Tho A; þauh V; þagh L; þoiȝe U. my] me N; I my A; *om* U. liflode] lyuelode HKM; levelade E; lyue lowe A. lakke] lake EWH³ (? *touched up* W); lak ChM; lacken H²H; I lacke K; fayle R; me faile U; lede A. leten] letyn JA; letten UDCh VHWM; lettyn KH³; leten it N; lette ȝut R; ȝet lett E; leue L. nille] nelle RChH²HNH³; nulle V; ne wyll EAM; ne wolle U; no wol L.
230 iche] H²JWN; eche DChKMH³; vche VL; iche a T; ilke E; eu*er*y RUHA. man] mon VL. shal] sall E; xal H³; ne schal H²K; ne sclal N. haue] han A; habben V. er . . . hennis] hen ar I M. er] or DChJLE AK; ar N; er or (er *cancelled for* owne *by late corrector*) H². I] ich V. hennis] henne DV; hynde E. wende] wy*n*de N.
231 And] *om* EAW. wiþ] why Ch; *om* W. residue . . . remen*aun*t] remenau*n*t & þe resydue H³; remanent & residew E; remembrans & residue A. &] of W; *om* M. þe(2)] *om* RKNM. remen*aun*t] remanau*n*t D; remnant J; *om* M. roode] rude E.
232 I wile] In wille M; Shal I W. wile] wol UChL; schal VH; seke] sekyn J; seche VHLH³. treuþe] truþe R; trwþe N; þerwiþ trouþ W; trweth þerwith M; sir trewth K; seynt Treuþe VHLE; *late corrector inserts* seint H²; seynt *in margin another hand* N. er . . . rome] to fynde W. er] or RDChH² HJLEAKM; ar N. se] RDHJANMH³; see UEK; seo VL; seke TChH².
233 Robert] roberd RUH²HJ; Robard LAK; Robyn W; *om* H³. þe] of E; *om* MH³. robbo*ur*] robber*e* RUDHJEAWH³; *om* M. on *reddite*] on *reddere* H³; *om* H. on] þan on W. lokide] lokyd EK; lokede RH²; loked DChJWN; he lokede V; he loked L; rufulliche loked H; ful reufully lokede H³; ful reufulli he lokid A; ful ruly he loked M.
234 Ac] Bot ChLAK; and RUVEWN MH³; *om* H. for] *om* A. þ*er*e . . . w*ith*] þat he was wicked H. was] nas DVK WNM. nouȝt] not RVJLW; non A; *om* KM. wherew*ith*] qwerw*ith* JH³; þ*er*w*ith* E; wher of with Ch; þer but A; to paye *added by late corrector* H². wepte] weped Ch; wepyd ENH³; wepd R; weppid J; weopte L; weep U. swiþe] wel RLW; ful VEAN; *om* ChJH³.
235 And] But VHLN. ȝet] ȝit RUDVJN; þus M; *om* ChHEAH³. þe] þat UJEM; *om* R. synful] sunfol V; senful M. shrewe] *same hand after cancelled* wreche H². seide] sayde RLEKW. to] tille Ch. selue] self ChKW; seluen VENM; seluyn H³; seoluen L; silue H.

'Crist, þ*at* on caluarie vpon þe [cros] diȝedist,
Þo dismas my broþ*er* besouȝte þe of g*race*,
And þou haddist m*er*cy on þ*at* man for *memento* sake,
Þi wil w[orþ]e vpon me, as I haue wel des*er*uid
To haue helle for eu*er*e ȝif þ*at* hope nere. 240
So rewe on þis robert þ*at* *red*[*dere*] ne hauiþ,
Ne neu*er*e wen[e] to wynne wiþ craft þ*at* [I owe], |
But for þi muchel m*er*cy mytygac*io*u*n* I beseche; *fol.* xxxvij *b*
Dampne me nouȝt at domisday for þ*at* I dede so ille.'
Ac what befel of þis feloun I can not faire shewe; 245

236 þ*at*] *om* A. on] vppon VAK. vpon] oppon Ch; apon L; on RUVEK; þat vpon A. þe] *om* JAW. cros] RVHJLEA KWNM; croys UH³; rode TDChH². diȝedist] diȝedest V; dyedest L; dydyst K; dydest W; dyed E; dyde M; deyȝide J; deydist A; deyddyst H³; deydest DH²N; deyde RUH; dedest Ch.
237 Þo] To N; When E; Whan þat W. besouȝte] he besouth A. þe] ȝow J; hi*m* RU. g*race*] mercy A.
238 And] as H; *om* JN. þou] ȝe J; *om* VWH³. haddist] haddest RUDHWNM; hadest L; had JA; hade E; heddest V; hast Ch; *om* H³. m*er*cy] rewthe (*above line similar hand*) W. on] of VEN; on hym D. man] mon VL. for] fo M. *memento*] RUDVJLEAWNM; *menento* K; *memento* is TChH²HH³. sake] salke M.
239 Þi . . . worþe] þou haue m*er*cye N. worþe] worthe JM; worþ VHLKWH³; worch Ch; wurche U; werche TH²A (*late corrector adds* not H²); wirche RD; wirke E. vpon] apon L; of N. as] for H. I . . . wel] wys I haue N. I] Ich V. wel] *om* UDJAM. des*er*uid] deseruyde J; dysseruyd A; des*er*ued RChHLWNM; deseruet V; s*er*uyd E.
240 haue] han A. ȝif] ȝef L. þ*at*] ne E; *om* JAMH³. hope] mercye (*after cancelled* h) K. nere] neore V; ne were RUDAK NMH³; ne war*e* J; no weore L; were E.
241 So] Swa E; to RChH³; Thou AN. rewe] rue K; reowe L. on] vpon W. þis] me VHKN; *om* W. robert] roberd RUDH²HA; Robart L; Robyn W; robber JH³; rybawde K. *reddere*] EH³; *reddere* non A; *redde* none N; no *redde* K; rederd M; no rede W; no red DVJ; no reed H; red non TRH²L (*late corrector alters to* reddere H²); reed non UCh. ne] no L; *om* UDVJAKW. hauiþ] haueþ RUDChH²LM; haues E; hath AKW; haue VHN.
242 Ne] No ChL. wene] HJLN; weene V; wenys E; weniþ TRAK; weneþ UDChH²; we M; wot H³; *om* W. to] *om* W. wynne] wynnyn J; wan W; haue K. wiþ] wit*h* no K; for VH. þ*at*] *om* K. I owe] N; I knowe VHJAKW MH³; I knawe E; he knowe L; he knoweþ RDCh; he knowiþ TUH².
243 But] *om* J. for] of WMH³; *om* A. muchel] much ChW; moche RD; mychel J; mychil K; mechele H³; meche A; meychel N; mekyll E; grete U; *om* H. m*er*cy mytygac*io*u*n*] mytigaciou*n* m*er*cy H. m*er*cy] *om* W. beseche] beseke RJH³; seke E; beteche A.
244 *line om* H. Dampne] And dampne L. nouȝt] nouth JH³; not RVLKW; nat A. at] atte N; on VLEK. þ*at* . . . ille] my euell dede E. þ*at*] *om* DVJLAWNMH³. dede] dide UH²W; dude VL; ded ChM. dyd KN; haue done J. so] *om* KW.
245 *line om* H. Ac] But UChJLEAKWM; And H³; *om* N. what] wath A; qwat JEH³. befel] befil H²; byfeol L; fel VJA; fyll M. of] on DAW. þis] þat EAW MH³. feloun] feolou*n* L; freke W; man M. can not] schal ȝou D. can] con V. not] nouȝt ChH²NM; noght U; nouth H³; no EKW. faire] ferrer E; ferþ*er* W; fard*er* K. shewe] schewen M.

Wel I woot he wep faste watir wiþ his eiȝen,
And knowelechide his [coupe] to crist ȝet eftsones,
Þat *penitencia* his pik he shulde pulsshe newe
And lepe *with* hym ou*er* lond al his lif tyme,
For he hadde leiȝe be *latro* luciferis [aunte]. 250
[A] þousand of men þ[o þ]rong[en] togid*er*is,
Wepynge & weylyng for here wykkide dedis;
Criede vpward to crist & to his [clene] modir
To haue g*ra*ce to seke treuþe; god leue þ*a*t hy moten!

246 Wel] But wel VEANMH³. I] Ich V. woot] wot RUDVLWH³; wote ChH²HJ AKNM; wate E. he] þat he H. wep] wepe DCh; wept HWNH³; wepte RUH²VA KM; wepyd E; weopte L; weptyd J. faste] *om* ChHA. watir] wat*ur* V. wiþ] at J; of E. his] boþen hie A. eiȝen] eyen DKWM; eyghnen L; eyne REH³; eyn N; iȝe*n* H; Iȝene J; yen A.
247 And] He H³. knowelechide] knowlechid H; knouhlechede V; knowleched ChJLM; knowlichid U; knowliched RD H²; knowlachyd H³; knoleched N; knolichid A; knowlegyd K; knewlaged W; knawleghde E. coupe] A; coulpe E; gilt TRUDChH²JKNMH³; gult VHL; gret gylt W. to crist] þ*er*to H; *om* U. to] fast to E; & fast on W. ȝet] ȝit RUD ChVJN; it M; *om* HEAW. eftsones] eft sone R; eft onys H³; ofte sythis A; of hys synnes E; called W.
248 Þat] And preyde þ*a*t M; Than A. *penitencia*] penaunce H; repentance E. his] is V; w*ith* hys E; *om* M. pik] pikke E; piked staf H; body H³; prest V; *om* M. he shulde] shulde RUDVLM; suld E; xulde H³; apertly schuld he J; shulde be H; myght W; *om* A. pulsshe] pulissh D; pullyche J; pulche R; polissche VEKW NM; pollyschon A; polischid H; polessche L; polsche Ch; pelychou*n* H³. newe] neowe L; al new H; it new E; him newe VWM; of(?) new K; efte sonys A; *om* J.
249 lepe] lepen M; lepyn JH³; lep R; leep U; lepid A; kepe D; go H. hym ou*er*] oure M. lond] land EK. lif] liue E.
250 *line om* M. hadde] haþ V. leiȝe] leiȝen V; leye RL; ley UDJ; leyn HN; lay ChH²; layne K; lyen W; lyn H³; loyn A; lyve E. be *latro*] by lator W; of lichore E. aunte] RUDHLEAKWNH³ (*over erasure* R); hyne TChH²; lemman J; brother V. *Here* K *adds a passage like* **C** VIII 70–154: *see above*, p. 31.
251 *line om* A. A] RUVJLEKNMH³; þo a H; And a DChH²; And TW. þousand] þousend UD; þousent V; thowsyng J. of] *om* RUHLEWMH³. men] mo men M; me*n* and mo RU; men sagh I W; *om* L. þo þrongen] thro*n*gen þo M. þo] RUChVJLKWNH³; þan E; þe TDH²; *om* H. þrongen] VHKW; throngy*n* H³; thrungen UN; thru*n*ge R; thrungu*n* J; thrange E; thryngen L; wrongen Ch; wrong TDH² (*late corrector adds* ed H²).
252 *line om* A. Wepynge] weopyng VL; Wepand E; wepten M. weylyng] wailing ChNH³; weylden M; walowand E; wringing H. here] her ChJKN; hir*e* H²; heore VL; þair E. wykkide dedis] mysdedis H.
253 Criede] kryeden L; Criedyn J; cried RDN; Cryidy*n* H³; Criȝed Ch; Cride W; Cryden UM; He cried A; Cryen K; c*r*iyng H; Criȝinge V; Cryand E. to(2)] *om* K. clene modir] moder dere Ch. clene] RUDVHJEAKWNH³; dere TH²M; leoue L. modir] moder RDH²VHEWH³; modre NM; moder*e* J; modur LA; mother K.
254 *marked with cross* N; *as first line of Passus* VI A; *as two lines divided after* wille L. To haue] Of M; For H³; *om* A. to(2) . . . moten] treuþ for to fynde W. seke] sekyn J; seche VHN; gon with a good wille To seche L; go to KH³; gon to AM; ga to E. treuþe] seint treuþe V; seynt treouthe L. god] got N; so god RUEK. leue] leve K; lenne E; g*r*aunte M. þat] at E; *om* H²VH. hy] he JA; þei UDChH²KNM; þai E; þei so VHLH³; ȝe R. moten] motyn J; mote RUDVH LAKNH³; myght E; meten H².

VI

Ac *þere* w[ere] fewe men so wys *þat* þe [wey] þid*er* couþe,
But blustrid forþ as bestis ou*er* [baches] & hilles
Til late & longe *þat* hy a lede mette,
Ap*ar*ailid as a paynym in pilgrim[ys] wyse.
He bar a burdoun ybounde wiþ a brood list, 5
In a [weþewindes] wyse [ywounden] aboute;
A bagge & a bolle he bar be his side;

1 *Here* H *inserts two lines: see above,* p. 46. Ac] Agh L; ȝit W; Now N; Bot ChVH EKM; Tha*n* H^3; *om* A. *þere* were] were *þere* W; wher*e* *þere* N; was *þer* H^3. *þere*] Here A. were] RUChVHJ; weore L; was TDH^2EA; ne was K; nas M. fewe men] wight none K; non AMH^3; nane E. men] *om* UN. so wys] *om* W. *þat*] at E; *om* UJWM. þe . . . couþe] couþe þe wei þider V; walked on fote Ch. þe wey] UHJANM; þe weyȝe H^3; þe way LEKW; þei TRH^2; *om* D. þid*er*] þidyr J; þeder DEWM; thedir RH^3; þedur A; thether K; *om* HL. couþe] couþe*n* H; cowthin J; coude $RUDAMH^3$; could K.

2 But] And E; *om* R. blustrid] blustred Ch; blusterid AH^3; blostred W; blustre RD; blustryn J; blustren U; blostreþ N; blustreyng M; bolstride H; Bloundere*d* E; bustelyng V; bleoseden L. forþ] forth blusteryng L; *om* HM. bestis] blynde bestis H. ou*er*] ower*e* J; oure E; þrogh W. baches . . . hilles] hulles & dales L. baches] W; valeis $TRUDChH^2VHJKN$; dales MH^3; bankes EA. &] or U. hilles] hull*es* RDV; hullis H; helles M. *Here* H *adds a line: see above,* p. 46.

3 Til] So E. late] was late V; late was N; hit was late HKW. longe] to longe A; till longe MH^3; so lang E. *þat*] at E; *om* AWH^3. hy] hij (*late corrector alters to* they) H^2; he J; þei $RUDChVHLKNMH^3$; þai EAW. lede] Leod VL; ludde W; ladde D; ma*n* $HJMH^3$. mette] metten VHLM; mettyn RJH^3.

4 Ap*ar*ailid] Parayled U; Perraylid A; Ip*ar*ailed LR. a] *om* H^2. paynym] payneme DM; *altered to* palmer *by late corrector* H^2; Palmere VHEK; palmare L. pilgrimys] pilgrymys $RChKH^3$; pilgrymes UDH^2V HJLAN; pilgremes M; pilgr*a*mes E; pilgrim T; palmeres W. wyse] wede EAKW; wedes V.

5 *line om* J. ybounde] ybounden L; bounde D; bondon E; bondy*n* H^3; boundyn aboute A; in his hond bounde H. brood] brod $RVLAH^3$; brode $DChH^2$ KWNM; brad E; *om* H.

6 *line om* RUA; *run together with following* J. In . . . wyse] In þe way of a wodewynde D; *om* J. In a] In an W; Alle on M. weþewindes] wethewyndes N; withwynd K; weþebondes V; wrethewyndes L; wyrnde wythys H^3; wrythen M; way wendis T; wodebyndes HE; wodebynde H^2; weyward Ch; yuyn W. ywounden] Iwounden ChLK; wou*n*den JW; Iwonde H^3; wonden EN; Ibounden M; bounden D; he bond hym TH^2; Iwriþen V; wriþen H. aboute] al aboute L; abowtyn him J; at bowte D.

7 A] Bothe a W. bagge] bage K. &] *om* J. bolle] botell E. he bar] *om* J. be] at W.

An hundrit of ampollis on his hat seten,
Signes of synay, ⁊ shilles of galis,
And many crouch [o]n his cloke, ⁊ keiȝes of rome, 10
And þe v*er*nicle beforn for men shulde knowe
And sen be his signes whom he souȝt hadde.
Þis folk fraynide hym faire [fro] whenis þ*at* he come.
'Fro synay,' he seide, '⁊ fro þe sepulcre.
At bedlem, at babiloyne, I haue ben in boþe; 15
In armonye, in alisaundre, in manye oþ*er*e places.
Ȝe mowe se be my signes þ*at* sitten on myn hat

8 An] A EKN; And an W. hundrit] hundrid J; hundred RUDH^2VLAKW; vndred M; hundreþ ChEN; honderd H^3; C H. of] *om* E. ampollis] ampollus R; ampullos H^3; hanpolles Ch; hampnels W; appoles N; apples H^2; saumples L; ensaumples E. seten] setyn MH^3; setten N; settyn JK; sette W; seeten V; saten H^2; sotyn A; wer sett E.
9 synay] sise M; asyce A; sissell E; þe holy lond H^3. ⁊] *om* J. shilles] schelles UDCh VLWM; schellys RJEAKH^3; chellis N. galis] gales UDChH^2WM.
10 And] *om* V. many] Moni VE; many a RUDChJAKWM; mony a L. crouch] croche K; cros RUVE; crosses H. on] RUChH^2VHJLEAKWNMH^3; in TD. cloke] cloth *corrected another ink* H^2. keiȝes] keyes UDChH^2HLW; keyys KNH^3; keys A; kyxes M; synes E.
11 *line om* E. þe] a L. vernicle] vernyclie H^3; vernacle K; vernache A. beforn] byforn DL; beforu*n* M; before KW; bifore V; hi*m* byforn RU; hy*m* before H^3; aforn Ch; afore N; tofore H. for] þat AH^3. shulde] shulden M; schuldyn J; xulde H^3; cholde N; schul A. knowe] knowyn K; yknowe H; Iknowen M; hy*m* knowe RUDVLA; knowe hym W.
12 *run together with following* E. And] I E. sen] se ChHEW; sene H^2AN; seen UKM; seene J; seyn D; seon L; seo V. his] þe A. signes] syngnys H^3; synes REA. whom . . . hadde] *om* E. whom] hom J; qwom H^3; wher Ch. hadde] hedde V.
13 *expanded to two lines divided after* made U. Þis . . . fro] *om* E. Þis] þes ChK; Thus A. fraynide] fraynyd JK; fraynede H^2V; frayned LWN; freynyd H^3; freyned RDChHA; freynden M; frayneth U. hym] *om* W. faire] feire VH; fast AWM; fryst H^3. fro] HLAW; fro*m* VKH^3; for hym þ*at* hym made Fro U; *om* TRD ChH^2JNM. whenis] whenes M; whens KW; whe*n*nes RUDChH^2LN; qwenns H^3; whene A; whe*n*ne V; when H; qwen J; qwyne E. þ*at*] *om* DKWNMH^3. come] coome V; come ⁊ whiderward he schulde U.
14 Fro] Fra E; fram H. synay] senay E. he seide] said he W. ⁊] þo ⁊ J. fro(2)] fram H. sepulcre] seynt sepulcre L; sepulcre of oure lord AKH^3.
15 At] Atte M; ac R; From V. bedlem] bedlehe*m* RL. at(2)] ⁊ at H; and RVE. babiloyne] babilony AH^3. I haue] haue y H. ben] be RCh; bene J; byn K; beon L. in boþe] bath E; also H. in] at AKWH^3.
16 armonye] ermonye RDHJLAKW; ermenye U; hermony ENM; ermenyȝe H^3; Ynde V. in(2)] ⁊ in DV; ⁊ E. alisaundre] Elisaundre H; alexandre H^3; Assye V. in(3)] and in VHK; and RCh ENH^3. manye] mony VL. places] place JEWN.
17 Ȝe] As ȝe M. mowe] mowen K; mown LH^3; may ChHEWNM. se] sen RAMH^3; sene J; see E; seen UK; seo V; seon L. be] on L. my] þe WH^3; *om* M. signes] syngnys H^3; synes R; synys A; senys E. sitten . . . hat] on myn hatte setten W. sitten] sitty*n* JAKNH^3; sitteþ VM; sette*s* E.

Þat I haue walkid wel wide in wet & in driȝe,
And souȝt goode seintes for my soule hele.'
'Knowist þou ouȝt a corseint,' *quaþ* þei, 'þ*at* men callen treuþe?
Canst þ*ou* wisse vs þe wey where þ*at* wy dwelliþ?'
'Nay, so [me god] helpe,' seide þe [gome] þanne.
'I sauȝ neu*ere* palm*ere* wiþ pik ne wiþ scrippe
Axen aftir hym, er now in þis place.'
'Petir,' quaþ a plouȝman and putte forþ his hed, 25
'I knowe hym as kyndely as clerk doþ his bokis.
Clene consience & wyt kende me to his place,

18 *transposed with following* K; *this is the* C-*text order. From here to line* 94 K *has a* C-*character, resembling* **C** VIII 175–260: *see above*, p. 31. **Collation of K now ceases and resumes at line** 95 **below.** Þat] Tht M; *om* A. walkid] walked RDChVHLWNM. wel] wil D; wol A; ful VHENH³; *twice* H²; *om* RUJWM. wide] wyde qwore J. wet] weet UV. in(2)] *om* Ch. driȝe] drie URDChH²HJ LEAWN; druye V; dreye M.
19 And] I haue E. souȝt] souȝth R; south H³; soth E; sekid A. goode] gude E; many a W. seintes] seynt W. soule] saule E; soulis N. hele] heile E; helthe JLN.
20 Knowist] Knawys E. þou] *om* WN. ouȝt] oute JAH³; aught UD; *om* RHM. corseint] corsante E; corpsent M; seint H. *quaþ* . . . treuþe] þai clepe sent trewþe quot þai A. *quaþ* þei] *om* VNM. þei] þai E; I W. þ*at*] *twice* M; *om* VE. men] me W. callen] callyn J; calle RN; calleþ DVW; callys E; clepyn H³; clepeth M. treuþe] trewethe M; truþe R; trwþe N; trouthe LW; seynt Treuþe V.
21 Canst þou] canstu R; Canstow N; kannustow M; Const þou VL; Constow Ch; Canstow oght W; kanstow out J; Can þou oght E; And canst þou H³. wisse] wissen VL; wyssyn JH³; wyschen A; teche H. vs] me W. wey] weyȝe H³. where] qwere J; quare E; þer LAMH³; þeder as W. þat] the H²E; *om* W. wy] wyghe L; wyte A; wyth H³; man M; he RUDVHJW. dwelliþ] dwelleþ DRChVLWM; dwellys E; walkeþ H.
22 so] sa E. me . . . helpe] God glade me V. me god] RUDJLENMH³; god me HAW; god mote me TChH². seide] seiþ N; seis U; q*uod* JW. þe] þat M. gome] RUVJLA; grome EWN (r *above line same ink* W); man TDChH²MH³; pilgrym H. þanne] þenne UVE; þen H.
23 *run together with following* A. I sauȝ] Sauh I V; Saw I U; Yit say I W. sauȝ] sawe ChLEN; sayhe J; say DH² (*late corrector alters to* saw H²); seye M; sey RAH³. wiþ . . . scrippe] wiþ scrip ne wiþ pyk H; *om* A. pik] sclaveyn W. ne] no ChL; no*n* H³. wiþ(2)] *om* W. scrippe] schrippe V; skreppe H³.
24 Axen . . . hym] Such a seint seche V. Axen] Axin J; Axe N; Asken LWM; askyn AH³; Aske DHE. aftir] euer after L. hym] seint treuþe HAN. er . . . place] *om* A. er] or DChH²JEW; ar NM; eer þan U; bote VH. in] here in DM; right in E; neuere in W; I come i*n* H³. þis place] my lyue W. þis] no diu*ers* J.
25 a] þe E. plouȝman] Plouȝ Mon VL. forþ] for U; out D. hed] hede JWM; heed H; heued UDChE.
26 knowe] knawe E. as(1)] als ChE; as so J. kyndely] kuyndeliche V; kendely ChM. as(2)] as a ChEAH³. clerk] clerk*es* R. doþ] doys E; done R. his] is A; her R; *om* D. bokis] bukeȝ E; boke H²JM.
27 Clene . . . wyt] Conscience and clene witte W. Clene] kynde H; *om* N. &] *om* H. wyt] wygte M; kynd wyt H²N (kynd *cancelled* H²); *om* H. kende me] me kenneth L. kende] kenned DN; kennyd E; kennyþ RA; kenne W; tauȝte VH; taugth H³; taugte M; taute J. to] riȝt to H. his] þis D.

And dede me sure hym [siþþe] to *ser*ue hym for eu*er*e;
Boþe sowe [and sette] while I swynke mi3te.
I haue ben his folewere al þis fourty wynt*er*; 30
Boþe sowen his seed, & sewide hise bestis, |
And kepide his corn, & cariede it to house, *fol.* xxxviij *a*
Dyke[d] & d[o]luen & do what he hi3te,
Wiþinne & wiþoute waytide his *pro*fit.
Þ*er*e is no labo*ur*er in his lordsshipe þ*at* he louiþ bet*er* 35
For, þei3 I sey it myself, I *ser*ue hym to pay.

28 *line om* W. dede] dedde M; dide H; did JEN; diden U; dude RVL. me sure] enseure me V. me] HJLANMH³; me to TRUDChH²E. sure] suren N; seure D; assur*e* H; asuryn J; ensur*e* H²; ensuren L; swere EH³; sweren M; sweryn A. hym(1)] *om* VEAMH³; *erasure* H. siþþe] sithen LAN; syþin J; seþþe V; sothe M; sothenesse H³; *om* TRUDChH²HE. to] for to RDA. *ser*ue] seruen NM; *ser*uyn JH³. hym(2)] *om* L. for] *om* RDAMH³.
29 Boþe] Bathe E; For Ch. sowe . . . sette] to sett & to sawe E; now and siþe RU. sowe] sowen N; sowyn J; to sowe ChHAWH³; to sowen VM. and sette] & sette LN; & settyn J; & to sette HAW MH³; and to setten V; & seden D; his seed TChH². while] wille M; qwyl JH³; whiles L; qwylse E. swynke] swynckyn J; swenke M; mi3te] moughte M.
30 *marked with cross* N. I . . . folewere] So haue I folwed forth W. ben] be R; bene J; bien H²; beon L. folewere] folower DChE; folwer*e* RAH³; falwere U; falwer J; felawe V; holder*e* H; *ser*uaunt NM. al] *om* VH. fourty] four*e* J; fiftene VH; seuenty N. wynter] wynt*er*s H; 3eres M.
31 Boþe] Bath E. sowen] sowyn JAH³; sawyn E; Isowen VHNM; to sowe Ch. his] *in margin, same hand* H³. seed] sedys H³. sewide] sewyd H²J; sewed RCh; seued D; suwed V; swed N; sywed L; folewid H; folwid AH³; folewed M; folwde E; kepid U; siþ kept W.
32 *line om* N; *touched up, another hand* L. And] and eek UVMH³. kepide] kepid RUH²EAH³; keped ChL; kepit D; kepe M; Ikept VH; kepid wele J; layd on and lad W. his] *om* W. &] *om* V. cariede] caried RUDChHLEA; caryid H³; cary3id J; Icaried V; carie M; broght W. it] *om* Ch. to] tou M. house] howse3 E.
33 Dyked] LN; I diked E; I dikid A; Idyket V; Idykete M; dychid JH³; And eke diked W; I haue dichid H; Dyken TRUChH²; Dykyn D. &(1)] *om* AM. doluen] URH²HLN; doluy*n* H³; duluy*n* J; Idoluen VM; I dalfe A; deluen TDCh; delved EW. &(2)] *om* VAM. do] don RLWN; Ido M; Idon V; dyd E; I dede A. what] qwat JE; þat ANH³. hi3te] hy3the RH²; hythe H³; hyth A; hyte J; hoted L; 3eygth M; bad H; me hi3t Ch; bad me E.
34 Wiþinne] *with*Innen V; withinnyn J; Boþe wiþin W; &] *om* M. wiþoute] *with*outen VN; withoutyn JH³. waytide his *pro*fit] his profite awaited W. waytide] waytyd H³; waited ChA; I wayted VHNM; & wayted L; I watyd E; to wayte R; to wayten U; wayten D; weele J. profit] *pro*fyth AH³; *pro*fete J; *pro*fett E.
35 Þ*er*e] *om* W. is] nys UDVM. no] non D; *om* M. labo*ur*er] laboure H; labore W. in] *with*inne R. his] þis VLWM; *om* H. lordsshipe] lordschep RChAH³; lond W; leod V. he] hi*m* RU. louiþ] loueth DCh VHLWNM; louet H²; loves E; louyd A; lykeþ RU. bet*er*] more VH.
36 þei3] thei H²JM; þou3 RDChHN; þogh W; þoghe U; þow AH³; þaugh L; þauh V; yf E. sey] seie U; say HLEW; sigge V. it] *om* A. self] seluen E; seluy*n* H³; seolf L. *ser*ue] serued ChL; seche W. pay] plese UW.

[I] haue myn here of hym [wel] & oþ*er*while more;
He is þe presteste payere þ*at* pore men knowen;
He [wiþ]halt non hyne his hire þ*at* he ne haþ it at eue.
He is as louȝ as a lomb & loueliche of speche. 40
And ȝif ȝe wilneþ wyte where þ*at* wy dwelliþ
I [wile] wisse ȝow wel riȝt to his place.'
'Ȝa, leue piers,' quaþ þe pilg*ri*mes & p*ro*fride hym hire.
'Nay, be þe p*er*il of my soule!' quaþ piers & gan to swere:
'I nolde fonge a ferþing for seint Thomas shryne, 45

37 I] RUDVHJLEAWNMH^3; And TCh H^2. here] er*e* M; hir*e* RUH^{2}JEAH^3; hure DVN; huyr*e* HL. of . . . wel] wele of hym E; at my wyl W. wel] RDVA NH^3; wele J; weel U; *om* TChH^{2}HLM. oþ*er*while] sumtyme AMH^3. while] qwile JE; whiles L. more] mare E.
38 W *corrupts to* He paieþ prest pore men and þat dar I proue. is] his E. þe] þeo L; *om* N. presteste] prestyste RUCh; p*ri*stest E; rediest H. payere] payȝer*e* R; maist*er* E. pore] pure E; *om* A. knowen] knowyn JAH^3; knoweþ RM; knowiþ H; knawen E; habbeþ V.
39 He wiþhalt] w*ith*holde he N. He] *om* W. wiþhalt] withhalt H^{2}VLH^3; withholt JW; wiþholdiþ H; w*ith*haldeȝ E; withhalde M; ne w*ith*holdith A; ne halt TRUD; ne holte Ch. non] noon Ch; no RHEAW. hyne his] mannys HA. hyne] hyȝen J; huwe N; hynes M; man W. his] here W. hire] her*e* M; hure D; huire VHL; *above line and in margin, similar hands* W. þat . . . it] he paieþ hem H; but ȝeueþ hit hym W. þ*at*] bot E. ne] no L; *om* VJEMH^3. haþ it] hit hath L; hit naþ V. haþ] hatȝ H^2; hat H^3; hase E; haue D; nath M. eue] euen ChVHEN; euyn JAH^3; ones W.
40 as(1)] als LE; *om* DMH^3. louȝ] louh V; low RUH^2; lowe DChHJLANM; lowlych W; louely E; lown H^3. as(2)] als E. a] *om* (*late corrector supplies*) H^2. lomb] lom H^3; lambe DChE. &] *om* DVHN. loueliche] louesume E.
41 *run together with following* W. And] *om* HAN. ȝif] ȝef ChL; ȝif þat UHN. ȝe] *om* (*late corrector supplies* ye) H^2. wilneþ] willeþ D; wolleþ V; willen M; wille U; wil REAH^3; wol ChHW; desyrin J. wyte] wite RUH; wete ChEW; weten M; wetyn AH^3; Iwite V; to wyte TH^{2}LN; to wityn J; to weten D. where] whare U; qwer H^3; qwar E. þ*at*] þe J; *om* H^{2}EW. wy] wyht J; wyte A; wytt H^3; man M; he RUDH^{2}VHLEW. dwelliþ] dwelleþ DRChVWN; dwellys E.
42 wile] wil W; wol V; shal TRUDCh H^{2}HJLANM; sall E; xal H^3. wisse ȝow] ȝow wisse W. wisse] wissen VLM; wissyn J; visse E; teche H. ȝow] ow VLE. wel] ful HEH^3; *om* UVWM. riȝt] right ENM; riht J; ryth H^3; ryȝth R; riȝt home HL; þe riȝt way TCh; þe wey right U; þe way DH^2; þe wey hom V; *om* AW. to] vnto E. his] his owyn AMH^3; his awne E. place] house H.
43 Ȝa] ȝe RDH^{2}HLNM; YE V; A ȝe J; *om* W. leue] leoue L; loue H. piers] *om* J. þe] þis V; *om* LH^3. pilg*ri*mes] pilgrym Ch WM; palmers VE. profride] p*ro*frid H; p*ro*frede H^2; p*ro*frede*n* V; p*ro*fred DW; p*ro*ferid AH^3; p*ro*fereden L; p*ro*feredyn J; p*ro*fered R; proferd ChENM. hym] *om* H^{2}JA. hire] huire VHL; her (*late corrector cancels and supplies* hym hyre *in margin*) H^2; ere M.
44 Nay . . . piers] Piers sone seyde nay M. Nay] *om* H. be . . . piers] q*uo*d he by my saule E. þe] *om* N. peril] perele A; pereille Ch. quaþ piers] *om* H^{2}H^3 (*late corrector supplies* H^2). piers] perus U; he H. &] *om* H^3. gan to] gan A; can L; began to DW; bigon to V; gan for to RUH^{2}JN; he ga*n* H^3; he gun E; fast he dide H. swere] swere fast EAMH^3; faste swere L.
45 nolde] ne wold AM; nold not W; nold nouth H^3; wald noght E. fonge] fongyn J; fange EA; take HMH^3. ferþing] ferdyng J; peny H^3. for . . . shryne] not for fyften shillyng W. shryne] shiryne N; scryne H^2.

For treuþe wolde loue me þe wers a long tyme aftir.
Ac ȝe þat wilneþ to wende, þis is þe weye þider:
Ȝe mote go þoruȝ meknesse, boþe men & wyues,
Til ȝe come into consience þat crist wyte þe soþe,
Þat ȝe loue hym leuere þanne þe lif in ȝoure hertis; 50
And þanne ȝoure neiȝebours next in none wise apeir[e]
Oþerwise þanne þou woldist men wrouȝte to þiselue;
And so bo[wiþ] forþ be a [brok], be buxum of speche,
Forto ȝe fynden a foorþe, ȝoure fadris honouriþ;

46–7 *transposed, but the correct order is indicated* U.
46 For] *om* VHJLEANMH[3]. treuþe] Trouthe LE; truþe R; Trweth M; Trwþe N; he W. wolde] wald E. þe] *om* H[2]. wers] worse DH; wores R; lasse VL; lesse N. long] gret VHM. tyme] while VHLAW; wyle M. aftir] þereaftir H[2] LN; hereafter HJW.
47 Ac] Bot ChVHLEWNM; And AH[3]. ȝe] if ȝe EM. þat] *om* EAMH[3]. wilneþ . . . wende] wendeþ to him V. wilneþ] wilnen L; willeþ DCh; wil REA; wole H; ȝernyn J; þenkyn M; thenke H[3]. to] to hym H; *om* REA. wende] wende þeder R; wenden þe weye M; wite JW. weye] weyȝe H[3]. þider] þidire J; þeder DChE; thedere M; thedyr H[3]; þedur A; *om* RW.
48 Ȝe] You E. mote] motyn J; most HAWM; bus E. go] gon DChJAH[3]; ga E; mete W. þoruȝ] thoru H[2]; þorow ChJN; þorgh L; þorw RV; þurȝ H; þurw U; pourȝt D; be EAMH[3]; wiþ W. meknesse] meokenesse L. boþe] bath E. men] man HAN; Mon V; maydenis R; ȝe W. wyues] wyfes DA; wyfs M; wyffeȝ E; wyf VH; ȝowre wyfs W.
VI 49–VII 2 *om* (**a leaf wanting**) H.
49 come] comen JM. into] to UChH[2] LEAWNMH[3]. þat] *om* EWH[3]. wyte] wete M; wot AWH[3]; wate E; knowe V.
50 *divided from following after* lyf W. Þat] And Ch; Than must W. loue] louen LM; louyn JAH[3]; loueþ V. leuere] *same hand after cancelled* bettre N; better H[3]. þanne] þen ChVE. þe . . . in] ȝe do E. þe] ȝowre W; ȝoure oune M. lif] liȝf N; lifes M. in . . . hertis] *om* M. in] of A. ȝoure] oure V. hertis] heortis L; hert EW.
51 *run together with following* M. And þanne] In ernest E. þanne] þenne V; *om* LWM. ȝoure] oure V. neiȝebours] neyȝbours D; neyȝbores R; neiȝborowes Ch; neihebors V; neyebores J; neytebours A; neyȝbour U; neghbour W; neygbore H[3]; neburrow M; nextbure E. next] nixte R; *om* EW. in . . . apeire] *om* M. none] no DEAWH[3]. wise] vise E. apeire] apeyre RVJLAWNH[3]; to apeire UD; apeiriþ T; apeyreth H[2]Ch; ȝe pare E.
52 Oþer . . . to] And no more harm to hym þan to A; euen as M. wise] wisse E; weys V; wayes W; *om* Ch. þanne] þen V; & E. þou] ȝe RULE. woldist] woldest DChH[2]VWN; wolde UL; wald E; wost J; wol R. men] he W. wrouȝte] wrouȝten V; wroute J; dyd E; dedyn H[3]. to] on J. þi] ȝou RUE; ȝor M; or L. selue] seluen ChVN; siluen H[2]; seolue L; *om* E.
53 And] *om* V. so] swa E; *om* H[2]ANM. bowiþ] bowith J; bowyt H[3]; boweþ RUNM; Bouweþ V; bowes ChL; bowe D; bouȝ T; shal ȝe bowe W; behofes yow E; vowe H[2]; wende A. forþ] furth E; *om* JWM. be(1)] to J; tyl N. brok] VLA; broke RDJWNM; brook UH[3]; bruke E; bank TChH[2]. be(2)] beo V; beþ UJNMH[3]; beoth L; hight W; *om* R. buxum] buxhomme M. of] of your E.
54 *line om* V; *marked with cross* H[3]. Forto] For til M; Til WN; Vnto E; Forþ til RUA; For D. ȝe] *om* J. fynden] fyndyn JA; fynde RUDChH[2]LWH[3]; fynd E. a] *om* J. foorþe] forthe H[2]MH[3]; forþ N; furth E; forde UDChLA; for W; ferde R; *om* J. ȝoure fadris] of A. ȝoure] ȝow W. fadris] fadir E. honouriþ] honoured ChR; honour A; ȝe honoure LE; ȝe honnourdd M; & hem ȝe honoure J; to honewre H[3].

Wadiþ in *þat* watir & wasshiþ ȝow wel *þere*, 55
And ȝe shuln lepe þe liȝtliere al ȝo*ure* lif tyme;
So shalt þou se swere nouȝt but it be for nede,
A[nd] nameliche an ydel þe name of god almiȝt;
Þanne shalt þou come be a croft, ac come þou nouȝt *þere*inne;
Þ[e] croft hattiþ coueite nouȝt menis catel ne h*ere* wyues, 60
Ne none of h*ere* s*er*uauntis, *þat* noiȝe hem miȝte;
Loke þou breke no bowis *þere* but it be þin owene.

55 Wadiþ] wadeþ RDChVNM; wades U; Wade E; Þan wadyth H³; And þan wadeþ W; wendith H². in] into LE. *þat*] þe ChEA; *om* W. &] *om* V. wasshiþ] wachith J; wasscheþ VN; waschetȝ H²; wassche UDLAWM; wasch Ch; ways R; weshe E. ȝow] ow V; ȝe ow L. wel] *om* RUEAWMH³. *þere*] thare H²; þerinne RUM; þan þare E.
56 *line om* A; *marked with cross* D. ȝe shuln] xul ȝe (*transposition indicated*) H³. ȝe] he M. shuln] schul UH²VJM; schule L; schulle R; shole W; schal DChN; sal E. lepe] lepyn J; kepe (k *cancelled*) D. liȝtliere] lyȝtlere H²; liȝtlyar N; lithlichere J; liȝter Ch; lytthere H³; lightlokere UDVW; lythtloker L; bettre M. ȝo*ure*] oure V. lif] live E. tyme] after LEWMH³.
57 So] þa*n*ne N; And than W; And þen E; Sone V; *om* A. shalt . . . nouȝt] Thou schalt not swere A. shalt] xalt H³; schal JLWN; sal E; shul RUM. þou] ȝe RUJLE WNM. se] see M; seo L; þenne Iseo V; gon be J; *om* ChE. swere] swereth M. nouȝt] not UVLWM. it . . . for] þou haue V; ȝyf þou se H³. it] ȝef hit L; if it EAWNM. be] beo L. for] *om* W. nede] neode V; gret nede W.
58 And] RUDChH²VJLEAWNMH³; A T. nameliche] nameleche A; nomeliche V. an] on RUDLW; In VJEANMH³. ydel] Idille Ch; þe ydel U; ydelnes EH³; Idylchepe A. þe name] non othe A. þe] *om* RU. name] nome V. god] *om* H³. almiȝt] *late corrector adds* y H²; almygth A; almyghte UD; almyȝty ChLEWN; almyȝthy R; Almihti V; almythy H³; almyhtyn J; almyten M.
59 Þanne] þenne V; *om* A. shalt þou] Thou schalt A. shalt] xalt H³; shal RDN; sall E; schul UVJ; schule L. þou(1)] ȝe RUVJLEN (*top margin same hand* L). come(1)] comen J; comy*n* H³. be] to N. ac] but DChVJLEWNMH³; *om* RUA. come] kome*n* M; comeþ RU JN. þou] ȝe V; *om* RUDJLEWNMH³. nouȝt] not RVJLEAWM; nat H².
60 *divided from following after* catell JL; *as two lines divided after* side W. Þe] UDVJ LEANMH³; Þat TRChH²W. croft] *om* W. hattiþ] hatteþ R; hatte UH²L; hatt N; hat Ch; hoteth M; hette V; hiȝte DW; hite JA; heght E. coueite] coueyteþ R; coueitise cast hym by side Coueite W. nouȝt] not RUVEM; nat H²; not no L; no JW; *om* A. menis] ma*n*nys RJ; mannes L; mans W. ne . . . wyues] his wif ne his hyne W. ne] no ChL; no*n* H³; & N. h*ere*] her ChJNH³; hire D; heore VL; þair E.
61 *line om* A. Ne . . . s*er*uauntis] His Norice ne no þing W. Ne] no L; Nou*n* H³. none of] *om* JL. h*ere*] her ChJNH³; hire H²; heore VL; þair E. s*er*uauntis] seruauns VL; s*er*uaundes JE; catel N. *þat*] at E. noiȝe hem] hem noyȝen J; hem noye U; þaim noye E; hym noie W; han any N. noiȝe] noiȝen ChH³; noye DM; nuyȝen V; nuyen L. hem] heom L; hym DM. miȝte] mought M.
62, 63 *transposed* A.
62 Loke] Luke E; And loke W. þou] ȝe R. breke] breyke J; plokke A. no] none UM. bowis] bowe AH³; bowhe J; Bouȝ V; boughe M; bogh L; bugh E; brau*n*che N; bonys W. *þere*] *þer*for (for *cancelled*) J; *om* ChEAW. but . . . owene] *as an independent line after cancelled* for peryl of þi soule U. it] ȝif hit VENMH³; ȝef hit L; þei RUCh. be] beo VL. þin] þi E; ȝo*ur* RU. owene] owyn RAH³; awyne J; nawne E.

Two stokkis þere stonde, but stynte þou not þere;
Þei hote stele nouȝt, ne sle nouȝt; strik forþ be boþe.
Leue hem on þi left half, & loke nouȝt þereaftir, 65
And hold wel þin haliday heiȝ til euen.
Þanne shalt þou blenche at a b[erw]e, bere no fals wytnesse;
He is fre[þ]id in wiþ Floreynes & oþere [fees] manye.
Loke þou plukke no plant[e] þere for peril of þi soule.
And þanne shalt þou [se] sey soþ, so it be to done; 70
[And] loke þat þou leiȝe nouȝt for no manis biddyng.
Þanne shalt þou come to a court, cler as þe sonne.

63 Two] To A; Twa E; Twei VW. stonde] stonden UDM; stondyn H³; stondeþ RVL; stondith A; stondes W; standyn J; standes E. but] *om* AWM. stynte] stunt V. þou] þe E; ȝe UN; ȝou R; *om* JWH³. not] nouȝt DChNM; noght ULE; nouth H³. þere] þare E.
64 Þei] Þai EA; þay L; Tho D; *om* W. hote] hoten UD; hatte RH³; hatten L; hattyn J; hat Ch; hetten V; Hight WN; higten M; hyten A; heght E. stele] stel RU; steyll E; steol L; Sle V. nouȝt(1)] not RVLEAW. ne] no ChL. sle] sla E; slo H³; stel V. nouȝt(2)] not RUH²VJLEAWM. strik] stryk VDJLNMH³; streke E; but strik TRUChH²W; stirte A. forþ] furþe Ch; *om* A. be] by hem DV; fro hem A. boþe] boþin J; bathe E.
65 Leue] lef RDVL; Leefe J. hem] heom L; þaim E; hym W; it M. þi] þe U. left] lyft RLA; luft V. half] hand EAH³. &] but J; *om* VEMH³. loke] luke E; loke þow Ch; loke hem VN. nouȝt] not RH²VJLAM; nat Ch; neuere W. þereaftir] aftre N; aftur V.
66 *line om* U. And] *om* EA. hold] hold so H³; Hald swa E; helde so M. haliday] holiday WN. heiȝ] heiȝe Ch; hey R; hye JL; heyliche D; hay (? haþ) H³; holly AW; euere V; alwey forþ N; fro morew M; it is þe way E. til] to DE WM. euen] DChVLEN; euyn JAH³; eue M; þe euen TH²; þe eue R; þe ende W.
67 *marked with cross* H³. Þanne] þenne V. shalt] xalt H³; schal NM; sall E. þou] ȝe N. blenche] blenchen RVJ; blynche D; bleinke E; see blenche U. at] be W; *om* RUA. a] *om* LA. berwe] DN; berwh L; bergh W; bowhe J; bourne T; borne Ch; burne H²; brok VM; brook H³; bak RU; brige E; *om* A. no] non H².
68 He] Þat EAMH³. freþid] frethid U; frithed RD; frettid TH²H³; frettyt J; fretted ChLM; frettet V; fetterd E; federid A; feffyd N; frayd W. in] *with*-Innen V; *om* JLEANMH³. wiþ] white D. Floreynes] floures D; flours W. oþere . . . manye] many oþer floures Ch. oþere fees] oþes V. oþere] *om* L. fees] RUJL MH³; feys E; foos W; foes N; federis A; flouris T; floures DH². manye] mony E; wel manye L; wel monye V.
69 Loke] RUVJLAWNMH³; Luke E; And loke TDChH². plukke] pulke J. no . . . þere] þerof no plant W. plante] ChJLEAMH³; plaunte N; plonte V; plantis TRUDH². þere] *om* A. soule] saule E.
70 *line om* AN. And] *om* RUVEWMH³. þanne] þenne V; *om* L. shalt þou] þou xalt H³. shalt] sall E. þou] *corrected from* ȝow W; *om* (*late corrector inserts*) H². se] RUDW; sen H³; seyin J; see EM; seo L; *om* TChH²V. sey] seye M; seyȝe H²; say EW; *om* DL. soþ] þe soth JE; sithe L. so . . . be] for þat is wel W. so] sa E; so þat V; if M. be] beo VL. done] do E.
71 *line om* N. And] RUVJLE; And þan W; *om* TDChH²AMH³. loke . . . nouȝt] In none manere ellis M; in na maner ellys E; In no maner ellis nout H³. þat] *om* RAW. leiȝe] liȝe ChV; lye RUDJ LAW. nouȝt] not RH²VLAW. no] nome U. manis] monnes V; manere W. biddyng] bidyng V; heste M.
72 Þanne] ÞEnne V. shalt] xalt H³; schal NM; sall EJ. þou] ȝe N. come] comen JM. cler] Cleer V; as cler RUJLWH³; as cliere D; as bryght A; is clire M. as] of M.

Þe mot is of m*er*cy þe Maner al aboute,
And alle þe wallis ben of wyt to holde wil þeroute; | *fol.* xxxviij *b*
Þe kirnelis ben of cristendom þ*at* kynde to saue, 75
And bot*er*asid wiþ beleue [so] oþ*er* þou [be]st not sauid;
Alle þe housis ben helid, hallis ⁊ chaumbris,
Wiþ no led but [wiþ] loue ⁊ louȝnesse, as breþ*er*en of o wombe.
Þe tour þ*er*e treuþe is hymself is vp to þe sonne;
He may do wiþ þe day sterre what hym dere likiþ; 80
Deþ dar not do þing þ*at* he defendiþ.
Grace hattiþ þe [gateward], a good man forsoþe,

73 Þe] þeo L. þe(2)] þat þe L. al aboute] encloseth L. al] *om* AWNMH^3. aboute] abouten V.
74 alle] *om* A. wallis] wall E. ben] bene J; been M; bien H^2; beon L; beþ RDVW; is E. wyt] wght M. holde wil] wonyn J. holde] holden L; holdyn A; hald E. wil] self wyl H^3; wel U; wele E; foule W. þeroute] oute AWH^3; *om* N; *defaced* M.
75 Þe] þeo L. kirnelis] kyrnalles E; kernelis H^2; kernelles M; cornelys RH^3; cornels DL; Carnels V; kernelle Ch; corneris AW. ben] bene J; bien H^2; beon L; beþ RDVW; er E. cristendom] cristalle Ch. þat] þe UV; o*ur* E; man M; to H^3. kynde] kuynde V; kende A; ken WH^3. to] for to E; is for to L; ȝou to W; to be H^3. saue] sauue M; sauere (?) J; kepen L.
76 And] þe N; *om* VWM. boterasid] boterased DL; boteraseded (-ed *cancelled*) J; Botrace it W; botraces N; boterace Ch; Ibotrasde M; burased R; briteschid U; britasyd E; Brutaget V. wiþ] wit W; of N. beleue] þe bileeue V; lef R; eliues A. so] RDJLA; wel W; *om* TUChH^{2}V ENMH^3. oþer . . . sauid] longe to stonden M. oþer þou] wher þorw we VN. oþer] or RChH^{2}LEWH^3; or elles UA; elles D; worth (*followed by cancelled* þou now) J. þou] *om* E. best] RUChH^{2}JAWH^3; bes L; beys E; be N; worst TD; moten beo V. not] nouȝt DCh; noght UE; nouth H^3; notes L; now J; *om* VN. sauid] saued RUDChH^{2}LEWN; sauet V.
77 *line om* N; *divided from following after* led AH^3; *run together with following* M. Alle] *om* A. þe] *om* U. housis] rofeȝ E. ben] bene J; bien H^2; beon L; beþ RD; beoþ V; ar E. helid] heled RDChW; hylyd J; hilde M; hyllyd H^3; heoled L; Ihulet V. hallis ⁊ chaumbris] *om* M. hallis] bath halleȝ E; halle U; alle A; boþe alle W. chaumbris] chambre W.
78 no . . . but] *above line similar hand* J; *om* M. no] *om* A. led] lede EN; leed UH^2; lord W. but] bod E; *om* A. wiþ] *with* RChH^{2}VLANH^3; al wiþ U; *om* TDJEW. loue] pure loue J; lownes W. ⁊ . . . wombe] wete þou þe sothe M. ⁊ louȝnesse] and lownesse RDAH^3; ⁊ lufsumnes E; ⁊ loue W; *om* UVJLN. as . . . wombe] of hert ChH^2; also E; echon oþer W. o] on D; one U; a JL.
79 Þe] þeo L. þere] qwer E; þat W; is A. treuþe] treouthe L; truþe R; Trweth M; trwþe N; troth E. is hymself] him selue is U. is(1)] is Inne VAWM. hymself] *om* VJWNM. self] selue H^2; seluen E; seolf L. is(2) . . . to] is vpon JN; Iset Is aboue V; sette by W. þe(2)] þat J.
80 do] don JA. day] *om* A. sterre] steorre L; sterne EA. what] qwat JEH^3; what so R; waat so W; what þat D. hym] he E. dere] deore VL; good U; *om* RDW. likiþ] likeȝ E.
81 Deþ] Ded N; And dede E; For þe daye (? days) M. not] nouȝt ChH^{2}N; noght E; nouth JH^3; *om* DW. do] don JL. þing] noþing RDW; *om* EAMH^3. defendiþ] defenditȝ H^2; defendeth DChV LWNM; defend*es* RE. *Here* EAMH^3 *insert* 3 *lines like* **B** V 601–2 *or* **C** VIII 240–1: *see above*, p. 31.
82 *marked with cross* H^3. hattiþ] hattyt H^3; hatteþ R; hatte UH^{2}L; hat DChEN; hette V; hoteth M; hite JA; is W. þe] that H^2; *om* W. gateward] RUJLEAWM; gatward N; ȝateward V; ganward (?) H^3; porter TDChH^2. good] goud R; gude E. man] mon VL.

His man hattiþ amende ȝow, for many man he knowiþ.
Tel hym þis tokne, "treuþe wot þe soþe:
I *perfourmde* þe *penaunce* þe prest me enioynide, 85
And am sory for my synnes & so shal I *euere*
Whanne I þenke *þere*on, þeiȝ I were a pope".
Biddiþ amende ȝow meke hym to his *maister* ones
To weue [vp] þe wyket þat [þe wif] shette
Þo *Adam* & Eue eten here bane, 90
For he haþ þe keiȝes & þe cliket þeiȝ þe king slepe.
And ȝif *grace graunte* þe to gon in [on] þis wise,

83 *line om* A. man] Mon V; knave W; name E. hattiþ] hattyt H³; hatteth H²; hatte RUL; hat ChEN; hette V; hoteth M; hight DW; hyhte J. amende] ame*n*det H³; amendes D. ȝow] þou VLE (? you E); *om* D. for] ful H³; *om* EM. many] meny R; mony VLE. man] men RVLEM. he] hi*m* RUDVE. knowiþ] knowyt H³; knowitȝ H²; knoweth RDChVLWNM; knawys E.
84 *line om* A. Tel] Telle DChH²; Tyll E. þis] þe H³. tokne] tokene DH²VLH³; tokyne N; tokyn J; takeny*ng* E. treuþe] treuthȝ H²; treouthe L; truthe R; trweth M; trwþe N; troth E; for treuþe V; þat treuþ W. wot] woot U; wate E.
85 *perfourmde*] *perfourmed* H²; *per*formed RDChLE; *per*formede V; *per*formyd JA; *per*forned UNM; *per*forme W. þe *penaunce*] *om* D. þe(1)] myn M. þe(2)] þat þe RUVEAWMH³. prest] *pr*ist E. me enioynide] me enIuned Ch; mengeoned W; on me leyde JMH³. me] *om* RE.
86 And] And y UEA; I RVWN. synnes] sunnes V; synne W. so] swa E; *om* (*inserted another ink*) H². shal] xal H³; sall E.
87 *line om* A. Whanne] when ChH²LE; whon V; Qwan JH³. þenke *þere*on] þeron þenke U. þenke] thinke RDE; thing J. *þere*on] *þer*vpon N; vpon hem W. þeiȝ] þei JNM; þouȝ DChH²; þogh W; þow RUH³; þauȝ V; yf E. were] weore VL. a] *om* W. pope] pape E.
88 *line om* A; *divided from following after* maist*er* TRUDChH²JLN. Biddiþ] Bidde V; Bide W; Byd EH³; Beddeþ N; Bedde M; he Byddyth (he *in margin, same or similar hand*) J; loke ȝe men þat ȝe Ch. amende] Amendis D. ȝow] þou L; ȝow þan W; ȝow þat he Ch; & D; *om* V. meke] Meken VM; mekyn RJH³; meokyn L. hym] ȝow (*similar hand above cancelled* him) J. ones] anes E; *om* W.
89 *marked with cross* H³. To] And W; Prey hym to A. weue] weve D; weyue N; wayue ChLW; weyn A; weyen H³; wy*n*ne RUV; wynny*n* J; wynneyn M; put E. vp] RUH²VJLEAWNMH³ (*above line same hand* R); out TDCh. þe(1)] a H³. wyket] weket JEA; wiket ȝat V. þat] at E; þe NM. þe wif] þe wy N; þe whye L; þe wyȝt R; þe wight U; he W; þe aungel A; þe wey VM; þe weyȝe H³; þe way E; he *with* TDChJ; he *with* wylle H². shette] schet A; scette H²; chette N; schutte V; schytte J; schetteþ UM; schettet D; schetyth H³; stekett E; stoppet W.
90 Þo] To N; þo þat V; when L; Whan þat W; Þ*er* was E. eten] etyn RJEH³; heten A; hetene M; eeten V. here] her ChJNH³; heore VL; þ*er* E; oure R. bane] bone V; hane E.
91 For] *om* AW. haþ] hat H³; hatȝ H²; hed E; bar*e* M. keiȝes] keyes RUDCh; keyȝe H³; keye VJLWNM; key EA. &] of VLEAWMH³. þe] þ*at* EA. cliket] cleket DChJEAWH³. þeiȝ] þeig N; thei H²J; þeghe U; þouȝ D; þogh W; þou A; þow RChH³; þauȝ V; þagh L; if E; þer M. slepe] slepyd E; clepe R; Clepe (C? *or badly written round* s?) U.
92 And] *om* JA. ȝif] ȝef ChL; if þat W; at E. *graunte* þe] þe graunte V. þe] yow E. to] *om* Ch. gon] gone J; go ChEANM. in on] RUJ; in in VLN; in TDChWMH³; on H²EA. wise] tyme L.

Þou shalt se treuþe hi*m*self wel sitte in þin herte
And lere þe for to loue & hise lawes holden.
Ac be war þanne of wraþþe, þat wykkide shrewe, 95
For he haþ enuye to hym þat in þin herte sitteþ
And pokiþ [forþ] pride to preise þiselue.
Þe boldnesse of þi bienfait makiþ þe blynd þanne,
And so worst þou dryuen out as dew & þe dore closid,
Ikeiȝid & ycliket to kepe þe þ*er*oute 100

93 Þou shalt] þanne schatow N. Þou] Ye E. shalt] xalt H^3; schal H^2A; sal E. se] sen W; sene A; see EM; seene J; seo V; seon L. treuþe] trouthe LE; truþe R; trweth M; trwþe N. hi*m*self] hy*m* seluy*n* H^3; himseolf L; þyself ChJM; þeselfe A; yowr selfe E; *om* N. wel] wil DJ; *om* RUVEAWMH^3. sitte] sitten UVM; sytty*n* JAH^3; syttyng N; sette DE; setten W. þin] your E. herte] heorte L; herte*s* E.
94 *line om* A. And . . . for to] þe*n*ne loke þ*at* þou V. And] To E; And he wyl M; *om* N. lere] lerne UChMH^3; lernyn J. þe] ȝow JEMH^3; þou L. for] *om* NMH^3. loue] louen DChH^2; louy*n* H^3; loue him LWN; louyn him J; loue hi*m* wel V; leuen M. lawes] lawe VW. holden] holdy*n* H^3; holde UVJW; halde RE; kepen N.
95 **Here collation of** K **resumes.** Ac] Bot ChVEAKWM; And LNH^3. be] beo L; be wel N; beo wel V; be þou wel ȝit W; he M. war] warr*e* M; waar D; Iwar V. þanne] þenne LK; *om* RUVJEAWNMH^3. of] *om* DEH^3. wraþþe] wreth A; wraþe nouȝt D; wretthe noght U; wratthe nouþ R; wrathe þe nouȝt N; wrath he wrathe þe not J; þ*at* wreth noye yow noght E; þ*at* wratthe neyth ȝou nouth H^3. þat] þe W; for he is a VA. wykkide] *om* VJAW. shrewe] sherewe N.
96 For] *om* AN. haþ] hat H^3; hase E. enuye] envyȝe H^3. to] till E; w*ith* A. þat] & A. in . . . sitteþ] sitteþ in þyn herte V; sytte in þi herte W; settyn hym in ȝo*ur* hertis A. þin] yow E. herte] hart K; heorte L. sitteþ] sittihȝ H^2; stondeth M; riste*s* E.
97 And] *om* E. pokiþ] pokeþ DLAM; poukiþ Ch; poke H^2; p*ro*kerryth J; wil prike W; Put EN; puiteþ V; lokith U; loke R. forþ] VJLAKN; forth for H^3; for UH^2; ye furth no E; for no R; þe for TDChM; þe wiþ W. pride] pruide VL. to] forto D. preise] preisen VLM; preysyn JH^3; prayse KWN; prays E. þi] þe A; yowr E; him J. selue] seluen VENM; seoluen L.
98 Þe] Þat E; Throgh W. boldnesse] baldnes E. þi] þ*at* RU. bienfait] benefait Ch; benfet D; benfeet U; benefeth A; beynfeate K; bienfaitȝ L; benfetes W; benefetys JH^3; benfes V; buffet R; lyffe fett E; kyme M. makiþ . . . blynd] blyndeth þe JN; blendeþ þin eiȝen V; mekenes & blynd hym E. makiþ] makitȝ H^2; make W. þanne] þenne U; sone W; *om* VE.
99 And] *om* ChLKWN. so] Than W. worst þou] worþestou V; bestow W; *om* A. worst] worþ RJKN; wordyst H^3; doys E. þou] þe R. dryuen] dryuyn JKH^3; dryue RE; Idriuen V; dreven W; dreuyn A. out] *om* LE. as dew] at dore K; *om* VM. &] qwen E; at H^3. dore] durr*e* M; dere H^3. closid] closed DChLWNM; closede J; yclosed R; Icloset V; is closyd E.
100 E *corrupts to* And kepe þe clene owt of howse for eu*er*. Ikeiȝid & ycliket] Boþe wiþ cleket and keye W. Ikeiȝid] ykeyȝed R; Ikeyȝede H^2; Ikeiȝet V; ykeied UDL ANM; Ykeyyd K; keyed J; Ikayȝed Ch; wyt keyȝe H^3. ycliket] yklyked N; cliked D; ycliketid U; Ikliketed VL; ycleketyd K; ycleketed RCh; Iklekedyd A; Iclekedit H^2; clekedyd J; w*ith* cleket H^3; Ihoked M. kepe] holde RUM; holden V; holdyn J. þe] ȝou AW; *om* (*late corrector supplies*) H^2. þeroute] w*ith*oute AMH^3.

Happily an hundrit wynt*er* er þou eft entre.
Þus miȝt þou lese his loue, to lete wel be þiselue,
And geten it aȝen þoruȝ g*race* ⁊ þoruȝ no gift ellis.
Ac þ*ere* arn seuene sistris þ*at* [seruen] treuþe eu*ere*,
And ben port*er*is to þe post*er*nis þ*at* to þe place longiþ: 105
Þ*at* on hattiþ abstinence, and [humylite] anoþ*er*,
Charite ⁊ chastite beþ hire chief maidenes,
Pacience ⁊ pees mekil [peple] þei helpen,
Largenesse þe lady let in wel manye.

101 Happily] Haply H^2; Hapliche V; hapley Ch; Appely M; And happely KW. hundrit] hundrid U; hu*n*dred RDChH^2 VJLAK; hundreth EW; hu*n*deryd H^3; vndred M; C N. wynt*er*] ȝer VEM. er] or DChLEAK; ar NM. eft entre] *after cancelled* est entere J; entre eft W. eft] ofte M; *om* A.
102 miȝt þou] myghtestow L; þou myght W; maihtou VJ. miȝt] mught M; may EN. lese] lesen K; lesyn JNH^3; leosen VL; lose E. his] þ*at* E. to . . . selue] þ*at* last*es* for eu*er* E. lete] leten VM; letyn J; letten K; lat N; late W; *late corrector alters to* sete H^2. wel] much W. be] of W. selue] seluen V; seluy*n* H^3; silue H^2; seoluen L.
103 And] Bote VE. geten it] hit geten L. geten] getyn JKH^3; gete RUVAWN; þou gett E. it] hy*m* H^3; *om* E. aȝen] aȝeyn VL; ageyn UKNH^3; agayne JAW; *om* EM. þoruȝ(1)] *with* DWM; bi V. ⁊] *om* W. þoruȝ(2)] *with* DM; bi V; be A; he wil W; *om* EKH^3. no] no*n* H^3. gift] gefte D; ȝift V; ȝefte L; ȝiftys J; thing RUM; gilt E.
104 Ac] But ChLEKWNM; And H^3; *om* A. arn] arne M; er E; beþ W; beoþ V; ben KN. seuene] seouen L. sistris] sustres LW; sust*er*s DK; sustren ChVNM; douȝt*res* R; doutres U. þ*at*] to A. seruen treuþe] VUDLM; s*er*uyn trewthe JKH^3; serue trewþe AW; s*er*ue truthe RN; s*er*uys trowth E; trewþe loueþ Ch; treuth louen H^2; treuþe louf (louf *above line, smaller hand*) T. eu*ere*] ellys E.
105 And] To E; He A; *om* WN. ben . . . to] kepen M. ben] be E; bene J; bien H^2; beon L; beþ RChW; arn A; *om* N. to] at UH^2V; of DChJEAWNH^3; ou*er* K. þe(1)] hys E; *om* H^2V. post*er*nis] postornes L; posterne U; postru*n* M. þe(2)] þat WM. longiþ] longeþ RDCh LNM; longyn K; longen VW; lang*es* E.
106 Þ*at*] þe UAMH^3; *om* E. on] ton UAM. hattiþ] hattitȝ H^2; hatte RUChL; hatt E; hat N; hette VM; hiȝte D; hight KW; hyte A; is callid J. and] *om* RUJN. humylite] RUVJLEAKWNMH^3; meknesse TDChH^2. anoþ*er*] is anoþer R; hat an other E; þ*at* oþ*er* DChK; þe tother AW; the toher*e* M; þe oþr H^3.
107 *line om* A. Charite ⁊ chastite] Chastite and charite UN. beþ] beoþ V; ben UCh KNH^3; been M; bien H^2; beon L; er E; boþin J. hire] hir K; here UD; h*er* RChJ; his LENMH^3; þe W; *om* V. chief] clene E; tweye L; tweyne ful Choyse V. maidenes] maydynnes E; *om* (*two minims only*) U.
108 *line om* RU. ⁊] and eke W. mekil] mechil A; meche H^3; mykul H^2; michel J; mich K; muchel L; muchul M; muche ChV; moche N; many D; þat þe W. peple] VEWN; peeple M; puple AH^3; people K; folk TDChH^2JL. þei] þai A; thay K; *om* VEWN. helpen] helpyn JEAKH^3.
109 Largenesse] Largesse H^2VNH^3; Larges JE; largice (? largite) U; And largesse WM. þe] þat UDAKWNH^3. lady] lauedy Ch; leuedy J; mayde W. let] lette M; letith U; lettyth K; lat L; latyþ ChAH^3; lateþ RW; lattith J; latt*es* E; ledeþ VN. wel] wol UA; ful VEWMH^3. manye] monye V. *Here* K *adds lines like* **C** VIII 276–7: *see above*, p. 31.

Ac whoso is sib to þis sistris, so me god helpe, 110
He is wondirliche welcome & faire vndirfonge.
But ȝif ȝe be sibbe to su*m*me of þis seuene
It is wel hard, be myn hed, any of ȝow alle,
To gete ingang at any gate but g*ra*ce be þe more.'
'Be crist,' q*ua*þ a cuttepurs, 'I haue no kyn þ*er*e.' 115
'Ne I,' q*ua*þ an apeward, 'be auȝt þ*at* I knowe.'
'Wyte god,' q*ua*þ a waffrer, 'wiste I þat forsoþe,
Shulde I neu*er*e ferþ*er*e a foote for no freris p*re*ching.' |
'Ȝis,' quaþ peris þe plouȝman & pukide hym to goode: *fol.* xxxix *a*

110 Ac] Bote VLK; And ChENMH[3]; *om* AW. whoso] ho so DAH[3]; hose V; wo so M; qwo so J; qwa sa E; who RLN; sche U. is sib] syb is E. is] be AH[3]. þis] þes ChK; þese DH[2]AW; tho M; þa E; þe RUH[3]. sistris] sustres RChLKWN; sustren VM; sosteres D. so . . . helpe] sothely to telle K. so me] & sa may E.
111 He] *om* VJ. wondirliche] wonder E; wonder wel W; riȝt N; worþi to be A; ther*e* M. welcome] wel comen VM; wolcome RDWH[3]; wolcomyd A; wilcom E; vnwolcome U. faire] vnfair U. vndirfonge] vndirfongen UM; vndirfongyn D; vnderfonged R; vnderfongyde J; vnd*er*fangyd E; vnderforgeyn N.
112 But] And bote VKWNM; Ac bot J. ȝif] ȝef Ch; þagh L; *om* RDH[2]VEKWNM. ȝe] *same ink above cancelled* he H[2]; he RUJAWMH[3]. be] ben DV; bien H[2]; byn K; beo L; *om* E. su*m*me of] *om* E. þis] þise N; þes RChK; þees E; þese UDH[2]AH[3]; þeos V; þeose L; þo M. seuene] seuyne JK; seouen L; sewen M; seuene sustr*es* R; seuen I tell you for sothe E.
113 *line om* A; *run together with following* E. It] He D. is] war (*altered from* was) E. wel] wol U; ful VEKMH[3]. be myn] to ben D. hed] heued UE; hod R; had D. any . . . alle] *om* E. any] eny V; ony RUDH[2]; to any L; for eny N; for ony M. ȝow] Ow V.
114 To] *om* U. gete] getyn JAKH[3]; come M. ingang] ingonge N; in ȝong L; in goynge VJ; ingang*es* H[2]; any Ingange Ch; ingate RUEKH[3]; in AWM. at . . . more] *om* E. at] atte DM. any] eny RULN; my H[2]; þat VM; þe JAH[3]; *om* D. gate] ȝate ChH[3]; ȝat V; *om* U. be] beo VL. more] better L.
115 a] þe D. haue] RUDChH[2]VJLEAK WMH[3]; ne haue TN. kyn] kun V; kenne M. þere] þare DH[2]; þore A.
116 Ne] No ChVJ. I] *om* V. an] a RE MH[3]; þe D; *om* H[2]. apeward] hapeward A; apewart L; peward E; Bereward M; pelo*ur* R. be . . . þat] bott at E. be] for VN. auȝt] ouȝt DH[2]N; ouȝth R; owght K; oght LW; oute JAM; nouth H[3]; nout V. þat] *twice* M. knowe] knawe H[2]E.
117 Wyte god] God wote W; Iwis VA. Wyte] wete Ch; Wate E; wot N; I vowe to M; I wow to H[3]. a] þe D; *om* R. waffrer] waufrere R; brewst*er* J. wiste] wust V. þat] þis VJAKWN; it M; *om* E. forsoþe] þe sothe RUE.
118 Shulde I] I shuld M; I wolde JN; I nold W. Shulde] Sculde H[2]; Suld E; Would K. I] *om* L. neuere] no D; *om* W. ferþere a foote] a fote ferþer Ch; a fote forther L; feyre A. ferþere] forþere UVJEH[3]; further M; forth KW. a] no KW. no] all þe E. freris] frere LEW.
119 Ȝis] ȝus VL; Yes K; þus D. þe] *om* RULEW. plouȝman] plouȝmon VL; *om* W. &] a*n* R. pukide] puked M; pookyde H[3]; pokid UK; poked RDJ (*cancelled for* prokerd *similar hand* J); pouked Ch; powkid N; pluckyd A; plocked L; pullid H[2]; p*re*chede V; p*re*chyd E; poreth W. hym] he*m* DH[3]; hire VJL; hir N; here AM. goode] god Ch; gude E.

'M*er*cy [is] a maiden [þere], haþ miȝt ou*er* [hem] alle; 120
And she is sib to alle synful, ⁊ hire sone alse,
And þoruȝ þe helpe of hem [two], hope þou non oþ*er*,
Þou miȝt gete g*ra*ce [þere] so þou go be tyme.'

120 is] ChVJLEAKWNMH^3; haþ TD; hatȝ H^2; had R; hadde U. maiden] maydy*n* H^3; maydou*n* J; mayde DW. þere] RUVJLKWN; þare D; *om* TChH^2 EAMH^3. haþ] hatȝ H^2; has E; and haþ VKM; ⁊ hat H^3; þat hath A; þat U; ⁊ W; she R. miȝt] maystre W. ou*er*] of W. hem] he*m* RUDChVJAKWNM H^3; heom L; þaim E; *om* TH^2.
121 And] *om* RVJEWN. she] Scho E; Heo VL; he M; *om* A. synful] synful men V. ⁊] an V. hire] hir ENH^3; her*e* UDAWM; her ChK; hure RH^2. alse] also UDChH^2ANMH^3; als JEW; both K.
122 þoruȝ] þourȝt D; þrogh W; thrugh K; þorou*r* (?) A. þe] *om* EAWMH^3. helpe] hope E. hem] heom L; them K; þaim E. two] RUVLWN; to AMH^3; too so K; bath twa E; so J; *om* TDChH^2. hope] howpe J. þou] þou my*n* H^3; now Ch. non] no E.
123 miȝt] maiȝt V; mayht J; mightyst K; may E; schalt N. gete] geten Ch; getyn JM; gett EK; se R. g*ra*ce þere] þ*er* grace H^3. g*ra*ce] ingate E; In M. þere] RDVJLKNM; *om* TUChH^2EAW. so] sa E; so þat V; ȝif A; ⁊ M. go] goo KH^3; ga E; come V. tyme] tymes U. *Here* K *adds lines like* **C** VIII 292–306: *see above*, p. 31.

VII

'Þis were a wikkide weye, but whoso hadde a gide
Þat mi3te folewe vs iche fote [forto] we were *þere*.'
Quaþ *per*kyn þe plou3man, 'be seint poule þe apostel,
I haue an half akir to er[e]n be þe hei3e wei3e;
Hadde y [erid] *þa*t half akir 5
I wolde wende wiþ 3ow til 3e were *þere*'.
'Þis were a long lettyng,' q*ua*þ a lady in a scleire;

1 *Between* Septimus passus de visione *and line* 1 W *copies* IV 1. Þis were] Now is þis N. Þis] This oþer A; his E. were] war E; weore VL. a] a wel LKW; a ful H³. wikkide] wylsu*m* J; kykkyd E. weye] wey3e H³; way ChH²EKW. whoso] ho so DChJMH³; hose VA; qwa sa E; ho L. hadde] hedde V; hase E.

2 Þat] *þa*t we JE; Þ*ou* H³. folewe] folowe DK; folow JEN; folow3e Ch; folwe RU H³; folwen V; folwyn A; foulyn M; gide W. vs] ous D; hi*m* J; *om* UEM. iche] eche RUDJKWM (*after cancelled* icchon J); vche N; eche a AH³; vch a VL; ilke a E; euery Ch. forto] DLK; forte þat V; til RUChJEAWNM; tel H³; til þat TH². we] he M; *om* ChH² (*late corrector supplies* H²). were] weryn J; war K; weore L; come VNH³.

3 *line om* D; **Here** H **resumes.** Quaþ] þe U. perkyn] piers W. plou3man] plughma*n* E; plou3mon V; ploghmon L. seint] Saynt EK; sent AH³; *om* VW. poule] paule E; peter VH; thomas R. þe] *om* JLE. apostel] postel ChAWH³.

4 *line om* D. an] one E. half] halue JA; *om* E. akir] aker ChVE; acre UH²HJLA KWNMH³. to eren] of erþe Ch; of hered lond L; *om* E. eren] H²; ere RHN; eryn J; ern T; erien M; erie UK; ery3e H³; here W; herie VA. be] by side H. hei3e] hey AWH³; he M; hiegh N; hy3e RChHL; hye JEK; hy U. wei3e] weye RUH²VHJLNM; wey A; way ChEKW.

5 *line om* DW; *run together with following* RUK; *divided from following after* wende VHJ; *after* 3ow N. Hadde . . . akir] weore he wel I Eried V; were it don N; y schal hye me in haste til I haue hit done L. y] *om* U. erid . . . akir] it heryed K. erid] H²HJE; ered R; erede M; eryid H³; eryed UCh; heried A; herd T. *þa*t] þe E; my*n* RU. half akir] *om* HJ. akir] akre RU; akir so me god helpe TChH²; acre ⁊ sowen it after M; aker ⁊ sawyn it after E; akre ⁊ Isowe it aft*er* H³; acre and also sowyn aftir A.

6 *line om* D. I . . . 3ow] wi*th* 3ow wold I wende J; þenne wi*th* ou wolde I wende V; þe*n* wolde y wiþ 3ou wende H; And þanne wol I wandre L. wolde wende] wende wolde H². wolde] wil R; schuld A; suld E; xulde H³; schal U; wolde fayn N; *om* W. wende] ga E; brynge U; *om* R. wiþ] forþ wiþ N; *om* U. til] And wissen ou þe rihte weye til V; And wysse 3ow ri3t wel til N; ⁊ teche 3ow þe ri3te wey til H; And techyn 3ow riht forth til *þa*t J; hadde I don til W; *om* U. 3e] we A; *om* U. were þere] fou*n*den treuþe V. were] weren M; be RW; bene J; beon L; come HA; *om* U. þere] ritht þere W.

7 Þis] þat VHH³. were] weore VL. a(1)] *om* N. long] lang E. lettyng] abydyng M. lady] lauedy Ch; leuedy J. in a scleire] ful clere E. in] wiþ H; *þa*t loured in L. a] hire L; here W; her Ch. scleire] skleir V; sklere M; sklaire N; sleyre RH²HA; slyre H³; chayere K; chare Ch; share W.

'What shulde we wom*m*en werche þe while?'
'Su*m*me shal sewe þe sak for shedyng of þe whete;
And wyues þ*at* han woll[e] werchiþ it faste, 10
Spynneþ it spedily, spariþ not ȝo*ure* fyngris
But ȝif it be holy day oþ*er* holy euen;
Lokiþ forþ ȝo*ure* lynen & labo*ure*þ þ*er*on faste.
Þe nedy & þe nakid, nymeþ hed how þei liggen;
Caste hem cloþis for cold for so wile treuþe. 15
For I shal lene hem lyflode, but ȝif þe lond faile,

8 What] Qwat JH^3. shulde] schule L; shul RUChVH; xul H^3; sall E. we] *om* DChW. wom*m*en] wymmen $DChH^2$ VHJLWM; wy*n*ne R. werche] werke H^2; worche ChVLN; worchen K; wurche UD; wyrke JE; & wyrke R; do or werchen M; do þ*ere* worche W. þe] þ*er* UDH^2 JAK; ony W; in þe mene L. while] qwyl JH^3; wiles WM; qwylse E.
9 Su*m*me] Go summe A; Nay somme W. shal] sall E; shul RUChVHJ; xul H^3; shuld M; *om* A. sewe] sewȝe Ch; sowe RUHLANM; sowen K; sowwe H^3; souwe V. þe(1)] *om* VHF. sak] sek AH^3; sakkes V; sackis H; sek*es* E; sakke q*uod* piers W. shedyng] chedyng N; schadyng E; spyllyng JM. þe(2)] *om* VLEW. whete] qwete JH^3.
10 wyues] ȝe wyues $VHJLEKNH^3$; þe wyfes A; oþ*er* wyues W. han] an (*late corrector prefixes* h) H^2; hauen LK; haue RJWM (*above line, similar hand* W); haueth UH; hath DCh; habbeþ V; nowe hase E. wolle] RUDVHLN; woll W; wol E; wollene TH^3; wollen ChH^2J; þe wollen A; lennyn K; lenen M. werchiþ] wercheth M; wyrchith J; wircheþ D; worchiþ H; worcheþ ChVN; worches L; worche W; werchen R; worchen K; wurche U; werky*n* H^3; wirke E; schul werche A. faste] ȝe schulle U; ȝe shole R.
11 *line om* V. Spynneþ] spynnet R; Spennytȝ H^2; And spenne W; Spynne ȝe E. it] *om* AH^3. spedily] spedly RCh H^2H; fast A. spariþ] sparetȝ H^2; spare A; and spare ChEW. not] nouȝt $DChH^2N$; noght UE; nouth MH^3. ȝo*ure*] here W.
12 ȝif] ȝef L; *om* $UChEAH^3$. be] beo VL; be on E; be an A; be ony M; be any H^3. holyday] halyday $UVJLMH^3$; halday A; halydays E. oþ*er*] or Ch; or elles UVHJLN (elles *after cancelled* hal U); or ony WM; or any H^3; or on E; or an A. holy] haly UJ; hey H^3. euen] euyn $JAKH^3$; eue ChH; euennys E.
13 Lokiþ] lokeþ RDChVHLKNM; Loketȝ H^2; Loke W; luke E. forþ] fortȝ H^2; vp W. ȝo*ure*] oure L; or V. lynen] lynene RH^3; lynnen DChHLAKN; lynnene UVJ; lyne towe W; wullou*n* M. &] *om* M. labo*ure*þ] labereþ V; laboure H^3; labo*ur* E; labore A; wercheth M. þ*er*on] on E; it (*above line same hand*) J. faste] *om* W.
14 Þe nedy] þ*er* nedy ben U. Þe(1)] To þe A. nedy] Neodi V; naked HN. þe(2)] *om* U. nakid] nedy HN. nymeþ hed] loke W. nymeþ] nymmeth K; ny*m* RUVJN; nemeþ D; nemyth H^2AH^3; takeþ Ch; takiþ H; take E. hed] ȝeme L; ȝeeme V; kepe HAN. how] qwow H^3. þei] þai EK; þe R; þi H^2; þat þat *corrected to* þat þay A. liggen] lyggyn J; ligge HAW; liggeth D; lygen M; lig E; legge H^3; lyen RU.
15 Caste] casteþ RDLK; Castyth J; And cast on V. hem] heom L; þaim E; him M. cloþis] clathes E. cold] could K. for] & A. so] sa E. wile] willeth D; wole H; wol UCh; wilneth L; wolde V; would K; byddyth A; bidd*es* E; techiþ N; comandeth MH^3. treuþe] trouthe LEKW; truthe RJ; trowþe ChN; Trwth M.
16 *run together with following* E. For] And JWN. lene] lenen MH^3; lenyn J; len E; lenden A; fynde H. hem] heom L; þaim E; hym DM. but . . . faile] *om* E. ȝif] ȝef L; *om* ChH^3.

As longe as I lyue for þe lordis loue of heuene.
And ȝe loueliche ladies wiþ ȝo*ur* [longe] fyngris,
Þ*at* han silk & sendel, sewiþ it whanne tyme is,
Chesiblis for chapell*is* chirches to honoure. 20
And alle maner of men þ*at* be þe mete libbiþ,
Helpiþ hem werche wiȝtly þ*at* wynne ȝo*ur*e foode.'
'Be crist,' q*ua*þ a kniȝt þo, 'þou [kenn]ist vs þe beste;
Ac on þe tem trewely tauȝt was I neu*er*e.
Ac kenne me,' q*ua*þ þe kniȝt, '& I wile [conne] eren.' 25
'Be seint poule,' q*ua*þ p*er*kyn, 'for þou p*ro*frist þe so lowe

17 As] Als LE; Also N. longe] lang E. lyue] lif J; leue DChEAWNH[3]. for . . . heuene] *om* E. þe] our UDVH; *om* JKW. loue] lof J; lowe W; *om* U. heuene] heuyn JAK; heouene L; euen M.
18 And] *om* N. ladies] lad*es* EK; leuedys J. ȝo*ur*] oure VL. longe] VHJLAKWN MH[3]; lang E; louely TRUDChH[2] (*late corrector cancels for* longe H[2]).
19 *line om* A. Þ*at*] ȝe MEH[3]. han] hauen UH; haue RDJEM; haueth K; habbeþ V; hathe Ch. silk] syke R; selk UH[2]V HM; seolk L. sendel] sandel RL. sewiþ] sewytȝ H[2]; seweþ ChW; sowith UH; soweþ RDN; souweþ V; sewe K; sowe L; to sewe M; to sew E; to sowwe H[3]; wyrche J. it . . . is] wha it is tyme M; qwa*n* it is tyme H[3]; it in tyme EW. it] *om* VH. whanne] whe*n* RHL; whon V; qwan J.
20 Chesiblis] Chesiples ChHJ; Chesepels H[3]; Werchit cheseplis A. chapell*is*] chapleynes ChVJLEKNMH[3]; churchis H. chirches] cherchis R; Churches D; chirche N; cherches for to M; chirche for Ch; and cherches U; And Churches V; & chapels H; holy chirche AKW; clerkys J.
21 *line om* A. of] oþ*er* N; *om* RHW. þ*at*] thet H[2]. be] on N. þe] *om* VW. mete] molde N. libbiþ] lybbeth DChH[2] LWM; libben U; libbes R; lyveth K; liuen VHN; leuyth H[3]; leuys E.
22 Helpiþ] Helpeth DH[2]VHWM; Helpe JLAN; Help RUChE. hem] heom L; þaim E; him VM; *om* W. werche wiȝtly] wel for to worche W. werche] wyrche RCh; worche DH[2]VLKN; wurche U; to werche AH[3]; to wirk E; þ*at* wyrchin J; forþ H. wiȝtly] wygtely M; wythtyly N; witly RJAH[3]. þ*at*] to J; and W; *om* A. wynne] wynneth UDChVHLW NM; wynnyth AK; wynnys E; wynnyn J. ȝo*ur*e] oure VM. foode] fodes E.
23 þo] *om* RUEH[3]. kennist] kennyst H[3]; kennest RUHLKNM; kennys JEA; techist TH[2]; techest ChVW; teches D. þe beste] right W.
24 Ac] Bot ChHLEKWM; Saue V; and RH[3]; For N; *om* A. on] o VH; or H[3]; *om* L. þe] þis RH[3]; þat A; a better L; *om* H[2]VHW. tem] teem ChH[2]J; theme E; teame K; tyme VHWH[3]; plough M. trewely] *om* L. tauȝt . . . neu*er*e] so was I neuere taght W. tauȝt] tauth A; tawte J; þus tauht V; so tauȝt H. I] me L.
25 H *substitutes* I wol helpe þee to labore whil my lyf lastiþ. Ac] Bote VJLKW MH[3]; And E; Now N; *om* RChA. kenne] kene R; ken UH[3]; tech V; ken þou W. me] me now L; *om* E. þe] *om* RH[2] (*late corrector supplies* H[2]). kniȝt] knyth H[3]; knyte A; kyng (*underlined*) D. & . . . eren] sum thyng for to werche A; for cristes loue of heouene L. &] *om* RD. I wile] Ichul V. wile] wol UCh; woll K; wel H[3]; shal M. conne eren] be þine ayr*e* E; fayn lern W. conne] V; lere to UD; lerne to TChH[2]; leye þ*er* to R; gon H[3]; comsen K; comse to N; gy*nn*e M; gynne to J. eren] eryn M; ere R; eryen DChH[3]; erye UVN; eryyne J; eiren K. *Here* L *adds a line: see above,* p. 47.
26 seint] sent AH[3]; saynt Saynt E. poule] paule E; peter VH. p*er*kyn] Pers V. for] & for MH[3]; *om* LW. p*ro*frist] p*ro*frest VHW; p*ro*ferist AH[3]; p*ro*ferest RDLK; p*ro*ferst ChNM; p*ro*fers JE. þe] me LH[3]; *om* AK. so] sa E; wel L; *om* M. lowe] law E; fayre A.

I shal swynken & sweten & sowe for vs boþe,
A[nd] ek laboure for þi loue al my lif tyme,
In couenaunt þat þou kepe holy[k]ir[k]e and myself
Fro wastours [and wikkide men] þat wolde me destroye, 30
And go hunte hardily [to] har[is] & [to] fox[is],
And [to] boris & [to] bukkes þat breken myn heggis,
And fecche þe hom fauconis þe foulis to kille,
For þise comiþ to my croft & croppiþ my whete.'

27 I shal] And þerfore schal I L; Now wil I W. shal] xal H³; sall E; *om* A. swynken & sweten] swete and swynke UW. swynken] swynkyn DJAK; swynke RChHLENH³; swenken M. &(1)] *om* L. sweten] swetyn DJAK; swete RChHE NH³; *om* L. sowe] sow J; sowen V; sowyn K; sowȝe Ch; saw E. boþe] bathe E.

28 And] RUDChH²VHJLEAKWNMH³; Ac T. ek] also N; take E; lelly W; *om* RU. laboure] labouren UL; laboren K; laboryn JA; labourne M; labre V; labour E; trauaile D. þi] ȝour R. loue] lufe E. lif] liȝf N; lyyfe J.

29 *divided from following after* holychirche TDChH²; *after* riȝt RU. couenaunt] couienaunt JAH³; conant E. þat] at E; *om* WMH³. þou . . . holykirke] holichirche þou kepe L. kepe] kepe wel RUW; wilt kepe D. holykirke . . . self] holy cherche riȝt And me RU; þe right of holycherche W. holy] haly E. kirke] N; kirk E; chirche TDChH²VJAKH³; cherche M; churche H. my] me AN; *om* D. self] seluen VEMH³; silue H; seoluen L; *om* DN.

30 Fro] Fra E; fram H; For A. wastours] wastour Ch; wateres R; watris U. and . . . men] and wickide men UDVHJLA KWN; and wikkemen R; fro wikedmen M; from wykkyd men H³; fra wykkyd men E; *om* TChH². wolde me] me wolde R; it wil W. wolde] wolden VL; wald E; wollen K; welyn H³. me] vs VHLKN; hem J. destroye] destroyen K; distroye RDChH²A; distroy E; destroiȝe H; dystroyȝe H³; destryen M; destruye L; destruyen V; destruene J; destrwe N.

31 go] ga E; go þou VW; go & M. hunte] hut H³. hardily] hardly E. to(1)] VHLKWNM; two J; at EA; for H³; þe TRUDChH². haris] HJAKH³; Hares VLN; hare TRUDChH²EM; fox W. to(2)] VHLWNM; two J; at EA; for H³; þe TUDChH²; *om* RK. foxis] JANH³; Foxes VHK; fox TRUDChH²LEM; hare W.

32 And] Bothe W; *om* VHLEANM. to(1)] RUDVHLAKWNM; At E; þe TChH²; *om* JH³. boris] bore Ch; bor W; bare E; beris HJ; beres R; Beores V; brokkys U; Roes L. &] in E; *om* HA. to(2)] UDVHAWNM; þe TChH²E; *om* RJLKH³. bukkes] bockis H²VH (*late corrector alters to* brockis H²); bukke W; bolis A; bole Ch; buskeȝ E. þat . . . heggis] *with* hornes & houndes (*following cancelled* & f) K. breken] brekyn ANH³; breke RH²; brekeþ VL; brekiþ H; brekes E; breky M; breykyn J; breke adoun D. myn] men Ch; menne V; mennys H. heggis] eggys J; *om* M.

33–85 *om* (**a leaf wanting**) A; *see above*, p. 1.

33 And] *om* J. fecche] fech RD; facche L; foche E; fette H²M; fayten K; sende W. þe hom] thy K; after W. þe(1)] *om* DL EM. fauconis] fauchones H²; fauconers W. þe(2)] þo H³; & the K; *om* UEM. to] *om* K. kille] kyllen M; kulle H²L; quelle V; fell E.

34 þise] þis J; þese UDH²H³; thes R; theose L; theys þese M; þei ChVHWN; þai E; thay K. comiþ] cometh DH²L; comyn UJH³; comen VHKWM; come RChEN. to] into UVM. my] myn NM; *om* H³. croft] croftes R. croppiþ] croppitȝ H²; croppeþ DL; croppeȝ E; croppyn JH³; croppen UChVKM; croppe RN; crop W; crepen H. my] in my H; of my N. whete] qwete JH³.

Curteisliche þ[e] kniȝt [conseyuede] þise wordis; 35
'Be my power, piers, I pliȝte þe my treuþe
To fulfille þe foreward whiles I may stande'. |
'Ȝa, ⁊ ȝet a poynt,' q*ua*þ p*er*kyn, 'I p*re*ye þe more: *fol.* xxxix *b*
Loke þou tene no ten*au*nt but treuþe wile assent,
And þei pore men p*ro*fre þe p*re*sauntis or ȝeftis 40
Nyme hem nouȝt, an aunt*er* þou mowe hem nouȝt des*er*ue.
For þou shalt ȝelde it aȝen at one ȝeris ende
In a wel p*er*ilous place þ*at* p*ur*catorie hattiþ;

35 L *substitutes* þe knyght konned him thonk and cortesly saide. Curteisliche] Ful Curteisliche V. þe] RUChVHJEK WMH^3; þanne þe N; þise T; þis DH^2. kniȝt] knyht þoo J; knyght þen E. conseyuede] RU; conseiued VW; conceyuet D; consaved E; conseiueþ Ch; conseyvith K; comsede H^2; comsed HN; compsiþ T; answeryd J; rehersede M; rehersyd H^3. þise] þese DH^{2}HM; þes ChK; þeise N; þeose V; þo H^3; þir E; his RU; al his W; to þe J.
36 Be] ȝys be M; By al N. piers] p*er*kyn N; piers q*uod* he W; *late corrector adds* quod he H^2. pliȝte] pleyth H^3. treuþe] treweth M; trouþe RH^{2}VLKW; trowþe N; troth E.
37 fulfille] fulfillyn J; fulfulle L; folfulle V; fulfell M; folewe H. þe] þis HLEKW NMH^3; þat U; þy DJ; my R. foreward] counand E. whiles] whilis R; qwylis J; qwilse E; while ChHKW; qwyl H^3; whiles þat U; while þat VL; wil þat N; wille þat M. I] my lyf HEWH^3. may stande] dureþ W. stande] stonde RUCh VHEKN; stondyn J; stoden M; lest H^3.
38 Ȝa] ȝe DHJLW; Yea K; *om* RUVNM. ⁊] But V; *om* HE. ȝet] ȝit DChVHJE WN; ȝut R; *om* U. a] O V. perkyn] pers V. preye þe] wil þe prayen W. þe] to þe N. more] of mare E; sire more H; no more H^{2}V (*late corrector alters* no *to* of H^2); forþere W.
39 Loke] Luke E. tene] teone VL. no] non J. ten*au*nt] teneande E; tenau*n*tis J. but treuþe] þat trewly E. wile] wol ChVL; wole H; woll EK. assent] acorde RU.
40 þei] þeiȝe U; though K; þouȝgh N; þogh W; þow H^3; þaugh L; ȝif VH; ȝef Ch; ȝif þat M; if þe D; gyff a sely E. men] man E. profre . . . or] p*re*sentiþ þee wiþ H. profre þe] þe profre W. profre] p*ro*fyre H^3; profern M; p*ro*feren K; p*ro*freþ V. þe] ȝou LN; ou V. p*re*sauntis] presens LN; *om* EMH^3. or] oþ*er* UH^2; and RDJLWN; *om* EMH^3. ȝeftis] ȝeftes H^{2}LK; ȝiftis HJH^3; ȝift*es* RUDChVW NM; gyfteȝ E.
41 Nyme] nym RChJW (*after cancelled* Nem J); Nymme K; Nymeþ N; Neme DH^{2}H^3; Neyhe E; take HM; Takeþ V. hem(1)] hit RDLKWNMH^3; *om* E. nouȝt] not UDVHLKWM. an] on LKN; in RVHJEWMH^3. aunt*er*] auenture VHNMH^3. þou] ȝe VN. mowe] mouwen V; may DLEW; maist H; mught M. hem(2) . . . deserue] *stained* L. hem] h*i*t RDEKWNMH^3. nouȝt] nauȝt Ch; not RVHEKWMH^3; *om* D. des*er*ue] deseruen V; deseruyn DM.
42 shalt] schat J; sall E. ȝelde it] hit ȝelde Ch. ȝelde] ȝelden H^{2}VWM; ȝeldyn H^3; ȝeilde L; ȝildyn J; ȝiue R. it] *om* EH^3. aȝen] aȝeyn VJLN; ayayn E; ageyn KM. at . . . ende] *illegible* L. one] o W; þe JE. ende] tyme M.
43 wel] wol U; full EH^3; *om* WM. p*er*ilous] p*er*lous DChEKM; p*er*lyous JH^3; p*er*lious ere R. p*ur*catorie] purgatorie RUDH^{2}VHJLEKNH^3; pugatorie M; purgatie (*missing contraction supplied in another ink*) W. hattiþ] hattithȝ H^2; hatteþ R; hatte UDHJKN; hatt E; hette V; hoteþ Ch; hotuth M; is hoten W; *illegible* L.

And mysbede nouȝt þi bondemen, þe bet shalt þou spede;
And þat þou be trewe of [þi] tunge, & talis þou hate, 45
But it be of wysdom or of wyt þi werkmen to chaste;
Holde wiþ none harlotis ne here nouȝt here talis,
And nameliche at mete suche men eschew[e],
For it arn þe deuelis disours I do þe to vndirstonde.
'I assente, be seint Iame,' seide þe kniȝt þanne, 50
'For to werche be þi woord while my lif duriþ.'
'And I shal apparaille me,' quaþ perkyn, 'in pilgrym[ys] wyse,
And wende wiþ ȝow þe wey til we fynde treuþe.'

44 And] *om* JEWN. mysbede] mysbeed U; Misbyd E; mysbeode L; misbeode þou V. nouȝt] not RDH²VHJLKWM. bondemen] bounde E. þe . . . þou] *illegible* L. bet] bette M; beter RV; betere U; better ChHEKWH³; bettur J. shalt þou] xalt þou H³; schaltow JN; schal þou D; þou schalt VLW; may þou E; þou myȝt RUH.

Here (fol. 26*b*) E **ends.** VII 70–213a **were however copied after** I 182 **and are collated in their place:** *see above*, p. 4.

45 And] *om* N. þat þou] þat þiself V; euere W; *om* RHMH³. þou] tow J. be] beo L. trewe] treowe L; trwe N. þi] RUChHJLKWNMH³; *om* TDH²V. &] *om* ChHJW. talis] ill tales (ill *above line same hand*) K. þou] þat þou H³; to Ch; *om* K. hate] hatye D.

46 *line om* K. But] But ȝif MH³; Bot ȝef L. be] beo VL. of(1)] be H³; *om* RVHJWNM. or] oþer R; & HN. of(2)] *om* RVHJWNMH³. wyt] wigtte M. þi] of þy Ch; *om* H. werkmen] workmen D; wicked men H. to] *om* Ch. chaste] chasten LM; chastyce H³; chastysyne J; charge W; *om* Ch.

47 *line om* K. Holde] hoold U. wiþ none] not wiþ H; not þou with V. none] no DWNM. harlotis] harlatys J. ne] no ChJL; *om* VHH³. here(1)] hure H; leue M. nouȝt] not VHLWM; non of R. here(2)] her ChJH³; heore V; hire H²; h R. talis] wordes W.

48 nameliche] nomeliche V. at] att H³; at þe UHL; atte H²V; at þy M. mete] mete tyme H³; eys M. suche] RDVLKWNM; siche H; swiche UJ; sweche H³; for suche TChH² (*late corrector alters* for *to* from H²). eschewe] LKWN; eschuwe V; eschue RM; echchwe J; þou eschewe U; eþchewe H; eschewen TDChH²; aschure H³.

49 For] *om* WN. it arn] it ben H³; it beþ H; þei ben VJNM; Thei beþ W; thay ar K. deuelis] deoles L. disours] dissours ChMH³; dishoures R. þe] hit þe R. to] *om* RVJMH³. vndirstonde] vndirstanden D.

50 I] Ich V; And I N. be . . . Iame] þe same N. seint] sent H³. Iame] Iem V; Iames K. seide] seyþ RU; quod LKW. þanne] þenne VL; þen H.

51 For] *om* N. werche] werchen M; worche RDChH²VLKW; worchen N; wurche U; wyrchyn J; werkyn H³. be] *om* M. woord] wordis HN. while] wil M; qwyl H³; whiles K; qwylis J; ȝe whil L. my . . . duriþ] þat I libbe W. lif] liȝf N; lyue J. duriþ] dureȝt R.

52 And] *om* JW. shal] xal H³; scal J; sal M. apparaille apareylyn J; diȝt N. me] þe D; *om* RU. perkyn] Piers WN. pilgrymys] pilgrimys RJ; pilgrimes UD VKWM; pilgryms L; a pylgrimys H³; palmers N; a palmerys H; pilgrym TChH². wyse] wede W.

53 wende] wendyn J; *om* U. ȝow] ou V; þee H. þe] on þe H. wey] weyȝe H³; way ChHKW; rihte wei V. we] ȝe UVM; I Ch. fynde treuþe] treuþe fynde VW. fynde] fyndyn J; fyne M. treuþe] truþe R; trwþe NM; *defective* H².

He caste on his cloþis, ycloutid ⁊ hole,
Hise cokeris ⁊ his cuffis for cold of his nailes, 55
And heng his hoper at his hals in stede of a scrippe:
'A busshel of breed corn br[yng m]e þereinne,
For I wile sowe it myself, ⁊ siþþe wile I wende.
And whoso helpiþ me to eren, or any þing swynke,
Shal haue be oure lord þe more here in heruist, 60
And make hym *mery* wiþ þe corn whoso it begrucchiþ.
And alle kyne crafty men þ*at* conne lyue in treuþe,
I shal fynde hem foode þ*at* feiþfulliche libbeþ,
Saue Iakke þe Iugel*our* ⁊ Ionete of þe stewis,

54 *divided from following after* cokeris H. He] Sone he W. caste] casteth K. cloþis ycloutid] cloutid cloþis H. cloþis] closys J; cloke Ch. ycloutid ⁊ hole] ⁊ his hode bothe M. ycloutid] yclouted RVN; cloutyd J; cloutyde U; clouted DChH²L; clutte W; ⁊ cloutyd H³; both Clowted K. ⁊ hole] as þei were W; *om* H. ⁊] an H³. hole] I hole V; olde D; *defective* H².
55 Hise] ⁊ his olde H. cokeris] colers D. cuffis] Coffus V; coffis also H. of . . . nailes] *defective* H². of] on H³.
56 And] he UVH; *om* N. heng] hang L; hong ChK; hyng H³; hieng U; henge on W. his(1)] an V. hoper . . . scrippe] *defective* H². hoper] hop*ur* R; cope hoper*e* M; sedlepe J. at] on RUVHJMH³. hals] alse M; bak RUV; rugge H. stede] stedde M; steode L; stude V. a] his RU.
57–78 defective H²: *see above*, pp. 6–7.
57 busshel] bucchel J; boyschel H; bushel q*uod* he W. bryng me] RUDJKWN; bryng me he bad L; bryng I H³; brouȝte he TCh M; he brouȝte H; he bringeþ V. þere] her L.
58 wile] wol UChVHLK. sowe] sowen DL; sowyn J; souwen V; sowȝe Ch. self] selue UJKM; seolf L; self quoþ he H. siþþe] siþe WH³; sithen UKN; seþþe Ch; seþþen V; sethe D; sethen M; sethin J; seothen L; swythe R. wile I] I wol L; *with* ou V. wile] wol UHK; wul M; wold Ch. wende] *altered from* wynde D.
59 And] For V; *om* N. whoso] ho so DJH³; hose V; who þat N. helpiþ] help H³. me] *om* UM. eren] eryn M; ere W; heren V; heryn J; eryen DChLK; erye RUH; eryȝe H³; herye N. any . . . swynke] hewe *with* þe hatchet H³; he with his hachete M. any] eny RVHN; ony D. swynke] swynken U; to swynke LKN; to swink H; to swynken V; to swing J.
60 Shal] Xal H³; He schal VHW. haue] haue leue MH³; be allowed N. be] beo V; byhynde W; *om* M. oure] hour*e* M; *om* LW. lord] lord god R; god W; heouene L. þe more] to leuyn MH³. þe] *om* K. here] hir*e* RDLKN; huyre V; hur*e* H; mede UJ. in] at U; tyl H³. heruist] erueste M; harvest K.
61 And] A W. make] maken LM; makyn J. hym] he*m* N; *om* M. *mery*] murie VL; *om* D. wiþ . . . corn] þerwith U; þerw*ith* mawgry H³; þer mydde mauggre M. þe] þat W. whoso] ho so DChJH³; hose V. it begrucchiþ] begrucche it N. it] *om* MH³. begrucchiþ] begrucheþ DChW; begrucche RUJL; grutchith K; grotchyth H³; grucche M; euere bigruccheþ V.
62 alle] al KW. kyne] kynne UDChJK; kyns W; ky*n*nes N; kennes M; ku*n*nes V; skynnes R; sky*n*nys H³; man*ere* H; maner of L. crafty] craftis H; Craftus V; Cristen WM. men] *om* W. conne lyue] trauail W; lybbeth M. conne] kony*n* J. lyue] lyuen VJK; leue RDCh; leuy*n* H³. in] *with* RVMH³; be Ch. treuþe] treweth M; trouthe LKWN; truþe RJ; trewe Ch.
63 fynde] fynden UDVKM; fyndyn J. hem] heom L; hem heore V. þat] *om* H. feiþfulliche] feyfully R; skilfulliche U. libbeþ] lybbith J; libben UChLWNM; lybbe R; lyuen VK; leuyth H³; to lyue*n* H.
64 Ionete] Ienett KW; Ienot H; Iohannet N. of þe] at þe RUJLKW; atte N. stewis] stywes U; stuwes N; stues DJ; stuyues V; styves HLW.

And robyn þe ribaudo*ur* for hise rusty woordis. 65
Treuþe tolde me ones & bad me telle it forþ:
Deleantur de libro; I shulde not dele wiþ hem,
For holy chirche is holden of hem no tiþes to asken,
Et cum iustis non scribantur.
Þei arn askapid good auntir, now god hem amende.'
Dame werche whanne tyme is piers wyf hatte; 70
His dou3*ter* hattiþ do ri3t [so] or þi da*mm*e shal þe bete;
His sone hattiþ suffre þi sou*er*eynes to hauen h*er*e wille
And deme hem nou3t for 3if þou dost þou shalt it dere abiggen,

65 robyn] Robert VH^3; Roberd H. ribaudo*ur*] rebaudrere H^3; rybawde KM. rusty] lusty Ch. woordis] talis J.
66 tolde] tauhte hit V. me] me hit L. ones] onys DJH^3; *þus* onys RU; of hem W. telle] tellen L; tellyn JH^3; teche H. it] *om* $DJWH^3$. forþ] forþe ChN; forþer VLM; ferther RUHJ.
67–68α: 67a *and* 68α *as one line*; 67b *and* 68a *as another*; 68b *expanded into an independent line* W. 67 *combined with* 68α *and copied after* 69 H.
67 *as two lines divided after viuencium* N. *Deleantur*] *Deliantur* DM. *libro*] *libro viuencium* $UVHJKWNMH^3$; *libro vite* Ch. I . . . hem] *om* VH. I] þey D. shulde] RUJLKWNM; schal D; xal H^3; ne shulde TCh. not . . . hem] helde w*ith* he*m* nou3t he bad me also N. not] noght UL; nouth H^3; *om* Ch. dele] delyn J; deale K. hem] heom L.
68 *run together with following* JL. For] *om* VH. holy . . . asken] of heom holy chirche askith no tithe L. chirche] Churche DVH; cherche WNM. is holden] *om* M. holden] holdyn K; holde RChH; howldyn J; hoty*n* H^3. hem] hym W; soche men M. no] none D. tiþes] tuþes D; tithe $UVHJH^3$; teche W. to asken] ne craueth M. to] *om* J. asken] askyn H^3; aske H; axen UDCh; axin J; axe N; taken RV; take here wynnyng is so wid W.
68α *divided from following after* aventure K; *see line* 67 W. *Et*] *om* H^3. *scribantur*] *scribentur* KW; *scribantur &c* N; *scribentur &cetera* H^3; *scribantur* they ben no bettere worthy M.
69 *line om* M. Þei] thay K; þat þey L; For þei N. arn] be KW; ben $UDVJNH^3$; beon L; beþ RH. askapid] escapid K; scapyd J; aschaped D. good] god*es* R; *om* N. auntir] auntо*ur* U; auenture LKH^3; þrift VHN. now] *om* $RUChVHH^3$. hem] heo*m* L. amende] amend & send hem bettre happe K.
70–213a *misplaced* RUE: *see above*, p. 14.
70 werche] worche ChLKW; worch R; wurche UD; wirche JN; wyrke E; *om* V. whanne] when HL; whon V; qwan JH^3; qwen E. piers . . . hatte] Hette Pers wyf V. piers] peirse E; piers is Ch; perkynes N. hatte] hat N; hette E; hight W; hyth H^3; is cleped L.
71 His] Hir J. dou3*ter*] dougtre M. hattiþ] hatte RUDChLM; hatt K; hat HJN; hette V; hight EW; hyth H^3. do] *om* R. so] $RUVHJLKWNMH^3$; *om* TDChE. or] lest W. þi . . . bete] þou schalt abugge L. þi] owr E. shal] xal H^3; wol VH; wille M; *om* W.
72 His] And hys E. hattiþ] hatte RUDCh JM; hat HN; hette V; hitte L; hight EK; hyth H^3; high W. suffre . . . wille] Sufferance to suffurre in tyme E. suffre] suffurre H^3. souereynes] soueraign W. to] for to VHJLKW. hauen] haue RCh $HJLKWH^3$; han V; *om* M. here] her ChJKN; heore L; heor V; his W. wille] willes K.
73 And] *om* NMH^3. deme . . . dost] if þow do noght E. deme] dem R; deeme V; dampne M; kurse N; tene J; greue W. hem] heom L; hy*m* RChW. nou3t] not DVHKW. 3if] 3ef L; 3eue Ch; *om* R. dost] doist H; do VJN. þou . . . abiggen] sore þou xal abygge H^3. shalt] shal EM. it] *om* ChE. dere] der E; deore V; sore RULW. abiggen] abigge HJKW; abyge M; abugge V; abegge D; abye RUChE; bigge N; *illegible* L.

Let god worþe wiþal for so his woord techiþ.
'For [now] I am old & hor & haue of myn owene 75
To pen*aun*ce & to pilg*ri*mage wile I passe *with* oþ*er*e;
Forþi I wile er I wende do w[r]yte my bequest.
In dei nomine Amen I make it myseluen:
He shal haue my soule þat best haþ dese*r*uid, | *fol.* xl *a*
And defende it fro þe fend, for so I beleue, 80
Til I come to his acountes as my crede me techiþ—
To haue reles & remissiou*n*, on þat rental I leue.
Þe [k]ir[k]e shal haue my caroyn & kepe my bones,

74 *line om* VE. Let] lat UJLNH^3; Late W; latte M; And let *altered to* but let *same hand* K. worþe] aworþe N; worche LKW; wurche UD; werche MH^3; wyrche R; wrþin J. wiþal] þerw*ith*alle RCh; al D. for] *om* J. his woord] þys world M. techiþ] teches RD. *Here* H^3 *adds a Latin line as e.g. after* **B** XI 88 *or* **B** XII 91 *or* **C** XIII 31: *see above*, p. 31.
75 For] *om* EN. now . . . old] I am old now W. now] RUVHJLEKMH^3; Now þat N; *om* TDCh. I am] I ame K; I hame M; Icham V; am I E. old] holde EM; elde K; boþe holde J. & hor] *om* HE. &(2)] & I E; & y now H; þoughe N. myn] myn of (of *cancelled*) M. owene] owe R; awne E.
76 &] or E. to(2)] *om* HJK. pilg*ri*mage] pylgermage R. wile I passe] passe I wil W. wile I] wel I Ch; I wil JNH^3; I wol UV HLK; I M. *with*] *with* þis VJN; wiþ þese HH^3; *with* thes KM; with þeose L.
77 Forþi] þerfor JN; For UEH^3; And ȝit W; And yet K. wile] wole V; wol UCh HL; woll K. er] eer W; or RDHJKNM; ar ChVL. wende] go J. do . . . bequest] my bequest make W. do] don L; *om* VHMH^3. wryte] RDChVHLKN; writen U; wrytyn J; writte E; wryth H^3; wrygte M; wyte T. bequest] bequyste M; byquyste L; bequest*es* R; byquestes U; queste DH^3; bequethe J; Testament VH; intest E; lyqueste N. *Here* H^3 *adds a line: see above*, p. 48.
78 *dei . . . Amen*] þe name of god (*in margin* In dei no:·) H make] makyd R; write W. it] *om* R. seluen] selue UCh JMH^3; self WN; seoluen L; siluen H.
79 Here H^2 resumes briefly. He . . . soule] My soule hym self shal haue W. He] VHJLKNMH^3; For he TRUDCh H^{2}E. haue] an J. soule] saule E. þat . . . haþ] he haþ best W; he hath it best K. þat] þat it JE. best] *om* H^2. haþ] hat H^3; hatȝ H^2; it haþ N. dese*r*uid] deserued RUChHLWN; deseruet V; seruyd J.
80 fro] fram H. fend] feond L; fynd M. for so] þat W. I] I wil W; is my RUEM. beleue] beoleeue V.
81 Til] To E; Til wanne N; *defective* H^2. his] myn VN; *om* JWMH^3. acountes] acount*us* R; acou*n*te H^3; countes Ch; acomptes H^{2}M; acompte EK. as] so W; for so E. my] þe Ch. me] *om* ChHLE WM. techiþ] techitȝ H^2; techeþ DChL WM; techys RE; telleþ V.
82 To haue] In þat re*n*tal to haue N; *defective* H^2. haue] ha V. reles & remissiou*n*] remission & seles E; remission þan & relesse W. reles] a reles JHLKH^3. &] & a HLH^3; of Ch. on . . . rental] *om* WN. on] of HKH^3. rental] rente R; trentale ChL. I leue] for eu*er* H. leue] beleue E; byleue U; beleeue V; trowe L; hope W.
83 Þe . . . shal] *defective* H^2. kirke] N; kyrke EW; kirk Ch; chirche TVLKH^3; cherche RUJM; Churche DH. shal] xal H^3; sal JE. haue] hauen M. caroyn] carayne H^3; careyne RUDChH^{2}VHJLK WM; caryon N; body E. kepe] kepyn JM; kepe þ*er* H; kepe alle N; kepyn of E.

For of my corn ⁊ my catel [he] crauide þe tiþ[e];
[I] payede hym *pre*stly for *per*il of my soule; 85
He is holden, I hope, to haue me in mynde,
And monewe me in his memorie among alle cristene.
My wyf shal haue of þ*at* I wan wiþ treuþe, ⁊ namore,
And dele among my frendis ⁊ my dere children,
For þeiȝ I deiȝe today my dettis ben quyt; 90
I bar hom þat I borewide er I to bedde ȝede.
And wiþ þe residue ⁊ þe remen*aun*t, be þe rode of chestre,
I wile worsshipe þ*er*ewiþ treuþe in my lyue,

84 For . . . ⁊] *defective* H^2. of . . . he] he of corn ⁊ of my catel L. my(1)] *om* W. corn . . . catel] catel ⁊ my corn H. ⁊] and of W. my(2)] *om* VEKW. catel] cateyle J. he crauide] þer gaf I W. he] RUDChHJEKNMH^3; heo V; I TH^2. crauide] cravyd K; crauede H^3; craued Ch; crawed L; crauyth UJ; craueþ RDV HN; cravys E; cleymeth M. þe] þeo L; my KW. tiþe] Tiþe VHJKWNMH^3; toyþe(?) L; tiþes TUDChH^2; tyþys R; tendes E.

85 I . . . peril] *defective* H^2. I] RVJLEKN MH^3; I haue H; And I DCh; It U; And TW. payede] paied ChHLKWN; payid H^3; payȝid J; payde RM; payd UD; prayd E. hym] hit him L; hem RD; it UJM; it hi*m* ful (it *above line*) N; it euere W; *om* E. *pre*stly] aprestly R; þe *pri*st E. soule] saule E.

86–109 defective H^2.

86 Here (p. 341) A **resumes.** He is] Be hys E. holden] holdyn J; holde E; halden L; beholdyn AH^3; byholde R. I] Ich V. hope] howpe J. me] men Ch. in] in his UEAMH^3. mynde] Muynde V; mende D; masse M; messe AH^3.

87 *line om* A. monewe] monewen M; mo*n*ne R; menewe U; menewyn D; menge W; mengen LN; mengyn JK; mene E; munge V; mynwe H; mynne Ch; mengyt H^3. me] *om* LN. his] *om* D. memorie] memory L; memore E; memories Ch; memento K. among] among*es* K.

88 of] half W; al R; *om* UVHEH^3. þat] at E. wan] won V; wan of L. wiþ treuþe] trewliche U; trewly EA; truly R. wiþ] wi*th* þe M. namore] nomore RDChVH JLEAKWNM; no*n* more H^3.

89 And] To H^3; For to A. dele] delen L; delyn J. among] among*es* K; emong E. my] her*e* M. frendis] freondis L; children H. my] also my A; her*e* M; hyr H^3. dere] der E; deore VL; *om* ChHA. children] chyldryn R; schildren M; childre W; childern K; child*er* E; chylderyn H^3; childeryne J; frendis boþe H.

90 For] *om* N. þeiȝ] þey DJ; þouȝ RChH; þogh W; þoghe U; þow AH^3; þauh V; þagh L; ȝif NKM; ⁊ E. deiȝe] deye RUDAM; dey J; dyȝe Ch; dye VLEK WN; deied H. today] þis day VMH^3. dettis] dete H^3. ben] beon L; beþ RHW; beoþ V; arn A; aru*n* J; ar N; is H^3. quyt] quyte W; qwytt E; quitte ChJAN; quyted D; Iquit V; yquytte UM; yquytted RK; aqwytyd H^3; paied L.

91 þat] *om* E. borewide] borewed L; borowyd JK; borowed DN; borowd E; borowȝed Ch; borwide U; borwid AH^3; Borwede VM; borwed RHW. er] eer W; or RDChHAKM; ar N. to . . . ȝede] ȝede to bedde AW; went to bedde H. ȝede] ȝeode L; eode V.

92 And wiþ] *om* W. þe(1)] *om* UM. residue] resude AN. þe(2)] *om* EK. remen*aun*t] remanent E; remelau*n*t H; remelaund A. be] *om* E.

93 wile] wol UDChVHL; wolde R; wold E. worsshipe] worschepe RChAH^3; worschupe V; wrchippy*n* J; werche M. þerewiþ treuþe] truthe therwith K. þerewiþ] þarwi*th* E; þe wi*th* D. treuþe] sent trewþe A. in] by RE; be U; to W. my] *om* E. lyue] lyfe AK; lyf N; leue D; lyues ende W; seluen E.

And ben his pilgrym at þe plouȝ for pore menis sake.
My plouȝpote shal be my pyk ⁊ putte at þe rotis, 95
And helpe my cultir to kerue ⁊ close þe forewis.'
Now is peris ⁊ þe pilg*ri*mes to þe plouȝ faren;
To erien þis half akir helpen hym manye;
Dikeris ⁊ delu*er*es dy[gg]eþ vp þe balkis.
*Þer*ewiþ was p*er*kyn payed, and p*re*isid hem ȝerne. 100
O*þer*e werkmen *þer*e were [þat] wrouȝte ful faste,
Eche man on his maner made hymself to done,
And su*m*me to plese p*er*kyn pykide vp þe wedis.

94 ben] be RUHEW; byn K; beon L. his pilgrym] þe pilg*ri*mage E. at þe] atte DVN; at W; at his U. menis] me*n* DH WM. sake] *illegible* L.
95 *line om* W; *as two lines divided after* staffe N. My . . . pyk] I xal now poyntyn my pekyd staf H^3. plouȝ] *om* M. pote] pot L; bat H; Foote K; staf AM; *om* RUE. shal] sal J. be] ben J; beon L. my] *om* M. pyk] pykstaf RUJLEK; pekedstaf D; pyked M; pilg*ri*mstaf HN; potent A. ⁊] to HJNM H^3. putte] put D; potten M; posse H; posschen V; pyke REAH^3; picche U; pyche L; pycchyn J; rende N. at . . . rotis] *illegible* L. at þe] atte DV; owt E. at] vp UANH^3; wp R; aweye (*after cancelled* þe) M. rotis] rotis of þistlys ⁊ þornes N.
96 helpe] helpen M; helpyn J; do xarpe H^3. kerue] keruen M; keruyn J; carve K. ⁊ close] *om* H^3. ⁊] ⁊ to E; to N. close] clense AKN; klensen M; clensyn J; clanse L. þe] my H^3; *om* E. forewis] forewes L; forowes ChKN; forwys RDHAMH^3; forwes W; furwes U; fowrys J; fores E; vorwes V.
97 *line om* H^3. Now] And þus W. is] *om* M. peris] p*er*kyn AM. ⁊] in E; as M; *om* H. þe(1)] his A; þys M. pilg*ri*mes] pilgryme H; pilg*ri*mage E. faren] faryne J; fare RA; Ifare V.
98 erien] erye D; eryn JKM; eere W; eyre E; heryen LA; herye RN; heren VH. þis . . . akir] ⁊ to wirke E. þis] þ*at* H^3; þe RUAM; his H. helpen hym] hym help W. helpen] helpyn RDKN; holpen L; holpyn JH^3; hulpen M; hopyn A; and helpen Ch. manye] monye L; mony E; right many W; ful monye V.
99 Dikeris] dyker*es* RD; Dikers ChVWN; Dikars K; Dycherys J; Dichers HL; Diggeris A; Diggers E; As dykerys H^3. dyggeþ] dyggen U; diggyn EK; digged N; dyggid A; dyggyng R; doluen L; doluyn J; duluen M; þ*at* deluy*n* H^3; dykeþ TCh; dyken D; dyke W; Dikeden V; diȝten H. vp] on R. balkis] bankis HJ; bankes RCh; rotys H^3; Rotes M.
100 Þ*er*ewiþ] Therof AW; wel H^3. payed] paiede K; payd DE; apayed VM; apayid H^3; apayde R; ypaied U; wel paid W; wele payyd J; wele Ipayd A; apayn (n *corrected to* d *same ink*) H. p*re*isid] preysed RUDCh HLKM; preisede V; p*re*syd H^3; p*ra*ysed JWN; prasyd E. hem] heom L; þaim E. ȝerne] ȝeorne L; ful ȝerne H; fast W; al E.
101 H^3 *corrupts to* Þat *þer* weryn werkyng ⁊ trauayle sore. werkmen] workme*n* K; wirkemen Ch. þere were] weren *þer*e M; was *þer* mony E. were] weren VH; weron K; weryn J. þat] þ*at* RUVHJLE AKWNM; ⁊ TDCh. wrouȝte] wrouȝt Ch; wrouȝten DVHN; wroughten UK; wrougten M; wrouȝthyn R; wroȝt E; wroght W; wroghten L; wrowhty*n* J; wroutyn A. ful] wel DLKWN; wol J. faste] ȝerne W; monye V.
102 Eche man] And so*m*me H^3. Eche] vche VL; euerey RUE. man] Mon VL. on] in VHKMH^3. his] þis H^3. made] mady*n* H^3. hym] he*m* H^3. self] seolf L; *om* RUVHEAWNH^3.
103 And su*m*me] *om* H^3. And] *om* AN. su*m*me] come Ch. to] For to H^3; *om* EA. plese] plesyn J; pleese L; pleysen K; plesid A; pleasyd E. pykide . . . wedis] carped of cof worde W. pykide] pykyd UJ; pykeden V; pyked DChHLN; pikkedyn A; pikyn K; pykened M; þei pekede H^3; ⁊ pykyd E; gaderyd R. vp] out RUE. wedis] weodes VL; weys A; stanes E.

At heiȝ prime peris let þe plouȝ stande
To ouersen hem hymself; whoso best wrouȝte 105
Shulde ben hirid þereaftir whan heruist tyme come.
Þanne seten somme & sungen at þe ale,
And holpen [to] ere þe half akir wiþ 'hey trolly lolly'.
'Be þe prince of paradis!' quaþ piers þo in wraþþe,
'But ȝe rise þe raþere, & rape ȝow to werche, 110
Shal no greyn þat here growiþ glade ȝow at nede;
And þeiȝ ȝe deiȝe for doel þe deuil haue þat recche!'

104 At . . . prime] An hast þen H; þan be thouth hym H³. At] At þe R; And at W; And at the K; And atte M. heiȝ] hey RAM; hiegh N; hygh L; hiȝe Ch; hye UJEKW. prime] prime tyme K; prime of þe day UJE. peris] perkyn VHEN. let] lete EWNM; lett K; lette VL; leet U; leete J; & let H³. stande] stonde VHLEK WNM; stodyn J; stonde stille Ch.
105 To] And H³; while þat he V. ouersen] ouersene ChJ; ouerseen UKN; ouerse HW; ouersey R; ouerseȝe V; ouerseon L; euer see E; lokyn H³. hem] heom L; þaim E; hym A; *om* VHMH³. hymself] himseolf L; ichon E; alle J; he þoght W; *om* A. whoso] ho so J; who þat HWM; ho þat V; qwo E; ho þer H³; For ho so N; so so A. wrouȝte] wrouȝt ChHKN; wroghte L; wroȝt EW; wrouhte V; wrowht J; wrouȝthe R; wrougte M; wrouth AH³.
106 Shulde] Suld E; He schulde VM; þei shulde HW; He schal A; For he xal H³. ben] bene J; beon L; be RChHE MH³; haue WN. hirid] hyred UDLEK; huyred V; hurid H; herid M; hered Ch; heryed R; hyre WN. þereaftir . . . heruist] in heruest þeraftir E. whan] when RHL; whon V; qwan JH³. tyme] *om* W. come] comith JA; to come E; were in W.
107 Þanne] þenne V; þen H; But þanne N. seten . . . ale] fond he losels þat lotred aboute W. seten] setyn JAH³; setten Ch M; sett E; sitten K; sete þer R. sungen] sungyn A; sungun J; sunge R; songyn H³; songe E. at þe] atte VJN; at D; faste at þe L. ale] nale UDChHJLEAKN.
108 And] *om* A. holpen] holpyn JEAKH³; holp W; hulpen U; hulpyn N; helped D; helpen R. to] RUChLEAWMH³; him to VHJN; *om* TDK. ere] eere W; eyre E; erye RUDChHN; erien M; eryȝen H³; herye A; herien VL; eryyn (*after cancelled* l) J; earye K. þe . . . akir] *om* VHJN. þe] þat RH³. hey . . . lolly] dieu sa dame emme U; dusadammeme R; dieu or dame Emme E. hey] hay H; ay M; hie W; hoy J.
109 Be] Now be VHWN. of] in L. quaþ] þo quaþ H³; þo quod Ch. piers] perkyn N. þo] þan W; al ChE; *om* DAH³. in] I R; in that D. wraþþe] wreth AWH³; wrothe E.
110 Here H² resumes briefly. But] RUVHEANH³; But ȝif TDH²JKWM; Bot ȝef ChL. ȝe] ȝ A. rise] risen DChVK; rysyn JA; arysen M; rise vp H. raþere] sunner J. rape] rapen K. werche] worche ChVLWN; worchen K; wurche D; wyrche UJ; werke E.
111 Shal] Xal H³; þere shal N; Schchl (? Schchil) A. greyn] grayne JW; gren E; greynin H³. þat] at E. here] heer V; *om* H. growiþ] groweþ RDChH²VLWNM; groys E. glade] glad JE; gladen V; gladden K; helpe A. ȝow] ow V. nede] neode V.
112 And] *om* AH³. þeiȝ] þey RDJ; þouȝ HK; þowȝ Ch; thogh W; Thou AMH³; þaugh L; þauh V; ȝif UE. deiȝe] deyȝin J; deye RUDH; dey A; deyen M; diȝe Ch; dye LEKN; dyen VW. doel] doyl W; dole DJEANM; dol R; dool UCh; doole K; dul H³; defaute VL; þe defaut H. deuil] deouel L. haue] hym haue D; haue hym A; hange RUE; honge W; him hang J. recche] rechith A; recke RD; rekkyth J; rakys E; *defective* H².

Þanne were faitours aferd & feynide hem blynde;
Somme leide here leg alery as suche lorellis cunne,
And pleynide hem to peris wiþ suche pitous wordis: 115
'We haue none [lymes] to laboure wiþ, lord, ygracid be ȝe;
Ac we preye for ȝow, peris, & for ȝoure plouȝ boþe,
Þat god of his grace ȝour greyn multiplie,
And ȝelde ȝow of ȝour almesse þat ȝe ȝiuen vs here,
For we mowe no[þer] swynke ne swete, such seknesse vs eileþ'.
'Ȝef it be soþ,' quaþ peris, 'þat ȝe seyn, I shal it sone aspie.

113 Þanne] þenne VL; þen H. were] werin JM; weore L; was E; were þo A; were þer H; weore þe V. faitours] fatours E; faightouris N. aferd] fele H. &] þat H. feynide] feynyd DJH^3; feynede V; feyned UHLEAWNM; faynede K; fayned RChH^2. hem] heom L; þaim E; hym W. blynde] *defective* H^2.
114 Somme] And summe VH. leide] leyden DVL; leydyn JH^3; layde W; lade E. here] her ChJ; heore L; þeire N; þe RUVHE. leg] legge EW; leges L; legges VKNM; leggis HJAH^3. alery] on lery A; alyry UVJW; alirrye M; on lyry L; on lyre H^3; of lery E. as] & H^3. suche] swiche U; sweche H^3; summe A; shuld W; *om* D. lorellis] lorelles ChM; lorels W; loselys RAH^3; loseles UDEKN; losels VHJL; lorell:::: H^2. cunne] knoweþ N; done KW; shuld E; *defective* H^2.
115 pleynide] pleynyd NH^3; pleynede H^2; pleyneden U; pleyned RDChHLAW; pleyndyn M; plenyde K; plenyd JE; playneden V. hem] þaim E; *om* ULKN. peris] perus U; perkyn EWN. suche . . . wordis] *defective* H^2. suche] siche H; swiche UJ; *om* EAWMH^3. pitous] petows Ch; petous AH^3; petuouse K.
116 haue] hauen L; han AK. none] no RUDChVHJLEAKWN; *om* M. lymes] RUVHLWN; lymys E; lymmes JK; lemys AH^3; lemmes M; hondis TH^2; handes DCh. to . . . ȝe] *defective* H^2. laboure] labouren L; labowryn J; labourne M; lobore R; harowȝe Ch. wiþ] *om* DM. lord] vr lord VH. ygracid . . . ȝe] gyff vs grace E; Ithanked be ȝe L; we hit þonken VH. ygracid] ygraced RUChKN; gracyd H^3; graced D; gracied M; grace A; þankyd J; þonked W. ȝe] thou KWM; þe UN.
117 Ac] Bot ChVHLKWNM; And EH^3 *om* A. preye . . . boþe] *defective* H^2. preye] preyen DLM; preyeþ V; praye RChW; pray ENH^3; prayen K; prayȝen J. ȝow] ou V; þee H. peris] perus E. for(2)] *om* Ch. ȝoure] ȝow N; oure V; þy H. boþe] boþen M; bothin J.
118–40 defective H^2.
118 *line om* H. of] for RDVE. his] *om* M. grace] grete grace JL. ȝour] oure VL. greyn] grene E; grayne JK; greynes M; goodes W.
119 *line om* HA. ȝelde] ȝeilde L. ȝow] ow V. of] for RVLK; *om* WH^3. ȝour] oure VL. almesse] almes ULKWN; almusse E; Almus VJ; almasse M. þat] *om* W. ȝe] yow K. ȝiuen] ȝyue R; ȝyfen J; ȝif N; ȝeuen ChLM; ȝeue D; ȝef W; gyf E; yeld K; do H^3. vs] to vs W.
120 we . . . eileþ] sekenes vs eylyth that we mow not laboryn A. mowe noþer] ne mow W; ne may M. mowe] mowen K; moun H^3; may HEN. noþer] noþer RHE; nouþer L; nouþur V; neyther UK; neythir J; neþer H^3; not TD; nat Ch; in no maner N. swynke . . . swete] swete ne swynke RUChE. swynke] swynckyn JH^3; swenkyn M. ne swete] *om* N. ne] no ChL; ner J; non H^3; ne for payne K. swete] swetyn JH^3. such . . . eileþ] so febyll we ben E; *om* K. such] siche UH; swyche J; sweche H^3. seknesse] sykenes DHWM; febelnysse R; feblesse U. eileþ] aileþ ChW; heiles M; a:::: L.
121 Ȝef] ȝif RUDVHJEAKWNMH^3. be] beo VL. soþ] so UJA; *om* R. quaþ . . . seyn] þat ȝe seyen quod pers VWM; as ȝe seyn quot peris A. quaþ peris] *om* LN. peris] perkyn E. þat . . . seyn] *om* UHE. þat] as J. seyn] seyne J; seye R; sayn L; sayen K. I . . . sone] sone I schal VH. shal] shalt M. it] *om* LK. sone] *om* AH^3. aspie] aspyen JM; aspyȝe H^3; espye K.

ȝe ben wastours, I wot wel, & treuþe wot þe soþe;
And I am his [h]olde hyne & auȝte hym to warne. |
Suche wastours in þis world his werkmen distroyeþ; *fol.* xl *b*
ȝe eten þat [hy] shulde ete þat eren for vs alle. 125
Ac treuþe shal teche ȝow his tem for to dryue,
Boþe to setten & to sowen, & sauen his telþe,
[Cacche cowes] from his corn, [and] kepen hise bestis,
Or ȝe shuln ete barly bred & of þe bro[k] drynke;
But he be blynd, or brokesshankid, or beddrede ligge: 130
Þei shuln ete as good as I, so me god helpe,

122 ȝe] Bot ȝe J. ben] be WN; beon L; beþ RH; beoþ V; arne M. wot] wene W. wel] *om* VHEW. &] *om* AMH³. treuþe wot] nowe I knaw E.
123 And] *om* VHA. I am] I ame K; Icham V; I haue M. his] is A; god*es* E. holde] VHJNM; hold LA; olde TRUCh K; old DWH³; awne E. &] I RUAM. auȝte] awght N; awht J; aght W; augthe H³; aut A; ouȝte DVK; hougte M.
124 *line om* W. Suche] Siche E; sWhyche R; Sweche AMH³; whuche V; whiche UK; wyche N; Qwyche J. in . . . world] *om* A. þis] þe H; *om* DVLNH³. world] wordle R; werlde JH³. werkmen] workmen K; wyrkme*n* D. distroyeþ] dystroye J; distroyen K; distroys E; distroyȝe H³; destroien U; destroiȝ*en* H; distruyȝen V; destrueþ N; distryeth L; dystroen A; to destroyin R; schende M.
125 ȝe eten] þat wastene M. eten] etyn JAH³. þat] at E. hy] hij N; þei UDChVHJ LKMH³; þai EAW; I TR. shulde] schulden VM; schuldyn A; xuld H³; suld E. ete] eten DChVLK; etyn JH³; etene M; hete W; *om* A. eren] eyre E; erien UDChHAK; erye R; ery N; heryen L; tilen W; swynken V; swynkyn JH³; *om* M. vs] vu*s* J; ȝow H.
126 Ac] Bot ChVHLKWNM; And EAH³. treuþe] treweth M; trouthe LEW; truthe RJK; trwþe N. shal] most W. teche] techen V; techin JH³; techn M. ȝow] ow V. tem] teem RUChEN; Teeme VJ; tyme H³; plough M. for to] to H³. dryue] dryuen M; dyne H³.
127 Boþe] Boþen M; Bothin J; Bot E; *om* A. to(1)] *om* UH³. setten . . . sowen] sowen and to setten V. setten] settyn JA; sette RHEWNH³; sett K. to(2)] *om* ULH³. sowen] sowyn JA; sowe RUDH LWNH³; sowȝen Ch; sawe E. &(2)] and to REAK. sauen] sauyn JAH³; saue REM; sawen (? *for* salven) W. telþe] tilþe RUVJLEAKWNMH³.
128 Cacche] AKNMH³; Chase TRUDCh E; Gaste VW; gast H; kaire L; To kepyn J. cowes] coos A; crowes LKNM; crowys J; Crowen VH; gees TRUDChEWH³. his] þe RUHJEAWN. and] & RUChVH JEKWMH³; & also N; *om* TDLA. kepen] kepyn JEAH³; kepe RChNM.
129 Or] oþ*er* H; Othir J. shuln] schul UChJM; schulen L; shull HKW; schulle V; sculle R; xul H³; schal DEAN. ete] eten RDChK; etyn JAMH³. barly] barlich K; barle E. bred] bryn A. of] *om* L. brok] RVLAH³; broke DChHJEKNM; brook UW; brod (*small* k (?) *above* od) T. drynke] drynken UChK; drinkyn JA.
130 But] But if K; Bote ȝef L. he] heo V; ȝe HEAWNM. be . . . or(1)] bryng a A. be] beo VL. or(1)] oþ*er* R; *om* W. brokesshankid . . . ligge] bedrede or ellis brokeshankid H. brokesshankid] brokynschankyd K; brokenschanked M; brokshanked N; broke schonket V; broke schank A; brokelymed JW; brokyn E. or(2)] oþ*er* R; & H³. beddrede] bedrede UDChLAWH³; bedred RJ; bedered N; bedreden V; beddryn E; Bredred M. ligge] liggen V; lyggyn AK; liggeth M; lygg*es* R; legg*es* E; *illegible* L.
131 Þei shuln] Schul þai A; þen shulle ȝe H; Than shul ȝe W. Þei] hij N; For þey M; ȝe RUEK. shuln] schul UChVM; schullyn J; schull K; schulle R; xul H³; schal DEN. ete . . . good] *om* R. ete] eten UDK; etyn JEM; haue VH. as(1) . . . I] as I seie U; as I sayd as E. as(2)] *om* L. me god] god me AW. helpe] help HE.

Til god of his *gr*ace gare h[e]m to arise.
Ankeris & heremytes þ*at* holde hem in here sellis
Shuln haue of myn almesse al þe while I libbe,
Inouȝ iche day at non, ac no more til on þe morewe 135
Lest his flessh & þe fend foulide his soule.
Ones at noon is ynouȝ þ*at* no werk vsiþ;
He abideþ wel þe bet*er*e þ*at* bu*m*miþ nouȝt to ofte.'
Þanne gan wasto*ur* arise & wolde haue yfouȝte;
To peris þe plouȝman he p*ro*fride his gloue. 140

132 *line om* UVHN. Til] To E; Til þat W. grace] grete gr*ace* JL. gare] gar DE AW; gere R; ger Ch; graunte JL; make KMH³. hem] RDChJAKMH³; hom L; hym TE; ȝow W. to] *om* ChWM. arise] ryse AH³.
133 heremytes] ermit*es* RCh; ermytys J; armetes W. þat] at E. holde] hold D; holden UChJLKW; holdyn MH³; holdeþ RVH; hald*es* E; wonyn A. hem] hom L; þaim E; *om* AW. in] to W. here] her RChJKH³; heore VL; *om* EN. sellis] selle WM.
134 Shuln] Schulen VL; Schul DHAW; Schullen ChK; Schully*n* J; Schulle U; Xul H³; Shal NM; Sal E; ȝe schal R. haue] haue*n* H³; hauyn J; habben V. almesse] almes ChHLAK; almusse E; Alm*us* VJ; halmes W. al þe] *om* HA. while] qwyle JEH³; whiles K. I] þat y HAM. libbe] *same hand after cancelled* bene (? beue) A; liue VHKN; leve EWH³.
135 Inouȝ] And now E; *om* A. iche] eche RUDChHAKWNMH³; vche VL; eu*er* I J. at . . . ac] eet none W. non] noone DHJE; nou*n* H³. ac] bot ChVJAKNM; & HLEH³. no more] namore U. til . . . morewe] aftre N. til] er ULWM; or DEK; ar R. on þe] on J; a VM; þe HW H³; *om* RUDLEAK. morewe] morowe DEK; morowh J; morwe RUVHLAW MH³; morne Ch.
136 Lest] þat J; þai lat E; In auenture þat bred A. his(1)] heore L; þe UVHJEWH³; *om* A. flessh . . . fend] feend and his flesche U; fende ne his fleche J; fend & þe flesh W; fend & her*e* flesch H; Fend and heore flesch V. fend] feond L. foulide] foulyd R; fouleden V; fouled DChLN; fowlen K; fowly*n* H³; folwele M; schuld foulyn A; defowle nouht J; folowed U; folow E; folewen H; greuen W. his soule] togidr*es* U. his(2)] her*e* HW; her A; heore VL; þe E. soule] sowele M; saule E; soules VL; soulis H.
137 *transposed with following* A. at] atte M; a N. noon] day N. is] it is J. ynouȝ] ynowȝ RDW; Inowh J; ynogh L; Inowȝe Ch; ynow UHANH³; Inowe M; enogh E. þat] to him þat J. werk] work K; craft N. vsiþ] vsyth JUDChLAWM; vsys E; vsyd H³; ne vsiþ TRVHKN.
138 abideþ] abit A; abitte M; abyd*es* E; bideþ N; vmbydyth J; beth H³. wel] *om* N. betere] bette A; bet V. þat] þat ne H. bu*m*miþ] bumbyth J; bibbith A; etyth H³. nouȝt] not RDVHLAKWM. to] *om* DJLKWN. ofte] ofþe R; oftyn J.
139 Þanne] ÞEnne V; Tho AH³. gan . . . arise] rose wasto*ur* N. gan wasto*ur*] wastours gu*n*ne V. gan] can L; bygan HH³; began A; beganne M; wald E. wasto*ur*] wastour UDHLEAKWMH³; a wasto*ur* J; þe wasto*ur* TCh; þe wastor*es* R. arise] arisyn J; ryse E; to rise H; *om* AMH³. wolde] wolde*n* V; wold þan A; wold fayn W; nedely wald E. haue] han VN; a AH³; *om* E. yfouȝte] Ifougten M; Ifowhtyn J; fouȝten E; fouthen H³; foutyn A; foght W.
140 To] And to A. peris] p*er*kyn EN. þe] þo J; *om* A. plouȝman] plouh Mon V. he] one H; and V. p*ro*fride . . . gloue] p*er*sued fast E. p*ro*fride] p*ro*frid H; pro-frede V; profred W; proferyd RAH³; p*ro*fered DJLKN; proferd ChM.

A breton*er*, a bragg*ere*, he bostide hym also,
And bad hym go pisse wiþ his plouȝ: 'pilide shrewe!
Wilt þou, nilt þou, we wile haue oure wil
Of þ[i] flo*ur*, and þi flessh fecche whanne vs likeþ,
And make vs m*er*ye þ*er*wiþ maugre þi chekis'. 145
Þanne peris þe plouȝman pleynede hym to þe kniȝt
To kepen hym as couen*au*nt was fro curside shrewis,
Fro wasto*urs* þat waite wynn*er*es to shende.
Curteisliche þe kniȝt þanne as his kynde wolde
Warnide wasto*ur* & wisside hym bet*ere*, 150

141 Here H^2 resumes briefly. A] And W. breton*er*] Bretinor M; bretonyr R; brytoner UH^{2}HEKN; Brutiner V. a(2)] & a H^3. bragg*ere*] bragour K; braggar NH^3. he] a HVJWNMH^3; *om* RUEK. bostide] bostid HJH^3; bostede RV; bosted DChKWNM; bosteth L; bost EA. also] Alse VLANM; als WH^3.
142 And] he Ch; *om* JAN. hym] *om* V. go] *om* J. pisse] pysse hym RChVHEMH^3; *om* J. wiþ] & H. his] all hys E; þe D; *om* H^2. pilide] pylede RUH^2; pyled DN; pillid K; pillede V; pilled ChJW; pelyd E; pelled L; olde pilede H; pynyd H^3; pyned M; foule pyne A. shrewe] sherewe N; screwe V; schre M; swerwe H^3; wreche A.
143 *divided from following after* flour TRU DChH^{2}HE. V *corrupts to* For we wolen habbe of þi Flour wol þou so nulle þou. Wilt þou] wiltow ChJK; wille þou R; Will þou E; Wil þou U; woltou HL; For wiltow WN; *defective* H^2. nilt þou] nyltou H^{2}JK; nyl þou U; nelt þou D; neltou H; nelle þou R; nell þow Ch; ne wiltow N; or nylt þou AMH^3; or nyltow LW; or nyll þou E. we wile] wyl we H^2. wile] willyn J; wullen M; wole H; wol UChK; woln L; wolle E; shul W. haue] han A. oure wil] þe wil D; ynow H; *om* U.
144 Of . . . flour] *om* (*see above*) V. Of] And of KM. þi(1)] þy RUHJLEAKW NMH^3; þis TDChH^2. and . . . likeþ] *om* E. and þi] *defective* H^2. and] And of VHJLAKNMH^3; *om* RU. flessh] fleche J; flees R; fysche A. fecche] VAKNMH^3; fette LW; to fechin J; fecche awey TD; fette away RChH^2; fetten awey U; & þy fysch H. whanne] wanne R; when HL; whon V; qwan JH^3; whan wan M. vs] so vs RU; þat vs DVH. likeþ] lykyt H^3.
145 *line om* V. And . . . vs] *defective* H^2. make] maken L; makyn J. m*er*ye] myry J; mury L; mrye M. þ*er*wiþ] þermyd M; with al L. maugre] mawgreth J.
146 Þanne . . . plouȝ] *defective* H^2. Þanne] þenne V; þen HE. peris] peirse E. þe(1)] *om* RDVAW. plouȝman] plouhmon V; ploghmon L; plouman A; *om* W. pleynede] pleyned RUDChH^{2}HLAW; pleynyd NH^3; playnede V; playned K; playnyd J; plened M; plenyd E. hym] *om* WN MH^3. to þe] *twice* E. kniȝt] knyth AH^3; knygh M; knyȝthys R; knygh & prayed hym to helpe W.
147 To . . . fro] *defective* H^2. kepen] kepyn JAM; kepe RUDChHEWNH^3. as] a ChL. couen*au*nt] conant WK; conand E. fro] fro þe H; for L. curside] cursid AK MH^3; cursede RV; cursed DChH^{2}JEN; corsed HLW. shrewis] sherewes N.
148–92 defective H^2.
148 *line om* N. Fro] fram H; Fro suche W; And from K; For A. waite] wayten UDVHLKWM; waytyn JH^3; waytid A; watyng E. wynn*er*es] werke men A. shende] schenden DLM; stroye W. *Here* A *adds a line: see above*, p. 48.
149 þe . . . þanne] þan þe knyght WMH^3; tho þe knyȝth RH. þanne] þoo J; *om* VA. as . . . kynde] be kende as he wel A. his] *om* K. kynde] kuynde V; kende DCh. wolde] wodde W.
150 Warnide] warneþ D. wasto*ur*] wastour UDJLEANH^3; wastor*es* RVH; þe wasto*ur* TChK; þe wastours W; þan wastour M. & . . . bet*ere*] to worche and wynne bettre L; bade hem go werche H. wisside] wissyd JAH^3; wyssede RV; wyssed DChKWNM. hym] hem RW; hem do V. *Here* M *adds a line: see above*, p. 49.

'Or þou shalt abigge be þe lawe, be þe ordre þat I bere'.
'I was not wonid to werche,' *quaþ* wasto*ur*, 'now wile I not
begynne,'
And let li3t of þe lawe & lesse of þe kni3t,
And countide peris at a pese & his plou3 boþe,
And manacide hym & his men whanne h[y] next metten. 155
'Now be þe p*er*il of my soule!' q*ua*þ peris, 'I shal appeire 3ow
alle,'
And houpide aftir hungir þat herde hym at þe ferste:
'Awreke me on wasto[urs],' q*ua*þ peris, 'þat þis world [shend]iþ.'

151 Or] Ethir J; Or ellys N. þou . . . bere] by þe ordre þat I beore þou schalt hit deore abugge L. þou] boye þou N; 3e RVW; þei H. shalt] xalt H³; schat J; schal RE; schul VW; shulde H. abigge] abige K; bygge W; abugge V; abegge D; aby3e R; abye UEAN; abyen J. be . . . lawe] *om* N. be] hit bi VKW. þe(1)] *om* V. lawe] law3e Ch. þe(2)] *om* M. ordre] orde J; lord RUE. þat] at E. I] he H. bere] welde RUDEA.
152 *as two lines divided after* wastour D; *after* worche W. was] nas W. not] nou3t ChN; noght U; nout H³; neu*er* EW. wonid . . . wasto*ur*] q*uod* wastour wont for to worche W. wonid] woned RH; wont UDVLENH³; wonte ChJAK; wo*n*ne M. to] for to E. werche] werchen M; worche RChVLKN; wurche UD; wyrchin J; wirke E. q*ua*þ wastour] *om* N. wasto*ur*] a wasto*ur* V; wastor*es* R. now . . . not] I wol not now A. now] ne nowe E; Ne now forsoþe D; 3it VH; And 3it W; & H³; it M. wile I] I wil W; I wol L; I nel H³. wile] wole H; wol ChV; woll K. not] nou3t N; no*u*t H³. begynne] begynne so me god helpe W.
153 let] lete DChHEANM; lette V; leet UH³; leete J. li3t] lygte M; lyth R; lyith H³; lightlich L; lytely A; lyt J; litil W; luy-tel V. of(*both*)] be J. þe lawe] his lore L. lawe] law3e Ch. lesse . . . kni3t] of þe knyght lesse W; eke of him seoluen L. lesse] lasse DRChVHJNM. kni3t] kny3th R; knyth H³; knygt M; knyte A; kynyth J.
154 And] He A; *om* M. countide] countyd EA; cou*n*tede RV; counted DCh; coump-ted K; acou*n*tid HH³; acountyt J; Aconp-tede M; acounteth L; sette WN; bad U. peris] peirse E. at a pese] go pisse U. pese] peese JK; pees N; peose VL; pere W. boþe] after L.
155 And] *om* A. manacide] manasid HJAH³; Manasede V; manaced UDCh LKM; mancede R; mansed N; manyshyd E; manases W. &] & eke LK; as D. men] man N; me Ch. whanne] when DHLW; qwan JH³; qwen E; whon þat V. hy] he TH³; þei RUDChVHJLWNM; þai EA; thay K. next] nyxt R; both K. metten] mettyn JAH³; mette RULEN.
156 *as two lines divided after* Mon V. Now] *om* AN. þe . . . soule] goddis pyte N. þe] *om* L. soule] saule E. peris] peirse E; Pers þe plouh Mon V. shal] xal H³. appeire 3ow] you pare E. appeire] apeiren V; apaire ChN; enpeire L; peyre J. 3ow] ow V. alle] alle for oure proude wordes V.
157 And] He A. houpide] houpyd E; houped D; howpide U; howpid KN (w *added above line same hand* K); hopyd R; hoped VL; hoppyd J; hopped W; hu*n*tid H; hawnted Ch; clepid M; wyschid A; wepyd H³. þat] þo þat V; he AWMH³. herde] harde AN; hard K; her H³. at . . . ferste] anon W. at þe] atte DVJL; atte þe M; at N. ferste] fyrste RUChJLKN; furste V; furst H; frist EAH³.
158 Awreke] Awreyke J; wreke UDH EA; And wreke Ch; To wreky*n* H³. me] hy*m* H³; *om* E. on] on þese UA; on þes RE; on þis VM; of JW; of þis H³. wastours] URDVHJLEAKWNMH³; was-to*ur* TCh. q*ua*þ peris] *om* NH³. peris] peirse E. þat] pat W. þis] þe UWH³; al þe N. world] wordle R; word W; werlde J; werd A; wreld H³. shendiþ] schendith UJL; sche*n*dyt M; schendeþ V; schenden DHKN; schende H³; schendis R; shend*es* E; schendt A; apeiriþ T; apaireiþ Ch; stroie W.

Hungir in haste þanne hente wastour be þe mawe,
And wrong hym so be þe wombe þat al watride his eiȝen, 160
And buffetide þe bretoner aboute þe chekis
Þat he lokide lik a lanterne al his lif aftir;
He beet hem so boþe he brast ner here mawis.
N[e] hadde peris [wiþ] a pese lof preyede hym beleue,
And wiþ a bene batte he[ȝe]de [hem] betwene, 165
And hitte hunger þerwiþ amydde hise lippes, |
And bledde into þe bodyward a bolle ful of growel, *fol.* xlj *a*

159 *run together with following line* U. Hungir . . . haste] And þus sone he W. Hungir] & hunger UN. in] on LM. þanne] þenne R; þoo J; þou D; *om* UVH LEWN. wastour] wastores RV; þaim E. mawe] wombe A.
160 And . . . wombe] *om* U. wrong] wrang REM. hym] hem R. so] *om* RJ. wombe] mawe RE. þat] at E. al . . . eiȝen] hys eyne watteryd H3; his eyen watred KW; his eyen waterden M; his Ien watturedyn J; boþe his eyn watrid N; boþe his iȝen watrid H; boþe his eȝen watreden V; bo his eynen wattred L. al] *om* E. watride] wattred D; wateryd EA; watered RUCh. his] her R; þair E. eiȝen] eyen RUD; eyneȝ E; yen A.
161 And] And he E; he N. buffetide] buffetid A; buffatid J; Buffetede V; buffeted RDChKWM; boffetid HH3; Bofete E; buffet N; boffet L. þe(1)] so þe AH3; so L. bretoner] bretener J; bretenner H3; brytoner UEKN; bretoun DM; Bragger Ch; boye V. aboute] abouþe R; abowtyn JH3; wel aboute L; so aboute KWM. þe(2)] boþe his VH.
162 Þat] *om* VW. lokide] lokyd JEAMH3; lokede V; loked RDChHLKWN. lik] lyik H3; liche J; as RM. lanterne] lantarne A; launtren E. lif] lyue UJ.
163 He] Hongre W; And UE. beet] bet RDJEAKN; bete HM; bette Ch; Beot VL; bote W; beth H3. hem so] so hem JN. hem] heom L; þaim E; hym UW; *om* VH3. so] so sore E; *om* U. boþe] bothin J; þe Boyes V. he(2)] VHJLAM; þat he TDChKNH3; and RUE; þat W. brast . . . mawis] here mouþ brosten W. brast] barst DVHL; brak RU; brake EM. ner] negh E; nee M; neigh N; neih V; nyȝe H; nigh K; nyth H3. here] her DChJKH3; heore VL; þair E. mawis] mawȝes K; mawȝe Ch; wombis A; Ribbes V.
164 Ne hadde] RUHM; Ne had ChJAK NH3; Ne hed E; Nadde D; Nedde V; No hadde L; Nhadde T; Til W. peris] perus U; Pers VJ; peirse E. wiþ] with RUVHJLEAKWNMH3; but TDCh. pese] peese J; peyse E; peose VL. lof] loue N. preyede] preied L; preyid H3; preide NM; preyȝid J; prayed RUKW; Ipreyed VH; a preyed A; þei preyede T; þey preyed DCh; help E. hym] hem HA; þaim E. beleue] bileue ChLK; belyue R; by lyue U; in hast E; to leue VWNH3; to lyue H; stynte M.
165 bene] beene J; beane K; benne (? for benen) H; benen W; Benene V; beny U. batte] bat DV; bach R; kake H3. heȝede hem] he ȝede hem M; he ȝed hem H3; he ȝede JN; he ȝede so W; ȝede hem H; had hyhyd K; busked heom L; he wente hem A; he hadde TRU; he had DCh; I bot hem V; þai abade E. betwene] betwenyn J; betwen his handes Ch; *om* E.
166 And] he Ch. hitte] hutte V; hard E. þerwiþ] þermyde DM; þer mellyd E; *om* U. amydde] amyddes DChEK; amyddys J; in myddis of A; þe meddys of H3; right so bytwyx W. hise] boþe his VH; bothe L; þe UJAKWNMH3.
167 And] And he V; þat he ChLWNMH3. bledde] made hym blede HK. into . . . bodyward] inward H. þe] his A. bodyward] bodywardes M; wombeward H3; body K. bolle ful] potel H3. growel] gruwel V; gruel DH; grwel N; grewelle ChJ; grovell K; benes M.

Ne hadde þ[e] fisician ferst defendite him watir
To abate þe barly bred ⁊ þe benis ygrounde,
Þei hadde be ded be þis day ⁊ doluen al warm. 170
Faitou*rs* for fer flowen into bernis
And fla[ppid]e on wiþ flailes fro morewe til eue,
Þ*at* hung*er* was not hardy on hem for to loke.
For a potel of pe[s]is þ*at* peris hadde mad
[A]n he[p] of heremites henten hem spadis, 175
And doluen drit ⁊ dung to ditte out hung*er*.

168 Ne hadde] No hadde L; Nadde H; Nad W; Nedde V; hadde N; Ne hadde hadde M. þe . . . ferst] ferste þe fisisian M; fryst þe feciscian AH^3. þe] RUDVHJLE KWN; a Ch; þi (*touched up*) T. ferst] first ChJ; furst VHL; first fast K; faster W; *om* RUEN. defendite] defendid HJN; defendet V; defended RDChLMH^3; defende U; defend E; a defende A; fette W; fett K. him] hem R; hym in E; hym fresh W.
169 abate] abatyn J; bate RE; abate wiþ W. bred] *om* K. þe(2)] *om* W. benis ygrounde] grounden benes W. benis] bones L. ygrounde] grounde UAM; grounde*n* H; groundyn J; gronde H^3; grynde E.
170 Þei] Þai E; Thay K; he ChM. hadde] hed E; hedden V. be] beo VL; ben RDJ EN; byn K. ded] dede RChMH^3; deed U; deyd E. be(2)] er W; or K. doluen] doluyn JH^3; dolfyn EA; ydolfe H. al warm] in erthe K; ful depe W. al] as J.
171 Faitou*rs* . . . fer] For ferede this faitours M; For ferd þo faytou*ris* H^3; For ferd þese wastouris A. Faitou*rs*] Fatou*rs* E; ÞEnne Faytors V; Sone wastours W. for fer] ben ferd a E. fer] fere RUVLN; feare K; ferde HW; drede J. flowen] flowyn RA; flowe W; flow D; fleyen H^3; þoo flowyn J; þo flow N; þen flowe H. into] to VAM. bernis] beernys U; barnes N; þe berne WH^3; hernes Ch.
172 flappide] flappid HJEANMH^3; flapten VL; flappyn R; flappen K; flappe U; flyp flapt W; flatte TCh; flatted D. on] *om* A. flailes] flaylys RJ; fleyles UDVAN; fleylys H^3. fro] fram H. morewe] morowe ChK; morow JEN; morowen D; morwe RVLWMH^3; morne UA; morn H. til] intil (in *cancelled*) J; to HE. eue] euen UDChVHLEWNM; euyn JAKH^3.
173 Þ*at* . . . was] Was not hungr*e* W; Ther*e* nas M. was] nas VHL. not] nouȝt ChN; noght UE; nouth H^3; non M. hardy] so hardy RUHJEWMH^3. on] ones on U; onys on R; onys of E; of M; vp V. hem] heom L; þaim E; *om* V. for to] to RUEKWM. loke] loken DLKWM; lokyn J.
174 potel] potful VJLKWN. pesis] pesys J; peoses L; pese E; pesyn RUNH^3; pesen DHWM; peson K; pesoun Ch; peosun V; pecis T; pece A. peris] peirse E; p*er*kyn N; piers wif W. hadde] hedde V; hade gert E; let H. mad] made JWN; Imad V; Imade Ch; ymaked RDLKM; ymakyd UH^3; make HE.
175 An hep] RUVJKH^3; ⁊ an hepe HA; A gret hepe LNM; Þen þe hepe E; And þan an hepe W; In helpe TD; In helpe þenne Ch. of] *om* Ch. heremites] ermyt*es* RUChK. henten] hentyn JMH^3; hente RA; hent W; hyntt E. hem] heom VL; þaim E; here H.
176 doluen] doluyn AH^3; dulphyn J. drit ⁊ dung] dong ⁊ dryt boþe W; depe into þe donge E; pp dunge (ng *rubbed*) M. drit] dirte K; driȝt N. ditte] dittyn J; dutte DVL; dryue RE; dryuen UCh; holde WM; holdyn AH^3; fil K. out hung*er*] away hungre E; hou*n*ger out RUDVAWNH^3; dugre (?) oute M; hungers throte K.

Blynde ⁊ bedrede were botind a þousand
[Þ*at* ley3e [blereyed] and brokelegged by þe hye waye];
Hungir hem helide wiþ an hot[e] cake.
And lame menis lymes wern li[þ]id þ*at* tyme, 180
And become knaues to kepe peris bestis,
And prei3ede *pur charite* wiþ peris for to dwelle,
Al for coueitise of his corn to [cacche] awey hungir.
And pieris was proud þ*er*of, ⁊ putte hem in office,
And 3af hem mete ⁊ monie as þei mi3te ass*er*ue. 185

177 *line om* K; *divided from following after* Ibotyd J. Blynde] Blinde men J; Boþe blynd W; Of blynde N. ⁊] ⁊ of N. bedrede] bedred JWN; bederede A; bedderede (*after cancelled* blere) D; Beddered M; bedreden L; Bedraden VH; blered E; blereyed R; blereey3ed U. were] weren UM; weryn þ*er* J; weore VL; leyu*n* H³. botind] botenyd D; botened ChL; Botned VH; boted WM; betyn A; Ibotyd J; wotned (*for* ibotned) N; aboute RUE; aboutyn H³. þousand] þousent V.
178 RUVHJLEAKWNMH³ (*text based upon* R); *line om* TDCh; *as two lines divided after* legget VHN; *after* leggys J. Þat] Thay þat K; Thei AN; And H³; *om* E. ley3e] leyen UHM; leyu*n* H³; leyn JA; Lay E; layen L; liggyd K; hadde laien W; had yleye N; ly3en V. blereyed] *see* RUE *variants, line* 177; blynde RJAK MH³; for blynd UVHLEN; *om* W. and] *om* W. brokelegged] brokenleggyd K; for brokelegged LN; for broke leggid H; for broke legget V; for brokyn leggys J; long lame W; bedrede A; bedderede H³; blered E. by . . . waye] vpo*n* soft sonedaies by þe hi3e weie HN; Vppon softe sonenday bi þe hei3e weye V; On softe segys on sonndayes be þe hye weye J.
179 hem helide] þoo helid hem J; heled hem so W; heled hem alle N. hem] heom L; þaim E. helide] helid AH³; helede RDV; heled ChK; held M; heelid H; heled wel sone L; halsyd E. an] a EKN. hote] ChJEAKWM; hot TRDV H³; ote ULN; oten H.
180 And . . . menis] That all here W. And] And manye RM; *om* VA. lame] Lome V. menis] men E. lymes] lemes W; lemys DH³; le*m*mys E; lomes M; leggis A. wern] weryn JM; wer ChE; wer*e* RUD HWH³; where AN; war K; weore VL. liþid] lithid JE; litid A; lyþed RUDCh HKN; lyþet V; liþnid T; lechyd H³; leched L; lissed M; louses and liþes W.
181 And] And many of hem W. become] becomyn JAH³; bycomen RHK. to] and AW. kepe] kepen KM; kepyn J; kepte W; cepte A. peris] peirse E; piers is Ch. bestis] hoggis J.
182 And] þei N. prei3ede . . . *charite*] for charite prayd E. prei3ede] preyeden DVL; preiden UAN; preide HM; pray3idyn J; p*r*aydyn H³; p*r*ayden K; prayde R; praied ChW. *pur*] *par* JNH³; for RVHA WM; pytously *par* L; hym for U. *charite*] cherite R. wiþ] *om* W. peris] peirse E; hym U. for to dwelle] to beleuyn J. dwelle] dwellen M; serue W.
183 Al] And alle M; and RDVE; *om* AW. coueitise] couatise ChE. his] þe W; *om* N. cacche] NKH³; cachen JM; cacchyn A; chache E; chase TRUDCh; kayre L; caste VH; kepe W.
184 And] Bot E; *om* VANH³. pieris] peirse E; p*er*kyn N. was . . . ⁊] þ*er*of was proud ⁊ L; wel appaied W. proud] prout H. þ*er*of] þ*er*fore H. hem] heom L; þaim E; hi*m* M. in] into R; to D. office] offyces DLN.
185 And] he N; *om* RA. 3af] yafe K; gaf NH³; gaff E. hem] heom L; þaim E; hi*m* M. monie] i *above line same ink* T; mony EMH³; mone RUJLAN; money DChHK; moneye V; monoie W. as] a M; lik as Ch. þei] þai EA. mi3te] mighten K; my3the R; myth H³; mygh W. ass*er*ue] asseruen D; serue ChE; deserue HJLKWNH³; deseruen VM; dysseruyn A.

Þanne hadde piers pite & preiȝede hungir to wende
Hom into his owene er[d]e & holde him þere euere.
'Ac ȝet I preye þe,' quaþ peris, 'er þou passe ferþere:
Of beggeris & bidderis what best is to done.
For I wot wel, be þou ywent, hy wile werche ille; 190
Meschief it makiþ h[y] ben so mek nouþe,
And for defaute of foode þus faste hy werchiþ.
And it ben my blody breþeren, for god bouȝte vs alle.
Treuþe tauȝte me ones to loue hem ichone

186 Þanne] þenne V; þen H. hadde piers] Piers hadde W. hadde] hedde V; bad E. piers] peirse E. pite . . . hungir] put hunger in preson E. pite] pete A; pety K; pece H³. preiȝede] preiede V; preied L; preid AN; preyde UChHM; prayȝid J; prayed KW; prayid H³; prayd D; prayde R. to] for to EA; *om* NM. wende] wynde N.
187 Hom] Or home E; *om* HA. into] to VEKWMH³. owene] awne E. erde] hurde V; lond AH³; ȝerd RJE; ȝerde U; erþe TDChHLK; hous WN; lord M. holde] holden VL; holdyn JH³; dwelle A. him] *om* AH³. euere] for euere VHLEA WNM; eueremore H³.
188 Ac] Bot ChHKWN; And RUVJLE MH³; *om* A. ȝet] ȝit UChVJEANM; ȝut R; þat L; *om* HW. þe] you E; *om* RL. peris] perus U; peirse E. er] or RUDCh HK; ar N. þou] ye E. ferþere] forthere DChHLNH³; farther K; henne V.
189 Of] Of þese A. beggeris & bidderis] Bidders and of beggers VN; bedreden & beggeris H. &] and of U. bidderis] bedderys H³. what] qwat JEH³. best is] best beo L; is best RUVHEAKWMH³.
190 For] *om* VHJWN. I . . . wel] wele I wot AMH³. wel] *om* H. be þou] whon þou art V. be] by U; beo L. þou] ȝe UE. ywent] went RUChHJLEAKWNMH³. hy] he A; þey RUDChVHJENMH³; þay LKW. wile] wilen M; wil RDJ; wille Ch; willyn A; will E; wol UVHLW; woll K; wolle N; xul H³. werche] worche RChLN; worchen V; wurche D; wurchen UK; wirchin J; wirke E. ille] ful ille VHWNH³; wel ille L; euell E; ful euyl A; alle M.
191 Meschief] Myschief D; Mescheif L; myschef RChEKW; Mischeue J; And Mischef V; For myschef NMH³; For myschep A; þy self H. it makiþ] makiþ it iwis H; mekeþ hem W. makiþ] maket M. hy] þey RUChVHJLANMH³; þai E; thay K; þat þey D; þe W; hym T. ben] be DNH³; bene J; beon L; beþ RW; beoþ V. mek] meoke L. nouþe] nowe JEAKNH³.
192 foode] helpe & fode A. hy] þey RU DChVHJLAWMH³; þay E; thay K; now þei N. werchiþ] werchyn AM; werchen H; werche H³; wurchet D; wurchen U; worchen VLK; worche Ch; wyrchin J; wyrche RN; wirke E; worche nowe W.
193 **Here** H² **resumes briefly.** And] *om* HN. it] þei HLH³; þai E; thay K; heo V; alle A; we W. ben . . . alle] *defective* H². ben] be D; beþ RHW; beon L; beoþ V; bene (*followed by* þey *above line another ink*) J. my . . . breþeren] brethren of blood W; myne breþeren of one blood H. my] may E; our H³. blody] bodely E; *om* AMH³. breþeren] breþerin DAH³; breþern Ch; brethirn J; bredern K; brethren L; breþryn R; brether E; breyeryn M. for] *om* ANH³. bouȝte vs] sent vs hider N. bouȝte] bouȝthe R; bouth H³; boute AM; made HL. alle] *rubbed out* H.
194 Treuþe] Trouth E; truþe RN; And trouþ W. tauȝte . . . ichone] *defective* H². tauȝte] tauȝthe R; tauhte V; taugthe H³; tauþt W; tauthe M; taut A; thaght E; touȝt ChK; told J. to] for to E. loue] louen UVK; louyn JAMH³. hem] heom L; þaim E. ichone] echone RUDChHA K; vchone VLN; ylchoun H³; all E.

And helpe hem of alle þing [aftir] þ*at* hem nedi[þ]. 195
[Now wolde I] wite, ȝif þ*o*u wistest, what were þe beste,
And how I miȝte amaistrie hem & make hem to werche.'
'Here now,' q*ua*þ hungir, '& holde it for a wisdom:
Bolde beggeris & bigge, þ*at* mowe here breed beswynken,
Wiþ houndis bred & hors bred holde vp here hertis, 200
And [a]baue hem wiþ b[e]nes for bollnyng of h*er*e wombe,
And ȝif þe [g]omes grucche bidde hem gon & sywnke,

195 A *corrupts to* Thei þat han nede helpe hem in alle þinge. helpe] helpen DVLK; helpyn JMH^{3}. hem(1)] heom L; þaim E. of . . . nediþ] *defective* H^{2}. of] at E. þing] thyng*es* K. aftir þ*at*] aftir þat NM; aftur þat VJ; aft*er* þat HLKH^{3}; aftr*e* W; what þat RU; qwat at E; þat TDCh. hem(2)] heom L; þey M; þai E. nediþ] nedyþ RUHJKNH^{3}; nedit M; nedeþ DLW; neodeþ V; nede E; of nedide T; of neded Ch.
196 Now . . . I] RUHJLAWNMH^{3}; Now would I K; Now wald I E; ȝit wolde I V; wold I D; I wolde TChH^{2}. wite] witen VLKN; wyty*n* J; wete ChEWH^{3}; weten D; wetyn AM. ȝif . . . wistest] of the KW. ȝif] ȝef L. þou . . . beste] *defective* H^{2}. wistest] wystyst RChH; wist EH^{3}; wistid A; wustest V; wost JNM. what] whad L; qwat JEH^{3}; wat here of N; wht M. were] wer ChJE; weore L; war K. þe] *om* N.
197 *line om* A. And] *om* RH. how] wherwiþ W. miȝte] myȝthe RN; mygthe M; myth H^{3}; may W. amaistrie . . . werche] *defective* H^{2}. amaistrie] amaystr*ie*n J; amaystry Ch; amaistre N; A Maystren VHL; amaystryn M; amaist*er* E; amastrye R; amastre K; maystrye D; maystre W; maystery*n* H^{3}. hem(*both*)] heom L; them K; þaim E. make] maken UV; maky*n* JH^{3}. to] *om* K. werche] worche VLWN; worchen K; wurche U; wyrche RChJ; wirke E.
198 *line om* H^{3}. Here] Heare K; Hire W. now] noon W. holde . . . wisdom] *defective* H^{2}. holde] goold U; hald E; held A. it] þat W. a] *om* VJEA. wisdom] wisdam VLM.
199 *run together with following* D. Bolde] Boold W; Hold E. beggeris] Bidders VH. &] þat A. bigge] Beggers VH; byddd*er*ys E; byddars K; beggyn A. þat . . . beswynken] *defective* H^{2}; *om* D. mowe] mowen UVM; mowne J; mou*n* H^{3}; may ChEKW. here breed] noght swete ne E. here] h*er* RChVJKN (*after for which is above line another ink*) J; hire W; heore L. breed] mete UVHJWH^{3}. beswynken] byswynke RVLN; byswink H; swinken ChM; swynke UEKWH^{3}; swynk JA.
200 Wiþ . . . hors] *om* D. houndis . . . &] benis & wit*h* M. houndis] honde E; hond W. bred(1)] *om* U. &] or H^{2}. holde . . . hertis] *defective* H^{2}. vp] þow H. here] her RChJKN; hire W; heore L; heor V; þair E. hertis] heortes L; hart*es* K; mawes H; lyues W.
201 And] *om* DHJAKN. abaue] DHJAK N; baue TUH^{2}EM; bayue H^{3}; abate L; bayte R; batten Ch; Ba*m*me V; fede W. hem] heom L; þaim E. wiþ] *om* H^{3}. benes] LEW; benys UJANMH^{3}; bones TChH^{2}V; bonys RDHK. bollnyng . . . wombe] *defective* H^{2}. bollnyng] bolnyg H^{3}; bolling ChVLKM; swellyng RUE; bornyng W. h*er*e] her RChJKN; hyre W; heore VL; þair E. wombe] wombes UVHKWM; wombys H^{3}; wonbys R; belyes N; *illegible* L.
202–22 defective H^{2}.
202 *line om* A. And] *om* H. ȝif] ȝef ChL. þe gomes] þei W. þe] þo DJH^{3}; eny H. gomes] V; gromes TRUDChHJLEKN MH^{3}. grucche] grucchen V; grucchin M; gruch Ch; grochen E; gr*o*chyn J; grotch H^{3}; groche þ*er*ewiþ W. bidde] bede M. hem] heo*m* L; þaim E; them K; hym DM. gon] go RUDChVHJLEKWNH^{3}. &] *om* UDVHJEWNH^{3}. swynke] swynken M; worche WN; work Ch.

And he shal soupe swettere whanne he it haþ deseruid.
Ac ȝif þou fynde any frek þat fortune haþ apeirid
Wiþ fuyr or wiþ false men, fond suche [to] knowen; 205
Counforte hem wiþ þi catel for cristis loue of heuene;
Loue hem & lene hem & so þe lawe of kynde wolde.
And alle maner of men þat þou miȝte aspien,
Þat nedy ben or nakid, & nouȝt han to spende,
Wiþ mete or [wiþ] mone let make hem [fare þe betere], | 210
[Or with werk or with word þe while þou art here].

203 *line om* A. And] for R. he] þei UVHN; *om* E. shal] xal H³; sal J; schul UH; schule V; scholyn M. soupe] soupin M; sowpyn J; sope ChE; supp K. swettere] sweitere W; þe swetter H; þe swettore V; betere M; þe betere UE. whanne] when RHL; whon V; qwan JH³; qwen E; than K. he] þei UVHNM. it haþ] haþ hit RLW; han hit V; hase it E. it] *om* HJH³. haþ] hat H³; han UNM; haue H. deseruid] deserued RChHEWNH³; deseruet V; *illegible* L.
204 Ac] Bot LKWM; And ChVHJENH³; *om* A. ȝif] ȝef ChL. fynde] fyndest V. any] eny VH; ony RUDEAM. frek] freyke DVJAH³; freek UH. haþ] hat H³; has AM; hase E. apeirid] apeyred RUDHAKN; apeiret V; aperyd M; apayryd J; appaired ChW; aparyd E; enpeired L.
205 fuyr] fure H; fyre RUChJEAKWN; fyir H³; feer D; fer M. or] oþer RH. wiþ] wit wit M. men] folk V. fond] fonde RDChHJWNM; founde E; fonden K. suche] siche H; swyche JM; sweche AH³; sike E; siche men U; swych men D; hem W. to] RUChVJLEAKWNMH³; forto H; *om* TD. knowen] knowe RUChVHJAWNH³; knaw E.
206 *line om* E. hem] heom L; hym RW. þi] *om* LN. cristis loue] Cristesake W. cristis] godis A. loue] lof J. heuene] heuyn JAK; heouen L.
207 Loue] Lof J. hem(*both*)] heom L; þaim E; hym W. lene] lenne E; lone U; lend K; lenede H³. &(2)] for RUHEAKMH³; *om* VWN. so] as WN; *om* A. þe] *om* RHKWNMH³. of] *om* J. kynde] kende ChH³; kuynde V; *om* J. wolde] wole VH; it wolle A; askeþ W; techith K; *om* E.
208–12 (*omitting* 211) *as three lines divided after* naked—mone RUDE.
208 And] And eke L. alle . . . þat] þo U; if E. maner] *om* R. of] *om* RDHW. men] suche men W. miȝte] myȝthe R; mygth M; myth H³; mayȝt V; mayt J; may EN. aspien] aspye RUVHEAKWM; asspyȝe H³.
209 nedy . . . nakid] be naked & nedy N. nedy ben] ben nedy H; beþ nedy W. nedy] neodi V; in nede A. ben] be E; beþ R; beon L. or] & H. nakid] naket V; nekyd H³. &] or A. nouȝt han] han noght U; haue noght W; naue not H. nouȝt] nouȝth R; noght LE; nouth JAH³; nowt M; nauȝt Ch. han] haue RDVEK. spende] spenden U; spendyn JM; despende L.
210 Wiþ] Of þi W; in E. or] oþer H; ne RUE; & W. wiþ(2)] with RUDChVHJLAKNMH³; in E; *om* TW. mone] monee L; mony EMH³; monye KN; money ChH; Moneye V; þi monoye W; drink J. let . . . betere] *om* RUDE. let] lete HN; lat AH³; late W; *om* ChV. make] *om* HJLAKWNMH³. hem] heom L; them K. fare . . . betere] VH; be þe bettere AKW; ben þe betere MH³; beene þe bettur J; beo þe bettre L; be releued N; at ese TCh.
211 LVHJAKWNMH³; *line om* TRUDChE. Or] oþer H; Oyþir J. with(1)] wiþ wiþ W. werk . . . word] word or with werk V. werk] work K. or(2)] oþer H. word] wordis H; dede A. þe while] the whiles K; while þat V; wyl þat N; whil AW; whils H; qwyl H³; qwylis J. here] þere N. *Here* M *copies* 212α *in margin.*

Make þe Frendis þermi[d] for so matheu vs techiþ: *fol.* xlj *b*
Facite vobis amicos.'
'I wolde not greue god,' quaþ peris, 'for al þe gold on ground.
Mi3te I synneles do as þou seist?' seide peris þanne.
'3e, I hote þe,' quaþ hungir, 'oþ*er* ellis þe bible lei3eþ. 215
Go to genesis þe geaunt, engendro*ur* of vs alle:
In sudore & swynke þou shalt þi mete tilen
& labouren for þi liflode, & so oure lord hi3te;
And sapience seiþ þe same, I sai3 it in þe bible:
Piger propter frigus no feld wolde tilie; 220

212 *transposed with following* H. Make] HJAKWN; Mak VLMH³; lat make RUD; Bot make E; And make TCh. þe] þi UE. Frendis] frend EH³. þermid] þ*er*myde UN; þer mydde A; þ*er* mede E; þ*er* miþ T; þ*er*with RDChVHJLKW; þer wit M H³. for] and RUDJLEAKNMH³; *om* W. so] so vs N; so seint V; as W. matheu . . . techiþ] seiþ þe gospel H. vs] þe W; *om* VEMH³. techiþ] techys R; teches D; techth H³; bydd*es* E.

212α *divided from following after* god TRU ChE; *after* greue DA; *in margin* JLM; *end of misplaced portion (see above,* p. 14) RUE; **collation of** E **ends with** 213*a*. *Facite*] *Facite amicos* A. *amicos*] *amicos &c* RChN; *amicos de mammona iniquitatis* VHJKW; *amicos de mamone iniquitatis* H³.

213 I] *om* RUE. wolde] ne wold A; nolde M; nold WH³. not] nou3t ChN; noght UE; nouth H³; *om* AM. greue god] god greue DA. greue] greuyn JM; gryue R; wraþþe H. quaþ . . . ground] *om* U. quaþ . . . gold] for al þe gold q*uod* peres R. peris] pers þanne M. al þe] no W. gold] gode ChHJLWN (*same hand after cancelled* gold J). on] in W; þat groweþ on RDCh. ground] grounde DVJNM; þis ground TRChH³; þe grounde AK; erþe HW; eorthe L.

214 Mi3te] Myth H³; Myte A; May UJ WM. synneles do] do synles H. synneles] su*n*neles V; senneles M; synelesly K. do] don RUDVLAM; do*n*ne J. as] þus as W. seist] now saiste K; seyde A; hast saide W; dost Ch. seide . . . þanne] *om* KWN. þanne] þenne UV; þen H.

215 3e . . . hungir] Therof be þou wel bold W. 3e] Yea K; 3a ChAH³; 3is D. I . . . þe] be goode M; hardyly R. hote] behote DVHLKH³. þe] god U. oþ*er*] or RUDChVHJLAKWNMH³. ellis] *om* W. bible] book H. lei3eþ] ly3eþ V; lyeth DChHJLAWNM; lyyth KH³; lyes RU.

216 *line om* A; *misplaced after line* 218 H. Go to] so seiþ H; In WN. to] to þe V. genesis] genosis H; genesy3e H³. geaunt] gyaunt JN; giant W; gent H. engendro*ur*] eng*en*drure V; gendrour M; gendrer H; þat gendred W; engenderid J. of] *om* W.

217 *line om* A; *divided from following after* mete TRUDCh. *In*] þ*er* he seyth *in* H³. *sudore*] VJLKWNMH³; *sudore &c* TDCh; *sudore uultus tui* RU; sweting H. &] & in K; *om* RU. swynke] swinking H; *labore* H³. þi] þey M. tilen] tile R; Tylien U; tilie VHJLNM; Telien Ch; Telye D; telle H³; tylthe K; wynne W. *Here* L *copies line* 221.

218 *line om* A. &] Bote L. labouren] labour*e* RHLKWNH³; labowryn JM; labre V. þi] yo*ur* K. liflode] lyslode H³. & so] for so VHKW; as R. oure] hour*e* N; yo*ur* K. hi3te] higthe M; hyte J; hieght N; hatte K; hy*m* hytthe H³; biddith UH.

219 *line om* H. And] *om* N. sapience] *Sapiens* VH³. seiþ] seit M; saith LKWN; seyde J. sai3] saih V; say DJ; seie U; sey AWH³; see M; se R; saw3e Ch; sawe K; saw LN. it . . . bible] þe book myself W. bible] bibbele M.

220 *frigus*] prigus U; *frigus noluit* H³. no . . . tilie] *arare noluit* H. no . . . wolde] he nolde his lond M. no] In Ch. feld] fold LH³; londe N; fote W; mete J. wolde] would K; wild J; nolde RDN; wolde he LW; wolde it A; nolde he V. tilie] tyle H³; telye DCh; telle A; tylthe K.

He shal go [begge & bidde] & no man bete his hungir;
Matheu wiþ þe manis face [mouþ]iþ þise wordis:
Seruus nequam had a nam, & for he nolde it vsen,
He hadde maugre of his mais*ter* eu*er*emore aftir,
And benom hym his nam for he nolde werche, 225
And ʒaf [it] hym in haste þ*at* hadde ten before,
And siþen he seide, his *ser*uaunt[s] it h[er]de:
"He þ*at* haþ shal haue to helpe þ*ere* nede is,

221 *copied here and after line* 217 L. He] þ*er*fore he HN. go] gon D; cone H³; *om* RHJN. begge & bidde] begge and bidde UDL(1)KWNMH³; beggyn & byddyn JA; beoge & bidde L(2); bygge and begge RH; bidde & begge TChV. & . . . man] to A. man] mo*n* VL(*both*). bete] bety*n* J; bet D; bett K; beete V; bote MH³; bete away A.
222 Matheu] Seint mathewe W. wiþ] *om* UVHJN. þe] *om* A. manis] ma*nnus* H; Mo*nnes* V. mouþiþ . . . wordis] þes word*es* þ*us* mowtheþ R. mouþiþ] mouthith UJ; mowthis N; mowþed HK; he mouþed W; mevith AH³; mowuyt (? mownyt) M; he Mommeþ V; nempniþ T; nempned Ch; nemened D; techeth L. þise wordis] vs þe same U. þise] þis JWN; þese DHH³; þes ChAK; þeose VL.
223 Here H² **resumes briefly.** *As two lines divided after* &c H. *Seruus* . . . nolde] *defective* H². *Seruus*] þat *seruus* RUJLAK NM; Serue H; Þat Serue H³; *rubbed* (? *original* seriens) Ch. *nequam* . . . nam] *nequam sciebas quia* &c þe wicked *ser*uau*nt* made a couenau*nt* H. had] haued D; hath JLA. nam] name R; naam J; Mnam KN; npnam (*glossed* talentum) V; man AH³; ilman W; besant M. &] *om* D. for] *om* AN. nolde] ne wolde RA. it vsen] worche W. vsen] vsyn JA; vse RUHLN; not vsen K; wise M; wysse H³.
224 *line om* KW. He . . . more] *defective* H². hadde] hedde V. maugre] RUChV HJNH³; a maugre TDLAM. euere] euer RUChVHAMH³; for euere TDJLN. aftir] þeraftir UHLNM. H *then adds a Latin line: see above*, p. 46.
225 *line om* W. And . . . nolde] *defective* H². And] He V; his lord K. benom] benomy*n* J; bynam RAK; byraft H. hym] *om* L. his] is A; þat UJ. nam] name L; na*m*me R; naam J; Mnam KN; mam M; namp H³; npnam (*glossed* besaunt) V; man A; besau*nt* H. nolde] ne wolde R; nolde not VH (not *same hand after cancelled* it vse H); wold not A. werche] werche*n* H; worche RChVL; worchen K; wirche U; wirchen N; wyrchin J.
226 *line om* U. And . . . ten] *defective* H². And] *om* W. ʒaf] yafe K; gaf N; The lord ʒaf W. it] hit ChVHJLAKWNMH³; *om* TRD. hym . . . haste] to a man W. in] on L. hadde] hedde V. before] ChVHJWMH³; afore N; þ*ere* before TRH²AK; ʒeer before D; of his owen L.
227 And . . . seruaunts] *defective* (nt *legible*) H². siþen . . . seide] *om* D. siþen] sitthe*n* R; sytthy*n* H³; siþþe H; siþ W; seþen Ch; sethin J; seþþen V; sone af*ter* M. he] sone he L; he þus V; hit R. his] þat his RDL AKMH³; hym to þat his H; hym also þat his W. *ser*uaunts] seruauntes UKH³; seruuauntis A; *ser*uau*nt*ʒ NM; seruau*ns* V; *ser*uandes J; *ser*uaunt TDChH²HLW; mayst*er* R. it] *om* LW. herde] JLWN; herden VH; herdyn UH³; harde A; hard K; hardyn M; hadde TRDChH². *Here* H *adds a tag: see above*, p. 46.
228 He . . . helpe] *defective* H². haþ] hat MH³. shal] xal H³. haue] hauen M; han J; haue more K. to] and ChH³. helpe] helpyn JAM. þere . . . is] hi*m* at is nede M. nede is] is nede W; it nediþ HN. nede] neod V.

And he þat nouȝt haþ shal nouȝt haue ne no man hi*m* helpe,
And þ*at* he weniþ wel to haue I wile it be hym bereuid". 230
Kynde wyt wolde þat iche wiȝt wrouȝte
Oþ*er* wiþ teching, oþ*er* telling, or trauaillyng of hondis,
Actif lif oþ*er* contemplatif; crist wolde it alse.
The sauter seiþ in þe salme of *Beati omnes*:
Labores manuum tuarum quia manducabis &c.
He þat get his fode here wiþ trauaile of his hondis, 235

229 And . . . nouȝt(2)] *defective* (ouȝt *legible*) H^2. And] *om* AWH^3. he] *om* ChW. nouȝt haþ] haþ not U. nouȝt(1)] nouth JAH^3; nout M; nauȝt Ch. haþ] hat MH^3; nath L. shal nouȝt] nouȝt schal VH^2HJLK; nouth xal H^3; nowgh shal W. nouȝt(2)] nout M; not RUA. haue] ha*n* RJ. ne] no Ch; no*n* M; ny L. no] no*n* M; none H. man] mon VL; *om* H. hi*m*] shal hy*m* HN. helpe] helpen U.
230 And . . . wel] *defective* H^2. And] *om* H^3. þ*at* he] he þ*at* DVHJNH^3. weniþ] venyth K; hopeþ V. wel] weele J; best W; *om* VAKM. to] forte V. haue] han J. I wile] y wol UChHL; shal W; it schal KN; it xal H^3; *om* V. it . . . hym] hit him beo V; þ*at* h*i*t hi*m* be R; hym be WH^3; hy*m* by N; þ*at* hit fro hi*m* beo L; from hym be K; hit hym ChAM. bereuid] bereued DW; byreued H; bireuet V; breuyd N; reuyd H^3; reued RLK; bereuen Ch; bereve AM. H^3 *then adds a Latin quotation: see above*, p. 48.
231 Kynde . . . wolde] *defective* H^2. Kynde] For kynde NM; For kuynde V. wyt] *om* A. wolde] would K; wold wel W. iche] eche RChHAKW; vche V; iche a J; eu*er*y U. wiȝt] wyȝth D; wit R; man UChHAKMH^3; mon V. wrouȝte] wrouȝthe R; wrougthe M; wrouth AH^3; for his fode wroghte U; scholde worche L.
232–52 defective H^2.
232 *line om* U. Oþ*er*] Eyþer Ch; Or RD LKNH^3; *om* VAWM. wiþ] wit M. teching] techenge D. oþ*er*(2)] or RDCh JWNM; oþ*er* wiþ H; or w*i*t*h* VLAKH^3. telling] telieng Ch; tyllyng K; tilynge VH; tylyyng JN. or . . . hondis] w*i*t*h* handis or w*i*t*h* trauelyng A. or] or w*i*t*h* K; oþ*er* wiþ H. trauaillyng] traualyng R; traueling ChJ; trauaill WM; t*r*auel H. hondis] handis MH^3; handes DChJKN; honde W; hande R. *Here* N *misplaces line* 236.
233 *line om* R. Actif . . . contemplatif] Contemplatife lyfe or actife lyfe A; Or co*n*te*m*platyf lyf or actyf lyf H^3; Or comte*m*platif or actif M. Actif] A stef D. lif] *om* JW. oþ*er*] or UDChVJLK; &c WN. contemplatif] contemplatif lif Ch. crist] cryst hy*m* selue H^3; crist oure lord A; so c*r*ist H; as crist hi*m* self M. wolde] would K; coueiteþ N; *om* W. it alse] *om* AMH^3. it] *om* N. alse] also ChK; als JWN; wer*e* H; were so U.
234 *run together with following* H^3; *divided from following after* hende M. The . . . seiþ] For so seiþ þe Sauter V; And so seit þe sautir M. The sauter] Oure lord A. The] þeo L; as þe H; As i*n* þe H^3. sauter] psauter K. seiþ] seith it UChKN; saiþ so W; hym self seiþ H. in . . . salme] *om* H^3. þe] a UHLM; *om* V. salme] psalme RUVHK; spalme ChL; salmes W; psalmis hende M. of . . . *omnes*] of *Beati omnes qui timent dominum qui ambulant* H^3; *om* H. of] *om* M.
234α–236 *as two lines divided after* fode A.
234α *line om* V. *Labores*] A vers þat bygynneth *labores* L. *quia . . . &c*] *&c* A; *manducabis beatus es et bene tibi erit* UH^3. *&c*] *om* DHLM.
235 get] geteþ ChLW; getith UHJK; wynnyth A; etyn H^3. his] here H^3. here] hire W; *om* HAMH^3. wiþ] Thorow A; þourgh M; throw H^3. trauaile] trauel H; trauaylinge V; his trauale M. of . . . hondis] in Treuþe V; *om* MH^3. hondis] hondes ChL; handys DJ; hand*es* RUKN; honde W; hand A.

God ȝiueþ [hem] his blissing þat here liflode so wynneþ.'
'Ȝet I preye þe,' quaþ peris, '*pur charite*, ȝif þou kenne
Eny l[e]f of lechecraft lere it me, my dere,
For summe of my seruauntis ben seke oþer while;
Of alle þe wyke [hy] werkiþ nouȝt, so here wombe akiþ.' 240
'I wot wel,' quaþ hunger, 'what seknesse hem eileþ.
Þei han mangid ouer muche, þat makiþ hem grone ofte.
Ac I hote þe,' quaþ hunger, 'as þou þin hele wilnest,
Þat þou drynke no day er þou dyne sumwhat,

236 N *misplaces after line* 232, *and here substitutes* Shal haue goddes benedictioun & so is he wel worthy. ȝiueþ] ȝiffyth J; ȝif M; ȝeueþ ChHL; ȝeuyth H3; yevith K; ȝeuet D; ȝefþ W; gyweþ N; geuyþ RA. hem] hem RDJNH3; heom L; hym UVHAKWM; *om* TCh. blissing] blessyng RUDChVHLN; blisse KW. þat . . . wynneþ] *om* A. þat . . . liflode] her lyflode þat J. here . . . so] so his lyuelood H; so wiþ treuþ W; him be hire M. here] her ChNH3; heore L; his UV. so] UDVJLKNH3; here so TR; her so Ch. wynneþ] wynnyt M; wynne RN; wynnyn J; geten W; swynkeþ V.
237 Ȝet . . . þe] I pray þe ȝit W. Ȝet] Yet K; ȝit RUChHJNM; Yit V; And ȝit A. þe] *om* U. quaþ . . . *charite*] *pur charite* quoþ peris H; *par charite* quod Piers W. *pur* . . . kenne] þat þu kenne me woldyst A; þat þou me techin woldist MH3. *pur*] *par* VJLN (? *pro* J); for RU. ȝif] ȝef L. kenne] kennys R; Conne VJLN; cunne U; Canne K; canst H.
238 Eny] Any ChLW; Ony UJA; Som H3. lef] WN; leff K; leef UL; leefe J; lif TChM; lyf RVH3; lyfe A; lessoun H; lyst D. of] or W. lere] lerne ChHJH3; þou lere L; lerne þou W; teche U; kenne A; ken R. it] *om* HAWH3. my dere] anone L. my] *om* HW. dere] deore V; leue W.
239 seruauntis] seruandys J; seruauns VL. ben] beþ DH; bet M; beoþ V; beon L; arn H3. seke] seek H3; sike UHK. oþer] som U. while] qwyle H3; whiles LM; tyme U.
240 Of] As D; *om* A. þe] *om* D. wyke] weke ChHLK; woke JAWMH3; wowke U; woke longe N. hy] heo V; þei UHJL ANMH3; thay K; *om* TRDChW. werkiþ] werkyn M; werke D; werche HAH3; worcheþ RChVL; worchen K; worche WN; wurchen U; wyrchen J. nouȝt] not RVHLAKW. here] her ChJAKNH3; heore L; heor V. akiþ] aketh RDChVL WN; akit M.
241 *line om* L. hunger] *om* M. what] qwat JH3. seknesse] syknesse RUHK. hem] þat hem J; hym D. eileþ] eilit M; aylith K; ailleþ W.
242 *line om* A. Þei] Thay K. han] haue UDHKWN. mangid] Imaunget V. ouer] to L. muche] mukel L; myche HN; mychel JK; mykel RM; mykil U; meche H3. makiþ] makyt H3; makeþ RDChV HLKN; maket M; make W. hem] heom L; *om* RU. grone oft] oft grone H. grone] gronyn J; sek W. ofte] fast J; aftre N.
243 Ac] But UChHLKWM; And H3; *om* AN. I] Ich V. hote] byhote N; bidde U; bid J. þe] *om* W. as] ȝif AMH3; ȝef H; and V. þou] *om* W. þin] *om* DH3. hele] heele J. wilnest] wylne V; willest D; willist M; woldest Ch; desirest U; desirist J; woldyst hauen H3; woldis hauyn A; weldest R.
244 Þat] Loke N. er] or DChLAKM; til UVHN. dyne sumwhat] somwhad dyne L. dyne] haue dyned N; haue dynet V; haue ydyned H; hast dyned W; dyen J; ete R. sumwhat] sumqwat JH3; *om* H.

And ete nouȝt, I hote þe, er hunger þe take 245
And sende þe of his saus to sauoure þi lippes,
And kep sum [til] soper tyme, & sit nouȝt to longe;
Aris vp er ap[e]ti[t] ha[ue] eten his fille;
Let nouȝt sire surfet sitten at þi bord;
L[o]ue hym nouȝt, for he is a lecchour & likerous of tunge, 250
And aftir many maner metis his mawe is alongid.
And ȝif þou diȝete þe þus I dar ley myn armes |
Þat fisik shal his furrid hood for his foode selle, *fol.* xlij *a*
And ek his cloke [of] calabre & þe knoppis of gold,
And be fayn be my feiþ his fesik to leten, 255

245–8 *as* 3 *lines divided after* sauce—tyme RD.
245 And] Ac W; *om* VHLKN. ete nouȝt] not ete R; nouth ȝet H³; not ȝet A. ete] Eet H; ȝit JM; *om* UD. nouȝt] not VHKW; nothyn L. I . . . þe] I þe hote W; *om* RD. I] Ich V. hote] bidde U; bid J. þe(1)] *om* JLAM. er] or ChJAK; ar NM; til DVH hunger þe] þe honger M. take] hente N.
246 sende] sent R. þe] þe sum V; *om* UWN. saus] sewis A. sauoure] sauourin M; sauerne J; sauer ChVHW. þi lippes] þe þe betere V. þi] wiþ þi UJMH³. lippes] lyppus R; lippis *same hand above cancelled* mawe J.
247 And] An W; *om* V. kep] keep V. sum] somwhat U; sumqwat J. til] RUDVHANH³; to ChJW; for TLKM. tyme] *om* M. &] *om* U. sit] fast H; Faste þou V. nouȝt] not RDVHJAKWM. to] *om* RUD.
248 Aris vp] And leue of N. Aris] Aryis H³; but rise D. vp] *om* U. er] or DChHAK; ar VLN. apetit] apetyt RUDChVHJLAKWNMH³; aptid T. haue] RUDChHJLKNM; habbe V; haþ TAW; hat H³. eten] etyn JAKMH³; eteyn U; Iȝeten V; *om* R. fille] Fulle VL; wille D.
249 *divided from following after* þyng M; *after* nouth H³. Let] Lat JLN; Late W; And let K. nouȝt] not RDChVHLAKW; *om* MH³. sire] sere A. surfet] surfer H³. sitten] syttyn JAM; sitte ChHWH³; sit RN. at . . . bord] *om* M. bord] bord ende H³.
250 *line om* A. Loue . . . nouȝt] *om* N. Loue] DChVHL; Loffe J; ne lof þou M; Leue TUKW; lef R; longe H³. hym nouȝt] not him R. hym] *om* W. nouȝt] not VHLKW; ryth nouth H³; no þyng M. for . . . &] þat lechour for he is W. for] *om* RH. a] *om* D. lecchour] lichere J. &] *om* D. likerous] lekerous M; lecorous Ch; liberous R; kekerous H³. of] of his R. tunge] mouþ W.
251 *line om* A. aftir] to M. many] mony VL. maner] maner RUDChJLKWNH³; maner of TM; *om* VH. his mawe] he K. is alongid] is alonget V; *om* H.
252 And] *om* AN. ȝif] ȝef ChL. diȝete] diete RUDN; dyote LW; dyith H³; dyht J; dight K; digthe M; vsest H; do A; ech day do Ch. þe] *om* ChA. ley] leye HLN; leyn RUMH³; lay K; legge V. myn] boþe myn V. armes] harmes N; eres UV; hede Ch; hed L; eie W; lyf H.
253 Here H² resumes briefly. Þat] *om* W. fisik] phisike K; fesyk DChA. shal . . . selle] *defective* H². shal . . . hood] his furhed hood schal U. shal] xal H³; *om* D. his(1) . . . foode] for his fode his forred hode W. hood] hodes L. foode] lyflode V. selle] sellyn JAM; sulle V; sille H; wil selle D.
254 ek] *om* AWH³. his] is A; þe U. cloke . . . gold] *defective* H². cloke] Clokes K; clokis UHH³. of] UVHJLANMH³; wiþ TRDChK; and his W. calabre] alabre R. &] *with* VJW. þe] his HAMH³; *om* VJWN. knoppis . . . gold] goold knappis M. knoppis] knappes V; knottes R; coppis HAH³.
255 *line om* UNH³. And] he schal A. be] ben M; byn K; beo VL. fayn] ful fayn HW. be my] in H. my . . . leten] *defective* H². feiþ] faiþ H; fay RChJLKWM. fesik] fysyk RVHJLKWM. leten] letyn RJ; lete VHW; leve KM; leuyn A.

And lerne to laboure wiþ lond lest liflode hym faile.
Þ*ere* arn mo liȝeris þan lechis, lord hem amende.
Þei do men diȝe þoruȝ here drynkes er destenye it wolde.'
'Be seint p*er*nel,' q*ua*þ peris, 'þise arn p*ro*fitable wordis.
Þis is a louely lessoun, lord it þe forȝelde. 260
Wende now whanne þi wille is, þ*a*t wel be þou eu*ere*.'
'I behote god,' q*ua*þ hung*er*, 'henis nile I wende
Er I haue dyned be þis day & ydronke boþe.'
'I haue no peny,' q*ua*þ piers, 'pulettis to biggen,
Noþ*er* gees ne gris, but two grene chesis, 265

256 *line om* A. lerne] lernyn J; leorne VL; leryn H³. to] him (*above line same ink*) R; *om* NMH³. laboure] labowryn JM; laboren ChL; labre V. wiþ . . . faile] *defective* H². wiþ] the K. lond] his hond W; hande J; hondes U. lest . . . hym] þat him no fode J. lest] lest his H; last h*is* R. hym] *om* VH.
257 *line om* N. arn] arne A; ar*e* R; ben U; be Ch; beþ W; beoþ V; ne beþ H. mo] more H³; no mo D; no*n* more H. liȝeris] liȝers ChV; lyeris AMH³; lyer*es* RUH²; lyers DJLW; liars K; losels H. þan . . . amende] *defective* H². þan] þen VH. lord] vr lord VHM; god RUChA. hem] heom L.
258 Þei] Thay K; And thei H². do] don RVHJLAH³; done K; doth M. men] me M. diȝe] dyȝen V; dye LWN; dyen K; deiȝe H²H; deye RUDM; deyyn J; dey A; deyn H³. þoruȝ . . . wolde] *defective* H². þoruȝ] *with* RUDAWNMH³. here] her RChJKNH³; heore L; heor V. drynkes] drynke RUVHAWNMH³. er . . . wolde] god hem amende A. er] or DChHKN. it] *om* RVHJMH³.
259 seint] sent AH³; saynt K. p*er*nel] poul RUChVJLKWN. peris] p*er*kyn UN. þise] þis HWM; þese UDH²JAH³; þes RChK; þeose L; þeos V. arn] ar*e* R; ar N; ben ChA; be W; beþ DH; beoþ V. p*ro*fitable wordis] *defective* H². p*ro*fitable] good W.
260 *line om* L. is . . . lessoun] lesson is me lef W. lord] oure lorde ChVHN; crist U. it þe] þe hit Ch. it] *om* HW. forȝelde] forþelde W; ȝelde DA; *defective* H².
261 now] þou L; *om* HA. whanne] whe*n* RHL; whon V; qwan J; wher ChW; qwer H³. þi . . . is] þou wilt D. is] RUCh H²VHJLAKWNMH³; *cancelled* T. þat . . . euere] *defective* H². þat] þere N; & M; for R; *om* VHAH³. wel . . . euere] eu*ere* be þow well W. be þou] þe be JN; þee be H; þe beo V. be] beo L. þou] þe UM. eu*ere*] for eu*ere* V.
262–84 defective H².
262 I] And I Ch; ȝe I N; *om* D. behote] beohote V; hote UChAKM. god] þe UChVHJLNH³. henis] heonnes V; þat hennes LN; ȝit W. nile] nyl UJAMH³; nyll K; nel DChH; nul VL; ne wil R; wil WN. I] RUDVHJLAKNMH³; I not TW (not *above line another script* T); I nauȝt Ch. wende] wendyn M; weende J.
263 Er] Or DChHAM; Ar N; Are K. dyned] dynyd JMH³; Idyned Ch; Idynet V. ydronke] ydrunke RM; Idronkyn J; ydrunken U; dronke H³; drunkyn A. boþe] boþin M; onys D.
264 I] & y H; I ne K. haue] naue H; na W. no] no*n* M. peny] penyes U. pulettis] pultys UJ. to] with to UJ. biggen] bigge UChHJAKWMH³ (*same hand after cancelled* bycche J); bugge RVL; begge D; bye N.
265 Noþ*er*] Nouther UVLK; Neyþ*er* RChJAWNMH³. gees] ges R; goos HAW; gos Ch; gose KN. ne] no DChL; no*n* H³; noþer N. gris] grices J. two] to A; too D; twey V; tweyne RW; a NMH³. grene] grete R. chesis] chese NMH³.

A fewe cruddis ⁊ crem, ⁊ [a]n [hauer] cake,
A lof of benis ⁊ bren ybake for my children;
And I sei3e, be my soule, I haue no salt bacou*n*,
Ne no cokenay, be crist, colopis to maken.
Ac I haue p*er*sile ⁊ poret, ⁊ many cole plantis, 270
And ek a cow ⁊ a calf, ⁊ a carte mare
To drawe on feld my dong while þe drou3t lastiþ.
Be þis liflode I mote lyue til lammasse tyme;
Be þat I hope to haue heruest in my croft,
Þanne may I di3te þi dyner as þe dere likeþ.' 275
Alle þe pore peple pesecoddis fetten;

266 *transposed with following* W. A] And a UChVHJA; ⁊ also N. fewe] *om* N. cruddis] kurdis Ch; curdes KN. crem] creem UJNM; creym H; crayme DV. ⁊] I can Ch. an hauer] LJM; an havere K; an hauir UAH^3; an auer R; two hauer*e* H; an hote W; an hot N; a þerf V; non oþ*er* TDCh. cake] cakis H; take Ch.
267 A lof] al of H. A] And a UVJH^3; But a D. of] *om* H. benis] banes N; bonys M. ⁊] and of ChH. bren] bran UHKWN; bryn A. ybake] Ibakyn M; bake DJWN; Imade A. children] childrin ChMH^3; childre (h *imperfect*) W; childeryn J; childern K; chideryn A.
268 And] And 3it UJWM; And 3et LKH^3; and 3ut R; 3it N; *om* ChA. I . . . soule] Be my soule I sey A. sei3e] sey RChJNH^3; say DLKWM; sigge V; seie þe UH. I haue] haue I A. haue] ne haue M; naue H; na W.
269 Ne] Ny L; *om* Ch. no] non AK. cokenay] cokeney RULKNM; cokney W; cokeneys HA; Cokeneyes V. be crist] *om* A. colopis] Colopus V; colhoppis H; coleps Ch. to] with to ULN. maken] makyn DAM; make RUChHJWN; frye L.
270 Ac] But ChVHLKWN; *om* AMH^3. I haue] *om* N. p*er*sile . . . poret] porettes ⁊ percyl V; porett*es* and p*er*sely H^3. p*er*sile] p*er*sil UD; percele K; p*er*sely RChN; p*er*sel AW; p*er*ceel J; p*er*soly HM. ⁊(1)] *om* U. poret] porettes N; porettis ChHM; portys J; plantes W. ⁊(2)] *om* R. many] moni VL. cole plantis] plante colis AMH^3. cole] cool R; caul H; colde Ch; cold W. plantis] plontis H; plontes V; pores W.
271 ek] *om* HAWNM. cow] cowhe A. mare] mere JWN; more D; and a mare Ch.
272 To] Tho A. drawe] drawyn JA. on . . . dong] dung afelde J. on] a RVHN; to H^3. feld] filde Ch. my] þe RHN; *om* U. while] qwyl H^3; whiles DLK; qwylys J. þe] my Ch; *om* D. drou3t] drouhþe V; drouthe RHAH^3; drye M. lastiþ] lastet M; lastes L; lestyþ RH^3; *lost in sewing* A.
273 *line om* UA. I mote] most I W. mote] most RHLM; must KH^3; mi3t Ch; *om* D. lyue] lyuen V; lyffyn J; leue DCh WM. til] to JN; vnto L.
274 *line om* UA. þat] þan JWH^3. I] Ich V. hope] howpe J. to] RDChJLKWNMH^3; for to TH; forte V. haue] haue*n* M. heruest] haruest K; la*m*masse R. in] at home in L; to Ch. croft] croft*es* D.
275 *line om* UA. Þanne] þa*n* RJWNH^3; þe*n*ne V; þen H; And þanne TDChK. may I] I may N; shal I W. di3te] dy3the R; dyth H^3; digthi*n* M; dyhetyn J. þi] þe a W; my H^3. as] atte fulle as L. þe] me MH^3. dere] deore VL; wel W. likeþ] liket M; lykyþ RJLH^3.
276 *transposed with following* A. Alle] Now al M; And W. peple] people LK; puple HAH^3; peple þan WN; puple þe R. pesecoddis] peosekoddes L. fetten] fetchen KM; feccheden N; þei fetten UHH^3; þei fette JL; þei fechedyn A.

Benes & [b]ake applis hy brouȝte in *here* lappe[s],
Chibollis, & chiriuell*is*, & ri[p]e chiries manye,
And *pro*fride peris [þis] *pre*sent to plese þ*ere*wiþ hungir.
Hungir [eet] þis in haste & askide aftir more. 280
Þanne þise folk for fer fetten hym manye
[Grene porret and pesen; to [peysen] him þei þouȝte].
Be þ*at* it neiȝide ner heruest [þat] newe corn com to chepyng.
Þanne was folk fayn, & fedde hung*er* w*ith* þe beste;

277 Benes] Bake Benes V; Bedes Ch. & . . . applis] in Bred V. &] *om* H[3]. bake] RChLKW; baken U; bakyn JM; bakon H[3]; bacoun H; bacou*n* & N; blake T; blak D; *om* A. applis] appillis A; appyls J; *om* H. hy] þei RUDChVJLAM H[3]; þai W; thay K; wiþ hem þei H; *om* N. brouȝte] broughten UHL; brougthen M; brouhten V; browhtyn J; broutyn AH[3]; *om* N. in . . . lappes] *om* H. here] her RCh JKNH[3]; heore L; heor V. lappes] RUV LKW; lappys JANMH[3]; lappe TDCh.
278 *misplaced after line* 281 H. Chibollis] Chebolle*s* W; Chespollys J. &] *om* VHN. chiriuell*is*] Chiryfellys D; chireuellis J; chiryuels L; cheruelys UKMH[3]; cheruelles ChWN; cheruel A; chesteyns H; Cheef mete V; skalonys R. ripe . . . manye] many rype cheries A. ripe] RUDChVHJLKW NMH[3]; riche T. chiries] chiris J; cheries RDChHWN; cherijs MH[3]; cherys U; cherise K. manye] monye V; also H. *Here* A *copies line* 282, *which is, however, repeated in the correct place.*
279 *line om* W. profride] profrid U; profred R; proferid A; p*ro*fered DLK; proferde V; proferd ChN; p*ro*ferydy*n* H[3]; p*ro*feredyn J; profedyn M; offride*n* H. þis] þ*is* RUDVHJLAKMH[3]; a TCh; to N. to] for to A. plese] plesyn JM; please K; p*re*sente D. þerewiþ] w*ith* DVHAMH[3]; myd N. hungir] *rubbed* H; *lost in sewing* A.
280 *line om* W. Hungir] UVHJLANH[3]; And hungir TRDChKM. eet] VHJL; ete RUDKN; hente TChAMH[3]. þis in] in þat L. þis] al þis UJN; hit H; *om* M. askide] askid HAKMH[3]; asked RDChV; axide U; axit J; axed LN.
281 *line om* W. Þanne] þenne V; & þanne M; & H. þise] þis RUDChVJLAH[3]; thes K; þe HN. for fer] sore aferde N; ferdy*n* forth & H[3]. fer] feer DJ; feare K; ferd HA. fetten] fettyn JKM; fecchid AH[3]; fecchede N. manye] monye V; mony Ch; suche monye L; more R; faste K.
282 URVHJLAKWNMH[3] (*text based upon* U); *line om* TDCh. Grene] Of grene L; Grete H[3]; *om* VH. porret] porets L; Poretes VKH[3]; poretis HNM; portes J; garly W. pesen . . . þouȝte] peris applis & plowmes H. pesen] pesyn RJA(*both*); peson K; peosen V; peoses L; poysy*n* H[3]; percely M; gresse W. to] for VWM; *om* JN. peysen . . . þei] þei him plese V. peysen] plesen L; ple W; poysen U; poysene H[3]; poysyn JM; poyson K; poysone R; apoysen N; apoysyn A(2); apoysened A(1). him] hem W. þei] þai W; thay K; þen M. þouȝte] þouȝthe R; thouth H[3]; þougthy*n* M; wolde LA (*both*) KWN; wolden V; wode J. *Here* V *adds a line: see above*, p. 50.
283 Be þat] by þa*n* RJ; by þe*n*ne U; Whan A; Til V. it] *om* LWN. neiȝide . . . heruest] heruest neghed W; to heruest hiȝede V. neiȝide] neyȝed DChH; neyhed RUJH[3]; nighhid K; nyghed L; neschid A; was comyn N; was M. ner] neor L; ney D; nye K; ny M; nyȝe Ch; *om* RHNH[3]. heruest] haruest A. þat] þ*at* UDVHJ LH[3]; and RAWNM; for K; *om* TCh. newe] *above cancelled* ne, *another script* W; neowe L; *om* A. com . . . chepyng] to cheping come K; riped H. com] cam DJAM; *om* N. chepyng] markett W; sellyn M; towne RU.
284 Þanne] ÞEnne V; þen H; And than K. was] were RChH; was þe JWN; war the K; was þ*at* V; wox M. fayn] feyn ChH. &] *om* N. fedde] fedden H; feddyn JMH[3]; gaf N. hunger] him JW; hem M. w*ith* . . . beste] ȝeorne V; fast H. w*ith*] of N.

Wiþ good ale & glotonye h[y] gart hym to slepe. 285
And þo nolde wasto*ur* not werche, but wandrite aboute,
Ne no begg*ere* ete bred þ*at* benis in come,
But coket, or clermatyn, or of clene whete,
Ne non halpeny ale in no wyse drynke,
But of þe beste & þe brunneste þ*at* breust*er*is sellen. 290
Laboureris þat haue no land [to] lyue on [but] here handis
Deyneþ nou3t to dyne a day ni3t olde wortis.
May no penyale hem paye, ne no pece of bacou*n*,

285 Here H^{2} **resumes.** Wiþ . . . gart] *defective* H^{2}. good] goud R. & . . . to] bad gloton go A. &] in N. hy] he TD; þei RUChLNM; þai W; thay K; þe*n* H^{3}; and VH; *om* J. gart] garte L; gartyn J; gert Ch; gere R; gratte K; grathe W; gret N; dyden U; made H; gat H^{3}; getyn M. to] swythe to L; on WH^{3}; o M. slepe] sclepe K.
286 And . . . but] *defective* H^{2}. And] *om* $RAWNMH^{3}$. þo] Than W. nolde] wolde $RChHAWNH^{3}$; would K; ne wolde no M; no wold J; wolde no U. wasto*ur* not] not wasto*ur* JW. wasto*ur*] þe wastor V; wastours U. not] nou3t Ch; nouth H^{3}; *om* UVLM. werche] worche ChVLW; wurche UD; w*ur*chen K; wyrche RN; wyrchi*n* J; slepe A. wandrite] wandride U; wandrid H; wandred DChKW; wand*er*yd JAH^{3}; wandren VL; wandr*e* $RH^{2}N$; wandry*n* M. aboute] abouty*n* M.
287 Ne . . . in] *defective* H^{2}. Ne] Ny L. begg*ere*] beggar JKN; beggerys M; lengere U. ete] eten V; etyn M; eetyn J. bred] no bred K; no breed U. benis] beny*n* R; benes or barlych L. in come] come inne R; comen ynne U; wer*e* in W. come] comen DM; comyn JN; coome V; kemyn H^{3}.
288 *line om* A. But . . . of] *defective* H^{2}. But] Hot H^{3}. coket] soket D. or(1)] and RVHJWNM. clermatyn] chermayn D. or(2)] oþir J; or els K; & HN; an V; mad L; *om* M. of] of þe M; *om* K. whete] qwete H^{3}; qwhete J.
289 *line om* H. Ne . . . in] *defective* H^{2}. Ne] Ny L. non] no ChLW. halpeny] halfpeny DVK; halfpany M. in] on R. no] none $RUChH^{2}VJLKNM$. drynke] drynken UDL; drinkyn JH^{3}.
290 *line om* H. But . . . brunneste] *defective* H^{2}. of] *om* J. þe . . . brunneste] alderbest N. &] and of ULK. þe(2)] *om* UWM. brunneste] brinest M. þ*at*] þ*at* þe H^{3}. breust*er*is] brewstars N; breowesters L; brewstere H^{3}. sellen] sellyn RJM; selle N; sell W; sullen V; sellyth H^{3}; seldyn A.
291 Laboureris . . . no] *defective* H^{2}. Laboureris] laboures M. haue] hauen L; han JMH^{3}; hadde UA. land] lond $RUChH^{2}VHLAKWNMH^{3}$. to] $RUDVJLKNH^{3}$; but $TChH^{2}HAWM$. lyue] liuen VL; lyuy*n* JK; leue DCh; leuy*n* MH^{3}; leuyd A. on . . . handis] by hem silue H. on but] $DVJLKNH^{3}$; by but RU; be ChAW; on $TH^{2}M$. here] her $RChJKNH^{3}$; heore VL. handis] hondes DLN; honden V; honde W.
292 Deyneþ . . . dyne] dynyd nout M; *defective* H^{2}. Deyneþ] Deyne V; deyne*n* HW; Deyned DUChLA; Deynedyn J; Dyneþ N; Loue H^{3}. nou3t] not RVW; now DK; *om* HLA. dyne] dynen UW; dynyn J; do dyne H^{3}. a day] o day R; on day Ch; on þe day A; on dayes L; on þe day but M; on þe day w*ith* no*n* H^{3}; wiþ U; *om* DJ. ni3t] ny3th RD; nygth A; nith M; w*ith* K; *om* H^{3}. olde] holde L; cold K.
293 May . . . penyale] *defective* H^{2}. May] Ther may R. no(1)] non M. hem] heom L. paye] payn A; payne J. ne] ny L; no Ch. no(2)] none $ChAMH^{3}$; *om* W. of] *om* M.

But ȝif it be fressh flessh oþ*er* fissh yfried,
And *chaud*, ⁊ *pluys chaud*, for chillyng of h[ere] mawe. 295
But he be heiȝliche hirid ellis wile he chide, |
Þat he was werkman ywrouȝt warie þe tyme, *fol.* xlij *b*
And þanne curse þe king ⁊ alle þe counseil aftir
Suche lawis to loke laboureris to chast[e].
Ac while hung*er* was here maist*er* wolde þ*er*e non chide, 300
Ne stryue aȝen þe statut, so sternely he lokide.
I warne ȝow werkmen, wynneþ while ȝe mowe,

294 ȝif . . . be] *om* W. ȝif] ȝef L; *om* RUCh H²VHAH³. be] beo L; weore V. fressh] freche J; freysch M; rostid U. flessh] fleche J. oþ*er*] or ChHLKWNMH³; or oþ*er* D; or elles UH²V; ⁊ A. fissh yfried] fryid fysch or rostyd H³. fissh] fyche J; fresch fysch HL. yfried] Ifriȝed Ch; IFriȝet V; þat is fried N; wel Ifryed K; Ifryd or Irostid M; fryed or rostid A; fried or rost W.
295 And] ⁊ þat M; And ȝit W; boþe RVH; Or H³; *om* JAN. *chaud*(1)] chaut DCh; chaufed R; chauyd A. ⁊] or WM. *pluys*] plus RUDVJLKWN; plu A; pur H³. *chaud*(2)] chaut DCh; chawd H; chaufed R. chillyng] chellyng D; Chele V. here] her*e* UDHAM; her RChKH³; heore VL; hire W; his TH²JN. mawe] mawes HKW; mawis AH³; chekys U; nailes L; nal*is* M.
296 *line om* A. But] RUVHJLM; And but ChKW; Ȝet but H³; But ȝif TDH²N. he(1)] þei HM; þay W. be] ben M; beo VL. heiȝliche hirid] at her*e* ese M. heiȝliche] heylyche RDH³; hyghliche LK; hieghlyche N; hiȝelich ChH; hylych JW; lylyche U. hirid] hired UDH²KW; hered R; hyryyd J; heryed N; Ihered Ch; Ihuret V; yhuyred HL. ellis] ȝit W; ȝet H³. wile] wel H³; wol UChVL; welyn M; wollen H. he(2)] þei HM; þai W; *om* (*late corrector inserts* we) H². chide] chyden LK; chidyn M; grucche R.
297 *line om* U. Þat] And þat H³. he] þei HW. was werkman] warkeman was N. was] were HW; *om* A. werkman] werkmon VL; workman DChK; werkmen HW; ewer*e* ma*n* R. ywrouȝt] wrouȝt RChLWN; wrout D; bycome HA. warie] waryen DK; waryyn J; waryȝe H³; wary N; waryn M; þei warie W; and weriȝe Ch; he weylid A.
298 *line om* U. And] *om* A. þanne . . . counseil] þe counseil cursyn ⁊ þe kyng M. þanne] *om* RVHAH³. curse] cursen K; c*ur*syn JH³; curseþ Ch; he curse H²; Thay cursyn A; þei corseþ W; Corse ȝerne V. alle] *om* JAH³. þe] his RVHW H³; that K. counseil] co*mu*n*e* N.
299 *line om* U. Suche] siche H; Swich M; Sweche AH³; þ*at* suche JW. lawis] lawe M. to] *om* JW. loke] loken LK; lokyn JAM; conne loke W. chaste] RDH²VN; chast HW; chasten L; chastyn JM; chastien K; chastise TChH³; chastesyn A.
300 *line om* U. Ac] But ChHLKWNM; And H³; *om* A. while] wil N; qwyl H³; whiles K; qwylis J. here maist*er*] Mayster heer VH. here] her RChWN; heore L; *om* H²AMH³. maist*er*] Mast*er* K. wolde . . . non] her non wolde R. wolde] þanne wolde M. þ*er*e non] þei not HWM. þ*er*e] here J; *om* AH³. chide] chyden K.
301 Ne] No L; And U. stryue] stryuyn J; steren Ch. aȝen] aȝeyn VJLN; aȝens UMH³; aȝeins W; ageyne AK. þe] his ChLKWH³; her J. statut] statutes UH; statutis JH³; statutȝ N; statues V; state Ch. so] and U. sternely] steorneliche VL. he] *om* U. lokide] lokid H²JAH³; lokede RVM; loked DChHLKWN; loken U.
302 ȝow] ȝou alle V; ȝow wel ȝe W. werkmen] workmen ChK; werkma*n* R. wynneþ] wynnythe J; wynnyt M; wyneth H²; wynnyn K; ernyth A; wercheþ H; worcheþ W; worche N. while] wil N; qwil JH³. mowe] mowen UKNM.

For hungir hiderward hastiþ hym faste.
He shal awake [þoruȝ] water wastours to chaste;
Or fyue ȝer be fulfild such famyn shal arise; 305
Þoruȝ flood [and] foule wederis fruytes shuln fa[i]lle,
And so seiþ satourne & sente ȝow to warne.

303 For] *om* V. hiderward] hitherward K; hederward Ch; hedyrward H[3]; is hidirward M; is hedirward D; is hedurward A; rit hidirword J; hieþ hym aȝen W. hastiþ] hastyt H[3]; & hastit M; & hastet D; he hastit A; and hast W; hyeth U; heyeth R; hithid J; aȝeyn hiȝeþ V. hym] *om* HAM. faste] ful fast H; wol faste M; for fast A; ȝeorne V.
304 He] and he U. shal] xal H[3]; wole VH. awake] wake W; wade H; awastyn J. þoruȝ] þorugh L; þorw V; þurȝ H; þourth M; th*our* R; thrugh K; ȝow þorow N; ȝow thorw H[3]; ȝour UJA; wiþ W; þis TH[2]; þes Ch; þese D. wat*er*] wat*ris* H; wateris A; weþer Ch; wele U. wasto*urs*] þees wast*ur*ys J; þe wastours alle V; his wasto*urs* U. to] *om* V. chaste] chasten UL; chasty*n* JM; chastien K; chastice ChH[3]; chasteysyn A; warne W; *om* V.
305 Or] Er RUH[2]VJNM; And er W. fyue] þe fyue W; fewe H; syn L. ȝer] wynt*er* R; *om* DLKWN. be] ben ChVJ MH[3]; beo L. fulfild] fulfilled DChKN; fulfyllid JAH[3]; fulfulled L; folfult V; fulfeled M; fuldfyld R; fulle W. such] siche H; swiche UM; sweche AH[3]; *om* Ch. famyn] famen Ch; famyng D; fomen L; foomen (*corrected to* famyn *another ink*) K. shal] schul Ch; wol H.
306 flood] flodes ChVLN; flodis H; tempestes U. and] RUVHJAWNMH[3]; & þorgh LK; or DCh; or thoru H[2]; oþ*er* þoruȝ T. wed*er*is] weder V; wedo*ur* K. fruytes] fruicthis M; froytes D; freutis A; frutes H[2]K; frutys J; froite Ch; fruth H[3]; cornes R; fodes W; flodis U. shuln] shul RUH[2]VHAW; schule L; schullin J; scholy*n* M; schal DChKN; xal H[3]. faille] fayle RVHJKNM; faylen AW; be dystroyid H[3]; falle TDChH[2]; fallen U; fal:: L.
307 so] þus LW. seiþ] seit M; saith KW; sey H[3]; seiȝ H[2]. sato*urne*] Saturnes V; satourn*us* M; sire Satorn W. sente] sende H; sendith U; sendyt M. ȝow] vs V. warne] werne N; sayn W.
In the right hand margin of T *in a Tudor hand:* here is lefte ovte v versis w*hi*ch is in the olde coppi & ar set benethe. *At foot of page same hand a version of* **B** VI 328–32: *see above*, p. 38.

VIII

Treuþe herde telle hereof, ⁊ to peris sente
To take his tem ⁊ [tilien þe erþe],
And purchac[ide] hym a p*ar*doun *a pena ⁊ a culpa*
For hym ⁊ for hise heires eu*er*emore aftir,
And bad hym holde hym at hom ⁊ erien his laiȝes. 5
And [alle] þat holpen to erien or to sowen,
Or any man*er* mest*er* þ*at* miȝte peris helpen,
Part in þ[at] p*ar*doun þe pope haþ hem g*ra*untid.
Kinges ⁊ kniȝtes þ*at* kepen holy chirche

1 herde] hard A. telle] tellyn JAM. here] þ*er* R. peris] trewthe H^3. sente] sende VH; to sente H^2.
2 To] For to UW. take] taken UDVLKWN; takyn RJAMH^3. his] to his H^2; him JA. tem] teem UChH^2N; teeme VJ; terme H^3. ⁊] to H^3; *om* H^2. tilien . . . erþe] tilyen þe erþe UK; tilie þe erþe HWNM; tilyen þe eorþe V; tilye þe eorthe L; telyen þe erde A; tely*n* þe erthe H^3; tr*u*ly tylyyn þe erthe J; his erþe tilien TH^2 (*late corrector inserts* to *before* tylien H^2); his erthe tylie R; his erþe telyen DCh.
3 And] He AN. purchacide] purchasid AH^3; purchasede V; purchased LKWN; p*ur*chasidyn J; purchace TRDH^2H; purchaise Ch; purchasen U; purchasyn to M. a] *om* U. *a*] of D. ⁊ *a*] ⁊ of D; *om* AM.
4 for(2)] *om* RUChK. heires] heyris AM; eyr*es* RUDH^2H; eyris JH^3; eiȝers Ch. eueremore] euermore RUChVHJAWH^3; for eueremore TDH^2LKNM. aftir] þeraftir U; þeraftur J.
5 *line om* A. And] He N. bad] baddyn K; *om* D. hym(1)] *om* DV. holde] holden UVL; holdyn JMH^3; hodde R; helden N. hym(2)] hem V; *om* H^2. erien] erie HN; eryyn J; eren W; heren V; eiren K. his] here H; heore V. laiȝes] layes RULW (*same hand after cancelled* lawes U); leyȝes ChV; leyes DHKM; leyys JN; leygthys H^3.
6 alle] UVHJLKWMH^3; alle þo N; þo TChH^2A; *om* RD. holpen] helpen Ch; helpyn D; holpen him U; holpy*n* hi*m* M; holp hym W; helpen hi*m* H^2; helpyn hym KH^3 (hy*m* *in margin same ink* H^3); hym holpyn A; him hulpyn J; hym helpen H; eu*er*e hulpen him V; holpen hendely L; ȝe shul helpe R. erien] erie RUA; eren H; eryn JM; eere W; earen K; heryen L; heren V. or] er J; or ellys D; and RHLAN. to(2)] *om* WN. sowen] sowyn H^3; sowyne J; sowe RUHA; sowȝen Ch; sowe or sette W.
7 Or] ⁊ H; Of L. any] eny DV; ony RUJAWM; alle H. maner] RDVHJLAKWNMH^3; man*er* of TChH^2; many U. mester] myst*er* RUDChH^2JAKW; mystyr H^3; mystyer N; myst*er* me*n* H. miȝte peris] piers myghte UN. helpen] helpyn D; helpe RHJAWH^3; availe L.
8 Part] Pert A; *om* Ch. in] of HWH^3. þat] RUDVHJLAKWNM; þ*ou* H^3; þe TChH^2. þe pope] Piers W; þe peple D. haþ] hatȝ H^2; hat MH^3. hem] hym Ch; *om* RVHLAH^3. g*ra*untid] ygraunted RVHLAH^3.
9 kniȝtes] knythis MH^3; knytis A; knyghtes boþe W. kepen] kepyn JANMH^3; kepe ChW; kepeþ R; helpen U. chirche] cherche RWNM; churche DVH; chirke chirche A.

And r[iȝt]fulliche in reaum rewliþ þe peple 10
Han p*ar*doun þoruȝ p*ur*catorie to passe wel sone,
Wiþ patriarkes in p*ar*adis to pleiȝe þ*er*eaftir.
Bisshopis þ*at* blissen, & boþe lawes kenne,
Loke on þ*at* o lawe, & lere men þ*at* oþ*er*,
And bere hem boþe on here bak as here ban*er* shewiþ, 15
And p*re*chen here p*er*sonis þe p*er*iles of synne,
How þat shabbide shep shu[l] h*ere* wolle saue,
Han p*ar*doun wiþ þe apostlis whanne þei passe hennis,
At þe day of dom at here deis to sitten.

10 *line om* A. riȝtfulliche] rightfulliche URDChVHJLKWNH[3]; rewfulliche TH[2] M. in . . . rewliþ] Rulen þe Reame V; reulen þe rewmes H. in] in þe J; in here U; in this H[2]; þe R. reaum] reame D; realme K; rewme RUJLH[3]; reme ChH[2]; rewwmes N; Revmes M. rewliþ] rewlen UL; rewlyn JMH[3]; rulen K. þe] and þe RVH; her*e* U. peple] pepille Ch; people LKM; puple HH[3].
11 Han] hauen H; haue RDK; By W. þoruȝ] thoru H[2]; þorow ChJAN; þurȝ H; þourth M; þorw RUVH[3]; thrugh K; þrowgh W; þoruȝt D; in L. p*ur*catorie] p*ur*gatorie RUDH[2]VHJLAKWNMH[3]. to] shold W. passe] passen VLK; passyn JA. wel] wol M; ful RVHANH[3].
12 *marked with cross* A. patriarkes] patryk M. p*ar*adis] purgatori in paradidice A. pleiȝe] pleiȝen H[2]; pleye R; pleyen DVM; pleyyn J; pleyn AH[3]; pleyne L; playen KN; play ChW; pleyen hem U.
13 Bisshopis] Buschopis AH[3]; Busschops V. blissen] blissyn JAMH[3]; blessen RUD H[2]VHLKN; blessin Ch. &] && M. boþe] boþy*n* M; boþe þe ChVH. kenne] kennen UCh; kene D; ku*n*ne R; cunnen V; konne LKNH[3]; conneþ W; conyn A; konnien M; knowen H.
14 Loke] Loken UHLAN; Lokyn DJM H[3]; Lokeþ VW. on] *om* D. þ*at*(1)] þe UAMH[3]. o] on DVHJ; one K; to UM; *om* LA. &] *om* Ch. lere] leren DH; lereþ V; lerne UAKMH[3]; lernyn J. men] *om* D. þat oþer] bettir A. þ*at*(2)] þe UWH[3]; *om* J. oþ*er*] toþer W; tothir U.
15 *line om* A; *as two lines divided after* bak Ch. bere] bere*n* UH; bereþ VKW; beoreth L; bernyn J. hem] heom L; *om* RJMH[3]. boþe] bothin JM; bonere W; *om* L. on] *om* W. here(*both*)] her RChJ KH[3]; heore VL. here(1)] her N. bak] *om* W. as . . . shewiþ] in bering & in dede N. as] And ChH[2]. ban*er*] dedis H. shewiþ] sheweth RChH[2]VKW; schewit M; shewyn H; swewyt H[3].
16 p*re*chen] p*re*chyn JAM (*altered from* prechen M); preche ChH[3]; precheþ V. here] her ChJNH[3]; hir*e* R; heore VL; to here W; to her K; þys M. p*er*sonis] p*ar*yschens UW; p*ar*yschou*n*s H[3]; people K. þe] þeo L. p*er*iles] peril RChVJWMH[3]; perel UHA. synne] sunne V; svnnne M.
17 How] And how L. þat] þat þe RK; þat a N; þat here H; þe LW; heore V; fro M. shabbide] schabbyd JA; shabbede RVM; schabbed ChH; scabbide U; scabbyd H[3]; Scabbed DLKWN; scallide H[2]. shep] *om* L. shul] RUCh; xul H[3]; shol W; schollin J; schal VLN; þey may M; shulde TH[2]H; schuld DAK. h*ere*] her ChKH[3]; heore VL; his N; þe W. wolle] wulle UD; wlle*n* M. saue] sauen L; kepyn M.
18 Han] haue RDHJK; þei han N; And haue Ch; And W; Þat H[3]. p*ar*doun wiþ] be piers wiþ W. þe] *om* H[2]LAWN. apostlis] postelis A. whanne] whon V; whe*n* RHLA; qwan JH[3]. þei] þai W; thay K; þe U; he A. passe] passe*n* RUD VLK; passyn J; p*ar*tyn AMH[3]; wende HW. hennis] hens KWH[3]; henne H[2].
19 At þe] RHLAH[3]; Atte J; On þe U; And at þe TDChH[2]KWNM; And atte V. day of] eie daye of M; dredful W. at here] w*ith* hem on V. at] on HWNMH[3]. here] her ChN; heore L; hys H[3]; hiȝe H; hey M; the hye K; þe A; *om* W. deis] des AW; desse K; dees H[3]; dayes JL. to] for to A; schal M; *om* VJWN. sitten] sittyn M; sitte UJANH[3]; setten DV.

Marchauntis in þe margyn hadde manye ȝeris, 20
But non *a pena* & *a culpa* þe pope wolde h[e]m g*ra*unte,
For þei h[o]lde nouȝt here haly dayes as holy chirche techiþ,
And for þei swere be here soule, & so god muste hem helpe,
Aȝens clene consience here catel to selle.
Ac vndir his secre sel treuþe sente h[e]m a l*ett*re, 25
And bad h[e]m begge boldely what [hem best] likeþ,
And siþen selle it aȝen & saue þe wynnyng,
And make mesonis deux þ*er*ewiþ myseis[e] to helpe,

20 Marchauntis] Marchaundys JA; Marchantȝ UNM; Marchauns L; Marchans V; marchau*n*t R. in . . . margyn] & her meyne H^{3}. þe] þ*at* RJ; þis V; here A; *om* Ch. margyn] margeyne J; m*er*gent K; marchaundice A. hadde] hadde*n* RHK; had ChJWN; haden L; hedden V; han AH^{3}; þey han M. manye ȝeris] ȝeris many H. manye] mony VL. ȝeris] ȝerdis A.
21 non] neyer M; *om* AWH^{3}. *a*] of D; *om* A. & *a*] *cancelled* T; & UN; & of D; ne *a* M; *om* A. wolde] nolde RVHLWN; wyl H^{3}. hem] DChVHJKWNM; heom L; he*m* no*n* H^{3}; hym TH^{2}; non A; *om* RU. graunte] g*ra*nten U.
22 þei] þai A; thay K. holde] RUHN; hold DAW; holden K; holdyn MH^{3}; holdeþ VL; helde TH^{2}; helden Ch; heldyn J. nouȝt] no*u*t H^{3}; not RVHJA KW; nat H^{2}; no*n* M. here] h*er* RChJKH^{3}; heore VL; þe U; *om* M. haly] holy RDH KN; *om* W. dayes] day UVAM. chirche] churche RVH; cherche UDWM; writt K. techiþ] techit AMH^{3}; techitt K; techitȝ H^{2}; techeþ DChVLW; techys R.
23 for] *om* AW. þei] he A. swere] sweren K; swereth L; sweryn JMH^{3}; swor A; sworen V. here] her ChKNH^{3}; heore V; his L. soule] soulis HM; sowles K. &] *om* UVHJ. god . . . hem] mote he*m* god H^{3}; he*m* god M. muste hem] hem moste V. muste] mote Ch; mot R; shulde H; *om* DW. hem] heo*m* L. helpe] helpy*n* J.
24 Aȝens clene] Clene aȝens W. Aȝens] Ayenst K; Aȝen DHM; Aȝeyne JL; Ageyne A; Agayn N; Aȝeyn heore V. here] her ChKNH^{3}; heore VL; *om* A. catel] ware UJ; chaffar*e* M. selle] sellen U; sellyn JM; sulle V.
25 Ac] But UChVHLKWNM; And RH^{2} AH^{3}. secre] secret RChJLKNH^{3}; sekir H^{2}A. sel] seel UChHJL; seal DVKWM; sell H^{3}. treuþe] trouthe L; truþe RJ; trwþe N; *om* H^{3}. sente] sende VH. hem] DK WNMH^{3}; heom L; hym TRChH^{2}A; *om* UVHJ. l*ett*re] bille M.
26 bad] byt D. hem] UDVHJKWNH^{3}; heom L; hym TRChH^{2}AM. begge] bigge UDH^{2}HAKWNM; byggyn J; Bugge VL; bye Ch; byen H^{3}. boldely] baldely RH^{3}. what] wat N; qwat JH^{3}. hem best] UVHJKNH^{3}; heom best L; þing hem best W; hi*m* best RAM; þ*at* hem D; þ*at* hym TChH^{2}. likeþ] likith UH^{2}LH^{3}; lykede RV; liked ChHKWN; lykyd JA; ligede M.
27 *line om* U. siþen] sithe H^{2}W; syth A; sytthyn H^{3}; siþþe H; sethen D; sethin J; seþþen V; seþþe Ch; swythe R; oft M. selle . . . aȝen] saue it to selle A. selle] sellen L; sellyn JH^{3}; sille H; sullen V; sellyt M. it] *om* DH^{2}M. aȝen] aȝeyn VJL; ageyn K; agayn N. saue] sau*en* M; sauy*n* J. wynnyng] wynnyng*es* M.
28 make] maken L; makyn JMH^{3}; makeþ W; *om* U. mesonis . . . þ*er*ewiþ] þ*er*with mesondeux Ch. mesonis deux] maisou*n*s dieus M; mesou*n* dieux HLKWN; mesendews H^{3}; meysou*n* deu RVJ; mescon dyeu A; þe mesou*n* dieu U; mensou*n* de dieu D. þ*er*ewiþ] þ*er*myd N; þ*er*mide W; þ*er*mede D; þat mede A. myseise] mysese RD; Meseyse V; þe myseyse UN; þe meseyse J; myseises TH^{2}; meseise men L; mischefs M; meseles ChHW; myssell*es* K; myssede men A; meysy*n* H^{3}. to] so to M. helpe] helpen UK; helpyn DJH^{3}.

Wykkide weyes wiȝtly to amende,
And bynde brugges aboute þ*at* tobroke were, 30
Marie maidenis also [or] maken hem nonnes, |
[Pore] wydewis þ*at* wiln not be wyues aftir, *fol.* xliij *a*
Fynde suche here foode for oure lordis loue of heuene,
Sette scoleris to scole or [to] su*m*me skynes craftis,
Releue religioun & renten hem bet*ere*; 35
'[And] I shal sende myself seynt Michel myn aungel

29 Wykkide . . . wiȝtly] Wightliche wikkide weyes U. Wykkide] wikkid AH^3; Wyckede R; wykked DLW; & wikkyd J; And wickede H^{2}VM; And wikked ChK; Also wikke N; & also wicked H. weyes] weiȝes Ch; ways W; wones V. wiȝtly] wytly RH^3; wytlyche D; wytely A; wyttylyche J; also witterly W; þ*er* *with* M; wide wher nedful weore L. to] RDVHLKWMH^3; for to TUChH^2 (for *above line another script* T); *om* JAN. amende] amenden D; amendyn JM; mende W; don amende U.
30 *line om* UA. And] *om* V. bynde . . . tobroke] broken brigges also þat aboute W. bynde] byende D; *late corrector alters to* byllde H^2; bigge H; bete NH^3; Beete V; boten K; amendyn M; makyn J; þinke on R; Feble L. brugges] bruges H^2; brygg*es* RDChHH^3; briggys J; bridgis K; breggis M; burgis N. aboute] abouten D; abowtyn JM. tobroke] tobroken HKN; broken M; þo broken D. were] weore L; wern M.
31 Marie . . . also] Maydens for to marien W; Maydenes mayntene & marye L. Marie] Mary DA; maryen RUChKMH^3; Maryyn J; & marien H; help mary N. maidenis] madens K. also] þ*er*with M; *om* UVHJANH^3. or] RUDVJLKM; or ellis H; elles N; & TChH^{2}AWH^3. maken] make RDChH^{2}HAWNM; makyn UJH^3. hem] heom L. nonnes] wyues U; wyfes W.
32–80 *om* (**a leaf wanting**) A.
32 *divided from following after* wyues J. Pore] RDVJKN; & pore HL; þat pore U; And H^3; As M; And warde W; *om* TChH^2. wydewis] wydewes UDVL; wydowes N; wydowys JK; wydous W; widues R; wedowȝes Ch; wedewys H^3. þat] *om* U. wiln . . . wyues] wyues willen none be*n* M; wyuys wyl be H^3. wiln] wil DH^{2}JW; willen K; wilnen L; wol UCh; wole N; wolde VH. not . . . wyues] no wyues to beon L. not be] nat be H^2; nouȝt be Ch; not to be K; ben no J; be no WN; beo none V; be R; be no more H; ben and none U; nede be D. aftir] UDV HLKWNM; Aftur J; no*n* ofter RH^3; helpe hem þ*ere* aftir TChH^2.
33 Fynde] Fynde*n* RN; Help to fynde W. suche] siche H; swiche UM; sweche H^3; hem WN; heom L. here] her ChKNH^3; heore VL; *om* W. oure] þe LKNH^3; *om* VJWM. lordis] lou*er*dys J; Godes V. loue] loues H^2. heuene] heouen L; heue J.
34 Sette] Setteþ Ch; & sette U; & sett H. scoleris] scolars JKN; Clerkes D. scole] sclole L. or] oþer ChH^2. to(2)] UDVHJ LKWMH^3; *om* TRChH^{2}N. su*m*me] *om* W. skynes] skynnes H^2; skynnys H^3; skennes D; kyns J; kynnes ChLN; kennys R; kyne K; ky*n*ne U; kynde W; man*er* M; oþer VH. craftis] crafte UVHM.
35 Releue] releyue R; Releven K; Releuy*n* H^3; & releue H; Reule WM; Rule V; Reule wel U. religioun] Religiouns Ch; pore religiou*n* L; religions (? religious) U; religious W; religio*us* R; religiouse H. &] *om* N. renten] rentyn H^3; rente H^{2}V HNM; rent JW; renteth L; rede U. hem] heom L. bet*ere*] bettur J; þe beste U.
36 And] RUVHJLKWNMH^3; *om* TDCh H^2. sende] sende hem ChH^2; sende ȝow HKWMH^3; sende ow V; sendyn ȝow J; ȝow N. myself] my seolf L; ȝow selue U. seynt] sent H^3; saynt K; *om* RJ. Michel] michael RJ; Mihel VH^3; myȝhel H; mighel K; Mechel N. aungel] archaungel M.

Þat no deuil shal ȝow dere, diȝe whan ȝe diȝe,
Þat I ne shal sende [ȝour] soule sauf into heuene,
And before þe face of my fadir fo*ur*me ȝoure setis.
Vsure, & auarice, & oþes I defende, 40
Þat no gile go wiþ ȝow but þe graiþ treuþe.'
Þanne were marchauntis m*er*ye; many wepe for ioye,
And ȝaf wille for his writyng wollene cloþis;
For he co[pie]de þus h*er*e clause þei [couden] hym gret mede.
Men of lawe hadde lest for le[ttr]id þei ben alle; 45
For so seiþ þe sauter & sapience boþe:

37 no] non M. deuil] deouel L. shal] xal don H^3. dere] deren U. diȝe . . . diȝe] whon ȝe dye schulle V; whan þat ȝe ben dede N; when ȝe beþ dede H; when ȝe to deth go L. diȝe(1)] dye DKW; deyȝe H^3; deye RUM; dey J. whan] wan M; whe*n* R; qwan JH^3. ȝe] ȝow JK. diȝe(2)] dye D; deiȝe ChH^3; deye RUJM; shull W; done K.
38 *line om* MH^3. Þat] for H; *om* N. I] he U. ne] no L; *om* DHN. sende] senden L; sendyn J. ȝour] UChHJWN; ȝor V; his TRDH^{2}LK. soule] saule D; soules UChV; soulis HJN. sauf] saue Ch; saf RUDH^2; safe K; saaf V; saafe J; sauely H. into] to H. heuene] heouen L; blysse W.
39 And] *om* ChHJWN. before] biforen V; beforin H^3; Afore N. þe . . . fadir] my fadir face U. fo*ur*me] furme N; fourmen VM; for me R; þat formyd J; frely H. ȝoure] or V; ȝou RDHW; his L. setis] seetys M; seetes VK; settys UD; sete L; sette RH; to sitte W.
40 Vsure] Vsurye DW; Vserie H; Vsirye K. &(1)] *om* R. oþes] oþere H^3. I] y ȝou H. defende] defende ȝowe W.
41 Þat] Late W. ȝow] ou V. þe] *om* H^3. graiþ] greiþ ChL; grathe W; grete RUH; grace of V; heye MH^3; hard J. treuþe] trouthe LW; truþe RJ; trwþe N; weye M.
42 Þanne] Þenne V; þe*n* H; And þan ChM. were] weren UKH^3; weryn JM; weore L; wer*e* many (many *cancelled*) H^2. marchauntis] marchauns LM; Marchau*n*des VH^3; marchaundys JN; m*er*chaunt*es* KH; marchaundise Ch. m*er*ye] myry D; Murie V; so mery W; wel murye L. many] & many DCh; svme M; and some R; þei VJ; þai W; and UHLK. wepe] wep Ch; wepyn UK; weopen L; wopen V; wepte H^2; wept DW; wepte*n* H; weptyn JMH^3. ioye] Ioyȝe H^{2}HH^3.
43 And] Thei N. ȝaf] ȝauen L; gaf N; ȝeue D; ȝeuyn UKM; ȝeeuen V; ȝouyn JH^3. wille] william H. writyng] wrythyng H^3. wollene] wollen ChJLWN; wolleyn K; wullen D; willene M; wel newe H.
44 For] RUDChVHJLKNMH^3; And for TH^{2}W. he] to H; þat W. copiede] Copiede V; copied UChJ; copyid H^3; copide M; copede R; coped DLKN; coupide T; coupid H^2; copie H; copy W. þus h*er*e] of þat W. h*er*e] her ChJKNH^3; hir*e* RH^2; heore VL; þis H. clause] Cause VH^3; a b c M. þei] hy R; *om* UMH^3. couden] coude*n* V; cowde U; could K; couþe HN; cowthin J; konne R; konned L; konnyt M; comandy*n* H^3; ȝeue TDW; ȝeuen H^2; ȝaf Ch. hym] hem W. mede] þonk V; þank H.
45 Men] and men U. hadde lest] wer*e* laft oute H. hadde] hadden H^2; haddyn JMH^3; hedden V; þei haddyn U. lest] lene (? leue) R; leue (? lene) N. lettrid . . . alle] þe ben alle l*ett*red N. lettrid . . . ben] heo beoþ lettred V; þai beþ lerned W; þey beþ loþ H. lettrid] UM; lett*er*yd JH^3; lettred LK; lered RD; lewid TH^2; lewd Ch. ben] be Ch; bien H^2; beon L. alle] *om* H. *Here* H *adds a line: see above*, p. 46.
46 N *corrupts to* To loke vpon he sawter sapience to teche. For] and RULKWH^3; An M; *om* VHJ. so] also W; Soo as J; as H. seiþ . . . sauter] þe saut*er* seiþ H. seiþ] seyt RMH^3; seiȝt ChH^2; saith KW. þe . . . sapience] sapience and þe sautr*e* W. sauter] psalter K. &] & þe H. boþe] boþyn M.

Super innocentem munera non accipies; a regibus & principibus—
Of p*r*inces & p*re*latis here penc*io*u*n* shulde arise,
And of no pore peple no peny[worþ] to take.
Ac he þ*a*t spendiþ his speche & spekiþ for þe pore
Þ*a*t is Innocent & nedy, & no man apeiriþ, 50
Counfortiþ hym in þat cas, coueitiþ nouȝt his goodis,
Ac for oure lordis loue lawe for hym shewiþ,
Shal no deuil at his deþ day derie hym a myte
Þat he ne worþ sauf sykirly, & so seiþ þe sautir.
Ac to bigge watir ne wynd, ne wyt is þe þridde, 55

46α *Super . . . accipies*] *om* H. *Super . . . munera*] *Munera super innocentem* H^{3}. *innocentem*] *Innocentes* V. *accipies*] *accipiens* ChL; *Accipiunt* V; *accepit* H^{3}; *acceperunt* M. *a*] *sed a* H^{3}. *regibus*] *regibus prelatis* H^{3}. *& principibus*] *&c* V. *&*] *et a* Ch. *principibus*] *principibus &c* D; *principibus erit* RU; *principibus erit merces eorum* JKWNMH^{3}; *erit merces eius &c* L; *principibus erunt merces super innocentem &c* H.
47 p*r*inces] p*re*latis H; parisches V. &] and of RUDJNM. p*re*latis] p*re*latus V; p*re*las M; princes H. here] her ChJNH^{3}; heore L; heor V. penc*io*u*n*] pensiones H^{2}H^{3}; peticiou*n*s M; mede W. shulde] shal RUDJLKM; xal H^{3}; most W. arise] arisyn M.
48 no(1)] þe VHLWN. peple] people LK; puple HH^{3}. no(2) . . . to] þai shold not W. no(2)] no*n* M; a H^{3}. penyworþ] HUDJLKNMH^{3}; peneworþ RV; peny TCh; money H^{2}. to] *om* M. take] taken W; takyn M.
49 Ac] Bot ChHLKWNM; And H^{3}; For U. he] ȝe W; *om* R. spendiþ] spendit H^{2}M; spendeþ ChVL; spende W. his] ȝoure W. &] to R. spekiþ] spekyt M; speked D; speykyth J; speke RW. pore] pore peple U.
50 Þ*a*t is] Also for an H. is Innocent] innoce*n*t is R; ben Innocentys J; Innocent ben M; i*n*nocentis ben U; is not nocent W. &(1)] but W; *om* H. nedy] neodi V; nedeþ W; *om* H. &(2)] þat UHJ. no] non JM. man] mon VL; men J. apeiriþ] apeirit M; apeyreth DChH^{2}HK; apeyre R; apaireþ W; apayryn J; he appaireth N; haþ apeyret V; hem apeire U; empeyreth L.
51 *line om* R. Counfortiþ] Counfortit M; Conforte U; Comforteth DChH^{2}VLK; Comforte W. hym] hem UH. þat] his VM; *om* H^{3}. coueitiþ] coueiteþ ChH^{2}V HLN; coueytet D; & coueitit M; and coueyte U; coueyth H^{3}; take W. nouȝt] not VHLKWM. his] here UHW.
52 *line om* R. Ac] But UChVHLKWNM; And H^{3}. oure . . . loue] loue of ou*r*e lord M. loue] loue of heue*n* H. hym] hem UHJW. shewiþ] schewyt MH^{3}; shewe W; cheweþ N.
53 Shal] Xal H^{3}. no] no*n* M. deuil] deouel L. his] the K; ȝoure W. deþ] ded H^{3}. day] *om* ChN. derie] dere HK WN; deren UV; deryn JMH^{3}; to dere L. hym] ȝow W. a] worþ a VH; haue L. myte] mythe H^{3}; mygthe M; myȝte D; myghte L.
54 he] ȝe W. ne] no L; *om* JK. worþ] wortȝ H^{2}; shul W. sauf sykirly] sikerly sauf UL; sykyrlyche saafe J; securly saff H^{3}; syker sauf N; siker saf H; siker saaf V; sikerly be sauf W; sone sauid M. sauf] saf RDChH^{2}; safe K. sykirly] sicuu*r*ly H^{2}; sekerly DCh. & so] & so þe LKH^{3}; as þe M; or the W; & N. seiþ . . . sautir] psalter saith K; saute*r* wittenesseth L; saute*r* witnessit M; sautyr schew*ith* H^{3}; sautre lieþ W; sent forþ to ioye N. seiþ] seiȝth Ch; seiȝ H^{2}. *Here* MH^{3} *add the Latin after* **B** VII 51; HW *another Latin line: see above*, pp. 31, 46, 50.
55 Ac] Bot ChHLKWM; No*n* H^{3}; *om* N. to] do R; *om* W. bigge] bugge RVL M; begge DH^{3}; selle W; sell K. ne(1)] no ChL; or H; & J; *om* UH^{3}. wynd] wynt V. ne(2)] no L; no*n* H^{3}; or UH; and RN; *om* V. is] *om* K. þe þridde] ydel y rede U. þridde] þirde DK; þredde HW; threde H^{3}; ridde N.

Ne wolde neue*re* holy writ, god wot þe soþe.
Þise þre for þrallis ben þrowe among vs alle
To waxen & wanyen where þ*at* god likiþ.
His p*ar*doun in p*ur*catorie wel [petit] is, I trowe,
Þ*at* any mede of mene men for motyng resceyueþ. 60
3e legistris & lawi[er]is, [3e] wyten 3if I lei3e;
Siþen 3e sen it is þus sewiþ to þe beste.
Alle libbyng labo*ur*eris þ*at* lyuen be h*ere* hondis,
Þat trewely taken, & trewely wynnen,
And lyuen in loue & [in] lawe, for h*ere* lou3 herte 65

56 Ne wolde] Nolde V. Ne] No L; *om* RWN. wolde] wyld J. writ] cherche U. god] crist N.
57 Þise . . . ben] For þe tresouris be*n* oure aldiris M; For þe tresour be*n* thralle*s* þat is H³. Þise] þies J; These RUDH²H; þes ChK; þeose L; þeos V; For þese W. þre] þreo VL. for . . . ben] beþ for þrall*is* W. for] fro L. þrallis] thrall J; thalles L. ben] be DJ; bien H²; beon L; beo V; beþ RH. þrowe] throwen ULKN; throwyn J; Iþrowen M; trowen H²; þriuen V; sowe*n* H³; p*ro*ued R; y3eue*n* H. among] amongs Ch; amonge*s* K; *om* H.
58 To] Boþe to W. waxen] waxin JM; waxe HW. &] and to WM; or to VHN. wanyen] wanyyn J; wanye H; wanen N; wany*n* U; wane W; wonien V; wayten L. where] were J; qwer H³; wheþer VH N; wheyþ*er* W; þe while R. þat] *om* RVN. likiþ] liket M; lykes W; will K.
59 *transposed with following* W. His] The W. in] & hys H³. p*ur*catorie] purgatorye RUDH²VHJLKWNMH³. wel . . . is] is petit V; is peti M; is ful petyful H³; petit W. wel] wol U; ful ChHN. petit] RLKN; litel TDChH²H; litil UJ. trowe] chowe H³.
60 *line om* H³. Þ*at* any] But whoso W. any] eny DVHN; ony RUJM; ay Ch. mede] monee N. of] for L. mene] meane K; mone U. motyng] motynge*s* M. resceyueþ] resceyue U; reseyue*n* R; reseruit M.
61 *line om* H³. 3e] The D; Of M. legistris] legistre*rs* UDCh; Registres M. &] of WM. lawieris] H²; lawyere*s* RUVHLW; laweyere*s* K; lawe3eris J; law3eres Ch; lawers NM; lawist*er*is T; lawsters D. 3e(2) . . . lei3e] lye I out trowe 3e M. 3e(2)] RUDV HJLKWN; *om* TChH². wyten] wyte RH; wytyn JN; wete D; wetiþ W; woten K. 3if] 3ef ChL; wher V; where H. I] y (*same hand after cancelled* 3e) U. lei3e] li3e ChH²VH; lye RUDJLKWN.
62 Siþen] Sythyn JM; Siþ W; Sytthy*n* H³; Siþþe H; Sethe D; Seþþe ChV; syn R. sen] se RH²H; sene JN; seen UK; seyn M; seon VL; say W. it] þat hit VH; þis W. þus] this K; so VH; soþ W. sewiþ] sewit M; sueth U; sweþ N; sheweþ RL; schewyth JH³; serueþ VH. to] *om* RKW.
63 Alle] All oþer W; *om* V. libbyng] Libbinde V; lyuynge RUHKN; lyffyng J; leuyng Ch; leuyg H³; lyues W. lyuen] lyuyn J; libben VL; libbet M; leuen Ch; leuy*n* H³; leue D. here] her JNH³; heore VL; 3oure W; yo*ur* K; oure (o *rubbed*) Ch. hondis] handdys JH³; hande*s* RChK; landys M.
64 taken] takyn U; token N; tokyn JH³; tydyth M. & trewely] with trouthe L; of þat þat þey M; for 3oure trauaill & in tyme W. wynnen] wynne K; wynnyt M; wonnyn JH³; wonne N; worche W; tiþen V.
65 And] An M; þat N. lyuen] lyuyn JK; lyue RLWN; leuen DCh; leuy*n* H³; ledyn M; y *corrected from* o *same ink* T. in(1)] both in K; *om* L. loue] luffe J; londe M. in(2)] i*n* RUDVHLKNMH³; *om* TChH²JW. lawe] law3e Ch. for . . . herte] *om* K. for h*ere*] and wiþ W. h*ere*] her ChJNH³; heore VL. lou3] low3e Ch; lowe RUDH²VHJLWNMH³. herte] hertes VWNH³; hertis HM; heortes L.

Hadde þe same absolucioun þat sent was to peris.
Beggeris ⁊ bidderis ben not in þe bulle
But ȝif þe suggestioun be soþ þat [shapiþ hem to] begge.
For he þat beggiþ or bit, but he haue nede,
He is fals wiþ þe fend ⁊ [defraudiþ] þe nedy, | 70
And [ek] giliþ þe gyuere ageyns his wille. *fol.* xliij *b*
Þei lyue nouȝt in loue, ne no lawe holden.
Þei wedde no womman þat hy wiþ delen
But as wilde bestis wiþ wehe, ⁊ worþ vp togideris
And bringen forþ barnes þat bois ben holden. 75

66 Hadde] hadden UH^{2}KN; Haddyn J; Hedde V; Han H^{3}; shul haue HW; Schal hauen M. same] *om* H. absolucioun] assaillyng W; pardon M. sent was] was sent U. peris] pers plowman U.
67 Beggeris ⁊ bidderis] Bidders and Beggers VH; Bidders ne beggars N. Beggeris] Beggars K. ⁊] ne U; no LM. bidderis] byddars K; borwers W. ben] be DH^{2}WN; beþ RChH; Beoþ VL; weryn J; ne byn K; ne beth M. not] nouȝt DChN; nouth H^{3}; nout M. þe] þat UJN. bulle] bille M; bill W.
68 ȝif] ȝef Ch; *om* RVHLKNMH^{3}. þe] here U; *om* H^{3}. suggestioun] suggestionys R; subiectioun K; cause M; destenye U. be] beo L. soþ] sotȝ M; so U; soght L; seyn D. shapiþ . . . to] schapith hem to J; schapit hem to MH^{3}; schapeþ hem to DVN; schapen hem to U; schapith them K; makith hom to L; him nede to R; þei fore TChH^{2}HW. begge] beggen H; bigge K; asken W.
69 beggiþ] beggit M; beggeþ RDChVL WN; biggith U. or] oþer N. bit] byd L; byddith KH^{3}; biddeþ RChVHN; bidit M; borweþ W. but] but ȝif RJ; til H; or N. haue nede] nede haue M. haue] habbe V; bide N. nede] neede K; neode V; gret nede L; nedr H^{3}.
70 fals] flas (*so also in catchword*) H^{3}. wiþ . . . fend] be myn hed M. wiþ] as UH^{3}. fend] feend UJ; feond L. ⁊] þat Ch; *om* N. defraudiþ . . . nedy] nedys dysseiuyt M. defraudiþ] defraudith UHJ KH^{3}; defraudeþ VLN; frawdeþ R; gyleþ DChH^{2}; defouleþ W; kiliþ T. þe nedy] þe neodi V; trouþ W.
71 And ek] And eke RUVHJLKMH^{3}; And TDH^{2}WN; he Ch. giliþ] begilit M; bygyleth LW. gyuere] geuere DChH^{3}; gevar K; ȝiuere V; ȝeuere HJM (*same hand after cancelled* ȝifar J); gyuer by god L; kende U. ageyns] ageyn U; agaynes L; agayne N; ageinst K; aȝeynys J; aȝens ChHWH^{3}; al aȝeyn V. his] godis UN; *om* L.
72 Þei] þay L; Thay K. lyue] lyven K; lyuyn J; lyueth L; libben V; leue DChH^{3}; leuyn M. nouȝt] nouth H^{3}; nout M; not RUHJLK; *om* VW. in] in no VWNM. loue] lawe V. ne] ny L; þat VH; *om* H^{3}. no] non M; non þe H^{3}; *om* N. holden] holdyn JH^{3}; holde ChH^{2}; haldyn U.
73 Þei] URDVHJLWN; Thay K; For þey MH^{3}; Þei ne TChH^{2}. wedde] wedden HLK; weddyn JM; weddeþ V. no] none UMH^{3}. womman] wommon V; women K; wymmen RJL; wyues U. hy] þei RU DChH^{2}VHJLWNH^{3}; thay K; þe M. wiþ] wit M. delen] delyn RUChNM; dele H^{3}; deele J; deleþ V.
74 as] as þe W. wilde] *om* V. bestis] *om* W. wiþ . . . ⁊] when heo L; *om* H^{3}. wiþ] þat wiþ UJ; þat V; *om* WM. wehe] whe he R; wouh Ch; woo H; wo UV; vche N. ⁊] *om* UChVHJKWN. worþ vp] worup (h *added after* r, *same ink*) H^{2}. worþ] worþen HLK; worthin J; wurthen U; worche W; worcheþ V; wurch D; werchyn H^{3}. vp] *om* VH. togideris] ⁊ ryde N.
75 And] Þei N. bringen] bryngyn H^{3}; bringgyn J; brynge RDH^{2}WNM; bringeth ChV. barnes] barons H^{3}; children U; no barnes L. þat] bot L; for M. bois] barnes R; barons W; barnes þey L; *late corrector alters to* bastardes H^{2}; bastardes UVHJNMH^{3}; þey D. ben] been J; beon VL; beþ HWM. holden] holdyn JMH^{3}; holde ChH^{2}; yholden RK; Iholde W.

Or his bak or his bon þei breken in his ȝouþe,
And gon & faiten wiþ here fauntis for eueremore aftir.
Þere ben mo mysshapen amonges hem, whoso takiþ hede,
Þanne of alle oþer maner men þat on þis molde wandriþ.
Þo þat lyuen þus here lif mowe loþe þe tyme 80
Þat euere he was man wrouȝt whanne he shal henne fare.
Ac olde men & hore þat helpeles ben of strengþe,
And wommen wiþ childe þat werche ne mowe,
Blynde & bedrede, & broken here membris,

76 Or] Oþer ChH; Othir J; Eethyr H[3]; Or ellis M; For L. his] here H. bak] legge N. or(2)] oþer H. his(2)] here H; somme N. bon] boon M; bones W; boonys H; lyme N. þei] he UJLKWN; heo V; *om* H[2]. breken] brekyn RMH[3]; breke D; brekeþ VLW; brekith UKN; breykys J; bien broke H[2]. his(3)] here H; heore V; þe Ch; *om* M. ȝouþe] ȝougþe DCh; ȝungth (*after cancelled* ȝinthe) J; þougthe M.
77 gon] gone K; goþ V; gooþ W; *om* UM. &] *om* UVM. faiten] fayte H[2]N; faytyn JM; faiteth UVW; fatten D; fayntyn H[3]. here] her RChKNH[3]; heore VL; þe W; swiche M. fauntis] faundis M; faunt ChW; fautys (? fantys) H[3]; Fautes (? Fantes) VL; fawte K; foode J. for . . . more] al her lyf N. for] *om* UChVH WH[3].
78 Þere] *om* W. ben] beþ RW; beon L; arn MH[3]. mo] more H[3]. mysshapen] myschapyn UJMH[3]; mysshape RChW; myschapmen H[2]; mis happes V; myshappis H; mischefes K. amonges] amongus VH[3]; among UDChHJLKWN; of M. hem] heom L. whoso] hoso JH[3]; hose V. takiþ] takyt M; takyd J; take R. hede] ende hede (ende *underlined*) U.
79 Þanne] þen VL. of] amonges W; with H[3]; *om* UJ. alle] *om* U. oþer] *om* ChH[2]H NMH[3]. maner] maner of UChH[2]JM; *om* VW. men] man R. on] in U. þis] the K; *om* VHW. molde] world U. wandriþ] wandryn RUM; wandren ChV H; wendryth H[3]; wenden N.
80 Þo] þei ChV. lyuen þus] þus lyuen L. lyuen] lyuyn JK; lyue WN; leuen DCh; ledyn MH[3]; haue R. here] her ChNH[3]; heore VL; here her K. lif] liȝf N. mowe] mowen UK; moun H[3]; may ChHWNM. loþe] loþen W; loþin M; lakkyn H[3]; curse U; cursyn J.
81 Here A resumes. euere] heuer Ch; *om* AK. he was] was he JL; þei were H; þei weore V. man] Men VH; wy Ch. wrouȝt] wrouȝth R; wrouth AH[3]; Iwrouȝt H[2]VH; Iwrowht J. whanne] when RHL; whon V; qwan JH[3]. he] þei VH. shal] schul V; shulle H; *om* DH[3]. henne] hennes ChLN; hennys RUHJM; henys A; hens KWH[3]. fare] fareth D; wende AK; *lost in sewing* N.
82 Ac] Bot ChVHLAKWNM; and RH[3]. olde] holde N; elde JM. &] *om* U. hore] hory A; oþer L; oþer boþe W; trewly U. helpeles ben] are helples R. helpeles] help W; feble M. ben] be W; bien H[2]; beon L; beþ ChH; beoþ V. of] *om* W. strengþe] strenght AKN; strenthe H[2]H[3]; strenkyth J; streynthe L; here strengh W.
83 *transposed with following* Ch. wommen] wymmen RUDVHJLKM; wymen also W. childe] children Ch. werche] werchyn H[3]; worche ChH[2]N; worchen VLKM; wyrche RD; werke U; wyrkyn J; worche þei W. ne] no L. mowe] mowen UCh VKNM; may H.
84 Blynde] þe blynde N; blynde men UJ M; Blynde folk W. bedrede] bedred J; Bedreden VHL; bederede W; bedderede M; Beddred D; þe bedred N; blereyed U; blereyde R. & broken] & brokyn JAKH[3]; þat han lost W. here] her ChJKN; heore VL; of here H; in here MH[3]; þe U. membris] lymes W.

Þat takiþ [þ]is meschief mekliche as myselis & oþ*er*e, 85
Han as pleyn p*ar*doun as þe plouȝman hymselue;
For loue of here louȝ herte oure lord haþ hem g*ra*untid
Here pen*aun*ce & here purcatorie vpon þis pur erþe.
'Piers,' quaþ a p*re*st [þo], 'þi p*ar*don muste I rede,
For I shal construe iche clause & kenne it þe on englissh.' 90
And peris at his p*re*you*r* þe p*ar*dou*n* vnfoldiþ,
And I behynde hem boþe beheld al þe b[u]lle.
In two lynes it lay & nouȝt o l*ett*re more,
And was writen riȝt þus in witnesse of treuþe:
Et qui bona egerunt ibunt in vitam eternam; 95

85 Þat] & þo þat H; And W. takiþ . . . meschief] her*e* misschef takyn M. takiþ] takeþ RD; takyn JH^{3}; taken UVHLK; take ChWN; takis H^{2}. þis] LH^{3}; her*e* RA; her ChK; his TDH^{2}; *om* UVHJWN. meschief] mescheif L; Meschef VW; myschief D; myschif H^{2}; myschef RCh JAKNH^{3}; meschefs H. mekliche] meokelich L; myldelych H^{2}. myselis] meselis RH^{2}J; meseles ChVHKWNM; mesels DL; me selfe A. & oþere] oþ*er* ellis H. &] & siche U; or V.
86 Han] haue*n* HK; haue RDJ; Thay han W. as] a D. pleyn] playn ChH^{2}; pleyn a N; playne a K; pleno*ur* A. þe plouȝman] plowme*n* R; piers WM. man] mon VL. hym] he*m* R. selue] self KWN; selue*n* RVMH^{3}; seoluen L; silne*n* H; selfe hath A.
87 For] For þe L; *om* R. loue of] Of R; *om* VA. here] her ChJKNH^{3}; heore VL. louȝ herte] lewtie K. louȝ] low RD; lowe UChH^{2}VHJLAWNH^{3}; loue M. herte] heorte L; hertes VH^{3}; hertis HAM. oure lord] þat god U. haþ] hat MH^{3}; hatȝ H^{2}. hem] heo*m* L; hym W. g*ra*untid] ygraunted R.
88 Here] her ChJKN; Heore VL; þe H. &] of HN. here(2)] her ChJKH^{3}; heore VL; *om* N. purcatorie] p*ur*gatorie RUD H^{2}VHJLAKWNMH^{3}. vpon] here vpo*n* HLAW; is her vppon V; ryth vpon H^{3}; her*e* in M. þis] *om* DVHLAW. pur] pore D; pley*n* R; *om* VHLAWMH^{3}. erþe] eorþe VL; erde A.
89 p*re*st] preost L. þo] UDVHJLKW NMH^{3}; þanne A; *om* TRChH^{2}. muste I] mot I J; y moste UM. rede] reden V; Redyn M.
90 For] & H; *om* RAN. I shal] *om* H. shal] xal H^{3}; wil J; wol UV. construe] LChVAKWNMH^{3}; co*n*struy R; construyn J; construe it TDH^{2}H; construen it U. iche] eche DKW; eche a H^{3}; vch a VL; eu*er*y RUH; euerich a Ch; the iche H^{2}; þe vche N. kenne] ken UChL; kenny*n* JM; teche H^{3}; knowen V; telle RA; vndo H. it þe] þe it N. it] *om* JA WH^{3}. þe] heo*m* L; *om* VH. on] i*n* UV HH^{3}. englissh] engelische A; englys R.
91 þe] þat UK; his R. vnfoldiþ] vnfoldeþ RDVL; vnfoldyd A; vnfolded JKN; vnfeldith M; vnfeld H; he onfolded Ch; vnlapped W.
92 And] Am N; *om* A. I] *om* UChW. behynde] bihynden VJL; beheld M. hem] heom L; hym W. boþe] boþin M. beheld] biheold V; byhuld L; beheld I W; he hylde U; & say M. al] *om* AH^{3}. bulle] RUDH^{2}VHJLAKWNH^{3}; bille T ChM.
93 In] And in W; I H^{2}. two] to RDAM. lynes] lynys RJMH^{3}; leues H^{2}W. nouȝt] not RVAKW; nat Ch; no H; *om* LM. o] on D; a RUChH^{2}VJLAKWNMH^{3}; *om* H. l*ett*re] lettur J; lettir A; litel L.
94 And] hit R. writen] Iwriten VL; Iwrityn JN; Iwriton K; Iwrite H; wreten W; wretyn A; Iwretyn MH^{3}. riȝt] ryth H^{3}; reyth M; *om* K. treuþe] trouthe LW; trowþe N; truþe RJK.
95 *and* **96** *as one line* H^{3}; *copied after line* 99 H.
95 *Et*] *om* UChHKWM. *ibunt*] *om* K.

Qui vero mala in ignem eternum.
'Petir,' quaþ þe prest þo, 'I can no pardoun fynde
But do wel & haue wel, & god shal haue þi soule,
And do euele & haue euele, & hope þou non oþer
Þat aftir þi deþ day to helle shalt þou wende.' 100
And piers for [pure] tene pulde it assondir
& seide '*Si ambulauero in medio umbre mortis*
Non timebo mala quoniam tu mecum es.
I shal cesse of my sowyng,' quaþ peris, '& swynke not so harde,
Ne aboute my [belyue] so besy be namore; 105
Of preyours & of penaunce my plouȝ shal ben hereaftir,
And beloure þat I [be]louȝ er þeiȝ liflode me faile.

96 *line om* W. Qui] *Et qui* AK. *in . . . eternum*] *&c* H. *ignem*] *ignum* Ch. *eternum*] *eternam* AH^3.
97 *line om* M. þe prest] peris H^2A (*late corrector alters to* the preste H^2); he to piers Ch. þe] þat J; a N. prest] preost VL. þo] *om* UHNH^3. can] con V. no . . . fynde] non oþer pardoun AH^3.
98 But] *om* A. do wel] dowe W. haue wel] hawel D. shal] xal H^3. haue(2)] hauen M. soule] saule D.
99 And] *om* AN. euele(*both*)] euyl RAKWH^3; yuel UH^2HJLN; vuel V. &(2)] *om* RUVH^3. hope] trust R. þou] to H.
100 Þat] þan RW; And JH^3; *om* A. deþ] ded AH^3; lyf W. day] days W; *om* M. to . . . wende] þou shalt wende to helle R; þe deuyl schal haue þi soule AMH^3. shalt þou] schalt þou DHK; schaltou VLN; ne shalt þou T; ne schal thou (ne *cancelled another ink*) H^2; Sne schalt þow Ch; þou schalt UJ; for to W.
101 *divided from following after* seide TRUDChH^2VJLAKWM. And] þo H; *om* JA. piers] peres þo R. for . . . tene] *om* W. pure] UHJLAKNMH^3; puire V; *om* TRDChH^2 (*late corrector supplies* H^2). tene] teone VL. pulde] pulled RChL; pullid UDH^2JAKNMH^3; pollede V; pollid H; plukked W. asondir] on sondir U; onsonder K; atwynen M; a two W; on tweyne AH^3.
102 *as two lines, the Latin being copied independently after line* 105 H; *run together with following* TA; *divided from following after* mala J. & seide] & siþþe he seide to hem þese semely sawis H; *om* N. &] an H^2; and to þe prest W. seide] sayde DChKW. *in*] *om* Ch. *umbre*] *om* N. *mortis*] *mortis &c* H; *tribulacionis* N.
103 *line om* HH^3. *quoniam . . . es*] *&c* UW; *om* A. *es*] *es &c* V; *es domine* J.
104 I shal] Now wil I W. cesse] cese URDChH^2VHLA; secyn JH^3; seisyn M. quaþ peris] *om* UHJAWNMH^3. swynke] swynkyn M; swyng W; swyckyn J. not . . . harde] *defective* L. not] nouȝt ChN; nouth JH^3; no more H. harde] sore KM (*same hand after cancelled* hard K).
105 aboute] aboutyn J. belyue] M; bylyff H^3; liflode TRUDChH^2VHJLAKWN. so . . . be] be so besi W. so] *om* A. besy] besye K; bisy VLNH^3; busy R. be] ben M; bene J; beo VL; me ChA. namore] nomore RDChH^2VHJAKWNMH^3; *illegible* L.
106 Here (*fol.* 125*b*) L **is badly faded:** *see above*, p. 11. preyours] preyere V. &] *om* R. of(2)] *om* ChHLAKWN. penaunce] penaunces DM. plouȝ] plouth M. shal] xal H^3; mot ChH^2; *om* W. ben] be RChHK; bene J; bien H^2M; beon L; beþ W.
107 *line om* AW. beloure] belowren DK; belowryn J; lowren U; beloue M. belouȝ er] er bylowhe U; er lowhe J. belouȝ] H^2DH; bylowe R; beolouh V; louȝ TL; lowgh N; lowȝe Ch; laughed H^3; lawghede M; love K. er] ere RChH^2VLM; er *cancelled* T; or H; er þat H^3; *om* DKN. þeiȝ] þeiȝe U; þey RH^2J; þouȝ DChK; þaugh L; þe N; *om* VHMH^3. liflode] myn liflode JH^3; my lyf V. me] *om* VJ.

Þe p*ro*phet his p[a]yn e[et] in pen*au*nce & in wepyng
Be þat þe sauter vs seiþ, & so dede manye oþ*er*e.
Þat louiþ god lelly, his liflode is þe more: 110
Fuerunt michi lacrime mee panes die ac nocte.
And but ȝif luk leiȝe he leriþ vs anoþ*er*,
[By foules, þat are not] besy aboute þe bely ioye: |
Ne soliciti sitis he seiþ in his gospel, *fol.* xliiij *a*

108 *line om* WM; *transposed with following* A. Þe . . . eet] þ*er* is p*ro*fyt in peyne H; And parfit In praiers Ch; *Oculus* xal be ocupyid H^3. p*ro*phet] prophetis A; p*ro*phetes V. his . . . eet] hadde his peynes H^2; were pyned A; peyneden hem V. his] is D; hym K. payn eet] UJLN; peyne haþ (peyne *altered from* penauns (?) *same hand*) R; peyned TK (d *added later*, ? *another script* T); fayn D. in(2)] *om* VJNH^3. wepyng] weopyng LN.
109 *transposed with following* M. Be þat] As VM; In A. vs] þus A; *om* W. seiþ] seiȝt ChH^2; saith KWMH^3; techith U. &] *om* UVJN. so . . . oþere] othere bokys manye M. so] *om* H. dede] ded ChH^3; dide UH^{2}K; did N; dydyn J; dude RV; duden L; don A; doþ HW. manye oþere] oþer manye AH^3. manye] moni VL.
110 *line om* N. Þat] He þat (He *in margin, same ink*) H^3; For he þat M. louiþ] luffith J; lovyd K. lelly] treuly M; trewlyche H^3; luffly J; wel U. his] is AM; her K; *om* H. is] are K. þe more] wel muche V; wel mochell K; wel mochil U; ful mechyl H^3; myche H; ful mete A; wel meth L; leche W.
110α *copied after line* 112 H^3; *added at bottom of page same hand* U. *lacrime mee*] *lacrime* K; *om* A. *panes . . . nocte*] *die ac nocte panes* M. *nocte*] *nocte &c* DAKW.
111 *divided from following after* foules LN; *after* birdes W; *after* folis AMH^3. And] *om* A. but] *om* N. ȝif] ȝef L; *om* ChVH NH^3. luk] also seynt luk N; lutȝ D; þe boke RV. leiȝe] lyȝe VH^{2}H^3; lye RU DHJLAKWM; liȝed Ch; *om* N. he] *om* N. leriþ] lerit M; lereth DChVL; lereȝt H^2; lernyth UJAK; lerneþ HN; telleþ R; byddeþ W. vs] *om* W. anoþ*er*] non oþ*er* H; *om* AWNMH^3.
112 *as two lines divided after* ben U; besy H; aboute J; eorþe V. By foules] RUJKN; by þe foules L; by birdes W; be folis A; to ben foles M; þ*a*t be*n* folys H^3; we folys D; *om* TChH^{2}VH. þ*a*t . . . besy] þat to bisi we ne schulde beo her vppon eorþe V. þ*a*t . . . not] R; we schuld not be A; We xuld nouth ben H^3; That we schul not be H^2; Þ*a*t we ne shuln nouȝt be T; þat we schul not D; That we be nowght to W; that we schulden not be to K; þat we schuld nat be to Ch; þat we no scholde not beo to L; That we ne sholde be to (ne *above line same script*) N; þat we ne schuldyn to J; he vs techith þat we schulde U; And bitd vs be nout so M; he biddeþ vs we shuld not her*e* be to H. besy] bysy LW; busey R; besyen D; besy ben UJ. aboute . . . ioye] For to make wombe ioye in þis wonynge here U; while we woneþ in þis world to make vs wombe Ioye V; In no man*er* wise aboute our*e* wombe ioiȝe H; aboute Ne t*r*auellyn to myche to makyn þe wombe Ioye J. aboute] aboutyn MH^3; to make N. þe] *om* DChAWMH^3. bely] wombe W; bodyly A; lif L. ioye] Ioyȝe H^3; ioyes A.
113–4 *as three lines divided after* scitis—fayre R; *after* &c—ous(1) D; *after* manducemus—ensample W.
113 *line om* H^3; *run together with line* 115 H. *Ne*] *Non* R. *soliciti*] *sollicite* H. *sitis*] *sitis &c* D; *scitis* RK; *sitis dicentes quid manducemus* W. he . . . gospel] *om* H. seiþ] seiȝt Ch; seyt R; saith DKW. in] RUD H^{2}VJLANM; it in TChKW. his] the K. gospel] godspel V.

And shewiþ it vs be ensaumple oureselue to wisse.
Þe foulis in þe firmament, who fynt hem a wynter? 115
Whan þe frost fresiþ foode hem behouiþ;
Haue þei no garner [to go] to, but god fynt hem alle.'
'What!' quaþ þe prest to perkyn, 'peter, as me þinkeþ,
Þou art le[ttr]id a litel; who lernide þe on boke?'
'Abstinence þe abbesse myn a b c me tauȝte, 120
And consience com aftir & kennide me betere.'
'Were þou a prest, piers,' quaþ he, 'þou miȝtest preche wh[an] þe liki[de];
Quoniam literaturam non cognoui, þat miȝte be þi teme.'

114 shewiþ] schewit M; schewt A; schew Ch. it . . . be] is an (an *over erasure, another ink and script*) W. it] *om* UHJANH[3]. vs] ous D; to vs Ch; *om* VA. be] fayre by R; in L; *om* N. ensaumple] an ensample H; on exaumple R; ex example H[3]; ensamples U. oure . . . wisse] To done on þe selue wise & wisdom it kenneþ W. oure] vs UJLAM; ous D. selue] selven K; seluyn H[3]; selfuyn M; soules VHN; seurly L. wisse] wyssen KM.
115 *line om* R. foulis] foul H[3]. who] ho DJAH[3]; he Ch; heo V. fynt] fynd L; feedeþ V. hem] heom L; *om* H[2]. a] in UVHJAKWNMH[3].
VIII 116–IX 96 *om* H[3].
116 Whan] whon V; when HL; Qwan J. frost] Forst V. fresiþ] fresit M; freseþ RDChVN; freosyth L; freseþ fast W; *above cancelled* fedith *same hand* K. hem] heom L. behouiþ] behoueþ DRChH[2]V HLKWN; behouet M.
117 Haue þei] þei haue RUJ. Haue] Hauen L; Ha M. no] I no U. garner] gerner RDChH[2]VHL; garnard K; gerne M; geuer N; berne U; fode J. to . . . to] RUVLAWN; to gon to JKM; greiþ H; þerto TDChH[2] (go *inserted after* ther *by late corrector* H[2]). but] ȝit V. fynt] fynd LK. hem] heom L.
118 What] Qwat J; Piers N; *om* RA. þe] a N. prest] preost L. to perkyn] þo WN. peter] by crist R. as] *om* W. þinkeþ] thynkyt A; thenkeþ R.
119 lettrid] UH; lettred LKWNM; letteryd JA; lettret V; lernid TH[2]; lerned RDCh. a] but A. litel] litill UAKM; litul H[2]; lyte N; luyte V. who] ho VJA; whor U. lernide] lernyd H[2]A; lerned DChHKN; lered RVLW; taugthe M; taute J. on] on þe W; in H.
120 þe] myn RLA. abbesse] aunte RA. myn] quoþ he myne HW; *after cancelled* þe a.b U; *om* L. tauȝte] tauȝthe R; taugthe M; taght W; tawte J; touthe A.
121 And] *om* A. com . . . &] *om* Ch. com] cam H[2]JAM; came K. aftir] aftirward UJLANM. &] an A. kennide] kennyd UJK; kennede M; kenned DCh H[2]LWN; tauȝte VH; tauȝthe R; tauth A. betere] michell better K; moche more RU.
122 *line om* K. Were] Where A; weore VL. a] *om* W. prest] preost L. piers] *om* VHM. quaþ he] *om* RJN. he] þe prest M. þou] þe D. miȝtest] mygthist M; mytist J; myȝt RDChH[2]HAWN. preche . . . likide] prewe þe soþe A. preche] prechyn JM. whan] UDNM; when RH LW; whon V; qwan J; where TChH[2]. likide] U; lykyd J; lykede R; lyked DH WN; likyt M; likiþ T; likeþ Ch; likeȝ H[2]; luste V; *lost in sewing* L.
123 *as two lines divided after* teme H. *Quoniam*] For þou knowist no lettrure miȝt be þy teme *Quoniam* H. *literaturam*] *letteraturam* K; *litteram* A. þat . . . teme] *om* (*see above*) H. þat] *om* RVJAWN. be . . . teme] þi teme be N. be] beo L; beene J. þi] my DV. teme] teeme Ch H[2]V; tyme K.

'Lewide lorel,' q*ua*þ peris, 'litel lokest þou on þe bible;
On salamonis sawis [seldom] þou beholdis: 125
E[j]ice derisores & iurgia cum eis ne crescant.'
Þe prest & perkyn aposid eiþ*er* oþ*er*,
And þoruȝ here wordis I wok & waitide aboute,
And sauȝ þe sonne euene souþ sitte þ*at* tyme,
Metel[es and money]les on malu*er*ne hilles.
Musyng on þis metelis a myle wey I ȝede; 130
Manye tyme þis metelis han mad me to stodie,
And for peris loue þe plouȝman wel pensif in herte,

124 Lewide] lewid HJ; Lewede VM; Lewed RUDH²LKWN; lewde Ch; A lewid A. lorel] losel HA. peris] he UV HN. litel] luite V; whi ne W. lokest] lokedist K. on] in H; *om* H²JAN (*supplied another hand* H²). þe] þy R; *om* K. bible] boke K.
125 On . . . sawis] The sawes of sire Salamon W. On] Of A; And M. salamonis] salamon D. seldom] UK; selden DLNM; seld W; litel TRChH²HJA; luitel V. beholdis] beholdes Ch; beholdist HJAM; beholdest RUDH²VLKWN. *Here* H *adds two lines: see above*, p. 47.
125α *Ejice*] *Ecce* (? for *Eice*) TRUDChH²V HJLAKWNM. *derisores*] *dirisores* A; *derisiores* D. *iurgia*] *uirga* RU; *virga* HA KW. *ne*] *non* DHAWM; *nunc* V; *om* L. *crescant*] *crescunt* V; *quiescam* HW.
126 Þe] The RVHJAWN; þeo L; þus þe UKM; And þe TDChH². prest] preost L. &] þanne & N. perkyn] Perkin þo V; sire perkyn þo W. aposid eiþer] eiþ*er* apposid UAM; þ*us* oythir aposyd J. aposid] aposed RDChHKWN; Apposeden V. eiþ*er*] here eyþ*er* R.
127 And . . . I] I trowe here wordis A; And I wit her wordys M. þoruȝ] thoru H²; þorow ChJ; þorw RUV; þorgh L; þrow W; thrugh K; þoruȝt D; wiþ N. here] her ChJKN; heore VL. wok] awok RVHKWNM; awook U. &] a*n* R. waitide] waitid HJAM; waytede H²; wayted RUDChLN; awayted K; lokede V; loked me W. aboute] abouten U; abowtyn JM.
128 And] I N. sauȝ] sauh V; sagh L; sawe Ch; saw RN; say UDHJA; se W; seen K; sith M. euene . . . tyme] þat tyme sitte eue*n* souþ H. euene . . . sitte] syttyn euyn south A; sitte souþ euene V. euene] euy*n* JK; eu*er*e R. souþ] souty M. sitte] sytten UDLK; syttyn J; sittyng N; suttyn M. þat] in þat A; atte M.
129 Meteles . . . moneyles] RUDVHK; Meteles & monyles AM; Meteles & moneles JWN; :::::::s & moneylas L; Metelis on m*er*ueilles T; Meteles on m*er*ueyles (*twice ineffectually corrected*) H²; Mynnyng on þe mervailes Ch. on] vpon R. hilles] hulles DVL; hullys RH.
130–155 (*fol.* 125*b*) **badly faded** L; **henceforth to be taken into consideration only when named.**
130 *run together with following* RDK. Musyng] Meusyng D; And musande W; Mamelyng R; Mony elynge V. on] out H². þis] þes AK; þat Ch. metelis] metels Ch; meting HW; mat*er* meteles J; mat*er*e U. a . . . ȝede] *om* RDK. wey] weies U. I ȝede] Ich ȝeode V.
131 Manye . . . metelis] *om* RDK. Manye] Mony V; And many a W. tyme] tymes Ch. þis . . . han] ȝit W. þis] þes Ch; þese A. metelis] metel N; meting H. han] haþ UDHJKN; had M; *om* R. mad] maked D; makeþ W; *twice, but second cancelled* T. to] for to W. stodie] studyen M.
132 And] An J; *om* VW. peris] peris his H. loue] lyf UJ; me*n* R; *om* KM. þe] *om* UJ. plouȝman] plouhmon V; ploghmon L; plouthman M. wel] ful VHAM; *om* UJ. pensif] pitously U; petusly J. in] in myn V; at K. herte] harte K.

For þat I saiȝ slepyng ȝif it so be miȝte.
Ac catoun construiþ it [nay] & canonistris boþe:
Sompnia ne cures.
Ac for þe bible beriþ wytnesse 135
How Dani[el] deui[n]ide þe drem[is] of a king
Þat nabugodonosor nempne þise clerkis—
Daniel seide, 'sire king, þi sweuene is to mene
Þat [vncouþe] kniȝt[is] shal come þi kingdom to cleyme;
Among l[ower]e lordis þi londis shuln be departid'. 140

133 For] Of N. saiȝ] say DJLA; seyth K; sey M; sauȝ H²H; sawgh W; sauh V; sawe Ch; saw RUN (*same hand after cancelled* seye U). ȝif] ȝef Ch; if þat UK; ȝ þat M. it] I M. so be] be so ChHL. so] *om* K. be miȝte] might be K. be] ben J.
134 Ac] Bot ChVHKW; But þat M; and RUH²N; As A. catoun construiþ] constreweþ Caton Ch. construiþ] construit RH²; construet D; construed U. it] *om* JWNM. nay] RUVHJAKWNM; nouȝt D; *om* TChH². & . . . boþe] but seyth þus hem selue D. &] An V. canonistris] canonistre UK; þe canon W; catonistris H. boþe] boþin M; eke W.
134α *run together with following* H². *Sompnia*] Caton saiþ him self *Sompnia* W; And saith hym self *sompnia* K; And seyn be hem selfe *sompnia* J; And siggen bi hem seluen *Sompnia* V; And hem seluen siggyn *sompnia* M; and by hem selue *Sompnia* U; And he hem selfe boþe *Sompnia* A; And Iugyn hem seluen *Sompnia* R. *cures*] *cures &c* RDChM; *cures ne mens humana* N; *cures nam mens est humana quod optat* H.
135–6 *as three lines* H: & seiþ þat we shulde charge no sweuenys but daniel dampneþ it & þe bible boþe & beriþ witnes þer of a kingis dremyng.
135 *line om* N; *divided from following after* how TRDCh; *after* prophete UJ; *after* deuynede VL; *after* dremys K; *after* oþer W. Ac] Bot ChJKWM; and RU; *om* A. for] For þus þe buke berith For þus A; *om* W. bible] book of þe bible M. wytnesse] witnesse and telleþ vs an oþer W.
136 *run together with following* V; *divided from following after* bible N; *after* Nabogodonosor L. How] How þat W; But N; *om* H². Daniel] ChH²VAKWNM; daniel þe prophete UJ; Dauid TRD (*cancelled for* daniel *another hand* R). deuinide] deuynede V; deuyned UChLA WN; Dyuynyd J; dyvyned K; demide T; demyd H²M; demede R; dremyd D. þe . . . king] of þe kynges dremes W. þe] a D; as witnesseþ þe bible þe N. dremis] dremys RUJK; dremes N; Dremels V; drem TDChA; dreem H²; dremeyd M. a] þe AM. king] kyng ones N; kyng onys UJ; knyȝth R.
137 Þat] Of A; *om* HWN. nabugodonosor] Nabegodonosor D; nabagodonosor R. nempne . . . clerkis] þese clerkis hym nempneþ H; ne myght no clerkis A; hette V; *om* N. nempne] nompne J; nemyth M; namen D; memned (*first minim cancelled*) R; so reden W. þise] þis RJ; þese UW; þes DChK; the H²M. clerkis] clerk R.
138 seide] said KW. sire] sere AK. þi] the K; þis W. sweuene] sweuyn JK; sweue R. to] þus to A. mene] meane K.
139 vncouþe] uncouthe UVHJKWNM; an vncouþe D; vnkyd R; an vnkynde TChH²; vnconyng A. kniȝtis] kniȝtys N; kniȝtes HKW; knihtes V; knytis A; kniȝt TRH²; kyngis J; kynges U; kyng DCh; men M. shal] schul UVHA. come] comyn JM. kingdom] kyndom H²; kyngdam M; kindam V. to] *om* R. cleyme] clayme ChVKW; cleue J; cle::::: (*lost in binding*) N.
140 lowere] lowere RUVHJLWN; lowar K; hyere A; lewide T; lewid H²; lewed D; lewde Ch; lether M. þi . . . shuln] it mot W. londis] lond ChVAKNM; kingdam R. shuln] schul UDH; schollyn J; shal RChVAKNM. be] ben JM. departid] departet V; partid J.

As daniel deui[n]ide in dede it fel aftir:
þe king les his lordsshipe, & lesse men it hadde.
And Iosep mette m*er*ueillously how þe mone & þe sonne
And þe enleuene sterris ha[i]lsiden hym alle.
'*Beau fitȝ*,' quaþ his fadir, 'for defaute we shuln, 145
I myself & my sones, seke þe for nede.'
It befel as his fadir seide in faraos tyme
þ*at* Iosep was Iustice Egipt to kepe—
Al þis makiþ me on metelis to þinke
Manye tymes at mydniȝt whan men shulde slepe, 150
On peris þe plouȝman, whiche a p*ar*dou*n* he hauiþ,
And how þe prest inpugnid it al be [pu]re resoun,

141 As daniel] And as he W. deuinide] deuyned WN; dyuynyd J; diuinede V; dyuyned UK; deuysed H; demide T; demyd A; demed RDChH²; dymde M. in . . . fel] hit fel in dede V. in dede] so A. it fel] fel it J. fel] feol L; byfel RUCh HW; befil H².
142 king] kynk J; lord U; *twice* D. les] lese Ch; lees H²M; loste UK; lost HJA WN; lafte V. lordsshipe] lordschep RCh JA; lordschupe V; lond H. &] *om* R. lesse] lasse RVHJKNM; false U. men] lordis HA. it hadde] hadden it H. it] *om* Ch. hadde] hadden UVM; haddyn A; heldyn K. **Here** H **ends.**
143–4 *as 3 lines divided after* alse—sterres V.
143 And] As A. Iosep] Ioseph UH²VJKN. mette] mete K. m*er*ueillously] meruelyusly R; maruaylously D; a meruaill W; Metels ful Meruilous alse V; also M. how] þat M; of AW. þe . . . sonne] þe sonne and þe Mone VW.
144 þe] how þat W; *om* UVKM. enleuene] elleuen DChH²JKWN; eleue A; xj RM; seuene U. hailsiden] haylseden DK; haylsedyn J; hailsede U; hailsed ChN; halsiden T; halside H²; hayled R; he heylid A; Falden bifore his Feet and heileden V; grettyn M; worshipt W. alle] al abowtyn U; also A.
145 *Beau*] bew RUVJAN. *fitȝ*] fiȝ UVM; fisȝ J; filtȝ N; sir*e* R; seris A. fadir] father K. for . . . shuln] defaute shal vs make W. defaute] nede M. we] *om* H². shuln] schullen H²; schullyn A; shulle RUDCh VJKN; scholen M.
146 I] Bothe W. seke] seken K; sekyn RJAM; seche VWN. for] at W. nede] neede K; neode V; defaute M.
147 It] And h*i*t RW. befel] befyl D; fel VA; felle J. his fadir] he K. his] þe RV AM. seide] saide WK. faraos] pharaoes UN; pharaoys RDJ; faraonis M; Pharaones V; pharo A; pharoo his K; fargos H².
148 þ*at*] þer V. Iosep] Ioseph VH²JKN. Egipt] egept Ch; al egipte U; & egipt W. to] he W. kepe] kepen VK; kepyn M; kept W.
149 *transposed with following* U. Al] and al KW. makiþ] makyt M. on metelis] svmtyme M. on] mochil on U; mychel on J; on t D. metelis] metyng W. þinke] thynken K; þinkyn M; thenke H²; þenken UV.
150 Manye] Mony V. tymes] tyme UVA WNM. whan] whe*n* R; whon V; qwan J. men] y UVJLWNM. shulde] schulden K. slepe] slepyn M; sclepe K.
151 On] Of AN; And Ch. peris] p*er*kyn N. þe] *om* R. plouȝman] plouhMon V; whiche] & whiche UK; and whuch V; & qwyche J; such Ch; swoche A; þat suche N; what M. a] *om* AWM. he] *om* N. hauiþ] haueþ RDCh; hath K; hadde UJWNM; had A; hedde V.
152 prest] preost V; *om* D. inpugnid] inpugnide H²; inpugned DCh; inpugnede V; enpugned RUWN; inpu*n*gnyd JK. enpugnedid M. it] him JK; *om* M. al] and al KM. be pure] by pure RUVJLK WN; to pure A; be pour*e* M; before TDChH².

And [dem]ide þat dowel indulgence passiþ, |
Bienalis & trienalis & bisshopis lettres. *fol.* xliiij *b*
Dowel at þe day of dome is digneliche vndirfongen; 155
He passiþ al þe pardoun [of] seint petris chirche.
Now haþ þe pope power pardoun to graunte
Þe peple wiþoute penaunce [to passe to Ioye]?
Þis is [a] l[e]f of oure beleue, as lettrid men vs [tech]iþ:
Quodcumque ligaueris super terram &c.
And so I leue lelly, lord forbede ellis, 160
Þat pardoun, & penaunce, & preyours do salue
Soulis þat han ysynned seue siþes dedly.

153 demide] demede M; demed RKWN; he leuide TH²; he leued Ch; he leueth D; deuyned A; dyuynyd J; diuinede V; dyuyned U. þat] how þat W. indulgence] Indulgences N; indulgencis J. passiþ] passide U; passede VM; passed JKWN; pasid A.
154 Bienalis] Byonalis UDA; Byannalis Ch; Trienal W. trienalis] trionalis UDA; triannalis Ch; quinal W. bisshopis] buschopis A; Busschopes V. lettres] letturs J; seles W; *after cancelled* seales *same hand* K.
155 at þe] atte WM. at] on V. þe . . . dome] Domesday VN. of] a ChM. is] *om* KM. digneliche vndirfongen] worthiere þan they alle W. digneliche] dinglyche J; deyneliche K; deneliche D; derly A; ferforþliche U. vndirfongen] vndirfongyn M; vndurfongyn A; vndirfonge D; vnderfonge RH²K; vnderfong Ch; vnderfongyd J; ::::urfonde L; praised N; Ipreiset V. **Here L ends.**
156 He] And W. passiþ] passit M; passitȝ H²; passydh J; pasith A. þe] *om* D. pardoun] pardouns VW. of] RUH²VJA KWNM; at TDCh. seint] sent A; Saynt K. petris] petres R; petrus V; peturs K; petre W; petir A; peter D; petur J; marie M. chirche] cherche RWM; Churche DV; chirche at rome U. *Here* U *copies line* 159α.
157 *run together with following* Ch. haþ] hat M; hatȝ H². pope] peple M. pardoun . . . graunte] *om* Ch. graunte] graunten U.
158 Þe . . . penaunce] *om* Ch. Þe] Al þe D. peple] people K; puple A. wiþoute] wiþouten UJ; withoutyn M; apertly withoute D; with a R. to . . . Ioye] RVK WN; to passen to ioie U; to passyn to Ioye J; to pasyn into Ioy A; for to gon to ioie M; *a pena & a culpa* TChH²; *om* D.
159 is] *om* R. a . . . of] *om* A. a lef] RDV WNM; a lefe K; a leef UJ; þe lif TChH². oure] *om* J. as . . . men] þat lettreure W. lettrid] lettred RDN; lettret V; letteryd JM; lettered Ch; letterd K; lernyd A. men] *om* J. techiþ] UJA; techit M; techeþ DVKW; techen N; teche R; shewiþ T; schewitȝ H²; scheweþ Ch.
159α *line om* W; *copied after line* 156 U. *super . . . &c*] *om* M. *&c*] *erit ligatum & in celis* UVJA.
160 so] also Ch; *om* UDJ. I leue] bileeue I V. leue] beleue W; byleue it UJ; loue DCh. lelly] lelely J; wel U; teuly (*altered from* leuly ?) M. lord] vr lord V; lordys J; god ChA; godis M. forbede] it forbede U; forbeode hit V; forbode JM.
161 *divided from following after* togidres UJ. pardoun . . . preyours] prayeres and pardoun and penauns R. penaunce . . . preyours] preiers & penaunce M. & preyours] oft tymes Ch. &(2)] *om* DA. do] don VA; doun N; doone K; doþe Ch; shal W; may M; togidres mown UJ; ben R. salue] saue UDChAKW; sauen VJM.
162 Soulis] to soules R. þat . . . dedly] of þat þe seuen dedly synnes W. þat] than K. han] haue DJK; haþe Ch; heue R. ysynned] synned RUDChKN; synnyd JA; sennyd M; sunget V. seue . . . dedly] dedly seuene syþys M. seue] seuen UVJ; seuene RDH²AN; sevyn K; In seuen Ch. siþes] synnes Ch.

A[c] to triste on þis trionalis, trewely, me þinkeþ,
It is not so sikir for þe soule, c*er*tis, as is do wel.
Forþi I rede ȝow renkes þ*at* riche ben on erþe 165
Vpon trist of ȝo*ur* treso*ur* trienal*is* to haue
Be þou neu*ere* þe bald*ere* to breke þe ten hestis;
And nameliche ȝe maistris, as meiris & iuggis,
Þ*at* han þe [welþe of þis] world, & wise men ben holden,
[To purchace p*ar*dou*n* and þe popes bulles], 170
At þe dredful dom whanne dede shal arisen
And come [alle] before crist acountes to ȝelden,
How þou leddist þi lif here & his lawe keptest,

163 Ac] RUJ; Bote VKWNM; And TD ChH^2; *om* A. to triste] be crist D. to] For to AN; *om* H^{2}V. triste] truste RK; trust ChWN; trustene V; traste U; tristnyn M; tr*o*stnyn J; storn trostyn A. on] to V; *om* D. þis] thes K; þese UD H^{2}J; his Ch; *om* VANM. trionalis] tryenal*es* RH^{2}VJKWNM; triannalis Ch. trewely] truly R; trwely N; soþely Ch; certes U. þinkeþ] þinkit M; þinkeþs W.
164 It] *om* UDVJAWN. not] nouȝt DCh; nout MJ; nouȝ N; non A. sikir] syker RUH^{2}VKN; sekyr M; seker DCh AW. for . . . is] sooþly as say I W. soule] saule D. c*er*tis] certus R; trewly U; *om* A. is] for to A; *om* RDChV.
165 *line om* A. Forþi] For why K; þ*er* fore UJN; Fo þey M; For þouȝ D. rede] red N. ȝow] ȝe DM; þat U; now R. renkes] lordes UJ; þenke D; þinkeþ RW; þinkyn M. þ*at*] þei þ*at* R; þan D. riche] *om* RW. ben] bene J; bien H^2; beþ W. on] in UW. erþe] eorþe V.
166 Vpon . . . of] Trostyth not vp A. Vpon] Vpyn M; Vp JN; For no W. trist] trust RUDChH^{2}VKWNM; trest J. ȝo*ur*] oure V; þat A. trienal*is*] tr*i*onales UDA; triannalis Ch; trenales N. haue] hauen M.
167 *line om* A. Be þou] Beth M. Be] Beo V. þou] ȝe ChVJWN; ye K. bald*ere*] baldar J; Baldore V; bolder RChH^{2}WNM; boldar K. breke] brekyn M; breykyn J.
168 *line om* A. nameliche] nomeliche V. ȝe] þe M; þese D. maistris . . . iuggis] Meires and ȝe Maister Iuges V. maistris] masters K. as . . . iuggis] Iustices & Maires W; þat men þ*at* Iuggeȝ holden U. as] *om* JNM. meiris] mairis H^2; maires ChN; mayers K.
169 *line om* A. Þ*at*] þei RU. han] haue RDJW; to haue U. þe] *om* U. welþe . . . world] VUKNM; welþe of þis word R; welth of þe werld J; wele of þis world W; world at wille TCh; wolrd at wylle H^2; world D. &] & for D; for RV; þat M; *om* U. wise] who so R. men] *om* W. ben] be RCh; beþ W; bien H^2; arn M. holden] holdy*n* JM; holde UCh; yholde RW.
170 RUVJAKWNM; *line om* TDChH^2. To] For to UJ. purchace] purchasen V; p*ur*chasyn JM. bulles] billis A.
171 At] And at W; For at M. þe] *om* D. dredful] *om* R. dom] AKWN; doom M; dom day T; domesday DChH^2; day of dome RUVJ. whanne] qwan J; þ*er* V. dede] RUChVJM; dead N; þe dede TD H^2; dedes W; deth K; men A. shal arisen] beþ Irekned W. shal] shul RChAM; schuln U; schullen V; sully*n* J. arisen] arise RUDChJNM; ryse A.
172 come alle] al shal come W. come] comen VK; comyn UDJAM; come forþ N. alle] RUVJKM; *om* TDChH^{2}AN. before] beforn AM; tofore DJ; afor N. acountes] acounptis M; accomptes K; acomptis N; and aCou*n*tes V; countes Ch; & cowntys J; and here acountes W. to] *om* VW. ȝelden] ȝeldyn M; ȝelde RDChH^{2}JAWN; yelde *after cancelled* ma K.
173–84 *om* U.
173 *marked with cross* D. þou] we W. leddist] leddest ChN; leddis A; ledest R; laddyst J; laddest VK; led han W; haddest D. þi] oure W. lif] lyue A. here] *om* VJWNM. &] & how A. his] þin J; the KN. lawe] lawis A. keptest] kept W; kepist A.

What þou dedist day [by day] þe dom wile reherce.
A pokeful of *pardoun* þ*ere*, ne þe p*rouincialis* l*ett*res, 175
Þei3 þou be founde in þe frat*er*nite among þe foure ordris,
And haue indulgence doublefold, but dowel þe helpe
I ne wolde 3iue for þi patent on pye hele.
Forþi I counseil alle cristene [to] cri3e god m*er*cy,
And marie his modir to be mene betwene, 180
Þat god 3iue vs g*ra*ce er we go hennis
Suche werkis to werche, whiles we ben here,
Þat, aftir oure deþ day, dowel reherse
Þ*at* at þe day of dome we dede as he hi3te.

174 *marked with cross* T. What] Qwat J; That H^2; And how AM. þou] we W; *om* M. dedist] dedest D; dedust R; didest N; dyddist K; dudest V; dost JA; haue done W. by day] RDChH^2VJAKWNM; *om* T. þe] þi A. dom] dou*m* R; doom H^2VM. wile] wol Ch; woll K; it wil A; þe wol V; schal M. reherce] rehersen DV; rehercyn M.
175 pokeful] powheful V; pound ful A; buysschelful M. *pardoun*] pardons K. þ*ere*] þore A; þanne W; *om* NM. ne þe] ne RJKWM; ne no A; ⁊ N; wi*th* V. p*rouincialis*] prouincial ChJKW. l*ett*res] lettre W; selis A.
176 Þei3] þei ChH^2JNM; þou3 RDK; Thogh W; þauh V; And þow A. founde . . . frat*er*nite] a breþyr M. founde] fou*n*den VJN; *om* AW. in] of W. þe(1)] *om* VWN. frat*er*nite] fruyte (? frnyte) D. among] of alle RWM; of D; in alle A. þe(2)] *om* AWM.
177 And . . . fold] Ne no man*er* indulgence W. haue] habbe V; *om* DM. indulgence] indulgences N; Idulgences M. doublefold] Idoubled V. wel] *om* (*late corrector supplies*) H^2. þe] 3ou RDJNM. helpe] helþyn K.
178 ne wolde] nolde RDVNM; nold ChJ AKW. 3iue] 3if JA; 3eue DChV; yeve K; 3ef W; 3euy*n* M; gyue N. þi] 3oure JNM; þe RDK. patent] patentis M; pardoun VJ N; pate*n*t of þi *pardoun* RD; patent*es* of thy *par*done K; patentis of *par*don A. on] one DVKN; o RJW; oon H^2; a A. pye] pi3e Ch; pies NM; pece A; fleis R. hele] hole A.
179 Forþi] For þey D; þ*er*for JAN; For why K; þi *above line same hand* T. counseil] rede A. alle cristene] to Crist W. cristene] cristen men A. to] RDVJAKNM; we W; *om* TChH^2. cri3e] crie RChH^2VAKN; crien JM; cry D; crie al W. god] crist VK; *om* W.
180 And] And to W. modir] mother K. to] *om* DJW. be] be*n* RAM; beo V. mene] meane K. betwene] betwy*n*ne R.
181 3iue] 3if RJ; 3eue DChH^2; 3ef W; gif N; geve K; graunte M; of A. vs] his A. g*ra*ce] such grace W. er] or ChH^2; her er R; here or DJAKN. go] gon RVJM; gone K; goon A; passe W.
182–4 N *corrupts to* To do so þat Dowel reherse it att Dome.
182 Suche] Swyche J; Sweche A; Swichiche M. werkis] workes ChKW; wurkes D. werche] worche RDVKW; wirche Ch; wyrchin J; werkyn M. whiles] wyle3 (y *over erasure*) W; qwylis J; while RDChH^2A; while þat VM. ben] be Ch W; bene JK; bien H^2; beþ D.
183 aftir] reith at M. deþ] ded A. reherse] wyl reherce J; may reherce A; reherche M.
184 J *corrupts to* þat we wrowtyn wysely as he vs bad ⁊ tawte Amen. Þ*at*] *om* AK M. at þe] atte VM. day of] dredful day at M; dredful W. we . . . hi3te] wi*th* crist for to wone A. we] that we K. dede] ded Ch; dedyn M; dyde KW; dude R; duden V. he] he us V; we RDK. hi3te] higthe Ame*n* Ame*n* M; ou3te D; avghten K; au3the Amen R. **Here collation from** N **ceases:** *see above*, p. 12.

IX

Thus, yrobid in rosset, I rombide aboute
Al a somer sesoun for to seke dowel,
And fraynide ful ofte of folk *þat* I mette
ȝif any wiȝt wiste where dowel was at Inne;
And what man he miȝte be of many man I askide. 5
Was neu*ere* wiȝt as I wen[t]e *þat* me wisse couþe
Where þis lede lengide, lesse ne more,
Til it befel on a Friday two Freris I mette,
Maistris of þe meno*urs*, men of gret wyt.
I hailside hem hendely as I hadde ylernid, | 10
And p*re*iȝede hem, *pur charite*, er þei passide ferþ*ere*, *fol.* xlv *a*

1 Thus] us V. yrobid] yrobit H²; yrobed RDChVW; Roberd M. I rombide] Romed I V. I] *om* W. rombide] romyd UJAM; romed RDChKW; rome H². aboute] abowtyn JM; al aboute U.
2 Al] A A. sesoun] sesyn J; season K. for . . . wel] dowel to sechyn M. for] *om* W. seke] sekyn J; seche RV. do wel] sire dowell W.
3 And] and I RU; I AM. fraynide] fraynyd J; fraynede H²; frayned RUDCh KW; freinid M; freyned A; askede V. ful ofte] fele men M. ful] wel RU. ofte] oftyn J; faste K. of] at Ch. folk] Men V. mette] mete H².
4 *line om* V. any] eny U; ony RDJA. wiȝt] wyȝth D; with M; man J; *om* RA. where] qwer*e* J. dowel] he J.
5 *line om* V. what man] qwat J. he] it UW. be] ben J. of many] ȝif ony A. many] meny R. man(2)] men ChKM. I] *om* A. askide] askid H²JA; askede M; asked DChKW; frayned RU.
6 Was] was þ*er* R. wiȝt] wyȝth R; wyte A; man JM. wente] VAM; went JKW; wene TRUDChH². me wisse] wisse me M. wisse] wissyn J. couþe] cowde RUD AM; coulde K.
7 Where] Qwere J. þis] þat AM. lede] ladde DV; dowel M. lengide] lengede H²; lenged ChJK; lengith U; longeþ R; loggede VA; logged DW; duellit M. lesse] UJAKW; lasse RDVM; þe lesse TChH². ne] RUDVKWM; no J; noþer A; and þe Ch; ne þe TH².
8 befel] befil H²W; fel RVJA; was M. on] vpon A; me on K. two] to A; twey ChV. Freris] friers K. mette] mete M.
9 Maistris] Masters K. wyt] wittes V.
10 I(1)] Ich V; and y U; and R. hailside] haylsed RUDJ; halside H²; halsed ChKW; heylid A; heilede V; grette M. hem] hom *added marginally, another ink* W; hem wol M. hendely] hendyly U. I(2)] Ich V. ylernid] Ileorned V; lernyd UJAM; lerned RChKW; serued D.
11 p*re*iȝede] preiede V; p*re*yed U; p*re*yde H²M; preyd A; p*r*ayȝid J; prayed DChW; p*r*ayyd K; prayde R. hem] for hem (for *cancelled*) M; *om* DW. *pur charite*] besili A. *pur*] *par* VJ (? *pro* J); for RUD. *charite*] cherite R. er] or DChAK. þei] I K. passide ferþ*ere*] furre passede V. passide] passid H²; passede M; passed RDChJKW; went A. ferþ*ere*] forþ*er* DCh; farder K.

ȝif þei knewen any cuntre or costis aboute
'Where þat dowel dwelli[þ], do me to wisse'.
'Marie,' *qua*þ þe maistris, 'among vs he dwelliþ,
And euere haþ [as] I hope, & euere shal hereaftir.' 15
'*Contra*,' *qua*þ I as a clerk & comside to dispute:
'*Sepcies in die cadit iustus.*
Seue siþes, seiþ þe bok, [synneþ] þe riȝtful;
Ac whoso synneþ, I seiȝe, sertis, me þinkiþ
[Þat] dowel & do euele mowe not dwelle togid*ere*.
Ergo he nis not alwey at hom among ȝow Freris; 20
He is oþ*er*while elliswhere to wisse þe peple.'
'I shal seiȝe þe, my sone,' seide þe Frere þanne,
'How seue siþes þe sadde man synneþ on þe day;

12 *line om* W. ȝif] ȝef Ch; Yef K. þei] þai A; any K. knewen] knewyn JA; knewe RUVK; knew DChM. any] eny D; ony RUH²JAM; *om* V. cuntre . . . costis] cost or cuntre J. cuntre] contrey Ch; countrey K. or] oþ*er* U. costis] coustis A. aboute] abowtyn J.
13 Where] Qwer J. þat] *om* U. dwelliþ] dwelleþ DVW; duellyþ RUJK; duellit M; dwellid H²A; dwelled Ch; dwellide T. do] doþ RJ. wisse] witte W.
14 Marie] Be marie M. þe] þo R; þese U; a V. maistris] men*our*ys JA; men*ours* K; Menour VWM. among] amongs Ch; at hom *with* RU.
15 And] *om* A. haþ] hat M; hatȝ H². as] RUVJAKWM; *om* TDChH². I] Ich V. hope] howpe J. shal] scha (l *added by late corrector*) H². hereaftir] aftre WM.
16 as . . . clerk] þo M. as] *om* H². clerk] clek W. &] I A. comside] gan RA; began M; wold J. to] *om* J. dispute] disputen RU; disputyn JA; despute K; desputen D; dispuite V; spute W.
16α *line om* V. *cadit*] *cadet* R. *iustus*] *iustus &c* RD.
17 Seue] Seuen UChJ; Seuene RDH²A WM; Sevyn K. siþes] sythis AK; siþe DW; tyme M. seiþ . . . bok] on þe day JAM. seiþ] seiȝt H²; sayþ D; on þe day seyþ RU; on þe day saiþ W; a day seiþ V; a day saith K. synneþ] W; synnyth AK; syngnyt J; sungeþ V; sennyth M; falliþ TRUDChH². riȝtful] rihtful mon V; Riȝtwisse Ch.
18 *divided from following after* ille J. Ac] Bot Ch; and RUDVJAKW; *om* M. whoso] hoso A; hose V; ho þat J. synneþ] synnes R; sennyt M; singnyt J; sungeþ V. I] as I A; he RU. seiȝe] saie Ch; say DJ AM; seiþ U; seide V; sayde RW; said K. sertis] I wot he doth ille Certys J. me] as me VKWM. þinkiþ] þinkyt M; thinkes R.
19 Þat] RUDVAKWM; *om* TChH²J. do euele] I nylle M. euele] Evill K; yuele UH²J; vuele V. mowe . . . dwelle] ne duellit not M. mowe] may ChKW. not] nouȝt Ch. dwelle] stond A; stondyn J.
20 *Ergo*] Ego M. nis] is RUChJAKW. not] nouȝt DChH²; nouth M; nowt R. alwey . . . hom] at hom alwey AM. at hom] a tom V; *om* UW. among] with K. ȝow] ow V.
21 He is] But M. oþ*er*while . . . where] ellis oþer while A. oþ*er*while] oþerqwyle J; oþirwhilis M; or while V; som tyme U. where] qwer*e* J; whare U. wisse] wissen R; wyssyn JAM. peple] people K; puple A.
22 seiȝe] seye UV; sey RDChJ; sein M; say AKW. sone] sawe RU. seide] saide W; said K; seiþ U. þanne] þenne UV.
23 seue] seuen UChVJ; seuene DH²WM; seuyn AK; vij R. siþes] siþe DH². þe . . . day] on þe day þe sadde man synnes RU. man] mon V. synneþ] synnetȝ H²; synned Ch; sennyt M; sungeþ V. on þe] in a V.

Be a forebisene,' q*ua*þ þe Frere, 'I shal þe faire shewen:
Let bringe a man in a bot amydde a brood watir; 25
Þe wynd, ⁊ þe watir, ⁊ þe waggyng of þe boot,
Makeþ þe man many tymes to falle ⁊ to stande.
For stande he neu*ere* so stif he stumbliþ in þe waggyng,
And ȝet is he sauf ⁊ sound, ⁊ so hym behouiþ.
For ȝif he ne arise þe raþ*ere* ⁊ [rauȝte þe stere], 30
Þe wynd wolde wiþ þe watir þe boot ou*er*þrowe.
Þ*ere* were þe manis lif lost for lacchesse of hymselue.
Riȝt þus [it] fariþ,' q*ua*þ þe Frere, 'be folk here on erþe.
Þe watir is liknid to þe world þ*at* waniþ ⁊ waxiþ;
Þe goodis of þis ground be lik þe grete wawes, 35

24 Be a forebisene] ȝif þou wilt suffir J. a] on M; *om* VW. forebisene] forbysen H^2W; forbyse D; forebysne RU; forbesene A; forbesen Ch; ensau*m*ple VM. q*ua*þ] seide DV; seyd J. Frere] frier K. faire] feire V. shewen] shewe RUDVAKW; schew J.
25 Let] lat ChJA; Late W. bringe] bryngyn J. man] Mon V. in] to D. amydde] amydd*es* RU; amyddys J; in myddis A; on Ch; in D. a(3)] the H^2. brood watir] brok watur A.
26 *line om* J. Þe] And þe VKW. wynd] wint V. watir] wawes KW. þe(3)] *om* K. waggyng . . . boot] wawes eke H^2. waggyng] waggeng R; waggig M.
27 Makeþ] Maketȝ H^2; Maky*n* M; Makis U; It makys J. þe . . . tymes] many tyme þe man U. þe] a JAM. man] Mon V. many] Mony V; *the* n *lacking one minim* A. tymes] tyme RVWM. falle] fallen H^2K; fallyn JAM; stomble V. stande] stonde ChA; stondyn JM; stomble KW; falle V.
28 For] But W. stande] stonde RUChH^2VM; stond JKW. stif] fast AM. stumbliþ] stumblit M; stu*m*bleþ RChV; stomblitȝ H^2; stombleþ DW; stumbelyth J; stombelith K; stomelith A. waggyng] wawyng K.
29 ȝet] ȝit RUChVJAWM. is he] he is RDH^2VJAK. sauf] saf RDChH^2M; safe K; saue A; saaf V; both hole J. ⁊ sound] *om* UW. sound] sounid M. behouiþ] behouyt M; byhoues R.
30 For] and U. ȝif] ȝef Ch. arise] rise VJ; rese A; rose K; ros ChW. þe] *om* RA. raþere] rayer M. rauȝte . . . stere] raughte þe stere U; rawte þe stere J; raught þe sterne WM; rauȝthe þe sterne R; rowght the sterne K; rauhte to þe steorne V; ȝede to þe sterne A; ariȝt stere D; ariȝt sterede T; ariȝt sterid H^2; riȝt stired Ch.
31 wynd] wynt V. wolde wiþ] ⁊ A. wolde] wilde J. ou*er*þrowe] ou*er*þrowȝe Ch; ouyrthrow*ith* A; ou*er*torne H^2.
32 Þere] þanne U. were] weore V; with H^2. manis] Monnes V. lost] ylost RV; Iloost M. for] þorw V. lacchesse] laches W; lachisse K; lacchans A; sleuþe V. selue] selue*n* M.
33 Riȝt] Rit J; Reith M; *om* A. it fariþ] fareþ hit Ch. it] hit RUDVJAKWM; *om* TH^2. fariþ] farit M. be] *with* R. folk] men A. here on] of þis AW. on] in U. erþe] eorþe V; erde A.
34 liknid] likned DW; liknet V; lykened AK; lekened Ch; lyk RU. to] here to K. þe] þis RAK. world] word R; werld JA. þat] and Ch. waniþ ⁊ waxiþ] waxith ⁊ wanyth A; waxeth and wanyeth U; waxeþ and wanyes R. waniþ] wanieþ ChH^2; wanyit M; wonieþ V. waxiþ] waxit H^2; wexit M.
35 Þe] þes J. of] on DChJW; in V. þis] þe RDChWM. ground] world V. be] ben ChVAK; beþ RW; bet M; arn U. lik] lykened A; liknyd M; lyknyth J. þe(2)] þis V; to þe RUDAW; to þes J; to ChM. grete] *om* RUDJA.

Þ*at* as wyndis & watris wa[l]wen aboute;
Þe boot is lik[nid] to þe body þ*at* britel is of kynde,
Þ*at* þoruȝ þe fend, & þe flessh, & þe false world,
Synnes þe sad man seuene [siþes] in þe day.
Ac dedly synne doþ he nouȝt, for dowel hym helpiþ, 40
Þ*at* is charite þe champiou*n*, chief helpe aȝens synne.
For he strengþeþ þe to stonde & steriþ þi soule
Þat, þeiȝ þi body bowe as bot doþ in þe watir,
Ay is þi soule sauf but þou þiself wilt
Folewe þi flesshis wil & þe fendis aftir, 45
And don dedly synne & drenche þiseluen.
God wile suffre þe to deiȝe so for þiself hast þe maistrie.'

36 Þ*at*] and RU; Riht V; *om* A. as] as þe W; þe M. wyndis] wynde ChJW. &] and þe WM. watris] water ChW; wawis AM. walwen] walwyn J; walweth KW; walwit M; waleweþ V; walkyn A; wawen TDChH²; wawes RU. aboute] abouty*n* M.
37 liknid] lyknyd J; liknet V; likened A; liken H²; leked Ch; lik TRUDKWM. to] til Ch. þe] þi J. britel] bretel Ch; Brutel V; bruttel K; brotel R; brotil WM; brisel J; brechel A. kynde] kuynde V.
38 Þ*at*] and RV. þoruȝ] thoru H²; þorow ChJA; þurw UV; þourgth M; þourȝt D; þrow W; thrugh K; þow R. þe(1) . . . flessh] þin flesch & þy*n* fend M. þe(2)] þi J; his ChV. þe(3)] þys M. world] werlde J; word RM; werd A.
39 Synnes] Synneþ UChH²W; Synnyth JAK; Senneþ D; Sennyt M; Sungeþ V; syþe*n* R. sad man] sadde Mon V; fals man M. seuene . . . day] on þe day seuen sythys J. siþes] sithes RUChVKW; syþis DAM; tymes TH². in] on RUDAKWM.
40 Ac] Bot ChVKWM; *om* A. synne] su*n*ne V. doþ he] he doth A. doþ] deoth M. he nouȝt] nat he Ch. nouȝt] nout A; not RVM; none K. helpiþ] helpit AM.
41 *divided from following after* alle RU. Þat] That RUVJAM; And þat TDChH² KW. is] *om* H². þe] *om* D. champiou*n*] champlioun A; chaunpliou*n* M; chapma*n* D. helpe] to helpe D; *om* JAK. aȝens] ayenst K; aȝen Ch; aȝeyn VJ; ageyne AM; of alle Aȝens U; of alle aȝen R; *om* D. synne] sunne V; vij RM; *om* D.
42 *line om* A. For . . . þe] *om* RU. streng-þeþ] strengthitȝ (g *above line same ink*) H²; strengþes Ch; strengþe D; strenthes K; strengkyth J; strengit M; streyngheth W. to] for to U; *om* H². stonde] stondy*n* M; synne U. &] he RUV. steriþ] steryȝt R; stireth UKW; stires Ch; stureþ V; helpit M. þi] þe RUD. soule] saule aȝen synne D.
43 *line om* A. Þat] For DCh; *om* JK. þeiȝ] þeiȝe U; þey RH²M; þouȝ DK; þow ChJW; þauȝ V. þi] þe RUD. bot] a bot RUVJW; þe boot M. doþ] *om* VM. in] on RK. þe] a J; *om* DChKW.
44 Ay] Euer VM. is] es J. þi] the RD. soule] sawle D. sauf] saue JA; saf RDCh M; saff H²; safe K; saaf V. þ*ou*] ȝif þu A; ȝif V; ȝef Ch; *om* U. þiself] *om* A. wilt] wilte K; will W; wille JAM; wolt UCh; wolle V.
45 Folewe] Folowe K; Folow Ch; Folowyn D; Folwe RUA; Folwen W; Folwyn J; Fouli*n* M. þi . . . wil] þe wil of þi flesche A. flesshis] flechis J; Flessh DW; fleschly RK. fendis] fend RUH²JKM.
46 don] do RUChVAM; done K; doon D. synne] sunne V. drenche] drenchen DK; drenchin J; drenge H². seluen] selue DH²JAM; self ChW; soule RUK.
47 wile suffre] sufferith A; suffrit M. wile] wol UChV; woll K. suffre] suffrin J. þe to] þe VK; þou W. deiȝe] deyȝin J; deye RD; dey U; deyn A; die ChVK WM. so] *om* UD. þiself] þou RUV. þi] þe A. self] selue J; seluy*n* M. hast . . . maistrie] is maiste*r* M; art þin owne Mayster V. hast] hath JK; to haue A. maistrie] mastrye K. *Here* M *adds a line: see above*, p. 49.

'I haue no kynde knowyng,' q*ua*þ I, 'to conseyue þi wordis,
Ac ȝif I may lyuen & loken I shal go lerne bet*ere*.
I bekenne [ȝow] crist þ*at* on þe crois deiȝede.' 50
And þei seide, 'þe same saue þe fro myschaunce,
And [g]iue þe g*ra*ce on þis erþe in good lif to ende'.
Þus I wente wydewhere dowel to seken,
[And] as I wente be a wode, walkyng myn one,
Blisse of þe briddis made me abide, | 55
And vndir a lynde vpon a launde lenide I me a stounde *fol.* xlv *b*
To lerne þe laies þ*at* louely [foulis] maden.
Blisse of þ[e] briddis brouȝte me a slepe;
Þe m*er*ueilleste metyng mette me þanne
Þ*at* euer*e* dremide driȝt in doute, as I wene. 60

48 *line om* A. kynde] ke*n*de M; kend Ch. q*ua*þ I] *om* U. to . . . þi] to to co*n*seyue*n* þys M.
49 *line om* A. Ac] But UChVKWM; And R. ȝif] ȝef Ch. lyuen] lyfuen J; lyue RUK; leue DChW; go liue*n* M. loken] lokyn J; loke RUDH²W. shal] wil J; wol U. go] *om* J. lerne] lern Ch; lernyn J; lere R. bet*ere*] ferþer R.
50 bekenne] beotake V. ȝow] ChJ; ȝou to V; þe TRUDH²KW; þe to AM. þe] *om* VJAW. crois] cros RDChH²AK WM. deiȝede] deyȝid J; deyde RUH²M; deyd A; diȝede V; diede W; died Ch; dyyd K; dyde D.
51 þei seide] eke W. þei] þai A; thay K; þe M; he D; I Ch. seide] seiden V; seydyn JM; saide DCh; saiden K. same] same God V. þe] ȝow Ch. myschaunce] myscheff K.
52 giue] gif RW; geve K; ȝiue TUV; ȝif DH²JA; ȝeue M; ȝef Ch. þe] ȝe D; *om* H². on þis] vppon V. erþe] erde A; grou*n*de VK. in] on M. ende] endy*n* M.
53 wyde] wyden V. where] whare U; qwer*e* J; for A. dowel] *sere* dowel M. seken] sekyn JA; seke Ch; sechen UK; seche RVWM.
54 *line om* A. And] RUH²VJKWM; *om* TDCh. as] als J. walkyng] wandryg M. myn one] my one M; me one K; me alone U; alone ChJ.
55 *line om* A. Blisse] The blysse W. þe] thise H². briddis] birdes ChK; p*r*iddis J. made] madene R. me] me to RV. abide] vnbyde J.
56 *line om* J. And vndir] Vpon A. a(1)] *om* RUD. vpon] on DW; in A. lenide] lenyd AK; lenede H²; lened RDChW; leonede V; ylened U; lend M. I] *om* U. me] *om* DVAKW.
57 *line om* J. To] For to V. lerne] leorne V; leren W; lyþen RU; listen K; lystyn A; lestny*n* M. þe] *om* Ch. þat] þat þe AK; þe RUWM. louely] *om* A. foulis] AM; foules VKW; briddis TRUDH²; birdes Ch. maden] madyn RA.
58 J *corrupts to* And wi*th* þe myrthe of her mowthe made me to slepyn. Blisse] The blysse A. þe] RUDChH²VAKM; þise T; þis W. briddis] birdes ChKW. brouȝte] broughten UV; brout A. a] on UDH²W. slepe] sclepe K; *after cancelled* me D.
59 merueilleste] m*er*ueylist H²; meruei-louste K; Meruiloste V; meruelest Ch; meruelyest A; meruelyouste R; m*er*ue-lousest J; maruoyllest D; most merueillous W; m*er*ueilouerste M. me] I me VJM; I A. þanne] þenne UV.
60 dremide . . . doute] dryȝt in doute drempte RU. dremide] dremyd DH²JA KM; dremede V; dremed ChW. driȝt] wyth A; I ȝit J; y dyd D; þing M. doute] drecchynge V; þoght W; drouth A; drougthe M; dede K. as] a W; *om* V.

A muchel man, me þouȝte, lik to myselue,
Com & callide me be my kynde name.
'What art þou,' *quaþ* I þo, 'þ*at* my name knowist?'
'Þ*at* þou wost wel,' *quaþ* he, '& no wiȝt bet*ere*.'
'Wot ich?' *quaþ* I; 'who art þou?' 'þouȝt,' seide he þanne. 65
'I haue sewide þe seue*n* ȝer; seiȝe þou me no raþ*ere*?'
'Art þou þouȝt, þo?' *quaþ* I; 'þou couþest me telle
Where dowel dwelliþ, & do me to wisse.'
'Dowel,' *quaþ* he, '& dobet, & dobest þe þridde,
Arn þre faire v*er*tues, & ben not f[e]r to fynde. 70
Whoso is mek of his mouþ, mylde of his speche,
Trewe of his tunge & of his two handis,

61 muchel] Muche VW; much Ch; moche D; michel JKM; meche A; mykil U; meke R. man] Mon V. þouȝte] þouȝþe R; þougthe M; þouth A; thowte J; þough W. lik] liche JKW. my] me K. selue] selue*n* RVK.
62 Com] Cam JM. callide] callid JAK; called DChW; calde RM; clepede V. kynde] kuynde V; kene M; righte UR ChH²AW; propir J. name] nome V; dame U.
63 What] Qwat J. þo] *om* RUDVAKM. þat] that thus K. name] nome V. knowist] konnest K.
64 Þat] *om* DAM. þou wost] wost þou RUJ wost] wotest K; *om* H². wel] wel Inow M; wel þy self D; *om* J. he] he þo J. no] no*n* M. wiȝt] wyȝth RD; bodi V; man AM.
65–8 *divided after* þanne—ȝere—I W.
65 Wot . . . I] I schuld wetyn M. Wot] woot UK; wost A. ich] icche A; I RUChVJ; q*uod* ych D. quaþ . . . þou] what þu art quot I A. who] ho ChV; hoo D; what W; *om* J. art þou] þou art DM. þouȝt . . . þanne] þanne Thoght q*uod* he W. þouȝt] thoutȝ R; thouth AM; thout J; þhouȝte V; y þouȝt D. seide . . . þanne] þan he seyde R. seide] I me seide V; *small* I *above line before* seide T. he] I VJ. þanne] þenne UV.
66 I] ȝe I J. sewide] sewyd H²AK; sewed DCh; suwyd J; suwed V; swyed U; s*er*uid M; s*er*ued RW. þe] þe þis RUD VW; the thes K; þe al þis A. ȝer] yer*es* K. seiȝe] seiȝ H²; seye UJ; sey RAM; se ChV; saw D; seest K; And saw W. þou] ȝe (*as one word with preceding*) V. no] non H²M. raþere] raye A.
67 Art] Ert Ch. þouȝt] þouth A; thout RJ; youth M. þo . . . I] q*uod* I þo VJM. þo] *om* RChAW. I] he U. þou couþest] coudest þou U; canst þu A; canstow J; const þou V; kant þou M. þou] þow hit Ch. couþest] coudest RDK. me telle] telle me W. me] ouht me J.
68 Where] Qwere J; wher þat VK. dwelliþ] dwellit H²AM. & . . . to] I preye þou me M. &] *om* UVJA.
69 quaþ he] *om* J. &(1) . . . dobest] dobest & dobet A. dobet] dobett *same hand above cancelled* dobeste K. þridde] þredde W; thirde K.
70 Arn] Arne JK; are RD; Ben U; Beoþ V. þre] þreo V. & ben] *om* J. ben] be DH²A; beþ RW; betȝ M; beoþ V. not] nouȝt H²; nouth J; noght U; nauȝt Ch. fer] RUDChVWM; ferre J; far K; for TH²; *om* A.
71 Whoso] Hoso JA; Who þat M; He V. is] be A. mek] milde M. mouþ] mouȝt H². mylde] and mylde RCh; meke M; & meke A.
72 *line om* A; *divided from following after* laboure W. Trewe] Treuthe H². his(1)] *om* R. of(2)] *om* W. two] tweie M. handis] hondes VW.

And þoruȝ his labo*ur* or his lond his liflode wynneþ,
Trusty of his tailende, takiþ but his owene,
And [is] nouȝt drunkelewe ne deyno*us*, dowel hym folewiþ. 75
Dobet þus doþ, ac he doþ muche more.
He is as louȝ as a lomb, louelich of speche,
Whiles he haþ ouȝt of his owene he helpiþ þ*er*e nede is;
Þe bagges & þe [bi]gerdlis, he haþ broken hem alle
Þat þe Erl auerous hadde, or his eires, 80
And wiþ mammones money he haþ mad hym frendis,
And is ronne to religioun, & haþ rendrit þe bible,
And p*re*chiþ þe peple seint poulis wordis:
Libenter suffert[*is*] &*c*.

73 *line om* A. þoruȝ] thoru H[2]; thorow J; þurw U; þorw R; þourȝt D; þourth M; bi V; trewe of W. his(1)] þe RUCh. or] or bi VK; Or þrow W; of RUChM. lond] land M; lond*es* K; honde Ch; hondes W; hand*es* RU. wynneþ] wy*n*nyt M; he wynnyth K.
74 *line om* UA. Trusty] Tristy Ch; And trusti VKW; And trwsty D; and tr*o*sty J; and trost R; Is trust M. of his] is of W; *twice* M. takiþ] & takyth J; and takeþ ChK; ne takyt M.
75 *line om* A. is] RUVJKWM; *om* TD ChH[2]. nouȝt] not RVKWM. drunkelewe] drunkelew H[2]; dronkeleuh V; dronklowe W; dronkloy K; drunlew J; dronken DM. ne] no Ch. deyno*us*] denyous R; dinous M; deignous of speche U. dowel . . . folewiþ] *om* U. folewiþ] folowyth K; foloweþ Ch; folwyþ RJ; folwit M; folweþ W; folewewith H[2].
76 *line om* UA. þus doþ] doþ þus VJKW; dot þus M. ac] bote VKWM; & J; *om* R. he] *om* J. doþ(2)] dotȝ M. muche] mochell K; mychel J; mechel M.
77 *line om* UA. as(1)] a H[2]; *om* DM. louȝ] louh V; lowe ChJKW; low RM; lowelich D. louelich] and louelich Ch; and louely R; louechiliche (chi *cancelled*) H[2].
78 Whiles] while UVK; whil RAM; Qwyl J. haþ] hat M. ouȝt] outh J; out M; *om* RUA. his] *om* D. owene] owyn RA. he(2)] *om* ChA. helpiþ] helpit AM; helpeth DChVW; delyþ RU. þere . . . is] þe nede A; the nedye K; þerwiþ many (many *over erasure of* (?) nedy) W. nede] neod V; most nede RU.
79 *line om* A. Þe . . . bigerdlis] To bidderis & beggeris M. bagges] bagge W. &] of R. bigerdlis] bygirdles U; bigerdelys R; bygerdels W; Bigirdelis ChJ; Bigurdeles VK; breigerdlis T; breigirdelis H[2]; begg*er* doles D. haþ] hat M; hatȝ H[2]. broken hem] hem broken V. broken] brokyn JM; broke RChW. hem] them K; *om* J.
80 Þat] The D. þe] eu*er* J; *om* RM. Erl] *om* VM. auerous] auarous RD; auarouse man M; auarice A; aueris J. hadde] hedde V. or] or eny of V; or ony of A; and RU. eires] eiȝers Ch; heires VK.
81 And] *om* A. wiþ] *om* D. mammones] ma*m*monas RVW; ma*m*moneis K; mammonaes J; ma*m*monays D; mamoynes Ch; mani mannis M. money] mone RUJ; mony M; monoye W. he] *om* UVA. haþ] hatȝ H[2]; had A; *om* M. mad] maked V. hym] hem W.
82 And] And he W; He A. is] his Ch. ronne] Ronnen VW; ronnyn AM; ru*n*nyn J. to] to þe R; into UDVJW. religioun] relygious R; religious (? religions) A. haþ] hatȝ H[2]; *om* AM. rendrit] rendrid UDM; re*n*dred RChW; Rendret V; renderid JK; renderith A. þe bible] is bille A.
83 *run together with following* ChH[2]VWM. p*re*chiþ] prechit AKM; prechitȝ H[2]; precheþ RDChVW. peple] people K; puple A. seint] sen A; saynt K.
83α *line om* UJ. *suffertis*] RVAKW; *sufferte* TDChH[2]; *suffe*:: M. &*c*] *insipientes* &*c* K; *insipientes* M; *om* ChV.

[ȝ]e wise suffriþ þe vnwise *with* ȝow to libbe,
And wiþ glad wil doþ hem good for so god [hiȝte]. 85
Dobest is aboue hem boþe ⁊ beriþ a bisshopis croce;
Is hokid at þ*at* on ende to holde men in good lif.
A pik is in þat potent to pungen adoun þe wykkide,
Þat waiten any wikkidnesse dowel to tenen.
And as dowel ⁊ dobet dede hem to vndirstonde, 90
Þei han crounide o king to kepe hem alle,
Þat ȝif dowel ⁊ dobet dede aȝens dobest
And were vnbuxum at his bidding, and bold to don ille,
Þanne shulde þe kyng come ⁊ casten hem in p*re*sou*n*,
And putten hem þ*er*e in pen*au*nce wiþoute pite or g*ra*ce, 95

84 ȝe] UVJM; Ye K; The TRDChH^{2}A W. suffriþ] suffrit M; suffreþ UDChW; suffretȝ R; sufferith JA; soffreþ V; suffre K. þe] *om* KM. ȝow] ow V. to] for to RUVJAKWM. libbe] leue A; dwelle K.
85 And] *om* JM. wiþ] *om* D. glad] good UAM. doþ] do RUChAK. hem] hym W. for] *om* AM. so god] god so W. so] *om* K. god] hem god J; our lord U. hiȝte] highte U; hyhte J; hi*m* hyȝte R; hem hiȝte D; himself hiȝte VWM; hymselfe hite A; hymself hete K; bit hym TH^2; biddiþ hym Ch.
86 aboue] abouen ChWM; abouyn JA. hem] *om* VJKWM. boþe] bothyn J; boþn M. ⁊] *om* JA. beriþ] berit M; beret D; *om* J. bisshopis] Busschopes VA. croce] crois ChW.
87 Is] His D; Yt is K; *om* RUW. hokid] hokit H^2; hoked DChK; hoket V; Ihokid U; yhoked RW. at þat] atte V. þat] þe UChJAKM. on] one K; ton UA; *om* VJ. ende] hende M. to . . . lif] in godelyfe men to holdyn J. holde] holden UV; holdi*n* M. men] hem U; hi*m* RV. in] to Ch.
88 *line om* A. pik] poynt W. is] *om* RJ WM. in] *om* H^2. þat] þe RUVKWM; þo D. potent] ende V. pungen] punge ChV; punchin J; pynge KW; pynche U; pycche R; puttyn M; put D. adoun] down KW. þe] *om* R.
89 *line om* A. waiten] waytyn JM; wayte DW; wayteth K; haunteþ RU. any] eny RV; ony UDH^2; ay Ch. wikkidnesse] wikkedly Ch. tenen] tenyn M; tene RU DChJ; teone V.
90 dede] ded Ch; dedyn A; dydyn J; dyddyn K; dude D; duden V; don RH^2; doþ U. hem] *corrected from* hym K; hi*m* RUDChJAWM. to] *om* DJAM. vndirstonde] vnderstondyn J; vnderstande W.
91 Þei] Thay AKW; He J. han] haue RUDAKW; hath J. crounide] crounid H^2; crouned RDChKW; corounyd AM; corouned U; ICorouned VJ. o] on ChW; one K; a RUDH^{2}VJAM. kepe] kepen UDChH^{2}VKW; kepin RJAM.
92 Þat] and RUChJM; *om* A. ȝif] ȝef Ch. ⁊] or DVAKM. dede] dedyn RChM; dide UW; dyden K; dydyn J; dude V; weryn A. aȝens] aȝenst R; aȝen UChW; aȝeyn VJA; ageyn KM.
93 *line om* VA. And] *om* M. were] weren Ch; weryn J; weron K; wern to hi*m* M. at . . . bidding] *om* M. and] or M. don] do H^{2}K.
94 Þanne] Þa*n*ne URJAM; þen V; Þat þanne TDChH^{2}KW. shulde . . . kyng] þe king shulde RU. come . . . p*re*sou*n*] in prysou*n* hi*m* caste M. come] comen V; comyn JA. casten] castyn J; caste RDH^{2}A; cast ChK; don W. hem] hi*m* H^{2}W. p*re*sou*n*] p*ri*sou*n* RUDVKW; Irnys J.
95 putten] puttyn J; putte RUW; putt K; put DChM; puiten V; cast (c *badly formed*) A. hem] them K; him VM. þere] *om* UAM. pen*au*nce] prisone U. wiþoute] w*i*thoute*n* V; w*i*thoutyn JM. pite or] pete or A; any M; ony J.

But dobest bede for hem abide þere for euere.
Þus dowel, ⁊ dobet, ⁊ dobest þe þridde,
Corounid on to be kyng ⁊ be h[ere] counseil werchen,
And rewele þe reaum be red of hem alle,
And oþere wise ⁊ ellis nouȝt but as þei þre assent[e].' | 100
I þankide þouȝt þo þat he me so tauȝte. *fol.* xlvj *a*
'Ac ȝet sauouriþ me nouȝt þi segging, so me god helpe;
More kynde knowyng I coueyte to lere,
How dowel, dobet ⁊ dobest don on þis erþe.'
'But wyt can wisse þe,' quaþ þouȝt, 'where þo þre dwellen, 105
Ellis wot no man þat now is o lyue.'

96 But] but ȝif RVKW; ⁊ but ȝif UJ. bede] beede V; bid ChK; bidde H^2JM; þe þredde bidde W; prey R. hem] him VWM. abide] þei abide Ch; abide shal he W; þei bedyn A; vnbydyn J.
97 Here H^3 resumes. Þus] Þan H^3. dowel] Dewel W. ⁊(1)] *om* KWH^3. þridde] þredde ChWH^3; þirde DK.
98 Corounid] Corouned U; crouned RCh KW; Crounede V; Crownedyn J; Croune D; Xul corond H^3. on] one JKW; oon H^2; hym A. be(1)] ben JM; beo V. ⁊] *om* J. be(2) . . . werchen] worche by hyre conseill W. be(2)] *om* A. here] DAM; her J; heor V; theire K; his TRU ChH^2H^3. werchen] werche DAMH^3; worche VK; wurche U; wirchen Ch; to wyrche J; wrouȝthe R.
99 *divided from following after* wise W. rewele] reule UDH^2AW; Rule VK; rewlen R; rewlyn JH^3; Reulin M; rewled Ch. þe] that H^2. reaum] reame DV; reume W; rewme RUJH^3; reme ChH^2AM; realme K. be] for U. red] reed U; reule A.
100 *line om* A. oþere] non oþer WM. ⁊] ne JWM; or D; not H^3; *om* VK. nouȝt] not RUVW; *om* JM. as] *om* W. þei] þai W; þese U. þre] þreo V. assente] URH^2; assenten V; assentyn H^3; assenteþ D; assentide T; assented ChK; asentedyn M; assended W; acordene J.
101 þankide] þankid UJAH^3; þanked RDChH^2KWM; þonkede V. þouȝt] þouȝth R; þouth AMH^3; thowte J; him feire V. þo] so U. þat] so þat R; *om* V. he] *om* Ch. so] so had H^3; *om* R. tauȝte] tauȝthe R; tauthe M; tauth A; taute J; taght W.
102 Ac] Bot ChVKW; and RUAMH^3. ȝet] ȝit RUVJAM; *om* WH^3. sauouriþ] sauoureþ RU; sauereþ ChVW; sauerid A; sauourde M; sauourd H^3; saide D. me nouȝt] not me V. me] it H^3; ous D. nouȝt] not RUAKWM. þi] hys H^3; in A. segging] siggynge UVWM; sayyng KH^3; seying J; seyng A; seggenges D. so] as so A.
103 *line om* A. kynde] kuynde V; kende D. coueyte] couet J; coueitid M. lere] lerne RUDJKWH^3; here V.
104 dowel] dowel and RUChH^2VAMH^3. dobet ⁊ dobest] dobest ⁊ dobet A; dobet U; ⁊ his feris J. don] done JK; beþ V. on] in H^3. þis] þe A; *om* VMH^3. erþe] eorþe V; erde A.
105 But] *om* H^3. wyt] wt M. can] con VJ; conne WM; kunne U; counne R; *om* A. wisse] wissyn J. þe] *om* Ch. quaþ] *om* RU. þouȝt] þouth AM; thout JH^3. where] whare U; qwere JH^3. þo] þey D; þes Ch; þese A; þeos V; þat þei W. þre] *om* AW. dwellen] dwellyn JA; dwelle DWH^3; dwelleþ V; duellyn RCh; dullin M.
106 wot] woot UH^2; not V; wot I DA H^3; þer can J. no] non (*twice*) M. man] Mon V. now] yit D. o] on RUDH^2 JAKWH^3; a ChVM. lyue] lyfe A; erthe R; *after cancelled* lyfe J.

Þou3t ⁊ I þus þre dayes we 3eden,
Disputyng on dowel day aftir oþ*er*,
Ac er we ywar were wiþ wyt gonne we mete.
He was long ⁊ lene, lyk to non oþ*er*, 110
Was no pride on his app*ar*ail ne no pou*er*t noþ*er*,
Sad of his semblaunt ⁊ of a softe speche,
I durste meue no mat*er* to make hym to iangle,
But as I bad þou3t þo be mene betwene,
To putte forþ sum p*ur*pos [to] p*ro*uen hise wittes. 115
Þanne þou3t, in þ*at* tyme, seide þis wordis:
'Where þ*at* dowel, ⁊ dobet, ⁊ dobest beþ in londe,
Here is wil wolde wyte 3if wit couþe hym teche.'

107 *run together with following* JAMH^3. þou3t] Thouth AMH^3; þus þou3t V; þ*us* thowt J. þus] also V; þese A; *om* JMH^3. þre . . . 3eden] we*n*te iij dayis H^3. þre dayes] þroly V. we] *om* JAWM. 3eden] 3edyn JA; 3ede RU; eodem V; *om* M.
108 *line om* Ch. Disputyng . . . dowel] *om* M. on] of UW; wi*th* H^3. day . . . oþ*er*] *om* J. aftir] be AM. oþ*er*] day A.
109 *line om* H^3. Ac] Bot Ch; And RUD VJKW; wentyn ⁊ M; *om* A. er] or DChH^{2}A; ar K. ywar were] wer*e* war UA; weoren war V; wyst J; war werey D. ywar] war RChKWM. were] wern M; ware K. wiþ] wit M; *om* RU. wyt] wyth M; wtite A. gonne we] we gu*n*ne J. gonne] gan RDChKWM; conne V. mete] meten K; metyn JM; meeten V.
110 He] le R. long] lond A. lene] lhene U. lyk . . . oþ*er*] to loken on ful symple V. lyk] lyche J; and lyk WM; ⁊ lyik H^3.
111 *line om* RUV; *run together with following* Ch. Was] þer was J. no] no*n* M. on] In ChJAKWMH^3. his] *om* M. app*ar*ail] aperele A; parayle DJM. ne . . . noþ*er*] *om* Ch. ne] *om* MH^3. no(2)] *om* DJAKW. pou*er*t] pouerte DJW; povertie K. noþ*er*] nouþer W; neyther K; neythir*e* JH^3; neþer A; neire M.
112 *line om* A. Sad . . . semblaunt] *om* Ch. his] *om* H^3. semblaunt] sembland R; semelaunt H^{2}H^3; semland J. of a softe] soft of his W; seft of his M. a] *om* ChVJ KH^3. softe] sad RU.
113 I] RUDVAKWMH^3; and I J; I ne TChH^2. durste] drost H^3. meue] meven M; meuy*n* J; moue UK; mene W. no] no*n* M. mat*er*] matir MH^3; mateere V; matiere U. to . . . hym] wi*th* hi*m* for J. make] maken K; makyn AM. hym to] hem W.
114 *line om* A. as] *om* H^3. I . . . þou3t] þou3t bad V. bad] badde H^2; hadde M. þou3t] þouth M; thowt JH^3. be] to be UM; to beo V. mene] meane K; me U. betwene] betwenyn J; bytwynne R.
115 To] and JM; 3if A. putte] puttyn J; pote H^3; put I A. sum] a A; *om* J. to] RUChH^{2}VAKW; ⁊ TDJMH^3. p*ro*uen] prouyn JH^3; p*ro*ve K; preuen VH^2; preuyn A. wittes] witte A.
116 Þanne] þe*n*ne V. þou3t] þou3th R; þouth AMH^3; thowt J; þaght W; i H^2. in . . . tyme] þan W. in] *om* V. seide] sayde RW; said K; seydyn J. þis] þise M; þes ChJK; þese RUDH^{2}AWH^3; þeose V.
117 Where] Qwere JH^3. þat] *om* DVJA MH^3. ⁊(1)] or J; *om* DKH^3. ⁊(2)] or J. beþ] beoþ V; ben DAWMH^3; be ChJ; bien H^2; byn K; wer*e* RU. in] in þis AW; *om* Ch.
118 Here . . . wolde] To hery*n* hys wytt wold I H^3; To heryn fawen woldy M. Here is] His A; Oure V. is] his RUCh. wil] wille UChH^{2}VJ; will KW. wolde] wilde fayne J. wyte] wete ChW; wetyn M; Iwite RU; Iwiten V; Iwetyn A; *om* H^3. 3if] 3ef Ch. couþe] coude RUDMH^3; coudd A; could K. hym] me A; *om* RD VKMH^3. teche] techen VA; techi*n* M.

X

'Sire dowel dwelliþ,' quaþ wyt, 'nouȝt a day hennes,
In a castel þ*at* kynde made of foure skenis þinges.
Of erþe & eir it is mad, medlit togid*er*is;
Wiþ wynd & wiþ watir wi[tti]liche enioynede.
Kynde haþ closid þ*er*einne, craftily wiþalle, 5
A le*m*man þ*at* he louiþ lik to hymselue.
Anima he[o] ha[tte]; to hire [haþ] enuye
A proud prikere of Fraunce, *Princeps huius mundi*,
And wolde wynne hire awey w*ith* wyles ȝif he miȝte.
Ac kynde knowiþ [þis] wel and kepiþ hire þe bet*er*e, 10

1 Sire] Sere A. dwelliþ . . . wyt] q*uod* witte dwellith KW. dwelliþ] dwellyt H^3M; dwelliȝ H^2; dwelleþ RDV; duellith Ch; *om* U. nouȝt] nouth H^3; not RVJAKWM. a] on Ch. day] myle K. hennes] henne A.
2 þat] of VW. kynde] kuynde V; kende DChA. made] Imad V; hath made J. of] rit of J. foure] *om* A. skenis] skynnys M; skynnes H^2; ke*n*nys R; kynnes Ch; kene H^3; kyn W; kynne UK; ku*n*ne V; kynde A; man*er* D; *om* J. þinges] thyng*us* H^3.
3 erþe & eir] eir of erthe M. erþe] herde A. &] & of UChH^2A; of RH^3. eir] eyir H^3; heyre A. it is] is hit DKW. medlit] medlid H^2J; medled RDChW; meddlid M; medelid AKH^3; ymedled U; Imedelet V.
4 Wiþ] wit M. wynd] wynt V. wiþ(2)] *om* DJW. wittiliche enioynede] enioyned wittily R. wittiliche] wittylych DKWM; wittyly UJ; wittely A; witlich Ch; ful wittiliche V; wyttyrly H^3; wiȝtliche TH^2. enioynede] enioyned UDChA; enIoynyd JK; Inioynyd H^3; enyoyned H^2; yioyned W; Ionyid M; IMeint V.
5 Kynde] Cuynde V; Kende DChM. haþ] hat MH^3. closid] closed RDChW; Closet V; Iclosyd H^3; Iclosed K. craftily] craftly ChH^2; crftely A; Curteisly M. alle] walle H^3.
6 *divided from following after* Anima M; *after* hatte W; *after* hette V; *after* hyte AH^3. le*m*man . . . louiþ] loueli lemmon V. louiþ] louyd A; louyn J. lik] liche J. to] *om* V. selue] selfuen M; self VKW.
7 *run together with following* VAWMH^3. *Anima* . . . hatte] þat hiȝt *anima* Ch. heo hatte] sche hatte UDW; sche hate K; heo hette V; sche hyte J; ȝhe hyte A; he hyth H^3; hit hatteþ R; he haþ TH^2; *om* M. to . . . haþ] he haþe to her Ch. hire] hyr H^3; her*e* RDAW; hem H^2. haþ] RUDVJK; hat H^3; had AM; hadde W; *om* TH^2. enuye] envyȝe H^3.
8 proud] *om* M. prikere] preker ChA. *Princeps . . . mundi*] sire pride he hatte Ch; *in margin* M. *Princeps*] sire *princeps* H^2.
9 And] He M. wynne hire] hir*e* wynne H^2. wynne] wy*n*nen VM; wy*n*nyn JH^3; a woned A. hire] hyr H^3; here DAW; her ChK; hure R. awey] away RDChH^2JKWH^3. ȝif] ȝef Ch. miȝte] myȝthe R; mygthe M; mygth A; myth H^3; mihti V.
10 Ac] Bote VKWM; and RChAH^3. kynde] kuynde V; kende ChA; *in margin same hand* W. þis] RUDM; hit VKW; hym Ch; hire TH^2; hyr H^3; here A; his wille J. kepiþ] helpyth H^3; knowt A. hire] hyr H^3; here UDAWM; her ChK; hur*e* R.

And haþ don hire to sire dowel, duk of þise marchis.
Dobet is hire damysele, sire dowelis [douȝter],
And s*er*uiþ þis lady lelly boþe late ⁊ raþe.
Þus dowel, ⁊ dobet, ⁊ dobest þe þridde,
Beþ maistris of þis man*er* þis maide to kepe. 15
Ac þe cunstable of þe castel, þ*at* kepiþ hem alle,
Is a wys kniȝt w*ith*alle, sire [inwit] he hatte,
And haþ fyue faire sones be his furste wyf:
Sire se wel, ⁊ sey wel, ⁊ here wel þe hende,
Sire werche wel wiþ þin hond, [a] wiȝt man of strengþe, 20
And sire godefrey go wel, grete lordis alle.
Þise sixe ben yset to saue þe castel;

11 *run together with following* V. haþ] hat H^3; hatȝ H^2; had AM; doþ W; *above line with caret* D; *om* RUK. don] done J; do RH^2; Idon V; doþ UK. hire] hyr H^3; here DAW; her ChK; hur*e* R. to sire] seke A. do . . . marchis] *om* V. duk] dwke A; dewke J. þise] þis J; þese UD; þes Ch; þe RAWMH^3; his K.
12 Dobet . . . sire] *om* V. hire] hyr H^3; here DA; her ChK; hur*e* R; a M. sire dowelis] and dobest here W. sire] sere A; *om* Ch. douȝter] RUDVKW; dowt*er* J; dowtir MH^3; douter A; sistir T; suster ChH^2.
13 s*er*uiþ] s*er*uit M; seruitȝ H^2; s*er*ueþ RUDChV; seruyd A; s*er*uen W. þis] þat V; þe DK; his M. lelly] louely J; treuly MH^3. boþe] boþ*in* M. *Here* J *adds two lines: see above*, p. 49.
14 Þus] þis J. ⁊(1)] *om* H^3. þridde] thride A; þredde ChW; threde H^3; þirde DK.
15 *repeated after line* 19 A. Beþ] Beoþ V; ben RUKMH^3; Bene JA(2); Bien H^2; Be A(1). þis(1)] thes K; þat J; þe U. man*er*] manoire W; mare R. þis(2)] thise H^2; þes A(2); þat VJ; þe UD. maide] mayden RVJA(2)K; maydi*n* MH^3. kepe] kepe*n* VM.
16 Ac] But ChVKW; And H^3; As A; *om* RM. þe(2)] þis ChH^{2}W; þat J; *om* A. kepiþ] kepit DM. hem] them K.
17 Is] his M. wys kniȝt] knyth wyse A. wys] wyis H^3; wondir wis M. w*ith*alle] sykyr J; *om* MH^3. sire] sere A. inwit] RUVJKWMH^3; þe wyt D; Iewet A; þouȝt TChH^2. hatte] hate K; hette V; hatteþ RCh; hattith H^{2}H^3; hotyt M; hiȝte D; hight W; hyhte J; hythe A.
18 And] he UM. haþ] hatȝ H^2; had A; hadde MH^3; haue D; *om* R. faire] fayir H^3; feire ChV. furste] firste UDChJKW; ferste M; frist AH^3. wyf] wyue RUDH^3.
19 Sire] Sere A. se] see RUK; seo V; sey J; do A. ⁊(1)] and sir Ch; ⁊ sere A; sire U. sey] say DKWH^3; se J. ⁊(2)] sire U. hende] ende RV; thrydde H^3; thride A; þredde M. *Here* A *repeats line* 15.
20 Sire] Sere A. werche] worche VKW; worch Ch; wurche U; wyrche J; wyrch R; werk D. wel] *om* J. wiþ] wit M. þin] *om* DK. hond] hand UDKMH^3. a] DChH^{2}VJKMH^3; ⁊ TRU; *om* AW. wiȝt] wyȝht D; with MH^3; w*ith* RA; wytty J. man] mon V. of] and W. strengþe] strenght K; strenthe H^3; strenth A; strong W.
21 *run together with following* K. And] *om* RU. sire] sere A. go wel] dowel R. grete . . . alle] *om* K. lordis] lord w*ith* A.
22 Þise . . . yset] *om* K. Þise] þis JW; þese RUDH^{2}AH^3; þes Ch; þeose V. sixe] sexe A; vij U; fyue ChM; v H^3; lordes W. ben] bene J; bien H^2; beþ RDCh; arn M. yset] ysette UCh; set DH^{2}M; sett H^3; sette JAW. to . . . castel] þe kastel to sauyn M. to] for to JA. saue] sauyn JH^3. *Here* J *adds a line: see above*, p. 49.

To kepe þise womman þise wise men ben chargid,
Til kynde come oþer sende [and] kepe hire hymselue.'
'What calle ʒe þat castel,' quaþ I, 'þat kynde haþ ymakid? 25
[And what [kenis] þing is kynde, conne ʒe me telle]?'
'Kynde,' quaþ he, 'is creatour of alle kenis bestis, |
Fadir & fourmour, þe ferste of alle þing. *fol.* xlvj *b*
And þat is þe grete god þat gynnyng had neuere,
Þe lord of lif & of li[ʒt], of lisse & of peyne. 30
Aungelis & alle þing arn at his wille,
Ac man is hym most lik of mark & of shap.
For þoruʒ þe woord þat he warp wexe forþ bestis,

23 To] And to H³; And W; Tho A. kepe] kepen K; kepyn AM; kepyn wele J. þise] þis RUChH²VJAKWMH³; þe D. womman] wommon V; wymman R. þise] þis DV; these H²AWH³; þes ChJK; þo M; *om* RU. wise men] sexe A. ben] be ChW; bien H²; arn MH³. chargid] charged RDChKW; Charget V; *corrected same hand from* charchyd J.

24 Til] Til þat V; To Ch. kynde] kuynde V; kende ChAWM. come . . . sende] send or come (*same hand after cancelled* come) K. oþer] or RUDChVJAWMH³. sende] sente R. and] RUDVJMH³; to TChH²AKW. kepe] kepen H²; kepn K. hire hym] hem hire H². hire] hyr H³; here RJAWM; her ChK; hem D. hym] hem A; to hym W. selue] seluen V; self KW.

25 What] wath A; Qwat JH³. calle] clepe MH³. þat] þis U; þe DH²VA; þe þat J. quaþ I] *om* A. kynde] kuynde V; kende ChA. haþ] hatʒ H²; haþ þus VK; hat þus MH³; þus W. ymakid] Imaket V; makid AMH³; maked D; makeþ W.

26 WRUH²VJAKMH³ (*text based on* W); *line om* TDCh. And] *om* UA. what] qwat JH³; of what RU. kenis] *compare line* 27; kennys R; kynnys AM; kynnes H²J; cunnes V; skyns H³; kynne U; kyn KW. is] *om* RU. kynde] kuynde V; kende H²AM; *om* RU. conne] con VH³; cunne UH²; canst A; *om* M. ʒe] þu A.

27 Kynde] kuynde V; kende ChA. quaþ he] quod he *above line same hand after* creatoure J. is] is a ChAWM. creatour] kreature AWH³; creatours U; ceatour RV. kenis] kennis H²; kennes Ch; kynnys M; kynnes RJ; skyns H³; kyn K; kynne UD; kunne V; kynde A; þing W. bestis] best VW.

28 Fadir] Father K. þe] *om* UDAWH³. ferste] firste UDChJKW; furste RVH²; fryst AH³. alle] *om* H². þing] þinges RK. *Here* M *copies line* 34α *in margin.*

29 And] *om* VAW. þat] þat he RU; he D. þe] *om* RUD. gynnyng . . . neuere] bigynnyng hedde neuere V; nere hadde gynnynge M.

30 of(2)] *om* AW. liʒt] light U; liht V; liʒte D; liʒthe K; lith H²AMH³; liþ TCh; lyt R; litthe J; lyst W. lisse] *late corrector prefixes* b H²; blysse RUVJWMH³; blyssis A. peyne] payne J; pyne UKM.

31 þing] þingis U; þinges DK. arn] arne A; ern W; ben V.

32 Ac] But ChVKWM; and RH³; As A. man] Mon V. hym . . . lik] most lik to hym W. hym] hymself H³; he M. lik] lyik H³; liche UJ. mark] merke ChAW H³; mar D; *after cancelled* martl *same hand* J. shap] Shape D; shappe RUChJ; schaft MH³; face A.

33 þoruʒ] thoru H²; þorow ChJ; þurw U; þourth M; þourʒt D; thur R; þrow WH³; thrugh K; wiþ V; be A. þe] his A; *om* V. woord] world D. þat . . . warp] & be is werke A; of his mouth M. warp] werpes D; wrap KH³; spak W. wexe] wex ChH²; wexen UDAH³; waxe R; wax W; waxen K; waxin J; woxen V; woxin M. forþ] forth al W; alle H³. bestis] þing W.

And al at his wil was wrouȝt wiþ a speche,
Dixit & facta sunt &c,
Saue man þat he made ymage to himselue, 35
ȝaf hym gost of his godhed & grauntide hym blisse,
Lif þat ay shal laste, & al his lynage aftir.
Þat is þe castel þat kynde made, *caro* it hatte,
As muche to mene [as] man *with* his soule,
Þat he wrouȝte wiþ werkis & *with* wordis boþe. 40
Þoruȝ miȝt of þe maieste man was ymakid:
Faciamus hominem ad ymaginem nostram.
Inwit & alle wyttes enclosid ben þerinne,
For loue of þat lady þat lif is ynempnid.
Þat is *Anima*, þat oueral in þe body wandriþ,
Ac in þe herte is hire hom heiȝest of alle. 45

34 And . . . at] *om* W. al] alle þing VJAKMH³; *om* D. was wrouȝt] he wrout A. wiþ] at J. a] on ChA. speche] word K.

34α *line om and* 41α *substituted* U; *copied with line* 34 V; *with line* 28 M. &c] *omnia &c* J; *ipse mandauit &c* A; *vniuersa* (?) M; *et vniversa mandauit et creata* H³; *om* ChH²VW.

35 man] Mon V. ymage] Image like K; like AM. selue] seluen RVM; self KW; silue H².

36 ȝaf] Gaf A; And gaf W; Þat he ȝaf H³. hym] *om* H³. gost] goost UM; *om* R. of his] and Ch. godhed] godhode W. grauntide] grauntyd JAWMH³; grauntede V; graunted RDChK.

37 Lif] Lyue A; & lyf J. ay] euer VJMH³. shal] xal H³; *om* M. laste] lasten DVK; lastyn J; lesten W; lestyn H³; lastith M. al] *om* UA. lynage] lenage H³; kynne J.

38 Þat is] Þis is U; *om* D. þat(2)] of RA. kynde] kuynde V; kende AW. *caro*] *corpus* H³. hatte] hatteþ R; hattith H²AH³; hate K; hette V; hotitȝ M; hyhte J.

39 As] Is as U; And is as V. muche] myche D; mychel JKM; mechil AH³. to] for to H²; is to H³; it is to M; is A. mene] menyn J; mean K; meny M. as] RUDChVJAKH³; as a WM; þat TH². man] Mon V. with] withoute A. his] a V; þe RUDAWMH³; *om* J. soule] saule D; body & with sowle J.

40 *line om* RU. werkis] wyrkes D; werk VJWMH³; worke K; word A. with] *om* Ch. wordis] word VJKH³; woord WM; werke A. boþe] boþin M.

41 Þoruȝ] Thoru H²; þorow ChJA; ÞOrw VH³; þurȝ R; þurw U; þourth M; Þoruȝt D; Throw W; Thrugh K. miȝt] myȝth R; myth H²MH³. þe] his VJH³. man] Mon V; whan U. ymakid] ymaked RDChK; Imaket V; maked W.

41α *line om* V; *copied after line* 34 U. *ymaginem*] *ymaginen* H². *nostram*] *& similitudinem nostram* UH³; *et similitudinem nostram &c* KM; *&c* J; *et similitudinem added above line another hand and ink* W.

42 enclosid ben] enclosed ben RDChKW; closid ben A; Iclosid bet M; ben closed U; ben closet V; bien Iclosid H²; closyd hem H³. ben] bene J; beþ Ch.

43 *divided from following after* anima W. loue of] *om* M. lady] leuedy J. lif] lyue A. ynempnid] ynempned RUCh; Inempnet V; nempnyd J; nempned W; nemnyd D; Inemyd H³; Inamyd M; namyd K; Imenyd A.

44 *divided from following after* home W. oueral] *om* W. in] *om* RU. wandriþ] wandrit M; wandreþ RDChKW; wandureþ V; wanderis A.

45 *line om* H³; *run together with following* W. Ac] Bot ChVJKWM; *om* A. herte] hart K. hire] here UDAW; her ChK; hure R. heiȝest] heyest RUDJ; heyst A; heiyrst M; hiȝest ChH²V; highest K; hiest W.

Heo is lyf ⁊ led*ere*, a lemman of heuene.
Inwyt is þe [allie] þat *anima* desiriþ;
Aftir þe g*ra*ce of god [þe grettest is Inwyt].
Inwyt in þe heuid is, ⁊ an help to þe soule,
For þoruȝ his connyng is kept *caro* ⁊ *anima* 50
In rewele ⁊ in resoun, but reccheles it make.
He eggiþ eiȝe siȝt ⁊ heryng to gode;
Of good speche ⁊ [going] he is þe begynn*ere*;
In manis brayn is he most ⁊ miȝtiest to knowe.
Þ*ere* is his bour bremest but ȝif blod it make; 55
For whan blood is brem*ere* þanne brayn, þan is Inwit bou*n*de,
And ek wantoun ⁊ wilde, wiþoute any resoun.

46 Heo] He RUH^2WH^3; Ȝhe A; Sche DChJKM. ⁊] a W; *om* A. led*ere*] ledar K. a] and a VW; and RUJH^3. lemman] lemmon V.

47 *run together with line* 49 M. allie] halle TChH^2; help RUDVJAKWH^3; moost helpe M. þat . . . desiriþ] *om* M. desiriþ] desyret R; dyshyrith A; *corrected same ink from* sedireth H^2.

48 *line om* M. þe(1)] *om* Ch. þe(2) . . . Inwyt] þe gretteste is Inwit VW; þat grettest is inwytte A; grettest is Inwitt KH^3; Inwyt is þe grettest TRUDChH^2; grettest of alle J. is] es U.

49 Inwyt . . . help] *om* M. in] is J. heuid] heued U; hed RDChVH^3; hede W; hedd K. is] *om* J. ⁊] *om* RUH^2. an] *om* DV JAW. help] helpeþ VW; helpith J. to] *om* V. soule] saule D.

50 þoruȝ] þouth M. his] is A. connyng] koniyng*es* (? komyng*es*) M. is kept] he clepeþ V. is] ben K. kept] keped Ch; keppyt J. ⁊] *et* H^2.

51 in(2)] *om* DAW. resoun] fourme K. reccheles] rechelesnesse W; rechylnesse H^3; rechchilnesse J; reklesnesse M; recches A. make] makyth A.

52 *divided from following after* speche W. He] It H^2. eggiþ] eggitȝ H^2; eggeþ RCh VW; eggyd J; eggide U; tisit M. eiȝe siȝt] he ese W. eiȝe] eye RD; ey K; þe eye A; þin eie M; eye to U; aye J; ȝe *after erased* y Ch; þe i þe V. siȝt] siȝth D; siht VJ; sygth AM; syth H^3. ⁊ . . . gode] to goode and heryng also A; to goode þy*n* eryng to þe same M. heryng] beryng W; Bringeþ V. gode] god W.

53 *divided from following after* most W. Of] Ofte H^2. good] *om* RU. ⁊] and of RUVA; Of W. going] RUJK; connyng TDChH^2; cu*n*nynge V; good dede AW MH^3. is . . . begynn*ere*] begy*n*nyt eu*ere* M. þe] þo J; *om* RDAW. begynn*ere*] gynnere W; begynnyng K; kynner*e* J.

54 *run together with following* W. manis] Monnes V. brayn] brane A. is he] he is RH^2VAKW. miȝtiest] myȝthiest R; mythyest H^3; mytiest A; su*n*nerist M. to knowe] Iknowen M.

55 is] he is V. his bour] brayn Ch; *om* V. bremest] bre*m*mest H^3; bry*m*mest J. ȝif] ȝef Ch; hot R; hoot U. blod it] it blod M. it] *om* H^3.

56 *divided from following after* brayn W. For] *om* JA. whan] who*n*ne V; Qwan JH^3. brem*ere*] Bremore V; bremar K; brimmer JAH^3; brent U. þanne] þen V; in U. þan . . . bou*n*de] bownedyn is Inwitte (ne *above line another script and ink*) J. þan] þe*n* V. is Inwit] Inwit is M; is þe wit RU. bou*n*de] bou*n*den RU; boundyn DH^3; Ibou*n*de V; Iboundi*n* M; wanton W; lowe (*same hand for cancelled* away) K.

57 And] *om* A. ek] *om* M. wantoun] bounden W. wiþoute] w*i*thoute*n* RUH^2 VJ; w*i*thoutyn AH^3; ek w*i*thouti*n* M. any] eny V; ony RUDH^2JAM. resoun] reasone K.

In ȝonge fauntes ⁊ folis, wiþ hem failiþ Inwyt,
And ek in sottis þ*ou* miȝt se, þ*at* sitten at þe nale.
Þei helde ale in here hed til Inwyt be drenchit, 60
And ben braynwood as bestis, so here blood wexiþ.
Thanne haþ þe pouk power, sire *princeps huius mundi*,
Ou*er* suche man*er* of men miȝt in here soulis.
Ac in fauntis ne in folis þe [fend] haþ no miȝt
For no werk þat þei werche, wykkide oþ*er* ellis. 65
Ac þe fadir ⁊ þe Frendis for fauntis shuln be blamid
But þei witen hem fro wauntounesse whiles þei ben ȝon[g]e.
And ȝif þei ben pore ⁊ cateles, to kepe he*m* fro ille, |

58 In] w*ith* A; wit M. ȝonge] *om* RU. ⁊] and in UW. wiþ . . . Inwyt] Inwit is awei M. wiþ] in RU; whan W. hem] them K. failiþ] faylyt H^3; fayleþ RUDCh H^{2}VW; wanyth J.
59 in] *om* A. sottis] wrecches V. þou] as þou M; as ȝe W; þat H^3. miȝt] mygth AM; myth H^3; mayt J; maist K; *om* W. se] sen M; sene J; see UK; seo V. þat] *twice* H^2; *om* D. sitten] syttyn JAH^3; sitteþ V; sittit M; *twice but the first cancelled* U. at þe] att þe H^3; atte VJWM; at D. nale] ale RH^{2}VH^3.
60 Þei] Thay K. helde] held Ch; helden RKW; heldyn M; heldeþ V; heeld U; holde H^2; holden DJ; holdyn AH^3. ale] al Ch; dring J. here] her ChJKH^3; heore V. hed] heede K; heued U; heuyd J; hedes W. be] beo V; bet H^3; is M. drenchit] drenchid RUH^{2}K; drenched DChW; drinchid J; dronchen A; Idrenchid M; Idrynchyd H^3; adreynt V.
61 ben] bene J; bien H^2; *om* V. braynwood] branwood M; brayned RU. here] her ChJKWH^3; heore V. wexiþ] wexit H^2; wexeþ D; waxith JH^3; waxit RM; waxeþ UChVA; waxed W.
62 Thanne] þenne V. haþ] hat MH^3; hatȝ H^2. pouk] fende J. power] pouere A. sire] sere AK. *princeps . . . mundi*] *om* U.
63 Ou*er*] Of M; Hath of A. suche] siche U; swiche RM; sweche A; swethe H^3. of] *om* RUDVKWH^3. miȝt] mygth A; myth H^3; myȝtis RU; ⁊ mith M; he hath myȝte D. here] her ChJKH^3; heore V. soulis] saules D; soule UJA.
64 *line om* W. Ac] But ChVKM; and R; *om* AH^3. in] Ofe A. fauntis] Infant*es* K. ne in] ne D; and In Ch; and RUAK. fend] RUVJAKMH^3; deuil TDChH^2. haþ] hat MH^3; hatȝ H^2. no] ne J. miȝt] mygth AM; myth H^3; wit RUD.
65 no] to U. werk] worke ChK; werkys J; faute H^3. þei] þai A; thay K. werche] werchy*n* RM; worche W; worchen VK; wurchen U; werke H^2; werkyn AH^3; wyrkyn J. wykkide] amys J. oþ*er*] oyther J; or RUDVAKWH^3; ne M.
66 *divided from following after* schull J. Ac] But RChVKM; And H^3; *om* A. þe(*both*)] her J. fadir] faderis JAM; Fadres VW. Frendis] childres W. for] for þe W; for her J. fauntis] fantys (? fautys) JH^3; Fantes (? Fautes) V; fante (? faute) M; fawtes K. shuln] shul RUChVAW; schull JK; xul H^3; schole*n* M; schal D. be] Bene J. blamid] blamed RUDChKW; Blamet V.
67 *line om* RW. But] UChVJAMH^3; But ȝif TDH^{2}K. þei] thay K; he A; ye D. witen] wyte A; weten D; kepyn J; kepe MH^3; wone U. fro wauntounesse] þe betere M. whiles] while ChA; qwyl H^3; whil þ*at* VM; þe wyld J; þ*er* while D. þei . . . ȝonge] *om* J. þei] þai A; thay K. ben] be ChH^{2}AK; beþ D. ȝonge] UDChH^{2}VAKMH^3; ȝouþe T.
68 And] ac U; *om* JA. ȝif] ȝef Ch; ȝif þ*at* V; *om* RDH^2. þei] thay K; he A; the H^2. ben] be RChH^{2}A; beþ W. pore] nowth M; kynles J. ⁊ cateles] of catel MH^3. ⁊] or V; for A. to] and RU. kepe] kepen UVK; kepy*n* RDJM. he*m*] hym D.

Þanne is holichirche owyng to helpe hem & saue *fol.* xlvij *a*
Fro folies, & fynde hem til þei ben wise. 70
A[c] iche wiȝt in þis world þat haþ wys vndirstonding
Is chief sou*er*eyn ou*er* hymself his soule to ȝeme,
And cheuissh[en] hym for any charge whan he childhod passiþ,
Saue hymself fro synne, for so hym behouiþ;
For werche he wel oþ*er* wrong, þe wyt is his owene. 75
Þanne is dowel a duc þ*at* destroyeþ vices,
And sauiþ þe soule þ*at* synne haþ no miȝt
To routen ne to resten ne ro[t]en in þin herte;

69 Þanne] þ*en*ne V; *om* J. is holichirche] holichirch is K. holichirche] holycherche RDWM; holy A. owyng] awynge U; awenge R; holden W; holdyn KM; holde Ch; beholdyn A; asignet V. helpe] helpen V; helpyn J; kepe AWH³; kepy*n* M. hem] hym DM. & saue] from ille and saue A; at nede J. &] *om* R. saue] sauen V.

70 Fro . . . hem] & fyndyn hem fro folyys (*second* y *of* folyys *added above line*) J; and for to fynde hem forþ U. folies] *corrected from* folees R; foleyys K; foles Ch; falsed & folyes A; falsnesse & folye M; falsnesse from folyis H³; falsnesse & fro folys W. &] & to W. fynde] fynde*n* RVK; fyndyn A; fende H²H³; techyn M. hem] *om* A. til] til þat VK; to M. þei] þai AW; thay K; *om* M. ben] be Ch; bene J. wise] wisere RUDJAH³; wysore V; wisare K.

71 Ac] RD; Bote VJK; And TUH²MH³; For W; *om* ChA. iche] eche URDChA KW; vche V. wiȝt] with M; wyit H³; wit R; wytte A; mon V. in] on K. þis] þe U. world] werld AH³; word R. þat haþ] haþ Ch; *with* J. haþ] hat MH³; *om* H². wys] wyis H³; his DKW; wit J; *om* RAM. vndirstonding] vndirstandyng DH²WM.

72 chief] Cheef V; chef RChH²WM; chefe JAK; cheff H³. ou*er*] of ChH²J; to H³; *om* V. self] selue JA. soule] saule D. to] for to V.

73 And] To J. cheuisshen] Cheuesschen V; chefueschy*n* R; chevessen K; cheuise W; cheuese D; cheuisshiþ TU; cheuys-scytȝ H²; cheuiseþ Ch; to cheuy*n* H³; clensyn M; clense A; kepyn J. hym] *om* RJ. for] fro AWM; from VJH³. any] ony RUD; eu*er*y JW; heuy (? heny) A; en M; *om* VH³. charge] charg RW. whan] whon V; when Ch; qwan JH³. he] his A; þ*at* D; *om* RJM. childhod] childhed A; childesse J. passiþ] passit M; passeþ RDChVW.

74 *line om* D. Saue] to saue U; And save KH³; and sauyn J; And saaf M. self] selue UJA. synne] sunne V; senne M. for] and AH³. behouiþ] behouyt M; byhoueth RChVKW; behowyth H³; behouid H².

75 For] For to Ch; and J. werche] worche VKW; wurche U; wirche ChJ; werk H³. he] *om* ChW. wel] wele JA; wil D. oþ*er*] oythir J; or UDChKMH³; or ellis A. wrong] worng A. þe] his M. wyt] wyte UChJ; wyȝth D. his] *om* M.

76 Þanne] ÞEnne V. duc] deuk H³; Duyk V. þ*at*] and RUM. destroyeþ] distroyeþ RChH²KW; distroyet D; dis-troiyth M; dystroyit H³; distruieþ V; distruȝit J; dystroet A.

77 *line om* U. sauiþ] sauyt M; saueþ RChH²VW; saue D. soule] saule D. synne] sunne V; senne D. haþ] hat MH³; hatȝ H²; haue Ch. miȝt] myȝth R; mygth A; mith MH³.

78 To] Ne U. routen] route RUVW; routyn AM; rowten DChK; rowtyn J; rowte H³. ne(1)] no*n* H³; & D. to(2)] *above line, similar hand* H². resten] restyn JAM; reston H²; reste RUVWH³. ne(2)] ne to UVW; to RA. roten] UD; rotyn JAKM; rote RWH³; Rooten V; roren TChH². þin] þe DVJKW. herte] harte K.

And þat is dred of god, dowel it makiþ.
It is begynnyng of goodnesse god for to douten. 80
Salamon it seide for a soþ tale:
Inicium sapiencie timor domini.
For doute men doþ þe bet; dred is such a maister
Þat he makiþ men meke & mylde of h*ere* speche,
And alle kynde scoleris in scole to lerne.
Þanne is dobet to ben ywar for betyng of þe ȝarde, 85
And þerof seiþ þe saut*er*, þe salme þou miȝt rede:
Virga tua & baculus tuus ipsa me consolata sunt.
Ac ȝif clene consience acorde þat þiself dost wel
Wilne þou neuere in þis world, [wy], for to do betere,
For *intencio indicat hominem &c.* 90

79 dowel] & dowel M; for Dowel V. makiþ] makit AM; makeþ RDChVW.
80 It is] þe M. It] Þat H³; and RU. is] is þe UJKWH³. begynnyng] gynnyng RJW; gynnere A. of goodnesse] *om* U. god . . . douten] for to drede god W. god] god frist A; is good M. douten] doute URJ; dredyn AM; drede VH³.
81 *line om* VW; *as one line with following* H³. Salamon . . . seide] and so seyth salamon J. Salamon] And salamon M. it] *om* A. seide] said K. for] *om* A. soþ] sooþ U; soot M. tale] sawe K.
81α *line om* W. *Inicium*] *Innicium* DV. *timor*] RUDChVJAKMH³; *est timor* TH². *domini*] *domini &c* R.
82 *line om* W. doþ] dootȝ M; don U; done J; do AK. þe] *om* D. bet] bett K; bette UCh; bett*er* D; bettyr A. dred] for drede RD. such] siche U; swich M; sweche AH³. maister] master K.
83 Þat he] and þat U. makiþ] makit MH³; makeþ RDChVW. meke & mylde] mylde and mek RW. meke] Meoke V. mylde] myilde H³. h*ere*] her RChJAH³; hire H²; heore V.
84 kynde] kynne UJK; kunne V; kyns W; skyn*n*ys R; skyns H³; skennis M; *om* A. scoleris] scolars JK; scholeris A. scole] schole A; Scoles V. to] for to A; forte V. lerne] lere RU; lery*n*n H³.
85 Þanne] þenne V; That W. is] *om* D. dobet] dowel U. to] seyþ D; *om* H². ben ywar] drede U. ben] be RDChW; bene J; byn K; beo V; *om* H². ywar] war RVAWMH³; ware DJ. þe] *om* VJ. ȝarde] ȝerde UDChAWMH³; ȝerd*es* RV; ȝerdys J. *Here* J *adds a line: see above,* p. 49.
86 *run together with following* W. And þerof] and þ*er* RU; Of þat A. seiþ] seitȝ H²; seit M; saith KW. saut*er*] sauȝter Ch. þe salme] In a Salme Ch; þe selue A; þi selue J; þi seluen V; thyself KWMH³. þou] *om* AKH³. miȝt] mygth A; migtht M; myth H³; mayt J; maiste K. rede] reden V; it rede AKWMH³.
87 *& . . . sunt*] *& b.* V. *tuus . . . sunt*] *om* W. *tuus*] *om* M. *ipsa . . . sunt*] *&c* R; *om* A. *sunt*] sunn Ch.
88 Ac] Bot ChVK; And DWMH³; *om* A. ȝif] ȝef Ch; ȝif þi U; *om* V. clene] *om* AW. þat] and R; Bote V. self] selue J; soule AWMH³. dost] doþ W; dot M; do RUVAKH³.
89 *run together with following* VW. Wilne] Wille RUCh; Wyl H³; & willet M; ȝerne J; whil AW. þou] *om* MH³. neu*er*e] all wey H³; al woi*e* M; art W; wonyst A. in . . . wy] why in this worlde K; weye ne worde J. world] word M; werld AH³. wy] why TRUChH² (*heavily cancelled* T); *om* DVAWMH³. for to] forte V; to J. do] don RAM; done J; dou*n* H³. bet*er*e] þe betere M; bettre do W.
90 *transposed with following* M. For] *Quia* M; Cor H². *intencio*] Intencioun DH². *indicat*] ? *iudicat. hominem*] *quemquam* K; *&c*] *om* RUChVAWMH³.

Be counseil of consience, accordyng holy chirche,
Loke þou wisse þi wyt & þi werkis aftir;
For ȝif þou comist aȝen consience þou combrist þiseluen,
[And so witnesseþ goddis worde and holiwrit boþe]:
Qui agit contra conscientiam &c.
Ac ȝif þou werchist be godis word I warne þe þe beste, 95
Whatso men worden of þe wraþþe þe neu*ere*;
Catoun counseilliþ—tak kep of his teching—
Cum recte viuas ne cures verba malorum,
But suffre & sit stille & sek þou no ferþ*ere*,
And be glad of þe g*r*ace þ*at* god haþ Isent þe. 100
For ȝif þou comsist to clymbe, & coueitest herre,

91 Be] w*ith* RU; For M. counseil . . . consience] concience of counseil M. counseil] conseyld H^3. of] & D. accordyng] acordyng w*ith* RUVKH^3; acordyng to J; acordyng of H^2; accordyng wil W; acordith w*ith* A; acordit wit M. chirche] cherche RJW (*after cancelled* wryht J); Churche DV.
92 wyt] witt*es* K. werkis] werk*es* RUD VW; workes ChK; werke J. A *adds* fro falsed & folies *below the line another hand.*
93 For . . . comist] for do þou J; þat gynnyt M. ȝif] ȝef Ch. comist] comest UChH^{2}V; co*m*sest RDKW; gynnyst H^3; do A. aȝen] aȝens UH^{2}WH^3; aȝenys A; ayenst K; aȝein VJ; ageyn M; agayn R. þou] *om* M. combrist] co*m*brest RDCh H^{2}W; cumbrest UV; co*m*berest K; comerist AH^3; acombrit M. þi] hi*m* M. seluen] seluy*n* H^3; selue JA; self KW; siluen H^2.
94 ChRUH^{2}VJAKWMH^3 (*run together with following* W); *line om* TD. And] *om* JA. so] *om* AW. witnesseþ] witnessit H^{2}MH^3; witnesse W. goddis . . . writ] holy wrytte and godis word AWMH^3. writ] chirche U; cherche R. boþe] boþy*n* M; after RU.
94α *line om* VJ. &c] *edificat ad iehennam* U; *edificat ad condemnationem* (?) &c R; *om* ChAWMH^3.
95 Ac] Bote VKM; And ChJWH^3; *om* A. ȝif] ȝef Ch; *om* M. werchist] worchest UCh; wirchest D; werche RA; worche VKW; wyrche J; werke MH^3; werchif H^2. godis] god*us* V. þe(2)] for þe UDVAKWH^3.
96 What] Qwat JH^3; þat Ch. so] so eu*er* K; *om* J. worden] wordyn MH^3; seyn U; spekyn J; wo*n*dryn R. of] on W. wraþþe] ne wrathe J; reche A. þe] the thou KW. neu*ere*] neu*er* þe rather*e* J.
97 Catoun] For Catou*n* M. counseilliþ] counseilith so K; Counseileþ so VJ; conceylytȝ so R; counseilit so M; concelyt þe so H^3; counseilleþ to D; conseileþ þe to U; techith so A; techeþ þe so W. kep] hede VJH^3. of] on U. his] þis RU. teching] þing RU; tunge W.
98 *viuas*] *viues* K. *cures*] *curas* M.
99 *line om* A. But] *om* H^3. suffre] suffir J; Suffurre H^3. &(2)] ne RM; *om* U. sek] seke RUDChH^{2}J; sech VM; seche K; sey H^3. þou] *om* W. no] no*n* M; not Ch. ferþere] farther K; furre V.
100 *line om* A. And] But J. be] beo V. þe(1)] þat R; *om* W. haþ . . . þe] þe hat sent H^3. haþ] hat M; hatȝ H^2. Isent þe] þe Isent V; þe sente RUKM; sente D; þe g*r*auntyd J.
101 For] *om* JA. ȝif] whan Ch. comsist] comsest RDKW; Cumse V; gynnyst MH^3; begynne A; couet J. to] for to J. clymbe] clyme AMH^3; *after cancelled* climbe J. coueitest] coueitist ChH^3; coueitiste K; Coueyte V; woldyst A; *om* J. herre] here K; heyer*e* MH^3; hyere R; hier Ch; hiȝere H^2; heyrere A; hie W; to ben heiere U; for to risyn heyer*e* J.

Þou mi3test lese þi lou3nesse for a litel pride.
I haue [lernid] how lewid men han [lerid] here children
Þat selde m[os]seþ þe marbil þat men ofte [t]reden,
And ri3t so be romberis þat rennen aboute 105
Fro religioun to religioun, reccheles ben þei eu*er*e;
Ne men þ*a*t conne manye craftis, clergie [it telliþ],
Thrift oþ*er* þedom *with* þo is selde ysei3e:
Qui circuit [*omne genus in nullo genere est*].
Poule þe apostel in his pistil wrot it

102 Þou mi3test] þan my3tist þow Ch. mi3test] mythist A; my3t RUD; miht V; mith MH^3; mayt J. lese] lesyn JAM; leose V. lou3nesse] louhnesse V; lownesse RUDChH^2JAKWH^3; lovnesse M. litel] lite D; luitel V. pride] pruyde V.
103 lernid] lernyd JAMH^3; lerned VW; herd TRUDChH^2; hard K. how] þe how JMH^3; 3ou H^2W; whe*n* R. lewid] lewed RUW; lewede V; lewd DChH^3; lewde K; lewynd A. han] haue RDK; *om* JAWMH^3. lerid] U; lered RDV; leryn JH^3; lernid TH^2; lerned ChK; lerne A; lerny*n* M; lerne 3e W. here] her ChJKH^3; heore V; he D; 3oure W. children] childr*e* W; childern K; childeryn JH^3.
104 *as two lines divided after* treden Ch; *after* tredyn M. Þat] And MH^3; *om* A. selde] selden VW; seldyn M; seldom JAH^3; seelde U; seldo R. mosseþ] mosseth K; Moseþ VW; mosyth JAH^3; men seþ TH^2; me*n* se RCh; men sen D; men seen U; men seyn M. þe] þat þe M. marbil] m*er*ble K; Marbelston V; stone W; marbel mosy R; marbil mose U; marbel þryuen D. men ofte] ofte me*n* RH^2. ofte] ofty*n* JAH^3. treden] DVKW; tredyn RH^3; trede A; tredith H^2; dreden T; on wenedyn J; mouen U; treden Be ouermolded with mosse men to beholde Ch; tredy*n* Is wol seldyn Isein wit mos begrowyn M.
105 And] But W; *om* Ch. ri3t] rith JH^3; reith M; *om* W. be] by þe Ch; be þese H^3; fareþ be W; *om* V. romberis] romeris J; romers DChKW; romours H^3; renneris AM; re*n*ner*es* RU; walkers V. rennen] renny*n* JAMH^3; renneþ Ch; rennyth R; walken V. aboute] abouten DV; abowtyn JMH^3.
106 reccheles] rechelys R; regeles Ch. ben þei] þei be*n* RU; þei bene J. ben] be DM. þei] þai AW; thay K; *om* ChH^2.
107–68 *om* (**a leaf wanting**) H^2.
107 *line om* Ch. Ne] þo M; And UVJ. conne] connen DW; connyn A; konnit M; con H^3; conynggen K; kennyn J. manye] mony V; alle RUDJAWM; of alle H^3; in al K. clergie . . . telliþ] as clerk*es* and oþer R; and clergie boþe U. clergie] clergy3e H^3; clargie A; as clergie M. it telliþ] WA; hit telleþ V; tellith JH^3; tellit M; it techith K; techiþ eu*er*e T; techeþ eu*er*e D.
108 *run together with following* V; *transposed with following* W. Thrift . . . þo] wit sweche þrift & þedam M. Thrift] þruft V; trift (? trist) R; þat thrifte JAW; þ*at* thryf H^3. oþ*er*] or RDVJKH^3; of or A. þedom] thedam RW; þeodam V. *with* . . . ysei3e] seldom hem schewyth J. *with* . . . selde] ar seldom *with* tho K. þo] hem V; hym W; yt H^3. is selde] selden is V; seldom is H^3; seldam is W. selde] selden R; seldom U; sildy*n* M. ysei3e] Iseygh K; yseye RV; seie U; yseyn WM; seyn DA; sene H^3.
108α *transposed with following* M. *omne . . . est*] JAWH^3; *omne genus de nullo genere est* &c K; *omne genus nullius est generis* U; *omne genus nullius generis est* M; *omne genus* &c RD; *omne genus* V; &c TCh.
109 *divided from following after* ensample W. Poule] Paul D; And powl M; 3e se wel H^3. apostel] postele AW. in . . . it] wrot it In his pistel M. wrot it] wroot it U; wrythet A. it] þis H^3; *om* V.

In ensaumple [þat] suche shulde not renne aboute, | 110
And for wisdom is writen & witnessid in chirches: *fol.* xlvij *b*
In eadem vocacione qua vocati estis state.
3if þou be man maried, monk, oþer chanoun,
Hold þe stable & stedefast & strengþe þiseluen
To be blissid for þi beryng, [3]e, b[e]ggere þei3 þou were. 115
Loke þou grucche nou3t on god þei3 he gyue þe litel;
Be paied wiþ þe porcioun, pore oþer riche.
Þus in dred liþ dowel, [and] dobet to suffre,
For þoru3 suffraunce se þou mi3t how soueraynes ariseþ,
And so leriþ vs luk þat lei3ede neuere: 120

110 ensaumple] exaumple RJAKH³. þat] þat RUJKM; how W; of TDChVAH³. suche] siche U; swiche RJM; sweche AH³; which D. shulde] xuld H³; schule M; *om* V. not] nouth H³; no man Ch; *om* V. renne] rennyn JMH³; Rennars V; romen W. aboute] abowtyn JAM.
111 *line om* U. And] *om* W. wisdom] wisdam VJMH³. is] hit is ChJAWM (is *above line* J). writen] writyn K; writun J; write Ch; wreten DW; wretyn AMH³. & . . . chirches] as witnesseþ Clerkes V. witnessid] witnessit M; witnessed RChW; witnessith K; wittenesseþ D; wyttens A. chirches] Cherches DJWM (*after cancelled* clergyes *same hand* J); chirche A; cherche R.
112 *line om* V; *copied after line* 115 H³. *eadem*] *ea* U. *state*] *states &c* K; *in eadem permaneatis* U; *om* R.
113 þou] 3ou W. be] beo V; bei (i *cancelled*) U. man] Mon V. maried] maryid H³; mari3id J; maryd M; Imariet V; named D. oþer] oþur V; oythir J; or MH³.
114 *run together with following* A. Hold] Heeld U. stable] strong J. stedefast] studefast V. & . . . seluen] *om* A. strengþe] strenght K; strenþ W. seluen] seluyn H³; selue J; selfue M; self W; soule RU.
115 To . . . beryng] *om* A. be] ben M; beo V. blissid] blissed UDChK; blessed R; blesset V. 3e . . . þou] 3if þou a beggere U. 3e] RVW; yea a K; þe TCh; a A; *om* DJMH³. beggere] beggere RDVJAKW MH³; biggere TCh. þei3] þei RJM; though K; þow3 Ch; þogh W; þow A; þou3t D; þauh V; 3yf H³. were] weore V; wel W.
116 nou3t] nouth H³; nout M; not RVJ AKW. on] *with* H³. þei3] þei3e U; þei JM; þou3 Ch; thoughe K; þogh W; þow AH³; þou3t D; þau3 V. gyue þe] þe 3eue V. gyue] 3iue U; 3if J; geue DChK; 3eue RAWMH³. litel] luytel V.
117 Be] Beo V. paied] payid H³; pay3id J; payd RUDK; paide ChW; apaid M. wiþ] of Ch. þe] þi UChVJAW; þyn MH³; that K. porcioun] possessioun AW. pore] pouere RM; be it pore U; porore V. oþer] oythir J; or UVMH³. riche] Ricchore V; ryche eythyr H³.
118 *line om* R. in dred] I þrede D. liþ] liþe Ch; liyth KH³; li3t D; bit3 M; by W; dobest A. and] UDVJAKWMH³; *om* TCh. suffre] suffren DKW; suffryn M; suffuren H³; suffyre J; soffren V.
119 þoru3] þus þurw U; þus in R. suffraunce] suffurrans H³. se . . . mi3t] þou mayt se J. se] see K; seo V; so H³; *om* M. mi3t] myth AH³; mayst K. how] to M; *om* H³. soueraynes] souereyn DVM; soueraignte W; souereynte AH³; soferaunce K; sufference (? sufferente) J. ariseþ] arise RM; arisen U.
120 *line om* UCh; *run together with following* W. leriþ] lered D; lerede V; lernyth AH³; lernyt M; lernyd K; lerned RJW. vs] *om* A. luk] leuk H³. lei3ede neuere] neuer ne liede K. lei3ede] ly3ede RV; liede DM; lyed JAW; lyid H³.

Qui se humiliat exaltabitur &c.
And þus of dred & h[is] dede dobest arisiþ,
Which is þe flo*ur* & þe fruyt fostrid of boþe.
Ri3t as a rose, [þ*at* red is and] swet,
Out of a raggit rote and a rou3 brere
Sp*ri*ngeþ & spurediþ, þ*at* spic*er*is desiriþ, 125
Or as whete out of weed waxiþ, out of þe erþe,
So dobest out of dobet & dowel gynneþ sp*ri*nge
Among men of þis molde þ*at* mek ben & kynde.
For loue of here lou3nesse oure lord 3iueþ hem g*ra*ce
Such wer[kis] to werche [þat] he is wiþ paied. 130

120α *line om (space is left for it)* U; *attached to line* 119 V; H^3 *substitutes: Qui se exaltabit humiliabitur et qui se humiliabit exaltabitur. exaltabitur*] *om* V. *&c*] *et qui se exaltat humiliabitur* J; *om* RVAKW.
121 *line om* W. And] *om* M. of . . . his] dred of A. of] thour a H^3; for K. &] & of RUDM. his] ChVJK; here T; oure RU; *om* DMH^3. dede] doubte M. dobest] dobet R. arisiþ] arisit M; ariseþ UChV; arisetȝ R; aryse D.
122 Which] whuch V; wheche A; Qwyche J; Qwech H^3; Suche W; And M. þe(1)] *om* VJ. flo*ur* . . . fruyt] frut and þe flo*ur* RK. þe(2)] þy M; *om* VJ. fruyt] froyt DChW; freute A; frute J; frend MH^3. fostrid] fostred RDW; fosterid JH^3; Ifostrid M; Ifostred VK; forstered Ch; fore fosterid A. of boþe] aboue A. of] of hem Ch; on U; vs D. boþe] boþin M.
123–5 *om* A; *as two lines divided after* rote TRUDChKWMH^3.
123 Ri3t] ri3th R; Rith WH^3; Reith M; Rith as redily J. a] þe DVM; *om* H^3. þat . . . and] RUVJH^3; that is redd & KW; þat red is M; riseth Ch; *om* TD. swet] swote V; *om* ChM.
124 Out of] spryngith of M. a(1) . . . brere] row brere & raggyd rote H^3. raggit] raggid UJM; ragged RDChVKW. and . . . brere] *om* M. a] of V; out of K; on a Ch; as a RU. rou3] row3 D; rowh J; rogh W; rowhe U; row R; Rouwe V; *om* ChK. brere] breer K; Breres V.
125 Sp*ri*ngeþ] þat spry*n*geþ RU; & it springit M. & sprediþ] & spredit M; *om* K. spic*er*is] spiso*urs* U; spicerie Ch. desiriþ] desirit M; desyryn J; desiren RUKW.
126 Or] Oythir J; *om* A. whete] qwete JH^3. out(1)] ou3t D. of(1)] of a V; of þe A. weed] weod V. waxiþ] waxit M; waxeþ RChVAW; waxet D; wexith K; wex H^3. out of (2)] of JAKM; on W; vppon V. þe] *om* DVJ. erþe] eorþe V; erde A.
127 dobest] dobet D. dobet] dobettir A; dobest D; Dowel V. &] ad A. dowel] Dobet V. gynneþ] gynnyth JK; gy*n*nyt MH^3; gynnytȝ R; begynnyth to A; doþ VW. sp*ri*nge] sprynggen H^3.
128 of] on DKW. molde] world V. ben] bene J; byn K; beþ WM. &] or V. kynde] kuynde V; kende ChWH^3; milde M.
129–31 *repeated at head of a new page* Ch.
129 loue] luffe J. here] her RCh(*both*) JKH^3; heore V. lou3nesse] low3nesse Ch(1); louhnesse V; lownesse UCh(2)A KWH^3; lounesse RDM; lowe hert J. oure lord] god H^3; oure W. 3iueþ] 3ifit J; 3yft R; 3if AM; yeveth K; 3euet D; 3euyth H^3; 3eue W; 3ef Ch(1); 3af Ch(2).
130 Such] Siche U; Swych DJM; Sweche H^3; *om* A. werkis] UJAMH^3; werkes V; work*es* K; werke DCh(2); werk RCh(1); werch T; worche W. to] for to AWM. werche] werchen DM; worche Ch(1)V KW; wurche U; wirche Ch(2); werky*n* H^3; wyrkyn J. þat] URDVJAKWMH^3; as TCh(*both*). is wiþ] þerw*ith* is A. is] his R; be U. wiþ] wit R; wel M. paied] payd U; pay3id J; ypaied W; Ipayid H^3; apaid M; apayet V; plesid A.

Formest & ferst to folk þat ben weddit
And lyuen as here law[e] wil[e]; it likeþ god almi3ty
Þat þoru3 wedlak þe world stant, whoso wile it knowen.
Þei be þe riccheste of reaumes & þe rote of dowel.
For of here kynde þei comen þat confessours ben nempnid, 135
Boþe maidenis & [mynchons], monkes & ancris,
Kinges & kni3tes, & alle kyne clerkis,
Barouns & burgeis, & bondemen of tounes.
Ac fals folk & feiþles, þeuis & lei3eris,
Ben conseyuid in cursid tyme as kaym was on Eue: 140
Aftir þat adam & [heo] eten þe appil

131 Formest & ferst] First & formest J; Ferst & formerst M; Furst and foreward V. Formest] RUDAKH3; Formast W; And formest T; And formist Ch(2); And formast Ch(1). ferst] first UCh (*both*)KW; frist AH3; r *above line another script* T. to folk] to men J; þise men M. ben] bene J; byn K; beþ W; bet M; ben wele A. weddit] weddid UDJAK; wedded RCh(*both*)W; Iweddyd MH3; Iweddet V.

132 And] That A; *om* J. lyuen] lyvyn K; lyueþ U; leuen DCh; leuyn MH3; leuyth A; libbeþ V. here] her ChJKH3; heore V; he W. lawe] UChVJAKWMH3; lawes RD; lawis T. wile] M; wil UA; will W; wole V; wol Ch; woll K; wel H3; will wele J; whil D; wiln TR. it] þat UA. likeþ] likit M; plesyt H3. almi3ty] almy3thi R; almythy H3; almity M; almyghte UD; almyht J.

133 Þat] and U; For VJKWMH3; *om* A. þoru3] þorow ChJA; þorw RV; þurw U; þoru3t D; þourth M; thour H3; þrogh W; thrugh K. wedlak] wedlok UDChJKW; wedlook M. world] werld H3; word RU JM; werd A. stant] stont VW; stonte K; stonde J. whoso] hoso AH3; hose V; qwo so J; who W. wile] wol ChV; wole W; *om* A. knowen] knowe RUDChJA KWH3; Iknowe V.

134 Þei] Thay K. be] be*n* RUChVAK MH3; bene J; beþ W. þe(1)] *om* ChVM. riccheste] reychest R; rechest W; ricches A; riche M. of] of þis J; of þi W; in VM. reaumes . . . wel] reste & þe lawe folwit M. reaumes] reames D; rewmes RU; rewmys H3; remes Ch; remys JA; realmes K; Reame V; reume W. &] *om* A. þe(2)] *om* JW. rote] roto W.

135 For] *om* A. here] her ChJKH3; heore V; þat A; *om* WM. kynde] kuynde V; kende M; kyn RU; kyng W. þei] þai A; thay K. comen] comy*n* RUJAH3; come DChV; kenny*n* M. ben] be AW; beþ V; bet M; arn J. nempnid] nempned DChVK; nemyd H3; nemed W; namyd AM; nemled R; callyd J.

136 Boþe] Boþin M. mynchons] Mynchons Ch; nonnes T; nu*n*nes RU; nonne D; Martires VJH3; marters K; martres WM; maystris A. &] an V; *twice* W. ancris] ankeris JAH3; ankere*s* RD; ankers K.

137 Kinges] king RH3. &] *om* J. kni3tes] kny3thes R; knyggtes W; knythis MH3; knytis A. kyne] kyn W; kynne UK; cunne V; kenne D; kyns J; ke*n*nys RM; sky*n*nys H3; kynde Ch; oþer A.

138 &(1)] *om* JH3. burgeis] burges J; burgeses K; burgois W. of] *in* H3. tounes] touunes A; thounys H3; towne U.

139 Ac] Bot ChJM; and R; As H3; *om* VAK. feiþles] feitles M; faythles JKW; faiþlese Ch; feithes U. þeuis] theuys RJ; þeues DW; thefes K; þeoues V; as þeuis TUA; as þeues Ch; schrewys H3; schewis M. lei3eris] ly3ers V; lyeris UAMH3; lyeres RD; liers ChJW; lyars K.

140 Ben] Be D; Bene J; Beþ W. conseyuid] *con*seyued RUDChW; Conseyuet V; conseiuedid M. cursid tyme] Cursydnesse (*touched up:* rs *another ink*) D. cursid] Curset V. on] of RJAWM; and UD.

141 þat] *om* RA. heo] she TDChKMH3; eue RUVJAW. eten] etyn JKM; etein W; had etyn A; haddy*n* etyn H3; hedden eten V. þe] of þe VWMH3.

A3ens þe hest of hym þ*at* hem of nou3t made,
An aungel in angir hi3te h[e]m to wende
Into þis wrecchide world to wonen & to libben
In tene & trauaille to here lyues ende; 145
In þ*at* curside constellac*iou*n þei knewe togid*er*is,
And brou3t forþ a barn þat muche bale wrou3te;
Caym þei hym callide, in cursid tyme engendrit.
And so seiþ þe saut*er*, se it whanne þe likiþ:
Concepit dolore[m] & peperit iniquitatem. 150
Alle þat comen of þat caym crist hatid aftir,
And manye mylions mo of men & of wo*m*men
[Þat] of seth & his sistir siþþe forþ come |

142 *line om* U. A3ens] A3enys A; Ayenst K; A3en RDCh; A3eyn VJW; Ageyns M. hest] hestys J. hem] he R; hy*m* M; 3ow J.
143 An] And an M; The A. in . . . hem] hi3t hem in anger Ch. angir] haste RU VK; a while M. hi3te . . . wende] þennes hem tornde V. hi3te] hyth H^3; het RJK; hete hete W; made A. hem] RUDJAK WH^3; hym TM. to] for to W. wende] wendy*n* M.
144 Into] In K. þis] þe RUCh. world] werld H^3; word RM; werd A. wonen] wonyn JAH^3; wone RU; wonyen DKM. to(2)] *om* DJH^3. libben] libbe RUJ; lyven K; lyue H^3; leue A.
145 *line om* V. &] and in RUChAKWM. to] into RAM; vnto W. here] her ChJ KH^3; hire W. lyues] lyf*es* K; lyfys D. ende] hende M.
146 In] And in J; *om* Ch. curside] cursid AKMH^3; cursede RU; cursed DChJ; Corsede V; corsed W. constellac*iou*n] constulac*iou*n D; tyme MH^3. þei] þai W; thay K; þat þei U. knewe] knewen V; knewyn JKM; knew hem W; knewy*n* he*m* H^3.
147 brou3t] brou3the R; brouth A; Brou3ten V; browtyn JH^3. a] *om* V. barn] baron A; barou*n* H^3; Barnes V; broþel M. muche] meche H^3; mychel K; michil M; mekil A; mykyl J. bale] wo H^3. wrou3te] wrou3the R; wrouth AM; wrowte JH^3; wrou3ten V.
148 þei] þai AW; thay K; men V. hym callide] cleped him V. hym] hem DW. callide] callydyn J; callid KH^3; kalledy*n* M; called DChW; calde R; clepid A. cursid] curside U; cursed RDChV; corsed W; acursyd J. engendrit] engendrid UD; engendret V; engendred RCh W; engenderid JAH^3; Ingendred K; getyn M.
149 *run together with following* VW. seiþ] seit M. se] see UK; seo V; seyth A. it] *om* AH^3. whanne þe] whon þe V; qwan þe J; won þu A; hoso H^3.
150 U *substitutes: Quare via impiorum prosperatur bene est omnibus qui peruerse & inique agunt.* dolorem] RChJAKWH^3; *in dolore* VM; *dolore* TD. & . . . *iniquitatem*] &*c* V. *iniquitatem*] RDChJAKW; *iniquitatem* &*c* TH^3; *iniquitate* M.
151 Alle] And alle VJKWMH^3. þat(1)] *om* Ch. comen] comy*n* H^3; come RCh VW; camyn J; cam AM. þat(2)] *om* ChJM. hatid] hated DChW; hatide hem U; hated he*m* R; hetid hem A; hem hated K; he*m* hatede V.
152 manye] Mony V; a A; *om* K. mylions] milyonys RJ; mylionos U. mo . . . men] of men mo M. of(2)] *om* W. wommen] wymmen DVJWM; wy*m*man R.
153 Þat of] Of that K. Þat] That DChVJ WMH^3; And TRU; Ther A. seth] seeth U; sed (*another* e *added above line*) M. &] & of UD. sistir] suster RDChVWM; susters K. siþþe] sytthy*n* H^3; sith W; siþen ChK; sythyn J; seþþen V; sethen DA; sitthe þei U; swiþe R; fele M. forþ] for A. come] comen DK; comyn AM; coome V; camyn J; kemy*n* H^3.

For þei mariede hem wiþ curside men of caymes kyn. *fol.* xlviij *a*
For alle þ*a*t comen of þ*a*t caym acursid þei were, 155
And alle þ*a*t couplide hem *with* þ*a*t kyn crist hatide [dedliche].
Forþi he sente to se[þ], & se[i]de hym be an aungel
To kepe his kynrede fro kaymes, þei couplide nouȝt togid*er*is;
And siþen se[þ] & his suster [sed] wern spousid to kaymes;
Ageyns godis hest girlis hy geten 160
Þat god was wroþ wiþ here werkis & [suche wordis seide]:
Penitet me fecisse hominem.

154 mariede hem] weryn maried M. mariede] Marieden V; maryedyn J; maried RUDChAKW; maryid H³. hem] them K; hym W; *om* VA. wiþ] wiþ þe U; to VK; vnmesourly to J. curside] cursed to R; cursyd blode to K; cursid hed *with* A; *om* JWM. of] þat come*n* of V. kyn] kyn*n*e RUDChA; kynde JK; kuynde V; kende MH³.
155 *run together with following* U. For] *om* A. comen] comyn UA; come R; camy*n* J; kemy*n* H³. þ*a*t(2)] *om* DChJA MH³. acursid . . . were] *om* U. acursid] acursed RVJ; acorsed W; cursyd AH³; cursed DChK. þei] þai A; thay K; *om* J. were] weren V; wern M; wery*n* H³; weryn eu*er*e J.
156 *line om* R. And . . . kyn] *om* U. And] *om* A. þ*a*t] þa W. couplide] couplede V; coupled ChW; cowpledyn J; coupillid A; cowpled K; cowplete M; copplyd H³; cowled D. hem] *om* DKM H³. *with*] to VJAWH³; *om* D. kyn] kun V; ken M; kynd K. hatide] hatid MH³; hated DChJW; hatide hem U; hatid hem A; he*m* hatede V; them hated K. dedliche] VJKWH³; eu*er*e TUD; after Ch; aftir AM.
157 Forþi] For þey D; þ*er*for J; For H³. he] y U. sente] sende V. to] DVJAKW H³; hym to TChM; he*m* to RU. seþ] sey Ch; seye RU; seyn T; Sem DVJAK WH³; se*n*de M. seide . . . aungel] þe aungil seyde to hym A. seide] seyde RUDChVMH³; sayd JKW; sende (*perhaps altered from* seide) T. hym] *om* ChWM. an] *om* U.
158 kepe] kepyn J. his kynrede] hi*m* M. kynrede] kynnerede A; kyndered K; cun V. kaymes] kaym RUK; þat þ*a*t kynde M. þei] þ*a*t þei RUDVKWH³. couplide] covpelid K; couplid A; couplede M; coupled ChVJ; couple UDWH³; cople R. nouȝt] no*u*t H³; not RUVJAK WM.
159 *divided from following after* spoused W. And] Ac J. siþen] siþin M; syþe R; syth AKW; siþþe U; sytth H³; seþen Ch; sethin J; seth D; seþþe*n* V. seþ] seth RChM; seeþ U; sem TDVAKWH³; seem J. suster sed] V; suste*r*ys seede JH³; sustre seth KW; suster TDChM; soster R; sister U; systir A. wern spousid] couplid weryn M. wern] were*n* V; wery*n* J; wer ChK; were RUDAWH³. spousid] spoused RUDChVKW. to kaymes] to kaymes kyn R; T kayms kyn W; wiþ caymes kynne U; to þ*a*t kynde M; togederis A.
160 *divided from following after* god W. Ageyns] Ageyn D; Agayn RJ; Aȝeyn V; Aȝens UChWH³; Aȝenys A; Ayenst K; & ageyn M. godis hest] þe hest of god AWMH³. girlis] gerlys H³; gerles RCh; Gurles V; garlis A; cherlys J; childry*n* M. hy] þei RUDChVJAWMH³; thay K. geten] getyn RM; gete D; geeten V; getten K; gette H³; gotyn A; beȝete J.
161 *divided from following after* werkes W. Þat] and RUJH³; *om* A. was] *om* W. wroþ] wrouth A. here] her ChJKH³; heor V. werkis] work*es* K; wirkes Ch; werk V. &] an A. suche . . . seide] suche wordes seide VKW; swyche wordys seyde J; sweche wordis seyde AH³; seide suche wordis TCh; seyde swich wordes D; sayde þese word*es* RU; seyde þyse wor M.
162 *attached to line* 164 V. *me . . . hominem*] *hominem me fecisse* M; *me &c* V. *hominem*] *hominem &c* DH³; *eos ·i· homines* R.

And is as muche to mene, among vs alle,
"þat I man makide now it me forþinkeþ".
And com to noe anon, and bad hym nouȝt lette 165
Swiþe to shapen a sship of shidis & bordis;
Hymself & his sones þre, & siþen here wyues
Busk[en hem] to þat boot & biden þ*ere*Inne
Til fourty dayes be fulfild, þat flood haue ywasshe
Clene awey þe cursid blood þat caym haþ ymakid. 170
"Bestis þ*a*t now ben shuln banne þe tyme
þat eu*ere* curside caym com on þis erþe;
Alle shuln deiȝe for his dedis be dounes & hilles,
Boþe fisshis & foulis, forþ mi[d] oþ*ere* bestis,

163 And] þ*a*t UAWM; þis H3. as] als Ch; þus V; *om* A. muche] meche H3; michel KM; mychyl J; *om* A. mene] mean K. among] Amonges VKW; rith among J. vs] ȝou V.
164 I] I haue W. man makide] makede Mon V. makide] makid A; makede M; maked RDChK; made UJW; mad H3. now] sore U. it] *om* JA. forþinkeþ] forthingkyth J; forþenkeþ R; ouyrthynkith A.
165 com] cam RJAM. noe] nowel U. anon] an noon D. nouȝt] not RUVAKWM. lette] letten U; lettyn M; lete Ch.
166 Swiþe] But swythe H3; *om* A. to] gyn to M; go DAKW; gon JH3; *om* Ch. shapen] shapyn RJAMH3; schape ChW. a] him a UA. sship] schup V. of] *om* H3. shidis] sides U. &] and of RUAK.
167 self] selue UJA. sones þre] iij sonys H3; sone þre W. siþen] siþin M; sytthy*n* H3; sethen D; sethyn J; seþþen ChV. here] her ChJKH3; heore V; alle her*e* U. wyues] wyfes K.
168 Busken] K; Buskyn JH3; Bosken D; Buskym A; Busked Ch; buskede R; Buskide TU; buskedy*n* M; Bringen V; Bring W. hem] UVJKW; hem breme M; hem brymme AH3; *om* TRDCh. to] *in*to H3. þat] þe UVM. boot] bote brime W. &] aid A; to U; *om* J. biden] bidi*n* M; byde RW; abydy*n* H3; abide U; vnbydyn J; holdym hem A.
169 Here H2 **resumes.** dayes] dawes V; *om* UD. be] ben ChVJKM; arn H3; were R; hath A. fulfild] fulfillid AK; fulfeld M; folfuld V; Ifyllyd H3. þat] that the K; þe UVJH3. flood] folood H2. haue] hath A; hat H3. ywasshe] Iwasch Ch; Iwaschen A; ywaschy*n* M; Iwaschyd H3; ywaschide U; wasshed KW.
170 awey] away RDChH2JKW. þe] þat DK. cursid] curside U; cursed RDChJK; Cursede V; corsed W. haþ] hatȝ H2; had H3; hadd M. ymakid] Imakyde J; ymaked RDChK; Imaket V; maked W.
171 ben] bene J; bien H2; beþ DW. shuln] schul DH2A; xul H3; schulle U; scholyn JM; shal RChKW; mouwen V. banne] banny*n* J; curse V. þe] þat A. tyme] stounde JAK.
172 curside] cursid H2AH3; cursede RM; cursed Ch; corsed W; þat *cur*syd J; þat Cursede V; þ*a*t cursed DK; þe curside U. com] come DChW; cam JAH3; came K; *om* M. on] vppon V; in H3; to RU. þis] þe UK; *om* ChVA. erþe] eorþe V; erde M; grounde A.
173 Alle] And alle D; For al M. shuln] shul RChA; schulen V; schulle U; schal DJWM; xal H3; schallen K. deiȝe] deyȝyn J; deye RUDCh; deien M; deyn A; dye VKW; byen H3. his] her J. dedis] dede DAK. be] bothe H3. dounes] townis M. hilles] hulles DV; helly*n* M.
174 Boþe] Bothin JM. fisshis] Fisch VW. foulis] foule W. forþ] *euen*forþ (? *em*forþ) U; for H2; *om* H3. mid] myd DM; w*ith* RUChH2VJAKWH3; miþ T. oþere] þe RU.

Outtake þe ei3te soulis, & of iche beste a couple 175
Þat in þe [shynglid] ship shal ben ysauid;
Ellis shal alle di3en & to helle wenden."
[Þus] þoru3 curside caym cam care vpon alle,
And al for se[þ] & his sist*er* children spouside eiþ*er* oþ*er*,
A3en þe lawe of oure lord le[i3en] togid*er*is, 180
And [were] marie[d] at meschief as men do now h*er*e children.
For su*m*me, as I se now, soþ for to telle,
For coueitise of catel vnkyndely be maried.
A carful concepc*iou*n comiþ of such weddyng

175 Outtake] Outtaken VK; Owttakyn JA; Outake Ch; Out3take H²; but take MH³. þe] 3e JMH³; *om* RVA. ei3te] Eihte V; eyte DJ; viij RChH³; seuene A; souen U; iij M. soulis] *om* J. &] þat U; *om* H³. of] *om* R. iche] eche RUDChK WH³; vche V; eche a A.
176 Þat] RUDVJAKWMH³; Put þat TH²; Putte Ch. þe] þat M; þis W; 3oure J. shynglid] schynglid KM; shyngled W; schynglede V; schyngelyd J; sengle RUDA; sollyd H³; same TChH². ship] schup V. shal] schal DJW; xal H³; shul RA; schullen V; schulde M; schulden K; þat shal TH²; þat I schal Ch; þat tyme schal U. ben] be RUA; bien H². ysauid] ysaued RDH²VKW; sauyd A; saued UCh.
177 shal] xal H³; shul RA; schulde U; schulden K. di3en] dyen ChK; dye VW; dei3en H²; deyen DAH³; deyin M; deye RUJ. wenden] wendyn AM; wende RUJKWH³; weende V.
178 Þus] RUDVJAKWMH³; *om* TChH². þoru3] þorou3 Ch; Thoru H²; þoru3t D; þorow JA; þorw V; þurw U; þourth M; thou*r* H³; þhur3 R; þrogh W; thrugh K. curside] cursid H²JAKMH³; Cursede V; cursed RDCh; corsed W. cam] AJM; came K; com UDVH³; come RW; þus cam TH²; þus come Ch. vpon] o M; to vs H³. alle] erþe W; loofte M.
179 *divided from following after* childres W. And] *om* VA. al] *om* V. seþ] seth RChM; seeth U; sem TDVAKW; seem H²JH³. sist*er*] suster DH²VK; soster Ch; sisterys JAH³; sustres W; sustri*n* M; *om* R. children] childryn D; childeryn JAH³; childern K; childres W; *om* UM. spouside] spousid UDH²AK; spouseden V; spousedi*n* M; spoused RChW; dyspousyd H³; leyne J. eiþ*er* oþ*er*] togydere J; togederis A; childry*n* togedere M. eiþ*er*] eþer ChW; eþir H³; here eyþ*er* RU; *om* D.
180 *line om* M; *divided from following after* lord W. lawe] leue Ch. lei3en] ley3en R; leyen UH³; layen DKW; ly3en V; lei3 hem H²; ley hem TCh; loyn A; spowsyd J. togid*er*is] eythir oþ*er* J.
181 *as two lines divided after* myschef W. were] were RUAWH³; weryn J; wern KM; weore*n* V; *om* TDChH². maried] RUDChH²VAKWM; mariyd JH³; mariede T. at] to A. meschief] mschef M. do] don UWH³; done K; doþ V; dot3 M; 3yuy*n* J. h*er*e] her ChJKH³; heore V. children] Childryn DM; childre W; childerin JH³; childern K.
182 *line om* U. For] For now H³. se] seo V; here K. now] *om* H³. soþ] þe sothe JAKMH³; for soþe Ch. telle] tellen V; tellyn M.
183 For] þat for U. coueitise] couatise Ch. vnkyndely] vnkuyndeliche V; vnkendly DChAWMH³. be] ben UChJKH³; beþ W; bien H²; beoþ V; arn M. maried] mariyd JH³; maryd M.
184 A] And VH³. comiþ] comeþ RUCh H²VW; komsit M. of] on A. such] swiche UDJM; sweche H³; swich a R; sweche a A. weddyng] mariage Ch; maryages H³.

As fel of þe folk [þat I] before shewide. 185
It is an vncomely copil, be crist, as [me þinkeþ],
To ȝiuen a ȝong wenche to an old feble,
Or wedde any wydewe for any wele of godis,
Þ*at* neu*er*e shal bere [barne] but it be in armes.
In gelosie, ioyeles, ⁊ ianglyng [a] bedde, 190
Manye peire siþen þ[e] pestilence han p[l]iȝt hem togid*er*e.
Þe fruyt þ*at* þei bringe forþ arn manye foule wordis.
Haue þei no children but ch[este], ⁊ choppis [betwene].
Þeiȝ þei don hem to dunmowe, but ȝif þe deuil helpe

185 *line om* A; *marked with cross* D. As] Also V. fel] befel ChVM; fele RDH^{2}W. þe] þo M; þis RU; þat VJ. folk] folk*es* K. þat] UVJKWMH^3; as TRDChH^2. I] RUDChVJKWH^3; *om* TH^{2}M. before] beforne JM; beofore V; before of KH^3. shewide] shewyd RH^{2}JKH^3; schewede UVM; schewed ChW; swewed (h *written over first* w) D.
186 an] a H^3; rith J; *om* A. vncomely] vnkyndly W; vnkendely AH^3; vnkende M. copil] couple RUDChH^{2}VKWMH^3; weddyng A; *om* J. as] *twice* U. me þinkeþ] VJAKWMH^3; I wene TRUDChH^2.
187 ȝiuen] ȝyue U; ȝif W; ȝeuen DH^{2}V; ȝeuyn AH^3; ȝeue RChK; weddyn M. wenche] *om* W. an . . . feble] a man of elde M. old] hold WH^3. feble] feble man H^{2}H^3; feble Mon V.
188 Or] Or to ChV. wedde] wedden DV; weddyn JKWMH^3. any(1)] eny D; ony RUJA; an Old V. wydewe] widue D; wydowe K; wydow J; wedewe H^{2}MH^3; wedue R; wedowe ChAW. any(2)] ony RUDA; *om* VJWM. wele] weale K; welþe ChJAW; weolþe V; lykyg M. of] of here WM; of her J; of hir*e* V.
189 *line om* R. neu*er*e shal] schal neu*er* H^{2}W. bere barne] barne bere KW; baron bere A; baru*n* bery*n* H^3; Child bere V. bere] beryn J; bern M. barne] J; barn DM; child TUChH^2. but] but ȝyf H^3; but if K. it] t *over erasure* H^2. be] beo V. in] in here DAW; in her ChJ; in hire VM. armes] harmis M.
190 In] *om* A. gelosie] Ielosye RH^{2}K; Jelousye DW; gelusie M; Ielusie U; Ielesye V; Ielisie A; iolosie Ch; gelesoyȝe H^3; Iolouste J. ioyeles] and Ioyeles VH^3; þey Ioilyn M. ⁊ . . . bedde] þai goon to here beddes W. ⁊] an A; *with* D; *om* K. ianglyng] Iangli*n* M; Iangelyn J; gangeling Ch. a] RUD; on ChJMH^3; in VAK; of TH^2.
191 Manye] Mony V; many a R; Sweche many H^3; Ofte D. peire] *om* DMH^3. siþen] sithe H^2; sith UK; siþþe W; syn RAH^3; seþ Ch; seþþen V; sen J; siþes D; siþis M. þe] RUVAKMH^3; þis TChH^2 W; þese D; *om* J. pestilence] pestilence time W; p*er*estolences D. han] haue D; hath K; hat M; arn H^3. pliȝt] Ch; plight UKW; pliht VJ; plyȝþ R; plith MH^3; plyt A; piȝt TH^2; put D. hem] *om* H^3.
192 *line om* W. Þe] þat H^3. fruyt] froyte DCh; frut RH^{2}JAKH^3; fruth M. þei] thay K. bringe] bringen V; bringyn JM. arn] er Ch; ben VH^3; buþ D. manye] mony V; but U.
193 *line om* A. Haue þei] þei haue R; ⁊ M. Haue] Han VH^3. þei] þai W. no] none VM. children] Childryn DChM; childr*e* W; childeryn JH^3; childern K. cheste] UDJKWM; chestes V; chost R; chiding TChH^{2}H^3. ⁊] *om* DH^3. choppis] choppes UChVK; chopp*us* H^2; choppyn J; chappis M; *om* DH^3. betwene] DUJM; betwythen R; hem bitwene VKWH^3 (*after cancelled* togyders *same hand* K); togid*er*e TChH^2.
194 Þeiȝ . . . hem] Thynk þei nouth H^3. Þeiȝ] þauȝ V; Though K; þouth M; þow ChJ; *om* RUDAW. don] done ChK; be don D; gon M; hien W; hiden RU. hem] hym wel fast W; *om* DM. dunmowe] do*n*mowe H^3; danmowe D; don now J; done al þat þei mowen V. but . . . helpe] *om* VW. ȝif] ȝef Ch; *om* UJ. þe deuil] dowel A.

To folewe aftir þe flicche, fecche þei it neuere; 195
But ȝif þei boþe be forsworn þat bacoun þei tyne.
Forþi I counseile alle cristene coueite not be weddit |
For coueitise of catel or of kynrede riche, *fol.* xlviij *b*
But maidenis & maidenis macche ȝow ysamme;
Wydeweris & wydewis werchiþ riȝt also; 200
And [þanne] glade ȝe god þat al good sendiþ.
For in [vn]tyme, treweliche, betwyn m[a]n & wom*m*[a]n
Shulde no bedbourd be; but þei were boþe clene
Of lif & of loue & of lawe also

195 folewe] folewen V; folowe DK; folow Ch; folowyn J; folwe RU; folwyn AMH[3]; fechen W. aftir] *om* W. flicche] flysh W; Flucchen V; flykke H[3]; flyk A; flesche R. fecche þei] for þei gete H[3]. fecche] fette UD; fatte A; cache W; flicche M. þei] þai AW; thay K.
196 ȝif] ȝef Ch; *om* UAWMH[3]. þei(1)] þai W; thay K; *om* A. boþe be] ben both H[2]. boþe] boþen A; bothin J; *om* M. be] ben VAM; byn K. forsworn] forsworyn JMH[3]; forswore DV; forswon R. þat . . . tyne] and Cursen þat tyme V. þei(2)] þai W; thay K; xal þe H[3]. tyne] tynun M.
197 *divided from following after* ben W. Forþi] For þey DM; þerfor J; *om* A. coueite] couetyth J; coueitid M; þei coueyte R; *om* H[3]. not] nouȝt DCh; nouth H[3]; noght U. be] ben VJ; to be RUChAKH[3]; to ben WM; to D. weddit] weddid UJAKMH[3]; wedded RChW; Iweddet V; wedde D.
198 or] ne VJKWMH[3]; & A. of(2)] for RUH[3]. kynrede riche] non riche ken M. kynrede] kenrede A; kyn ChJW; kun V.
199 maidenis(1)] maydons H[3]; sengil J. &] *om* A. maidenis(2)] maydons H[3]; madenys J; vnMaydens V; *om* A. macche . . . ysamme] ȝou to same take U; ȝow to same takyn R; clene ow save V. macche] macchit M; makkyth J; meke A; marie H[2]. ysamme] same J; þe same D; togeder Ch; togeders K; togederis AMH[3]; togidre W; togyderis H[2].
200 Wydeweris] wydeweres U; widewers V; wydowers KW; Wedueris A; Weduer*es* R; wedewers M; weduers D; wydewys JH[3]; widowes Ch. wydewis] widewes UV; widowes ChK; wedewis M; wedues RDA; wodewes W; wydoweris J; wedewerys H[3]. werchiþ] werchit M; wyrchith J; wircheþ Ch; wurcheth D; worchet K; werche ȝe RA; wurche ȝe U; worche ȝe W; worschupeþ V. riȝt] rith JH[3]; *om* RUH[2]VAWM. also] so ChK; the same H[2]AWMH[3]. *Here* J *adds a line like* **B** IX 175: *see above*, p. 31.
201 *line om* A. And] *om* RU. þanne] URChJKWMH[3]; þenne V; *om* TDH[2]. glade] gladyn J; gladden K. þat] and W. al . . . sendiþ] good sendyth al H[3]. al] alle RUVJW. good] goodes V; god*es* R; godis UJ. sendiþ] sendit M; sendeþ RDChV; saintȝ W.
202 *line om* A. in] *om* U. vntyme] VJK; no tyme WH[3]; no*n* tyme M; my tyme TRUChH[2]; tyme D. betwyn] betwyxin J. man] URJKWMH[3]; Mon V; men TDChH[2]. womman] UJKWH[3]; wommon V; wymman RM; wommen TDCh; wymmen H[2].
203 *line om* A; *divided from following after* were J. Shulde] Xuld H[3]. no] no*n* M. bedbourd] bed borded D; berd in bedde M. be] ben M. but] but ȝif J; but if H[2]K; but ȝef Ch. þei] þai W; thay K; he H[3]; *om* V. were boþe] werin boþy*n* M; bothin wer*e* J; Boþe weore V.
204 *line om* A; *as one line with following* W. Of] boþyn of M. lif] lyue J. of(2)] eke in V. loue] luffe J; soule M. &(2)] *om* W. of(3)] in VKW; i*n* þe H[3]. also] alse V; als J; leuyng W; lyuende M; leuedyn H[3].

Þat dede derne do no man ne shulde. 205
As betwyn sengle ⁊ sengle, siþþe lawe haþ yg*ra*untid
Þat iche man haue a make in [mariage] of wedlak
And [werche] on his wyf ⁊ on no wo*m*man ellis,
Þ*at* oþ*er*e gatis ben geten for gadelynges ben holden;
And þat ben fals folk, ⁊ fals eires also, foundlynges ⁊ [leiȝeris],
Vng*ra*cious to gete loue or any good ellis,
But wandriþ [as wolues] ⁊ wastiþ [ȝif] þei mowe;
Aȝens dowel hy don euele, ⁊ þe deuil plesen,

205 *line om* A; *divided from following after* sengle KMH^3. Þat] Sweche H^3. dede derne] derne dede RUDJKW; dede MH^3. do . . . shulde] xuld no ma*n* do H^3; schuld not be don M. do] to done J. man] mon V. ne] no J; *om* UDChVKW.
206–8 *divided after* make-werke A; *as two lines divided after* make M.
206–7 *as one line* AKH^3; *as three lines divided after* sengle-make V.
206 As . . . siþþe] *om* A. As] As is vset V; Ac RU; But J; *om* H^{2}M. betwyn] betwyx W; betwyxin J. sengle ⁊ sengle] ij° sengle K. sengle(1)] single W. siþþe] sith H^{2}W; Sithen K; Seþþen V; seþ Ch; sethin J; siþin M; swich R; But H^3; *om* D. lawe] þe lawe DK. haþ] hat H^3; hatȝ H^2; had M. yg*ra*untid] ygrau*n*ted RUChK; grauntid A; grau*n*ted DW; grandyd H^3; it g*ra*untyd J; Iloket V.
207 Þat] *om* AKH^3. iche] eche DChAK WH^3; vche V; eue*r*y RU. man] mon V. haue] to haue AKH^3. in] ⁊ J. mariage] RUDVJAKWMH^3; mane*r* TChH^2. of wedlak] of wedlok RUDChH^{2}JWM; and Matrimoyne IMedlet togedere V; *om* KH^3.
208 And . . . wyf] *om* M. And] *om* A. werche] wirche R; wurche U; worche þat V; wyrche þat werk J; worche þat werk W; worche that worke K; werke þ*at* werk H^3; werche þu þat werke A; do þ*at* werk TChH^2; þe werlc (?) D. on(1)] wit*h* V; of D. his] þi A. wyf] wyue J; *same hand after cancelled* lyf D. on(2)] wit*h* V; of DWM; *om* UAK. no] no*n* MH^3; no mo J. wo*m*man] wommon V; wy*m*man R; wymmen J. ellis] *om* J.
209 *line om* A; *run together with following* V. Þat] Þo þat H^3; For þat U. gatis] gate MH^3; wise ChKW. ben(1)] be H^3; beþ RW; bet M. geten] getyn J; getton K; goten Ch; goty*n* H^3; ygeten UV; Igeti*n* M; ygote*n* R. for . . . holden] *om* V. for] *om* RCh. gadelynges] gedelyng*us* H^3; gadlynge H^2. ben(2)] beþ W; **arn** K. holden] holdyn RJMH^3.
210–11 *as three lines divided after* eyrys—werkys J.
210 *line om* A; *divided from following after* also RDK; *after* foundelynges W. And . . . also] *om* V. And] *om* U. þat] þo RW; *om* H^3. ben] bene J; beþ ChW; *om* D. fals] þis fals J; many fals M. ⁊(1)] ⁊ eke þis J; *om* W. eires] heires UKW; heris M; eiȝers Ch. also . . . leiȝeris] maky*n* M. also] als H^2; as ChH^3; and W; *om* J. foundlynges] Fondelyng*es* DChK. fu*n*delyng*es* R; ben fyndlynges V; *om* U. ⁊(2)] *om* UJ. leiȝeris] lyȝers V; lyerys H^3; lyer*es* RD; lyers JW; liars K; folis TChH^2; *om* U.
211—XI 47 *om* (**a leaf wanting**) U.
211 *line om* A. to] of werkys for to J. gete] getyn J; gett K. loue . . . ellis] any good or love K. loue] ony loue J. or] oþir M. any] eny RV; ony DH^{2}JM.
212 *line om* A. wandriþ] wandrit M; wandritȝ H^2; wandreþ Ch; wandry*n* R; wandren VK; wanderin JH^3; wandres D; wandren aboute W. as wolues] RVKW; as woluys H^3; os woluys J; as wlfis M; ⁊ walwes D; *om* TChH^2. wastiþ] wastit M; wasteþ Ch; wastyn JH^3; wasten VK; waste RDW. ȝif] RVJ; if DK; what þat TChH^2; what W; þat MH^3. mowe] mowe*n* MH^3; mouwen V.
213 Aȝens] Ayenst K; aȝen RH^3; Aȝeyn VJA; ageyn M. hy] þei RDChH^{2}VJM; þai AW; thay K; *om* H^3. euele] euyl A; eyuel R; yuel H^2; vuele V; ill KWH^3; hille M; *om* J. plesen] plesyn JAMH^3; plese R; pleasen K.

And aftir here deþ day shuln dwelle *with* þe same
But ȝif god [g]iue h[e]m *gra*ce here to amende. 215
Þanne is dowel to dreden, & dobet to suffre,
And so comiþ dobest aboute, and bringeþ doun mody,
And þat is wykkide wil þ*a*t many werk shendiþ.'

214 And] *om* A. here] her ChJH³; heore V; þe DK. deþ] detȝ H²; ded AH³. shuln] shul RDChVA; xul H³; schulle*n* M; scholyn J; shal W; schallen K. dwelle] dwellyn J; dulle*n* M. þe] þat ChH²J. same] schrewe VJK.
215 *line om* AWMH³. ȝif] *om* ChVK. giue] geue ChK; ȝiue TH²V; ȝif RDJ. hem] DRChVJK; hym TH². here] hem here J. to] for to D.
216 Þanne] þenne V. dreden] dredyn RAMH³; drede H²JW; þreden D. dobet] dobest A. suffre] suffren RDCh H²VKW; suffryn M; sufferyn A; suffury*n* H³.
217 And] *om* A. comiþ] komyt M; cometȝ H². dobest] *om* R. aboute] aboutyn AMH³; *om* J. bringeþ] bryngit MH³. doun] adoun VM; don W.
218 And] *om* H³. þat] *om* RAW. is] his AW; *om* H². many] Mony V. werk] worke Ch; werk*es* RW; ma*n*nis werkis M; wight K; men V. shendiþ] sche*n*dit M; shendeþ RDChVW.

XI

þanne hadde wyt a wyf þ*at* hatte dame studie,
þat lene was of lich & of lo[u3] chere.
She was wondirliche wroþ þ*at* wyt so tau3te,
And sterneliche staringe dame studie seide:
'Wel art þou wys, wyt,' q*ua*þ she, 'any wisdomis to telle 5
To flat*er*eris or to folis þ*at* frentyk ben of wittis,'
And blamide hym [and bannide hym] & bad hym be stille—
Wiþ suche wise wordis to wisse any foolis!
And seide, '*Nolite mittere*, Man, marg*er*ie p*er*lis
Among hogges þ*at* hauen hawen at wille. 10

1 þanne hadde] þEnne hedde V. wyt] wyth H[3]; he A. þ*at* hatte] hyr name was H[3]; þai clepid A. þat] & M; was RDVW. hatte] hi3t Ch; hyte J; heithe M; hote RDKW; hoten V.
2 lene . . . lich] euer was Iliche V. lene] low3 D; leef M. of(1)] as a H[3]. lich] leche H[3]; lithe K. of lou3] lowe of W; lout3 of M. lou3] louh V; low R; lowe DJAKH[3]; loþly TChH[2]. chere] hir*e* chere M.
3 She] Heo V. was . . . wroþ] wondurly wroth was A. wroþ] wrouth H[3]; wrot3 M; wro3t H[2]. wyt] wit*h* M. so] so me H[2]; þ*us* me RAW; me þus VJKMH[3]. tau3te] tau3þe R; taugthe H[3]; tauthe M; tauth A; taght W; tawte J.
4 And] and al RVJAWM. sterneliche . . . studie] staring dame stodye st*er*nelyche JK; starinde Dam Studie steorneliche V; scornynge dam stodie st*er*neliche M; schornely dam stodie sternely A; skorn-fullych dame stody to vs bothe H[3]; scornyng sternly she W. seide] sayde RDChKW.
5 Wel] wil D. wys] wyce J; wyis H[3]; witti V. wyt . . . she] q*uod* sche to witt KMH[3]. wyt] *om* VJAW. she] scheo H[2]; 3he A; heo V. any] eny D; ony A; my R; *om* VJM. wisdomis] wysdom*us* H[2]; wysdams H[3]; wisdom VAKW; wisdam RM.
6 flatereris] flateris M; faytouris A; Fayturs V. or] & A. to(2)] *om* JM. frentyk] Frantike KW; wilde M. ben] be Ch; beþ W. of] in RDJKW. wittis] witte AW; wordys H[3].
7 blamide] blamyd H[2]JAKMH[3]; Blamede V; blamed RDChW. hym(1)] hem DA. and . . . hym] & bannyd hym KMH[3]; and ba*n*ned hi*m* RDW; and bannyd hem A; bitt*er*ly TChH[2]; for his Beere V; *om* J. hym(3)] hem A. be] ben AMH[3]; beo V.
8 *divided from following after* saide W. suche] swyche RJM; sweche AH[3]. wise wordis] wordys wyse M. wisse] wissen RKWM; wyssyn JA; wysy*n* H[3]. any] eny RV; ony DJA.
9 *run together with following* W. *Nolite*] *noli* RVJKW (*te erased* J). *mittere*] *amittere* H[3]. Man] þese H[3]; *om* ChVAWM. margerie] mergery K; *margaritas* Ch. p*er*lis] the perles Ch; perle D.
10 Among] Among*es* K. hauen] hauy*n* RH[3]; haue K; han VJAWM. hawen] hawes RVKW; hawys DJAH[3]. at] at here AM; at her JH[3]; at heore V.

þei do but drauele þeron; draf were hem leuere
þanne al þe precious perrie þat in paradis wexiþ.
I say be þo,' quaþ she, 'þat shewen be here werkis
þat hem were leuere lond, & lordsshipe on erþe,
Or ricchesse or rentis, & reste at here wille, 15
þanne alle þe soþe sawis þat salamon seide euere.
Wisdom and wyt now is not worþ a risshe
But it be cardit wiþ coueitise as cloþeris don here wolle;
þat can construe deseites, & conspire wrongis,
And lede forþ a loueday to lette þe treuþe, 20
þat suche craftis conne [to counseil ben yclepid],

11 þei] Thay AK. do] don RVAWM; done K; doun H[3]; ben J. but] *om* J. drauele] drauelyn RAM; dreuele DChW; dreuelyn H[3]; drevile K; dreueler J. þeron] þer vpon R; on þe D. were . . . leuere] wher be þey leue D. were] wer K; weore V. hem] hym Ch.
12 þanne] þen V. al] *om* J. precious] preciousest J. perrie] perre RJAMH[3]; Peerles V. wexiþ] wexit H[2]; wexeþ Ch; waxith JK; waxit H[3]; waxeþ RD; waxxes W; waxen V; growith A; growit M.
13 say] sey RChJAMH[3]; sigge V. be(1)] it be AVKWH[3]; *corrected from* þe D. þo] þoos Ch; þulke V; hem JW. she] scheo H[2]; ȝhe A; heo V. shewen . . . werkis] bi heore werkes schewen V. shewen] schewyn KH[3]; shewe RD; schewith A; schewit M; werchin J. be(2)] *om* H[2]. here] her ChJKH[3]. werkis] workes K; wordis AWMH[3].
14 hem . . . lond] wern leuere lond to hem M. hem] *om* W. were] weore V; war K. lond] londes W; *om* J. &] or D; þat R; *om* J. lordsshipe] lordschupe V; lordschep ChJ; lordchep AH[3]; lordschipes H[2]; lorschips W; wirchepe R. on] in H[2]. erþe] eorþe V; erde AM.
15 Or] *om* VAWMH[3]. ricchesse] Rytches H[3]; Richessis M. or(2)] and WH[3]; *om* V. rentis] rent AH[3]. &] or VJK. reste] rist W. here] her ChJKH[3]; heore V.
16 þanne] þen V. alle] *om* R. euere] RDChH[2]VJKWMH[3]; *in another ink after punctuation mark* T; *om* A.
17 *line om* W. Wisdom] wisdam RVMH[3]. and] an A. now is] is now A; ys KH[3] (*same hand after cancelled* not K). not] nouȝt DChH[2]; nouth H[3]. risshe] Russche VJAK; rosche H[3]; roysche R; ressche D; reissche M.
18–20 *as two lines divided after* desaytes W.
18 *run together with following* AMH[3]. it] ȝif it AM. be] beo V. cardit] cardyd DJ; cardet A; carded RChK; carket V; caried W; carpyd H[3]; menkt M. wiþ] wyt H[3]. coueitise] qweyntyse H[3]; conciens R. as . . . wolle] *om* AWMH[3]. cloþeris] clothears K. don] do H[2]; doþ ChV. here] her RChK; heor V; *om* J.
19 þat . . . deseites] and desaytes W; *om* AMH[3]. þat] That þat D; Thay þat K; He þat J; Tha H[2]. can] *om* DVJK. construe] contryven K; counterfetyn J; Conterfeteþ V. deseites] deseytes R; disceytes DVJK; þe deseites TChH[2]. &] & to A; To WH[3]. conspire] conspiren RK; Conspiret V. wrongis] wrong WH[3].
20 lede forþ] forþre D. lede] leden K; ledyn JA; ledeþ V. a] þe R. to] and A. lette] letten K; lettin M; lettyn with J; leuyn A. þe] *om* JW. treuþe] truþe RJK.
21 þat] he þat H[3]. suche] swyche JM; sweche H[3]; swedche A; swichani R; shch W. craftis] craft M; *om* RA. conne] connen D; con H[2]; cunnen V; kan RJK; kan do M; can doun H[3]; do can AW. to . . . yclepid] to counseil beoþ Iclept V; to counceile is cleped K; to councel es clepyd J; to counsel is callid MH[3]; to consaill is called W; ben yclepid to counseil TH[2]; ben clepid to councel A; ben cleped to conceile Ch; be cleped to Counceyl D; is cleped to counseyl R.

And ben seruid as sires þat serue þe deuil.
Iob þe ientile in his gestis seide it:
Quare via impiorum p[ros]peratur, [bene] est omnibus qui praue agunt ⁊ inique? |
And he þat haþ holy writ ay in his mouþ, *fol.* xlix *a*
And can telle of tobie ⁊ of þe twelue apostlis, 25
Or prechen of þe penaunce þat pilat[u]s wrouȝte
To iesu þe gentil þat Iewis todrowe
On crois vpon caluarie, as clerkis vs techiþ,
Litel is he louid or lete by þat suche a lessoun techiþ,
Or daun[cel]id or drawe forþ; þise disours wyte þe soþe. 30

22 ben] bene J; bien H^{2}; arn M; is R; *om* ChW. seruid] serued RH^{2}VW; Iseruyd H^{3}; Iserued Ch. as] as a RW. sires] seris A; sire RW. þat] and H^{2}. serue] seruen DCh; seruyn JA; serueþ RV; servith K; sewit M; sweyn of H^{3}; folweþ W. þe] þat M. deuil] deuylis lore H^{3}; deuels lore W; deuelis loris A; lore M.
23 *line om* R. Iob] But Iob H^{3}; Forþy iop M. in . . . it] seide in his geste M. in] ⁊ D. gestis] gest JW; geeste H^{2}. seide] saide W; said K; seyden D. it] it for a sawe K; *om* VAWH^{3}.
23α *copied in place of* X 150 U. *Quare*] *In* H^{3}; *sempiternum* (?) M. *via impiorum*] *impiorum uia* R. *via*] *om* K. *prosperatur*] UVJ; *prosperabitur* M; *preparatur* TDH^{2}; *preperatur* Ch; *preparabitur* AW; *properatur* RK; *probabitur* H^{3}. *bene*] RUVJAM; *quod bene* H^{3}; *ve ve* D; *ve* TChH^{2}KW (*same hand over erasure of longer word* W). *est*] *est in* A; *om* ChW. *qui*] *que* A. *praue*] *praui sunt* W; *peruerse* U; *preuare* (?) *sunt* J. *agunt ⁊ inique*] *⁊ inique agunt* RUVJWMH^{3}; *⁊ inique agerunt* A.
24 And] Ac V; *om* AMH^{3}. he] *om* W. haþ . . . writ] holi writte haþe ChVJ. haþ] hat MH^{3}; hatȝ H^{2}; had W; *om* D. ay] euer VW; alday M; *om* AK. in] hyn A. mouþ] mouȝt H^{2}.
25 can] con V. telle] tellen V; tellyn JA. tobie] tobyȝe H^{3}; theologie R. of(2)] *om* VAW. þe] is A; *om* DM. twelue] twelf Ch. apostlis] apostelis AH^{3}; apostolys RH^{2}; appostoles K.
26 Or] Other K; And VA. prechen] prechin RJAMH^{3}; preche ChK. þe] *om* W. pilatus] RDChVAKW; pylat JMH^{3}; pilatis TH^{2}. wrouȝte] wrouhte V; wrouȝthe R; wrougthe M; wrowht J; wrouth AH^{3}.
27 To] Of D. þat] that the K. Iewis] Iues J. todrowe] todrowen MH^{3}; todrowyn JA; todrewen W; todrewyn K.
28 On] As on H^{3}. crois] cros RVAKW MH^{3}. vpon] on ChW. caluarie] calwarie R. techiþ] techit M; techitȝ H^{2}; techeþ DCh; techyn RAH^{3}; techen KW; telleþ V.
29 *line om* Ch. Litel] Luytel V. he] *om* A. louid or] to M; *om* J. or . . . by] *om* W. lete] leten V; letyn JM; lettyn K; late RDA; sett H^{3}. suche] swych DJM; sweche AH^{3}. a] *om* M. lessoun] lessyn J; sermoun A; sarmon WH^{3}; sermouns M. techiþ] techitȝ H^{2}; techeþ D; teches R; lerith J; Redeþ V; schewith AH^{3}; schewit M; sheweþ W.
30 Or . . . or] But hoso can daunce ⁊ H^{3}. dauncelid] dauncelyd D; daunselit M; Daunseled V; dawenseld J; daunsels W; damseld R; dauntid TH^{2}; daunted K; daunteþ Ch; honourid A. drawe] drawen DVK; drawyn J; draweþ ChW; drawit M. forþ] for W. þise] þis RVW; these H^{2}AH^{3}; þes ChJK; *om* D. disours] dyssours H^{3}. wyte] witen VK; wytyn J; witit M; wote W; wot A; knowith H^{3}. þe] ȝe for Ch.

For ȝif harlotrie ne halp[e] hem betere, haue god my trouþe,
More þanne musik, or makyng of god almiȝt,
Wolde neuere king, ne kniȝt, ne canoun of seint poulis
Ȝiue hem to here ȝerisȝiue þe value of a grote.
Menstralsie & merþe among men is nouþe 35
Leccherie & losengerie & loselis talis;
Glotonye & grete oþis, þise arn games nowadayes.
Ac ȝif þei carpen of crist, þise clerkis & þise lewid,
At mete [in here] merþe, whanne mynstralis ben stille,

31 *divided from following after* good W. ȝif] ȝef Ch; *om* M. harlotrie] harlottryȝe H[3]; harlatrie A; harlot D. ne] no H[3]; *om* D. halpe] Ch; halp TJ; holpe RVH[3]; holp M; helpe DH[2]AW; help K. hem] hym Ch; *om* K. betere] bet J; þe bettere AKW; þe bet V; nouth more H[3]. haue . . . trouþe] so god me helpe A. haue . . . my] to haue good In W; þan þe M; þan grace or H[3]. haue] so haue R. trouþe] truþe RJ; treuthe MH[3]; trewþe DK; soule V.
32 More] & more MH[3]. þanne] þen V. musik] ony musyk J. god] Crist V. almiȝt] almyȝte D; almyȝty ChH[2]K; almyȝthi R; almithi MH[3]; almyti A; *om* VJ.
33 Wolde] Nold J. neuere] neþer AW; neiþer þe M; *om* J. ne(1)] no ChJ; noun H[3]; *om* M. kniȝt] knyth AH[3]; *om* M. ne(2)] no Ch; nor A; non H[3]. canoun] chanoun RChJAKWH[3]; chanouns M. seint] sent H[3]; saynt K; sen A; *om* WM. poulis] poule D.
34 Ȝiue] ȝyuyn J; ȝif AW; ȝeue RDH[2] KH[3]; ȝeuen VM; ȝef Ch. hem] hym W. to] for K. here] her ChJK; hyre W; heore V. ȝerisȝiue] service K. ȝiue] ȝeue RDChJ; ȝifte AMH[3]; ȝeft W. þe] *om* W. value] valour K; worth W; ȝift J. of] *om* W. grote] *defective* H[2].
35 Menstralsie] Mynstralcy ChH[2]A; Ac menstracie R; Ac mynstralcie W; but menstralsie M; But mynstralsyȝe H[3]; BOte Munstralsye V; For mynstralcy J; But mynstrelles K. &] or J; *om* K. merþe] myrthe H[2]AH[3]; murþe DV; mirthes K. among . . . nouþe] is now among men W. among] amonges K; amongys J. men] *om* H[3]. is nouþe] *defective* H[2]. is] ar K; *om* J. nouþe] nouth A; nowe JH[3]; nouye M; nouȝt Ch; Cowthe K.
36 *divided from following after* glotonye K. Leccherie] But lechorie Ch; Is lychery J; Losengerie WM; Losenrye A; Bouseuryȝe H[3]. &(1)] *om* J. losengerie] losengrie RChVK; lecherie WM; rebaudie A; bysmeryȝe H[3]. &(2)] *om* K. loselis] losell (*rest of line defective*) H[2]; broþelles R.
37 Glotonye] Gloteny J; and glotonye RDKM; And glotenie W; And glotenyȝe H[3]; And geten gold V. &] with RDVJ KM. þise . . . adayes] *defective* H[2]. þise] þis W; þese H[3]; þes RChK; *om* DVJA. arn] are R; beoþ V; buþ D; arn her Ch; is J. games] gamys A; gamus V; gamenys RM; gamyn J; *om* W. now] *om* H[3]. adayes] o dayes RJ; on dayis H[3]; on days A; *om* M.
38 Ac] Bot ChVK; and RJWMH[3]; *om* A. ȝif] ȝef Ch. þei] þai A; thay K; he H[3]. carpen] carpyn ChJAMH[3]; carpe W. of] on A. þise . . . lewid] *defective* H[2]. þise(1)] þis VW; þese DA; þes RChJK; þe H[3]. þise(2)] þis VW; þese DAM; þes RChJK; þe H[3]. lewid] lewed RD; lewede VM; lewd ChH[3]; lewde K; lewid men A; lewed men W.
39 At] RDChJAKWH[3]; Atte VM; At þe TH[2]. in here] in here RWM; in her JKH[3]; in heor V; & at TDChH[2]A. merþe . . . stille] *defective* H[2]. merþe] myrþe ChH[3]; myrth A; murþe DV; merthes KW; merthys J; monye M. whanne] qwan JH[3]; whon V; þece A. mynstralis] mynstralles Ch; mynstrals D W; mystrelis H[3]; menstralis M; menstrales R; menstrelles K; Munstrals V. ben stille] faylen R. ben] be D; beþ W; bet M; beoþ V; arn A.

Þanne telle þei of þe trinite how two slowe þe þridde, 40
And bringe forþ a ballid resoun, t[a]k[e] bernard to witnesse,
And putte forþ presumpcioun to proue þe soþe.
Þus þei dryuelen at here deis þe deite to knowe,
And gnawen god in [þe gorge] whanne here guttis fullen.
Ac þe carful may crigen & carpe at þe gate, 45
Boþe for hungir & for þrest, & for chele quak[e];
Is non to nymen hym In ne his [noye] amende,
But hunsen hym as an hound & hoten hym go þenne.

40 Þanne] þenne V. telle] tellen KM; tellyn JAH³; telleþ V. þei] þai A; thay K; hym H³; *om* J. of . . . þridde] *defective* H². trinite] trenite A. how . . . þridde] qwow þat it is in iij H³; a tale or twoo K. two] þe to A. slowe] slowen VM; slowyn J; slew Ch. þridde] þredde RW.
41 W *corrupts to* And take bernard to witnesse & bryng forþ a balled reson. And . . . resoun] A ballyd resoun þei bringyn forth J. And] *om* A. bringe] bryngen DH²K; bryngyn M; bringeþ ChV; Bryngith A; bryngyt H³. forþ . . . witnesse] *defective* H². a] *om* V. ballid] balled RDChK; Ballede V. resoun] reason K; Resouns V; *om* R. take bernard] barnard I take A. take] D; tak V; takyth H³; & take K; & takyn JM; and takeþ Ch; tok T; tokne R. bernard] barnerde K; barnard H³.
42 putte] putten RK; puttyn JA; putteþ Ch; puttit M; put H²; potyn H³; puyteþ V. forþ] forth a A; a KW; *om* DH³. presumpcioun] persomcyoun H³. proue] prouen RKW; prouyn JM; preue ChV; preuyn AH³.
43 *line om* A. þei] thay K. dryuelen] dryvylyn K; dreuelen W; dreuelyn DCh JH³; drauelen V; drauelyn RM. at here] at þe W; atte M; on heore V. deis] dees W; des RCh; dese K; dysch H³. þe] *om* JM. deite] deitis M; deuynyte J; dette D; detre H³. knowe] knowen DM; knowyn H³.
44 gnawen] gnawyn JA; gnawe R; knawe D; gabbyn H³; demeþ V. god] *om* H³. in] into V; be M. þe] RDVJAM H³; here TH²; her ChK; *om* W. gorge] RVJAKWH³; goorge M; þrote TDH²; þrotes Ch. whanne] whon V; when RCh; qwan JH³. here] her ChK; heore V; þe JH³. guttis] Gottus V; þrotes R. fullen] fullin M; fulle H²; follen V; fillen ChK; fillyn AH³; fyllyth J; ben fulle W.
45 Ac] Bot ChVKM; And H³; *om* A. þe(1)] *om* V. carful] carful man A; Carful Mon V. may] mowen K. crigen] crien RDChH²VJAKMH³; carpen W. &] *om* A. carpe] carpen DChK; carpyn JMH³; crien W; clepen V; *om* A. at þe] atte VWM. gate] gate RKWMH³.
46 Boþe] Boþin M; *om* A. for(1)] of DV. for(2)] of DV; *om* K. þrest] thrist RH²J AKH³; þirst Ch; þurst DV. chele] chele of his nayles K; cold JAH³. quake] VRJ KW; quakyn AMH³; quakiþ TH²; quakeþ DCh.
47 Is] Nis V; þer is RJH³; Is þer AWM. non] no Mon V. to . . . ne] him neih V; with Inne þat A. nymen] nyme W; neme Ch; nemyn JH³; nemle R; takyn M; meuen D. hym] *om* H². In] *om* DJ. ne] no Ch; & MH³; *om* W. his] is A; *om* R. noye] AW; nuy V; anoye K; noyce J; disease M; anguyssh TChH²; angwys RD; anyr H³. amende] amendyn DM; to Amende VJ; wil amendyn A; to mende Ch.
48 Here U **resumes.** But] *om* A. hunsen] honesshen DV; hounshe R; honysche U; huschen K; hoynyn J; hold AW; comaundin MH³. hym(1)] on him J; hym out AWM; out H³. as] as on J. an] a J. hound] houne M. hoten] hotyn JMH³; hote RUKW; hunte A. hym(2)] hem Ch; *om* M. go] so A. þenne] þennes UDChV; þennys RJM; þenis A; þens WH³; hennys K.

Litel louiþ he þat lord þat leniþ hym al þat blisse,
Þat þus partiþ wiþ þe poore a parcel whanne hym nediþ. 50
Nere mercy in mene men more þan in riche
[Mendynaunt ȝ] meteles miȝte go to bedde.
God is muche in þe [gorge] of þis grete maistris,
Ac among [mene] men hise mercy & his werkis,
And so seiþ þe sauter, se[ke] it in *Memento*: 55
Ecce audiuimus eam in effrata, inuenimus eam in campis silue.
Clerkis and k[ete] men carpen of god faste,
And han [hym] muchel in here mouþ, ac mene men in herte.
Freris and faitours han founden vp suche questiouns
To pleise wiþ proude men, siþen þe pestilence tyme,

49 Litel] lite D; Luyte V; liteþ Ch. louiþ] louen M. leniþ] leneþ RUDChV; lent A; lonyt M; leueþ W; levith K. hym] hem M; *om* R. al] *om* UDVJW. þat] þys M; the K; his A.
50 partiþ] parteþ RDChV; partin MH³; parten W. a] no K. whanne] whon V; qwan JH³. hym] hem JK. nediþ] nedit M; nedeþ RUDChW; neodeþ V; lyste A.
51 Nere] Neore V; ne were RUJAMH³. mene] meane K. men] man A. þan] þen V.
52 *line om* A. Mendynauntȝ] *compare line* 201; Mendicans J; Many mendynantȝ W; Many mendinantes K; Manye mendynauns R; Manye mendenawtes U; Many pore men DM; Manye men TChH²H³; Wiþ Mony V. meteles] metelys R; defauti Meeles V. miȝte] myth H³; migthin M; Mihte þei V. go] gon JMH³; goon K.
53 is] his U. muche] mochel K; mychel J; michil M; meche A; mechel RU; mechyl H³. þe] his U; here AM; *om* W. gorge] RUChH²VJAKWH³; þrote TD; mouth M. of] amonges K; among W; with Ch. þis] thise H²; þies J; þes RChK; þese UA; þeose V; þe H³. maistris] masters K.
54 *line om* U. Ac] Bot ChVJKM; and RDH³; *om* A. among] amonges K; amongys J. mene] RDChVJAWMH³; mean K; *om* TH² (*late corrector inserts* meane H²). hise] is K; is his WH³. mercy] grace J. & his] is in R. werkis] workes K; werchyng A.
55 And] *om* JA. so] As A. seiþ] seit M; saith KW. seke] DW; sek R; seek U; sekyth JA; seche H³; sech VKM; se TCh H². it] *om* JAM. in] *om* A. *Memento*] *mementote* R; *Me memento* M.
55α *eam*(1)] *eum* RChJ; *om* U. *in*(1)] *om* R. *effrata*] *eufrata* RU. *inuenimus . . . silue*] *om* A. *eam*(2)] *eum* ChV. *silue*] siluet H³.
56 kete] VKW; kedde RU; ked D; kydde Ch; kid TH²; grete MH³; courte A; cowrte J. carpen] carpyn JMH³; spekyn A. god] *after cancelled* men *same hand* H². faste] ofte V.
57 han] haue DChK. hym] DChH²VJA WMH³; *om* TRUK. muchel] muche VW; much Ch; mochel K; moche D; mychel JM; mechel RU; mechil AH³; mekul H². here] her RChJKH³; heore V; *om* D. mouþ] muþ W; mowtȝ R. ac] bot ChVJKM; and RWH³; an A. mene] mean K; many R; fewe MH³. men] *om* H³. in] in her ChH³; in here (here *cancelled*) H². herte] harte K; hertys H³.
58 Freris . . . faitours] *erased* H³. Freris] Fryres U. han] haue DK. founden] foundyn JAM; founde RCh; fonden UH²; fondyn H³. vp] *om* H²VM. suche] swche H³; swyche J; swych UM; a A. questiouns] questioun A; questiounouns M.
59 To] Forto J. pleise] plese RUDH²VW; plesen ChK; plesyn JAM; plesse H³. proude] prude R; þis proude V; þe proud A; poure Ch; pore M. siþen] syþin M; sithe H²W; siþ UK; sethin J; seþe D; seþ Ch; seþþe V; syn RAH³. þe] þis H³; *om* DVJM.

Þat defouliþ oure f[eiþ] at fest[is] þ*er*e þei sitten. 60
For now is iche boy bold, & he be riche,
To tellen of þe trinite to be holden a sire,
And fyndiþ forþ fantasies oure feiþ to apeire,
And [ek] defame þe fadir þat vs alle made,
And carp[en] aȝens clergie crabbide wordis: 65
"Why wolde oure sauio*ur* suffre such a worm in his blisse |
Þat he gilide þe wo*m*man & þe wy aftir, *fol.* xlix *b*
Þoruȝ whiche a werk & wille þei wenten to helle,
And alle here seed for here synne þe same wo suffride?"

60 Þat] þei V; Thai W. defouliþ] defoulit M; defouleþ RD; defoulen UChVW; defoulid A. feiþ] feyth UAKMH^3; fayth JW; faiþe Ch; Fey V; feyþ als R; false T; face D; *heavily corrected from* fa:::e *to* (?) fase H^2. festis] UJAMH^3; fest*es* RChVKW; þe feste TDH^2. þei] þai AW. sitten] sittyn JAMH^3.
61 For] *om* A. iche] ich WM; vche V; eche AKH^3; ech RD; eu*er*y Ch. boy] body D. & . . . riche] Broþel an oþer V. &] ȝyf H^3; ȝif þat AWM.
62 To] for to RJA. tellen] tellyn JAMH^3; telle RUW; talken V. trinite] trenite A. to] and to Ch; and A. be] be*n* RJAMH^3; beon V. holden] holdyn AH^3; holde RUW; howldyn J; Iholdi*n* M. sire] sere A.
63 fyndiþ] fyndeþ RDChV; fynte A; fynt WH^3; fyndyn JM; fyde U. forþ] for H^3; newe M. fantasies] fantsyes D; fawtys J. feiþ] faiþ WChJK. to] for to UD. apeire] apaire Ch; apery*n* M.
64 And . . . defame] *defective* H^2. And] A W. ek] eke RVJAWMH^3; to U; *om* TDChK. defame] ::::fame H^2; defameþ DChVK; defamith AH^3; defamit M; famyn J. þe] oure D. fadir] fader RUCh H^{2}VJW; fadur A; father K. vs . . . made] formyd vs alle J; formed vs alle Ch. vs] ones W. made] makyde U; makeþ D.
65 And carpen] *defective* H^2. carpen] carpe*n* RUChK; carpyn JM; carpeþ DW; carpith AH^3; carpide T; Craken V. aȝens] aȝen R; aȝeyn VJ; ageyn KM; ageyne A; of U. clergie] þe Clergie VK; clergise A. crabbide] crabbyd JKH^3; crabbede RH^{2}V; crabbed DChW; crappede M; crambit A. wordis] wordis an sayth A.
66–9 *as five lines divided after* worm—woman—will—synne W.
66 Why . . . sauiour] *defective* H^2. Why] Qwy JH^3. oure sauiour] God vr saueour V; god M. suffre] suffry*n* M; suffur J; suffurre H^3. such] susche D; swych UJM; swech H^3; þat A. a] *om* UA. worm] werm RUM; wyrm H^3. in . . . blisse] *om* V.
67 V *corrupts to* In such a wrong wyse þe wommon to bigyle. Þat . . . þe(1)] *defective* H^2. Þat] To A; *om* W. he gilide] he gyled D; begylyd H^3; begilede M; begiled RChK; begyles U; begile AW; deceyuyd J. þe(1)] suche a W. wy] why Ch; wey RD; man UJAKMH^3; worm W.
68 V *corrupts to* Boþe hir hosebonde and heo to helle þorw him wenten. Þoruȝ . . . &] *defective* H^2. Þoruȝ] Thorow JA; þourth M; Þoruȝt D; þorgh W; Thorw H^3; Þ*our* U; Thurȝt R; Thrugh K. whiche . . . wille] who is wilis & his werkys M. whiche] wiche DCh; wheche A; qweche H^3; swyche UW; such K; wykkyd J. a] *om* RChJAKH^3. werk] work ChK; werkys J; *om* A. wille] wile K; while A. þei] þai A; thay K. wenten] wentyn JAM; wenton H^2; we*n*te RUD H^3; went W. helle] helle aftre W.
69 And . . . synne] *defective* H^2. alle] *om* VJ. here(1)] *after cancelled* þat sed U; her ChJKH^3; heore V; ou*re* R. for] aft*er* for J. here(2)] her ChJKH^3; þat RUV; *om* W. synne] su*n*ne V. þe] that H^{2}W. suffride] suffrede U; suffred RCh; sufferid A; suffurd H^3; suffryn JM; suffren K; suffreþ D; drien V; such suffre moten W.

Suche motifs þei meuen, þise maistris in here glorie, 70
And make men to mysbeleue *þat* musen on here wordis.
Ac austyn þe olde for alle suche *pre*chide,
And for suche tale telleris suche a teme shewide:
Non plus sapere quam oportet.
Wilneþ neu*ere* to wyte why that god wolde 75
Suffre sathan his sed to bigile,
Ac beleue lelly o[n þe] lore of holy chirche,
And *pre*ye hym of *par*doun & pen*au*nce [in] þi lyue,
And for his muchel m*er*cy to amende vs here.

70 Suche . . . þise] *defective* H². Suche . . . þei] þat W. Suche] swiche RUJM; Sweche AH³. motifs] Motyues V; moteyuys M; motyngys J; motetys H³; motes U; notes R; maisties A. þei] thay K; *om* J. meuen] meuyn JAM; meue H³; mouen D; moue U; meuy3t R; menen W. þise] þ*is* RVW; þese UH³; þes DChAK; þies J. maistris] masters K. here] her ChJKH³; heor V.
71 And . . . musen] *defective* H². make] maken ChK; makyn JAH³; makeþ V. men] me R. to] in JAKWMH³; *om* UDV. mysbeleue] misse beleue A; nice beleue W. þ*at*] and Ch. musen] musyn J; musit M; mousen RU; mousin A; mowsy*n* H³; leuen W; leeuen V. on] in RV. here] her ChJAKH³; heore V.
72 Ac] Bot ChVJKM; And H³; As A. olde] elde A; old clerk K; hor*e* R; bold W; holy man M. for] of A. suche] siche U; swiche RJM; sweche A; sweche me*n* H³. prechide] *pre*chid H²K; *pre*chede MH³; *pre*ched DCh; prechet U; *pre*cheþ RVW; *pre*cheris J; prechouris A.
73 *line om* Ch. for] for al W; *om* A. suche(1)] siche U; swyche JM; sweche AH³. tale telleris] teliers M. suche(2)] siche U; swyche JM; sweche AH³; this K; in his W. a] *om* KW. teme] teeme VJ; Theme K; tyme H³. shewide] schewid H²KH³; schewede M; schewed DW; shewyþ RUJ; scheweþ V; iseyde A.
74 *Non*] *Nolite* U. *quam oportet*] *&c* (*followed by scribble in another hand*) A. *oportet*] *oportet &c* JWM; *oportet sapere* RUDH²; *oportet sapere &c* ChK; *oportet sapere et sapere ad sobrietatem* H³; *oporteþ sapere* V
75 *divided from following after* why TRUD ChH²AKMH³; *after* godde W. Wilneþ . . . wyte] & bad no*n* man asky*n* wherfore ne M. Wilneþ neu*ere*] þ*at* hys wyl is ne were H³; That þis were A. Wilneþ] þis wilneþ 3e V; That is wil 3e W; þat is to say wilneþ RK; That is to seyn ne wilneþ TH²; That is to seyne willeþ D; Þat is to seie ne wilnehþ U; þat is to sey me willeþ Ch; Coueytyth J. to] RUDV JAH³; for to TChH²K; *om* W. wyte] wyten W; witten K; wete UCh; wetyn AH³. why] qwy JH³. wolde] *om* M.
76 Suffre] suffurre H³; Forto suffyr J; sufferede M; *om* A. sathan] Sathanas W. sed] sedis M; fod H². to] for to A.
77 *line om* A. Ac] Bot ChVKMH³; And U. beleue] belef M; beleef U; bylef R; beleueþ W; leeueþ V. lelly] treuliche M; trewly H³; holych W; holely J; *om* V. on þe] UDKWH³; on þat RV; in þe J; þe M; of TChH². lore] lord RU; leue J; *late corrector alters to* lord H². of] þat lereþ V. chirche] Churche D; cherche RJW.
78 *line om* A. preye] pray RUDJKWH³. hym] *om* H². of] of his U. & penaunce] *om* W. in] VJKM; here in WH³; be TUDChH²; by R. lyue] lyf W.
79 *line om* A. And] *om* Ch. for] of K. his] þe M. muchel] muchele V; muche H²W; much Ch; mochel K; moche RD; mychel JM; meche UH³. amende] amenden V; amendyn JM; mende Ch. vs] vs all K.

For alle þat wilneþ to wyte þe [whyes] of god almiȝt, 80
I wolde his eiȝen wern in his ars & his hele aftir
Þat euere eft wilneþ to wyte why [þat] god wolde
Suffren sathan his sed to bigile,
[O]r Iudas þe Iew Iesu betraye[n].
—Al was as he wolde; lord yworsshipid be þou, 85
And al worþ as þou wilt, whatso we telle—
And now comiþ a conyon & wolde cacche of my wittes
What is dowel fro dobet; now def mote he worþe,
Siþen he wilneþ to wyte which þei ben alle.

80–84 *disordered thus* J: 79—80+82—83—81—84.
80 *run together with line* 82 J. For] *om* A. wilneþ] willeþ RD; willet M; welyn H³; wole A; ȝernyth J. to] two V; so M; *om* AKWH³. wyte] wete DChH³; wetyn AM; *om* V. þe . . . almiȝt] *om* J. þe] al the K; *om* V. whyes] whyys K; weyes RV; weyis UH³; weys A; ways W; priuytes M; werkes TCh; werkis H²; wordes D. almiȝt] almyȝte U; almyȝty ChKW; Almihti V; almyȝthi R; almythy H³; almyti A; *om* M.
81 his(*all*)] here W; her K. eiȝen] eyȝe H³; eȝe V; eye RUDAKWM; Ie J. wern] were RUDChH²JAWMH³; wer K; weore V. ars] ers RH²VJ; hars U; eres D; taile K. hele] honde J.
82 *divided from following after* why RUD; after godde W. Þat . . . wyte] *om* J. euere] *om* M. eft wilneþ] wilneþ eft Ch. eft] oft H³; *om* RUAM. wilneþ] willeþ D; willit M; wylyn H³; wold A. to] for to UD; *om* AWH³. wyte] wete UCh; wetyn AMH³; *om* W. why] qwy UJMH³. þat(2)] þat RUDVJAKW MH³; *om* TChH². wolde] woolde M; *om* R.
83 Suffren] Suffryn JM; suffre UDH²W; Suffer Ch; Suffur H³; Soffre V; To suffre A; Suffre so K; suffrede R. sathan] sory sathan J; þat schrewe satan M; satan þe vnsaut H³; Sathan vnsaght W. sed] seed UH²VKH³; sedis M. to] for to A.
84 Or] RUDChVJAKM; Oþer W; Eythyr H³; Er TH². Iudas] qwy þat Iudas to J. Iew] Iue AKW; Ieuȝ V; Iues J. Iesu] his sone M. betrayen] (*after cancelled* ben) U; betraye ChV; to betraye AKWM; to betrayȝe H³; betrayede TRH²; betrayed D; betrayȝyd J.
85 Al] For al M. as] *om* M. he wolde] þow woldest Ch. lord . . . þou] þat lord be heried M. lord] *om* A. yworsshipid] Iworschipped K; yworshipt W; Iworscheped Ch; yworcheped R; Iwyrchepid U; worschiped D; worcheped H³; now worchepid A; Iheried V; thankyd J. be þou] þou be RU. þou] þe D; to the H³; he AW.
86 And] *om* A. al] *om* UDJW. worþ] wrouth A; beo V; was Ch. as . . . wilt] at his wille M. wilt] wolt VK. what] qwat JH³. so] so euere W; euer H³; sum euer A. telle] tellen V; tellyn M.
87 And] But WMH³; *om* DA. now] noun U. comiþ] comeþ RDChH²VW; comyn H³; komut (? konnit) M. a] þies J; *om* RU. conyon] Congyoun D; congeoun W; congoun ChKH³. & wolde] to J. &] *om* DM. cacche] cacchen V; cacchyn JM; cache H³; kaithe K; wete Ch; wetyn A. my] me VK; mennys J; him M; þuy (*for* þyn ?) H³.
88 What] Qwat JH³. is dowel] dowel is Ch; is wel A. fro] from MH³; & K. dobet] dobest Ch. now] *om* UM. def] deefe JM; daffe V. he] the H²K; *om* W. worþe] worthyn JAM.
89 Siþen] siþin M; Sith W; Sytthyn H³; Siþþe U; Sethyn J; Seþe D; Seþ Ch; Sþe A; Swiþe R; Sire V. wilneþ] willeþ UDCh; willit M; wil AH³; wiþneth W; ȝernyth J. to] *om* AH³. wyte] wytyn J; wete ChW; wetyn AMH³. which] wyche M; whuche V; qwyche J; qweche H³; what ChA. þei] þai W; thay K; hee H³; he A. ben] bene J; beþ Ch.

But he lyue in þe leste degre þat longiþ to dowel 90
I dar be his bolde boruȝ do bet wile he neuere,
Þeiȝ dobest drawe on hym day aftir oþer.'
And whanne þat wyt was war how his wif tolde
He beco[m] so confus he couþe nouȝt mele,
[And] also doumb as a dore drouȝ hym asid. 95
Ac for no carping I couþe, ne knelyng to þe ground,
I miȝte gete no g[r]ayn of hise grete wyttes,
But al lauȝinge he loutide & lokide vpon studie
In signe þat I shulde beseke hire of grace.
And whanne I was war of his wil to his wif gan I knele, 100

90 But] but ȝif RUK. lyue] lyf J; lyue lely U; leue RDChAWH^3; loue M. in] *om* M. leste] leest H^{2}J; last U. degre] day RU. longiþ to dowel] to dowel longit M. longiþ] longyt H^3.
91 I] For I UJKWM. dar] wol Ch. be] ben DVJAM. bolde] *om* V. boruȝ] borwȝ R; borgh W; borowe ChK; borow JA; borwe U; borw DVH^3; bourth M. do bet] þat do bet RVM. wile] wil RUDJW; wele M; wol Ch; nyl K; nul V; schal A; xal H^3. he] we R.
92 Þeiȝ] Þeiȝe U; þey ChH^{2}JM; þouȝ DK; Thogh W; þow RH^3; Thou A; þauȝ V. drawe] draw UDJW; drawen Ch. on] *om* Ch. day . . . oþer] halfe a day after J. aftir] after RUDChK; aftre W; aftur VH^3. oþer] oþur V; day RU.
93–4 *in another hand* K.
93 And] *om* A. whanne] qwan JH^3; whon V. þat] *om* AH^3. was] whas U; *om* W. war] ware DChJW; Iwar VKMH^3. his] is A. tolde] tolle H^2.
94 becom . . . confus] lost so his cowntenaunce J. becom] become DRChH^{2}AKW H^3; bicom V; bekam M; becomiþ T; come U. confus] confuse UK; confous R; confius M; confusyd DA; confoundet V; coy Ch; confers W. he] þat he JWH^3. couþe] coude RDH^{2}AMH^3; could K. nouȝt] nouth H^3; nowt U; not RDH^{2}VJKWM; *om* A. mele] speke H^3; spekyn M; carpe J; medle V; speke no more A.
95 *line om* M. And] RUVJKWH^3; *om* TDChH^{2}A. also] Als so H^2; As ChVJA KW. doumb] dowme J; dome K; dom RAW; dounbe U. dore] dornaile ChH^2 AK. drouȝ] drogh W; drow RUJAK; and drouȝ H^2; & drow H^3. asid] on syde AH^3; be syde J.
96 Ac] Bot ChVJKM; And UH^3; *om* A. no] non M. carping] Craft V. I] þat i UVKWH^3; þat he RM. couþe] cowde RUAMH^3; could K. ne] no Ch; ne for no A. to] on J. þe] *om* DVJA.
97 I] *after cancelled* He U; I ne M. miȝte] migthe M; myth H^3; myte A; couþ W. gete . . . grayn] no grayn gete H^3; no greyne getyn J. gete] getyn AM; Gettyn K. no] non M. grayn] W; grayne A; greyn RUDVM; greyne K; graunte Ch; gayn TH^2. hise] hire V; here W.
98 lauȝinge] laghyng W; lawhyng ChA; lauȝwhinge V; lawqwyng J; lauwynge M; lawyng D; louryng UK; *om* R. he] *om* R. loutide] loutid AJH^3; loutydde U; loutede RV; louted DChKW; lokede M. lokide] lokyd UH^{2}JAMH^3; lokede V; loked RDChKW. vpon] on A; on dame K. studie] stode R.
99 signe] syngne ChJH^3. I] h U. shulde] xulde H^3. beseke] besekyn JW; beseche UK; bisechen V; besechin M; seken R; prey A. hire] hir JH^3; here UDAW; her ChK; hure R. grace] URChH^{2}VJAK WMH^3; here grace D; his grace T.
100 *as two lines divided after* wille AWMH^3. And] *om* ChJA. whanne] whon V; Qwan J; whanne þat M; qwan þat H^3. was war] wuste V. of] þat it was A; þat such was W; þat swich was M; þat sweche was H^3. his(1)] is A; here W. gan] con V; *om* UJ. I knele] i knelyd UJ; I gon & kneled to the grounde W; I goun & knelyd to þe gronde H^3; I gon and knelid to ground A; I gon & knelede to þe erþe M.

And seide, 'm*er*cy madame, ȝo*ur* man shal I worþe
For to werche ȝo*ur* wil [while] my lif duriþ,
[To] kenne me kyndely to knowe what is dowel'.
'For þi meknesse, man,' q*ua*þ she, 'and for þi mylde speche,
I shal kenne þe to my cosyn þ*at* clergie is hoten. 105
He haþ weddit a wif wiþinne þise woukes sixe,
Is sib to þe seuene ars þ*at* script*ur*e is nempnid.
Þei two, [as] I hope, aftir my besekyng,
Shuln wisse þe to dowel, I dar wel vndirtake.'
Þanne was I [as] fayn as foul of fair morewen, 110
Gladd*er*e þanne þe gleman þ*at* gold haþ to ȝifte, |

101 seide] sayde RW; said K. ȝo*ur*] *om* M. man] mon V; *om* M. shal] xal H[3]; wile M. worþe] worthen K; beo V. *Here* J *adds a line: see above*, p. 49.
102 *line om* A. For to] To V; and K. werche] werchy*n* M; wyrche U; wirch Ch; wyrchin J; worche H[2]; worchen VK; wurche D. while] DRChVW; wil U; qwyl JH[3]; the while KM; þ*er* whiles TH[2]. my] ȝo*ur* R. duriþ] lastith M; lasteth K.
103 To] to RUDJAKWMH[3]; *om* TChH[2] V. kenne] kenny*n* J; ken W; Teche VH[3]; techyn M. kyndely] kuyndely V; kendely UDChAMH[3]. to] *om* A. knowe] knowen V; knowyn JM; knawe H[3]; *om* A. what] qwat JH[3]; wath A.
104 meknesse] myldenes A. man] Mon V; *om* JAH[3]. she] ȝhe A; heo V. for] *om* A. mylde] myild H[3]; melde Ch; faire M.
105 shal] xal H[3]. kenne] kenny*n* J; teche VH[3]; techi*n* M. cosyn] cosynys howse J. is] *om* RUAMH[3]. hoten] hotyn J; hote ChK; Ihoten V; hoteþ UW (*touched up* W); hotith AH[3]; hotit M; hotuþ R. *Here* J *copies lines* 108–109 *but cancels and repeats them below*.
106 haþ] hatȝ H[2]; hayþ U; had M. weddit] weddyd UH[2]JAKM; wedded RDChVWH[3]. wiþinne] wit innyn M. þise] þis RUVW; these H[2]AH[3]; þes ChK; *om* DJ. woukes] wokes DChKW; wokis MH[3]; wougys J; wykes RUH[2]V; wekis A. sixe] sexe RUChJAH[3]; sexxe W; vj M.
107 Is sib] þ*at* sibbe is J. Is] Þat is U. seuene] sefne RU. ars] artes ChKW; artys JAM. þ*at*] ꝧ JM. nempnid] nempned ChW; Inempnyd U; Inempnet V; nemned D; namyd KM; nemyd H[3]; ynempled R; Inemelid A; hotyn J.
108 Þei] Thai A; þe J(2). two] twoo K; to UAMH[3]. as] VJ(*both*)AKWMH[3]; *om* TRUDChH[2]. I] Ich V. aftir] þorow A. besekyng] besekyn W; beseching RChV M; byddyng J(*both*); wissynge K.
109 Shuln] shul RUDChH[2]VW; Xul H[3]; Schulyn J(2); Scholyn J(1); Schal AKM. wisse] wissen K; wyse A; techyn J(2); techene J(1). to] *om* M. wel] it J(*both*); *om* DVAM. vndirtake] vndertakyn J(1); ondertakyn *altered to* vndertakyn J(2).
110 Þanne] ÞEnne V; ꝧ þan M. as(1)] RUVJAKWMH[3]; a D; *om* TChH[2]. as(2)] as a H[3]. of] of a H[3]; on ChVA. fair] feir V; erne A. morewen] morwen RH[2]V; morwy*n* H[3]; morwe UM; morowen Ch; morowe DJK; morne A; morn W.
111 Gladd*er*e] Gladdore V; Gladdar K; ȝa gladdere M; And gladd*er*e H[3]. þanne] þen V. þe] a MH[3]; *om* DChJKW. gleman] glewman MH[3]; gleo Mon V; gluma*n* RJ; glewmen W. þat . . . to] is of his grete V. gold haþ] hath gold A; han gold W. haþ] hat MH[3]; hayt U. ȝifte] yefte K; ȝeft Ch; ȝiftes V.

And axide hire þe heiȝe wey where clergie [dwell]ide, *fol.* 1 *a*
'And tel me sum tokne to hym, for tyme is þ*at* I wende'.
'Axe þe heiȝe wey,' q*ua*þ heo, 'from henis to suffre
Boþe wele & wo ȝif þ*at* þou wile lerne, 115
And rid forþ be ricchesse, ac reste þou not þ*er*einne,
For ȝif þou coupl[e] þe w*ith* hym to clergie comist þou neu*ere*;
And ek þe longe launde þ*at* leccherie hatte,
Leue hym on þi left half a large myle or more,
Til þou come to a co*ur*t, kepe wel þi tunge 120
F[ro] lesinges & li[þer] speche & likerous drinkes.
Þanne shalt þou se sobirte, & simplite of speche,

112 And] I M. axide] axed J; axkid A; axked R; askyd KH^3; askede VM; asked DChW. hire] hyr H^3; here U; her ChK; herre W; hur*e* R; *om* DJA. þe] þo þe H^3. heiȝe] heye U; hey RDAH^3; eie M; hiȝe ChH^2; hye JKW. wey] way RChH^2KW. where] qwere JH^3; wher that K; þer A. dwellide] dwelt W; duellyd JH^3; duellede M; wel dwellid A; dwelleþ V; wonide T; wonyd D; wonede H^2; woned ChK; wonde RU.
113 And] *om* DJ. tel] Telle DChH^2JA MH^3. sum] *om* A. tokne] token A; tokene DH^2WH^3; tokyn ChJK. to] of RH^2A (*corrected to* to *similar hand* H^2). for . . . is] it is tyme A. þat] *om* DJH^3.
114–16 *as two lines divided after* woo W.
114 Axe] Axke RA; Aske DChKWMH^3; Axe þanne J; I schal teche þe V. heiȝe] heye U; hey RDH^3; eie M; hiȝe ChH^2; hye JKW; *om* A. wey] way RH^2KW. q*ua*þ heo] *om* J. heo] ȝhe A; she RUDCh KWMH^3. from] fro RUDChH^2WH^3; *om* JAM. suffre] suffure H^3.
115–16 *transposed, but the original scribe indicates the right order* R.
115 Boþe] Bothyn J; Bothe in H^3; boþin in M. wele] weele KW; weole V. &] & *in* MH^3. ȝif] ȝef Ch. þat] *om* DChJAK WMH^3. wile] wilt RDJAWH^3; willt U; wolt ChVK; wit M. lerne] leorne V.
116 And] *om* JA. rid] ride RUDChH^2 JAKWM; *om* H^3. ac] ar *corrected to* ac *by original scribe; late corrector cancels this for* and H^2; bot ChAH^3; & KM; *om* RUVJ. reste] byde A; trust Ch. þou] þe RVKH^3; *om* JAW. not] nouȝt DChV; nouht J; nouth H^3; nowt U. inne] *om* A.
117 For] *om* A. ȝif] ȝef Ch; *om* U. couple] RVJA; couplest DW; couplist TH^2; cowpelest K; coplest Ch; copplyst H^3; comple U; compleinyst M. þe] *om* A. w*ith*] *late corrector prefixes* þ*er* H^2; to VM. to clergie] þ*er* J.
118 ek] leue A. þe] be þe M. longe] *om* A. launde] lande A; lane M. þat] *same hand above cancelled* of U. leccherie] lechorie Ch; rebaudie A. hatte] hate W; hette V; hotte K; hatteþ R; hattyth H^3; hauntith A; hauntid M; *in margin, another hand* hath H^2.
119 Leue] lef RDH^2; Lete A. hym] it W; *om* M. þi] þe U. left] lyft RJAKW; luft V. half] halue J; hande WMH^3; side Ch. large] *om* JW. or] oþ*er* W; othir J; and RUChH^3; an A.
120 Til] Foor til U; Forte V; Whan AW; And qwa*n* H^3. to] tyl D. a] þe M. co*ur*t] corwt H^3; court of M. kepe] kep RUVAH^3.
121 Fro] fro RUDChJAWMH^3; From VK; For TH^2 (*cancelled for* from *by late corrector* H^2). &(1)] fre A; *om* J. liþer] lither KW; lethyr JH^3; lether M; ledur A; liȝeris TH^2; lyȝeres V; liȝers Ch; liere*s* RUD. speche] speches Ch; spechys J; *om* UD. &(2)] & fro A; *om* J. likerous] lekerous U; lecerous Ch. drinkes] drinke V.
122 Þanne] þe*n*ne V; And þa*n* H^3. shalt] salt J; xalt H^3; schal A. þou] *om* U. se] sen MH^3; sene J; see K; seo V; *om* A. sobirte] soberte RUChH^2M; sobrete DJ W; sobryete H^3; sobernes K; sobre V. &] of U. simplite] symplete D; sympulte H^2; symplenesse RMH^3; sympilnes A; symplesse UJKW; sympel ChV.

Þ*at* iche wi3t be in wille his wyt þe to shewen;
So shalt þou come to clergie þ*at* can many wyttes.
Sey hym þis signe, I sette hym to scole, 125
And þ*at* [I] grete wel his wyf for I wrot hire þe bible,
And sette hire to sapience & to hire saut*er* yglosid.
Logik I lerid hire, & al þe lawe aftir,
And alle þe musons of musik I made hire [to] knowe.
Plato þe poete, I putte hym ferst to boke; 130
Aristotel & oþ*ere* mo to arguen I tau3te;
Gram*er* for girles I garte ferst write,
And bet hem wiþ a baleis but 3if þei wolde lerne.

123 Þ*at*] Qwat J; And K. iche] eche UD ChAKW; eu*er*i V. wi3t] wy3th D; wyth AH^3; wit R; man M; mon V. be] beo V. his] hit R. þe to] to þe H^3; for to ChH^2. shewen] Schewyn DAM; shewe RUVJK WH^3.
124 shalt þou] schaltow J; shal þou RA. come] comy*n* JM; couþe A. clergie] clergy3e H^3; clergice A. can many] con mony V. wyttes] þing*es* RVKWM; thingis JA; thyng*us* H^3; thenges U.
125 Sey] Say KW; and sey RUH^3. þis] þes D; þe A; *om* U. signe] syngne J; syne A; tokene VM. I] þat I V. scole] schole A.
126 *line om* U. And] *om* A. þat] if H^2; *om* ChW. I] RDVJAKWMH^3; þou TH^2; *om* Ch. grete] gret JAW; grette V; gete R. his] is A. for] *om* DJAM. wrot] wroth A. hire] hyr H^3; here DAW; her ChK; hi*m* R. þe] a V. bible] bibille Ch; bille WMH^3; Bulle V.
127 sette] sent H^3. hire(1)] hir KH^3; here UDJAW; her Ch; hur*e* R. &] an A; *om* ChJ. to(2)] *om* JK. hire(2)] hyr H^3; here D; her ChJ; þe RUAKWM. yglosid] Iglosyde J; yglosed RChW; Igloset V; glosyd UMH^3; glosed DK.
128–66 *misplaced after line* 206 D.
128 Logik] logek Ch; Lo logyk V; Long K. lerid] lered V; lernyd JAM; lerned RDChWH^3; servyd K. hire] hyr H^3; here UDJAW; her ChK; hur*e* R. lawe] lawes D.
129 And] *om* M. þe] *om* VH^3. musons] musonys UJ; musionis H^2; mosou*ns* R; moysons H^3; musun A. of] In VJAW. musik] mosyk R; nusik A; mesik Ch. hire] *small e in another script above* i W; hyr H^3; here UJA; her DChK; hur*e* R. to knowe] RUVJAKWMH^3; knowe alse TH^2; knowe also Ch; knowe aft*er* D.
130 þe] and RUCh. poete] Poyete V; poyet ChJ. I] *om* A. hym] he*m* RUCh; *om* JH^3. ferst] first DChJKW; furst RH^2V; frist AH^3. boke] scole MH^3.
131 Aristotel] Aristodil A; Aristtele M. to . . . tau3te] I tavghten to argewe K; I tau3the furst to argue R; I tawte ferst to argue U. arguen] arguy*n* JH^3; argue AWM; argeu (? argen) Ch. I] first I J. tau3te] taugthe MH^3; tauth A; taght W; tawte J.
132 for . . . ferst] ferst for gerlys I gerd forto J. girles] gerles DCh; gerlis RA; gurles H^2; Children V; childryn M; childery*n* H^3. garte] gert Ch; gar R; made WMH^3; gan A; gon V. ferst] first DChK; furst H^2; ferst to M; first to W; furst to RV; frist to AH^3. write] writen KW; wrytyn JM; whryte U.
133 bet] bett K; bette ChA; beet UM; Beot V. hem] hi*m* M. baleis] balice W; bayles A. but 3if] but 3ef Ch; but DAM; til W. þei] þai A. wolde] woldyn JM; wuld D. lerne] lernen V.

[Of] alle kynne craftis I contreuide tolis,
Of carpenteris & kerueris; [I] kende ferst masons, 135
And lernide h[e]m lyuel & lyne þei3 I loke dymme.
Ac theologie haþ tenid me ten score tymes,
For þe more I muse þeron þe mistlokere it semiþ,
And þe deppere I deuynide þe derkere me þou3te;
It is no science forsoþe for to sotile þereinne. 140
Ne were þe loue þat liþ þerein a wel lewid þing it were.
Ac for it lat best be loue I loue it þe betere,
For þere þat loue is lord lakkiþ neuere grace.

134 *line marked with cross* H^3; *divided from following after* here TDChH^2; *after* lerne R; *after* lere U. Of] VJKWM; Off H^3; For A; And TRUDChH^2. kynne] kyn H^2; kynnes Ch; kyns W; skynnys H^3; kenne R; ken D; kennes M; Maner V; knyuis A. contreuide] contreuid M; contreved W; contryvyd KH^3; contryued D; contrued A; contrewed Ch; construed RU; counterfetyd J; con Counterfeten V. tolis] A; toles W; toolys M; talys H^3; here Tolis TDH^2; her toles K; heor tooles V; firste her tolys (firste *same hand after cancelled* fert) J; here to lerne Tolus R; hure ferst to lere Tolis U; here Ch.

135 *divided from following after* lerned J. Of] As H^3; *om* ChJ. &] of AKM; *om* D. kerueris] keruirs M; carueris A; carvers K; kerue RU. I] RUDVJA; & I K; & TCh H^2WMH^3. kende] kenned ChW; kennyd DJAKH^3; tau3te V; tau3þe R; tauþte U. ferst] first ChKW; furst H^2V; fryst AH^3; & DJ.

136 And . . . lyne] Leuel & lyne I hem lernyd AH^3; Leuel and lyne I hem lerned W. And . . . hem] *om* M. &] I J. lernide] lernyd H^2; lerned RUChJK; lered DV. hem] URDChVK; hym TH^2; To wyrchyn with J. lyuel & lyne] lyne and leuel RU. lyuel] leuel DChJKM. þei3] þei JM; þou3 DK; þou3e U; þogh W; þow RCh AH^3; þau3 V. loke] lokede R; lokyd U.

137–8 J *corrupts to* But in teology rit dyrke þat semyth.

137 Ac] Bot ChVKM; And RH^3; *om* A. theologie] thologie R. haþ] hat AMH^3; hat3 H^2; hayt U; þat RK. tenid] tened RUDChKW; teoned V; tenyn A. ten] oftere þan x M. score] schore DA. tymes] tyme DM; tynne A.

138 For] *om* A. þe(1)] *om* D. I] þat I M. muse] mouse U; musid A; studie V. þeron] þer In AWMH^3. mistlokere] mystoloker W; mistlikere R; mystlyere H^3; misteliere M; mistiere A; derkore V. semiþ] semit M; semeþ RDChH^2VKW; semyd A.

139 *line om* A. And] *om* JM. deppere] deppore V; depar K; dippere M; sporere H^3. I] þat I W. deuynide] deuynid H^2; deuyned Ch; dyuynyd J; diuinede V; dyuyned UDK; dyuened W; deuyne H^3; deuyne hit R. derkere] dyrker J; darkar K; drykere H^3; deppere RU; Mistiloker V. me] me hit R; hit Ch; I U. þou3te] þou3þe R; þougthe M; þoght W; þowte UJ (e *over an* h J); thynkyt H^3; semed Ch.

140 no] non M. for to] to RUDV. sotile] sotilen V; sotylyn J; sotelen DW; sotelyn AMH^3; sotelye K; sutyle U. þereinne] Inne JAKWMH^3.

141 *line om* U. Ne were] Nere W; Neore V. þe] *om* DH^3. þat] þe more þat W. liþ] lyhþ V; li3th D; lith3 M; lieth K; li3t H^2. þerein] þrynne D. a] *om* J. wel] ful H^3; *om* DVJAM. lewid] lewed RVW; lewd DChH^3; lewde K. were] weore V.

142 *line om* A. Ac] Bot ChVJK; & MH^3. for] *om* H^3. lat] lateþ W; let J; letteth K; laft R; last UH^3; set V. loue(2)] leeue V.

143 þere] *om* VAK. þat] as M; *om* A. is] is þe V; is a A. lakkiþ] lackyt H^3; lakkeþ UD; lackyd JK; lakked Ch; lakkede H^2M; þer lackith A; þer lakkeþ W; þat lakkede V; balkeþ R. neuere] no A.

Leue lelly þeron ȝif þou þenke do wel,
For dobet & dobest ben drawen of louis s[co]le. 145
In oþer science it seiþ, I saiȝ it in catoun,
Qui sim[u]lat verbis, nec corde est fidus amicus,
[*Tu quoque fac simile: sic ars deluditur arte*].
Ac theologie techiþ not so, who[so] takiþ heed;
He kenniþ vs þe contrarie, aȝens catonis wordis, 150
And [biddiþ] vs ben as breþeren, & blissen oure enemys,
And louen hem þat liȝen on vs, & lenen hem at here nede,
And do good a[g]ens euil; god hymself hotiþ
And seide it hymself in ensaumple for þe beste:

144 Leue] lef U; Leef V; Leue nowe WMH³; Now leue þu A. lelly] leuely J; trewliche M; wel VH³; *om* A. þeron] þer vppon VWMH³. ȝif . . . wel] dowel ȝif þou þinke M. ȝif] ȝef Ch. þenke] thinke RD; þink Ch; thinke to J; thynk to AKWH³.
145 ben] byn K; beþ W; beoþ V. drawen] drawyn JAMH³; drawe RUH²W. of] out of M. louis] loues RDW; loue J; leue U; lowest A; lore in V. scole] RUVJ; scoole K; skile TH²; skille Ch; skele D; lore AWMH³.
146 science] sciences K. seiþ] seyt H³; saith KW; seþ UA. I . . . catoun] *in* Caton þou migth redyn M; *in* catoun þou myth rede H³; in Caton þou might it rede W; in caton þu may rede A. I] *om* V. saiȝ] say RD; seyh J; see K; seo V; sawȝ Ch; saw U. in catoun] my self K. in] *om* U.
147 *simulat*] RUChVKW; *similat* TDH² JMH³; *similiat* A. *nec*] *uel* R; *non* W; *hic non* H³. *corde est*] *est corde* W; *cordis est* A; *est* H³. *fidus*] *fidelis* V; *fidis* ChH².
148 RDJKWM; *line om* TUChH²VAH³. *deluditur*] *diluditur* W.
149 Ac] Bot ChVJKM; And H³; *om* A. techiþ] techith JA; techeþ V; techiþ vs T; techeþ vs RUD; techit it H²; techeþ it Ch; tellyth H³; tellit M; telleþ W; teneth K. not] nouȝt DCh; nouth H³; nowt U. whoso] RUDChKWM; hoso JAH³; hose V; who TH². takiþ] takit AMH³; takeþ RDChV; take UW. heed] kepe VK; kepp A; hende H³.
150 *line om* M. kenniþ] kenneþ RDCh H²W; kennes U; kennys A; techeþ V; techyth H³. vs] *om* UH³. aȝens] aȝenys A; ayenst K; aȝen RU; aȝeyn V; & aȝens W; of J. catonis wordis] Caton voordes W.
151 And] He MH³. biddiþ] biddith H²JKH³; biddeþ VW; bidit M; byt RU; bid A; bidded Ch; *om* TD. vs] *om* V. ben] be U; to ben D. blissen . . . enemys] oure foomen blissen M. blissen] blissyn JAH³; blysse UW; blessen H²VK; blessyn D; blesse R. enemys] enemyes D; ennymyes K; enmys R; enmyys J; enmyes Ch; fomen AWH³.
152 *line om* A. louen] louyn JH³; loue UChW. hem] *om* U. þat] þan Ch. liȝen] lyȝyn J; lyen RUDKWH³; lyin M; leiȝen H². & . . . hem] lellyche V. lenen] lenyn M; lene RUDChH²KW; lenyin J; lenden H³. here] her ChK; heor V; oure R; *om* JWH³. nede] neode V. *Here* H³ *adds a Latin tag as after* **C** VI 58: *see above*, p. 31.
153 And] An H². do] don M; done J; so Ch. agens] ageins Ch; ageynes A; ageynst K; aȝens TRUDH²WMH³; aȝenys J; aȝeyn V. euil] yuel UH²; vuel V. god] so god WM; & so god AH³. hymself] *om* A. self] selue UJ. hotiþ] hotit M; hoteþ DChVW; hotes RU; biddyth AH³.
154 seide] said K; seided U; schewed M; schewid A; sheweþ W; swewith H³. it . . . self] himself hit V. it] *om* UW. hym] hem W. self] selue UDJA; seluyn MH³. ensaumple] exaumple RJAH³. for] of RUJAK. þe beste] þe bestes J; lownes A.

Necesse est vt veniant scandala.
Astronomye is hard þing & euil for to knowe; 155
Geometrie & geomesie is gynful of speche;
Þat þinkeþ werche wiþ þo þre þriueþ wel late, |
For sorcerie is þe souerayn bok þat to þat science longiþ. *fol. 1 b*
Ȝet arn þere febicchis of Forellis of many manis wittes,
Experimentis of alkenemye of albertis makyng, 160
Nigromancie & per[i]mansie þe pouke to reisen;
Ȝif þou þenke do wel deile þerewith neuere.
Alle þise sciences, sikir, I myself

154α *in margin, another hand* W. U *substitutes: Dilige dominum deum tuum ex toto corde tuo &c. Necesse*] *Necesce* Ch. *est*] *est enim* KW. *veniant*] *uenient* AK; *veniunt* Ch; *ueniat* H². *scandala*] *schandala* A; *scandala &c* K.

155 Astronomye] Ac astronomye RUW; Bote Astronomye VK; And astronony3e H³; but ascorne (?) M. is] is an J. þing] heuy þing A; *om* W. euil] euel RChM; yuel UH²; vuel V. for] *om* VK. knowe] knowyn M.

156 Geometrie] Geomatrye K; Gemetrie VA; gemettrie R; Geemetry3e H³. geomesie] gemessie RUA; geemessye H³; Gemensye V. is] *om* J. gynful] gilefull K; gynner J; greful R; gryfful U; synful ChAW. speche] spece (*same hand after cancelled* speche) J.

157 Þat] Hee þat H³. þinkeþ] thinkyth J; þinkit M; þinken W; thynkyn KH³; thynk A; thynkist H²; þenkeþ UD; *om* V. werche] RD; worche W; to werche UA; to werchin MH³; to worch K; to wyrchyn J; dele H²; worcheþ V; *twice* T; *om* Ch. þo] *same hand after cancelled* woo D; þis W; þeose V; hem A. þre] 3re U; þreo V. þriueþ] thryuet3 H²; þryuit M; thryven KW; thryuyn JH³; thryfyn A. wel] wol UJM; ful AH³; he V.

158 *run together with following* V. For] *om* U. sorcerie] sorsorie Ch; socerye H². is . . . þat] *om* A. þe] *om* W. souerayn] souereinge K. bok . . . longiþ] *om* V. to . . . science] þerto J. to þat] *om* (*late corrector inserts* to the) H². þat] þis AW; þe UD; tho K; *om* M. science] sciences K. longiþ] longit M; longeþ RUDChW.

159 *run together with following* U. Ȝet . . . Forellis] *om* V. Ȝet] 3it UDChJAWM; 3ut R. arn] ar W; are R. þere] þer þre J; þer iij H³; þre R; þe D. febicchis] febucches H²; fybychys J; fybicches R; fibiches KW; fibeches UD; fybytthys H³; febuthis M; fybecythis Ch; febeles A. of(1)] in JAWMH³; & K. Forellis] forelles D; forelis U; forels RKW; forolis M; forelle Ch; *om* A. of(2) . . . wittes] *om* U. of(2)] *om* A. many] mony ChV; *om* AH³. manis] mans K; mannys RH²H³; mannes D; menys J; mens W; mennis M; mennes V.

160 Experimentis . . . alkenemye] *om* U. Experimentis] Experimens J; Expermens D; Expimentis Ch; Of experimentis A; of experimens R. of] for J; and ChH³. alkenemye] alkenamy Ch; alkonomye RDVJW; alconamy3e H³; alknamye H²; alcamie A; alcomie M. albertis] albertes RUDK; albertus W; Alberdes V; beerdis M.

161 perimansie] H²UV; peramancie KW; permansie TRDJAMH³; pernirancy Ch. pouke] deuyl J. reisen] reysyn H³; reise URK; areysen H²; areisyn M; areise ChJ; Rise makeþ V.

162 *line om* Ch. þenke] thinke RUDAM H³; think JKW; þenche V. do wel] to dowel AKMH³; to doun wele J. deile] dele DH²VJKMH³; del RUW; medil A. þerewith] with hem VAWMH³. neuere] neyther A.

163 *divided from following after* foundit TRUDChH²; *after* made K; *after* formed W; *after* formest AH³; after formerst M. þise] þis W; þies J; þese RUDH²AMH³; þes ChK; þeose V. sciences] science AW H³. sikir] siker VM; sicre W; seker DCh; sikerly RUK; sekyrly AH³. self] selue UJA; seluen V; sef M.

Foundit hem formest folk to desceyue.
I bekenne þe crist,' q*ua*þ she, 'I can teche þe no bet*ere*.' 165
I seide 'g*ra*unt m*er*cy madame,' & mekly hire grette
And wente wiȝtly my wey wiþoute more lettyng,
And fond as she foretolde & forþ gan I wende,
And er I com to clergie coude I neu*ere* stynte.
I grette þe goode man as þe gode wyf me tauȝte, 170
And aftirward his wyf I worsshipide boþe,
And tolde hire þe toknes þ*at* me ytauȝt were.
Was neu*ere* [gome] vpon þis ground, siþþe god makid heuene,
Fairere vndirfonge ne frendliere mad at ese

164–6 *as two lines divided after* she W.
164 Foundit . . . formest] formest he*m* foundyd in feyth H³; formest Hem foundyd in feth A; form*er*st he fondeth in feith M; first hem formed In fayþ W. Foundit] foundite H²; foundide U; fou*n*ded RJ; Haue Ifou*n*ded V; founded And founden Ch; founded And made D; made Fownded K. hem] Þurw hem U. formest] t *cancelled* Ch; furst V. to] RUDChVJAKWMH³; for to TH². desceyue] deseyuen RUK; dysseyuyn AH³.
165 *line om* A. bekenne] betake V. þe] þe to VWM. q*ua*þ she] *om* JM. she] scheo H²; heo V. can] con V. teche . . . bet*ere*] þe no bett*er* techyn J. teche þe] seyn M.
166 *line om* A. I] And I U. g*ra*unt m*er*cy] gram*er*cy RUDChWMH³; grem*er*cy J. madame] ma *above line another script* J. mekly] meche U; mychel J. hire] hyr H³; her*e* UDH²JW; her ChK; hure R. grette] grete KM. *Here* W *adds: Tercius passus de dowel; see above*, p. 41.
167 And] I AWM. wente] wend þid*er* D. wiȝtly] withly M; witly R; wytely A; whithly Ch; wiȝth in U; liȝtliche D; forþ on V. wey] way RChH²KWH³. wiþoute] w*ith*outen V; withouty*n* JAM. more] ony A.
168 fond] fone M; *om* K. she] scheo H²; ȝhe A; heo V. foretolde] aforn tolde M; had told H³; fayre tolde RU. &] so K. gan] gon V.
169 er] ar DVK; or Ch; til J. com] come UH²H³; coome V; cam RJA; came K. to] at J. clergie] clergyȝe H³. coude] could K; couþe VChJW. stynte] styndte (d *cancelled*) H²; stunte V; stente D. stondyn A.
170 I] and UW. grette] grete KM; gret ChJA. þe] þat AMH³. man] mon V. þe(2) . . . me] me þe gode wif R; stody me JM. wyf] man A. tauȝte] tauȝthe R; taugth H³; tauthe M; tauth A; taght W; taute J.
171 *line om* R. aftirward] aftir M. his] þe AWMH³. wyf] gode wyf JAWMH³. I] & U. worsshipide] worschipped DK; worshipt W; worsschepede M; worscheped Ch; worchepyd JAH³; worschupet V; wyrschepid U. boþe] hem bothe UV; he*m* boþi*n* M; als W.
172 tolde] tould K. hire] hyr H³; here UDH²AW; her K; hi*m* R; hem ChJ. þe] *om* UA. toknes] tokenes DVWH³; tokenys ChA; toknesse H²; tokne M; tokynyng J. þ*at*] as R. ytauȝt] Itauȝte H²; Itawȝte U; tauȝt ChDK; tauȝth R; taugth H³; tauth M; taut A; taute J; told W. were] weren K; wery*n* H³; wern M.
173 neu*ere* gome] grome neu*er* K. gome] RChVJAW; grom TUDH²; man MH³. vpon] on DChAWM. þis] þe R; *om* ChVJ. ground] moolde M. siþþe] syth UH²W (*after cancelled* syþþ U); sithen K; sythin JM; syn RAH³; seþ DCh; seþþe*n* V. makid] made RUChH²VJKWMH³; mad A; makeþ D. heuene] heuyn JAK; hefne U; þe world Ch.
174 Fairere] Feirore V. vndirfonge] vndyrfonge*n* H³; vndirfongi*n* M; vnderfonged R; vnderfongyd J. ne] or Ch. frendliere] frendliar K; frendliker*e* RM; frendlekere U; frendloker DChH²VJW. mad] maad V; *om* JKW. ese] ease K.

Þanne myself soþly so sone [as] heo it wiste 175
Þat I was of wyttis hous ⁊ wiþ his wyf dame stodie.
Curteisliche clergi[e] c[o]llide me ⁊ kiste,
And axide how wyt ferde ⁊ his wif studie,
And I sei[d]e, 'soþliche, þei sente me hider
To lere at ȝow dowel ⁊ dobet þereaftir, 180
And siþen aftirward to se sumwhat of dobest'.
'It is a wel lel[e] lif,' quaþ she, 'among þe lewide peple;
Actif it is hoten; [husbondis] it vsen,
Trewe tilieris on erþe, taillours ⁊ souteris
And alle kyne crafty men þat cunne here foode wynne, 185

175 *line om* A. Þanne] þen V; þei I sey it J. my] I my VWMH^{3}; hym Ch. self] selue UJ. soþly] *om* J. so] as UWM (*in another hand* W); *om* H^{3}. sone] son H^{3}. as] RUDVKM; so JW; *om* TChH^{2}H^{3}. heo] he Ch; she RUDJK; þey MH^{3}; þai W. it] me H^{3}; *om* DVJKWM. wiste] wysten M; wystyn H^{3}; wuste V; weste U.
176 *line om* A. Þat] þan H^{3}. I] *om* (*late corrector supplies*) H^{2}. of] In Ch. wyttis] wit U. wiþ] of D; *om* RUH^{3}. dame] *om* J.
177 *line om* RDW. Curteisliche] Curtessely A; Curtaisly Ch. clergie] UChH^{2}VJAK; clergyȝe H^{3}; clergise T; clerkys M. collide me] me collyd J. collide] H^{2}; colled Ch; Clupte V; callide T; callid AKH^{3}; calde U; kalledin M. kiste] kyssyd J; custe UV; kyssid me A; me kyssed K; kestyn M.
178 *line om* RDW. axide] axid J; axede H^{2}; axkid A; askyd KH^{3}; asked UChV; askedin M. how] me how UJM. ferde] fared K; *om* U. ⁊] and eke V. wif studie] studye U; goode frendis M. studie] dame studie H^{2}; eke J.
179–81 *as two lines divided after* dowell W.
179 seide] ChH^{2}VAMH^{3}; seyd J; saide W; sayd DK; seyde him R; seyde hem U: seiȝe T. soþliche] sootȝly M; sikerly R. þei] þai W; thay K. sente] senten K; sentyn JM; sende V. hider] hydyr JM; hyddyr H^{3}; hedyr D; hedur A; þeder U.
180 lere] lerne ChAKWMH^{3}; lernyn J; leorne V. at] with M; *om* W. ȝow] the K; *om* W. dowel] to dowel UKW. þere] *om* VW.
181 siþen] syþin M; siþe RU; sytthyn H^{3}; seþen Ch; sethyn J; seþ D; seþþen V; *om* AW. aftirward] aftir U; after K; *om* W. se] sen M; see K; seo V. sumwhat] sumwaht JA; sumqwat H^{3}.
182 wel] weel K; wol UWM; ful JH^{3}; *om* Ch. lele] JA; leel Ch; lelle W; leal K; lely RUD; lelly TH^{2}; trewe MH^{3}; feir V. lif] loue Ch; *om* R. quaþ she] *om* J. she] scheo H^{2}; heo V; he ChAWMH^{3}. þe] *om* J. lewide] lewyd RUH^{2}JA; lewed VK; lewd DChH^{3}; lowed (*altered to* lewed *another ink*) W; comoun M. peple] people K; puple AH^{3}.
183–7 *as four lines divided after* erthe—men—trauaill W.
183 Actif] A lyf V. it is] is it AH^{3}; is V. hoten] hotyn JAMH^{3}; hote Ch; yhoten RUV. husbondis] A; husbondes K; housbondes UD; husbandys J; vsbondis M; hosbondes RW; hosebondes V; husbondryȝe H^{3}; lewide men TChH^{2}. vsen] vsyn JA; vseþ U; vsyth H^{3}; vsit M. **Here V ends.**
184 tilieris] tilieres RK; tiliers DH^{2}JWM; telieris AH^{3}; telieres U; teliers Ch. on] of JKMH^{3}. erþe] herþe U; the erthe KWMH^{3}; þe erde A. taillours] tayliourys J; talyours H^{3}; talliouris A; talioures R; as taliouurs U; or tailours M. ⁊] or DM. souteris] *same hand after cancelled* oþere U; Toukers W; towkkars K; toucheris AH^{3}; touchers M.
185 *run together with following* A. kyne] kyn DH^{2}W; kynne JK; kynnes Ch; kynnys A; kenne U; kennes M; skynnys H^{3}; kynde R. crafty] craftes W. þat . . . wynne] *om* A. cunne] konnen M; can ChK; *om* H^{3}. here] her RChJKH^{3}; with here U. foode] craft RU. wynne] wynnen WM.

Wiþ any trewe trauaille toille for here foode,
Diken or deluen, dowel it hatte.
To breke beggeris bred & bakken hem *with* cloþis,
Counforte þe carful þat in castel ben fetterid,
And seken out þe seke & sende hem þat hem nediþ, 190
Obedient as breþeren & sustren to oþere,
Þ[i]s be[þ] dobet; so beriþ witnesse þe sauter:
Ecce quam bonum & quam iocundum habitare Fratres in vnum.
Sike *with* þe sory, singe *with* þe glade,
Gaudere cum gaudentibus Et flere cum flentibus,
[Dredles] þis is dobet; [dobest wot þe soþe].

186 Wiþ . . . trauaille] *om* A. any] ony RUJ; eny D; alle H³; here W. toille] tilie U; Tylien WM; tylyin J; telye R; þat telyn H³; to leuyn A. for] *om* M. here] her ChJKH³.
187 Diken] dykyn R; Dichen K; Dychin JM; Dychoun H³. or] and Ch. deluen] deluyn JAMH³. hatte] hattith H²H³; hyȝte U; hyte J; hoteþ Ch; hotith A.
188 To] And Ch. breke] breken K; brekyn M; breykyn J; brekere U. beggeris] beggere U. &] an M; to R. bakken . . . cloþis] also for to cloþun hem A. bakken] bakkyn H³; bakke W; bak D; bachem U; baskyn R; coueryn J; happin M. hem] hym D; *om* U.
189 Counforte] Counfortyn JM; Confort W; comforte RUDChKH³; Comforth A; Confortid H². þat] *om* DJM. in] in þe RUA. castel] castyl H³; Castels W; Castelles K; castelys J. ben] bien H²; is U; lythe A; *om* JM. fetterid] feteryd KH³; fetered UH²; fettryd D; fettred Ch; fetrid R; fetred W; Ifettrid M; federid A.
190 seken] sekyn RJM; seke AH³; sechen ChK; seche W. out] vp H³. þe] þo (o *above* þ, *another ink ?*) D. seke] sike KM; seke fulk H³; *om* D. sende] senden M; sendyn J. hem(1)] him M. þat] what U. hem(2)] h M; *om* AH³. nediþ] nedit M; nedeþ RDW; neden K.
191–92α *as two lines divided after* dobet A; *after* askeþ W.
191 H³ *corrupts to* Obedyent to beryen þes seke *and divides from following after* dobet; M *to* Millde among his euene cristene *and divides after* vsit. as] also A; also as JK. breþeren] brethern K; brothren H²; broþer D. & . . . oþere] *om* AW. sustren] sustern K; susteryn J; sostren R; sistres U. to oþere] to alle othir H²; *om* J.
192 Þis] RM; Þese UWH³; þies J; Thes K; Þus TDChH²A. beþ] ben A; ben þat U; beþ þo þat R; be þo þat H³; ben tho that KW; ben þoo þat J; is þat M; byt D; bad Ch; bed þe T; bad the H². dobet] doun bet J; dobet askeþ W; dowel vsit M. so] & so JMH³; þus U. beriþ . . . sauter] þe sautre bereþ witnes W; witnessit dauid in þe sauter book M. beriþ] beriȝt H²; seyth J; *om* A. witnesse] *om* J.
192α *transposed with line* 193α U. &] *om* H³. *habitare . . . vnum*] &c JW; *om* A. *Here* H³ *adds two lines: see above*, p. 48.
193 *transposed with following* M. Sike] Syk R; Sykyn J; Seke A; Loke þou so be H³. þe(1)] *om* U. sory] sore K. singe] and syng WH³; syngyn J; & singen M.
193α *in margin same hand* W. Ch *alters to* Flere cum flentibus gaudere cum gaudentibus. Gaudere] Gaudete UA. Et] *om* RJA.
194–6 *so divided* AWMH³; *after* sayen—worthy K; *as two lines divided after* benefices TRDH², *after* benefice Ch; *imperfect* U. J *attaches* god . . . dobet *to line* 193α *and divides lines* 195–6 *after* worthy.
194 Dredles] WMH³; Sekyrly A; God wot TRUDChH²JK. þis] þat J; it M; *om* H³. dobet] dobest UKM. dobest . . . soþe] AWH³; dobet wot þe sothe M; & therfor I sayen K; *om* TRUDChHJ².

Sire dobest haþ ben [in office], so is he best worþi 195
Be þat god in þe gospel grauntiþ & techiþ:
Qui facit & docuerit magnus vocabitur in regno celorum.
Forþi is dobest [a] bisshopis pere,
Prince ouer godis peple to prechen or to chaste.
Dobet doþ ful wel, & dewid he is also, | *fol.* lj *a*
And haþ possessions & pluralites for pore menis sake; 200
For mendynaunt3 at meschief þ[o] men were dewid,
And þat is ri3tful religioun, none renneris aboute,
Ne no leperis ouer lond ladies to shryue.
Gregory þe grete clerk, a good pope in his tyme,
Of religioun þe rewele he reherside in his morals, 205

195–6α *in margin, another hand and ink* W.
195 Sire] Sere A; So K. dobest] dobet H³. haþ] hat H³; haiþ U; had M; hast A. ben in office] AMH³; be in office W; benefices TRUDK; benefycys J; bienefices H²; benefice Ch. so . . . worþi] *om* U. so] And so RAKWM; & JH³. is he] he is WM; is RJAK.
196 *line om* U. þat . . . þe] god þat D. þe] *om* R. grauntiþ] grauntit A; grantit3 H²; hit graunteþ D; boþin grauntit M. & techiþ] & techit AM; and techit3 H²; *om* RD.
196α *line om* U; *transposed with following* A. *facit*] *fecerit* J. *docuerit*] *docuit* DAMH³. *magnus*] *hic magnus* JKW; *hic maior* H³; *magis* A. *in . . . celorum*] &*c* W.
197–9 *as two lines divided after* peple W.
197 Forþi] þerfore J; For þis RU; For þus Ch. is dobest] dobest is RUAW. is] is sire M; is now K. a] RUDChJAMH³; *om* TH²KW. bisshopis] buschops H³; boschopes A. pere] peire U.
198 ouer] ouer alle Ch; of UJWH³. peple] people K; puple AH³. to(1)] & J. prechen] prechyn JM; preche RChAH³. or] oþer Ch; othir H²; and RUJAWMH³. to(2)] *om* J. chaste] chasten W; chastyn JM; chastien K; chastice Ch; teche RA; techyn U.
199 doþ] dot3 M; doiþ U; do A. &] *om* A. dewid . . . is] is a dewyd J. dewid] dewed Ch; dued H³; dowed K; endued A; doutid M; dowel RUDW. he is] is he AKM; is ChH³; *om* W. also] alse JM; als A.
200 And] *om* A. haþ] hat MH³; hat3 H²; haiþ U; *om* A. possessions] poscesciouns Ch; posessiones U; possession W. & pluralites] many J. &] in AW; *om* U. pluralites] pluraltes DChM; pluralite A; pluralte W. menis] men W; mannys H².
201 mendynaunt3] mendynauntes H²KH³; mendinantis U; mendynans M; mendicans J; mendevauntis Ch; mendinant R; amendement A. at] & M. meschief] messchef U; myschief D; myschyff H³; myschef RChH²JAKW; michefs M. þo] RUJAKWMH³; þes Ch; þe TH²; þat D. were] weryn AM. dewid] dued A; dueed Ch; dowed W; Idewyd J; ydewed R; Idued U; Idowed K; Induyd H³; dubbid M; sumtyme D.
202 And] *om* A. ri3tful] rythful UJ; reitful (*after cancelled* ry) M; right W; ryth H³. none] no ChWH³; and non A; but not M. renneris] rennere A. aboute] aboutyn AJMH³.
203 *line om* W. Ne] And A. no] none RDH²JKMH³. leperis] lepars K; lippers H². lond] lande ChJ; londys H³. ladies] ladijs RUKMH³. shryue] schryven KM H³; serue A.
204 þe] a DH³. a good] *om* J. pope] clerk M; *cancelled for* busshop, *later hand* H³. his] is U.
205 Of . . . rewele] þe rewle of religyoun J. rewele] rewle RH²KH³; reule UDAW; rule M; rewþe Ch. he] *om* JAMH³. reherside] rehersyd DH²MH³; rehersed Ch; rehersit U; rehersyth JAK; reherseþ RW. morals] moralis UH²JAMH³; morales RK; morale Ch; moral W.

And seide it in ensaumple þat þei shulde do þe betere:
"Whanne fisshes faile þe flood or þe fresshe watir
Þei di3e for þe drou3te, whanne þei drei3e lengen;
Ri3t so be religioun, it roileþ ⁊ steruiþ
Þat out of couent ⁊ cloistre coueiten to libben". 210
Ac now is religioun a ridere ⁊ a rennere [be stretis],
A ledere of l[oue]d[a]ies ⁊ a lond biggere;
Poperiþ on a palfrey [fro] toune to toune;
A bidowe or a baselard he beriþ be his side;
Godis flessh, ⁊ his fet, ⁊ hise fyue woundis 215
Arn more in his mynde þan þe memorie of his foundours.
Þis is þe lif of þis lordis þat lyuen shulde wiþ dobet,

206 seide] said K; seit M; seyþ RUJA; saiþ W; sent H^3. it] him RU; *om* A. in] be A; *om* D. ensaumple] example RJAH^3. þat] *om* JA. þei] þai W; men RU. shulde] shulden K; xuld H^3; scholdyn J. do] don AM; doun J. þe] *om* D. *Here D copies* XI 128–66.
207 Whanne] When R; Qwan JH^3. fisshes] fyssh DAK (*above line same hand* K). faile] faylen RChKW; faylyn JMH^3; fayleþ UD; faylith A. þe(1)] *om* AH^3. or] other KW; oþ R; eyther A; of ChH^2; ⁊ JH^3. þe fresshe] fysche þe A. watir] waterys J.
208 Þei] Thay K. di3e] dyen KW; dey3e Ch; deye U; deyen RMH^3; deyin D; deyn JA. þe] þat J; *om* DWH^3. drou3te] drougthe M; drouthe RA; drowte UH^3. whanne] when R; qwan JH^3. þei] thay K; þe A; it U. drei3e] dreie M; drye RDChJAKWH^3; dryheþ U. lengen] longe RU; long Ch; leggen H^2; liggen KW; lyggyn DJMH^3; lyggith A.
209 Ri3t] Ry3th R; Ryth UH^3; Rit J; Ryeth M. be religioun] *twice* A. be] farit be M. it] þat UH^3. roileþ] roylith H^2JH^3; roilit M; reylith A; rolleþ W; roxleþ U; roxlet R; relexith K. ⁊ steruiþ] al aboutyn M. steruiþ] steruyt A; sterueþ UKW; steryth H^3; stereþ D; streueþ Ch.
210 ⁊] an A; ⁊ of M; or H^2; in R. cloistre] cleyster A. coueiten] coueitin M; coueyte DAW; coueyteþ R; coueytiþ UJH^3. libben] libbe RUChJW; lyve K; leuyn H^3; leue **A**
211 Ac] But RChKH^3; And UM; *om* JA. religioun] sire Religioun M. ridere] ridedere A. ⁊] *om* JAM. rennere] romer JAKWM. be stretis] UJAMH^3; by stretes RKW; be strete D; aboute TChH^2.
212 A] And a Ch; And H^3. ledere] ledar J. louedaies] ChH^2; louedays RJ; lufdayes U; ladies TDAW; ladyis MH^3; ladys K. ⁊] *om* M. lond biggere] biggere of londis M. lond] lowde Ch. biggere] byggar K; byere RA; bugghere (*same hand after cancelled* beggere) U; beggere D; begger Ch.
213 Poperiþ] Poperit A; Popereþ DK; Popreþ RU; He popreth W; Prykyth J; Rydyth H^3; Ridit M. a] his AWMH^3. fro] RUDChH^2JAWH^3; from K; for M; to T. toune(1)] thon H^3; parkes Ch. to] RUDChH^2JAKWMH^3; ⁊ to T. toune(2)] townes Ch; thon H^3. *Late corrector adds* ⁊ manour to manour H^2.
214 bidowe] bidewe K; bedowe ChJ; bedew RAH^3; bidev M. or] ar D; and A. his] is A.
215 fet] blode his fet W; feyth A. hise] þe H^3. fyue] fyf R.
216 Arn] Arin A; Buþ D; Is W. mynde] mende UChAM. þe] *om* RUDJKH^3. his(2)] *om* R. foundours] founders ChK; founderys J; foundour RU; foundere M; frendis A.
217 lif] lyue A. þis(2)] þes RChA; þese UDH^2; þo JK; þe WMH^3. lyuen shulde] shulde lyue RW; xuld leuyn H^3. lyuen] lyuyn J; leuen Ch; leuyn M; leue UD; leuyn ⁊ A. wiþ] *om* A.

And welawey wers and I [wo]lde al telle.'
'I wende þat kinghed, ⁊ kniȝthed, ⁊ caiseris wiþ Erlis
Wern dowel, ⁊ dobet, ⁊ dobest of hem alle, 220
For I haue seiȝe it myself, ⁊ siþþen red it aftir,
How crist counseilliþ þe comune ⁊ kenneþ hem þis tale:
Super cathedram moisi sederunt principes.
Forþi I wende þat þo wyes wern dobest of alle.'
'I nile not scorne,' q*ua*þ script*ure*, 'but scryueyns liȝe, 225
Kinghod ⁊ kniȝthod, for auȝt I can aspie,
Helpiþ nouȝt to heuene[ward] at one ȝeris ende,
Ne ricchesse, ne rentis, ne realte of lordis.

218 welawey] welawo M; dowel awey Ch; leuyn wel J; wele A. wers] worse DKW; were Ch. and] if þat W; þan M; *om* J. I wolde] wold I J. wolde] R; wold DAWH^3; would K; wele M; shulde TUChH^2. al telle] telle alle Ch. al] it A; *om* WM.
219 wende] wend DJAK; went W. þat] *om* RU. kinghed . . . kniȝthed] knyȝthod ⁊ kynghod D. kinghed] kynghode ChJAK WH^3; king*es* R; kyngis U; *om* M. ⁊(1)] *om* M. kniȝthed] kniȝthode ChJK; knygthode W; knythod MH^3; knyttehod A; kniȝt*es* R; knythis U. ⁊(2)] q*uo*d I ⁊ KAW; *om* J. caiseris] keyseris R; keysers W; cayser A. wiþ] and UA. Erlis] herlis M.
220 *line om* A. Wern] weren ChH^2; Weryn J; wer*e* RUWH^3; wer DKM. ⁊(1)] *om* KW. of] ouer RU. hem] *om* ChJKWMH^3.
221 seiȝe it] it sen U. seiȝe] sey R; seyn DChH^{2}JM; sen AWH^3; seen K. self] selue UChH^{2}JAK. siþþen] sithen H^{2}AK; siþin M; siþ W; sytthy H^3; seþþen Ch; sethen D; sethin J; suþþe U; swithe R. red] redd K; Redde ChH^{2}W; radd M; yrad RU. it(2)] *om* RU.
222 counseilliþ] conseilyth H^{2}H^3; cou*n*seylyd J; conseylede U; counseilde M; consailled W; kennyd A. comune] comunes Ch. kenneþ] kennes U; kennede M; telleþ W; tellith J; tauth A. hem] *om* M. þis] þese U. tale] talis R; lawes U.
223 *line om* (*a space left for it*) U. *moisi*] *moyli* R. *principes*] *principes ⁊c* H^3; *principes qui dicunt facite* RAM; *principes qui dicunt facite ⁊c* K; *principes qui dicunt facite ⁊c* J; *scribe ⁊ pharisei que dicunt facite ⁊c* (*scribe ⁊ pharisei over erasure, another hand*) W.
224 Forþi] þerfor JH^3; For þ*er* R; For A. I] þai A. þat] *om* UA. þo wyes] þoughtes W. þo] þese H^3; þis Ch. wyes] weyes RDH^{2}A; weyys J; weyhes U; ways K; wythys H^3; *om* M. wern] weren ChAH^3; weryn JK; wer*e* RUDW. do] *om* A.
225 *marked with cross* H^3. nile] nyl H^2 WH^3; nel D; wil JA; wol ChK; wele U; wolde R. not] nat ChH^2; nouȝt D; nouth H^3; nowth U. scorne] schorne A; skorne þe H^3; *om* M. but . . . liȝe] þe soth I wyl seyne J. but] but if K; but if þat W; *late corrector adds* if H^2. scryueyns] skreueynis R; schreueneris A; skriueners W; scriuers (? scriners) M; screuoys (? screnoys) H^3. liȝe] lyȝen Ch; lye RUDA W; lien M; leiȝe H^2.
226 *line om* K. ⁊] ne JWM. kniȝthod] kniȝthhod R; knythod AMH^3. for] be AWMH^3. auȝt] ouȝt Ch; ouȝth R; oute JA; nouȝt D; nouth H^3; not W; not þat M. aspie] aspyȝe H^3; spye J; speye A.
227 Helpiþ] Helpit M; helpeþ RDCh H^{2}W; thay helpeth (thay *above line another script*) K. nouȝt] not RJAKWM. heuene-ward] RWMH^3; heuynward JAK; hefne-ward U; heuene TDChH^2. at] atte J; *om* AKWMH^3. one] *om* J. ȝeris] heris MH^3; heres K; heers W. ende] hende M.
228 Ne] No ChH^3. ne(2)] no Ch; no*n* H^3. rentis . . . realte] ryalte no rente H^3. rentis] rente RUKWM. ne(3)] no Ch. realte] rialtie K; rialte RDChJW; royalte U. lordis] londis AM; londes W; þis landys H^3.

Poul *p*rouiþ it is vnpossible, riche men in heuene.
Ac pore men in pacience & penaunce togid*ere* 230
Hauen eritage in heuene, ac riche men non.'
'*Contra*,' *qua*þ I, 'be crist! þ*at* can I þe wi[þsigg]e,
And *p*rouen it be þe pistil þ*at* petir is nempnid:
Qui crediderit et baptizatus fuerit saluus erit.'
'Þat is *in extremis*,' *qua*þ scrip*ture*, 'as sarisines & Iewis 235
Mowe be sauid so, & so is oure beleue.
Þat arn vncristene in þ*at* cas may cristene an heþene,
And for his lele beleue, whanne he his lif tyneþ,
Haue eritage in heuene as an hei3 cristene.
Ac cristene men, god wot, comiþ not so to heuene, 240

229 Poul] Paul D; For poul M. *p*rouiþ] prouit M; preueþ Ch. it is] it DChJK WH³ (*above line same hand* W); *om* RU AM. vnpossible] onpossible ChH²; inpossible RUWMH³; impossible AK (? unpossible A). riche] þe riche RU; þat riche (þat *above line another script*) W. men] man D; *om* RU. in] to comen in U; to com to J; to H³. heuene] hefne U. *Here* H³ *adds a Latin line as after* **B** XIV 211 or **C** XII 203; *see above*, p. 31.
230 Ac] But JKM; And H³; Bot for Ch; *om* A. men] *om* D. in] and RAWM. pacience & penaunce] penau*ns* & pacience M. pacience] pacient A. &] in A. penaunce] pacience U; pacient R. togid*ere*] togydyr*e* J; togedere W; togeder Ch; togedur A; togideres D; togeder*es* RUK; togederis MH³.
231 Hauen] hauy*n* M; Han H²JAW; Haue KH³; han here U; haue her*e* R. heuene] hefne U. ac] but ChJK; and RUAMH³. riche] reche M.
232 þat] and þat A; *om* U. can I] i kan U; wil I W; I dar A. þe] *om* RDJAKW MH³. wiþsigge] *compare* IV 142 *above*; wiþsay RKW; wi*th*seye UJ; withseyn M; wi*th*sey3e H³; wel say A; wisse TDChH².
233 And] I A. *p*rouen] *p*roue RH²AWH³; *p*rouyn JKM; preue Ch. þe] a U. pistil] pistel DChH²H³; pistole W; postil U; postel R; apostel J; gospel M. petir . . . nempnid] crist hi*m*sel made M. is] it D; hat H³. nempnid] nempned ChW; Ine*m*pnyd J; Inempned K; Inemelid A; ynemled R; nemnyþ D; Imenyd (? Imeuyd) H³.
234 *saluus*] *om* U. *erit*] *erit qui vero non &c* JK; *erit Qui vero non condempnabitur* W; *erit Qui vero non crediderit condempnabitur* M; *om* U.
235 is] *om* U. *extremis*] extrems R. as] wi*th* J; among RUAWMH³; among*es* K. sarisines] sarisenis H²; sare3ines Ch; Sarasynes D; sarsynes U; sar3ynes RK; sar3inis A; sarseynys J; sara3enys H³; sarsyns W; saranis M. &] & wi*th* J.
236 *line om* A. Mowe] Thei mowe WH³; Thay mowen K; þei mou*n* J; þey may M. be] be*n* RJM; bien H². sauid] ysaued R; saf H³; sauy M. so(2)] þat RU. is] it is H³; *om* U.
237 arn] buþ D; an ChK; *om* RUAWM H³. vncristene] onc*r*isten K; on c*r*istene R; oon cristen U; iche cristene M. þat] *om* RU. cristene . . . heþene] becomen c*r*istene J. cristene] crystene*n* H³. an] on A; a H³; and RH²W; at Ch.
238 And] As A; *om* KH³. lele] leel UCh; leal RDK; trewe MH³; gode J. beleue] *after cancelled* lyf *same hand* U. whanne] qwan JH³; whar (?) A. he] *om* W. his] is AM; *om* J. lif] lyue A. tyneþ] tynyth JH³; tynyt3 R; ty*n*nit M; tenyth A; endeth W.
239 Haue] Han J; And haue H³; Haue an U. an hei3] ony J; a man þat is AWH³; he þat is M. hei3] hei3e U; hey D; hie ChK; her R. cristene] cristened W.
240 Ac] Bot ChJKM; And H³; *om* A. cristene men] c*r*istenene J. god] god it AKWM; c*r*ist J. comiþ] comeþ UH²; come ChAK; com RD; comy*n* H³; ne come W. not] nou3t Ch; nouth H³; nowt U. to] i*n* M. heuene] heuyn AKH³; hefne U.

For cristene han a degre ⁊ is þe comun speche:
Dilige deum ⁊c, Et proximum tuum sicut teipsum.
Godis word witnessiþ we shuln ȝiue ⁊ dele
Oure enemys | and alle men þat arn nedy ⁊ pore, *fol.* lj *b*
⁊ suche [[shewiþ] þis sermoun þat [sewiþ] aftir]: 245
Dum tempus est operemur bonum ad omnes, maxime autem ad domesticos fidei.
Alle kynne creatures þat to crist be[n] l[yche]
We be holde heiȝly to herie ⁊ honoure,
And ȝiuen hem of oure good as good as oureseluen,
And sou*er*eynliche to suche þat sewen oure beleue:
Þat is, iche cristene [creature] be kynde to oþ*er*, 250

241 cristene] cristen me*n* ChAKWH³; þei JM. han] hauy*n* H³; haue RDChK. a] on Ch; anoþir M. degre] decre KH³; *dirige* U. ⁊] þat H³. is] *om* U. þe] here AM; her JKH³; oure RU; he W; on Ch. comun] comyn J.
242 *here* U *reads line* 263α. *Dilige*] *Diligite* J; *Diliges* RM. *deum*] *deuum* (?) Ch; *dominum* J; *dominum deum tuum* RAWM; *dominum deum tuum ex toto corde tuo* H³. ⁊*c*] *om* RDJK. *tuum . . . teipsum*] ⁊*c* J. *sicut teipsum*] *sicut* H³; ⁊*c* M. *teipsum*] ⁊*c* W.
243 *divided from following after* enemys TRUDChH². word] word*es* K. witnessiþ] witnessit H²MH³; witnesseþ RDChW; wittnessith K; wittnesseþ U. we] þat we RUKW. shuln] schullyn J; shul RDChH²; xul H³; schuldy*n* M; schuld A; shold W; schal UK. ȝiue] ȝeue DChAKW; ȝeue*n* M; ȝeuyn JH³; þeue U; *om* R. ⁊] *om* R. dele] delyn JM.
244 *divided from line* 245α *after* suche TRUDChH²; *after* seyth J; *after* syke K. enemys] enymyes K; enmys JH³; enmyes R; euene crstene M. arn nedy] nedy arn J. arn] ar Ch; ben K; buþ D. nedy ⁊ pore] pore nedy K. ⁊] as RUChH²; *om* D. pore] JAWMH³; pore men TRUDChH².
245 suche] siche U; seyth J; syke K; *om* AWMH³. shewiþ . . . aftir] AWMH³ (*based upon* A); *om* TRUDChH²JK. shewiþ] schewyt H³A; sheweþ W; schewit vs M. sewiþ] sone sewit M; sone seweþ W; sone sueth A; sone schewi*th* H³.
245α *Dum . . . est*] *om* U. *est*] *habemus* RKMH³. *operemur*] *operiemur* A. *maxime autem*] *maxime* AM; ⁊ K. *fidei*] *fidei* ⁊*c* RD; ⁊*c* A; *rubbed* T; *om* H².
246 kynne] kyn H²W; kynnes Ch; kynde RUAM; kende H³. creatures] creaturis AH³; creaturs W; creatoures R; creatouris M; creatours UD. to] on Ch; *om* UA. ben lyche] RK; bene liche J; ben like AWH³; bet lik M; ben ylyche U; beleuiþ TH²; beleueþ Ch; longen D.
247 We] *om* D. be] ben RUDChAKMH³; bene J; beþ W. holde] hold A; holden ChJKW; holdy*n* MH³; yholde RU. heiȝly] heiȝely H²; heyliche RUDH³; hyelich KW; hylyche J; holy A; holliche M; leely Ch. herie] herien KM; heryyn J; heryn A; heyre H³. ⁊] and to H²KH³. honoure] honouren DK; honuren M; lonowryn (? *imperfect* h) J.
248 ȝiuen] ȝif RAW; ȝeuen UDM; ȝeuy*n* H³; ȝeue ChK. oure] here D. good] good*es* KW; godes Ch. good as] god haþ to W. as(2)] as to H³. oure] hem D. seluen] seluyn H³; selue UJA; self Ch; siluen H²; sefluy*n* M.
249 And] *om* W. suche] syche U; swyche JDM; sweche AH³; such men Ch. þat] as UKWMH³. sewen] sewyn A; sewit M; suen U; sueþ R; schewyn vs J; swynk H³. beleue] bylyf H³.
250 Þat is] þat U; *om* J. iche] eche UJAKW; ech RD; euerich Ch. cristene] *om* H³. creature] AJKWH³; creatour M; man TRUDChH². kynde] kende U. to] til JAM; eche to W.

And siþen he[þen] to helpe in hope hem to amende.
To harme hem ne slen hem god hiȝte vs neu*er*e,
For he seiþ it hymself in his ten hestis;
Ne *mecaberis*, ne sle nouȝt, is þe kynde englissh;
For *Michi vindictam et ego retribuam.* 255
I shal punisshen in p*ur*catory or in þe put of helle
Eche man for his misdede but m*er*cy it make.'
—Ȝet am I neu*er*e þe ner for nouȝt I haue walkid
To wyte what is dowel witt*er*ly in herte,
For howso I werche in þis world, [wrong] oþ*er* ellis, 260
I was markid wiþoute m*er*cy, & myn name entrid
In þe legende of lif longe er I were,

251 *line om* A. siþen] siþin M; sytthy*n* H[3]; syþþe U; siþ W; sethen D; sethin J; seþþen Ch; swithe R. heþen] hethen KW; hethyn J; heyene M; hem TRUD H[2]; hym Ch; t*r*auaylyn H[3]. to(1)] *om* D. helpe] helpyn DMH[3]. hem to] hym to ChH[3]; to he*m* R; he*m* D; of J. amende] amendys J; amen W.
252 *run together with following* A. To] Tho A; Neiþ*er* to MH[3]. harme] harmy*n* M; hirtyn J. hem(1)] hym WM. ne] no Ch; ne to H[2]JAWM; or R; or to U; no*n* to H[3]. slen] sle UChWH[3]; sclee K; slo A; harme J; teche R. hem(2)] *om* M. god . . . neuere] *om* A. god] for god M; good Ch. hiȝte] hyȝth R; higtid M; hit Ch; hett K; hyt it H[3]; biddith J. vs] is Ch; *om* M.
253 *divided from following after mecaberis* W. For . . . self] *om* A. For] *om* U. he] cryst M. seiþ] saiþ ChKW; seide M. it] *om* J. self] selue UJ. in] and R. his] þe JH[3]. hestis] heestes H[2]K; behestis A.
254 *line om* M; *run together with following* W. Ne] *Non* RUDChAKWH[3]; *om* J. *mecaberis*] *occides* H[3]; *om* J. ne(2)] þat is to seyn J; *om* K. sle nouȝt] thou schalt not scle K. nouȝt] nouth JH[3]; not RAW. is] in J. þe] þis H[3]. kynde] kende UCh; *om* DAH[3]. englissh] englys R; ynglysh W.
255 For] *No vindicabis quia* M; *om* JAH[3]. *retribuam*] *retribuam &c* RK; *retribuam dicit dominus* J.
256 shal] xal H[3]. punisshen] punysche H[2]W; punschi*n* M; punchyn J; punshe RH[3]; ponyschen A; ponisch K; ponesch Ch; pyne U. in] he*m* i*n* H[3]. p*ur*catory] purgatorie RUDH[2]JAKWMH[3]. put] pit RUChJAK; pet M; peyne (*altered from* penne) H[3].
257 Eche] Iche H[2]M; eu*er*y RU. man . . . his] ma*n*nys J. misdede] mysdedys JAH[3]. but] but ȝif AM. it] *om* M. make] lette AWM. *Here* H[3] *adds a tag: see above*, p. 48.
258 Ȝet] ȝit RUChH[2]JWM; And ȝit A. am I] ame I K; i am U. I(1)] I q*uod* I M; *om* W. þe] *om* M. for nouȝt] for nouth JMH[3]; for nowth U; for out A; q*uod* I for oght W; q*uod* I though K. I(2)] þat I RUChMH[3]. haue] *om* W. walkid] walked RDCh; Iwalked K; hawed W.
259 wyte] wytyn J; witten K; wete DCh H[3]; wetyn AM. what] wath A; qwat JH[3]. is] *om* W. witterly] & vitterly W. herte] harte K.
260 how] ho A; who*m* R; what M. so] *om* J. I] *om* A. werche] werke M; wirche DJ; worche ChKW; wrouth H[3]. in . . . world] *om* U. world] wordle R; word M; werlde JAH[3]. wrong] RUDAKWMH[3]; amys J; *om* TChH[2]. oþ*er*] or UChAH[3].
261 markid] marked RD; m*er*kyd JAH[3]; merked Ch; maked K; mad W. wiþoute] *with*outy*n* MH[3]; *with* UCh; to J. m*er*cy] merke A. entrid] entred RUDChKH[3]; enterid A; yentred W.
262 þe] *om* H[2]. legende] legande R. lif] lyue JA. er] or DChK; ar H[2]J. were] were bory*n* H[3]; ded were R; ded ware U.

Or ellis [vn]writen for wykkid as witnessiþ þe gospel:
Nemo ascendet ad celum nisi qui de celo descendit.
And I leue on oure lord & on no *let*trure bet*ere*.
For salamon þe sage, þ*at* sapience made, 265
God ȝaf h[i]m g*ra*ce & ricchesse togid*ere*
For to reule his reaum riȝt at his wille;
De[m]de he not wel & wisly, as holy [writ] techiþ,
Boþe in werk & in woord, in world in his tyme?
Aristotle & he, who wrouȝte bet*ere*? 270
And al holy chirche holden hem in helle.
And was þ*ere* neu*ere* in þis world to wysere of werkis,
For alle cunnyng clerkis siþþe crist ȝede on erþe

263 Or] and R. ellis] eft H^3. vnwriten] W; vnwrityn JK; vnwrite U; onwryte*n* R; vnwretyn AMH^3; vndirwriten TD; vnd*ur*writen H^2; writen Ch. wykkid] wikke W; wykednes K; wiled RU. as] þus U. witnessiþ] witnessit M; witnessitȝ H^2; witnesseþ RDCh; wittenessit A; wytnesse W; seiþ UH^3.
263α *in margin, original hand* (*cp. line* 242) U. *ascendet*] *ascendit* RU(*both*)DKWMH^3; *assendit* A. *ad*] *in* RU(*both*)AKWMH^3. *qui*] *ille qui* H^3; *que* Ch. *de . . . descendit*] *descendit de celo* JW; *discendit de celo* DM; *decendit de celo* A; *descendit de celo &c* K; *&c* U(1). *de celo*] *om* H^3. *descendit*] *discendit* Ch; *descendit &c* R.
264 And] *om* AW. I] *om* H^2A. leue] beleue H^2J. on(1)] it be DJK; it wel be AWM; it wel H^3. oure . . . on] *om* H^3. &] *om* JA. on(2)] *om* RJAKW. no] non KM. *let*trure] lettereur ChJ; lettere UAM; lettre K; lettyr H^3.
265 þe] þat A.
266 ȝaf] gaf W; gave K; ȝif R. him] hi*m* RUDChJAKWMH^3; hem TH^2. togi*dere*] togideres DU; togedere A; togeder Ch; togederes RW; togederis MH^3; together K.
267 reule] rewlyn J; rewelyn A; rulyn M. reaum] reame D; realme KM; reume UW; rewme RH^3; Reme ChH^2; rem A; reeme J. riȝt] riȝth R; rigth M; ryth AH^3. at] as Ch. his] is U.
268 Demde . . . &] And he dyd J. Demde] Dede TRDChH^2AM; ȝet dede H^3; dide UKW. not] nouȝt DCh; nouth H^3; nout M; nowt U. wel & wisly] wisly & wel M. &] ne D. writ] ChJKWMH^3; chirche TH^2A; cherche RUD. techiþ] techit A; techitȝ H^2; techeþ RDChW; teches U; tellyth H^3; tellit M.
269 Boþe] Bothin JM. werk] worke K. in(2)] *om* JA. in world] inward A. in(3)] & *in* H^3; in the KW. world] wordle RU; werld H^3. in his] and In Ch. tyme] teme A.
270 Aristotle] Aristodil A. who] ho ChJH^3; he A. wrouȝte] wrouȝt Ch; wrouȝthe R; wroughten K; wrowht J; wroute U; wrouty*n* H^3; wrote W: wretyn A; dedyn M.
271 al] ȝet H^3; *om* U. chirche] cherche RUDWM. holden] holdyn A; hold D; holdeþ R; holdiþ UH^3; holdit M; helt J. hem] hym D.
272 And] *om* JA. was] wern M. þere] *om* UJAMH^3. world] werlde JH^3; wordle U; word RM; *om* A. to] two RDChH^2JW; twoo K; ij MH^3; no U. wysere] wisar K. of] *om* A. werkis] clerkis A; clerkes W; witte Ch.
273 For] of R. cunnyng] konyg H^3; comou*n* (? coniou*n*) J; kennys M. clerkis] clergkys J. siþþe] sytthy*n* H^3; sithe H^2; syþ UW; sithen K; syþin M; syn RA; seþe D; seþ Ch; sethin J. crist] god A. ȝede] ȝode J; went A. on] in U. erþe] herthe U; erde A.

Taken ensaumpl[e] of *here* sawis in sarmonis þ*at* þei maken,
And be here werkis & here wordis wissen vs to dowel, 275
And ȝif I shal werke be here werkis to wynne me heuene,
And for here werkis & here wyt wende to pyne,
Þanne wrouȝte I vnwisly wiþ alle þe wyt þ*at* I lere.
A goode friday, I fynde, a feloun was sauid
Þ*at* hadde lyued al his lyf wiþ lesinges & þeft[e], 280
And for he kneuȝ on þe crois & to crist shr[o]f hym,
Sonn*ere* hadde he saluac*io*u*n* þanne seint Ion þe baptist,
Or ad*am*, or ysaye, or any of þe p*ro*phetis
Þat hadde leyn w*ith* lucifer manye longe ȝeris; | *fol.* lij *a*
A robbere hadde remission raþ*ere* þanne þei alle, 285
Wiþoute pen*au*nce of purcatorie to haue p*ar*adis for eu*ere*.

274 Taken] Takyn JAM; Take UDWH³. ensaumple] ChRH²KWM; exau*m*ple JA H³; exsanple U; ensaumpl*is* T; ensamples D. of] at K. h*ere*] her ChKH³; hire H². in] & RH³. sarmonis] sermonys A; sermones Ch; s*er*mons KH³; s*er*mowni*s* R. þei] ȝei U. maken] makyn RAM; make UChJW; maden H²; made H³.
275 And] *om* AW. werkis] work*es* K; werk RW. &] & by W. here(2)] *om* ChA. wissen] wyssyn JAH³; wisse W. vs] hem K. dowel] goode M.
276 And] *om* JA. ȝif] ȝef Ch. shal] xal H³; schuld Ch; schulde J. werke] werky*n* MH³; werche A; wirke R; wyrkyn J; wirch Ch; work K; worche W; wurche U. be] *om* A. here werkis] he*m* M. werkis] werkes Ch; workes K; werk RUJWH³; wordes D. to] & A. wynne] wynnen K; wy*n*nyn JM; wyn Ch; wony*n* H³; bryng W. me] me to W; *in* H³.
277 And] And thay K; and I RUAH³. for(1)] w*ith* A. here(1)] her ChJKH³. werkis] work*es* K. & . . . wyt] *om* UW. here(2)] her*e* RM; her Ch; for here TDH²; *om* JAKH³. wende] wynde D; wenten K; þei went Ch; þei wentyn J; wony*n* H³; wynne me AWM. to] *in* H³; *om* AWM. pyne] peyne H³; payne R; helle Ch.
278–83 *as five lines divided after* fryday—lyf—crosse—sauacion W.
278 wrouȝte] wrouȝthe R; wrougthe M; wrouth AH³; wroutt U; wrowht J. wroght W. vnwisly] vnwittily RU. þe] *om* JWM. wyt] wittis A; *om* JM. þat] *om* D. lere] lerne JH³; lernede M.
279 A] On RJAKWMH³. a(2)] þat a A. sauid] saued DCh; ysaued RUKW.
280 *line om* U. Þat] And RK. hadde] *om* H³. lyued] lyuede M; lyuyd J; llyvyd K; leued Ch; leuede H³; leuyd DAW; ylyued R. his] is A. lyf] lyue ChA. wiþ] be J; in AM. lesinges] lesyng*us* H³; lesyng JW. þefte] MJAKWH³; þefthe R; þeftis TD; þeftes Ch; theeftis H².
281 And] *om* UJAM. kneuȝ] knew DCh H²H³; knewe it K; beknew AWM; beknewe J; kneled R; knelyd U. on] to RU. crois] cros RUChAKWMH³. shrof] RUJAWH³; schroff K; shroue Ch; shref TDH²; schsof M.
282 hadde . . . saluac*io*u*n*] was he sauid M; was sauyd J. he] *om* UD. saluac*io*u*n*] sauacyou*n* RUDAW. seint] sent H³; saynt K; seyn M; sen A. þe] *om* K.
283 ad*am*] habraham M. any] ony RU JAM; eny D. þe] þoo J; those H²; þese UA. p*ro*phetis] other J.
284 *line om* AWMH³. hadde] hadde*n* R. leyn] lay H²; lien K; yleye R. w*ith*] be UJ.
285 hadde] hade U; had ChJAKW. raþ*ere*] sonn*ere* M. þei] þai W; ȝei U; he A.
286 Wiþoute] w*ith*outen UJ; w*ith*outyn AH³; Witoutyn M; W*ith* RW. of] in U; or JWMH³. purcatorie] p*ur*gatorie RUD H²JAKWMH³. to] *om* JA. haue] han U; haiþe A; *om* JMH³.

Þanne marie þe maudeleyn who miȝte do wers?
Or who dede wers þanne dauid þat vrie destroyede,
Or poule þe apostil þat no pite hadde
Cristene kynde to kille to deþe? 290
And arn no[ne], forsoþe, soueREYNES in heuene
As þise þat wrouȝte wykkidly in world whanne þei were.
And ȝet [haue] I forget[e ferþer] of fyue wyttis teching
Þat clergie of cristis mouþ comendite [was hit] neuere,
For he seide it hymself to summe of his disciplis: 295
Dum steter[it]is ante [reges &c] presides nolite cogitare,
And is as muche to mene, to men þat ben lewid,

287 Þanne] And J. þe] of R; *om* UDJAK. maudeleyn] Magdeleyne DH^{2}; magdalen JWH^{3}. who] ho JAH^{3}. miȝte] myȝthe R; migth M; myth H^{3}. do] don RM; doun JH^{3}. wers] wors ChW; worse RD.
288 Or . . . wers] And also J. who] ho AH^{3}; she W; *om* RU. dede] dide $UH^{2}K$; dude R. wers] wors ChKW; worse RD; wurse U. þanne] or W. dauid] dauit A. vrie] vrry Ch. destroyede] destroyed RW; destruȝyd J; distroyed $DChH^{2}K$; destruyed U; dystroyid H^{3}; distroide M; dystroed A.
289 poule] paul D; pawle J. apostil] postil D; postel RA. no] non M. pite] pete JAH^{3}; petie K. hadde] RUDCh $JAKWH^{3}$; ne hadde $TH^{2}M$.
290 Cristene] Mychel cristen J. kynde] kende UCh. kille] kyll KW; killen Ch; kyllyn JM. to] to the KW. deþe] dede M.
291 And] *om* UA. arn] Arne A; ar Ch; buþ D. none] UM; non DRJ; þer none H^{3}; þer non AW; now $TChH^{2}K$. souereynes] so souereyn J; more souereyn D; souereynlych H^{3}; so souereyne liche A; so souerainlych W; so souereynglich K; so sikirly M; so fer RU. heuene] heuyn AK; hefne U.
292 As] And Ch. þise] þies J; þese RUD AM; þes $ChKH^{3}$. wrouȝte] wrouȝthe R; wroght W; wrouȝten $H^{2}K$; wrougthin M; wroute U; wroutyn AH^{3}; weryn J. wykkidly] so wikkedly W; wykkyd J. in] in þis A. world] werld AJH^{3}. whanne] wan A; qwen J; tho K; qwyl H^{3}; wher W. þei] þai W. were] weren K; wern M; weryn AH^{3}.
293 *line om* U. And] but M; *om* J. ȝet] ȝit $RChH^{2}JAWM$. haue] $ChKH^{3}$; am RDJM (? ani D); arn W; any TH^{2}; *om* A. I] þai W. forgete] ChH^{3}; forget TDH^{2}; forgat A; forȝote R; forged K; forgyd J; forked W; aferd M. ferþer] ferther JAH^{3}; farther K; forþere W; for soþe R; for TH^{2}; *om* DChM. of fyue] of vyue R; of þe v M.
294 *line om* UW. Þat] wat A; þanne M. clergie] clergyȝe H^{3}; clergise M. mouþ] moutȝ R; mouȝt H^{2}. comendite] comendyd JA; comended Ch; comaundid MH^{3}; commaunded K; comonded D; commdeþ (? comindeþ) R. was hit] Ch; was it KM; was JAH^{3}; hit D; what is TRH^{2}. neuere] euer ChK; *om* A.
295 *line om* UA; *as one line with following* W. seide] said KW; seyth J. it] þus H^{3}. self] selue J.
296 *Dum*] *Cum* U. *steteritis*] $RUChH^{2}JA$ $KWMH^{3}$; *steteris* TD. *reges &c*] UJAK MH^{3}; *reges* $H^{2}W$ (*cancelled* H^{2}); *om* TRD Ch. *&c . . . cogitare*] *&c* W. *presides*] *principes* K. *cogitare*] *cogitare &c* RChJK MH^{3}; *cogitare quid loquamini* U.
297 And] That R; Þis H^{3}; It U; *om* A. as] *om* H^{2}. muche] mochell K; meche UAH^{3}; mychel J; michil M. mene] menyn M. to(2)] as A. ben] bene J; be AH^{3}.

'Wh[anne] ȝe ben aposid of p*r*inces or of p*r*estis of þe lawe
For to answere hem haue ȝe no doute,
For I shal g*r*aunte ȝow g*r*ace of god þ*at* ȝe s*er*uen, 300
Þe help of þe holy gost to answere hem [alle]'.
Þe douȝtiest docto*ur* or dyuyno*ur* of þe trinite,
Þat [was] austyn þe olde, & hiȝeste of þe foure,
Seide þis for a sarmou*n*, so me god helpe:
Ecce ipsi ydiot[*e*] *rapiunt celum vbi nos sapientes* 305
in infernum mergemur.
And is to mene in oure mouþ, more ne lesse,
Arn none raþ*er*e yrauisshid fro þe riȝte beleue
Þanne arn þise [k]ete clerkis þ*at* conne many bokis,
Ne none sonn*er*e ysauid, ne sadd*er*e of consience,

298 Whanne] wha*n* RUAKWM; qwan JH^3; whar D; Wheþ*er* TChH^2. ȝe ben] be ȝe Ch. ȝe] þei A. ben] bene J; be H^2H^3. aposid] aposed RJ; apposid UH^2M; apposed DChKW; posid A. of p*r*inces] of kyng*es* K; *om* M. or of] othir of H^2; or UDJ; and RAKWH^3; of M. p*r*estis . . . lawe] p*r*incis in the hall K. þe] *om* W.
299 answere] answeryn JAMH^3. hem] them K; hem alle M; hym D. no] no*n* M. doute] douȝte D.
300 I shal] I xal H^3; he wile M. g*r*aunte] grauntyn J. of] þe M. s*er*uen] seruyn DJAMH^3; serue ChW.
301 þe(2)] *om* D. answere] answeryn JAMH^3. alle] RUDJAKWMH^3; at wille TChH^2.
302 douȝtiest] douȝctyest D; douthyest H^3; douthiyste M; doutiest A; douttyest R. docto*ur* . . . dyuyno*ur*] dyuynour*e* or docto*ur* J. or] & H^3; *om* RU. dyuyno*ur*] deuino*ur* (? demnour) R; dempno*ur* U. þe] *om* J. trinite] trenite A; lawe U.
303 Þat was] RUJKWM; Þat TDH^2A; was H^3; As Ch. þe] *om* W. olde] hold M; owlde J; elde A; holden W; old frere (frere *cancelled*) K. &] & þe UChW; þe JA. hiȝeste] hyeste K; hyest RChJW; heyest DAH^3; heist U; heyirst M. þe] hem alle A; *om* JH^3.
304 Seide] sayde RDW; Said K; He seyde H^3; And seide U. þis] þ*us* RUJAKMH^3. for] in AH^3. sarmou*n*] sermou*n* RChA KH^3. so] as so A.
305 *ipsi*] *om* H^3. *ydiote*] UW; *ydioti* TRD ChH^2JKM; *ideoti* H^3; *indocti* A. *rapiunt celum*] *celum rapiunt* U. *rapiunt*] *rapient* R; *rapuerunt* ChH^2. *vbi . . . mergemur*] *vibi eium* (? *enim*) &*c* J. *vbi*] & U. *nos*] *om* H^3. *sapientes*] *cum doctrinis nostris* U. *in . . . mergemur*] *demergemur in infernum* U. *infernum*] *infermo* W; *infenum* K. *mergemur*] *mergimur* WM; *merguntur* H^3; *dimergimur* &*c* R; *margimur* A; *merg*::::: K.
306 And] And it J; It A; þat H^3. mene] menyn JM; meane K. in . . . mouþ] *om* J. in] on W. mouþ] mouȝthe H^2; mowtȝ R; mouthis M. more . . . lesse] noþer lesse ne more A. more] neþ*er* more H^3; nethyr more J. ne] no Ch. lesse] lasse JM.
307 Arn] Arne A; Ben H^3; Buþ D; Arn þ*er* W; þ*er* bene J. raþ*er*e] raþir U. yrauisshid] IRauesched Ch; rauyschid UJM; rauyssched DW; raueshid R; rauesched A. fro] from AKM; for D. þe] *om* J. riȝte] ryȝtthe R; rigthe M; rith UJAH^3.
308 arn] ar*e* R; buþ D; *om* U. þise] þis W; þies J; þese UH^2H^3; þes RChAK; *om* D. kete] KW; grete TRUDChH^2 JAMH^3. conne] connen KW; connyn J; cun A; koniyn M; know H^3.
309 Ne] Ben H^3. ysauid] Isaued ChW; sauyd UDJA; saued R. ne] no*n* H^3. sadd*er*e . . . consience] of consciens sadd*er*e J. consience] cosience H^2.

Þanne pore peple, as plouȝmen, and pastours of bestis, 310
Souteris & seweris; suche lewide iottis
Percen wiþ a *paternoster* þe paleis of heuene
Wiþoute penaunce at here partyng, into [þe] heiȝe blisse.

310 Þanne] þan þe J. peple] people K; puple AH³. as] & M. plouȝmen] plouthmen M. and . . . of] þat pasture her A. and] or D. pastours] paustores U; pasturers H³; pasturars K; pastorrerys J.
311 Souteris] Saweris AMH³; Sawiers W. &] an U. seweris] seweres U; Sewers DH²; soweris AMH³; soweres K; sowers ChW; souestreres R. suche] swiche M; sweche A; and suche RChKW; and swiche UJ; & sweche H³. iottis] Iuttis U; Iuttes R; peple J. *Here* H³ *inserts four lines: see above*, p. 48.
312 Percen] Percyn ChJ; Percien K; Mon persyn A; Perchen R; Pasen U; þey departyn M; *om* H³. wiþ] wit M. a] her Ch. þe] to þe H³. paleis] pales A; palais M.
313 Wiþoute] withouten U; withoutyn JH³; witoutyn M; I withoute A; & without (& *in margin*) K. penaunce] gret penans H³. here] her ChJK; hys H³. into] passyn into (into *above line same hand*) K; to comyn to H³. þe] RUChH²JAWM; *om* TDKH³. heiȝe blisse] blisse of heuyn Amen A. heiȝe] heye UDM; hye RChJKW; *om* H³. blisse] blisse amen (amen *cancelled*) K. *Here* M *adds 6 lines; see above*, p. 49.

APPENDIX

XII

'Crist wot,' q*uo*d clergie, 'knowe hit ȝif þe lyke, *fol.* 40 *a*
I haue do my deu*er* þe dowel to teche,
And whoso coueyteþ do*n* beter*e* þa*n* þe boke telleþ,
He passeþ þe apostolis lyf, and [peryth] to au*n*gelys.
But I se now as I seye, as me soþ thinkytȝ, 5
þe were lef to lerne but loþ for to stodie;
þou woldest konne þ*at* I can and carpe*n* hit after;
P*re*sumptuowsly, p*ar*auentur*e*, apose so manye
That myȝthe turne m[e] to tene & theologie boþe.
ȝif I wiste witterly þou woldest don þerafter, 10
Al þat þou askest asoylen I wolde.'
Skornfully þ[o] scriptur*e* she[t] vp h[ere] browes,
And on clergie crieþ on crist*es* holy name
That he shewe me hit ne sholde but ȝif [I schriue*n*] were
Of þe kynde cardinal wit, and cristned in a font, 15
And seyde so loude þ*at* shame me thouȝthe,
þat hit wer*e* boþe skaþe and sklau*n*dre to holy cherche

1 lyke] likeþ U.
2 do] don UJ.
3 And] An J. who] ho J. coueyteþ] coueite U. do*n*] to don U; bene J. telleþ] tellyth J.
4 passeþ] passyth J; pasith U. þe] *om* U. apostolis] apostillis J; apostlis U. lyf] lyue J. peryth] J; put hi*m* R; put hem U. to] in to U.
5 as(1)] *om* J. thinkytȝ] thinkyth J; þynkeþ U.
6 *line om* U. lef] leue for J.
7 woldest] woldist UJ. konne] kunne U; cony*n* J. carpe*n*] carpyn UJ.
8 apose] aposyn J.
9 myȝthe] myht J; it myȝte U. turne] t*ur*nun J. me] UJ; me*n* R. boþe] bothin J.
10 woldest] woldist U; wyldyst J.
11 askest] axist J. asoylen] asoylyn J.
12 þo scripture] sc*r*ipture þo J. þo] U; þe R. shet] schet J; set U; sherte R. here] U; her J; his R.
13 crieþ] cryede U; c*r*iyd J. crist*es*] godis U. name] halue (*same hand after cancelled* name) J.
14 shewe . . . hit] schewiȝt U; it schewe me (it *above line over erasure in a smaller script*) J. ne] nout J. ȝif] if it U; *om* J. I schriue*n*] J; stryf RU.
15 kynde] *om* U. wit] *om* J. cristned] c*r*istenyd UJ.
16 seyde] seide it U. loude] lowyd J. thouȝthe] thowte J; it þoute U.
17 boþe] *om* UJ. sklau*n*dre] slaundre U. to] to al J.

Sitthe theologie þe trewe to tellen hit defendeþ;
'Dauid godes derling defendyþ hit also:
Vidi preuarica[nt]es & tabescebam.
"I saw synful," he seyde, "þerfore I seyde no þing 20
Til þo wrecches ben in wil here synne to lete."
And poul precheþ hit often, prestes hit redyn:
Audiui archan[a uerba] que non licet homini loqui.
"I am not hardy," quod he, "þat I herde with erys,
Telle hit with tounge to synful wrecches."
And god graunted hit neuere; þe gospel hit witnesseþ 25
In þe passioun, whan pilat aposed god almyȝthi, |
And asked Iesu on hy þat herden hit an hundred. *fol.* 40*b*
"*Quid est ueritas?*" quod he; "verilyche tel vs."
God gaf him non answere but gan his tounge holde.
Riȝt so I rede,' quod she, 'red þou no ferþer; 30
Of þat he wolde wite wis him no betere;
For he cam not by cause to lerne to dowel
But as he seyþ, such I am, when he with me carpeþ.'
And when scripture þe skolde hadde þis [skele] ysheued
Clergie into a caban crepte anon after, 35
And drow þe dore after him and bad me go do wel
Or wycke ȝif I wolde, wheþer me lyked.
Þan held I vp myn handes to scripture þe wise
To be hure man ȝif I most for eueremore after,

18 Sitthe] Sethin J; scihoþ U. þe trewe] þat trewe is UJ. to] *om* U. tellen] tellyn J. defendeþ] deffendeþ U; defendyth J.
19 defendyþ] deffendeþ U.
19α *preuaricantes*] UJ; *preuaricationes* R. **Here U ends.** *Variants from* J *are henceforth given without sigil.*
20 saw] sayhe.
21 here] her.
22 precheþ] preched. often] oftyn.
22α *archana uerba*] J; *archane* R.
23 þat] of þat.
24 Telle] Tellyn. wrecches] schrewys.
25 graunted] grauntyd.
26 whan] how. aposed] aposyd. almyȝthi] almyht.
27 asked] axed. þat] þer. herden] herdyn. hundred] hunderith.
29 gaf] ȝaf.
30 Riȝt] Rit. red] rede.
31 wolde] ȝernyth to.
32 not] nouth. lerne] lernyn.
33 he] ho. such] swyche. when] qwan. me] men. carpeþ] Iangelyth.
34 when] qwan. skele] scole J; wyt R. ysheued] schewyd.
35 a] *om.* crepte] crepe.
36 after] to.
37 wycke] wykly. wheþer] qwethir þat. lyked] lykyd.
38 vp] *preceded by cancelled* h. handes] hondes.
39 be] bene. hure] her.

With þ*a*t she wolde me wisse wher þe tou*n* were 40
Kynde [wit] hur*e* co*n*fesso*ur*, hur*e* cosyn was Inne.
Þat lady þ*a*n low and lauȝthe me in her*e* armes
And sayde, 'my cosyn kynde wit knowe*n* is wel wide,
And his loggyng is *with* lyf þ*a*t lord is of erþe,
And ȝif þou desyre *with* hi*m* for to abyde 45
I shal þe wisse [wynlyche] wher*e* þ*a*t he dwelleþ'.
And þa*n*ne I kneled on my knes and kyste h*er* [fete] sone,
And þanked hur*e* a þousand syþes *with* þrobbant herte.
She called me a clerioun þ*a*t
Hyȝt *omnia probate*, a pore þing *with*alle; 50
'Þou shalt wende *with* wil,' q*uo*d she, 'whiles þ*a*t hi*m* lykyþ,
Til ȝe come to þe burg[h] *quod bonum est tenete.*
Ken hi*m* to my cosenes hous þ*a*t kinde wit hyȝth.
Sey I sente hi*m* þis segge, and þ*a*t he shewe hy*m* dowel.'
Þ*us* we lauȝþe our*e* leue, lowtyng at onys, 55
And wente forþ on my way *with omnia probate*,
And er*e* I cam to þe court *quod bonum est tenete*
Many ferlys me byfel in a fewe ȝeris. |
The fyrste ferly I fond afyngrid me made; *fol.* 41 *a*
As I ȝede thurgh ȝouþe, aȝen prime dayes, 60
I stode stille in a stodie and stared abowte.
'Al hayl,' q*uo*d on þo, and I answered, 'welcome, & *with* who*m* be ȝe?'
'I am dwellyng *with* deth, and hu*n*ger I hatte.

40 wisse] wissyn. wher] qwer*e*.
41 Kynde] þat kynd. wit] wytte J; *with* R. hur*e*(1)] þe. hur*e*(2)] her. cosyn] ky*n*nysman.
42 low] lowhe on me. lauȝthe] lawht.
43 sayde] seyd. knowe*n*] knowyn. wel] ful.
44 his . . . is(1)] is lyggyng.
45 abyde] dwelle.
46 wisse] wyssyn. wynlyche] J; *om* R. wher*e*] qwere. dwelleþ] dwellyth.
47 kneled] knelyd. kyste] kyssyd. fete] J; wel R.
48 And . . . syþes] A thowsyng tymes I thankyd hir*e*. þrobbant] throbbyng.
49–50 *as one line* R; *divided after* hite J.
49 called] callyd. me] *om*. clerioun] clergyn. þ*a*t] þan þat.
50 Hyȝt] hite.
51 wende] wendyn. wil] wille. whiles] qwyl. þ*a*t] *om*.
52 burgh] burgh*er* R; bowhe J.
53 cosenes] cosynys. hyȝth] hite.
55 *line om*.
56 And] I. on] in. way] wey.
57 And] *om*. court] cuntreyys.
58 ferlys] ferlyys.
59 afyngrid] an hunger it.
60 As I ȝede] And I þan. aȝen] aȝeyn.
62 hayl] heyle. and] *om*. answered] seyd. who*m*] hom. ȝe] ȝowe.
63 hatte] hyte.

To lyf in his lordshepe longyt my weye
[To kyllyn him ȝif I can, þei kynde wit helpe]. 65
I shal felle þ*a*t freke in a fewe dayes.'
'I wolde folwe þe fayn, but fentesye me hendeþ;
Me folweþ such a fentyse, I may no ferþer walke.'
'Go we forþ,' q*uo*d þe gom, 'I haue a gret boyste
At my bak of broke bred þi bely for to fylle, 70
A bagge ful of a begger*e*.' I bouȝþe h*it* at onys.
Than mau*n*ged I wit[h him] vp at þe fulle;
For þe myssyng of mete no meso*ur* I coude,
[But ete as hung*er* me hete til my belly swellyd.
Þ*er* bad me hung*er* haue gode day but I helde me stille; 75
For gronyng of my guttys I durst gon no ferther].
W*ith* þat cam a knaue w*ith* a co*n*fesso*ur*es face,
[Lene ⁊ rewlyche, w*ith* leggys ful smale].
He halsed me, and I asked hi*m* after
Of whe*n* þat he wer*e*, and wheder þ*a*t he wolde. 80
'W*ith* deþ I duelle,' q*uo*d he, 'dayes and nyȝt*es*.
Mi name is feu*ere* on þe ferþe day; I am aþrest euer*e*.
I am masag*er* of deþ; men haue I tweyne:
Þat on is called cotidia*n*, a co*ur*rour of our*e* hous;
Tercian þ*a*t oþ*er*; trewe drinker*es* boþe. 85
We han lett*er*es of lyf, he shal his lyf ty[n]e.
Fro deþ þat is our*e* duk swyche dedis we brynge.'
'Myȝth I so, god wot, ȝour*e* gat*es* wolde I holden.'
'Nay, wil,' q*uo*d þ*a*t wyȝth, 'wend þou no ferther,
But lyue as þis lyf is ordeyned for the. 90

64 in] ⁊. longyt] longyth.
65 J; *line om* R.
66 felle] fellyn. freke] freyke.
67 folwe] folwyn. fayn] fayne q*uo*d I. fentesye] fayntys. hendeþ] hentith.
68 folweþ] folwyth. fentyse] fayntyse. no ferþer] not forth.
70 At . . . of] Of battys ⁊. broke] brokyn. for to] to.
71 begger*e*] beggar. bouȝþe] bowht.
72 mau*n*ged] mau*n*gyd. with him] w*ith* him J; wit R. at] to.
73 þe] *om*. no] none. coude] cowthe.
74–6 J; *ll. om* R.
78 J; *line om* R.
79 he . . . I] I haylsyd hym hendely ⁊ (haylsyd *after cancelled* haysyd, hym *above cancelled* me, *both in original hand*). asked] axid.
80 whe*n*] qwennys. wheder] qwedyr.
81 dayes] dayys. nyȝt*es*] nyhetys.
82 aþrest] athrist.
83 masag*er*] mensenger. tweyne] twayne.
84 called] callyd.
85 oþ*er*] othyr. trewe] true. boþe] bothen.
86 han] haue. of] of his. tyne] J; tyme R.
88 Myȝth] Myht. so] se q*uo*d he. gat*es*] gatys. holden] holdyn. **Here J breaks off.**

Þ[ou] tomblest wiþ a trepget ȝif þou my tras folwe,
And ma*n*nes me*r*þe w[or]þ no mor þa*n* he deseruyþ her*e*
Whil his lyf and his lykhame lesten togedere.
And þ*er*for*e* do aft*er* dowel whil þi dayes duren, | *fol.* 41 *b*
Þat þi play be plentevous in p*ar*adys w*ith* au*n*gelys. 95
Þou shalt be lauȝth into lyȝth w*ith* loking of an eye
So þat þou werke þe word þat holy wryt techeþ,
And be prest to preyer*es* and p*ro*fitable werk*es*.'
Wille þurgh inwit [wiste] wel þe soþe,
Þat þis speche was spedelich, and sped hi*m* wel faste, 100
And wrouȝthe þ*at* her*e* is wryten and oþ*er* werk*es* boþe
Of per*es* þe plowma*n* and mechel puple also.
And wha*n* þis werk was wrouȝt, er*e* wille myȝte aspie,
Deþ delt hi*m* a dent and drof hi*m* to þe erþe
And is closed vnder clom, crist haue his soule. 105
And so bad Iohan but busily wel ofte
Whe*n* he saw þes sawes busyly alegged
By Iames and by Ierom, by Iop and by oþ*er*e,
And for he medleþ of makyng he made þ*is* ende.
Now alle ke*n*ne creatur*es* þ*at* cristene wer*e* euere 110
God for his goudnesse gif he*m* swyche happes
To lyue as þ*at* lord lykyþ þ*at* lyf in he*m* putte:
Furst to rekne Richard, kyng of þ*is* rewme,
And alle lord*es* þ*at* louy*n* hi*m* lely in herte,
God saue he*m* sound by se and by land. 115
Marie moder and may, for man þou byseke
Þat barn bryng vs to blys þ*at* bled vpon þe rode ame*n*.

91 Þou] þe R.
92 worþ] wrouȝþ R.
99 wiste] þou wost R.

CRITICAL NOTES

Prologue

1 *softe was the sonne / I south wente*. See above, p. 154. The difficulty is to account for the rejected variant. Neither of these readings is likely to have given rise to the other. It is possible that *softe was the sonne*, which receives overwhelming manuscript support, is an author's variant replacing an earlier form; equally, that it is a **B**/**C** reading which has almost completely ousted *I south wente*.

2 *schrubbes*. See above, p. 120. The variant *schregges* (Ch) was possibly introduced for emphasis.

10 *swiȝede* is challenged only by *sweiued* (EJ), a possible form of *swayve*, 'move to and fro, flow'. The reading *sownede* of VH derives from *swiȝede*.

13 *Ac / But / And*. See above, p. 159.

14 *triȝely*. See above, p. 133.

20 *to / to þe*. For the sense of *putte* in this line see *NED* s.v., 27(*a*). In both uses the first recorded instance is from *Piers Plowman*. The use with infinitive seems more difficult than that with noun or participle, and therefore more probably original.

22 *Wonne þat*. The variants *whanne þat* and *Whom þat* derive from the adopted reading, possibly as visual errors encouraged by the abrupt repetition of the verbal notion. RE's *Þat* reflects omission of an awkward word; *þat many of* was produced by padding after such omission.

26 *wel / ful*. See above, pp. 138–9.

29 *cairen / caryen*. The rejected reading is either an inferior spelling or a homœograph for this evidently difficult term from alliterative poetry.

31 *chosen hem to / chosen to / chosen*. See above, pp. 159–60.

34 *giltles / synneles*. The reading adopted, which is the only possible original of all the variants, is also metrically superior.

41 *bely ... bagge / belyes ... bagges*. The older, distributive singular construction is retained as presumably original. Substitution of the plural would have been suggested to scribes by the possessive pronoun.

42 *Flite þanne / Fayted*. See above, p. 160.

63 *hy / he / þei*. See above, p. 157.

73 *gyuen*. See above, p. 157.

74 *leniþ / leuiþ*. These words are indistinguishable in most fourteenth-century and many fifteenth-century hands. The present phrase is, however, a variation of *gyuen . . . glotonis* in line 73, and I find no meaning of *leuiþ* to fit that relation. I therefore transcribe *leniþ*, 'bestow' (*NED* s.v. *Lend* v.^{2} 2).

75 *Were / But were*. See above, p. 158.

79 The line is metrically difficult. See above, p. 154.

86 *poundide / poundys*. The pattern of variation argues a more difficult original than a noun *poundys,* from which the readings *poynteþ* and *ponderys* can hardly be derived. An original *poundide,* 'shut up, confined', perhaps bearing the special sense 'distrained' (cp. *NED* s.v. *Poind* v.), and with a play on *barre* in line 85, can have given rise to all the variants.

96 *bondage / bondeagys / Bonde men*. The last of these variants is too easy to have generated the other two. Of those the plural has a meaning unsuited to the context: compare *The English Register of Godstow Nunnery*, i, ed. A. Clark, EETS 129 (London, 1905), p. 257, *demaynes rentis homagis wardes relefis villenagis or bondages and all other availes that comyn out of the londe.* The remaining variant is therefore adopted, as an extension of the use of the abstract noun signifying a condition of tenure, to the class which holds by that tenure.

102 *dede / dedes*. The singular, with the meaning 'task, stint of work' (*NED* s.v. *Deed* 3) is the more difficult reading, and the less likely substitution.

Passus I

1 *merke / derke*. Manuscript support for *derke* is less impressive than might at first appear, amounting to the presumptive family {⟨[(TH^2)Ch]D⟩RU}, having the weight of a single manuscript, K and V. H's *deope* suggests that the reading of the exclusive common ancestor of VH was probably not *derke*. The variation points to independent substitution for a difficult original reading; such a reading is the regional word *merke*.

8 See above, p. 154.

18 *of liflode / to liflode*. The minority reading of TRCh, supported by that of HM, is adopted as necessary to the sense.

23 Variation in this line was probably caused by the difficult metre: *þa tón is vestúre · fro chéle*. But see Chambers (*MLR*, xiv, p. 151 n. 1) and Day (*MLR*, xxiii, p. 12).

37 *wolde þe / þe to*. In the majority of manuscripts this line is unmetrical. The variants are explicable on the assumption that original *wolde* was lost early in the **A** tradition because of its proximity to *world*; that *to* was next inserted to strengthen the now incomplete line, and that EM were at some stage corrected.

48 *ilike / lik(e*. That the original word had the prefix is suggested by *ymagis* of T, *Image is* of ChL, and *ymage was* of VH.

61 *wy/wiȝt*. The harder, alliterative word is unlikely to have been inserted by southern scribes of the fourteenth century or by any scribes of the fifteenth. Its use here by the poet with an ironic flavour (its connotations are usually good) would make it even more difficult.

62 *foundide / foundit*. See above, p. 169.

78 *sennes*. For T's more usual form see I 177, III 255, etc.

104 *such seuene & anoþer*. See above, p. 160.

105 See above, pp. 154–5.

107 *trouþe*. Elsewhere in this passus spelled *treuþe* by T; e.g. at lines 12, 83, 95, 97 etc.

122 *troniþ hem / tronen hem*. The identity of the original verb is hardly in doubt; its precise form is less certain. The context, however, seems to require the sense 'Truth will enthrone them' rather than 'their souls will enthrone themselves'.

137 *plante*. See above, p. 155.

148 *him heiȝe / him by*. See above, p. 106. The line refers to Luke xxiii. 34, *Pater, dimitte illis: non enim sciunt quid faciunt*, not to Luke xxiii. 40–3, the source of the legend of Dismas. Confusion of reference would be created by the currency of this legend (compare V 237–8 below), and possibly increased by the similarity of the letters *b* and *h* in some hands.

159 *ioynide / Iuggid*. The reading adopted is the more pregnant, implying both judgement and injunction, and therefore the harder. It is also obviously the more likely original of all the variants, whereas *Iuggid* can scarcely have produced *bond hit* or its own unmetrical synonym *demys*, let alone *ioynide*. *Iuggid* is probably a homœograph for the aphetic reading adopted (see *NED* s.v. *Join* v.[2]); *bond hit* preserves the meaning of this after a fashion; *demys*, *hath wryten* and *Seyth it* are resourceless substitutions.

162, 168 *cheynide / schryned*. The rejected reading, the only serious rival to that adopted, is found in RUL in line 162, and RU in line 168. It might appear to have a more difficult meaning; in fact, however, to 'enshrine' a thing in an inappropriate place seems to have been a current mode of abuse (compare Chaucer, *Complete Works*, ed. F. N. Robinson, Cambridge, Mass., 1933, 'Pardoner's Tale', line 955), and not a distinguished irony. *cheynide* should stand then, according to the direction of the manuscripts.

173 *lering*. See above, pp. 151–2.

179 *graiþ*. See above, pp. 162–3.

PASSUS II

31 *lord / our lorde*. The reading adopted is the more probable original for two reasons, which together seem conclusive: as a less usual expression it is unlikely to have replaced the familiar *our lorde*; and it receives the strongest manuscript support. The originals of WN, L and E almost certainly did not read *our lorde*; that the agreement of VH and M is coincidental is suggested by the text of Ch, where the process of substituting a more familiar locution can be observed. Compare also VII 260.

35 *assent*. An ambiguous original form meaning either 'summoned' or 'in agreement' is adopted as the likely original on the indication of the two directions of variation shown by *of sent* and *of asseent*. See *NED* s.vv. *assent* pa. pple, *assent* v. 2b.

37 *þermyd / þerwiþ*. See above, p. 157.

43 *cuntre / þe cuntre.* The adopted reading, meaning 'native of the region', is less explicit and therefore somewhat harder. For the use see *English Gilds*, ed. T. Smith and L. T. Smith, EETS 40 (London, 1870), p. 76.

51 *boun / bounde.* See above, p. 169.

83 *mendis.* The only possible original of the other variants. See above, p. 99.

87 *mede / hire.* See above, p. 106. The adopted reading is that of the archetype of the surviving manuscripts. The quite unmetrical *mede* cannot derive from *hire*, which would in any case have satisfied most scribes by affording an *aa bb* alliteration. The original may have been deliberately unmetrical, to draw attention to a meaning of the word *mede*. The author uses such a trick at VI 71, for another purpose. See the critical note to that line, p. 445 below.

94 *feyntles / feythles.* It is hardly conceivable that so easy and obviously apt an original as *feythles* could have given rise to variants like *faylere*, *fals* and *feyntles*. Similarly *faylere* and *fals* are patently unoriginal. The remaining variant, while apparently uncommon, has the excellent sense 'tireless, unflagging'; see *MED* s.v. *feintles* for another example.

127 *fette / fette forþ.* The rejected reading appears to have originated in scribal desire to increase alliteration. See above, pp. 142–3.

130 *feintliche / fetisliche.* Support for the rejected variant is limited to TRULKWN; moreover *quentyliche* (H^2) echoing *feintliche*, *sotely* (Ch) preserving some of its meaning, and *fastlyche* (D), show further that the original of ⟨[(TH^2)Ch]D⟩ did not read *fetisliche.* Original *fetisliche*, apt, emphatic and with an easy general meaning would scarcely have been liable to corruption. Against that, original *feintliche,* 'feignedly', would have been more difficult because of its ambiguity and less obvious value in the context.

144 *fobbis / folis.* The range of variation here suggests a difficult original; no variant except K's *fobbars* has this qualification. The **C** text here (III 193) reads *fobbes,* v. ll. *fobberus, robbers, fablours, freres*; two **B** manuscripts (II 182) read *fobberes.* Assumption of an original like that of **C** will account for the variation in the **A** manuscripts. See *MED* s.v. *fob* n. (2.)

iotten / trotten / rennen / ganges. The original was in any case not *rennen,* a reading too easy to have been thus corrupted, and not *ganges,* a reading typical of its manuscript. Between *iotten* and *trotten,* the former is the likelier original, since *trotten* may well have acquired its initial sound from the preceding word. The reading *iotten* is probably a past tense of the verb 'to go'; see *NED* s.v. *Yode, Yede* v. γ^2, and compare also *Pearl,* ed. E. V. Gordon, Oxford, 1953, p. 46.

147 *tom / tong / tyme.* See above, pp. 162 ff.

158 *of / on.* The minority reading is adopted as having the fuller, and therefore more difficult sense 'earthly, mortal' (see *NED* s.v. *Mould* sb.^{1} 4b).

leste / beste. The rejected reading, meaning those morally best, or of highest standing and most likely to find surety, may seem better. But *leste,* signifying the smallest number, or the lightest offender, or the most insignificant, is the harder because the less obviously apt reading.

169 *doom / dyne.* Earlier argument about this crux seems inconclusive. The context can be enlisted to support either of these equivalent readings (Day, *MLR*, xxiii, 4; Chambers and Grattan, *MLR*, xxvi, 31–4; Day, op. cit., 336–8). Three **A** manuscripts read forms of 'din': *dyne* J, *deone* L, *dune* V. Between two of them there is a possible relation (above, pp. 109 ff.). None of the three is 'good', each having its peculiar forms of corruption; all may blandly conceal much corrected originals. None of the three is impressive alone, and while indeed they have more weight together this is diminished first by their character and second by the strong possibility that their agreement was induced by the suggestion of the **C** version. For this reason full weight cannot be given here to the unlikelihood of three scribes independently substituting the same variant: this is just the occasion where identical variation could occur without the coincidence of substitution being extreme. The most important factor is the possibility that *dyne* is a memorial contamination from a manuscript of **C**. Palæographically a 'doom' to 'din' corruption is as easy as the reverse. Finally, neither reading is identifiably the harder: *doom* may look easy to the modern scholar with a printed text before him and a close knowledge of this, but the medieval copyist paying little attention to sense might be puzzled by its reference. Nor would original *din* necessarily be difficult; in *Piers Plowman* it has the extended sense of 'commotion, upheaval, clamorous tumult', which here is apt enough (compare **B** XVIII 62; **C** XXI 65). The reading of the basic text must then stand as neither demonstrably easier than *dyne,* nor successfully challenged by the combined evidence of VJL.

Passus III

6 *world / molde.* The rejected variant is a mistaken attempt to improve alliteration; the line, with rhetorical stress, scans *Whát wórld wére.*

13 *somme / sone.* The adopted reading, meaning either 'band, company' (*NED Sum* sb.[1] 2) or possibly 'all together, in a body' (*NED Sam* adv.), is the harder.

17 *shape / make.* The adopted reading with the sense 'contrive, plan', seems to be the harder because of the presence of the added notion of scheming (*NED* s.v. *Shape* v. 13 and 14).

27 *þi / oure.* The context requires the reading adopted: 'as long as there is money to be made'. The variant *oure,* 'as long as we live', records a natural and thoughtless surrender to the obvious.

49 *heuene to haue.* See above, p. 158.

58 *þi soule.* The possessive adjective seems more likely to have been omitted than inserted: the balanced construction *in siȝt ne in soule* would seem easier because the differences of grammar and meaning between the two elements would be concealed by its symmetry. With the pronoun expressed, however, tension is created between the objective genitive notion accompanying *siȝt* and the simple possessive before *soule. þi* is therefore retained against strong manuscript evidence as the harder reading.

62 *giue.* See above, p. 157.

63 *here / hire.* See above, p. 169. Although the scribe of T may perhaps have used these spellings impartially for both adverb 'here' and noun 'hire' (compare *here* noun in VI 37),

in this line his second *hire* (the adverb) is probably affected by the form of the preceding *hire* (the noun) and therefore not a true form.

65 *maceris* / *maistris*. Two considerations favour the adopted reading: *maistris*, as a general, more emphatic term, is the likelier substitution; and *maceris*, 'minor officials', is, on reflection, actually apter in a context of tradesmen's offences and municipal law.

67 *pynyng*. See above, p. 169.

84 *tok hym* / *tolde hem*. The adopted reading with the sense 'chose for himself' is harder because it requires a shift of interest from the object of rebuke not merely to the authority by which the offence is condemned but to that authority subjectively visualized as a preacher. An early stage of corruption can be seen in {⟨[(TH^2)Ch]D⟩RU}, where R and Ch have substituted a plural for the singular pronoun. The split of VH here indicates that their exclusive common ancestor did not read the easy *tolde hem*.

89 *or ȝerisȝiuys* / *for here seruice*. The rejected reading, attested only in {⟨[(TH^2)Ch]D⟩RU} is unlikely to have given rise to the one adopted. The variants of W, H and E, and the omission by V indicate a more difficult original than *for here seruice*. The adopted reading, by making the distinction between occasional presents and annual gifts or retaining fees, is relatively difficult; scribes might also object to it because it caused a jingle, which they would not tolerate if they did not see the value of the offending word.

95 *wy* / *womman* / *ywys*. See above, p. 164.

99 *kniȝt* / *kniȝt hatte*. The rejected variant illustrates the scribal tendency to more explicit utterance; possibly it also records objection to the stress pattern *a kníȝt cónsience*.

102 *ellys* / *sone*. Originality must lie between these two variants; *in haste* and *hye* are to be rejected out of hand. Manuscript support for the eligible readings is nearly balanced: although at first sight *ellys* is attested only by RUJ, in fact it was almost certainly present in ⟨[(TH^2)Ch]D⟩ to cause omission of the line by *homoteleuton*, and in H, which varies independently of V. The decision is finally made on the consideration that scribes were finical about ending successive lines with the same word, and would therefore more likely have removed *ellys* than inserted it.

201 *ȝerne* / *renne*. See above, p. 161.

206. 'Beggars ask reward of men in return for their prayers.' The sense of this line, which was missed by some scribes, is made clear in VII 117–19.

209 *kenne . . . hem* / *ben . . . hym*. The rejected variants receive support only from {⟨[(TH^2)Ch]D⟩RU}, E and K; and traces of the phrase adopted survive in K's cancelled *of hem*. The readings *knoweþ* of V and *kunnynge* of H derive from *kenne* rather than *ben*, as obviously does *techyn* in M. On grounds of manuscript support alone, then, *kenne* is to be adopted. It is also difficult, because of the abrupt transition required by it from the preceding instance in Meed's argument.

216. See above, p. 140.

259 *non* / *an.* The reading adopted seems the harder because it calls for more precise knowledge of the sense of *culorum* than is shown in *an ende wile I make.* This consideration is decisive in the near balance of manuscript support.

Passus IV

5 *raþer* / *erst.* Although the adopted reading receives less manuscript support its claim to originality is the better one: scribes objected to the occurrence of the same expression in successive lines, and would 'improve' their copy by substituting a synonym for the second one. Here the process can actually be observed, for the exclusive common ancestor of VH read neither *arst* like V, nor *leuere* like H, since substitution of one of these variants for the other would be pointless. Moreover, H's variant argues strongly that the VH ancestor's reading was *raþer.*

14 *renneþ* / *rideþ.* The harder reading is adopted as the less likely substitution. Within its family, meanwhile, H² can be observed substituting the easier *rydyth.* For the somewhat uncommon meaning of *renneþ*, 'speeds on horseback', see *NED* s.v. *Run* v. 6.

29 *myle wey* / *myle.* The manuscript evidence is indecisive, and neither reading is demonstrably the harder.

34 *þe parlement.* See above, p. 153.

47. The sense is 'Because of him I scarcely have the courage to raise my eyes'. Manuscript evidence for the adopted form of the line is strong: the reading of JHLK, difficult enough to make coincidence of substitution improbable, is supported by the several attempts to increase intelligibility in V and EAM; and the untidy inversions of RWN point to an original like the form adopted. For this meaning of *loke*, 'raise the head, look up, lift the eyes and see what is going on' compare V 46. The common element in these two passages is the attitude of submission.

57 *my* / *þi.* This is a typical minor crux. The choice, in the balance of manuscript evidence, is between meanings: either, 'I, Wisdom, say on the authority of my (allegorized) self'; or 'I say, with your case as an instance'. The former seems more difficult, since it requires application of the allegory, which scribes were prone to forget.

61. The text of this difficult and much corrupted line is not offered with much confidence. The problem is to account for the loss of *penys he proffride* from so many manuscripts. The only explanation to recommend itself has been that these words were lost from the archetypal manuscript by mutilation or some other physical cause, and restored in the exclusive common ancestor of [(TH²)Ch] by correction. Support for this conjecture is found in the quality of these three manuscripts, which are generally not sophisticated. Their form of the line, moreover, is distinct from that of **B** and **C.** But the doubtful character of the text here must be noticed.

63. See above, p. 158.

91. See above, p. 158.

94 *ofte* / *eft.* What seems the harder reading is adopted as the probable original. *ofte*, with the sense 'on many future occasions', leaves the temporal distinction between the two phases of behaviour implicit; *eft*, 'subsequently', seems too easy to have been corrupted. It is, however, possible that the variation is simply palæographic.

104 *heþyng* / *hyne.* See above, pp. 161–2.

113 *coyn* / *coroune.* The minority reading, meaning 'stamp, impress' (*NED* s.v. *Coin* sb. 4) is distinctly the harder and less obvious, and therefore the less likely substitution.

120 *be* / *for.* The rejected variant would weaken the allegory. The sense of *be myself*, 'upon my own authority, that of the faculty of mind which, as a personification, I represent', is more complex, less obvious, and more difficult than that of *for myself*, 'for my part, as far as I am concerned'. This consideration decides against the tendency of the manuscript evidence. Compare the note to line 57 above.

153 *raike* / *ryde.* See above, pp. 161–2.

Passus V

1 *kirke* / *chirche.* See above, p. 157.

9 *mekel* / *meke.* The rejected reading is perhaps a genuine form and not just a spelling error. Compare *mike* in *Havelok*, ed. W. W. Skeat and K. Sisam, Oxford, 1915 (repr. 1939), lines 960, 1744, and *mik*, op. cit., line 2342; also *The Story of Genesis and Exodus*, ed. R. Morris, EETS 7 (London, 1865), line 292; and *Cursor Mundi*, ed. R. Morris, EETS 57 (London, 1874), and following, part v, p. 1485, Cotton MS, line 26113.

10. For the omission see above, p. 123. Objections to the second *tolde* are registered in the variants of five manuscripts.

35 *proue* / *& proue.* See above, p. 160.

36 *leue* / *loue.* The only criterion to determine originality here, between two readings of almost identical shape, distinguished only in letters which are often confused, is the meaning. The rejected reading *loue* would give the line the sense 'we shall the less resent your telling us what to do, and cherish you more', which is, to the speaker, a secondary consideration. The reading adopted has the meaning 'show, by your conduct, your conviction that what you preach to us is the most desirable way of life and we shall find your sermon the more convincing'. This is appropriate to *proue* of the preceding line in both the senses 'make trial of' and 'establish the truth of'.

54 *to* / *on.* The readings are equivalent: see above, p. 152, and *NED* s.v. *Cry* v. 2a.

55. It is not possible to emend this metrically unsatisfactory line from manuscript evidence. It may, however, originally have ended with *mysdede*, the remainder being either padding or the vestige of a lost or cancelled line. For an equally awkward case see VI 78.

59 *cope comsiþ* / *gylt begynneþ.* The first indication of originality here is afforded by *car-fulliche*, which suggests the original alliteration. The second is the relative difficulty of one group, *cope* and *comsiþ* being without doubt the harder. (Only three instances of the

occurrence of *coupe* outside this poem before Caxton seem to be recorded: *The Parson's Tale*, cited by *NED* s.v. *Culp(e*; *The Pauline Epistles*, ed. M. J. Powell, EETS ES 116 (London, 1916), Hebrews viii. 7; *Knyghthode and Bataile*, ed. R. Dyboski and Z. M. Arend, EETS 201 (London, 1936), line 1002). Finally in each case there is one variant likely to have generated the others, and therefore the probable original: *cope* would produce the homœographs *counte* and *compte* and the synonyms or near-synonyms *gylt*, *synnes*, *wilis*; so *comsiþ* would generate *com for* and *couettes* as homœographs, and the synonym *begynneþ*. No other hypothesis of originality would account for all the variants. The substitutions *gylt* and *begynneþ* are to be explained as an ingenious attempt to make an easier line.

60 *pelet* / *palet* etc. The spelling of the basic manuscript is here improved. For the probable meaning of this word see *NED* s.v. *Pellet* sb.^{2} 2.

67 *wroþ* / *wrong*. The tendency of manuscript evidence has been obscured by substitution within families. These words are equivalent, but *wrong*, 'in very frequent use from *c.* 1300' (*NED* s.v. *Wring* v. 3b) would seem to be the commoner and easier. Another consideration is that scribes would be more likely to remove an unpleasing homonym, as in the adopted text, than to create one. In any case there is not sufficient evidence to disturb the reading of the basic manuscript.

71 *auȝte* / *sholde* / *miȝte*. The adopted reading, suggesting the shape of *miȝte* and containing the meaning of *sholde*, is the likeliest original of the other variants.

87. A line corresponding to this one was almost certainly present in the original **A** version. The occasion of its loss will have been the phrases *for þe peple* (86) and *for all þe peple* (87). Possibly the presence of the line in EAM and W is due to restoration, the archetype of the surviving manuscripts having retained only the vestigial *Aftir*, as this appears in TRUDH^{2}JK. But coincidence of loss caused by the same circumstance need not be ruled out. The explanation chosen is not material; for *Aftir* is unmistakably the vestige of a lost line, and not an insertion.

89 *broken* / *broke* / *brode*. Day (*MLR*, xxiii, p. 15) rejects *broken*: 'Thieves would not take away the torn sheet, if there was any choice'. Either the bowl and the torn sheet are meant to be objects of little value, showing the unreasonable degree of resentment, or the line, reading *broke*, means 'who stole my bull and fouled my brook'.

90–2. These lines were evidently corrupted early in the tradition of copying the **A** version. In accounting for the corruption the wrong division of lines is to be viewed as a result rather than a cause: the likeliest explanation being the omission of a word at the beginning of line 90. That word was possibly *Awey*, as in **B** V 109, its omission from **A** being connected with its occurrence in **A** V 89. Or else the original might have been difficult; *Awey fro þe weued wende I myn eiȝe* suggests itself, in which case the corruption would have occurred during scribal modernizing (*weued* occurs only once in the **A** manuscripts, as a variant to III 50). The redivision and the restoration of line 92b are confidently made; likewise, *and his wyf anoþer* is easily rejected as padding. But determining precisely what was lost at the beginning of line 90 is another matter.

93 *liȝtiþ / likeþ*. The reading adopted both is the harder, and accounts for the other variants as homœographs or synonyms. ⟨[(TH^2)Ch]D⟩'s omission of a verb from the second half line, and RU's substitution of *smyle* are attempts to smooth a corrupt original. The reference of *liȝtiþ* is to the speaker's physical state (lines 66–72 above). See *NED* s.v. *Light* v^1 1, 3.

98 *lyk / as*. Scribal tendency to increase alliteration notwithstanding, the single substitution necessary to account for the variation of [(TH^2)Ch] is the more probable.

100 *an vnche / vnneþe*. The adopted reading is patently that of the archetypal **A** manuscript; on grounds of sense it is also the likely original. The context (lines 101–2 below) requires in line 100 the sense 'the least amount' (*NED* s.v. *Inch* sb.^{1} 2) rather than 'scarcely, hardly, barely' (*NED* s.v. *Uneath* adv. 1c); *an vnche*, moreover, has particular aptness to the speaker's condition (lines 69–72 and 99 above). The thoughtless variant *vnneþe*, attested only in two manuscripts here otherwise corrupt, is to be rejected out of hand.

106 *mat / mad*. The minority reading is adopted as the more difficult, the reference here being symbolical, like those to Envy's physical ailments. The force of this line, with the preceding, is then ironical in the manner of **B** V 233–4.

109 *betilbrowid / bittirbrowid*. See above, p. 169.

110 *leþerene*. See above, p. 169.

132 *myn owne / myn*. The minority reading *owne* is adopted as original because its presence makes the line metrical and because its poor representation can be explained by the ease with which its similarity to the following word might cause it to be lost.

134 *pilewhey*. This word and its variants do not seem to be elsewhere attested. The reading adopted appears once in a proper name, *Gilbertus Pylewhey* (1327, in *Somerset Record Society Publications*, iii, 1889, p. 85).

135 *hym / hem*. The sense seems decisive here: the diluted *penyale* was kept separate. Whoever had first drunk the strong drink, and was too foxed to know what passed his throat, then had this mixture brought in to him from another room by the cup at an outrageous price. *þerof* and *it* would be distinguished by gestures in reading (see Chaytor, *From Script to Print*, pp. 55 etc.).

141 *Sheo*. It is possible that this unusual form is anomalous, and that the scribe of T had *heo* before him, as at V 131, 133, 149 etc.

142. See above, p. 164.

147 *coupe / synne*. See note to V 59 above.

153 *Hast þou / Hast þou ouȝt / Hast þou ouȝt in þy pors*. Knott (*MP*, xii, p. 398) argued for an 'erroneous omission' of *ouȝt in þy pors*. Scanned thus, *Hást þou quaþ hé any hóte spíces*, the text adopted, which receives good manuscript support, is excellent in sense and metre, and as the sparest of the three forms of the line, the least likely to be of scribal origin.

The additions are to be explained as attempts to make the question more explicit, or possibly as reminiscences of its form in **B** manuscripts.

157 *glotoun in / in glotoun*. See above, p. 151.

160 *Tymme / Thomme*. Manuscript support for these two readings is fairly evenly distributed, when it is taken into account that *Symme* of TRDH²H³ derives from original *Tymme*. In addition the tendency to substitute proper names (above, p. 137) makes it particularly difficult to determine originality here. The reading of the basic manuscript, corrected to the alliterating form, is therefore allowed to stand.

162, 165. After each of these lines VHEANMH³ read an additional verse which I exclude from the text as not belonging to the **A** version. The main consideration is that, supposing these lines to have been original, no palæographic or other reason for their loss suggests itself. Treating them as original would therefore require assuming coincidence of apparently causeless, accidental omission from the same manuscripts on two distinct occasions, which is very difficult. By comparison, the assumption of several independent insertions from memory of another version, in an evidently popular passage, is relatively easy, for the necessary element of coincidence is much reduced. Memorial contamination should not surprise us; the remarkable thing is that it happened so infrequently in this text.

171 *bed*. See above, p. 169. The commoner spelling occurs at IX 114.

174 *Þo / Thei*. An original older form of the pronoun accounts for all the variants: it is modernized to *Thei*; mistaken for the numeral; and taken for an adverb of time, a new pronoun being supplied.

187 *vmbewhile / sumwhile*. The adopted reading, with the meaning 'at intervals', appears to have been a word of diminishing currency in the fourteenth century. It is therefore unlikely to have been substituted for the easier *sumwhile*, which would have the added attraction for scribes of increasing the alliteration. Compare **B** V 345.

194. The loss of a half line from TRDChH²JK may possibly have followed redivision of lines 194 and 195 by scribal editors to whom the second seemed unduly light.

198 *þrumblide / stumblide*. The adopted reading is taken from the corresponding line of the **C** version (VII 408) rather than on the authority of V. The presence of *þrew* in six other manuscripts supports its introduction. Independent substitution of the obvious variant *stumblide* is not hard to assume. Before 1500, *þrumblide* is recorded only in V's reading here and in the corresponding **C** line. Nevertheless the earlier currency of the word is altogether probable. It seems to mean 'jostle, push or bump with the shoulders', rather than 'stumble'. See *NED* s.v. *Thrumble, thrimble* v.² b.

After line 198 UEMH³ read five additional verses. The arguments of the note to V 162, 165 above apply *a fortiori* here. This is another case of memorial contamination.

205 *witide / blamide*. The variants here divide themselves into the homœographs *wyssyd* and *warnede* and the synonym *blamide*, the only likely source of both being the reading adopted. Variation from their exclusive common ancestor takes the two distinct forms

in V and H; the imperfect word in H probably records the scribe's distraction. W and L have attempted to repair the damage to the metre.

217 *synne / synnes.* The singular, as the more precise and meaningful, is the harder reading. Glutton is made to repent of his besetting sin, but it evidently seemed to scribes that since he was a grievous sinner the plural was more appropriate.

232 *treuþe / seynt treuþe.* The attractive reading *seynt treuþe* is probably not original; there is no reason why it should have been corrupted, and it can hardly have given rise to the variants *sir* and *þerwith.* The insertion of *seynt* by VHLE and the independent correctors of H² and N was probably suggested by V 41 above. The poet's intention of contrast, however, has its full effect in the original *séke tréuþe sé róme.*

241 *reddere / redde none / no rede / red non.* The hardest, and therefore probably original, reading is the Latin infinitive used figuratively to signify 'means of restitution'; it is more probable than the imperative, which could have been suggested by *redde quod debes* of **B** XIX 388. The form *redde*, moreover, might be only the infinitive after loss of an *er* suspension. Neither of these variants is likely to have been generated by an original *no rede* or *red non*, 'no help, no remedy' (*NED* s.v. *Rede* sb.¹ 3c, 4), which is easy enough.

242 *owe / knowe.* The adopted reading appears original as the only one which promotes the argument of the poem and is hard enough to have been corrupted. The common error of the **A** scribes, here and in line 241, was apparently to assume that Robert referred to his poverty and nothing more: 'and have no hope of prospering with any trade that I know'. Actually the poet is concerned solely with Robert's inability to earn what he needs to make restitution (see lines 227–30 above); this is what threatens him with damnation. With such meaning the original requires *owe*, not only difficult because of its ambiguity (*NED* s.v. 1 and 2), but also liable to corruption because of the metre of the line, which scans *wéne wýnne wíþ.*

Passus VI

2 *baches / valeis.* The rejected unmetrical variant of TRUDChH²VHJKN indicates the meaning of the original. But original *valeis*, as in these manuscripts, would scarcely have generated the variant *dales* of L and MH³, which does not seem easier and is not metrically preferable. Nor would original *valeis* have been likely to generate *bankes*, of opposite meaning and quite dissimilar shape. Original *baches*, however, could have generated both *valeis* and *dales* as easier synonyms on the one hand, and *bankes* as a homœograph on the other. It therefore appears the likeliest original.

6 *weþewindes.* Judging by the variation the original here was a word which could be understood to mean either 'woodbine' or 'wrapping of withies'. Evidence of these interpretations appears in *weyward, yuyn,* and *wyrnde wythys, wrethewyndes.* The reading adopted seems the likeliest to have been taken ambiguously in this way.

22 *gome / man.* The reading adopted, a difficult word of restricted currency, is the central variant, having generated the synonym *man* in some copies, and the homœograph *grome* in others.

37 *here* / *hire*. In this line T's spelling seems genuine. See, however, the note to III 63 above, and the commoner *hire* at lines 39 and 43 below.

41 *wy* / *wyht* / *he*. Of the three variants, *he*, which receives majority support, is unoriginal on metrical grounds alone. Between *wy* and *wyht*, the more restricted currency of the former makes it seem the harder reading, of which *wyht* is probably a homœograph.

42. The variations of this line argue that its original form was not so straightforward as *I shal wisse ȝow wel þe riȝt way to his place.* An original line, however, where the first stave was *wile*, 'I am willing', and where the cæsural pause fell before *wel*, would be sufficiently difficult and unusual to give rise to variation. Scribes who failed to see the necessity of stressing *wile* heavily for both sense and metre would weaken it to *shal*; next the cæsura would be shifted to a position after *wel*; then *way* would be inserted to provide a stave for the second half line. It is also possible that an original *wel riȝt* might appear difficult. (For analogous formations see *NED* s.vv. *Well* adv. 18 b, and *Right* adv. 7.) The form of line adopted is offered on these arguments as the likeliest to have given rise to the numerous variations, but is admitted to be conjectural: certainty ends with knowledge that all surviving forms of the line are corrupt.

46. In this very easy line the source of confusion can only have been metrical, but it is impossible to determine originality with any confidence. One thing, however, seems clear: if the original metrical form was *aa ax*, *lóue lésse lóng*, there is no conceivable reason why the line should have been corrupted. The text of the basic manuscript is then allowed to stand, as a possible source of the variations.

54 *Forto*. The homœographs *Forþ til* and *For* and the synonyms *Til* and *Vnto* point to the originality of the form adopted. See note to VII 2 below.

67 *berwe* / *bergh* / *bourne*. The evidently harder reading of DLN is adopted. Whether it here means 'mountain, eminence' (*NED* s.v. *Barrow* sb.[1]), or else 'grove, shady place' (*NED* s.v. *Berwe*), as an ambiguous and uncommon word it is the likeliest source of variation.

68 *freþid* / *frettid*. The difficulties of TChH²VJMH³ with *berwe* in the preceding line are reflected in the substitution of forms of *frettid* for *freþid* here. The corruption is in any case an easy, auditory one. The shady grove or eminence is enclosed; compare *Catholicon Anglicum*, ed. S. J. H. Herrtage, EETS 75 (London, 1881), p. 143, *Frithed felde*: *excipium*. The exact term is a harder reading than the indefinite 'ornamented'.

71 *manis*. This line seems to be deliberately unmetrical; contemporary readers or hearers would, from the context, substitute the word *lordis* which, with a show of discretion, the poet refrains from making his third stave. Compare **B** III 313–15.

89 *þe wif* / *þe wy* / *þe wyȝt* / *he with*. A reading not attested in any **A** manuscript is here adopted as original on grounds of sense and the direction of the other versions. The conjectured original *wif* is not itself difficult, but its difficult reference is assumed to be the cause of substitution. Scribes will have thought that when Adam and Eve were driven out of the garden it was certainly not Eve who shut the door; they will then have tried in various ways to make good an apparent error of their original. But that the author

had in mind precisely Eve as the agent appears in the **B** version, where he quotes *per euam cunctis clausa est* (**B** V 612α). In the light of this intention the necessary original of the **A** variants is the reading adopted.

97 *þokiþ forþ pride.* 'prompts Pride'. The preposition and pronoun object of some readings were inserted or substituted because the personification of the vice was not noticed.

PASSUS VII

2 *forto* / *til.* Originality here is with the minority reading which, as a more difficult word, passing out of common currency in the fifteenth century, is unlikely to have been substituted for a more familiar synonym. Compare VI 54 above.

5. This is an unusually short line. Whether the form adopted is original can hardly be established, but it does seem that the variant readings of TChH^2 and EAMH^3 filling out the line are unoriginal. Evidently neither of these variants is a substitution for the other; therefore, if one of them was original, it must first have been lost before the other, unoriginal one was supplied. This necessarily assumed loss is difficult, since no reason for it appears. There is the further consideration that both TChH^2 and EAMH^3 are probable genetic groups. To treat the reading of one of these groups as original then requires assuming loss of its reading in all remaining manuscripts for no evident reason. The line adopted is meanwhile metrical, indeed following a classical pattern.

erid / *herd.* T's form is corrected because it seems not a true spelling, but induced by the nearby word *half.* Compare line 25 below.

20 *chapellis* / *chapleynes.* See above, p. 153.

25 *conne* / *gon* / *comsen* / *lere.* Homœographs and synonyms here require the adopted reading as their common source. *conne* with the sense 'get to know, study or learn' (*NED* s.v. *Con* v.[1] 3) does not seem to have been a frequent fourteenth-century use, and as the neologism appears the most difficult.

31, 32 *hunte to* / *hunte.* Manuscript evidence here argues that the verb was used with a preposition.

32 *boris* / *beris.* The rejected variant occurs as a spelling for 'boar' in Minot, *Poems*, ed. J. Hall, Oxford, 1887, App. ii, p. 101, line 117. The wild bear was extinct in fourteenth-century England (Sir Cyril Fox, *The Personality of Britain*, Cardiff, 1947, p. 62).

35 *conseyuede* / *comsede.* The adopted reading is shown to be original by the homœographs of TH^{2}HN and the attempts of MH^3 and J to produce equivalents. The word means 'receive into the mind, grasp and apprehend', as at IX 48 below (see *NED* s.v. *Conceive* v. 9); the knight's speech which follows is parallel to line 35 but not governed by its verb, and *þise* of line 35 refers to Piers's speech in lines 26–34.

48 *eschewe* / *eschewen.* The form of T is attested only in the subgroup ⟨[(TH^2)Ch]D⟩. The insertion of *for* records an attempt to make the corrupted text intelligible.

60. Although the adopted form of this line seems to rest securely on manuscript evidence its originality is by no means certain. The variants *haue leue* (MH^3), *be allowed* (N),

byhynde (W), may be accounted for as memorial reflections of manuscripts of the **B** version. But one circumstance is disturbing: the ease with which the adopted **A** form of the line might have derived from an original *haue leue . . . to lese here*, simply through early omission of *leue*. In a line so affected, reading *Shal haue be oure lord to lese here in heruist, to lese* would quickly become *þe lesse*, and this nonsense, on the suggestion of the context, would be corrected to *þe more*, as in the form adopted.

61. This line, which is apparently unmetrical, should perhaps be scanned with two staves, *hým whóso*. The variant *mauggre* of MH[3] would improve the metre, but its originality is made to seem doubtful by the absence of any reason for its omission.

66 *forþ / forþer*. The adopted reading, which gives its phrase the two senses 'go on saying' and 'proclaim' is the more difficult. The variant records efforts to remove the ambiguity.

70–3. There is no manuscript evidence of any kind for regarding these lines as spurious.

74 *worþe / worche*. The same choice confronts the editor at V 239. The minority reading *worþe*, with the general sense 'leave the matter to' is the harder; its likelihood of being corrupted was doubtless increased by the ease of confusing *ch* and *th*. For a very clear instance of the present sense of *worþe* see *William of Palerne*, ed. W. W. Skeat, EETS ES 1 (London, 1867; repr. 1890), lines 2566–7: '*I ne wot in wat wise to worche be best.*' '*nor ich, iwisse, . . . but worþe god wiþ alle.*'

76 *wile I / I wile*. See above, p. 152.

95 *plouȝpote / -fote / -bat / -staf*. The reading of T receives the support of the manuscripts. *-bat* and *-staf* are equivalents; *-fote*, with a distinct and inappropriate meaning, is a homœograph or visual error. A *plouȝpote* or plough-pusher is to be seen in the picture of Cain ploughing on fol. 6 of *The Holkham Bible Picture Book*, ed. W. O. Hassal, London, 1954.

pyk / pykstaf. The minority reading seems the harder, as a word used in a number of senses; it is assumed that the variants arose from efforts to make the meaning explicit. The variant of A reflects one meaning of the original (see *NED* s.v. *Pike* sb.[1], the scribe having in mind the similar shape of 'pick' and 'potent'); that of the remaining manuscripts another (op. et loc. cit. 3).

putte at / pyke at. The rejected reading looks as if scribes, having altered *pyk* to *pykstaf* etc., now substituted for the general verb 'push' (*NED* s.v. *Put* v.[1] 1) required by *plouȝpote*, a more explicit one (*NED* s.v. *Pick* v.[1] 1).

96 *close / clense*. The context seems to require the adopted reading. When the coulter cuts, the soil falls into the furrow last opened as the share lifts and the mouldboard turns it, but if the roots are not all severed it may drop back into its original lie instead of being turned over for the stubble to rot. This is bad ploughing, and on the next round another furrow will lie badly in consequence. To help the coulter is to make sure that the sods fall true, and thus close the furrows.

99 *dyggeþ / dykeþ*. The rejected reading originated in scribal lack of attention to meaning; *dykeþ vp þe balkis* would mean 'throw up earth to make ridges or selions', but the context requires 'dig up the ridges (left between furrows)'. See *NED* s.v. *Balk* sb. 4.

114 *lorellis* / *loselys.* See above, p. 152.

116 *ygracid* / *þankyd.* See above, p. 101. The adopted reading is required by the evidence of the **A** manuscripts. It was, moreover, obsolescent, and therefore more difficult (*NED* s.v. *Grace* v. 1). Fowler here takes leave of Knott, who would read *þankid.*

123 *holde* / *olde.* The ambiguous form, as the harder reading, is adopted in the balance of manuscript support.

128 *cowes* / *crowes* / *gees.* The variant adopted seems the hardest (see *NED* s.v. *Chough* 1 β). An easy reading like *crowes* would scarcely have generated the patently unoriginal, unmetrical variant *gees.*

141 *he bostide* / *a bostide.* I can find no instance of a verb *abosten* recorded in Middle English apart from the variants of this line and the corresponding ones in **B** and **C.** It seems likely, then, that this is the simple verb preceded in some manuscripts by an unstressed pronoun.

160 *al . . . eiȝen* / *boþe . . . watrid* / *hys . . . watteryd.* The evidence of the manuscripts being indecisive here, the reading of the basic text is retained. It is, incidentally, good in metre and sense, *al,* 'profusely', being superior to the superfluous 'both'. The addition of the latter word by some scribes in lines 161, 166 below should be noted.

177 *botind.* See above, p. 169.

178. A line is evidently wanting in TDCh here (H^2 is defective). Its restoration is attempted on the basis of R; *blereyed* is introduced on the indication of RU's variant in line 177 and that of E in 178. It appears to have been a new word in the fourteenth century, and may well have been found hard enough to prompt general substitution of the obvious *blynde.* The originality of *blereyed* or *blereide* is further supported by the consideration that its original presence would account for the loss of the line from TDCh(H^2), since it resembles *bedrede* of line 177 in shape and would come below it in line 178. Finally I exclude *for* from this line as a more explicit and therefore easier reading which in any case does not receive very strong manuscript support.

179 *hote* / *ote.* From the variation it seems as if the archetype of the **A** manuscripts at least had an ambiguous form.

187 *erde* / *erþe* / *ȝerd* / *lond.* The pattern of variation can be explained by assumption of originality in the reading adopted: *erþe* is either a homœograph or a confusion of the two words (see *NED* s.v. *Earth* sb.^{1} 11); *ȝerd* is a homœograph by scribes ignorant of the meaning of *erde*; *hurde* is a personal or dialect spelling of *erde*; *lord* a careless error; and *hous* a brave guess with an eye to the alliteration of the line.

201 *abaue* / *baue* / *abate.* The rejected aphetic form *baue,* otherwise unrecorded and probably anomalous, seems here to have originated by assimilation of the prefix to the preceding conjunction; the compound form survives in DHJAKN where the conjunction has been lost. The variants of RChLW are attempts to gloss; that of V a homœograph, possibly for *bauue.* The presence of the conjunction in the original is taken to have been the first source of corruption; the difficulty of *abaue,* or possibly of *baue,* the second. *abaue,*

'discomfit, confound', is recorded about a dozen times in the fourteenth and fifteenth centuries.

benes / bones. The rejected variant is well attested. It seems as if some scribes took *for bollnyng of here wombe* to mean 'in order to prevent flatulence', in which case *benes* would naturally seem wrong, and an obvious homœograph be supplied. It is remotely possible that *bones* is an otherwise unrecorded northern form; compare Old Norse *baun*. The original is, of course, *benes*, and the *bollnyng* to be prevented is the swollen belly of famine.

210. The reconstruction of the second half of this line is conjectural. Neither manuscript evidence nor sense affords any decisive indication of originality.

211. The occasion of loss of this line from TRUDChE appears to have been the occurrence of the phrase *or with* here and in line 210.

212 *þermid*. See above, p. 169.

223 *Seruus / þat seruus*. The conjunction is excluded as the more explicit reading. See above, p. 131.

231 *wiȝt / man*. It is possible that T's reading here is the product of scribal desire to increase alliteration. Against this there is the consideration that *iche man*, as an extremely common word group, is the likelier substitution. Since manuscript evidence is also indecisive the reading of the basic manuscript stands unaltered.

232. This very difficult line reads as the manuscripts direct, but its form may nevertheless be unoriginal: it is possible that *of hondis* was caught up from line 235 below, and that the original read *trauaillyng in preyeres* like **B** VI 250. In that case *teching* would refer to the Mixed Life, *telling* to an Active Life of husbandry, and *trauaillyng in preyeres* to Contemplation. It is hard to find the Triad in the line as it stands.

238 *lef / lif*. The rejected reading of T may be an inferior spelling, but is more likely the result of failure to see the figure of speech.

259 *pernel / poul*. The distribution of manuscript support for these names does not help to determine originality. It is possible to argue that the reading of the basic text is the less common and therefore more probably original; also that a palæographic variation *pernel*] *poul* by loss of an *er* contraction is the easier.

282 *peysen / poysen*. Although the noun *poison* meant in its first sense a medicinal draught or potion (*NED* s.v.) the meaning 'administer a potion' is apparently not recorded for the Middle English verb in even its earliest occurrences. The choice is then between *peysen*, 'content, satisfy', and *poysen*, 'administer poison to'. The necessary originality of the reading adopted is shown in lines 284–5. It was evidently not the author who thought of malignant attempts on Hunger, but scribes, misunderstanding the allegory, who took the sense to be 'they intended to put an end to hunger, to destroy him'. The allegory may have received a humorous turn here from bynames like *Pesewombe* (*Register of Edward the Black Prince*, ed. M. C. B. Dawes, London, 1930, i, 131, 1347).

291 *to lyue on but / but lyue on (by)*. Originality is here to be identified in the strong metaphor of the adopted text, which is the hardest reading.

Passus VIII

30 *bynde / bete / bigge*. See above, p. 160. For semantic analogies with the adopted reading see *NED* s.vv. *Tie* sb. 7, and *Girder* [1] 1b. The verb *bigge*, though somewhat locally restricted, is recorded in so many fourteenth- and fifteenth-century instances that it seems too easy to have given rise to such an assortment of variants.

41 *graiþ / grete*. Compare I 179 and the discussion on pp. 162–3 above. Here *grete* and *grace of* are homœographs; *heye* and *hard* attempts to produce an easier equivalent.

44 *copiede / copide / coupide*. The text is not altogether secure here. While it may be argued that TH²'s variant *coupide* was influenced by a form *couden* in the vicinity, and that the required sense is 'copied' because not Will but Truth makes the bargain, the suggestion of the variants *copide*, *copede*, *coped* that the original read a form of 'cope' or 'coup' is hard to dismiss. These two words would have been difficult in the fifteenth century; but judging from available information, so would 'copy': the first instance of its use as a verb in *NED* is from Trevisa's Higden. It may be, of course, that the author intended a pun, and that awareness of this is reflected in the variation.

couden / ȝeue. The rejected variant apparently originated in scribal rejection of the somewhat unusual *couden mede*, an assimilation of *connen þonk* (*gre*) to *don* (*beden*, *ȝiue*, *quyte*) *mede*.

61 *lawieris / lawisteris*. See above, pp. 121–2.

62 *þus / so*. The line is metrical without *so*, which is to be explained as a scribal attempt to increase alliteration.

74. Disregarding minor variation, three possibly original types of this difficult line are attested: the one adopted, read by TRDH² and (omitting *wiþ*) M; a second, *But as wilde bestis þat wiþ wehe worþ* etc., read by JU; and a third, *But as wilde bestis wiþ wehe worþ* etc., read by K and Ch. The remaining manuscripts are evidently corrupt here. It does not seem possible to determine originality between these types, and the reading of T therefore stands. In fact, by making *But as wilde . . . wehe* modify *wedde* it gives excellent sense: 'They marry only as beasts do, with a wild cry (instead of a sacrament)——'.

75 *bois / bastardes*. The adopted reading is supported by the variants of R, W and L, which reflect one of its meanings. *bois*, with the sense 'worthless persons, rogues' (*NED* s.v. Boy sb.[1] 4) is the harder reading; *bastardes* records scribal desire to be explicit in terms of the context.

105 *belyue / liflode*. The adopted reading, which is apparently not recorded after *Piers Plowman*, would seem to be the harder, and would not have been substituted for *liflode* by late fourteenth- or fifteenth-century scribes.

107 *belouȝ / louȝ*. The archaic word, meaning not 'mock, deride' (as *NED bilauh* v.) but 'smile upon, look with favour on', is adopted as the harder reading. For this sense see *The Poems of William of Shoreham*, ed. M. Konrath, EETS ES 86 (London, 1902), p. 98, lines 9–10, *Senne makeþ by wepe þat somman er by loȝ*.

112. The corruptions of the manuscripts here are explicable on the assumption that R has, whether preserved or restored, the original text. They will have occurred because such an original, taken without reference to what follows and read in ignorance of its allusion (explained in line 115 below) is not easy, and they are of a kind likely to have occurred independently. The common element in all the variant readings except that of R is a notion of obligation, which is the most natural and obvious way of making sense of the line out of context. Once this idea of obligation is present, whether as *we schuld*, *he techith* or *he biddeþ*, the other corruptions develop from it: loss of the now superfluous *foules* from TChH[2] and VH; its corruption into 'fools' in DAMH[3], perhaps from recollection of **B** XX 60; the incorrect line division; and the various other minor changes likely to be made when copy does not seem right to the scribe.

125 *seldom* / *litel*. While it is improbable that any scribe would deliberately substitute unmetrical *litel* for an easy reading like *seldom*, it is more than likely that several would be induced to error by the sight of *litel* in the text directly above the word which they were copying, or by the sense of parallelism with *litel lokest þou*.

130. Here again, although the text rests with apparent security on the support of the majority of manuscripts, its originality is actually in doubt. R's variant *Mamelyng*, 'chewing, musing', fits the sense of the preceding line very well, and V's *Mony elynge* is likely to be a homœograph for this word. The consideration which restrains the editor here is that in V 21 most scribes had no difficulty with *mamele*.

134α. The disagreements between R and U, and V and H, among the augmentations of this line, suggest that their readings are independent corruptions. Such measure of agreement as there is, is not impressive, 'say' and 'self' being sufficiently obvious words for padding this Latin.

136, 141 *deuinide* / *demide*. See above, p. 121.

Passus IX

1 *rombide*. See above, p. 169.

6 *wente* / *wene*. The more difficult variant, meaning ambiguously 'thought' or 'proceeded' is adopted.

17. The variation in this easy line seems to have originated in scribal desire to reproduce the preceding Latin accurately. One attempt introduced *on þe day*, another substituted *fallip*.

30 *stere* / *sterne*. The variant *ariȝt sterede* of ⟨[(TH[2])Ch]D⟩ derives from the adopted reading, which thus receives slightly stronger manuscript attestation. The **A** manuscripts afford poor support for treating *to* as original.

36 *walwen* / *wawen*. Originality is identified in the adopted reading for two reasons: *wawen* is supported only by a presumptive genetic group; and the form of this variant may well have been induced by *wawes* in the line immediately preceding.

50 *ȝow* / *þe*. The reason for adopting the variant with poorer manuscript support here is

found in the context. It is clear that lines 50 and 51 are spoken by different persons. Since line 51 is unmistakably what the friars said, line 50 must belong to the Dreamer, who would use the plural because he was taking leave of two people.

52 *giue* / *ȝiue*. To read *grounde* instead of *erþe* here for reasons of alliteration is unauthorized; the line is made metrical by the justifiable emendation to *giue*. Other things being equal, scribes tended to increase the alliteration. Therefore, between two words of such common currency, a *grounde*⟩*erþe* substitution would be quite unlikely in this position, and *erþe* is therefore very probably original, as indeed manuscript representation indicates. At the same time free substitution of one regional form of 'give' for another was altogether natural and likely. See above, p. 157.

57 *lerne* / *lyþen*. The two groups of variants, taking *listen* as a synonym for *lyþen*, are equally well represented. They are both difficult: *lerne* because of its pregnant character; *lyþen* as a literary word of presumably restricted currency. But *lyþen* is so clearly the apt word that it is not easy to see why it should have been lost; conversely it would be difficult to assume coincident substitution of *lerne*. Finally, original *lerne* might well have been ousted by *lyþen* through the influence of manuscripts of the other versions. On these grounds originality is presumed to lie with *lerne*.

107. See above, p. 156.

PASSUS X

24 *and* / *to*. The conjunction seems necessary because, from the sense, line 24b is parallel to the whole phrase *come oþer sende*, not governed by its second element.

30 *liȝt* / *liþ*. Compare a similar phrase in **B** XVIII 59. The various corruptions can have arisen either by way of the ambiguous spelling *lith* or else by confusion of this phrase with a Middle English form of the group 'lith and limb'. (See *NED* s.v. *Lith* sb.[1] 2.) The spelling *liþ* for 'light' does not seem to be recorded in Middle English.

47 *allie* / *help* / *halle*. See above, pp. 164–5.

53 *going* / *connyng* / *good dede*. All indications point to the originality of the adopted reading. It receives the strongest manuscript support, from RU, J and K, *connyng* being attested only in ⟨[(TH²)Ch]D⟩ and V, and *good dede* in AWMH³, four manuscripts in some genetic relation. Unlike *connyng* it is metrically suitable. Its meaning is not immediately obvious; nevertheless, on examination it makes the best sense in the larger context. It is relevant to the discussion of the proper use of the faculties (see lines 59–61 below), and may even allude to Glutton's misadventure (V 194–8); in the corresponding C passage (VII 421) it is actually Inwit, governor of the faculties, who reproaches Glutton. Finally it is the only one of the three variants which could have generated both the others: original *good dede* would hardly have been corrupted, and original *connyng* would hardly have produced a variant *good dede*; whereas *going*, with its obscurer significance, might easily have given rise to *connyng*, either as a homœograph or on the suggestion of line 50 above, and to a resourceless general variant like *good dede*. Its difficulty is in its contextual meaning 'faculty of locomotion'; to scribes who did not see this it would seem a trivial and unsuitable word.

86 *þe salme / þi selue.* See above, p. 153.

89 *wy / why.* The variant *why* is to be rejected as unoriginal, but not to be ignored; its presence must be accounted for. Since *why* would not have been waywardly introduced by scribes, it must be a substitution for some other reading. Its obvious original is the traditional alliterative form of address, which some manuscripts have simply omitted.

91 *accordyng / acordyng with.* See above, p. 161.

93 *comist / comsest.* See above, pp. 153–4.

97 *counseilliþ / counseilith so.* The adverb is probably an intruder, either from the scribal tendency to more explicit statement, or because it was not grasped that the Latin could be the object of *counseilliþ*, although separated from it by the interjected admonition. The construction without *so* is the harder.

104. The source of difficulty here was apparently the verb *mossen*, of which this seems to be the earliest recorded intransitive use. Ignorance of the actual proverb, and the general ease of *o*><*e* confusion may have aided the corruption.

107 *manye / alle.* Despite stronger manuscript support for *alle*, originality is to be identified in *manye* for two reasons: because it is the less emphatic statement, and so less likely to be of scribal origin; and because of the possible suggestion of *omne* in the next line but one.

110 *þat / of.* The rejected variant seems to have originated in subconscious anticipation of a construction *ensaumple of suche þat þei shulde* etc.

136 *mynchons / Martires.* See above, p. 162.

141 *heo / she / eue.* Of the two variants an original *she* might have been replaced by *eue* but not by *heo*; original *eue* would hardly be ousted by the less explicit pronoun in any form; original *heo*, however, would be subject to variation both because of its difficulty in the fifteenth century, and in favour of a more explicit reading.

156 *dedliche / euere.* Originality is presumed to lie with *dedliche*, because of the distribution of manuscript support, and because it is possible to see a reason for variation from original *dedliche*, but not from original *after* or *euere*. The idea of Christ being capable of mortal hatred appears to have been displeasing; it may even account for the omission of this line from R.

157, 159, 179 *seþ / sem.* These confusions which, on the indication of line 153 above, are not to be imputed to the author, had two sources: scribal ignorance of pseudepigraphical history, and the ease of the palæographic corruptions *seþ*>*sey* and *seyn*>*sein*>*sem*.

174 *mid / miþ.* As *miþ* does not seem to be attested in fourteenth-century Middle English outside this line and VII 212 above (of T), I take the present instance to be an aberrant scribal combination of *mid* and *wiþ*.

193 *betwene / hem bitwene.* The adverbial use, meaning 'at intervals, in the intervals', (*NED* s.v. *Between* B adv. 3) seems both the less explicit and harder. The irrelevant *hem*, excluding the circumstance that the *choppis* involved a third party, is a scribal

recourse to the obvious at the end of a line doubly difficult because of its metaphor and the pun in *cheste.*

199 *ysamme* / *togeder.* T's variant, supported by the readings of RU, J and D, and reflected in the homœograph of V, is the harder, and therefore more likely original.

212 *as wolues.* Manuscript evidence requires adoption of this reading. D's variant *& walwes* indicates that it was present in a corrupt form in the exclusive common ancestor of ⟨[(TH²)Ch]D⟩. *what þat* in TChH² is almost certainly padding to compensate for its omission.

215 *giue* / *ȝiue.* See above, p. 157.

PASSUS XI

2 *louȝ* / *loþly.* The rejected variant of TChH² probably originated in failure to perceive that in the context an original *louȝ chere* meant not 'humble mien' but 'unhealthy appearance' (compare *NED* s.v. *Low* a. 8).

3 *so* / *þus* / *so me* / *þus me* / *me þus.* It seems impossible to determine originality among these equivalent readings; at most it may be argued that *þus me*, *me þus*, and *so me*, as the more explicit, are the likelier to be of scribal origin.

11 *drauele* / *dreuele.* Manuscript evidence about the original form of this word has been obscured by independent substitution. *NED* treats *drauele* in this passage as a form of *Drivel* v. 1. The Vulgate, however, to which the present line alludes, has *ne forte conculcent eas pedibus suis* (Matthew vii. 6), suggesting a connexion with Middle English *drabelen*, 'to make wet or dirty by contact with mud' (*NED* s.v. *Drabble* v. 2).

30 *dauncelid* / *dauntid.* Decision between these near-synonymous variants is made on grounds of manuscript representation. For the rejected variant see *NED* s.v. *Daunt* v. 6.

43 *dryuelen.* Here the meaning is clear. See *NED* s.v. *Drivel* v. 5.

52. The variant *Many* here is a product of scribal desire for emphasis (above, pp. 138–9), or a record of objection to a metrically difficult line.

56 *kete* / *kid* / *grete* / *courte.* Identification of originality in the reading adopted explains the remaining variants: *kid*, *ked* etc., and *grete* as homœographs, and *courte* as an attempt to reproduce the sense more intelligibly.

64 *vs alle made* / *formyd vs alle.* I do not know why the author should not have used the obvious, metrical *formyd vs alle* here. But if he did, how is the loss of such an easy, wholly suitable reading, from the majority of the manuscripts, to be explained? This consideration makes it necessary to accept the direction of manuscript evidence that *formyd vs alle* is probably not original.

67 *gilide.* See above, p. 156.

75–6. The correct division of these lines is unmistakable despite extensive variation. I assume the first corruption to have been wrong division after *why*, either because of resistance to the run-on line, and desire for conformity between grammatical unit and verse unit, or because the insertion of forms of *id est* by scribes at the beginning of line 75 lengthened it so that redivision seemed necessary. The latter is perhaps the more probable course. It should be noted that in the very similar lines 82–3, where there is no insertion of the *id est* notion, correct division is generally maintained.

78 *in* / *be*. The reading of the majority is adopted. Compare a maxim in the Antiquaries' Manuscript, M, on page 381: *penitencia in inferno sine mesura sine remedio sine fine penitencia in purgatorio dura longa sine mercede penitencia in mundo iusta lenis meritoria*; also **C** IV 101.

80. See above, pp. 163–4.

103 *To kenne* / *Kenne*. Manuscript evidence points to the originality of the infinitive sign. The grammar of the text adopted is difficult; perhaps the infinitive depends on *gan knele* with an unexpressed notion of supplication; more probably it introduces a quasi-legal formula of condition (compare Einenkel, *Geschichte der Englischen Sprache*, ii, *Historische Syntax*, pp. 20–1), relating to the offer of allegiance in lines 101–2.

112 *dwellide* / *wonide*. Two considerations affect determination of originality here: that *wonide* is less well supported; and that it may have been introduced to increase alliteration in a metrically difficult line.

121 *liþer* / *liȝeris*. The rejected variant probably originated in the suggestion of *lesinges* and the easy *þ*>*y* confusion, perhaps through *leþer*>*leyer*.

124 *wyttes* / *þinges*. The minority reading, with the meaning 'departments of knowledge', is adopted as the harder. See *NED* s.v. *Wit* sb. 11 a, and, most aptly, Louelich, *Grail*, ed. F. J. Furnivall, EETS 20 (London, 1874) and following, XVII 89–90: *I have Seyn . . . Of Alle wittes the Fowndyng*.

148. Manuscript evidence for this line is not strong, but the context seems to require an explicit statement of the teaching in question, and this the first line of the distich does not give.

177 *collide* / *Clupte* / *callide*. This is a particularly good instance of the relation of synonym and homœograph to the original reading. See above, pp. 162 ff.

182 *lele* / *lelly*. The rejected variant appears not to be attested as an adjective in Middle English.

192 *þis beþ* / *þus bed þe*. The injunction is probably unoriginal; the syntactical parallels in lines 188–91 are less likely to be governed by *bed þe* than to form part of an extended descriptive definition. Scribal proneness to homily accounts for the corruption. Meanwhile the text is given the forms which might most easily submit to the change.

195 *ben in office* / *benefices*. The adopted reading (*NED* s.v. *Office* sb. 4, 4b) seems the harder, by referring beyond local context to the doctrine of the Mixed Life. Moreover it makes sense of the following line and Latin, which the scribe of U has, by the way, omitted, to smoothe his corrupt original. *benefices* may be a homœograph, or, alternately,

a substitution prompted by misinterpretation of lines 199–200, especially of the force of *also*. This word, however, applies to the two halves of line 199.

208 *lengen* / *liggen*. The reading of T, supported by the variants of H², RU and Ch, is adopted as much the harder. *lengen*, with the sense 'remain or continue in some state' has a restricted currency, being attested outside *Piers Plowman* mainly in northern and principally alliterative texts; it is therefore likely to have been replaced by a commoner word. By the same token there is no evident reason why original *liggen* should have been corrupted. With the present use compare *Purity*, ed. R. J. Menner, New Haven, 1920, line 412: *Þer alle ledez in lome lenged druye.*

212 *louedaies* / *ladies*. See above, pp. 138–9. The copyists who introduced the variant no doubt had in mind the sort of behaviour described at **B** XX 345.

227 *at one ȝeris ende* / *one heris ende*. The reading of the majority of manuscripts, as also the more pregnant and therefore harder, is the probable original. *one heris ende* means simply 'the very least amount'; the phrase adopted, a legal formula (compare II 69 above) here has the meanings 'in due course, as a sure consequence, at the day of judgement'. *heris* was introduced either because this was not perceived, or because the alliteration *Hélpiþ héueneward óne* was missed.

237 *arn* / *an*. These variants are of equal value, and in the absence of decisive manuscript evidence the reading of T accordingly stands.

245. The evidence for the originality of this line is not merely its presence in AWMH³, but also the readings & *suche* of TRUDChH², & *seyth* of J; and & *syke* of K, which, as hypermetric matter, are more probably vestiges of a lost original than independent insertions. The occasion of the omission may have been the occurrence of *alle* in lines 244 and 246.

254 *Ne* / *Non*. The minority reading of TH² is adopted as the first element of a correlative use (*NED* s.v. *Ne* adv. and conj. B 1) in which *mecaberis* (from *mœchor*, *mecor*) is understood as not translated by *ne sle nouȝt* but parallel to it. The reference is then to Luke xviii. 20 (*non occides*, *non mœchaberis*) and the author is assumed to be citing one element of the pair of commandments in Latin to indicate his authority, while translating the second, relevant one into English.

268 *Demde* / *Dede*. The sense of the difficult context seems to require the adopted reading; compare also **B** X 382. The corruption assumed, by very early loss of *m* suspension, is easy and likely. The allusion of *in werk* may be to III Kings iii. 16–28; *in woord* is taken up in *wrouȝte* of line 270.

281 *shrof* / *shref*. The rejected variant is a doubtful form likely to have originated palæographically.

293 *haue I forgete*. The reading of TH² here is almost nonsense; those of RDJM are difficult to understand as Middle English, and appear to be scribal attempts at patching. In these circumstances the minority reading *haue* of ChKH³ is adopted as the most intelligible. The source of difficulty may well have been early corruption of some form

of original *ferper*. The sense of the adopted text is 'And yet I have left out an additional point from the evidence of my five senses, namely that' etc.

Passus XII

3 *don / bene*. Adoption of J's reading would improve the alliteration, but *don* makes better sense, following *dowel* in the preceding line.

4 *peryth / put him*. The less familiar word, and therefore presumably the harder, is adopted. Compare **B** XV 410.

12 *shet / set / sherte*. See *NED* s.v. *Shoot* v. 17. The *r* of *sherte* may have entered through influence of an original following *here*.

here / his For the gender of Scripture see XI 106–7 above.

14 *I schriuen / stryf*. The source of corruption will have been a spelling *scriue(n)*, followed by *c*>*t* confusion. For the sense compare *confessour* in line 41 below, and the extension of the trope, in *confessoures face* of line 77.

34 *þis*. Skeat read *þus*, but the suspensions are distinguished in this part of R; compare lines 55 and 113 below.

41 *wit / with*. R's error is orthographical. The adopted reading is supported by line 43 below.

49 Both manuscripts are manifestly corrupt here. In the spirit of the passus a half-line could be supplied from II 160 above, but there are numerous other possibilities; see for instance Skeat's conjecture (*A-Text*, p. 139*).

65, 74–6, 78. No conclusive argument about the originality of these lines is possible. J has, however, been several times used to correct R, and is not appreciably inferior to the latter except in length. This consideration must be admitted to improve the one chance in two that the lines are original.

67 *fentesye / fayntys*. The adopted reading, also the harder, seems to relate to lines 58–9 above, especially to *The fyrste ferly*.

86 *tyne / tyme*. Skeat (*A-Text*, p. 140*) made this emendation without knowledge of J, on the analogy of XI 238.

99 *wiste / þou wost*. The emendation is made on the ground that the admonition ends with line 98, and that a scribe who failed to observe this changed the form of the verb to carry it on. But compare Skeat's reading (*A-Text*, p. 140*).